THE DYNAMICS OF
WORLD POWER

Latin America

THE DYNAMICS OF WORLD POWER

A DOCUMENTARY HISTORY OF UNITED STATES FOREIGN POLICY 1945–1973

General Editor
ARTHUR M. SCHLESINGER, JR.
Albert Schweitzer Professor
in the Humanities
City University of New York

Volume III
Latin America

ROBERT BURR
Professor of History
University of California
at Los Angeles

New York

CHELSEA HOUSE PUBLISHERS
IN ASSOCIATION WITH
McGRAW-HILL BOOK COMPANY
New York   Toronto   London   Sydney

1973

Managing Editor: *KARYN GULLEN BROWNE*

Consulting Editor: *LEON FRIEDMAN*
Editorial Staff: *BETSY NICOLAUS, ALICE SHERMAN, GRACE CORSO,
ELLEN TABAK, IRVING RUDERMAN*

Library of Congress Cataloging in Publication Data
Schlesinger, Arthur Meier, 1917-   comp.
The dynamics of world power.
CONTENTS: v. 1. Western Europe, edited by R. Dallek.
— v. 2. Eastern Europe and the Soviet Union, edited
by W. LaFeber. — v. 3. Latin America, edited by
R. Burr. — v. 4. The Far East, edited by R. Buhite.
— v. 5. The United Nations, edited by R. C. Hottelet.
Subsaharan Africa, edited by J. Herskovits.
1. United States—Foreign relations—1945—
— Sources. I. Dallek, Robert. II. LaFeber, Walter.
III. Burr, Robert N. IV. Title.
E744.S395   327.73   78-150208
ISBN 0-07-079729-3
1234567890 HDBP 76543

CONTENTS

Volume III
Latin America

The General Introduction to this Series
by Professor Arthur M. Schlesinger, jr. appears
in Volume I.

INDEX

Volume I
Western Europe

Volume II
Eastern Europe
and the Soviet Union

Volume IV
The Far East

Volume V
The United Nations
Subsaharan Africa

UNITED STATES LATIN AMERICAN POLICY
1945-1972

Introduction

Following the end of the Second World War, relations between the United States and the Latin American nations became subject to growing tensions which were the result of two fundamental changes. One of these changes related to the structure of world power, and forced the United States to replace its traditional policy of political isolation in the Western Hemisphere with a policy of worldwide engagement. As a result, Washington policymakers, who before the Second World War had considered Latin America to be the region of paramount political interest to the United States, now assigned it a secondary role. The other of these changes concerned a sharp shift in the social and economic situations of the previously relatively static, elitist, under-developed societies of the Latin American nations. Pressed by the rising aspirations of underprivileged citizens and by growing nationalistic sentiment, the leaders of Latin America embarked upon programs of rapid modernization to raise the standard of living of their masses and to transform their weak dependent states into strong, respected, viable nations. Latin American leaders looked to the United States for help with this task at the very time that the United States was looking away from Latin America. In order to understand the significance of these two changes for the post-1945 period reflected in the following documents, it is necessary very briefly to review the pre-1945 history of United States policy toward Latin America.

Since the early nineteenth century, when most of the Latin American nations became independent, United States governments have sought to develop relations with them which would help to achieve two broad major objectives of United States foreign policy: to assure the physical security of the United States and to protect and advance the interests of United States citizens abroad, particularly in commercial and economic matters. Although these objectives have remained constant, the relative importance of Latin American relations for achieving them and the specific policies adopted with respect to Latin America for advancing the interests of the United States have varied—in response both to the international power position of the United States and to the desires of Latin American leaders to protect and advance what they have perceived to be the interests of their own nations.

For a century and a half before the Second World War a major tenet of United States policy was what has been called "isolationism." This policy did not imply that the United States wanted to discontinue economic and cultural relations with the rest of the world but rather that it sought to avoid involvement in the perennial conflicts among the great powers of Europe. The United States—largely because of a desire to protect the interests of its citizens—did become peripherally involved in the Napoleonic wars and directly involved in the First World War. Nevertheless, its isolationist policy was generally viable because three conditions contributed to United States security and made it possible for the United States to "go it alone." In the pre-air power era, two ocean barriers buttressed the defenses of the United States. Moreover, rivalries among the great European powers caused them to focus their attention upon maintaining a balance of power among themselves and generally discouraged them from sustained involvement in the Western Hemisphere—involvement which might upset that balance and lead to a European conflagration. Finally, during the century and a half before the Second World War the power position of the United States *vis-a-vis* the world's great powers improved steadily as a result of the rapid growth of its population, wealth, and industrial and military might.

During this long pre-World War II era, the Latin American policy of the United States was in effect a corollary of its isolationist outlook. Isolationism was a two-way street. While the United States might by its own acts avoid entanglement with the European great powers, this would be to no avail if those powers took the offensive by establishing new military and naval bases in areas of Latin America which were considered of strategic importance for the defense of the United States. If this were to happen, not only might the security of the United States be threatened but the United States might be drawn into the vortex of the European balance-of-power system in search of allies against potentially hostile intruders. Therefore, as a corollary to its isolationist policy, the United States developed a Latin American policy of containing or reducing European political influence in Latin America while at the same time advancing its own political and economic interests in that area.

The fundamental principles of this policy—a policy which later became known as the Monroe Doctrine—were outlined by President James Monroe in 1823. Monroe's policy was based upon the assumption that two distinctive and irreconcilable political systems existed in the Atlantic world. One of these systems existed in Europe, where legitimate monarchical governments, having withstood the onslaught of the French Revolution and its Napoleonic aftermath, were now resolutely determined to oppose revolution and republican governments based upon the concept of the sovereignty of the people; the other was in the Western Hemisphere where the United States and the Latin American nations had achieved independence as a result of revolutions against European monarchies and, with the exception of Brazil, had established republican governments. On the basis of this assumption, Monroe, foreshadowing the "domino" theory, in effect concluded that because United States citizens had given their resources and their blood to establish their system, which was like that of the Latin American states, the United States government would consider any attempt on the part of the European monarchies ". . . to extend their system to any portion of the hemisphere as dangerous to our peace and safety. . . ." Moreover, Monroe, against a backdrop of the long wars in which the United States and the Latin American nations had achieved their independence from the monarchies of Europe, announced ". . . that the American continents, by the free and independent condition which they have assumed and maintain, are henceforth not to be considered as subjects for future colonization by any European powers."

Monroe's policy was one of containment. While on one hand he proclaimed that the United States would oppose the extension of European political influence or territorial control in the Western Hemisphere, on the other he stated that "with the existing colonies or dependencies of any European power [in the Western Hemisphere] we have not interfered and shall not interfere." Moreover, Monroe related his policy to United States "isolationist" doctrine when he pointed out that it was United States policy not to take part ". . . in the wars of the European nations in matters relating to themselves," or "to interfere in the internal concerns. . ." of the European nations. Finally, by positing that Europe and America formed distinctive political systems, Monroe provided an ideological basis for United States-Latin American cooperation both to contain European influence in the New World and to promote their common interests.

Over the half-century after the announcement of the Monroe Doctrine two aspects of United States Latin American policy stand out in bold relief: the United States augmented its power by acquiring vast territories formerly belonging to Mexico; the United States sought to implement Monroe's containment policy when its interests appeared threatened by the expansion of European political influence. In the mid-1840's when Great Britain appeared interested in acquiring California from Mexico, the United States publicly announced its opposition to the establishment of any new European colony in America. Furthermore, to prevent Great Britain from gaining exclusive control over potential inter-oceanic canal routes in Central America the United States made two moves. In 1848, it approved a treaty guaranteeing the sovereignty of New Granada (Colombia) over the isthmus of Panama. Two years later the United States negotiated with Great Britain the Clayton-Bulwer Treaty by which both powers agreed neither to acquire territory in Central America nor to gain exclusive control over an inter-oceanic canal route in that area. Then, in the 1860's, during the United States Civil War, France openly flouted the Monroe Doctrine by using military force to establish and maintain a puppet European monarch in Mexico. When the Civil War ended, the United States issued an ultimatum which—combined with a deterioration in France's position in Europe—resulted in the withdrawal of French troops, the collapse of the monarchy and the reestablishment of an independent republic in Mexico.

In the late nineteenth and early twentieth centuries, as its population, wealth and industrial production expanded, the United States became increasingly determined to uphold the Monroe Doctrine. Moreover, no longer content to rely solely on a negative policy of containment, the United States took positive steps to bring the Latin American nations more directly within its orbit and at the same time to reduce, rather than merely to contain, European political influence in Latin America.

Beginning in the 1880's, the United States sought to foster a "special" relationship with the Latin American nations by promoting the Pan American movement. It was hoped that this movement would not only facilitate the expansion of United States economic relations with Latin America but that it would also contribute to the prevention of wars among the Latin American states, thereby depriving European powers of any reason for intervening in Latin America to protect the interests of their citizens. Moreove, Pan Americanism, by emphasizing the so-called "special" relationship between the United States and the Latin American nations, would provide support for the isolationist policy of the United States—a policy based upon the assumption that Europe and America constituted two mutually exclusive political systems.

At the same time that the United States was promoting a positive relationship with Latin America through the Pan American movement, it was expanding its concept of its strategic interests to conform to its growing wealth and power. Whereas in 1850 the United States had been willing to settle for joint control of an inter-oceanic canal with Great Britain, in the 1880's it became a policy of the United States to construct a canal under the exclusive jurisdiction of the United States. Moreover, the United States took positive steps to reduce, rather than merely to contain, European political influence in Latin America. As a result of the Spanish-American War, Spain was deprived of its remaining American colonies: Puerto Rico became a dependency of the United States; Cuba, although it achieved nominal independence, was forced to include provisions (Platt Amendment) in its constitution which made it a United States protectorate. Both islands now became potential naval bases to augment United States naval power in the Caribbean. Then, in 1901, after years of desultory negotiation the United States induced Great Britain—whose European relations were deteriorating—to agree to abrogation of the Clayton-Bulwer Treaty. Not only did Britain now approve the building of a canal exclusively controlled by the United States but it also reduced its naval forces in the Caribbean, thus enhancing the relative power position of the United States.

With the British neutralized, the United States now proceeded to negotiate a treaty with Colombia to build a canal through its province of Panama. But when the treaty was rejected by the Colombian Senate, the United States supported a revolution for the independence of Panama, which broke out in 1903. The revolutionary government promptly signed a treaty with the United States which not only granted Washington sweeping rights to build and defend a canal but which for all practical purposes made Panama a United States protectorate.

Henceforth, the United States became increasingly concerned with defending the canal. A major danger envisaged by United States policymakers was that a hostile European great power, following the practice generally accepted under international law, might use the pretext of protecting the rights of its citizens to intervene with force in one of the turbulent tiny republics of the Caribbean region. Such intervention might lead to the establishment of a naval base which might be hard to dislodge once forces had been landed. Because Washington could not deny the right of other nations to intervene to protect the rights of their citizens, and because it wanted to avoid such intervention, the 1905 Roosevelt Corollary to the Monroe Doctrine was formulated. Under its provisions the United States would become the policeman of the Western Hemisphere. It would intervene in the affairs of any nations unable to handle their own affairs—intervene for the purpose of eliminating conditions which might encourage European intervention. By the time the United States entered the First World War, implementation of the Roosevelt Corollary had added the Dominican Republic, Nicaragua, and Haiti to the list of its protectorates.

European political influence in Latin America was further reduced as a result of the First World War. Having exhausted their resources on more than four years of devastating war, the great powers of Europe had neither the strength nor the desire to challenge the vigorous and expanding United States in the Western Hemisphere. The European great powers tacitly accepted the Monroe Doctrine in the Covenant of the League of Nations; and Great Britain, which for more than a century had adhered to a policy of maintaining worldwide naval preeminence, accepted naval parity with the United States at the Washington Conference of 1922, thereby giving the United States naval hegemony in the Western Hemisphere.

Moreover, the power position of the United States in the Western Hemisphere was enhanced by the rapid expansion of its economic relations with Latin America at the expense of Great Britain which had been preeminent in the economic life of that area during the nineteenth century. As New York replaced London as the financial center of the world, United States private investments grew from approximately a billion and a quarter dollars in 1913 to more than five and a half billion in 1929—an increase of nearly 350 percent, while British investments expanded by only 18 percent during the same period. From 1913 to 1927, while Great Britain's share of Latin America's total world trade decreased from approximately 23 percent to 13 percent, the share of the United States increased from 27 percent to 35 percent. In the 1920's, the United States penetrated with special vigor into South America. United States private investments in South America increased from 14 percent to 41 percent of the total of United States investments in Latin America between 1913 and 1929, and the United States' share of the total foreign trade of South America rose from 13 percent to 26 percent between 1913 and 1927.

Over the course of a century the United States had been successful in minimizing European influence in Latin America and maximizing its own power there. But in the 1920's the very success of the United States in achieving these objectives began to threaten its vital interests. Having veered temporarily from its tradition by entering the European war, the United States reacted against the idea of becoming permanently involved in the European political system, rejecting membership in the League of Nations and attempting to return to its isolationist policy. The Pan American movement, which had been downgraded while the United States was involved in Europe, now assumed great importance. Because Panamericanism was based upon the idea that the nations of the Americas formed a political system distinctive from that of Europe, the strengthening of the movement would buttress the renewed isolationism of the United States. Moreover, if the Pan American movement could make progress toward its proclaimed objectives of maintaining peace and promoting cooperation among the American nations, the United States could demonstrate to the world that it practiced those high ideals which it had proclaimed to justify its entrance into the First World War. But while Panamericanism was becoming more important to the United States in the 1920's, its very existence was threatened by a conflict of interest between the United States and the Latin American nations.

In the early nineteenth century, the weak Latin American states shared a major common interest with the United States; like the United States, all of them feared the intervention of European great powers and desired to contain or reduce European political influence in the New World. Although at times, such as during the Mexican War, Latin American leaders felt uneasy about the rapidly growing English-speaking republic to the north, most of them were more concerned about potential dangers from Europe. Although some Latin Americans resented the paternalism implied in the Monroe Doctrine, they generally viewed the growing power of the United States as a useful counterpoise to the imperialistic European great powers.

However, in the early twentieth century when Washington embarked upon an imperialistic course which made five of the ten Caribbean nations protectorates and made the United States the dominant power in the region within less than two decades, Latin American leaders became suspicious and fearful of United States intentions and began to denounce "Yanqui imperialism." Latin American fears and suspicions were intensified in the 1920's when the United States, which had justified its Caribbean interventions on the grounds that they were necessary to prevent European intervention, failed to liquidate its own interventions even when it became obvious that no European threat existed. Faced with a great power without counterpoise which was expanding its economic influence in the Western Hemisphere, Latin American leaders began to fear that some or all of the remaining independent nations of the area might fall under United States domination. The Latin American countries faced a dilemma. As developing nations they wanted the stimuli to their economies which, considering the economic exhaustion of Europe, could best be provided by expanding trade with the United States and by increased United States investments in Latin America; but at the same time they feared that increased economic ties with the United States might lead to political dependence.

To deal with this dilemma and to avoid political domination by the United States, in the 1920's the relatively weak Latin American nations—like the United States a century before when faced with a threat from Europe—sought to contain or reduce United States political influence in Latin America while at the same time encouraging the expansion of United States economic relations in the area. This was not an easy task. The European great powers could no longer be played off against the United States for the protection of Latin America. Moreover, nationalistic rivalries within Latin America impeded the development of an alliance of Latin American nations which might have acted as a bulwark against United States expansion. Finally, the Pan American movement offered no protection to the Latin American nations because its organizational structure was dominated by the United States; in fact, the Pan American movement might become merely another instrument for extending United States political influence.

To meet such problems, in the 1920's a number of Latin American nations sought to implement two policies designed to contain and reduce the political influence of the United States. One was to reduce United States influence over the Pan American movement by restructuring it into an organization in which all members would have an equal voice, so that the Latin American majority might at the least be able to contain Washington's efforts to use the Pan American movement to enhance United States political power. During the 1920's, the United States, anxious to preserve Pan American harmony, responded to Latin American pressures by moving in the direction of relinquishing its dominant position in the Pan American movement.

The second policy pursued by a number of Latin American nations in their desire to contain and reduce United States influence concerned legal doctrine. The Latin Americans wanted the United States to accept as a principle of Western Hemisphere international law the Latin American doctrine of non-intervention. This doctrine stated in essence that no nation has the right to intervene in the domestic or foreign affairs of any other nation. If the United States could be forced to accept this doctrine as the basis of its relations with the Latin American nations the latter would reap several positive advantages. United States political influence would be contained because by agreeing not to intervene the United States would in effect be relinquishing the use of the superior military force which it commanded in its relationships with the Latin American nations. United States political influence would also be reduced because it would be forced to liquidate its protectorates in the Caribbean which were based upon interventions. Moreover, if the United States accepted the doctrine of non-intervention, the Latin American nations would be freer to intensify their economic relations with their northern neighbor because they would have greater assurance that their growing economic dependence would not lead to political intervention and domination.

But the United States strongly resisted the doctrine of non-intervention and when a number of Latin American nations forced the issue at the Havana Pan American conference in 1928, a controversy developed which was so serious that observers predicted the end of the Pan American movement with the Havana meeting as the last Pan American conference.

Such dramatic predictions were not to be fulfilled. Aware that the existence of the Pan American movement was threatened and that United States political and economic interests in Latin America might be endangered, Washington began to reassess its Latin American policy. During the following decade the United States formulated what came to be known as the "Good Neighbor Policy"—a policy which sought to reconcile Washington's interests with those of the Latin American nations and to secure the latters' cooperation in achieving the main objectives of United States policy.

Harmonious relations were reestablished by assuring the Latin American nations that they were not threatened by United States imperialistic designs. Aware that the threat of European intervention in Latin America was now remote, the United States gradually moved toward acceptance of the Latin American doctrine of non-intervention. The Roosevelt Corollary to the Monroe Doctrine was repudiated by President Herbert Hoover's administration; President Franklin D. Roosevelt not only announced that his policy would be that of a "Good Neighbor" but also committed his administration to the doctrine of non-intervention and showed his good faith by permitting the Cubans to remove Platt Amendment provisions from their constitution and by withdrawing United States Marines from Haiti.

A further step in the development of the "Good Neighbor Policy" was related to a marked deterioration in world politics. The 1932 Japanese invasion of Manchuria, the rise of Nazi Germany, and the Italian conquest of Ethiopia all demonstrated the weakness of the League of Nations as a peacekeeping instrument and made it appear that there would occur another major war. At the same time the Leticia conflict between Colombia and Peru and the exceptionally bloody Chaco War between Paraguay and Bolivia disrupted the peace of the Western Hemisphere, making clear the ineffectiveness of Pan American peacekeeping machinery.

In response to these many threatening events, the United States government made two moves. The United States Congress approved elaborate neutrality legislation which it was hoped would prevent United States involvement in what appeared to be an imminent European or world conflict. The United States sought the cooperation of the Latin American nations in isolating the entire Western Hemisphere from any future external war and transforming it into a community of nations peaceful in contrast to the growing conflict in the rest of the world.

At the suggestion of President Roosevelt, a special Inter-American Conference for the Maintenance of Peace was held at Buenos Aires in 1936. There the United States assured Latin America of its good intentions by committing itself unequivocally to non-intervention. In a treaty later ratified by the Senate with only one abstention, the United States and the Latin American nations proclaimed that ". . . the High Contracting Parties declare inadmissible the intervention of any one of them, directly or indirectly, and for whatever reason, in the internal or external affairs of any of the other parties."

Although the United States, in spite of its demonstration of good intentions, did not succeed in convincing the Latin American nations to adopt neutrality legislation similar to its own, at Buenos Aires the American nations did adopt what became a major component of the "Good Neighbor Policy"—the extremely important principle of consultation. In the Convention for Maintenance, Preservation and Re-establishment of Peace, approved by the Buenos Aires Conference, the United States and the Latin American nations agreed to consult with each other with respect to policies which they might adopt in the event of a threat of war either among the American nations or among non-American nations which might threaten the peace of the Western Hemisphere. Two years later, at the Eighth Pan American Conference in Lima, a mechanism for implementing the principle of consultation was adopted. It was agreed that at the request of any American nation the foreign ministers of the American republics would meet to consult on possible common action to deal with any external or internal threat to the peace of the hemisphere.

The adoption of the doctrine of non-intervention and of the principle of consultation by the United States marked a turning point in United States-Latin American relations. By assuring the Latin American nations that it would not use its superior military force in its relationships with them, and by agreeing to consult with them on matters of hemispheric concern, the United States seemed to relinquish its traditional position as a dominant, paternalistic power which decided matters of hemispheric security unilaterally. It now accepted the Latin American nations as juridical equals which merited consultation on hemispheric questions in which their interests were just as much involved as were those of the United States.

Latin Americans responded to the new United States policies with enthusiasm, and the basis was laid for transforming the ineffecutal Pan American movement into a genuine inter-American peace and security system through which the United States could achieve its traditional policy objectives while at the same time maintaining the friendship of the Latin American nations. When war broke out in Europe in 1939 and the United States was still determined to remain uninvolved, a Consultative Meeting of American Foreign Ministers was held in Panama—a meeting which declared the neutrality of the Western Hemisphere nations and which established an inter-American committee to deal with the dislocations to the economies of the Latin American countries which it was assumed would result from the European conflict. Then, in 1940, when the German "blitzkrieg" conquered Denmark, Norway, Belgium, Holland, and France, leaving Great Britain as a precarious bulwark against fascist domination of Europe, a second Consultative Meeting of American Foreign Ministers was held in Havana, Cuba. Fearing that Germany might attempt to take over colonies of its conquered foes in the Caribbean and to use them as naval bases, the American Foreign Ministers declared their opposition to the transfer of the colony of one European nation to another, and authorized any American nation to intervene to prevent such a transfer from taking place. Moreover, realizing that if Germany were to defeat Great Britain it might next turn its attention to the Western Hemisphere, the American Foreign Ministers declared that an attack by any non-American state against one American nation would be considered as an act of aggression against all of them. The United States, by means of the honey of its "Good Neighbor Policy," had secured the

Latin American nations' multilateral sanction of its old policy of intervening in the Caribbean to prevent European intervention and had received their promise to support the United States if it were attacked.

Until 1940, the policies of the United States and the Latin American nations had been isolationist in the sense that they had sought to keep the Western Hemisphere out of the war and the war out of the hemisphere. However, when isolationist policies were nullified by the Japanese attack on Pearl Harbor and the entry of the United States into the war in 1941, most of the Latin American nations promptly changed their policies in order to support the United States. Within a few days twelve Latin American governments either declared war or broke off relations with the Axis powers. All of the Latin American nations sent representatives to the Third Consultative Meeting of American Foreign Ministers which took place at Rio de Janeiro in January, 1942, and which adopted a series of resolutions which laid the basis for supporting the United States war effort and further developed the rapidly growing inter-American system. An Inter-American Defense Board to coordinate military activities and an Inter-American Committee for Political Defense to combat Axis subversion were established. Agreements were approved prohibiting economic and commercial relations with the Axis powers and mobilizing the resources of the hemisphere in support of the war effort. Moreover, the Rio meeting recommended unanimously that all American nations break relations with the Axis powers. By the time the conference ended all except Chile and Argentina had done so. Fearing Japanese reprisals against its 2300-mile-long undefended coast, and under pressure from domestic forces which favored neutrality, the Chilean government did not break off relations until early 1943 at which time it fully committed itself to cooperation against the Axis. Argentina severed relations with the Axis in 1944, but it made little difference, for Argentina had in fact been a center of Axis activities before 1944 and continued to be so until the end of the war and even beyond.

The resolutions of the Rio Conference intensified United States-Latin American cooperation. The United States contributed military equipment to the Latin American nations and granted financial support and technical assistance to speed up production of their strategic materials and to help them solve the economic and social dislocations which they suffered as a result of the war. The Latin American nations made strenuous efforts to supply the United States war machine and to combat subversive activities. Several permitted the United States to establish strategic bases on their territories. Brazil prepared an expeditionary force which participated in the invasion of Italy and Mexico contributed units of its air force to fight in the Far East.

Nevertheless, as the war progressed, the Latin American nations began to have misgivings about United States policy. The United States, which had given top priority to Latin America through the Rio Conference, now became pre-occupied with Europe and the Far East. In wartime this was understandable; but it soon became apparent that United States interest in non-hemisphere areas was not merely a wartime aberration but rather represented a fundamental change in United States foreign policy. By the time the United States entered the Second World War it had become obvious that its traditional policy of hemispheric isolationism was no longer viable. To achieve its basic objectives of assuring its physical security and protecting and advancing the interests of its citizens, the United States now moved to establish a worldwide collective security organization. Plans for such an organization were developed by the

United States, Great Britain, the Soviet Union and China at the Dumbarton Oaks Conferences in 1944.

The Latin Americans were disturbed by the results of this conference for three reasons. In the first place, although the United States had committed itself to consult with the Latin American states on matters concerning the peace of the Western Hemisphere, it had not done so prior to the Dumbarton Oaks Conferences which obviously had dealt with this matter. Moreover, the weak Latin American nations disliked the fact that the Dumbarton Oaks proposals provided for a great-power-dominated security organization which was in contrast to the inter-American system based upon the principle of juridical equality. Finally, the Latin American nations, which had begun to realize that a healthy inter-American system could provide them with assistance in solving their economic problems and offer them protection from great power intervention, did not like the fact that the Dumbarton Oaks proposals appeared to restrict the activities of regional security systems.

In response to Latin American misgivings about its policy and in an effort to elicit their views on postwar world organization, Washington agreed to participate in a special Inter-American Conference on the Problems of War and Peace which was held at Chapultepec Castle in Mexico City in the Spring of 1945. Because only those American nations participating in the war were invited, Argentina did not attend. The Chapultepec Conference was to set the course for United States-Latin American relations in the immediate post-World War II period. In the first place, the delegates decided not merely to retain the Inter-American system as it was, but rather to improve its organization, extend its social and economic activities, and expand its security functions. Outstanding among the agreements reached was the Act of Chapultepec (Doc. 1) which provided for collective action against aggression from either a non-American or a hemispheric nation during the remainder of the war and which pledged the signatories to negotiate a permanent Inter-American collective security treaty once the war had ended. At the Chapultepec Conference the American nations agreed to cooperate to obtain recognition of their improved system as a part of the proposed world organization which was in the process of formation.

At the United Nations Conference on International Organization held in San Francisco a month after the Chapultepec meeting, there was opposition to the recognition of regional systems from the Soviet Union, which considered the Latin American states as satellites of the United States, and from those who claimed that the problem of maintaining peace was global and could not be dealt with on a regional basis. The Latin American nations fought stubbornly to provide for an important place for regional systems within the United Nations. The chief Colombian delegate, Alberto Lleras Camargo, effectively presented their point of view in a long address to the Conference—an address which described the accomplishments of the Inter-American system and which called for a United Nations charter which would permit regional systems to act without first being authorized to do so by the United Nations Security Council (Doc. 2). The Latin American delegates, with the support of the United States, won the day. Articles 52, 53, and 54 of the Charter recognized the right of United Nations members to enter into regional arrangements and deal with regional security problems without prior approval of the United Nations Security Council (Doc. 3).

When the war ended, arrangements were made to hold an Inter-American Conference in Rio de Janeiro in October, 1945, to implement the Act of Chapultepec by negotiating a permanent regional security treaty. However, less than three weeks before the scheduled date of the proposed meeting the United States requested a postponement on the grounds that it could not accept a proposed military treaty which included the Argentine government (Doc. 4). A few months later the United States government issued a detailed explanation of its position. Charging that Argentina not only had failed to live up to inter-American obligations but had actually collaborated with the enemy during and after the war, the United States government stated that it did not have sufficient confidence in the Argentine regime to negotiate a military treaty with it (Doc. 7). Furthermore, the United States gave its approval when Uruguay's foreign minister proposed that the American nations adopt a policy of collective intervention to preserve democracy and to protect human rights (Doc. 5)—a proposal that was obviously aimed at the existing dictatorial regime in Argentina. Although United States officials publicly talked of the "Good Neighbor Policy" (Doc. 6) and even requested Congress to provide funds for military assistance to the Latin American nations to help implement the Act of Chapultepec (Doc. 8), the proposed meeting to negotiate a regional security treaty did not take place for nearly twenty-two months after it had been originally scheduled.

While the main reason for the delay of the Rio Conference was the deterioration of United States-Argentine relations, a contributing factor was the major change which had taken place in United States world policy—the change from hemispheric isolationism to worldwide commitment. In the immediate postwar years the affairs of the Western Hemisphere nations, with the exception of Argentina, appeared to be on a relatively sound footing; but two interrelated sets of non-American problems demanded urgent attention. One was the peace settlement which included thorny questions such as the status of Austria and Germany. The other was the functioning of the new United Nations which the United States hoped would establish a new world order through which it could achieve its basic foreign policy objectives. The need to concentrate on these problems tended to deflect United States interest away from Latin America and to make it less concerned with the proposed inter-American security conference.

However, by the Spring of 1947, conflicts within the United Nations between the Soviet Union and the western powers led by the United States over the use of the veto power and disarmament made it clear that the United Nations was not going to live up to the expectations of the United States. Moreover, basic disagreements among the same powers over the terms of the final peace settlement had produced a dangerous impasse. More importantly, Washington had come to realize that these conflicts were reflections of a fundamental change in the international power structure which necessitated the formulation of a new United States policy.

In the past the United States had lived on the periphery of a polycentric power system in which the rivalries among several great powers had forced them to concentrate on their relations with one another and had deflected their interests from the United States. But the Second World War had destroyed the power of Germany, Japan, and Italy, and had reduced France and Great Britain to second rank status. The United Nations had not succeeded in creating a new world order in which power politics would be subordinated to international cooperation. There had evolved a bipolar system of power politics in which the United States—for the first time in its history—found itself face to face with a potentially hostile superpower, the Soviet Union, a power without counterpoise which appeared intent upon expanding its influence into the vacuum created by the collapse of the former great powers, not only in Europe but in the underdeveloped world which had formerly been dependent upon the European great powers and which now began to demand political independence and social and economic equality.

In response to this new situation the United States, while continuing to support the United Nations, also embarked upon a policy of worldwide engagement. Its aim was to develop a new international power structure which would be favorable to the achievement of its foreign policy objectives. This was to be accomplished by a policy of "containing" the Soviet Union. During the next two decades the United States not only built up its own military strength but also provided military and economic assistance to other nations in order to strengthen their capacity to resist Soviet expansion.

In 1947, the United States began to implement its policy of containment. President Harry S. Truman, realizing that Turkey was being pressed for territorial concessions by the Soviet Union and that the government of Greece was threatened by domestic communist forces supported from abroad, announced ". . . that it must be the policy of the United States to support free peoples who are resisting attempted subjugation by armed minorities or by outside pressure." Congress responded promptly to the "Truman Doctrine" by approving military assistance for Turkey and economic and military aid for Greece. Then, because western Europe's economic dislocations had created conditions in which communist activities could thrive, the United States devised the Marshall Plan which provided massive economic assistance to strengthen the lagging economies of the western European states.

In the light of deteriorating United States-Soviet relations, the long contemplated western hemisphere security conference assumed greater importance to Washington as a means for strengthening its world position and for containing possible Soviet expansion in the Americas. Moreover, United States-Latin American relations were not as cordial now as they had been at the end of the war. Latin American leaders tended to interpret the refusal of the United States to deal with the *de facto* Argentine government and Washington's support of the concept of collective intervention as indications of a tendency toward intervention. More importantly, the Latin Americans, whose support had been strenuously sought by the United States in the 1930's and early 1940's and who had responded with cooperation, had begun to feel neglected because of United States concentration on other areas of the world. They were particularly disturbed when the United States offered massive economic assistance to Europe but seemed to have no interest in the acute economic problems of its loyal allies in the Americas.

The United States government therefore sought to improve its image in the Western Hemisphere. It removed the major reason for the postponement of the long-delayed security treaty meeting by reestablishing satisfactory relations with Argentina so that in August, 1947, the Inter-American Conference for the Maintenance of Continental Peace and Security finally convened in Petropolis, Brazil. There, after the United States, in response to Latin American pressures, had modified its views on the obligatory nature of collective measures (Doc. 9) and after rejection of an Argentine proposal to restrict collective action against aggression from non-American nations, the Conference adopted the Inter-American Treaty of Reciprocal Assistance (Doc. 10).

This document, which became known as the Rio Treaty, established an Inter-American regional security organization within the framework of the United Nations. Under its terms, the United States and the Latin American nations agreed to act collectively against aggression against any one of them whether it was an armed attack or some other type of threat to their territory, sovereignty and independence. Collective action would be taken not only against non-American aggressors but also against any member of the regional community which threatened the peace. Decisions on the application of sanctions against aggressors approved by a two-thirds vote of a Consultative Meeting were to be binding on all the signatories of the treaty, but no nation could be required to use armed force without its consent.

At the Rio Conference the United States was primarily interested in negotiating this security pact, but the Latin American nations had concerns that they considered far more important. Suffering from serious economic problems, they had hoped that these too would be discussed and that the United States would be willing to commit itself to provide the Latin American nations with economic aid of the type it was now offering to Europe under the Marshall Plan. The Latin Americans were disappointed. The United States position was explained to the conference by President Truman who sympathized with the problems of Latin America and indicated the willingness of the United States to cooperate in their long-term development (Doc. 11). Nevertheless, Truman claimed that the United States had only limited resources which had to be allocated to the rehabilitation of wartorn Europe rather than to the less urgent problem of America. He therefore called upon the Latin Americans to cooperate in the rehabilitation of Europe which he considered essential to the welfare of all American nations. In view of this explanation it was agreed that the Rio Conference would refrain from discussing the economic problems of Latin America, but that a special conference to deal with them would be held in the near future.

Having reached agreement on the security treaty, the American nations moved to strengthen further the Inter-American system which had previously rested upon a series of unintegrated resolutions adopted at various conferences since 1889. In April, 1948 at the Ninth International Conference of American States at Bogotá, Colombia, agreements were reached which gave the system a new name—The Organization of American States (OAS)—streamlined its organization, and outlined its functions and ideals. The most important agreement was the Charter of the Organization of American States (Doc. 15) which placed the system on a treaty basis and which in effect provided it with a constitution which set forth its guiding principles, defined the rights and duties of its members, and described its organizational structure. Less significant agreements reached at Bogotá were the American Treaty on Pacific Settlement (Doc. 16) which defined principles and procedures for maintaining peace among the American nations, and the Economic Agreement of Bogotá (Doc. 17). The latter, because of the generality of its provisions and the reservations attached to it, was in reality a statement of the aspirations of the American nations for economic and social development rather than a concrete program for action.

The establishment of the Organization of American States—a fullfledged international organization with political, military, economic and social functions—was the culmination of a half century of efforts to develop inter-American cooperation. This event might have been expected to usher in a period of harmonious relationships between the United States and the Latin American nations, and superficially this was the appearance during the next decade. In 1949 and 1950, the American nations cooperated to use their international organization to prevent incipient wars between Costa Rica and Nicaragua and between the Dominican Republic and Haiti (Docs. 18, 19, 20). Representatives of the United States and the Latin American nations met to discuss common problems at a series of conferences such as the Consultative Meeting of Foreign Ministers (1951), the Tenth Inter-American Conference (1954), the Meeting of American Ministers of Finance (1954), the Summit Conference of American Presidents (1956), and the Economic Conference of Buenos Aires (1957). Programs of economic, technical, and military assistance were developed. With respect to bilateral relations between the United States and the separate Latin American nations, there were problems with Argentina which under the leadership of President Juan Perón sought to develop a "third position" bloc in opposition to the United States, and with Panama where nationalistic sentiment pressed to gain greater benefits from the United States for its use of the canal and to reduce the special privileges of United States citizens in the Canal Zone. The Argentine problem was solved when Perón abruptly sought a rapprochement with the United States (1953) and was then succeeded by regimes more willing to cooperate with the United States. United States-Panamanian relations were temporarily improved by the negotiation of a new Canal treaty which made concessions to the Panamanian position (Docs. 58, 59). However, the problems with Argentina and Panama seemed like aberrations from the general rule because, on the whole, bilateral relations between the United States and the other eighteen Latin American nations appeared to be on a satisfactory basis.

Yet in spite of this superficial evidence of harmony, the fact was that during the decade following 1948 United States-Latin American relations deteriorated seriously. The main reason was the growing contrast between the United States' concerns and those of the Latin American nations. The Cold War between the United States and the Soviet Union became increasingly intense as communist regimes were established in Czechoslovakia and mainland China, as the Soviet Union sought actively to attain influence in the world's underdeveloped areas, and as the military power of the Soviet Union was enhanced by its development of atomic and nuclear weapons. To contain Soviet expansion the United States built up its own military power, formed military alliances such as the North Atlantic Treaty Organization (NATO-1949) and the South East Asian Treaty Organization (SEATO-1954), and provided military and economic assistance to nations around the world to strengthen their ability to resist Soviet influence and to encourage them to cooperate with the United States.

The United States' vital concern with the Cold War in the decade after 1948 determined its priorities with respect to Latin America in two ways. In the first place, because the Soviet threat seemed greatest in Europe, the Near East, and Asia, while United States-Latin American relations appeared to be on an even keel, the United States government, which prior to the Second World War had considered Latin America to be the area of its paramount political interest, now began to view Latin America as a relatively secure region and to assign to it a secondary priority. Not only did the Cold War reduce the importance of Latin America in the eyes of United States policymakers but it also convinced them that the top priority of United States-Latin American policy should be to persuade Latin American leaders to adopt political and military measures which would: (1) prevent Soviet penetration of Latin America and (2) assure Latin American support for United States policies in the Cold War.

Latin American leaders had different priorities—priorities related to the pressures which faced them in their own nations. Under the impact of technological innovation, expanding economic activity, and urbanization, the traditional Latin American societies in which small, moneyed, elites ruled a vast underprivileged minority had, since the late nineteenth century, been undergoing a transformation. By the end of the Second World War the less privileged elements in many of those societies—i.e., middle class and laboring groups—had acquired political leverage and, under the impact of the revolution of rising expectations which coursed through the underdeveloped world, were intensifying their demands for a higher standard of living, education, and social justice. In the post-World War II period Latin American governments found it increasingly difficult to meet those demands because their underdeveloped economic systems did not grow rapidly enough to feed the exploding population characteristic of all Latin America.

Moreover, since the early twentieth century, nationalism had been on the rise throughout Latin America. The nationalists had been reacting with mounting intensity against the historical dependence of their nations upon the world's more highly developed states. Since the time of independence, the Latin American economies had come increasingly to revolve around the production of foodstuffs and primary raw materials to meet the needs of the more highly developed nations. In return, Latin Americans received manufactured goods which they did not produce, technical skills, and investment capital. As a result of this interchange, foreign investors had gained control of significant segments of Latin America's export industries as well as of its communications systems and public utilities. The dangers of this dependence upon the developed nations for markets and manufactures were made clear to the Latin Americans during the depression of the 1930's when conditions beyond their control brought their nations to the brink of economic disaster. Prices for Latin American exports which were determined on the world market plummeted. Foreign investments and loans dried up. Manufactures, customarily purchased with the exchange from exports, became scarce. Unemployment became widespread. Government revenues, derived to a large extent from taxes on exports, declined drastically at the very time they were needed to cope with the problems of depression.

As a result of the trauma of the depression, Latin American leaders moved to make their economic systems more self-sufficient and independent. They sought to develop their own industries, to exploit hitherto untapped resources, and to reduce foreign influence over their economies. It soon became apparent that to achieve such goals it was necessary to raise the standard of living and the education level of the less privileged—this so that there would be the markets necessary for national manufacturing and the skills necessary to participate in more sophisticated economic processes. Some Latin Americans began to claim that the wretched conditions of the less privileged resulted from the exploitation of their nations which stemmed from the dependence of Latin America on more highly developed nations. The linkage of social change with the desire to reduce dependence led to an intensification of nationalism. No longer an elitist sentiment exclusively, nationalism now became a more broadly popular feeling. The less privileged and the privileged now had the common goal of reducing foreign influence and making the nation strong. Governments were pressed to take action to achieve that goal.

For Latin American leaders in the post-World War II era, development was the solution to the domestic pressures which confronted them. Through developing the productive capacities and physical and human resources of their nations they could satisfy the burgeoning demands of the less privileged and reduce foreign influence over the destinies of their nations—all of which would go far toward satisfying growing nationalistic sentiment.

The overriding concern of the Latin Americans with development determined their priorities in their relations with the United States. Although Latin American officials strongly opposed Soviet penetration, they did not believe that the political and military measures advocated by the United States should have top priority. Latin American leaders claimed that Soviet influence could best be contained by eliminating social and economic inequalities and creating strong, independent, viable nations. These objectives could best be attained through rapid development, they believed. The top priority of the Latin Americans, therefore, was to obtain United States development assistance. Moreover, having been convinced by the United States in the 1930's that a "special" relationship existed among the nations of the Western Hemisphere and having cooperated with the United States on the basis of this assumption during and after the Second World War, the Latin Americans believed that this special relationship entitled them to special assistance from the United States in solving the problems which they considered most urgent. They therefore deeply resented the fact that the United States had demoted Latin America to a secondary position of importance.

Thus, while the priorities of the United States were determined by domestic forces demanding the containment of Soviet influence, Latin American priorities were determined by equally strong domestic pressures for development. Each side recognized that the objectives of the other were valid, but each side believed that its own objectives merited top priority. The result was that the relations of the United States with Latin America during the decade following 1948 consisted of a tug-of-war over these differences. During that decade the United States was generally successful in implementing its own priorities, but at each stage the Latin Americans resisted and became increasingly disillusioned concerning their relationships with the United States.

During the decade after 1948, the United States justified its opposition to possible Soviet penetration of the Western Hemisphere on the basis of the Monroe Doctrine, which was still considered to be a fundamental policy of the United States (Docs. 21, 55). However, Washington also sought support of its policies from Latin America on other grounds. It claimed that growth of the OAS and the Rio Treaty made dealing with the Soviet threat, the collective responsibility of all the American nations (Doc. 21). The United States also claimed that if the Latin American nations wished to preserve their freedom and the principles upon which their governments were based, it was in their national interests to oppose the imperialism of the authoritarian Soviet regime (Docs. 28, 29).

To implement its policy of containing the Soviet Union, the United States took several steps in its relations with Latin America in the decade after 1948. When the Korean War broke out in 1950, the United States asked for a Consultative Meeting of the American Republics to discuss the coordination of efforts to deal with the world situation (Docs. 25, 26). Realizing that the Latin American nations would want to discuss their economic development, before the meeting the United States government made it clear that it believed it appropriate to consider economic questions only within the limits imposed by the war emergency (Doc. 27). Moreover, when the Consultative Meeting finally occurred in March, 1951 President Truman and several other high government officials called upon the Latin Americans to subordinate their economic development plans to cooperative defense measures against the claimed worldwide threat of international communism (Docs. 28, 29, 30). The United States prevailed. Although the Final Act of the Consultative Meeting recognized in general terms the importance of Latin American development, its concrete proposals were measures for mobilizing military, political and economic resources for defense against the communist challenge (Doc. 31).

In accord with the agreement of the Consultative Meeting, the United States proceeded to implement a military assistance program with the Latin American nations. Its aim was to develop their defense capabilities to the point where they could defend themselves, thereby releasing United States forces for duty in other areas of the world (Doc. 32). Military assistance agreements similar to the one negotiated with Chile (Doc. 33) were negotiated with twelve Latin American governments. The *quid pro quo* in each of these agreements was that the United States provided military equipment and technical aid to the Latin American nation and that the latter in return agreed to sell any strategic materials it produced to the United States and to refrain from furnishing such materials to communist-bloc nations.

The United States' next step in implementing its containment policy with respect to Latin America was precipitated by developments in Guatemala. There—following a long period of dictatorship—a democratic reform regime had come into power in 1944 and had begun to deal with Guatemala's social and economic problems in a positive manner. In 1951, with the election of President Jacobo Arbenz, the Guatemalan government moved toward the left; communists began to exert greater influence on government policies. Expropriation of vast properties of the United Fruit Company, which claimed that it was not being adequately compensated, focused United States government attention on that Central American nation.

Claiming that international communism was establishing a beachhead in Guatemala, the United States took the opportunity provided by the Tenth Inter-American Conference, held in Caracas, Venezuela in March, 1954, to try to shore up the political defenses of the Western Hemisphere. Secretary of State John Foster Dulles warned the Latin American delegates that international communism posed a serious threat to all of the American nations and called upon them to adopt a United States resolution to meet that threat (Doc. 40, 41). The Conference responded by approving the Declaration of Solidarity for the Preservation of the Political Integrity of the American States Against International Communist Intervention (Doc. 46) which Dulles characterized as making the Monroe Doctrine an all-American policy (Doc. 45). This Declaration of Solidarity stated that the control of the political institutions of any American state by the international communist movement would constitute a threat to the independence and peace of the American nations and would call for a consultative meeting in accord with the provisions of the Rio Treaty for collective security.

In winning approval of the Declaration of Solidarity the United States achieved its objective at Caracas, but many Latin Americans were unhappy about the conference results. They feared that the Declaration of Solidarity might be used by the United States to justify collective intervention in the domestic affairs of nations whose reform policies the United States disapproved. They did not like the fact that the Declaration made no reference to development as a protective measure against communist penetration (Doc. 44). Moreover, the Latin Americans were disappointed by the subordinate role given to the discussion of economic problems at Caracas. In response to Latin American concerns, the conference approved the Declaration of Caracas which affirmed the right of the American nations to decide upon their own domestic institutions and emphasized, in general terms, the importance of economic and social development (Doc. 47). However, in spite of professions of concern for Latin American development (Docs. 40, 42, 43) the United States was unwilling to accept proposals which the Latin Americans considered to be of great importance (Doc. 48).

The Declaration of Solidarity provided a mechanism for dealing with the Guatemalan question through collective action, but instead of consulting with the Latin American nations on that matter the United States acted unilaterally against the Guatemalan regime. Claiming the arrival in Guatemala of a large arms shipment from East Germany as justification (Doc. 49), the United States airlifted military equipment to Guatemala's neighbors, Honduras and Nicaragua. The United States also supported a revolt against the Guatemalan government. The government of Guatemala took its case to the United Nations Security Council where the Soviet Union vetoed a resolution supporting the claim of Washington that the Guatemalan affair should be handled by the Organization of American States—a position supported by a Concurrent Resolution of the United States Congress (Doc. 52). Finally, after a long Security Council debate, the case was turned over to the OAS (Docs. 50, 51, 53). The United States then requested a Consultative Meeting of the American States (Doc. 54), but before that meeting could convene the Arbenz government was felled and a regime more to the liking of Washington was set up in Guatemala (Doc. 55).

In spite of the importance which it assigned to political and military measures for containing the Soviet Union, the United States did consider the economic development of Latin America as one of its policy objectives during the decade after 1948. On many occasions, United States officials attested to the importance of solving the economic and social problems of the Latin American nations, and spoke of Washington's desire to cooperate in that effort (Docs. 13, 35, 43, 56). The administration of President Dwight D. Eisenhower demonstrated its interest in these problems by sending the president's brother, Milton, on an investigatory mission to South America in 1953—a mission which resulted in a comprehensive report (Doc. 38).

The United States also took positive steps to assist Latin American development. It strongly supported the World Bank for Reconstruction and Development and the International Monetary Fund (IMF) from which the Latin American nations, along with the other countries of the world, could borrow funds for development purposes or to ease monetary crises. Through its own Export-Import Bank, the United States tried to provide loans to support economically sound development projects in Latin America (Docs. 14, 72). Funds were furnished for technical assistance programs with the Latin Nations (Docs. 22, 24). When a new government seized power in Bolivia in 1952 and undertook a revolutionary program of social and economic reform, the United States embarked upon a program of massive aid which it hoped would stabilize conditions in Bolivia and prevent communist elements from seizing control (Docs. 34, 36, 37).

In addition, United States representatives participated in three inter-American conferences specifically concerned with economic and social questions—the Meeting of American Ministers of Finance, held in Brazil in 1954 (Docs. 56, 57); a summit Meeting of American Presidents in Panama in 1956 (Docs. 64, 65) which appointed an

Inter-American Committee of Presidential Representatives to consider ways of making the action of the OAS more effective with respect to economic and social cooperation (Docs. 66, 67); and the Economic Conference of the OAS in Buenos Aires in 1957 (Docs. 68, 69, 70).

United States efforts to contribute to Latin American development failed to satisfy Latin Americans. They charged that in allocating financial aid the United States gave much higher priority to other areas of the world than to the needs of its loyal Western-Hemisphere allies. United States leaders responded that other areas of the world needed assistance more urgently than did Latin America which, in the long run, would benefit from its worldwide program (Doc. 60). More importantly, Latin Americans disagreed fundamentally with the theoretical approach of the United States government to Latin American development.

That fundamental disagreement revolved around the relative merits of the "free enterprise" system advocated by Washington and the government-directed, planned, economic systems favored by Latin American officials (Docs. 13, 42, 43, 56, 57, 60, 68, 70). In support of its position, the United States claimed that its own remarkable economic growth was the result primarily of "free enterprise." The Latin Americans, who had been educated and socialized in a tradition of government intervention in economic and social matters which dated back to the times of the Spanish and Portuguese empires, and who for over a generation—under the pressure of nationalistic impulses—had been striving to reorient their societies by means of state guidance, were cool to the United States argument. They believed that what was good for the United States in the early nineteenth and twentieth centuries was not by any means necessarily good for Latin America in the complex post-World War II environment. They were convinced, moreover, that the United States had no understanding of their problems and was merely attempting to make Latin America over in its own image. Finally, they believed that their own problems were so urgent that they could only be solved through strong centralized government action which would mobilize and direct their limited available resources.

Latin Americans supported their arguments with data and theory developed by the United Nations Economic Commission for Latin America (ECLA) headed by the Argentine economist Rául Prebisch (Doc. 12). A major premise of the ECLA group was that a progressive deterioration of the terms of trade for nations which were dependent upon the exportation of primary materials was inherent in the existing international trading system. If this system were not changed, the underdeveloped nations including those of Latin America would become progressively poorer while the developed nations would become progressively richer. According to ECLA theory, this situation could be changed through concentrated efforts by the Latin American governments to develop their nations with financial aid from the developed nations.

The basic disagreement between the United States and the Latin American nations produced conflict on three specific issues. One was the question of how Latin American development should be financed. The United States agreed that some public foreign aid financing was necessary but it claimed that sufficient funds for the purpose were already available through the Export-Import Bank, the World Bank, and the IMF. However, it was the position of the United States that the great bulk of the capital needed for Latin American development should be provided by private investors, both foreign and domestic. According to Washington, sufficient private capital would become available if the Latin American governments would create conditions attractive to investors by eliminating nationalistic restrictions and reducing governmental economic controls.

Latin American officials agreed that foreign and domestic private investment had a role to play in development but they believed that private investors were not interested in essential long-term projects which had no chance of producing immediate profit. Existing agencies which provided public financing were obviously useful but according to Latin Americans they reflected United States policy in their lending decisions and did not allocate a sufficiently high proportion of their funds to Latin America. Moreover, because these agencies loaned money only for "economically sound" projects they would not help finance programs for housing, health, and education which the Latin Americans considered essential for solving their problems. To meet their needs, Latin Americans proposed that the United States join with their governments to establish an inter-American development bank which would concern itself exclusively with the Western Hemisphere, and which would have less rigid lending policies than existing institutions and in the management of which Latin Americans would play a significant role. The United States rejected that proposal (Docs. 61, 71).

A second issue was the question of what should be done about the price levels of Latin America's export commodities. Latin American governments were heavily dependent upon satisfactory prices to provide them with foreign exchange for development purposes. When a general downward trend in prices began in 1953, Latin American officials proposed that the United States join them in devising an inter-American, or an international system of price supports. Although the United States was willing to talk about this proposal, its basic position was the price supports interfered with the operation of the free-enterprise system and that prices for primary commodities should be determined by supply-and-demand in a free competitive market. The Latin Americans found this position particularly odious because, at the same time that Washington was espousing it, the United States placed restrictions on the importation into the United States of Latin American primary commodities such as lead, zinc, petroleum, and wheat—restrictions which Washington justified on the grounds of United States national interest.

A third issue arose when Latin American leaders, stimulated by the example of the European Common Market, sought the support of the United States for economic integration. Such integration, it was believed, would create larger markets than those provided by the limited populations of the individual Latin American nations—markets which would enable industry to enjoy advantages inherent in large-scale production. The United States, however, claiming that the Latin American nations had not reached a sufficiently advanced stage of development to emulate the Europeans, was unsympathetic to the idea of a Latin American common market. It did, however, agree to talk about the matter (Doc. 71).

Difference of view over questions of Latin American development was the single major cause of the deterioration of United States-Latin American relations in the decade following 1948; but there were other contributing factors. Many Latin Americans interpreted the United States' unilateral action in Guatemala as a return to the detested policy of intervention and as an indication that the United States was fundamentally opposed to any regime which undertook radical social and economic reforms. Democratic elements in Latin America were disturbed by the fact that while the United States professed an interest in promoting democracy in Latin America (Doc. 23), it not only gave assistance to dictatorships such as those of Fulgencio Batista in Cuba and Rafael Trujillo in the Dominican Republic but even demonstrated approval of anti-democratic regimes by giving special awards of merit to military dictators in Peru and Venezuela. Many Latin Americans were now convinced that the United States was more interested in maintaining stable anti-communist regimes than in supporting democratic institutions, or contributing to their establishment.

Although fully aware of such differences, United States officials—pressed by what they considered to be more urgent business in other parts of the world—tended to minimize the importance of their disagreements with Latin Americans and to emphasize what the United States claimed were the positive aspects of inter-American cooperation. They pointed to the OAS as a world model for international cooperation (Docs. 60, 62) and stressed the mutually beneficial relationships which had developed among the American nations and the positive values which would result from continued cooperation to solve common problems (Docs. 68, 71). Rising criticism of United States policies was often attributed to Latin American misunderstanding of the objectives of capacities of the United States (Doc. 38) or to communist or radical agitators (Docs. 37, 39). Little was done to adjust United States policy to respond to the concrete proposals which the Latin Americans considered vital to their national interests.

The seriousness of the deterioration of United States-Latin American relations was dramatically called to the attention of the United States public in 1958 when Vice President Richard Nixon, on a goodwill tour of South America, was met in several countries with hostile and sometimes angrily violent demonstrations (Doc. 73). Although these expressions of anti-United States sentiment were attributed by some to the machinations of communist agitators (Doc. 74), it was generally realized that they represented the expression of more fundamental problems (Docs. 75, 76, 77).

The Nixon incidents marked a turning point in the history of United States Latin American policy. During the next five years the United States government, in search of a rapprochement with the Latin American nations, not only raised Latin America to a position of top priority but also changed its policies on several basic issues on which it had differed with Latin Americans. Washington now accepted the view of the Latin Americans that the development of their nations was a matter of the greatest importance from the point of view of the security of the Western Hemisphere. Moreover, although the United States government continued to insist upon the virtues of the "free-enterprise" system and the importance of private investment, it changed its approach to Latin American economic development in three important ways. First, the United States not only agreed to the need for larger scale public financing of development but also committed itself to provide it. Second, the United States accepted and actually encouraged government direction of development by insisting upon national planning by Latin American governments as a prerequisite for financial assistance. Third, the United States cooperated with the Latin American governments toward the establishment of international price supports for two major Latin American exports—coffee and tin. In addition, the United States began to favor Latin American integration and to throw its support to democratic regimes in Latin America.

Such changes in United States policy commenced as an attempt to restore inter-American harmony by responding to the demands of the Latin American nations for assistance with their development. But the interest of the United States in promoting Latin American development and the energy which it devoted to that task were immensely heightened by the events which followed Fidel Castro's seizure of power in Cuba in January, 1959. Castro not only embarked upon a far-reaching social and economic revolution which aimed at restructuring Cuban society and eliminating Cuban dependence upon the United States but, beginning in 1960, when he sought and received Soviet assistance, Castro rapidly moved Cuba into the Soviet orbit. Moreover, when Castro began actively to promote his type of revolution as a model for the solution to the problems of the other Latin American nations, he became a symbol of the aspirations of many underprivileged Latin Americans as well as of those who were opposed to the United States on other grounds.

As a result of the Cuban revolution, the United States was encouraged to provide its own alternative for the solution of Latin America's problems by intensifying its efforts to promote Latin American development. Moreover, the United States, which through-out its history had been able to minimize the influence of hostile powers in the Western Hemisphere, now faced a Soviet satellite, ninety miles from its shores, which appeared to be spearheading a communist penetration of Latin America. After the rise of Castro, United States policy had two interrelated objectives. One was to intensify United States efforts to contribute to Latin American development which had already commenced, but now with the hope that those efforts would not only restore harmonious relations with Latin America but that they would also provide an alternative to Castro's proposed solutions. The second was to make sure that Cuba, either because of its influence in Latin America or because of its strategic geographical position, would not threaten the security of the United States.

In the wake of the hostile demonstrations against Vice President Nixon, the United States government took a new look at its Latin American policy and moved to develop more mutually satisfactory relations. President Eisenhower responded promptly and sympathetically in May, 1958 when President Kubitschek of Brazil—after referring to the unpleasantness surrounding the Nixon trip—suggested that ". . . something must be done to restore composure to the continental unity." (Docs. 78, 79). In August, Milton Eisenhower, returning from a mission to Central America, recommended that action be taken to provide loans to the Latin American governments and to develop a stable relationship between the prices of Latin America's exports and those of the manufactured goods which it had to purchase from the industrialized countries.

When Brazil proposed "Operation Panamerica"—a crash program to expedite Latin American development (Doc. 81)—the United States convened an informal meeting of American foreign ministers to discuss the suggestion. The foreign ministers proclaimed that ". . . action to promote the greatest possible economic development must be intensified." To accomplish this they recommended that a Special Committee of the Council of the OAS be established (Doc. 82). At its first meeting in December, 1958 U.S. Under Secretary of State, Douglas Dillon, indicated the high priority which Washington now assigned to Latin America when he told the Special Committee that "no matter what our commitments in other areas of the world . . . the United States will never forget the needs of its sister republics." (Doc. 83). The Special Committee recommended that study should be given to the problem of export prices and that an inter-American economic development institution should be established (Doc. 84). These recommendations were supported in a lengthy analysis of United States-Latin American relations by Milton Eisenhower who also made a number of other suggestions (Doc. 85). Among them were recommendations that the United States should make clear its sympathy for democratic regimes in Latin America and that it should support the creation of regional common markets there. Within a few months the Central American Common Market and the nine-member Latin American Free Trade Association were established and the United States and the Latin American nations agreed to set up the Inter-American Development Bank (Doc. 87). Two years after the demonstrations against Vice President Nixon, President Eisenhower, upon returning from a goodwill tour to Argentina, Brazil, Chile, and Uruguay, was able to report that his reception had been warm and enthusiastic (Doc. 88).

While the United States was moving toward a rapprochement with most of the Latin American nations, its relations with Cuba were sharply deteriorating. Shortly after Castro had assumed power in Cuba, the United States denied the accusation that it had been supplying arms to help the Batista regime suppress the revolution (Doc. 86) and adopted a policy of watchful waiting with respect to the new Castro regime. However, when Cuba entered into an economic agreement with the Soviet Union and began to receive Soviet military assistance, the United States acted to punish and weaken the Castro government. Cuba's chief market for sugar, its major export, had for many decades been the United States. In July, 1960 the United States market was for all practical purposes closed to Cuban sugar by a presidential decree drastically reducing the Cuban sugar quota (Docs. 89, 90). In response, Cuba unsuccessfully charged the United States with economic aggression before the United Nations (Doc. 91). Next, the United States took advantage of an already-scheduled Consultative Meeting of American Foreign Ministers to seek inter-American action against the Castro regime. The scheduled meeting was the culmination of a series of international conflicts in the Caribbean region revolving around Cuba, the Dominican Republic, and Venezuela, each of which accused another of intervening in its domestic affairs. Specifically, the Sixth Consultative Meeting of American Foreign Ministers met in San Jose, Costa Rica in August, 1960 to consider Venezuelan charges that the Dominican Republic—ruled by dictator Rafael Trujillo—had not only intervened against the democratic government of Venezuela but had gone so far as to try to assassinate Venezuela's President Romulo Betancourt. Having reached a decision on this accusation, the Foreign Ministers remained in Costa Rica for a Seventh Consultative Meeting to review the charge of the United States that Soviet penetration of Cuba posed a threat to Western Hemisphere security. Although the United States won praise from democratic elements in Latin America for agreeing at the Sixth Meeting to condemn the Trujillo dictatorship (Docs. 92, 94), the Latin Americans were unwilling to take any specific action against Cuba at the Seventh Meeting. Under pressure from domestic forces sympathetic to the Cuban revolution, and fearing to set a precedent for collective action against nations at odds with the United States, the Latin Americans would only go so far as to join the United States in a general condemnation of the intervention of non-American powers in the affairs of any American nation (Doc. 93).

Failing to win Latin American support against the Castro regime, the United States acted alone. Plans similar to those previously carried out with success against the left-leaning government of Guatemala were developed for overthrowing the Cuban government and all United States exports to Cuba, except for specified foodstuffs and medical supplies, were prohibited (Doc. 98). At the same time the United States increased its financial assistance to Latin America for the purpose of broadening the dimensions of its development program. At a meeting of the Special Committee of the OAS in Bogotá, Colombia in September, 1960, Under Secretary of State Dillon pointed out that if Latin America's democratic institutions were to be strengthened there was an urgent need for social development to raise the standard of living of Latin America's underprivileged masses. For this purpose, Dillon committed the United States to provide 500 million dollars with the understanding that the Latin Americans would undertake basic reforms in their land tenure systems and their taxation policies which it was hoped would increase their capacities to help themselves (Doc. 95). The United States then joined the other members of the Special Committee in approving the Act of Bogotá which delineated the measures which they would cooperatively adopt in the fields of rural life, housing, and education to expedite Latin America's social development (Doc. 96). Fidel Castro, speaking to the General Assembly of the United Nations on the purpose of the Cuban Revolution, denounced at length United States policy toward Cuba and Latin America and asked if the new concern of the United States for social development had any connection with the Cuban revolution (Doc. 97).

The administration of President John F. Kennedy followed the general policy lines set by its predecessor of contributing to Latin American economic and social development and of making sure that neither Cuba nor any other Latin American nation threatened United States security. But President Kennedy's policy with respect to Latin America was to be more dramatic, more highly integrated and coordinated with the efforts of the Latin Americans, and more developed in the sense that it gave greater emphasis to the promotion of democracy. With respect to Cuba and the security of the United States, the Kennedy administration faced graver problems than did its predecessor.

In the early days of his administration, President Kennedy demonstrated the importance attached to Latin America by his government—and his dramatic flare—by inviting the Latin American ambassadors in Washington and distinguished United States leaders to a White House reception. There, declaring that the challenge to the Western Hemisphere nations was to demonstrate that economic progress and social justice could best be achieved through democratic institutions, the president called upon the Latin American nations to join the United States in an Alliance for Progress—an alliance which through a massive collaborative effort would raise the standards of living in Latin America according to a ten-year plan, the details of which would be worked out later (Doc. 99). The president demonstrated his good faith by requesting Congress to appropriate the 500 million dollars for Latin American social development promised by the Eisenhower administration (Doc. 100).

In respect to Cuba, under the direction of the United States Central Intelligence Agency (CIA) preparations for an armed invasion of that island by Cuban exiles, with United States air support, had been underway since the last months of the Eisenhower administration. The Kennedy administration decided to proceed with the proposed invasion but without air support. On April 3, 1961—a short time before the invasion—the United States State Department issued a detailed denunciation of the Castro regime for having betrayed the Cuban revolution and having delivered Cuba over to the

Sino-Soviet bloc (Doc. 101). Rumors that United States armed forces were about to intervene in Cuba were denied both by the president and Adlai Stevenson, U.S. Representative to the United Nations (Doc. 102). But in mid-April, a force of about 1500 armed Cuban exiles, intent upon overthrowing the Castro government with the help of its domestic enemies, departed from Florida and landed at the Bay of Pigs in Cuba. Within a few days all had been killed or captured and Castro emerged stronger than before. Cuban charges of United States aggression produced a heated debate in the United Nations (Docs. 103, 107, 108), brought the Soviet Union into the conflict on the side of Cuba (Doc. 105), and led to an exchange of angry views between President Kennedy and Chairman Khrushchev of the Soviet Union (Docs. 104, 106, 111, 112). In the course of this exchange, Chairman Khrushchev stated that the Soviet Union would provide all the assistance necessary for Cuba to repulse an armed attack while President Kennedy declared that if an outside power intervened militarily in Cuba the United States would protect the hemisphere. The president also announced to the nation that he was determined that United States security would not be lost piece by piece through subversion in Cuba (Doc. 109). The United Nations took no action on Cuba's charges other than to exhort its members to act to relieve existing tensions (Doc. 110).

The Bay of Pigs invasion produced a surge of anti-United States sentiment in Latin America, and elicited strong protests not only from those who admired the Cuban revolution but also from elements sympathetic to the United States who decried its failure to abide by its commitment to non-intervention. In this unpropitious atmosphere, the United States temporarily abandoned efforts to win Latin American support for political action against Cuba and concentrated on its development policy. As a result, in August, 1961 a Ministerial Conference of the Inter-American Economic and Social Council of the OAS, meeting in Punta del Este, Uruguay, adopted the Declaration and Charter of Punta del Este which established the Alliance for Progress (Doc. 113).

The Charter of the Alliance set forth the economic and social development goals which the American nations hoped to achieve during the next decade and described the means for attaining those goals. It was specifically stated in the Charter that national development programs would "... be carried out in accordance with democratic principles." The Alliance was a compromise which attempted to coordinate and direct toward common goals the divergent ideas concerning development which prevailed in the United States and in Latin America. In return for massive financial assistance and agreement to cooperate to promote Latin America's economic integration and to solve its export problems, the United States secured Latin America's commitment to increase the amount of its own resources devoted to development, to encourage free enterprise, and to undertake basic structural reforms. Above all, the Alliance for Progress provided an instrument for carrying out peaceful social and economic revolution in Latin America—a program which might prevent other Latin American nations from following the Castro model and thereby posing a threat to the security of the United States.

With the Alliance for Progress set in motion, the United States government now tried again to convince Latin America to act against Cuba. In January, 1962 at the Eighth Consultative Meeting of American Foreign Ministers in Punta del Este, Uruguay, the United States easily won support of a resolution which declared the principles of communism incompatible with those of the Inter-American system (Doc. 114). However, when Washington asked for expulsion of the Castro regime from the OAS and for prohibition of arms sales to Cuba, it did encounter some resistance. Fearing political repercussions from Castro sympathizers within their own countries, and disliking the setting of a precedent of a small nation's being expelled from the OAS as the result of a conflict with the United States, six nations including Argentina, Brazil, Chile, and Mexico abstained in a show of disapproval. Nevertheless, the resolutions were adopted and Cuba was expelled from the OAS.

At the same meeting the Foreign Ministers approved a resolution reaffirming the democratic basis of the Alliance for Progress and calling upon all governments not based upon representative processes to hold free elections. The United States, demonstrating its adherence to that resolution, not only broke off diplomatic relations with Peru but also deprived it of all forms of assistance when a military coup overthrew the government (Docs. 115, 116, 117). Relations were not restored until the military junta set a date for the holding of free elections (Doc. 118).

The exclusion of Cuba from the OAS had little or no effect upon its position. In the months that followed, Cuba continued to promote subversive activities in other Latin American nations and to receive an increasing flow of Soviet military equipment and personnel. In September, 1962 President Kennedy reported that these activities did not constitute a serious threat; nevertheless, he warned that if Cuba should become a menace the United States would do whatever might be necessary for its own security and that of its allies (Doc. 119). Congress supported the President's position with a strongly worded resolution (Doc. 120).

However, a few weeks later, when it was discovered that the Soviet Union was secretly installing sophisticated missile bases in Cuba, President Kennedy reported to the nation by radio and television that a serious threat had developed and that he was ordering a quarantine of all offensive weapons being shipped to Cuba—a quarantine which would be enforced by a blockade (Docs. 121, 122). Support for the United States action came the next day from the OAS Council which without opposing votes not only called for the withdrawal from Cuba of all weapons with offensive capabilities but also recommended that its members do whatever necessary—including the use of force—to prevent Cuba from receiving further shipments of war material (Doc. 123). For a few days the world waited in fear that a confrontation between the United States and the Soviet Union might precipitate a nuclear holocaust. The crisis was, however, resolved through an exchange of views between the chiefs of state of the two superpowers in the course of which the Soviet Union committed itself to remove all offensive weapons from Cuba and the United States agreed to end the blockade and pledged itself not to invade Cuba (Docs. 124, 125, 126, 127, 128).

The Cuban crisis eased, the United States pushed ahead with the Alliance for Progress. In March, 1963, President Kennedy met with the presidents of the Central American Republics and assured them of his support for their economic integration efforts (Doc. 129). In October, when military coups overthrew constitutional regimes in the Dominican Republic and Honduras, the United States cut off military and economic assistance and reaffirmed its support of democratic regimes (Doc. 130, 131). The United States also sought to counter rising Latin American criticism of the Alliance. Because no mechanism had been created to decide upon the allocation of public funds for development, the basic decisions had come to be made by the United

States as the chief source of external financing. The Latin American countries charged that instead of being a cooperative program the Alliance was becoming merely another AID program which made decisions on the basis of United States interests rather than those of the Latin American nations. To allay this criticism the United States, in November, 1963, agreed to the establishment of the Inter-American Committee of the Alliance for Progress. This Committee was, in effect, an executive committee entrusted with making recommendations concerning the allocation of public funds for development (Doc. 132). Because the Committee's chairman and six of its seven members were Latin Americans, Latin America's role in Alliance decision-making was greatly enhanced.

The increase of their influence in the Alliance pleased many Latin Americans, but it did not solve all of the problems in United States-Latin American relations. Shortly after Lyndon B. Johnson became president, he faced a serious crisis with Panama. Since 1955 when the last modification in the canal treaty had been made, there had been growing dissatisfaction among the Panamanian nationalists concerning rental paid by the United States, discrimination against Panamanians in the Canal Zone, and questions of the nature of Panama's sovereignty and its right to fly the Panamanian flag in the Zone. In January, 1964 a group of United States students, acting against instructions, raised the United States flag at a high school in the Zone. Rioting broke out which resulted in over 200 casualties including 24 deaths. Although the United States troops used to restore order were not moved outside the Canal Zone, the Panamanian government charged aggression and broke off relations with the United States, at the same time asking for OAS assistance (Doc. 134). The United States appealed in its turn to the OAS, and the Inter-American Peace Committee went into action immediately (Doc. 135). At the same time, the United States dispatched Assistant Secretary of State Thomas C. Mann to the Canal Zone (Doc. 136). The United Nations Security Council accepted the suggestion of Washington that the OAS should continue to handle the dispute (Docs. 137, 138).

The Inter-American Peace Committee not only took steps to prevent further violence in Panama but it also made progress toward reestablishing relations between Panama and the United States (Docs. 139, 140, 142). But Panama broke off negotiations and asked that the conflict be considered at a Consultative Meeting of the OAS—a request which was granted (Docs. 143, 145, 146, 147). During the long crisis, the United States adopted a generally conciliatory attitude, but was firm in its insistence that it would defend the physical security of the canal (Docs. 141, 144, 149). Finally, nearly two months after the riots, the OAS announced that Panama and the United States had agreed to reestablish relations (Doc. 151).

At the end of the year, President Johnson announced that the United States was going to pursue the possibility of constructing another inter-oceanic canal either in Panama or in a nearby territory and that he was going to propose to Panama the negotiation of an entirely new treaty on the existing canal (Doc. 153). The linking of a potentially competitive new canal with the problems surrounding the existing canal undoubtedly strengthened the bargaining position of the United States in the ensuing negotiations with Panama. In June, 1967 after more than two years of discussions, the two nations agreed upon a treaty which recognized Panamanian sovereignty over the Canal Zone and gave Panama more influence in the management of the canal. But in 1970, Panama rejected the treaty.

Although the Panamanian crisis posed a serious problem, in reality it lay on the periphery of the main concerns of the United States—concerns which continued to be the interrelated objectives of preventing communist penetration of Latin America and promoting Latin American development. In pursuing these objectives, the Johnson administration followed the general lines set by its predecessor, but hardened its policy by placing greater emphasis upon political and military measures for preventing communist subversion and by supporting anti-communist regimes in Latin America whether they were democratic or authoritarian and dictatorial. The Johnson administration restored relations with regimes in the Dominican Republic and Honduras—regimes which the Kennedy administration had refused to recognize on the grounds that they were undemocratic (Doc. 133). Moreover, when military elements overthrew a democratic government in Brazil—a government which the Johnson administration considered to lean to the left—the United States did not suspend relations, and President Johnson went so far as to send a message to the new Brazilian president commending the willingness of the Brazilian community to resolve its difficulties ". . . within the framework of constitutional democracy" (Doc. 150). Then, in October, 1968, when military elements overthrew the constitutional government of Peru, the United States—without referring to the democratic assumptions of the Alliance for Progress—delayed but two weeks in granting recognition to a military junta which made vague promises to restore constitutional government (Docs. 183, 184).

With respect to Cuba and communist penetration in Latin America, the Johnson administration also followed a hard line. Greater emphasis was given to the policy developed by the previous administration of using the United States military assistance program to train Latin American armed forces in anti-insurgency tactics so that they might prevent internal subversion (Doc. 175). When Cuba shut off the water supply to the United States base at Guantanamo Bay, the White House issued a stern warning (Doc. 148). Then, in 1964, when the democratic government of Venezuela, plagued with Castro-supported subversion, convoked a Consultative Meeting of American Foreign Ministers, the United States and fourteen other OAS members supported a strong resolution applying diplomatic and economic sanctions against Cuba in conformity with the terms of the Rio Treaty (Doc. 152).

But the clearest evidence of the Johnson administration's hard line was its reaction to a revolt which broke out in the Dominican Republic in April, 1965. While the fighting was still in progress President Johnson—without consulting the OAS—landed 400 United States soldiers in the Dominican Republic, increasing their number to 20,000 in the days that followed. The administration first justified this intervention as necessary for the protection of United States and other foreign nationals residing in the violence-torn land (Docs. 154, 155, 161), but Washington soon admitted that the major motive for its intervention was to prevent communist elements from taking advantage of the existing turmoil to seize control of the government and to establish another communist state in the Western Hemisphere (Doc. 163).

Although the United States had obviously violated its agreements concerning non-intervention, the Johnson administration claimed that it was abiding by the principles of the inter-American system (Docs. 157, 163)—a claim which it sought to make good by shifting to the OAS the responsibility first for restoring peace and then reestablishing constitutional government in the Dominican Republic (Doc. 159). Many Latin Americans were profoundly shocked by the intervention of the United States—

intervention which they considered a brazen flouting of United States agreements with their nations. They were hostile to the idea of cooperating with the United States in liquidating problems which it had brought upon itself in such a manner. At Chile's request, a Consultative Meeting of the OAS was convoked (Doc. 156) where two resolutions calling for the withdrawal of the United States forces were presented without success. The United States prevailed in the OAS, which first worked for a ceasefire in the Dominican Republic (Docs. 157, 158), then appointed a committee to reestablish normal conditions there (Docs. 160, 162), and finally approved the creation of an inter-American military force to maintain order on the island until a new government could be established (Docs. 164, 169).

During the intervention, the Soviet Union called upon the United Nations Security Council to condemn the United States action and demand the withdrawal of its troops. Although the suggestion was not approved, the United States received a setback when the Security Council—for the first time—ignored the United States position that the OAS had prior jurisdiction over regional disputes and sent a representative to report first-hand on the events in the Dominican Republic (Doc. 165). Senator J. William Fulbright, in an extended critique of the United States intervention in the Dominican Republic, charged that "United States policy . . . was characterized initially by overtimidity and subsequently by overaction. Throughout the whole affair it has also been characterized by a lack of candor (Doc. 166)."

The forceful action of the United States in the Dominican Republic did not reduce Fidel Castro's interest in promoting revolution. In fact, Cuba now intensified its activities. In January, 1966, under Castro's auspices, a Conference of Solidarity Among the Peoples of Asia, Africa, and Latin America was held in Havana. That conference, which was attended by a number of Latin American leaders of the left, took steps to intensify revolutionary activity in the Western Hemisphere as well as in other parts of the world. Moreover, Cuba not only continued its campaign of violence against the Venezuelan government but it also secretly sent master tactician of guerilla warfare Che Guevara to Bolivia to organize a revolt. In response to these developments, the United States not only joined the other members of the OAS in denouncing the Havana Solidarity Conference (Doc. 168) but also—at a Consultative Meeting of American Foreign Ministers in Washington in 1967—proposed that the American nations attempt to weaken Cuba's economic base by convincing their free-world friends to restrict their economic relations with Cuba until it stopped its aggressive behavior (Doc. 172). The Foreign Ministers transformed this proposal into a resolution which was adopted along with others aimed at restraining the Cuban government (Docs. 173, 174).

The efforts of the Johnson administration were not confined to political and military measures to prevent further communist penetration of Latin America. The United States joined the Latin American nations in amending the Charter of the OAS to improve its effectiveness (Doc. 167, 171, 180). President Johnson also approved United States adherence to the Treaty of Tlatelolco—an agreement among the Latin American nations to ban nuclear weapons from their territories (Doc. 176) and continued to support the Alliance for Progress. President Johnson participated in a 1967 summit meeting of American Chiefs of State and a 1968 meeting of Central American Presidents. At the former, the president declared his support for the creation of a Latin American common market and joined his Latin American colleagues in approving a number of resolutions to expedite Latin American development (Docs. 170, 178). At the latter, the president promised continued United States financial support for the development of the Central American common market and its integration into the proposed Latin American Common Market (Docs. 181, 182).

But in spite of its efforts to promote Latin American development, the Johnson administration became increasingly less interested in Latin America as it approached its end. This decline of interest was largely a reflection of new trends which, beginning in the late 1960's and continuing into the early 1970's, led to a reorientation of the Latin American policy of the United States.

Decreasing United States interest in Latin America was related to several inter-related developments. For one thing the sense of the urgency of solving Latin America's problems as a means for preventing Soviet penetration diminished as the Soviet Union—seeking to concentrate its energies on its growing conflict with China—abandoned a policy of supporting revolution in Latin America in favor of one of gradually advancing the communist program through peaceful collaboration with reformist groups in Latin America. Although Castro continued his support of revolution in Latin America, his effectiveness was reduced by Soviet opposition to his policy and by the growing problems of the Cuban economy.

The preoccupation of the United States with the Vietnam War, the Near East crisis, and with racial tensions, student riots, and environmental problems at home, deflected interest from Latin America. Moreover, in the United States there was growing disillusion with the entire concept of foreign assistance to the underdeveloped world—disillusion which sprang from the feeling that over the course of nearly two decades such assistance had neither solved the world's problems nor made friends for the United States. The Alliance for Progress had aroused high hopes for the fast resolution of Latin America's problems. Although substantial achievements could be credited to the Alliance, it was criticized in the United States on two grounds: by objective criteria it had failed to reach its stated goals of raising living standards and strengthening democracy in Latin America (Docs. 175, 177); and instead of contributing to harmonious relations with Latin America, the Alliance, in the late 1960's, was arousing growing discontent.

Latin American objections to the Alliance for Progress were due in part to the frustrations they were experiencing as a result of the societal dislocations which accompanied the rapid modernization to which the Alliance contributed. These frustrations nourished an intensification of nationalistic sentiment among Latin Americans—sentiment which made them increasingly sensitive to United States influence over their development plans and led to charges that the United States was trying to make the Latin American nations over in its own image rather than allowing them to work out their own destinies.

More concrete objections to United States policy under the Alliance for Progress included the following: (1) because the United States insisted that its aid funds be used to purchase goods and services from the United States, the Latin Americans were forced to pay significantly higher prices than those prevailing on the world market; (2) the existing terms for international financing of Latin American development were so onerous that the Latin American nations were incurring mounting debts, the payments on which were reducing their ability to finance their own development; and (3) the restrictions of the United States and other developed nations against the importation of Latin American products were damaging the export trade of the area—trade which produced the foreign exchange so important for development. The Latin Americans proclaimed, in the light of the foregoing criticisms, that they desired trade, not aid.

In this atmosphere of declining United States interest in Latin America and increasing criticism of United States Latin American policy both at home and abroad, Richard M. Nixon assumed the presidency in January, 1968. Before making any major policy statement with respect to Latin America, the new president sent Governor Nelson Rockefeller of New York as the head of a committee to observe at firsthand conditions in Latin America and to make recommendations for policy changes. While the governor was carrying out his mission, the unsatisfactory state of United States-Latin American relations was brought forcefully to the president's attention by two developments. In May, 1969 representatives of all the Latin American nations, meeting in Viña del Mar, Chile, prepared a long report analyzing their development problems and detailing charges against the United States. Known as the Consensus of Viña del Mar, this report was personally presented to President Nixon. Then, when the Rockefeller mission began to travel in Latin America it was greeted in many countries by hostile demonstrations. Anger was so widespread that three Latin American governments asked the commission to cancel its proposed visit to their countries.

The Rockefeller Report which was the result of that mission was submitted to President Nixon in August, 1969. It was a comprehensive analysis of the social, economic, and political turmoil observed in Latin America, and of the implications of that turmoil for United States policy. According to the report, a major challenge for the United States was "... to find ways in which its tremendous human and material resources can effectively supplement the efforts of the other American nations themselves, in a climate of growing instability, extremism and anti-United States nationalism (Doc. 185)." A series of recommendations was made for meeting that challenge. Although the mission's findings were not made public until following the president's first major Latin American policy address in October, 1969, in that address the president gave credit to the Rockefeller Report for "substantially shaping" the new approaches which his administration was adopting (Docs. 186, 187).

In his October address, President Nixon reaffirmed the United States' commitment both to the inter-American system and to providing assistance to Latin America. The new approach which he outlined was a response both to Latin American nationalism and to sentiment in the United States for reducing the nation's worldwide commitments. Implied in the new policy was the relaxation of the intense involvement of the United States in Latin American development problems. President Nixon proposed that the United States and Latin America establish what he called a "mature partnership" in which the United States would step down from its dominant, paternalistic position while the Latin Americans would assume greater responsibility for the development of their individual nations. According to the president, the United States would "lecture less and listen more."

Translating this approach into more concrete terms, President Nixon specified that his administration would: (1) give assistance to Latin American-initiated programs rather than to programs initiated in the United States; (2) increasingly channel United States assistance through a multilateral inter-American agency, thus increasing the influence of the Latin Americans over their own development; and (3) submit in advance for the consideration of an inter-American agency proposed United States economic policies which affected Latin America. In addition, the President announced that among other things the United States would take steps to help the Latin Americans expand their foreign trade, deal with their debt-servicing problems, and promote their economic integration.

During the next three and one-half years, the Nixon administration sought to implement this policy (Doc. 195). The United States accepted the Latin American decision that the Inter-American Committee on the Alliance (CIPA) should be the agency endowed with increased responsibility for decisions on development assistance. Not only did the United States provide funds to strengthen CIPA and the Inter-American Development Bank (Doc. 188) but in October, 1970 it submitted its economic policies relating to Latin America for review by CIPA (Doc. 190). In addition, the United States began to decrease its direct aid to individual Latin American nations while increasing its support for multilateral agencies. The United States also supported the study of Latin America's debt problems and took two steps to promote the expansion of Latin America's foreign trade. Not only did it relax—but not eliminate—restrictions on the spending of United States dollar loans but it also worked to get other developed nations to adopt general systems of tariff preferences which would facilitate the entrance into their markets of Latin American products. Assuring the Latin Americans of the importance the United States attached to their nations, Secretary of State William Rogers told the General Assembly of the recently reorganized OAS that "Neither our other international interests nor our domestic concerns will reduce or tarnish the firmness of our commitment to the hemisphere (Doc. 189)."

But beginning in 1971 serious problems tested the "mature partner" relationship. A conflict which had been developing for some time over the rights of United States citizens to fish in areas claimed by several Latin American nations to be their territorial waters came to a head in January when the administration, implementing congressional legislation, suspended military sales and credits to Ecuador in retaliation for that nation's repeated seizures of United States fishing vessels. Ecuador—charging economic aggression—appealed to the OAS for help and expelled the United States military mission from its territory (Doc. 63, 194).

Even more serious were the problems encountered in dealing with the urgent demands of the Latin Americans for assistance in expanding their foreign trade. Although Japan and the European Common Market nations had, at the behest of the United States, adopted preferential tariff systems favorable to Latin American trade, the United States did not itself adopt such a system. In fact, because of domestic economic problems and protectionist sentiment in Congress, the administration had not even submitted to Congress the legislation which the Latin Americans desired. Latin Americans who had become increasingly disturbed by this lack of action became even more disturbed when in August—without previously consulting CIPA—President Nixon announced emergency economic measures which included a ten percent surcharge on all imports. Latin Americans, at a meeting of the Inter-American Economic and Social Council, demanded the removal of the surcharge on their products.

Events which occurred in Chile posed a further problem. Although the Nixon administration had not been pleased by the election to the presidency of Chile of Salvador Allende—a socialist supported by a coalition which included a strong Communist party—the two nations had continued to maintain satisfactory relations.

However, in October, 1971 the Chilean government announced that the major United States copper-mining companies whose Chilean properties had previously been expropriated would for all practical purposes remain uncompensated. When the United States suggested that Chile's action might impair its ability to secure future international financing of its development, it was accused of threatening Chile (Docs. 191, 192).

By this time United States-Latin American relations had deteriorated to the point where Assistant Secretary of State Charles A. Meyer felt it advisable to answer publicly the charge that the United States had no Latin American policy.

Nor did the situation improve in early 1972. Not only did Congress drastically reduce the president's foreign assistance budget, but it also showed itself still hostile to the idea of preferential tariffs for underdeveloped nations. The chief of the United States delegation to the second annual CIPA review of United States economic policies found it necessary to explain that because of strong protectionist sentiment in the United States, the administration did not feel the time to be ripe for submitting the desired tariff legislation to Congress (Doc. 196). At this point the question was whether the United States would find means for restoring harmonious relations with Latin America, or whether it would slide into another period of neglect and indifference with respect to its Latin neighbors in the Western Hemisphere.

Robert N. Burr
Los Angeles

August, 1972

THE UNITED STATES
AND LATIN AMERICA

1. Inter-American Conference on Problems of War and Peace, The Act of Chapultepec*

March 6, 1945

Whereas:

The peoples of the Americas, animated by a profound love of justice, remain sincerely devoted to the principles of international law;

It is their desire that such principles, notwithstanding the present difficult circumstances, prevail with even greater force in future international relations;

The inter-American conferences have repeatedly proclaimed certain fundamental principles, but these must be reaffirmed at a time when the juridicial bases of the community of nations are being re-established;

The new situation in the world makes more imperative than ever the union and solidarity of the American peoples, for the defense of their rights and the maintenance of international peace;

The American states have been incorporating in their international law, since 1890, by means of conventions, resolutions and declarations, the following principles:

a) The proscription of territorial conquest and the nonrecognition of all acquisitions made by force (First International Conference of American States, 1890);

b) The condemnation of intervention by one State in the internal or external affairs of another (Seventh International Conference of American States, 1933, and Inter-American Conference for the Maintenance of Peace, 1936);

c) The recognition that every war or threat of war affects directly or indirectly all civilized peoples, and endangers the great principles of liberty and justice which constitute the American ideal and the standard of American international policy (Inter-American Conference for the Maintenance of Peace, 1936);

d) The system of mutual consultation in order to find means of peaceful cooperation in the event of war or threat of war between American countries (Inter-American Conference for the Maintenance of Peace, 1936);

e) The recognition that every act susceptible of disturbing the peace of America affects each and every one of the American nations and justifies the initiation of the procedure of consultation (Inter-American Conference for the Maintenance of Peace, 1936);

f) The adoption of conciliation, unrestricted arbitration, or the application of international justice, in the solution of any difference or dispute between American nations, whatever its nature or origin (Inter-American Conference for the Maintenance of Peace, 1936);

g) The recognition that respect for the personality, sovereignty and independence of each American State constitutes the essence of international order sustained by continental solidarity, which historically has been expressed and sustained by declarations and treaties in force (Eighth International Conference of American States, 1938);

Report of the Delegation of the United States of America to the Inter-American Conference on Problems of War and Peace (Washington D.C., 1946), pp. 72-75.

h) The affirmation that respect for and the faithful observance of treaties constitute the indispensable rule for the development of peaceful relations between States, and that treaties can only be revised by agreement of the contracting parties (Declaration of American Principles, Eighth International Conference of American States, 1938);

i) The proclamation that, in case the peace, security or territorial integrity of any American republic is threatened by acts of any nature that may impair them, they proclaim their common concern and their determination to make effective their solidarity, coordinating their respective sovereign wills by means of the procedure of consultation, using the measures which in each case the circumstances may make advisable (Declaration of Lima, Eighth International Conference of American States, 1938);

j) The declaration that any attempt on the part of a non-American state against the integrity or inviolability of the territory, the sovereignty or the political independence of an American State shall be considered as an act of aggression against all the American States (Declaration XV of the Second Meeting of the Ministers of Foreign Affairs, Habana, 1940);

The furtherance of these principles, which the American States have constantly practised in order to assure peace and solidarity among the nations of the Continent, constitutes an effective means of contributing to the general system of world security and of facilitating its establishment;

The security and solidarity of the Continent are affected to the same extent by an act of aggression against any of the American States by a non-American State, as by an act of aggression of an American State against one or more American States;

Part I

The Governments Represented at the Inter-American Conference on Problems of War and Peace
Declare:

1. That all sovereign States are juridically equal among themselves.

2. That every State has the right to the respect of its individuality and independence, on the part of the other members of the international community.

3. That every attack of a State against the integrity or the inviolability of the territory, or against the sovereignty or political independence of an American State, shall, conformably to Part III hereof, be considered as an act of aggression against the other States which sign this Act. In any case invasion by armed forces of one State into the territory of another trespassing boundaries established by treaty and demarcated in accordance therewith shall constitute an act of aggression.

4. That in case acts of aggression occur or there are reasons to believe that an aggression is being prepared by any other State against the integrity or inviolability of the territory, or against the sovereignty or political independence of an American State, the States signatory to this Act will consult among themselves in order to agree upon the measures it may be advisable to take.

5. That during the war, and until the treaty recommended in Part II hereof is concluded, the signatories of this Act recognize that such threats and acts of aggression, as indicated in paragraphs 3 and 4 above, constitute an interference with the war

effort of the United Nations, calling for such procedures, within the scope of their
constitutional powers of a general nature and for war, as may be found necessary,
including: recall of chiefs of diplomatic missions; breaking of diplomatic relations;
breaking of consular relations; breaking of postal, telegraphic, telephonic, radio-
telephonic relations; interruption of economic, commercial and financial relations; use
of armed force to prevent or repel aggression.

6. That the principles and procedure contained in this Declaration shall become
effective immediately, inasmuch as any act of aggression or threat of aggression during
the present state of war interferes with the war effort of the United Nations to obtain
victory. Henceforth, and to the end that the principles and procedures herein stipulated shall conform with the constitutional processes of each Republic, the respective
Governments shall take the necessary steps to perfect this instrument in order that it
shall be in force at all times.

Part II

The Inter-American Conference on Problems of War and Peace
Recommends:

That for the purpose of meeting threats or acts of aggression against any American
Republic following the establishment of peace, the Governments of the American
Republics consider the conclusion, in accordance with their constitutional processes,
of a treaty establishing procedures whereby such threats or acts may be met by the
use, by all or some of the signatories of said treaty, of any one or more of the
following measures: recall of chiefs of diplomatic missions; breaking of diplomatic
relations; breaking of consular relations; breaking of postal, telegraphic, telephonic,
radio-telephonic relations; interruption of economic, commercial and financial relations; use of armed force to prevent or repel aggression.

Part III

The above Declaration and Recommendation constitute a regional arrangement for
dealing with such matters relating to the maintenance of international peace and
security as are appropriate for regional action in this Hemisphere. The said arrangement, and the pertinent activities and procedures, shall be consistent with the purposes
and principles of the general international organization, when established.

This agreement shall be known as the "ACT OF CHAPULTEPEC."

2. *Speech by Alberto Lleras Camargo, Colombian Delegate,
to the U.N. Conference on International Organization, on
the Inter-American System**

April 30, 1945

It is already easy to understand, from the addresses we have heard in the first few
days of the Conference, the spirit which moves us.

*United Nations Conference on International Organization, *Selected Documents* (Washington D.C.,
1945), pp. 326-31.

We are under the tremendous influence of the most devastating war which human-ity has ever endured. We sense the anxious vigilance of the soldiers and sailors of the United Nations, of our peoples, of the humble folk of the world, watching over each and every one of our acts and words. Fresh in our minds is the memory of—one might better say remorse for—the dismal failures of the prior world organization in the preservation of peace. For that very reason we are more realistic and far-seeing and, at the same time, we feel obliged to be more audacious in our experiments. We do not believe today, as in 1919, that this has been the last war; rather, we share the prudent fear that others may occur if we do not act here with care and energy. For the purpose of preventing another war we are prepared to subordinate sentiments, and even principles, which we deemed, and still deem, to be fundamental. We are ready to deposit part of our individual sovereignty as nations in the common treasury in order to build up capital against possible future aggressors.

Furthermore, with the aim of adjusting our conduct to reality, we have talked of international hierarchy more than at any previous conference. It almost seems as though none of us has used the word "nations" without explaining that there are large, middle-sized, and small nations. We have said that some have more responsibility and greater duties than the rest for the security of the world, and must consequently, be in possession of better means to comply with their responsibilities adequately. Juridical equality seems thus to be subordinated to political responsibility. We small nations well understand that otherwise the world organization would be feeble and we are ready to accept the fact that security, which is based on the force to be employed against the violators of international law, should be likewise a question of hierarchy in responsibility.

Nevertheless, I have thought that it would not be completely lacking in interest to present the point of view of an American nation, a small nation, of course, as to the possible agreements which may emerge from our deliberations. Colombia early entered into the fraternity of the United Nations. It has not been neutral in the war since December 1941. Like the other republics of the hemisphere, it declared its solidarity with the United States, attacked at Pearl Harbor. Its little Army, recruited from a people dedicated to the arts of peace, has not had the painful privilege of fighting at the side of the large armies. Its cities have not been bombarded, its women have not suffered the sad absence of their men under arms, its territory has not been invaded nor its people enslaved. It has offered but modest cooperation to the war effort of the United Nations, compared with the sacrifice of other countries, but it has given everything that has been asked of it. On the other hand, as is the case with any other republic of our continent, we can affirm without fear of contradiction that the peace and security of the world would have never been endangered by any conflict which originated in intrigues or machinations on the part of the American nations or through their foreign policy, nor has any person beyond the seas found any reason for anxiety in our political structure. It is true that there is no way of giving sufficient recognition to the spirit and sacrifice of the peoples who have fought the war to reestablish justice. But, in considering a world peace organization, it is well also to remember the importance in preserving peace, of the fact that there is a whole continent which has known how to maintain it and is, day by day, perfecting the rules of international law in order to apply them rigorously in the relations of its states among themselves, as well as with the other states of the globe.

Our contribution to the war has been of two sorts: one moral and inestimable, when we declared our solidarity with the United States at a moment when the outcome of the war was not only uncertain but seemed to indicate clearly the triumph of the powers of despotism. The other, strategic: when all of the American states formed a united front and established strict vigilance over the activities of the Axis in America, we discouraged any effort to breach the defenses—then still weak—which the United States was endeavoring to erect throughout the world to check the attacks of Germany and Japan. If there had been an opening in America for the pacific or military penetration of an enemy who at that time had the most ambitious of plans for world dominion, who can say that the course of the war would not have been longer or perhaps more doubtful?

But we do not wish to overestimate our role nor even that of the Latin American troops and the Latin American aviators who are fighting overseas. As a whole, we are a group of small nations from the military point of view. But peoples who are growing, like ours, do not have a static place in the international community and they should be thought of as a potential force, still undefined but capable of transforming themselves, as the United States did in a century, to a higher scale of development.

From another point of view, war comes closer to our shores as the world gets smaller through the expansion and growing rapidity of communications. It is not easy to understand why, as we become more actively and intensively linked to the western civilization from which we drew our language, our tradition, our religions, our culture, we should pay greater tribute to force and uncertainty, but we accept it as an inescapable fact. In the Napoleonic wars in the last century, which were also world wars, we took advantage of the European bedlam to obtain our independence. But in the first World War of this century some of us American states were belligerents and other neutrals. In the present war there was no neutrality nor could there be any. In the next one, if unfortunately there should be one, we would be unconditional belligerents and we are fully aware of the fact that the devastation and suffering which have been inflicted on most of the countries here represented would fall on all of the Americas, without exception, from pole to pole. Our concern with universal peace and security is, therefore, no less than that of those countries which have known insecurity and war in its most cruel manifestations. The countries of Latin America experienced violence and instability in a century and a half of domestic strife over the political principles to dominate in each state; if they hate war it is because they have undergone it; there is little difference between dying from a bayonet wound on an Andean plateau and being smashed by an ingenious robot bomb. But we have been able in general to banish war from our international relations. And we know full well that another world war, breaking out in another continent for whatever reason foreign to our direct interests, would still be our war. It is our unequivocal duty to sit with you to discuss the best means of making such a war impossible precisely because we are small, almost defenseless, countries as compared with the great powers but with an undeniable place in the front ranks of peace-loving nations, that is, of those nations who neither seek nor welcome wars and renounce them as an instrument of national policy.

The Dumbarton Oaks Proposals are based on an exact and practical evaluation of this truth; the small nations cannot guarantee the peace and security of the world; only the large ones can. We are all in agreement. But the basis for this truth lies in the fact that it is only the great powers which can menace the peace and security of the world. When, in the fall of 1944, the Dumbarton Oaks Proposals were discussed and approved it did not seem as clear as it does today that the three aggressor nations of the Axis would not again be in a position to attack for a long time, perhaps never. The mechanism set up in the draft Charter is influenced by the war effort against a definite enemy; it is and always will be sufficient to deal with that enemy. But is there any among us who believes that, when the capacity of Germany, Japan, and Italy is destroyed another war will be impossible? No. We are realists and we fear another war the source of which is absolutely unforeseeable. The mechanism should be effective for any war, against any aggressor. The pointing out of deficiencies in the Proposals which has taken place here is only the indirect expression of the fact that none of our governments believes that aggression can be banished from the world simply by the unconditional surrender of the present aggressors.

But Colombia, like the other countries of America which expressed their thought in the resolutions of Mexico City, has confidence in the will for peace of the United Nations, large and small, victorious in this war. It believes that, in general, the mechanism of Dumbarton Oaks assures a long peace but a provisional one. Colombia believes that the generation which waged the war, which led it and backed it, is capable of keeping the peace. But it also believes that this system is a compromise, as has been said here, between the realities of 1945 and the aspirations of humanity. No American state can think otherwise because the inter-American system, functioning, of course, in a less complex continent, is unquestionably more perfect. The inter-American system proscribes all violence, all acquisition of territory by force, all intervention or interference of one country in the internal affairs of another, all aggression and, furthermore, unequivocally defines the aggressor. Should the latter appear on the scene, the Pan American community would condemn it and apply sanctions by the democratic majority of its representative bodies; there is no privileged vote nor right of veto against such a decision. In accepting a different and less perfect system, we citizens of the Americas would not renounce our system; on the contrary, we would conserve the hope that the whole world might some day be ruled by the principles and procedures which have guaranteed peace, security, justice, and respect to all our nations and which have permitted us to live unarmed. But we are fully aware that if we did not join this world organization, inadequate and imperfect though it might be, we should not be contributing to the peace of the world and that, in any event, we should have to face any war which might break out beyond our hemisphere, through no fault or responsibility of ours.

It was with this criterion that we participated in good faith in the League of Nations. It may not be out of order to recall that the only two interventions of that organization which stand out as examples of efficiency took place in two cases centering in the Americas: In the conflict between Colombia and Peru, countries which submitted to the decision of the League and one of which had part of its territory administered by authorities of the League until the end of the incident, and the other, with less brilliant results, in the Chaco War.

But, so far as Colombia is concerned, it understands that no regional system like the inter-American one, or any other that might be established on a similar basis, can and should suffer any setback or detriment as long as, like ours, it shows that it is fully consistent with the aims of the general organization and, in addition, shows its efficacy in maintaining the peace and security of part of the world. The inter-American regional system is an old and excellent political institution and it was so recognized very clearly, although badly defined, by the Covenant of the League of Nations as the typical regional system. We citizens of the Americas will never ask for special privileges for our system and I believe that we all agree that, if there were three or four similar ones which guaranteed regional peace with the efficiency which ours has shown, great progress would be made toward permanent universal peace. The regional system must be coordinated with the sole world system and it cannot have different objectives than those of the world organization. But the regional methods, pacific and coercive, which the regional system may employ to guarantee peace or to prevent and punish aggression, so long as they are applied within the spirit of the procedures of the world organization and with the sole purpose of preserving a just peace and the rule of justice, should not be subject to the veto of a single nation if, as is the case with the Pan American system, this right of veto is not granted to any of the nations in the regional group. If there were to be an act of aggression in or against the Americas, all of the countries of the American system should come to the aid of the victim in accordance with our undertakings at Mexico. No nation of the Americas, still less if it were the aggressor, could veto the action taken to prevent or repulse the aggression. On the other hand, within the world organization, a nation foreign to the conflict could do so and arrest the action at any moment with only a single negative vote. Some of us of the American States have well-grounded fears that the presumption that the regional group would be in error and that, on the contrary, the state which has the right to paralyze the group's action cannot be wrong, is too forced a presumption to be a guarantee of peace, and would instead contribute to disorder.

It is clear that the defect lies in the voting procedure in the Security Council and not in the relations of the world organization and the regional one. But Colombia is prepared to concede that this voting procedure may be necessary to maintain the unstable equilibrium of another part of the world, destroyed by the barbarity of Nazism, which will enter once more, from now on, into a new experiment to try to find a solution for its age-old conflicts. In this part of the world, miraculously spared from catastrophe and miraculously stable, which has settled its territorial problems, which relies on perfected and respected public treaties, which consequently is in a position to ascertain who is the aggressor and when there is aggression, such a procedure might unleash war instead of assuring peace. In accord with its undertakings at Chapultepec, Colombia believes that if the system of voting in the Security Council be approved as recommended, because it is deemed necessary for the security of the world, autonomy of regional arrangements like the Inter-American one should be amplified so that its decisions could not be vetoed by a single nation in the Security Council.

I am well aware that the old nations whose beginnings and history are interwoven with the history and the beginnings of mankind may listen with certain explicable doubts to us of the American states when we proclaim our confidence in the juridical and political methods which we have adopted in the international field. Nevertheless, these doubts are not justified. In reality, we are only a young branch of the civilization of Christianity and of the West. There is nothing in our culture nor in the forms of our political and social life in which a man of the old world cannot recognize the basic roots, which are the nature or the will of his own forebears. However, through an understandable phenomenon, the great antitheses which were created in the political thought of the West were resolved without great struggles in American syntheses and in an atmosphere more favorable to the unlimited growth of man. The first clashes in modern times between democracy and autocracy took place in England; while the struggle continued fiercely and cruelly on the other side of the Atlantic, here, in the broad reaches of the British colonies the conflict was settled with marvelous ease. None of the concepts of international law which govern the relations of the peoples of this hemisphere can be termed a typically American creation. But how much effort, how many wars, how much pain, how much misery has it cost European civilization for centuries to implant a principle which, among us, is accepted at a Pan American meeting as a natural accord of wills without opposition from any important national interest? We are not, because of this, better or worse but only more fortunate. And we do not feel, nor shall we feel, it to be unjust or arbitrary that every time that the old hemisphere is shaken by a new conflict, caused by complications dating back through the centuries, the American continent should interest itself in its settlement, including the shedding of its blood. If classical civilization were to undergo a disaster, ours, which is identical, would be tied to its destiny. The short experience of America is that the past and present of Europe are the immediate future of America and not the reverse. Thus, we have the privilege of foretelling our destiny by reading the pages of the history of our civilization as it was unfolded on the other side of the ocean. We are not and should not be regionalists and we could not be, even if we wished. We speak today of the continent as of a unit, it is true, but this is for one reason: because we will not be able to say that the world is a unit until the task which we are beginning now, in San Francisco, becomes perfected and a long peace permits us to have a little more confidence in our capacity to make it a permanent one—without need for recourse to force.

But, Fellow Delegates, any explanation as to the feelings of America regarding the problems of the world is unnecessary. One by one, the representatives of all the nations meeting here have rendered tribute to the memory of Franklin Delano Roosevelt. Each one has found a special reason for affection, for admiration, for gratitude, interpretating the sorrow of his nation because Roosevelt was a friend of all the nations and the good neighbor of humanity. Franklin Delano Roosevelt was an American, the greatest of our times, the most American of all. We owe the development of our regional system to his generous, straightforward and fortunate policy as a true American but the old world owes him more, the victory of the United Nations, the liberation of many oppressed peoples and the peace which we must guard zealously at this Conference.

3. United Nations Charter, Excerpts Concerning Regional Arrangements*

June 26, 1945

CHAPTER VIII
REGIONAL ARRANGEMENTS

Article 52

1. Nothing in the present Charter precludes the existence of regional arrangements

---

*United Nations Conference on International Organization, *Selected Documents* (Washington D.C., 1945), p. 954.

or agencies for dealing with such matters relating to the maintenance of international peace and security as are appropriate for regional action, provided that such arrangements or agencies and their activities are consistent with the Purposes and Principles of the United Nations.

2. The Members of the United Nations entering into such arrangements or constituting such agencies shall make every effort to achieve pacific settlement of local disputes through such regional arrangements or by such regional agencies before referring them to the Security Council.

3. The Security Council shall encourage the development of pacific settlement of local disputes through such regional arrangements or by such regional agencies either on the initiative of the states concerned or by reference from the Security Council.

4. This Article in no way impairs the application of Articles 34 and 35.

Article 53

1. The Security Council shall, where appropriate, utilize such regional arrangements or agencies for enforcement action under its authority. But no enforcement action shall be taken under regional arrangements or by regional agencies without the authorization of the Security Council, with the exception of measures against any enemy state, as defined in paragraph 2 of this Article, provided for pursuant to Article 107 or in regional arrangements directed against renewal of aggressive policy on the part of any such state, until such time as the Organization may, on request of the Governments concerned, be charged with the responsibility for preventing further aggression by such a state.

2. The term enemy state as used in paragraph 1 of this Article applies to any state which during the Second World War has been an enemy of any signatory of the present Charter.

Article 54

The Security Council shall at all times be kept fully informed of activities undertaken or in contemplation under regional arrangements or by regional agencies for the maintenance of international peace and security.

4. Suggestion by Dean Acheson, Acting Secretary of State, on Postponement of the Inter-American Conference for Maintenance of Peace and Security *

October 3, 1945

In view of recent developments in Argentina, the United States Government does not feel that it can properly negotiate or sign with the present Argentine regime a treaty of military assistance. Since the conference to be convened in Rio de Janeiro on October 20 is exclusively for the purpose of negotiating such a treaty, this Government has communicated with the host Government of Brazil suggesting that that

*Department of State Bulletin, Oct. 7, 1945, p. 552.

conference be postponed but emphasizing that, in view of the great importance which this Government attaches to the negotiation of such a treaty, it has urged that negotiations proceed as rapidly as possible to the end of concluding and signing such a treaty in Rio de Janeiro at the earliest possible moment.

5. Note from Alberto Rodríguez Larreta, Foreign Minister of Uruguay, to the Governments of the American Republics on Collective Intervention *

November 22, 1945

In the note of this Ministry under date of October 19, I stated that the "parallelism between democracy and peace must constitute a strict rule of action in inter-American policy." And I added that the highest respect for the principle of non-intervention by a state in the affairs of another, a principle established during the last decade, does not shield without limitation "the notorious and repeated violation by any republic of the elementary rights of man and of the citizen, nor the non-fulfilment of obligations freely contracted by a state with respect to its external and internal duties and which entitle it to be an active member of the international community."

I

This Ministry is deeply aware of the urgent need of developing these concepts, and of proposing to the American governments an exchange of views in an effort to arrive at formulas and solutions that will bring into concrete reality this sense of right which is so firmly held in the Americas. If before the war the interdependence of democracy and peace was a recognized concept in inter-American relations, that concept has, since the terrible experience of the war, acquired the force of an absolute truth.

At the Conference for the Maintenance of Peace held in Buenos Aires in 1936, President Roosevelt said:

> First, it is our duty by every honorable means to prevent any future war among ourselves. This can best be done through the strengthening of the processes of constitutional democratic government—to make these processes conform to the modern need for unity and efficiency and, at the same time, preserve the individual liberties of our citizens. By so doing, the people of our nations, unlike the people of many nations who live under other forms of government, can and will insist on their intention to live in peace. Thus will democratic government be justified throughout the world."

Since the representatives of the other American republics assembled at Buenos Aires unanimously shared these basic principles, there was proclaimed "the existence of a solidary democracy in America."

At every inter-American meeting held since that time, identical concepts have been stated.

In Panama, in 1939, it was said that—

> "On more than one occasion the American Republics have affirmed their adherence to the democratic ideal which prevails in this Hemisphere;

Department of State Bulletin, Nov. 25, 1945, pp. 864-68.

"This ideal may be endangered by the action of foreign ideologies inspired in diametrically opposite principles; and

"It is advisable, consequently, to protect the integrity of this ideal through the adoption of appropriate measures."

In Habana, in 1940, resolution VII refers to the "Diffusion of Doctrines Tending to Place in Jeopardy the Common Inter-American Democratic Ideal or To Threaten the Security and Neutrality of the American Republics," and recommends a series of measures against propaganda originating abroad or carried out by foreign elements within the republics of the continent.

In Rio de Janeiro, 1942, measures intended to "prevent or punish as crimes, acts against democratic institutions" were confirmed and strengthened.

II

In March 1945, at the Conference of Mexico City the American republics, still under the impact of the tragic experience of a war which had already lasted five years, gave vital force and meaning to these concepts in numerous declarations. In resolution VII the American republics "affirmed their adherence to the democratic ideal," and declared that "it is desirable to safeguard this ideal" and that "the dissemination of totalitarian doctrines in this Continent would endanger the American democratic ideal."

The Declaration of Mexico (resolution XI) confirmed these concepts and sought to give them force and effect throughout the continent, by proclaiming: "The purpose of the State is the happiness of man in society. The interests of the community should be harmonized with the rights of the individual. The American man cannot conceive of living without justice, *just as he cannot conceive of living without liberty*."

And in resolution XL on International Protection of the Essential Rights of Man it was resolved, "To proclaim the adherence of the American Republics to the principles established by international law for safeguarding the essential rights of man, and to declare their support of a system of international protection of these rights."

It is highly important to note that these concepts are extended to protect the individual as such in his essential rights, and that the necessity of a system of international protection of those rights is proclaimed.

III

The Conferences of Mexico City and San Francisco, which took place at the close of this war, gave a still firmer and more definite proof of the common determination to make effective, to any necessary extent, the defense of the democratic ideal and of the individual, as the essential objective. Thus the nations became bound, not only by international duties but also by internal duties having an international effect. The persistent and repeated violation of the essential rights of man and of the citizen affects both the American and the international sense of justice. (Introductions articles 1, 2, 13, 55, 62, 68, etc., of the Charter of the United Nations.)

And as a sanction against the violation of such principles, article 6 provided that: "A member of the United Nations which has persistently violated the Principles contained in the present Charter *may be expelled from the Organization by the General Assembly upon the recommendation of the Security Council.*"

IV

The repeated violation of such rules is not only disastrous in itself, but sooner or later produces grave international repercussions. A nazi-fascist regime, acting through its characteristic methods, attacks the rights of man and of the citizen, develops the ideology of force, creates false notions of superiority and is a fatal ferment for future external conflicts. It is a system which, prompted by the instinct of self-preservation in an environment which is hostile to it, must spread out in order to survive. Its will to endure forces it, in times of crisis, toward international conflict, in the hope of filling out its weakened ranks through a wave of patriotism. It is, furthermore, a system which seeks to spread contagion and which tends thereto by the very potency of the virus which it injects into the social organism.

Hence it was that in Mexico and in San Francisco, new international concepts were brought into being to meet this danger. The maintenance of these concepts was deemed indispensable if the plans prepared for the preservation of peace and security are to be effective.

V

The principle of non-intervention by one State in the affairs of another, in the field of inter-American relations, constitutes in itself a great advance achieved during the last decade; this principle was inspired by noble and just claims. We must maintain and affirm that principle whenever the need arises. It must, however, be harmonized with other principles the operation of which is of fundamental importance for the preservation of international peace and security.

First there is the principle which I have defined as the "parallelism between peace and democracy." Second, there is the conviction acquired through tragic experience, that "peace is indivisible," that is, that conflicts cannot be isolated or continue indefinitely, without serious danger, as centers of disturbance, in a world devoted to work and the pursuit of well-being. Such disturbance will, in the long run, be fatal to the peaceful world which we desire. Finally, there is the principle of the defense of the elementary human liberties—of the four freedoms of Roosevelt, of the minimum human liberties within a civilized continent—wherever they are notoriously and persistently infringed or ignored.

It is not difficult to harmonize such principles. "Non-intervention" cannot be converted into a right to invoke one principle in order to be able to violate all other principles with immunity. Therefore a multilateral collective action, exercised with complete unselfishness by all the other republics of the continent, aimed at achieving in a spirit of brotherly prudence the mere reestablishment of essential rights, and directed toward the fulfillment of freely contracted juridical obligations, must not be held to injure the government affected, but rather it must be recognized as being taken for the benefit of all, including the country which has been suffering under such a harsh regime.

It is pertinent to recall that when the principle of non-intervention was being most firmly defended and obtained its full recognition, multilateral action, exercised under the conditions and with the aims stated above, was not prohibited. That was the Uruguayan thesis at Habana in 1928. In 1933, at Montevideo, and at Buenos Aires, in 1936, it was clearly specified that it is the action of one state against another state, of one party against another, which is prohibited, the text of the two conferences emphasizing the individual, and therefore presumptively selfish, character of the action condemned. "It is declared that the intervention of any *one* of them in the affairs of another is inadmissible." (Article 1 of the additional Protocol of 1936.) "No state has the right to intervene in the internal or external affairs of another." (Convention on Rights and Duties of States, Montevideo, December 1933.)

Principles to which the war has restored all their vital force and whose operation is indispensable to the creation of a better world, do not conflict therefore with this rule [of non-intervention] and the latter would, in any event, remain unchanged.

The free and harmonious working of these principles must be effected on the basis that "non-intervention" is not a shield behind which crime may be perpetrated, law many be violated, agents and forces of the Axis may be sheltered, and binding obligations may be circumvented.

Otherwise, at the very time when, since Mexico and after San Francisco, we should be creating a new international and humanitarian conception, we would find ourselves tolerating a doctrine capable of frustrating and destroying that very conception.

VI

The views set forth above are far from constituting an innovation. They respond to the demand of the peoples, the platforms of political parties, and to the judgment of those organizations and institutions which are devoted to the study of juridical and political problems. They echo the views of the free press, and the insistent plea of the young generations which do not wish to be defrauded again.

Its only novelty consists in being expressed in a diplomatic document, which many would prefer devoid of any sentiment, and in the fact that the need is stressed for transforming into realities—whenever circumstances require—oft repeated and pro-claimed principles and standards.

These concepts, the observance of which, since the war, has acquired the nature of a "state of necessity" in the judgment of civilized man, have not come into being by chance, or in vain. The American republics have, in this respect, a responsibility for leadership, which has been and must continue to be their role in the task of building a free and peaceful world. Our continent is today the hope of the peoples of the world for a better life. Pusillanimity or unenlightened selfishness may counsel a passive attitude, but the result would then be that the mission of the Americas would transform itself into that of making our continent a refuge for evil doctrines, practices, and interests and into a field favorable to their future rebirth.

This Ministry is certain that no people and no government of the continent wishes such a sad fate for America. And it is in this certainty that it takes the liberty of addressing itself to Your Chancellery, and submitting that, in view of notorious events, there is a need for a collective multilateral pronouncement, using for that purpose some of the means already counseled; either by means of an advisory committee [Comisión dictaminante] or by an express consultation, or by including the subject in the proposed Conference of Rio de Janeiro.

6. *Address by Spruille Braden, Assistant Secretary of State,*
   on "Our Foreign Policy and Its Underlying Principles
   and·Ideals"*

February 13, 1946

Let us examine the principles which guide our foreign relations and the basic policies which result therefrom. Also what are the general applications and expressions we give to those policies?

It goes without saying that the first duty of our Government, and consequently its most fundamental policy, must be to protect and promote the interests of the United States, of the people who make up the United States. There is nothing cynical or sinister about this practical policy. For one thing, we know now, if we never knew it before, that our national welfare, far from being in conflict with the welfare of the other nations, must be coordinate with it. It is not as if there were just so much welfare to be had in the world, so that the more we enjoy the less there is left for others. On the contrary, we shall prosper in the long run only as the world prospers. Our policy of self-interest, if it is in a sense selfish, must also be altruistic and our interests always legitimate. It must be a policy, if you will permit me to say so, of altruistic as well as legitimate self-interest.

Secondly, we recognize—to use a homely phrase—that honesty is not only the best—it is the only sane policy. Unless we are consistently honest we will not be trusted in the world, and we will have little influence where we are not trusted. Unless what we say can be and is believed, what we say will have little weight with other nations. The strength and effectiveness of a nation resides as much in its honorable character and reputation as in the number of guns it has available. I may say here, by way of example, that the mediation of the Chaco dispute would never have succeeded if the parties to it had had any reason to mistrust the honesty and impartiality of the mediators. It is perfectly clear that we must hew to the line of honesty and absolute good faith if we, as one of the great nations of the world, are to discharge in the atomic age our responsibilities to ourselves and to mankind. It must be our basic policy to work for the permanent establishment in international relations of those principles of morality and religion that we uphold in our domestic relations. The alternative is not to be contemplated.

Thirdly, we must take full account in our international relations of the political and social principles upon which this nation was founded, enunciated in our Declaration of Independence and in our Constitution, including the Bill of Rights. The day has passed when we can remain unconcerned at slavery and tyranny outside our borders. With the advances that have been made in technology, the contacts between nations are more numerous, more frequent, more critical. The affairs of nations have become so mutually interrelated and entwined in good times and so entangled and embroiled in

**Department of State Bulletin*, Feb. 24, 1946, pp. 294-97.

bad times that we must increasingly regard the international community as a whole. We should apply to the whole world the dictum applied by Abraham Lincoln to our own union of States: that it cannot endure half slave and half free. Consequently, as a matter of self-preservation and the survival of the principles for which we stand, while we do not undertake to impose our system of government on others, we must necessarily feel a greater and more active friendship for those governments that rest on the freely and periodically expressed will of the governed than for governments that depend for their existence on a denial of such popular expression.

These three fundamental and guiding principles that govern our international relations have found their expression in certain broad policies to which this nation has explicitly and consistently committed itself.

First among these, in the historical order, is the Monroe Doctrine, enunciated by President Monroe in 1823, when he declared: (1) that the American Continents were not to be considered as subjects for future colonization by any European power; and (2) that the United States would consider any attempt on the part of those powers to extend their political system to any portions of this hemisphere as dangerous to our peace and safety. Thus the United States warned the overseas powers against any attempted acquisition of territory in the New World, and likewise against any attempt at propagating their autocratic political system in the soil of the New World. While to begin with we lacked the power to enforce the Monroe Doctrine and at times we may have allowed ourselves temporarily to pervert it, on net balance our record compares favorably with that of any other nation and for some years past the Doctrine has meant what it was originally intended to mean. It is a national protective doctrine that in no way injures or threatens the legitimate interests of any other nation. Its essential character and high purpose have been implicitly recognized by the American republics generally, which at Habana in 1940, at Rio de Janeiro in 1942, and on other occasions have joined in their determination that this hemisphere shall be defended against such territorial ambitions or such attempts at the imposition of undemocratic political systems as have been manifested by aggressor nations overseas. Thus the Monroe Doctrine, while it continues to represent the unilateral policy of the United States, is in complete harmony with the joint, multilateral policy adopted by the American republics and expressed in the inter-American system.

This hemisphere need no longer fear any attempt from overseas at territorial conquest or colonization. But we must remain fully alert to prevent the infiltration of any foreign system or theory of government.

Secondly, in keeping with our determination to govern our international relations by our basic national principles and ethical tenets, we have developed and given expression to the policy of the good neighbor. Like the Monroe Doctrine, this policy has on occasion been misinterpreted or only partially understood. It is not, for example, a policy of purchasing friendship by spending money abroad. As originally enunciated by President Roosevelt in his first inaugural address, it is the policy of "the neighbor who resolutely respects himself, and, because he does so, respects the rights of others—the neighbor who respects his obligations and respects the sanctity of agreements in and with a world of neighbors." I call your attention to the fact that the root of this policy is *self-respect* and the trunk which grows out of it is *mutual respect*. From this trunk, in turn, grow the branches and the fruits of international collaboration. In other words, the premise of collaboration under the good-neighbor policy is that the collaborating nations respect one another because they are themselves, in the deepest meaning of the terms, respectable and self-respecting. The policy of the good neighbor inevitably implies a community of good neighbors, self-respecting neighbors. Consequently, it is a matter of the utmost gratification that the American republics have adopted the policy as a common one and have, in the great majority of cases, lived up to its high standards. Inherently a part of the good-neighbor policy is this country's policy and its obligation to refrain from intervening in the internal or external affairs of any other American state. There was a time when it was considered that in the absence of a competent international authority, an authority representing the community of nations, a state had the right to intervene in the affairs of its neighbors for the purpose of protecting its just interests. One trouble with this doctrine was that, in practice, it enabled the strong, on their own account, to judge in their own cause and to enforce judgment in their own cause against the weak. Under this doctrine, while any other American republic might have as much right to intervene in the affairs of the United States as the United States had to intervene in its affairs, it did not, like the United States, have the power to exercise such a right. The conscience of the United States, as of the other American republics, was in the long run unwilling to accept a right of unilateral intervention that, in the nature of things, was bound to frustrate an even-handed justice. In our domestic affairs, except in cases of self-defense, a citizen must appeal to the authority of the community for the enforcement of justice against his neighbor, but he cannot be allowed to practice such enforcement for himself and by himself. Consequently, even if we were not committed as we are to refrain from unilateral intervention, such intervention would still be obnoxious to us as being contrary to the principles of equity that we wish to see established in the world. One of the clear principles underlying the United Nations Organization is that the international enforcement of justice is a prerogative of the international community, not of any individual member thereof.

The United States recognizes that the preponderance of its power in the inter-American community of nations imposes on it a special responsibility to exercise the most scrupulous restraint, to lean over backward—so to speak—in honoring its policy and obligation with respect to non-intervention. It is clear that, since we are bound to be engaged in continuous transactions and intimate contacts with our fellow American republics—since we all live in the same continental abode—whatever we refrain from saying and whatever we refrain from doing may constitute intervention no less than what we do or say. The carrying on of ordinary diplomatic relations and their amenities with another government may, in default of some positive and explicit indication from us, be taken as approval and encouragement of that government's policy, and thus may constitute intervention in favor of that government's policy. Therefore, as I have so repeatedly stated, we must be scrupulous to avoid intervention by action and by inaction alike.

I would be giving a very partial and thus misleading picture of this Government's broad policy if I did not emphasize its positive aspects. We, the United States, represent certain explicit ideals and principles that we have defended at a terrible cost in life and treasure on the battlefields of the world, and that we are determined shall be realized, by every legitimate means in our power, throughout the world. These positive ideals, these objectives, these principles have been given clear and eloquent expression in the United Nations Charter and in the 12 points of foreign policy set forth by President Truman in his speech of October 27, 1945. They are the principles of democracy itself, and thus represent an acceptance in the international sphere of the basic principles embodied in our Declaration of Independence and Constitution. They form the common basis on which the American republics have associated themselves, and without which their association could not exist. They are our common ground. That is why, when any American government, in contravention of its commitments and the aspirations of its own people, violates those principles, it attacks the very foundation of the inter-American system.

I shall not enumerate these principles here. Let me emphasize, however, that they are all expressions of our regard for the inviolable dignity of the human individual, by virtue of which we conceive governments to be instruments devised by the people for the protection of their basic human rights and the enhancement of opportunities for the exercise of those rights. Consequently, in the most fundamental sense, no government that denies those rights and uses force to prevent their expression can be considered in our eyes to be a legitimate, and thus a respectable, government. Our own conscience demands that we make as clear a distinction as possible between, on the one hand, the legitimate governments "deriving their just power from the consent of the governed," and, on the other hand, those governments which usurp power from the people.

*　　　　　　*　　　　　　*

Within the framework of these broad principles and policies, we have certain specific policies bearing on particular situations and adjusted to meet those situations.

I have already indicated that the good-neighbor policy, based on mutual respect between self-respecting nations, is expressed through collaboration and mutual assistance. It is thus our policy to give active help to our fellow American republics in their efforts to raise their standards of living, of education, and of health. We recognize that in doing this we are, in actuality, contributing to our own well-being. Here is a concrete instance of what I have called altruistic self-interest. For by helping to raise these standards in the other American republics we are strengthening the foundations of our own security by providing the essential conditions of orderly and democratic government among our neighbors, and we are also strengthening ourselves economically by building better markets for our own products.

*　　　　　　*　　　　　　*

Our cooperation is not confined, however, to the general economic front. The American republics aspire to a continuing social and cultural advancement, all the aspects of which are inevitably interconnected and in a large degree interdependent. By our active programs for the exchange of books, students, and teachers with the other American republics, we are constantly strengthening the foundations of democracy in the hemisphere and promoting peace through mutual understanding. We are thus helping one another to progress on all fronts for our common benefit.

In short, the community of American nations is trying, through cooperative effort, to establish a workable system of peace, security, and prosperity. It is a system that does not in the least threaten legitimate national interests anywhere else in the world.

On the contrary, to the extent that it is successful it provides an area of order and progress, of freedom under law, that contributes effectively to international stability and the realization throughout the world of those ultimate objectives proclaimed by all the great religions of mankind.

In this lies our hope. For the atomic bomb and the other terrible and devastating implements now in our hands are dangerous only in so far as men use them dangerously. Let us make no mistake about it. The atomic bomb is not a problem in itself. It merely aggravates an old moral problem, which is the problem of man himself.

7. Excerpts from a State Department Memorandum on the Argentine Situation*

February 24, 1946

PART I: INTRODUCTORY STATEMENT

I

On October 3, 1945 the Department of State initiated consultation among the American republics with respect to the Argentine situation. All of the other American republics agreed to participate in this consultation.

During the intervening period, this Government has made a careful study and evaluation of all the information in its possession with regard to Argentina. An enormous volume of documents of the defeated enemy, in many cases found only with much difficulty and after prolonged search, have now been studied and verified. German and Italian officials charged with responsibility for activities in and with Argentina have been interrogated. Although this work of investigation continues, the Government of the United States at present has information which establishes that:

1. Members of the military government collaborated with enemy agents for important espionage and other purposes damaging to the war effort of the United Nations.

2. Nazi leaders, groups and organizations have combined with Argentine totalitarian groups to create a Nazi-Fascist state.

3. Members of the military regime who have controlled the government since June, 1943 conspired with the enemy to undermine governments in neighboring countries in order to destroy their collaboration with the Allies and in an effort to align them in a pro-Axis bloc.

4. Successive Argentine governments protected the enemy in economic matters in order to preserve Axis industrial and commercial power in Argentina.

5. Successive Argentine governments conspired with the enemy to obtain arms from Germany.

This information warrants the following conclusions:

1. The Castillo Government and still more the present military regime pursued a policy of positive aid to the enemy.

2. Solemn pledges to cooperate with the other American republics were completely breached and are proved to have been designed to protect and maintain Axis interests in Argentina.

*Department of State Bulletin, Feb. 24, 1946, pp. 285-89.

3. The policies and actions of the recent regimes in Argentina were aimed at undermining the Inter-American System.

4. The totalitarian individuals and groups, both military and civilian, who control the present government in Argentina, have, with their Nazi collaborators, pursued a common aim: The creation in this Hemisphere of a totalitarian state. This aim has already been partly accomplished.

5. Increasingly since the invasion of Normandy, and most obviously since the failure of the last German counteroffensive in January, 1945, the military regime has had to resort to a defensive strategy of camouflage. The assumption of the obligations of the Inter-American Conference on Problems of War and Peace to wipe out Nazi influence and the repeated avowals of pro-democratic intentions proceeded from this strategy of deception.

6. By its brutal use of force and terrorist methods to strike down all opposition from the Argentine people the military regime has made a mockery of its pledge to the United Nations "to reaffirm faith in human rights, in the dignity and worth of the human person."

II

Prior to the Inter-American Conference on Problems of War and Peace, twenty American republics concluded unanimously that the Argentine Government had not collaborated in the war effort and could not therefore properly participate in the Conference. At the conclusion of the meeting, they deplored the fact that "the circumstances existing before the meeting have undergone no change that would have justified the Conference in taking steps to re-establish continental unity." No more clear-cut judgment has ever been rendered by a community of nations with regard to the conduct of the *government* of one of its members. And lest its judgment be misconstrued, the Conference carefully distinguished—as we must distinguish today—between the people of Argentina and the ruling regime: "the unity of the peoples of America is indivisible . . . the Argentine nation is and always has been an integral part of the union of the American republics."

It was in large measure a response to this spirit of unity among the peoples of the American republics and a response to that faith which animates the inter-American system, which prompted the American republics once again to accept the pledged word of the Farrell-Perón Government.

By its adherence to the Final Act of the Mexico Conference, the Farrell regime took a necessary step to qualify for participation in the treaty contemplated by Part II of the Act of Chapultepec. But enjoyment of the benefits of the Act of Chapultepec, as well as of other rights under the Final Act of the Conference, was conditioned upon good faith by the Farrell Government both in the assumption and in the execution of the agreements and declarations approved by the Conference.

Recognition of the Farrell regime and admission to the United Nations Organization were not based on a finding that the regime had satisfied its obligations. Recognition and admission to the United Nations Organization were based on an undertaking by the Farrell Government to comply with the agreements of the Mexico Conference. As stated on May 28, 1945 by Secretary of State Stettinius, Chairman of this Government's delegation both at Mexico City and at San Francisco:

"By voting to admit Argentina in these circumstances, the United States, . . . has by no means changed its position that Argentina is expected to carry out effectively all of her commitments under the Mexico City Declarations. On the contrary, we consider that her admission to the San Francisco Conference increases her obligation to do so. We expect the Argentine nation to see that this obligation is fulfilled."

Several months later the Assistant Secretary of State in charge of American Republic Affairs and the alternate delegate of the United States to the Mexico City Conference, Mr. Nelson Rockefeller, declared:

"This record shows that while steps have been taken toward carrying out the commitments there are many important failures which have serious implications. Too often steps have been begun or promised and not carried through to completion. The fact remains that many vital commitments in which Argentina joined with her American Neighbors still remain unfulfilled by her Government."

The acceptance of the pledged word of the Farrell Government repeated a process in which the American republics, in a spirit of genuine good will towards the Argentine people, had patiently participated during four years of war. From shortly after Pearl Harbor until the unconditional surrender of the enemy, successive Argentine governments had coupled assertions of full compliance with solemn promises of future performance. This record, in itself, demonstrated insincerity and would strongly have supported a charge of deliberate deception. Today we *know* the reasons for the important failures, the apparent reluctance, the unfilled vital commitments, the promises to keep promises. Behind the record of broken promises and repeated pledges of cooperation we have proof positive of complicity with the enemy.

This complicity compels us to doubt the motive, the plan and purpose of every act of the present Argentine regime. Such lack of trust will not be cured by decrees or administrative orders, by signatures to charters or by adherence to final acts of conferences. It can be cured only when our brother people of Argentina are represented by a government which inspires full faith and confidence at home and abroad.

III

The information in support of these charges is respectfully submitted to the Governments of the American republics for their consideration in relation to the Treaty of Mutual Assistance to be negotiated at the forthcoming conference at Rio de Janeiro.

By its terms the Act of Chapultepec lays the basis for a mutual assistance pact which will obligate the member governments to assist one another to meet an attack or a threat of aggression from any source whatsoever. Furthermore, pursuant to Resolution IV of the Conference on Problems of War and Peace, the pact would be implemented by the creation of a permanent military agency which would be charged with the preparation of proposals for a closer military collaboration among the republics. This implementation would require a close cooperation in the development of security plans of vital importance to every American republic. It would also require cooperation in the maintenance of adequate military establishments for the defense of the continent.

Such a defense structure can be built only on a foundation of absolute trust and confidence. Because the Government of the United States did not have such trust and confidence in the present Argentine regime, it took the position in October, 1945 that it could not properly sign a military assistance treaty with that regime.

It is submitted that the information transmitted to the Governments of the American republics in this memorandum makes abundantly clear a pattern which includes aid to the enemy, deliberate misrepresentation and deception in promises of Hemisphere cooperation, subversive activity against neighboring republics, and a vicious partnership of Nazi and native totalitarian forces. This pattern raises a deeper and more fundamental question than that of the adequacy of decrees and administrative measures allegedly enacted in compliance with Argentina's obligations under Resolution LIX of the Mexico Conference. The question is whether the military regime, or any Argentine government controlled by the same elements, can merit the confidence and trust which is expressed in a treaty of mutual military assistance among the American republics.

The early sections of this memorandum demonstrate conclusively that "the totalitarian machine in Argentina is a partnership of German Nazi interests with a powerful coalition of active Argentine totalitarian elements, both military and civilian."

Part II produces specific and documentary evidence of Argentine-Nazi Complicity, declaring that the
basic source of this complicity consists of the preference for an Axis victory which those individuals who have held the powers of government in Argentina throughout this whole period have (except for its disclosure to Nazi Germany) secretly entertained. . . .

*   *   *

In May 1942, acting President Castillo frankly conveyed to Germany through authorized channels that he believed in and hoped for "the victory of the Axis Powers"; that he had "based his policy upon that" desired result; and that, rather than sever relations with the Axis, he had determined, if necessary, "eventually to come out openly on the side of the Axis powers." Those who seized the reins of power in June 1943 shared this attachment even more deeply and implemented it in many ways more fully described below.

The consequence of this basic choice between the forces of fascism and of democracy was an intimate and integrated pattern of mutual understandings, cooperation, and assistance begun in the days of Castillo and carried forward and completed under the present military regime until it embraced every significant sphere of interest in Argentine-German relations:

Simply stated, the basic accord of which all these ramifications were but details was that those governing Argentina sought from Nazi Germany the military and political support for Argentina's policy of isolation not elsewhere obtainable, and the Nazis obtained freedom from any action tending materially to interfere with their operations or prejudice their interests in Argentina, both during and after the war. The growth, perfection, and implementation of this conspiracy is hereinafter described, under topical headings corresponding to these various areas of interest.

Argentina's effort "to procure military assistance from Germany" is pointed out as "One of the most striking areas of such collaboration."

After the military *coup d'etat* of June 1943, the Ramirez regime immediately resumed these negotiations, assuring the Nazis of their purpose not to break relations and of their need for military equipment to reinforce them in this position. When these requests were advanced, the Ramirez regime referred also to the plan of subversion against neighboring countries which it had determined to set in motion. These negotiations continued throughout the summer of 1943, and culminated in October 1943 in the ill-starred Hellmuth mission. In this affair, the Argentine Government and Himmler's secret intelligence (Sicherheitsdienst) agents in Argentina selected Osmar Hellmuth, an Argentine national, as their common representative to enter into broad négotiations with the German Government in Berlin, not only for arms, but for many other types of mutual assistance. This mission failed, but only because of Hellmuth's arrest *en route* by the Allies.

Upon the basis of these various negotiations and conferences, the German Government understood at the time of Hellmuth's departure that his mission was designed to accomplish the following objectives:

One
Assure Germany that Argentina had no intention of breaking relations.

Two
To arrange a safe-conduct for the Buenos Aires.

Three
To negotiate regarding arms and other war material.

Four
To arrange for shipment to Argentina of German armaments technicians.

Five
To arrange for replacement of the Argentine Chargé d'Affaires in Berlin, Herr Luti, who was not pro-Nazi and therefore trusted neither by the Argentines nor by the SD.

Six
To discuss other matters of mutual interest (e.g., exchange of information between the two governments with the help of the SD).

Argentina disclosed to the Nazi Government another scheme to defend its pro-Axis policy: the "essence of this scheme was the undermining and subversion of pro-Allied Governments in neighboring countries and to draw them into a pro-Axis 'bloc' headed by Argentina." A common plan was "activated with respect to Bolivia, Brazil, Chile, Paraguay, and Uruguay." In each of those countries Argentine–SD collaboration with domestic pro-Axis forces was "pressed forward, under guidance and with aid, or promises of it, from the Argentine military government." During the Ramirez regime Col. Juan D. Perón, Chief of the Secretariat of the Argentine War Ministry, was the principal leader of the Argentine conspirators.

In the section devoted to Argentina's political and social collaboration with the Nazi Government, evidence is produced of Argentine aid and protection of Axis espionage throughout the American republics, of the "devotion" of the Argentine confidential agents and intermediaries to the Axis cause which is established by later reports from Erich Otto Meynen, the German Chargé d'Affaires with the rank of Minister in Argentina during President Castillo's regime, which stated that " 'effective execution of our political tasks is contingent upon the ever-heightened effort among our political friends.' "

Other examples of Argentina's complicity with the Nazis are cited in this part of the memorandum: Argentine failure to repatriate Nazi agents; that country's protection and assistance to pro-Axis press and manipulation of public opinion; the protection of Nazi schools and organizations; and Argentine preservation of Nazi economic power in its failure to control Axis firms and in its transmission of funds for the Nazi Embassy.

Part III, Nazi-Fascist Character of the Argentine Regime, is analyzed briefly as follows:

General Analysis

The internal administration of the military regime has passed through two phases. In the first phase, which continued from the accession to power until roughly the end of 1944, the military rulers of Argentina clearly revealed a Fascist-totalitarian mentality both in their public statements and in their public acts. Their efforts to organize and consolidate their revolutionary regime paralleled those made earlier by the rising dictators of Italy, Germany, and Spain. They set out to create a Fascist state in the Western Hemisphere, openly anti-democratic and authoritarian both in its basic ideology and in its operation. Following Nazi-Fascist-Falange methods they suppressed individual liberties, liquidated democratic institutions, persecuted their opponents by terroristic methods, created a state propaganda machine for the dissemination of Nazi-Fascist ideals, established a "corporate" labor organization subservient to the government, and adopted a program of military and naval expansion obviously out of all proportion with the requirements of the country's security. They dissolved the national Congress, outlawed all political parties, and successfully resisted all pressure to hold national elections. During this period the Argentine authorities arbitrarily interfered with the independence of the courts and through the appointment of special Federal officials, thwarted the normal development of the judicial and educational systems, and of labor. Federal appointees replaced the normally elected provincial authorities, and were also used to control universities and labor organizations.

Certain policies and acts of an outstandingly totalitarian character have continued to form an integral part of the program of the Argentine Government from June 1943 to the present. These include the suppression of individual liberties, police repression and terrorism, and the corporate organization of labor. On the other hand, from roughly the eve of the Mexico City Conference on Problems of War and Peace (February 21–March 8, 1945) to the present, while the Argentine authorities were trying first to win recognition from the other American republics, then to gain a seat at the United Nations Conference in San Francisco, and finally to establish their claim to the full confidence of the other American republics, they have ostensibly followed a less ardently Fascist policy.

The fact is that this opportunistic "change" of policy to the second phase came only after the failure of the last German counteroffensive in early January 1945, when the inevitability of the Nazi defeat became obvious to all. It having become apparent that the program and ideals, which the military rulers were trying to impose upon the nation, were suffering defeat in Europe and in the Pacific at the hands of the United Nations, the Farrell Government began to modify its policy to one of defensive camouflage whose principal characteristic was avowal of pro-democratic intentions. Officials of the Government became less outspokenly pro-Axis and Fascist-totalitarian in their public statements. The purpose has been obvious: to conceal and preserve a nucleus of Fascist-totalitarian economic and political positions with sufficient strength to serve as a basis for reversion to the earlier program at some better future opportunity. Acting always and only under pressure either from democratic elements within Argentina or from abroad, the leaders of the military government qualified those policies which were most conspicuously Fascist-totalitarian and which had aroused the most virulent domestic opposition.

The conclusion is irresistible, however, that if the present Argentine Government were relieved of these pro-democratic pressures it would quickly expand the area, and intensify the nature, of its Fascist activities. Individual rights guaranteed in the Argentine constitution and endorsed by Argentina in the resolutions of the Mexico City Conference and the United Nations charter are being violated by the Argentine authorities today; police terrorism directed particularly against pro-democratic groups continues; and the only labor organizations legally recognized by the Government are those established by the Ministry of Labor and Social Security after the Nazi-Fascist cooperative system. The elected representatives of the Argentine people have not been allowed to assemble for more than two and a half years. The state of siege has been continued with an interruption of only a few weeks in August–September 1945. The Fascist-totalitarian and pro-Axis character of the policy-making personnel of the Government remains essentially unchanged. Many known Axis sympathizers, who have long worked for the establishment of a Fascist-totalitarian state in Argentina, have either been appointed to or have continued in public office. The forced installation of a predominantly civilian cabinet in October did not change the character of the Government.

PART IV: CONCLUDING STATEMENT

In October 1945, when consultation concerning the Argentine situation was requested by the United States, it had substantial reason to believe from the evidence then at its disposal that the present Argentine Government and many of its high officials were so seriously compromised in their relations with the enemy that trust and confidence could not be reposed in that government.

Now the Government of the United States posesses a wealth of incontrovertible evidence. This document, based on that evidence, speaks for itself.

The Government of the United States looks forward to receiving from the governments of the other American republics the benefit of their views in the premises.

8. *Statement by James F. Byrnes, Secretary of State, before the House Foreign Affairs Committee, on Inter-American Military Cooperation**

May 29, 1946

I appreciate the opportunity of meeting with the members of the Committee on

*Department of State Bulletin, June 9, 1946, pp. 1001-03.

Foreign Affairs today in regard to the Inter-American Military Cooperation Bill, H. R. 6326.

The subject matter of the bill which you are considering has been given extended consideration by the State, War and Navy Departments. Representatives of the War and Navy Departments have discussed with you the purposes of the bill in the light of military and naval policy, and have presented from the military viewpoint the principal explanation of why passage of the bill is considered desirable in the interests of the United States. I must, of course, limit my remarks to consideration of the objectives and purposes of the bill as they affect the foreign relations of the United States in general.

The purpose of the proposed legislation is to clarify the authority of the President, and through him of the executive departments of the Government, to extend training facilities, and to transfer military equipment, subject to certain conditions, to other American states, as a means of implementing the cooperation of the American nations in military and naval matters. Present legislation authorizes such activities only to a limited and inadequate extent.

The long range objective of the military cooperation which this bill would authorize is the continued and closer coordination of the efforts which the American nations have made over many years to promote their mutual security and preserve their peace.

The basis for the cooperation among the American states in the military field lies in the obligations they have assumed for their mutual defense and for the maintenance of peace in the Western Hemisphere. In the Act of Chapultepec which was signed by the American republics in March of 1945, these 21 countries stated that an attack by any state against any one of them would be considered an attack against all of them. If such an attack occurs, the Act of Chapultepec provides, the American republics will consult with each other to agree upon measures it may be advisable to take. The measures which the Act of Chapultepec authorized the American republics to take included, for the first time in inter-American agreements, the use of armed force if necessary.

The Act of Chapultepec thus represents a distinct advance over previous inter-American security arrangements. It created for the first time a system for maintaining the peace and security of the American republics regardless of whence an attack might come.

The Act of Chapultepec also provided that the arrangements made under it should be consistent with the United Nations, the Charter of which had not yet been drafted when the Act of Chapultepec was signed. Since that time the United Nations has become a reality. The Charter of the United Nations recognizes that regional arrangements for the maintenance of peace and security, which are consistent with the Charter, may exist, and stipulates the conditions under which such regional arrangements as the Inter-American System may act in the maintenance of international peace and security.

In case of an armed attack, all members of the United Nations may exercise, under the Charter, their rights of individual and collective self-defense until the Security Council acts. If aggression is threatened—without an armed attack having occurred—it is possible for regional arrangements to be directed by the Security Council to enforce the peace or to be authorized to take enforcement action on their own initiative. The chief restriction upon the activity of a regional arrangement such as the Inter-American System is that it may not, except in the case of an armed attack, undertake any enforcement measures without the authorization of the Security Council. By virtue of this provision the Security Council remains the supreme authority in regard to the enforcement of international peace and security.

I am sure that you are familiar with the fact that the complete fulfillment by this Government of the terms of the Act of Chapultepec depends upon the exercise of the war powers of the executive. The American republics have announced their intention, which this Government shares, of signing a treaty, as called for by the Chapultepec agreement, which will, when ratified, give permanent validity to the principles of mutual defense and collective action for the maintenance of peace and security in the Americas as a regional arrangement under the United Nations.

The Act of Chapultepec places upon each of the American republics a responsibility to collaborate in the common effort to maintain the peace and security of all the Americas. The perfection of the entire structure of this regional arrangement is still in the future in that there remains to be concluded the basic treaty called for in the Act of Chapultepec. However, the advantage of cooperative relations among the military establishments which the American governments will continue to maintain, and of the acceptance of common technical standards as a means of facilitating those relations, is obvious. I trust that the passage of this legislation will do much to place this Government in a position to play its part in this general cooperative undertaking. It will be an indication to the other American states that the United States desires to go forward with such collaboration subject to the overriding considerations of our general foreign policy—particularly our support of the United Nations as the supreme international authority for the maintenance of peace and security.

The bill has been drafted so as to permit this Government to extend the same cooperation to Canada, with whom our relations in all matters, including defense, are of special importance.

The President clearly indicated, in his message of May 6 to the Congress concerning the legislation under discussion, other aspects of our foreign policy which bear upon this inter-American military cooperation. I should like to express very strongly the opinion that it would not be in the interests of the United States to enter upon an extensive program of adding to the armaments of other countries. It would be in conflict with our peaceful aims to stimulate an arms race with all the disastrous consequences which such a development might bring about. It is a purpose of our foreign policy to work for a regulation of armaments in the light of requirements for the maintenance of internal order and of international peace and security. We desire to see the world freed from both the fears and the economic burdens which the maintenance of unnecessarily large armed forces imposes upon peoples, whose energies and resources must be directed to world reconstruction and improvement of living standards. There has not yet been time since the cessation of hostilities to establish any such system of arms regulation. I am confident, however, that this objective which we so sincerely desire can be achieved. With respect to the American republics, the cooperation which this Government will be empowered to extend if the bill under discussion is passed will be guided by our purpose of keeping armaments down to the minimum. The authority to extend such cooperation will, I hope, place this Government in a better position to work out with the other American governments arrangements both for the regulation of armaments and for the maintenance of continental peace and security.

The bill itself explicitly recognizes that any operations which this Government carries out under it will be subordinate to any international agreement for the regulation of armaments to which the United States is a party. It further calls for the exchange wherever possible of non-standard arms for those which this Government may make available, indicating that the objective of such transfers shall be the standardization, rather than the increase, of arms in the possession of other countries.

The initiative in planning specific activities under this bill will, of course, rest with the War and Navy Departments. However, the Department of State will have a part in that it will negotiate with other countries the agreements called for in the bill. Moreover, the Department of State will continue to work in the closest collaboration with the War and Navy Departments with regard to any activities under this bill which may touch upon our foreign policy. On the basis of the discussions which the three Departments have had in the past on this subject, I am sure that I can speak not only for the State Department, but for the War and Navy Departments also, in saying that any activities which we may recommend to the President in the event this bill is passed will be governed by the basic objectives of our policy toward the countries immediately concerned. Those objectives include, along with the protection of the peace and security of the Americas, assistance to our sister American nations in the raising of living standards for their peoples and in the progressively greater achievement of the political, economic and cultural objectives of a democratic society. Through continuing consultation among the State, War and Navy Departments I am confident that these objectives can be given constant and full consideration in planning the cooperation in military affairs which the proposed bill would authorize.

9. Statement by George C. Marshall, Secretary of State, before the Inter-American Conference for Maintenance of Continental Peace and Security, Modifying the United States Position on Hemisphere Defense

Petropolis, Brazil, August 15, 1947

In their replies to the recent consultations concerning the treaty to be signed at Rio de Janeiro, a majority of the American republics expressed the opinion that decisions for collective measures should be obligatory on all parties to the treaty.

The United States is anxious to contribute in every possible way to the formulation of a treaty of maximum effectiveness and has been encouraged by the results of the consultation to review its position regarding obligatory decisions.

It is now the intention of the United States Delegation to submit a revised draft in which it will propose that those collective measures specifically mentioned in the Act of Chapultepec shall be obligatory on all contracting parties when agreed upon in consultation by a vote of two thirds of the parties, with the sole exception that no state shall be required to furnish armed forces without its consent.

Department of State Bulletin, Aug. 24, 1947, p. 367.

10. *Inter-American Treaty of Reciprocal Assistance Issued by the Inter-American Conference for the Maintenance of Continental Peace and Security* *

September 2, 1947

In the name of their Peoples, the Governments represented at the Inter-American Conference for the Maintenance of Continental Peace and Security, desirous of consolidating and strengthening their relations of friendship and good neighborliness, and

Considering: That Resolution VIII of the Inter-American Conference on Problems of War and Peace, which met in Mexico City, recommended the conclusion of a treaty to prevent and repel threats and acts of aggression against any of the countries of America;

That the High Contracting Parties reiterate their will to remain united in an inter-American system consistent with the purposes and principles of the United Nations, and reaffirm the existence of the agreement which they have concluded concerning those matters relating to the maintenance of international peace and security which are appropriate for regional action;

That the High Contracting Parties reaffirm their adherence to the principles of inter-American solidarity and cooperation, and especially to those set forth in the preamble and declarations of the Act of Chapultepec, all of which should be understood to be accepted as standards of their mutual relations and as the juridical basis of the Inter-American System;

That the American States propose, in order to improve the procedures for the pacific settlement of their controversies, to conclude the treaty concerning the "Inter-American Peace System" envisaged in Resolutions IX and XXXIX of the Inter-American Conference on Problems of War and Peace;

That the obligation of mutual assistance and common defense of the American Republics is essentially related to their democratic ideals and to their will to cooperate permanently in the fulfillment of the principles and purposes of a policy of peace;

That the American regional community affirms as a manifest truth that juridical organization is a necessary prerequisite of security and peace, and that peace is founded on justice and moral order and, consequently, on the international recognition and protection of human rights and freedoms, on the indispensable well-being of the people, and on the effectiveness of democracy for the international realization of justice and security,

Have resolved, in conformity with the objectives stated above, to conclude the following Treaty, in order to assure peace, through adequate means, to provide for effective reciprocal assistance to meet armed attacks against any American State, and in order to deal with threats of aggression against any of them:

Article 1

The High Contracting Parties formally condemn war and undertake in their international relations not to resort to the threat or the use of force in any manner inconsistent with the provisions of the Charter of the United Nations or of this Treaty.

*Organization of American States, *Annals*, Vol. I, No. 1, 1949, pp. 87-90.

Article 2

As a consequence of the principle set forth in the preceding Article, the High Contracting Parties undertake to submit every controversy which may arise between them to methods of peaceful settlement and to endeavor to settle any such controversy among themselves by means of the procedures in force in the Inter-American System before referring it to the General Assembly or the Security Council of the United Nations.

Article 3

1. The High Contracting Parties agree that an armed attack by any State against an American State shall be considered as an attack against all the American States and, consequently, each one of the said Contracting Parties undertakes to assist in meeting the attack in the exercise of the inherent right of individual or collective self-defense recognized by Article 51 of the Charter of the United Nations.

2. On request of the State or States directly attacked and until the decision of the Organ of Consultation of the Inter-American System, each one of the Contracting Parties may determine the immediate measures which it may individually take in fulfillment of the obligation contained in the preceding paragraph and in accordance with the principle of continental solidarity. The Organ of Consultation shall meet without delay for the purpose of examining those measures and agreeing upon the measures of a collective character that should be taken.

3. The provisions of this Article shall be applied in case of any armed attack which takes place within the region described in Article 4 or within the territory of an American State. When the attack takes place outside of the said areas, the provisions of Article 6 shall be applied.

4. Measures of self-defense provided for under this Article may be taken until the Security Council of the United Nations has taken the measures necessary to maintain international peace and security.

Article 4

The region to which this Treaty refers is bounded as follows: beginning at the North Pole; thence due south to a point 74 degrees north latitude, 10 degrees west longitude; thence by a rhumb line to a point 47 degrees 30 minutes north latitude, 50 degrees west longitude; thence by a rhumb line to a point 35 degrees north latitude, 60 degrees west longitude; thence due south to a point in 20 degrees north latitude; thence by a rhumb line to a point 5 degrees north latitude, 24 degrees west longitude; thence due south to the South Pole; thence due north to a point 30 degrees south latitude, 90 degrees west longitude; thence by a rhumb line to a point on the Equator at 97 degrees west longitude; thence by a rhumb line to a point 15 degrees north latitude, 120 degrees west longitude; thence by a rhumb line to a point 50 degrees north latitude, 170 degrees east longitude; thence due north to a point in 54 degrees north latitude; thence by a rhumb line to a point 65 degrees 30 minutes north latitude, 168 degrees 58 minutes 5 seconds west longitude; thence due north to the North Pole.

Article 5

The High Contracting Parties shall immediately send to the Security Council of the United Nations, in conformity with Articles 51 and 54 of the Charter of the United Nations, complete information concerning the activities undertaken or in contemplation in the exercise of the right of self-defense or for the purpose of maintaining inter-American peace and security.

Article 6

If the inviolability or the integrity of the territory or the sovereignty or political independence of any American State should be affected by an aggression which is not an armed attack or by an extra-continental or intra-continental conflict, or by any other fact or situation that might endanger the peace of America, the Organ of Consultation shall meet immediately in order to agree on the measures which must be taken in case of aggression to assist the victim of the aggression or, in any case, the measures which should be taken for the common defense and for the maintenance of the peace and security of the Continent.

Article 7

In the case of a conflict between two or more American States, without prejudice to the right of self-defense in conformity with Article 51 of the Charter of the United Nations, the High Contracting Parties, meeting in consultation shall call upon the contending States to suspend hostilities and restore matters to the *status quo ante bellum*, and shall take in addition all other necessary measures to reestablish or maintain inter-American peace and security and for the solution of the conflict by peaceful means. The rejection of the pacifying action will be considered in the determination of the aggressor and in the application of the measures which the consultative meeting may agree upon.

Article 8

For the purposes of this Treaty, the measures on which the Organ of Consultation may agree will comprise one or more of the following: recall of chiefs of diplomatic missions; breaking of diplomatic relations; breaking of consular relations; partial or complete interruption of economic relations or of rail, sea, air, postal, telegraphic, telephonic, and radiotelephonic or radiotelegraphic communications; and use of armed force.

Article 9

In addition to other acts which the Organ of Consultation may characterize as aggression, the following shall be considered as such:

a) Unprovoked armed attack by a State against the territory, the people, or the land, sea or air forces of another State;

b) Invasion, by the armed forces of a State, of the territory of an American State, through the trespassing of boundaries demarcated in accordance with a treaty, judicial decision, or arbitral award, or, in the absence of frontiers thus demarcated, invasion affecting a region which is under the effective jurisdiction of another State.

Article 10

None of the provisions of this Treaty shall be construed as impairing the rights and obligations of the High Contracting Parties under the Charter of the United Nations.

Article 11

The consultations to which this Treaty refers shall be carried out by means of the Meetings of Ministers of Foreign Affairs of the American Republics which have ratified the Treaty, or in the manner or by the organ which in the future may be agreed upon.

Article 12

The Governing Board of the Pan American Union may act provisionally as an organ of consultation until the meeting of the Organ of Consultation referred to in the preceding Article takes place.

Article 13

The consultations shall be initiated at the request addressed to the Governing Board of the Pan American Union by any of the Signatory States which has ratified the Treaty.

Article 14

In the voting referred to in this Treaty only the representatives of the Signatory States which have ratified the Treaty may take part.

Article 15

The Governing Board of the Pan American Union shall act in all matters concerning this Treaty as an organ of liaison among the Signatory States which have ratified this Treaty and between these States and the United Nations.

Article 16

The decisions of the Governing Board of the Pan American Union referred to in Articles 13 and 15 above shall be taken by an absolute majority of the Members entitled to vote.

Article 17

The Organ of Consultation shall take its decisions by a vote of two-thirds of the Signatory States which have ratified the Treaty.

Article 18

In the case of a situation or dispute between American States, the parties directly interested shall be excluded from the voting referred to in the two preceding Articles.

Article 19

To constitute a quorum in all the meetings referred to in the previous Articles, it shall be necessary that the number of States represented shall be at least equal to the number of votes necessary for the taking of the decision.

Article 20

Decisions which require the application of the measures specified in Article 8 shall be binding upon all the Signatory States which have ratified this Treaty, with the sole exception that no State shall be required to use armed force without its consent.

Article 21

The measures agreed upon by the Organ of Consultation shall be executed through the procedures and agencies now existing or those which may in the future be established.

Article 22

This Treaty shall come into effect between the States which ratify it as soon as the ratifications of two-thirds of the Signatory States have been deposited.

Article 23

This Treaty is open for signature by the American States at the city of Rio de Janeiro, and shall be ratified by the Signatory States as soon as possible in accordance with their respective constitutional processes. The ratifications shall be deposited with the Pan American Union, which shall notify the Signatory States of each deposit. Such notification shall be considered as an exchange of ratifications.

Article 24

The present Treaty shall be registered with the Secretariat of the United Nations through the Pan American Union, when two-thirds of the Signatory States have deposited their ratifications.

Article 25

This Treaty shall remain in force indefinitely, but may be denounced by any High Contracting Party by a notification in writing to the Pan American Union, which shall inform all the other High Contracting Parties of each notification of denunciation received. After the expiration of two years from the date of the receipt by the Pan American Union of a notification of denunciation by any High Contracting Party, the present Treaty shall cease to be in force with respect to such State, but shall remain in full force and effect with respect to all the other High Contracting Parties.

Article 26

The principles and fundamental provisions of this Treaty shall be incorporated in the Organic Pact of the Inter-American System.

In witness whereof, the undersigned Plenipotentiaries, having deposited their full powers found to be in due and proper form, sign this Treaty on behalf of their respective Governments, on the dates appearing opposite their signatures.

Done in the city of Rio de Janeiro, in four texts respectively in the English, French, Portuguese and Spanish languages, on the second of September nineteen hundred forty-seven.

Reservation of Honduras:
The Delegation of Honduras, in signing the present Treaty and in connection with Article 9, section (b), does so with the reservation that the boundary between Honduras and Nicaragua is definitively demarcated by the Joint Boundary Commission of nineteen hundred and nineteen hundred and one, starting from a point in the Gulf of Fonseca, in the Pacific Ocean, to Portillo de Teotecacinte and, from this point to the Atlantic, by the line that His Majesty the King of Spain's arbitral award established on the twenty-third of December of nineteen hundred and six.

(Here follows the list of Plenipotentiaries.)

*11. Address by President Harry S. Truman before the
Inter-American Conference for the Maintenance of
Continental Peace and Security, on Economic
Rehabilitation is Collective Responsibility**

Petropolis, Brazil, September 2, 1947

Mr. President, Delegates to the Inter-American Conference for the Maintenance of Continental Peace and Security, Ladies and Gentlemen:

It is a distinguished privilege to address the final session of this historic Conference. You are assembled here as the representatives of the nations of this hemisphere which have been banded together for over half a century in the inter-American system. You have successfully accomplished the task of putting into permanent form the commitments made in the Act of Chapultepec. You have made it clear to any possible aggressor that the American republics are determined to support one another against attacks. Our nations have provided an example of good neighborliness and international amity to the rest of the world, and in our association together we have strengthened the fabric of the United Nations. You can be justly proud of the achievements of this Conference, and I commend the noble spirit which has inspired your efforts.

The cordial and gracious invitation of President Dutra to visit this beautiful land has allowed me to fulfil a desire I have long cherished. I consider it most fortunate that I am enabled also to meet with the Foreign Ministers and other leaders of the American republics. Thus, in a sense, I am visiting not only Brazil, but I am visiting all of your countries, since each of you carries his country in his heart.

While we are assembled here together, I wish to discuss with you the responsibilities which our nations share as a result of the recent war. For our part, the United States is deeply conscious of its position in world affairs. We recognize that we have an obligation and that we share this obligation with other nations of the Western Hemisphere. Therefore, I take this occasion to give you a frank picture of our view of our responsibility and how we are trying to meet it.

The people of the United States engaged in the recent war in the deep faith that we were opening the way to a free world and that out of the terrible suffering caused by the war something better would emerge than the world had known before.

The postwar era, however, has brought us bitter disappointment and deep concern.

We find that a number of nations are still subjected to a type of foreign domination which we fought to overcome. Many of the remaining peoples of Europe and Asia live under the shadow of armed aggression.

No agreement has been reached among the Allies on the main outlines of a peace settlement. In consequence, we are obliged to contemplate a prolonged military occupation of enemy territories. This is profoundly distasteful to our people.

Almost everywhere in Europe, economic recovery has lagged. Great urban and industrial areas have been left in a state of dependence on our economy which is as painful to us as it is to them. Much of this economic distress is due to the paralysis of political fear and uncertainty in addition to the devastation caused by war.

Department of State Bulletin, Sept. 14, 1947, pp. 498-501.

This situation has impeded the return to normal economic conditions everywhere in the world and has hampered seriously our efforts to develop useful forms of economic collaboration with our friends in other areas.

We did not fully anticipate these developments. Our people did not conceive, when we were fighting the war, that we would be faced with a situation of this nature when hostilities ceased. Our planning for peace presupposed a community of nations sobered and brought together by frightful suffering and staggering losses, more than ever appreciative of the need for mutual tolerance and consideration, and dedicated to the task of peaceful reconstruction.

In view of the unfortunate conditions which now prevail, we have faced some difficult problems of adjustment in our foreign policy. I would not say that we have made no mistakes. But I think that the elements of the policy we have evolved thus far are sound and justifiable.

The fundamental basis of the policy of the United States is the desire for permanent world peace.

We are determined that, in the company of our friends, we shall achieve that peace.

We are determined because of the belief of our people in the principle that there are basic human rights which all men everywhere should enjoy. Men can enjoy these rights—the right to life itself, and the right to share fully in the bounties of modern civilization—only when the threat of war has been ended forever.

The attainment of world-wide respect for essential human rights is synonymous with the attainment of world peace. The peoples of the earth want a peaceful world, a prosperous world, and a free world, and when the basic rights of men everywhere are observed and respected, there will be such a world.

We know that in the hearts of common people everywhere there is a deep longing for stability and for settled conditions in which men can attain personal security and a decent livelihood for themselves and their children. We know that there are aspirations for a better and a finer life which are common to all humanity. We know—and the world knows—that these aspirations have never been promoted by policies of aggression.

We shall pursue the quest for peace with no less persistence and no less determination than we applied to the quest for military victory.

There are certain important elements in our policy which are vital in our search for permanent peace.

We intend to do our best to provide economic help to those who are prepared to help themselves and each other. But our resources are not unlimited. We must apply them where they can serve most effectively to bring production, freedom, and confidence back to the world. We undertook to do this on an individual basis in the case of Greece and Turkey, where we were confronted with specific problems of limited scope and of peculiar urgency. But it was evident, at the time that decision was made early this year, that this precedent could not be applied generally to the problems of other European countries. The demands elsewhere were of far greater dimensions. It was clear that we would not be able to meet them all. It was equally clear that the peoples of Europe would have to get together and work out a solution of their common economic problems. In this way they would be able to make the most of their own resources and of such help as they might receive from others.

The representatives of 16 nations are now meeting in Paris in an effort to get to the root of Europe's continued economic difficulties and to chart a program of European recovery based on helping themselves and each other. They will then make known their needs in carrying this program to completion. Unquestionably it is in the interest of our country and of the Western Hemisphere in general that we should receive this appeal with sympathy and good will, prepared to do everything we can, within safe limits, that will be helpful and effective.

Our own troubles—and we have many—are small in contrast with the struggle for life itself that engrosses the peoples of Europe. The nations of free Europe will soon make known their needs. I hope that the nations of free America will be prepared, each according to its ability and in its own manner, to contribute to lasting peace for the benefit of mankind.

Another important element of our policy vital to our search for peace is fidelity to the United Nations. We recognize that the United Nations has been subjected to a strain which it was never designed to bear. Its role is to maintain the peace and not to make the peace. It has been embroiled in its infancy in almost continuous conflict. We must be careful not to prejudge it by this unfair test. We must cherish the seedling in the hope of a mighty oak. We shall not forget our obligations under the Charter, nor shall we permit others to forget theirs.

In carrying out our policy we are determined to remain strong. This is in no way a threat. The record of the past speaks for us. No great nation has been more reluctant than ours to use armed force. We do not believe that present international differences will have to be resolved by armed conflict. The world may depend upon it that we shall continue to go far out of our way to avoid anything that would increase the tensions of international life.

But we are determined that there shall be no misunderstanding in these matters. Our aversion to violence must not be misread as a lack of determination on our part to live up to the obligations of the United Nations Charter or as an invitation to others to take liberties with the foundations of international peace. Our military strength will be retained as evidence of the seriousness with which we view our obligations.

This is the course which our country is endeavoring to follow. I need not tell you how important it is to our success that we have your understanding, support, and counsel. The problem is in the deepest sense a common one for this hemisphere. There is no important aspect of it which does not affect all of us. No solution of it can be fully successful in which we do not all cooperate.

I have already mentioned our collective responsibility for economic assistance. By the grace of God and by our united armed efforts our countries have been saved from the destruction of war. Our economies are intact, our productive powers undiminished, our resources not even yet fully explored. In consequence, our collective importance in the affairs of a distressed world has become immense.

The Western Hemisphere cannot alone assure world peace, but without the Western Hemisphere no peace is possible. The Western Hemisphere cannot alone provide world prosperity, but without the Western Hemisphere no world prosperity is possible.

In so far as the economic problems common to the nations of North and South America are concerned, we have long been aware that much remains to be done. In reaching a solution there are many subjects which will have to be discussed among us. We have been obliged, in considering these questions, to differentiate between the urgent need for rehabilitation of war-shattered areas and the problems of development elsewhere. The problems of countries in this Hemisphere are different in nature and cannot be relieved by the same means and the same approaches which are in contemplation for Europe. Here the need is for long-term economic collaboration. This is a type of collaboration in which a much greater role falls to private citizens and groups than is the case in a program designed to aid European countries to recover from the destruction of war. You have my solemn assurance that we in Washington are not oblivious to the needs of increased economic collaboration within the family of American nations and that these problems will be approached by us with the utmost good faith and with increased vigor in the coming period.

If acceptable solutions of these economic problems can be found, and if we can continue to work with mutual confidence and courage at the building of that great edifice of political security to which this Conference has made so signal a contribution, then I believe that we can look with high hopes on the further development of our community life in this Hemisphere.

I have no desire to overlook the difficulties that have been encountered in the past and will continue to be encountered in the future. All of us are young and vigorous nations. At times we have been impetuous in our relations with one another. There has been a natural tendency for us to exhibit the same exuberance in our differences and our criticisms as in our friendships. Wide differences of background and tradition have had to be overcome.

But I believe that we may view with sober satisfaction the general history of our Hemisphere. There has been steady progress in the development of mutual respect and of understanding among us. As the United States acquires greater maturity, as its experience becomes deeper and richer, our people gain in appreciation of the distinguished cultural traditions which flourish among our neighbors in the Western World. I hope that as your acquaintance with us broadens, you will appreciate our fundamental good-will and will understand that we are trying to bear with dignity and decency the responsibility of an economic power unique in human history.

There are many concrete problems ahead of us on the path of inter-American relations. They will not be solved with generalities or with sentimentality. They will call for the utmost we can give in practical ingenuity, in patience, and good will. But their solution will be easier if we are able to set our sights above the troubles of the moment and to bear in mind the great truths upon which our common prosperity and our common destiny must rest.

This Western Hemisphere of ours is usually referred to as the New World. That it is the New World is clearer today than ever before. The Old World is exhausted, its civilization imperiled. Its people are suffering. They are confused and filled with fears for the future. Their hope must lie in this New World of ours.

The sick and the hungry cannot build a peaceful world. They must have the support of the strong and the free. We cannot depend upon those who are weaker than we to achieve a peace for us to enjoy.

The benefits of peace, like the crops in the field, come to those who have sown the seeds of peace.

It is for us, the young and the strong, to erect the bulwarks which will protect mankind from the horrors of war—forever.

The United States seeks world peace—the peace of free men. I know that you stand with us. United, we can constitute the greatest single force in the world for the good of humanity.

We approach our task with resolution and courage, firm in the faith of our Lord whose will it is that there shall be Peace on Earth.

We cannot be dissuaded, and we shall not be diverted, from our efforts to achieve His will.

*12. U. N. Economic and Social Council Terms of Reference
For the Economic Commission for Latin America**

February 25, 1948

The Economic and Social Council

Having considered the report of the *ad hoc* Committee appointed to study the factors bearing upon the creation of an Economic Commission for Latin America, and

Having noted General Assembly Resolutions No. 119 (II) and No. 120 (II),

Establishes an Economic Commission for Latin America with terms of reference as follows:

1. The Economic Commission for Latin America, acting within the framework of the policies of the United Nations and subject to the general supervision of the Council, shall, provided that the Commission takes no action in respect to any country without the agreement of the Government of that country:

(a) initiate and participate in measures for facilitating concerted action for dealing with urgent economic problems arising out of the war and for raising the level of economic activity in Latin America and for maintaining and strengthening the economic relations of the Latin-American countries both among themselves and with other countries of the world;

(b) make or sponsor such investigations and studies of economic and technological problems and developments within territories of Latin America as the Commission deems appropriate;

(c) undertake or sponsor the collection, evaluation and dissemination of such economic, technological and statistical information as the Commission deems appropriate.

2. The Commission shall direct its activities especially toward the study and seeking of solutions of problems arising in Latin America from world economic maladjustment and towards other problems connected with the world economy, with a view to the cooperation of the Latin-American countries in the common effort to achieve world-wide recovery and economic stability.

3. (a) Membership of the Commission shall be open to Members of the United Nations in North, Central and South America, and in the Caribbean area, and to France, the Netherlands and the United Kingdom. Any territory, or part or group thereof, within the geographic scope of the Commission's work, may, on presentation of its application to the Commission by the Member responsible for the international relations of such territory, part or group of territories, be eligible for admission by the

*United Nations, Economic and Social Council, Unrestricted E/712/Rev. 1, Mar. 6, 1948, Original: English.

Commission as an associate member of the Commission. If it has become responsible for its own international relations, such territory, part or group of territories, may be admitted as an associate member of the Commission on itself presenting its application to the Commission.

(b) Representatives of associate members shall be entitled to participate without vote in all meetings of the Commission, whether sitting as Commission or as Committee of the Whole.

(c) Representatives of associate members shall be eligible to be appointed as members of any committee, or other subordinate body, which may be set up by the Commission and shall be eligible to hold office in such body.

4. The geographical scope of the Commission's work is the twenty Latin-American States Members of the United Nations, participating territories in Central and South America which have frontiers adjoining any of these states, and participating territories in the Caribbean area.

5. The Commission is empowered to make recommendations on any matters within its competence directly to the Governments of members or associate members concerned, Governments admitted in a consultative capacity, and the specialized agencies concerned. The Commission shall submit for the Council's prior consideration any of its proposals for activities that would have important effects on the economy of the world as a whole.

6. The Commission shall invite any member of the United Nations not a member of the Commission to participate in a consultative capacity in its consideration of any matter of particular concern to that non-member, following the practices of the Economic and Social Council.

7. (a) The Commission shall invite representatives of specialized agencies to attend its meetings and to participate, without vote, in its deliberations with respect to items on its agenda relating to matters within the scope of their activities; and may invite observers from such other inter-governmental organizations as it may consider desirable in accordance with the practices of the Council;

(b) The Commission shall make arrangements for consultation with non-governmental organizations which have been granted consultative status by the Economic and Social Council, in accordance with the principles approved by the Council for this purpose.

8. The Commission shall take measures to ensure that the necessary liaison be maintained with other organs of the United Nations and with the Specialized Agencies with special attention to the avoidance of the duplication of efforts.

9. The Commission shall cooperate with and take the necessary measures to coordinate its activities with the appropriate organs of the Inter-American System and as may be necessary with the Caribbean Commission to avoid any unnecessary duplication of effort between those organs and itself; to this end the Commission is empowered to and shall seek to make working arrangements with the appropriate organs of the Inter-American System regarding the joint or independent study or execution of economic problems within its competence, and the fullest exchange of information necessary for the coordination of efforts in the economic field. The Commission shall invite the Pan American Union to nominate a representative to attend meetings of the Commission in a consultative capacity.

10. The Commission may after discussion with any Specialized Agency concerned, and with the approval of the Council, establish such subsidiary bodies as it deems

appropriate, for facilitating the carrying out of its responsibilities.

11. The Commission shall adopt its own rules of procedure, including the method of selecting its Chairman.

12. The Commission shall submit to the Council once a year a full report on its activities and plans, including those of any subsidiary bodies, and shall make interim reports at each regular session of the Council.

13. The administrative budget of the Commission shall be financed from the funds of the United Nations.

14. The Secretary-General of the United Nations shall appoint the staff of the Commission, which shall form part of the Secretariat of the United Nations.

15. The headquarters of the Commission shall be Santiago de Chile. The first session of the Commission shall be held during the first half of the present year in that city. The Commission shall at each session decide upon the place of meeting for its next session with due consideration for the principle that the countries of Latin America be chosen in rotation.

16. Not later than 1951 the Council shall make a special review of the work of the Commission with a view to determining whether the Commission should be terminated or continued, and if continued what modification if any should be made in its terms of reference.

13. Address by Secretary Marshall, before the Ninth International Conference of American States, on Interdependence of the Americas*

Bogotá, Colombia, April 1, 1948

It is a genuine pleasure for me to meet again with the distinguished delegates of the American republics, and especially so under the hospitable auspices of the Republic of Colombia. I wish to express through His Excellency Doctor (Laureano) Gómez, Foreign Minister of Colombia, our distinguished presiding officer, the very sincere appreciation we feel for the Government of Colombia as our host, our respectful admiration for His Excellency President Ospina Pérez, and our strong feeling of friendship and regard for the people of Colombia.

It is my privilege and duty to convey to the conference warm greetings from President Truman with his earnest wish that our efforts here will be successful in behalf of all the peoples of the Americas.

Ten years have passed since the Eighth International Conference of American States was held in Lima. The momentous events of that period delayed this Ninth Conference but did not halt progress in inter-American cooperation.

The emergency meetings of the Foreign Ministers, which enabled us to coordinate our wartime efforts, were followed by the all-important conference at Mexico City in 1945 which resulted in the Act of Chapultepec, and the Conference on the Maintenance of Continental Peace and Security so successfully concluded last August at Rio de Janeiro with the treaty of reciprocal assistance.

We are here to consolidate and to carry forward the decisions of these previous conferences. We have to consider a lengthy agenda to give effect to the provisions of

*Department of State Bulletin, Apr. 11, 1948, pp. 469-73.

the ninth resolution of the Mexico City conference, pertaining to the reorganization, consolidation, and strengthening of the inter-American system. This is no small undertaking, for what we do in this respect will have an important bearing on the future of all our joint undertakings. The proposed organic pact will be the very heart of our hemispheric organization.

Cooperation among our countries has been greatly broadened and intensified during recent years. We need for this cooperation an organizational structure which will on the one hand be adequate to the increased responsibilities placed upon it, and on the other hand, efficiently administered so that duplication of effort may be avoided. The inter-American conferences and meetings of Foreign Ministers are the instruments through which the inter-American system formulates policy and reaches decisions on questions of major importance. The drafters of the organic pact have wisely concluded that to insure that these policies and decisions are effectively carried out, the Pan American Union, as the central permanent agency of the inter-American system, must be given a greater responsibility and commensurate staff. Under the direction of the inter-American conferences and meetings of Foreign Ministers the Pan American Union should play an increasingly significant role in the effective functioning of the inter-American system.

I am sure we all are agreed that the development of the inter-American system is within the concept of the United Nations and contributes to the attainment of its objectives.

The urgent need of effective methods of economic cooperation presents us with problems that call for the utmost good will and understanding in order to accommodate complex interests.

Agreement on a convention setting forth the procedures for the pacific settlement of disputes is one of the necessary aims of this conference. By this means we will establish a broad juridical basis for the peaceful adjudication of any differences that may arise among the American states. At the same time we will set an example to a distracted world in the maintenance of peace among neighbor states under an accepted system of law that assures justice and equity to all nations, large and small.

Significant questions related to social progress and the rights of the individual man are to receive full consideration in the deliberations of the conference. These are matters in which all our peoples are deeply concerned. They rightfully expect us to take positive action for their protection and welfare. That, in reality, is the purpose of our endeavors.

The overwhelming desire of the people of the world is for peace and security, freedom to speak their thoughts, freedom to earn a decent living in their own way. It is the earnest, the very genuine desire of the people of my country to continue to assist, so far as they are able to do so, the other people of the world to attain these objectives.

We have encountered, as you are aware, the determined and open opposition of one group of states. If the genuine cooperation of the Soviet Union could be secured, world recovery and peace would be assured. Until such cooperation is secured, we must proceed with our own efforts.

My Government has assumed heavy responsibilities in this undertaking, but we cannot do the job alone. We need the understanding and the cooperation of other nations whose objectives are the same as ours.

We must face reality. Allow me to talk to you frankly regarding the tremendous problems the United States is facing. After four years of supreme effort and a million casualties, we had looked forward to a state of tranquillity which would permit us to reorganize our economy, having made vast expenditures in natural resources and money. Instead my people find themselves today faced with the urgent necessity of meeting staggering and inescapable responsibilities—humanitarian, political, financial, and military—all over the world, in western Europe, in Germany and Austria, in Greece and Turkey, in the Middle East, in China, Japan, and Korea. Meeting these unprecedented responsibilities has demanded tremendous drafts on our resources and imposed burdensome taxes on our people. These are heavy exactions—far heavier than seems to be realized.

The basic economic trouble has been the collapse of European economy. Europe was formerly the most important center of international trade, and the disastrous impact of the war on the European economy has been felt everywhere in the world. The Western Hemisphere, for example, formerly enjoyed a substantial business with Europe and the virtual breakdown of that commerce has adversely and directly affected the American republics. The recovery of Europe is therefore a prerequisite to the resumption of trade relationships.

In the planning of the European Recovery Program, the United States gave and will continue to give careful consideration to the interests of the countries represented at this conference, both as to the procurement of materials to be purchased and the need of goods in short supply.

The difficulties you have experienced in obtaining certain materials from the United States to meet the needs of your industrial and agricultural development are understood. The problem of shortages is not yours alone. I am constantly under the necessity of explaining and defending this situation to manufacturers and particularly to farmers in the United States, who are themselves short of tools of production, of fertilizers, of steel, and other vital elements of our economy. The pressure on your production comes from every direction.

The Recovery Program provides the economic means of achieving a purpose essentially moral in nature. We propose to provide the free nations of Europe with that additional marginal material strength they require to defend the free way of life and to preserve the institutions of self-government. If human rights and liberties are blotted out in Europe, they will become increasingly insecure in the new world as well. This is a matter of as much concern to your countries as it is to mine.

The United States cannot continue to bear alone the burdens on its own economy now necessary to initiate a restoration of prosperity. We have to look to other nations whose interests correspond with ours for active cooperation. All that are able should contribute. All will share the benefits. We have poured out our substance to secure the victory and prevent suffering and chaos in the first years of peace, but we cannot continue this process to the danger of exhaustion.

The rewards of freedom are economic as well as political. Only in such freedom can opportunity and incentive give full rein to individual initiative.

We have already agreed to certain principles that are stated in the Economic Charter of the Americas, signed in Mexico City in 1945. In that document the American republics proclaimed their common purpose to promote the sound development of national economies. The charter pointed the way toward realization of this aim through the encouragement of private enterprise and the fair treatment of foreign capital.

Our specific task here is to find workable methods by which our principles may be effectively applied in practical affairs. In a few moments I shall discuss the proposals of the United States Delegation for achieving this objective. But first I wish to draw attention to the general background from which they proceed. I do so because I believe that the experience of my country in its economic development offers some useful precedents.

One of the principal needs of the United States after it achieved independence was private capital for development of its resources and for western expansion. From overseas, and this is the point I wish to emphasize, at first cautiously and often with misunderstanding on both sides, the venture capital of Europe was invested in the new United States of America.

The great benefits accruing to the people of the United States from its material development were attributable in an important degree to this assistance received from abroad which together with the economic and political freedom of action enabled our people to capitalize rapidly upon the great natural resources of the country, and thus develop the production which has enabled us to bear today the heaviest responsibilities ever placed upon a single nation.

By 1900 the people of the United States themselves were becoming large investors in enterprises abroad. But internal development continued unabated. Despite the transformation from debtor to creditor nation and the accumulation of capital for foreign investments of its own, the United States continues to welcome money and technical assistance from other countries.

The point I wish to make is that even after the United States had achieved economic maturity and had become a major source of venture capital foreign investors continued to participate in the industrial and commercial growth of the nation without discrimination.

This policy has enabled the United States to prosper. The large-scale exchange of capital, goods, and services; the system of free enterprise; the confidence of other people in our future and the protection afforded foreign investments; the contributions made by skilled, energetic immigrants—all these helped immeasurably in making our nation not only productive and vigorous, but free. I repeat, this policy has enabled the United States to prosper, and I wish here to stress that it has enabled the United States to do a great deal for other countries, including the protection of their freedoms along with our own.

May I at this time invite your attention to a fact of particular significance related to the broad benefits to which I have just referred? That is, the fact that these benefits have been transferred into human values through the elevation of the real wages of labor to a point higher than has been achieved under any other system of enterprise in the history of mankind. These benefits automatically transfer themselves into the cultural and physical advancement of all of the people.

The United States is qualified, I submit, by its own historical experience to respond understandingly to the purpose of other American republics to improve their economic status. We understand the wish to achieve balanced economies through the development of industries, mechanization of agriculture, and modernization of transportation.

My Government is prepared to increase the scale of assistance it has been giving to the economic development of the American republics. But it is beyond the capacity of the United States Government itself to finance more than a small portion of the vast development needed. The capital required through the years must come from private sources, both domestic and foreign.

As the experience of the United States has shown, progress can be achieved best through individual effort and the use of private resources. Encouragement should therefore be given to the increase of investment capital from internal as well as external sources. It is obvious that foreign capital will naturally gravitate most readily to countries where it is accorded fair and equitable treatment.

For its part, the United States fully supports the promotion of economic development in the American republics. We advocate the prompt preparation of sound development programs, which will set specific and realistic goals to be accomplished in the next few years.

The United States supports the International Bank for Reconstruction and Development as an important source of long-term capital for developing the economies of the American republics. My Government confidently expects the role of this institution to be one of increasing usefulness.

The President of the United States is submitting to Congress a request for an increase in the lending authority of the Export-Import Bank which will be available for sound projects. These Government funds will be in addition to the private financing which will be needed for a much greater number of development projects.

The United States has studied the proposals regarding the taxation of foreign investments, with a view to avoiding double taxation and to encouraging the flow of private capital into other countries desiring it. I am glad to report that the President has under consideration measures to liberalize taxes on capital invested in foreign countries. These measures are designed to encourage not only initial investment but also the retention and reinvestment abroad of earnings derived from such capital. These measures also would liberalize the tax treatment of United States citizens residing abroad, and should therefore encourage technical experts to accept employment in other countries.

My Government attaches special importance to efforts to improve health, sanitation, education, and agricultural and industrial processes throughout the Hemisphere. We look forward to an expansion of the cooperative efforts of the American republics in these fields. We are surveying the availability of technical experts who may collaborate in the progress and development of the American republics, as recently authorized by the Congress on a more flexible basis.

The economic advancement and security of the Hemisphere are supremely important to all countries, large and small, and to every citizen of our countries. Through joint endeavor, with each country accepting its share of responsibility and seeking faithfully to carry out its obligations, I am confident that the American republics will consistently move forward and attain the objectives which we all so earnestly desire.

Before concluding I wish to call attention to the close relationship between the solemn pacts we are here to conclude at Bogotá and the treaty of reciprocal assistance signed at Rio de Janeiro last September. Together, these pacts, when ratified, will form a harmonious whole guaranteeing the social, cultural, and economic progress of the Americas and at the same time the preservation of their independence, security, and sovereignty. I am informed that ten countries have already ratified the treaty of reciprocal assistance and that several other nations plan to take positive action along this line. It is to be hoped that during our labors here we may receive the gratifying word that the required number of ratifications have been deposited to enable the treaty to enter into effect. Such action is particularly important in the present world situation. We need the other vital measures we are to consider here as indispensable contributions to the welfare of the Americas. The peoples for whom we speak are impatient to launch this promising cooperative endeavor, for they see in it their greatest hope for achieving a better life for themselves, their children, and their children's children. They look to this conference to set in motion the concerted effort that will make their constant dream of peace and plenty a living, satisfying reality. We must not fail them.

[*Following the conclusion of his formal address to the conference, Secretary Marshall spoke extemporaneously substantially as follows*]

As has been the case with my predecessors here, it has been necessary for me to speak formally from a prepared statement. Much of what is said here goes far beyond this table to ears other than ours. Now my friends, I wish to speak to you personally and directly. I feel that in the discussions, particularly of economic matters, so much of detail necessarily becomes involved that the great purpose for which we are assembled and the situation in which we find ourselves becomes somewhat submerged, if not at least partially lost sight of.

I feel that what has already been said and, I suppose, much of what has yet to be said refers directly or indirectly, but specifically in many instances, to my country, to its international actions and present undertakings. I also have the feeling that there is a very limited understanding of the tremendous responsibilities and the equally tremendous burdens that the Government of the United States has been compelled to assume and which is very pertinent to our discussions here in this conference. For example, at the present moment our Legislature is under the necessity of considering at the request of the President the strengthening of our armed forces which would involve the expenditure of additional billions. Now you have a direct interest in that, because we hope that through such a process we can terminate this subversion of democratic governments in western Europe, and we can reach an understanding to maintain the peace and security, the tranquillity, and the future trade developments of the entire Western Hemisphere and not alone the United States. But the great burden of such action has rested on the people of the United States, and it is a very heavy burden.

I think that I can to a reasonable degree understand your reactions and your views because I had a considerable experience along very similar lines immediately preceding and during the war years. As Chief of Staff of the United States Army from the fall of 1939 up until almost the end of the war, I was under continual and the heaviest possible pressure from almost every part of the world, from rulers of countries, from our own military commanders in those regions, and from groups or sections at home or their representatives in Congress who felt very deeply regarding a particular situation. Now if we had not resisted those multitudes of pressures, all of which were based on the logical belief to a reasonable extent of the people concerned of the importance, the necessity, and urgency of their situation, the duration of the war and the situation at the end of the war would probably have been quite different.

The United States today with its tremendous responsibility, which involves us all over the world, has to proceed with great wisdom in all it does and what it feels it must do in the future. I ask you to have this in mind and to realize what a tremendous burden the people of my country have undertaken. You profit by it as much as we do.

I was sitting here yesterday and regarding this very decorative and impressive mural painting (the mural of Liberator Simón Bolívar) which illuminates this room. It suddenly occurred to me that it had a peculiar significance in relation to an event far distant from us here—in the far Pacific, as a matter of fact. The last territory that we wrested from the hands of the Japanese was a small island called Okinawa, between Formosa and Japan. That was the last big fight. One hundred and ten thousand Japanese were killed. The only captured were those wounded to the extent that they could not commit suicide. We had very heavy casualties. That operation was carried out by the 10th United States Army. But the point that occurred to me yesterday was this: the Commander of that Army was Simon Bolivar Buckner. He died in the last days of the fight—on the front line. Surely, that has some significance here in this room dominated by this painting in the rear of me; that out in the Pacific that man who made a great contribution and finally gave his life for the peace and security of the Pacific, that it would no longer carry a threat to your western shores, should have born the name of your great liberator. Certainly that indicates something of our common purpose and much more of our common bonds.

14. Message by President Truman to Congress on the Role of the Export-Import Bank in Financing Latin American Development*

April 8, 1948

In recent months the United States has been considering a number of measures to further the achievement of the primary objective of our foreign policy—the establishment throughout the world of the conditions of a just and lasting peace.

One of the essential requirements for the attainment of that objective is continuing cooperation among the American republics and collaboration in the development of their resources and industries.

Genuine friendship has long existed between the people of the United States and our neighbors to the south. This friendship has been marked by cultural and economic association and close cooperation. The people of the United States have strongly supported the policy of the Good Neighbor and have a special regard for the peoples of the countries to the south of us.

The United States has long recognized the importance of economic and political stability in the Western Hemisphere. Such stability rests substantially upon the continuation of a satisfactory rate of economic progress. In this respect, we must fairly recognize that the economies of the other American republics are relatively undeveloped. In these countries, natural resources are abundant, but the expansion of production has been restricted due to the lack of capital and of modern production methods. Production can be increased only by means of a considerable volume of capital investment in transportation and power facilities, processing plants and other installations.

To some extent the need for capital in these countries is met by domestic savings, but such savings in general are insufficient to secure the necessary equipment and

*Department of State Bulletin, Apr. 25, 1948, pp. 548-49.

technical skills. Substantial and continued progress in the development of the resources and industries of the other American republics therefore requires foreign financing. The United States, by reason of its close relations with these countries and its strong economic position, is the principal source to which the other American republics look for equipment, materials, and technology as well as for their financing.

I recommend, therefore, that the Congress increase the lending authority of the Export-Import Bank by 500 million dollars. The proposed increase in the lending authority of the Bank would not involve any change in the statutory requirements under which the Bank has been operating.

This increased lending authority would place the Bank in a position to assist in meeting essential requirements for the financing of economic development in the other American republics. It would permit the Bank to make loans for well-planned development projects which are economically justified and to cooperate most effectively with private funds.

Such an increase would not, of course, be a substitute for necessary action that the other American republics can and should take to attract private investment capital and to mobilize fully their own investment resources.

The proposed increase represents, I believe, an important step which this Government should take to assist the economic development of the countries to the south of us.

It is of great importance to the United States, as a member of the American community, that there be continued expansion of production, increasing trade activity, and rising standards of living in the other American republics. It is in our mutual interest to help develop in the countries to the south those essential materials which are becoming less abundant in the United States, as well as others regularly imported from distant regions.

Above all, it is in our mutual interest to assist the American republics to continue their economic progress, which can contribute so much to the cooperative strength of the independent American republics.

I request the Congress, therefore, to give favorable consideration to the proposed increase in the lending authority of the Export-Import Bank.

15. Charter of the Organization of American States Issued by the Ninth International Conference of American States*

Bogotá, Colombia, April, 1948

In the name of their peoples, the States represented at the Ninth International Conference of American States,

Convinced that the historic mission of America is to offer to man a land of liberty, and a favorable environment for the development of his personality and the realization of his just aspirations;

Conscious that that mission has already inspired numerous agreements, whose essential value lies in the desire of the American peoples to live together in peace, and,

*Organization of American States, *Annals*, Vol. 1, No. 1, 1949, pp. 76-86.

through their mutual understanding and respect for the sovereignty of each one, to provide for the betterment of all, in independence, in equality and under law;

Confident that the true significance of American solidarity and good neighborliness can only mean the consolidation on this continent, within the framework of democratic institutions, of a system of individual liberty and social justice based on respect for the essential rights of man;

Persuaded that their welfare and their contribution to the progress and the civilization of the world will increasingly require intensive continental cooperation;

Resolved to persevere in the noble undertaking that humanity has conferred upon the United Nations, whose principles and purposes they solemnly reaffirm;

Convinced that juridical organization is a necessary condition for security and peace founded on moral order and on justice; and

In accordance with Resolution IX of the Inter-American Conference on Problems of War and Peace, held at Mexico City, have agreed upon the following:

CHARTER OF THE ORGANIZATION
OF AMERICAN STATES
PART ONE

Chapter I

Nature and Purposes
Article 1

The American States establish by this Charter the international organization that they have developed to achieve an order of peace and justice, to promote their solidarity, to strengthen their collaboration, and to defend their sovereignty, their territorial integrity and their independence. Within the United Nations, the Organization of American States is a regional agency.

Article 2

All American States that ratify the present Charter are Members of the Organization.

Article 3

Any new political entity that arises from the union of several Member States and that, as such, ratifies the present Charter, shall become a Member of the Organization. The entry of the new political entity into the Organization shall result in the loss of membership of each one of the States which constitute it.

Article 4

The Organization of American States, in order to put into practice the principles on which it is founded and to fulfill its regional obligations under the Charter of the United Nations, proclaims the following essential purposes:

a) To strengthen the peace and security of the continent;

b) To prevent possible causes of difficulties and to ensure the pacific settlement of disputes that may arise among the Member States;

c) To provide for common action on the part of those States in the event of aggression;

d) To seek the solution of political, juridical and economic problems that may arise among them; and

e) To promote, by cooperative action, their economic, social and cultural development.

Chapter II

Principles
Article 5

The American States reaffirm the following principles:

a) International law is the standard of conduct of States in their reciprocal relations;

b) International order consists essentially of respect for the personality, sovereignty and independence of States, and the faithful fulfillment of obligations derived from treaties and other sources of international law;

c) Good faith shall govern the relations between States;

d) The solidarity of the American States and the high aims which are sought through it require the political organization of those States on the basis of the effective exercise of representative democracy;

e) The American States condemn war of aggression: victory does not give rights;

f) An act of aggression against one American State is an act of aggression against all the other American States;

g) Controversies of an international character arising between two or more American States shall be settled by peaceful procedures;

h) Social justice and social security are bases of lasting peace;

i) Economic cooperation is essential to the common welfare and prosperity of the peoples of the continent;

j) The American States proclaim the fundamental rights of the individual without distinction as to race, nationality, creed or sex;

k) The spiritual unity of the continent is based on respect for the cultural values of the American countries and requires their close cooperation for the high purposes of civilization;

l) The education of peoples should be directed toward justice, freedom and peace.

Chapter III

Fundamental Rights
and Duties of States
Article 6

States are juridically equal, enjoy equal rights and equal capacity to exercise these rights, and have equal duties. The rights of each State depend not upon its power to ensure the exercise thereof, but upon the mere fact of its existence as a person under international law.

Article 7

Every American State has the duty to respect the rights enjoyed by every other State in accordance with international law.

Article 8

The fundamental rights of States may not be impaired in any manner whatsoever.

Article 9

The political existence of the State is independent of recognition by other States. Even before being recognized, the State has the right to defend its integrity and independence, to provide for its preservation and prosperity, and consequently to organize itself as it sees fit, to legislate concerning its interests, to administer its services, and to determine the jurisdiction and competence of its courts. The exercise of these rights is limited only by the exercise of the rights of other States in accordance with international law.

Article 10

Recognition implies that the State granting it accepts the personality of the new State, with all the rights and duties that international law prescribes for the two States.

Article 11

The right of each State to protect itself and to live its own life does not authorize it to commit unjust acts against another State.

Article 12

The jurisdiction of States within the limits of their national territory is exercised equally over all the inhabitants, whether nationals or aliens.

Article 13

Each State has the right to develop its cultural, political and economic life freely and naturally. In this free development, the State shall respect the rights of the individual and the principles of universal morality.

Article 14

Respect for and the faithful observance of treaties constitute standards for the development of peaceful relations among States. International treaties and agreements should be public.

Article 15

No State or group of States has the right to intervene, directly or indirectly, for any reason whatever, in the internal or external affairs of any other State. The foregoing principle prohibits not only armed force but also any other form of interference or attempted threat against the personality of the State or against its political, economic and cultural elements.

Article 16

No State may use or encourage the use of coercive measures of an economic or political character in order to force the sovereign will of another State and obtain from it advantages of any kind.

Article 17

The territory of a State is inviolable; it may not be the object, even temporarily, of military occupation or of other measures of force taken by another State, directly or indirectly, on any grounds whatever. No territorial acquisitions or special advantages obtained either by force or by other means of coercion shall be recognized.

Article 18

The American States bind themselves in their international relations not to have recourse to the use of force, except in the case of self-defense in accordance with existing treaties or in fulfillment thereof.

Article 19

Measures adopted for the maintenance of peace and security in accordance with existing treaties do not constitute a violation of the principles set forth in Articles 15 and 17.

Chapter IV

Pacific Settlement of Disputes
Article 20

All international disputes that may arise between American States shall be submitted to the peaceful procedures set forth in this Charter, before being referred to the Security Council of the United Nations.

Article 21

The following are peaceful procedures: direct negotiation, good offices, mediation, investigation and conciliation, judicial settlement, arbitration, and those which the parties to the dispute may especially agree upon at any time.

Article 22

In the event that a dispute arises between two or more American States which, in the opinion of one of them, cannot be settled through the usual diplomatic channels, the Parties shall agree on some other peaceful procedure that will enable them to reach a solution.

Article 23

A special treaty will establish adequate procedures for the pacific settlement of disputes and will determine the appropriate means for their application, so that no dispute between American States shall fail of definitive settlement within a reasonable period.

Chapter V

Collective Security
Article 24

Every act of aggression by a State against the territorial integrity or the inviolability of the territory or against the sovereignty or political independence of an American State shall be considered an act of aggression against the other American States.

Article 25

If the inviolability or the integrity of the territory or the sovereignty or political independence of any American State should be affected by an armed attack or by an act of aggression that is not an armed attack, or by an extra-continental conflict, or by a conflict between two or more American States, or by any other fact or situation that might endanger the peace of America, the American States, in furtherance of the principles of continental solidarity or collective self-defense, shall apply the measures and procedures established in the special treaties on the subject.

Chapter VI

Economic Standards
Article 26

The Member States agree to cooperate with one another, as far as their resources may permit and their laws may provide, in the broadest spirit of good neighborliness, in order to strengthen their economic structure, develop their agriculture and mining, promote their industry and increase their trade.

Article 27

If the economy of an American State is affected by serious conditions that cannot be satisfactorily remedied by its own unaided effort, such State may place its economic problems before the Inter-American Economic and Social Council to seek through consultation the most appropriate solution for such problems.

Chapter VII

Social Standards
Article 28

The Member States agree to cooperate with one another to achieve just and decent living conditions for their entire populations.

Article 29

The Member States agree upon the desirability of developing their social legislation on the following bases:

a) All human beings, without distinction as to race, nationality, sex, creed or social condition, have the right to attain material well-being and spiritual growth under circumstances of liberty, dignity, equality of opportunity, and economic security;

b) Work is a right and a social duty; it shall not be considered as an article of commerce; it demands respect for freedom of association and for the dignity of the worker; and it is to be performed under conditions that ensure life, health and a decent standard of living, both during the working years and during old age, or when any circumstance deprives the individual of the possibility of working.

Chapter VIII

Cultural Standards
Article 30

The Member States agree to promote, in accordance with their constitutional provisions and their material resources, the exercise of the right to education, on the following bases:

a) Elementary education shall be compulsory and, when provided by the State, shall be without cost;

b) Higher education shall be available to all, without distinction as to race, nationality, sex, language, creed or social condition.

Article 31

With due consideration for the national character of each State, the Member States undertake to facilitate free cultural interchange by every medium of expression.

PART TWO

Chapter IX

The Organs
Article 32

The Organization of American States accomplishes its purposes by means of:
a) The Inter-American Conference;
b) The Meeting of Consultation of Ministers of Foreign Affairs;
c) The Council;
d) The Pan American Union;
e) The Specialized Conferences; and
f) The Specialized Organizations.

Chapter X

The Inter-American Conference
Article 33

The Inter-American Conference is the supreme organ of the Organization of American States. It decides the general action and policy of the Organization and determines the structure and functions of its Organs, and has the authority to consider any matter relating to friendly relations among the American States. These functions shall be carried out in accordance with the provisions of this Charter and of other inter-American treaties.

Article 34

All Member States have the right to be represented at the Inter-American Conference. Each State has the right to one vote.

Article 35

The Conference shall convene every five years at the time fixed by the Council of the Organization, after consultation with the government of the country where the Conference is to be held.

Article 36

In special circumstances and with the approval of two-thirds of the American Governments, a special Inter-American Conference may be held, or the date of the next regular Conference may be changed.

Article 37

Each Inter-American Conference shall designate the place of meeting of the next Conference. If for any unforeseen reason the Conference cannot be held at the place designated, the Council of the Organization shall designate a new place.

Article 38

The program and regulations of the Inter-American Conference shall be prepared by the Council of the Organization and submitted to the Member States for consideration.

Chapter XI

The Meeting of Consultation of
Ministers of Foreign Affairs
Article 39

The Meeting of Consultation of Ministers of Foreign Affairs shall be held in order to consider problems of an urgent nature and of common interest to the American States, and to serve as the Organ of Consultation.

Article 40

Any Member State may request that a Meeting of Consultation be called. The request shall be addressed to the Council of the Organization, which shall decide by an absolute majority whether a meeting should be held.

Article 41

The program and regulations of the Meeting of Consultation shall be prepared by the Council of the Organization and submitted to the Member States for consideration.

Article 42

If, for exceptional reasons, a Minister of Foreign Affairs is unable to attend the meeting, he shall be represented by a special delegate.

Article 43

In case of an armed attack within the territory of an American State or within the region of security delimited by treaties in force, a Meeting of Consultation shall be held without delay. Such Meeting shall be called immediately by the Chairman of the Council of the Organization, who shall at the same time call a meeting of the Council itself.

Article 44

An Advisory Defense Committee shall be established to advise the Organ of Consultation on problems of military cooperation that may arise in connection with the application of existing special treaties on collective security.

Article 45

The Advisory Defense Committee shall be composed of the highest military authorities of the American States participating in the Meeting of Consultation. Under exceptional circumstances the Governments may appoint substitutes. Each State shall be entitled to one vote.

Article 46

The Advisory Defense Committee shall be convoked under the same conditions as the Organ of Consultation, when the latter deals with matters relating to defense against aggression.

Article 47

The Committee shall also meet when the Conference or the Meeting of Consultation or the Governments, by a two-thirds majority of the Member States, assign to it technical studies or reports on specific subjects.

Chapter XII

The Council
Article 48

The Council of the Organization of American States is composed of one Representative of each Member State of the Organization, especially appointed by the respective Government, with the rank of Ambassador. The appointment may be given to the diplomatic representative accredited to the Government of the country in which the Council has its seat. During the absence of the titular Representative, the Government may appoint an interim Representative.

Article 49

The Council shall elect a Chairman and a Vice Chairman, who shall serve for one year and shall not be eligible for election to either of those positions for the term immediately following.

Article 50

The Council takes cognizance, within the limits of the present Charter and of inter-American treaties and agreements, of any matter referred to it by the Inter-American Conference or the Meeting of Consultation of Ministers of Foreign Affairs.

Article 51

The Council shall be responsible for the proper discharge by the Pan American Union of the duties assigned to it.

Article 52

The Council shall serve provisionally as the Organ of Consultation when the circumstances contemplated in Article 43 of this Charter arise.

Article 53

It is also the duty of the Council:

a) To draft and submit to the Governments and to the Inter-American Conference proposals for the creation of new Specialized Organizations or for the combination, adaptation or elimination of existing ones, including matters relating to the financing and support thereof;

b) To draft recommendations to the Governments, the Inter-American Conference, the Specialized Conferences or the Specialized Organizations, for the coordination of the activities and programs of such organizations, after consultation with them;

c) To conclude agreements with the Inter-American Specialized Organizations to determine the relations that shall exist between the respective agency and the Organization;

d) To conclude agreements or special arrangements for cooperation with other American organizations of recognized international standing;

e) To promote and facilitate collaboration between the Organization of American

States and the United Nations, as well as between Inter-American Specialized Organizations and similar international agencies;

f) To adopt resolutions that will enable the Secretary General to perform the duties envisaged in Article 84;

g) To perform the other duties assigned to it by the present Charter.

Article 54

The Council shall establish the bases for fixing the quota that each Government is to contribute to the maintenance of the Pan American Union, taking into account the ability to pay of the respective countries and their determination to contribute in an equitable manner. The budget, after approval by the Council, shall be transmitted to the Governments at least six months before the first day of the fiscal year, with a statement of the annual quota of each country. Decisions on budgetary matters require the approval of two-thirds of the members of the Council.

Article 55

The Council shall formulate its own regulations.

Article 56

The Council shall function at the seat of the Pan American Union.

Article 57

The following are organs of the Council of the Organization of American States:
a) The Inter-American Economic and Social Council;
b) The Inter-American Council of Jurists;
c) The Inter-American Cultural Council.

Article 58

The organs referred to in the preceding article shall have technical autonomy within the limits of this Charter; but their decisions shall not encroach upon the sphere of action of the Council of the Organization.

Article 59

The organs of the Council of the Organization are composed of representatives of all the Member States of the Organization.

Article 60

The organs of the Council of the Organization shall, as far as possible, render to the Governments such technical services as the latter may request; and they shall advise the Council of the Organization on matters within their jurisdiction.

Article 61

The organs of the Council of the Organization shall, in agreement with the Council, establish cooperative relations with the corresponding organs of the United Nations and with the national or international agencies that function within their respective spheres of action.

Article 62

The Council of the Organization, with the advice of the appropriate bodies and after consultation with the Governments, shall formulate the statutes of its organs in accordance with and in the execution of the provisions of this Charter. The organs shall formulate their own regulations.

A) The Inter-American Economic and Social Council
Article 63

The Inter-American Economic and Social Council has for its principal purpose the promotion of the economic and social welfare of the American nations through effective cooperation for the better utilization of their natural resources, the development of their agriculture and industry and the raising of the standards of living of their peoples.

Article 64

To accomplish this purpose the Council shall:

a) Propose the means by which the American nations may give each other technical assistance in making studies and formulating and executing plans to carry out the purposes referred to in Article 26 and to develop and improve their social services;

b) Act as coordinating agency for all official inter-American activities of an economic and social nature;

c) Undertake studies on its own initiative or at the request of any Member State;

d) Assemble and prepare reports on economic and social matters for the use of the Member States;

e) Suggest to the Council of the Organization the advisability of holding specialized conferences on economic and social matters;

f) Carry on such other activities as may be assigned to it by the Inter-American Conference, the Meeting of Consultation of Ministers of Foreign Affairs, or the Council of the Organization.

Article 65

The Inter-American Economic and Social Council, composed of technical delegates appointed by each Member State, shall meet on its own initiative or on that of the Council of the Organization.

Article 66

The Inter-American Economic and Social Council shall function at the seat of the Pan American Union, but it may hold meetings in any American city by a majority decision of the Member States.

B) The Inter-American Council of Jurists
Article 67

The purpose of the Inter-American Council of Jurists is to serve as an advisory body on juridical matters; to promote the development and codification of public and private international law; and to study the possibility of attaining uniformity in the legislation of the various American countries, insofar as it may appear desirable.

Article 68

The Inter-American Juridical Committee of Rio de Janeiro shall be the permanent committee of the Inter-American Council of Jurists.

Article 69

The Juridical Committee shall be composed of jurists of the nine countries selected by the Inter-American Conference. The selection of the jurists shall be made by the Inter-American Council of Jurists from a panel submitted by each country chosen by the Conference. The Members of the Juridical Committee represent all Member States of the Organization. The Council of the Organization is empowered to fill any vacancies that occur during the intervals between Inter-American Conferences and between meetings of the Inter-American Council of Jurists.

Article 70

The Juridical Committee shall undertake such studies and preparatory work as are assigned to it by the Inter-American Council of Jurists, the Inter-American Conference, the Meeting of Consultation of Ministers of Foreign Affairs, or the Council of the Organization. It may also undertake those studies and projects which, on its own initiative, it considers advisable.

Article 71

The Inter-American Council of Jurists and the Juridical Committee should seek the cooperation of national committees for the codification of international law, of institutes of international and comparative law, and of other specialized agencies.

Article 72

The Inter-American Council of Jurists shall meet when convened by the Council of the Organization, at the place determined by the Council of Jurists at its previous meeting.

C) The Inter-American Cultural Council
Article 73

The purpose of the Inter-American Cultural Council is to promote friendly relations and mutual understanding among the American peoples, in order to strengthen the peaceful sentiments that have characterized the evolution of America, through the promotion of educational, scientific and cultural exchange.

Article 74

To this end the principal functions of the Council shall be:

a) To sponsor inter-American cultural activities;

b) To collect and supply information on cultural activities carried on in and among the American States by private and official agencies both national and international in character;

c) To promote the adoption of basic educational programs adapted to the needs of all population groups in the American countries;

d) To promote, in addition, the adoption of special programs of training, education and culture for the indigenous groups of the American countries;

e) To cooperate in the protection, preservation and increase of the cultural heritage of the continent;

f) To promote cooperation among the American nations in the fields of education, science and culture, by means of the exchange of materials for research and study, as well as the exchange of teachers, students, specialists and, in general, such other persons and materials as are useful for the realization of these ends;

g) To encourage the education of the peoples for harmonious international relations;

h) To carry on such other activities as may be assigned to it by the Inter-American

Conference, the Meeting of Consultation of Ministers of Foreign Affairs, or the Council of the Organization.

Article 75

The Inter-American Cultural Council shall determine the place of its next meeting and shall be convened by the Council of the Organization on the date chosen by the latter in agreement with the Government of the country selected as the seat of the meeting.

Article 76

There shall be a Committee for Cultural Action of which five States, chosen at each Inter-American Conference, shall be members. The individuals composing the Committee for Cultural Action shall be selected by the Inter-American Cultural Council from a panel submitted by each country chosen by the Conference, and they shall be specialists in education or cultural matters. When the Inter-American Cultural Council and the Inter-American Conference are not in session, the Council of the Organization may fill vacancies that arise and replace those countries that find it necessary to discontinue their cooperation.

Article 77

The Committee for Cultural Action shall function as the permanent committee of the Inter-American Cultural Council, for the purpose of preparing any studies that the latter may assign to it. With respect to these studies the Council shall have the final decision.

Chapter XIII

The Pan American Union
Article 78

The Pan American Union is the central and permanent organ of the Organization of American States and the General Secretariat of the Organization. It shall perform the duties assigned to it in this Charter and such other duties as may be assigned to it in other inter-American treaties and agreements.

Article 79

There shall be a Secretary General of the Organization, who shall be elected by the Council for a ten-year term and who may not be reelected or be succeeded by a person of the same nationality. In the event of a vacancy in the office of Secretary General, the Council shall, within the next ninety days, elect a successor to fill the office for the remainder of the term, who may be reelected if the vacancy occurs during the second half of the term.

Article 80

The Secretary General shall direct the Pan American Union and be the legal representative thereof.

Article 81

The Secretary General shall participate with voice, but without vote, in the deliberations of the Inter-American Conference, the Meeting of Consultation of Ministers of Foreign Affairs, the Specialized Conferences, and the Council and its organs.

Article 82

The Pan American Union, through its technical and information offices, shall, under the direction of the Council, promote economic, social, juridical and cultural relations among all the Member States of the Organization.

Article 83

The Pan American Union shall also perform the following functions:

a) Transmit *ex officio* to Member States the convocation to the Inter-American Conference, the Meeting of Consultation of Ministers of Foreign Affairs, and the Specialized Conferences;

b) Advise the Council and its organs in the preparation of programs and regulations of the Inter-American Conference, the Meeting of Consultation of Ministers of Foreign Affairs, and the Specialized Conferences;

c) Place, to the extent of its ability, at the disposal of the Government of the country where a conference is to be held, the technical aid and personnel which such Government may request;

d) Serve as custodian of the documents and archives of the Inter-American Conference, of the Meeting of Consultation of Ministers of Foreign Affairs, and, insofar as possible, of the Specialized Conferences;

e) Serve as depository of the instruments of ratification of inter-American agreements;

f) Perform the functions entrusted to it by the Inter-American Conference, and the Meeting of Consultation of Ministers of Foreign Affairs;

g) Submit to the Council an annual report on the activities of the Organization;

h) Submit to the Inter-American Conference a report on the work accomplished by the Organs of the Organization since the previous Conference.

Article 84

It is the duty of the Secretary General:

a) To establish, with the approval of the Council, such technical and administrative offices of the Pan American Union as are necessary to accomplish its purposes;

b) To determine the number of department heads, officers and employees of the Pan American Union; to appoint them, regulate their powers and duties, and fix their compensation, in accordance with general standards established by the Council.

Article 85

There shall be an Assistant Secretary General, elected by the Council for a term of ten years and eligible for reelection. In the event of a vacancy in the office of Assistant Secretary General, the Council shall, within the next ninety days, elect a successor to fill such office for the remainder of the term.

Article 86

The Assistant Secretary General shall be the Secretary of the Council. He shall perform the duties of the Secretary General during the temporary absence or disability of the latter, or during the ninety-day vacancy referred to in Article 79. He shall also serve as advisory officer to the Secretary General, with the power to act as his delegate in all matters that the Secretary General may entrust to him.

Article 87

The Council, by a two-thirds vote of its members, may remove the Secretary General or the Assistant Secretary General whenever the proper functioning of the Organization so demands.

Article 88

The heads of the respective departments of the Pan American Union, appointed by the Secretary General, shall be the Executive Secretaries of the Inter-American Economic and Social Council, the Council of Jurists and the Cultural Council.

Article 89

In the performance of their duties the personnel shall not seek or receive instructions from any government or from any other authority outside the Pan American Union. They shall refrain from any action that might reflect upon their position as international officials responsible only to the Union.

Article 90

Every Member of the Organization of American States pledges itself to respect the exclusively international character of the responsibilities of the Secretary General and the personnel, and not to seek to influence them in the discharge of their duties.

Article 91

In selecting its personnel the Pan American Union shall give first consideration to efficiency, competence and integrity; but at the same time importance shall be given to the necessity of recruiting personnel on as broad a geographical basis as possible.

Article 92

The seat of the Pan American Union is the city of Washington.

Chapter XIV

The Specialized Conferences
Article 93

The Specialized Conferences shall meet to deal with special technical matters or to develop specific aspects of inter-American cooperation, when it is so decided by the Inter-American Conference or the Meeting of Consultation of Ministers of Foreign Affairs; when inter-American agreements so provide; or when the Council of the Organization considers it necessary, either on its own initiative or at the request of one of its organs or of one of the Specialized Organizations.

Article 94

The program and regulations of the Specialized Conferences shall be prepared by the organs of the Council of the Organization or by the Specialized Organizations concerned; they shall be submitted to the Member Governments for consideration and transmitted to the Council for its information.

Chapter XV

The Specialized Organizations
Article 95

For the purposes of the present Charter, Inter-American Specialized Organizations are the inter-governmental organizations established by multilateral agreements and having specific functions with respect to technical matters of common interest to the American States.

Article 96

The Council shall, for the purposes stated in Article 53, maintain a register of the Organizations that fulfill the conditions set forth in the foregoing Article.

Article 97

The Specialized Organizations shall enjoy the fullest technical autonomy and shall take into account the recommendations of the Council, in conformity with the provisions of the present Charter.

Article 98

The Specialized Organizations shall submit to the Council periodic reports on the progress of their work and on their annual budgets and expenses.

Article 99

Agreements between the Council and the Specialized Organizations contemplated in paragraph c) of Article 53 may provide that such Organizations transmit their budgets to the Council for approval. Arrangements may also be made for the Pan American Union to receive the quotas of the contributing countries and distribute them in accordance with the said agreements.

Article 100

The Specialized Organizations shall establish cooperative relations with world agencies of the same character in order to coordinate their activities. In concluding agreements with international agencies of a world-wide character, the Inter-American Specialized Organizations shall preserve their identity and their status as integral parts of the Organization of American States, even when they perform regional functions of international agencies.

Article 101

In determining the geographic location of the Specialized Organizations the interests of all the American States shall be taken into account.

PART THREE

Chapter XVI

The United Nations
Article 102

None of the provisions of this Charter shall be construed as impairing the rights and obligations of the Member States under the Charter of the United Nations.

Chapter XVII

Miscellaneous Provisions
Article 103

The Organization of American States shall enjoy in the territory of each Member such legal capacity, privileges and immunities as are necessary for the exercise of its functions and the accomplishment of its purposes.

Article 104

The Representatives of the Governments on the Council of the Organization, the representatives on the organs of the Council, the personnel of their delegations, as well as the Secretary General and the Assistant Secretary General of the Organization, shall enjoy the privileges and immunities necessary for the independent performance of their duties.

Article 105

The juridical status of the Inter-American Specialized Organizations and the privileges and immunities that should be granted to them and to their personnel, as well as to the officials of the Pan American Union, shall be determined in each case through agreements between the respective organizations and the Governments concerned.

Article 106

Correspondence of the Organization of American States, including printed matter and parcels, bearing the frank thereof, shall be carried free of charge in the mails of the Member States.

Article 107

The Organization of American States does not recognize any restriction on the eligibility of men and women to participate in the activities of the various Organs and to hold positions therein.

Chapter XVIII

Ratification and Entry into Force
Article 108

The present Charter shall remain open for signature by the American States and shall be ratified in accordance with their respective constitutional procedures. The original instruments, the Spanish, English, Portuguese and French texts of which are equally authentic, shall be deposited with the Pan American Union, which shall transmit certified copies thereof to the Governments for purposes of ratification. The instruments of ratification shall be deposited with the Pan American Union, which shall notify the signatory States of such deposit.

Article 109

The present Charter shall enter into force among the ratifying States when two-thirds of the signatory States have deposited their ratifications. It shall enter into force with respect to the remaining States in the order in which they deposit their ratifications.

Article 110

The present Charter shall be registered with the Secretariat of the United Nations through the Pan American Union.

Article 111

Amendments to the present Charter may be adopted only at an Inter-American Conference convened for that purpose. Amendments shall enter into force in accordance with the terms and the procedure set forth in Article 109.

Article 112

The present Charter shall remain in force indefinitely, but may be denounced by any Member State upon written notification to the Pan American Union, which shall communicate to all the others each notice of denunciation received. After two years from the date on which the Pan American Union receives a notice of denunciation, the present Charter shall cease to be in force with respect to the denouncing State, which shall cease to belong to the Organization after it has fulfilled the obligations arising from the present Charter.

In witness whereof the undersigned Plenipotentiaries, whose full powers have been presented and found to be in good and due form, sign the present Charter at the city of Bogotá, Colombia, on the dates that appear opposite their respective signatures.

(Here follows the list of Plenipotentiaries.)

16. *"Pact of Bogotá," American Treaty on Pacific
     Settlement, Issued by the Ninth International Conference
     of American States**

April 30, 1948

In the name of their peoples, the Governments represented at the Ninth International Conference of American States have resolved, in fulfillment of Article XXIII

*Organization of American States, *Annals*, Vol. I, No. 1, pp. 91-98.

of the Charter of the Organization of American States, to conclude the following Treaty:

CHAPTER ONE

GENERAL OBLIGATION TO SETTLE DISPUTES BY PACIFIC MEANS

Article I

The High Contracting Parties, solemnly reaffirming their commitments made in earlier international conventions and declarations, as well as in the Charter of the United Nations, agree to refrain from the threat or the use of force, or from any other means of coercion for the settlement of their controversies, and to have recourse at all times to pacific procedures.

Article II

The High Contracting Parties recognize the obligation to settle international controversies by regional pacific procedures before referring them to the Security Council of the United Nations.

Consequently, in the event that a controversy arises between two or more signatory states which, in the opinion of the parties, cannot be settled by direct negotiations through the usual diplomatic channels, the parties bind themselves to use the procedures established in the present Treaty, in the manner and under the conditions provided for in the following articles, or, alternatively, such special procedures as, in their opinion, will permit them to arrive at a solution.

Article III

The order of the pacific procedures established in the present Treaty does not signify that the parties may not have recourse to the procedure which they consider most appropriate in each case, or that they should use all these procedures, or that any of them have preference over others except as expressly provided.

Article IV

Once any pacific procedure has been initiated, whether by agreement between the parties or in fulfillment of the present Treaty or a previous pact, no other procedure may be commenced until that procedure is concluded.

Article V

The aforesaid procedures may not be applied to matters which, by their nature, are within the domestic jurisdiction of the state. If the parties are not in agreement as to whether the controversy concerns a matter of domestic jurisdiction, this preliminary question shall be submitted to decision by the International Court of Justice, at the request of any of the parties.

Article VI

The aforesaid procedures, furthermore, may not be applied to matters already settled by arrangement between the parties, or by arbitral award or by decision of an international court, or which are governed by agreements or treaties in force on the date of the conclusion of the present Treaty.

Article VII

The High Contracting Parties bind themselves not to make diplomatic representations in order to protect their nationals, or to refer a controversy to a court of international jurisdiction for that purpose, when the said nationals have had available the means to place their case before competent domestic courts of the respective state.

Article VIII

Neither recourse to pacific means for the solution of controversies, nor the recommendation of their use, shall, in the case of an armed attack, be ground for delaying the exercise of the right of individual or collective self-defense, as provided for in the Charter of the United Nations.

CHAPTER TWO

PROCEDURES OF GOOD OFFICES AND MEDIATION

Article IX

The procedure of good offices consists in the attempt by one or more American Governments not parties to the controversy, or by one or more eminent citizens of any American State which is not a party to the controversy, to bring the parties together, so as to make it possible for them to reach an adequate solution between themselves.

Article X

Once the parties have been brought together and have resumed direct negotiations, no further action is to be taken by the states or citizens that have offered their good offices or have accepted an invitation to offer them; they may, however, by agreement between the parties, be present at the negotiations.

Article XI

The procedure of mediation consists in the submission of the controversy to one or more American Governments not parties to the controversy, or to one or more eminent citizens of any American State not a party to the controversy. In either case the mediator or mediators shall be chosen by mutual agreement between the parties.

Article XII

The functions of the mediator or mediators shall be to assist the parties in the settlement of controversies in the simplest and most direct manner, avoiding formalities and seeking an acceptable solution. No report shall be made by the mediator and, so far as he is concerned, the proceedings shall be wholly confidential.

Article XIII

In the event that the High Contracting Parties have agreed to the procedure of mediation but are unable to reach an agreement within two months on the selection of the mediator or mediators, or no solution to the controversy has been reached within five months after mediation has begun, the parties shall have recourse without delay to any one of the other procedures of peaceful settlement established in the present Treaty.

Article XIV

The High Contracting Parties may offer their mediation, either individually or jointly, but they agree not to do so while the controversy is in process of settlement by any of the other procedures established in the present Treaty.

CHAPTER THREE

PROCEDURE OF INVESTIGATION AND CONCILIATION

Article XV

The procedure of investigation and conciliation consists in the submission of the controversy to a Commission of Investigation and Conciliation, which shall be established in accordance with the provisions established in subsequent articles of the present Treaty, and which shall function within the limitations prescribed therein.

Article XVI

The party initiating the procedure of investigation and conciliation shall request the Council of the Organization of American States to convoke the Commission of

Investigation and Conciliation. The Council for its part shall take immediate steps to convoke it.

Once the request to convoke the Commission has been received, the controversy between the parties shall immediately be suspended, and the parties shall refrain from any act that might make conciliation more difficult. To that end, at the request of one of the parties, the Council of the Organization of American States may, pending the convocation of the Commission, make appropriate recommendations to the parties.

Article XVII

Each of the High Contracting Parties may appoint, by means of a bilateral agreement consisting of a simple exchange of notes with each of the other signatories, two members of the Commission of Investigation and Conciliation, only one of whom may be of its own nationality. The fifth member, who shall perform the functions of chairman, shall be selected immediately by common agreement of the members thus appointed.

Any one of the contracting parties may remove members whom it has appointed, whether nationals or aliens; at the same time it shall appoint the successor. If this is not done, the removal shall be considered as not having been made. The appointments and substitutions shall be registered with the Pan American Union, which shall endeavor to ensure that the commissions maintain their full complement of five members.

Article XVIII

Without prejudice to the provisions of the foregoing article, the Pan American Union shall draw up a permanent panel of American conciliators, to be made up as follows:

a) Each of the High Contracting Parties shall appoint, for three-year periods, two of their nationals who enjoy the highest reputation for fairness, competence and integrity;

b) The Pan American Union shall request of the candidates notice of their formal acceptance, and it shall place on the panel of conciliators the names of the persons who so notify it;

c) The governments may, at any time, fill vacancies occurring among their appointees; and they may reappoint their members.

Article XIX

In the event that a controversy should arise between two or more American States that have not appointed the Commission referred to in Article XVII, the following procedure shall be observed:

a) Each party shall designate two members from the permanent panel of American conciliators, who are not of the same nationality as the appointing party.

b) These four members shall in turn choose a fifth member, from the permanent panel, not of the nationality of either party.

c) If, within a period of thirty days following the notification of their selection, the four members are unable to agree upon a fifth member, they shall each separately list the conciliators composing the permanent panel, in order of their preference, and upon comparison of the lists so prepared, the one who first receives a majority of votes shall be declared elected. The person so elected shall perform the duties of chairman of the Commission.

Article XX

In convening the Commission of Investigation and Conciliation, the Council of the Organization of American States shall determine the place where the Commission shall meet. Thereafter, the Commission may determine the place or places in which it is to function, taking into account the best facilities for the performance of its work.

Article XXI

When more than two states are involved in the same controversy, the states that hold similar points of view shall be considered as a single party. If they have different interests they shall be entitled to increase the number of conciliators in order that all parties may have equal representation. The chairman shall be elected in the manner set forth in Article XIX.

Article XXII

It shall be the duty of the Commission of Investigation and Conciliation to clarify the points in dispute between the parties and endeavor to bring about an agreement between them upon mutually acceptable terms. The Commission shall institute such investigations of the facts involved in the controversy as it may deem necessary for the purpose of proposing acceptable bases of settlement.

Article XXIII

It shall be the duty of the parties to facilitate the work of the Commission and to supply it, to the fullest extent possible, with all useful documents and information, and also to use the means at their disposal to enable the Commission to summon and hear witnesses or experts and perform other tasks in the territories of the parties, in conformity with their laws.

Article XXIV

During the proceedings before the Commission, the parties shall be represented by plenipotentiary delegates or by agents, who shall serve as intermediaries between them and the Commission. The parties and the Commission may use the services of technical advisers and experts.

Article XXV

The Commission shall conclude its work within a period of six months from the date of its installation; but the parties may, by mutual agreement, extend the period.

Article XXVI

If, in the opinion of the parties, the controversy relates exclusively to questions of fact, the Commission shall limit itself to investigating such questions, and shall conclude its activities with an appropriate report.

Article XXVII

If an agreement is reached by conciliation, the final report of the Commission shall be limited to the text of the agreement and shall be published after its transmittal to the parties, unless the parties decide otherwise. If no agreement is reached, the final report shall contain a summary of the work of the Commission; it shall be delivered to the parties, and shall be published after the expiration of six months unless the parties decide otherwise. In both cases, the final report shall be adopted by a majority vote.

Article XXVIII

The reports and conclusions of the Commission of Investigation and Conciliation shall not be binding upon the parties, either with respect to the statement of facts or in regard to questions of law, and they shall have no other character than that of recommendations submitted for the consideration of the parties in order to facilitate a friendly settlement of the controversy.

Article XXIX

The Commission of Investigation and Conciliation shall transmit to each of the parties, as well as to the Pan American Union, certified copies of the minutes of its proceedings. These minutes shall not be published unless the parties so decide.

Article XXX

Each member of the Commission shall receive financial remuneration, the amount of which shall be fixed by agreement between the parties. If the parties do not agree thereon, the Council of the Organization shall determine the remuneration. Each government shall pay its own expenses and an equal share of the common expenses of the Commission, including the aforementioned remunerations.

CHAPTER FOUR
JUDICIAL PROCEDURE

Article XXXI

In conformity with Article 36, paragraph 2, of the Statute of the International Court of Justice, the high Contracting Parties declare that they recognize, in relation to any other American State, the jurisdiction of the Court as compulsory *ipso facto*, without the necessity of any special agreement so long as the present Treaty is in force, in all disputes of a juridical nature that arise among them concerning:

a) The interpretation of a treaty;

b) Any question of international law;

c) The existence of any fact which, if established, would constitute the breach of an international obligation;

d) The nature of extent of the reparation to be made for the breach of an international obligation.

Article XXXII

When the conciliation procedure previously established in the present Treaty or by agreement of the parties does not lead to a solution, and the said parties have not agreed upon an arbitral procedure, either of them shall be entitled to have recourse to the International Court of Justice in the manner prescribed in Article 40 of the Statute thereof. The Court shall have compulsory jurisdiction in accordance with Article 36, paragraph 1, of the said Statute.

Article XXXIII

If the parties fail to agree as to whether the Court has jurisdiction over the controversy, the Court itself shall first decide that question.

Article XXXIV

If the Court, for the reasons set forth in Articles V, VI and VII of this Treaty, declares itself to be without jurisdiction to hear the controversy, such controversy shall be declared ended.

Article XXXV

If the Court for any other reason declares itself to be without jurisdiction to hear and adjudge the controversy, the High Contracting Parties obligate themselves to submit it to arbitration, in accorance with the provisions of Chapter Five of this Treaty.

Article XXXVI

In the case of controversies submitted to the judicial procedure to which this Treaty refers, the decision shall devolve upon the full Court, or, if the parties so request, upon a special chamber in conformity with Article 26 of the Statute of the Court. The parties may agree, moreover, to have the controversy decided *exaequo et bono.*

Article XXXVII

The procedure to be followed by the Court shall be that established in the Statute thereof.

CHAPTER FIVE
PROCEDURE OF ARBITRATION

Article XXXVIII

Notwithstanding the provisions of Chapter Four of this Treaty, the High Contracting Parties may, if they so agree, submit to arbitration differences of any kind, whether juridical or not, that have arisen or may arise in the future between them.

Article XXXIX

The Arbitral Tribunal to which a controversy is to be submitted shall, in the cases contemplated in Articles XXXV and XXXVIII of the present Treaty, be constituted in the following manner, unless there exists an agreement to the contrary.

Article XL

(1) Within a period of two months after notification of the decision of the Court in the case provided for in Article XXXV, each party shall name one arbiter of recognized competence in questions of international law and of the highest integrity, and shall transmit the designation to the Council of the Organization. At the same time, each party shall present to the Council a list of ten jurists chosen from among those on the general panel of members of the Permanent Court of Arbitration of The Hague who do not belong to its national group and who are willing to be members of the Arbitral Tribunal.

(2) The Council of the Organization shall, within the month following the presentation of the lists, proceed to establish the Arbitral Tribunal in the following manner:

a) If the lists presented by the parties contain the three names in common, such persons, together with the two directly named by the parties, shall constitute the Arbitral Tribunal;

b) In case these lists contain more than three names in common, the three arbiters needed to complete the Tribunal shall be selected by lot;

c) In the circumstances envisaged in the two preceding clauses, the five arbiters designated shall choose one of their number as presiding officer;

d) If the lists contain only two names in common, such candidates and the two arbiters directly selected by the parties shall by common agreement choose the fifth arbiter, who shall preside over the Tribunal. The choice shall devolve upon a jurist on the aforesaid general panel of the Permanent Court of Arbitration of The Hague who has not been included in the lists drawn up by the parties;

e) If the lists contain only one name in common, that person shall be a member of the Tribunal, and another name shall be chosen by lot from among the eighteen jurists remaining on the above-mentioned lists. The presiding officer shall be elected in accordance with the procedure established in the preceding clause;

f) If the lists contain no names in common, one arbiter shall be chosen by lot from each of the lists; and the fifth arbiter, who shall act as presiding officer, shall be chosen in the manner previously indicated;

g) If the four arbiters cannot agree upon a fifth arbiter within one month after the Council of the Organization has notified them of their appointment, each of them shall separately arrange the list of jurists in the order of their preference and, after comparison of the lists so formed, the person who first obtains a majority vote shall be declared elected.

Article XLI

The parties may by mutual agreement establish the Tribunal in the manner they deem most appropriate; they may even select a single arbiter, designating in such case a chief of state, an eminent jurist, or any court of justice in which the parties have mutual confidence.

Article XLII

When more than two states are involved in the same controversy, the states defending the same interests shall be considered as a single party. If they have opposing interests they shall have the right to increase the number of arbiters so that all parties may have equal representation. The presiding officer shall be selected by the method established in Article XL.

Article XLIII

The parties shall in each case draw up a special agreement clearly defining the specific matter that is the subject of the controversy, the seat of the Tribunal, the rules of procedure to be observed, the period within which the award is to be handed down, and such other conditions as they may agree upon among themselves.

If the special agreement cannot be drawn up within three months after the date of the installation of the Tribunal, it shall be drawn up by the International Court of Justice through summary procedure, and shall be binding upon the parties.

Article XLIV

The parties may be represented before the Arbitral Tribunal by such persons as they may designate.

Article XLV

If one of the parties fails to designate its arbiter and present its list of candidates within the period provided for in Article XL, the other party shall have the right to request the Council of the Organization to establish the Arbitral Tribunal. The Council shall immediately urge the delinquent party to fulfill its obligations within an additional period of fifteen days, after which time the Council itself shall establish the Tribunal in the following manner:

a) It shall select a name by lot from the list presented by the petitioning party.

b) It shall choose, by absolute majority vote, two jurists from the general panel of the Permanent Court of Arbitration of The Hague who do not belong to the national group of any of the parties.

c) The three persons so designated, together with the one directly chosen by the petitioning party, shall select the fifth arbiter, who shall act as presiding officer, in the manner provided for in Article XL.

d) Once the Tribunal is installed, the procedure established in Article XLIII shall be followed.

Article XLVI

The award shall be accompanied by a supporting opinion, shall be adopted by a majority vote, and shall be published after notification thereof has been given to the parties. The dissenting arbiter or arbiters shall have the right to state the grounds for their dissent.

The award, once it is duly handed down and made known to the parties, shall settle the controversy definitively, shall not be subject to appeal, and shall be carried out immediately.

Article XLVII

Any differences that arise in regard to the interpretation or execution of the award shall be submitted to the decision of the Arbitral Tribunal that rendered the award.

Article XLVIII

Within a year after notification thereof, the award shall be subject to review by the same tribunal at the request of one of the parties, provided a previously existing fact is discovered unknown to the Tribunal and to the party requesting the review, and provided the Tribunal is of the opinion that such fact might have a decisive influence on the award.

Article XLIX

Every member of the Tribunal shall receive financial remuneration, the amount of which shall be fixed by agreement between the parties. If the parties do not agree on the amount, the Council of the Organization shall determine the remuneration. Each Government shall pay its own expenses and an equal share of the common expenses of the Tribunal, including the aforementioned remunerations.

CHAPTER SIX
FULFILLMENT OF DECISIONS

Article L

If one of the High Contracting Parties should fail to carry out the obligations imposed upon it by a decision of the International Court of Justice or by an arbitral award, the other party or parties concerned shall, before resorting to the Security Council of the United Nations, propose a Meeting of Consultation of Ministers of Foreign Affairs to agree upon appropriate measures to ensure the fulfillment of the judicial decision or arbitral award.

CHAPTER SEVEN
ADVISORY OPINIONS

Article LI

The parties concerned in the solution of a controversy may, by agreement, petition the General Assembly or the Security Council of the United Nations to request an advisory opinion of the International Court of Justice on any juridical question.

The petition shall be made through the Council of the Organization of American States.

CHAPTER EIGHT
FINAL PROVISIONS

Article LII

The present Treaty shall be ratified by the High Contracting Parties in accordance with their constitutional procedures. The original instrument shall be deposited in the Pan American Union, which shall transmit an authentic certified copy to each Government for the purpose of ratification. The instruments of ratification shall be deposited in the archives of the Pan American Union, which shall notify the signatory governments of the deposit. Such notification shall be considered as an exchange of ratifications.

Article LIII

This Treaty shall come into effect between the High Contracting Parties in the order in which they deposit their respective ratifications.

Article LIV

Any American State which is not a signatory to the present Treaty, or which has made reservations thereto, may adhere to it, or may withdraw its reservations in whole or in part, by transmitting an official instrument to the Pan American Union, which shall notify the other High Contracting Parties in the manner herein established.

Article LV

Should any of the High Contracting Parties make reservations concerning the present Treaty, such reservations shall, with respect to the state that makes them, apply to all signatory states on the basis of reciprocity.

Article LVI

The present Treaty shall remain in force indefinitely, but may be denounced upon one year's notice, at the end of which period it shall cease to be in force with respect to the state denouncing it, but shall continue in force for the remaining signatories. The denunciation shall be addressed to the Pan American Union, which shall transmit it to the other Contracting Parties.

The denunciation shall have no effect with respect to pending procedures initiated prior to the transmission of the particular notification.

Article LVII

The present Treaty shall be registered with the Secretariat of the United Nations through the Pan American Union.

Article LVIII

As this Treaty comes into effect through the successive ratifications of the High Contracting Parties, the following treaties, conventions and protocols shall cease to be in force with respect to such parties:

Treaty to Avoid or Prevent Conflicts between the American States, of May 3, 1923;

General Convention of Inter-American Conciliation, of January 5, 1929;

General Treaty of Inter-American Arbitration and Additional Protocol of Progressive Arbitration, of January 5, 1929;

Additional Protocol to the General Convention of Inter-American Conciliation, of December 26, 1933;

Anti-War Treaty of Non-Aggression and Conciliation, of October 10, 1933;

Convention to Coordinate, Extend and Assure the Fulfillment of the Existing Treaties between the American States, of December 23, 1936;

Inter-American Treaty on Good Offices and Mediation, of December 23, 1936;

Treaty on the Prevention of Controversies, of December 23, 1936.

Article LIX

The provisions of the foregoing Article shall not apply to procedures already initiated or agreed upon in accordance with any of the above-mentioned international instruments.

Article LX

The present Treaty shall be called the "PACT OF BOGOTÁ."

In Witness Whereof, the undersigned Plenipotentiaries, having deposited their full powers, found to be in good and due form, sign the present Treaty, in the name of their respective Governments, on the dates appearing below their signatures.

Done at the City of Bogotá, in four texts, in the English, French, Portuguese and Spanish languages respectively, on the thirtieth day of April, nineteen hundred forty-eight.

RESERVATIONS

Argentina

"The Delegation of the Argentine Republic, on signing the American Treaty on Pacific Settlement (Pact of Bogotá), makes reservations in regard to the following articles, to which it does not adhere:

1) VII, concerning the protection of aliens;
2) Chapter Four (Articles XXXI to XXXVII), Judicial Procedure;
3) Chapter Five (Articles XXXVIII to XLIX), Procedure of Arbitration;
4) Chapter Six (Article L), Fulfillment of Decisions.

Arbitration and judicial procedure have, as institutions, the firm adherence of the Argentine Republic, but the Delegation cannot accept the form in which the procedures for their application have been regulated, since, in its opinion, they should have been established only for controversies arising in the future and not originating in or having any relation to causes, situations or facts existing before the signing of this instrument. The compulsory execution of arbitral or judicial decisions and the limitation which prevents the states from judging for themselves in regard to matters that pertain to their domestic jurisdiction in accordance with Article V are contrary to Argentine tradition. The protection of aliens, who in the Argentine Republic are protected by its Supreme Law to the same extent as the nationals, is also contrary to that tradition."

Bolivia

"The Delegation of Boliva makes a reservation with regard to Article VI, inasmuch as it considers that pacific procedures may also be applied to controversies arising from matters settled by arrangment between the Parties, when the said arrangement affects the vital interests of a state."

Ecuador

"The Delegation of Ecuador, upon signing this Pact, makes an express reservation with regard to Article VI and also every provision that contradicts or is not in harmony with the principles proclaimed by or the stipulations contained in the Charter of the United Nations, the Charter of the Organization of American States, or the Constitution of the Republic of Ecuador."

United States of America

"1. The United States does not undertake as the complainant State to submit to the International Court of Justice any controversy which is not considered to be properly within the jurisdiction of the Court.

2. The submission on the part of the United States of any controversy to arbitration, as distinguished from judicial settlement, shall be dependent upon the conclusion of a special agreement between the parties to the case.

3. The acceptance by the United States of the jurisdiction of the International Court of Justice as compulsory *ipso facto* and without special agreement, as provided in this Treaty, is limited by any jurisdictional or other limitations contained in any Declaration deposited by the United States under Article 36, paragraph 4, of the Statute of the Court, and in force at the time of the submission of any case.

4. The Government of the United States cannot accept Article VII relating to diplomatic protection and the exhaustion of remedies. For its part, the Government of the United States maintains the rules of diplomatic protection, including the rule of exhaustion of local remedies by aliens, as provided by international law."

Paraguay

"The Delegation of Paraguay makes the following reservation:

Paraguay stipulates the prior agreement of the parties as a prerequisite to the arbitration procedure established in this Treaty for every question of a non-juridical nature affecting national sovereignty and not specifically agreed upon in treaties now in force."

Peru

"The Delegation of Peru makes the following reservations:

1. Reservation with regard to the second part of Article V, because it considers that domestic jurisdiction should be defined by the state itself.

2. Reservation with regard to Article XXXIII and the pertinent part of Article XXXIV, inasmuch as it considers that the exceptions of *res judicata*, resolved by settlement between the parties or governed by agreements and treaties in force, determine, in virtue of their objective and peremptory nature, the exclusion of these cases from the application of every procedure.

3. Reservation with regard to Article XXXV, in the sense that, before arbitration is resorted to, there may be, at the request of one of the parties, a meeting of the Organ of Consultation, as established in the Charter of the Organization of American States.

4. Reservation with regard to Article XLV, because it believes that arbitration set up without the participation of one of the parties is in contradiction with its constitutional provisions."

Nicaragua

"The Nicaraguan Delegation, on giving its approval to the American Treaty on Pacific Settlement (Pact of Bogotá) wishes to record expressly that no provisions contained in the said Treaty may prejudice any position assumed by the Government of Nicaragua with respect to arbitral decisions the validity of which it has contested on the basis of the principles of international law, which clearly permit arbitral decisions to be attacked when they are adjudged to be null or invalidated. Consequently, the signature of the Nicaraguan Delegation to the Treaty in question cannot be alleged as an acceptance of any arbitral decisions that Nicaragua has contested and the validity of which is not certain.

Hence the Nicaraguan Delegation reiterates the statement made on the 28th of the current month on approving the text of the above-mentioned Treaty in Committee III."

(Here follows the list of Plenipotentiaries.)

17. Economic Agreement of Bogotá, Issued by the Ninth International Conference of American States*

May 2, 1948

Whereas: It is the desire of the American States to maintain, strengthen and develop in the economic field and within the framework of the United Nations the special relations that unite them;

The economic welfare of each State depends in large measure upon the well-being of the others;

At the Inter-American Conference for the Maintenance of Continental Peace and Security, they considered that the economic security indispensable for the progress of all the American peoples is at all times the best guarantee of their political security and of the success of their joint effort in behalf of the maintenance of continental peace;

In the Economic Charter of the Americas they have established the essential principles that should guide their economic and social policy;

They have adopted as their own the economic and social principles and aims of the Charter of the United Nations;

The American States Represented at the Ninth International Conference of American States Have Resolved:

To authorize their respective representatives, whose Full Powers have been found to be in good and due form, to sign the following articles:

CHAPTER I
PRINCIPLES

Article 1

The American States, represented at the Ninth International Conference of American States and which hereinafter shall be called the States, declare that it is their duty to cooperate toward the solution of their economic problems, and to conduct their international economic relations in the American spirit of good neighborliness.

*Organization of American States, *Annals,* Vol. I, No. 1, 1949, pp. 99-108.

Article 2

The purposes of the cooperation to which this Agreement refers and the principles that inspire it are those set forth in the Charter of the United Nations, the Economic Charter of the Americas, and the Charter of the Organization of American States.

Article 3

The States declare their intention to cooperate individually and collectively and with other nations to carry out the principle of facilitating access, on equal terms, to the trade, products, and means of production, including scientific and technical advances, that are needed for their industrial and general economic development.

At the same time, they reaffirm their resolution that, as a general policy, there should be taken into account the need to compensate for the disparity that is frequently noted between the prices of raw materials and the prices of manufactured products, by establishing the necessary balance between them.

Article 4

The States agree that encouragement should be given to such bilateral or multi-lateral agreements as will contribute to their economic welfare and common security, as provided for in this Agreement.

Article 5

The States reiterate that the productive use of their human and material resources is of interest and benefit to all countries, and that

a) General economic development, including the exploitation of natural resources, the diversification of economies, and technological advancement, will improve employment possibilities, augment the productivity and income of labor, increase demand for goods and services, help balance economies, expand international trade, and raise the level of real income; and

b) Sound industrialization, particularly that of those States which have not succeeded in fully utilizing their natural resources, is indispensable for the achievement of the aims mentioned in the foregoing paragraph.

Article 6

The extent and character of economic cooperation shall, for each participating country, be determined by its resources, the provisions of its own laws and by its commitments made through international agreements.

Article 7

The States recognize their common interest in maintaining economic conditions favorable to the development of a balanced and expanding world economy and to a high level of international trade, in such a way as to contribute to the economic strengthening and progress of each State.

Article 8

No State may apply or encourage coercive measures of an economic and political character in order to force the sovereign will of another State and to obtain from the latter advantages of any nature.

CHAPTER II
TECHNICAL COOPERATION

Article 9

The States undertake through individual and joint action to continue and to expand technical cooperation for carrying out studies; preparing plans and projects directed toward intensifying their agriculture, cattle raising, and mining; developing their industry; increasing their trade; diversifying their production and generally strengthening their economic structure.

Article 10

In order to realize the objectives set forth in the preceding Article, the Inter-American Economic and Social Council which, in the text of this Agreement, is hereinafter called the Council, shall within the sphere of its competence be responsible for the development and coordination of the activities necessary to:

a) Make a study of the current economic situation and prepare an inventory of the economic potential of the States, consisting of studies of their natural and human resources and of the possibilities of agricultural, mineral and industrial development, with a view to the full utilization of these resources and the expansion of their economies;

b) Promote such laboratory research and experimental work as it considers necessary;

c) Promote the training of technical and administrative personnel in all economic activities through such means as teacher and student exchange between technical educational institutions in the Americas; the exchange of specialized administrative officials; the exchange of specialists between governmental, technical and economic agencies; the apprenticing of skilled workers, foremen and auxiliary personnel in industrial plants and technical schools; and lectures and seminars;

d) Prepare studies on technical problems in public administration and finance, relating to trade and economic development;

e) Promote measures to increase trade among the States and between them and other countries of the world. Such measures should include the study and promotion of the adoption of sanitary standards with respect to plants and animals, for the purpose of reaching an international understanding to prevent the application of sanitary regulations as an indirect means of imposing barriers to international trade. The said study should be undertaken in cooperation with other appropriate organizations;

f) Place at the disposal of the interested country or countries the statistical data, information, and general plans that it is possible to develop in connection with the above-mentioned program;

g) Study, at the request of the Member States, specific proposals for development or for immigration with a view to giving advice in regard to their practicability and their utility in the sound economic development of the country concerned, and to assist in preparing for their later presentation to private capital, or to governmental or inter-governmental lending agencies for possible financing;

h) Place technical advice at the disposal of countries requesting it and make arrangements for the exchange of technical aid in all fields of economic activity, including social security and welfare.

Article 11

In order to perform the functions assigned to it in Article 10, the Council shall organize a permanent Technical Staff. This Staff shall be directed by a technical chief, who in matters within his competence shall participate and have a voice in the deliberations of the Council and shall execute the decisions of the latter.

The Council shall absorb existing inter-American organizations having similar functions and shall utilize the services of the Pan American Union.

Article 12

The Council shall maintain permanent contact with the Economic Commission for Latin America of the United Nations Economic and Social Council, in order to assure close collaboration and a practical division of functions so as to avoid duplication of work and expense.

In carrying out its activities, the Council shall maintain communication and exchange of information with the agencies in each country that are engaged in the study of economic problems or that serve as directing and planning agencies for the national economy, as well as with educational, technical, and scientific institutions, and with private national and international organizations of production and trade. The Council shall transmit to the governments concerned copies of its correspondence with such entities.

Article 13

In carrying out its functions the Council may request of the respective governments the facts which in its judgment it needs. The Governments may decline to give any information they consider to be confidential in character. The Council may perform its functions in the territory of a country only if authorized by that country.

Article 14

The Member States may request special studies by the Council, which shall determine whether the studies requested are within its competence and which may also indicate whether it would be more appropriate for the respective requests to be directed, in whole or in part, to other national or international institutions or to private entities.

Article 15

The States, in fixing the budget of the Pan American Union, shall take into account the amounts necessary to cover the increased expenditures of the Council and of its Technical Staff, in order that they may be able to perform the functions set forth in Article 10.

Article 16

Whenever one or more countries request the preparation of specific projects on economic development or immigration, such projects shall be drawn up by the Council with its own staff or with experts especially engaged for the account and at the cost of the country or countries requesting them, it being left to the Council, in the latter case, to determine the proportion of the costs to be borne by those countries.

Only in cases determined to be exceptional by the Council itself may the costs of specific studies on reconstruction or economic development be chargeable to the general budget.

Article 17

Nothing in this Chapter shall interfere with other arrangements entered into by the States for the reciprocal granting of technical cooperation in the economic field.

CHAPTER III
FINANCIAL COOPERATION

Article 18

The States, in accordance with Article 6 of this Agreement, undertake to grant reciprocal financial cooperation for accelerating their economic development.

Without prejudice to the obligations of each country to take the domestic measures within its power for such development, they may request financial cooperation of other States.

Article 19

The States reaffirm their purpose to bring about a high level of international trade among themselves and with the rest of the world and to promote general economic and social progress by providing stimulation for the local investment of national savings, and for private foreign capital, and they undertake to continue their efforts toward the realization of this purpose.

The States that are members of the International Monetary Fund reaffirm the aims of the Fund and in normal circumstances will utilize its services to achieve those aims. that will facilitate the accomplishment of the objectives mentioned above.

All the States agree, in appropriate cases, to supplement financial cooperation for the aforesaid objectives:

a) By means of non-discriminatory bilateral stabilization agreements on mutually advantageous bases; and

b) By the utilization of whatever institutions it may be desirable to create in the future and of which they may be members.

Article 20

The States that are members of the International Bank for Reconstruction and Development reaffirm the objectives of the Bank and agree to coordinate their efforts to make it an increasingly effective instrument for the realization of such objectives, especially those concerned with promoting their mutual economic development.

All of the States declare, furthermore, that in appropriate cases they will continue to extend medium and long-term credits to one another through governmental or inter-governmental institutions for economic development and the expansion of international trade, for the purpose of complementing the flow of private investments. Sufficient economic reasons shall exist for the particular purposes to be served by such credits, and the projects to be undertaken shall be adapted to local conditions and be able to survive without the need of excessive permanent protection or subsidy.

Furthermore, the States agree that with respect to such loans a criterion shall be established whereby it will be possible to grant facilities to debtor countries with respect to conditions and/or currencies in which they should make payment, in cases where such countries suffer an acute shortage of foreign exchange, which prevents them from complying with the terms stipulated in the loan.

Article 21

The States recognize that the lack of domestic savings, or the ineffective use thereof, has contributed to inflationary practices in many countries of America, which may ultimately endanger the stability of their rates of exchange and the orderly development of their economies.

The States agree, therefore, to stimulate the development of local money markets to provide, from non-inflationary sources, the funds needed to cover investment expenditures in national currency. The States agree that, in general, international financing should not be sought for the purpose of covering expenditures in local currency. However, they recognize that as long as available national savings in local money markets or elsewhere are not sufficient, expenditures in local currency may, in justified circumstances, be considered for the financing referred to in Article 20.

CHAPTER IV
PRIVATE INVESTMENTS

Article 22

The States declare that the investment of private capital and the introduction of modern methods and administrative skills from other countries, for productive and economic and socially suitable purposes, are an important factor in their general economic development and the resulting social progress.

They recognize that the international flow of such capital will be stimulated to the extent that nationals of other countries are afforded opportunities for investment and security for existing and future investments.

Foreign capital shall receive equitable treatment. The States therefore agree not to take unjustified, unreasonable or discriminatory measures that would impair the legally acquired rights or interests of nationals of other countries in the enterprises, capital, skills, arts or technology they have supplied.

The States shall reciprocally grant appropriate facilities and incentives for the investment and reinvestment of foreign capital, and they shall impose no unjustifiable restrictions upon the transfer of such capital and the earnings thereon.

The States agree not to set up within their respective territories unreasonable or unjustifiable impediments that would prevent other States from obtaining on equitable terms the capital, skills, and technology needed for their economic development.

Article 23

The States declare that foreign investments should be made with due regard not only for the legitimate profit of the investors, but also with a view both to increasing the national income and accelerating the sound economic development of the country in which the investment is made and to promoting the economic and social welfare of the persons directly dependent upon the enterprise in question.

They further declare that, with respect to employment and the conditions thereof, just and equitable treatment should be accorded to all personnel, national and foreign, and that the development of the technical and administrative training of national personnel should be encouraged.

The States recognize that, for private capital to contribute as much as possible to their development and progress and to the training of their nationals, it is desirable to permit enterprises, without prejudice to the laws of each country, to employ and utilize the services of a reasonable number of technical experts and executive personnel, whatever their nationality may be.

Article 24

Foreign capital shall be subject to national laws, with the guarantees provided for in this chapter, especially Article 22, and without prejudice to existing or future obligations between States. The States reaffirm their right to establish, within a system of equity and of effective legal and judicial guarantees:

a) Measures to prevent foreign investments from being utilized directly or indirectly as an instrument for intervening in national politics or for prejudicing the security or fundamental interests of the receiving countries; and

b) Standards with respect to the extent, conditions, and terms upon which they will permit future foreign investments.

Article 25

The States shall take no discriminatory action against investments by virtue of which foreign enterprises or capital may be deprived of legally acquired property rights, for reasons or under conditions different from those that the Constitution or laws of each country provide for the expropriation of national property. Any expropriation shall be accompanied by payment of fair compensation in a prompt, adequate and effective manner.

Article 26

The States declare their intention to promote sound investment by developing, whenever possible and in accordance with the laws of each country, uniform principles of corporate accounting, as well as of standards for the reports that may or should be used by private investors.

Article 27

Each State, in order to stimulate private investment for the purpose of economic development, shall, within the framework of its own institutions, seek to liberalize its tax laws so as progressively to reduce or even eliminate double taxation as regards income from foreign sources and to avoid unduly burdensome and discriminatory taxation, without, however, creating international avenues for tax avoidance.

The States shall also seek to conclude as soon as possible agreements to prevent double taxation.

CHAPTER V

COOPERATION FOR INDUSTRIAL AND
ECONOMIC DEVELOPMENT

Article 28

In accordance with Article 5 of this Agreement, the States:

a) Recognize that they are committed to cooperate with one another, by all appropriate means, so that their economic development shall not be retarded but rather accelerated as much as possible, and when suitable, to collaborate with inter-governmental agencies to facilitate and promote industrial and economic development in general, including the expansion of agriculture, mining, and the production of other raw materials with which to meet their needs;

b) Shall seek to utilize such industries and production in general as are of present or potential efficiency, so that they may be able to participate in joint economic plans of interest to the Americas; and

c) Also consider it desirable that progressive development of production be carried forward in accordance with the agricultural and industrial potentialities of each country, in order fully to meet the requirements of consumer nations at prices that are fair to them and that offer the producers reasonable returns.

Article 29

Progressive industrial and economic development requires, among other things, adequate supplies of capital, materials, raw materials, modern equipment, technology, and technical and administrative skill. Therefore, to promote and assist in supplying such facilities:

a) The States, in accordance with the objectives of economic cooperation of this Agreement, agree to do as much as possible, within the limits of their powers, to facilitate the acquisition and exportation, for their mutual benefit, of the capital, machinery, raw materials, services and other elements needed for their economic requirements.

b) The States undertake not to impose unreasonable or unjustifiable obstacles that impede the acquisition from one another, on fair and equitable terms, of the elements, materials and services mentioned in the preceding paragraph.

c) If exceptional circumstances make it necessary to apply restrictions on exports, priorities for purchases and exports, or both, the States shall apply such measures on a fair and equitable basis, taking into account their mutual needs and other appropriate and pertinent factors; and

d) In applying the restrictions mentioned in the preceding paragraph, the States shall seek to make the distribution of and the trade in the restricted products approximate as nearly as possible the amounts that the various countries could have obtained in the absence of such restrictions.

CHAPTER VI
ECONOMIC SECURITY

Article 30

The States agree to cooperate among themselves and with other producing and consumer nations, for the purpose of concluding inter-governmental agreements to prevent or correct dislocations in international trade in regard to raw materials that are basic and essential for the economies of the producing countries of the Hemisphere, such as tendencies and situations of persistent disequilibrium between production and consumption, of accumulation of substantial surpluses, or of sharp fluctuations in prices, without prejudice to the provisions of the second paragraph of Article 3.

Article 31

States with common boundaries or those belonging within the same economic region, may conclude preferential agreements for purposes of economic development, each State respecting the obligations that it has undertaken by virtue of existing international bilateral agreements or multilateral agreements that have been or may be concluded. The benefits granted in such agreements shall not be extended to other countries by application of the most-favored-nation clause, except in case of a special agreement in that respect.

The development of the principle contained in this Article is assigned to the Specialized Economic Conference to be held during the second half of the present year.

CHAPTER VII
SOCIAL GUARANTEES

Article 32

The States, within the economic objectives expressed in this Agreement, agree to cooperate in the most effective manner in the solution of their social problems, and to adopt measures appropriate to their political and social institutions in accordance with what is provided in the Inter-American Charter of Social Guarantees, and tending:

a) To assure the effective reign of social justice and good relations between workers and employers;

b) To foster opportunites for useful and regular employment, at fair wages, for all persons who want and are able to work;

c) To reduce the disruptive effect of illness, old age, temporary unemployment and occupational hazards on the continuity of earnings;

d) To safeguard the health, welfare, and education of the entire population, with special regard to maternal and child health;

e) To provide in each country suitable administrative machinery and personnel to implement these programs;

f) To ensure a legal system of paid annual vacations for all workers, taking into special account the suitable period in the case of minors; and

g) To ensure permanence of tenure to all wage earners, and prevent the possibility of discharge without just cause.

CHAPTER VIII
MARITIME TRANSPORTATION

Article 33

The States agree to encourage and coordinate the most effective use of their transportation facilities, including ports and free ports, so as to satisfy their economic needs at the lowest possible cost compatible with reliable and adequate service.

Article 34

The States agree to encourage the reduction of transportation costs by all means possible, through the improvement of port conditions, regulations affecting the working of ports and vessels, customs requirements, and the lowering of fees and other charges and imposts that unduly restrict inter-American maritime trade.

Article 35

The States shall endeavor to remove discriminatory action and unnecessary restrictions by governments affecting shipping engaged in international trade, so as to promote the availability of shipping services to the commerce of the world without discrimination; assistance and encouragement given by a government for the development of its national shipping and for purposes of security does not in itself constitute discrimination, provided that such assistance and encouragement is not based on measures designed to restrict the freedom of shipping of all flags to take part in international trade.

CHAPTER IX
FREEDOM OF TRANSIT

Article 36

The States consider that, to encourage international trade among them, there should be freedom of transit through their respective territories.

Regional and general agreements shall regulate the application of this principle among the States of the Continent.

CHAPTER X
INTER-AMERICAN TRAVEL

Article 37

The States declare that the development of inter-American travel, including tourist travel, constitutes an important factor in their economic development which contributes to expanding trade, facilitating technical cooperation, and increasing economic harmony. They undertake, therefore, to promote national and international action to reduce restrictions on non-immigrant travelers of the States, without discrimination among visitors because of the object of their visit, whether for pleasure, health, business or education.

The States consider that one of the most effective means to encourage inter-American travel is to reduce the cost of fares.

CHAPTER XI
ADJUSTMENT OF ECONOMIC DISPUTES

Article 38

The States agree, individually and collectively, to resort only to orderly and amicable means in the settling of all economic differences or disputes between them. They agree, when such controversies arise, to enter into consultations through diplomatic channels for the purpose of reaching a mutually satisfactory solution. If such consultations prove ineffective, any State that is a party to the controversy may request the Council to arrange for further discussions sponsored by the Council for the purpose of facilitating an amicable settlement of the controversy between the parties.

If necessary, the States shall submit the solution of economic disputes or controversies to the procedure set forth in the Inter-American Peace System or to other procedures set forth in agreements already in existence or which may be concluded in the future.

CHAPTER XII

COORDINATION WITH OTHER INTERNATIONAL AGENCIES

Article 39

The Council, in accordance with the provisions of the Charter of the Organization of American States, shall take all necessary measures to coordinate the activites within its jurisdiction with the activities of other international agencies, in order to eliminate duplication of effort and to establish a basis for effective cooperation in areas of common interest. To this end the Council shall maintain the fullest exchange of information necessary for such cooperation and coordination of efforts, and establish working arrangements with other international agencies regarding the preparation and execution of studies and programs.

CHAPTER XIII

RATIFICATION, ENTRY INTO FORCE AND AMENDMENTS

Article 40

The present Economic Agreement of Bogotá shall remain open to signature by the States, and shall be ratified in accordance with their respective constitutional procedures. The original instrument, whose texts in Spanish, English, Portuguese and French are equally authentic, shall be deposited with the Pan American Union, which shall transmit certified copies to the Governments for purposes of ratification. The instruments of ratification shall be deposited with the Pan American Union, which shall notify the signatory Governments of such deposit. Such notification shall be considered an exchange of ratifications.

Article 41

The present Agreement shall enter into effect among the ratifying States when two-thirds of the signatory States have deposited their ratifications. The present Agreement shall enter into effect with respect to the remaining States in the order in which they deposit their ratifications.

Article 42

The present Agreement shall be registered in the Secretariat of the United Nations through the Pan American Union, upon the deposit of the ratifications of two-thirds of the signatory States.

Article 43

Amendments to the present Agreement shall be proposed, with the necessary advance notice through the Council, for consideration, together with the respective reports, if any, of the Council, by the Inter-American Conference or a Specialized Conference.

Such amendements shall enter into force as among the States accepting them when, in fulfillment of the provisions of Article 40, two-thirds of the Member States at that time parties to the Agreement, have deposited the document containing their acceptance with the General Secretariat of the Organization of American States, which shall send certified copies of such document to the Governments of all the signatory States.

RESERVATIONS

Reservation of the Delegation of Ecuador to the Economic Agreement of Bogotá

The Delegation of Ecuador, on signing this Agreement, makes the following reservations:

First: The principle established in the third article, of facilitating access to trade under equal conditions, must be understood in harmony with Article 31, according to which preferential agreements are permitted for the purposes of economic development.

Second: Article 24 must not be understood in the sense of limiting the principle according to which foreign capital is subject to the national laws.

Third: Article 25 must be understood in the sense that the rule therein established must be subordinated to the constitutional provisions in force at the time of its application, and that it is exclusively within the jurisdiction of the courts of the country within which the expropriation takes place to determine, in accordance with the laws in force, everything relating to the circumstances under which such expropriation must be carried out, the sum to be paid, and the means of executing such payment.

Fourth: Article 31 must be understood in the sense that preferences between Spanish-American States are permitted, either for economic reasons—due to the need for the development of their economies and because they belong to the same region—or because such preferences concern States united among themselves by special ties based on a community of language, origin, and culture.

Fifth: Article 35 must be understood in the sense that the disciminatory measures mentioned therein do not refer to the preferences that may well be granted by Spanish-American States for the development of their merchant marines, preferences the establishment of which Ecuador does not renounce. Ecuador especially reserves to itself the right to consider as national vessels those of the Flota Mercante Grancolom-biana, S. A., regardless of whether they fly the flags of Venezuela, Colombia, or Panama.

Chapter I

Reservation of the Delegation of the United States of America

The Delegation of the United States of America finds it necessary to enter a formal reservation to the second paragraph of Article 3 of the Economic Agreement of Bogotá referring to the relationship between the prices of primary products and manufactured products.

Chapter IV

Reservation of the Delegation of Mexico to Articles 22, 24 and 25 of the Economic Agreement of Bogotá

1. The Delegation of Mexico makes an express reservation to the last part of Article 25, to the effect that the principle established there should be subordinated to the constitutional laws of each country.

2. Although in agreement with the spirit of equity that inspires Article 22, paragraph 3, and the first paragraph of Article 24, the Delegation of Mexico at the same time makes an express reservation on the texts thereof, since, in their present wording, they could be interpreted as a limitation to the principle that aliens, as well as nationals, are subject to the laws and courts of the country.

Reservation of the Delegation of the Argentine Republic

Argentina wishes to record in the Minutes that—as it stated in making known its vote on Article 25 of the Economic Agreement of Bogotá on the amendment proposed thereto by the Delegation of Mexico—it confirms the fact that it gave its approval to the above-mentioned text primarily with the understanding that that text does not in any way indicate that international treaties or agreements shall prevail over the constitutional texts of the American countries, nor that foreign capital investments shall be subject to any jurisdiction other than that of their own courts. It further understands that the concepts expressed with regard to the above-mentioned article apply to all pertinent provisions of the Agreement.

Declaration of the Delegation of Uruguay

The Delegation of Uruguay understands that Chapter IV grants foreign capital entering its country no guarantee not already afforded it by constitutional provisions. And, with regard to Article 25, it considers that the express reference to the constitution, in matters relative to the system of expropriation and payment therefor, is unnecessary, because constitutional provisions always govern the settlement of all situations, since all inhabitants are subject to the jurisdiction of the national courts.

Reservation of the Delegation of Guatemala

The Delegation of Guatemala makes an express reservation to the last part of

Article 25 in the sense that the principle established there should be subject to the constitutional rules in force in each country.

It also makes an express reservation regarding the third paragraph of Article 22, and the first paragraph of Article 24, insofar as they restrict the principle that aliens, as well as nationals, are subject to the laws and courts of the country.

Declaration of the Delegation of Cuba
The Delegation of Cuba has voted affirmatively on Article 25 with the understanding that the last paragraph thereof, interpreted dogmatically, contains provisions in accordance with the Constitution of Cuba.

Reservation of the Delegation of Venezuela
Venezuela makes an express reservation to Article 25 for the reasons set forth during the debate. Regarding the rest of Chapter IV, it states that in no case will it admit the preeminence of international treaties or agreements over the text of its constitution, nor will it accept any jurisdiction for foreign investments other than that of its own courts.

Reservation of the Delegation of Honduras
The Delegation of Honduras declares that it has voted affirmatively on Article 25 of the Economic Agreement of Bogotá, with the interpretation that the application of the last part of that article—like the application of the other parts thereof—remains subject to the primacy of the National Political Constitution.

Chapter VI

Reservation of the Delegation of the Dominican Republic
The Delegation of the Dominican Republic makes express reservation to Article 31 on the ground that the procedures set forth in the Charter of Habana for preferential agreements did not serve as essential guide in its formulation, and since it may give rise to a policy of privileges at variance with the desire of the American people to offer one another mutual advantages.

Reservation of the Delegation of the United States of America
The Delegation of the United States of America finds it necessary to enter its formal reservations to Articles 30 and 31 of the Economic Agreement of Bogotá.

Chapter VII

Reservation of the Delegation of Colombia
The Delegation of Colombia makes a reservation regarding clauses f) and g) of Article 32 of the Economic Agreement of Bogotá, as these concern points that were submitted for the consideration of the respective committee at the last moment, without time for study or consultation on the part of the Delegation.

Reservation of the Delegation of the United States of America
The Delegation of the United States of America finds it necessary, for the same

reasons as those set forth in its reservation to the Charter of Social Guarantees approved at this Conference, to enter a formal reservation to the subparagraphs f) and g) of Article 32 of the Economic Agreement of Bogotá.

Chapter VIII

Reservation of the Delegation of Venezuela

The Delegation of Venezuela wishes to have it recorded in the Minutes that, in approving Chapter VIII of this Economic Agreement of Bogotá, and the annexed declaration, it did so with the assurance that the phrase "questions having to do with maritime transport" includes the problem relating to discriminatory practices and similar problems that appear in the maritime transport contracts that the conferences or associations of ship owners have in use, as was expressly approved in the work group to which the study of this chapter was assigned.

It also understands that the foregoing sentence includes the study of the freight rates at present in effect and the means for ensuring that such rates be fair and equitable.

Reservation of the Delegation of Cuba

The Delegation of Cuba states that measures adopted as defense against discriminatory measures taken by other States are not themselves to be considered as discriminatory.

Statement of the Delegations of Ecuador, Venezuela, and Colombia

For the purposes of the provisions of Chapter VIII—Maritime Transport—of the Economic Agreement of Bogotá, the Delegations of Ecuador, Venezuela, and Colombia state that they consider the Flota Mercante Grancolombiana, S.A., as their national merchant marine because of the participation of capital of Ecuador, Venezuela, and Colombia in that enterprise, regardless of whether the vessels of the company fly the flag of Ecuador, Colombia, or Venezuela.

Reservation of the Delegation of Chile

The Delegation of Chile, in view of the declaration made by the Delegation of Ecuador at the meeting of Subcommittee IV C held during the current month of April, on the application of certain discriminatory measures as a means of giving support to their national merchant marine, declares: that it wishes to record in the Minutes its opinion that certain governmental disciminations and restrictions exist in inter-American maritime commerce and that in its desire to bring about the elimination thereof, it reserves the right to make proposals and to participate in any other debates on this topic at future meetings of the American States.

Chapter IX

Reservation of the Delegation of Honduras

The Delegation of Honduras, in voting affirmatively on the article contained in Chapter IX—Freedom of Transit—does so with the reservation that freedom of transit cannot be established at present or in the very near future for merchandise that arrives at any of its Atlantic ports for transshipment across Honduran territory to another country, whether or not utilizing the Pacific ports of Honduras.

Chapter X

Reservation of the Delegation of Argentina

Argentina explains that its reservation to Article 37 refers exclusively to the latter part thereof, to the effect that there shall be no discriminations for reasons of health. Argentina understands that this matter must obviously be subject to sanitary provisions in force in each country.

In witness whereof, the respective Plenipotentiaries sign and affix their seals to the present Economic Agreement of Bogotá, at the City of Bogotá, on the second day of May of 1948, in texts in the English and Spanish languages, which shall be deposited in the archives of the Pan American Union, to which they shall be transmitted through the Secretary General of the Conference, in order that certified copies may be sent to the Governments of the American Republics.

(Here follows the list of Plenipotentiaries.)

18. The Costa Rica-Nicaragua Incident: Effective International Action in Keeping the Peace*

June 5, 1949

On December 3, 1948, the Inter-American Treaty for Reciprocal Assistance, more familiarly known as the Rio treaty, entered into force. A scant week after the elaborate ceremony at the Pan American Union, Costa Rica, on December 11, requested that the treaty be invoked. This first test of the Rio machinery resulted in the establishment of numerous precedents in inter-American organization and in the interpretation of this mutual defense agreement. In view of the importance of these precedents and the general similarity between the Rio document and the North Atlantic pact, it may be of interest to review in some detail the steps taken in the initial implementation of the Rio accord.

The Costa Rican action was taken in a letter of December 11, 1948, to the chairman of the Council of the Organization of American States (COAS) from Mario A. Esquivel, Ambassador of Costa Rica to Washington and representative of his government on the Council. As is generally known, among the principal features of the treaty are stipulations concerning specific obligations on the part of the American Republics in the event either of an armed attack or other threats to the integrity of any of one of their number. The Costa Rican Ambassador's communication charged that on the night of December 10 Costa Rican territory had been invaded by armed forces proceeding from Nicaragua. The Ambassador stated that in the opinion of his government this violation of the territory of a sister republic with the aim of overthrowing its established government had precipitated a situation within the scope of article 6 of the

Department of State Bulletin, June 5, 1949, pp. 707-12; 725.

Rio treaty. The Ambassador went on to request an immediate convocation of the Council of the Organization of American States to consider the situation. In his communication Ambassador Esquivel refrained from alleging official participation on the part of Nicaraguan Government, confining himself to statements that the invasion had resulted from preparations carried on openly in Nicaragua by a group of Costa Ricans and that the movement had proceeded from Nicaragua to Costa Rican territory. In response to this request and in view of the urgency of the situation, the chairman of the COAS, Ambassador Enrique V. Corominas of Argentina, called an extraordinary session of the Council for 3 p.m. on Sunday, December 12.

As the representatives of the American Republics assembled that afternoon, there was general awareness of the significant implications of the situation. The machinery provided in the Rio treaty was to be put into operation for the first time. The decisions taken, the procedures followed would serve as precedents for the future and would establish a pattern for the consideration of future controversies. Concurrent, therefore, with the rapid response to the Costa Rican call and the urgent consideration of practical steps to serve the immediate situation, careful assessment of the juridical aspects of the problem and of their import for future situations was required. Some felt that the application of the Rio treaty should be confined to conflicts between states and, since not even the aggrieved party here had charged direct action by the other state, there were perhaps no grounds for calling the treaty into action.

Pertinent Treaty Articles

A citation of pertinent articles of the treaty is here given. The first paragraph of article 3 provides as follows:

> The High Contracting Parties agree that an armed attack by any State against an American State shall be considered as an attack against all the American States and, consequently, each one of the said Contracting Parties undertakes to assist in meeting the attack in the exercise of the inherent right of individual or collective self-defense recognized by Article 51 of the Charter of the United Nations.

Article 6 reads as follows:

> If the inviolability or the integrity of the territory or the sovereignty for political independence of any American State should be affected by an aggression which is not an armed attack or by an extra-continental or intra-continental conflict, or by any other fact or situation that might endanger the peace of America, the Organ of Consultation shall meet immediately in order to agree on the measures which must be taken in case of aggression to assist the victim of the aggression or, in any case, the measures which should be taken for the common defense and for the maintenance of the peace and security of the Continent.

The consensus was that, if the Rio treaty were to be invoked, article 6 was the provision applicable to the situation. It was then necessary to consider whether the application of article 6 would require a meeting of the Foreign Ministers to examine the problem and to decide on appropriate action. Article 11 of the treaty states that consultations

> shall be carried out immediately by means of the Meetings of Ministers of Foreign Affairs of the American Republics which have ratified the Treaty ...

The calling together of the Foreign Ministers would have been, indeed, a serious step and would have brought with it many attendant complications and inevitable delays. Following the discussion on December 12, the Council came to the conclusion that there was insufficient information at hand to justify the immediate convocation of the Foreign Ministers as the Organ of Consultation provided. In conclusion, therefore, the Council adopted a resolution providing for urgent study of the Costa Rican complaint and authorizing the chairman to seek full information from all appropriate sources. It was agreed that the Council would meet again on December 14, 48 hours later.

In pursuance of the authority given him, the chairman of the Council dispatched on the evening of the twelfth telegraphic messages to the Presidents of the 21 American Republics to apprise them of the situation and to bespeak the full cooperation of their respective governments in the maintenance of inter-American order, as well as their collaboration in such curative measures as might be decided on by the Council with respect to the instant case. On December 13 a circular telegram was addressed by the chairman to the 21 Foreign Ministers, in which they were requested to furnish any pertinent information on the problem.

On December 14, the Council assembled again in extraordinary session. On the basis of information supplied to the chairman, including a memorandum transmitted by the United States, and after lengthy discussion the meeting adopted the following resolutions:

1. To convoke the meeting of Consultation of Ministers of Foreign Affairs to study the situation existing between Costa Rica and Nicaragua, the place and date of the meeting to be fixed later.

2. The Council of American States to constitute itself Provisional Organ of Consultation as provided in Article 12 of the Treaty.

3. To authorize the Chairman of the Council to appoint a committee to investigate on the scene the alleged events and their antecedents.

4. To request all the American governments and the Secretary General of the OAS to extend full cooperation to the work of the committee which should undertake its task immediately.

Investigating Committee Named

The Provisional Organ of Consultation met the following afternoon, December 15. The chairman of the Council announced that he had that morning designated a Committee of Information from among the members of the Council to proceed at once to Costa Rica and Nicaragua. Its membership was as follows:

Ambassador José María Bello of Brazil
Ambassador Silvio Villegas of Colombia
Ambassador Luis Quintanilla of Mexico
Ambassador Juan Bautista de Lavalle of Peru
Ambassador Paul C. Daniels of the United States

The Peruvian member was unable to serve, so the Committee was composed of the four Ambassadors, together with their political and military advisers and a secretariat made available by the Pan American Union. The entire group consisted of 14 persons.

The Foreign Ministers of the American Republics were informed of this action by the chairman, and, in accord with article 15 of the treaty, a communication was immediately addressed to the chairman of the Security Council of the United Nations to inform that body of the situation under consideration by the Provisional Organ of Consultation. The chairman also placed in the minutes of the meeting a copy of the letter of appointment of the five members of the Committee of Information. This communication did not give detailed instructions to the Committee but called on it to organize immediately and to adopt such measures as it might consider necessary for the fulfillment of its duties. The Committee was thus given wide discretion as to the exercise of its functions.

The Committee departed from Washington on the evening of December 16 in a special plane made available by the United States Government and flew directly to Costa Rica, arriving at San José in the afternoon of December 17. After 2½ days in Costa Rica the Committee flew to Managua, Nicaragua, for a 2-day visit, whence the return to the United States, by way of Mexico was made. The group arrived back in Washington in the early morning of December 23, less than a week after its departure for Central America.

Committee Activities in Costa Rica and Nicaragua

The reception given the international Committee by the two affected parties to the dispute afforded a heartening indication of the respect accorded the institutions of the inter-American system by the governments and peoples of the member states. At San José, for instance, a quite unexpected welcome awaited the Committee. In addition to the President and members of the Costa Rican Cabinet, who were assembled at the airport, a crowd estimated at 40 thousand overflowed the plaza at the air terminal and lined the highway from the airport to the city. The roadway had been strewn with flowers, and small white flags were waved by the thousands along the route. This unusual reception, which had nothing of regimentation or forced participation in its spontaneous enthusiasm, was eloquent testimony to the prestige enjoyed by the Organization of American States among the general public, quite aside from any official attitude of the Government.

The Committee took testimony for one full day in Costa Rica for which the Government made available the principal salón of the *Casa Amarilla*, the Costa Rican Foreign Office. In addition, headquarters of the Committee secretariat had been set up in the Grand Hotel. At the Foreign Office the Committee met with President Figueres and the members of his Cabinet for an exposition of the Costa Rican viewpoint in the controversy. The Committee was invited to go anywhere in Costa Rica that it wished and to talk with anyone whom it desired. Private persons were invited to come forward with testimony and did so. The Costa Rican Government conducted to the Foreign Office prisoners who had been captured in the fighting near the frontier, and some of these individuals were interrogated in executive session with no members of the Government present. At the request of the Committee there appeared for questioning certain officials of the so-called Caribbean Legion, an organization of exiles of various Caribbean countries alleged to be plotting the overthrow of their home governments. Since Costa Rica and Nicaragua continued to exercise full diplomatic relations, an interview was had by the Committee with the Chargé d'Affaires of Nicaragua in San José. On the last day of the Committee's stay in Costa Rica a flight was made to Liberia, the field headquarters of the Costa Rican armed forces. Testimony was taken from officers of the Costa Rican forces, Red Cross personnel, and private individuals, and there was opportunity to gain impressions of the general atmosphere.

In sum, the Committee enjoyed complete freedom of action in Costa Rica and pursued its investigations with full acceptance on the part of the local government of the unlimited scope of its authority as an international investigating body.

Similar cooperation was shown the Committee and its mission in Nicaragua. In Managua headquarters were established at the Grand Hotel, and persons from whom testimony was desired were requested to meet with the Committee. The Costa Rican Minister at Managua was interviewed, and discussions were held with other members of the Diplomatic Corps on an informal basis. Members of the Foreign Office presented the Nicaraguan Government's version of the case and supplied pertinent data. Another witness was the former President of Costa Rica, Teodoro Picado, now residing in Nicaragua. In further cooperation the Nicaraguan Government arranged to have escorted to the Committee headquarters a Nicaraguan political prisoner and a leading officer of the invasion forces, who had subsequently been interned by the Nicaraguan Government. In the cases of both these individuals their military escort withdrew before the Committee's questioning began.

The Committee obtained additional information in calls on President Roman y Reyes of Nicaragua, on the Acting Foreign Minister, and on the Minister of War. Conversations also were had informally with officers of the Nicaraguan Army relative to events along the border. One of the military advisers to the Committee made a visit to the scene of the actual fighting in the border area and took testimony from active participants. In short, every effort was made to get at the basis of the situation and to obtain confirmed facts regarding events which had occurred in a remote frontier region and which already in less than 2 weeks' time had come to be shrouded in confusion and obscurity.

The work of the Committee and the preparation of its report provided an excellent example of the physical exigencies of modern-day diplomacy. The Committee left Managua early in the morning of December 22 and, with the exception of a 3-hour stopover in Mexico City, flew steadily for 23 hours arriving in Washington early on the morning of December 23. This day-long flight was the final lap in a journey of 6,500 miles, which involved almost continuous travel and lengthy sessions without interruptions for meals, nor should the late hours necessitated by official demands in the two capitals be discounted. Notwithstanding the physical demands of the week, the members of the Committee wished to have their report in at least preliminary form upon arrival in Washington; accordingly, the long night hours of December 22 were spent in discussion and drafting aboard the plane. A statement for release to the press on the return to Washington was prepared at 4:15 a.m. during a brief operational stop at Nashville on the morning of the twenty-third. All decisions of the Committee were taken unanimously.

Conclusions of the Committee of Information

The Committee assembled on the afternoon of December 23 with the chairman of the Council of American States and officials of the Pan American Union to give an informal report and to make arrangements for presentation of their impressions to the

Provisional Organ of Consultation, which was called to meet on December 24. It was agreed that actual minutes of testimony and other documents involving individuals, as well as the data furnished the Committee by the two Governments should not be published at that time. There was general agreement that certain of the material was of such a nature as to prove incriminating or embarrassing to individuals involved. It was, accordingly, decided that the documents should be held in confidential files of the Pan American Union until sufficient time will have elapsed to bring about the elimination of these considerations.

The Council of the Organization of American States, acting as the Provisional Organ of Consultation under the Rio treaty, assembled once again in extraordinary session on Christmas Eve, at 10:30 a.m. This meeting lasted until 5 p.m., with only one 10-minute recess in the late afternoon. It was voted to make the session open to the press and the public. The Committee of Information presented its report which follows below in substance:

[Translation]

Conclusions Unanimously Adopted by the Committee of Information of the Provisional Organ of Consultation (Council of the Organization of American States)

1. The members of the Committee do not doubt that the revolutionary movement which broke out in Costa Rica was organized principally in the territory of Nicaragua. It was in Nicaragua that a large group of Costa Rican political exiles, headed by Calderón Guardia, prepared the expedition which later crossed the frontier between Nicaragua and Costa Rica. There is not the least doubt that the Government of Nicaragua did not take adequate measures to prevent the development of revolutionary activities directed against a neighboring and friendly country.

2. From December 10, it appears that the Government of Nicaragua actually began to take the necessary measures to the end that the rebels, who had already crossed the frontier, might not continue to receive assistance from Nicaragua; but the principal nucleus of the revolutionaries, composed of Costa Ricans and Nicaraguans, had already entered the territory of Costa Rica when the measures to which we refer were taken.

3. The Committee did not find any proof that the armed forces of the Government of Nicaragua had participated, on Costa Rican territory, in this revolutionary movement against the Government of Costa Rica, although, as a result of its investigations, it has the impression that certain military elements in Nicaragua, perhaps on their own account, might have furnished technical assistance to the groups which later were to cross the frontier.

4. The Committee had no knowledge of any contact between armed forces of Nicaragua and armed forces of Costa Rica.

5. As certain Costa Rican elements have declared, the failure to fulfill the pact of amnesty which was solemnly signed explains to a great extent why the large majority of the exiles were obligated to resort to desperate and violent measures, with serious international repercussions.

6. On the other hand, it is undeniable that for many months before the invasion, the so-called Legion of the Caribbean or Caribbean Legion, with the material and moral support of the Government of Costa Rica, received official favor and facilities to develop its programs and activities, both of which were directed, according to the prevailing opinion in the Caribbean region, toward the overthrow of certain Governments, including the present Nicaraguan regime.

7. The existence of active military centers of international agitation constitutes, as it is natural to suppose, a justifiable ground for preoccupation on the part of the Governments affected.

8. This situation, which is abnormal and dangerous for American international peace, explains why the majority of the Central American and Caribbean Republics have been living in an atmosphere of mutual distrust, constant anxiety, and open hostility for some time.

9. The situation is all the more regrettable since, because of the characteristics which we have pointed out, the international relations of the republics involved must, of necessity, become more strained each day, as the fear of the intentions of one neighboring country obliges the other to take the precautions which it considers necessary, with serious detriment to its own economy and with grave danger to institutional life.

Luis Quintanilla
Representative of Mexico, Chairman
Jose María Bello
Representative of Brazil
Silvio Villegas
Representative of Colombia
Paul C. Daniels
Representative of the United States

Action by the Provisional Organ of Consultation

After discussing the Committee's conclusions, the Provisional Organ of Consultation adopted the following resolution:

[Translation]

Resolution of the Provisional Organ of Consultation
The Council of the Organization of American States, acting as the Provisional Organ of Consultation, after carefully examining the detailed report of the Commission which was in Costa Rica and Nicaragua for the purpose of investigating the facts and antecedents of the situation created between these sister Republics.

Resolves:
I. To request that the Governments of Costa Rica and Nicaragua, in fulfillment of the Inter-American Treaty of Reciprocal Assistance, give the Provisional Organ of Consultation full guaranties that they will abstain immediately from any kind of hostile acts toward each other.

II. To inform the Government of Nicaragua respectfully that, in the light of the data gathered by the Committee of Investigation especially appointed for the purpose, that Government could and should have taken adequate measures in due time for the purpose of preventing: (*a*) the development, on Nicaraguan territory, of activities aimed at overthrowing the present government of Costa Rica, and (*b*) the departure from Nicaraguan territory of revolutionary forces which crossed the frontier and are now prisoners or fighting aginst the Government of Costa Rica.

III. To inform the Government of Costa Rica respectfully that it can and should take adequate measures to prevent the existence on its territory of domestic or foreign groups militarily organized with the deliberate purpose of conspiring against the security of Nicaragua and other sister Republics and of preparing to fight against their Governments.

IV. To request both Governments very earnestly to observe loyally by all the means in their power the principles and rules of non-intervention and solidarity contained in the various Inter-American instruments signed by them.

V. To continue in consultation until they receive from the Governments of Costa Rica and Nicaragua clear assurances that, they undoubtedly are resolved to do, they will be bound strictly by those lofty principles and rules that constitute the juridical basis of American relationships.

VI. To recommend to all American Governments that they actively collaborate for the better fulfillment of the principles by which this Resolution is inspired.

VII. To inform all States Members of the Organization of the steps taken in this case, for their better information.

(Approved on December 24, 1948.)

Appointment of a Committee of Military Experts

In addition to the principal resolution the Provisional Organ also voted to designate an inter-American committee of military experts to be composed of not more than three representatives from each of five member states. This committee was directed to proceed to Costa Rica and Nicaragua at the earliest possible date for the purpose of "contributing to the effective fulfillment of the resolution adopted on this date," that being the resolution of December 24. Brazil, Colombia. Mexico, Paraguay, and the United States were subsequently requested by Chairman Corominas to appoint representatives of their armed forces to this committee. These actions were duly reported to the governments of the American Republics and to the President of the Security Council.

In his letter of instruction to the members of the military committee, Chairman Corominas called attention to the confusing situation existing along the frontier between Costa Rica and Nicaragua and outlined the duties and obligations of both governments under the 1928 Habana convention on the duties and rights of states in the event of civil strife. The committee of military experts was directed to inform the Provisional Organ of Consultation immediately of any violation of the December 24 resolution, and it was authorized, on prior agreement of the Governments of Costa Rica and Nicaragua, to give assistance to those Governments in the application of the measures called for in that resolution. The committee was informed that the duration of its mission would be determined by the Provisional Organ of Consultation.

The Mexican and United States members departed for Costa Rica on December 28 and were joined there by the other representatives. Members of the Committee spent more than 2 months in Costa Rica and Nicaragua. They traveled between the two countries, visited the border areas involved in the military action, and were in continuing communication with the two governments concerning compliance with the terms of the December 24 resolution. The Committee sent periodic reports to and received instructions from the Provisional Organ of Consultation. In a report transmitted from Managua on January 31 the Committee expressed the view that the official measures taken by the Costa Rican and Nicaraguan Governments in pursuance of the December 24 resolution were sufficient to comply with the terms of the resolution.

Pact of Amity—Termination of the Incident

This report gave impetus to the efforts under way in Washington through the Provisional Organ of Consultation to bring about a final solution of the controversy. A committee was appointed to draw up a brief document which might be signed by the Governments of Costa Rica and Nicaragua to indicate their compliance with the directives of the Council and their desire to bring an end to the existing situation. The representatives of Costa Rica and Nicaragua on the Council participated in the work of the committee. There resulted a Pact of Amity, which was signed at the Pan American Union on February 21, 1949, by the Costa Rican and Nicaraguan Ambassadors on behalf of their governments. In the pact the two governments bound themselves to avoid such controversies in the future and to submit any disputes to pacific settlement in accord with existing inter-American agreements. The two governments agreed to negotiate an accord providing for appropriate internal measures and border controls with the purpose of preventing a repetition of incidents tending to disturb the tranquil relations of the two countries. It was provided that the pact would be ratified by the two governments. Copies of the document were sent at once by the Pan American Union to the 21 American Republics and to the Secretary-General of the United Nations.

Following this peaceful solution of a controversy which had at one time threatened open armed conflict between two members of the American community, the Council took a final resolution in termination of the incident. Summarizing the steps which had been taken since the establishment of the Provisional Organ of Consultation on December 14, including the naming of the Committee of Information and the later committee of military experts, the resolution concluded that the circumstances which had brought the convocation in the December 14 resolution of a consultation of Foreign Ministers no longer existed. Accordingly, the call for consultation was revoked, and with it the labors of the military committee and that of the Provisional Organ of Consultation were terminated. A paragraph of this final action in the Costa Rica-Nicaragua incident resolved "to present this noble conduct of American solidarity and of respect for pacific solution as a new and high example for all the peoples of the continent."

19. State Department Memorandum to the Inter-American Peace Committee*

August 18, 1949

The situation existing in the political areas of the Caribbean, on which the Inter-American Peace Committee has requested information and suggestions from all of the American states, contains a number of elements which warrant close examination by that Committee, in order that it shall fulfill its continuing responsibility, under Resolution XIV of the Second Meeting of Ministers of Foreign Affairs, of keeping constant vigilance to insure that states between which any dispute exists or may arise may solve it as quickly as possible. Furthermore, this study deserves the full cooperation of all of the American governments which are in a position to contribute to the success of the Committee's work.

*Department of State Bulletin, Sept. 26, 1949, pp. 450-54.

Although a few striking and well-publicized incidents have attracted general attention, long-continued tensions and evidences of political unrest have threatened to produce, or have actually produced, conflicts which have a deeper significance than would appear from the surface manifestations of isolated instances of plotting or revolutionary activity.

In the period since the cessation of hostilities of World War II, citizens of one or another of the countries in the Caribbean area have engaged in preparations for, and have participated in, movements whose purpose has been to accomplish by intimidation or armed invasion political changes in governments of the area. Despite the exercise of vigilance by the Government of the United States to prevent the violation of applicable United States laws, citizens of the United States have from time to time been involved in activities aimed at other governments. These movements have been inspired and carried on, at least in part, by political exiles whose aim is to return, by force if necessary, to active political life in the countries of their origin. Whatever may be the motivation of these individuals, some of whom declare that the cause of their exile is the absence of democratic practices in their home countries, the methods they have chosen may involve violation by established governments of their international obligations with consequent disruption of friendly relations among the countries in the area.

In some instances, the real, apparent or rumored threat of revolutionary activities has served to create international tensions, and there have even been open accusations from government to government. Three times, within a period of a year, the procedures of inter-American peaceful settlement have been called upon to deal with situations thus created. While the success of these instruments in improving the atmosphere for amicable negotiation, or in actually achieving pacific settlement of the specific situations which gave rise to the use of inter-American machinery, has been conspicuous, other situations have continued or new ones have appeared which indicate that all tensions have not been removed, and that means must still be sought for achieving a renewal of international confidence and a feeling of security among members of the American community.

The unfortunate results of these conditions cannot fail to be a matter of concern to the states involved as well as to all the American nations. It is obvious that recurring suspicion and lack of confidence among governments do not provide a proper climate for those mutually beneficial relationships, including economic relationships, which are of importance to the fullest development of the American states. Some of the governments concerned have found the situation sufficiently disturbing to cause them to acquire considerable amounts of armament, which they feel to be necessary for their self-defense, as well as to institute rigorous measures of internal control. Heavy expenditures for armaments for these purposes hinder economic improvement in the area and contribute to an accentuation of discord. The proper functioning of the Organization of American States and the effort to realize the ideals and principles to which all have subscribed in the charter require that methods be found for getting at, and eliminating if possible, the causes of international friction and discord.

In searching for these methods, the Inter-American Peace Committee has wisely chosen to seek full information on those matters which will contribute to its better appreciation of the problem. In fulfillment of its desire to cooperate with the Committee in every appropriate way, the Government of the United States herewith furnishes certain items of information which relate to the activities of its citizens or which have come to its attention in the course of official investigations of activities alleged to have been carried on by its citizens or within its jurisdiction. If further pertinent information which the United States is able to make available is developed, this will be furnished to the Committee.

Browder-Eisenhardt Case

Early in 1947 the theft of certain United States Government-owned arms was discovered. United States citizens Edward Browder and Karl J. Eisenhardt subsequently pleaded guilty to the theft. Browder received 18 months in prison and Eisenhardt was fined 10 thousand dollars. During the investigation and court proceedings in this case it was brought out that the arms in question were destined for revolutionary purposes in the Caribbean area, particularly against the then Government of Venezuela; and that the movement was financed in considerable part by foreign sources. It was also publicly asserted during these proceedings that a Dominican consular officer in the United States was involved in the movement. The officer concerned was subsequently recalled by his government.

Cayo Confites Plot

In connection with the revolutionary expedition organized in Cayo Confites in Cuba in July-August-September 1947 against the Dominican Republic, the United States Government took the following action:

1. Revocation in August 1947 of the export license granted for the export of the *LCI Patria* to one Cruz Alonzo in Cuba, when it became known that the ship was destined for the use of the revolutionaries.

2. Recommendation by the United States Embassy in Habana in September 1947 to American pilots recruited to participate in the revolution that they abandon this undertaking and return to the United States.

3. Statements to the United States press on August 2 and September 20, 1947, of the intention of the United States Government to meet its international obligations in connection with revolutionary activites in other countries. This included a statement that as early as January 1947 the appropriate law-enforcing agencies of this government had been taking special precautions to prevent violation of United States neutrality and export control statutes with reference to possible revolutionary activity in the Caribbean.

4. Indictment by a Federal grand jury in Florida on November 25, 1947, of Manolo Castro (who was the then Cuban Government Director of Sports), Miguel Angel Ramirez (Dominican), Hollis B. Smith (American), and two American fliers, on a charge of conspiracy to violate the export control act. Manolo Castro was killed in Habana before the trial began; Miguel Angel Ramirez has never returned to the United States to stand trial; Hollis B. Smith was given a 2-year suspended sentence and put on probation for 3 years by a Federal court in Jacksonville, Florida, in March 1948.

5. On another charge of conspiracy to violate the export control laws in connection with the export of arms to Cuba during the Cayo Confites activity, Reinaldo

Rosell (Cuban), and United States citizens Louis Dell, Frank Adkins, and Luis Bordas were given 2-year suspended sentences and were placed on probation for 3 years by a Federal court in Miami, Florida, in May 1948.

James G. Hurst Jr.

Hurst, a United States Air Force pilot during the recent World War, arrived in Guatemala City on January 1, 1948, in a war surplus bombing plane which he had flown out of the United States without obtaining an export license as required by law. In the investigation it was brought out that the plane had been purchased by him with funds made available from foreign sources for use in connection with plans for a revolution against the Government of Nicaragua. In response to a request of the United States Embassy, the Guatemalan Government impounded the bomber, which was later returned to the United States. In May 1949, Hurst was found guilty of violation of Section 452, Title 22, United States Code (Neutrality Act). He was sentenced to 2 years in the penitentiary and fined one thousand dollars. The penitentiary sentence was suspended for a period of 5 years to be conditioned on Hurst's good behavior.

Edward Browder, Jr., Harry A. Snow
Olin D. Mason, and Others

In January 1948, two military aircraft were illegally flown out of the United States by Snow, Mason, and three other United States citizens to Puerto Cabezas, Nicaragua. Investigation revealed that Browder, who, as reported above, had previously been involved in the theft of United States Government property in connection with a revolutionary plot against the Venezuelan Government, was attempting in January 1948 to engage pilots to fly "to an unknown spot" outside the United States to load bombs and then to fly to Venezuela to bomb the city of Caracas. The American pilots stated to investigating authorities that, upon their arrival at the Nicaraguan airport, they were met by 33 Venezuelan citizens who had arrived that same week from the Dominican Republic. In addition to the Venezuelan citizens who had arrived from the Dominican Republic, subsequent investigation revealed that other individuals connected with the same movement had arrived in Nicaragua during January 1948, from Costa Rica, Panama, and the United States.

Following urgent action by United States Embassy officials in Nicaragua, the American airmen were transferred from their hotel in Managua to the United States Air Force Base at Managua and returned at an early date to the Canal Zone and the United States. Legal action was promptly taken against them in the United States Federal courts. Browder pleaded guilty to separate indictments involving organizing a military expedition and violating the United States Neutrality Act. He was sentenced to 18 months imprisonment on each charge, the sentences to run concurrently. Snow, Mason, and the other individuals involved pleaded either guilty or *nolo contendere* to one or both of the above charges and received appropriate sentences.

Paul W. Warren

Paul Warren, a citizen of the United States, has for sometime resided in Costa Rica, where he has engaged in the business of obtaining animals for sale in the United States. In 1948, Mr. Warren became a vigorous partisan of the Caribbean Legion and an active participant in certain of its activities. On various occasions during September, October and November 1948, Warren made trips to Cuba, Guatemala and Honduras. In response to questions of United States authorities, he indicated that his travels were connected with activities of the Caribbean Legion. United States obligations under the Habana convention of 1928 and information as to certain United States statutes were communicated by United States officials to Warren. When it proved difficult to dissuade Warren from his activities, the United States Embassy at San José was directed to take up Warren's passport and inform him that it would be made valid only for his return to the United States. It was made clear to Warren that this government did not object to his remaining in Costa Rica for the carrying on of legitimate business but that the United States is strongly opposed to interference by its citizens in the internal political affairs of other nations.

Costa Rican-Nicaraguan Incident

The invasion of Costa Rica from Nicaraguan territory in December 1948 and the resulting action by the American states is a matter of recent record. This government supported wholeheartedly the inter-American action taken in solution of that controversy and is of the opinion that the course followed in connection with the Costa Rican-Nicaraguan incident offers a valuable precedent for problems of a similar nature. In that connection, the resolution of the Provisional Organ of Consultation of December 24, 1948, is considered by this government to have pertinence to the current problem. The United States has been happy to note the improved relations which have existed between Costa Rica and Nicaragua since the signing by the two governments on February 21, 1949, of the pact of friendship which terminated the incident, and which has subsequently been ratified by both governments.

The Luperon Incident

Information available to this government indicates that on the night of June 19, 1949, a PBY Catalina aircraft bearing United States registration No. N-1096-M was destroyed at Luperon on the north coast of the Dominican Republic after the persons on board endeavored to disembark munitions and attack the local authorities. All 15 persons aboard were either killed or captured. Of those killed, three were identified as American citizens, namely, John W. Chewning, Habet Joseph Maroot, and George R. Scruggs. The plane was registered in the United States in the name of Jesse A. Vickers of Miami Springs, Florida, who had applied for a license in May to export it to Mexico. This application was not approved by the United States Government. On June 4, however, the plane departed for Vera Cruz, and the circumstances surrounding the departure are now under investigation by the proper agencies of the United States

Government to obtain information as to possible violations of United States statutes in this connection.

Reports received by United States officials in the course of this investigation indicate that other aircraft landed in Yucatan on June 18 and 19, destined for the Dominican Republic. According to these reports, two of these, which landed in Yucatan on June 18, were transports of Mexican registry, C-46 XB-HUV and C-47 XA-HOS. They are known to have been at the Air Force Base at San José, Guatemala, for several weeks prior to June 19, their presence there having been confirmed by the Guatemalan Government in a note to the United States Embassy. Two other aircraft, which landed on June 19, were Guatemalan army transports T-1 and T-2; they were reported to have returned to Guatemala on June 26.

The Chief of the Guatemalan Air Force subsequently informed the press that Air Force plane T-1 had not been outside Guatemala and that T-2 had just returned from Houston, Texas. Official United States Government records disclose that T-2 did not have permission to enter the United States, nor was it reported at or in the vicinity of Houston during this period.

The reports also indicate that there were disembarked from these planes in Yucatan some 50 armed persons, several of whom made statements that they were destined for the Dominican Republic to overthrow the Dominican Government. Among the persons disembarked were two individuals who said they were United States citizens and gave their names as Marion R. Finley and Earl G. Adams. Also disembarked were the reported leaders of the expedition, Juan Rodriguez Garcia and Miguel Angel Ramirez (Dominicans), and Eufemio Fernandez (Cuban). Action by Mexican Government officials in taking into custody these armed men and military equipment prevented further movement of this group.

Conclusions

The formulation of recommendations for methods of dealing with the situation in the Caribbean area which fall within the duties and competence of the Inter-American Peace Committee would appear to depend to a very large extent upon the results of its study of the information which will be received in response to its request for cooperation from the American governments.

In the meantime, however, this government calls attention to the relevance to this situation of inter-American and other international agreements on nonintervention, and, specifically, to the 1928 Convention on the Rights and Duties of States in the Event of Civil Strife. It is suggested that the Committee may wish to give consideration to the question of whether obligations assumed in the 1928 convention and other agreements are being observed with sufficient positiveness by all states which have ratified them. It may wish also to consider whether a recommendation should be made that all states which have signed pertinent international agreements should take the steps necessary to complete their ratification. Such suggestions might also include reference to the desirability of there being domestic laws and enforcement machinery adequate to insure compliance with international obligations.

In view of the lapse of time and on the basis of experience regarding its applicability over intervening years, it is conceivable that the terms of the 1928 Convention may not be sufficiently clear or precise to cover situations to which it was intended to apply, or situations of a kind which could not have been fully foreseen when that Convention was negotiated. The Committee may, therefore, wish to consider the desirability of recommending that the Convention should be reviewed, with a view to its being clarified and strengthened, as necessary, or to determining whether a new convention should be drafted.

It is pertinent to recall that, during consideration of the Costa Rican-Nicaraguan case by the COAS, acting as Provisional Organ of Consultation, the Committee of Information designated by that body presented a report which included, among other conclusions, the following which are particularly relevant to the broader problem:

"7. The existence of active military centers of international agitation constitutes, as it is natural to suppose, a justifiable ground for preoccupation on the part of the Governments affected.

"8. This situation, which is abnormal and dangerous for American international peace, explains why the majority of the Central American and Caribbean Republics have been living in an atmosphere of mutual distrust, constant anxiety, and open hostility for some time.

"9. The situation is all the more regrettable since, because of the characteristics which we have pointed out, the international relations of the republics involved must, of necessity, become more strained each day, as the fear of the intentions of one neighboring country obliges the other to take the precautions which it considers necessary, with serious detriment to its own economy and with grave danger to institutional life."

Furthermore, the Provisional Organ of Consultation approved, on December 24, 1948, a resolution which contains the following particularly relevant articles:

"IV. To request both Governments very earnestly to observe loyally by all the means in their power the principles and rules of non-intervention and solidarity contained in the various Inter-American instruments signed by them.

"VI. To recommend to all American Governments that they actively collaborate for the better fulfilment of the principles by which this Resolution is inspired."

It is suggested that the Committee may wish to invite the attention of all of the American states to the action which was taken at that time.

20. State Department Statement Concerning the Cases of Haiti and the Dominican Republic Being Considered by the Organization of American States*

February 10, 1950

On January 3, 1950, the Government of Haiti, through its representative on the Council of the Organization of American States, requested that body to put into application inter-American machinery for dealing with its charges that the Government of the Dominican Republic had taken part in the development of a plot, within Haiti, directed against the President of that country. On January 6, 1950, the Council met in extraordinary session to deal with this request. After hearing a further statement from

*Department of State Bulletin, Feb. 20, 1950, pp. 279-82.

the Haitian representative and a statement by the Dominican representative containing charges and countercharges that Haiti, Cuba, Guatemala, and other countries had, over a considerable period of time, tolerated or supported activities hostile to his Government, the Council approved a resolution making applicable to the two cases before it the Inter-American Treaty of Reciprocal Assistance.

In accordance with the terms of this resolution, the Council determined that it would act provisionally as Organ of Constitution and that a full examination of the facts and antecedents of the charges made by Haiti and the Dominican Republic would be made by an Investigating Committee of five members chosen by the Chairman of the Council, Ambassador Quintanilla of Mexico. The Chairman, subsequently, selected as members of this Committee the representatives on the Council of Bolivia, Colombia, Ecuador, Uruguay, and the United States.

After several meetings in Washington, this Committee, under the chairmanship of Ambassador Mora of Uruguay, began a series of visits to countries where it was felt that significant information might be obtained, including Haiti, the Dominican Republic, and Cuba. The Committee, when it shall have completed this investigation, is required, by the terms of the resolution referred to above, to submit a report to the Council, acting provisionally as Organ of Consultation under the Inter-American Treaty of Reciprocal Assistance, adopted at Rio de Janeiro in 1947. This body will then determine whether there are steps which need to be taken in order to maintain peace and security in the area.

The action of the consultative organ of the OAS on the cases presented by Haiti and the Dominican Republic is the most recent, and in some respects the most extreme, of a series of actions taken with regard to the general problem of illegal revolutionary activities in the Caribbean, and the international tensions which they have created, over a period of almost 2 years. These actions have involved the application of two procedures afforded by the inter-American system for handling disputes which exist or may arise between American governments. Although the treaties, resolutions, and agreements which have been approved in inter-American conferences for many years past contain other procedures for the peaceful settlement of disputes, the methods resorted to in connection with the troubled Caribbean situation have been: (a) that provided for in the Rio treaty and (b) that made possible by utilization of the Inter-American Peace Committee. The following outline indicates briefly the origin and nature of the Peace Committee and the treaty, and the application in recent instances of resultant procedures to Caribbean problems.

Inter-American Peace Committee

The Inter-American Peace Committee is a five-member group, the creation of which was provided for in Resolution XIV of the 1940 Habana Meeting of American Foreign Ministers. The five countries which appoint representatives (United States, Cuba, Mexico, Brazil, and Argentina) were selected in December 1940 by the Pan American Union Governing Board, now the Council of the Organization of American States. Interest lagged, however, governments were slow in appointing representatives, and the Committee was not actually installed before the summer of 1948, when it met to consider a dispute between the Dominican Republic and Cuba placed before it by the Dominican Republic.

By the terms of Habana Resolution XIV, the Committee is limited to the functions of (1) "keeping constant vigilance to insure that states between which any dispute exists or may arise . . . may solve it as quickly as possible" and (2) "suggesting the measures and steps which may be conducive to such a settlement."

The Committee has, up to the present dealt, with two disputes and has carried on a general examination of the "situation" created by illegal revolutionary activities in the Caribbean. Besides suggesting actual measures and steps aimed at peaceful settlement of disputes, the Committee has at times operated in the capacity of a "good offices" instrument—on one occasion, its members visited the capitals of Haiti and the Dominican Republic in that capacity. It has not been deemed warranted or desirable that the Committee should act as a formal international investigating body.

The Committee is required by Resolution XIV to submit reports on its activities to each meeting of Foreign Ministers and inter-American conference. Although it has provided information to other governments through their representatives on the Council of the Organization of American States, it is not dependent upon that body. The Committee existed only on paper at the time of the Bogotá conference in 1948; and there was no attempt at that meeting to clarify its relationship to the Organization of American States. Nevertheless, it seems generally agreed that the Committee has demonstrated that it has a valuable role to perform.

The present members of the Committee are the representatives of Brazil, Mexico, Argentine, Cuba, and the United States on the Council of the Organization of American States. Ambassador Accioly of Brazil is its chairman.

Examples of Peace Committee Activities

Since its installation, in 1948, the Peace Committee has dealt with a number of problems. Its work may be illustrated by the following examples:

In March 1949, the Haitian Government requested Peace Committee cognizance of a situation resulting chiefly from activities of a former Haitian Army officer in the Dominican Republic. These activites, it held, were directed against the stability of the Haitian Government and were not only being tolerated but encouraged by the Dominican Government. After hearing the parties to the dispute and extending good offices in a number of ways, including a visit to the capitals of both countries by three of its members, the Peace Committee achieved agreement between the parties on the text of a declaration in which each government stated that it did not and would not in the future tolerate activities within its territory which had the purpose of disturbing the domestic peace of the other country. This declaration was issued simultaneously in Port-au-Prince and Ciudad, Trujillo on June 10, 1949.

In view of the continued rumors, allegations, and actual instances of organized armed revolutionary activity, including an attack by aircraft near Luperon in the Dominican Republic in June 1949, the Peace Committee gave consideration, during August and early September 1949, to the general situation thus produced in the Caribbean area. This situation involved, as was pointed out, several actual or potential conflicts. Information regarding illegal activities and suggestions regarding methods for dealing with the situation were requested from all the American governments, and the United States submitted a detailed memorandum. After extensive discussions among representatives of the Committee and with representatives of other governments, the

Committee on September 14, 1949, issued a document containing its conclusions regarding the situation and methods whereby it might be improved. The 14 points in this document were largely a reaffirmation of principles, standards, and inter-American commitments, the vigorous observance of which, it was pointed out, would not only keep such a situation from arising but would "avoid even the slightest symptom of disturbed relations among the American States."

Inter-American Treaty of Reciprocal Assistance

The Inter-American Treaty of Reciprocal Assistance, the Rio treaty, was concluded at the Inter-American Conference for the Maintenance of Continental Peace and Security held in 1947. While the treaty's chief significance is often felt to be its insurance of Western Hemisphere solidarity against armed attacks or aggression from outside the hemisphere, the treaty applies with equal force to armed attacks or aggression which may occur between two or more American states. It is not only a protection against possible aggressors from across the seas, but it is also an effective instrument for the maintenance of peace within the hemisphere.

The effectiveness of the provisions of the Rio treaty has been demonstrated in actual practice. There are two general types of situation which call for its application. The first is an "armed attack by any State against an American State." When such an armed attack by any state against an American state is launched within the hemisphere, the parties to the treaty are obligated, under article 3 of the treaty, to assist immediately in meeting the attack in the exercise of the right of self-defense.

Although a state is free to determine the immediate measures which it will individually take, the obligation to assist in some way is entirely clear. So, also, is the obligation to consult immediately with all the other parties in order to determine the collective measures which may be taken until the Security Council of the United Nations has taken the measures necessary to maintain international peace and security.

In this consultation on collective measures set forth in the treaty, decisions are to be taken by a two-thirds vote which is binding on all parties including those not concurring, except that no state is required to use armed force without its own consent. In other words, a party to the treaty may be required to take part in a number of specified steps, such as complete interruption of economic relations with the aggressor, even though it has not originally favored such action. It may not, however, be required under the treaty to use armed force without its own consent.

Fortunately, no occasion has arisen since this Rio treaty has been in effect which has required the invoking of the obligations found in this article.

The second type of situation contemplated under the treaty is concerned with an act or threat of aggression which is not an armed attack or in which there may be any other fact or situation that might endanger the peace of the Americas and that affects the inviolability, territorial integrity, sovereignty, or political independence of an American state. It is provided that, when any such situation arises, the Organ of Consultation shall meet immediately in order to agree on the measures which must be taken in case of aggression to assist the victim or, in any case, the measures which should be taken for the common defense and for the maintenance of the peace and security of the continent. Although the formal Organ of Consultation is a meeting of Ministers of Foreign Affairs, the treaty provides that, prior to an actual formal meeting of this kind, the Council of the Organization of American States may act provisionally as the Organ of Consultation.

On December 11, 1948, the Costa Rican representative on the Council of the Organization of American States charged, in a letter of the Chairman of the Council, that an armed force was invading its territory from the neighboring territory of Nicaragua. It should be noted that Costa Rica specifically requested that the provisions of article 6 of the Rio treaty be invoked. These provisions, which concern the second kind of situation discussed above, do not automatically require all nations to come to the immediate assistance of the victim, but they do require an immediate consultation among the parties to the treaty. The decision on whether to invoke the treaty is made by the Council of the Organization of American States.

Events moved rapidly. The Chairman of the Council of the Organization of American States immediately called a meeting of the Council for Sunday, December 12. Only a few days earlier, the Rio treaty had come into legal effect, with final deposit of the ratification of Costa Rica, herself, fulfilling the requirement that two-thirds of the states complete their ratifications. Failure to stop the dispute involving Costa Rica and Nicaragua, or any delay in its solution, could get the Organization—and the treaty—off to a bad start from which it might never recover. At the same time, any premature action might fan the flames. This was a time for prompt decision but not for snap judgment.

As is often the case in such disputes, complete and accurate information was lacking. Consequently, the next 48 hours was devoted to obtaining information. On the following Tuesday, an important decision was taken, the importance of which may not even today be fully appreciated. With the information at hand, the Council invoked the Rio treaty, declaring itself to be provisionally the Organ of Consultation under the treaty. The Council's first official act as consultative organ was to send immediately an investigating commission to San José and Managua in order to obtain on-the-spot accurate, complete information. This commision included representatives of Mexico, Brazil, Colombia, and the United States, with civilian and military advisers.

In San José and Managua, officials of both countries showed the utmost cooperation. All parties concerned were most anxious to settle the difficulty. It was obvious that neither country had any intention of declaring war. The actual incident which had initiated the Costa Rican request—the crossing of its border by an armed force chiefly revolutionary in character—had not developed into a serious threat to the stability of that Government, but there was evidence that both the Costa Rican and Nicaraguan Governments had each been remiss in discouraging revolutionary groups whose aim was to overthrow the government of the other. Unquestionably, a serious misunderstanding had arisen.

Within a few days, the Commission was back in Washington with its report to the Council. The latter met immediately to study the report and, on December 24, 1948, approved a resolution which called upon each of the Governments to eliminate those conditions which had led to the dispute and made specific recommendations to both for settling it.

There followed a relatively short period when the Council, still acting provisionally as the Organ of Consultation, continued to maintain its direct interest in the situation and to encourage a peaceful solution. This "watch and wait" period lasted until February 21, 1949, when the two Governments, through their representatives in Washington, signed a treaty of friendship—*Pacto de Amistad*. This treaty, in the view of the Council and of the countries involved, represented an effective basis for a mutually satisfactory solution. It was subsequently formally ratified by both Governments.

In our relations with Latin America, the year 1949 was thus marked by increasing recognition of the significant role which the regional international organization—the OAS and its ancillary bodies—has to play in strengthening the sinews of peace. Of particular interest was the fact that international procedures were utilized on several occasions for the purpose of relieving tensions or otherwise improving the chance for solution of disputes or other difficulties between American states.

The existence of such disputes or difficulties is, of course, unfortunate since there has been considerable basis in recent years for the optimistic view that the sovereign nations of the Western Hemisphere have achieved juridical and political relationships making direct conflict among them a thing of the past. But aggression by state against state is not the only cause of disputes; and the inter-American machinery has been tested and has shown its usefulness in dealing with situations which, in the absence of an international method for settlement, might have become more threatening.

We have seen how the dispute between Costa Rica and Nicaragua was dealt with through the first invocation of the Rio treaty—the hemisphere pact which is directed at means for insuring peace among the American states as well as mutual defense against aggression from without—with the result that the two countries agreed upon a treaty of friendship as the means for resolving the difficulties between them. Other situations, likewise resulting from activities of armed adventurers and, perhaps, of a few sincere political exiles holding that they had been deprived of the opportunity to achieve their ends peacefully in their own countries, have been placed before the Inter-American Peace Committee. That body has suggested measures and steps which, when followed, have been helpful in improving relations among the countries concerned. It would be unrealistic to say that all of the conditions leading to controversy have been removed; but the extent to which inter-American procedures have been used and the degree of their success hold hope for the future.

The first regional conference of United States Ambassadors in the Caribbean area meeting at Habana in January 1950 was marked by full and frank discussion of the most important current problems both administrative and substantive. Following are excerpts from the conference report:

> The Conference afforded an excellent opportunity to reassess and reaffirm the interest of the United States in the inter-American system and in the Organization of American States as the most important expression of law and order in the hemisphere.
>
> The Conference took a very serious view of the state of political tension that has existed between some countries in the Caribbean area for the past several years as emphasized by the Haitian and Dominican complaints to the Organization of American States. The Conference expressed satisfaction over the manner in which the entire situation was now being handled by the Council of the Organization of American States in Washington. The members of the Conference felt that progress towards a solution of present problems in the Caribbean area, or the relaxation of present tension, would follow from a thorough ventilation of all the facts. The Conference felt that through the examination and possible elimination of many factors and charges which may have been unduly exaggerated, the matter would be reduced to its proper proportions.
>
> All present felt that the United States should fully support the present

efforts of the Council of the Organization of American States and in this way help that organization to achieve ever greater progress in the direction of becoming the true and lasting guarantor of peace and tranquility in the hemisphere.

The Conference also felt that much could be done toward the easing of the present situation if the nations involved show a real and sincere desire to engage in direct discussions for the purpose of composing their differences in a spirit of mutual conciliation.

21. Address by Edward G. Miller, Assistant Secretary for Inter-American Affairs, before the Pan American Society of New England, on Nonintervention and Collective Responsibility *

April 26, 1950

I mean to address myself this evening to certain basic features of our inter-American policy and to deal with them in rather broad historic terms. We have to keep in mind the historical perspective when we are dealing with international policy, or we cannot possibly maintain the consistency and clarity that are essential to its development. To the extent that a foreign policy is truly a national policy, it is, in its essence, traditional. It represents the attitude of a whole nation as it has been forged over the generations, as it has been expressed in the words and actions of successive administrations, and as it has been applied to the solution of successively new international problems. We have such a national policy in the inter-American field, and it is this policy that I shall examine this evening.

Monroe Doctrine in Force

In his proclamation of what later came to be known as the "Monroe Doctrine," President Monroe declared that the political system of the powers in the Old World was essentially different from that of America, and "that we should consider any attempt on their part to extend their system to any portions of this Hemisphere, as dangerous to our peace and safety." We are no longer concerned today with the political system of the Holy Alliance, based on monarchy and the exploitation of peoples kept in colonial servitude. We are concerned, however, with the alien political system of Communist Russia, based as it is on totalitarian dictatorship and the enslavement of populations at home and abroad. The Monroe Doctrine has not lost its meaning with the passage of a century and a quarter, for, today, we consider any attempt to extend the Communist system to any portions of this hemisphere as "dangerous to our peace and safety." This attitude is still basic to our policy.

The enforcement of the Monroe Doctrine was never purely a military problem, since the imperialism that it proscribed could realize its objectives by other than military means. Extreme weakness in the political and social structures of small states has always made them vulnerable to diplomatic pressures and to penetration by political and economic means. Such internal weakness characterized many of the Latin

*Department of State Bulletin, May 15, 1950, pp. 768-70.

American states during the nineteenth and early twentieth centuries. It invited, and at times seemed to justify, the interference of overseas powers. To forestall that interference, which would have been contrary to the Monroe Doctrine, the United States felt constrained to undertake certain protective interventions in the Caribbean in the first quarter of this century.

It is easy for us today, in the light of present thought and present circumstances, to assume a high moral attitude toward those protective interventions and to regard our statesmen of those times as guilty of political immorality. We should do them the justice, however, of appreciating some of the hard facts that they themselves had no choice but to appreciate.

The Monroe Doctrine was, of course, not designed to exclude the legitimate business interests of Old World powers from the hemisphere. Those interests, and the nationals who represented them, were, under the law of nations, entitled to certain protection by the states in which they operated. There are standards of civilization and civilized treatment that all states are obliged to maintain. All states, through their governments, have this responsibility. The internal weakness of certain Caribbean states a generation ago, manifesting itself in utterly chaotic conditions, sometimes made them unable to sustain this responsibility and so confronted United States policy with a serious dilemma. Rightly or wrongly, but certainly with reluctance, the United States finally felt itself obliged to intervene temporarily in certain extreme cases for the restoration of order. Its purpose was the exclusion of European states that might themselves intervene to redress their just grievances and enforce the standards of behavior on which the international world was agreed. The danger was that, having once intervened, the European states might make their own interventions permanent.

Whatever may be said against our protective interventions of these times, they accomplished an objective equally vital to all the states of the Western Hemisphere. They played their part in bringing about the situation that we have today, in which no American state has become the protectorate of a foreign power, in which the weakest are free to enjoy their sovereignty along with the strongest. For the United States itself—and history has proved this—had and has no desire to establish protectorates of its own. We regarded our interventions as necessary evils to be ended as soon as circumstances allowed us to end them. It is fair to ask what other great power in the history of the world has made such a record of willing forebearance.

Alternative to Intervention

No American state was more anxious than the United States to find a practicable alternative to the interventions of the early twentieth century, bearing in mind the necessity of maintaining the independence of the hemisphere. We can now see, in the long perspective of events, what form that alternative took. After a period of uncertainty, it presented itself in the gradual assumption by the American states, as a regional community, of a common responsibility for the maintenance of peace and order in the hemisphere and the defense of its independence.

The record of history does not, on its surface, show the close relationship between the nonintervention agreement of the American states and the assumption by them of collective responsibility. To see the relationship, however, you have only to look closely at the logic and at the coincidence of events. In 1933, at the Montevideo conference, the United States, mindful of its responsibilities rather than desirous of conquest, felt compelled to make some reservation in agreeing to the doctrine of nonintervention. In 1936, at Buenos Aires, it accepted that doctrine unreservedly when it was presented jointly with another instrument in which the American governments provided for consultation and collaboration of their 21 nations in the event of any act susceptible of disturbing the peace of America. In the years since Buenos Aires, the American states have defined their responsibility more circumstantially and have greatly strengthened the organization of their community for meeting it. In the treaty of Rio de Janeiro, they now have a common defense pact and procedures for carrying out a common defense against any aggression or threat of aggression, whether from overseas or from one of their own number. If the circumstances that led to the protective interventions by the United States should arise again today, the organized community of American states would be faced with the responsibility that the United States had once to assume alone.

Now, all this seems very clear and simple to me. Like so much else in international affairs, however, it has been the subject of serious confusion in the use of words. Some people have gone to the dictionary, instead of to the historical context, for their definition of "intervention" and have consequently concluded that any official correspondence with another state about some action on its part constitutes a violation of the nonintervention commitment. Others have said that, on the contrary, the absence of any manifestation of official concern with affairs of another state may constitute a negative intervention that violates the commitment. By debating such propositions we can, in time, make what is really very simple seem unutterably complicated and abstruse.

The worst confusion, however, has been that by which the action of the international community in the discharge of its collective responsibility has, on occasion, been identified with the word "intervention." At Montevideo and again at Buenos Aires, "intervention" had been carefully identified with the unilateral action of a single state. The Montevideo convention said: "No state has the right to intervene in the internal or external affairs of another." The Buenos Aires protocol said: "The High Contracting Parties declare inadmissible the intervention of any one of them . . . in the internal or external affairs of any other of the Parties." It is true that the Bogotá charter of the Organization of American States says, "no state or group of states has the right to intervene . . ." but an exception is made in the case of "measures adopted for the maintenance of peace and security in accordance with existing treaties . . . ." The fact is that the doctrine of nonintervention never did proscribe the assumption by the organized community of a legitimate concern with any circumstances that threatened the common welfare. On the contrary, it made the possibility of such action imperative. Such a collective undertaking, so far from representing intervention, is the alternative to intervention. It is the corollary of nonintervention.

Intervention was repugnant to the people of the United States as of all the American countries. Its occasional practice, morever, made it impossible for us to put our relations with the other American states on a footing that reflected the community of our interests. It actually prevented the development of a community responsibility and a community organization for the maintenance of peace and security. Under all these circumstances, it died a universally unlamented death. We are well rid of it today.

The Situation in the Hemisphere Today

The basic situation in the hemisphere today is this. The 21 American states together face the challenge of Communist political aggression against the hemisphere. This aggression bears directly on the purpose of the Monroe Doctrine, which is as much our national policy today as it ever was. It bears directly on the purpose of the treaty of Rio de Janeiro, which in some of its aspects represents a Monroe Doctrine of our inter-American community. The ability of our community to meet that challenge depends on its own inward strength and, of course, on the inward strength of its individual members. By this, I do not mean just military strength or especially military strength. I mean primarily moral and political strength. Governments should be self-reliant and able to command the support of their people so that they can maintain intrinsic order and deal effectively with Communist attempts at subversion. They should be uncompromised in their determination to achieve this end. States that are strong in this sense will almost surely constitute a strong and effective regional community, alert to the common responsibilities, and able to maintain a peaceful order among its members. Such a community, in turn, by acting intelligently and courageously, can promote the political and social health of its members and make the hemisphere impervious to clandestine Communist penetration. That is its basic responsibility, and the basic responsibility of its members.

The United States is committed to this purpose and these means for its attainment. It places its faith in them, believing that the time is well past when it had to look to itself alone for the defense of a hemisphere, the independence of which is essential to its own independence. The last war justified that faith. It is even more justified by subsequent developments culminating in the purposeful way in which the Council of the Organization of American States, acting on the terms of the Rio treaty, has come to grips with the recent threat of impending conflict in the Caribbean.

The American states have made and continue to make their contribution to international cooperation and peace. The world has drawn on their experience and their example for its most constructive attempts at the establishment of a world-wide order. If all of us continue purposefully along the path on which we have set our feet, the historians of a future age may have reason to say that the subversive challenge of communism, instead of weakening the hemisphere, strengthened it in the unity of its purpose and enabled it to triumph over its common problems.

22. *Address by Willard F. Barber, Deputy Assistant Secretary
    of State for Inter-American Affairs, before the Second
    National Conference of World Areas, on Point 4 and
    Research in Latin America**

May 5, 1950

It has been more than a year since the President enunciated his now famous Point 4 of United States foreign policy. Authorizing legislation to carry out the policy has now been approved by the House of Representatives and, with certain modifications, by the Senate Foreign Relations Committee. A fundamental purpose of the policy is the

*Department of State Bulletin, May 22, 1950, pp. 804-05.

furnishing of aid to foreign governments through experts, technicians, and trainees in such a way as to promote a balanced increase in the productive capacities of underdeveloped areas.

When President Truman called for "making the benefits of our scientific advances and industrial progress" available to underdeveloped countries, as a security measure in our enlightened self-interest he but underlined the considerable debt that we owe to those elements in our society which have already engaged in various fields of research. To a large extent, it is to the tradition and encouragement of research in this country that we may attribute the skills and technical know-how that we are preparing to share with other countries. This research element is now an integral part of our business enterprises, our educational institutions, and the Government. Its role and responsibilities under Point 4 are of vital importance. Scores of business organizations, universities, and private foundations (the Carnegie, Rockefeller, and, more recently, the Armour Research Foundations) have furnished technical assistance to other countries for a long time. The amount of theoretical and practical research accomplished by some mining and manufacturing enterprises before making investment commitments involves thousands of man-hours and a considerable expenditure. The counsel and cooperation of each of these groups are necessary to the success of the Point 4 Program.

The concrete results which may be derived from Point 4 activities might be gauged from the experiences we have had during the past 10 years in working with the countries of Central and South America. This work was carried out by the Institute of Inter-American Affairs and by a number of departments and agencies of the Government working through the Interdepartmental Committee on Scientific and Cultural Cooperation.

Record of Accomplishments

The Institute and its predecessor agencies have expended approximately 59 million dollars as the United States participation in technical cooperation with Latin American governments from 1940 to 1949. There is an impressive record of accomplishments in the three fields in which they function: agriculture, health and sanitation, and education. Since 1942, food supply programs have been carried on in 10 countries of Latin America. In four countries, current joint activities include methods of soil conservation and cultivation, food storage and marketing, agricultural education. In cooperative health and sanitation, the Institute employs 8,000 physicians, sanitary engineers, and nurses. Five hundred and fifty projects are now going on in 14 countries in this field. Its cooperation in vocational and rural education is conducted in seven countries of the hemisphere.

Through the Interdepartmental Committee on Scientific and Cultural Cooperation, the Government spent approximately 18 million dollars from 1940 to 1948. During this period, more than 1,550 United States Government experts were sent to the other American Republics on technical cooperation projects. These covered an exceptionally wide range, as indicated by the following partial list: plant entomology, forestry, public health, social welfare, vocational rehabilitation, geological surveys, reclamation and irrigation, fisheries, tidal and magnetic observations, census and statistical procedures, civil aviation, highway planning and construction, industrial safety, labor inspection and legislation, housing, telecommunications, taxation, and fiscal policy.

The simple recital of the various fields in which we have worked with other governments gives little idea of the accomplishments. I note the virtual eradication of typhoid fever and dysentery in a large valley in Brazil; the provision of a sewage system to a metropolitan district of 200,000 persons in Chile previously without adequate sanitation; safe drinking water in Venezuelan communities and the development in Cuba of a new fiber (kenaf) as a substitute for jute. These are concrete and even spectacular instances of our aid. They have been repeated many times.

There are in the laboratories of the Mexican Government two mining engineers, supplied by the United States Bureau of Mines, who are helping the Mexicans work out processes for extracting or reducing ores, so as to make mining less expensive.

The Civil Aeronautics Administration has field parties in five Latin American countries, advising other governments on the location and construction of airfields and the maintenance of airways communications.

We have a solid background and experience of cooperative endeavor. Prospects are promising for passage of legislation which will enable this work to be broadened in scope and extent.

The legislation, furthermore, would authorize our participation in a multilateral as well as in a bilateral way. The United Nations is about to expand in this field. The specialized inter-American agencies have engaged in these tasks for several years. Studying the possibility of extending much needed technical assistance on a multilateral and regional basis, the Inter-American Economic and Social Council, at an extraordinary session in March-April 1950, agreed to set up a special board and separate budget to handle technical cooperation. In both these international bodies, the United States will participate actively, recognizing that the multilateral approach, in some cases, offers advantages the bilateral does not possess. The salient fact remains, however, that the member nations of these organizations offer their research facilities and the services of their trained personnel to a joint endeavor.

The Role of Research

Research will have an important function in the expanded program as in the past. It will, for instance, be essential, in most cases, to have a clear idea of a country's economic potentialities. This undertaking would demand basic research on problems of population, natural resources, agriculture, fuel and power, mining, trade, labor, transportation, fiscal policy, and in many other disciplines. An example of a comprehensive survey of a nation's needs and its possibilities was the Joint United States Brazilian Economic Committee (the Abbink Mission) which was, in essence, a research body. Other examples are the Klein Mission in Peru and the Bohan Mission, of several years ago, to Bolivia. Detailed research on soil surveys and extensive laboratory tests may be a prerequisite to proper technical assistance on farm management problems. The intensive research and experimentation in the Inter-American Institute of Agricultural Sciences at Turrialba, Costa Rica, has already led to improved techniques in soil erosion control, land drainage, the drying and storage of seeds and grains. Turrialba has brought out new plant strains of greater productivity, resistant to disease or drought.

These are but a few instances of the role research has been and will be called upon to play in the development of the Point 4. Its full and effective participation is basic to success.

In many countries in Latin America there is insufficient information and analysis upon which a comprehensive and specific country program for economic development can be based. A number of countries also lack sufficient trained personnel of their own to make all the necessary economic, sociological, and engineering studies.

I believe that considerable emphasis should be put on the trainee portion of the Point 4 Program. This training would assist the collaborating countries in expanding the number of their own citizens not only with proper technical training but also with an appreciation of the research methods necessary in a modern economy. In turn the training would be a contribution both to the self-help principle involved in Point 4 and to the long-run economic development of the other countries.

Finally, not only must research be made of specific practical projects adapted to local conditions but research must also properly relate those projects to the external regional and world economy. It would be wasteful to encourage a large expansion of an agricultural crop for export when that crop is approaching a world market surplus position perhaps due to expended production elsewhere.

As Point 4 gets under way in other parts of the world, the demand on United States specialists in agriculture, sanitation, education, engineering, and science will become greater. These specialists must be more than simply technicians. They need to know how to work effectively in the foreign countries which need them. There is, thus, an immediate and urgent need that the foreign area studies of the universities be made at once comprehensive and practical. The incentives are obvious. There is every reason, therefore, for this Conference to go forward at once with its timely and important work.

23. Address by Assistant Secretary Miller before the Pennsylvania Federation of Labor, on the American Way and Standards of Democracy *

May 9, 1950

Organized labor is making its presence felt in Latin America. The movement has grown slowly and has encountered stiff opposition at times, as it did in this country; but especially in the last few years, it has made itself increasingly heard in political matters. Nobody knows how large the labor movement is in Latin America; I have heard estimates that vary by more than 100 percent. But, even if we accept that so far the movement is small in total numbers, we must allow that its importance is great. This is particularly true in those countries where the great bulk of the people are uninformed and politically inarticulate. Organized labor speaks in the name of the people and must take special care to work for the true aspirations of the people.

You, I know, are interested in the promotion of democratic ideals and institutions in this country and abroad. So am I. So is the Department of State. But liberal groups here and in Latin America have sometimes not understood some of our policies. I think it is because they do not fully appreciate the reasoning behind those policies. I won't say, as I might be tempted to, that it is the fashion today to jump on the State Department. Just remember that most of the tough situations in the world have complex and deep-rooted causes. They can't be solved overnight. Precisely because our policies are misunderstood by some groups that claim to champion democratic ideals,

Department of State Bulletin, May 22, 1950, pp. 797-99.

I'd like to talk to you for a few minutes about two matters of public concern: one is why we maintain diplomatic relations with governments that are not so democratic as we'd like them to be; the other is why we cooperate in the economic field with governments of this type.

Our policies are the result of long and serious study, of trial and error, of practical application of our fundamental principles. I believe that they are sound, that they are designed to get us where we all want to go as fast as the hurdles in our way will let us travel.

One basis for establishing diplomatic relations with a government has to do with whether it can maintain civil order. That is, of course, the first test of any government. Also, we want to know whether the government can be depended on to respect its international obligations, which is to say, to honor its treaties, to abide by the principles of international law. Generally speaking, whether we approve of the form of that government has nothing to do with the matter. When a government has been overthrown by force, we are faced with the problem of whether to recognize the new government that takes its place. It is our policy to consult with the other governments of the hemisphere, so that in so far as possible the action of the American community of nations may be united. We have had great success with this sort of consultation, and I believe that our countries have been brought closer together by such negotiations. Moreover, this method has brought greater public understanding of the problem and of our policy.

To argue against this policy would immediately bring up the question as to what is "intervention in the internal affairs" of a country, and I do not intend to go into that hotly debatable question. Let me just say that diplomatic recognition of a government should not be used as a moral force to bring about internal reform. It is obvious that we do and that we should maintain relations with many countries whose governments do not conform to our ideals. The fact that we do not agree on principles is all the more reason for keeping open the channels for interchange. The progress of civilization has come from the movement of people and ideas. Let us lower no Iron Curtain. If we are to work toward international understanding, we must have the way open.

Some of our friends in Latin America have been unhappy because we have not offered aid to them on the scale of our Marshall Plan for Europe or our aid to certain Asiatic areas. These same friends, and some people in this country, have protested because we have not confined to those countries, whose governments fit our standards of democracy, the aid we could give. These questions bring up a fundamental point which I shall discuss in a moment. But first, let me point out some special differences between Latin America and Europe.

Differences Between Latin America and Europe

In the first place, our hemisphere is truly united by something we call the Inter-American system, represented by the Organization of American States. Unless we look at the evolution of this organization in the perspective of history, we may underestimate the very real and great achievements that have been made in welding our community since the days when James G. Blaine and his collaborators throughout the hemisphere founded the Pan American Union. Indeed, to go further back, it is safe to say that the great South American leader Bolivar would approve most enthusiastically what has been done to realize his ideal of a united hemisphere. In the conferences at Montevideo in 1933, at Buenos Aires in 1936, at Lima in 1938, at Panamá in 1939, and at Habana in 1940, great steps were taken toward unity among the American nations. At Rio in 1942, at Mexico city in 1945, at Rio again in 1947, and at Bogotá in 1948, the solidarity of the community was proved time and again.

The effectiveness of the system that we have created has survived its first great test in the notably successful way in which the Organization of American States, acting under the Rio treaty, has dealt with recent disputes in the Caribbean. This achievement could not have been realized if the American community were divided into blocks based upon ideological differences among the member nations. We believe in the system, and by we, I mean the Department of State and the people of the United States. We are determined to strengthen it, to see that our hemispheric hostilities and frictions are resolved peacefully for our mutual benefit, to raise the general well-being. we intend to do nothing to set us one against the other.

We all remember the tragic emergency that made us adopt measures to help Europe. The war had devasted Western Europe, an industrial area with a complex economy. The factories in which the workers made their living were destroyed. There was no capital to rebuild the factories. The workers were destitute. They could not go out and grow food; there was not space. They had to be fed. We helped to feed them. They had to have work that they could do; we helped to restore the factories, so trade could begin again, and the farmers and the workers could exchange their products. Thus, we helped to avert a catastrophe.

The situation in Latin America is entirely different. There, the problem is not to rebuild great industrial nations but to help to stimulate the full growth of economies. This growth takes time. Permanent institutions such as the Export-Import Bank, the International Bank, and the International Monetary Fund, whose lives will not expire upon the expiration of an emergency, as in the case of the Economic Cooperation Administration, afford one form of help. We believe that these institutions offer the financial assistance which can properly be made available from governmental sources for development.

Another great need of Latin America is technical assistance. For 8 years, our Government has supported the Institute of Inter-American Affairs. The work of this organization is highly regarded in Washington, and its life was extended for 5 years in the last session of Congress without a dissenting vote. The Institute of Inter-American Affairs and the Interdepartmental Committee on Scientific and Cultural Cooperation have been a proving ground of President Truman's Point 4 Program. An expanded program of technical assistance, along the lines now before the Congress, will offer to Latin America, as it will to other parts of the world, an opportunity to obtain, at little expense, technical assistance to develop agriculture and industries with either local or foreign capital. In the absence of overriding political considerations, our financial assistance to Latin American countries has been intended to further development and prevent the stagnation of trade without trying to impose our views on their internal affairs.

At this point, I should like to say that during my 10 months as Assistant Secretary of State for Inter-American Affairs, I have thought very hard about the role that governments play in international relations. In the world of today, the relations between countries are not confined to governments but transcend government at every moment. Our commercial relations, our tourist relations, our cultural relations, the indirect effect of our actions on public opinion, all are beyond the power of government to dictate.

In my opinion, there is a tendency in our thinking, in our political writing, to overemphasize the role of government and to confuse a people or country with the government that happens to be in power. If our programs of cooperation in this hemisphere are to be effective, they must be continuous. We must not be misled by distaste for a government that comes into power. I dare say that there is nothing we could do in this hemisphere which would go further to make our enemies happy than to shackle ourselves with self-righteousness. If we believe in our power to do good in the American community, we must use it.

Strengthening Democracy in Latin America

This brings me to a big question: How do we think democracy can be strengthened in Latin America? Let me confess right here, gentlemen, that I recognize the impossibility of fully explaining democracy. Democracy is more than the sum of its parts—it is of the spirit. It cannot be created by any simple campaign of mind or matter. But, if I put first things first, I believe that true democracy depends on self-confidence, on the belief by a people that they are the masters of their fate. We cannot force democracy on a docile and supine people by refusing to do business with its government. It is true that if we were to deny recognition to the government of a small country and were to resort to economic sanctions against it, we might cause the overthrow of that government. But, this action would not remove the causes that produced the government in the first place. Moreover, as we have learned from sad experience, nationalism distorts the judgment and makes people stubborn, so that our expressions of disapproval of their government may make them cling all the more desperately to it.

Democracy does not come merely by the violent overthrow of government. As we all know, some unhappy countries in Latin America have seen innumerable changes without any rapid advance toward democratic freedoms. Democracy also requires lawful progress, the expansion of the idea of freedom. It requires, as I said before, the self-confidence of the people, their faith in their ability to take care of themselves to their best advantage, their passion for independence. Democracy depends on education, on an informed electorate, on an economy of opportunity. These are the things we are attempting to offer to Latin America today—technical assistance in education, in agriculture, and in industry. What we offer Latin America is an opportunity to help itself.

Any political discussion, these days, eventually gets around to communism. At the end of the last war, the Communists held many of the most vital positions in the labor movement in Latin America. But, ever since then, they have been losing ground, until, now, they control mainly those splinter labor federations that openly and clearly acknowledge their Communist leadership. There are notable exceptions, as we all know. In some countries, the fight is engaged; in others, the Communist leadership is, for the moment, in a strong position, although we do not consider these governments or peoples as true adherents to communism, nor do we expect the Communists to long retain control of the labor movements in them.

In this connection, I take pleasure in noting the growth of the Inter-American

Confederation of Labor since its organization in 1948. The growth of the CIT has certainly been an important factor in the steady decline of the Moscow-directed CTAL. Now that the AFL and the CIO are collaborating in the ICFTU and are extending this cooperation to their relations with Latin American unions, the situation is still more improved. I should like to take this opportunity to express my deep hope that the AFL and the CIO will continue to expand their cooperation in the international labor movement.

I have rejected the idea that we express our disapproval of an autocratic government by denying it diplomatic recognition or economic cooperation. This idea is a negative answer to our problem; and, so, I feel I must ask myself: How do we exert moral force for democracy in Latin America? Naturally, we must affirm and ever reaffirm our belief in democratic principles, and we must use our influence to further them. We play our part by working for more and better democracy at home. We should continue to demonstrate to the world that our system is the best in practice. We must continue to work by peaceful and friendly means with the people of Latin America to develop their countries to a place where all the men of the Americas may face life confident in their strength and in their faith in our way of life.

24. *United States, Title IV of the Foreign Assistance Act of 1950**

June 5, 1950

Sec. 401.

This title may be cited as the "Act for International Development."

Sec. 402.

The Congress hereby finds as follows:

(a) The peoples of the United States and other nations have a common interest in the freedom and in the economic and social progress of all peoples. Such progress can further the secure growth of democratic ways of life, the expansion of mutually beneficial commerce, the development of international understanding and good will, and the maintenance of world peace.

(b) The efforts of the peoples living in economically underdeveloped areas of the world to realize their full capabilities and to develop the resources of the lands in which they live can be furthered through the cooperative endeavor of all nations to exchange technical knowledge and skills and to encourage the flow of investment capital.

(c) Technical assistance and capital investment can make maximum contribution to economic development only where there is understanding of the mutual advantages of such assistance and investment and where there is confidence of fair and reasonable treatment and due respect for the legitimate interests of the peoples of the countries to which the assistance is given and in which the investment is made and of the countries from which the assistance and investments are derived. In the case of investment this involves confidence on the part of the people of the underdeveloped

*Public Laws—Ch. 220, Public Law 535-64 Stat. 198.

areas that investors will conserve as well as develop local resources, will bear a fair share of local taxes and observe local laws, and will provide adequate wages and working conditions for local labor. It involves confidence on the part of investors, through intergovernmental agreements or otherwise, that they will not be deprived of their property without prompt, adequate, and effective compensation; that they will be given reasonable opportunity to remit their earnings and withdraw their capital; that they will have reasonable freedom to manage, operate, and control their enterprises; that they will enjoy security in the protection of their persons and property, including industrial and intellectual property, and nondiscriminatory treatment in taxation and in the conduct of their business affairs.

Sec. 403.

(a) It is declared to be the policy of the United States to aid the efforts of the peoples of economically underdeveloped areas to develop their resources and improve their working and living conditions by encouraging the exchange of technical knowledge and skills and the flow of investment capital to countries which provide conditions under which such technical assistance and capital can effectively and constructively contribute to raising standards of living, creating new sources of wealth, increasing productivity and expanding purchasing power.

(b) It is further declared to be the policy of the United States that in order to achieve the most effective utilization of the resources of the United States, private and public, which are or may be available for aid in the development of economically underdeveloped areas, agencies of the United States Government, in reviewing requests of foreign governments for aid for such purposes, shall take into consideration (1) whether the assistance applied for is an appropriate part of a program reasonably designed to contribute to the balanced and integrated development of the country or area concerned; (2) whether any works or facilities which may be projected are actually needed in view of similar facilities existing in the area and are otherwise economically sound; and (3) with respect to projects for which capital is requested, whether private capital is available either in the country or elsewhere upon reasonable terms and in sufficient amounts to finance such projects.

Sec. 404.

(a) In order to accomplish the purposes of this title, the United States is authorized to participate in multilateral technical cooperation programs carried on by the United Nations, the Organization of American States, and their related organizations, and by other international organizations, wherever practicable.

(b) Within the limits of appropriations made available to carry out the purposes of this title, the President is authorized to make contributions to the United Nations for technical cooperation programs carried on by it and its related organizations which will contribute to accomplishing the purposes of this title as effectively as would participation in comparable programs on a bilateral basis. The President is further authorized to make contributions for technical cooperation programs carried on by the Organization of American States, its related organizations, and by other international organizations.

(c) Agencies of the United States Government on request of international organizations are authorized, upon approval by the President, to furnish services and such facilities as may be necessary in connection therewith, on an advance of funds or reimbursement basis, for such organizations in connection with their technical cooperation programs. Amounts received as reimbursements from such organizations shall be credited, at the option of the appropriate agency, either to the appropriation, fund, or account utilized in incurring the obligation, or to an appropriate appropriation, fund, or account currently available for the purposes for which expenditures were made.

Sec. 405.

The President is authorized to plan, undertake, administer, and execute bilateral technical cooperation programs carried on by any United States Government agency and, in so doing—

(a) To coordinate and direct existing and new technical cooperation programs.

(b) To assist other interested governments in the formulation of programs for the balanced and integrated development of the economic resources and productive capacities of economically underdeveloped areas.

(c) To receive, consider, and review reports of joint commissions set up as provided in section 410 of this title.

(d) To make, within appropriations made available for the purpose, advances and grants in aid of technical cooperation programs to any person, corporation, or other body of persons, or to any foreign government or foreign government agency.

(e) To make and perform contracts or agreements in respect of technical cooperation programs on behalf of the United States Government with any person, corporation, or other body of persons however designated, whether within or without the United States, or with any foreign government or foreign government agency: *Provided*, That with respect to contracts or agreements which entail commitments for the expenditure of funds appropriated pursuant to the authority of this title, such contracts or agreements, within the limits of appropriations or contract authorizations hereafter made available may, subject to any future action of the Congress, run for not to exceed three years in any one case.

(f) To provide for printing and binding outside the continental limits of the United States, without regard to section 11 of the Act of March 1, 1919 (44 U.S.C. 111).

(g) To provide for the publication of information made available by the joint commissions referred to in section 410, and from other sources, regarding resources, opportunities for private investment capital, and the need for technical knowledge and skill in each participating country.

Sec. 406.

Agreements made by the United States under the authority of this title with other governments and with international organizations shall be registered with the Secretariat of the United Nations in accordance with the provisions of article 102 of the United Nations Charter.

Sec. 407.

In carrying out the programs authorized in section 405 of this title—

(a) The participation of private agencies and persons shall be sought to the greatest extent practicable.

(b) Due regard shall be given, in reviewing requests for assistance, to the possibilities of achieving satisfactory results from such assistance as evidenced by the desire of the country requesting it (1) to take steps necessary to make effective use of the assistance made available, including the encouragement of the flow of productive local and foreign investment capital where needed for development; and (2) to endeavor to facilitate the development of the colonies, possessions, dependencies, and non-self-governing territories administered by such requesting country so that such areas may make adequate contribution to the effectiveness of the assistance requested.

(c) Assistance shall be made available only where the President determines that the country being assisted—

> (1) Pays a fair share of the cost of the program.
> (2) Provides all necessary information concerning such program and gives the program full publicity.
> (3) Seeks to the maximum extent possible full coordination and integration of technical cooperation programs being carried on in that country.
> (4) Endeavors to make effective use of the results of the program.
> (5) Cooperates with other countries participating in the program in the mutual exchange of technical knowledge and skills.

Sec. 408.

The President is authorized to prescribe such rules and regulations as may be necessary and proper to carry out the provisions of this title.

Sec. 409.

The President shall create an advisory board, hereinafter referred to as the "board," which shall advise and consult with the President or such other officer as he may designate to administer the program herein authorized, with respect to general or basic policy matters arising in connection with operation of the program. The board shall consist of not more than thirteen members to be appointed by the President, one of whom, by and with the advice and consent of the Senate, shall be appointed by him as chairman. The members of the board shall be broadly representative of voluntary agencies and other groups interested in the program, including business, labor, agriculture, public health, and education. All members of the board shall be citizens of the United States; none except the chairman shall be an officer or an employee of the United States (including any agency or instrumentality of the United States) who as such regularly receives compensation for current services. Members of the board, other than the chairman if he is an officer of the United States Goverment, shall receive out of funds made available for the purposes of this title a per diem allowance of $50 for each day spent away from their homes or regular places of business for the purpose of attendance at meetings of the board or at conferences held upon the call of the chairman, and in necessary travel, and while so engaged they may be paid actual travel expenses and not to exceed $10 per diem in lieu of subsistence and other expenses. The President may appoint such committees in special fields of activity as he may determine to be necessary or desirable to effectuate the purposes of this title. The members of such committees shall receive the same compensation as that provided for members of the board.

Sec. 410.

(a) At the request of a foreign country, there may be established a joint commission for economic development to be composed of persons named by the President and persons to be named by the requesting country, and may include representatives of international organizations mutually agreed upon.

(b) The duties of each such joint commission shall be mutually agreed upon, and may include, among other things, examination of the following:

(1) The requesting country's requirements with respect to technical assistance.

(2) The requesting country's resources and potentialities, including mutually advantageous opportunities for utilization of foreign technical knowledge and skills and investment.

(3) Policies which will remove deterrents to and otherwise encourage the introduction, local development, and application of technical skills and the creation and effective utilization of capital, both domestic and foreign; and the implementation of such policies by appropriate measures on the part of the requesting country and the United States, and of other countries, when appropriate, and after consultation with them.

(c) Such joint commissions shall prepare studies and reports which they shall transmit to the appropriate authorities of the United States and of the requesting countries. In such reports the joint commissions may include recommendations as to any specific projects which they conclude would contribute to the economic development of the requesting countries.

(d) The costs of each joint commission shall be borne by the United States and the requesting country in the proportion that may be agreed upon between the President and that country.

Sec. 411.

All or part of United States support for and participation in any technical cooperation program carried on under this title shall be terminated by the President—

(a) If he determines that such support and participation no longer contribute effectively to the purposes of this title, are contrary to a resolution adopted by the General Assembly of the United Nations that the continuance of such technical cooperation programs is unneccesary or undesirable, or are not consistent with the foreign policy of the United States.

(b) If a concurrent resolution of both Houses of the Congress finds such termination is desirable.

Sec. 412.

The President may exercise any power or authority conferred on him by this title through the Secretary of State or through any other officer or employee of the United States Government.

Sec. 413.

In order to carry out the purposes of this title—

(a) The President shall appoint, by and with the advice and consent of the Senate, a person who, under the direction of the President or such other officer as he may designate pursuant to section 412 hereof to exercise the powers conferred upon him by this title, shall be responsible for planning, implementing, and managing the programs authorized in this title. He shall be compensated at a rate fixed by the President without regard to the Classification Act of 1949 but not in excess of $15,000 per annum.

(b) Officers, employees, agents, and attorneys may be employed for duty within the continental limits of the United States in accordance with the provisions of the civil-service laws and the Classification Act of 1949.

(c) Persons employed for duty outside the continental limits of the United States and officers and employees of the United States Government assigned for such duty, may receive compensation at any of the rates provided for the Foreign Service Reserve and Staff by the Foreign Service Act of 1946 (60 Stat. 999), as amended, may receive allowances and benefits not in excess of those established thereunder, and may be appointed to any class in the Foreign Service Reserve or Staff in accordance with the provisions of such Act.

(d) Alien clerks and employees employed for the purpose of performing functions under this title shall be employed in accordance with the provisions of the Foreign Service Act of 1946, as amended.

(e) Officers and employees of the United States Government may be detailed to offices or positions to which no compensation is attached with any foreign government or foreign government agency or with any international organization: *Provided*, That while so detailed any such person shall be considered, for the purpose of preserving his privileges, rights, seniority, or other benefits, an officer or employee of the United States Government and of the United States Government agency from which detailed and shall receive therefrom his regular compensation, which shall be reimbursed to such agency from funds available under this title: *Provided further*, That such acceptance of office shall in no case involve the taking of an oath of allegiance to another government.

(f) Experts and consultants or organizations thereof may be employed as authorized by section 15 of the Act of August 2, 1946 (5 U.S.C. 55a), and individuals so employed may be compensated at a rate not in excess of $75 per diem.

(g) Such additional civilian personnel may be employed without regard to subsection (a) of section 14 of the Federal Employees Pay Act of 1946 (60 Stat. 219), as amended, as may be necessary to carry out the policies and purposes of this title.

Sec. 414.

No citizen or resident of the United States, whether or not now in the employ of the Government, may be employed or assigned to duties by the Government under this Act until such individual has been investigated by the Federal Bureau of Investigation and a report thereon has been made to the Secretary of State: *Provided, however,* That any present employee of the Government, pending the report as to such employee by the Federal Bureau of Investigation, may be employed or assigned to duties under this Act for the period of three months from the date of its enactment. This section shall not apply in the case of any officer appointed by the President by and with the advice and consent of the Senate.

Sec. 415.

The President shall transmit to the Congress an annual report of operations under this title.

Sec. 416.

(a) In order to carry out the provisions of this title, there shall be made available such funds as are hereinafter authorized and appropriated from time to time for the purposes of this title: *Provided, however,* That for the purpose of carrying out the provisions of this title through June 30, 1951, there is hereby authorized to be appropriated a sum not to exceed $35,000,000, including any sums appropriated to carry on the activities of the Institute of Inter-American Affairs, and technical cooperation programs as defined in section 418 herein under the United States Information and Educational Exchange Act of 1948 (62 Stat. 6). Activities provided for under this title may be prosecuted under such appropriations or under authority granted in appropriation Acts to enter into contracts pending enactment of such appropriations. Unobligated balances of such appropriations for any fiscal year may, when so specified in the appropriation Act concerned, be carried over to any succeeding fiscal year or years. The President may allocate to any United States Government agency any part of any appropriation available for carrying out the purposes of this title. Such funds shall be available for obligation and expenditure for the purposes of this title in accordance with authority granted hereunder or under authority governing the activities of the Government agencies to which such funds are allocated.

(b) Nothing in this title is intended nor shall it be construed as an expressed or implied commitment to provide any specific assistance, whether of funds, commodities, or services, to any country or countries, or to any international organization.

Sec. 417.

If any provision of this title or the application of any provision to any circumstances or persons shall be held invalid, the validity of the remainder of the title and the applicability of such provision to other circumstances or persons shall not be affected thereby.

Sec. 418.

As used in this title—

(a) The term "technical cooperation programs" means programs for the international interchange of technical knowledge and skills designed to contribute to the balanced and integrated development of the economic resources and productive capacities of economically underdeveloped areas. Such activities may include, but need not be limited to, economic, engineering, medical, educational, agricultural, fishery, mineral, and fiscal surveys, demonstration, training, and similar projects that serve the purpose of promoting the development of economic resources and productive capacities of underdeveloped areas. The term "technical cooperation programs" does not include such activities authorized by the United States Information and Educational Exchange Act of 1948 (62 Stat. 6) as are not primarily related to economic development nor activities undertaken now or hereafter pursuant to the International Aviation Facilities Act (62 Stat. 450), nor pursuant to the Philippine Rehabilitation Act of 1946 (60 Stat. 128), as amended, nor pursuant to the Foreign Assistance Act of 1948 (62 Stat. 137), as amended, nor activities undertaken now or hereafter in the administration of areas occupied by the United States armed forces or in Korea by the Economic Cooperation Administration.

(b) The term "United States Government agency" means any department, agency, board, wholly or partly owned corporation or instrumentality, commission, or independent establishment of the United States Government.

(c) The term "international organization" means any intergovernmental organization of which the United States is a member.

25. *Announcement by Secretary Acheson on a United States*
    Request for a Consultative Meeting of the
    Foreign Ministers of the American States*

December 16, 1950

Pursuant to instructions from President Truman, I have today instructed the representative of the United States in the Council of the Organization of American States [OAS] to request that a meeting of consultation of Ministers of Foreign Affairs be held in accordance with article 39 of the Charter of the Organization, which provides that such meetings shall be held "to consider problems of an urgent nature and of common interest to the American States."

The aggressive policy of international communism, carried out through its satellites, has brought about a situation in which the entire free world is threatened. The free world is meeting that threat by resolute action through the United Nations, in keeping with the principles of the United Nations Charter. As President Truman announced in his speech last night, the United States, for the purpose of organizing its strength in support of these principles, has embarked on an emergency program of economic and military preparedness.

Within the United Nations, the United States is also part of the established regional community represented by the Organization of American States. All 21 members of that community have jointly dedicated themselves to the cause of freedom. This common cause, even more than geography, has prompted them to work together for their common security. Their cooperation is based on the principle that the defense of any one of them is inseparable from the defense of all of them. What is at stake in the present situation, with respect to this inter-American community of ours, is the survival of all that it stands for in the world.

The United States, having embarked on urgent mobilization for the common defense, wishes to consult its fellow members in the inter-American community with respect to the situation which we all face and on the coordination of the common effort required to meet it. That is the reason why it is requesting that a meeting of consultation be held.

In the near future this Government, after consultation with Congressional leaders and the governments of the other American Republics, will have proposals to make respecting the date and place of the meeting and its agenda.

26. *Letter from Paul C. Daniels, United States Representative*
    on the Council of the Organization of American States,
    to Ambassador Hildebrando Accioly, Chairman of the
    Council, Requesting a Consultative Meeting of the
    Foreign Ministers of the American States†

December 20, 1950

My Dear Mr. Chairman: Confirming the request which I made to you Saturday, December 16, I have been instructed by my Government to request that a Meeting of

*Department of State Bulletin, Jan. 1, 1951, p. 8.
†Department of State Bulletin, Jan. 1, 1951, pp. 8-9.

Consultation of Ministers of Foreign Affairs be held in accordance with Article 39 of the Charter of the Organization of American States, which provides that such Meetings shall be called "to consider problems of an urgent nature and of common interest to the American States." I am, therefore, hereby requesting, in accordance with Article 40 of the Charter, that this matter be considered at the next meeting of the Council of the Organization of American States which will, I understand, be held on Wednesday, December 20, at 10:30 a.m.

The aggressive policy of international communism, carried out through its satellites, has brought about a situation in which the entire free world is threatened. The free world is meeting that threat by resolute action through the United Nations, in keeping with the principles of the United Nations Charter. As President Truman has announced, the United States, for the purpose of organizing its strength in support of these principles, has embarked on an emergency program of economic and military preparedness.

The twenty-one American Republics have jointly dedicated themselves to the cause of freedom. Our common cause, even more than geography, has prompted us to work together for common security. Our cooperation is based on the principle that the defense of one is inseparable from the defense of all. What is at stake in the present situation with respect to this inter-American community of ours is the survival of all that it stands for in the world.

Having embarked on urgent mobilization for the common defense, the United States wishes to consult its fellow members in the Organization of American States with respect to the world situation which we all face and on the coordination of the common effort required to meet it.

Should this request receive the approval of the Council, my Government in the near future, but after there has been adequate time for prior consultation, especially among our respective governments, will present for the consideration of the Council, in accordance with Article 41 of the Charter of the Organization of American States, specific proposals, falling within the scope of the subject mentioned above, with regard to the program of the meeting.

27. *Letter from John C. Dreier, United States Representative on the Council of the Organization of American States, to Alberto Lleras Camargo, Secretary General of the Organization of American States, Concerning the Agenda of the Fourth Consultative Meeting of Foreign Ministers of American States**

January 31, 1951

Under instructions from my Government, I wish to submit the following comment concerning the proposed agenda for the Fourth Consultative Meeting of Ministers of Foreign Affairs, which was transmitted by the Council of the Organization of American States to the Governments on January 17, 1951.

With respect to Point III (b), my Government has taken particular note of the discussions which led up to the adoption of the language of the draft agenda submitted

*Department of State Bulletin, Feb. 12, 1951, p. 266.

by the Council to the Governments for consideration. It appears that there has been some doubt concerning the scope of this agenda item.

It is the desire of the United States Government to remove all doubt concerning the scope of this item. My Government particularly wishes to make clear that it believes that Item III (b) on the agenda should permit the discussion, among others, of problems regarding the continuation of basic economic activity and the expansion of basic productive facilities within the limits imposed by the present emergency situation.

My Government recognizes the interest of the other American Republics in plans for increased economic activity. It is manifestly impossible and inappropriate for the Meeting of Foreign Ministers to consider all aspects of the economic future of the American Republics. However, the Government of the United States considers it appropriate and desirable for the Meeting to discuss frankly both the possibilities and limitations of the present emergency with respect not only to existing economic activities, but to plans for increased production for both civilian and defense purposes.

Accordingly, my Government suggests that Item III (b) on the agenda of the Fourth Meeting of Consultation of Ministers of Foreign Affairs be revised to read as follows:

"Production and distribution of products and services in short supply to meet, within limits imposed by the emergency, the requirements of the American Republics for the continuation of basic economic activity and expansion of basic productive facilities."

With every good wish, believe me,

28. *Address by President Truman before the Fourth Consultative Meeting of Foreign Ministers of the American States, on Cooperation in the World Struggle for Freedom**

March 26, 1951

It is an honor to open this meeting of the Ministers of Foreign Affairs of the American Republics. I am happy to extend to you a wholehearted welcome to our country and to our capital city. On behalf of the United States, I hope that this will be a most satisfactory and successful meeting.

This is the fourth meeting of the Ministers of Foreign Affairs of the American Republics. This meeting, like the earlier ones, is held at a time of international danger. When the first meeting was held, in 1939, war had just broken out in Europe. As that conflict spread to nation after nation and threatened to extend to all parts of the world, the Foreign Ministers of the American Republics held two more meetings, in 1940 and 1942, to plan a common course of action against the common danger.

As a result of our concerted efforts, our countries did not become a theater of war. The nations of this hemisphere succeeded in protecting the American continents from invasion. And, as a result of our common efforts, the people of the Americas were able to contribute power and resources which turned the tide against aggression and brought victory to the forces of freedom.

Today, we meet again to consider our common defense. We meet again to work out

*Department of State Bulletin, Apr. 9, 1951, pp. 566-68.

ways and means by which our united strength may be employed in the struggle for freedom throughout the world.

The Heritage of Common Principles

The American republics all owe their national beginnings to the same set of ideals—the same concepts of human and international freedom. We have all followed and we will continue to follow two basic principles. First, we believe that international affairs should be based upon cooperation among free and independent nations, and not upon coercion or force. Second, we believe that the aim and purpose of government is to promote the welfare of all the people—not just the privileged few.

These principles have long been the basis of relations among the American Republics. The same principles are now embodied in the Charter of the United Nations, where they have become the foundation of a new society of nations. The statesmen of the American Republics have shown their continuing devotion to these principles by the great and constructive work they have done in creating and strengthening the United Nations.

Today, these principles are under relentless attack from a center of power which denies the whole concept of human freedom—whether it be spiritual freedom, or economic freedom, or political freedom.

World Threat of Soviet Expansion

Communist imperialism attacks and undermines national independence and international cooperation. In their place, it substitutes the rule of force. Communist imperialism also seeks to destroy the system of government that serves the welfare of the people. Instead, it sets up a system under which the people exist only to serve the purposes of the government. As a result, the Soviet system is one of unbridled power, imposing slavery at home and aggression abroad.

The aggressive expansion of Soviet power threatens the whole world. In Europe, we see it trying to engulf the nations from which we have drawn our cultural heritage. If Soviet subversion and Soviet armed force were to overthrow these nations, the consequences for all of us in the Western Hemisphere would be disastrous. We would lose those cultural and religious ties which mean so much to us. The international trade on which we are so dependent would be violently disrupted. Worst of all, we would be confronted by a hostile power on the shores of the Atlantic, capable of using the great economic resources of our conquered friends to strike across the ocean at our own independence.

We must not and will not let that happen. We in the Western Hemisphere must help the free men of Europe who are resisting Soviet expansion.

In the Far East, Communist imperialism presents us with another threat. There, we see many new nations emerging, as our own countries once did, from colonial status to full independence. For these new nations, we of the Western Hemisphere have the greatest feeling of fellowship. But Communist imperialism has fallen upon these new nations with its weapons of internal subversion and external attack. It seeks to overpower them before they are strong enough to stand alone.

If Soviet communism were to be successful in this venture, it would be a terrible blow to the bright promise of the principles of freedom and peace which we uphold. The great manpower of Asia would become one of the instruments of the aggressive expansion of the Soviet system toward our own hemisphere.

Both to the East, therefore, and to the West, we are confronted by great perils. Our future progress, our very survival, lie in the defense of the world order of free nations of which we are a part. Our very existence depends upon the success of those principles which our countries stand for, and which we have supported in the United Nations. There is no safety for any of us in abandoning these principles. There will be no security in the world without the United Nations. Powerful and productive as the Western Hemisphere is, we cannot make it safe by building a wall around it.

Instead of withdrawing into our hemisphere in a hopeless attempt to find security through retreat, we must concert our defenses and combine our strength in order to support men in Europe and Asia who are battling for freedom. That is the only course that can lead to security or peace or freedom for us or for men anywhere in the world.

Recognition of this fact lies behind the aid the United States has given to the rebuilding of Europe. It lies behind the struggle the free nations are now waging in the hills of Korea. The resistance of the United Nations to aggression in Korea—a resistance that has the firm approval of all the nations represented here—is of momentous importance. It has shown that the free nations are determined to defend their ideals of national independence and human welfare.

The issue in Korea is the survival of the principles on which we have built our countries. The principle of national independence and self-government is at stake there, as well as the principle that government shall be for the welfare of the people. If justice and order do not prevail in Korea, they will be in danger everywhere.

Heroic sacrifices are being made in Korea to check the forces of aggression and protect us against the terrible destruction and vastly greater sacrifices of a world conflict. By standing firm in Korea and by preparing to meet aggression elsewhere, we are doing our best to prevent a third world war.

Steps to Establish World Peace

This meeting in Washington, therefore, must consider not only what should be done to improve the defense of this hemisphere but also what measures we can best undertake to support and strengthen the United Nations in its effort to establish world peace.

We meet here as a region which has already, in the solemn treaty of Rio de Janeiro, announced its intention to defend itself through cooperative action. We are pledged to resist the common foe.

We must now plan as a primary task for the strengthening and the coordinated use of our defense forces in this hemisphere. We must also consider how we may best use our strength to support the cause of freedom against aggression throughout the world.

The success of our defense program depends upon our economic strength. In these troubled times, defense production must have prior claim upon our economic re-sources. We shall have to increase the production of strategic materials. We shall have to divert manufacturing capacity to defense purposes.

These necessities will create many difficult practical problems for our countries to solve. There will be shortages of basic materials and other commodities. There will be limitations on certain kinds of capital expansion.

The first step in solving these problems is to face them in a spirit of cooperation. We must recognize that we are engaged, as good neighbors, in a common enterprise that is vital to our survival as free and democratic nations. We must establish the principle of sharing our burdens fairly. We must act together to meet essential civilian needs, and, at the same time, we must act together to be sure that scarce supplies are limited to essential uses. We must try to prevent wild and speculative price movements in our international trade, whether in raw materials or manufactured products.

Our defense needs are not, of course, limited to the things that go into the making of weapons. We need to build up our economic strength in a much broader way. It is essential to our security that we constantly enlarge our economic capacity. Our defense needs include, in many areas, more food, better education, and better health services. They include, in certain cases, the building of roads, dams, or power plants.

We must remember that the real strength of the free nations lies in the will and determination of their peoples. The free nations stand for economic progress and social advancement. They grow in strength by going forward along the road of greater economic opportunity for all.

Over the last 10 years, our countries have made great economic progress. In most of the countries represented here, national income is at least twice what it was in 1939.

An important factor in our advance is the program of technical cooperation which we have joined together to carry out. Joint projects for spreading technical knowledge have already made notable achievements in improving the health, education, and living standards of our people. We intend to press on with this kind of activity.

The American Republics are full of breathtaking possibilities for future economic development. These possibilities can be made realities only if we work and plan together for a long time ahead. I like to think, for example, of the possibility of developing vast areas of wilderness, such as the eastern slopes of the Andes, and turning them into new and fertile farm land.

I like to think of a project about which I talked to the President of Chile, which contemplates the diversion of water from those high mountain lakes between Bolivia and Peru for making a garden on the coast of South America to the west for Chile and Peru, and in return, giving Bolivia a seaport on the Pacific.

I had a very pleasant conversation with the President of Chile on that subject, and I like to think of the development of the Parana, Paraguay, and Uruguay rivers. Think that wonderful possibilites are in those great waterways for development, and those are only samples, for all over the continent of South America there are greater resources underdeveloped than were ever in these United States of America. And I know that we can develop them for the welfare of the whole world, as well as for ourselves.

I like to think of the possibilities of industrial development in your countries. I remember with pride the part which this country played, even during the troubled times of the last war, in helping to create a steel industry in Brazil. I think with satisfaction of the progress that has been made by Chile and other countries in setting up factories and hydroelectric projects in recent years.

Our countries do not have unlimited resources to devote to creative developments such as these. We cannot do as much, in the midst of a defense emergency, as we could in normal times. But we must do all we can.

Our Goal—A Better World

It is the genius of our democratic type of society that we are constantly creative and constantly advancing. We hold out to all people the prospect of bettering their condition, not in the dim future, not after some terrible and bloody upheaval, but steadily through the years, in the simple activities of their daily life.

In our countries, we do not measure our prosperity by the power of the state. We do not measure the progress of our society in terms of military might. We do not measure our advancement in terms of the profits or the luxuries of the few. Our yardstick is the welfare of the many. We think in terms of the average man—how he lives, what he can buy, and the freedom he enjoys. These are the standards by which we measure our development.

And, by these standards, we are marching steadily forward. We shall continue that march!

Our vision of progress is not limited to our own countries. We extend it to all the peoples of the world.

We know that people are very much alike in their basic aspirations, wherever they may be or whatever language they may speak. We recognize that the people of Russia, the people of the Soviet satellite states, are very much like us in what they want for themselves and their children. We hope that some day they will find it possible to turn their leaders from their present path of tyranny and aggression.

Our goal is self-development, not imperialism.

Our goal is peace, not war.

Our goal, not only for ourselves but for all peoples, is a better world—materially, morally, and spiritually.

29. Address by Secretary Acheson before the Fourth Consultative Meeting of Ministers of Foreign Affairs of the American States, on Freedom—the Key to Hemisphere Solidarity and World Peace*

March 27, 1951

I look forward with considerable pleasure to the prospect of working closely together with my colleagues of the Americas in this important meeting.

Our distinguished Brazilian colleague, Minister Neves da Fontoura, has already eloquently set before us the significance of this meeting in terms of our long inter-American tradition. That tradition dates back to the first International Conference of the American States to which this country had the honor to be host 60 years ago. Since then we have managed, by our determination, to preserve and greatly strengthen our freedom in spite of all perils.

More than that, we have built up a brotherhood of nations that time has tested. In the course of the decades, the foundations of our system have had time to set. Can anyone doubt that the men who worked to bring us together in the first Washington Conference would find their vision more than vindicated by the great Organization of American States as it exists today?

*Department of State Bulletin, Apr. 9, 1951, pp. 569-73.

The significance of this meeting is appreciated, I believe, by free men all over the world.

It rests not alone on the work we have come together to do, as important as that is to our future and to theirs. Even more important than this is the fraternal way in which the American Republics have grown accustomed to working together.

We meet freely. We talk frankly, as people who understand each other and like each other. We have problems between us, and some of them are difficult. But there are no problems between us that will not yield to the good will and friendship we all bring to this meeting.

It is our hope that our consultations here and our cooperative actions will have a dual effect.

We hope that what we do here will produce sound and constructive results. We hope also—indeed we know—that this meeting, as a demonstration of the kind of friendship among nations which may someday prevail universally, will convey inspiration and encouragement to men everywhere.

Partnership of the Free World

The larger significance of our meeting arises from the fact that we are a part, inescapably, of the partnership of the free world.

What is the partnership of the free world? It is something new in the world, and its meaning should be made clear to all.

Is it an alliance, like those which crisscrossed Europe in the last century? No, it is not like the old alliances, because it is not directed against anyone, nor does it aspire to rule or to conquest.

Is it a sphere of influence arrangement or a satellite system? No, it most assuredly is not, for no rulers in a master state dictate to the free nations.

The partnership of the free world is something different from any of these. It is a spiritual confederation of peoples as well as nations. It is a partnership which encompasses many differences. The states in it do not all have the same political or social institutions. They do not conform to any standard pattern. They do not have a single "way of life."

Each has its own set of hopes and anxieties, its own domestic problems, its own national traditions and desires.

What binds the nations of the free world together into a partnership is that they have a powerful interest in common: their concern for freedom.

Freedom is the key. This is what free nations have, and other nations do not. This is the heart of the matter, for without freedom, neither real peace, nor real security, nor any real progress is possible.

To the nation, freedom means national independence, freedom to work out its destinies in its own ways.

To the people, freedom is not only the very breath of life itself but it is also the gateway of opportunity. Free men have the opportunity to better their lives, to abolish poverty, and to live in human dignity.

Freedom is the climate in which men can work to fulfill all the affirmative aspirations and values of their lives.

When people ask us, "What is it you are for, you men of the free world?" Then we say, "We're for freedom, because freedom is the key to everything else we want."

Where there is freedom, we can make peace prevail, we can govern ourselves the way we want, we can improve our land and grow more food. We can live side by side with people who think differently, who worship differently, who talk a different language—so long as they and we are both free, we have that one important thing in common.

This is not to say that any of us has fully realized our ideals of a free society. Our progress toward this goal is not always even, from week to week, or from month to month. But it is the ideal and the objective toward which, over the decades and the generations, we have been moving steadily forward.

The Communist Threat to Freedom

And now this freedom of ours is faced with a mortal threat.

The small group of men who rule the Soviet Union and pull the strings of the international Communist movement have a doctrine which is opposed to freedom.

Their doctrine is a blueprint for a Communist world, governed from the Kremlin.

This is the new imperialism. Its instruments are a formidable machine of war and the international Communist movement. With one or the other, and sometimes both, the new imperialism reaches out for more power and for rule over more people.

Never before have we faced a menace of this magnitude. Never before has there been so great a challenge to our determination to preserve our independence as nations.

But it is not only against the independence of governments that this new imperialism is directed. The freedom of people, of the individual man, is also its target.

Although the Communists have played upon the hopes of people for a better life, they have in practice been the enemies of progress. The new imperialists have contributed nothing but propaganda to the great cooperative efforts to improve standards of living among the peoples of the world. Instead, they use human misery as a political tool, callous to the cost.

This is the threat which jeopardizes freedom. It is a threat which has for us the greatest urgency, a threat which calls upon us as people and as nations to defend our freedom.

It calls upon us for action now.

No free man anywhere can safely disregard this threat. There is no free nation anywhere, large or small, whose freedom is secure. Freedom does not come in different sizes. Large states do not have more of it, nor small states less, according to their size. The defense of freedom is an obligation which falls upon all who are worthy of it.

And it is in this sense that the partnership of the free world is a spiritual confederation among those who value their freedom, and each, according to his capacity, will do his utmost to defend it.

This is the meaning of the great effort which the free nations are making. Its purpose is to assemble sufficient force to make it plain in advance that further aggression will not succeed.

In the face of the challenge of the new imperialism, the rapid increase of this deterrent force is the only real road to peace—the kind of peace in which the survival and growth of our free institutions will be possible.

The task is a great one. To perform it, each must do his full share. We are well begun, but the greater part lies still ahead of us.

Progress in the Defense of Freedom

In Korea, the principle of collective security has been put to the test. It has stood the test. Aggression has not been allowed to succeed. This is a history-making battle, a landmark, we may hope, on the road to world peace.

The forces of the United Nations are fighting a battle which is of vital significance to the security of all free nations. The cause of freedom owes a great debt to the men of many lands who are bearing arms in Korea and making heavy sacrifices under the banner of the United Nations. And the lessons learned in the defense of Korea should enable the United Nations to develop a collective security system that will be better prepared to meet aggression in the future, if it occurs.

Heartening progress is also being made in another sector in the defense of freedom: in recent months, major steps have been taken toward strengthening the defenses of free Europe. The work that is now going forward to build an integrated and effective defense organization under General Eisenhower contributes to the security of this hemisphere.

It is a happy and a significant coincidence that the visit of the President of France, M. Auriol, to this country comes while this meeting is in progress and that we shall have the pleasure of hearing him address this assembly. This fortunate circumstance symbolizes to the world the relationship between our efforts in this hemisphere and those of our brothers in Europe, in behalf of our common aspirations for peace and freedom.

Impact of Mobilization on Economy

In this country, the mobilization of our strength is beginning to have a substantial impact upon our economy and upon the lives of our citizens. By last week, the size of our armed forces had been doubled over the level that prevailed before the attack upon Korea, and many more young men and women are being called into military service.

Although total production is increasing, the requirements of defense are such that curtailment of many goods and services has been necessary. The burden of taxation is being heavily increased. We are seeking to hold in check the strong inflationary pressures which have been generated by the defense program.

It is our intention to prepare an economic base that will have the stamina to sustain this substantial defense program over as long a period as may be necessary, and which would be capable of further rapid expansion if war should be forced upon us.

The scale and complexity of this endeavor, side-by-side with the changes wrought throughout the hemisphere by the defense mobilization, inevitably creates many difficulties for us all.

We in the United States have been mindful of the many difficult questions raised for our neighbors of this hemisphere by our mobilization program.

Looking ahead to the intensification of this program in the future, it is evident that the closest working relationship must be established among all of us in the Americas in order that our common effort for our common defense may realize the best that is in all of us. Together, we must seek ways of avoiding any uncontrolled and unfair distribution of the sacrifices that our peoples face.

With this in mind, on the day that the United States entered upon its emergency program of economic and military preparedness, it made known its proposal that this emergency meeting of consultation be held.

We have before us, at this meeting, a realistic agenda that sets forth the questions to which we, the American Republics, must jointly find the answers.

We shall find these answers in the spirit of cooperation that is basic to our inter-American tradition. We are cooperators. Our great tradition illustrates the principle that the spirit of cooperation and the spirit of bargaining are mutually incompatible. They exclude each other. For in bargaining, each man tries to reap advantage for himself to the detriment of the man he deals with. It is the genius of our inter-American system—and the effectiveness of our defense rests on it—that mutual cooperation, instead, has been the means by which all have benefited.

This is the spirit with which we address ourselves to the problems on our agenda.

Measures Necessary for Defense

One question which each of us faces, in the light of our hemispheric position, is: In what way can each of us best develop our military capabilities in order that we may have the most effective individual and collective self-defense against armed attack?

We may wish to consider measures which can be taken by our respective Governments to enable the Inter-American Defense Board to carry on its functions most efficiently and to prepare, at the earliest possible time, a coordinated defense for this hemisphere.

In considering the military defensive strength of the hemisphere, it is evident that any disturbances to the peaceful relations among the American Republics can only have the effect of weakening our total defensive capabilities. As part of the effort to bulwark our defenses against aggression, it may serve a useful purpose for us to strengthen our determination to make fullest use of available machinery for the peaceful settlement of disputes.

In view of the effect upon our hemispheric security of the danger of aggression in other parts of the world, a related question requires our attention. That is, how we, the American Republics, can best support the United Nations in strengthening its capacity to deal with aggression.

The interests of the Republics of this hemisphere in the building of a world of law and order are greatly served by the progress which the United Nations has been making in strengthening its collective security system. The success of this effort depends upon our willingness to back up the United Nations.

Our deliberations here will measurably strengthen our common security if they lead to action on the part of the American Republics in helping to fulfill the purposes of the uniting-for-peace resolution of the United Nations.

The use of subversion and other forms of indirect aggression by the international Communist movement requires us, as a vital part of our defense program to examine carefully our present internal security procedures and improve them where necessary.

It is equally important that we should consult as to the practical steps we may take, together and individually, to insure the maximum protection and strengthening of our basic democratic institutions. They are the heart of what we are seeking to defend against Communist undermining, and to safeguard these institutions, while we prevent their abuse, requires our constant vigilance.

These are some of the matters which are involved, either directly or indirectly, in strengthening our military security.

Economic Problems

The economic problems before us pervade our whole effort and touch upon the life of every individual in the hemisphere. We must gather up our joint economic forces for the common defense, not only in one country or some countries but throughout our interlocking economic community.

This means vital adjustments for all of us. These would fall to us even though some among us did not participate in our endeavor. For the sacrifices that the United States and its people are now making inevitably have their effect upon all whose economies are related to our own.

Are these effects, then, to fall indiscriminately and without control on peoples everywhere? Or are we going to provide, by cooperation, that the essential needs of all our peoples are met; that production for defense is pushed to a level which will serve to accomplish the purpose of averting a third world war; and that the sacrifice of unessentials is fairly distributed? The Government of the United States had this question very much in mind when it requested the convening of this meeting.

In this country, we are already allocating materials required for defense production so that they will be available only in limited quantities for normal civilian demands.

Your countries, I know, are also facing the problems of increased production for the defense of our hemisphere, production on which the survival of freedom for every one of us depends. In most cases, your chief problem is to effect emergency increases in the production of essential materials without, at the same time, inviting disaster when a more normal situation returns. The United States understands this problem. We do not underestimate it. Certainly, we must consider what practicable means there may be, within the terms of our great purpose, to deal with this risk together.

The problem of curbing inflation is no less important to each of our countries and to our common purpose. The danger of uncontrolled inflation in any country threatens its people. It also weakens the economic stability of the hemisphere as a whole. We must make the most strenuous effort together to take the steps that are necessary to keep inflationary tendencies under control. This must be done not only by international action but by each of our Governments within its own jurisdiction.

Undoubtedly, we shall not be able to foresee all the measures which our respective Governments will find it necessary to take in dealing with the economic defense program. As much as circumstances permit, we should endeavor to consult with one another and act cooperatively in this field, particularly, to our mutual and our common benefit.

In his address to the meeting yesterday, President Truman spoke of the concern felt by this country for the need of carrying forward the programs of economic cooperation.

It is my hope that we shall all continue to give as much support as we can to these measures by which our people are enabled to improve the conditions of their life.

The programs of economic development and technical cooperation, in many ways, effectively support the emergency defense program. Such programs as those which increase food supply, combat disease, increase the output of materials in short supply, and improve working conditions and labor standards are of double importance in this period.

Insofar as we can, we must seek to fulfill both the immediate requirements of the defense program and our long-range objective of economic development and social progress.

High Purpose of Meeting

We must always keep our goals in mind. While we work together here to find solutions for these difficult problems with which the rapid development of our political, economic, and military strength confronts us, we must never allow ourselves to forget the real nature of the endeavor which brings us together.

Our cause is above all the cause of freedom, of international morality. It is, therefore, the cause of peace, and of the well-being of man himself.

So that the world at large and our own peoples shall not mistake the greatness of our purpose, it is my hope that this historic meeting will create a declaration of the principles for which we stand and which we are determined to defend.

May our meeting send forth a beacon of hope and inspiration from the New World to all mankind.

30. Statement by Willard L. Thorp, Assistant Secretary of State for Economic Affairs, before Committee III of the Fourth Meeting of Consultation of Ministers of Foreign Affairs of the American States, on the Economic Problems of Today*

March 27, 1951

We are faced with a clear and present danger, and we have no choice except to build our defenses. This means simply that we must devote whatever energy and resources are required to the task of rearmament. Unhappily, once again we in the free world must look to our military strength to insure the preservation of our fundamental institutions.

But, building military strength is not our only goal. Even more basic is the objective that the civilization which we seek to preserve should become more and more responsive to the needs and aspirations of mankind. We must make ever more worthy that which we undertake to defend.

These are great and difficult tasks. No one of our countries alone can protect itself nor can it build its future by itself. We must put our energies, our abilities, and our economic resources into the common effort in order that each of us may continue to

*Department of State Bulletin, Apr. 30, 1951, pp. 693-98.

develop and grow in ways of life conforming to our ideals. The strength of the whole is much greater than the strength of its parts. We can meet the challenge if we meet it together.

In no area does the emergency raise as many difficult questions as in the economic field. The vast new military production effort necessitates many readjustments, and perhaps the most difficult part of our task lies in the working out of appropriate economic arrangements and policies both within and among our countries, and also with other countries of the free world.

The Questions Before Us

The specific questions we are called upon to deal with in this Committee can, I think, be summed up about as follows: What common steps are required for us to build up most rapidly and effectively our defensive military strength? How, while doing so, can we best meet the requirements of our civilian populations for goods and services? How can we maintain our economies on an even keel? How can we reconcile the requirements of the defense program with the aspirations of all our countries for improved standards of living and for futher economic development?

These are the questions to which we must find the answers. They are more than questions. They are challenges. By accepting them as such, we will go a long way toward meeting them.

In thinking about these problems, I am sure that many of us are tempted to recall the experiences we all went through during World War II and to seek solutions from the history of the war years. The lessons of wartime can certainly be of use to us, but I am sure that we will be making a serious mistake if we try to apply them too closely to our present situation. For there is an important difference between the objectives we now seek and the objectives we sought then, and there are marked changes between the world economic situation as it was then and the economic conditions which exist today.

I should like to discuss these points a bit further.

Our Objective

First, it is clearly not the objective of the free world to enter upon that full-scale economic mobilization which is necessary for the actual carrying on of war. It is true that this may be forced upon us if the Kremlin persists in a course of aggression. But our purpose now is to discourage the aggressor. Our purpose is to prevent war. We in the free world hope to do this by building around ourselves a military shield of sufficient toughness to deter aggression and to create behind that shield an expanding and dynamic economy which can serve both the purposes of peace and the purposes of war if war should be forced upon us.

This is a goal that is both easier and more difficult than we faced before. It is easier because it will not require that we devote as much of our total energies to military production as we did in wartime. It is more difficult because it depends upon maintaining in peacetime a resolute and unwavering determination that the defensive shield be forged quickly and that, once it is forged, it be kept strong over as many years as may be necessary, perhaps for an indefinite period.

Our Capacity

If the task be less today because it is not the task of full war mobilization, it is also easier because of our present economic potential. We in the free world have much greater economic capacity today than we had before the last war.

In the United States, the total output of the economy—that is, the gross national product—for the last quarter of 1950 ran at the rate of 300 billion dollars per year. We are achieving this output on the basis of an average work week of less than 42 hours. If we adjust this figure for changes in the price level, such an annual rate of the gross national product of the United States is about 60 percent greater than in 1940. The index of our industrial production is more than 70 percent above the 1940 average. Our civilian labor force has grown by more than 7,000,000 workers in the last 10 years, from 55,600,000 in 1940 to 63,000,000 in 1950. We are today producing, without substantial strain, somewhat more than we were producing, under the greatest strain, during the wartime years of peak production.

In the other American Republics, we also see great economic advances. In the last 10 years, it is estimated that the national income in various Latin American countries has increased by percentages ranging from 20 percent to more than 60 percent. Industrial output for the region as a whole has doubled in this period.

In Canada, our neighbor to the north, output has grown by almost one-third during the last decade, from 13.6 billion to 17.7 billion dollars, Canadian dollars, in current prices.

In Western Europe, economic recovery from the devastation of war is all but complete. Real output, even on a per capita basis, is substantially higher than it was at the beginning of World War II. By the end of 1950, the countries of Western Europe had increased the physical volume of their industrial production by 42 percent above the level achieved in 1938.

So that today, we in the free world can begin the hard and disagreeable, but necessary, task of rebuilding our military defenses with the knowledge that we start from a stronger economic base, with greater productive capacity, greater manpower, and enhanced skills to carry us forward.

In part, because we have a greater capacity to produce, we will need to devote less of it to build our defensive military shield than we spent for military purposes during World War II. Again turning to statistics for the United States, during the wartime years of peak production, 45 percent of our gross national product went for military purposes, whereas by the end of 1951 we expect that about 18 percent of our gross national product will go for the purpose of security. Assuming that we are successful in our objective of preventing war and barring a further serious deterioration in the international situation, the percentage of output going into military production is not likely to become greatly higher than this figure. In spite of the burden of armament production, the production for civilian consumption at home and abroad should, therefore, be at a substantially higher level than that of the wartime years. It must be recognized, however, that unless and until new capacity becomes available, certain segments of industry, where the impact of military production is felt most directly, will of necessity have to curtail their output for civilian consumption.

There are other differences between today's economic situation and that prevailing during the war period, which will necessarily affect our international economic relationships.

During the war, the countries of Latin America were almost wholly cut off from sources of supply in Western Europe. The continent of Europe after 1940 was in enemy hands. The export trade of the United Kingdom was drastically curtailed. The United States, which had supplied about one-third of Latin America's imports before the war, and Canada, became virtually the sole suppliers of the goods required to maintain the economies of the other American Republics.

Today, Western Europe has again become an important source for the industrial and other commodities making up the import trade of the Latin American countries. In 1947, the export trade of the countries participating in the Organization for European Economic Cooperation, excluding intra-European trade, amounted to only 75 percent of their exports during the prewar year 1938. During 1948, the prewar level was reached and, in 1949, was slightly exceeded. By the end of 1950, Western European exports had increased to 60 percent above the 1938 level.

Again, there is more shipping available today to carry the commerce of the free world and the trade routes are free of the submarine menace. During World War II, shipping space was the scarcest commodity on the market and, even when goods were available, they could not always be moved.

All of these are comforting comparisons to make. They are mainly useful because they help us to set our sights and steer our course with confidence.

The Task Ahead

The facts about our increased capacity do not mean that we can preserve our liberties without economic sacrifice. Our levels of consumption have greatly increased since the end of the war. Our civilian populations cannot continue to consume all they produce and still build tanks, planes, and guns. There is no way in which we in the free world can build our military defenses without economic pain. We must bear the cost as taxpayers and as consumers. All of us will have to do with less than we would like. But, if we are successful in deterring aggression and avoiding war, we will be substantially better off, even with these cuts, than we were during World War II. Many of our luxuries and some of our comforts and conveniences may have to go, but we should have more of the essentials which we need than we had before.

This, then, is not the mobilization for war of 1943-44. But neither is it "business as usual." It is a time for soberness and sacrifice, as well as a time for keeping our progressive goals steadily before us and alive in our minds. It is a time for sharpening our swords to defend our homes as we go about the task of making those homes better places to live in.

We can view the period ahead of us with confidence, if we also approach it with determination. We have the productive powers, the skills, and the economic resources. We must develop the economic programs and policies which are necessary to deploy our total resources so as to build our military defenses, sustain our essential civilian economic activities, and move forward as circumstances permit toward further economic growth and social progress These policies and programs should be designed to encourage a greater output of basic materials and foods; provide for the effective and equitable international distribution of scarce goods in support of the defense effort and of civilian economies; hold in check the inflationary pressures which threaten our economic stability; and press forward with programs of technical cooperation and economic development within the limitations imposed by the emergency.

Again, these are common tasks, to which all of us must make our full contribution, each according to his abilities and circumstances. A major purpose of this meeting of our Foreign Ministers must be to forge our wills to these ends and make known to the world our joint purpose and determination.

I should like to turn now to a number of specific economic problems which we face. These are all problems which have been in the minds of many of us for a long time. They have been discussed in international meetings and in single speeches. They have been discussed in aide-mémoires and in the communications of diplomats. Many of the things which I shall say have been said before by many of you or by your representatives. I have tried to approach these problems not from the point of view of a single country but as a consensus of the thinking, so far as I know it, of all the countries here represented.

Requirements and Supplies

First, I must speak about the problem of physical commodities—copper and cotton, coffee and automobiles, manganese and machine tools—the raw materials and the manufactured goods which are the lifeblood of any economy.

One of the most serious limiting factors affecting the ability of the free world to build its defenses and supply its civilian populations is the shortage of basic materials. The availability of materials, more than any other single thing, will determine how quickly we can strengthen our military defense and how well we can supply the manufactured goods, both durable and nondurable, upon which our civilian populations depend. All of us, I am sure, are aware of the recent spectacular increases in the prices of many of these materials which are so vitally important to the economies of all of us. No one is to blame for these price increases. They are simply the result which one gets when demand outruns supply. They are a measure of the fact of shortage. We, the Governments of the American Republics, and the Governments of other free world countries, will be at fault if we do not cooperate to bring this situation under control.

It is essential that we do our utmost to increase production. The American Republics are among the world's most important producers of the basic materials which supply the factories of the free world. It is appropriate, therefore, that they should take the lead in this effort. We are aware that the stimulation of production of basic materials for emergency purposes may encounter difficulties unless the producers of these materials can look forward to adequate and fair compensation for their efforts and can be assured of a market for their increased output over a reasonable period in the future. One approach which the Government of the United States is prepared to follow is to cooperate with the other American Republics in providing financial assistance, on reasonable terms, where such assistance is necessary to increase output needed in the common defense. It is also prepared, where necessary, to cooperate in the conclusion of medium or long-term undertakings for the purchase of basic materials at reasonable prices.

Unfortunately, it is clear that, despite efforts to increase production, there will still be shortages. At the manufacturing level, the immediate requirements of military production will necessitate the curtailment of civilian production. The curtailment may be severe in some particular items. None of us, during this period of building up our common defenses, will be able to have everything we want to satisfy the needs and desires of our civilian populations. It will often be necessary for our Governments to place limits on various forms of civilian production and consumption and, to a substantial degree, to direct and channel the flow of goods in international trade.

How, then, shall we go about determining the best way in which to share the limited supply of goods that is available?

Two points, I think, are clear. First, we must give highest priority to the requirements for military production in our common defense. Second, we must stand ready to meet the minimum requirements for the maintenance of essential civilian supply in our respective countries and in the free world. Military strength can be effective only if it is firmly and squarely based on strong and healthy economies.

Military production and essential civilian needs—these are the twin urgencies which must have a prior claim on our economic resources. With respect to less essential civilian requirements, each country should make its full contribution in reducing consumption, and the principle of relative equality of sacrifice among countries should prevail.

We must also take steps to see that we do not strengthen the hand of aggressors or potential aggressors by making available to them goods of strategic significance or by depriving the countries of the free world of the goods which they need.

Many of these matters, which I have been discussing, will appear in the form of individual actions by one country or another. But that is not enough. In the case of key commodities, we have already begun the development of international machinery through the establishment in Washington of the International Materials Conference. The International Materials Conference, consisting of a series of International Materials Committees and a Central Group, is designed to provide an organization through which all of the countries of the free world having an interest in certain commodities, whether as producer or consumer, can cooperate in bringing about a sensible distribution of materials in short supply, in stimulating their production, and in agreeing to reduce their consumption for nonessential or less essential purposes. The Organization of American States is a member of the permanent Central Group and, as such, plays an important role in its deliberations. The Governments of Brazil and of the United States are also members of the Central Group. Other Governments of the American Republics are represented on the several committees relating to specific commodities. Countries which are not members of particular committees will be afforded a full opportunity to present their views to the committees and will be kept informed as to the work of the committees as it proceeds.

The commodity problems of which I have been speaking are interrelated. Obviously, there will be situations in which some one country will be tempted to seek its own advantage at the expense of the common effort. However, cooperation cannot be turned on and off in accordance with short-run gain or loss. Our cooperation should be built solidly upon a continuing spirit of common purpose, common need, and common sacrifice. Our aim should be to conserve and develop the economic strength of all of us.

Control of Inflation

One of the greatest economic dangers we face is the threat of inflation. If we place unlimited and uncontrolled demands upon our economic resources, we shall multiply manifold the costs of our defense program and undermine our basic economic stability.

Here again cooperation and concerted action among the American Republics is called for. Each of us must be willing to adopt and enforce, both within our own countries and internationally, the stern measures which may be necessary if runaway inflationary tendencies are to be kept under control. For all of our countries, this will mean appropriate internal fiscal, credit and tax policies to reduce excessive requirements for goods of which there is no longer an abundance. For others of us, it will also mean some form of direct control over the prices of goods.

As you know, the United States has already adopted controls over prices, both for goods entering into international trade and for goods consumed domestically. Our price controls have been introduced at a time which, when compared with past periods, is highly favorable to countries which trade with the United States. In other words, the base period selected for the price control is one in which the prices of goods which the United States imports are high in relation to the prices of goods which the United States sells abroad. The index of unit values in the foreign trade of the United States (1936-38 equals 100) shows that, during December 1950, the unit value of our imports stood at 276, whereas the unit value of our exports was 195. This is certainly a wide price differential.

The price controls which now exist over exports from the United States can be of substantial benefit to the other American Republics in the fight against inflation. But this benefit can easily be wasted and dissipated if parallel measures are not taken in the importing countries to prevent speculative price rises for these same commodities after they have left our shores. We see in this one illustration, therefore, an important opportunity for the American Republics to concert their efforts against inflation, so that the actions of each of them will supplement and reinforce the actions of the others.

Price controls necessarily have an impact on international trade flows, on income from goods produced and sold, and on competitive relationships. Certain basic principles seem to be the subject of general agreement. It should be the aim to manage such price controls as are adopted so as to achieve their central purpose of stabilization while stimulating the production and flow of goods into desirable channels. Price control systems should apply equally to raw materials and manufactured goods. If imposed on imports, they should also be extended to exports. They should not be designed to favor domestic producers or to discriminate against producers in other countries. These are principles by which we can be sure that price controls will be just and equitable in our international dealings with each other.

International Consultation

The emergency economic controls which we must adopt in defense of our liberties will, of course, give rise to many knotty problems and difficulties among our countries on which there will frequently be differences of view. The only true solvent for these problems is full and frank consultation among us. I am sure that the Government of the United States is no different from the other countries represented here when I say that we are prepared at all times to consult fully with each and all of the other American Republics in seeking the right answers to these problems in the light of our common purposes and our historical relationship of mutual friendship. The urgencies of the defense program and the large number of countries involved will not always permit international consultation to go forward before it becomes necessary for a particular government to impose emergency controls. Even in such cases, however, consultation can often lead to appropriate adjustments so that hardships can be lightened and inequities removed.

Economic Development and Technical Cooperation

These, then, are the emergency problems we face—how to increase the production of basic materials and use them best in the common defense; how to go about the allocation of goods in short supply; how to avoid giving strength to aggressors and potential aggressors; how to keep down inflation and maintain our economic stability; and how to resolve the differences which may arise among us.

But what about the role of economic development during this emergency period? Do the urgencies of defense mean that we must forego all progress toward a better life—that we must shelve for the time being all our plans for improving our health, our education, our industrial and agricultural organizations, our working conditions, our standards of living?

The answer, I think, is clearly, "No." Economic development of the under-developed regions of the free world is not a luxury. It cannot be made a casualty of the defense program. Like our other free institutions, it is part and parcel of the way of life in the free world which we are determined to defend.

But neither can we, in this critical time, have all of the economic development that we would wish to have. Like the other aspects of our economic life, it too must be made subject to necessary limitations and priorities.

Let us, then, press forward with our programs of economic development and technical cooperation, advancing them as best we can, subject only to the higher priorities which we must give to the needs of military production and the essential requirements of our civilian economies. In this effort, we should give emphasis to those programs which will stimulate the production of food and of basic materials, raise nutritional standards, reduce the incidence of disease, and improve labor standards and working conditions.

There is, I think, one thing that all of us can do immediately which would stand both as a symbol and as a concrete demonstration of our intention to move forward in the field of economic development. I refer to the need for supporting the Technical Cooperation Program for 1951, which has already been approved by the Council of the Organization of American States. This program, even though of moderate proportions, is being held up for lack of national contributions from the various American Republics. I hope that all our Governments will find it possible to contribute their funds promptly so that this worthwhile program will not be delayed.

Draft Resolutions

In my remarks today, I have, I believe, touched on each of the main economic problems with which we have been called upon to deal. The United States delegation has prepared and distributed to the Conference a series of draft resolutions on these various points. These resolutions are the product of many consultations between my Government and other Governments here represented. They also reflect much of the work and discussion which have gone into the excellent technical report prepared for us by the Inter-American Economic and Social Council. In drawing up these resolutions, the United States delegation has sought to put forward a set of principles and policies which would reflect our common aspirations and meet our common problems. It is our hope, therefore, that they will facilitate the work of the Conference in expressing the agreement of all of us as to the economic policies which should guide us in the difficult, yet hopeful, years ahead.

31. *Organization of American States, Fourth Meeting of Consultation of Ministers of Foreign Affairs, Final Act**

April 7, 1951

I. Declaration of Washington

Whereas: the present Meeting was called because of the need for prompt action by the Republics of this Hemisphere for common defense against the aggressive activities of international communism;

Such activities, in disregard of the principle of nonintervention, which is deeply rooted in the Americas, disturb the tranquility of the peoples of this Hemisphere and endanger the liberty and democracy on which their institutions are founded;

All the said Republics have stated, in formal acts and agreements, their will to cooperate against any threat to or aggression against the peace, security, and territorial integrity or independence of any one of them;

It will be impossible for such cooperation to be effective unless it is carried out in a true spirit of harmony and conciliation;

In view of the common danger, the present moment is propitious for a reaffirmation of inter-American solidarity;

That danger becomes more serious as a consequence of certain social and economic factors;

In this last connection there is now, more than ever, need for the adoption of measures designed to improve the living conditons of the peoples of this Hemisphere; and,

On the other hand, in any action for the defense of the Hemisphere and its institutions, the essential rights of man, solemnly proclaimed by the American Republics, should not be lost sight of,

The Fourth Meeting of Consultation of Ministers of Foreign Affairs

Declares:

1. The firm determination of the American Republics to remain steadfastly united, both spiritually and materially, in the present emergency or in the face of any aggression or threat against any one of them.

*Department of State Bulletin, Apr. 16, 1951, pp. 606-13.

2. A reaffirmation of the faith of the American Republics in the efficacy of the principles set forth in the Charter of the Organization of American States and other inter-American agreements to maintain peace and security in the Hemisphere, to defend themselves against any aggression, to settle their disputes by peaceful means, improve the living conditions of their peoples, promote their cultural and economic progress, and ensure respect for the fundamental freedoms of man and the principles of social justice as the bases of their democratic system.

3. Its conviction that strong support of the action of the United Nations is the most effective means of maintaining the peace, security, and well-being of the peoples of the world under the rule of law, justice, and international cooperation.

II. Preparation of the Defense of the American Republics and Support of the Action of the United Nations

Whereas: the American Republics, as Members of the United Nations, have pledged themselves to unite their efforts with those of other States to maintain international peace and security, to settle international disputes by peaceful means, and to take effective collective measures to prevent and suppress acts of aggression;

International peace and security have been breached by the acts of aggression in Korea, and the United Nations, despite its efforts to find a peaceful solution, was obliged, pursuant to resolutions of the Security Council and the General Assembly, to take action to restore peace in that area; and

In order to ensure that the United Nations has at its disposal means for maintaining international peace and security, the General Assembly, on November 3, 1950, adopted the resolution entitled "Uniting for Peace,"
The Fourth Meeting of Consultation of Ministers of Foreign Affairs of American States

Declares:

That the present world situation requires positive support by the American Republics for: (1) achievement of the collective defense of the Continent through the Organization of American States, and (2) cooperation, within the United Nations Organization, to prevent and suppress aggression in other parts of the world; and

Recommends:

1. That each of the American Republics should immediately examine its resources and determine what steps it can take to contribute to the defense of the Hemisphere and to United Nations collective security efforts, in order to accomplish the aims and purposes of the "Uniting for Peace" resolution of the General Assembly.

2. That each of the American Republics, without prejudice to attending to national self-defense, should give particular attention to the development and maintenance of elements within its national armed forces so trained, organized and equipped that they could, in accordance with its constitutional norms, and to the full extent that, in its judgment, its capabilities permit, promptly be made available, (1) for the defense of the Hemisphere, and (2) for service as United Nations unit or units, in accordance with the "Uniting for Peace" resolution.

III. Inter-American Military Cooperation

Whereas: the military defense of the Continent is essential to the stability of its democratic institutions and the wellbeing of its peoples;

The American Republics have assumed obligations under the Charter of the Organization of American States and the Inter-American Treaty of Reciprocal Assistance to assist any American States subjected to an armed attack, and to act together for the common defense and for the maintenance of the peace and security of the Continent;

The expansionist activities of international communism require the immediate adoption of measures to safeguard the peace and the security of the Continent;

The present grave international situation imposes on the American Republics the need to develop their military capabilities in order, in conformity with the Inter-American Treaty of Reciprocal Assistance: 1) to assure their individual and collective self-defense against armed attacks; 2) to contribute effectively to action by the Organization of American States against aggression directed against any of them; and, 3) to make provision, as quickly as possible, for the collective defense of the Continent; and

The Ninth International Conference of American States, in its Resolution XXXIV, charged the preparation of collective self-defense against aggression to the Inter-American Defense Board, which, as the only inter-American technical-military organ functioning, is the suitable organ for the preparation of military plans for collective self-defense against aggression,

The Fourth Meeting of Consultation of Ministers of Foreign Affairs

Resolves:

1. To recommend to the American Republics that they orient their military preparation in such a way that, through self-help and mutual aid, and in accordance with their capabilities and with their constitutional norms, and in conformity with the Inter-American Treaty of Reciprocal Assistance, they can, without prejudice to their individual self-defense and their internal security: a) increase those of their resources and strengthen those of their armed forces best adapted to the collective defense, and maintain those armed forces in such status that they can be immediately available for the defense of the Continent; and, b) cooperate with each other in military matters, in order to develop the collective strength of the continent necessary to combat aggression against any of them.

2. To charge the Inter-American Defense Board with preparing, as vigorously as possible, and keeping up-to-date, in close liaison with the Governments through their respective Delegations, the military planning of the common defense.

3. That the plans formulated by the Inter-American Defense Board shall be submitted to the Governments for their consideration and decision. To the end of facilitating such consideration and decision, the Delegations of the American Republics to the Inter-American Defense Board shall be in continuous consultation with their Governments on the projects, plans, and recommendations of the Board.

4. To recommend to the Governments of the American Republics: a) that they maintain adequate and continuous representation of their armed forces on the Council of Delegates, on the Staff of the Inter-American Defense Board, and on any other organ of that organization that may be established in the future; b) that they actively support the work of the Board, and consider promptly all the projects, plans, and

recommendations of that agency; and c) that they cooperate in the organization, within the Board, of a coordinated system of exchange of appropriate information.

IV. Importance of Maintaining Peaceful Relations Among American States

Whereas: it is desirable that the energies of each American Republic be devoted to strengthening its ability to contribute to international peace and security in the Western Hemisphere and to the prevention and suppression of international communist aggression; and

Any breach of friendly relations among the American Republics can only serve to provide aid and comfort to the leaders of such aggression as well as to weaken the peace and security of the Western Hemisphere,
The Fourth Meeting of Consultation of Ministers of Foreign Affairs

Reaffirms:

The solemn obligations undertaken by all the American Republics to refrain in their international relations from the threat or use of force in any manner inconsistent with the Charter of the United Nations or the Inter-American Treaty of Reciprocal Assistance, and to settle their international disputes by peaceful means;

Recommends:

That the American Republics will make every effort to settle any disputes between them which threaten friendly relations, in the shortest possible time, by direct bilateral negotiations, and will promptly submit such disputes as they may be unable to settle by negotiation to other available procedures for the peaceful settlement of disputes; and

Declares:

That the faithful observance by the American Republics of the commitments not to intervene in the internal or external affairs of other States and to settle any disputes among them by peaceful means makes it possible for each of the Republics to concentrate the development of its capabilities upon the tasks best adapted to the role each is most qualified to assume in the collective defense against aggression.

V. Provisions Concerning Military Conscription of Students

Whereas: the strengthening of the cultural ties between the American countries is one of the most effective means to promote their knowledge of one another, and therefore, sentiments of union and friendship among them;

Student exchange has proved to be a positive contribution in the realization of this high purpose;

Likewise, the exchange of professional men and women, technical experts, and skilled workers who are to carry out advanced studies in scientific or industrial establishments, is equally desirable not only because of the cultural ties thus created, but also because of the benefits accruing therefrom to the development of productive activities in the various countries; and

In order to continue providing encouragement and facilities for this exchange, which is contemplated in various Pan American instruments and bilateral treaties, this exchange should be carried out under conditions which would make it more effectual and continuous rather than hindering it,

The Fourth Meeting of Consultation of Ministers of Foreign Affiars

Recommends:

1) That the Governments of the American Republics consider in connection with programs of military service the desirability of adopting or continuing measures to assure that students from other American Republics who have enrolled in duly recognized centers of education may be permitted to continue their programs of studies without interruption;

2) That the Governments of the American Republics consult among themselves regarding their respective legal provisions concerning military conscription to assure, insofar as possible, that these provisions will not affect advanced studies being carried out in scientific or industrial establishments in one American country by students, trainees, teachers, guest instructors, professors and leaders in fields of specialized knowledge or skills of another, when their stay is temporary and has as its purpose the above-mentioned professional or technical training objectives;

3) The recommendations contained in the two foregoing paragraphs in no way change the obligations arising under the Convention on the Status of Aliens, signed at the Sixth International Conference of American States.

VI. Reaffirmation of Inter-American Principles Regarding European Colonies and Possessions in the Americas

Whereas: the first Meeting of Consultation, held in Panama during October 1939, approved Resolution XVII, which contains provisions to be applied in case of a transfer of sovereignty in geographic regions of the Americas under the jurisdiction of non-American States;

At the Second Meeting of Consultation, held in Habana during July 1940, the Governments of the American Republics signed the "Act of Habana," which provided emergency measures to determine the action those Republics should take in the face of any situation that might, because of World War II, affect the status of non-American possessions located in this Hemisphere;

At that Second Meeting of Consultation the "Convention on the Provisional Administration of European Colonies and Possessions in the Americas" was also signed, which later entered into force as prescribed in the Convention; and

The American Republics declared, in Resolution XXXIII of the Ninth International Conference of American States, the Continental aspiration that colonialism would be brought to an end in the Americas,

The Fourth Meeting of Consultation of Ministers of Foreign Affairs

Declares:

The firm adherence of the American Republics to the following principles adopted at the First and Second Meetings of Consultation:

1. The non-recognition and non-acceptance of transfers or attempts at transferring

or acquiring interest or right, directly or indirectly, in any territory of this Hemisphere held by non-American States, in favor of another State outside the Hemisphere, whatever the form used to accomplish this purpose;

2. That in case it should be necessary to apply the measures prescribed in the "Convention on the Provisional Administration of European Colonies and Possessions in the Americas," the interests of the inhabitants of those territories should be taken into account, so that the gradual development of their political, economic, social, and educational life may be promoted.

VII. The Strengthening and Effective Exercise of Democracy

Whereas: topic II of the program of the Meeting is "Strengthening of the internal security of the American Republics," and, for the achievement of that purpose and the application of the proper measures, it is essential for each Government, as the mandatory of its people, to have their confidence and support;

In order to achieve such identification of the people with their government, it is imperative that each country have an effective system of representative democracy that will put into practice both the rights and duties of man and social Justice; and

The American Republics and their origin and reason for being in the desire to attain liberty and democracy, and their harmonious association is based primarily on these concepts, the effectiveness of which it is desirable to strengthen in the international field, without prejudice to the principle of nonintervention,

The Fourth Meeting of Consultation of Ministers of Foreign Affairs

Delcares:

That the solidarity of the American Republics requires the effective exercise of representative democracy, social justice, and respect for and the observance of the rights and duties of man, principles which must be increasingly strengthened in the international field and which are found in Article 5 (d) of the Charter of the Organization of American States and Resolutions XXXII (The Preservation and Defense of Democracy in America) and XXX (American Declaration of the Rights and Duties of Man) adopted by the Ninth International Conference of American States; and

Resolves:

1. To suggest that the Tenth Inter-American Conference consider, within the framework of Articles 13 and 15 of the Charter of the Organization of American States, the provisions necessary in order for the purposes stated in Resolutions XXX and XXXII of the Ninth International Conference of American States to acquire full effectiveness in all the countries of America.

2. To instruct the Inter-American Council of Jurists to draw up, as a technical contribution to the ends contemplated in the preceding paragraph, draft Conventions and other instruments; and, to that end, likewise to instruct the Inter-American Juridical Committee to make the pertinent preliminary studies, which it will submit to the said Council at its next meeting.

3. To urge the Governments of America, pending the adoption and entry into force of the aforementioned provisions, to maintain and apply, in accordance with their

constitutional procedures, the precepts contained in the aforementioned Resolutions XXX and XXXII of the Ninth International Conference of American States.

VIII. Strengthening of Internal Security

Whereas: the American Republics at the Ninth International Conference of American States, with specific reference to "the preservation and defense of democracy in America" and using as a basis Resolution VI of the Second Meeting of Consultation, resolved to condemn the methods of every system tending to suppress political and civil rights and liberties, and in particular the action of international Communism or any other totalitarian doctrine, and, consequently, to adopt, within their respective territories and in accordance with their respective constitutional provisions, the measures necessary to eradicate and prevent activities directed, assisted or instigated by foreign governments, organizations or individuals tending to overthrow their institutions by violence, to foment disorder in their domestic political life, or to disturb, by means of pressure, subversive propaganda, threats or by other means, the free and sovereign right of their peoples to govern themselves in accordance with their democratic aspirations;

To supplement those measures of mutual cooperation assuring collective defense as well as the economic and social well-being of the people, upon which the vitality of political institutions so much depends, it is necessary to adopt laws and regulations for internal security;

In their concern to counteract the subversive activity of international Communism, they are imbued with the desire to reaffirm their determination to preserve and strengthen the basic democratic institutions of the peoples of the American Republics, which the agents of international Communism are attempting to abolish through the exploitation and abuse of the democratic freedoms themselves:

Within each one of the American Republics there has been and is being developed through democratic procedures a body of laws designed to assure its political defense;

It is in accordance with the high common and individual interests of the American Republics to ensure that each of them will be able to meet the special and immediate threat of the subversive activities of international Communism; and

Since the said subversive activities recognize no boundaries, the present situation requires, in addition to suitable internal measures, a high degree of international cooperation among the American Republics, looking to the eradication of any threat of subversive activity endangering democracy and the free way of life in the American Republics,

The Fourth Meeting of Consultation of Ministers of Foreign Affairs

Resolves:

1. To recommend to the Governments of the American States:

(a) That, mindful of their unity of purpose and taking account of the contents of Resolution VI of the Second Meeting of Consultation in Habana and Resolution XXXII of the Ninth International Conference of American States in Bogotá, each American Republic examine its respective laws and regulations and adopt such changes as it considers necessary to ensure that subversive activities of the agents of international Communism, directed against any of them, may be adequately forestalled and penalized;

(b) That, in accordance with their respective constitutional provisions, they enact those measures necessary to regulate in the countries of the Americas the transit across international boundaries of those foreigners who there is reason to expect will attempt to perform subversive acts against the defense of the American Hemisphere; and

(c) That, in the application of this resolution, they bear in mind the necessity of guaranteeing and defending by the most efficacious means the rights of the individual as well as their firm determination to preserve and defend the basic democratic institutions of the peoples of the American Republics.

2. To instruct the Pan American Union, for the purpose of facilitating the fulfillment of the objectives of this resolution, to assign to the proper Department, which might be the Department of International Law and Organization, with the assistance, if deemed advisable, of experts on the subject, the following duties:

(a) To make technical studies concerning the definition, prevention, and punishment, as crimes, of sabotage and espionage with respect to acts against the American Republics and directed from abroad or against the defense of the Americas;

(b) To make technical studies of general measures by means of which the American Republics may better maintain the integrity and efficacy of the rights of the individual and of the democratic system of their institutions, protecting and defending them from treason and any other subversive acts instigated or directed by foreign powers or against the defense of the Americas;

(c) To make technical studies concerning measures to prevent the abuse of freedom of transit, within the Hemisphere, including clandestine and illicit travel and the misuse of travel documents, aimed at weakening the defense of the Americas.

The Pan American Union shall transmit the reports and conclusions resulting from its studies to the American Governments for their information, through their representatives on the Council of the Organization of American States, and should any of the said Governments so request and the Council by a simple majority of votes so decide, a specialized conference on the matter shall be called pursuant to the terms of Article 93 of the Charter of the Organization of American States.

IX. Improvement of the Social, Economic, and Cultural Levels of the Peoples of the Americas

Whereas: in the name of their peoples, the States represented at the Ninth International Conference of American States declared their conviction that the historic mission of America is to offer to man a land of liberty and a favorable environment for the development of his personality and the realization of his just aspirations, and for that reason they set forth in the Charter of the Organization of American States as one of their basic principles that of promoting, through cooperative action, their economic, social, and cultural development;

The aforesaid Charter entrusts to the Inter-American Economic and Social Council and to the Inter-American Cultural Council the promotion of such well-being in their respective fields, and these Councils, in turn, should carry out the activities assigned to them by the Meeting of Consultation of Ministers of Foreign Affairs;

It is a right of man to obtain the satisfaction of the economic, social, and cultural needs essential to his dignity and to the free development of his personality;

The failure to satisfy this right produces a discontent that may mistakenly lead men to accept doctrines incompatible with their own interests and the rights of others, the security of all, the general well-being, and democratic ideals,

The Fourth Meeting of Consultation of Ministers of Foreign Affairs of American States

Resolves:

1. To recommend to the American Republics that, in order to strengthen their internal security, they act with due decision to forward the great undertaking of raising the social, economic, and cultural levels of their own peoples, taking care that, to the greatest degree possible, they satisfy the rights set forth in this regard in the American Declaration of the Rights and Duties of Man, the Universal Declaration of the Rights of Man, and the Inter-American Charter of Social Guarantees.

2. To recommend to the Inter-American Economic and Social Council and to the Inter-American Cultural Council that, within their respective spheres, they prepare as soon as possible plans and programs of action for promoting effective cooperation among the American Republics in order to raise the economic, social, and cultural levels of their peoples. These Councils shall present periodically to the General Secretariat of the Organization of American States, for the same ends, a report on the execution of the aforesaid plans and programs, and their opinion regarding any changes that might be made in them.

3. The aforesaid plans, programs, and reports shall also be transmitted to the American Governments through the Secretary General of the Organization of American States.

X. Economic and Social Betterment of the Working Classes

Whereas: the democratic institutions that have been inherent characteristics of the American Republics since the beginning of their life as free States are based upon the principles of human equality and solidarity and upon the principle of the welfare of their inhabitants; and

The propagation of ideologies alien to the spirit of America and its civil liberties finds favorable development in materially and culturally underdeveloped countries, for which reason it is necessary to fight poverty and ignorance as an effective means of protecting Democracy and the Rights of Man,

The Fourth Meeting of Consultation of Ministers of Foreign Affairs

Resolves:

To repeat and broaden the resolutions adopted at previous inter-American meetings in such a way that in the measures introduced during the present international emergency, as well as in permanent peacetime economic programs, the economic and social betterment of the working classes of America shall be a matter of constant concern, by securing for them a satisfactory wage level, protecting them from unemployment, and making every effort to assure the progressive improvement of their culture and the hygienic and sanitary conditions in their homes and places of work.

XI. Betterment of the American Worker

Whereas: many Resolutions adopted by the American Republics in the Seventh, Eighth and Ninth International Conferences of American States as well as Resolution

LVIII of the Inter-American Conference on Problems of War and Peace, have manifested the great concern of the Governments to raise the standard of living of their peoples;

The objective proposed is of transcendental importance because the internal security of the American Republics, based on the proper functioning of a representative democracy, cannot be permanently strengthened unless it is based on an increasing production, the yields from which are distributed equitably among the members of the community; and

The Inter-American Charter of Social Guarantees, approved at Bogotá, establishes, in general terms, the minimum standards governing the conditions under which American workers shall carry out their work,

The Fourth Meeting of Consultation of Ministers of Foreign Affairs

Recommends:

1. That those American nations that have not already done so, and within the limitations imposed by their respective Constitutions, adopt in their respective legislations appropriate measures to give effect within each such country to the principles contained in the Inter-American Charter of Social Guarantees approved at Bogotá.

2. That each American nation inform the Inter-American Economic and Social Council annually of any legislative and administrative measures it has put into effect.

XII. Economic Development

Whereas: the present international state of emergency and the dangers it contains for all free countries demand efficacious cooperation among the American Republics for the effective defense of the Hemisphere;

One of the most serious factors in social decline, one that best suits the purposes of aggression, is the existence of low standards of living in many countries that have been unable to attain the benefits of modern techniques;

It is therefore necessary to establish rational bases that will make it possible to maintain the equilibrium and, to the extent that the emergency permits, the development of the economies of the underdeveloped American Republics and to improve the standard of living of their peoples in order to increase their individual and collective capacities for the defense of the Hemisphere and contribute to the strengthening of their internal security; and

The programs of economic development and technical cooperation have proven to be the most successful instruments for strengthening internal economies and improving living standards; and the present emergency situation and the greater needs for defense that it imposes are additional and urgent reasons for increasing international cooperation in this field of activity,

The Fourth Meeting of Consultation of Ministers of Foreign Affairs

Declares:

That the economic development of underdeveloped countries should be considered as an essential factor in the total concept of Hemisphere defense, without disregarding the fact that it is the prime duty of the American States in the present emergency to strengthen their defenses and maintain their essential civilian activities; and

Resolves:

1. That the American Republcs should continue to collaborate actively and with even greater vigor in programs of economic development and programs of technical cooperation with a view to building economic strength and well-being in the underdeveloped regions of the Americas and to improving the living levels of their inhabitants.

2. To this end, the American Republics shall supply, subject to the provisions of Resolution No. XVI, the machinery, mechanical equipment, and other materials needed to increase their productive capacity, diversify their production and distribution, facilitating in appropriate cases financial and technical cooperation for carrying out plans for economic development.

3. Such financial and technical collaboration shall be carried forward with the purpose of modernizing agriculture, increasing food production, developing mineral and power resources, increasing industrialization, improving transportation facilities, raising standards of health and education, encouraging the investment of public and private capital, stimulating employment and raising managerial capacity and technical skills, and bettering the conditions of labor.

4. During the present emergency period, preference among economic development projects should be given in the following order: Projects useful for defense purposes and projects designed to satisfy the basic requirements of the civilian economy; projects already begun, the interruption of which would entail serious losses of materials, money, and effort; and other projects for economic development.

5. Each American state will take steps to coordinate its respective plans and programs for economic development with the emergency economic plans, bearing in mind its own tendencies and possibilities, for the continuity of its development.

XIII. Increase of Production and Processing of
Basic and Strategic Materials

The Fourth Meeting of Consultation of Ministers of Foreign Affairs

Resolves:

That the American Republics should adopt in their respective countries practical and feasible measures for increasing the production and processing of basic and strategic materials required for the defense emergency, for the essential needs of the civilian population, and for operation of the basic public services. To achieve this end they undertake:

a) To accord one another, by means of administrative measures, the priorities and licenses required to obtain necessary machinery and material to increase the production, processing, and transportation of these necessary basic and strategic materials;

b) To render one another special and adequate technical and financial assistance when necessary and appropriate, by means of bilateral negotiations or multilateral agreements, when necessary, or through special joint organs, in order to increase the production, processing, and transportation of these basic and strategic materials;

c) To be prepared to enter into long-term or medium-term purchase and sale contracts at reasonable prices for these basic and strategic materials, and in conformity with any international agreement of general scope in which they might have participated.

XIV. Production, Utilization and Distribution of Scarce Essential Products

Whereas: some nations have sponsored the creation of international organizations for the purpose of obtaining the cooperation of the free countries, in order to increase the production of scarce essential products during the present emergency situation and to make the best distribution and use thereof; and

The activities of those organizations will of necessity affect the economy of the Western Hemisphere, for which reason the American Republics should have suitable and adequate representation therein,

The Fourth Meeting of Consultation of Ministers of Foreign Affairs

Declares:

That the American States shall have suitable and adequate representation in any international organization created during the emergency to deal with the production, utilization and distribution of scarce essential products, it being necessary that the different geographical regions and the relative importance of their production and population be taken into account.

XV. Defense and Security Controls

Whereas: it is essential for the American Republics, as a part of the free world, to build up their economic strength relative to that of the forces supporting international aggression,

The Fourth Meeting of Consultation of Ministers of Foreign Affairs

Declares:

1. That the American Republics agree to cooperate fully with one another in the adoption of effective measures of economic defense and security controls in the field of their international economic relations, including measures to increase the availability of products in short supply to the countries of the free world.

2. That where one country imposes security controls which affect activities of private entities located in another country, full opportunity for consultation shall be afforded between the two countries with the purpose of developing cooperative measures to attain the objective of the security controls with a minimum of economic dislocation in the country where the affected private activities are carried on or the respective asset is located.

3. During the emergency and the period of adjustment following it, the principle of relative equality of sacrifice shall apply in the reduction or limitation of civilian needs, and an endeavor shall be made not to impair the living standards of the low-income population groups. Allocations and priorities for elements of production and consumption shall be established, in accordance with the principles contained in the General Statement of this Resolution, in such a manner as not to impair productive activity and economic development unnecessarily, or jeopardize political and social stability and effective collaboration among the American nations.

4. When producer countries establish export allocations to meet essential foreign requirements, such countries should adopt effective administrative measures to facilitate the fulfillment of such allocations for export.

5. Once export quotas have been established, it shall be the responsibility of the

importing country to determine the essentiality of the use of the products and to control their distribution. It shall be the responsibility of the exporting country to distribute the quota among exporters from the exporting country. In case of conflicts or difficulties in the operation of the controls, there shall be consultation between the interested Governments.

XVI. Allocations and Priorities

The Fourth Meeting of Consultation of Ministers of Foreign Affairs

Resolves:

That in order to meet the emergency situation and the subsequent period of adjustment, the American States shall do all in their power to provide one another with the products and services necessary to sustain the common defense effort, and declare that the maintaining of essential civilian activities and public services and the economic development of underdeveloped countries are considered as an essential element in the total concept of defense of the American hemisphere, without disregarding the fact that the strengthening of their defenses is the principal duty of the American States in the present emergency.

Whenever the emergency situation makes it imperative to apply the system of allocations and priorities, the American States will observe the following principles:

1. The essential needs for the functioning of civilian economic activities should be met.

2. In the case of products which are the subject of allocations, or priorities affecting their domestic consumption and export, priority be given to the utilization of such products for defense production in the common cause, including the maintenance of adequate stockpiles of strategic materials, pursuant to the principles of the General Statement.

3. The Governments of the American Republics shall accord one another ample opportunity for consultation concerning the effect of the establishment of substantial revision of allocations and priorities on international trade. Whenever, owing to special circumstances caused by the emergency, it is impossible for an American Government to hold a consultation before establishing allocations or priorities, such measures shall be discussed, after their adoption, immediately upon the request by any country for their re-examination on the ground that its interests are adversely affected, for the purpose of endeavoring to make an adjustment by mutual agreement.

XVII. Prices

The Fourth Meeting of Consultation of Ministers of Foreign Affairs

Resolves:

1. That the Governments of the American Republics should adopt adequate internal measures and controls, including reciprocal measures to make them more effective, in order to prevent inflationary tendencies which would endanger the common defense program and basic economic stability and which would be detri-

mental to mutual economic relations. In addition, they will consider those international actions or cooperative measures which may be necessary to mitigate inflationary pressures.

2. That, with a view to assuring the proper administration of price regulations in such a way as to provide equitable treatment for both imported and exported products subject to controls, any American Republic which maintains a price control system will afford to any other member nation full opportunity to be heard with reference to any measures of price control affecting its products, and shall give consideration to such adjustments as may be pertinent, on the basis of data submitted by the member nation, but without being limited thereto. Such information may include increases or decreases in the cost of production (including the cost of manufactured articles, raw materials, wages, and any other elements making up an integral part of the cost of production), in the cost of transportation, and in the margin of profit, and the effect of the price regulation on the supply available to the country of importation.

Whenever, owing to special circumstances, it is not feasible for an American Government to hold consultation prior to the establishment of such price controls, such measures shall be the subject of consultation, after their adoption, immediately upon the request by any country for their re-examination on the ground that its interests have been prejudiced.

3. When a Government adopts a general price control system, it should apply such controls to the prices of raw materials as well as to those of manufactured products, and if it applies them to imports, it should also apply them to exports.

4. The establishment and administration of price controls, whether general or selective, shall conform to the principles of national and most-favored-nation treatment.

5. With respect to policies governing price controls during the emergency period, there should be taken into account the desirability of establishing in international commerce an equitable relationship between the prices of raw materials, foodstuffs, strategic materials, and the price of manufactured products. It is understood that the obligations under the resolution are directed toward international consultation regarding appropriate means of solving such problems. As a result of such consultation it may be agreed to take appropriate measures to solve those problems.

6. That, having in view the maintenance of the purchasing power of the currencies of the American Republics and the real incomes of their peoples, recognition should be accorded to the principle that price stabilization measures should be continued so long as the threat of serious inflation persists.

The Inter-American Economic and Social Council should convoke as soon as possible an *ad hoc* committee of technical experts from central banks, treasuries or similar fiscal agencies, which, in collaboration with the appropriate organs and specialized agencies of the United Nations, should study, making pertinent recommendations to the Governments of the American States, the problem of maintaining the purchasing power of their currencies and monetary reserves.

7. That the Inter-American Economic and Social Council, in collaboration with the appropriate organs and specialized agencies of the United Nations, should study, making pertinent recommendations to the Governments of the American States, the continued operation and administration of systems of price control instituted by the American Republics, their effect on the economies of the American Republics, and the need for appropriate adjustments in the operation of such systems.

XVIII. Study Groups on Scarce Raw Materials

The Fourth Meeting of Consultation of Ministers of Foreign Affairs

Resolves:

1. To recommend to the Inter-American Economic and Social Council, which will hold an Extraordinary Meeting within two months following the closing of the Fourth Meeting of Consultation, the special consideration of the different basic aspects imposed by the present emergency situation on the future economy of the countries of the Americas, and particularly the policy to be followed by the American countries with respect to the International Materials Conference.

2. To instruct the Inter-American Economic and Social Council to make a preliminary study of the status of those raw materials that are of particular importance to the American Republics, in their capacity as exporters or importers, in order to determine whether it is desirable:

(a) In the case of raw materials for which an international committee already exists, to establish an Inter-American Study Group for each one, to draft recommendations whenever necessary for transmittal to the pertinent international committee;

(b) In the case of raw materials for which there is no international committee, to establish Inter-American Study Groups to decide whether the Central Group of the International Materials Conference should be sent a recommendation on the establishment of the pertinent international committees.

3. To recommend that the Inter-American Economic and Social Council convoke the necessary Inter-American Study Groups, in accordance with the considerations of paragraph 2 above.

4. To recommend that for this purpose the Inter-American Economic and Social Council decide that the members of the said Study Groups may be the members of the Organization of American States having a substantial interest as producers of the corresponding scarce raw materials or indicating that they have a national interest in the consumption of those materials.

5. To recommend that the Inter-American Economic and Social Council request the interested Governments to appoint technical representatives to the Inter-American Study Groups on scarce raw materials that are organized pursuant to this resolution, so that the work of those Groups may be done on a sound technical level.

6. To suggest to the Inter-American Economic and Social Council that the recommendations made by the Study Groups referred to in this resolution be transmitted to the Central Group by the representative of the Organization of American States thereto, and in the case of recommendations to any Commodity Committee, that it be requested to call a Special Meeting or a series of meetings so that a representative of the appropriate Study Group may have an opportunity to present such recommendations personally and with all the necessary details.

XIX. Transportation

The Fourth Meeting of Consultation of Ministers of Foreign Affairs

Resolves:

1. That the American States shall collaborate to ensure the availability and most

efficient utilization of inter-American transportation facilities and cooperate in their improvement when necessary.

2. That the Inter-American Economic and Social Council be requested to undertake immediate studies in order to prepare and recommend to the Governments of the American Republics, for their adoption, in case of an emergency, measures leading to the most effective equitable utilization of all transportation facilities of the Americas. In particular, such measures shall include information as to the availability of transportation facilities, the minimum requirements for the defense program and for the essential civilian needs of each Republic.

3. With a view to maintaining the equilibrium necessary to the economy of the maritime transportation system, the Inter-American Economic and Social Council, through appropriate channels, shall study the system of freight and insurance rates applicable to inter-American trade, and make recommendations on the pertinent problems and their solution.

4. If the state of emergency causes difficulties in the trade of the American States, bilateral and multilateral adjustments shall be made to assure as far as possible the flow of exports from the countries supplying raw materials and foodstuffs, and the correlative importation of essential materials.

5. If the state of emergency should make it necessary to establish transportation quotas, not only shall the volume of their trade be taken into account to assure such quotas, but also the special characteristics of the principal export products used to maintain their trade and monetary equilibrium, so that, in so far as possible, the means of transportation that may be counted on will be adequate to their particular national needs.

XX. Gradual Absorption of Production Factors Applied to Activities of a Temporary Nature

The Fourth Meeting of Consultation of Ministers of Foreign Affairs

Resolves:

That the Inter-American Economic and Social Council study measures to assure that once the emergency is over, production factors applied to activites of a temporary nature will be gradually absorbed in permanent activities.

XXI. Temporary Nature of Restriction and Control Measures

The Fourth Meeting of Consultation of Ministers of Foreign Affairs

Declares:

That the emergency restriction and control measures contemplated in various resolutions of this Fourth Meeting of Consultation should be considered as temporary measures required because of the common defense effort, and therefore recognizes the advisability of their being eliminated as soon as the circumstances that gave rise to their establishment no longer exist.

XXII. Liquidation of Emergency Stocks

The Fourth Meeting of Consultation of Ministers of Foreign Affairs

Resolves:

To establish a common policy so that the return to normalcy will not cause dangerous disturbances in the markets and prices of the products of American countries accumulated by the governments during the emergency. The liquidation of the emergency stocks shall be carried out gradually and step by step, in consultation with the producer countries, in order to avoid abnormal disturbances in the world markets of the aforesaid products.

XXIII. Study on the Shortage and Distribution of Newsprint

Whereas the scarcity of newsprint gravely affects the normal development of the organs of the press in the American countries, which is the foundaion on which freedom of expression must rest;

It is necessary to join forces to give every possible facility to the newspapers of America, in order that they may participate in the struggle to perfect the democratic system in America;

The Fourth Meeting of Consultation of Ministers of Foreign Affairs

Recommends:

1. That the Secretariat of the Organization of American States prepare, with the advice of the newspaper organizations of the Western Hemisphere, a technical report containing recommendations for facilitating the access of newspaper publishers to the sources of production and distribution of newsprint under price conditions that are equitable for all the American countries, with no discrimination whatsoever. The conclusions of the said study shall be submitted to the American States for consideration.

2. That governmental measures for the distribution and transportation of newsprint must be applied with due regard for the social function of journalism and with the same fundamental sense of general sacrifice as that underlying the system of allocations and priorities, and without preference or limitation that would affect the freedom of the press.

XXIV. Plants Producing Synthetics

The Fourth Meeting of Consultation of Ministers of Foreign Affairs

Resolves:

In disposing of Government-owned industrial plants for the production of substitute or synthetic products built for defense purposes, due consideration should be given to the effects of the terms of such disposal upon the countries producers of natural materials, in order to avoid unfair competition.

XXV. Manufacturing Plants and Rubber Plantations

The Fourth Meeting of Consultation of Ministers of Foreign Affairs

Recommends:

That the Inter-American Economic and Social Council study and submit reports to the interested American Governments dealing with the increase of natural-rubber production in the Hemisphere and the encouragement of plantations of rubber-producing trees and plants; and with economic and technical assistance for: (a) the establishment of plants manufacturing tires, inner tubes and other articles of rubber whether or not they have the raw material for meeting the needs for these products; (b) the expansion of manufacturing plants in the American countries that already possess such plants; and (c) the installation and extension of plants producing natural-rubber goods.

32. *United States Department of State, Military Assistance to Latin America**

March 30, 1953

1. There has been some criticism of the military assistance program in Latin America on the grounds that it violates the best interests of the Latin American countries themselves. Is this charge valid?

2. 100 percent of our vanadium imports come from Latin America. How many other strategic materials in short supply do we get from our Good Neighbors?

3. Enemy submarines scored heavily in this hemisphere during World War II. What steps are being taken to prevent this from happening again?

4. A major problem of hemisphere defense is the military weakness of most Latin American nations. What are we doing in this important area to create stronger defensive forces?

This survey provides the answer to these and other questions relating to cooperative military assistance arrangements in the Western Hemisphere.

During World War II, the security of the Western Hemisphere was safeguarded by the collective efforts of the American Republics. A submarine offensive against American shipping early in World War II came perilously close to driving American vessels from the Atlantic sea lanes. Its success would have resulted in the virtual isolation of every American country, and in the modern world no nation can survive in isolation.

The economies of many American Republics were in danger of collapse. Those nations, for example, which depend on petroleum from the United States and Venezuela would have been without oil. Those which depend on wheat imports would have been short of bread. Despite its wealth of natural resources, the United States would have faced economic problems of extreme gravity.

The American nations were spared these disasters only because they united to build strong defenses. When the Axis threat was turned back, these countries resolved that

*Department of State Bulletin, Mar. 30, 1953, pp. 463-67.

they would set up permanent defenses to guard against future aggression. They had learned that the preservation of peace and security in the Americas depends on cooperation.

The Foreign Ministers of the American Republics who met at Washington in 1951 laid the foundation for effective military cooperation by putting the lessons of World War II to valuable use. They directed the Inter-American Defense Board, on which each country is represented, to plan for the general defense of the hemisphere. They also recognized that preparations for defense, in the event of attack, would require self-help and mutual aid on the part of American Republics in the military and economic fields.

The United States mutual security program includes provisions for assisting Latin American countries to carry out their responsibilities with respect to these decisions of the Foreign Ministers. In the Mutual Security Act of 1951, the Congress voted $38,150,000 for direct military assistance to Latin America. In 1952 the Congress added $51,685,750 to that sum. The money will be used to provide U.S. military assistance to those American Republics whose participation in missions important to the defense of the Western Hemisphere has been found by the President to be required in accordance with defense plans. Before providing assistance to any country, the United States enters into a bilateral military assistance agreement with that country.

Reasons for Military Assistance

The United States is giving military aid to Latin American countries because of three fundamental facts:

1. This hemisphere is threatened by Communist aggression from within and without;

2. The security of strategic areas in the hemisphere and of inter-American lines of communication is vital to the security of every American Republic; and

3. The protection of these strategic areas and communications is a common responsibility.

A major problem of defense is the present limited military capability of the nations of Latin America. Although many are willing to do their share of the defense job, they are unable to develop and support adequately equipped and trained forces. Therefore, if these American Republics are to assume a greater share of the burden of continental defense, we must help them strengthen their forces. By doing this we can release thousands of U.S. soldiers for other duty.

Types of Military Assistance

We have offered three types of military assistance to Latin American nations:

1. Direct grants of equipment and other assistance to certain countries to prepare their forces for specific hemisphere defense missions;

2. Opportunities for purchasing U.S. weapons and equipment which Latin American countries require for their own and hemisphere defense; and

3. The establishment of U.S. Army, Navy, and Air Force missions to help train Latin American armed forces.

The money which the Congress has appropriated for direct aid to Latin America will provide training and military equipment to protect key installations and communications and help to assure the production and delivery of strategic materials in emergency periods. This aid is granted only for specific programs consistent with the defense plans of the Inter-American Defense Board. Our military advisers will assess the military and equipment requirements in each of the countries.

Latin American countries receiving equipment have specifically agreed to use it exclusively for missions important to the defense of the hemisphere. It consists of specialized items for air and marine antisubmarine patrol; for defense of coastal regions against naval, air, and submarine attack; and for the protection of strategic installations.

Agreements with five American Republics—Chile, Colombia, Cuba, Ecuador, and Peru—have already entered into force. Agreements with Brazil and Uruguay have been signed but require ratification before they become effective. Negotiations for an agreement with the Dominican Republic are in progress.

The second type of assistance permits purchases of our military equipment for cash when approved by U.S. officials, as authorized in the Mutual Defense Assistance Act of 1949. Procurement help in filling military requirements is also offered. For example, in 1951, Argentina, Brazil, and Chile each bought two light cruisers. Peru acquired three destroyer escorts and Uruguay, two. Colombia bought a U.S. frigate. These and other sales of equipment from excess U.S. stocks, at low prices, were permitted after explicit assurances that the vessels purchased would be devoted to hemisphere defense requirements. The presence of stronger naval forces in South American waters will free U.S. naval units for North Atlantic patrol and convoy duties, if the need arises.

The third form of military assistance is the establishment of U.S. training missions in Latin America, at the request of the other governments. Training missions are now operating in most countries. These missions are purely advisory, and the principal costs are borne by the local governments.

The over-all cost of these programs is small compared with our total foreign commitments. But these comparatively small programs make a major contribution to free-world strength by preparing Latin America to defend itself.

The security of the peoples of Latin America and their political independence would be gravely endangered by an attack on any one of them. No country in the Western Hemisphere is self-sufficient; none could survive cut off from its neighbors and the rest of the free world. Each has a stake in the security of one of the world's richest storehouses of strategic materials. Thus the economic and political vulnerability of our Latin American neighbors imposes the burden of hemisphere defense on them as well as on us.

Peace in the Americas

Peace in the Western Hemisphere depends not only upon peaceful relations among the American Republics but also upon their peaceful relations with other nations. The first requisite for peace in the Americas has been established and guaranteed by the Inter-American Treaty of Reciprocal Assistance (the Rio Treaty of 1947) and by other inter-American agreements. Through these agreements, the American Republics have pledged themselves to settle their disputes by negotiation rather than by war. They have forbidden the use of force or the threat of force in bargaining for economic or other concessions from a neighbor government. Each American state is equal under law, and the rights of each are respected by the others.

The second requisite—world peace—is yet to be realized. There is no guaranty of world peace so long as the Soviet Union and its satellites refuse to honor their international commitments under the United Nations Charter. It is therefore essential that the Americas keep their guard up and their defenses strong.

Continental Defense in World War II

As early as 1936, at Buenos Aires, the American Republics realized what an Axis attack would mean to this hemisphere. At other inter-American meetings from 1938 to 1942, they agreed to act together to repel any threat to the American continents.

It was not long before events showed the decision to be wise. Although the battle lines of World War II never penetrated Latin American shores, the fighting spread to hemisphere waters. Axis submarines sank thousands of tons of merchant shipping vital to the war effort and to the American economy.

On February 16, 1942, a Nazi submarine shelled shore installations on the Caribbean island of Aruba. On the same date, in the vicinity of the island, enemy raiders torpedoed two British tankers, one U.S. tanker, one Dutch tanker, and three light draft tankers from Venezuela. All seven vessels carried Venezuelan oil urgently needed for hemisphere defense.

To the south, after losing a dramatic engagement with two British cruisers, the crew of the German pocket battleship, the *Graf Spee*, scuttled her in the Rio de la Plata.

Ashore, Axis agents engaged in espionage and sabotage and evoked vigorous countermeasures from Latin American governments. The handwriting on the wall became apparent even to the doubters.

The torpedoing of a Mexican vessel in the Gulf of Mexico, May 13, 1942, was followed within a few days by Mexico's declaration of war. After losing five ships to Axis torpedoes in early August 1942, Brazil also declared war on August 22.

Defense Measures

To meet the threat, the United States diverted to Latin America a substantial part of its merchant marine and segments of its fleet and air force. During the early days of the war that diversion meant great sacrifice because of the shortage of merchant carriers, warships, and planes. Many ships and a large number of lives were lost. For months no one was certain that we could maintain all the vital lines of communication. It was only with the military assistance of a number of the other American Republics that the submarine campaign was stopped.

With the consent of the nations concerned, over 100,000 members of U.S. military forces were stationed south of this country during World War II. Our southern neighbors freely volunteered the use of important air and naval bases as part of their contribution to the Allied cause. (These bases, incidentally, were just as freely returned to their owners by the United States at the conclusion of the war.)

The best-known air bases were on the southern air route to Africa and Europe, particularly those on the Brazilian "hump." The North African and Mediterranean campaigns could hardly have been so successful without them. The naval bases were a significant factor in beating off the Axis submarines that, in 1942, had threatened to cut surface contact with Europe.

Latin American armed forces were strengthened with the assistance of U.S. military and naval missions. A Brazilian infantry division fought valiantly in Italy, and Mexico made an air unit available for action in the Pacific. Latin American naval forces and facilities also contributed to the Allied war effort.

In short, security was a hemisphere concern in World War II. All the American Republics were fully aware that none could be safe without the support of the others. Nothing has happened since to alter that principle.

The Communist Threat

The actions of the Soviet bloc show little promise of an early end to the obstructionist tactics of the Communists. They refuse to comply with traditional democratic standards of fair play and honest compromise of disagreements. They pay lip service to the United Nations Charter, but they violate its spirit. They talk of negotiation but refuse to honor their pledges to refrain from aggression. They frequently speak of their desire for peace, but they persist in using naked force in Korea.

Although the Soviet armies may not pose an immediate military threat to this hemisphere, we must always be prepared to meet naval and air attacks. Such attacks would seek to destroy, by blockade and isolation, the economy of every American Republic. Furthermore, the agents of communism, active throughout the Americas, constitute an internal menace.

The Communists can, with tongue in cheek, endorse any aspiration of the Latin American people without fear of involving the Soviet Union. They can back any program, however irresponsible, because they will not have to carry it out while they are not in power. Their purpose is to promote neutralism and break up the unity of the hemisphere.

One of their main targets is the United States military assistance program. Their propaganda against it has been loud and long. They have even convinced some responsible Latin American leaders that it violates the interests of the American Republics. Our best method of countering both propaganda and opinions based upon inadequate facts is to explain the military assistance program to the people of Latin America and to coordinate it with technical assistance for economic development. In this way the people can judge for themselves how much they have to gain through inter-American cooperation.

Charges Against the Program

Numerous false charges have been leveled against the program of military assistance to Latin America. Some critics make these charges because they do not understand the nature and scope of the program; others, because they hope to profit from a propaganda campaign of distortion and misrepresentation. Among the charges most frequently heard are the following—

The Charge:
The military agreements will require the sending of Latin American troops to Korea.

The Truth:
The commitments are limited strictly to hemisphere defense.

The Charge:
They oblige Latin American troops to defend the United States.

The Truth:
They relate only to defense problems south of the United States.

The Charge:
They are solely for the convenience of the United States.

The Truth:
They directly involve the highest national interests of every American Republic, since their purpose is to protect communications, to defend coastal areas, and to protect strategic areas vulnerable to enemy attack.

The Charge:
The military agreements invite aggression.

The Truth:
They deter potential aggressors and help preserve the peace, because they increase the ability of the American Republics to repel aggression.

The Charge:
The agreements expand the obligations assumed by the American Republics under the Rio Treaty.

The Truth:
They merely increase the ability of the countries receiving aid to carry out those obligations.

The Charge:
The United States is acting contrary to the principles of inter-American solidarity in entering into these agreements.

The Truth:
None of these agreements runs contrary to the principles, practices, or obligations of hemispheric solidarity.

The Charge:
Our military assistance will give some of the countries of Latin America an unfair advantage over others.

The Truth:

The program is directed toward encouraging unity among the American Republics and strengthening them for a common defense against aggression.

U.S. military assistance is no one-way street. The guiding principle of inter-American military relations is that defense must be a collective responsibility. The aim is to raise the ability of Latin American states to carry their share of the load. Every Latin American patrol vessel, every antiaircraft battalion, every fighter squadron which is committed to hemisphere defense and adequately equipped and trained is a step toward full security.

This is not a question of whether the Latin American countries or the United States gain more from such cooperation. Just as security is indivisible, so are its specific benefits. For Latin America, it is important to protect the flow of essential civilian supplies. For the United States and the rest of the free world, the strategic materials of Latin America are vital.

Latin American countries import from the United States machinery, iron, steel, chemicals, foodstuffs, vehicles, electrical and agricultural equipment, and textiles. Our four major imports from Latin America are coffee, sugar, copper, and petroleum. In addition, Latin America supplies us with many other strategic materials necessary to defense production.

Percentage of Total U.S. Imports of Selected Strategic
Materials in Short Supply Received from
Latin America (1950)

Percent	Material
100:	vanadium, quebracho
Over 90:	quartz crystals
Over 80:	castor bean oil, crude petroleum, fuel oil
Over 70:	cordage sisal
Over 60:	antimony, copper
Over 50:	beryl, bismuth, lead, cadmium
Over 40:	tungsten, zinc

Note—A significant percentage of imports of chromite, manila fibers, manganese, tin, wool, iron ore is also received from Latin America.

The adjacent table shows a few of these vital materials we get from Latin America. It illustrates graphically why sizable U.S. forces were diverted during World War II to protect hemisphere sea lanes and key installations. We and our neighbors in countries south of the Rio Grande are working hard to insure the future safety of these strategic areas and shipping lanes. This is the goal of current hemisphere defense arrangements.

The Rio Treaty of 1947 provides the basis for inter-American mutual defense. The Washington meeting of Foreign Ministers in 1951 applied the concept of collective defense to the realities of the present critical world situation. The actual putting into force of practical military measures for assuring adequate defense requires that the American Republics continue to work closely together. This is the essence of the U.S. military assistance program—to make it possible for the American Republics to play an increasingly active role in collective measures for the preservation and security of the hemisphere.

33. *Republic of Chile and the United States of America, Military Assistance Agreement**

April 9, 1952

The Governments of the Republic of Chile and of the United States of America:

In accordance with their pledges under the Inter-American Treaty of Reciprocal Assistance and other international instruments to assist any American State subjected to an armed attack and to act together for the common defense and for the maintenance of the peace and security of the American Continent;

With the intent of fostering peace and security within the framework of the Charter of the United Nations and of cooperating fully with the purposes and endeavors of the United Nations, through measures which will increase the ability of nations interested in accomplishing the purposes and furthering the principles of the Charter to participate effectively in arrangements for individual and collective self-defense;

Reaffirming their determination to give their full cooperation to the collective security efforts of the United Nations in accordance with the Charter and the international endeavors to obtain agreement on universal regulation and reduction of armaments under adequate guarantee against violation;

Taking into consideration the support that the Government of the United States of America has brought to these principles by enacting the Mutual Defense Assistance Act of 1949, as amended, and the Mutual Security Act of 1951, which provide for the furnishing of military assistance to nations which have joined with it in collective security arrangements;

Desiring to set forth the conditions which will govern the furnishing of such mutual assistance;

Have agreed as follows:

Article I

1. Each Government will make or continue to make available to the other, and to such additional governments as the parties hereto may in each case agree upon, such equipment, materials, services, or other military assistance as the Governments furnishing such assistance may authorize in accord with their respective Constitutions and in accordance with such terms and conditions as may be agreed for the fulfillment of this Agreement. The furnishing of any such assistance as may be authorized by either party hereto shall be consistent with the Charter of the United Nations. Such assistance shall be so designed as to promote the defense of the Hemisphere and be in accordance with defense plans which may be accepted by both Parties under which both Governments will participate in missions important to the defense of the Hemisphere within the region defined in Article 4 of the Inter-American Treaty of Reciprocal Assistance. Assistance made available by the Government of the United States of America pursuant to this Agreement will be furnished under the provisions, and subject to all the terms and conditions of the Mutual Defense Assistance Act of 1949, the Mutual Security Act of 1951, acts amending and supplementing the same and pertinent appropriation acts. The two Governments will, when necessary, negotiate detailed arrangements to carry out the provisions of this paragraph.

*Department of State, *Treaties and Other International Acts Series* 2703.

2. The Government of the Republic of Chile undertakes to make effective use of assistance received from the Government of the United States of America pursuant to this Agreement for the purpose of implementing defense plans, which may be accepted by the two Governments, under which they will participate in missions important to the defense and maintenance of the peace of the Western Hemisphere, and, unless otherwise mutually agreed, will devote such assistance exclusively to the purposes indicated in Paragraph 1 of this Article.

3. Arrangements will be entered into under which equipment and materials furnished pursuant to this Agreement and no longer required for the purposes for which it was originally made available (except equipment and materials furnished under terms requiring reimbursement) will be returned to the Government which furnished such assistance for appropriate disposition.

4. In the common security interest of both Governments, the Government of the Republic of Chile undertakes not to transfer title to or possession of any equipment, materials or services furnished to it by the Government of the United States of America under this Agreement.

5. All funds or materials of any nature allocated to or derived from any program of assistance undertaken by the Government of the United States of America under the laws cited in this Article shall not be subject to garnishment, attachment, seizure or other legal or administrative process by any person, firm, entity, corporation, organization or government.

6. Each of the Governments, in accord with the other, will take security measures in order to prevent the disclosure or compromise of classified military articles, services or information furnished by the other Government pursuant to this Agreement.

Article II

Each Government will take appropriate measures consistent with security to keep the public informed of operations under this Agreement.

Article III

The two Governments will, upon the request of either of them, negotiate appropriate arrangements between them providing for the methods and terms of the exchange of patent rights and technical information for defense, which will expedite such exchanges and at the same time protect private interests and maintain necessary security safeguards.

Article IV

1. Subject to the provision of the necessary appropriations, the Government of the Republic of Chile undertakes to make available to the Government of the United States of America sums in local currency, in an amount to be agreed upon, for the use of the latter Government for its administrative and operating expenses in connection with carrying out this Agreement in Chile.

2. The Government of the Republic of Chile will, except as otherwise agreed, grant duty-free treatment and exemption from internal taxation upon importation or

exportation to products, property, materials or equipment imported into its territory in connection with the Agreement or any similar agreement between the United States of America and any other country receiving military assistance.

Article V

1. Each Government agrees to receive personnel of the other Government who will discharge responsibilities of the other Government in connection with the implementation of this Agreement. Such personnel will be accorded reasonable facilities to observe the progress of assistance furnished pursuant to this Agreement. Such personnel will operate as part of the Embassy, under the direction of the corresponding Chief of Diplomatic Mission, and shall have the same immunities and prerogatives as other personnel of the Embassy with corresponding rank.

2. In order to carry out the provisions of the preceding paragraph, the two Governments, by common accord, will establish regulations governing the classification of such personnel. Such personnel will consist exclusively of nationals of the sending country. It is understood between the two Governments that the number of such personnel will be kept as low as possible.

3. The Government of the Republic of Chile shall accord the United States personnel sent pursuant to this Article the same privileges as are conferred on members of the United States Navy and Air Force Missions to Chile under Article XVII of the Agreements of February 15, 1951.

Should it become necessary to send Chilean personnel to the United States in connection with the provision of military assistance by Chile to the United States, the Government of the United States of America shall grant, upon request of the Chief of the Chilean Diplomatic Mission, exception from customs duties on articles imported for the personal use of such personnel and of members of their families.

Article VI

Existing Agreements relating to armed forces missions of the United States of America will not be affected by this Agreement and will remain in full force.

Article VII

In conformity with the principle of mutual aid, under which the two Governments have agreed as provided in Article I, to furnish assistance to each other, the Government of the Republic of Chile agrees to facilitate insofar as possible the production and transfer to the Government of the United States of America for such period of time, in such quantities and upon such terms and conditions as may be agreed upon, of raw, semi-processed and processed strategic materials required by the United States of America as a result of deficiencies or potential deficiencies in its own resources, and which may be available in the Republic of Chile. Arrangements for such transfers shall give due regard to requirements for domestic use and commercial export of the Republic of Chile.

Article VIII

In the interest of their mutual security, the two Governments by mutual accord, will take measures designed to control trade with nations which threaten the security of the Continent.

Article IX

The two Governments reaffirm their determination to join in promoting international understanding and good will and maintaining world peace, to proceed as may be mutually agreed upon to eliminate causes of international tension, and to fulfill the military obligations assumed under multilateral or bilateral agreements and treaties to which both are parties. The Government of the Republic of Chile will make the full contribution permitted by its manpower, resources, facilities and general economic conditions to the development and maintenance of its defensive strength as well as that of the free world, and will take all reasonable measures which may be needed to develop its defense capacities.

Article X

Whereas this Agreement has been negotiated and concluded on the basis that the Government of the United States of America will extend to the other party thereto the benefits of any provision in a similar agreement concluded by the Government of the United States of America with any other American Republic, it is understood that the Government of the United States of America will interpose no objection to amending this Agreement in order that its provisions may conform, in whole or in part, to the corresponding provisions of any similar Military Assistance Agreement, or agreements amendatory thereto, concluded with an American Republic.

Article XI

1. This agreement shall enter into force on the date of receipt by the Government of the United States of America of notification in writing from the Government of the Republic of Chile of ratification of the Agreement in accordance with the constitutional procedures of Chile, and shall continue in force until one year after the receipt by either party of written notice of the intention of the other party to terminate it. In any event, notwithstanding the denouncement or termination of this Agreement, the provisions of Paragraphs 2, 3, 4, 5 and 6 of Article I will continue in force until the Parties agree to the contrary. The arrangements referred to in Article III shall terminate in conformity with the stipulations established in said arrangements.

2. The two Governments shall, upon the request of either of them, consult regarding any matter relating to the application or amendment of this Agreement.

3. This Agreement shall be registered with the Secretary General of the United Nations.

34. Letter from V[ictor] Paz Estenssoro, President of
    Bolivia, to President Dwight D. Eisenhower,
    Requesting Economic and Technical Assistance *

October 1, 1953

Your Excellency: On August 13, 1953, the Government of Bolivia delivered to the Department of State and to other agencies of the Government of the United States of America a copy of a "Plan for the Diversification of Production."

That plan was formulated after the visit to this country of your brother, Dr. Milton Eisenhower, and his advisors, Messrs. Cabot, Overby, and Anderson of the Departments of State, the Treasury, and Commerce, respectively.

The qualities of an educator which Dr. Eisenhower possesses, his extraordinary comprehension, and his sympathetic grasp of the problems of my country made it possible for the conversations held with him and his advisors to be carried out with complete frankness and on the level of the broadest cordiality and mutual understanding. I therefore wish to express again to Your Excellency my appreciation for your vision in having asked Dr. Eisenhower to visit Bolivia as your representative.

The plan presented after those conversations for the study and consideration of the high officials of the Government of the United States of America deals with the technical and economic assistance which my country needs in order to diversify its economy, which is now dependent almost completely on tin, as well as to overcome the economic crisis caused by the low price of that mineral.

Since that moment the Bolivian financial situation has deteriorated dangerously. Our availabilities in foreign currency have diminished so considerably through the fall in the price of tin and other minerals that we find ourselves in the insurmountable difficulty of not being able to provide food and other essential articles for the people, since in order to import them we need foreign currency.

This circumstance impels me to address Your Excellency to ask you that those parts of the above-mentioned plan which refer to providing food and other essential articles for the people of Bolivia and to additional technical assistance indispensable for developing a program of emergency food production be considered and resolved urgently.

Such assistance, granted in time, will serve on the one hand to spare the people of Bolivia from the menace of hunger which hangs over them, and on the other hand will permit the alleviation of the present disequilibrium in our balance of payments.

Such measures as Your Excellency may take in this matter will constitute yet another step in the program of technical and economic collaboration which Bolivia has been receiving from the United States of America and which has made possible the construction of the important Cochabamba-Santa Cruz highway and of certain works in our petroleum and agricultural industries.

The Bolivian currency which would be obtained from the sale to the public of the food and other essential articles furnished us could be utilized to put into effect that part of the plan of diversification of the Bolivian economy which might be carried out through the use of local currency.

I believe that Your Excellency will receive this letter with sympathy and good will

*Department of State Bulletin, Nov. 2, 1953, pp. 182-83.

since it concerns the furnishing of aid to a people who, as is the case in Bolivia, are sincerely pledged to improve the democratic institutions inherent in the free world, to which they firmly adhere, and who furthermore are solidary with the principles of mutual security which govern the nations of the Western Hemisphere.

In thanking Your Excellency in advance in the name of the people of the Government of Bolivia for the measures which you may be good enough to take so that this assistance may reach us opportunely, I express sincere wishes for the happiness of the great American people, whose destiny Your Excellency guides so wisely, as well as for your personal well-being.

35. Address by Nelson A. Rockefeller, Under Secretary of Health, Education and Welfare made at the Pan American Union on Economic Growth and Human Welfare in the Western Hemisphere*

October 12, 1953

Today's anniversary is perhaps even more significant for us in this generation than for the generations that preceded us. For there are more likenesses than may be at first apparent between our world and the world of the daring Genoese. If in 1492 men were on the verge of tremendous discoveries which were to change not only the geographic pattern of the earth but were to alter in many ways the world's designs for living, so are we now near ever vaster discoveries in the realm of science and ever further flights into the unknown.

On this anniversary let us recall the prophetically appropriate words of Columbus in his letter reporting the Discovery: "The eternal Almighty God, our Lord, it is, Who gives to all who walk in His way victory over things apparently impossible."

Indeed, it will be with the strength which comes from the unity through faith and belief in Him that we, as Columbus, can navigate successfully the uncharted waters of today.

All of us are grateful to the Citizens Committee of the Knights of Columbus, the Ambassadors, and the Pan American Union for this special Columbus Day program. Any group dedicated to the tradition of unity based on the spiritual affinity among the peoples of the Americas will always find a warm response in the United States. The tradition of Simon Bolivar has become an integral part of our rich heritage, a heritage which is a bulwark in these times of international turmoil.

President Eisenhower's personal concern for the vitality of this relationship was evidenced when he sent his brother Milton on the recent tour of the hemisphere. It is particularly significant, first because of the confidence the President has in his brother and secondly because of Dr. Milton Eisenhower's outstanding ability and deep human understanding.

In the great tome of the written and unwritten history of mankind there are pages bright with the record of human progress alternating with others dark with the evidence of cruelty, selfishness, and degradation of the human spirit.

The record of no nation, no people, no area is free of shadowed pages, but I believe

*Department of State Bulletin, Nov. 2, 1953, pp. 581-84.

that in the long perspective of history the Western Hemisphere will be judged to have made a great contribution toward increasing the stature of man. Its accomplishment may be discounted by some as weighted on the side of materialism, but I believe that the contribution will be recognized as an enlargement of the human spirit. The Western Hemisphere has offered a new frontier of opportunity by demonstrating that the world's resources could yield an increasing return for the many rather than the few. It has given new vitality and faith to the concept that the goal of society is to provide every individual with an opportunity to develop his highest potential as a citizen, as a productive member of society, and as a spiritual being. An expanding horizon of material opportunity is not an end in itself but the means for offering an environment in which there can thrive a generosity of the human spirit that equates the development and welfare of each individual with the development and welfare of all.

It is, then, more than an historical accident that the discovery by Columbus of the Western Hemisphere with its rich resources provided a laboratory for the development of the institutions of democracy, the concepts of the dignity and worth of the individual, and the conviction that material, cultural, and spiritual growth could be general to all. The Western Hemisphere, by providing both a rich soil of opportunity for the growth and development of these concepts and by providing an expanding frontier for European migration and trade, gave new life and vigor to these values in the European society that had cradled them.

Because of my present association with the new Department of Health, Education, and Welfare, a Department whose sole concern is the well-being of the individual citizen, I should like to take the liberty of focusing on the basic factors affecting the well-being of the individual citizens throughout the 21 American Republics.

Economics in Terms of Human Welfare

Human welfare is the true goal of economic progress. This is a particular concern of President Eisenhower's. I know that he shares with us a faith in the inherent dignity and worth of the individual and in the capacity and desire for self-improvement of human beings of whatever nationality, race, creed, or color. Basic to this well-being is economic growth and a rising standard of living.

In view of this conviction, it is important to define in more specific terms what is meant by economic growth and to examine the record of that growth in the Western Hemisphere.

Since democracy is concerned with the welfare of individuals and not with the aggrandizement of the State, it is insufficient to measure increases in national income in terms of money alone.

Genuine economic growth occurs only when the average man is earning more money and can buy more of the things he needs and wants. To achieve this, total income in terms of buying power must be increasing at a faster rate than the growth of the population and must be distributed in a pattern that allows all to benefit from expanding total production. This type of economic growth is basic to what is popularly known as a rising standard of living.

In examining the growth record, thus defined, of the Western Hemisphere, it is interesting to compare what has been happening in three separate areas—the Latin American Republics, the United States, and Canada.

The United States has taken justifiable pride in a long-term growth record that from about 1880 to the present shows a steady improvement in per capita income to the extent of doubling living standards for everyone each 40 years. Over the same period, the average work week of production workers has been cut from 65 hours in 1880 to 41 hours in 1952, and the pattern of income distribution has assured that a more than proportionate share of the increased return has gone to those in the lower brackets of income.

In recent years the growth trend in Canada, expressed in the same terms, has been equally dramatic. Between 1938 and the end of 1951, Canada's real output in terms of production has increased at an average rate of 5.6 percent per year against a population growth of 1.7 percent per year. Thus, the real increase in the standard of living of the people of Canada during this period has been at an average rate of 3.8 percent per year. This is considerably higher than the long-term increase in the United States, which has averaged about 2 percent per year. Canada is going through one of the most dynamic developments that the world has ever known.

Until recently, there has been insufficient data upon which to base any comparable appraisal of the growth trend of the 20 Republics of Latin America considered as a whole. This can now be done, thanks to two pioneering studies of the United Nations Economic Commission for Latin America published in March of this year.

These studies show that the economy of Latin America is on the march. Over the past two decades the real per capital income for Latin America has been increasing at an average rate of 2¼ percent per year. In the postwar period, from 1946 through 1952, the rate of increase is even better—2½ percent per year, a rate which is higher than that of the United States.

The magnitude of this achievement is better appreciated when it is noted that at the same time Latin America's population was increasing by more than 2 percent a year. This population growth is about twice as great as the world average. It means that, in terms of physical output, Latin American progress has had to be twice as great as in other areas to make comparable advances in living standards. In physical terms, total production of Latin America in the postwar period has shown an annual increase of almost 5 percent, which has provided the 2½ percent annual increase in the per capita income of its rapidly growing populace. This record surpasses the United States and Canada for the postwar years.

It is an extraordinary record indeed and one which few of us in the Americas recognized was in the making because of our preoccupation with the many problems of postwar readjustment. Even more significant is the potential increase in standards of living which it indicates is possible for the future.

However, magnificent as this accomplishment is, it does not mean that Latin America has solved its economic problems. Her start on the road to economic dynamism was late, and the distance is long to catch up with the levels already achieved in Canada and the United States. Further, the balance and maintenance of a dynamic economy is always precarious and something that must be guarded and continuously reinvigorated through the maintenance of strong individual incentives and wise government policy.

This rapid expansion in production, coupled with the steady growth in population, has highlighted some of the basic underlying economic weaknesses which exist in the hemisphere. These must be faced realistically and dealt with promptly if we are to achieve our common goals of human dignity and well-being for all the peoples of the Americas, goals which are still far short of realization.

Seven Major Problems

In my opinion there are seven such problems that may be listed as of major importance. They are as follows:

1. *The possibility that the relatively high prices recently enjoyed by many of Latin America's exports will not be maintained.*

Since this favorable price position acted as a powerful stimulant to Latin America's recent development progress, a further shrinking of this advantage would have increasingly sharp repercussions.

There is need for constructive and imaginative thought upon effective methods of dealing with this problem, in a way that reflects the best interests of all.

2. *In many of the Republics there is a serious lack of adequate transportation, power, and domestic fuel supply.*

These shortages are major bottlenecks to continuing economic growth and should be decisively dealt with.

3. *The failure of agricultural production in Latin America as a whole to keep pace with population growth.*

Compared with the excellent record of growth in the industrial and commercial fields, there has been a lag in food production. A healthy, well-balanced development requires progress on all fronts. While the postwar emphasis on industrial progress was justified, it is now clear that agriculture must be stepped up to a growth trend that will provide better standards of nutrition for fast-growing populations.

The industrialization of tropical agriculture based on the use of chemicals and mechanization gives promise of tremendously increased yields. Such a development requires large capital outlays. However, the possibility of greatly increased productivity and earnings should attract much-needed investments and permit a sharp rise in the standard of living of rural workers.

4. *The increasing need for investment capital, both domestic and foreign.*

In the postwar period the Latin American nations have done well on this score with capital investment of all types amounting to 16½ percent of the total output of the area. The record is an excellent one, particularly since 95 percent of all postwar investment in Latin America has been made with local capital. However, continuing capital investment is so crucial a key to economic development that measures to insure its availability in sufficient volume and to channel it into the most productive paths must be unremitting.

The Latin American Republics need modernized investment institutions and organized capital markets to encourage the increased flow of domestic and foreign capital for continuing growth. High on the list of requirements is control of inflation that distorts the investment pattern and encourages speculation.

5. *Persistent shortages of foreign exchange to purchase imports essential to continuing economic growth.*

In some areas of Latin America this shortage is sufficiently acute to require severe belt-tightening procedures. In the long run, the best solution lies in building up the volume of export products and in the control of inflation that fosters trade deficits.

The United States is also importantly involved in this problem. As the American Bankers Association put it:

> A nation can sell abroad only as it buys abroad. We believe that the United States should live up to its international responsibilities as the world's greatest creditor and producing Nation by continuing to open its markets increasingly to foreign goods. Such a policy will help to create a larger volume of world trade, the eventual restoration of freely convertible currencies, and stronger economies in the United States and other nations of the free world.

6. *The shortage of educational facilities to train manpower in administration, management, and the professions adequate to the needs of modern society.*

The scale and complexity of present-day government, industry, and, increasingly, agriculture require a tremendous number of highly trained and experienced men and women. Shortages in this field will become an increasing obstacle to expanding development and to the achievement of increased efficiency essential to improve services and lower costs to the people. This scarcity of adequately trained personnel also affects the growth and improvement of health and welfare services.

A large-scale educational effort is essential throughout the hemisphere. The experience of one area can be of great usefulness to others. However, the problem is of such pressing magnitude that it can only be met through major expansion and improvement of educational facilities within the respective American Republics. A cooperative effort in this field can be rewarding to all.

7. *The limitations to economic growth imposed by restrictive national frontiers that cut across the natural lines of economic interdependence.*

Despite a very strong nationalistic tradition, this problem has been clearly recognized in Europe and the Schuman Plan now in operation represents a tangible evidence that the European countries are willing to take action to meet it.

The community of economic interest in the Western Hemisphere is no less compelling, and there is a strong case for giving thought to how its nations might collaborate to reduce barriers and promote common interests.

It is my understanding that these seven major problems are already being considered for the agenda of the forthcoming 10th inter-American conference to be held next March at Caracas.

They are common problems and must importantly be met within a framework of common understanding. The representatives of the 21 American Republics meeting in Caracas next March have a unique opportunity to lay the foundation for their joint solution in accord with the long-established tradition of the Americas.

My confidence that they can and will be met is reenforced first by the conviction that most of them are easier to handle in the framework of an expanding inter-American economy and secondly by the evidence that the economies of the Latin American Republics are going forward at a pace comparable to the rest of the Western Hemisphere.

There must be a working partnership among all of the nations of the Western Hemisphere to preserve and continuously strengthen this area's traditional role in the world as a frontier of expanding opportunity. Each of the nations that make up this hemisphere has deeply established ties to the European cultures from which we derived basic infusions of population and ideology. It is natural that our earliest ties of cultural and economic exchange should have run east and west rather than north and south.

Many scholarly accounts have repeated as a truism the statement that our basic resource patterns were competitive, rather than complementary, and that inevitably our economies would continue this east-west focus; that there would be relatively little economic exchange between us; and that our political and intellectual orientation would follow the lines of our economic interests.

Now that we all are coming of age, this concept is being uprooted both by the formidable force of mutual interest and by the inexorable force of common understanding. The truism is evaporating, simply because it is not true.

The increasing community of Western Hemisphere economic interest is dramatically attested by our foreign trade figures.

In closing, I should like to give you these briefly:

In 1938 trade with Canada and Latin America accounted for 34 percent of the foreign commerce of the United States. In 1952 it represented 47 percent of our total foreign trade.

In 1938 trade with the United States and Latin America accounted for 51 percent of Canada's foreign commerce. In 1952 it was 70 percent.

In 1938 trade with the United States and Canada made up 36 percent of Latin America's total foreign trade. In 1952 the proportion had mounted to 55 percent.

In 1938 the total trade between the three major divisions of the Western Hemisphere represented 25 percent of all world trade. In 1952 it represented 36 percent of all world trade.

The cementing of our political, intellectual, and cultural ties has been no less solid, if less amenable to statistical demonstrations. This meeting is one evidence of their validity.

I hope and I believe that the scope and the depth of Western Hemisphere collaboration upon all planes will continue to grow. Ours should be a genuine partnership—a demonstration that mutual respect, trust, and recognition of common interest can keep alive the concept of opportunity and growth, not for the aggrandizement of a hemisphere or for any one group but for the nourishment that an atmosphere of growth affords to man's spirit, to his physical well-being, and to the institutions of freedom and democracy.

36. Reply from President Eisenhower to President Paz Estenssoro*

October 14, 1953

I have received your letter of October 1, 1953, in which you describe the very grave economic emergency now threatening Bolivia and in which you request financial and technical assistance from the United States.

Department of State Bulletin, Nov. 2, 1953, pp. 585-86.

The people of the United States feel deep concern for the welfare of the people of the sister Republic of Bolivia. The friendly spirit of cooperation between our two nations has in the past motivated the programs of technical assistance and the Export-Import Bank loans for economic diversification to which your letter refers. Our concern for the welfare of the Bolivian people motivated the recent decision to make a further purchase of Bolivian tin at a time when this country had no immediate need for additional tin. This concern is founded today not alone on the traditional friendship between our two peoples but also on the realization that the security of the entire Free World is threatened wherever free men suffer hunger or other severe misfortunes.

We appreciate fully the fact that the present emergency in Bolivia is one which the Government and the people of Bolivia are unable to meet without the assistance of friends. The Government of Bolivia is already taking wise and courageous measures of self-help looking toward the diversification and stabilization of the Bolivian economy, but unfortunately these measures cannot produce their full effect in time to prevent severe suffering by the people of Bolivia in the immediate future.

To assist Bolivia in this emergency, and to help accelerate the economic diversification of your country, the Government of the United States will provide the following emergency aid in response to your request:

(a) As announced on October 6, I have determined that up to $5 million of Commodity Credit Corporation stocks of agricultural products shall be made available to meet the urgent relief requirements of Bolivia;

(b) In addition, the Director of the Foreign Operations Administration is allocating up to $4 million of Mutual Security Act funds to be used in providing additional essential commodities and services required by the people of Bolivia;

(c) In accordance with your request, most of the Bolivian currency funds accruing from the sale of these commodities to Bolivian consumers are to be used by your Government for projects which will contribute to the economic development of Bolivia;

(d) The United States contribution to the cooperative technical assistance program in Bolivia has been more than doubled, and the additional funds, together with the matching contribution of your Government, are to be used for a program of emergency food production.

In closing I wish to express my deep personal appreciation for the kind reference in your letter to the visit to Bolivia of my brother, Dr. Milton Eisenhower. He has given me a first-hand account of the situation in Bolivia, and he has been among the strongest advocates of assistance to your country.

37. *Address by John M. Cabot, Assistant Secretary of State for Inter-American Affairs, before the General Federation of Women's Clubs, on Inter-American Cooperation and Hemisphere Solidarity* *

October 14, 1953

In reading comments on international affairs, one is often reminded of the differ-

*Department of State Bulletin, Oct. 26, 1953, pp. 554-59.

ence in the image one sees in looking through the two ends of a telescope. Our differences with other nations frequently arise because we do not see a given situation in the same light. Yet if we are to live in constructive friendship with the other nations of this world, surely the first essential is mutual understanding. Surely in this era of hydrogen bombs it is better to sacrifice something of one's own viewpoint to the honest views of another if that will maintain the peace.

Since the dawn of history the way of the peacemaker has been hard. In international affairs it is easier to arouse hatred than understanding, suspicion than confidence, selfishness than collaboration. Those who appeal to emotion rather than reason can point to historical examples to sow whatever evil weed they may wish to implant in the public's mind. Unhappily the public is not told so often, nor does it so vividly remember, the times it has been deceived by appeals to its narrow prejudices and selfish emotions. Yet wars have almost never started in modern times from nothing; they have resulted from an accumulation of grievances, real or fancied, on both sides. It is the task of diplomacy to allay those grievances before they reach the danger point.

In the Americas there are happily but few cases in which there is danger that grievances may reach the explosion point. Whatever the shortcomings in our mutual relations, we can proudly maintain as a group of free peoples that in our relations we have been a beacon light to the rest of the world. The Pan American Union antedates by half a century the United Nations and furnished the U.N. Charter the vital concept of regional organizations; the concept of Point Four had already been in successful operation for years in Latin America when it was announced as an essential contribution of the United States to the maintenance of peace in the world. The basic principle of the NATO treaty had previously been embodied in the Rio Treaty of 1947. Thanks to the cooperative concepts we had built up over the years in this hemisphere, we were spared the material destruction of the Second World War, and we were able to devote all of the resources of the Americas to maintaining inviolate our lives, our homes, our beliefs, and our institutions against foreign tyranny, nihilism and imperialism. Let us never for a moment forget the horrors from which our continental solidarity happily saved us.

In the years which have passed since our common victory in the Second World War, rifts have appeared in our continental solidarity, and today it is not so firm and unquestioned as it was 8 years ago. For the most part, I do not believe that these rifts are serious. Even between the closest friends an occasional misunderstanding is inevitable. It is the duty of friendship to examine such misunderstandings with candor and tolerance; only thus can they be prevented from rankling.

Let us examine some specific problems we have recently faced in our Latin American relations.

Bolivia

We have just made a unique grant of aid in Bolivia. We have not done this because we have uniquely close relations with Bolivia. We do not necessarily approve all that the present Bolivian Government has done; on the contrary, we have had to make strong representations to it regarding its attitude towards American interests. Why then this aid?

First, let me point out that the present Government unquestionably came to power by the will of the Bolivian people. If we believe in democracy, it is surely our duty to deal with regimes solidly based on the consent of the governed, even if they differ somewhat from us in their concepts of government.

Second, the present Government has shown much courage in facing the problems it inherited. I shall not discuss the question of the nationalization of the tin mines. Bitter charges have been flung back and forth, but it would not be proper for me to discuss them. What is important is to note that preliminary agreements have been reached between the Bolivian Government and the former owners of the tin mines regarding compensation.

The present Government inherited an impossible economic situation. In an effort to keep down the cost of food, the previous governments had imported staple items at an unrealistically low rate of exchange. As a result foodstuffs disappeared over the frontiers even after importation, while domestic farmers were ruined. The proportion of foodstuffs imported rose to 40 percent of consumption. As long as tin prices remained high, the necessary exchange could be found to pay for food imports, but this year the price in world markets dropped abruptly from $1.21 to about $0.80 a pound. At the same time we filled our stockpile and were no longer interested in the low-grade ores which could be smelted only by us in an uneconomic smelter. This combination of circumstances spelled disaster for Bolivia.

With drastically curtailed foreign exchange receipts, famine in Bolivia was a mathematical certainty. Given the traditional political pattern there and the grave stresses to which the country is subject, chaos seemed certain and a swing to communism probable if we sat on our hands. Taking its political life in its hands, the Government has drastically modified the economic controls which have been ruining the country's economy and has tried to put things on a sound economic basis. You will appreciate the tragic sacrifices it means for people who have barely enough to live on when the prices of necessities are suddenly jumped far more than wages.

It seems to me that our attitude toward this question is basically a test of the sincerity of our adherence to the true ideals of pan-Americanism and hemispheric solidarity. As 21 sovereign Republics we shall have differences—serious differences—in this hemisphere. We have common interests vastly more important than our differences. We face alike the implacable challenge of communism. The true test of our hemispheric solidarity, upon which our security so importantly depends, is our willingness to sink our differences and to cooperate with regimes pursuing a different course from ours to achieve common goals. If we have our reservations regarding some of the present Bolivian Government's measures, we believe it is sincere in desiring social progress and in opposing Communist imperialism. We are therefore cooperating with it, for history has often described the fate of those who have quarreled over nonessentials in the face of a mortal peril.

Let us turn to a somewhat similar case which is very different in its basic implications.

Guatemala

Our relations with the Guatemalan Government are today not those which we would like to have with it and with every other government in this hemisphere. Profoundly believing, as we do, in hemispheric solidarity for both spiritual and material reasons, I think we should strive as dispassionately as we can to seek the causes for the situation which has arisen. I also feel that we have the right and duty to defend ourselves and explain our position in answer to years of wanton attacks on this country and its citizens from official Guatemalan sources.

We find it difficult, for example, to be patient, after all the blood and treasure we have poured out in Korea to safeguard the free world, when the official Guatemalan newspaper follows the Communist line by accusing us in effect of bacteriological warfare just after our airmen have returned to tell us of the tortures to which they were subjected to extract fabricated confessions. We are also surprised that the Guatemalan Ambassador should misrepresent a perfectly proper note I handed him explaining our juridical views regarding the expropriation of American property in Guatemala. All that we have asked of Guatemala is that it respect its obligations, legal and moral, within the family of nations. We wish to discuss questions outstanding with Guatemala on the basis of the facts, our inter-American responsibilities, and international law; and we are awaiting their answer to see if they also are prepared to discuss outstanding questions on that basis.

I shall not at this point discuss the question as to whether activities of the international Communist conspiracy to destroy free governments are prejudicing the independence of Guatemala and that of neighboring Republics, since this is essentially a matter of inter-American rather than unilateral concern. The American Republics have on numerous occasions, notably by Resolution XXXII of the Bogotá Conference of 1948, made clear their opposition to activities of this nature.

With any regime's purpose of social reform, insofar as it is sincere, we have no quarrel. On the contrary, we applaud measures which raise the living standards of the underprivileged. Having myself served in Guatemala and observed conditions, I personally would have great sympathy with any such purpose. But when we are resisting Communist aggression and subversion all over the world, no regime which is openly playing the Communist game can expect from us the positive cooperation we normally seek to extend to all of our sister Republics. We know indeed that despite its hypocritical appeals on behalf of the underprivileged, communism does not give a snap of the fingers for the welfare of the masses. It will liquidate them or send them to slave labor camps by the millions to advance its tyrannical power.

When we seek to defend the rights of our citizens under international law in Guatemala or elsewhere, we are often accused of opposition to any form of social progress. Such an argument is so obviously absurd, so monstrous in the light of our entire history, that I find it difficult to know where to start refuting it. Am I to recite our Declaration of Independence or our Bill of Rights? Am I to invoke the shades of Jefferson, Lincoln, the two Roosevelts? Am I to describe the innumerable curbs which by law we have effectively placed on abuses of the power of wealth, or must I point out that our society is far less divided into classes than that of Soviet Russia? Need I remind our Latin friends of the freedom which we helped to win for Cuba and the Philippines and yielded to them spontaneously with our warmhearted blessing? Is it for nothing that we have in the United States the highest standard of living in the world, that under wise laws the benefits of our material advancement are so widely spread throughout the community? Have other countries so soon forgotten what private American efforts have done to relieve the sufferings resulting from disaster wherever it has struck in the world, or the enormous contributions which our private foundations have made towards wiping out pestilence? What selfish purpose are we supposed to be serving by the aid we have given millions of the underprivileged through our Point Four work? Over what people, territory, or class does the Star Spangled Banner wave as a symbol of oppression or exploitation? No national record could show more clearly our sympathy for the weak, the stricken, and the oppressed, our desire for the greatest good of the greatest number.

Argentina

Let us turn to another situation. Our relations with Argentina have often been troubled. I am not going to analyze the causes and the course of the difficulties which arose between us; I doubt that any good purpose would be served by raking over the dead leaves of the past.

The Argentine Government follows a different political and economic philosophy from ours; whether it is well adopted to Argentine domestic conditions I shall not venture to say, for it frankly is none of our business. It is, however, clear that the present Government of Argentina came to power by the will of the Argentine people. The Government of the United States has repeatedly pledged itself not to intervene in the internal affairs of its sister Republics, and it must and will respect its pledges; they are the cornerstone of our inter-American relations. . . . Reviewing the sorry history of past years, I hope you will agree that this is not only practically sound but morally right.

We cannot take the attitude that what is good for us is necessarily good for other nations under vastly different circumstances; that Uncle Sam knows best what is good for others and will assume the responsibility for seeing that they get it; that it is wrong for Soviet Russia to impose communism on foreign nations but permissible for us to impose democracy on them; that in the present grave state of international affairs we can afford to feud with every government whose internal politics don't altogether meet our approval. If it is not obvious to us that democracy (unlike communism) can never be imposed on a foreign nation by force, then we should and did learn from past interventions that they never produced democracy. If we are to have hemispheric solidarity, with all that it means to our security, we must scrupulously respect the principle of nonintervention in our relations with our sister Republics.

In his inaugural address President Eisenhower stated that, much as we cherished our own political and economic institutions, we should never try to force them on others. President Perón on his part indicated to the new administration his hope for better relations between our two nations. Thanks to the tact, ability, and understanding of Dr. Milton Eisenhower, a marked change in the tenor of our relations took place as a result of our visit to Buenos Aires in July.

In our talks with President Perón, he made it clear he wished for good relations with the United States based upon mutual respect. The purpose of our visit was to make it equally clear that the principle of mutual respect was likewise the basis of our policy. In today's world, Argentine and United States interests coincide far more than they clash. Logic and common sense point to the course which we should take.

President Perón has taken steps toward improving relations by settling outstanding controversies with us. There have been mischievous stories circulated that, in return for better relations, he demanded concessions, notably large loans, of us. The fact is the exact reverse; he told us that Argentine friendship had no price tag on it. We welcome the constructive attitude President Perón has shown. Obviously I cannot predict what the future of our relations with Argentina will be; some of the factors which have troubled them still exist. But this much I can state: we, on our part, shall strive earnestly to consolidate the improvement which has taken place in our relations with Argentina. . . . Though remembering past disappointments, let us on our part do all we can to prevent another. Let us demonstrate our profound belief and faith in pan-Americanism and hemispheric solidarity.

Mexico

In thinking of the future of our relations with Argentina, let us take heart from the story of our relations with Mexico. In the past 26 years, some exceptionally able American diplomats have handled our relations wisely and have resolutely adhered to first principles. Their efforts have been greeted with equal statesmanship by their Mexican colleagues. Our relations have been completely transformed, and today they are those of friendship, respect, understanding, and trust. If there are times, in the innumerable questions which inevitably rise between neighbors, that we cannot agree, we can disagree without rancor or suspicion. The forthcoming meeting between President Eisenhower and President Rúiz Cortines at the Falcón Dam will symbolize the sincere friendship and effective cooperation which characterizes our relations with our good neighbor to the south.

I have described to you the story of three major problems which we have had recently in our relations with our sister Republics. Do not think that they are typical. Our relations in this hemisphere suffer in a sense from the fact that they are not more dramatic. If we are friendly with our neighbors, if we cooperate with them, if they are going about their own business without creating major problems for us, that is not news—tragic though that may be as a commentary on human relations. Let us, however, take comfort from the fact that we can develop our relations with our sister Republics in an atmosphere other than one of lurid crisis.

For here is a frontier of human development similar to that which raised us in a century to our present grandeur. Here is a blackboard where history is yet to be written. Here is a group of nations where our present policies can greatly influence our future relations for good or ill. Here is a continent in a period of amazing develop-ment—a development so rapid that our Latin friends complain more of growing pains than they take satisfaction in their increasing stature.

Now is the moment when we must decide whether we are to keep this rendezvous with destiny. We can foresee for Latin America a development in the next century as portentous for world history as our development was in the last century. While this is going on, while Latin America is going through a period of febrile development, we should not be surprised if it centers its attention on its domestic problems. We did. Let us remember how deeply we appreciated the helping hands which were extended to us when we were younger and weaker, and let us cooperate in friendship and under-standing in the development of our sister Republics. History beckons us.

Brazil

Take, for example, our relations with Brazil. With no nation in the world have we a record of longer, more loyal friendship. Greater than the United States in area, more populous than any other Latin land in America or Europe, Brazil is going forward as though Aladdin had rubbed his lamp. If there are today certain maladjustments in Brazil's economy, can anyone doubt Brazil's majestic future? Reason and sentiment have alike cemented our friendship in the past. No nation has brighter promise for the future than Brazil, and no nation can better help Brazil to achieve that future than the United States. If the problems of our collaboration are often complex and prosaic rather than glamorous, let us press forward together in continuing, constructive friendship.

Panama

Or take our relations with the Republic of Panama. We are holding discussions with representatives of that Government in regard to certain readjustments in our relations which they desire. Given the immensely complex relations which exist between Panama and the Canal Zone, this is a highly intricate, involved subject. Differences of opinion will, of course, arise as to whether or not some of the Panamanian aspirations are just and practical, and some of their demands seem excessive, but we on our part are examining them in a spirit of understanding with a desire to promote continuing friendship and mutually beneficial relations. Not only must we bear in mind that close collaboration is essential to the defense of the Canal, but also we should always remember the example we set for the world in our dealings with smaller states.

We hear quite a bit in the United States of the occasional troubles of American companies operating in certain parts of Latin America, but we hear little of the economic statesmanship shown by many of our sister Republics, notably Venezuela and Peru. We hear of dictators, but we scarcely hear, for example, of the sturdy democracies of Uruguay and Costa Rica. We have as neighbors a group of sister Republics with defects and problems, but in a period of pulsating change and progress. As we seek to solve our day-to-day problems, as crises elsewhere distract us, let us lift up our eyes to the brilliant future which cooperation with them can so mightily advance.

And finally a word which I trust our sister Republics will not take amiss. Communist imperialism recognizes the United States as the citadel of the free world. So long as we stand intact and free, they cannot proceed unhampered with their conspiracy to subjugate the world to their godless tyranny. So long as the mendacities of Communist propaganda can be exposed, it will not be particularly effective. As the principal obstacle in their aggressive path, we must be eliminated; and to that purpose they are devoting every resource at their command which they feel it prudent to use. In Latin America they are seeking through a tremendous campaign of calumny to destroy our prestige, to weaken our economy and that of our sister Republics by vicious attacks on our private companies operating in Latin America. Not a few honest people have been misled to a greater or lesser degree by this campaign. Recognizing a few words of truth in a lengthy Communist diatribe, irritated with the United States by the frustrations we all face in this ever-narrowing world, they unwittingly lend aid and comfort to their mortal enemies.

As free men and free nations in this hemisphere, let us disagree if we choose as to how we are to achieve our goals; but let us disagree with friendly tolerance, and let us remember that our goals, of governments and peoples, are substantially the same. As sovereign Republics, we seek national development in accordance with respective national geniuses; seek rising living standards; we emphasize the rights and dignity of the individual. In a shrinking world we wish in our international relations to secure mutual benefits on the basis of mutual respect. We want peace, and we know how mighty a force for peace our hemispheric solidarity has proved. In short, although there are some conflicts of interest between us as there are even in the most closely knit families and although the Communists ceaselessly try to exploit these conflicts, our interests, aspirations, and goals in the Americas are so closely paralleled that they should indissolubly cement our continental solidarity. Let us then deal with each other with understanding hearts.

38. Report by Milton S. Eisenhower, Special Ambassador, to the President on United States-Latin American Relations*

November 18, 1953

At your direction, I have in recent months sought ways in which the traditional bonds of friendship between the United States and the nations of Latin America might be strengthened.

Early in April, 1953, you asked me to do three things:

First, to express to the governments and peoples of Latin America the sincere conviction of the United States that sound economic, military, political, and cultural relationships between our countries are necessary to our common future;

Second, to obtain a broad continental perspective of those conditions which affect the relationship of the United States with the republics of Latin America; and

Third, to consider what, if any, changes might be desirable in United States policies and programs in order to contribute to the meaningful unity we all desire.

During the month of May I consulted with the Secretary of State, John Foster Dulles, regarding the selection of mission members who could best help carry out this assignment. We chose John M. Cabot, Assistant Secretary of State; Andrew N. Overby, Assistant Secretary of the Treasury; Samuel W. Anderson, Assistant Secretary of Commerce, and W. Tapley Bennett, Jr., Deputy Director of the Office of South American Affairs, Department of State. These officials with both specialized and general knowledge of Latin America accepted the invitation to accompany me and to share in the responsibility of my assignment. Because of time limitations the field portion of this task was limited to the republics of South America.

We left Washington on June 23 and returned on July 29, 1953.

In those thirty-six days we held friendly and informative discussions with the

*Department of State Bulletin, Nov. 23, 1953, pp. 695-717.

Presidents and cabinet ministers of the ten republics of an entire continent. We talked with their leaders of agriculture, industry, finance, labor, and education. We visited factories, homes, farms, and schools. In all, we traveled about 20,000 miles and met with several thousand persons, individually or in groups.

Everywhere our mission was greeted with friendliness and understanding. Everyone was genuinely concerned in making certain that we should have the opportunity to obtain all the facts, ideas, and attitudes we sought. Exceptional courtesy was the rule everywhere. A few efforts by communists to mar the cordiality of the welcome were conspicuously futile and indicated that the communists feared the mission would succeed in establishing better understanding among the leaders and peoples of the American republics.

The members of the mission are deeply appreciative of the great kindnesses and courtesies which were extended to us everywhere.

I am happy to tell you that all with whom we talked share your desire to strengthen relationships between the United States and the ten republics we visited, as well as among all the nations of the Western Hemisphere.

Upon our return home, we began the task of synthesizing our data and crystallizing our views. We also began holding discussions with many governmental and other leaders who are vitally concerned with both public and private policy in the United States as it affects relations with the Latin American countries.

Here, to contribute to public understanding, it seems well to emphasize that the development and implementation of foreign policy is today a tremendously complicated undertaking, requiring wisdom and a great deal of patience as the many phases of a consistent policy are coordinated and implemented.

Thus, all may agree that sound, mutually helpful economic relations with a particular country will contribute to our own national welfare. Everyone, in principle, may favor a policy of economic cooperation. But to bring the policy alive may require a great many public and private decisions and actions which are difficult to coordinate. Hypothetically, it may require a favorable decision by the Office of Defense Mobilization for the purchase, from a given country, of critical materials for stockpiling purposes; it may call for loans by the International Bank for the expansion of transportation and power facilities, and here the decision is outside the sphere of authority of the United States Government; it may necessitate short-term loans by the Export-Import Bank, a possibility of interest not only to the Bank and the Secretary of State, but also to the Secretary of the Treasury and the Director of the Budget, for the funds drawn by the Export-Import Bank come from the Treasury and are a charge against the annual cash budget of the United States; the achievement of the mutually agreed upon policy may be dependent on changes in the domestic laws and policies of the country concerned, a matter on which only that country can take the initiative; and some or all the foregoing actions may be essential to increase the flow of private capital to the other country—private capital which must, it seems to me, be primarily depended on for helping to develop the great economic potentials of the nations of Latin America.

Even then, this single instance of promoting mutually helpful economic relationships may not be complete. At this point there may be a profitable two-way trade between the United States and that country. We may buy many millions of dollars worth of products from it each year, and it may, most likely will, buy an equivalent amount from us. But then the foreign country or the United States may, as a result of domestic considerations, increase a tariff, or impose quantitative restrictions, or fix uneconomic exchange rates which affect adversely the level of trade in both directions. Such actions may not only cause great economic dislocation within the foreign country but may also injure United States traders who have been dealing with that country, and may threaten the soundness of both public and private investments which have been made in an effort to further economic growth in both countries.

In the face of these ramifications in formulating and effectuating policy, we have, as I have indicated, been holding many conversations with public officials and private leaders, for we are convinced that better and more stable relations with the countries of Latin America will result only from wise decisions, day after day, by a great many individuals.

This process of consultation could, of course, be much extended, but I am now submitting this report, believing that the inter-agency and governmental-private consultations which are needed continuously are properly the function of the established departments and agencies of the Government.

For my associates and me it has been a rare privilege and rewarding experience to represent you, the Government, and the people of the United States on what we deem to have been a mission of vital importance. We believe deeply that we must constantly be alert to maintain and to build better political, economic, military, and cultural relations with our neighbors to the South. Good relations in this Hemisphere are crucially important to our own future, and to theirs, and indeed to the future progress of the entire world.

II. The Importance of Latin America and the United States to Each Other

Stable, satisfactory relations between the United States and the nations of Latin America are vital as we seek to build a cooperative peace characterized by freedom and rising levels of well-being.

The Economic Aspect

The trade of the United States with the Latin American republics was about $3.5 billion in each direction in 1952.

As a market for our commercial exports, Latin America is as important to us as all of Europe and more important than Asia, Africa and Oceania combined. Our sales to Latin America encompass the entire range of our national production. As a source of United States imports, the Latin American republics have even greater relative importance, standing well ahead of Europe or the other continents.

Reciprocally, the United States is of key importance to every one of the Latin American countries, both as a market for their products and as a source of essential imports.

The copper, tin, zinc, iron ore, manganese, and other minerals which we obtain from Latin America are vital constituent parts of the machinery which we in turn ship there. The dollars we provide through purchases of coffee, sugar, tropical fruits, and wool, as well as metals, finance their purchases of transportation and industrial equipment and consumer goods. The industrial and military items which the United

States turns out to help defend the free world, including the American republics, require a continuing supply of a great variety of strategic materials from Latin America.

Such trade is mutually advantageous.

Almost 30 percent of all United States private, long-term foreign investment is in Latin America; this investment of some $6 billion is larger than the amount invested in any other part of the world except Canada. Such an investment is important not only to the United States as earning assets but also to Latin America as a stimulant to productivity and economic progress. Its contribution to the general development of individual countries is daily made evident in practically every field of economic endeavor, from electric power and heavy industry to the manufacture of finished goods and their distribution to consumers.

This United States direct investment ordinarily earns a good return; at the same time, of course, it develops the desert and the jungle, provides work at good wages, offers sound technical training for hosts of young people, carries with it technical and managerial skills and, by increasing the output of minerals, foods and manufactured goods, helps build prosperity in our sister republics.

While we might cite instances in which this capital has not been fairly treated, we could also call attention to many cases in which reasonable treatment has redounded to the benefit of both countries and has promoted an additional flow of productive investment.

The economic well-being of every section and every special interest group in the United States is affected by our relations with Latin America. The dollars she gets from her sales here are used largely for direct purchases here. If, because of tariff or other changes, we should buy less from any of the countries to the South, their purchases from us would decline. The effects of such change would be felt in every part of our country.

Unfortunately, the people of the United States do not seem generally to comprehend the full significance to us of stable economic relations with Latin America; moreover, some of our actions have caused leaders in those countries to adopt the mistaken view that we turn our attention to them only in times of crisis.

On the other hand, many Latin Americans appear to disregard the importance to them of their economic relations with the United States. The fact is, of course, that our market is indispensable to the well-being of the other American republics. Our record is such that, no matter how disturbed Latin Americans become over some of our trade and tariff policies, they do have considerable confidence in our basic fairness in the conduct of international trading. However, this preponderant importance of United States consumption as regards so many Latin American products is precisely the reason why our actions, however minor they may be in our view, can have such significant effects on the economies of other republics in the Hemisphere.

The Military Aspect

The military relations between Latin American countries and the United States are closely related to their economic interdependence, to the significant role being played by the United States in the defense of the free world and to the strategic location of our countries with respect to one another.

The present military strength of the nations of Latin America is relatively small, for the most part designed for the maintenance of internal order. This fact may suggest to some that these republics are, therefore, not significant in the system of collective security which the free world is constructing.

This is a fallacious, dangerous assumption.

In the event of a general war, some of the essential resources of the world might well be in the hands of the enemy. The resources of Latin America would then be of enhanced importance. A Latin America under the control of or allied with our enemies could deny these resources to us and even open broad lines for direct attack upon us.

But a friendly Latin America can do more than provide strategic materials. It can help guard the lines of communication and shipment, including the Panama Canal. It can, as occurred in World War II, provide air and sea bases. It can, as Brazil and Mexico did in World War II and Colombia did in the struggle in Korea, supply forces trained in the use of standardized weapons.

Perhaps the greatest military importance of Latin America, in the coalition of the free world, is in its rapidly growing potential: We believe that some of the nations of Latin America will in the relatively near future develop into potent allies and thereby significantly augment the free world's ability to uphold collective security.

Here again, the mutuality of interest merits emphasis: If the nations of Latin America have a military importance to the United States, the United States is vital militarily to them. With no other American republic having a military establishment remotely comparable to our own, and with the United States standing between Latin America and today's potential aggressors, it must be abundantly clear that catastrophic consequences for the freedom and independence of the other nations of this Hemisphere will be avoided only if the United States remains strong.

To comprehend the interdependence of the nations of this Hemisphere in the event of war, one need only recall the determined attempt of enemy submarines in World War II to sink all shipping between the Americas and how near to success they came. On one day, February 17, 1942, seven tankers carrying Venezuelan oil for use in other nations of the Hemisphere were torpedoed. For months no one could be certain that lines of communication could be kept open. In another war, the interruption of shipping with vital cargoes would present serious problems to the United States, which is the most self-sufficient of the American republics; for other nations more dependent on imports, failure of lines of communication might well mean that even essential production would be in danger of complete collapse.

The Political Aspect

The United States and the other American republics have had close relations since the earliest days of their independence.

The doctrine enunciated in 1823 by President Monroe was designed to protect the newly won independence of all the nations of this Hemisphere and to permit the community to grow to maturity free from domination by any transoceanic power. The Monroe doctrine was obviously based upon considerations of our own security; if the arguments to justify it were strong in 1823, they are truly mighty in the shrunken world of today.

The possible conquest of a Latin American nation today would not be, so far as anyone can foresee, by direct assault. It would come, rather, through the insidious process of infiltration, conspiracy, spreading of lies, and the undermining of free institutions, one by one. Highly disciplined groups of communists are busy, night and day, illegally or openly, in the American republics, as they are in every nation of the world. While many persons may now think of Latin America as not being in the line of attack in the modern world struggle, success by the communists in these nations could quickly change all the maps which strategists use in calculating the probabilities of the future.

One American nation has succumbed to communist infiltration. With this exception, however, the other American republics share our desire for peace, freedom, and independence and continue to cooperate effectively in the political councils of the world.

In this Hemisphere we have frequently developed principles and techniques of international collaboration which have later come to be adopted in other parts of the world. Thus, the present global student exchange and technical cooperation programs were initiated by cooperative action of the United States and other American republics well before World War II. The NATO Treaty of 1949 was foreshadowed by the Act of Chapultepec of 1945 and the Treaty of Rio de Janeiro of 1947. The inter-American system preceded the United Nations.

We in this Hemisphere have significantly developed the principle of the sovereign equality of nations; indeed, we can proudly say that we have long been building a system under which all nations, great and small, may live together in peace, mutual respect, and cooperation. The bases of this sytem have found expression and meaning in the Charter of the Organization of American States. Despite differences and serious misunderstandings from time to time, the record of the American nations in settling disputes by peaceful means has been unique, and has largely saved this Hemisphere from the destruction and bloodshed which so often have occurred in other parts of the world.

Today, Latin American influence at the United Nations in support of freedom, peace, international justice, and effective cooperative processes is a powerful force in the difficult construction of a better world.

Abiding political relationships between the United States and the republics of Latin America are of supreme importance to every citizen of this Hemisphere: If we with our long record of cooperation should begin to falter in such relationships, there would seem to be little hope for success with the cooperative processes toward peace in a larger world whose record is less persuasive.

The Cultural Aspects

The building of permanent peace involves the establishment of abiding cooperation among nations of great cultural diversity. This is not an insurmountable task. We have cultural diversity in the United States, but there are sufficient common beliefs, allegiances, and purposes among all the people to make democratic cooperation effective.

Admittedly, the greater the differences in the cultures of nations, the more arduous cooperation becomes. This is the basal difficulty between the communist countries of the East, with their rejection of God and their adherence to a militant dialectic materialism, and the West with its long adherence to the cardinal principles of the Judeo-Christian philosophy.

The cultural diversity of the Western Hemisphere, while notable, is primarily within the philosophic framework of Western civilization—a civilization which seeks to establish and maintain institutions and processes conducive to the attainment of the supreme human purposes and rules of conduct proclaimed by its religious concepts.

It is true, of course, that the culture of the Latin American countries has until recently been oriented primarily toward Europe. The leaders of our neighbors to the South came in great numbers from Spain and Portugal, but also in significant numbers from England, France, Germany, Holland, Italy, Ireland and other countries. For generations, many of them sent their children to Europe to be educated.

During the past twenty-five years this has changed markedly. Today, seventy-five percent of the students of South America who go abroad for study come to the United States; five thousand students from one country alone are now in the secondary schools and universities of the United States. Their tourist travel is predominantly this way. Large numbers of United States citizens live in Latin America, and increasing numbers of our tourists are enjoying the rewarding experience of travel in Latin America. Bi-national institutes and courses in the schools are rapidly making English the second language of Latin America. Reciprocally, Spanish is today the leading foreign language taught in American schools, and the teaching of Portuguese is increasing.

The predominantly Ango-Saxon culture of the United States and the predominantly Latin cultures of the other American republics, the latter often blended with strong and proud Indian influences, are today cross-fertilizing each other, to their mutual enrichment.

The true significance of cultural interchange is this: Abiding cooperation among nations toward common goals must be based on genuine understanding and mutual respect; economic cooperation, political cooperation, and military cooperation may break down under the strain of crisis unless there is much more than superficial understanding of one another's cultures, problems, and aspirations.

Fortunately, while there are wide variations in the types of institutions and degrees of democracy among the American nations, their peoples are all spiritually motivated, desire independence, want to live in peace and to work for rising economic, educational, social and spiritual levels among their peoples. This is their common cultural heritage, their common aspiration.

In this Hemisphere, despite great cultural diversity, there is no real impediment to the development of that understanding on which effective cooperation among our peoples can surely be built.

III. Our Approach to our Assignment

In stating our convictions regarding the transcendent importance of sound relations among the American republics, we have already indicated to some extent the approach we employed in trying to carry out the assignment you gave us. We should like, however, to state in more detail the views we held, prior to the trip to South America, concerning the factors that must be considered in building better relations among the American republics.

We were and still are deeply convinced that abiding cooperation between the United States and the other nations of this Hemisphere will not be the result of wishful thinking or mere accident. Rather, it will flow only from adherence to consistent programs, honorably and consistently observed.

The *first* requisite for good relations among nations is, as we have said, genuine understanding—understanding among governments and peoples.

Cooperation between two or more individuals, between two or more economic groups in a single society, or between two or more nations must be based on understanding. Otherwise the best that we can get is appeasement in a particular situation, and appeasement blows up in our faces at crucial times and places.

Governments must understand one another's problems, methods, purposes, actions and failures to act. They need to understand the difficulties of finding solutions to problems of common interest. They need to know whether good or bad faith is involved. They must understand the consequences which are likely to flow from a particular solution to a problem or from its non-solution. But since the ultimate power in all republics resides in the people, no matter what their degree of democracy, it is equally imperative that there be understanding among peoples as well as governments. National policy today is rarely formed by small cliques. It is made by agricultural, labor, industrial, educational, and civic organizations, and by individual citizens—all of whom find a myriad of ways, day by day, to make their judgments felt in the legislative and executive branches of national governments and in international councils.

The efforts of those who are concerned with developing good relations among nations must be directed first of all to the multitude of methods by which there may be developed among peoples and governments that understanding on which economic, political, military and cultural cooperation may successfully proceed. This is one of the highest tasks of diplomacy.

A *second* requisite for good relations among nations is mutual respect. This is especially important in relations between large and small countries. Nations, like people, have dignity and pride. Only if each respects the rights, interests, aspirations, cultures, and sensibilities of the others can there be true friendship and cooperation between disparate nations.

A *third* closely related requisite for dependable relations among nations is that of the sovereign equality of states. The concepts of respect and equality are inseparable. The whole inter-American system is and must be based on the reality of juridical equality and the concept of consent, not coercion.

A *fourth* requisite to abiding relations in our threatened world is mutual security. This concept is embodied in the Treaty of Rio de Janeiro of 1947: an attack on one American republic is now considered an attack on all. This broadening of the concept of the Monroe doctrine is vital to all the American republics, since it constitutes a curb on aggression within the Hemisphere as well as on aggression by a transoceanic power.

A *fifth* requirement for sound cooperative relations is firm adherence to mutual goals. Generally, the nations of the Americas do have common goals: goals of permanent peace, freedom, independence, rising levels of economic well-being, the advancement of democratic processes, the attainment of spiritual values.

Achieving these goals calls for cooperation in essentially every phase of human activity.

Fortunately, essential cooperative processes are working well in most areas, though not in all.

Political and cultural cooperation is on the whole proceeding satisfactorily. Military cooperation is newer, has unique problems, but is outside the scope of our report.

Economic cooperation involves especially difficult problems. In recent years the economic factors affecting our relations with the nations of Latin America have increased greatly in importance and complexity and now occupy a position of great prominence. Hence, this report will pay particular attention to economic conditions, which in some respects are unsatisfactory both to our friends in Latin America and to us.

This, then, was our approach to our assignment. So we conceived our major task in the field to be that of developing evidence to show how each of the requisites for successful cooperation among nations might be met.

IV. What We Found

It had been our hope that we might visit all twenty Latin American republics. However, since time did not permit this, it was decided that we should visit only the ten republics of South America. Assistant Secretary Cabot had just completed a trip to the Central American and Caribbean countries, you had announced a meeting with the President of Mexico, and it did not seem wise to be selective in the Middle American area among nations which are all vital to our welfare. For these reasons, the trip was scheduled to include Venezuela, Colombia, Ecuador, Peru, Bolivia, Chile, Uruguay, Argentina, Paraguay and Brazil.

Regarding Basic Understanding

We found misunderstanding of the United States in South America—misunderstanding especially of our economic capacity and an underestimation of the degree of the sacrifices the people of the United States have made since 1941.

A great deal of this misunderstanding is a natural consequence of our assistance programs in Europe, the Middle East, and the Far East. The leaders and peoples of Latin America have seen the spending of billions of dollars by our Government under the European Recovery and Mutual Security Acts. Disturbed by the fact that they did not have a large direct share in post-war recovery programs, Latin Americans have tended to forget that they enjoyed an unprecedented boom during the war and post-war period so that there was no need for emergency programs for that area.

In their current thinking they have minimized the fact that the tremendous volume of dollars made available to the free world by the United States tended to sustain directly and indirectly their export markets with Europe and other parts of the world. They have also seemingly minimized the fact that the high level of activity in the United States has resulted in recent years in dollar imports from Latin America which are at least six times pre-war levels, while our imports from Europe have risen to only three times pre-war levels. There has been, in other words, an entirely different situation in the older industrial areas which suffered from wartime destruction and consequent shortages and post-war scarcity of foods and raw materials, and where the problem has been one of restoring production. In Latin America the war and post-war period brought the opposite situation—a tremendous stimulus to production and trade, the greatest in Latin American history.

Nevertheless, our assistance to other areas came precisely at the time that need for foreign capital was growing rapidly in Latin America, and loans to them, though substantial, did not fully satisfy their aspirations. The unfortunate result has been that the peoples of Latin America have sometimes come to the view that the United States considers other areas of the world to be more important to its future than the countries of Latin America. Not realizing that the burdens we have borne during and since the war have strained even our great resources, the feeling persists in Latin American countries that the United States has such vast riches that it could, if it wished, have made substantial funds for development available to them at a time when it was providing billions of dollars to other parts of the world.

Their dissatisfaction is enhanced by the fact that they seek primarily not financial *grants* but *loans*—loans desired to satisfy their driving demands for a broad and immediate development of their economies.

They view with skepticism all explanations of our need to reduce our own public expenditures, including expenditures in the form of loans by the Export-Import Bank. To them our financial capacity appears unlimited.

A tremendous social ferment exists today throughout Latin America. Leaders of the nations to the South, recognizing that too many of their people are desperately poor, that widespread illiteracy is a handicap to progress, that educational and health facilities are woefully inadequate, and that improvement calls for capital for machinery, tools, highways, schools, hospitals, and other facilities, look to the United States for help. They acknowledge that no other part of the world is now developing as rapidly as theirs: that their construction of buildings, roads, power dams, and factories must amaze even the most sophisticated observer. But these achievements are, in discussion at least, made to seem unimportant. They want greater production and higher standards of living, and they want them *now*. The key to both industrial and agricultural improvement, they feel, is capital, capital in great volume.

Unhappily, the need for foreign capital is accompanied throughout most of Latin America by a rising tide of nationalism.

In some respects this surge of nationalism is praiseworthy, for it indicates a growing pride in achievement and an impatient desire to raise dramatically and immediately their standards of living.

But ultra-nationalism, with its blindness to true long-time interests, is a major retrogressive influence in some countries, often closing the door to the very help and cooperation which are so desperately needed. It leads to laws and practices which prevent the entrance of foreign capital essential to development.

Ultra-nationalism is being fostered by communist agitators. Sometimes political leaders who in no sense agree with ultimate communist purposes accept communist support to obtain temporary political advantage. Thus, the two may be joined for a time in the fallacious contention that foreign capital investment, private or public, is in reality a form of imperialism.

The situation is uneven: In some countries, we found a favorable attitude toward the investment of United States capital in local enterprises, and a full recognition of its contribution to economic development. In others we found mild resentment; for example, there was criticism of the fact that certain United States enterprises had originally invested relatively few dollars locally, had expanded over the years through the reinvestment of earnings and the use of some local capital, and now, when exchange difficulties pose a major problem, seek to take out of the country substantial amounts of dollars earned on the total investment. In a few instances we found that the communist propaganda had gained support—propaganda to the effect, as we have said, that the use of foreign capital for productive purposes somehow impinges upon the sovereignty of the nation in which the capital is invested.

But here we met a great inconsistency: While some condemn foreign investment as an actual or potential evil and while some adopt practices and legislation that frighten or make almost impossible the entrance of foreign capital, *all* strongly insist that a greater volume of public and private capital from abroad is needed if they are to meet their just aspirations.

We found misunderstanding of the policies and practices of the International Bank for Reconstruction and Development, and to a lesser extent of the Export-Import Bank of the United States, both of which have important roles in Latin American development. Though most of the countries we visited are members of the International Bank and therefore should understand its authority and operations as an international body, nonetheless among many officials and industrial leaders we discovered a belief that the United States essentially controls the Bank; that a failure of the Bank to make loans in the desired volume is really a decision of the United States Government; that conditions for loans laid down by the Bank—such as the requirement for reestablishment of their credit standing by settling defaulted external debts—are in fact United States requirements and thus constitute intervention in their affairs.

We found attitudes toward United States business enterprises now operating successfully in Latin America to be mixed. Most thoughtful Latin Americans realize that the days when some foreign-owned enterprises might exploit local populations are gone. Today, United States enterprises usually pay higher wages to their employees than local employers do, and also provide better housing, working conditions, schools, hospitals and highways. They pay very substantial sums in taxes, and provide excellent technical training programs in many instances. Most of the United States managers and staff are well-educated, speak Spanish or Portuguese, work for the improvement of conditions in the host country, and are, in general, effective, friendly representatives of the United States and its people.

But they are also the targets of communists and ultra-nationalists. They and their companies are foreign. They represent large amounts of capital. As such, they sometimes suffer from unwarranted attacks which on occasion are directed at our Government.

Where United States enterprises own and operate utilities, an earning rate sufficient to provide for expansion sometimes has not been permitted. This has in some cases led to a rationing of power, which in turn has closed industries part of each day or week, thus throwing men out of work and curtailing production. The facts have been misrepresented to the point that the United States Government is blamed for the failure of the utilities to expand in harmony with the growing industrial requirements Incidentally this situation has occasionally put a premium on public power development.

There is also considerable misunderstanding of the operation of wartime price controls and of post-war terms of trade. We heard many times the claim that a large part of the purchasing power of Latin American exchange reserves accumulated during the war, when availability of imports from the United States was restricted by shortages of goods and shipping, was lost when goods again came into free supply, but at higher prices. There is also the belief that raw materials prices are low in relation to the prices of manufactured goods. However, an examination of the unit value indexes of United States exports to and imports from the other American republics shows that the terms of trade shifted in favor of Latin America from a base of 100 for the 1936-38 average to 120 for 1947 and to 171 for the first quarter of 1953. Preliminary data for the second quarter of 1953 indicate that there was further improvement to an index of 177. In practically every product of trade importance, the Latin American seller stands today in a better position than before World War II.

These complaints likewise do not take into account similar shortages and decline in the purchasing power of savings suffered by United States consumers during and after the war and the serious, and, on the whole, successful effort made by the United States Government, both during the war and during the Korean emergency, to assure continuing supplies of essential goods to the other republics on a basis of equality with our domestic consumers. Nevertheless, the feeling persists in Latin America that the United States should assume some responsibility for maintaining favorable prices of basic commodities which form the bulk of Latin American exports, or, as an alternative, that the United States should refrain from imposing price controls on raw commodities at times when demand for such commodities is abnormally high.

In view of the magnitude of trade and investment relationships between the United States and Latin America, it is not surprising that there are some misunderstandings and disagreements in the economic field. Disagreements are bound to arise in an area of such activity, as indeed they do between sectional interests within the United States.

Fortunately, the misunderstandings we found with respect to economic affairs are not matched in other areas. We were delighted to find a growing understanding of the United States as a nation and as a people. By no means are the peoples and leaders of the area uninformed of our ways of thinking and of our institutions, our democratic philosophy, and our aspirations.

The press of South America daily carries much news from the United States—far more than our newspapers carry about their affairs. Schools teach English and offer courses in American history and literature. Bi-national institutes are teaching English and related subjects to vast numbers of young people. In São Paulo, Brazil, we visited a bi-national institute with 7,000 students; the funds are almost wholly local, the United States Government putting in only a few thousand dollars each year; with local funds, a ten-story building is being built to house the institute, and its sole purpose is to help the people better understand the United States and to build international friendship. We visited a similar institute in Asunción, Paraguay, where 1,200 students are studying English; many of them were in class when we arrived to visit an evening session. They literally overwhelmed us with their friendliness.

American schools in Latin America, which enroll approximately 70,000 students each year and in which the United States invests only about $125,000 annually, are focal points for developing detailed understanding of us as a people and as a nation. American libraries are making a notable contribution. We visited one library with only 8,000 volumes, but it had 48,000 check-outs last year.

The small investment that our Government puts into these cultural and educational activities pays large dividends in understanding and goodwill.

The personnel of United States embassies and specialized agencies are capable, well-informed, and respected. They are intimately a part of the life of the countries to which they are accredited, and thus are able to promote essential understanding. The technical cooperation program, while having as its primary purpose the improvement of agricultural, health, educational, and related conditions, is one of the most successful methods of promoting mutual understanding, for here persons of similar interests are working closely together. Understanding flows from their common interests and purposes.

Thousands of young men and women from Latin America are studying in the high schools and universities of the United States. Most of these, upon their return home, become good ambassadors, promoting inter-cultural understanding.

Some democratic labor leaders have traveled and studied in the United States, and usually they are effective in promoting democratic concepts. We talked with such labor leaders wherever we could. In one country we held a three hour conference with thirty leaders. They told us that at that very time many labor leaders of the country were, at Soviet expense, behind the Iron Curtain, receiving indoctrination. They pleaded with us to find a way to permit a greater number of democratic leaders to come and learn from us. In this connection we noted with concern in more than one country the Soviet practice of extending numerous invitations, with all expenses paid, to communist propaganda conferences and to student, labor and other meetings in Europe and elsewhere. The Communists appear to have ample funds for such purposes.

While, as we have said, the press of South America carries an abundance of news from the United States, unfortunately the functioning of our free press and its value as an independent medium of news and opinion are not too well understood. A good many leaders with whom we talked, while indicating their comprehension of our free, competitive press and news agencies, nonetheless expressed the belief that the United States Government could, if it wished, influence the attitude of the press insofar as their news stories and editorials impinge upon foreign relations. They seem to believe that press criticism of their domestic policies, sometimes based on inadequate understanding of their local conditions, reflects a governmental attitude and that thus, while maintaining an official policy of non-intervention, we do in fact intervene by indirect means.

On the whole, however, we learned that in South America there is a growing understanding of the United States, its methods, and its philosophy, save in the economic field where misunderstanding and lack of information represent a challenge to all of us to work for improvement.

We must in all candor say that many in the United States do not understand adequately the economic difficulties and potentialities in South America—in Latin America as a whole.

In short, overcoming the present lack of information and understanding on both sides with respect to economic problems constitutes in our judgment the greatest single opportunity to strengthen relationships between the United States and the republics of Latin America.

Regarding Mutual Respect and Equality of States

We were pleased to find that our political relations with Latin America are on the whole quite good. They are based upon a concept of mutual respect. The cornerstone of our inter-American relations is the principle of juridical equality of states. An essential concomitant of this principle is that of non-intervention in the internal affairs of others. We respect their right to be different. We must restrict our official negotiations to situations in which the actions, attitudes, or policies of other nations impinge upon our interests or welfare.

This principle of mutual respect is embodied in several inter-American agreements and is firmly accepted in official circles, though it is sometimes misunderstood by the public at large. Acceptance of the non-intervention principle—the real essence of the Good Neighbor Policy—gave impetus to the Pan-American movement in the 1930's by eliminating the most serious obstacle to confidence between the United States and her Hemisphere neighbors. The United States now consistently emphasizes that our common American destiny rests on the freely extended cooperation of the American nations—each the master of its own house but all working together for mutual benefit and progress.

In every country we visited we found genuine pride in the inter-American system, with 21 nations meeting regularly at a council table to discuss their mutual problems, as the forerunner of efforts toward organized international cooperation. We found also that there is general adherence, even devotion, to the series of principles which have evolved through the years as the guiding rules of inter-American conduct: In addition to non-intervention, they include the juridical equality of American nations, solidarity in defense of the continent, solution of inter-American disputes by peaceful means, consultation in matters of common interest before action is taken, and cooperation in economic, social, political and cultural programs of mutual benefit.

The concept of hemispheric solidarity, we learned, is cherished by all the American republics. This solidarity is the Hemisphere's strongest assurance of its own security; it is, indeed, a great contribution of the Americas toward peace in the world.

Regarding Mutual Security

Although, as we have said, an analysis of military cooperation is outside the scope of this report, we were gratified to find everywhere a recognition of the strength and vitality of the mutual security principles embodied in the Rio Treaty. We were informed of steps being taken to translate these principles into instruments of effective common action. Though much remains to be done before the military defense of the Hemisphere against external aggression can be assumed as a collective responsibility, substantial gains are being made. Some of these gains have come through the actions of individual governments. Important progress is also being made through the assistance we are giving to the military establishments of those countries with which we have military assistance agreements. In the wider international scene, the Latin American states have joined with us in giving support to United Nations objectives for the security and defense of the free world against aggression.

Acceptance of the principle of peaceful settlement of difficulties *is a fact* among the American republics.

The importance of this cannot be over-emphasized. It is unique in the history of mankind.

It must not be thought that tensions do not sometimes develop between basically friendly nations in this Hemisphere. They do. On our trip, some existing ones were explained to us in detail. But in each of these situations we were assured that the nations feeling aggrieved would abide by their pledge "not to resort to the threat or use of force" in any manner inconsistent with the U.N. Charter or the Rio Treaty. The leaders and peoples of the American nations are convinced that employing the machinery of the inter-American system for the peaceful settlement of disputes provides the best method for solving intergovernmental problems within the Hemisphere. Again and again, we were told that recourse to anything other than peaceful settlement of a controversy is unthinkable.

Regarding Common Goals

The American nations have, since achieving independence from their mother countries, struggled with uneven success toward democratically-functioning republican forms of government. If democracy is not perfect in any of them, including the United States, it is nonetheless an ideal which neither reactionaries nor radicals find it feasible to ignore. There is a strong feeling among the peoples of all the Americas for the dignity and worth of the individual.

While there is a wide gulf between the most authoritarian and the most democratic of the regimes—Uruguay, for example, justly takes pride in the advanced development of its political democracy—virtually all the nations of Latin America seek the goals of permanent peace, independence, rising levels of economic well-being, and the attainment of the basic values of Western civilization.

In our conversations we developed the conviction that common dedication to the achievement of these goals is the greatest single guarantee we have that the nations of this Hemisphere will continue to work amicably together. This cooperation can be made more effective as understanding among our peoples and governments increases. It can be fortified by our unswerving adherence to the principles we have discussed in this report.

Attaining some of the goals is the responsibility of each individual nation. This is true, for example, of gradually extending the blessings of democracy to all the people of a country. Despite all difficulties, varying degrees of progress toward genuine democracy are being made in most of the nations of the Hemisphere.

But most of the goals the nations of the Americas seek can be reached only by cooperative effort. We have already discussed cooperative efforts toward some of these. We now wish to concentrate on the problem of mutually-beneficial economic cooperation designed to help the peoples of the Western Hemisphere improve their levels of well-being. Economic improvement is the greatest single desire of the leaders and peoples of Latin America. And economic cooperation is without question the key to better relations between the United States and the nations to the South. Everything else, no matter how important, must take secondary place, at least in the absence of war.

Regarding Economic Development

Despite the difficulties and misunderstandings which we have enumerated in the economic field, no one could return from a trip such as ours without deep feelings of faith and optimism in the future of Latin America. The outstanding impressions left with us are of the tremendous vitality and activity found everywhere—of a continent in transition, in various stages in different countries—of the sights and sounds of construction in every city—of green fields on what short years ago were deserts. South

America is truly a spectacle of enormous variation, with giant skyscrapers and new factories standing beside early Indian and Spanish structures, and with modern agricultural experiment stations operating in areas still characterized by primitive practices and feudalistic systems of farming.

Abundant Resources Available

Human and physical resources are great. A rapidly growing population of willing and active workers is an asset, though promising to be a problem unless production, especially of foodstuffs, is substantially increased. New leadership in business and agriculture has manifested itself in many countries. There is a growing awareness of the many things which must be done if the aspirations of the people for a better life are to be achieved.

The vast agricultural and mineral resources of Latin America are only partially developed. If the energies of people are properly joined with capital, with incentives for self-betterment, and with stable political and economic conditions, we shall witness an enormous agricultural, mineral, and industrial development in Latin America in the next twenty-five years.

The Growth of Population

One profoundly significant fact which will affect Latin America in its long-time future, but which was seldom mentioned to us by the leaders we interviewed, is the growth of the population. In 1950 the population of Latin America exceeded that of the United States for the first time since the colonial era. In each decade since 1920, Latin America's population has risen at a progressively faster rate. The present rate of 2.5 percent per year exceeds that of any other major region of the world and is at least twice the world average.

If this rate continues, Brazil's present population of 53,000,000—already more than that of the United Kingdom or of any Latin nation of Europe—will double in about 35 years. Within 50 years Latin America's population, now about equal to that of the United States and Canada, may reach 500,000,000, or double the total anticipated for the latter two countries.

The future problem is even greater than is suggested by these figures, for the rapid introduction and spread of public health measures will have an appreciable effect on the death rate. As malaria, yaws, typhus, tuberculosis, and other diseases are conquered, the rate of population increase may well accelerate. We visited numerous health projects and learned how malaria is being eliminated by spraying with DDT and yaws is being conquered by the use of penicillin. In every country we found determined efforts to reduce or eliminate diseases which for centuries have plagued South America.

Thus, the problem is not merely that of increasing production to improve the lot of the existing population—and in the countries we visited the per capita annual income ranged from a low of less than a hundred dollars a year to a high of about four hundred dollars a year. The problem is also to win a race with growing numbers. If the contest is to result in a higher average standard of living, increases in production must appreciably outstrip population growth.

Fortunately, since the war the annual increase in production has averaged nearly five percent. Thus, despite the rapid growth of population, an over-all increase of approximately 2.5 percent in per capita output per year has been achieved. This compares with an average annual per capita growth of 2.1 percent in the United States during the period 1869-1952. It is evident, then, that a long-sustained production increase equal to that of the post-war years could accomplish wonders in Latin America.

The Dependence on Raw Commodities

The export economies of most of the other American republics have been built around their ability to provide certain primary materials for consumption in the United States and Europe. Their supply of imported consumer goods and other materials depends upon their ability to sell these products to the rest of the world. This has been a major reason for the intense desire of the leaders to industrialize and diversify the economies of their countries. We encountered everywhere a widespread desire for steel mills, metal fabricating plants, food processing plants, textile industries and a wide variety of consumer-goods fabricating facilities.

Industrialization has gone so apace in some countries, notably in Brazil and Chile, that it has outstripped the production of food and fibre, as well as the fundamental services of transportation, communication and power. This imbalance has been recognized, but it is difficult and will take time to correct. It is a serious roadblock in the way of balanced economic development.

On the basis of our observations we believe that the much-needed balance in economic development will be more rapidly and soundly achieved if the relatively free play of market forces and competitive-price mechanisms are allowed to operate in all countries, as they are now operating in several countries of the continent. The allocation of resources, labor, and capital will then be permitted to occur in the interest of efficient production, distribution, and consumption, and at lower prices.

Agricultural Production

This is particularly pertinent with regard to the pressing need in most Latin American countries for a rapid increase in food production. Larger, more efficient production is absolutely basic to the continent, but agricultural improvement is usually a relatively slow process. In Latin America, improvement in farm production calls not only for price incentives (to which we shall refer again), but also for the establishment of agricultural research stations and extension systems, for far-reaching programs in fundamental education to decrease illiteracy in the rural areas, and for capital to finance the purchase or importation of machinery.

We were encouraged by what we saw on our visit to the modern, effective agricultural experiment station and agricultural college at Palmira, Colombia—projects aided by the United States in the technical cooperation program. We were similarly stimulated by what we saw of the work of SCIPA [*Servicio Cooperativo Inter-americano de Producción de Alimentos*] in Peru and STICA [*Servicio Técnico Inter-americano de Cooperación Agrícola*] in Paraguay—outstandingly successful examples of our technical cooperation. Indeed in every country we visited where our technical program is operating, we saw evidence which convinced us that the funds the United States is putting into "servicio"-managed agricultural projects is one of the best expenditures made by our Government. At long last science is being introduced to the agriculture of the entire continent. One new variety of corn will produce four times as much as the native variety. Research in genetics, entomology, livestock selection and breeding, fertilization, crop rotations, conservation and so on is showing spectacular results. And the discoveries in the stations are already being applied on many farms, though general adoption may have to await progress in fundamental education to decrease illiteracy, the building of practical extension services, and the widening of rural vocational training.

Agriculturally, Latin America is today reminiscent of the United States in the late 19th century. Primitive and inefficient practices are just beginning to be replaced by modern scientific farming.

Major credit for the accomplishments to date belongs to the local peoples and their governments, and of course theirs is the major task in the future. The technical assistance we have provided has been of enormous help. United States specialists in all branches of agricultural science have been skillful in training local leaders in research and extension work. Now many American republics have agricultural colleges for the training of expert personnel.

Fortunately, several of the countries recognize that to stimulate domestic food output they must restore the incentive that can flow from the price mechanism. Through inflation, price controls, and subsidy exchange rates, some governments have greatly discouraged domestic agricultural production and encouraged the use of scarce foreign exchange for food imports. So serious has this been that some countries which formerly produced enough of such products as wheat and sugar to meet most of their domestic requirements have recently been importing more and more of these very commodities.

Ceilings placed on domestic prices of foodstuffs as an emergency attempt to control inflation have exerted a regressive influence on domestic producers. Especially favorable exchange rates for food imports have sometimes made it impossible for the local farmer to compete. This has led in some instances to situations of sheer folly—to scarce foreign exchange being used to import food which in turn has been illegally re-exported in large volume at good profit by contraband traders.

Such policies have caused a shift in land resources in the affected areas from much-needed production to less economic and less basic production. As a result, the real standard of living of the people has suffered. Such policies also tend to vitiate, temporarily at least, the positive benefits of United States technical cooperation in agricultural experimentation and demonstration, and work extended for agricultural machinery, irrigation, and related purposes.

In view of the foregoing, we were indeed encouraged to learn from a number of governmental and financial leaders that they have become aware of the self-defeating nature of the policies which have been followed in some countries and that they are taking steps to make possible more realistic domestic prices and exchange rates for agricultural products.

The Need for Transportation

A government official in Ecuador told us that his country has three urgent needs: Roads, roads, and more roads. At present in Ecuador, as in other countries, mountainous terrain often cuts off rich agricultural regions from population and industrial centers. Next to an increase in agricultural production, development of transportation is the paramount need in most of the Latin American countries. The two are, in fact, inextricably linked. We found this dramatically exemplified in Bolivia. For many years, Bolivia was preoccupied with the mining of tin. She neglected her agriculture to such an extent that today she must import about fifty percent of the food required to meet the meager diet of the population. Bolivia is today trying to diversify, and to expand agriculture. The major opportunity to increase agricultural production is on the virgin lands of the Santa Cruz region, which only now is becoming economically accessible as a result of the construction of a new highway, financed in large part with an Export-Import Bank loan.

In many of the countries we visited, we found that there is real opportunity for assisting in planning and executing sound transportation-improvement projects, as has already been done in Colombia, Ecuador, and Bolivia, not only with loans, but also with technical assistance. Better highway, rail, harbor, inland waterway, and air transportation facilities will often create conditions which would make possible the development of mining, manufacturing, agricultural, and other enterprises, most of which could be financed privately.

The Need for Power and Fuel

Another serious impediment to a well-balanced development of the other American republics is the shortage of power and fuel. The demand for power in an expanding economy is almost insatiable. All over South America we witnessed the spectacle of severe power shortages and of potential shortages, even where herculean efforts were being made to develop new sources. Power facilities, especially hydroelectric facilities, are gluttons for capital. Hence, it is going to be difficult for countries short of capital to keep up with the demands for power.

Private electric power enterprises in several countries have demonstrated a readiness to expand generating facilities. They have given assurances of their willingness to bring in the necessary foreign capital to pay for imports of generating machinery. Nevertheless, we noted cases in which the rates that the companies are permitted to charge for electricity have been frozen at low levels while inflation and exchange depreciation have forced operating costs upward. In such a squeeze the private companies cannot finance expansion programs. It lies within the power of the respective governments to remedy the situation by establishing rates adequate to permit private financing.

The International and Export-Import Banks have demonstrated their willingness to provide reasonable support for power generation. There is an opportunity, certainly, to do more. Foreign capital support is indispensable, not only because of the magnitude of the problem, but also because most of the essential equipment must be imported. The financial support should in our judgment be forthcoming provided (*a*) that the assured rate structure will permit long-time amortization of the loans, and (*b*) that improved methods of local financing and better fiscal policies are adopted so that the large amounts of local capital necessary for power facilities do not cause distortions in the economy.

No large nation can have a satisfactory industrial development in the absence of a cheap, indigenous source of energy. Hydroelectric energy can make a contribution, but its capital requirements are high. Certainly no economy in South America can expect to function exclusively on electric energy. It must have coal, oil, or other combustibles.

Colombia, Ecuador, Peru and Venezuela have oil, and both Colombia and Peru have coal resources. Chile has coal mines, some oil, and attractive hydroelectric possibilities. Argentina and Bolivia may have an indigenous supply of oil to protect them for at least the near future. While exploration has not proceeded far enough to provide assurance, the best opinion is that there should be oil resources of exploitable size in Brazil. Today, Brazil has a production of about 2,500 barrels a day as against about a 125,000-barrel daily requirement. Last year, Brazil imported more than $250,000,000 worth of petroleum products. At the present rate of growth in consumption of petroleum products, it would not be long before the foreign exchange requirements for fuel would become an impossible burden. Thus, the need for oil development in Brazil is fundamental.

The manner in which Brazil solves this problem will be of crucial importance. Based on experience elsewhere in the world, and even under the most favorable circumstances for oil exploration—and with good luck—it will be many years before Brazil can be self-sufficient. The capital needs are difficult to estimate, but are very large. It may be pertinent to note that private companies will have spent in Canada more than $800,000,000 before 300,000 barrels a day are produced, transported, and refined in that country.

The Need for Industries

Another aspect of balanced economic development in South America relates to manufacturing activities. Countries lacking basic and secondary manufacturing industries understandably seek to remedy that deficiency. The development of healthy, competitive industry in South America should aid substantially in promoting higher standards of living. In nearly every country we visited we saw new industrial plants under construction. The city of São Paulo, Brazil, for instance, is the fastest growing metropolitan center in the world, with hundreds of new plants and businesses, and Medellín, Colombia, has notably modern, industrial establishments and manufacturing techniques.

In some countries there is, in fact, some danger of excessive industrialization— industrialization for its own sake, at any cost, rather than for the sound contribution it can make to economic progress. In a highly developed country possessing adequate resources and capital, unwise industrial development is serious enough; in a country which is short of capital and other resources, it can have critical consequences. Availability of local raw materials and of fuel resources are vital. If adequate fuel resources are lacking, increased industrialization, raising as it must the demand for fuel imports, places a still greater burden on an already overburdened balance of payments. In such a situation, a due regard for the balance-of-payments impact of specific industrialization would require evidence that the new industry directly or indirectly earn or save foreign exchange, and could operate without continued subsidy. High cost and uneconomic industries that absorb transportation, power, raw materials and other scarce resources may affect adversely the entire economy.

Many manufacturing industries, mines, processing plants, and businesses in South America are wholly or partly owned by United States enterprises. In some countries they are operating with no difficulty and are making good profits. In others, where exchange difficulties exist, they may have trouble in importing essential products or in exporting earnings, even though locally their operations are profitable. We met with large numbers of United States businessmen in nearly every country. We were happy to find that they wish to carry on their work for the benefit of their stockholders. They impressed us with a highly developed sense of business and political statesmanship. One company head told us of a development which may be, probably is, typical. When his company first went into business in South America, it imported annually more than 450 different processed items in quantity. Gradually the company has stimulated the development of local, small industries to supply its needs. Today, practically all items are locally manufactured.

We found a growing tendency for private United States investors to join with local investors in establishing and operating industries and businesses. This seemed to gain favorable reactions in most countries.

During the recent past, we learned, a number of European groups have made direct investments in South America along lines quite parallel to United States investments. These groups are supplying know-how and some capital and constitute active competition with their United States counterparts. There is also developing in South America rather keen competition especially in the sale of capital goods. In this competition, European suppliers are able, in large part through the support of their governments, to offer term payments usually considerably longer than is customary with American suppliers of comparable equipment. This is visible evidence of the export drive so much in vogue in the European industrial countries.

The Menace of Inflation

A vital contribution which can be made to sound development in the other American republics, as in any country, is the prevention of inflation and the maintenance of high levels of economic activity with relative price stability—in short, the maintenance of honest money. Inflation has often distorted economic development and disturbed living standards in Latin America as it has in other parts of the world. It has sometimes destroyed confidence in the currency, impaired the growth of sorely -needed local savings for development, led to the flight abroad of domestic capital, and encouraged speculation in local real estate rather than investment in productive enterprises of benefit to the population. Some Latin American governments, not unlike other governments, have tried to deal with the symptoms of inflation rather than its causes. In so doing they have resorted to various forms of control of prices, trade, and investment, as well as to varying degrees of government intervention, even to the point of government ownership of enterprises which directly compete with private industry and capital.

Inflation cannot be controlled effectively over any sustained period; it must be prevented. This requires unpopular measures in the field of budget expenditures, taxation, and credit policies to assure that the growth in the money supply and in money incomes does not outstrip growth of production. Policies designed to promote efficient production and at the same time keep money honest are as difficult to adopt and maintain in Latin America as they are in the United States and other countries. It is noteworthy, however, that several of the American republics have succeeded on various occasions in balancing their budgets while maintaining reasonable, sound rates of economic development. Some have been successful in stabilizing bank credit expansion, or at least in keeping its growth within satisfactory limits, by means of effective central bank policy and the judicious enforcement of appropriate requirements on commercial bank reserves. These general restraints, while often unpopular with would-be borrowers, are vital to the maintenance of a sound currency, a balanced economy, and a satisfactory growth of domestic savings.

We visited with financial experts, in and out of government, who said that among the *general* restraints which their governments might appropriately employ is the price deterrent on imports by appropriate upward adjustment of rates of exchange so that domestic prices are more nearly in line with world prices. Efforts to avoid this unpleasant necessity by direct licensing of imports and by multiple and unrealistic exchange rates have often created new difficulties worse than the shortages these devices were designed to remedy. Where inadequate imports are allowed and where unduly cheap rates for such imports prevail, the fortunate recipient of an import permit is often able to sell his goods at great profit. This situation leads to undue energy being expended on efforts to get permits, and on efforts to get reclassification of goods or special exemptions from the authorities, and can easily lead to favoritism in the issuance of permits. In addition, it often leads to prices for imported goods at the consumer level even higher than they might be with a realistic import exchange rate.

Mention has been made of the value of realistic domestic prices and import rates of exchange to encourage adequate agricultural production and to give consumers and businessmen more freedom in buying abroad. Of equal or greater importance is the function of realistic export rates of exchange in giving incentive to the producer and exporter to increase sales abroad, thus expanding the national earnings of foreign exchange and enlarging the country's ability to buy needed articles from foreign suppliers for further economic development and consumption. Penalizing certain major exports by permitting them to move only at unfavorable rates of exchange, while producing an apparent short-run advantage to the government in the form of "cheap" acquisition of exchange, may prove costly in the long run by discouraging a proper expansion of basic exports. In extreme situations this use of a multiple exchange rate system has tended to price the country's goods out of the market abroad and to discourage domestic production while stimulating domestic consumption. We learned that several South American governments have discovered this to be a costly experiment.

Well-trained experts of most of the South American countries are fully aware of these fundamental facts, and in a number of the countries attempts are being made to deal effectively with the conditions discussed. Candor compels us to say that the decisions involved frequently pose difficult and unpalatable political choices.

The Need for Capital

It is difficult to exaggerate the need of South America for capital to promote sound economic development. Agricultural and mineral resources, as well as industries, are awaiting the capital, the know-how, and the right conditions for expansion. The greater part of this capital must come from private investment, chiefly from local savings. For the development of local savings and local capital markets great emphasis must be placed on sound budgetary, fiscal and credit policies and the restoration of confidence in the value of the local currency.

We found no well established capital markets in South America in the sense we know them in this country. Constructive efforts are being made in Brazil, Colombia, and Venezuela; Argentina, Uruguay, and Chile have markets for bonds and stocks. But much remains to be done.

Foreign private capital, from the United States and other countries, has played and, under appropriate conditions, will continue to play an important complementary role in South American development. There are certain limited encouragements to private foreign investment within the power of the United States Government; we understand that consideration is now being given to what in this connection might appropriately be recommended to the Congress.

Basically, however, it is abundantly clear that private capital cannot be induced by the United States Government to flow to other countries, even to the most friendly. It must be *attracted* by the nation desiring the capital. United States private capital will be invested where conditions of political and economic stability and fair and equitable treatment provide it an opportunity for reasonable profit and assurance of remitting earnings. The fact is often overlooked that there is too much opportunity at home for United States capital for it to go abroad unless it is wanted and is sure of fair treatment.

Measures which can be taken by foreign governments to attract private capital are too well known to require extensive discussion: They include adequate opportunities for fair profit, reasonable provisions for transfer of earnings and amortization, equitable labor and management laws and regulations, and freedom from fear of discriminatory treatment, expropriation with inadequate compensation, or unfair Government intervention. Inflation and financial instability also play a part in many countries in discouraging or repelling private investment. A genuine belief in the value to the community of private competitive enterprise and private profit is perhaps the most fundamental requirement.

Private investment by United States capital in South America has been substantial and continues to be made in impressive volume in some countries where experience and prospects are favorable. Venezuela, Brazil, Colombia and Peru are examples of countries where substantial investments have been made and where United States companies appear interested in making further investments. In some other countries the experience of private capital has caused it to become timid, if not actually anxious to leave the country. In several instances, United States private capital has had unhappy experiences—experiences of "creeping expropriation," of inadequate opportunites to make reasonable returns due to government intervention, and of inability to transfer earnings into dollars. In considering private investment abroad, prospective investors will naturally seek the opinion of those who already are operating in a country.

Most of the conditions which affect the flow of private capital must be considered also by those who weigh the possibilities of extending public loans. That there is need for further development which might be met by public loans is evident in nearly every country we visited. International Bank and Export-Import Bank loans have played an important part in the unprecedented development now under way in all of Latin America. In its relatively brief period of operations the International Bank has authorized over $400 million in loans to Latin American countries, primarily for electric power, highways, railways, and agricultural development. The Export-Import Bank, with a longer history of operations, had outstanding credit authorizations to Latin American countries of over $1,350 million as of September 30, 1953. The experiences of the two banks have been highly favorable. As will be indicated later, public loans can often help provide the basic facilities in economic development that can foster further development through private capital investment.

The Need for Better Management

One of the significant facts about South America which impressed itself upon us is the shortage of trained management personnel in many fields. This deficiency varies considerably from country to counrtry. It is most noticeable in such state-owned enterprises as railroads and communication systems. In the private business community, there is discernible an increasing improvement in management due to training provided by technical schools at home and to an increase in overseas education. The infusion of experienced business men from abroad has also helped. In the field of management and other technical training lies one of the great opportunities we have to help Latin America. Some aid is now provided by the United States in the technical cooperation program.

Their Concern about Trade Restrictions

This part of our report—on the economic situation in South America—would not be complete without reference to what governmental, industrial, agricultural, and other leaders told us about those United States practices and attitudes which vitally affect their welfare. We have referred to some of these in a previous section.

They expressed to us the hope that the United States will continue a high level of prosperity, for they realize that economic difficulty here would seriously affect their welfare and endanger the whole free world. They stated emphatically their conviction that a constantly expanding trade between our countries would be mutually advantageous and they expressed the hope that the people of the United States would not favor restrictive legislation which would impede the further development of trade.

Everywhere leaders expressed concern about our future tariff policies. They pointed out that they are paying customers, and therefore they feel that the United States should welcome imports from them. They spend in United States markets most of the dollars thus earned.

Serious apprehension was expressed over measures introduced in our Congress which would increase restrictions on United States imports of petroleum, lead, zinc, and fish. The possibility of further restrictions on wool and other agricultural products concern them. They have, we found, a real appreciation of the problems of our domestic producers of these products, but they are nervous about what they believe to be a tendency in the United States to increase tariffs on these and other products.

Wherever we went, leaders of South America asked that we urge upon our Government and people the need at least for *stability* in the rules of international trade. There can be no doubt that they would be greatly injured economically, and their friendship and faith in us weakened, if we did less than stabilize the measures which affect their trade with us.

V. What Should Be Done?

In the light of the total situation in South America as we found it, my associates and I have, since we came home, considered carefully what the Executive Branch of our Government, the Congress of the United States, and leaders in private life might do to strengthen relationships between our country and the friendly neighboring nations to the South.

Since the other four members of the special mission are officers of the Federal Government, and may therefore make their convictions known from time to time in the official policy councils of government, it seems appropriate that this concluding section should reflect my personal views.

Strengthening Understanding and Mutual Respect

It seems evident that the first requirement is a better understanding in the United States of the importance of firm and abiding relationships between the United States and the nations of Latin America. Sentimentally, at least, the people of our country want good relations with their neighbors. But good relations may call for new policies, actions, or legislation. These will come to fruition only if there is a broad comprehension of the great need for stable political, cultural, military, and economic cooperation, as my colleagues and I have explained in this report.

While knowledge of us is greater in Latin America than is our knowledge of them, there are nonetheless many serious misunderstandings on their part which need to be overcome. The task of developing the essential understanding is a mutual one.

(1) Existing programs of intellectual and cultural cooperation—including scholarships, bi-national centers and language institutes, libraries, and exchange of persons—should be expanded.

The United States should increase its support of the American schools in Latin America which now have some 70,000 students enrolled. Our total budget for this purpose during the current fiscal year is about $125,000. This sum should be increased modestly, to $150,000 or $175,000 a year.

We should encourage more visits and lecture tours in Latin America by United States citizens who are eminent in the sciences, arts, and letters, for Latin Americans have a high appreciation of the cultural values of life.

We should encourage publishers, editors, business, agricultural and labor groups, students and others to travel more extensively in Latin America, and Government departments should maintain information services for groups planning such trips.

We should increase the number of invitations to leading Latin Americas to visit the United States, arranging, with the assistance of universities, lecture tours for them to help defray expenses.

We should also seek to arrange cultural exchanges in all branches of the arts.

Especially should we invite more democratic labor leaders of the Latin American nations to this country, helping them to arrange tours so that they may understand fully the functioning of our private competitive enterprise system and the key place free workers occupy in our society. We should expand our program of providing training courses for promising labor leaders.

With the cooperation of the American Council on Education and the National Education Association, we should encourage universities and schools to establish close cooperative relations with comparable institutions in Latin America. This practice is common between American universities and schools, on the one hand, and Middle Eastern and Far Eastern universities and schools on the other. One of the best demonstations in building understanding and good will my associates and I found on the trip was in Colombia where the agricultural college and experiment station at Palmira have close ties with Michigan State College.

(2) The press, radio, and motion picture programs of the United States Information Agency in Latin America, though limited in scope, are effective. In the conditions prevailing virtually throughout Latin America, local radio and motion picture pro-

grams have been particularly successful in getting our measures to the masses. They should be continued and expanded, for truthful information widely disseminated is one indispensable means of countering communist propaganda activities aimed at disrupting hemispheric solidarity and free world unity.

(3) The United States National Commission for UNESCO, which cooperates with the Secretary of State in promoting understanding among the peoples of the world, might well be requested to expand its program with respect to Latin America. If the Commission were willing to do this, pertinent educational and informational materials could be distributed by the nation-wide organizations represented on the Commission, and informative group discussions on Latin America might develop in the cities and towns and on the farms all over the country. Universities, secondary schools, and elementary schools could be encouraged by the Commission to do more in their curricular and extracurricular activities.

(4) It is my hope that several of the large foundations of the United States will make additional scholarships available to students of Latin America, especially to students in those countries where exchange difficulties make travel to and study in the United States difficult. Further, one or more of the foundations, with the cooperation of a university, could perform a valuable service by establishing as a pilot project a bi-national institute in the United States, modeled on those now functioning in several Latin American nations. The institute should be largely self-supporting, and should teach Spanish, Portuguese, and Latin American history and literature. Students should be of both school and post-school age.

(5) United States business firms now operating in Latin America might help their public relations and promote understanding by increasing their support of the American schools and the bi-national institutes in their host countries, and by offering scholarships and training grants to talented young Latin Americans.

(6) Attitudes toward United States business enterprises now operating successfully in Latin America have been discussed earlier in this report. United States companies in Latin America are playing an important role in promoting better understanding and friendship among the peoples of the American republics. They should seek constantly to ensure that their staffs are good ambassadors as well as good businessmen. By their actions and their relations with the public they can do still more to increase the understanding of the contribution which enlightened business methods are making to the local economies.

(7) In addition to the officially-sponsored exchange-of-persons programs, there are opportunities for distinguished American scholars who speak Spanish or Portuguese to lecture in universities in many of the American republics. On our trip we met three Emeritus Professors from the United States who were doing this. This may, indeed, be an attractive field for the great number of scholars, now retired from American universities, who still wish to be of great service to their country and who, with retirement benefits, can afford to undertake assignments at the modest salaries offered by most Latin American institutions.

(8) In Massachusetts, New York, Florida, Louisiana, California and Texas—and no doubt in other states—are private associations whose major purpose is to develop better understanding in the United States of Latin American culture, histories, problems, and aspirations. Some have active business, educational, and cultural services. They provide forums for distinguished Latin American visitors who come to the

United States. This type of association merits the thoughtful consideration of states and cities not now having such institutions. The large number of Foreign Policy Associations in a multitude of American communities might well give special attention to our relations with Latin America.

(9) We should look to the free mass communication media of the United States, and especially to the press associations and newspapers and magazines with Latin American correspondents and circulations, as a major means of promoting essential understanding. Certainly the information media of the United States have a profound effect on attitudes in both the United States and Latin America, and thus on official and unofficial relationships. It would be helpful if these media regularly found it possible to do more than report the spectacular occurrences in the Latin American countries. A revolution will merit widespread attention by the press, radio and television, but the long-term underlying causes may not. Yet the basic causes may have more to do with the future welfare of our country—and with international relationships—than did the revolution which brought new leaders to power.

I believe deeply that adequately-informed peoples in the Americas can find cooperative and mutually-advantageous solutions to hosts of problems, but partially-informed citizens are likely to foster tensions, disputes, and serious ill will.

It is recognized that the primary function of the press is to convey news, not to promote understanding and good will among nations as such; but in the modern world struggle, in which we need all the friends we can get, citizens must depend greatly on mass communication media for the evidence relevant to valid judgments. The media which have correspondents in Latin America should consider that part of the world so important to the United States that they will assign their best men and women there, as indeed some of them now do.

Similarly, United States dispatches to Latin America can faithfully interpret or grossly misrepresent our intentions and actions. As stated previously in this report, the press and radio of South America daily bulge with news gathered and dispatched by our great free information system.

In mass communications between the United States and Latin America, several considerations may be pertinent:

Varying degrees of authoritarianism exist in Latin America. There are also countries with democratic practices equal to ours. Most American nations which still have degrees of feudalism and dictatorship are moving gradually toward democratic concepts and practices. Commendation for their achievements may not be as newsworthy as criticism of their failures, but it could surely contribute to understanding and good will.

It would be helpful if the United States public better understood that our Government must distinguish carefully between actions and policies which are wholly within the jurisdiction of a single nation, and those policies and actions which impinge upon our welfare or the welfare of the community of nations.

(10) The Tenth Inter-American Conference, which is scheduled to be held at Caracas in March 1954, will present a timely opportunity to the United States to emphasize our positive interest in strengthening efforts to increase intercultural understanding as the foundation of mutually advantageous cooperation in all relevant areas.

Strengthening Economic Cooperation

Before undertaking to make specific recommendations on strengthening our economic cooperation with the countries of Latin America, I feel impelled to express the view that the greatest contribution which the United States can make to the well-being of the world as a whole is the maintenance of a high level of economic activity in this country at relatively stable prices.

In this report, my associates and I have described conditions which affect economic development in Latin America. We have also discussed practices in certain countries which deter the flow of private and public capital needed for balanced development. Whether such conditions are changed is up to the nations involved. Some of my recommendations for strengthening economic relationships must be made on the assumption that deterrents to the flow of capital will be altered, or must be considered only with respéct to those nations where serious deterrents do not exist.

I specifically recommend:

(1) That the United States adopt and adhere to trade policies with Latin America which possess stability, and with a minimum of mechanisms permitting the imposition of increased tariffs or quotas. I consider this matter of stability and consistency the outstanding requirement.

The nations of Latin America pay for what they obtain from us. Their purchases from us are governed almost wholly by the volume of our purchases from them.

Occasionally the importation of a particular commodity may cause temporary difficulty for one of our industries. But if we raise the tariff on that commodity, the export sale of other United States commodities is certain to decline. The question then becomes: Which United States industry, if any, should be temporarily disadvantaged? And the change in our tariff may seriously weaken the entire economy of a Latin American nation.

In a mature economy, and especially in a creditor country, it often develops that policies which are clearly in the national interest are nonetheless detrimental to one or more economic groups. This fact is not peculiar to problems of trade with Latin America. A solution to it would be widely beneficial and would enhance the probability of maintaining stable economic relations between the United States and Latin America.

(2) That the United States adopt a long-range basic-material policy which will permit it to purchase for an enlarged national stockpile certain imperishable materials when prices of such materials are declining.

We import from Latin America many minerals and other primary products whose prices on the world market are subject to wide fluctuation. To a country which sells the products of its mines and then purchases processed goods and food from abroad, a sharp decline in the price of its minerals can be calamitous, leading not only to lower standards of living, but also to political instability.

The United States could not, even if it wished, control world prices of such commodities, and it is clear that private enterprises will buy wherever they can get materials of the needed quality at the least cost.

However, in the light of the findings of the Report of the President's Materials Policy Commission, which predicted increasing United States deficiencies in important materials, serious consideration should be given to a new policy looking toward building more massive stockpiles when world prices of the storable commodities are declining. Such a policy would, in my opinion, be of immense benefit in protecting the long-term economic future of the United States, and would provide at least some degree of stability in world market prices of raw materials.

I recognize that the implementation of such a policy would presumably have to await the time when United States fiscal resources are not severely strained by defense expenditures; further, this policy is now partly in effect in the defense stockpiling program.

(3) That the United States carefully examine whether or not it would be appropriate to amend present tax laws to remove existing obstacles to private investment abroad.

(4) That public loans for the foreign-currency costs of sound economic development projects, for which private financing is not available, go forward on a substantial scale, provided, of course, that the borrowers take the necessary measures to ensure that they are good credit risks.

It is generally agreed that the International Bank for Reconstruction and Development should have the principal responsibility for making development loans, as compared with the shorter-range lending operations of the United States Export-Import Bank. However, it seems essential that the United States maintain a national lending institution to make sound development loans which are in our national interest, but which might not be made by an international agency.

One difficulty here is that the Administration's efforts to balance the budget would be affected by large loans made by the Export-Import Bank, since such loans are a charge against the annual cash budget. The Bank should, therefore, consider using the means available to it to raise more of its funds from the private capital market.

(5) That the United States stand ready to give appropriate technical help to the Latin American countries that express a desire to work out more orderly ways of determining how their resources, including their borrowing capacity, can make the greatest contribution to their economic development. It is noteworthy that the International Bank has made valuable contributions in this field.

Often, public loans for transportation, power, and harbor development, for example, will lay the foundation for sound industrial development and thereby encourage private enterprise, both local and foreign. The lack of coordination in planning and lending now, however, is notable in some countries.

The purpose of technical assistance in this area should be to establish priorities of need, to develop project plans in ways that satisfy lending institutions, and to do this within the credit worthiness of each nation.

(6) That, in very unusual circumstances, the President of the United States be in a position to make grants of food from our surplus stocks to Latin American countries.

Everyone recognizes the validity of food grants to meet problems caused by famine. But a no less serious human emergency exists when a nation which normally imports a substantial percentage of its food is unable to buy and its people are on the verge of starvation.

If food grants should be made, it would be appropriate to require the government receiving the grants to set aside counterpart funds, equal to the value of the grant, to be used in expanding its domestic agricultural production.

(7) That the technical cooperation program in Latin America be expanded.

The provision of expert technical assistance has been and continues to be an effective method of helping the people of Latin America attain better health, higher industrial production, better education, improved agricultural production, and higher standards of living. It has made firm friends for the United States among governments and individual citizens throughout the Hemisphere.

We should continue the "servicio" type of administration—a device in which local people and United States technical personnel share responsibility for the work.

The consultative part of the task should, wherever possible, be assigned to an American university which, like Michigan State College in its relations with agricultural development in Colombia, is willing to assume the responsibility for technical guidance. Such an arrangement has many advantages. A typical American university has every type of specialist who can be called on for short or long-time assignments. Further, Latin Americans cherish relationships with our leading educational institutions.

In each "servicio" project, the policy of the United States should be to withdraw when that project has become well established, local personnel have been trained, and the local government is able to carry on. Thus, when an agricultural experiment station or a health center has been operating successfully for a time and local personnel are ready to take over full management, United States funds should be put into a new project where a pioneering contribution can be made.

This is the general policy now, though it is not always followed. My colleagues and I saw it in operation in public health work in Brazil, where originally the bulk of the total cost was borne by the United States. Today, the United States portion of the cost of a greatly expanded program is very small.

For most of the technical cooperation work in Latin America today, the governments of the countries in which the work is done provide two to three times as much of the funds as does the United States. In some countries the local contribution runs eight or nine to our one.

With the transfer of the technical cooperation program from the State Department to the Foreign Operations Administration, some have warned of the danger of submerging technical cooperation under the vast emergency programs which are administered for the benefit primarily of parts of the world other than Latin America. This should not happen. Fortunately, the Director of the Foreign Operations Administration is greatly interested in the technical assistance program, and I am therefore confident that it will be carried forward efficiently and in the spirit of cooperation which has made it so successful.

(8) That we continue our vigorous support of the various technical agencies operating as an integral part of our activities in the Organization of American States.

Particularly should we continue to support the work of the Inter-American Economic and Social Council and to encourage that organization to expand its successful multilateral technical cooperation program among the nations of the Hemisphere.

(9) That our Government also continue to support the work of the International Monetary Fund which has extended helpful short-term financial aid and valuable technical assistance to the nations of Latin America on their monetary and exchange problems. We should also give continuing support to the work of United Nations agencies such as the Economic Commission for Latin America, with headquarters in Chile, which is helping the Latin American governments to further their economic development through use of their own resources.

Finally, I urge the Administration, the Congress, and the people of the United

States to take a long-range view as we consider how we may strengthen our economic relations with the nations of Latin America.

There is no doubt in my mind about the future of Latin America. Her people are on the march. They are determined to improve their standards of living. They have the resources and the manpower to do so.

Latin America is destined to be an economically powerful area of the globe. While it will always have economic relations with Europe and other parts of the world, its firmest and most extensive relations can and should be with the United States.

In the long view, economic cooperation, extended to help the people of Latin America raise their level of well-being and further their democratic aspirations, will redound to their benefit and to ours.

Working together, the nations of this Hemisphere can, if history should so decree, stand firmly against any enemy in war, and prosper mightily together in times of peace.

39. Address by Assistant Secretary John M. Cabot, before the Export-Import Club of the Columbus Chamber of Commerce, on Mutual Economic Progress in the Americas*

December 16, 1953

How much news regarding our sister American nations does the public in the United States read? And what kind of news?

If in recent years we have paid much more attention to problems in the Old World than to those of Latin America, our relations with our sister republics of this hemisphere are none the less vital to us. Since the Monroe Doctrine was first enunciated, we have considered it the most fundamental principle underlying our national security that no predatory foreign power establish its sway in any part of this hemisphere. In this shrunken world we live in, and in view of the astonishing growth and development of our sister republics, what was essential to us in 1823 is certainly no less essential today.

Already the voices of our sister republics speak with increasing authority in world councils and contribute vitally to the moral forces which Western civilization is mustering to maintain peace and security in the face of the Communist menace. With Brazil already surpassing the Latin nations of the Old World and the New in population as well as area, with Argentina, Mexico, Venezuela, and our other sister republics developing so fast that one can scarce credit one's eyes, the growing stature of our sister republics is bound to be an increasingly significant factor in world affairs. If only in obvious self-interest, we must strive to keep it as friendly a factor in the future as it has been in the past.

Our economic relations are no less important. Our $7 billion of trade with our sister republics is greater than our commercial trade with Europe or any other part of the world. Our $6 billion of investments in Latin America surpass those in any other single area except Canada. From Latin America we get most of our coffee and foreign-

*Department of State Bulletin, Jan. 11, 1954, pp. 48-53.

produced sugar and many other products such as bananas, cacao, wool, and tobacco; we also get many materials which we needed for our victory in World War II, such as copper, tin, lead, zinc, oil, and vanadium, and which, with the steady depletion of our own national resources, we are likely to need even more exigently in the future. In Latin American markets we sell some $3½ billion of our products annually.

The interplay of our cultures enriches our lives throughout the hemisphere. We on the balance have made liberal exports not only of the autos, movies, and bathtubs with which our culture is so often disdainfully associated but also of political ideas, books, education, science, medicine. In return, we have received painting, architecture, exotic dishes, dances, and the cultural stimulus which comes from so rich, varied, and different cultures in lands so close to us. When you travel to Mexico or the Caribbean to get away from it all (probably carrying a fat briefcase with you) most of you aren't thinking alone of warm sunshine, majestic scenery, and nightclubs; consciously or unconsciously you are thinking also of the colorful civilizations of the lands you are visiting. May I add that, as traveling ambassadors, I hope you see to it that you are good ones.

I shall not dilate further on the basic importance of Latin America to us. Everyone in the United States is aware of it; everyone wants friendly relations with our sister republics. The difficulty is that, like the sky, sea, and air of a beautiful day, we are at times not as inclined as we should be to think about it and appreciate it. Just because we don't have to argue about it, let us nonetheless never forget it.

For from the moment you drink your morning coffee—blended Brazilian and Colombian or other milds—till your wife opens for supper a can coated with tin from Bolivia, Latin America is always with you. If you don't sleep in a brass bed made from copper from Chile, the oil to produce the electricity for your home may come from Venezuela, the lead for your automobile battery from Mexico, the sugar for your cereal from Cuba, your bananas from Costa Rica, and that nice rum in the cocktails before dinner from Haiti. The soft scarf you're wearing may well have some alpaca wool from Peru, and quite possibly your suit some Uruguayan wool. On these cold, dark winter mornings you may step out of bed onto a carpet made of Argentine wool. And your child may take with his school lunch a chocolate bar made from Ecuadoran cacao.

Dependence on Latin American Products

And do not forget that your job may depend on these and other imports from Latin America. Antimony isn't a very large import in value—only some $3.2 million in 1952—but we imported nearly 80 percent of it in that year from Latin America and it is a vital defense item. The manganese ore we get from our sister republics—some 2.2 million pounds in 1952—may not be large in value, but remember that we can't make steel without manganese.

In short, your well-being here in Ohio depends very significantly on our relations with Latin America. Without it, many of your great factories would be crippled. If you could get many materials at all, it would be only at sharply higher prices. Your breakfast table without coffee and sugar would be dreary indeed, but how would you like your boy to have to fight without the arms made with Latin American materials?

Let us glance at our relations with Latin America on an individual basis, for, after all, our relations with our sister republics are determined by the 160 million individuals in the United States and the roughly equal number in Latin America. The western wool grower, to take a specific example, is in competition with the Uruguayan wool grower. Though existing duties add to the cost of the suits you and I are wearing, the domestic wool grower naturally enough from his viewpoint wants more protection. Perhaps he is just facing cut profits, but perhaps he is facing real loss—the need for getting out of an unprofitable business.

Now, no one likes to see that domestic wool grower hurt. We must nonetheless remember that we did not grow into the greatest economic power on earth by preserving high-cost production. Within the United States no protection is possible against more efficient production in other sections of the country. In New England our economy has had to go through four stages since colonial times. It is our proud boast that we have no natural resources except rocks and ice—and that we exported them both! Modern technology has stricken even these items from our export list. Today the textile era in New England is following the farming and shipping eras into history—but New England is still prosperous.

Surely this example—which has brought loss and misery to quite a few individuals yet healthy growth to New England as a whole—nevertheless has a lesson for the country. The New England farmer, textile worker, and investor may have suffered temporarily, but the country at large has cheaper and more abundant food and clothing. Moreover, within our great economy it is possible to adapt oneself to changing conditions.

But let us look at the position of the Uruguayan wool grower. His is a democratic country—a staunch friend in two world wars and in many ideological battles; but it is a small country whose obvious natural resources are largely agricultural as in New England, and it does not have the advantage of great domestic markets. The national economy is built on wool—which constitutes about 50 percent of Uruguayan exports. If we do not raise the tariff on wool, it may be tough for the domestic wool grower. If we do, it may be tough not only on the Uruguayan wool grower as an individual; it may be disastrous for Uruguay as a nation. It may also decrease sales in Uruguay of auto tires and jeeps and steel and cash registers and electrical goods and a lot of other things made in Ohio. A protective tariff may shield individual domestic producers from hurt; but it will do this only at the hurt of other domestic producers. If we cut off imports of Uruguayan wool or Chilean copper or Venezuelan oil or Bolivian tin or Mexican lead or Cuban sugar or Peruvian tuna, we shall simply reduce their purchases from us by the same amount. They can buy from us only what they sell to us.

Let us turn to the Bolivian tin miner. His job notably contributes to your wife's convenience when she prepares your supper; it also contributes an element essential to war production, for example of engine bearings. Twice in the past 15 years he has been asked to produce a vital ingredient to keep the free world free. As virtually the only secure source of tin for half the world, the price of tin from Bolivia then soared to fantastic heights despite our efforts to control it; and since goods of all sorts were simultaneously scarce, this stimulated inflation in Bolivia. Having bought tin furiously during the crises, we stopped buying once they were over, and tin dropped as precipitously in price as it had risen.

With the national economy dependent on tin, even the wisdom of Solomon would not suffice to direct Bolivian economic affairs under such circumstances. If the

Bolivians forget that we also controlled the prices of products we sold them, that the dollar saved by our citizens—and the one borrowed by Bolivia—sank as much in purchasing power as the dollar Bolivia saved from tin sales during the crises, we should emphatically not forget the impression it makes, in terms of hard economics as well as psychology, when we beg the Bolivians to produce all the tin they can at one moment and at the next won't buy it at any price. I shall leave the intricacies of price stabilization and the controversy regarding expropriation to the competent international forums, but I do want to say that, regardless of rights or wrongs, I do not think we should permit people in Bolivia to go hungry, and I think we would be very unwise to drive the unpent social forces in Bolivia into the gently smiling jaws of communism.

We should remember that the story of the Bolivian tin miner could be told almost equally well of the lead and zinc miners in Peru and Mexico, countries moreover with which we have particularly friendly relations. If the impact of great fluctuations in the prices of those metals has been less severe on those countries, it has been because their economies are more diversified and their governments have shown much statesmanship in handling national economic affairs. The story might also be told of the Chilean copper miners—which brings us to another story.

In Santiago de Chile an American utility company has until recently been unable to obtain from the Chilean authorities rates which would permit it to earn a fair return on their investment. Santiago is a rapidly developing city, and its demands for electricity are growing by leaps and bounds. If that demand is to be met, new capital must be obtained. It cannot be obtained from earnings if earnings are insufficient; and it cannot be obtained from investors if they do not think the company is a good investment. The Chilean may feel inadequate electric rates not only in dim lights and a quavering radio; it may rob him of his job when there isn't enough power to run the factory.

But, the Chilean will naturally think, this is a rich and greedy foreign monopoly which is trying to rob me. Remember that his income is only about one-eighth of that of an American and that his family budget has been just as hard hit by the chronic inflation in Chile as has that of the utility company. He thinks of the company as big, wealthy, and foreign; he forgets that it is owned by thousands of American stockholders who like him are trying to raise families on painfully tight budgets. If the Chilean is not altogether fair, let us remember that John Q. Public in the United States too has not always been fair in his views regarding business. If American companies have not always been fairly treated in Latin America let us remember that, as in the United States, they have not always acted fairly.

The record of American business in Latin America has been increasingly good. Upon the respective Latin American governments, rather than ours, devolves the responsibility of seeing that any remaining abuses are checked and that business in their countries is conducted in the national interest. Today I believe that it is a fact that foreign business in Latin America is more sinned against than sinning; that in some sectors several Latin American governments have gone so far in harassment and restrictive measures as to discourage the further foreign investment which is so essential to their national development. I am not referring to crass confiscation under Communist inspiration; I refer to the multiple, onerous economic controls which, in Dr. Milton Eisenhower's words, spell creeping expropriation.

Latin American voices to which we listen with the highest respect in the United

States have suggested recently that they do not favor further American investments in their respective countries. Let me make it unmistakably clear that the Government of the United States is not trying to force American investments on any country which does not wish to receive them. We consider that a country's policies in regard to new foreign investment are for its sole determination in accordance with its conception of the national interests.

Fair Treatment of Investments

We do expect fair treatment of our investments already made in good faith. We feel it proper to make representations on their behalf if they have been denied a remedy or suffered discrimination under national law or if valid contracts with governments have been unilaterally breached and justice denied. Obviously our policy in inter-American relations does not place the protection of our private investments at the top of our objectives—our national security, for example, takes precedence—but it is an important objective and duty. We believe it should be an even more important objective of our sister republics, given their present stage of development, to cultivate a reputation of treating foreign capital fairly. A reputation is acquired over the years—and can be destroyed in a day.

No one, for example, raises an eyebrow when a government buys out a foreign company by mutual agreement, but a country may do itself great disservice by a unilateral expropriation. The sovereign right of a nation to expropriate foreign property in its jurisdiction cannot be questioned—but we do insist on prompt, adequate, and just compensation. By the same token, any nation has the undeniable sovereign right to declare war on any other nation if it so chooses, but it would scarcely be argued that the exercise of such a sovereign right would entail no international responsibilities. In other words, the question of the treatment of foreign capital is not essentially one of right, and it should not be considered in terms of absolutes; it is a question of what is fair, what is wise, what is practical, what is in the national interest, what will preserve the international comity.

It has been suggested that there is no capital in the United States which would seek investment abroad. How then explain the outflow of direct capital investments to Latin America of some $1.7 billion between 1946 and 1952? How explain that our citizens made a net direct investment of over $1 billion in Canada in the same span of years, not to mention portfolio investments?

It has been suggested that foreign capital milks a country economically, leaving nothing for the people. How then explain that some 70 percent of Chilean, some 97 percent of Venezuelan and at least 55 percent of Costa Rican exports are produced by foreign companies? Without those exports what would become of those countries? And can there be any really clear cases cited where American companies have paid lower than prevailing wages, or provided poorer than standard working conditions? Obviously they couldn't get workmen if they did; obviously the fact that they do improves wages and working conditions.

It has been suggested that foreign capital tends to dominate a country's political life. At the present time there are American investments in Canada of some $8 billion—considerably larger than our investments in all Latin America, though the population of Canada is less than one-tenth that of Latin America. Our good neighbors to the north would deeply resent and know to be untrue any suggestion that our investments influence their political life.

Is it altogether an accident that, while some $25 billion of foreign and domestic capital were being invested in Canada in the years 1946 to 1952, per capita income in the period 1939-52 tripled in terms of dollars and rose 60 percent in terms of goods, even though the average work week was dropping from 48 to 43 hours? Is it without significance that Canada's oil production, largely developed by foreign capital, rose from 21,000 barrels daily in 1947 to 169,000 barrels in 1952 and that in four years Canada thereby saved $300 million in foreign exchange?

Canada has wisely used native capital to the greatest feasible extent but has not hesitated to use foreign capital when this was convenient. The new capital, native and foreign, invested in Canada has helped the Canadian workman to rival the American's standard of living. May I add, for people in the United States who think that the development of foreign countries will hurt our foreign trade, that Canada's foreign trade in this extraordinary period of internal development has risen by five times!

Finally, it is to be noted that Canada has had to grant no special privileges to foreign capital. Capital has flowed in because over the years and decades it has learned to count on fair treatment. That this has not been without its advantages for Canada is suggested by the fact that the interest rate on government bonds averages about 3 percent as against 8-10 percent in most of Latin America. That extra return is primarily the cost Latin America pays because of the added risks which foreign capital must face there.

In short, we can and should do several things to help our sister republics in the economic sphere; but for the most part their economic future rests in their own hands.

If some of our Latin American friends say that Canada is a special case, I would invite their attention to Puerto Rico. Here is a tiny land, increasingly overpopulated, lacking in natural resources and the elements for heavy industry. Despite a long-standing law limiting landownership to 500 acres, sugar companies formerly controlled vastly greater acreages. The sugar companies were forced to divest themselves of their large landholdings—but they always obtained just compensation.

A wise and energetic government has attracted some 1,388 industries to the island in the past 12 years; and the per capita income has trebled to $400 per year, higher than that in most Latin American republics. Puerto Rico proudly considers itself a bridge between North and Latin America; and certainly its economic experiences might be studied advantageously by nations with such similar problems. Its example has shown what even a naturally handicapped economy can do by prudent policies to raise living standards and is being increasingly studied in other countries.

Communist Attack on Capital

We must never forget that the Communists attack capital in Latin America—and particularly foreign capital—because, on the one hand, it is a subject which lends itself to their false propaganda and, on the other, they recognize that capital, by promoting national development and raising living standards, is a potent enemy of their agitation. There can be individual conflicts between capital and labor, between foreign companies and national interests, but in general cooperation and fair play between government, capital, and labor are necessary to the interests of each of them.

Let us think of that labor—or rather that Latin American laborer employed by a U.S. company. He is probably not well educated, and he is desperately poor. He may well have imbibed with his mother's milk a sense of oppression and exploitation—and a consequent suspicion of foreigners. He can see that the foreign company employing him has great resources, else how could it do what it does? Why should the foreign managers live so much better than he?

Now, you and I of course know the answers. The great resources are the pooled savings of thousands of investors. Foreign capital will in its own interest employ natives of the country to the full extent they are available, but it will wish to employ its own representatives in key jobs, and it will have to bring in trained employees for specialized jobs it cannot for the moment fill locally—and those people will obviously have to be paid at United States, not local, rates. As for labor organization, United States companies increasingly recognize that responsible organized labor is a stabilizing force with which it is to their self-interest to cooperate, and many American managers are likely to remember instinctively in Latin America the more advanced labor relations practices they learned in the United States. It is not, however, the role of American companies to reform foreign lands; it is their elementary duty to respect the laws and authorities in countries in which they operate.

Let us think equally of the Latin American intellectual who is troubled by the economic influence of the United States in his country. He sees irreplaceable natural resources—oil, copper, zinc, lead, iron ore—being extracted by foreign companies. The companies doing this often are more important proportionately in his country than our greatest corporations are in the United States. As the internal economy of his country may depend in important measure on United States companies, so its economic prosperity may depend on the market for its exports in the United States. He naturally resents the booms and busts of his national economy which arise from relatively small economic fluctuations in the United States, and he deeply resents the occasions on which we try, by protecting domestic producers, to export our misery and thereby add to his. Everywhere he turns in seeking to raise living standards—and remember, per capita income in Latin America is but one-eighth of ours—he encounters some economic interest of ours, and it is not surprising if he mistakenly thinks it is blocking his way.

It does not occur to him that natural resources are worth nothing till developed, that, for example, the Guayra Falls, probably the greatest potential source of hydraulic power in the world, beside which Niagara is only a leaky faucet, will be of value only when capital is used to develop it—and they are so remote that we may be using atomic power plants first. He may equally forget what living standards in his country would be if foreign capital had not come to it, or how much higher they would be if his government's policies had been wiser. He forgets that Henry Ford made good profits and certainly did the United States no harm.

Need for Reciprocal Understanding

In short, our problems in our inter-American relations are largely economic, and they largely boil down to the question of how we are going to cooperate in the economic sphere to our mutual benefit. The first requisite of such cooperation is reciprocal understanding. We must understand what our trade policy, our loan policy, our other economic policies mean to them, and that what is a trifle to us may spell disaster to them. In turn, our sister republics should appreciate the immense burdens which world leadership has placed on our shoulders and should realize that the treatment they give to foreign capital is far more important to them than it is to the United States. We have learned in the United States that capital and labor can work together to their mutual profit; we must not be deterred either by selfishness or misguided agitation from working together with our sister republics in the economic field for our mutual benefit. Our sister republics will follow our leadership in world affairs only if they think it to their national advantage. As to the possibilities of going it alone, I think of Secretary Dulles' wise words in this regard. I trust that through shortsightedness we shall never be compelled to defend our national existence along our national frontiers.

That is the meaning of our relations with our sister republics. We do not believe that our concerns end at the Rio Grande. We know that through our continental solidarity we were spared throughout this hemisphere the devastation of World War II, and we firmly believe that holds a lesson for the future. We seek so to order our hemispheric relations that we shall enrich ourselves and our good neighbors, spiritually and materially, by living with them in this hemisphere in understanding and harmony. If we were to heed the voices of selfishness, or to let Communist agitation corrode our common sense, we could easily destroy our future and ourselves. But I am confident that the Americas will not follow any such shortsighted path. The Americas are visibly on the march toward a better, brighter future, and we must go forward together in attaining it. Destiny has thrust upon this new world—this American Continent—a vital role in the future of mankind. The future history of the world will be increasingly written in the 21 sister republics of the Americas. May it be not only the story of understanding and cooperation for the benefit of our children's children but also an example which will help to bring peace on earth, good will to men—everywhere!

40. Address by John Foster Dulles, Secretary of State, before the Tenth Inter-American Conference, on the Spirit of Inter-American Unity*

Caracas, Venezuela, March 4, 1954

I am happy to be attending this Tenth Inter-American Conference. I have looked forward to this ever since becoming the United States Secretary of State. The recent Four Power Conference at Berlin was, at my request, arranged to conclude so as to make possible my presence here. I wanted to be here because in my opinion this Conference reflects the finest traditions of foreign policy. It produces solidarity among many nations on a basis of sovereign equality. That relationship has been tried and tested for many years. It survives as an example which others would do well to follow.

At Berlin there was a good deal of discussion about this unity of the American states. Mr. Molotov proposed that it should be copied in Europe. He produced a draft

*Department of State Bulletin, Mar. 15, 1954, pp. 379-83.

of a European security pact which he claimed was modeled on our inter-American treaty made at Rio de Janeiro in 1947.

As I read his draft I saw that many words were indeed taken from our treaty. However, I said to Mr. Molotov that he could never reproduce in Europe what we had in the Americas merely by copying words. I directed his attention to the Preamble of the Rio Pact which proclaims that "peace is founded on justice and moral order and, consequently, on the international recognition and protection of human rights and freedoms." I said that whenever the Soviet Union made such words a living reality then indeed much could be done to end the era of danger in which we live.

The fact is that Soviet communism stands for the liquidation of the values upon which our fraternal association is based. It denies the very existence of justice and of a moral law. It believes that peace is not founded on righteousness but on power. It does not believe in law as a shield which protects all, whatever be their status, but rather that law is the means whereby those in power liquidate their enemies. It does not believe in human rights and freedoms but rather that human beings are designed to serve their masters and to create the means of extending their masters' power. It is a mockery for those who hold these beliefs to pretend that they can reproduce on a European basis that which we have joined to create here on an American basis.

The death of Stalin has brought no basic change in Soviet policy. It remains expansive not merely out of greed but because it fears freedom. That was the most distressing aspect of the Berlin Conference. We discussed with Mr. Molotov time after time, both in formal meetings and privately, the granting of liberty to the peoples of East Germany and Austria. Mr. Molotov said, and I believe he said with conviction, that the Soviet Government could not tolerate an extension of freedom because it feared that freedom might be abused.

To Soviet Communists, freedom is frightening. To them it is inconsistent with order. Also they know that freedom is contagious. That is why they feel that they will not be safe until they have liquidated freedom as a major force in world affairs.

The Threat to the Americas

We here in the Americas are not immune from that threat of Soviet communism. There is not a single country in this hemisphere which has not been penetrated by the apparatus of international communism, acting under orders from Moscow. No one of us knows fully the extent of that conspiracy. From time to time small parts are detected and exposed.

The earliest postwar exposure of major importance was made in Canada by a Royal commission. It showed how Communist efforts directed from Moscow had drawn many well intentioned persons into a conspiracy to undermine the free Government of Canada. In the United States there has been a succession of exposures and judicial convictions which prove that international communism plots against our form of government. I venture to say that every delegate here knows of similar activities within his own country which are being conducted from Moscow or way stations.

This Communist conspiracy is not to be taken lightly. Its agents operate under the iron discipline of the Soviet Communist Party, acting as the self-proclaimed "General Staff of the World Proletariat." The agents themselves, in order to gain a following, pretend to be reformists seeking to eradicate the evils which exist in any society.

None of us want to be maneuvered into the position of defending whatever Communists attack. We do not carry on political warfare against ideas or ideals. But equally we must not be blind to the fact that the international conspiracy I describe has in 15 years been primarily responsible for turning what were 15 independent nations into Soviet colonies, and they would if they could duplicate that performance here.

In the past century battleships were the symbol of aggression against the hemisphere. Today the apparatus of an alien political party endangers the independence and solidarity of the Americas. From the earliest days of the independence of our countries we have all stood resolutely for the integrity of this hemisphere. We have seen that that integrity would be endangered unless we stood resolutely against any enlargement here of the colonial domain of the European powers. We have made our position in this matter so clear that it is known to and accepted by all the world. What was a great danger has thus receded.

We have not made it equally clear that the integrity of this hemisphere and the peace, safety, and happiness of us all may be endangered by political penetration from without and that we stand resolutely and unitedly against that form of danger. Because our position has not been made clear, the danger mounts. I believe that it is time to make it clear with finality that we see that alien despotism is hostile to our ideals, that we unitedly deny it the right to prey upon our hemisphere, and that if it does not heed our warning and keep away we shall deal with it as a situation that might endanger the peace of America.

What I suggest does not involve any interference in the internal affairs of any American Republic. There is ample room for natural differences and for tolerances between the political institutions of the different American states. But there is no place here for political institutions which serve alien masters. I hope that we can agree to make that clear.

Of course there will be some in other lands who will not like that. *Pravda*, the official organ of the Soviet Communist Party at Moscow, carried an important editorial on March 2 which was addressed to us here. It protested against the possibility that this Inter-American Conference might adopt an anti-Communist resolution. I suggest that rather than listen to those words we listen to the words of Simon Bolívar, in whose birthplace we meet. He symbolizes the independence to which we all are dedicated. Addressing the Congress of our host nation more than a century ago, he said, "Slavery is the offspring of darkness; an ignorant people is a blind tool, turned to its own destruction; ambition and intrigue exploit the credulity of men foreign to all political, economic or civil knowledge; mere illusions are accepted as reality, licenses taken as liberty, treachery for patriotism, revenge for justice."

The Conference has been shocked by the dastardly attack on Members of the United States Congress by those who professed to be "patriots." They may not themselves be Communists. But they had been subjected to the inflammatory influence of communism, which avowedly uses extreme nationalism as one of its tools. What they did is precisely in the Soviet Communist pattern. It should harden our resolve to be alert to danger and to detect and thwart the plotting of those who in the name of "nationalism" and "patriotism" do what in fact destroys liberty and turns men and nations into slaves.

The United States recognizes that the freedom and independence which we all covet, and which we are resolved to preserve, is based not only on political and moral considerations but also on economic and social well-being. The United States Government is confident of its ability to maintain the health and vigor of its own national economy. President Eisenhower, in his recent economic report to the Congress, said that "the arsenal of weapons at the disposal of the Government for maintaining economic stability is formidable."

The Economic Problem

This is important not only for ourselves but also for others. A high level of economic activity within the United States creates a demand for imports and provides the means for continued economic development in this hemisphere and elsewhere. It is, of course, a fact and properly a fact that no government operates primarily in the interests of other peoples. The first responsibility of every government is to its own people, for whom it acts in a trustee capacity. Nevertheless it is also true that no government adequately serves its own people unless it also is concerned with well-being in other countries.

Nations generally have it within their own power to do most of what is required for decent and healthy social conditions for their people. The task is thus primarily a domestic one. But there is need for international conditions which facilitate a mutually advantageous exchange of goods and a mutually advantageous flow of capital from the more developed countries to the countries which are less developed. This is for all a matter of enlightened self-interest.

I can assure you that President Eisenhower sees as clearly as any living person that the welfare of the United States is related to that of others. When last year our President asked his brother to visit the South American countries it was primarily that this message might be brought to you in a manner so authentic that no one could doubt it.

Dr. Milton Eisenhower's report has been brought to the attention of our Government Departments with a request that they do all within their power to carry out its recommendations. Much has already been done in this respect and more is in prospect. For example, the Commission on Foreign Economic Policy, the Randall Commission, has made specific recommendations which would give effect to that part of the report which stressed the importance of stabilizing the rules of international trade. Also, funds for technical assistance and cultural cooperation are being increased. The latter is particularly significant in view of Dr. Eisenhower's recommendation for "strengthening efforts to increase intercultural understanding as the foundation of mutually advantageous cooperation in all relevant areas."

There are five specific matters which I might mention at this time.

Coffee

1. First let me speak about coffee. I know that it is not the desire of the coffee-producing countries of the Western Hemisphere that prices should be so high as to discourage consumption and build up habits of drinking other beverages. Present prices are, I believe, primarily due to natural causes beyond human control. Possibly to some extent natural conditions are aggravated by artificial trading on United States commodity exchanges.

But that is not a responsibility of the producers. We are looking into that phase of the problem, and I am sure that all will welcome any relief that can be found in that quarter. The consumers of the United States do not like it when prices go up just as you do not like it when prices of your exported commodities go down. We accept it that in a free system there are bound to be fluctuations in both directions. And I can assure you that there is no plan afoot to attempt to deal arbitrarily with the problem of prices by imposing some artificial price ceiling.

Wool

2. Another matter which I know concerns you is that of wool. The United States Tariff Commission has recommended to the President an increase in the tariff on wool. The President, however, has another plan which he has submitted to Congress which will, it is hoped, adequately support the wool industry of the United States without imposing increased duties on imported wool. The President told me last week that he had no intention of acting favorably on the Tariff Commission's recommendation, pending congressional consideration of his own proposal.

Technical Cooperation

3. There has been some speculation with reference to the future of some of our governmental policies, principally with respect to the Technical Cooperation Program and the activity of the Export-Import Bank. We in the United States consider that the Technical Cooperation program is an important way of bettering conditions of living elsewhere. It spreads knowledge, and knowledge is the great liberator. The Technical Cooperation Program operates on a modest basis with more dependence on quality than quantity. The quality of its work has, I believe, improved with experience.

In Latin America the evidence is that this fact is accepted by the governments concerned, which have multiplied their own financial support of this program and taken over projects for further independent development. In such fields as public health and agriculture we can all feel a real satisfaction in the knowledge that these cooperative efforts have assisted in broadening and strengthening the basis for economic development by providing more and better food for a more healthy population. The Government of the United States firmly supports the continuance of our bilateral technical assistance programs as well as the programs carried on by the Organization of American States.

Much important work in the field of public health and agriculture is done by private organizations, as, for example, the Rockefeller Foundation. It has made an immense contribution of technical knowledge which has assisted Latin American Governments in stamping out many forms of disease. It is assisting in promoting agricultural knowledge. The United States Government encourages these private efforts. But also it intends at a governmental level to supplement them.

Capital Flow

4. The United States was developed with the help of private foreign capital, and it would like to see its own capital now help to develop the great resources of other countries of this hemisphere. There exists in the United States ample capital which is ready, willing, and able to perform its development function not only at home but also abroad.

The spectacular development of Canada during this century has been primarily due to cooperation between the private investors of the United States and those in Canada. Approximately 5 billion dollars of private United States capital have been invested in Canada and have made a significant contribution to producing for Canada one of the highest standards of living in the world.

We can see here in our host country the results of international cooperation. No one who has spent even a few days in this great and growing city can fail to be impressed by the atmosphere of creative vitality. I am told that nearly 2 billion dollars of private foreign capital have come to Venezuela on a mutually advantageous basis.

The results are open for anyone to see. There are other countries into which substantial United States capital has also flowed. The total of United States private direct investments in Latin America amounts, I believe, to about 6 billion dollars. This is a large figure, particularly when it is borne in mind that domestic capital always provides the greater part of any country's financing. Indeed, I understand that over 90 percent of the total investment undertaken in Latin America is now derived from domestic sources, a happy augury of the growing strength of this great area.

Some countries have seen fit to put artificial obstacles in the way of what would be the normal and natural flow of capital between highly developed and less developed countries. That is, of course, their privilege. In these matters every nation is sovereign.

The United States Government has not the slightest desire or intention to extort for its people opportunities which are not freely accorded. We would, however, like to see the economies of our American friends and neighbors more vigorous than in some cases they are. We would like to see living standards raised, employment increased, and wages such as to provide the workers with greater rewards. For these reasons we hope that no country will impose restrictions which unnecessarily inhibit cooperation for development.

In the United States private capital and free enterprise constitute the great source of our own economic well-being. That is a source which we do not try to keep at home. It is free to go abroad, and we welcome its international activities. Indeed, President Eisenhower in his recent Budget Message to the Congress recommended certain modifications in our tax laws which will encourage our capital and business people to work abroad. However, private capital cannot be driven. It has to be attracted. Therefore, the decision rests with you.

The Export-Import Bank

5. There are some development projects which may not be suitable for or attractive to private capital, domestic or foreign. The International Bank for Reconstruction and Development, which most of us here participated in establishing and to which the United States has made important capital contributions, is the primary instrument through which the free world can cooperate in the public financing of economic development.

We have also in the United States in the public financing field the Export-Import Bank, a national institution of my own Government. One important function of this institution will continue to be that of affording export credits either through direct loans or guarantees.

There has been speculation as to whether this bank has withdrawn from the field of economic development. I am glad to be able to clarify this matter. The Export-Import Bank will consider on their merits applications for the financing of development projects which are not being made by the International Bank and which are in our common interest, are economically sound, are within the capacity of the prospective borrower to repay and within the prudent loaning capacity of the bank.

Spiritual Unity

I have spoken of political and economic matters. Let me in conclusion speak of what is most important of all, that is, understanding and cooperation in spiritual and cultural matters.

It has been my happy experience to have been associated many times with the representatives of the Latin American countries at such gatherings as the Assembly of the United Nations. Also I recall gratefully the cooperation of the American Republics at the two San Francisco Conferences—that of 1945, which drafted the United Nations Charter, and that of 1951, which concluded the Japanese peace treaty.

The unity which generally prevails between us at international gatherings is nothing that is artificial. It is not, indeed, primarily geographic. It is a unity which exists because of a harmony of the spirit.

It has been my experience that the Governments of the American Republics usually act alike internationally because their peoples believe in the same fundamentals.

We believe in a spiritual world; we believe that man has his origin and destiny in God; we believe that this fact requires human brotherhood.

We believe that, just as every human being has dignity and worth, so every nation great or small has dignity and worth and that international relations should be on the basis of mutual respect and equal dignity.

We believe that nations, like men, are subject to moral law and that in the international field the task is to develop international law and to conduct international affairs in accordance with the standards of moral law.

That is the conception of my Government. I believe that it is a conception which the nations here generally share. Of course we are all fallible. None of us realizes fully his ideals. But the essential is to have ideals and to try to practice them. I expect that we shall do so here.

In that conviction I look to our Conference with eager anticipation. It will, I believe, be both a source of satisfaction to ourselves and also a symbol which will show men everywhere how good can be the fruits of freedom.

41. Statement by Secretary Dulles, before the Politico-Juridical Committee of the Tenth Inter-American Conference, on Intervention of International Communism in the Americas *

Caracas, Venezuela, March 8, 1954

The United States has introduced a resolution under the agenda item "Intervention of International Communism in the American Republics." Our proposal is before you.

Its preamble first recalls the prior resolutions finding international communism to be a threat and then records our judgment that this threat still persists.

The first operative portion declares that, if the international Communist movement

*Department of State Publication 5556, Inter-American Series 48, Washington D.C., 1954, pp. 1-7.

should come to dominate the political institutions of any American State, that would be a threat to the sovereignty and political independence of us all, endangering the peace of America and calling for appropriate action.

In accordance with existing treaties, the second operative portion calls for disclosures and exchanges of information, which would expose and weaken the Communist conspiracy.

What is international communism? In the course of the general debate, one of the Foreign Ministers (the Minister of Guatemala) asked, "What is international communism?" I thought that by now every Foreign Minister of the world knew what international communism is. It is disturbing if the foreign affairs of one of our American Republics are conducted by one so innocent that he has to ask that question.

But since the question has been asked, it shall be answered. International communism is that far-flung clandestine political organization which is operated by the leaders of the Communist Party of the Soviet Union. Since 1939, it has brought 15 once independent nations into a state of abject servitude. It has a hard core of agents in practically every country of the world. The total constitutes not a theory, not a doctrine, but an aggressive, tough, political force, backed by great resources, and serving the most ruthless empire of modern times.

Most of the leaders of the Soviet Communist Party appear before the eyes of the world as responsible officials of the Soviet Government. In this capacity they conduct relations with the other Governments through the traditional institutions of diplomacy. But at the same time they operate and control this worldwide clandestine political organization to which I have referred.

Until the Second World War, Moscow's control over this organization was exercised openly through the central headquarters of the Communist International, the so-called "Comintern." That was a political association to which all of the Communist parties belonged and it had its seat in Moscow. During the war the Comintern was officially abolished. Since that time the control over the foreign Communist parties has been exercised by the Moscow leaders secretly and informally, but for the most part no less effectively than before.

As proof of this fact one does not need to search for the precise channels through which this control proceeds, although some of them in fact are known. If one compares Soviet propaganda with the political positions taken by individual Communist officials and agents around the world, both from the standpoint of substance and timing, it becomes clear, beyond possibility of doubt, that there is this highly disciplined hierarchical organization which commands the unquestioned obedience of its individual members.

The disciplinary requirements include a firm insistence that loyalty to the movement, which means in effect loyalty to the leaders of the Communist Party of the Soviet Union, shall take precedence over every other obligation including love of country, obligation to family, and the honor of one's own personal conduct.

These conclusions are not speculation; they are established facts, well known to all who have seriously studied the Communist apparatus.

The fact that this organization exists does not mean that all members of all Communist parties everywhere are conscious of its existence and of their relationship to it. Only a small proportion of Communist Party members are initiated into complete awareness of the nature of the movement to which they belong and the real sources of its authority. Most national Communist parties masquerade as normal patriotic political parties, purporting to reflect indigenous political impulses and to be led by indigenous elements.

Actually, every one of these parties represents a conspiracy within a conspiracy; the rank-and-file members, while serving the purpose of duping others, are to a considerable extent duped by their own leaders. The leaders do not reveal fully to the rank and file either the nature of their own allegiance or the sources of their own authority and funds.

The overall purpose for which this organization is maintained and operated is to act as an instrument for the advancement of the worldwide political aims of the dominant group of Moscow leaders.

This, then, is the answer to "What is international communism"?

It may next be asked whether this international Communist apparatus actually seeks to bring this hemisphere, or parts of it, into the Soviet orbit. The answer must be in the affirmative.

I shall not here accuse any government or any individuals of being either plotters or the dupes of plotters. We are not sitting here as a court to try governments or individuals. We sit rather as legislators. As such, we need to know what will enable us to take appropriate action of a general character in the common interest. Therefore, I shall confine myself to presenting well-established facts of that character.

When the Comintern was operating openly, it trained at Moscow, largely in the Lenin School, numerous persons from the Americas. Some of them are still active.

International Front Organizations

There was a special Comintern headquarters, and there were secret field offices which controlled and supported Communist activities in Latin America. The Comintern also developed a series of international front organizations designed to enable its agents to get popular backing from special groups such as labor, youth, women, students, farmers, etc. These front organizations also served as cover for the Soviet intelligence services.

When the Soviet Communist Party went through the form of abolishing the Comintern, these same front organizations were carried on in a different form, with headquarters shifted from Moscow usually to satellite capitals. The Communist International of Youth emerged as the World Federation of Democratic Youth, with headquarters in Budapest, and as the International Students Union, with headquarters in Prague. There is the Women's International Juridical Association. There is the World Peace Council, located in Prague. There is the World Committee Against War and Fascism. Most powerful of all is the World Federation of Trade Unions, seated under Soviet auspices in Vienna. There is the All Union Society for Cultural Relations Abroad which channels propaganda through its local outlets, the various Soviet friendship societies.

These front organizations carry on important activities in many of the American

States. Their members in this hemisphere go back and forth to the Soviet bloc countries, using funds which are supplied by the Soviet Communist Party.

The basic facts I outline are well known. They could be supplemented by masses of detail, but that is unncessary for our present purposes. It is enough to know that international communism operates strongly in this hemisphere to accomplish the political purposes of its leaders who are at the same time the leaders of the Soviet Communist Party and of the Soviet Union.

International communism is not liberating but enslaving. It has been suggested that, even though the international Communist movement operates in this hemisphere, it may serve a liberating purpose, compatible with principles of the American States. Few, I believe, would argue for that openly. The thesis is advanced rather by innuendo and insinuation.

Such suggestions lose all plausibility when we recall what this Communist movement has done to the nations and the peoples it has come to dominate. Let us think first in terms of nations.

Many of us knew at the United Nations Jan Masaryk, the son of the great author of Czechoslovak freedom. He was a Foreign Minister who believed, until almost the end, that the Communist movement in his country was something different; that it could be reconciled with the national freedom to which his father and he were so passionately dedicated. But in the end his broken corpse was offered to the world as mute evidence of the fact that international communism is never "different" and that there can be no genuine reconciliation between it and national freedom.

Czechoslovakia was stripped of every vestige of sovereignty, as we in the Americas understand that term. It was added to the list of victims, which already in Europe included Latvia, Estonia, Lithuania, Poland, East Germany, Albania, Hungary, Rumania, and Bulgaria. These ten European nations, once proud and honorable examples of national freedom, have become Soviet serfdoms or worse.

Within all the vast area, now embracing one-third of the world's people, where the military power of the Soviet Union is dominant, no official can be found who would dare to stand up and openly attack the Government of the Soviet Union. But in this hemisphere, it takes no courage for the representative of one of the smallest American countries openly to attack the government of the most powerful.

I rejoice that that kind of freedom exists in the Americas, even if it may be at times abused. But the essential is that there be a relationship of sovereign equality. We of the United States want to keep it that way. We seek no satellites, but only friendly equals. We never want to see at the pan-American table those who speak as the tools of non-American powers. We want to preserve and defend an American society, in which even the weak may speak boldly, because they represent national personalities which, as long as they are free, are equal.

It is the purpose of our resolution to assure that there will always be in this hemisphere such national personalities and dignity.

If now we turn to see what international communism has done to the individual human beings, we find that it has stripped them, too, of their sense of dignity and worth. The professional propagandists for communism talk glibly of lofty aims and high ideals. That is part of the routine—and fraudulent—appeal of the international Communist movement. It is one of the principal means by which the dissatisfied are led to follow false leaders. But once international communism has gained its end and subjected the people to the so-called "dictatorship of the proletariat," then the welfare of the people ceases to be a matter of practical concern.

Communism and the Worker

Communism, in its initial theoretical stage, was designated primarily to serve the workers and to provide them, not with spiritual values, for communism is atheistic, but at least with a material well-being. It is worthwhile to observe what has actually happened to this favored group in countries subjugated by Communist power.

In these countries the workers have become virtual slaves, and millions of them are literally slaves. Instructive facts are to be found in the United Nations Report on Forced Labor, which was presented to the United Nations Assembly at its last session. The authors of this report were three eminent and independent personalities from India, Norway, and Peru. The report finds that the Soviet Union and its satellites use forced labor on a vast scale. Prior evidence presented to the United Nations indicates that approximately 15 million persons habitually fill the Soviet labor camps.

The Forced Labor Report calls the Soviet method of training and allocating manpower "A system of forced or compulsory labor." The Soviet workers are the most underpaid, overworked persons in any modern industrial state. They are the most managed, checked-on, spied-on, and unrepresented workers in the world today. There is no freedom of movement, for the Russian worker is not allowed to leave his job and shift to another job. He is bound to his job by his labor book. Except for the relative few who have class privileges, wages provide only a pitiful existence. Now, 37 years after the October revolution, unrest and discontent have so mounted in Soviet Russia that the rulers are forced publicly to notice them and to promise relief.

Conditions in the Soviet satellite countries are even worse than in Russia. The captive peoples have been subjected to sharply decreased living standards, since they lost their freedom, and to greater exploitation than prevails in Russia. The workers' outbreak in East Germany of last June showed in one revealing flash how desperate the people have become. Young boys armed only with stones dared to face up to Soviet tanks.

When I was in the East Sector of Berlin last month, the Soviet Foreign Minister referred to that outbreak, and he said that steps had been taken to be sure that it did not happen again. I saw those steps. They consisted of thousands upon thousands of heavily armed soldiers, with machineguns and tanks.

Traditions of liberty have been established in this hemisphere under the leadership of many great patriots. They fought for individual human rights and dignity. They lighted the guiding beacons along freedom's road, which have burned brightly in the healthy air of patriotic fervor. These beacons must not be stifled by the poisonous air of despotism now being fanned toward our shores from Moscow, Prague, and Budapest.

These places may seem far away. But let us not forget that in the early part of the last century the first danger to the liberties and independence which Bolivar, San Martin, and their heroic associates had won for the new Republics stemmed precisely from the despotic alliance forged by the Czar of Russia.

Sometimes, it seems, we recall that threat only in terms of colonialism. Actually, the threat that was deemed most grave was the desire of Czarist Russia and its allies to extend their despotic political system to this hemisphere.

I recall that President Monroe, in his message to Congress of December 2, 1823, addressed himself particularly to that phase of the problem. He spoke of ending future colonization by any European power, but he spoke with greater emphasis and at greater length of the danger which would come if "the Allied Powers should extend their political system to any portion of either continent" of this hemisphere.

What he said was being said in similar terms by other great American patriots and defenders of human liberty. Those sentiments have long since ceased to be merely unilateral. They have become an accepted principle of this hemisphere. That is why, it seems to us, we would be false to our past unless we again proclaimed that the extension to this hemisphere of alien despotism would be a danger to us all, which we unitedly oppose.

The Price of Freedom

My Government is well aware of the fact that there are few problems more difficult, few tasks more odious, than that of effectively exposing and thwarting the danger of international communism.

As we have pointed out, that danger cloaks itself behind fine sounding words; it uses the cover of many well-intentioned persons, and it so weaves itself into the fabric of community life that great courage and skill are required to sever the evil from the good. The slogan of "nonintervention" can plausibly be invoked and twisted to give immunity to what is, in fact, flagrant intervention.

The fact, however, that the defense of freedom is difficult, and calls for courage, is no adequate excuse for shutting our eyes to the fact that freedom is in fact endangered.

Freedom is never preserved for long except by vigilance and with dedicated effort. Those who do not have the will to defend liberty soon lose it.

Danger to liberty constantly recurs in everchanging form. To meet that danger requires flexibility and imagination. Each of our nations has in the past had to take some difficult and dangerous decisions, of one kind or another, on behalf of the independence and integrity of this hemisphere. During the 19th century, more than one American nation, including my own, risked the hazard of war against great military powers, rather than permit the intrusion into this hemisphere of the aggressive forces of European imperialism. During this 20th century, when evil forces of militarism and fascism twice sought world domination, the United States paid a great price in blood and treasure which served us all. Each of our American Republics has contributed to what has now become a glorious tradition.

Today we face a new peril that is in many respects greater than any of the perils of the past. It takes an unaccustomed form. It is backed by resources greater than have ever been accumulated under a single despotic will. However, we need not fear, because we too have greater assets. We have greater solidarity and greater trust born out of our past fraternal association. But just as the danger assumes an unconventional form, so our response may also need to be different in its form.

We need not, however, solve all these matters here. What we do need to do is to identify the peril; to develop the will to meet it unitedly, if ever united action should be required; and meanwhile to give strong moral support to those governments which have the responsibility of exposing and eradicating within their borders the danger which is represented by alien intrigue and treachery.

Of course, words alone will not suffice. But words can be meaningful. They can help to forge a greater determination to assure our collective independence, so that each of our nations will, in whatever way that is truly its own, be the master of its destiny. Thus, we will have served our common cause against its enemies.

It is in that spirit and in that hope that the United States presents its resolution.

42. Statement by Secretary Dulles, before the Committee on Economic Affairs of the Tenth Inter-American Conference, on Pan-American Relations*

March 10, 1954

I have sought the privilege of sitting with this economic committee because the problems which we face here in the Americas are as much economic as they are political.

It is sometimes said that we must seek economic welfare for the reason that that is the best defense against communism. I, myself, would put it differently. We seek economic welfare because, here in the Americas, we believe that all human beings, without regard to race, religion, or class should have the opportunity to develop in body, mind, and spirit. That can happen only in a healthy society. Therefore, we seek it as something which is good in itself, not merely as a defensive mechanism against communism.

Different nations develop their economies in different ways. This is natural and as it should be. We do not believe in a world of conformity. We believe that there is a richness in diversity. Just as this universe in which we live was created as a universe of diversity, so the human institutions which man builds are properly diverse, to take account of human and geographical differences.

In the United States we have a political system and an economic system which we believe to be good. At least, we are convinced that they serve well our particular needs.

We do not claim that our economy is perfect. In the past, business cycles, sometimes of great severity, have brought misery upon many people at home and abroad for reasons which they themselves could not control. There have been segments of our people who have not received adequate opportunity and who have not been rewarded in accordance with their merits.

We are constantly striving to make our society better by applying the lessons of experience. We do not believe that there exists, any more, the risk of great depressions as part of an inevitable cycle. Also the abundant productivity of our economy is steadily being spread to benefit more and more people.

All this is being done within the framework of a free enterprise economy which places a primary responsibility upon private effort. In this way we seek to develop a population of individuals who work hard, who invent, who save, who share. We recognize that, as social and economic problems grow in magnitude and complexity, so

*Department of State Bulletin, Mar. 22, 1954, pp. 426-27.

government has to assume increasing supervisory tasks. Nevertheless, the United States continues to place its primary dependence upon individual effort and upon private capital.

Our society is by no means a self-contained society. We know that for our present well-being, and the increasing of that well-being with others, foreign trade plays an important part in our economy. We know that it plays an even more important part in the economy of many friendly nations. We shall, therefore, strive to give to trade the dependability which it deserves.

Many of you feel that some adjustments of United States economic policies would be mutually beneficial. You may be right. Certainly, these are matters which we are prepared to consider openmindedly. That, indeed, is one of the reasons why we have come here with an important economic and financial delegation, representing not only the Department of State but also the Treasury, Commerce, and the Export-Import Bank. We are here to discuss, to study, and to learn, in line with the traditional United States policy of constantly taking new ways whenever we can be confident that the change is for the better.

We recognize that, in the economic field, it is more difficult to combine unity with diversity than it is in the political field.

In many of the American Republics, government plays a much more important role in economic affairs than we think desirable for ourselves. Some of you may think in terms of governmental capabilities, where we think in terms of private activity. Action which some of your governments would undertake as a normal function might seem to us a major departure from our standards of peacetime activity. Equally, opportunities and safeguards for private activity which we treat as a matter of course may seem to some of you to be extraordinary.

No one of our Republics should expect another to abandon its economic creed, in which its people believe and which seems adapted to its particular environment. Nevertheless, we must find more and better ways to cooperate. Happily, there are vast areas within which there are no basic obstacles, as evidenced by the very large amount of business which we do with each other. There is, and will continue to be, a vast exchange of goods between our countries to our mutual advantage. There will, I hope, be a substantial flow of capital which will help develop the vast potential resources of many of our southern neighbors.

But what now is, is not good enough to be accepted as satisfactory. We must do better. We must eradicate some of the difficulties and obstacles for which none of us can properly be held exclusively responsible.

We have heard here at this Conference a number of economic complaints directed against the United States. I take no offense at that. This is the place where we should talk frankly as friends, and it is best that we should say what is on our minds. However, I ask you to believe that these matters are not as simple as they sometimes sound. The difficulties may seem relatively small, but they can establish precedents which would have vast scope and consequences.

The situation requires that we should not be self-righteous, either in defense or attack, but that we should go forward with good will, tolerance, and patience to find an understanding. When I mention patience, I am not referring to delay but to effort which in order to be successful must be careful and painstaking.

The United States is eager to see within this hemisphere people who everywhere share the health of a good economy in the form appropriate to their own society and their own ideals; who have the opportunity to engage usefully in congenial work of their own choosing; and to enjoy, with their families and their neighbors, in peace and tranquillity, the fruits of their labor.

The United States will not continue to be satisfied merely with good political relations in this hemisphere. We also want good economic relations. We shall seek them on a basis of mutual respect for the economic and social, as well as the political, beliefs of each other. That is the pledge I give you.

43. Statement by Samuel C. Waugh, Assistant Secretary of State for Economic Affairs, before the Committee on Economic Affairs of the Tenth Inter-American Conference, on Economic Relations*

March 10, 1954

The members of the United States delegation who arrived 10 days ago have reported with enthusiasm the cordial reception they have received in this beautiful capital of our host country. Since arriving a few days ago, I have caught this same spirit.

We all look forward during the Conference to renewing old friendships as well as making new friends. It is our most sincere hope that, working jointly with you, we will be able to make some worthwhile contributions toward solving some of our mutual problems.

In his opening address last week, Secretary Dulles mentioned the report of the Randall Commission with which you are all familiar. In the very near future—possibly while we are still here—our President will send to the Congress a message outlining his recommendations for a foreign economic policy in the light of that report. The Secretary also discussed the flow of capital and technical assistance, our position on the coffee situation, and the action our President has just taken on the wool tariff. I might add that on Monday our Government announced a reduction in countervailing duties on wool tops from 18 to 6 percent. I am also pleased to refer to the heartening news of the progress made in several recommendations in the Eisenhower report.

The Secretary clarified certain questions about the future lending policy of the Export-Import Bank and mentioned the importance we place on the International Bank for Reconstruction and Development.

The statements which have been made in this Commission have been presented in a spirit of frankness and good will. This spirit we wish to reciprocate. Great care has gone into the preparation of your statements, and they deserve the serious considera-tion of all. In the committee meetings to follow, our delegates will sit down with you and discuss these and other important economic subjects in more detail.

The economic development of the entire hemisphere is of major interest to the United States. We are all partners in seeking common economic goals. These common purposes were perhaps most simply and clearly expressed in the economic charter of the Americas: "To live decently and work and exchange productively in peace and

Department of State Bulletin, Mar. 22, 1954, pp. 427-29.

security." The economic growth of each of us strengthens and broadens the basis for stable democratic societies of free men. One of the best assurances of a workable inter-American system is the continued success of our efforts toward greater economic development.

The basic philosophy of the United States emphasizes individual freedom. Our economic beliefs rest on confidence in what President Eisenhower recently called "the expansive power of individual enterprise." This is the revolutionary idea which, recognized or not, was so important in releasing human energies from the restraints of feudalism. The expansive power of individual enterprise again played a dramatic role when hemispheric trade came to flourish with the breaking of the bonds of colonialism. We reaffirm our faith in this constructive and expansive force.

The reaffirmation of these beliefs has led us to reexamine the proper role of government in modern society. Many of you have read the words of our President in his Economic Report to the Congress.

May I quote from one section:

> The Government can greatly help to maintain prosperity. But it is well to recall the accumulated experience of generations which has taught us that no Government can of itself create real and lasting prosperity. A thriving economy depends fundamentally on the enterprise of millions of individuals, acting in their own interests and in the interests of their families and communities.

The President then went on to say:

> The best service that the Government can render our economy, besides helping to maintain stability and insuring a floor of protection for the population, is therefore to create an environment in which men are eager to make new jobs, to acquire new tools of production, to improve or scrap the old ones, design new products and develop new markets, increase efficiency all around, and thus be able and willing to pay higher wages and provide better working conditions. The Federal Government is fostering and will continue to foster this kind of environment.

We believe that the role of government in the economy is to nurture and promote individual effort and not to replace it. In carrying this principle into action, the United States Government is pledged to maintain fair and equitable conditions under which our business enterprises, large and small, and our workers can operate most efficiently.

The dignity and worth of each individual in our society is one of our most sacred values. My Government shares with the Governments of the other American countries the objective of making these values a living reality.

In your statements you have indicated an interest in the economic situation and outlook in the United States.

U.S. Economic Conditions

Our economy in 1953 achieved a gross national product of $367 billion—the highest on record, and 5 percent larger than in 1952. Civilian employment averaged 61.9 million for the year. Unemployment, although increasing at the end of the year, averaged 1½ million, the lowest of all postwar years. Thus the economy had some of the characteristics of a business boom. As we move into 1954, production is down about 10 percent from its highest point and there is some increase in unemployment, though not beyond a figure which in times past was considered normal. What we have been experiencing is a transition from a wartime economy to one more nearly adjusted to peace. We appear to be making that adjustment without disturbance.

Farm production in 1953 was high but prices fell for the second successive year. Lower agricultural exports added to our domestic farm problem.

In foreign trade, United States exports of non-military goods to all countries in 1953 were $12.2 billion, about $1 billion less than in 1952. At the same time that our exports declined, our total imports rose slightly to $10.9 billion in 1953. Our exports to Latin America were about 15 percent less than in 1952, amounting to $3.1 billion, while our imports were $3.4 billion, about the same as in the previous year. Latin America thus continued to provide about one-third of our total imports, exceeding those from any other area in the world.

Our banking system, our insurance companies, and other financial institutions have operated conservatively and are in a strong position. The general price level has been stable. Plans of United States private business for new investment in plant and equipment, and projects of States and municipalities, indicate continued heavy expenditures for new capital investment.

These and other factors provide the basis for confidence in the economic outlook.

Your interest in the growth and stability of our country is equaled by our abiding interest in economic conditions in your countries. We fully recognize the problems facing various countries as their delegates have described them in these meetings. We are profoundly impressed, however, by the great progress which country after country has made toward the solution of these problems, each working with its problems in its own way.

Output in Latin America in the postwar period has increased by almost 5 percent annually. This is nothing short of spectacular. It exceeds the recent rate of growth in the United States. These gains have been based largely on the utilization of domestic resources. Your own people provided most of the capital, and their enterprise put the capital to work.

Foreign capital can hasten the development process. It will be attracted by conditions that promise fair treatment, stability, and a return which is interesting in relation to the returns elsewhere.

Tax and Treaty Matters

To provide incentives for an increased flow of private capital abroad, President Eisenhower has proposed specific changes in the United States tax laws. Among these are proposals (1) to tax income from foreign subsidiaries, or foreign branches that operate and elect to be taxed as subsidiaries, at a rate 14 percentage points lower than the regular corporation rates and (2) to broaden the definition of foreign taxes which may be credited against the United States income tax. We feel that these recommendations, if enacted into law, will represent positive unilateral action by the United States Government to encourage foreign investment.

Bilaterally, there are further steps the United States is prepared to take. I refer to treaties for the alleviation of double taxation. These treaties are an integral part of the

United States program to create a favorable tax climate for international trade and business. As of today, the United States is a party with foreign countries to 15 treaties relating to income taxes. Unfortunately, we have no treaty with any Latin American Republic. We trust that, in furtherance of their expressed desire for foreign private capital, the Latin American Republics will be receptive to our offer to meet and attempt· to work out mutually equitable arrangements to clarify international tax relations and minimize double taxation.

The United States also continues to be interested in negotiating with other governments more general treaties which will define the terms under which private capital may enter and operate in foreign countries. Discussion on a bilateral basis looking toward the establishment of common rules for the treatment of foreign investments would be mutually advantageous.

We are ready to discuss these treaty matters in the appropriate committee.

You have made clear at this Conference your concern about the relative prices of primary products and manufactured goods in international trade and the instability of raw material prices. We agree on the importance of these problems. They are, however, highly technical subjects which are difficult to treat adequately in this statement. I feel these are matters for fuller discussion in the appropriate committee.

In the field of primary production we have problems in my own country. The United States has always been a major producer and exporter of agricultural products. Today we are confronted with large surpluses arising in part from the great efforts to relieve shortages of farm products resulting from the devastation and destruction of World War II. It is worth noting that one of the primary causes of these surpluses has been our attempt to maintain too rigid a relationship between the prices of farm products and other prices. One result has been to price our agricultural products out of many foreign markets.

It takes time to adjust our agricultural economy to the more normal demand which has now developed. Legislation has been recommended to the Congress which, it is hoped, will hasten these adjustments. In the meantime, my Government is keeping its international responsibilities very much in mind in dealing with this problem. It is taking precautions to prevent, so far as possible, the disposal of our surpluses from interfering with normal marketings of friendly countries.

Our interest in the economic subjects under discussion at this Tenth Inter-American Conference is reflected in the fact that, in addition to the representatives of the Department of State, my Government is also represented by W. Randolph Burgess, Deputy to the Secretary of the Treasury; Samuel W. Anderson, Assistant Secretary of Commerce; our representative on the Inter-American Economic and Social Council, your longtime friend, Ambassador Merwin L. Bohan; Maj. Gen. Glenn E. Edgerton, Managing Director of the Export-Import Bank, together with members of their staffs. These gentlemen are here to participate in our committee discussions.

Many of our problems are not susceptible of easy or once-and-for-all solutions. This much can be said with assurance: Not only during this Conference but in the months and years to come there will be continuing and friendly consultations among us. We will constantly seek to develop with you constructive economic policies based on the mutuality of our interests.

It is for these reasons that we welcome and support the suggestion made here for a special Economic Conference. Possibly the extraordinary meeting of the Inter-

American Economic and Social Council, planned for this year, would serve this purpose.

In friendship and with a feeling of common destiny, we shall strive to work out with you constructive solutions to our common problems.

44. Statement by Secretary Dulles, before the Politico-Juridical Committee of the Tenth Inter-American Conference*

March 11, 1954

The U.S. delegation has listened with close attention to the important observations which other delegations have made with reference to intervention of international communism in the American Republics.

I have been impressed by the spirit of solidarity and unity. One's faith in our inter-American association cannot but be strengthened by this experience. It is a new chapter in practical cooperation for a common purpose.

There has been, it seems to me, an extraordinary degree of unanimity as to basic objective and means. I am confident that this unity of view will be incorporated in the document we approve.

There appears to be general acceptance of two basic propositions, i.e. (1) that international communism, which our American Republics have twice denounced with unanimity, is still a danger to hemispheric integrity, and, (2) that it is important for us at this time solemnly to warn the authors of this threat to keep their hands off this hemisphere.

The U.S. proposal for giving effect to these two principles has been generally accepted. However, certain amendments have been proposed or suggested.

The United States has given very careful consideration to these amendments and I should like to express, at this time, my views concerning them.

The concern most often expressed is that our declaration might be interpreted as intervention, or justifying intervention, in the genuinely domestic affairs of an American State. This concern is, we believe, due to natural historical fears rather than to any language in the U.S. proposal.

As several of my colleagues have pointed out, in view of the specific purpose and scope of the proposal and the safeguards of existing treaties within which it would operate, it is not conceivable that the declaration could be used for other than its intended purpose. I refer particularly to the admirable addresses of the Brazilian and Colombian Foreign Ministers. The U.S. proposal does not and obviously cannot enlarge or change in any way existing treaties.

The U.S. proposal, as submitted, is a foreign policy declaration directed against those in non-American lands who operate the subversive apparatus of international communism. They have used that apparatus to gain control over 800 million persons, to blot out indpendence in 15 nations in Europe and Asia, and they demonstrably are putting that apparatus into use against this hemisphere. We would warn them that we are aware of their design, that we oppose it, and that they cannot expect to gain a real

*Department of State Bulletin, Mar. 22, 1954, pp. 423-25.

success within this hemisphere because, if they should get control of any American State, we would all unite to deprive them of the fruits of their aggression and to restore the sovereignty and political independence to the American State that had been robbed of it.

Our proposed declaration in this sense is, I repeat, a foreign-policy declaration. Our admonitions are not addressed to any one of our Republics or to the Western Hemisphere.

Proposed U.S. Admendment

The delegations of Argentina and Mexico have suggested some verbal changes which they believe make this aspect of the declaration more clear. It seems to us, however, that the apprehension expressed comes not primarily from the present text but from historical fears and that the better and more adequate way to meet them is to add to the declaration as drafted by the United States an additional paragraph which would read as follows:

> This declaration of foreign policy made by the American Republics in relation to dangers originating outside this Hemisphere is designed to protect and not to impair the inalienable right of each American State freely to choose its own form of government and economic system and to live its own social and cultural life.

Such a supplement to the declaration proposed by the United States will, we believe, dispose of all the fears which have been expressed. Certain proposals have been made by the Mexican delegation which are unacceptable to the United States because they would, in our opinion, basically alter the concept of the declaration and turn it from a foreign-policy declaration into a declaration of domestic import. These Mexican amendments fall under four headings:

1. They would, in general, substitute the words, "agents of foreign international communism," where the U.S. proposal speaks only of "international communism." It is of course important that each of our states should take steps to detect and eradicate the secret agents which international communism has introduced into our midst. Such internal measures were recommended at the Fourth Meeting of the Ministers of Foreign Affairs. However, it was not the purpose of the United States to suggest that we should now merely repeat what was then said. We believe that we ought to give a simple, clear, and direct warning to the principals of these secret agents who for the most part reside in Moscow or satellite capitals and who from there dominate and direct the international Communist movement.

It is the fact that we direct our warning to them that gives the proposed declaration its status as a declaration of foreign policy. We would be reluctant to see our declaration altered so that it was essentially a doctrine of internal import as it would be if we directed ourselves only against the agents here of international communism.

2. It is suggested that we should introduce, at various points, references to our respective constitutional procedures. This would, of course, be appropriate if the declaration were designed to prescribe our own internal conduct. The United States would, however, be reluctant to adopt language which seemed to imply that that was the purpose of this declaration. Of course each of us will act in accordance with our

constitutional processes. However, a warning to potential enemies to keep their hands off of us has nothing whatever to do with our own domestic constitutional procedures.

3. One of the Mexican amendments would basically alter what is the heart of the proposed declaration, namely, that part which says that

> the domination or control of the political institutions of any American State by the international Communist movement, extending to this Hemisphere the political system of an extra-continental power, would constitute a threat to the sovereignty and political independence of the American States, endangering the peace of America, and would call for appropriate action in accordance with existing treaties.

In place of this clear, precise warning, which all can understand, the Mexican delegation would substitute a legalistic paragraph which attempts obscurely to define what we will do "when" the political institutions of any American State are subverted by the intervention of extra-continental or of any Communist power.

It seems to the United States unthinkable that the American States should adopt a declaration dealing with what we shall do "when" one of our American Republics is made the puppet of international communism. The whole purpose of our declaration is to prevent that from happening. A declaration which merely says what we shall do after it has happened would, I think, be wholly unacceptable to most of us. Certainly it is unacceptable to the United States.

The United States believes that, as suggested by the Brazilian and Colombian delegations, the declaration contained in its draft could usefully be amended by inserting before the words "appropriate action" the words "for consultation and," so as to make it perfectly clear that meetings of consultation would precede action—as is indeed prescribed both by the Rio Pact and by the charter of the American States.

4. The Mexican delegation has proposed certain amendments to the second section of the U.S. draft which contains recommendations which relate primarily to exposures and exchanges of information. For reasons which were very ably expressed by the chairman of the Haitian delegation, the United States believes that the Mexican amendments in this respect are inadvisable.

References to Social and Economic Measures

A considerable amount of discussion has related to the possible inclusion in the proposed declaration of references to social and economic measures which it is believed would help our American Republics in their fight against international communism. In this connection an amendment has been proposed by the Mexican delegate and a suggestion made by the Panamanian delegation.

The U.S. delegation believes that this Conference should make clear in no uncertain terms the dedication of our Republics to human rights and freedoms and to healthy economic and social conditions. In a statement which I made yesterday before the Economic Committee, I pledged my Government to support economic proposals in this sense, and we will equally support an appropriate declaration dealing with human rights and with the inherent dignity of the individual without regard to race, nationality, religion, or class. We entertain grave doubt, however, as to the wisdom of including such a declaration in our message of warning to the Communist dictators.

There are two reasons for our opinion that our declaration in these respects should be made elsewhere.

In the first place, it is, we believe, unfortunate to give the impression that we are interested in human rights, individual dignity, and opportunity and economic welfare only because we thereby combat communism. If there were no Communist threat in the world today, we would still believe that this Conference should renew its dedication to human welfare and its enhancement. It seems to us to degrade that which is most sacred and fundamental, to treat it as merely an anti-Communist tactic.

In the second place, it seems inappropriate to include a reference to our economic and social needs in a warning addressed to alien dictators. Surely we do not want to say to them in effect that their intervention would be acceptable in the case of an American State which did not achieve an ideal political, social, or economic order. The United States believes that the principle of non-intervention is an absolute principle and that we should avoid anything which could be interpreted to indicate that we would compromise it under any conditions.

For both reasons the United States believes that the declaration of our dedication to, and concern for, social and economic welfare should be expressed in another resolution rather than in a declaration of foreign policy directed to the alien despots who plot against us.

Mr. Chairman and Fellow Delegates, there are one or two around this table who seem to have expressed the thought that our collective American system is incapable of dealing with the kind of threat which now faces us and the formidable character of which has been demonstrated in respect to many countries and many people.

It is said that we cannot show a collective front against this danger because we cannot trust ourselves. It is suggested that the doctrine of non-intervention is so lightly regarded by the American States themselves that two-thirds of them might unite to practice intervention against a fellow American State. This danger is said to be so much greater than the danger of Communist intervention, that the American States should leave themselves exposed to international communism rather than run the risk that the doctrine of collective security might be turned by American States themselves into a doctrine of collective intervention.

Mr. Chairman, I have greater faith than that in the American system. I believe that there is not a single American State which would practice intervention against another American State. It is incredible to me that it should even be suggested that 14 of our 21 American States could be found to abuse the charter of the American States and the Rio Pact and to pervert those great enlightened political instruments into instruments of evil.

I can think of nothing more disastrous than for such mutual distrust to be exhibited to all the world so that our enemies may seek to take advantage from it.

I believe that the great disasters come about largely through miscalculation. Aggressors assume that they can with little risk make great gains. The purpose of the declaration proposed by the United States is to give a warning which will prevent such miscalculation. We believe that if the American Republics clearly and unitedly warn the alien plotters to keep away, the effect of that warning will be greatly to diminish the danger.

We believe, on the other hand, that if we fail to utter that clear and united warning, if we show distrust among ourselves, then the danger will go on mounting, and presently our beloved America will be ravaged by those evil forces which have turned Europe and Asia into continents of strife and misery.

45. News Conference Statement by Secretary Dulles on the Caracas Conference and the Monroe Doctrine*

March 16, 1954

I returned last Sunday from Caracas after 2 weeks of attendance at the Tenth Inter-American Conference. The Conference is still in session. It has many important matters to deal with, particularly in the social and economic field. Already, however, the Conference has made history by adopting with only one negative vote a declaration that, if the international communism movement came to dominate or control the political institutions of any American State, that would constitute a threat to the sovereignty and political independence of all the American States and would endanger the peace of America.

That declaration reflects the thinking of the early part of the nineteenth century. At that time, Czarist Russia was aggressive. Czar Alexander had made a claim to sovereignty along the west coast of this continent and had organized the so-called Holy Alliance which was plotting to impose the despotic political system of Russia and its allies upon the American Republics, which had just won their freedom from Spain.

In 1823, President Monroe, in his message to Congress, made his famous declaration. It contained two major points. The first related to the colonial system of the allied powers of Europe and declared that any extension of their colonial system in this hemisphere would be dangerous to our peace and safety. The second part of the declaration referred to the extension to this hemisphere of the political system of despotism then represented by Czarist Russia and the Holy Alliance. President Monroe declared that "it is impossible that the Allied Powers should extend their political system to any portion of either continent without endangering our peace and happiness. It is equally impossible, therefore, that we should behold such interposition, in any form, with indifference."

The first part of President Monroe's declaration against extending the European colonial system in this hemisphere has long since been accepted and made an all-American policy by concerted action of the American States. However, the same could not be said of President Monroe's declaration against the extension to this hemisphere of a European despotic system. It seemed to me, as I planned for the Caracas conference, that the threat which stems from international communism is a repetition in this century of precisely the kind of danger against which President Monroe had made his famous declaration 130 years ago. It seemed of the utmost importance that, just as part of the Monroe declaration had long since been turned from a unilateral declaration into a multilateral declaration of the American States, so it would be appropriate for the American States to unite to declare the danger to them all which would come if international communism seized control of the political institutions of any American State.

*Department of State Publication 5556, Inter-American Series 48, Washington D.C., 1954, pp. 10-11.

That matter was debated at Caracas for 2 weeks and a declaration in the sense proposed by the United States was adopted by a vote of 17 to 1, with 2 abstentions.

I believe that this action, if it is properly backed up, can have a profound effect in preserving this hemisphere from the evils and woes that would befall it if any one of our American States became a Soviet Communist puppet. That would be a disaster of incalculable proportions. It would disrupt the growing unity of the American States which is not reflected by the Charter of the Americas and by the Rio Treaty of Reciprocal Assistance.

It was time that we should have acted as we did because international communism is making great efforts to extend its political control to this hemisphere. The declaration adopted at Caracas, and particularly the sentiments which were expressed during the course of the debate, show an awareness of the danger and a resolution to meet it.

It is significant of the vitality of our American system that no one of the American Republics, even the most powerful, wanted to deal single-handedly with the danger, but that it was brought to the Inter-American Conference table as a matter of common concern. Furthermore, the declaration, as adopted, contained in substance the words of President Eisenhower, expressed in his great peace address of April 16, 1953, that the declaration "is designed to protect and not to impair the inalienable right of each American State freely to choose its own form of government and economic system and to live its own social and cultural life."

46. *Tenth Inter-American Conference Declaration of Solidarity for the Preservation of the Political Integrity of the American States against International Communist Intervention* *

March 28, 1954

Whereas:

The American republics at the Ninth International Conference of American States declared that international communism, by its anti-democratic nature and its interventionist tendency, is incompatible with the concept of American freedom, and resolved to adopt within their respective territories the measures necessary to eradicate and prevent subversive activities;

The Fourth Meeting of Consultation of Ministers of Foreign Affairs recognized that, in addition to adequate internal measures in each state, a high degree of international cooperation is required to eradicate the danger which the subversive activities of international communism pose for the American States; and

The aggressive character of the international communist movement continues to constitute, in the context of world affairs, a special and immediate threat to the national institutions and the peace and security of the American States, and to the right of each State to develop its cultural, political, and economic life freely and naturally without intervention in its internal or external affairs by other States.

*Department of State Publication 5556, Inter-American Series 48, Washington D.C., 1954, pp. 8-9.

The Tenth Inter-American Conference

I

Condemns:

The activities of the international communist movement as constituting intervention in American affairs;

Expresses:

The determination of the American States to take the necessary measures to protect their political independence against the intervention of international communism, acting in the interests of an alien despotism;

Reiterates:

The faith of the peoples of America in the effective exercise of representative democracy as the best means to promote their social and political progress; and

Declares:

That the domination or control of the political institutions of any American State by the international communist movement, extending to this hemisphere the political system of an extra-continental power, would constitute a threat to the sovereignty and political independence of the American States, endangering the peace of America, and would call for a meeting of consultation to consider the adoption of appropriate action in accordance with existing treaties.

II

Recommends:

That without prejudice to such other measures as they may consider desirable special attention be given by each of the American governments to the following steps for the purpose of counteracting the subversive activities of the international communist movement within their respective jurisdictions:

1. Measures to require disclosure of the identity, activities, and sources of funds, of those who are spreading propaganda of the international communist movement or who travel in the interests of that movement, and of those who act as its agents or in its behalf; and

2. The exchange of information among governments to assist in fulfilling the purpose of the resolutions adopted by the Inter-American Conferences and Meetings of Ministers of Foreign Affairs regarding international communism.

III

This declaration of foreign policy made by the American republics in relation to dangers originating outside this hemisphere is designed to protect and not to impair the inalienable right of each American State freely to choose its own form of government and economic system and to live its own social and cultural life.

47. Tenth Inter-American Conference Declaration of Caracas*

March 28, 1954

The Tenth Inter-American Conference

Reaffirms:

The fundamental principles and aims of the Charter of the Organization of American States, the American Declaration of the Rights and Duties of Man, the Universal Declaration of Human Rights, and the resolutions of the Organization that refer to those principles and aims,

Reiterates:

Recognition of the inalienable right of each American state to choose freely its own institutions in the effective exercise of representative democracy, as a means of preserving its political sovereignty, achieving its economic independence, and living its own social and cultural life, without intervention on the part of any state or group of states, either directly or indirectly, in its domestic or external affairs, and, particularly, without the intrusion of any form of totalitarianism.

Renews:

The conviction of the American States that one of the most effective means of strengthening their democratic institutions is to increase respect for the individual and social rights of man, without any discrimination, and to maintain and promote an effective policy of economic well-being and social justice to raise the standard of living of their peoples; and

Resolves:

To unite the efforts of all the American States to apply, develop, and perfect the above-mentioned principles, so that they will form the basis of firm and solidary action designed to attain within a short time the effective realization of the representative democratic system, the rule of social justice and security, and economic and cultural cooperation essential to the mutual well-being and prosperity of the peoples of the Continent; and

Declares:

This resolution shall be known as the "Declaration of Caracas."

48. Report by William G. Bowdler, Advisor to the United States Delegation, on the Tenth Inter-American Conference†

April 26, 1954

The Tenth Inter-American Conference met at Caracas, Venezuela, from March 1 to 28. All the American Republics participated with the exception of Costa Rica, but provision was made under which that Government may adhere to the Final Act. The

*Department of State Bulletin, Apr. 26, 1954, p. 639.
†Department of State Bulletin, Apr. 26, 1954, pp. 634-38.

Conference dealt with an agenda of 28 items covering the whole range of inter-American relations—juridical-political, economic, social, cultural, and organizational matters. It adopted 117 resolutions and 3 conventions. The Conference was also the forum in which Colombia and Peru announced the conclusion of a satisfactory agreement on the Haya de la Torre asylum case, a dispute which had been a constant source of tension between the two countries for the past 5 years.

Juridical-Political Matters

One of the principal objectives of the United States delegation to the Tenth Inter-American Conference, which was headed by Secretary Dulles, was to achieve maximum agreement among the American Republics upon a clear-cut and unmistakable policy determination against the intervention of international communism in the hemisphere, recognizing the continuing threat which it poses to their peace and security and declaring their intention to take effective measures, individually and collectively, to combat it. The United States proposed a resolution to this effect entitled "Declaration of Solidarity for the Preservation of the Political Integrity of the American States Against International Communist Intervention" ... The distinguishing feature of the resolution adopted, which marks a significant advance over the stands taken previously in inter-American meetings at Bogotá in 1948 and Washington in 1951, is the declaration:

> That the domination or control of the political institutions of any American State by the international communist movement, extending to this hemisphere the political system of an extracontinental power, would constitute a threat to the sovereignty and political independence of the American States, endangering the peace of America, and would call for a meeting of consultation to consider the adoption of appropriate action in accordance with existing treaties.

Seventeen of the American Republics voted in favor of the resolution. Mexico and Argentina chose to abstain, while Guatemala cast the only negative vote and also took the occasion to renounce its adherence to the anti-Communist resolutions adopted at Bogotá and Washington.

Amendments to this declaration prepared by other delegations suggested that it did not make adequate provision for promoting respect for human rights, for the effective exercise of representative democracy, and for the development of economic and social well-being as means for combating communism. Other proposed amendments implied concern that application of the declaration might in some way infringe upon the principles of self-determination and nonintervention. As a means of removing any doubt that the declaration is aimed at preventing, and not promoting, intervention, the United States proposed inclusion of a clear statement that the action taken is designed to protect and not impair the inalienable right of each state to choose its own form of government and economic system. The reaffirmation of traditional concepts of human rights and fundamental freedoms was included in a separate resolution entitled "Declaration of Caracas" ... , as well as in other actions taken, such as the Panamanian proposal relating to the abolition of racial discrimination as a means of fighting communism.

The topic "Colonies and Occupied Territories in America" received considerable attention from a number of the delegations. Three resolutions were presented and adopted. Two of these, submitted by Argentina and Brazil, respectively, were concerned with the general subject of colonialism in the Western Hemisphere and with the areas which are the subject of dispute between American and non-American states. The third, proposed by Ecuador, dealt with the American Committee on Dependent Territories (ACDT). The general resolutions for the most part repeat the views expressed in previous resolutions on this subject, namely, that colonialism in the Americas should be promptly brought to an end and that just claims of American States to territories in dispute should be supported. The resolution on the ACDT contemplates the continuation of the Committee, its convocation being left up to the Council of the Organization of American States (OAS) "when circumstances make this advisable." In conformity with the position generally taken on these issues, the United States explained its inability to go along with conference action upon matters involving so clearly the interests and responsibilities of friendly governments not represented. The delegation abstained in the vote on the two general resolutions and voted against the one on the American Committee on Dependent Territories.

*   *   *

Under the chapter of the agenda dealing with juridical-political matters, six instruments were submitted to the Conference for review and approval. Due to the exigencies of time, the Committee handling these items was able to complete action on only two of them: Convention on Diplomatic Asylum and Convention on Territorial Asylum. Each of these conventions was opened for signature at Caracas, but the United States, in view of its traditional position regarding the practice of diplomatic asylum and considering a treaty on the subject of territorial asylum to be unnecessary, did not sign either instrument. The other instruments—American Treaty of Pacific Settlement, Statute for an Inter-American Court of Justice, Statute of the Inter-American Peace Committee, and Protocol to the Convention on Duties and Rights of States in the Event of Civil Strife—were returned to the Council of the OAS variously for consultation with the governments, study by the corresponding technical organ, and appropriate action by the Council itself. In returning the proposed revision of the Statute of the Inter-American Peace Committee to the Council, the Conference confirmed the continuation of the Committee and applauded its fruitful work in the interest of the peace of the continent.

Economic Matters

From the speeches delivered in the opening debate it was evident that economic issues were of major importance to the Latin American delegates, particularly such problems as public financing of economic development; raw material prices and terms of trade; stability of, and access to, export markets; and technical cooperation. In many of the proposals introduced by Latin American delegations, it was clear that the United States was expected to provide assurances or make commitments which it was thought would provide solutions to these problems. The United States was not in a position to accept certain of those proposals, owing to the incompleteness or lack of clarity in the terminology, their one-sided provisions, or the fact that U.S. policy had not been firmly established in some fields.

One of the principal accomplishments in the economic field, as expressed by Assistant Secretary Holland, was the frankness and clarity with which the delegations presented their positions on various problems and the understanding achieved with respect to their respective viewpoints. He also pointed out that accords were being reached today on issues that had been in dispute in past years, and that the period ahead would yield agreement on problems for which solutions could not be found today. With a view to examining further, on the basis of new studies and developments, the possibility of achieving fuller agreement on practical measures for solving these problems, the Conference decided to convene a meeting of Ministers of Finance or Economy during the last quarter of 1954 in Rio de Janeiro, which will also be the IV Extraordinary Session of the Inter-American Economic and Social Council (IA-ECOSOC).

In addition to this decision, the Conference adopted 27 other resolutions relating to economic development, private investment, public financing of economic development, prices and terms of trade, trade restrictions, agricultural surpluses, agrarian reform, technical assistance, the economic resources of the continental shelf, and the future work of the Inter-American Economic and Social Council. In some of the more important resolutions on these subjects, the Tenth Conference took the following action:

1. Regarding foreign private capital, recommended that the American governments maintain and adopt suitable economic measures to attract such capital;

2. Regarding trade in strategic materials, recommended that consideration be given to the effect of decisions relating to these materials on the economies of the American States and that procedures be introduced permitting the exchange of views in order to study any practical measures relative to the adverse effects of such decisions;

3. Regarding public financing of economic development, recommended that the governments suggest to existing public-financed institutions that they give special consideration to measures to increase effectively their operations in the field of economic development in Latin America;

4. Regarding technical cooperation, decided to consider the OAS Program "as an activity of a continuing nature" and to urge the participating governments to maintain and possibly increase their present level of contributions;

5. Regarding economic resources of the continental shelf, requested the Council of the OAS to convoke a special conference in 1955 to consider as a whole the different juridical and economic aspects of this question; and

6. Regarding the Inter-American Economic and Social Council, made a series of suggestions with respect to its internal operations aimed at making it a more effective instrument for dealing with economic and social problems of the American States.

In the economic field the United States voted against the resolutions on Reductions of Restrictions on Inter-American Trade, and Terms of Trade and Prices; abstained on those dealing with Agricultural Surpluses, Agrarian Reform, and Economic Development, and Taxes on Passenger Fares in the Caribbean and Central America. The United States objection to the resolution on inter-American trade was based on the one-sided nature of the recommendation. On the terms of trade and prices resolution the United States objection was directed at the section referring to "an equitable level of remunerative prices to permit a balance in terms of trade," which seemed to imply a commitment which the United States could not accept. U.S. abstention on the last three of the resolutions listed above was explained as follows:

1. In the case of agricultural surpluses, the variable nature of the problem made it necessary for the United States not to commit itself definitively on a matter currently under intensive study in the executive and legislative branches of our government.

2. On agrarian reform, the resolution, in focusing solely on redistribution of land, followed too narrow an approach to this broad and important subject; and

3. On the question of taxes on passenger fares, that this is a matter which, for the United States, the Congress must decide.

Social Matters

The Conference considered six broad topics in the social field, covering social aspects of economic development, human rights, housing, cooperatives, rural exodus, and social welfare. Twenty-two resolutions relating to various aspects of these topics were adopted.

The discussions revealed general awareness of the social problems accompanying economic development and of the need for governments and international agencies to give proper attention to measures in the fields of health, housing, education, and social welfare in planning and executing economic development programs. Resolutions adopted on this subject, as well as on the related topics of rural migration and social welfare work, reflect a recognition of this need and urge the governments and the appropriate organs of the OAS through training courses, seminars, specialized conferences, and technical studies to give increased attention to the development of basic social services in rural areas and the training of personnel for planning and administering sound programs. In the field of labor, an important aspect of economic development, the resolutions adopted declare the intention of governments to continue to encourage the development of free and genuinely democratic labor unions; to recommend periodic information courses for workers to provide them with a knowledge of their rights and duties; and to urge closer coordination between the Organization of American States and the International Labor Organization.

The widespread interest in the Americas in housing and in cooperatives as a means for raising economic and social standards was manifest in the various proposals adopted for encouraging further development in these fields. Measures recommended for improving housing include the convening of meetings of housing experts to advise IA-ECOSOC on activities to be carried out; the appointment of a committee of three experts to work with IA-ECOSOC on a continuing basis; and the establishment of the present Inter-American Housing Center on a permanent basis. Studies were requested on the use of standardized construction materials and the effects which the establishment of a private inter-American bank for housing would have on the problem of low-cost housing. With respect to cooperatives, the Conference requested the Pan

American Union to make studies covering cooperative legislation and experience gained in the cooperative field and to provide, within its financial resources, technical assistance to the governments through training of leaders in the cooperative movement, regional seminars, and expansion of its secretariat services in connection with rural credit, consumer, low-cost housing, and multiservice cooperatives.

In addition to the declaration of Caracas and the racial discrimination resolution referred to above, the Conference adopted certain resolutions regarding human rights. One of these, entitled "Strengthening of the System for the Protection of Human Rights," appeared to the U.S. delegation to give appropriate attention to the point of view that the best methods for promoting respect for human rights are often found in education and example rather than through legal compulsion. In this resolution, various steps were proposed which governments might take to encourage observance of, and wider dissemination of information on, basic rights and duties of man. In the same resolution, the Pan American Union was requested to obtain periodically from the governments information relating to the progress made in promoting human rights, to effect exchange of pertinent legislation among the American States, and to undertake studies in comparative law concerning such legislation, giving preference to those rights centering around freedom of expression. A separate resolution, introduced by Uruguay, requesting the Council of the OAS to study the possibility of creating an Inter-American Court for the Protection of Human Rights, was opposed by the United States, on the grounds that such a court is premature and does not constitute an effective instrument for advancing the objective of greater respect for human rights.

Cultural Matters

Action of the Tenth Conference in the cultural field centered primarily on three important aspects: revision of the Convention for the Promotion of Inter-American Cultural Relations, the need for greater efforts to promote general education, especially the eradication of illiteracy, and guidance to the organs of the OAS dealing with cultural matters in the development and execution of their programs.

Revision of the Convention for the Promotion of Cultural Relations marked a significant step in the field of cultural relations and educational exchange. This convention, which is concerned with the exchange of students and professors, was sponsored by the United States at the Buenos Aires conference in 1936. Experience with its application since that time has demonstrated that many of its detailed provisions for the selection and support of exchangees are excessively rigid and cumbersome. Revision of the convention was directed, therefore, at introducing greater flexibility in the awarding of fellowships and grants. Thus, for example, allowance is made for the parties to carry out exchange programs through direct bilateral agreements. The procedures for selecting exchangees are simplified and the financial responsibilities of the participating governments are specified more precisely and realistically. A new provision was also introduced into the convention entrusting the Pan American Union with the responsibility for compiling and circulating annually to the states members of the OAS reports on the nature and extent of the participation of each in exchange programs. All the governments represented at Caracas signed the revised convention.

In the field of education the Conference recognized that the eradication of illiteracy is of the utmost importance and requested that special attention be given to this matter in the cultural activities for which the Council of the OAS is directly responsible as well as in the OAS Technical Cooperation Program. The governments were likewise urged to intensify their national campaigns against illiteracy, endeavoring to coordinate them with the activities of the OAS. In other resolutions bearing on education the Tenth Conference recommended to the governments the establishment of specialized educational centers for rural areas, requested the Committee for Cultural Action to undertake studies on vocational education in the American States and on the equivalence of academic degrees, commended the Pan American Union for the work it has done in organizing seminars in education and urged the governments to lend their support to development of demonstration libraries. The Conference also endorsed the idea that there should be held a meeting of Ministers and Directors of Education simultaneously with the next meeting of the Cultural Council and requested the Cultural Council to consider the desirability of holding periodic meetings of rectors, deans, and professors. Various other resolutions, including a possible convention on exchange of publications, participation in the 1946 Inter-American Copyright Convention, and support of the work of the Pan American Union in literary publications, the United States was not able to support for a variety of reasons.

A significant action of the Tenth Conference was to trace the guide lines which the governments, the Council of the OAS and the Cultural Council should follow in developing and carrying out inter-American cultural programs. The "Declaration on Cultural Cooperation" sets forth the areas in the educational, scientific, and cultural fields in which they are urged to intensify their efforts. In a resolution entitled "Inter-American Cultural Organizations" the Conference recommended to the governments a greater utilization of the cultural organs of the Organization of American States, to the Council of the OAS an increased effort to improve the functioning and coordination of its cultural organs, and to the Inter-American Cultural Council a series of points, emphasizing coordination and the establishment of priorities, which it should bear in mind in developing its program.

Organizational Matters

In a speech delivered during the opening debate the Secretary General of the OAS, Dr. Alberto Lleras, announced his decision to resign his post and went on to make a penetrating analysis of the Organization of American States and its future development. In particular, he singled out the tendency of the Council of the OAS to become absorbed in trivia and to avoid matters of substance, a trend which was at times evidenced during the preparatory period for the Tenth Conference. The address paved the way for one of the more important resolutions to emerge from the Caracas meeting: Resolution XLVI entitled "Matters Assigned to the Council of the Organization of American States." The resolution, based largely on suggestions which was proposed by the United States, is designed to strengthen the Council as the permanent executive body of the Organization by specifically assigning to it several important functions.

Consideration was also given by the Conference to the functioning and composition of two other organs: the Inter-American Juridical Committee and the Committee for Cultural Action. Following the recommendation of the Council of Jurists, the Conference decided that the Juridical Committee should hold annual sessions for a fixed period of time (3 months) and that it should, as appropriate, make greater use of the Department of International Law of the Pan American Union in furnishing background material and preparing preliminary studies. The Conference rejected the concept that the members of the Committee should have no other duties than those pertaining to the Committee, but did recognize that it was essential that they devote themselves exclusively to the work of the Committee while it is in session. The following nine countries were selected to membership in the Juridical Committee: Argentina, Brazil, Chile, Colombia, Dominican Republic, Mexico, Peru, United States, and Venezuela. The Conference did not enter into a detailed study of the functioning of the Cultural Action Committee, limiting its action to entrusting such a study to the Council of the OAS in consultation with the Inter-American Cultural Council and to establishing Mexico City as the seat of the Committee. Brazil, Cuba, Haiti, Mexico, and the United States were elected to membership in the Committee.

In other decisions on organizational matters the Conference revised the Statute of the Inter-American Commission of Women, adopted several resolutions relating to the civil, political, and economic rights of women, and entrusted to the Council of the OAS the study of administrative and fiscal policy of the Organization proposed by Brazil.

Quito, Ecuador, was designated as the site for the Eleventh Inter-American Conference, which, in accordance with the charter of the Organization, is to be held in 5 years.

49. News Conference Statement by Secretary Dulles, on Communist Influence in Guatemala*

May 25, 1954

The Guatemalan nation and people as a whole are not Communists. They are predominantly patriotic people who do not want their nation to be dominated by any foreign power. However, it must be borne in mind that the Communists always operate in terms of small minorities who gain positions of power. In Soviet Russia itself only about 3 percent of the people are Communists.

In judging Communist influence in Guatemala three facts are significant:

1. Guatemala is the only American State which has not completed ratification of the Rio Pact of the Americas.

2. Guatemala was the only one of the American States which at the last inter-American Conference at Caracas voted against a declaration that "the domination or control of the political institutions of any American State by the international communist movement, extending to this hemisphere the political system of an extra-continental power, would constitute a threat to the sovereignty and political independence of the American States, endangering the peace of America". . . .

*Department of State Publication 5556, Inter-American Series 48, Washington D.C., 1954, pp. 12-13.

3. Guatemala is the only American nation to be the recipient of a massive shipment of arms from behind the Iron Curtain.

It has been suggested from Guatemala that it needs more armament for defense. Already Guatemala is the heaviest armed of all the Central American States. Its military establishment is three to four times the size of that of its neighbors such as Nicaragua, Honduras, or El Salvador.

The recent shipment was effected under conditions which are far from normal. The shipment was loaded at the Communist-administered Port of Stettin. The ship was cleared for Dakar, Africa. The operation was cloaked under a series of chartering arrangements so that the real shipper was very difficult to discover. When he was discovered he claimed that the shipment consisted of nothing but optical glass and laboratory equipment. When the ship was diverted from its ostensible destination and arrived at Puerto Barrios, it was landed under conditions of extraordinary secrecy and in the personal presence of the Minister of Defense. One cannot but wonder why, if the operation was an aboveboard and honorable one, all of its details were so masked.

By this arms shipment a government in which Communist influence is very strong has come into a position to dominate militarily the Central American area. Already the Guatemalan Government has made gestures against its neighbors which they deem to be threatening and which have led them to appeal for aid.

The Guatemalan Government boasts that it is not a colony of the United States. We are proud that Guatemala can honestly say that. The United States is not in the business of collecting colonies. The important question is whether Guatemala is subject to Communist colonialism, which has already subjected 800 million people to its despotic rule. The extension of Communist colonialism to this hemisphere would, in the words of the Caracas Resolution, endanger the peace of America.

50. Statement by Henry Cabot Lodge, Jr., U.S. Representative to the U.N. Security Council, Concerning the Guatemalan Complaint*

June 20, 1954

The United States believes in the basic proposition that any member, large or small, has the right to an urgent meeting of the Security Council whenever it feels itself to be in danger. This is so even when, as is sometimes the case, the Security Council may not itself be in the best position to deal directly with the situation.

Guatemala charges that other governments are pursuing a policy of hostility and aggressiveness against it. The specific Guatemalan allegations involve two of its immediate neighbors, Honduras and Nicaragua, who are charged with disturbing the peace in a particular part of Central America. These charges are indeed serious and certainly warrant urgent examination.

But the question arises as to where the situation can be dealt with most expeditiously and most effectively.

The situation appears to the U.S. Government to be precisely the kind of problem which in the first instance should be dealt with on an urgent basis by an appropriate agency of the Organization of American States. The very fact that the Government of

*Department of State Publication 5556, Inter-American Series 48, Washington D.C., 1954, pp. 14-17.

Guatemala as a member of the Inter-American System has already requested that the Organization of American States take action strengthens this view.

It would perhaps be in order for me to inform the Council that, while the reports that we receive on the situation in Guatemala are incomplete and fragmentary, the information available to the United States thus far strongly suggests that the situation does not involve aggression but is a revolt of Guatemalans against Guatemalans. The situation in Guatemala, out of which this problem arises, has caused grave concern to the U.S. Government and to the other members of the Organization of American States. Consequently, the members of the Organization of American States have for some time been conferring intensively among themselves on the Guatemalan situation with a view to deciding upon what steps should be taken for the maintenance of peace and security of the continent.

No Charge Against U.S.

I am very glad that the Guatemalan representative made it crystal clear that he makes no charge whatever against the U.S. Government, because it is certainly true that the United States has no connection whatever with what is taking place.

I am constrained to note that, although he made no charges against the United States, the Guatemalan representative did cite a number of unfavorable comments made by others concerning Secretary Dulles, Ambassador Peurifoy, and Ambassador John M. Cabot. In fact, more of the time of his speech was given up in citing these statements that others had made—newspaper articles and hearsay—than in the actual charge that he made. Those tactics, of course, always give one the impression that instead of being interested in getting the answer to the question, "What is the truth?", the speaker is more interested in getting the answer to the question, "What is the headline going to be?"

Now, I do not think it is necessary for me here in the United Nations to make a lengthy speech about Secretary Dulles. Secretary Dulles has worked here for years. He is very well known personally to most of the men in this room. The merest inference that he could be actuated by any consideration other than that of duty is one which certainly reflects no credit on him who utters it. To anyone who knows President Eisenhower—and many of you know him—it must be crystal clear that there is a man who is utterly devoted to the principles of democracy, to the rights of man, and who abhors all forms of imperialism, who led a great army in World War II against Nazi imperialism, and who has shown by every word and deed of his life since the day when he was a small boy in Kansas that his heart is always on the side of the little man who is trying to get by in life.

The Secretary of State did nothing at Caracas which was not in accordance with the facts. As a matter of fact, the only authorities which the Guatemalan representative cites are the U.S. press. The U.S. press, estimable though it is and deeply as I respect it, does not speak for the U.S. Government, and I am sure the U.S. press will agree with me in that respect. You can find as many different opinions in the U.S. press as you care to look for.

Then the Guatemalan representative cites American companies, and, of course, they do not speak with the voice of authority.

Finally, he refers to Mr. Patterson [Richard C. Patterson, Jr., U.S. Ambassador to Guatemala from October 1948 until March 1951]. Well, Mr. Patterson does not hold office under this administration. He has never held office under this administration. Whatever he says is entirely on his own authority as an individual, and just as I will not judge the opinion of the Guatemalan Government about the United States on the basis of what some individual Guatemalan may say, so I will ask the Guatemalan representative not to judge the U.S. opinion about Guatemala on the basis of what some individual citizen of the United States may say.

I would like to point out that the Guatemalan representative has never produced any names or dates or other specific indications showing that the State Department has ever acted in an improper manner.

Now, this discussion began with a speech of Ambassador Castillo-Arriola which, as I say, was correct in tone. Then came the unspeakable libels against my country by the representative of the Soviet Union, which, in the words that Sir Gladwyn Jebb used last autumn, make me think that his reason must be swamped when he says things like that about the United States.

Then, as a climax, we had the crude performance in the gallery—a sequence which I fear is not without significance. Of course, anyone is capable of filling the galleries with paid demonstrators, and we hope that the Communists who think this is such clever politics will outgrow it after a while. It may take time.

No Satellites in OAS

The representative of the Soviet Union said that the United States is the master of the Organization of American States. When he says that, he is not reflecting on us. He is reflecting on himself, because it shows that he cannot conceive of any human relationship that is not the relationship of master and servant. He cannot conceive of a relationship in which there is a rule of live and let live, in which people are equals and in which people get along by accommodation and by respecting each other.

He can just imagine what would happen to somebody who raised his voice against the Soviet Union in Poland, Czechoslovakia, or Estonia, or one of those countries, and compare that with the way in which representatives of smaller countries in the United Nations constantly disagree with the United States—and they are welcome to do it. We have no satellites and we do not want any; and we do not desire to set up a monolithic structure in the free world.

Then the Soviet representative said that the United States prepared this armed intervention. That is flatly untrue. I will challenge him to prove it—and he cannot do so.

It is interesting to me, who spent 13 years of my life in the United States Senate, to come here and find that in the person of the representative of the Soviet Union we have such an outstanding authority on the United States Senate. Apparently, he knows all. Though he never has set foot inside the place, he apparently knows much more about the United States Senate than men who have been members of it for many years. When he infers that the Senators of the United States allow their official actions to be determined in accordance with their private financial interests, he is making an accusation which not only reflects no credit upon himself but which reflects a grave doubt on the wisdom and the good intent and the sincerity of every policy which his Government advocates here today.

I will call his attention to the fact that I was in the Senate at the beginning of World War II when the Senate voted the Lend-Lease Bill whereby the United States aided the Soviet Union in its fight to repel Nazi imperialism. At that time we did not hear anything out of the Soviet Union criticizing the motives of the Senators of the United States who were then voting to help the Soviet Union.

Now, the men who are in the United States Senate today are precisely the same kind of men who voted to help the Soviet Union. If they were good enough then to help the Soviet Union, they are good enough now to stand up for the interests of their country.

I notice the representative of the Soviet Union is smiling, which leads me to believe that he does not really believe the things that he has said and that he has said them under instructions. I trust that is the case.

Now, he has told us that he intends to veto the pending resolution. That will be the second veto by the Soviet Union in 3 days. We had veto No. 59 on Friday, and now we are going to have veto No. 60 on Sunday. And, vetoing what? Vetoing a move to ask the Organization of American States to solve this problem, to try to bind up this wound in the world and then report back to the Security Council—not to relieve the Security Council of responsibility. This resolution does not do that. It just asks the Organization of American States to see what it can do to be helpful. Here it says in paragraph 2 of article 52, "the Members of the United Nations entering into such arrangements"—that is, regional arrangements—"or constituting such agencies shall make every effort to achieve pacific settlement of local disputes through such regional arrangements or by such regional agencies before referring them to the Security Council."

Now, at the very least, that is a harmless provision. It is an intelligent provision. It is a constructive provision. Why does the representative of the Soviet Union, whose country is thousands and thousands of miles away from here, undertake to veto a move like that? What is his interest in it? How can he possibily—how can this action of his possibly fail to make unbiased observers throughout the world come to the conclusion that the Soviet Union has designs on the American Hemisphere. There is no other explanation of it. And the recent articles in *Pravda* and *Izvestia* which have appeared in the last 2 or 3 days give color to that assertion.

I say to you, representative of the Soviet Union, stay out of this hemisphere and don't try to start your plans and your conspiracies over here.

51. Statement by Ambassador Lodge to the U.N. Security Council, Concerning the Guatemalan Complaint*

June 22, 1954

I note specifically the cable from Mr. Toriello does not ask for another meeting of the Council.

*Department of State Publication 5556, Inter-American Series 48, Washington D.C., 1954, pp. 17-18.

As President of the Security Council I was very glad to respond to his request for an urgent meeting of the Council last Sunday.

The Security Council, after exhaustive discussion, by a vote of 10 to 1, voted last Sunday [June 20] that the right place to go to get peace in Guatemala is the Organization of American States, where there is both unique knowledge and authority. The one vote against this was that of the Soviet Union.

In the face of this action, therefore, those who continually seek to agitate the Guatemalan question in the Security Council will inevitably be suspected of shadow boxing—of trying to strike attitudes and issue statements for propaganda purposes.

I can understand that the Soviet Union, which, by its cynical abuse of the veto, has crudely made plain its desire to make as much trouble as possible in the Western Hemisphere, should constantly seek to bring this matter before the Security Council.

But the Government of Guatemala should not lend itself to this very obvious Communist plot, lest they appear to be a cat's paw of the Soviet conspiracy to meddle in the Western Hemisphere. In fact, as it is, many persons will wonder whether the whole imbroglio in Guatemala was not cooked up precisely for the purpose of making Communist propaganda here in the United Nations. This I am sure Mr. Toriello would not want.

The fact that it has become increasingly plain that the situation in Guatemala is clearly a civil—and not an international—war, makes it even more appropriate that the Security Council should not intervene further.

The Security Council showed last Sunday by a vote of 10 to 1 that it emphatically believed that the Organization of American States was the place to try to settle the Guatemalan problem. To fly squarely in the face of this recommendation would raise grave doubts as to the good faith of those who make such requests.

52. United States Senate Concurrent Resolution 91 Supporting the Caracas Declaration of Solidarity*

June 25, 1954

Whereas for many years it has been the joint policy of the United States and the other States in the Western Hemisphere to act vigorously to prevent external interference in the affairs of the nations of the Western Hemisphere; and

Whereas in the recent past there has come to light strong evidence of intervention by the international Communist movement in the State of Guatemala, whereby government institutions have been infiltrated by Communist agents, weapons of war have been secretly shipped into that country, and the pattern of Communist conquest has become manifest; and

Whereas on Sunday, June 20, 1954, the Soviet Government vetoed in the United Nations Security Council a resolution to refer the matter of the recent outbreak of hostilities in Guatemala to the Organization of American States: Therefore be it

Resolved by the Senate (The House of Representatives concurring), That it is the sense of Congress that the United States should reaffirm its support of the Caracas

*Department of State Publication 5556, Inter-American Series 48, Washington D.C., 1954, p. 24.

Declaration of Solidarity of March 28, 1954, which is designed to prevent interference in Western Hemisphere affairs by the international Communist movement, and take all necessary and proper steps to support the Organization of American States in taking appropriate action to prevent any interference by the international Communist movement in the affairs of the States of the Western Hemisphere.

53. Statement by Ambassador Lodge, to the U.N. Security Council, Concerning the Guatemalan Complaint*

June 25, 1954

Now, Gentlemen, the Government of the United States joins its colleagues in the Organization of American States in opposing the adoption of the provisional agenda. We have taken this position only after the most careful consideration. We believe that there should be great liberality with reference to the consideration of items by either the Security Council or the General Assembly, but in the present case, we believe that an issue was involved which is so fundamental that it brings into question the whole system of international peace and security which was created by the charter at San Francisco in 1945.

When the charter was being drafted, the most critical single issue was that of the relationship of the United Nations as a universal organization to regional organizations, notably the already existing Organization of American States. There were a good many days in San Francisco when it seemed that the whole concept of the United Nations might fail of realization because of the difficulty of reconciling these two concepts of universality and regionalism. Finally, a solution was found in the formula embodied in articles 51 and 52 of the charter. Article 51 recognized the inherent right of individuals to collective self-defense, and article 52 admitted the existence of regional arrangements for dealing with such matters related to the maintenance of international peace and security as are appropriate for regional action. Article 52 provided that the Security Council had the inherent right to investigate any dispute or situation under article 34 which might lead to international friction. While any member of the United Nations might bring any dispute or situation to the attention of the Security Council under article 35, nevertheless members of the United Nations who had entered into regional arrangements should make every effort to achieve pacific settlements of local disputes through such regional arrangements before referring them to the Security Council. The Security Council should thus encourage the development of pacific settlement of local disputes through regional arrangements.

Now, Gentlemen, by that formula a balance was struck between universality, the effectiveness of which was qualified by the veto power, and regional arrangements. The adoption of that formula permitted the charter of the United Nations to be adopted. Without that formula there would never have been a United Nations.

If the United States Senate in 1946 had thought that the United Nations Charter in effect abrogated our inter-American system, I say to you as a man with 13 years'

*Department of State Publication 5556, Inter-American Series 48, Washington D.C., 1954, pp. 18-23.

experience in the Senate, the charter would not have received the necessary two-thirds vote. And, in my judgment, the American people feel the same way today.

Translating a Formula Into a Reality

Now for the first time, the United Nations faces the problem of translating that formula from one of words into one of reality. The problem is as critical as that which faced the founders at San Francisco in 1945. Let us not delude ourselves. If it is not now possible to make a living reality of the formula which made possible the adoption of the charter, then the United Nations will have destroyed itself in 1954 as it would have been destroyed still-born in 1945 had not the present formula been devised primarily under the creative effort of the late Senator Vandenberg and the present Secretary of State, Mr. Dulles, working with Secretary Stettinius and other administration leaders. It was this formula which secured bipartisan support in the United States in 1946. And I note by a completely bipartisan vote the Senate today declared that the international Communist movement must be kept out of this hemisphere.

So much for the part of the United States in what happened at San Francisco.

The great weight of the effort at San Francisco, however, was made by the other American Republics, as you have heard Ambassador Gouthier and Ambassador Echeverri say before me. The representatives of the other American Republics were determined that the United Nations should be supplementary and not in substitution or impairment of the tried and trusted regional relationships of their own.

The United States, which took such an active part in drafting the charter provisions in question, soberly believes that, if the United Nations Security Council does not respect the right of the Organization of American States to achieve a pacific settlement of the dispute between Guatemala and its neighbors, the result will be a catastrophe of such dimensions as will gravely impair the future effectiveness, both of the United Nations itself and of regional organizations such as the Organization of American States. And that is precisely what I believe to be the objective of the Soviet Union in this case. Otherwise, why is he so terribly intent upon doing this?

The present charter provisions were drafted with particular regard for the Organization of American States, which constitutes the oldest, the largest, and the most solid regional organization that the world has ever known. The distinctive relationship of the American States dates back to the early part of the last century. Throughout this period of over 130 years, there has been a steady development of ever closer relations between the 21 American Republics. They have achieved a relationship which has preserved relative peace and security in this hemisphere and a freedom from the type of wars which have so cruelly devastated the peoples of Europe and Asia. The Organization of American States is an organization founded upon the freedom-loving traditions of Bolivar, of Washington, and of Abraham Lincoln.

The 21 American Republics have been bound together by a sense of distinctive destiny, by a determination to prevent the extension to this hemisphere of either the colonial domain of European powers or the political system of European despotism. They have repeatedly pledged themselves to settle their own disputes as between themselves and to oppose the interposition into their midst of non-American influences, many of which were abhorrent to the ideals which gave birth to the

American Republics and which sustained them in their determination to find a better international relationship than has yet been achieved at the universal level.

Evidence of Communist Intervention

There has recently been evidence that international communism, in its lust for world domination, has been seeking to gain control of the political institutions of the American States in violation of the basic principles which have from the beginning inspired them freely to achieve their own destiny and mission in the world.

Now it is our belief that the great bulk of the people of Guatemala are opposed to the imposition upon them of the domination of alien despotism and have manifested their resistance just as have many other countries which international communism sought to make its victim. The Government of Guatemala claims that the fighting now going on there is the result of an aggression by Honduras and Nicaragua. It claims that it is a victim. It asks for an investigation. It is entitled to have the facts brought to light. The procedures for doing that are clearly established within the regional Organization of American States. These states have established a permanent Inter-American Peace Committee to handle problems of this nature. Guatemala, Honduras, and Nicaragua all applied to that Committee for assistance in resolving this problem. The Committee has agreed to send a fact-finding committee to the area of controversy for that purpose. Guatemala has attempted to interrupt this wholesome process by first withdrawing its petition, and, second, by withholding its consent for the fact-finding committee to proceed with its task. Nevertheless, because the members of the Committee feel that it is inconceivable that Guatemala will obstruct the very investigation for which she has been clamoring for days, the Committee is firmly and vigorously preparing to proceed to the area of controversy.

The Government of Guatemala has regularly exercised the privileges and enjoyed all the advantages of membership in the Organization of American States, including those of attending and voting in its meetings. It is obligated by article 52, paragraph 2 of the charter, to "make every effort to achieve pacific settlement of local disputes through regional arrangements." Its efforts to bypass the Organization of American States is in substance a violation of article 52, paragraph 2.

We hear today that Guatemala, after years of posing as a member of that Organization, now for the first time claims that she is not technically a member thereof. To have claimed and to have exercised all the privileges of membership for a number of years and then to disclaim the obligations and responsibilities is an example of duplicity which surely the Security Council should not condone. Either Guatemala is a member of the Organization of American States and therefore bound by article 52, paragraph 2, or else it is guilty of duplicity such that it cannot come before the Security Council with clean hands.

Now, if we adopt the agenda, we in effect give one state, in this case Guatemala, a veto on the Organization of American States. It is not possible to do both. You do one at the expense of the other in this case.

In any event, the United States is a member of the Organization of American States, and as such we are clearly bound by article 52, paragraph 2 of the charter. The

United States is also bound by article 20 of the charter of the Organization of American States which provides:

> All international disputes that may arise between American States shall be submitted to the peaceful procedures set forth in the Charter before being referred to the Security Council of the United Nations.

Well, that has been so for a long time.

The United States does not deny the propriety of this danger to the peace from Guatemala being brought to the attention of the Security Council in accordance with article 35 of the charter, and that has been done. As I said, I called the meeting the day after I received the message. The United States is, however, both legally and as a matter of honor bound by its undertakings contained in article 52, paragraph 2, of the charter and in article 20 of the charter of the Organization of American States to oppose Security Council consideration of this Guatemalan dispute upon the agenda of the Security Council until the matter has first been dealt with by the Organization of American States, which through its regularly constituted agencies is dealing actively with the problem now.

The United States is in this matter moved by more than legal or technical considerations, and I recognize that. We do not lightly oppose consideration of any matter by the Security Council. We are, however, convinced that a failure by the Security Council to observe the restraints which were spelled out in the charter will be a grave blow to the entire system of international peace and security which the United Nations was designed to achieve.

The proposal of Guatemala, supported most actively by the Soviet Union, which in this matter has already passed its 60th veto, is an effort to create international anarchy rather than international order. International communism seeks to win for itself support by constantly talking about its love of peace and international law and order. In fact, it is the promoter of international disorder.

Gentlemen, this organization is faced by the same challenge which faced the founders at San Francisco in 1945. The task then was to find the words which would constitute a formula of reconciliation between universality and regionalism. And now the issue is whether those words will be given reality or whether they will be ignored. If they be ignored, the result will be to disturb the delicate but precious balance between regional and universal organizations and to place one against the other in a controversy which may well be fatal to them both.

The balance struck by the charter was achieved at San Francisco in the face of violent opposition of the Soviet Union at that time. It sought from the beginning to secure for the Security Council, where it had the veto power, a monopoly of authority to deal with international disputes. Today international communism uses Guatemala as the tool whereby it can gain for itself the privileges which it was forced to forego at San Francisco. I say with all solemnity that, if the Security Council is the victim of that strategy and assumes jurisdiction over disputes which are the proper responsibility of regional organizations of a solid and serious character, then the clock of peace will have been turned back and disorder will replace order.

The Guatemalan complaint can be used, as it is being used, as a tool to violate the basic principles of our charter. It is to prevent that result, which would set in motion a chain of disastrous events, that the United States feels compelled to oppose the adoption of the provisional agenda containing the Guatemalan complaint and appeals to the other members to join with us in avoiding a step which, under the guise of plausibility and liberality, will, in fact, engage this organization in a course so disorderly and so provocative of jurisdictional conflict that the future of both the United Nations and of the Organization of American States may be compromised and a grave setback given to the developing processes of international order.

54. Statement by John C. Dreier, United States Representative to the Council of the Organization of American States, on the Guatemalan Problem *

June 28, 1954

I speak today as the representative of one of 10 American countries who have joined in a request that a Meeting of Ministers of Foreign Affairs be convoked to act as Organ of Consultation under articles 6 and 11 of the Inter-American Treaty of Reciprocal Assistance. On behalf of the United States I wish to support this request with all the force and conviction that I can express, feeling profoundly as I and my countrymen do that this is a critical hour in which a strong and positive note of inter-American solidarity must be sounded.

The Republics of America are faced at this time with a serious threat to their peace and independence. Throughout the world the aggressive forces of Soviet Communist imperialism are exerting a relentless pressure upon all free nations. Since 1939, 15 once free nations have fallen prey to the forces directed by the Kremlin. Hundreds of millions of people in Europe and Asia have been pressed into the slavery of the Communist totalitarian state. Subversion, civil violence, and open warfare are the proven methods of this aggressive force in its ruthless striving for world domination.

Following World War II, in which millions of men died to free the world from totalitarianism, the forces of Communist imperialism took on a freshly aggressive aspect. The first objectives of this new drive for domination were the countries of Eastern Europe and the Balkans. Efforts to overcome Greece and Iran failed because of the heroic resistance of peoples whose courage not only gave them strength to defend their independence but also brought them the moral and material support of other countries directly and through international organizations.

Communist forces then turned their attention to Asia. Following the fall of China came the stark aggression of the Korean war where once more the united forces of the free world, acting through the United Nations, stemmed the tide of Soviet Communist imperialism.

More recently, we have seen the combination of Communist subversion and political power, backed with weapons from the Communist arsenal, strike deep into Southeast Asia and threaten to engulf another populous area of the world as it emerges from colonialism.

And now comes the attack on America.

*Department of State Publication 5556, Inter-American Series 48, Washington D.C., 1954, pp. 25-29.

Until very recently we of the Americas, here in our continental bastion, have felt ourselves relatively far from the field of open conflict. To be sure, in all our countries the international Communist organization has for some time undertaken its insidious work of attempting to undermine our institutions and to achieve positions of influence in public and private organizations. But only within the last few years has there been evidence of a real success on the part of the international Communist organization in carrying to this hemisphere the plagues of internal strife, and subservience to a foreign imperialism, which had previously been inflicted upon other areas of the world. That success marks the problem for which the treaty of Rio de Janeiro is now invoked as a measure of continental defense.

Mr. Chairman, this is not the time and place in which to enter into a discussion of the substance of the problem which will be placed before the Organ of Consultation when it meets. At this time it is the function of the Council merely to consider the validity of the request that the Organ of Consultation be convoked.

In support of the request for a meeting, I should like to cite briefly the following compelling arguments.

Anti-Communist Declarations

First, the American Republics have several times during recent years clearly and unequivocally stated their opposition to the objectives and methods of the international Communist movement which, by its very nature, is incompatible with the high principles that govern the international relations of the American States. This viewpoint was clearly enunciated at the Ninth Inter-American Conference, which in Resolution 32 declared that by its antidemocratic nature and its interventionist tendency the political activity of international communism was incompatible with the concept of American freedom. This thought was echoed at the Fourth Meeting of Foreign Ministers which, furthermore, pointed out that the subversive action of international communism recognized no frontiers and called for a high degree of international cooperation among the American Republics against the danger which such actions represented.

Only a few months ago at Caracas the American States expressed their determination to take the necessary measures to protect their political independence against the intervention of international communism, and declared that the domination or control of the political institutions of any American State by the international Communist movement would constitute a threat to the sovereignty and political independence of the American States, endangering the peace of America.

There is no doubt, Mr. Chairman, that it is the declared policy of the American States that the establishment of a government dominated by the international Communist movement in America would constitute a grave danger to all our American Republics and that steps must be taken to prevent any such eventuality.

Communist Penetration in Guatemala

Second, I should like to affirm the fact that there is already abundant evidence that the international Communist movement has achieved an extensive penetration of the political institutions of one American State, namely the Republic of Guatemala, and now seeks to exploit that country for its own ends. This assertion, which my Government is prepared to support with convincing detail at the right time, is clearly warranted by the open opposition of the Guatemalan Government to any form of inter-American action that might check or restrain the progress of the international Communist movement in this continent; by the open association of that Government with the policies and objectives of the Soviet Union in international affairs; by the evidences of close collaboration of the authorities in Guatemala and authorities in Soviet-dominated states of Europe for the purpose of obtaining under secret and illegal arrangements the large shipment of arms which arrived on board the *M/S Alfhem* on May 15, 1954; by the efforts of Guatemala in the United Nations Security Council, in collaboration with the Soviet Union, to prevent the Organization of American States, the appropriate regional organization, from dealing with her recent allegations of aggression, and finally by the vigorous and sustained propaganda campaign of the Soviet press and radio, echoed by the international Communist propaganda machine throughout the world in support of Guatemalan action in the present crisis.

The recent outbreak of violence in Guatemala adds a further sense of urgency to the matter. We well know from experience in other areas into which the international Communist movement has penetrated the tragic proportions to which this inevitable violent conflict may ultimately extend.

The above facts, Mr. Chairman, I submit, are more than enough to demonstrate the need for a prompt meeting of the Organ of Consultation as has been proposed in the note which was read at this meeting today.

Within the last 24 hours it appears that there has been a change in the Government of Guatemala. It is not possible, however, in the opinion of my Government, to arrive at any considered judgment of how this change may affect the problem with which we are concerned. Under the circumstances, it would appear to be essential that we do not relax our efforts at this moment, but proceed with our plans in order to be ready for any eventuality. At the same time, we should of course all watch developments in Guatemala carefully and be prepared subsequently to take whatever steps may prove necessary in the light of future events.

I should like to emphasize the fact that the object of our concern, and the force against which we must take defensive measures, is an alien, non-American force. It is the international Communist organization controlled in the Kremlin which has created the present danger. That it is rapidly making a victim of one American State increases our concern for that country and our determination to unite in a defense of all 21 of our American nations. We are confident that the international Communist movement holds no real appeal for the peoples of America and can only subdue them if allowed to pursue its violent and deceitful methods unchecked. Having read the tragic history of other nations seduced by Communist promises into a slavery from which they later could not escape, we wish to leave no stone unturned, no effort unexerted, to prevent the complete subordination of one of our member states to Soviet Communist imperialism. For when one state has fallen, history shows that another will soon come under attack.

Now, Mr. Chairman, in the Americas we have established ways for dealing with these problems that affect the common safety. We are pledged to maintain continental peace and security through our solidarity expressed in consultation and joint effort. In the Inter-American Treaty of Reciprocal Assistance we have the vehicle through which we can merge our individual efforts in order to take the measures necessary for the maintenance of continental peace and security. The meeting of the Organ of Consultation which we request here today is in fulfillment of the principles and procedures which the American Republics have laid down for dealing with threats to their independence, sovereignty, and peace. If that system of international relations of which the peoples of this hemisphere are so rightfully proud is to endure, it must resolutely meet the challenge which Soviet Communist imperialism has now thrown down to it.

If we take a valiant course and courageously face the danger which menaces us we will again prove, as America has proved in the past, the power of our united will. That, I am sure, we shall do because of what is at stake. There hang in the balance not only the security of this continent but the continued vitality and existence of the Organization of American States and the high principles upon which it is founded. In our decisions at this hour we may well profoundly affect the future of our American way of life.

Mr. Chairman, I urge that this Council promptly approve the proposal that the Organ of Consultation be invoked; that the date be set as of July 7 next; and that the decision be taken here and now so that the entire world may be given evidence of our determination to act effectively in the present crisis.

55. *Radio and Television Address by Secretary Dulles, on International Communism in Guatemala* *

June 30, 1954

Tonight I should like to talk with you about Guatemala. It is the scene of dramatic events. They expose the evil purpose of the Kremlin to destroy the inter-American system, and they test the ability of the American States to maintain the peaceful integrity of this hemisphere.

For several years international communism has been probing here and there for nesting places in the Americas. It finally chose Guatemala as a spot which it could turn into an official base from which to breed subversion which would extend to other American Republics.

This intrusion of Soviet despotism was, of course, a direct challenge to our Monroe Doctrine, the first and most fundamental of our foreign policies.

It is interesting to recall that the menace which brought that doctrine into being was itself a menace born in Russia. It was the Russian Czar Alexander and his despotic allies in Europe who, early in the last century, sought control of South America and the western part of North America. In 1823 President Monroe confronted this challenge with his declaration that the European despots could not "extend their political system to any portion of either continent without endangering our peace and happiness. We would not," he said, "behold such interposition in any form with indifference."

*Department of State Publication 5556, Inter-American Series 48, Washington D.C., 1954, pp. 30-34.

These sentiments were shared by the other American Republics, and they were molded into a foreign policy of us all. For 131 years that policy has well served the peace and security of this hemisphere. It serves us well today.

In Guatemala, international communism had an initial success. It began 10 years ago, when a revolution occurred in Guatemala. The revolution was not without justification. But the Communists seized on it, not as an opportunity for real reform, but as a chance to gain political power.

Communist agitators devoted themselves to infiltrating the public and private organizations of Guatemala. They sent recruits to Russia and other Communist countries for revolutionary training and indoctrination in such institutions as the Lenin School at Moscow. Operating in the guise of "reformers" they organized the workers and peasants under Communist leadership. Having gained control of what they call "mass organizations," they moved on to take over the official press and radio of the Guatemalan Government. They dominated the social security organization and ran the agrarian reform program. Through the technique of the "popular front" they dictated to the Congress and the President.

The judiciary made one valiant attempt to protect its integrity and independence. But the Communists, using their control of the legislative body, caused the Supreme Court to be dissolved when it refused to give approval to a Communist-contrived law. Arbenz, who until this week was President of Guatemala, was openly manipulated by the leaders of communism.

Guatemala is a small country. But its power, standing alone, is not a measure of the threat. The master plan of international communism is to gain a solid political base in this hemisphere, a base that can be used to extend Communist penetration to the other peoples of the other American Governments. It was not the power of the Arbenz government that concerned us but the power behind it.

If world communism captures any American State, however small, a new and perilous front is established which will increase the danger to the entire free world and require even greater sacrifices from the American people.

The Declaration at Caracas

This situation in Guatemala had become so dangerous that the American States could not ignore it. At Caracas last March the American States held their Tenth Inter-American Conference. They then adopted a momentous statement. They declared that "the domination or control of the political institutions of any American State by the international Communist movement . . . would constitute a threat to the sovereignty and political independence of the American States, endangering the peace of America."

There was only one American State that voted against this declaration. That State was Guatemala.

This Caracas declaration precipitated a dramatic chain of events. From their European base the Communist leaders moved rapidly to build up the military power of their agents in Guatemala. In May a large shipment of arms moved from behind the Iron Curtain into Guatemala. The shipment was sought to be secreted by false manifests and false clearances. Its ostensible destination was changed three times while en route.

At the same time, the agents of international communism in Guatemala intensified efforts to penetrate and subvert the neighboring Central American States. They attempted political assassinations and political strikes. They used consular agents for political warfare.

Many Guatemalan people protested against their being used by Communist dictatorship to serve the Communists' lust for power. The response was mass arrests, the suppression of constitutional guaranties, the killing of opposition leaders, and other brutal tactics normally employed by communism to secure the consolidation of its power.

In the face of these events and in accordance with the spirit of the Caracas declaration, the nations of this hemisphere laid further plans to grapple with the danger. The Arbenz government responded with an effort to disrupt the inter-American system. Because it enjoyed the full support of Soviet Russia, which is on the Security Council, it tried to bring the matter before the Security Council. It did so without first referring the matter to the American regional organization as is called for both by the United Nations Charter itself and by the treaty creating the American organization.

The Foreign Minister of Guatemala openly connived in this matter with the Foreign Minister of the Soviet Union. The two were in open correspondence and ill-concealed privity. The Security Council at first voted overwhelmingly to refer the Guatemala matter to the Organization of American States. The vote was 10 to 1. But that one negative vote was a Soviet veto.

Then the Guatemalan Government, with Soviet backing, redoubled its efforts to supplant the American States system by Security Council jurisdiction.

However, last Friday, the United Nations Security Council decided not to take up the Guatemalan matter but to leave it in the first instance to the American States themselves. That was a triumph for the system of balance between regional organization and world organization, which the American States had fought for when the charter was drawn up at San Francisco.

The American States then moved promptly to deal with the situation. Their peace commission left yesterday for Guatemala. Earlier the Organization of American States had voted overwhelmingly to call a meeting of their Foreign Ministers to consider the penetration of international communism in Guatemala and the measures required to eliminate it. Never before has there been so clear a call uttered with such a sense of urgency and strong resolve.

Attempt To Obscure Issue

Throughout the period I have outlined, the Guatemalan Government and Communist agents throughout the world have persistently attempted to obscure the real issue—that of Communist imperialism—by claiming that the United States is only interested in protecting American business. We regret that there have been disputes between the Guatemalan Government and the United Fruit Company. We have urged repeatedly that these disputes be submitted for settlement to an international tribunal or to international arbitration. That is the way to dispose of problems of this sort. But this issue is relatively unimportant. All who know the temper of the U.S. people and Government must realize that our overriding concern is that which, with others, we recorded at Caracas, namely the endangering by international communism of the peace and security of this hemisphere.

The people of Guatemala have not been heard from. Despite the armaments piled up by the Arbenz government, it was unable to enlist the spiritual cooperation of the people.

Led by Col. Castillo Armas, patriots arose in Guatemala to challenge the Communist leadership—and to change it. Thus, the situation is being cured by the Guatemalans themselves.

Last Sunday, President Arbenz of Guatemala resigned and seeks asylum. Others are following his example.

Tonight, just as I speak, Col. Castillo Armas is in conference in El Salvador with Colonel Monzón, the head of the Council which has taken over the power in Guatemala City. It was this power that the just wrath of the Guatemalan people wrested from President Arbenz, who then took flight.

Now the future of Guatemala lies at the disposal of the Guatemalan people themselves. It lies also at the disposal of leaders loyal to Guatemala who have not treasonably become the agents of an alien despotism which sought to use Guatemala for its own evil ends.

The events of recent months and days add a new and glorious chapter to the already great tradition of the American States.

Each one of the American States has cause for profound gratitude. We can all be grateful that we showed at Caracas an impressive solidarity in support of our American institutions. I may add that we are prepared to do so again at the conference called for Rio. Advance knowledge of that solidarity undoubtedly shook the Guatemalan Government.

We can be grateful that the Organization of American States showed that it could act quickly and vigorously in aid of peace. There was proof that our American organization is not just a paper organization, but that it has vigor and vitality to act.

We can be grateful to the United Nations Security Council, which recognized the right of regional organizations in the first instance to order their own affairs. Otherwise the Soviet Russians would have started a controversy which would have set regionalism against universality and gravely wounded both.

Above all, we can be grateful that there were loyal citizens of Guatemala who, in the face of terrorism and violence and against what seemed insuperable odds, had the courage and the will to eliminate the traitorous tools of foreign despots.

The need for vigilance is not past. Communism is still a menace everywhere. But the people of the United States and of the other American Republics can feel tonight that at least one grave danger has been averted. Also an example is set which promises increased security for the future. The ambitious and unscrupulous will be less prone to feel that communism is the wave of their future.

In conclusion, let me assure the people of Guatemala. As peace and freedom are restored to that sister Republic, the Government of the United States will continue to support the just aspirations of the Guatemalan people. A prosperous and progressive Guatemala is vital to a healthy hemisphere. The United States pledges itself not merely to political opposition to communism but to help to alleviate conditions in Guatemala and elsewhere which might afford communism an opportunity to spread its tentacles throughout the hemisphere. Thus we shall seek in positive ways to make our Americas an example which will inspire men everywhere.

56. *Address by Henry F. Holland, Assistant Secretary of*
     State for Inter-American Affairs, before the Pan
     American Society of the United States, on a
     Preview of the United States Position at the
     Meeting of American Ministers of Finance*

October 27, 1954

The bond that unites our American States is in its essence a spiritual tie born of our common struggle for liberty and of our consecration to identical moral and ethical standards. It is a relationship which we believe ennobles all those who share it. Its genius is our knowledge, proven again and again by experience, that through patience, understanding, and tolerance this kinship becomes steadily more meaningful—a source of strength and growth for all of us. Tonight I shall undertake a second report on the economic aspects of that relationship. The first was made in a talk given last April in New Orleans. I still adhere to the convictions expressed then and shall recall one or two of them to you.

Our basic goal in the economic field in this hemisphere is to make an effective contribution to the establishment in each American Republic of a strong, self-reliant, and durable economy, one that will mean better living standards for all our peoples. We recognize and we shall vigorously defend the right of each American State to determine the methods by which it will seek that goal. Correspondingly, in our contributions we shall try to be consistent with those sound principles which experience has demonstrated to be the basis of strong economies.

One of these is the principle that governments should invade the field of business only when absolutely necessary and then, if possible, only on a temporary basis. Where private enterprise is willing to undertake the task, it should be made responsible for the production, distribution, and marketing of goods and services. The role of governments in the economic field, we believe, is to create those conditions under which private enterprise can perform its task with maximum effectiveness and with full respect for its obligation to society and humanity. These conditions include guaranties of property and contract rights; an opportunity to earn a reasonable rate of return adequate to attract new capital; a stable and expanding international trade; the establishment of sound currencies; clearly enunciated and stable economic policies; the encouragement of strong and independent labor movements. They also include constant vigilance for the physical and spiritual needs of our people.

In April I emphasized the importance of the Conference of Ministers of Finance or Economy to be held next month in Rio de Janeiro. That conference gives us an opportunity to define economic goals, to compare our policies, and to coordinate them as far as possible. At Rio we can work toward the establishment of that kind of economic relation that should exist normally and permanently between mature, peaceful, and self-respecting nations, nations which are genuinely and deeply interested in each other's welfare. The time has come for us to concentrate on the kind of help which we can give to each other consistently, dependably, and on a long-term basis, shifting our emphasis from temporary and emergency measures.

*Department of State Bulletin, Nov. 8, 1954, pp. 684-90.

In New Orleans I said that in preparation for the Rio Conference we would undertake to clarify and define our Government's policies and would discuss them with our sister states well in advance of the meeting. In other words, we do not view that conference as an occasion for any dramatic disclosures of new policies. We are considerably more interested in performance and accomplishment. That calls for extensive consultation not only at the conference but before and after it. The economy of this hemisphere is a whole composed of interrelated parts. The more smoothly those parts fit together, the stronger is the whole. This process of inter-locking is not a task to be undertaken and concluded at the Rio Conference. It is a long-term job, in which that conference should be only an episode, albeit a very important one.

Preparations for Rio Conference

Taking this approach we began in April to prepare for the conference. A sub-Cabinet committee comprised of representatives from every interested department and agency of our Government met twice weekly over a period of months to review our past economic policies in the hemisphere and to make specific recommendations for the future. The work of that group was largely concluded by the latter part of August, and its recommendations have been accepted. A number of us have spent much of the intervening time discussing those plans and policies with the governments of our sister republics. Let me outline them for you.

We have reemphasized that our mutual American goal must be a world at peace, in which the free democratic peoples can prosper and in which every man may have a chance to provide for his family improved standards of living and better opportunities for the future. Perhaps the most important single economic development in the hemisphere is the growing determination among men everywhere somehow to achieve better living standards, to feed, clothe, house, and educate themselves and their families better. That determination, if encouraged, can become a powerful factor in our progress. If the Rio Conference is to have any significance, it must be remembered as a time when the American family assembled to rededicate itself to a joint and several effort to better the lives of its men, women, and children.

Americans everywhere as they go about their daily work must have the confidence that here work and self-discipline will achieve the kind of housing, clothing, food, and education that make for dignity in living. Our children must look at their future with the same confidence. As nations, as peoples, as business and industrial communities, every step that we take toward achieving this goal will be richly rewarded. Let me emphasize that, while that achievement will surely help in our united effort to eliminate communism from the Americas, our purpose would be the same if there were no Communist problem. It is our own interest in making of this hemisphere a better home for ourselves and our children that makes us steadfast in this purpose. An acceptable standard of living should be sought as an end in itself, not as a defense against communism.

The primary burden in each state must be borne by its own people and its own government. Nothing that the government or people of one country can do will raise living standards in another unless the internal conditions essential for progress are already there. If they are, we can, however, hasten the process somewhat by our own helpful policies. These to a considerable extent depend upon economic and legislative actions by our governments. This is particularly true with respect to the elimination of unnecessary controls and regimentation of economies. An outstanding example is the recovery made by Peru in the last 5 years where unsound controls and regulations were removed and export and import trade were progressively allowed to set the exchange rates without artificial manipulation. As was to be expected, the initial effects were disquieting, but the long-term advantages of a free economy are now fully apparent.

So each of us must be ready to carry his own load. That does not mean, however, that he must carry it alone. We know now that, just as there is an American political security, there is an American economic security in which we are all partners, and that whenever in any American State that freedom and that security are impaired, every other member of the family suffers. The long-term self-interest of each of us justifies our helping others to progress steadily toward a solution of this basic economic problem. The fight against hunger, disease, illiteracy, and human misery in this hemisphere must become more of a joint and several effort, each facing his own problem squarely but each trying in good faith to make some contribution to the efforts of others. We attach great importance to the combined aspect of this effort. The problem is not how one nation can help 20 others to raise their living standards. It is how every American State without neglecting its domestic responsibilites can find some way to help the other 20. The problems of none of us are so great but that each can find some way to demonstrate his sincere interest in the welfare of every other.

What have we concluded will be our own contribution? We believe that it can be most effective in three fields—commerce, finance, and technical assistance. In each, we have tried to define policies which are consistent with our laws and with what we believe to be practically possible in the United States today. Anything else would be pure theory, and we are interested in accomplishment. We shall, of course, take active interest in other fruitful fields of cooperation such as the encouragement of tourist travel.

Strengthening Commerce

In the field of commerce our policy will be that announced by President Eisenhower in his message on foreign economic policy sent to Congress last March. By those means which our laws permit and which are practically achievable we shall attempt to achieve more free and healthy trade and payments, to stabilize and strengthen our international commerce, and gradually and selectively to reduce those artificial barriers which obstruct it both here and abroad.

It may be hard to develop a policy, but it is harder still to apply it in the individual test cases. Here in this country when an issue is to be decided those on each side support their views tenaciously and energetically. That is wholesome even though it produces some pretty hot contests, particularly in the field of tariffs and quotas. Moreover, even people who wholeheartedly support a general policy of expanding foreign trade will fight hard for higher tariffs to protect their own interest. We would be unrealistic if we expected people to act in a less human fashion.

One thing is certain. Again and again the President's policy on foreign trade will be put to test, and each time it is, these clashes between opinions and interests will occur.

No one can prophesy with certainty their outcome in specific cases and under specific circumstances. It is obvious from experience in a world of affairs that our performance in the application of our announced policy in the field of international and inter-American trade will not be uniform. However, I believe that we can say with conviction that the great majority of our decisions will be consistent with the President's policy and that the exceptions will be based upon good and valid reasons. In my judgment there has never been a time when the people of the United States and their representatives in the legislative and executive branches of our Government have been more aware of the crucial importance of international trade to our survival. To preserve the strength of our economy this Nation must export and import. To export we must accept the goods of other nations in payment for ours. It is just as simple as that. Unless we buy more from our neighbors in this hemisphere and sell more to them, neither our economies nor theirs will develop rapidly.

I am asked what guaranties we can give of the stability of this foreign trade policy. The answer is obvious. The best guaranty of that policy lies in spreading to every corner of our country a clear understanding of the stake that each United States citizen has in our foreign trade. If we reduce our purchases of sugar from Cuba, by the same dollar amount we reduce our sales to her of automobiles, farm implements, rice, and other agricultural products. If we do not buy oil from Venezuela, we correspondingly reduce our tremendous volume of exports to her. The same happens if we reduce our purchases of wool from Uruguay or of coffee from Brazil, Colombia, and the other coffee-producing countries, if we do not buy lead and zinc from Canada, Mexico, and Peru, copper from Chile, tin from Bolivia. The same truth holds throughout the hemisphere.

Capital for Economic Development

The second field in which we shall try to make an effective contribution toward raising living standards is that of finance. To progress economically a nation must have capital. It must come, of course, from either public or private sources. By far the more prolific is the last. Private investors in the aggregate are able at any time to produce quantities of capital that enormously exceed the maximum that governments can contribute. Today much private capital is available here and in other nations which accumulate it.

This being true, if a government wants to attract capital for economic development, what better can it do than institute those policies and create those conditions that will logically encourage all private investors, both domestic and foreign. Both groups on the whole will react in the same way to a given set of conditions. Anything that discourages a Mexican investor is likely to discourage one from the United States or Argentina. By the same token conditions that attract one will attract the other.

I am afraid we may have placed too much emphasis on measures to attract the foreign investor. A government that wants foreign investors should first take a careful look at the local investor. If he is exporting his capital or investing it only in such nonproductive things as real estate, then it is a reasonable certainty that the foreign investor will be reluctant to enter. But if the domestic businessman is demonstrating his own confidence by investing in the sound and productive economic development of his country, then in order to attract the foreign investor it is necessary to add only two factors. The first is assurance of equal treatment to domestic and foreign investors, and the second is reasonable assurance of an opportunity to repatriate profits. Where the local situation is such that the domestic investor is active, add these two factors and the foreign investor will come if he is wanted.

We believe that in the 20th-century American businessman, be he Brazilian, Mexican, North American, or what you will, lies the greatest hope for prosperity in our hemisphere. Private enterprise went through a period of evolution when its lack of interest in basic human welfare brought it into ill repute and led nations to experiment with other systems. Those experiments have generally failed miserably, producing high costs, inferior goods and services, financial and political instability. They tended to make people lose confidence in currency, their savings, and their ability to take care of themselves and to devote their attention instead to plans to insure that governments would take care of them. We may now be emerging from that period of experiment. If so, it was not in vain.

In the last decades and particularly since World War II, I believe a new kind of buinessman has developed throughout the American hemisphere, a 20th-century businessman, one with a social conscience, who understands that a business which habitually fails to pay its workers a decent livelihood is not an asset to its owners, to its community, or to its nation. This new businessman has demonstrated a willingness to discipline himself and to submit to just discipline from his government. At the same time he has preserved that relentless drive, inexhaustible resourcefulness, and fierce pride in excellence of performance that no other system has even approached. He deserves the support of our governments.

I am told that we place too much emphasis on the role of private enterprise in solving our economic problems. The system has no peculiar sanctity. Our attitude toward it derives from the fact that it is the only economic system that fully preserves our philosophy of the dignity of every man; because better than any other system yet devised by man it has demonstrated the ability to make vast quantities of goods and services available at reasonable prices. Only private enterprise is equal to the task of developing the huge resources of this vast hemisphere, resources which could support a greatly increased population and at a much higher standard of living.

Government Financing

Yet we know that private enterprise cannot do the job without some government help. There are development projects that are essential to the progress of our countries and for which private capital will not be available even under the most favorable circumstances. That is true here in the United States as well as in Latin America.

For those projects governmental financing is needed. In some cases the local government will be equal to the task. In others it will be unable itself to provide the required amount of capital but will be able to service a long-term international loan.

Here we think first of the International Bank. It was created to perform precisely this task. On the whole its record has been excellent. Its personnel is highly trained and experienced. It has capital available to lend. It would be shortsighted not to make maximum use of the bank. However, we recognize that there will be projects, both public and private, for which foreign financing will be required and which will lie outside the normal scope of International Bank lending.

To meet this need the United States proposes to intensify and expand the activities of the Export-Import Bank. Through it we shall do our utmost to satisfy all applications for economic development loans that fulfill certain sound and logical standards. First, the project must be one for which private capital would not reasonably be available, even under favorable conditions. Preference will be given to applications from countries which have taken measures which would reasonably encourage private capital. The project must be one for which it cannot be reasonably expected that capital will be available from the local government or from the International Bank.

Secondly, the loan itself must be economically sound. We feel that unsound loans, those which a reasonable man must assume will not be repaid, do more harm than good. A defaulted loan impairs a nation's credit and makes it harder for it to negotiate loans which would otherwise be perfectly sound. A defaulted loan creates resentments at home and abroad. Several Latin American governments have expressed to us strong opposition to accepting so-called soft loans, pointing out that the liquidation of old debts which should never have been incurred imposes an unjustified burden on a national economy. On the other hand, acceptance of a sound loan standard encourages us all to follow those wholesome policies that not only increase the borrowing capacity of governments but lead to the establishment of strong business enterprises which can themselves qualify for loans that do not encumber the credit of their governments.

Third, the project to which the loan relates must be one in the mutual interest of the two governments and their peoples. The credit of a government should not be burdened for a project which has no bearing on the welfare of the taxpayers who must eventually repay it.

Lastly, the amount of the loan should not exceed the prudent lending capacity of the Export-Import Bank. After thoughtful consideration, we believe that the bank's capacity is and will continue to be adequate fully to support this policy. In reaching this conclusion we are entirely aware that this policy implies a substantial increase in the bank's activities.

Technical Assistance

I now come to the field of technical aid. This hemisphere is richly endowed with natural and human resources which are as yet but inadequately developed. Through technical assistance and training, these presently available resources can more quickly and effectively be put to use. Through technical assistance, agricultural lands which barely feed their occupants can be made to produce marketable supplies for cities as well. Technical assistance can correct substandard housing by making information available on construction methods and economical materials. Through technical assistance, disease can be reduced and life expectancies raised. In the field of technical assistance almost every nation can find some way to make its contribution to a vast attack on human misery. Our policy will be to strengthen and to diversify our contribution in the field of technical assistance, but only, of course, if this is desired and requested by the governments concerned.

The policies which I have outlined mark, as you might expect, a compromise between the sincere convictions of those within our Government who would not have gone so far and those who would have gone farther. A number of proposals submitted from within our own Government or from abroad have not been accepted. We are not foreclosing the discussion at Rio of any proposal supported by any delegation. We shall participate in all discussions and in good faith. However, we feel that it is constructive to announce our own views far in advance of the conference and to invite those of the other governments so that the work of coordinating our policies and our efforts can begin long before we arrive at Rio.

Price Stabilization

The governments of Latin America are interested in devising means to stabilize prices for the products which they sell in world markets. The problem is one which concerns us as well, for we also have exports whose prices fluctuate widely. We have attempted by various means to solve this problem here at home. None has proved entirely successful. This does not mean that we will abandon our efforts to find a solution or that we will be unwilling to consider those proposed by other American States. However, our own experience leads us to believe that a hemisphere-wide program which would simply shift to this Nation a large part of the risk for price fluctuations is not justified by the nature of the problem. The cost would exceed our capacities whether the program contemplated direct payments or buffer stocks created to support prices.

We are reluctant to guarantee to finance whatever portion of the cost of development projects a local government may find itself unable to carry because of a drop in prices of its goods. Such programs would tie up part of the government's borrowing capacity without any certainty that it would ever in fact be used.

There are practical ways to reduce the magnitude of the problem, even if it cannot be eliminated. Maintaining high and stable levels of economic activity and income will help. Assurance to producers everywhere of greater and more dependable access to the world's markets will neutralize some of the factors that produce these violent fluctuations in prices. If we maintain more accurate methods of estimating future supply and demand, those unforeseen shortages and excesses that distort prices can be minimized.

Another proposal which has been made is that we create an inter-American bank whose capital would be largely furnished by the United States and which would make loans directly to foreign companies without the guaranty of their governments. We feel that such a bank would either compete with private lending institutions or would largely duplicate services available through the Export-Import Bank. The latter is now authorized to extend credit to private borrowers whether domestic, foreign, or mixed, and it does not always require a guaranty from the local government. So flexible is the service offered by the Export-Import Bank that there are few lending operations which it cannot undertake within the limits of the policy we have outlined. We feel, therefore, that the benefits from creating still another independent banking institution would not justify the expense and time required to organize it, assemble and train its personnel, and establish operating procedures. Better, quicker, and more effective, we feel, is the achievement of those same benefits through intensified activity of the Export-Import Bank.

We have heard but little support either at home or abroad for massive programs of grant aid in this hemisphere. I believe that it is generally recognized that, save in cases of real emergencies and such special projects as the Inter-American Highway, these programs are neither needed nor wanted by the other American States.

I should mention at least briefly the question so often asked as to whether our policy is not really to discourage industrialization in Latin America, forcing it to supply us with raw materials which we will fabricate and resell as manufactured goods. Such a policy would be directly contrary to our own best interests. One of our problems is to sell our own foods and raw materials, as well as our manufactured goods. We export more than four times as much to Canada as to any other country in the world. Canada is rapidly industrializing, and the more she industrializes the more she buys from us and we from her. The same is true in Latin America. Mexico, Venezuela, and Cuba are industrializing rapidly. They are, respectively, our third, fifth, and sixth most important customers. Obviously, we serve our own interests by encouraging sound industrialization in Latin America.

These, then, are the policies which we are submitting to the Latin American Governments and to the Cabinet Ministers who will head their delegations at Rio. I have heard surprise that they include no dramatic, startling new element that will create a theatrical impact at Rio. I am grateful for that. It lets us center emphasis and attention where it should be centered, on our great need to define our basic problem—how to better the lives of our people—and to set about solving it.

The reaction of the South American Governments and business communities to these policies is in my opinion profoundly significant. In the 10 South American capitals whence I have just returned we found general receptiveness to our belief that if vigorously and energetically pursued by our Government these policies will meet the need that exists in this hemisphere. Latin Americans are clear and intensely realistic thinkers, and I found everywhere a willingness to face their problems squarely and analyze them with commendable courage. Our sister republics are not waiting passively for us or for anyone else to come and solve their problems for them. The other members of this American family look to us for economic policies and conditions of trade which fully protect our own interests but which are stable, dependable, and generous. They look to us as a source of capital on sound terms and conditions. They are anxious to participate with us in programs of technical assistance that will pool and extend our common resources in that field. They agree with us that the 20th-century private businessman, whatever may be his nationality, can do more for this hemisphere than can all our governments combined, and that he deserves our support.

The great question mark that I found everywhere was not as to the adequacy of these policies but as to how we will apply them. These policies require self-restraint and some sacrifice from us. They will prove more controversial here at home than programs whose only significance is their dollar cost. These policies are aimed squarely at the basic needs of Latin America—stable and expanding markets, access to sound development loans, technical assistance. Their effect in this hemisphere can be tremendous. If we are loyal to them, if we apply them vigorously and generously, we will have done our part. With these assurances from us any American State that is resolved to combat inflation through sound fiscal and monetary policies, and to clear the way for an enlightened private enterprise, can reasonably expect to make steady progress toward the goal to which I have so often referred. I am confident that the governments and the peoples of this hemisphere are disposed to adopt that course and to pursue it steadfastly. This conviction leads me to submit that, if we as a people and we as a Government determine that these undertakings which we propose to make to Americans everywhere shall be fairly and generously fulfilled, then truly we stand in this hemisphere on the threshold of an era of great progress which will make of our lands a better inheritance for our children and will earn for us the gratitude of future generations.

57. *Address by George M. Humphrey, Secretary of the Treasury, before the Meeting of American Ministers of Finance, on Economic Cooperation in the Americas**

November 23, 1954

I am happy to participate in this Meeting of Ministers of Finance and Economy. Many of us have met on other occasions, most recently at the annual meetings of the International Bank and International Monetary Fund 2 months ago. I am delighted to extend my acquaintance with you and to meet with you here.

Just before leaving Washington we discussed with President Eisenhower the views of the United States delegation on the problems we shall discuss here. He emphasized to us his deep interest in this historic meeting and asked that we convey a personal message to our colleagues here. With your kind permission I shall read it:

I am very pleased to send greetings and best wishes to the Meeting of Ministers of Finance and Economy of the American family of nations, convened in Rio de Janeiro, the capital of our great sister nation, Brazil. I am happy to send this message through our Secretary of the Treasury, Mr. Humphrey, who, as Chairman of the United States Delegation, speaks for our nation and will authoritatively present our policies.

I am confident that this conference will advance still further the unique relationships which have developed among the peoples and nations of this hemisphere. As those relationships evolved and grew, the people of the United States learned to call their own attitude toward their sister nations the policy of the good neighbor. Today, the bonds which unite us as sovereign equals who are working side by side for the betterment of all of us—nations and citizens—have elevated this neighborly relationship to one of genuine partnership.

No longer is it sufficient to maintain the mutual respect and cordiality of neighbors, useful and pleasant as that is. In the world of today, the well-being and the economic development—as well as the security—of all peace-loving nations are so closely interrelated that we must be partners. If this is true in the larger context, it is especially true among the American republics where we share the same traditions and many of the same favorable circumstances for progress.

As the conference discusses a wide variety of measures for economic and financial cooperation in this hemisphere, and endorses those that are sound and durable, I

*Department of State Bulletin, Dec. 6, 1954, pp. 863-69.

earnestly hope that the meeting as a whole may join with the delegation of the United States in common dedication to the policy of the good partner.

To this may I add my best wishes for the success of the conference and warm personal greetings to each of its members.

Let me say that every member of the United States delegation shares those convictions.

While this gathering was called in response to a resolution of the Tenth Inter-American Conference held in Caracas earlier this year, this Conference is in reality the realization of a desire expressed repeatedly throughout the rise and development of the inter-American system. It is the desire to strengthen the continental economy so as to benefit all the nations that share the hemisphere.

That desire was first manifested in the act of the United States Congress that convened the first Pan American Conference in Washington 65 years ago. The same desire created the Pan American Union, which has now become the Organization of American States. Today it finds expression in the statutes of the Inter-American Economic and Social Council which provide that it shall "promote the economic and social welfare of the American nations through effective cooperation among them for the best utilization of their natural resources."

We are not gathered here, then, because of an emergency situation, nor is this meeting an impulse of the moment. It is not an isolated or disconnected event in inter-American relations; but it is a new endeavor, one more step in the search for economic cooperation and solidarity toward which your countries and mine will continually strive.

We have come here with the same spirit of cordial solidarity with which the delegates of our nations arrived in this city of proverbial hospitality for the Third Pan American Conference. To describe it I shall borrow the eloquence of a great fellow countryman, Elihu Root, at that time Secretary of State, who said:

> I bring from my country a special greeting to her elder sisters in the civilization of America. . . . There is not one of all our countries that cannot benefit the others; there is not one that cannot receive benefit from the others; there is not one that will not gain by the prosperity, the peace and happiness of all.

And so it is today. Our country is part of the inter-American system; our Secretary of State, John Foster Dulles, recently affirmed that this is the cornerstone of our foreign policy.

We take our places with pride in this association of states which has established the complete equality of all members, has consecrated the principle of nonintervention, and has built a juridical system that has put an end to war among American nations.

We have bound ourselves, moreover, by pacts that stipulate that an attack on one American nation is an attack on all of them, and that any threat to the political integrity of one is a threat to all.

Our presence here at this Conference is a declaration that we also consider economic solidarity as part of the common defense.

None of us expects that we can at this meeting solve all of the economic problems of a hemisphere. But we can confidently expect that 21 nations, each motivated by a deep and brotherly interest in the welfare of every other, can accomplish enough here to convince us all that our efforts were richly rewarded, that our accomplishments justify our looking forward to future meetings.

We all have our own ideas as to how the economic interests of the entire continent could be promoted. We in the United States naturally subscribe to those principles that in our own country have proved effective in raising the living standards of the people and promoting the prosperity of the Nation. We shall present them here with the same friendly frankness with which we are ready to listen to the opinions of other delegations.

No one of us alone has the wisdom and experience necessary to solve all our problems. That is what this Conference is for: to exchange ideas, to draw closer together, to arrive at a promising and practical basis for cooperation, and to pave the way for constructive steps toward our goals.

It is with that spirit that my country's delegation has come to this Conference. We look forward with great interest to hearing your views, and we welcome the opportunity to lay before you our ideas on the problems that now engage our mutual attention.

But we shall never lose from sight the hemispheric interest, the welfare of the American family of nations, the need to fortify the inter-American system that past generations have bequeathed to us and that it is our duty to pass on, intact and improved, to future generation. When we shall have finished our work here, it should be possible to speak of this meeting in the same words as those used by a great American, the Baron of Rio Branco, in commenting on the Third Pan American Conference, when he said:

Here concessions represent conquests of reason, amicable compromises or compensations counselled by reciprocal interests.

We would first hope for a clear definition of the economic goals toward which we shall press. We are profoundly aware that we are here not so much as representatives of political entities; instead we are here as the spokesmen for 330 millions of men, women, and children whose problems, whose sufferings, and whose aspirations must constantly be present in our thoughts and in our deliberations. When we speak of economic development, international trade, and the other subjects of our agenda, we must be mindful that each is significant only in so far as it has a direct relation to our peoples, to their families, to their homes, and to their work.

I believe that we are capable of putting into words here at this meeting just what it is that our people would have us accomplish, and I believe that we can adopt that definition as our goal. It seems to us that the men and women of the Americas, living as they do among our mountains, on our plains, and along our seacoasts, are united and clear in their aspirations. They do not ask the impossible, but they do demand of us, who as government officials are their servants, that we promote those conditions which will give maximum assurance that everywhere in our Americas man has an opportunity to better himself, give his children even greater opportunities, and enjoy meanwhile those freedoms which we have achieved in the Americas and which are denied to so many millions elsewhere in the world.

I believe that we must face another problem in which our people are vitally interested. All of us are exposed to an insidious disease that stealthily robs us of our strength. It is the evil of inflation which makes the prices of food, of clothing, of all the necessities of life climb upward in a grim spiral which again and again snatches away the benefits of progress.

Our goal must be twofold—to unite our efforts to achieve the kind of economic development that means higher living standards for our people, and to take those wise and prudent measures which will avoid the evil of inflation. If here we make progress toward these goals, we shall have earned the gratitude of our people.

This is a goal that is achievable in the Americas. God has endowed this hemisphere with abundant and varied natural resources, with vast and fertile lands that are capable of affording an ever better life to our rapidly multiplying peoples. There is peace throughout our hemisphere. In a troubled world ours is a situation so privileged, so favorable, that it becomes our duty to examine critically the responsibilities that must accompany such advantages. Each of us singly and all of us jointly must strive to accomplish those things which will best and most effectively employ these lands and those resources to benefit our peoples.

Our agenda is admirably fashioned to help us appraise not only our place today on the road which has already brought us so far toward our goal, but also the measures which we can take jointly and severally to hasten our progress on that road. It is our conviction that to accomplish this purpose two basic principles should underlie all our thinking. The first is our belief that the road which will lead most surely and most directly to the goals which we seek is that of the vigorous free enterprise system. This system in its modern form builds new industries, new enterprises, and opens new areas to development. And it does all these things without endangering those free institutions which are the very foundation of the social and human progress which we have achieved in this hemisphere.

The other is our belief that we as governments should reduce to a minimum the scope and the duration of our own intervention in the fields of commerce and industry. We best serve our people when we encourage them to produce the goods and services required for our progress, when we stimulate them to bring new regions and new resources into productive use, rather than when we compete with them or otherwise take over the functions of private enterprise. Government intervention deprives the people of the full benefits of their earnings. Experience has demonstrated that almost without exception, in my own country and elsewhere, such intervention lowers production and raises costs.

We shall support and defend the right of every state to define its own economic course. Our own belief in the principles I have stated derives from the fact that wherever they have been applied in the Americas and elsewhere in the world they have brought improvement in the lives of our peoples, improvement that can be measured in terms of lower costs; greater per capita income; higher production; improvement that is visible in new factories, industries, and increased agricultural production; and intensified conversion of idle and undeveloped natural resources into jobs and usable wealth. These are the marks of vigorous, expanding, and self-reliant economies. These are the economic ends that we pursue.

The detailed discussion of each agenda item is the function of our committees. I would like, however, to say a word or two regarding our views on some of the more vital ones.

U.S. Views on International Trade

The first is international trade. We intend to the utmost of our ability to maintain a strong, healthy economy in the United States. This will insure a growing volume of trade with your countries at a steadily increasing level of demand. This will help sustain a high level of demand for the world's goods and so foster trade on a mutually beneficial basis. My Government is convinced that a strong, stable, and expanding international trade is the best single guaranty of economic strength in our hemisphere.

We are happy to see that our trade with each other is a most important and growing factor in the international commerce of every American State. It is in the interest of each of us that this wholesome interchange be strengthened and expanded. For your economic development you count heavily upon markets in the United States for your products. We value just as highly the strong markets which you afford for our own agricultural and manufactured exports. We hope to see our inter-American trade, which has increased so greatly in recent years, further expanded and the markets available to producers in all our countries strengthened by the gradual elimination of those artificial barriers that hinder access to them. Such a trade policy will increase mutually beneficial trade. This emphasis on expanding trade opportunities continues to be a fundamental part of President Eisenhower's foreign economic program, which it is his announced intention to press in the forthcoming session of the Congress in January.

Our tariffs on imports from Latin America are low. Two-thirds of all our imports from this area are on the free list, and tariffs on the remaining third are among the lowest in the world.

We have also made marked progress in freeing imports into the United States from unnecessary and cumbersome customs requirements. Our Congress passed customs simplification acts in 1953 and again in 1954. The first authorized the Treasury to eliminate many technical requirements which were a burden on imports. The act passed this year continued this program and also directed the Tariff Commission to undertake a study of our complicated tariff classification structure with a view to its clarification.

These congressional steps have been accompanied by an intensive management-improvement program and by administrative simplification within the framework of existing law, both contributing to speedier customs action. We are continuing our efforts along these lines and plan to submit to the next Congress further legislative proposals consistent with the President's program of last March. As an example of the progress we are making, just a few weeks ago we announced a further relaxation of requirements for consular invoices—an action made possible by the 1953 simplification act.

The problem of international trade is closely related to that of prices. We are aware of your intense and very understandable interest in this problem as it relates to the prices for your products sold in world markets. We share that interest, not only because of the importance to you of adequate and stable prices but also because our own producers suffer when the prices of their exports fluctuate widely.

Our experience convinces us that if we as governments follow policies which will give our producers everywhere maximum assurance that consumption of their products will enjoy a steady and healthy growth and that their access to international markets will be facilitated, then we will have gone far toward solving this basic problem of prices which so concerns us all.

Financing Economic Development

The subject of financing for economic development is one of the most important which we shall consider. My Government has devoted much study to its policies in this field and, within the framework of the general principles to which I have referred, has reached certain decisions of whose nature you are already aware and whose effect we believe will prove to be far reaching.

When we speak of the great need for economic-development financing in this hemisphere, what we are really saying is that throughout our countries there are profitable and attractive opportunities for the establishment of productive enterprises that will provide steady employment to our people, that will provide more of the goods and services which we need for higher standards of living, and that will diversify our economies. These opportunities cannot be converted into realities without capital, technical knowledge, and experience. As governments, we owe it to our people to promote those conditions which will help make available the capital and technical knowledge required.

I think that every one of us here can agree that in this field our greatest opportunity and our greatest responsibility lies in creating in our several countries those conditions which will give maximum access to the great reserves of private-investment capital that are available throughout the world. The reason is obvious. The aggregate amount of private capital that is available today in your countries, in mine, and in the rest of the world is many times greater than any that we as governments could possibly provide. Economic development in those countries which have successfully established access to the world's supplies of private capital is going ahead with a rapidity that is astonishing.

We all recognize that the movement of private capital cannot be forced; that private investors of all nationalities enter only where the circumstances are attractive. So numerous are the investment opportunities through the free world today that he who seeks investment capital must compete for it. But here again the position of Latin America is privileged and fortunate. Throughout your countries there are challenging and attractive opportunities for new investments such as are found only in young and rapidly developing economies. These factors give you very real advantages in competing for investment capital.

It is easy to understand, therefore, why the American States whose governments have established those conditions which have always proved attractive to private investors everywhere in the world have experienced little difficulty in finding ample supplies of capital, both domestic and foreign. This has been demonstrated so dramatically that there can be no longer any doubt but that in this favored area of the world, where nature has done its part so well, each government can, if it will, attract a volume of private investment that will compare most favorably with that of any other area of the world.

One of the things which our governments must do to encourage free enterprise is to insure that those projects necessary for economic development, but for which private capital is not reasonably available, are adequately supported by public investment. We view this as a necessary support to an economy which relies principally upon private enterprise as supplementing and encouraging, rather than as displacing, free enterprise. I am sure that each government will shoulder as much of its burden as it reasonably can, but we agree with you that substantial foreign lending will be necessary if we are to achieve our goals in this hemisphere. We shall do our part generously and loyally in meeting that need.

To that end we have reviewed the whole scope of our public-lending policies and have arrived at certain changes which we consider significant.

Changes in U.S. Lending Policies

The first relates to the United States Export-Import Bank, whose activities are to be intensified and expanded.

This past summer, the Congress of the United States by specific legislation increased the lending authority of the bank from $4½ billion to $5 billion, in anticipation of its increased lending activity. In his report to the Senate on this legislation, Senator Capehart, Chairman of the Banking and Currency Committee, stated:

> The Export-Import Bank has played an important role in our foreign economic policy and must continue to do so on an activated scale. Promotion of trade among the free nations of the world, and in particular, with the nations of the western hemisphere, is of utmost importance to the common welfare, the common defense, and the solidarity of the free world.

Within the last few months the Export-Import Bank has authorized loans of $130 million to nations in this hemisphere, and other important loans are under consideration. The loans which have been authorized will help two important Latin American cities develop municipal waterworks systems and will make possible the development of one of the world's largest copper deposits. The bank has made loans to finance the sale in Latin America of machine tools, of aircraft, of electric equipment, of textile equipment, and of wheat. It has facilitated the development of sulphur production. The range of its activities has been as wide and varied as the production process itself, from the extraction of basic materials to the fabrication of complex industrial products. Since its organization the Export-Import Bank has authorized loans in excess of $2¼ billion to Latin America.

Within the past few weeks, the Export-Import Bank has opened up new sources of credit for the countries of Latin America that wish to import equipment from the United States. With the assistance of lines of credit from the Export-Import Bank, United States exporters will be able to offer medium-term credit on equipment of a productive nature. This program will be in addition to long-term capital and should help to accelerate the flow of trade and ease temporary credit problems.

In addition, a large New York bank announced last week that it proposes to form a multimillion dollar export financing company. The Export-Import Bank will also participate in this new venture. This enterprise will add further to the supplies of medium-term credit available to Latin American importers of capital goods.

In the field of economic development, of course, the International Bank has a primary role to play in helping to promote the economic growth of the American

Republics. Most of the countries represented here were founding fathers of the International Bank. Your countries and my own participated in its establishment, and we have contributed importantly to its personnel and capital. The International Bank is our common institution. It was established to carry the major burden of financing reconstruction and development loans at a governmental level. While the International Bank in the early postwar years was primarily concerned with reconstruction, it has accelerated the tempo of its operations and has, more recently, concentrated its major efforts on economic development. The International Bank has financed a steady succession of high-priority development projects in Latin America. The total now exceeds $500 million for the last 5 years. Its first development loan was in Latin America, and today its investment in this hemisphere is greater than in any other developing area. Its loans have been made primarily for basic facilities and public works on which further fruitful investment depends: for electric power, for transportation, and for communication facilities. The loans of the International Bank are important not only in themselves but in their secondary effects. Electric-power installations, new road and communication systems, new port facilities, all have encouraged new industries and lowered costs. Development is a cumulative process, setting in motion innumerable individual efforts with multiplying effect.

In his report to the Conference, Eugene Black, President of the bank, states:

> It is my personal judgment that, given a continuance of present trends in Latin America, there is every reason to expect expanded lending activity by the bank in that area during the period which lies ahead. The bank has the resources to do so and it has the will to do so. The extent to which it may be able to translate its will into action depends largely on conditions within the control of the Latin American countries themselves.

At the meeting of the Board of Governors of the International Bank last September, representatives from many of the American Republics strongly urged support for the establishment of an international finance corporation to encourage private investment. The subject has been under study for several years.

Proposed International Finance Corporation

The matter has been given most careful consideration by the United States Government, and we are going to ask the Congress to support United States participation in such a corporation. We have in mind an institution organized as an affiliate of the International Bank, with an authorized capital of $100 million to be contributed by those members of the International Bank who wish to subscribe.

The corporation would be able to make loans without the guaranty of member governments. It would not directly provide equity financing. It would, however, be empowered to hold securities bearing interest payable only if earned, as well as debentures convertible into stock when purchased from the corporation by private investors. In that way it would operate in the area of venture capital without holding equity right of control. It would not compete with the International Bank or the Export-Import Bank, and indeed it would facilitate private investment.

If the international finance corporation is established, we shall then have three major financial institutions to help promote economic development. We shall have the Export-Import Bank that has had a long history of useful work in Latin America and whose activities are to be intensified. We shall have the International Bank, in which we are partners, to help finance basic resource development. We shall have an international finance corporation in which we would work together to assist and encourage private enterprise.

In the spirit of the resolution on private investment and taxation adopted at the Caracas Conference, the United States continues to explore feasible measures to remove tax impediments to increased foreign investments. The administration and the Congress, as well as numerous private groups in the United States, have given the matter intensive study. This has disclosed the complexity of the problems involved. In the light of this experience, the administration will again submit to the Congress proposals with respect to the reduction of taxation of foreign income along the general lines recommended by the President last year. We trust these proposals will find acceptance by the Congress.

We desire to complement these unilateral legislative steps with bilateral tax treaties. To that end, we are prepared to explore with individual countries the possibilities of the tax treaty as a medium for creating a more favorable tax climate for international trade and investment. For example, one of the matters which might be considered in treaty discussions is how the United States might give recognition to tax concessions made to foreign capital by the country where the investment is to be made. Under proper safeguards, we would be prepared to recommend giving credit for general foreign income taxes which are waived for an initial limited period as we now grant credit for taxes which are imposed. Such a measure as this will give maximum effectiveness to your own laws designed to encourage new enterprises.

Our agenda includes the subject of programing. Individual nations will no doubt continue to develop their overall approaches to their own economic-development problems. If any such nations wish to exchange views on their plans with other nations undertaking similar development plans, it may well be that this organization can provide such a meeting place.

We recommend that each of us expand and further diversify our joint activities in the vital field of technical cooperation. The interchange of people under this program draws us closer together and provides a better understanding of each other's problems. Through technical cooperation we pool our accumulated experience and knowledge to utilize the human and natural resources available to us as we seek to match resources against our needs. The enormous mutual benefits already produced by our efforts in this field justify our confidence in its future expansion.

We approach our talks here together with a sense of mission, which I am sure is common to us all. The challenge of the years ahead is a tremendous one. How we meet it may determine our place in history. We have great faith and confidence in the peoples and the lands that share this hemisphere. The human and physical resources are here out of which to build a glorious future.

The President of my country has very rightly called us partners in this great enterprise. He has declared the policy of our Government to be that of the good partner.

I know that the American States can be good partners, determined to work for the betterment of all our people. If we are energetic and practical, I am confident that we stand on the threshold of a great tomorrow. As good partners we can make this coming together at Rio a momentous one in the bright and lengthening record of inter-American relations.

*58. Press Release Issued by the State Department Concerning
a Treaty between Panama and the United States**

January 25, 1955

Representatives of the United States and the Republic of Panama signed today a Treaty of Mutual Understanding and Cooperation and Memorandum of Understandings Reached concerning relations between the two countries arising from the construction, operation, maintenance, and protection of the Panama Canal by the United States in accordance with existing treaties. The signing of these two instruments results from negotiations between the two countries which commenced in September 1953.

The two instruments were signed in Panama City by Foreign Minister Octavio Fábrega for Panama and by Ambassador Selden Chapin for the United States.

The principal provisions of these agreements are the following: The annuity will be increased from $430,000 to $1,930,000; Panama will be able to levy income tax on employees of Canal Zone agencies who are Panamanian citizens and others who are not U.S. citizens and who reside in territory under the jurisdiction of Panama; transfer to Panama of certain lands, with improvements, in territory under Panamanian jurisdiction, previously acquired for Canal purposes, including Paitilla Point and the Panama Railroad yard and the station in Panama City and the gradual turnover of the New Cristobal, Colon Beach, and Fort de Lesseps area in Colón and the Canal Zone; restriction of commissary and import privileges of non-U.S. citizen employees of Canal Zone agencies who do not reside in the Zone; abrogation of the U.S. treaty monopoly with respect to the construction of trans-Isthmian railroads and highways; abrogation of the U.S. treaty right to prescribe and enforce sanitary measures in the cities of Panamá and Colón; the U.S Congress will be requested to enact legislation authorizing the establishment of a single basic wage scale for all U.S. and Panamanian employees of the U.S. Government in the Canal Zone and providing for uniform application of the Civil Service Retirement Act to citizens of Panama employed by the U.S. Government in the Canal Zone; the United States agrees to put into effect certain administrative practices designed to enable the Panamanian economy to obtain an increased share in the business of supplying the Canal Zone market including the withdrawal, as of December 31, 1956, of U.S. agencies from the business of selling supplies (except fuel and lubricants) to non-U.S. Government owned or operated ships and the termination, under certain conditions, of manufacturing and processing in the Canal Zone of goods for sale to or consumption by individuals; the U.S. Congress will be requested to authorize the construction of a bridge across the Canal at Balboa referred to in point 4 of the General Relations Agreement of 1942; Panama grants to the United States the right to use, for a period of 15 years without cost, a military training and maneuver area in the province of Cocle; Panama waives certain treaty rights to enable the United States to restrict heavy vehicular traffic over a proposed new strategic highway within the Canal Zone; Panama waives certain rights acquired by treaty to free transportation on the Panama Railroad; Panama waives certain treaty provisions to enable the United States to extend limited post exchange privileges to friendly foreign military personnel visiting the Canal Zone under auspices of the

*Department of State Bulletin, Feb. 7, 1955, p. 237.

United States; Panama agrees to lease to the United States, for a period of 99 years without cost save for a recited nominal consideration, two parcels of land contiguous to the U.S. Embassy residence in Panama City; and Panama agrees permanently to reserve as a park area certain land in front of the U.S. Embassy office building in Panama City.

59. Republic of Panama and the United States of America, Treaty of Mutual Understanding and Cooperation with a Memorandum of Understandings Reached*

January 25, 1955

The President of the United States of America and the President of the Republic of Panama, desirous of concluding a treaty further to demonstrate the mutual understanding and cooperation of the two countries and to strengthen the bonds of understanding and friendship between their respective peoples, have appointed for that purpose as their respective Plenipotentiaries:

The President of the United States of America:

Selden Chapin, Ambassador Extraordinary and Plenipotentiary of the United States of America to the Republic of Panama,

The President of the Republic of Panama:

Octavio Fábrega, Minister of Foreign Relations of the Republic of Panama, who, having communicated to one another their respective full powers, found in good and due form, and recognizing that neither the provisions of the Convention signed November 18, 1903, nor the General Treaty signed March 2, 1936, nor the present Treaty, may be modified except by mutual consent, agree upon the following Articles:

Article I

Beginning with the first annuity payable after the exchange of ratifications of the present Treaty, the payments under Article XIV of the Convention for the Construction of a Ship Canal between the United States of America and the Republic of Panama, signed November 18, 1903, as amended by Article VII of the General Treaty of Friendship and Cooperation, signed March 2, 1936, shall be One Million Nine Hundred Thirty Thousand and no/100 Balboas (B/1,930,000) as defined by the agreement embodied in the exchange of notes of March 2, 1936, between the Secretary of State of the United States of America and the Members of the Panamanian Treaty Commission. The United States of America may discharge its obligation with respect to any such payment in any coin or currency, provided the amount so paid is the equivalent of One Million Nine Hundred Thirty Thousand and no/100 Balboas (B/1,930,000) as so defined.

On the date of the first payment under the present Treaty, the provisions of this Article shall supersede the provisions of Article VII of the General Treaty signed March 2, 1936.

Notwithstanding the provisions of this Article, the High Contracting Parties recog-

*Department of State Bulletin, Feb. 7, 1955, pp. 238-43.

nize the absence of any obligation on the part of either Party to alter the amount of the annuity.

Article II

(1) Notwithstanding the provisions of Article X of the Convention signed November 18, 1903, between the United States of America and the Republic of Panama, the United States of America agrees that the Republic of Panama may, subject to the provisions of paragraphs (2) and (3) of this Article, impose taxes upon the income (including income from sources within the Canal Zone) of all persons who are employed in the service of the Canal, the railroad, or auxiliary works, whether resident within or outside the Canal Zone, except:

(a) members of the Armed Forces of the United States of America,

(b) citizens of the United States of America, including those who have dual nationality, and

(c) other individuals who are not citizens of the Republic of Panama and who reside within the Canal Zone.

(2) It is understood that any tax levied pursuant to paragraph (1) of this Article shall be imposed on a non-discriminatory basis and shall in no case be imposed at a rate higher or more burdensome than that applicable to income of citizens of the Republic of Panama generally.

(3) The Republic of Panama agrees not to impose taxes on pensions, annuities, relief payments, or other similar payments, or payments by way of compensation for injuries or death occurring in connection with, or incident to, service on the Canal, the railroad, or auxiliary works paid to or for the benefit of members of the Armed Forces or citizens of the United States of America or the lawful beneficiaries of such members or citizens who reside in territory under the jurisdiction of the Republic of Panama.

The provisions of this Article shall be operative for the taxable years beginning on or after the first day of January following the year in which the present Treaty enters into force.

Article III

Subject to the provisions of the succeeding paragraphs of this Article, the United States of America agrees that the monopoly granted in perpetuity by the Republic of Panama to the United States for the construction, maintenance and operation of any system of communication by means of canal or railroad across its territory between the Caribbean Sea and the Pacific Ocean, by Article V of the Convention signed November 18, 1903, shall be abrogated as of the effective date of this Treaty in so far as it pertains to the construction, maintenance and operation of any system of trans-Isthmian communication by railroad within the territory under the jurisdiction of the Republic of Panama.

Subject to the provisions of the succeeding paragraphs of this Article, the United States further agrees that the exclusive right to establish roads across the Isthmus of Panama acquired by the United States as a result of a concessionary contract granted to the Panama Railroad Company shall be abrogated as of the date of the entry into force of this Treaty, in so far as the right pertains to the establishment of roads within the territory under the jurisdiction of the Republic of Panama.

In view of the vital interest of both countries in the effective protection of the Canal, the High Contracting Parties further agree that such abrogation is subject to the understanding that no system of inter-oceanic communication within the territory under the jurisdiction of the Republic of Panama by means of railroad or highway may be financed, constructed, maintained, or operated directly or indirectly by a third country or nationals thereof, unless in the opinion of both High Contracting Parties such financing, construction, maintenance, or operation would not affect the security of the Canal.

The High Contracting Parties also agree that such abrogation as is contemplated by this Article shall in no wise affect the maintenance and operation of the present Panama Railroad in the Canal Zone and in territory subject to the jurisdiction of the Republic of Panama.

Article IV

The second paragraph of Article VII of the Convention signed November 18, 1903, having to do with the issuance of, compliance with, and enforcement of, sanitary ordinances in the Cities of Panamá and Colón, shall be abrogated in its entirety as of the date of entry into force of this Treaty.

Article V

The United States of America agrees that, subject to the enactment of legislation by the Congress, there shall be conveyed to the Republic of Panama free of cost all the right, title and interest held by the United States of America or its agencies in and to certain lands and improvements in territory under the jurisdiction of the Republic of Panama when and as determined by the United States to be no longer needed for the operation, maintenance, sanitation or protection of the Panama Canal or of its auxiliary works, or for other authorized purposes of the United States in the Republic of Panama. The lands and improvements referred to in the preceding sentence and the determinations by the United States of America respecting the same, subject to the enactment of legislation by the Congress, are designated and set forth in Item 2 of the Memorandum of Understandings Reached which bears the same date as this Treaty. The United States of America also agrees that, subject to the enactment of legislation by the Congress, there shall be conveyed to the Republic of Panama free of cost all its right, title and interest to the land and improvements in the area known as PAITILLA POINT and that effective with such conveyance the United States of America shall relinquish all the rights, power and authority granted to it in such area under the Convention signed November 18, 1903. The Republic of Panama agrees to save the Government of the United States harmless from any and all claims which may arise incident to the conveyance of the area known as PAITILLA POINT to the Republic of Panama.

Article VI

Article V of the Boundary Convention, signed September 2, 1914, between the United States of America and the Republic of Panama, shall be replaced by the following provisions:

"It is agreed that the permanent boundary line between the City of Colón (including the Harbor of Colón, as defined in Article VI of the Boundary Convention of 1914, and other waters adjacent to the shores of Colón) and the Canal Zone shall be as follows:

Beginning at an unmarked point called "E," located on the northeasterly boundary of the Colón Corridor (at its Colón extremity), the geodetic position of which, referred to the Panamá-Colón datum of the Canal Zone triangulation system, is in latitude 9°21' N. plus 0.00 feet (0.000 meters) and longitude 79°54' W. plus 356.09 feet (108.536 meters).

Thence from said initial point by metes and bounds:

Due East, 2662.83 feet (811.632 meters), along North latitude 9°21' plus 0.00 feet (0.000 meters), to an unmarked point in Folks River, called "F," located at longitude 79°53' W. plus 3700.00 feet (1127.762 meters);

N. 36°36'30" E., 2616.00 feet (797.358 meters), to an unmarked point in Manzanillo Bay, called "G";

N. 22°41'30" W., 1192.00 feet (363.322 meters), to an unmarked point in Manzanillo Bay, called "H";

N. 56°49'00" W., 777.00 feet (236,830 meters), to an unmarked point in Manzanillo Bay, called "I";

N. 29°51'00" W., 2793.00 feet (851.308 meters), to an unmarked point in Manzanillo Bay, called "J";

N. 50°56'00" W., 3292.00 feet (1003.404 meters), to an unmarked point in Limon Bay, called "K";

S. 56°06'11" W., 4258.85 feet (1298.100 meters), to an unmarked point in Limon Bay, called "L," which is located on the northerly boundary of the Harbor of Colón.

Thence following the boundary of the Harbor of Colón, as described in Article VI of the Boundary Convention signed September 2, 1914, to monument "D'," as follows:

N. 78°30'30" W., 2104.73 feet (641.523 meters), on a line to the light house on Toro Point, to an unmarked point in Limon Bay, called "M," located 330 meters or 1082.67 feet easterly and at right angles from the centerline of the Panama Canal;

S. 00°14'50" W., 3074.46 feet (937.097 meters), parallel to and 330 meters or 1082.67 feet easterly from the centerline of the Panama Canal, to an unmarked point in Limon Bay, called "N";

S. 78°30'30" E., 3952.97 feet (1204.868 meters), to monument "D," which is a concrete monument, located on the easterly shore of Limon Bay.

Thence following the boundary between the City of Colón and the Canal Zone, as desribed in Article V of the Boundary Convention signed September 2, 1914, to monument "B" as follows:

S. 78°30'30" E., 258.65 feet (78.837 meters) through monuments Nos. 28 and 27 which are brass plugs in pavement, to monument "D" which is a concrete monument, the distances being 159.96 feet (48.756 meters), 28.26 feet (8.614 meters), and 70.43 feet (21.467 meters), successively, from beginning of the course;

N. 74°17'35" E., 533.60 feet (162.642 meters), along the centerline of Eleventh Street, through monuments Nos. 26, 25, 24 and 23, which are brass plugs in the pavement, to "C," which is an unmarked point beneath the clock pedestal on the centerline of Bolivar Avenue, the distances being 95.16 feet (29.005 meters), 91.02 feet (27.743 meters), 166.71 feet (50.813 meters), 158.66 feet (48.360 meters) and

22.05 feet (6.721 meters), successively, from beginning of the course;

S. 15°58'00" E. 965.59 feet (294.312 meters), along the centerline of Bolivar Avenue, through monuments Nos. 22, 21, 20 and 19, which are brass plugs in the pavement, to monument "B," which is a brass plug, the distances being 14.35 feet (4.374 meters), 143.13 feet (43.626 meters), 238.77 feet (72.777 meters), 326.77 feet (99.600 meters) and 242.57 feet (73.935 meters), successively from beginning of the course. (Monument "B" is the point of beginning referred to in Article I of the Convention between the United States of America and the Republic of Panama regarding the Colón Corridor and certain other Corridors through the Canal Zone, signed at Panamá on May 24, 1950.)

Thence following the boundary between the City of Colón and the Canal Zone, to monument "A," as described in Article I of the Corridor Convention referred to in the next-preceding paragraph:

S. 15°57'40" E., 117.10 feet (35.692 meters) along the centerline of Bolivar Avenue to Monument No. A-8, which is a brass plug located at the intersection with the centerline of 14th Street projected westerly, in North latitude 9°21' plus 1356.18 feet (413.364 meters) and West longitude 79°54' plus 1862.57 feet (567.712 meters);

N. 73°59'35" E., 172.12 feet (52.462 meters) along the centerline of 14th Street to Monument No. A-7, which is a brass plug located at the intersection with the line of the west curb of Boundary Street projected northerly in North latitude 9°21' plus 1403.64 feet (427.830 meters) and West longitude 79°54' plus 1697.12 feet (517.283 meters);

Southerly along the westerly curb of Boundary Street and its prolongation to Monument No. A-4, which is a brass plug located at the intersection of two curves, in North latitude 9°21' plus 833.47 feet (254.042 meters) and West longitude 79°54' plus 980.94 feet (298.991 meters) (this last mentioned course passes through a curve to the left with a radius of 40.8 feet (12.436 meters) and the intersection of its tangents at point A-6 in North latitude 9°21' plus 1306.23 feet (398.140 meters) and West longitude 79°54' plus 1669.37 feet (508.825 meters), and a curve to the right with a radius of 1522 feet (463.907 meters) with the point of intersection of its tangents at point A-5 in North latitude 9°21' plus 958.14 feet (292.042 meters) and West longitude 79°54' plus 1105.89 feet (337.076 meters));

Through a curve to the left with a radius of 262.2 feet (79.919 meters) and the intersection of its tangents at point A-3 in North latitude 9°21' plus 769.07 feet (234.413 meters) and West longitude 79°54' plus 955.43 feet (291.216 meters); a curve to the right with a radius of 320.0 feet (97.536 meters) and the intersection of its tangents at point A-2 in North latitude 9°21' plus 673.38 feet (205.247 meters) and West longitude 79°54' plus 836.40 feet (254.935 meters); and a curve to the left with a radius of 2571.5 feet (783.795 meters) and the intersection of its tangents at point A-1 in North latitude 9°21' plus 302.15 feet (92.096 meters) and West longitude 79°54' plus 680.96 feet (207.557 meters) to Monument No. "A," which is a 1½ inch brass plug located in the old sea wall, in North latitude 9°21' plus 45.60 feet (13.899 meters) and West longitude 79°54' plus 487.65 feet (148.636 meters);

S. 21°34'50" W., 29.19 feet (8.897 meters), to an unmarked point called #1;

Southeasterly, 23.26 feet (7.090 meters), along a curve to the left with a radius of 2596.48 feet (791.409 meters) (the chord of which bears S. 37°28'20" E., 23.26 feet (7.090 meters) to an unmarked point called #2, located on the southwesterly boundary of the Colón Corridor at North latitude 9°21' plus 0.000 feet (0.000 meters)).

The directions of the lines refer to the true meridian.

The above described boundary is as shown on Panama Canal Company drawing No. 6117-22, entitled "Boundary Line Between the City of Colón and the Canal Zone," scale 1 inch to 600 feet, dated December 23, 1954, prepared for the Canal Zone Government, attached as an annex hereto and forming a part hereof."

Article VIII of the General Treaty signed March 2, 1936, as amended by Article III of the Convention between the United States of America and the Republic of Panama regarding the Colón Corridor and certain other corridors through the Canal Zone, signed May 24, 1950, is hereby modified by removing from the Colón, or westerly, end of the Colón Corridor the portion thereof lying north of North latitude 9°21' and incorporating such portion within the boundary of the City of Colón as described above.

This Article shall become effective upon completion of the withdrawal by the United States of America from the sections of the city of Colón known as New Cristobal, Colón Beach and the de Lesseps Area, with the exception of the lots retained for consulate purposes, except that it shall in no case become effective prior to the exchange of the instruments of ratification of this Treaty and the exchange of instruments of ratification of the Convention signed May 24, 1950, referred to in the preceding paragraph.

Article VII

The second paragraph of Article VII of the Boundary Convention signed September 2, 1914, between the United States of America and the Republic of Panama, shall be abrogated in its entirety as of the date of entry into force of the present Treaty.

The landing pier situated in the small cove on the southerly side of Manzanillo Island, constructed pursuant to provisions contained in the second paragraph of Article VII of the Boundary Convention of 1914 between the two countries, shall become the property of the Government of the Republic of Panama as of the date of entry into force of the present Treaty.

Article VIII

(a) The Republic of Panama will reserve exclusively for the purpose of maneuvers and military training the area described in the maps (Nos. SGN-7-54 and SGN-8-54, each dated November 17, 1954) and accompanying descriptions prepared by the Comisión Catastral of the Republic of Panama, attached as the Annex hereto, and will permit the United States of America, without cost and free of all encumbrances, exclusively to utilize said area for the indicated purpose for a period of fifteen (15) years, subject to extension thereafter as agreed by the two Governments. This authorization includes the free access to, egress from, and movements within and over, said area. This utilization will not affect the sovereignty of the Republic of Panama, or the operation of the Constitution and the laws of the Republic over the mentioned area.

(b) The United States Armed Forces, the members thereof and their families actually residing with them, and United States nationals who, in an official capacity, are serving with or accompanying the Armed Forces of the United States and members of their families actually residing with them will be exempted within the said area from all taxation by the Republic of Panama or any of its political subdivisions.

(c) Prior to the expiration of the period envisaged in this Article and within a reasonable time thereafter the United States shall have the right to remove from this training and maneuver area, or otherwise to dispose of, without limitation or restriction all structures, installations, facilities, equipment and supplies brought into, or constructed or erected within this training and maneuver area by or on behalf of the United States. The Republic of Panama will not be required to reimburse the United States for any structures, installations, facilities, equipment and supplies not removed or otherwise disposed of as provided herein.

(d) The United States shall be under no obligation to restore this training and maneuver area or the facilities and installations thereon to their original condition upon the termination of this Article, except for the landing strip which will be returned in at least as good condition as compared with an employee who is a resident of the area.

(e) The employee who is a citizen of the United States will also be eligible for greater annual leave benefits and travel allowances because of the necessity for periodic vacations in the United States for recuperation purposes and to maintain contact with the employee's home environment.

Legislation will be sought to make the Civil Service Retirement Act uniformly applicable to citizens of the United States and of the Republic of Panama employed by the Government of the United States in the Canal Zone.

The United States will afford equality of opportunity to citizens of Panama for employment in all United States Government positions in the Canal Zone for which they are qualified and in which the employment of United States citizens is not required, in the judgment of the United States, for security reasons.

The agencies of the United States Government will evaluate, classify and title all positions in the Canal Zone without regard to the nationality of the incumbent or proposed incumbent.

Citizens of Panama will be afforded opportunity to participate in such training programs as may be conducted for employees by United States agencies in the Canal Zone.

2. With reference to that part of Article V of the Treaty signed today which deals with the conveyance to the Republic of Panama free of cost of all the right, title and interest held by the United States of America or its agencies in and to certain lands and improvements situated in territory under the jurisdiction of the Republic of Panama, steps will be taken as provided in this Item.

(a) Legislation will be sought to authorize and direct the transfer to the Republic of Panama of all the right, title and interest held by the United States or its agencies in or to the following real property:

1. The J. N. Vialette and Huerta de San Doval tracts in the city of Panamá and the Aspinwall tract on the Island of Taboga.

2. Las Isletas and Santa Catalina Military Reservations on the Island of Taboga. This transfer will include the cable rights-of-way which have a width of 20 feet (6.10 meters) and extend between the Ancon Cove Military Reservation and the Santa Catalina Military Reservation, and between the El Vigia Military Reservation and the Las Isletas Military Reservation.

3. The lot in Colón now reserved for consulate purposes.

4. Certain lands on the westerly shores of the city of Colón described roughly as extending from the southerly boundary of the de Lesseps area (4th Street extended) to the Colón-Canal Zone boundary and bounded on the east by the east wall of the old freight house and, below that structure, by a line 25 feet (7.622 meters) west of the center line of the most westerly railroad track. This transfer will include the certain improvements consisting of the old freight house and Colón Pier Number 3.

(b) Legislation will be sought to authorize and direct the Panama Canal Company to remove its railway terminal operations from the city of Panamá and to transfer to the Republic of Panama free of cost all of the right, title and interest of the Panama Canal Company in and to the lands known as the Panama Railroad Yard, including the improvements thereon and specifically including the railway passenger station. This action will also relieve the Government of the Republics of Panama of its obligation under Point 10 of the General Relations Agreement between the United States of America and the Republic of Panama signed May 18, 1942 to make available without cost to the government of the United States of America a suitable new site for such terminal facilities.

(c) With respect to those areas in the city of Colón known as de Lesseps, Colón Beach and New Cristobal (with the exception of two lots in the de Lesseps area which the United States intends to use for consulate purposes), legislation will be sought to authorize and direct the gradual withdrawal fom these areas and the conveyance or transfer to the Republic of Panama free of cost of all the right, title and interest of the United States and of its agency, the Panama Canal Company, in and to the lands and improvements thereon. Under this process of gradual withdrawal the United States Government, and/or its agencies, will not be obligated to install any new structure in such areas and, as severable parts of the areas cease to be needed, the lands and improvements would be conveyed or transferred. The severability of parts of the areas depends upon a number of practical considerations including those having to do with the present obligations of the United States, with respect to the subject areas, concerning water and sewerage facilities, street cleaning and paving, water supply, et cetera, as stipulated in the Instrument of Transfer of Water and Sewerage Systems, executed between the Governor of the Panama Canal and the Foreign Minister of Panama on December 28, 1945.

(d) With respect to the railroad passenger station and site in the city of Colón, legislation will be sought to authorize and direct the withdrawal from such site and structure at such time as the withdrawal from the areas known as de Lesseps, Colón Beach and New Cristobal, contemplated by the next preceding subparagraph, shall have been fully completed, and the conveyance to the Republic of Panama free of cost of all the right, title and interest of the United States and of its agency, the Panama Canal Company, in and to such site and structure. However, the railroad tracks and trackage area in Colón, being required for switching purposes serving the Cristobal piers, will be retained for such purposes.

(e) All tansfers or conveyances of lands and improvements contemplated by this Item, subject to legislative authorization and direction, will necessarily be made subject to any leases which may be outstanding in the respective areas, and will also contain provisions fully protecting the Government of the United States of America against any claims by lessees for damages or losses which may arise as a result of such transfers or conveyances.

(f) The transfers or conveyances contemplated by this Item, subject to legislative authorization, are in addition to the conveyance of Paitilla Point as specifically covered by Article V of the Treaty signed today, and to the transfer of real property effected by Article VI of said Treaty.

3. Articles, materials, and supplies that are mined, produced or manufactured in the Republic of Panama, when purchased for use in the Canal Zone, will be exempted from the provisions of the Buy American Act.

4. Referring to the exchange of notes dated March 2, 1936, accessory to the General Treaty between the United States of America and the Republic of Panama signed on that date, relative to the sale to ships of goods imported into the Canal Zone by the Government of the United States of America, the United States of America agrees, effective December 31, 1956, and in benefit of Panamanian commerce, to withdraw wholly from, and thereafter to refrain from, any such sales to ships, provided that nothing in this Item shall apply.

(a) to sales to ships operated by or for the account of the Government of the United States of America,

(b) to the sale of fuel or lubricants, or

(c) to any sale or furnishing of ships stores which is incidental to the performance of ship repair operations by any agency of the Government of the United States of America.

5. Legislative authorization and the necessary appropriations will be sought for the construction of a bridge at Balboa referred to in Point 4 of the General Relations Agreement of 1942.

6. The United States of America agrees, effective December 31, 1956, to withdraw from persons employed by agencies of the Government of the United States of America in the Canal Zone who are not citizens of the United States of America and who do not actually reside in said Zone the privilege of availing themselves of services which are offered within said Zone except those which are essential to health or necessary to permit them to perform their duties.

7. It is and will continue to be the policy of the Panama Canal agencies and of the Armed Forces in the Canal Zone in making purchases of supplies, materials and equipment, so far as permitted under United States legislation, to afford to the economy of the Republic of Panama full opportunity to compete for such business.

8. In general connection with the matter of the importation of items of merchandise for resale in the sales stores in the Canal Zone, it will be the practice of the agencies concerned to acquire such items either from United States sources or Panamanian sources unless, in certain instances, it is not feasible to do so.

9. With respect to the manufacture and processing of goods for sale to or consumption by individuals, now carried on by the Panama Canal Company, it will be the policy of the United States of America to terminate such activities whenever and for so long as such goods, or particular classes thereof, are determined by the United States of America to be available in the Republic of Panama on a continuing basis, in satisfactory qualities and quantities, and at reasonable prices. The United States of America will give prompt consideration to a request in writing on the part of the Government of Panama concerning the termination of the manufacture or processing of any goods covered in this Item as to which the Government of Panama may consider the criteria specified in this Item to have been met.

10. Prompt consideration will be given to withdrawing from the handling of

commercial cargo for transshipment on Canal Zone piers so soon as Panamanian port facilities are in satisfactory operation in Colón.

11. The United States agrees that the term "auxiliary works" as used in the Treaty includes the Armed Forces of the United States of America.

On the part of the Republic of Panama:

1. The Republic of Panama will lease to the United States of America, free of all cost save for the recited consideration of one Balboa, for a period of 99 years, two parcels of land contiguous to the present United States Embassy residence site, as designated on the sketch (No. SGN-9-54, dated November 19, 1954) and accompanying descriptions prepared by the Comisión Catastral of the Republic of Panama, attached herto.

2. The Republic of Panama assures the United States of America that the property, shown and described on the attached map (No. SGN-6-54, dated October 1954) and accompanying description prepared by the Comisión Catastral of the Republic of Panama, in front of the United States Embassy office building site and between the Bay of Panama and Avenida Balboa as it may be extended between 37th and 39th Streets, will be preserved permanently as a park and not developed for commerical or residential purposes.

3. So long as the United States of America maintains in effect those provisions of Executive Order No. 6997 of March 25, 1935 governing the importation of alcoholic beverages into the Canal Zone, the Republic of Panama will grant a reduction of 75 percent in the import duty on alcoholic beverages which are sold in Panama for importation into the Canal Zone pursuant to such Executive Order.

4. In connection with the authorization granted to the United States of America in Article VIII of the Treaty, the United States shall have free access to the beach areas contiguous to the maneuver area described in said Article VIII for purposes connected with training and maneuvers, subject to the public use of said beach as provided under the Constitution of Panama.

The provisions of this Memorandum of Understandings Reached shall enter into force upon the exchange of instruments of ratification of the Treaty signed this day by the United States of America and the Republic of Panama. . . .

60. Address by Secretary Dulles made at the Pan American Union on Pan American Day*

April 14, 1955

A little over 6 weeks ago, at Bangkok, I reminded the Manila Pact Council that the foreign policy of the United States of America has always rested on two propositions. One is that we want peace and liberty for ourselves. The other is that we ourselves cannot be sure of either liberty or peace unless other nations have them likewise. And I pointed to the Rio Pact and the Organization of American States as being rooted in that primary and constant international policy of the United States Government.

When President John Quincy Adams accepted the invitation for the United States to take part in the first international conference of American States, the Congress of

*Department of State Bulletin, May 2, 1955, pp. 728-32.

Panama, 129 years ago, he stated an inter-American policy which is still our policy today. In a message to the United States House of Representatives, President Adams enunciated three principles upon which he deemed it would be wise to lay the cornerstone of all our future relations with the other independent American peoples, of which there were then only eight.

First and paramount of these, he said, was a refusal to look only to our own selfish advantage. Next was cordial good will, and third, fair and equal sovereignty. And he said of our proposed participation in that first inter-American conference—I quote his words:

> It may be that, with the lapse of centuries, no other opportunity so favorable will be presented to the Government of the United States to subserve the benevolent purposes of Divine Providence, to dispense the promised blessings of the Redeemer of mankind, to promote the prevalence in future ages of peace on earth and goodwill to man, as will now be placed in their power by participating in the deliberations of this Congress.
>
> That the Congress of Panama will accomplish all or even any of the transcendent benefits to the human race which warmed the conception of its first proposer [continues President Adams' message] it were, perhaps, indulging too sanguine a forecast of events to promise. It is, in its nature, a measure speculative and experimental. The blessing of Heaven may turn it to the account of human improvement. Accidents unforeseen and mischances not to be anticipated may baffle all its high purposes and disappoint its fairest expectations. But the design is great, is benevolent, is humane.

We all know that there has been no lack of those unforeseen accidents and unanticipated mischances. All the American peoples have suffered them time and again in major proportions during the intervening generations. As a matter of fact, on a smaller scale, they struck at our own participation in the Congress of Panama itself. One of our two delegates died on the way, and the other arrived only after the Congress had adjourned. Nevertheless, President Adams made clear our moral presence at that meeting.

Neither he nor Bolívar would have been surprised, their faith being what it was, in our presence here today. This House of the Americas is outward evidence of the kind of solidarity, based on mutual trust among nations, which has become a guaranty of security to the free peoples of America and indeed one of the safeguards of freedom in the world.

Anniversary of Pan American Union

I am happy to recall also that this Pan American Day which we are celebrating is the 65th anniversary of the first meeting, here at Washington, of what became the International Union of American Republics, later to be known as the Pan American Union—a term now limited to the secretariat—and finally, as the tremendously significant Organization of American States.

This great inter-American system, which was first a vision and a dream and then an expression of faith, has become in our own time the most solid international organization of free peoples on earth. It is the family tree of America—its multiple roots deep in our common New World history—its 21 branches each a proud, independent nation, its rich fruits beneficial to all mankind. After more than a century and a quarter,

Bolívar's prophetic declaration that in the freedom of the Americas lies the hope of the world has lost neither veridity nor immediacy.

It is historic fact that the active, effective cooperation of the American Republics during the past half-century has established working models for other areas. The structure of the United Nations itself benefited from our experience in the Americas, and the Organization of American States continues to be one of the regional groups which contributes to making the principles of the United Nations Charter more effective and more stable.

Similarly, the Rio Treaty, our Inter-American Treaty of Reciprocal Assistance, has served as a prototype for the North Atlantic and other mutual defense arrangements. The two fundamental features of the Rio Treaty are the provisions relating to collective self-defense and common action in the event of armed attack, and to the steps which should be taken when we are confronted with situations that threaten the peace and security of the American States but that fall short of an armed attack. The framework of many collective defense treaties which free nations have built since 1947 is based upon these two features.

The most recent example of free peoples joining together to safeguard their independence is the Southeast Asia Collective Defense Treaty signed at Manila on September 8, 1954. In the preparation of this treaty it was recognized that perhaps the greatest threat confronting the parties in the area was that of subversion; that is, of aggression short of open, armed attack. Article 6 of the Rio Treaty was found to contain a most useful formula for covering this situation. The drafters of the Manila Pact consequently borrowed heavily from its idea and also from its actual language.

Thus it is clear that the Rio Treaty has contributed by precept and example toward fortifying the collective security of free men in both hemispheres. In this progressive action, regional cooperation of the kind in which this Organizaion has had over a half-century of experience is one of the surest bulwarks of global security and peace. We may all take satisfaction in the fact that, with the deposit of its ratification by Guatemala on April 6, the Rio Treaty is now in effect among all 21 Republics.

In his State of the Union Message in January, President Eisenhower emphasized the importance of two inter-American meetings held in 1954: the Tenth Inter-American Conference at Caracas and the Inter-American Economic Meeting at Rio de Janeiro. At the one, the American States closed ranks against international communism. At the other, they strengthened hemisphere economic ties.

Now I would like to discuss in our meeting here in the Hall of the Americas some policies of my Government which support and reinforce the objectives held in common, for our own countries separately and for the hemisphere, in our Organization of American States. They are policies which are rooted deep in United States history.

Hemisphere Security

The first major statement of United States foreign policy was a statement in behalf of hemisphere security. You know it well: President Monroe's message, which became a Doctrine, that there should be no further European colonization or the extension of the despotic political system of Europe to the American Hemisphere. Thus early we recognized the profound truth that, when one American people is endangered, all are in peril.

At Caracas last year the Tenth Conference of American States gave the truth a further historic application. It there recognized that, if international communism should gain control of the political institutions of any one American State, that would be a threat to the security of us all. Mutual refusal to compromise with communism, mutual awareness that extension of Communist colonialism to this hemisphere would endanger the peace of America, heartened the people of a sister State so endangered and enabled them to recover their lost freedom.

Again the American States found it possible to take an advanced position, which other free areas of the world may find it possible in due course to follow.

The Government and the people of the United States are resolved to stand fast with the other American nations in actively maintaining solidarity against all and every danger. Consequently, we participate in specific programs to that end with our neighbor Republics electing to insure their own military defense and that of the hemisphere.

Comparisons of Dollar Aid

You have all heard and read, time and again, criticism of the United States on the score that we give far more dollar aid to other areas—Europe, the Near East, the Far East—than to our close neighbors and traditional friends, the sister Republics of this hemisphere. In fact, you have read and heard far more; for instance, that the economic ills of the other American Republics are due primarily to failure—or refusal—on the part of the United States to make loans to them and give them other help in building up their economies in anything like the measure in which the United States gives such help to Europe and the Far East.

I have never been able to comprehend so complete a misunderstanding of the nature and the purpose of our foreign aid. We have had to pour enormous sums into Europe as loans, grants, and expenditures because Europe is geographically nearer to military peril. As such, it is a frontier, not for the defense of Europe alone but for defense of the United States, for defense of Argentina, Bolivia, Brazil, Chile, Colombia, Costa Rica, Cuba, the Dominican Republic, Ecuador, El Salvador, Guatemala, Haiti, Honduras, Mexico, Nicaragua, Panama, Paraguay, Peru, Uruguay, and Venezuela.

Vast sums sent by the United States to Europe and to the Far East have had to be used for reconstruction of devastated regions in order to enable free men once again to take their part in the development, the maintenance, and the extension of the free world. Similarly, the United States has had to make enormous expenditures for the military installations which insure defense in Europe and elsewhere against mighty forces whose mere existence, poised and ready, is an unceasing threat to us all. For the same reason we have had to maintain abroad detachments of our own armed forces in great number, at an expense undreamed of in less perilous epochs of history.

The United States has had to make available great funds for grants, loans, manpower, equipment, military assistance on front after front. These have been emergency expenditures, whether for reconstruction or defense. At every moment and in every particular, they have been expended to safeguard security and peace for my country—and for yours.

We cannot make any valid comparison in terms of dollars between that kind of assistance in rebuilding, reestablishing, and reinforcing war-stricken nations continually in danger of new armed attacks and the type of assistance which we extend to Latin America. Let us rather thank God that this fortunate hemisphere has had no need for stationing such multitudes of troops within its confines; that there is no war devastation to be undone; that there is no need for constructing such extensive military installations as deterrents to a war which, if it came, would destroy civilization as we know it.

Our hemisphere has been spared the terrific devastation of large-scale modern war. We have not had to undergo the harsh rigors of manmade devastation affecting entire peoples. Alliance and interest for our common good motivate inter-American cooperation; and in general we are not building together in this hemisphere against war so much as for peace. It is our hope that our economic and technical assistance in Latin America will help stablize national economies and raise living standards. It is our purpose to do our part in maintaining in America, which has long been freedom's dwelling place and the natural habitat of peace and prosperity, the good partnership of the American peoples.

Eximbank Loans

There is one further thing I would like to say with respect to the economic relations of the United States with Latin America. The present figures indicate how much importance we assign them. The Export-Import Bank has adopted the policy of making sound economic development loans for which funds are not available from the International Bank nor from private sources on reasonable terms. The amount of our governmental loans in this hemisphere depends primarily, therefore, on the number of sound loan applications filed by other Republics. As a result of this liberalized policy, the Export-Import Bank loans for the Latin America area since January first of the present year represent 90 percent of its total credits; that is to say, out of total credits of $184 million, Latin America has received $167 million. To emphasize the amount of increase, it may be recalled that during the first 6 months of 1954, total Export-Import Bank credits were $76 million, of which Latin America received $39 million.

Our programs of technical cooperation have always seemed to me one of the most praiseworthy aspects of inter-American relationships. They bring improved conditions of health, of education, of utilizing the land. They make the hemisphere a better environment for us all, and they enlarge the horizons of opportunity for our children and our children's children.

Increasing the hemisphere's economic strength is an essential factor in inter-American solidarity. Economically, the national approach is basic and is preliminary to international cooperation whether bilateral or multilateral. Recognizing and acting upon the common need, inter-American programs of technical assistance have also been trailblazers for other peoples of the world. They serve as seedbed and experimental stations for trans-Atlantic and trans-Pacific programs of my own Government's Foreign Operations Administration, as well as for international cooperation in this important field. Bilateral hemispheric programs of technical assistance, one nation with another, and the multilateral programs of the Inter-American Economic and Social Council and the United Nations promote both the security and the peaceful development of our peoples, contributing as they do to democratic progress by improving our national economies and raising our standards of living.

The final declaration of the Inter-American Economic Conference at Rio stated the agreement of the American nations on their economic objectives as follows:

> These may be summarized as a determination to speed up the progress of each and every one of them within the framework of freedom and justice, through substantial intensification of our inter-American economic, financial, and technical cooperation.

Importance of Self-Reliance

At Rio, the United States delegation was forthright in presenting our approach to economic problems confronting the American Republics. We hold that each one of the American peoples has it within his power to maintain a strong and self-reliant economy. It is our purpose, as steadfast partner for the common objective of better living standards throughout the hemisphere, to cooperate toward achieving that strength, without loss of awareness on the part of any of us, that apparent strength is illusory unless there be also self-reliance.

In attaining our mutual objectives, we believe, for our own country as for each of yours, that private enterprise rather than government will take the initiative in pioneering and developing industrial fields. That has traditionally been the history of industrial development in America. President Eisenhower in his foreign economic policy message to Congress expressed clearly the attitude of the United States. He said:

> The Nation's enlightened self-interest ... require[s] a foreign economic program that will stimulate economic growth in the free world through enlarging opportunities for the fuller operation of the forces of free enterprise and competitive markets.

Through technical cooperation and development loans we hope to help the other American Republics diversify their economies and eventually to help lessen dependence on only a few commodities.

There is widespread recognition in my country of the preeminent importance of trade in the economies of the neighboring Republics. There is corresponding recognition of the great importance to our own economy of the Latin American export market for United States products. We know that this market is made possible on a large scale only by United States purchases from Latin America.

The United States is prepared to consider on their merits proposals made on Latin American initiative that look toward regional trading arrangements, provided these meet certain criteria, especially provision for the maintenance of truly competitive conditions within any trading area that might be established.

I believe that just as a national economy must be viewed as a whole, not as a series of unrelated entities, so must we view inter-American economic relations. That is the logical and the practical viewpoint. The Organization of American States is taking this overall view and, through its agencies and specialized organizations, is making a concerted approach to improve the conditions and opportunities of life for the peoples of the hemisphere. The United States is establishing partnership with its neighbors in these enterprises, with full conviction that improvement of the American economy as a whole benefits our own national economy.

The cooperation characteristic of the inter-American system avoids on the one hand the snares and delusions of alien domination and on the other the pitfalls of narrow nationalism. The Organization of American States is also conscious that often the welfare of the many is the most certain good for the one. We are all aware of, all act in accordance with, what my distinguished predecessor, the late Charles Evans Hughes, termed "the inescapable relations created by propinquity ... the privileges and obligations of neighborhood."

The inter-American system contributes to human development and progress our mutual guaranties of assistance which insure and preserve security. It contributes our mutual endeavors to maintain peace as the natural climate of the Western Hemisphere and our mutual concern that the American family of nations reap the greatest possible harvest from the seed sown in cooperation and nurtured in good will. The United States of America is proud to be a member of this association of free and independent nations who hold steadfast to their great design of making peace a reality and freedom secure.

61. United States Departments of State and Treasury, Position on the Proposed Inter-American Bank for Economic Development*

July 1, 1955

The proposal for the establishment of an Inter-American Bank was made by a Committee of Experts consisting of representatives of nine Latin American Central Banks and the Secretariat of the Economic Commission for Latin America. This Committee was established by a resolution of the Meeting of Ministers of Finance or Economy in the Fourth Extraordinary Session of the Inter-American Economic and Social Council held at Rio de Janeiro, Brazil, in November-December 1954, to make specific plans for an inter-American financing institution.

The United States Delegation at that Meeting abstained from voting on the resolution, stating that the United States had given a great deal of thought to the problem of Latin American needs for credit and investment facilities, and had concluded that in its opinion the facilities available through the International Bank for Reconstruction and Development, the Export-Import Bank, the proposed International Finance Corporation, and private organizations, will be adequate to meet all demands for sound purposes. It also indicated that if we find at some later date that this program is not achieving the results which we believe it can, we shall be glad to discuss other solutions. The United States Delegation therefore expressed its regret that it could not at that time join in the proposed inter-American regional financing institution, and indicated it would abstain from participating in drafting specific plans for it. There have been no developments which would justify a change in the position expressed by the United States Delegation at that time.

*Department of State Bulletin, July 25, 1955, p. 140.

62. *Address by Assistant Secretary Holland, made at the Conference on American Foreign Policy of Colgate University, on the Responsibility of the American Republics in World Affairs**

July 11, 1955

We live in an age in which man has the power to blast himself from the earth. The very survival of humanity depends upon our ability to devise a structure of international relations within which widely divergent nations can live at peace with sufficient mutual respect and understanding to insure the peaceful settlement of disputes arising between them.

Perhaps it is unfortunate that man's capacity to destroy himself as a species should have been achieved at a time when the nations of the world still differ so widely as regards size and population, as well as their degree of industrial, political, military, and cultural development. These wide differences between us complicate our efforts to devise a workable international system adequate to maintain peace. On the other hand, this same awesome capacity for self-destruction may prove to be the catalyst without which such a system could never be developed.

The United Nations Organization has proved invaluable as a device for focusing the influence of world opinion on the peaceful solution of international problems, as a testing ground where the real facts regarding these problems can be established through debate and impartial investigation, as a forum in which large and small nations can speak with more nearly equal voices than when engaged in bilateral negotiation. The United Nations and its subsidiary organizations mark the closest approach yet achieved by man to that worldwide law and order which is today so clearly essential to our survival.

Much has been said of the world leadership which history has in our times imposed upon the United States. But there is another need whose urgency increases—that for a community of leaders. The free nations of the world are struggling to establish a workable international system which will maintain peace. The frustrations and obstacles we encounter are discouraging. If somewhere in the world a group of nations can give a continuing, successful demonstration of such a system actually working on a regional basis, the inspiration to the remainder of the world will be great. What any substantial group of nations actually achieves can eventually and surely be achieved by a worldwide community of nations if they so will.

We know that a peace sustained by force is not lasting. There can be no lasting peace until all nations voluntarily identify themselves with an international structure erected upon principles guaranteeing the indepedence, security, and integrity of the individual members. Such an international organization, once established, will not survive unless men are convinced that it will eventually be successful in meeting and solving the problems arising among its members. Should the United Nations fail, man's disillusionment may well be such that years could pass before desperation again drove him to undertake another worldwide organization for the peaceful solution of disputes between nations.

*Department of State Bulletin, July 25, 1955, pp. 135-40.

Evolution of a World Organization

From our experience in the United Nations we know now that an international structure embracing the whole world and functioning effectively can be achieved only by years of trial and error, by a process of evolution. The United Nations as it exists today, with all of its virtues and its defects, must be conceded to mark no more than a transitional stage in a process of evolution which must extend for we know not how many more years before a satisfactory result is achieved. Peace today is uneasily preserved by the harsh certainty that the combined military power of free nations is adequate to crush any combination of forces that Soviet Russia might lead or inspire. Such a peace falls far short of our aspirations. Yet such a peace preserved by the growing military strength of the free nations of the world does afford us time in which to perfect the essential framework of a successful worldwide system.

Ten years of work in the United Nations have put behind us a part of the tortuous and often discouraging road which we must travel if men are to reach that goal which lies somewhere in the future. The fact that thorny and stubborn problems have been solved in the United Nations gives us courage to attack those which, like the heads of the dragon, seem to replace each that is removed. So, too, does the somber conviction that the alternative to such efforts may be the frightful one of nuclear warfare.

These limited achievements, these frightful alternatives will suffice, I believe, to keep the free world constant in its course despite the strain and cost. But how much more willing would be our own effort and that of others, with what rising enthusiasm would the free world press forward if our ultimate goal could seem but nearer at hand! Mankind needs urgently a demonstration that the goal we have set for ourselves can in fact be achieved.

Nations at times become disheartened by the number and complexity of the problems, domestic and international, which obstruct their progress to a more abundant and dignified life. They need the incentive that can best derive from a living example of the rewards which can be achieved through the essentially spiritual and religious philosophy of the free world. These are rewards assured not only to powerful nations but to all nations, great and small, that identify themselves with an international order based upon these principles.

The Example of the American Republics

If our present evolutionary process is not to stagnate, if it is to avoid retrogressive phases, it becomes imperative that there emerge today a group of nations which all men can recognize as an example of that larger global community which must be our ultimate goal. That group of nations does exist in the 21 American Republics. Their association for military, political, cultural, and economic collaboration is the most successful and advanced yet achieved by man.

Not until some such relationship as that which for a century has been evolving in this hemisphere is extended to embrace all nations can we hope for more than a passing "peace in our time."

The success of the American Republics in the conduct of our international relations is of vital importance to all Americans. But today I want to talk of its importance to the rest of the world. It may well determine the direction in which world history will move in the years ahead. Why should such decisive influence with its correlative responsibility be vested in the 21 American Republics? Until recent decades no American State identified itself intimately with the trend of world events. The answer is that our relations with each other over the past century have been in a sense a pilot plant. Its successful operation through the stresses and shocks of international relations has offered a real incentive to the world at large to entrust its hopes to the United Nations. The visible, measurable success of the inter-American system, which included more than a third of the founders of the United Nations, gave that projected organization a basis in demonstrated experience rather than theory. The knowledge that 21 of the 51 nations assembled at San Francisco had made such an international system succeed, and had done so under conditions of adversity not unlike those existing elsewhere in the world, must have afforded a powerful incentive.

A century ago we undertook in this hemisphere to demonstrate that widely dissimilar states can devise a way of life which gradually eliminates harmful or unnecessary differences between them, while preserving and even perfecting those differences held sacred by their various peoples. Many of the problems which today imperil the success of the United Nations likewise, to a greater or lesser degree, obstructed our path at that time.

Here, as in the United Nations now, were countries ranging from the earth's smallest to its largest; states peopled by men of different race, culture, language, religion, and history. There were states separated by what traditionally would have represented a century of progress along the road of economic development and industrialization. There were nations whose relations were constantly troubled by the strain of old, unsettled disputes; people separated from each other by distances almost as great at those from pole to pole, by some of the world's highest mountain barriers, or by vast expanses of untraversable wilderness.

Any system of international relationships which could weld 21 such states into a tightly knit group which proudly refers to itself as a "family" must offer great hope to a troubled world which desperately seeks some device to preserve peace without sacrifice of freedom, honor, or national sovereignty, some means of averting a third world war from which civilization could not hope to recover.

The American Republics are a living example of the fruits of an international system designed to insure the peaceful settlement of disputes, to insure to each state an opportunity to achieve its economic, cultural, and political aspirations with the active assistance of other members of the community.

Regional Organizations

In 1945 when the United Nations Organization was established, the inter-American system had not yet reached its present state of development. Even so, its demonstrated success exerted an influence so powerful that many of the principles upon which it was founded were carried forward as keystones of the larger structure. Ten years ago in San Francisco the representatives of the American States were so convinced of the crucial importance of regional structures such as theirs that they joined in a gallant and successful fight to overturn the principle of universalism accepted at Dumbarton Oaks and to establish the concept of regional organizations within the United Nations. That concept is now embodied in such mutual security organizations throughout the world as the North Atlantic Treaty Organization and the Southeast Asia Treaty Organization. Without them the postwar threat of Communist subversion and imperialism might not have been met and checked.

Many of us feel deeply that for civilization to survive, to avert a spiritual and moral retreat that would sacrifice centuries of progress, the world as a whole must proceed along some such path of development as that down which we in this hemisphere have toiled for more than a century. Mankind may be willing to do that so long as, and only so long as, we in our lives as nations demonstrate that this road does in fact lead to the fulfillment of man's ancient yearning for peace with freedom and dignity. If we succeed in our own quest, then others will surely follow us. If each new decade reaffirms that in the Americas it is law and not force or threat of force which sustains the sovereignty and integrity of nations, then, though elsewhere international despotisms may arise, they will not endure. These principles which here have proved effective to guarantee to the smallest and weakest state that same degree of national dignity and sovereignty which is the most cherished achievement of the strongest will surely spread to the rest of this world.

What is the genius of our relationship in this hemisphere? First, perhaps, it is the knowledge that neither as individual states nor as a community have we yet achieved a level of progress which is acceptable to us as free and religious men. Yet, singly and collectively, the material and spiritual growth we can record at each successive inter-American conference makes us content to press forward confidently toward the next.

The Spiritual Bond

It is the essentially spiritual stuff of which our bond is made which has given it the strength to preserve its intended design despite the shocks of global wars and the constant erosion of those lesser disagreements which must occasionally arise among so large a group of vigorous and progressive nations.

Our relationship contemplates that all will, if necessary, by force of arms protect whichever may find itself attacked. Yet it is not primarily a military alliance. By treaties, resolutions, and international contracts we are committed to the principle that the economic development of each benefits the entire community. Yet we are far more than a trading or economic community. Our procedures for the peaceful settlement of disputes arising between us are among the finest achievements of our relationship. Yet the determination which more than all of these unites us and gives meaning and direction to our bond goes far beyond these which I have mentioned. It is to establish and constantly to strengthen throughout this new world and its 350 million peoples those principles of the sanctity of the individual and his freedom, of the brotherhood of man, which are common to all the different faiths that we profess.

On many things our views may differ. Our right to hold such differences is one of those which we most cherish. But on these basic tenets of our American creed we are solidly united.

There are, I believe, other convictions shared by all of us and which should be mentioned here. They and others of like nature are preserved in our inter-American treaties and resolutions.

Nonintervention in Domestic Affairs

As a man has the right to pursue the fulfillment of his aspirations without unlawful interference from his fellows, we are as states each irrevocably committed to the principle of nonintervention in the domestic affairs of every other. As the most powerful member of the community we are prone to think that the principle of nonintervention is one which restrains the United States for the benefit of the other American Republics. On the contrary, there is not a one of us but has felt both the benefits and the obligations of this principle.

Each of our governments is from time to time subjected to strong pressure from its own domestic groups to criticize or meddle in the domestic activities of some other American State. Were we to be swayed by these pressures, I doubt that our inter-American system could long endure. It was not until the doctrine of nonintervention was firmly established that the system achieved real grandeur.

An important companion to the principle of nonintervention is our conviction that the well-being of every American State is basically important to that of every other. The misfortunes of each member of this community vitally concern every other. In the military field this has led us to adopt the principle set out in article 3 of the Rio Treaty of 1947, which provides that "an armed attack by any State against an American State shall be considered as an attack against all the American States." That article served as the inspiration for article 5 of the North Atlantic Treaty of 1949, which provides that "an armed attack against one or more of them [the subscribers to the treaty] in Europe or North America shall be considered an attack against them all." This interpretation of an attack on one as an attack on all marks a milestone in our defensive security arrangements.

In the political field, our universal concern with the well-being of every member state inspired the Caracas Resolution, which declares that domination by international communism of the political institutions of any of our states imperils the peace of America. In the economic field, it leads each of us in its own realistic self-interest to seek means effectively to contribute to the well-being of every other.

Our belief in the sovereign equality of the American States recognizes the obvious fact that the dimensions of our statesmen are not determined by those of the sovereign territories they represent. In this hemisphere we deal as equals, as adult and mature states. We have no caste system. In our councils, from the smallest of us to the largest, we debate with the vigor and conviction of equals. And well we might, for all have contributed, and importantly, in forging the structure within which we reside. We are, I believe, all proud that the inter-American system as it exists today was neither an Anglo-Saxon nor a Latin vision. It is, instead, a marvelous composite which might never have existed had it not drawn upon the finest concepts of these two cultures.

Lastly, in referring to the basic convictions underlying our inter-American system, one is impressed by the profound assurance in the minds of Americans everywhere that we are in fact on the right road. Our inter-American system affords all the assurance that any nation needs that industry, resourcefulness, and self-discipline mean sure and steady progress toward the fulfillment of its just aspirations.

Successes of the Inter-American System

This kind of confidence can only come from success. What are our successes which would justify such a conviction?

In the political field our experience during the past years justifies our belief that the Organization of American States is capable of dealing with any inter-American problem brought before it. It is no reflection upon the liberation movement which so gallantly overcame the Communist-dominated regime in Guatemala to recall that for weeks earlier the Organization of American States had been readying an extraordinary meeting of Foreign Ministers to decide upon the measures which might be required to eliminate this threat to the peace of the Americas.

Earlier in this year that same organization, determined that its actions would be worthy of the trust reposed in it to preserve our peace, undertook in the Costa Rican outbreak a whole series of unprecedented measures. It established an international aerial patrol, coordinating aircraft supplied by several states. When circumstances required, it affirmatively requested the other American Governments to make war planes available to the Government of Costa Rica. If, loyal to our tradition and our trust, we resolve to go even beyond these unprecedented measures should the nature of the problem require, then we can indeed feel that aggression will never prevail in our hemisphere.

In the economic field our progress is as heartening as in the political. We hear talk of "underdeveloped nations" both in the hemisphere and out. I have often wondered just what those who use this phrase mean. If it means a nation whose progress is unjustly obstructed by its neighbors, then we can proudly sustain that there are no underdeveloped countries in this hemisphere. Here, as I have said, each of us in its own self-interest seeks to further the economic development of every other. Our own contribution to this joint effort is being made through expanded opportunities for inter-American trade, through substantially greater access to sound loans for developmental purposes, and through intensified programs of technical assistance. I believe that these contributions are recognized as constructive by the other members of this family of nations.

On the other hand, if an "underdeveloped nation" is one which has not yet attained that level of economic development to which its human and its natural resources give it the right to aspire, then we can thank God that we are all underdeveloped nations in this hemisphere. The feeling that in this sense we are underdeveloped is a wholesome one and furnishes a constant incentive to make greater use of our resources for the benefit of our people. It is true that we are experiencing an era of development which, judged by any standard, exceeds anything which the world has ever seen in a comparable area. Nevertheless, there is not a country in the hemisphere whose resources are not abundantly adequate to provide substantially higher living standards to its people.

Some of us are passing through temporary periods of adversity, but there are no cripples among us. There is not a stagnant economy in the hemisphere. On all sides there is activity and progress.

We are certainly not immune to the problems of inflation and instability of currencies which have plagued the entire world. In each of our states continued progress will depend upon the degree of courage and self-discipline which we demonstrate in meeting and solving these purely domestic problems. They are difficult, and their solution at times raises domestic political obstructions which may seem insurmountable. Their solution is complicated by the fact that the very people who cry out against the suffering which such problems cause often resist the measures of self-discipline inevitably required for their solution.

No Insurmountable Obstacles

Without minimizing the thorniness of our economic problems we must never lose sight of the fact that they are all of a kind that can be solved. They are often a product of that rapid development which will in the end enormously benefit our peoples. We can take courage from the fact that there is not one nation in the hemisphere whose further substantial and lasting progress is obstructed by really insurmountable obstacles. Every one of us has progressed enormously in the last quarter of a century. Yet every one of us has access to all the elements necessary for further substantial progress.

I have said that our future here in the United States and throughout the hemisphere must depend on work, self-discipline, and a willingness to undertake sacrifices where necessary for the greater good. These have produced for us the progress we have achieved. It has abundantly justified the cost. We would be foolhardy indeed if we allowed ourselves to be persuaded that like progress in the future can be had at any different price.

What I have said of the responsibility of the American States to serve as an example and an inspiration to the world is not new. I recall with some pride that at the San Francisco meeting commemorating the tenth anniversary of the United Nations the 21 American Republics met separately to exchange views. Also, just last week President Eisenhower and Secretary Dulles met with the Ambassadors of the other American Republics to discuss problems which will be raised at the forthcoming four-power conference and solutions which may be advanced for them. Such meetings evidence the growing conviction of our Governments and peoples that as partners in this hemisphere we owe a responsibility not only to our own people but to the entire world. We must succeed in our stewardship of our inter-American affairs, not only because of what it means to this hemisphere but because of the inspiration which such an example will afford to the rest of the world.

Those who attended the San Francisco meeting were deeply impressed by the speeches of the 37 Foreign Ministers and other heads of delegations who attended. They demonstrated beyond all question that national leaders today are keenly aware that the alternative to some reasonably effective international system may well be the destruction of the human race.

63. *State Department Comment on Action taken by the Third Meeting of the Inter-American Council of Jurists at Mexico City on Territorial Waters and Related Matters**

February 20, 1956

At its meeting at Mexico City, January 17-February 4, the Inter-American Council of Jurists adopted a resolution on the subject of territorial waters and related matters by a vote of 15 to 1, with 5 abstentions (Annex 1). This resolution, entitled "Principles of Mexico on the Juridical Regime of the Sea," was vigorously opposed by the United States Representative, who, in a statement included in the Final Act of the meeting, attacked the resolution on the grounds of both its substance and the manner in which it was adopted (Annex 2).

The Tenth Inter-American Conference (Caracas, 1954) in Resolution LXXXIV resolved, among other things, that the Council of the Organization of American States should convoke a Specialized Conference for the purpose of studying as a whole the different aspects of the juridical economic system covering the submarine shelf, oceanic waters, and the natural resources in the light of present-day scientific knowledge, and that the Council request pertinent inter-American organizations to render necessary cooperation in the preparatory work that the Specialized Conference requires.

Pursuant to this decision, the Council of the OAS convened the Specialized Conference for March 15, 1956, at Ciudad Trujillo. In preparation for the Conference, it requested the Inter-American Council of Jurists, its technical advisory organ on legal matters, to make a preparatory study on the legal aspects of the matters to be considered at Ciudad Trujillo. It was made clear that the purpose of this study was to furnish the Specialized Conference with pertinent background information and that any conclusions or decisions were to be reserved by the Conference. The agenda item for the Third Meeting of the Inter-American Council of Jurists covering this matter was formulated by the Council of the OAS in the following terms:

"Topic I (a)—Regime of Territorial Waters and Related Matters: Preparatory Study for the Inter-American Specialized Conference Called for in Resolution LXXXIV of the Caracas Conference."

Situation Confronting the council of Jurists

The Council of Jurists found itself handicapped at the very outset of its consideration of the topic by lack of any kind of working document on the subject. The

---

**Department of State Bulletin*, Feb. 20, 1956, pp. 296-99.

Inter-American Juridical Committee, the Council's permanent committee, had been requested to prepare a preliminary study but for a variety of reasons declined to do so. In view of the complete absence of preparatory materials, which as a method of precedure the Council of Jurists had consistently maintained to be necessary to enable it to proceed on a sound basis in the consideration of a topic, the United States early in the general debate indicated that in its opinion the most constructive contribution which the Council of Jurists could make to the work of the Specialized Conference under the circumstances would be: (1) to have an exposition of views of the respective governments on the general subject and to transmit the proceedings of the discussions to Ciudad Trujillo; and (2) to request the appropriate technical agency of the OAS to undertake a collection and systematic organization of pertinent background materials, particularly national and international acts and practices.

General Debate

During the first week of the meeting, action on the topic was limited to informal conversations among the delegations. This procedure was agreed upon considering that it would be advisable to allow time for an exchange of views on the controversial issues involved before taking them up in public session.

During the general debate on the subject, 17 delegations took the opportunity to present the views and attitudes of their respective governments on various aspects of the general problem. This general debate served the useful purpose of affording an opportunity for a very substantial number of the American governments for the first time to state their views on principal aspects of this important subject. The debate, however, did not include a discussion of the issues raised, being confined to the presentation of the general statements of governments, nor were any draft resolutions submitted for consideration.

Nine-Country Resolution

As the general debate came to an end, copies of a draft resolution sponsored by eight countries (Argentina, Chile, Ecuador, El Salvador, Guatemala, Mexico, Peru, and Uruguay, later joined by Costa Rica) were distributed in Committee I. The proposal incorporated, in extreme terms, one of the two principal points of view expressed during the general debate. In its presentation no statement was made by any of the proponents in explanation or justification of its contents.

The resolution declared that the three-mile limit of territorial waters "does not constitute a rule of general international law." In its place, according to the resolution, "each State is competent to establish its territorial waters within reasonable limits, taking into account geographical, geological, and biological factors, as well as the economic needs of its population, and its security and defense."

The extreme character of the resolution is also reflected in its articles dealing with the conservation of living resources. The coastal States have, the resolution asserts, "the right of exclusive exploitation of species closely related to the coast, the life of the country, or the needs of the coastal population"—a formula which is sufficiently elastic to suit the requirements of the most extravagant claims.

On the highly technical subject of base lines and bays, the resolution also came to firm conclusions despite the fact, as the United States Representative pointed out in the one session when an opportunity was given to comment upon the resolution, that there had been virtually no consideration of these highly technical points during the entire session of the Council.

United States Declaration and Reservation

The reasons for the United States opposition to the resolution are summarized in the declaration and reservation included in the Final Act. The United States delegation made this important statement after consultation with, and upon the authorization of, the Department of State.

As the U.S. declaration points out, the resolution suffers from serious substantive defect in that it seeks to lay down rules which fail to take into consideration fundamental and well-accepted principles of international law, such as the principle of freedom of the seas, and the rights and interests derived from international law and treaty by States other than the adjacent coastal State. Furthermore, the resolution contains pronouncements based on scientific and economic assumptions for which no supporting evidence was presented.

Perhaps of greater concern to the United States is the manner in which the resolution was adopted. On the day after the resolution was introduced in Committee I, the delegates of Cuba, the Dominican Republic, the United States, and Venezuela raised various questions and considerations regarding the resolution. The proponents refrained from answering these observations and on the following day, rejecting appeals for more time to consider the proposal, put the resolution through by a vote of 15 in favor, 1 against (United States), and 5 abstentions (Bolivia, Colombia, Cuba, the Dominican Republic, and Nicaragua). The same vote was repeated in the plenary session.

In signing the Final Act, 11 countries entered reservations to the "Principles of Mexico" resolution. These included the United States and the five countries which abstained on the resolution, as well as five which had voted in the affirmative.

Cuban Proposal

Immediately following the vote on the nine-country resolution, the Cuban delegate introduced a resolution providing that the proceedings of Committee I relating to territorial waters and related matters, together with any conclusions reached through the discussions, be transmitted to the Specialized Conference with the character of a preparatory study. Although objected to by proponents of the first resolution on the grounds that it modified the declaratory nature of their document, the Cuban resolution was approved by a vote of 11 to 9 (Annex 3). This resolution served, at least from a procedural standpoint, to bring the nine-country resolution more within the terms of the assignment made to the Council of Jurists by the Council of the OAS.

ANNEX 1

Resolution XIII

Principles of Mexico on the Juridical Regime of the Sea

Whereas:

The topic "System of Territorial Waters and Related Questions: Preparatory Study for the Specialized Inter-American Conference Provided for in Resolution LXXXIV of the Caracas Conference" was included by the Council of the Organization of American States in the agenda of this Third Meeting of the Inter-American Council of Jurists; and

Its conclusions on the subject are to be transmitted to the Specialized Conference soon to be held,

The Inter-American Council of Jurists

Recognizes as the expression of the juridical conscience of the Continent, and as applicable between the American States, the following rules, among others; and

Declares that the acceptance of these principles does not imply and shall not have the effect of renouncing or weakening the position maintained by the various countries of America on the question of how far territorial waters should extend.

A
Territorial Waters

1. The distance of three miles as the limit of territorial waters is insufficient, and does not constitute a rule of general international law. Therefore, the enlargement of the zone of the sea traditionally called "territorial waters" is justifiable.

2. Each State is competent to establish its territorial waters within reasonable limits, taking into account geographical, geological, and biological factors, as well as the economic needs of its population, and its security and defense.

B
Continental Shelf

The rights of the coastal State with respect to the seabed and subsoil of the continental shelf extend also to the natural resources found there, such as petroleum, hydrocarbons, mineral substances, and all marine, animal, and vegetable species that live in a constant physical and biological relationship with the shelf, not excluding the benthonic species.

C
Conservation of Living Resources of the High Seas

1. Coastal States, following scientific and technical principles, have the right to adopt measures of conservation and supervision necessary for the protection of the

living resources of the sea contiguous to their coasts, beyond the territorial waters. Measures that may be taken by a coastal State in such case shall not prejudice rights derived from international agreements to which it is a party, nor shall they discriminate against foreign fishermen.

2. Coastal States have, in addition, the right of exclusive exploitation of species closely related to the coast, the life of the country, or the needs of the coastal population, as in the case of species that develop in territorial waters and subsequently migrate to the high seas, or when the existence of certain species has an important relation with an industry or activity essential to the coastal country, or when the latter is carrying out important works that will result in the conservation or increase of the species.

D
Base Lines

1. The breadth of territorial waters shall be measured, in principle, from the low-water line along the coast, as marked on large-scale marine charts, officially recognized by the coastal State.

2. Coastal States may draw straight base lines that do not follow the low-water line when circumstances require this method because the coast is deeply indented or cut into, or because there are islands in its immediate vicinity, or when such a method is justified by the existence of economic interests peculiar to a region of the coastal State. In any of these cases the method may be employed of drawing a straight line connecting the outermost points of the coast, islands, islets, keys, or reefs. The drawing of such base lines must not depart to any appreciable extent from the general direction of the coast, and the sea areas lying within these lines must be sufficiently linked to the land domain.

3. Waters located within the base line shall be subject to the regime of internal waters.

4. The coastal State shall give due publicity to the straight base lines.

E
Bays

1. A bay is a well-marked indentation whose penetration inland in proportion to the width of its mouth is such that its waters are *inter fauces terrae* and constitute something more than a mere curvature of the coast.

2. The line that encloses a bay shall be drawn between its natural geographical entrance points where the indentation begins to have the configuration of a bay.

3. Waters comprised within a bay shall be subject to the juridical regime of internal waters if the surface thereof is equal to or greater than that of a semicircle drawn by using the mouth of the bay as a diameter.

4. If a bay has more than one entrance, this semicircle shall be drawn on a line as long as the sum total of the length of the different entrances. The area of the islands located within a bay shall be included in the total area of the bay.

5. So-called "historical" bays shall be subject to the regime of internal waters of the coastal State or States.

*(Approved at the Fourth Plenary
Session, February 3, 1956)*

ANNEX 2

Declaration and Reservation of the United States of America on Resolution XIII, "Principles of Mexico on the Juridical Regime of the Sea"

For the reasons stated by the United States Representative during the sessions of Committee I, the United States voted against and records its opposition to the Resolution on Territorial Waters and Related Questions. Among the reasons indicated were the following:

That the Inter-American Council of Jurists has not had the benefit of the necessary preparatory studies on the part of its Permanent Committee which it has consistently recognized as indispensable to the formulation of sound conclusions on the subject;

That at this Meeting of the Council of Jurists, apart from a series of general statements by represenatives of various countries, there has been virtually no study, analysis, or discussion of the substantive aspects of the Resolution;

That the Resolution contains pronouncements based on economic and scientific assumptions for which no support has been offered and which are debatable and which, in any event, cover matters within the competence of the Specialized Conference called for under Resolution LXXXIV of the Tenth Inter-American Conference;

That much of the Resolution is contrary to international law;

That the Resolution is completely oblivious of the interests and rights of States other than the adjacent coastal States in the conservation and utilization of marine resources and of the recognized need for international cooperation for the effective accomplishment of that common objective; and

That the Resolution is clearly designed to serve political purposes and therefore exceeds the competence of the Council of Jurists as a technical-juridical body.

In addition, the United States Delegation wishes to record the fact that when the Resolution, in the drafting of which the United States had no part, was submitted to Committee I, despite fundamental considerations raised by the United States and other delegations against the Resolution, there was no discussion of those considerations at the one and only session of the Committee held to debate the document.

ANNEX 3

Resolution XIV
System of Territorial Waters and Related Questions

The Inter-American Council of Jurists

Suggests to the Council of the Organization of American States that it transmit to the Specialized Conference provided for in Resolution LXXXIV of the Caracas Conference the Resolution entitled "Principles of Mexico on the Juridical Regime of the Sea" approved by this Council, together with the minutes of the meetings in which this subject has been considered during the Third Meeting, with the character of the preparatory study called for in Topic I (a) of its Agenda, "System of Territorial Waters and Related Questions."

(Approved at the Fourth Plenary
Session, February 3, 1956)

64. Address by President Eisenhower, to the Meeting of Presidents of the American Republics Commemorating the First Inter-American Conference *

July 22, 1956

To address a thought to the Heads of the American States here assembled is indeed a unique opportunity and a unique honor. I profoundly appreciate it.

We here commemorate the most successfully sustained adventure in international community living that the world has ever seen. In spite of inescapable human errors in our long record, the Organization of American States is a model in the practice of brotherhood among nations. Our cooperation has been fruitful because all of our peoples hold certain basic spiritual convictions. We believe:

That all men are created equal;

That all men are endowed by their Creator with certain inalienable rights, including the right to life, liberty, and the pursuit of happiness;

That government is the creation of man, to serve him; not man's master, to enslave him;

That those who demonstrate the capacity for self-government thereby win the right to self-government;

That sovereign states shall be free from foreign interference in the orderly development of their internal affairs.

Inspired by our faith in these convictions, our nations have developed in this hemisphere institutional relations and a rule of international law to protect the practice of that faith.

Our association began as we experienced the solemn but glorious transition from colonialism to national independence. Our association was intensified as we sought to maintain that independence as against recurrent efforts of colonial powers to reassert their rule. More recently it has been perfected to protect against encroachments from the latter-day despotisms abroad.

We are pledged to one another by the Inter-American Treaty of Reciprocal Assistance of 1947 to treat an armed attack by any state against an American State as an attack against all of us and are joined in the 1954 Declaration of Solidarity for the Preservation of the Political Integrity of the American States Against International Communist Intervention.

Department of State Bulletin, Aug. 6, 1956, pp. 219-21.

Preserving Peace Within America

Furthermore, we are organized to assure peace among ourselves. The time is past, we earnestly believe, when any of our members will use force to resolve hemispheric disputes. Our solemn promises to each other foresee that the community will take whatever measures may be needed to preserve peace within America.

In all of these matters our nations act as sovereign equals. Never will peace and security be sought at the price of subjecting any nation to coercion or interference in its internal affairs.

Thus, much has been done to assure the kind of national life which was the lofty vision of those early patriots who, in each of our countries, founded our Republics and foresaw the values inherent in hemispheric cooperation.

May it not be that we can now look forward to a new phase of association, in which we shall dedicate to individual human welfare the same measure of noble effort that heretofore has protected and invigorated the corporate life of our nations?

I do not suggest that the initial task is ended. A nation's peace and liberty can never be taken for granted. We must constantly be vigilant, individually and collectively. But we can, I believe, in the coming years, consecrate more effort to enriching the material, intellectual, and spiritual welfare of the individual.

Since the day of creation the fondest hope of men and women has been to pass on to their children something better than they themselves enjoyed. That hope represents a spark of the Divine which is implanted in every human breast.

Too often, from the beginning, those hopes have been frustrated and replaced by bitterness or apathy.

Of course, the problems thus presented are primarily those of the particular country in which the affected individuals reside. But I believe we can be helpful to each other. The possibilities of our partnership are not exhausted by concentration on the political field. Indeed, our organization has already begun to apply the principle that the material welfare and progress of each member is vital to the well-being of every other. But we can, I think, do more.

Increasing Effectivensss of OAS

On this matter a simple thought which I have had an opportunity to express to some other American Presidents here has been viewed generously by them. It is that each of us should name a special representative to join in preparing for us concrete recommendations for making our Organization of American States a more effective instrument in those fields of cooperative effort that affect the welfare of our peoples. To those representatives we could look for practical suggestions in the economic, financial, social, and technical fields which our Organization might appropriately adopt. As one useful avenue of effort, they could give early thought to ways in which we could hasten the beneficial use of nuclear forces throughout the hemisphere, both in industry and combating disease.

The coming year will bring to mankind limitless ways in which this new science can advance human welfare. Let us progress together, as one family, in achieving for all our people these results.

Our Organization can never be static. We are here to commemorate a dynamic concept initiated at the first Inter-American Conference of 1826, convoked by Simón Bolívar. We here pay tribute to the faith of our fathers, which was translated into new institutions and new works. But we cannot go on forever merely on the momentum of their faith. We, too, must have our faith and see that it is translated into works. So, just as our nations have agreed that we should join to combat armed aggression, let us also join to find the ways which will enable our peoples to combat the ravages of disease, poverty, and ignorance. Let us give them, as individuals, a better opportunity not only to pursue happiness but to gain it.

A great family history has drawn together this unprecedented assemblage of the Presidents of the Americas. Perhaps, in our day, it may be given us to help usher in a new era which will add worthily to that history. Thus, we too will have served the future, as we have been greatly served by the past that we honor here today.

65. *Presidents of the American Republics, Declaration of Panama** *

July 22, 1956

We, the Presidents of the American Republics commemorating in the historic City of Panama the Assembly of Plenipotentiaries of the American States of 1826, convoked by the Liberator Simón Bolívar, which constituted the first collective manifestation of Pan Americanism; and recognizing the continuing validity of the ideals which inspired the precursors of continental solidarity, subscribe to the following Declaration:

1. The destiny of America is to create a civilization that will give tangible meaning to the concept of human liberty, to the principle that the State is the servant of man and not his master, to the faith that man will reach ever greater heights in his spiritual and material development and to the proposition that all nations can live together in peace and dignity.

2. The full realization of the destiny of America is inseparable from the economic and social development of its peoples and therefore makes necessary the intensification of national and inter-American cooperative efforts to seek the solution of economic problems and to raise the standards of living of the Continent.

3. The accomplishments of the Organization of American States, and assurance of peace among the Member States and of security for the Continent, demonstrate how much can be achieved in the various fields of international endeavor through a loyal cooperation among sovereign nations, and move us to strengthen the inter-American organizations and their activities.

4. In a world in which the dignity of the individual, his fundamental rights and the spiritual values of mankind are seriously threatened by totalitarian forces, alien to the tradition of our peoples and their institutions, America holds steadfastly to its historic mission: to be a bulwark of human liberty and national independence.

5. An America united, strong and benevolent will not only promote the well-being

Department of State Bulletin, Aug. 6, 1956, p. 220.

of the Continent but contribute toward achieving for the whole world the benefits of a peace based on justice and freedom, in which all peoples, without distinction as to race or creed, can work with dignity and with confidence in the future. . . .

66. *Statement by Milton S. Eisenhower, U.S. Delegate to the Inter-American Committee of Presidential Representatives, on the Beneficial Use of Nuclear Forces throughout the Hemisphere**

September 17, 1956

The President of the United States in his address at the signing of the Declaration of Principles at the Meeting of Panama last July laid stress upon the work that might be initiated to ". . . hasten the beneficial use of nuclear forces throughout the hemisphere, both in industry and in combating disease."

Much thought has been given by the United States Government to ways and means by which all of the American Republics jointly might accelerate the use of this new force to bring greater health and happiness and abundance into the lives of all our peoples.

There are numerous ways in which nuclear energy may be put to the service of human welfare. Our Governments were represented at the U.N. Conference on the Peaceful Uses of Atomic Energy in Geneva last year, and there a vision was caught of the boons which might be gained by mankind through utilization of this new force. The United States is interested in the attainment of these benign results as soon as feasible.

Many of the Governments of the other American Republics have negotiated agreements for cooperation with the United States which will bring aid to their programs of nuclear research and new knowledge from this research to benefit their citizens. Such agreements have been negotiated with 11 of the American Republics; three more are under discussion. Under one agreement already completed, the President's offer of aid in financing the construction of a research reactor has been accepted and the United States commitment to pay a $350,000 contribution has been given.

President Eisenhower announced in February of this year that the United States initially will make available for distribution abroad 20,000 kilograms of uranium 235, the refined fissionable material that serves as the fuel for nuclear-power reactors. Under United States laws, our Government can provide nuclear fuels for research and power reactors only to those friendly nations with which we have concluded agreements for cooperation.

Such agreements for cooperation in the field of nuclear power are under discussion with three of the other American Republics—Argentina, Brazil, and Cuba. Discussions have not yet been undertaken by other member nations of the Organization of American States. The United States hopes they soon will be, for it is the desire of this Government that the American Republics made use of their full share of the stocks of

**Department of State Bulletin,* Oct. 1, 1956, pp. 511-13.

nuclear fuel which have been already allocated, and the additional supplies that shall hereafter be set aside, to aid in the development of atomic power in friendly nations.

However, there are some helpful things that can be done while waiting for research and power-reactor agreements of cooperation to be concluded, and the United States is ready, willing, and able to accelerate the application of nuclear energy to human welfare in the American Republics. In this spirit, the United States Atomic Energy Commission has recently taken two steps and soon will take a third.

The first of these steps was the inauguration last month of a special program of assistance to the University of Puerto Rico to enable it to establish programs of training and instruction in the Spanish language in the field of atomic energy. A second step was the formulation earlier this month of a program to cooperate with the Inter-American Institute of Agricultural Sciences at Turrialba, Costa Rica. A third project is the convening early next year of a symposium in which scientists and atomic energy officials of the 21 American Republics would exchange information and ideas on the peaceful applications of atomic energy.

The increasing use of radioisotopes in biology, medicine, agriculture, and industry, the development of nuclear propulsion for ships, and the inevitable large growth in electric power plants using nuclear energy instead of conventional sources of power are expected soon to put heavy demands on manpower resources for atomic-energy research and development.

The United States attaches great importance to the solution of the problem of how best to develop enough competent atomic scientists, engineers, and technicians in the immediate future. The world has not yet reached high noon in the atomic age but is only at the beginning of the dawn of a marvelous new era, the opportunities and responsibilities of which can hardly be imagined by any people now living.

The United States Atomic Energy Commission has progressively expanded its training programs and undertaken new ones to augment the supply of scientists and engineers in this country. It is also providing training assistance to friendly nations. There are now two schools supported by the Commission in which foreign students are trained—the International School of Nuclear Science and Engineering at Argonne, near Chicago, and the Oak Ridge Institute of Nuclear Studies in Tennessee. Only 16 students from the other American Republics of this hemisphere are now enrolled in these schools.

New Program in Puerto Rico

One of the most recent actions taken by the United States Atomic Energy Commission to alleviate the impending shortage of nuclear scientists and technicians was the inauguration of a special program of assistance to and collaboration with the University of Puerto Rico. The Commission is providing a training research reactor and laboratory equipment and other forms of aid to the university to enable it to begin practical training, education, and research in the field of atomic energy not later than the beginning of the next college year. This program of assistance to the university will include aid to its School of Medicine, School of Science, College of Agriculture and Mechanical Arts, and Agricultural Experiment Station.

The Commission and Puerto Rican officials are now planning the installation of a

20,000-kilowatt nuclear-power plant to supply more electric power for commercial purposes and to serve as an ancillary training facility for students attending the university. The implementation of this plan is, of course, subject to congressional approval.

This program will provide the University of Puerto Rico with unique nuclear training and research facilities within 3 or 4 years. Because these planned facilities would be truly outstanding and because instructions would be in Spanish, the University of Puerto Rico might well become a nuclear research and training center of interest to many of the countries of the hemisphere. In this connection, it is of interest to note that about 300 students from Central and South America are now attending the university, some of them under the technical assistance program of the United States International Cooperation Administration. If there should be evidence of a desire on the part of other students in the American Republics to enter the nuclear training and research courses at the University of Puerto Rico, the United States Government would, of course, cooperate in a program to include such students.

Earlier this month, the United States Government sent a team of three experts in the agricultural applications of atomic energy to Turrialba, Costa Rica, to discuss how atomic energy might be put to work in the program of the Inter-American Institute of Agricultural Sciences. They found that the Institute is peculiarly adaptable to utilizing radioisotopes and radiation in tropical agricultural research. They reported that implementation of a program in the Institute utilizing atomic energy for training and research in agriculture could be expected to make substantial contributions in plant nutrition and breeding, preservation of foodstuffs, and protection against disease and pests.

Aid to Institute at Turrialba

Four programs to assist the Institute are now being organized by the Atomic Energy Commission.

First, the Oak Ridge Institute of Nuclear Studies in Tennessee, an organization of colleges and universities maintained by the Commission, will accept applications for the course starting in early 1957 for those staff members for whom the Director of the Institute at Turrialba considers additional training desirable.

Second, the United States is prepared to make available to the Institute equipment for a radioisotope laboratory.

Third, if the Institute desires to set up a so-called "cobalt field" to study the effects of external radiation on a variety of plants, the United States would be willing to supply the radiation source and to give help in the technique of its use. Also the United States could provide radioisotopes for other research purposes.

Fourth, irradiation of plants and seed to obtain beneficial effects in new varieties and to acquire new knowledge of plant growth and development will be carried on for the Institute at the Brookhaven National Laboratory if the Institute so desires.

Inter-American Symposium

The United States Atomic Energy Commission is engaged in planning for an Inter-American Symposium on Nuclear Energy proposed to be held early next year at the Brookhaven National Laboratory on Long Island, N. Y. These plans anticipate that both the scientific and economic aspects of nuclear energy would be discussed at first hand by appropriate representatives of the 21 American Republics. Among the topics proposed to be considered are:

(1) the uses of radioisotopes in industry, agriculture, and medicine,

(2) nuclear-reactor types and uses, with collateral discussion on the prospects of economic nuclear energy as a source of commercial power, and

(3) factors to be considered in the organization and development of an effective nuclear energy program.

Following this 4- or 5-day symposium, several days of tours would be arranged to permit practical, close-at-hand inspections of our Atomic Energy Commission facilities and of hospitals, universities, and industrial establishments where the peaceful atom can be observed at work.

Believing this symposium to be a desirable forum to stimulate the use of nuclear energy throughout the American Republics, the United States Government, through its embassies, will shortly extend personal invitations to individuals who are prominently identified with the nuclear energy programs in the Latin American countries. It is hoped that there will be derived from this symposium an increased realization that this new servant of man—the atom—can improve the health and well-being of all the American peoples.

67. Inter-American Committee of Presidential Representatives, Final Communiqué*

September 19, 1956

The first session of the Inter-American Committee of Presidential Representatives adjourned on the afternoon of September 19 after three days of intensive work. Representatives of 21 countries met five times in closed session characterized by informal and frank discussions.

The Committee was created pursuant to a suggestion made by President Dwight D. Eisenhower of the United States, at the Meeting of Presidents at Panama, July 21-22, 1956, and accepted by the Presidents of the other American Republics. This proposal was that each President appoint a representative to consider together ways of making the Organization of American States a more effective instrument of inter-American cooperation in economic, social, financial and technical fields, including attention to the problem of the peaceful uses of atomic energy.

The objective of this first meeting was to identify the problems for the solutions of which recommendations will subsequently be drafted and submitted to the Presidents of the American States in fulfillment of the foregoing mission. As a first step in the Committee's deliberations, a general discussion was held concerning the approach to the Committee's task which the various Representatives considered appropriate.

The general discussion yielded a widespread recognition of the importance of the task assigned to the Committee and a universal desire to proceed with the effective strengthening of the Organization of American States. It was felt that ultimate

*Department of State Bulletin, Oct. 1, 1956, pp. 513-14.

recommendations should emphasize practical steps which the Organization of American States might take to promote the economic and social welfare of the peoples of the American continents. It was generally believed that the effective raising of the living standards of the American countries constitutes a long-range problem, to the solution of which the OAS could at this time make effective contributions.

The Committee then focused its attention upon the specific problems which in the opinion of the respective Representatives merited further study. The specific problems suggested for study fell under the main headings of economic, social, financial, technical, administrative and organizational, and nuclear energy. In all these fields emphasis was placed upon activities which might be considered under the general heading of technical-assistance activities and training and educational work. Great interest was also displayed in the possibility of developing through the OAS more effective and useful attention to specific economic and financial problems facing the various governments.

While Representatives at this stage did not feel in a position to express themselves definitively on any of the proposals which were advanced, the Committee can state that as a result of its three-day discussion, it has decided to proceed with study of the problems arising under the subjects summarized below:

A. Economic

1. *Agriculture:* Enlargement and wider dissemination of technical information; technical advice for governments; problems of development and trade in connection with agricultural products.

2. *Industry:* Industrial development and increase in industrial productivity.

3. *Commerce:* Expansion and facilitation of trade.

4. *Transportation:* Expansion of, and greater facilities for, land and water transport.

B. Social

1. *Public Health:* Elimination of major diseases.

2. *Education:* Expansion and improvement in educational facilities; wider public participation in activities of the OAS.

3. *Housing:* Methods of solving social problems of housing; development of low-cost housing.

4. *Social Security and Welfare:* Advice to governments on establishment and improvement of social security and welfare programs and other activities of special concern to workers.

C. Financial

Obtaining capital from public and private sources.

D. Technical

Improvement and coordination of present technical assistance programs.

E. Organization and Administrative

Adequate administrative organization of the OAS and strengthening of IA-ECOSOC [Inter-American Economic and Social Council] , in the light of new recommendations for substantive work.

F. Atomic Energy

Possibility of using nuclear materials in scientific research, and coordinating national training activities.

The Committee has decided to meet again early in January, after the governments have had an opportunity to give further consideration to the problems mentioned above. The purpose of the second meeting will be to prepare a list of topics, drawn from the various suggestions discussed at the present meeting, which will constitute the agenda for a third and final meeting later in 1957.

The Secretary General of the OAS is being requested to prepare factual reports on a number of subjects discussed during the present meeting and to present such additional observations on various topics as he may consider desirable. A secretariat for the Committee is being established by the Chairman of the Committee to provide a central point of coordination and information for all committee activities.

At the final meeting, probably in March or April 1957, definitive recommendations regarding certain topics will be drafted for submission to the twenty-one American Presidents.

68. *Address by Robert B. Anderson, Secretary of the Treasury, to the Economic Conference of the Organization of American States**

August 19, 1957

This conference follows in logical succession from the conference at Quitandinha in 1954. I was deeply impressed by the enthusiasm with which my predecessor, Secretary Humphrey, viewed the Quitandinha meeting. He was convinced at that meeting that there was unanimity among the delegates as to the great and inspiring objectives which we seek in this hemisphere. These objectives are clear and can be defined simply: We want our people all around the Americas to live better; we want them to pursue more healthful lives; we want their lives filled with hope, enriched with progress, and inspired toward the improvement of standards of well-being. Above all, we seek these goals while preserving the freedom of our peoples. It was most encouraging to me that in his eloquent address inaugurating this conference, President Aramburu [of Argentina] strongly reaffirmed the validity of these views.

As practical men with responsibility for helping to shape our nations' economic policies, we shall try to see our tasks as they really are, and not as we might wish them to be. They are many; they are difficult; and they are continuing. They are not to be dealt with by words alone, nor can they be laid to rest once and for all by some dramatic pronouncement at this or any other conference. Patience, persistence, and good will are the qualities of mind and heart which we must bring to our tasks.

I have recently talked at length with President Eisenhower about these matters. He shares the conviction that direct personal contacts and intimate exchanges between those of us who carry public responsibilities are the surest guaranty that our efforts will be successful and our objectives transformed into practical and satisfactory realities.

*Department of State Bulletin, Sept. 16, 1957, pp. 463-69.

You will all recall the unprecedented meeting of the Chiefs of State of the American Republics which took place in Panama in July 1956, and the Inter-American Committee of Presidential Representatives which developed from it to consider ways of strengthening the Organization of American States in fields of cooperative effort which directly affect the welfare of the individual. As a result of the Committee's deliberations, a series of recommendations was drawn up and submitted to the various Chiefs of State. President Eisenhower on May 26 publicly expressed his hope that many of the recommendations would be put into effect as promptly as possible.

We should not regard the meeting in Quitandinha, the conference in Panamá, or this conference as ends in themselves. Rather, each conference evidences greater strides forward to our common objectives. What is really important is the fact that we continue to demonstrate that 21 nations collectively, forming one of the world's most important communities, have come to the same conviction—that the welfare and progress of each member is related to the welfare and progress of each other member. Our approach has been, and will continue to be, that of good partners.

How then shall the Ministers of Finance or Economy of our Governments go about the task of increasing the effectiveness of their cooperative efforts? It would be presumptuous for me, one of the newest members of the group, to claim extensive personal familiarity with the details of the questions which we shall discuss. The delegation of the United States will express its views on the matters of our agenda, and I earnestly hope you will find them forward looking and constructive.

Before we came here, my Government reviewed and considered carefully the views that were expressed by the delegations in 1954 and weighed them in the light of the progress we have made in the interval of nearly 3 years since that meeting. We welcome this opportunity—indeed we feel it a responsibility—to express to you the fundamental approach which we bring to the questions before us.

This conference represents another important step in the continuing evolution of a long history of economic cooperation and business partnership. We are dealing with fundamental and long-range questions on which we can take stock and fruitfully exchange thoughts and points of view, but we recognize that in the economic field the march of day-to-day events and the cumulative effect of specific decisions in business and in government play the major role.

A country achieves material progress by developing its human and material resources. There is no other way to do it. The question that faces this conference, therefore, is how can our countries most rapidly and most efficiently develop their resources.

At inter-American meetings of this kind when we consider economic development we sometimes tend to talk as though Latin America were one great homogeneous area. In fact, the economic development of Latin America is the sum total of the economic development of each of the individual countries in the area.

When we examine the economic characteristics of the Latin American countries one by one we find a natural diversity. Some countries have limited natural resources. Others are among the most favored nations in the world in this respect. Some countries are almost entirely producers of raw materials. Others produce not only raw materials but also a wide variety of manufactured goods.

But amidst this diversity let there be this unity: however we develop our economies, however we use our resources or make our goods or provide opportunities for work, let us above all else guard freedom in all its aspects, for freedom is indivisible.

There are certain profound convictions with which I come to our meeting. They are convictions which I have held throughout a lifetime.

Common Objectives

The first conviction is this: No difference exists between us as to the objectives we seek. They are objectives that can be defined only in terms of human well-being and progress. We all agree that man does not exist to enhance the importance and power of the state, as the Communists would have us believe. The state exists for man—to respect his dignity as a child of God, to preserve his rights as an individual, and to provide opportunities which will enable him to develop, freely and fully, in all the ways that enrich human life and exalt its spiritual meaning and dignity. And this is what we mean when we speak of promoting commerce, industry, agriculture, and the development of all of our resources. We promote them because they make for the better employment of our citizens, better homes for our families, better education for our children, greater satisfaction of our aspirations—in short, a better America for all of us.

History has demonstrated the vital role of the competitive enterprise system in the economic life of our hemisphere. Its promise for the future is even greater. Just as truth flourishes best in the climate of political freedom, so in the economic field the system of competitive enterprise promises to yield most in the satisfaction of man's material needs. This system produces most of what people want most. I hope that at this conference we can contribute to the growth and strengthening of this system.

It is wholesome that we should explore the various ideas presented to us. No one knows better than a minister of finance or economy how difficult it is to choose between alternative measures. No one knows better than we that the fields of economy and finance are not exact sciences. Let us, therefore, approach our discussions with the hope that from a sincere and thoughtful exchange of views will come ways of doing things which are perhaps better than those which any of us alone might have brought to this conference.

This leads me to a second conviction which I hold strongly and which has been substantiated in actual experience. This is that there is no question incapable of resolution if we, as reasonable men of good will and as the representatives of our respective peoples, bring to bear on it the best and united effort of all of our peoples. President Eisenhower has characterized the Organization of American States and its predecessors as "the most successfully sustained adventure in international community living the world has ever known."

In this hemisphere we have had the courage to approach openly many problems for which solutions had not been found in international society. Some of these problems have found their first solution in the Americas. On other problems we have made the greatest progress toward an eventual solution that has yet been achieved. Why is this true? I believe that it is because we do not let differences of opinion divide us or breed distrust among us.

When we encounter a new problem or engage in a new field of discussion we seek a road we can all follow and which will ultimately bring us to our common objective. This method of approach has been a salient part of our cooperative effort during the past 50 years and against the background of history has been little short of remarkable.

Collective Security

For example, we developed in the Americas a hemispheric approach to security which was sealed in the Rio treaty of 1947. We unanimously agreed that an attack on any one state would be considered an attack on all. This concept of collective security has served as a pattern for the strengthening of the entire free world.

Our purpose is peace, both with the rest of the world and among ourselves. The repeatedly successful application of the Rio treaty to settle disputes between American states and the outstanding services of the Inter-American Peace Committee for peaceful settlement have established beyond doubt the desire and ability of the countries of the Americas to live peacefully together.

This fact has great economic significance. The assurances now provided by our common defense system offer us a dramatic opportunity to give greater emphasis to those economic activities that can better the lot of our peoples. Military expenditures, by their very nature, act as a brake on rising living standards, and for that reason they should be held to a level that will provide an adequate posture of defense. All of us in the Americas look forward to the day when a changed world situation will permit a substantial reduction of our large military expenditures. In the meantime, however, we must all do everything we can to control reasonably our expenditures in this area. All of us, I am confident, will continue to scrutinize our military budgets in an effort to accomplish savings that would make resources available in each of our economies for the kind of constructive development that advances economic well-being.

My third great conviction is that the progress and welfare of every American state is directly related to the progress and welfare of each. None of us can ever be indifferent to the problems and the suffering of another. Each of us has a personal and strong interest in the welfare of each of our partners. Often in the economic fields our problems are particularly subtle and stubborn.

Our best interests as members of this great American community clearly lie in pursuing a policy of cooperation. A basic aspect of this policy of cooperation is a firm determination on the part of my country to preserve a climate that will lead to the maintenance of a growing prosperity in the United States, which continues to represent the largest, most stable, and expanding market for the increasing production of the hemisphere. To seek to avoid any return to the depressed conditions of an earlier decade with the costly shrinkage it meant in our own economy and with the harmful reduction of your markets is a fixed point in the policy of my Government and of our whole people.

A further aspect of this policy of cooperation relates to the important areas of trade and investment. Needless to say, each of us occasionally is compelled to take action on the basis of important domestic considerations. Such departures from the general policy should be held to an inescapable minimum and should be justified by rigorous standards of necessity. In that way we can maintain our basic course with respect to international economic cooperation and maintain as well the integrity of those occasional departures from it which legitimate national considerations require.

Results of Cooperation

What are the results of our cooperative efforts during the past 4 years?

Today the people of the American states are contributing more to the economic progress and well-being of the world than at any previous time in our history. The output of goods and services is rising continuously at the rate of about three percent a year in the United States and at even higher rates in other American Republics. The average annual increase in the real gross national product for Latin America, as a whole, is estimated by the Economic Commission for Latin America at 4.3 percent for the 4 years 1953 through 1956. In several countries the rate of growth has been even higher.

Rarely, if ever, in history have we witnessed such a sustained and vigorous level of prosperity as we have been enjoying recently in the free world. Indeed in this decade we find we have a striking contrast to the world of 20 years ago. Then trade had shrunk, prices were depressed, and economic activity was feeble and discouraging. Today there is an increasing concern of an opposite character. In country after country the pressure of monetary demand is so great that inflation is either an unpleasant reality or a constant threat. In my country we are well aware of this fact. We are exerting our best efforts to keep our prosperity healthy and to avoid the adverse effects of inflation fever.

Many of you have experienced the effects of this economic illness and as finance ministers know all too well what it brings. You know how it not only complicates the task of the finance minister but enters as a disturbing factor into all the operations of business and the affairs of everyday life. You know how it can lead a whole people into competitive efforts to seek protection of their assets rather than employing them for the benefit of the community. You know how difficult it is for domestic and foreign capital to play an effective role in productive investment when there is continual worry and preoccupation with the dangers of a depreciating currency. You are familiar with the exchange difficulties and the constant tendency to excessive imports which inflation brings in its train. You know how exports may be discouraged when price relationships become distorted.

The United States applauds the efforts that are being made in many of the other American Republics to deal with this menace and to achieve greater financial stability and realistic and freer rates of exchange. We are happy that the International Monetary Fund has supported well-conceived programs for combating inflation in a number of these countries. The Treasury Department and other agencies of my Government have also supported these efforts.

We recognize that foreign trade and foreign investment is only one limited aspect of this broad panorama of economic development. Inter-American transactions are themselves a segment of the broader fabric of economic relations in the free world. Let me speak briefly, however, of the trade and investment transactions between my own country and the other American Republics. Through these transactions dollars become available to be effectively used by our sister republics. The flow of these dollars is generated, first, by our imports from the rest of the American States; second, by our investments; and third, by our loans for economic development. In each of these categories we have in recent years reached the highest levels yet recorded.

When we met at Quitandinha in 1954, imports into the United States from Latin America had reached the impressive annual rate of $3½ billion. In 1956 they reached the record level of $3.8 billion. About 30 percent of our total imports of goods from foreign countries are shipped from Latin America.

The increase of United States and other foreign private investment in Latin America has been most impressive. The flow of private investment from the United States, as shown by our balance of payments, has greatly increased in the past 5 years. During the first 2¼ years following our meeting at Quitandinha the figure amounts to about $1.4 billion or more than three times the corresponding rate during a comparable period preceding the meeting at Quitandinha. This is largely due to a very sharp expansion in direct investments, particularly in 1956. In that year direct investments exceeded $600 million, and total private investment amounted to more than $800 million.

Role of Private Enterprise

I should like to refer to some aspects of the role of private enterprise and private capital in the development of the American Republics.

It is reasonable that the governments and people of Latin America should expect our United States investors, to whom they extend a hospitable welcome, to be constructive members of the communities in which they operate. Certainly it is our earnest desire that they shall be. These same investors, we believe, are substantially determined that they shall be a factor toward progress in human welfare.

In the field of foreign investment we think there is a danger that undue attention may be given to the very partial figures which appear in balance-of-payments statements. From these figures it might be inferred that the investment of foreign capital brings no advantage, on balance, to the international accounts of the country receiving such investment. We believe such a conclusion would be incorrect for several reasons.

First, the balance-of-payments data do not show the complete picture. They do not show, for example, the total amount of new investment which has taken place on behalf of private investors. The Department of Commerce of my Government made a special study of the operations of a large group of United States enterprises operating in Latin America. The study covered the year 1955 and included companies holding nearly $6 billion of assets in Latin America. These companies represent about 85 percent of all United States operations in Latin America. The study showed that whereas the net capital these companies received from the United States amounted to $129 million, their total investment expenditures were about four times that amount, or $570 million. The difference between these two figures was financed out of retained earnings, depreciation, and other sources of funds.

The study showed further that the operations of these companies resulted in direct foreign-exchange income to Latin America of $2.3 billion, or $1 billion more than the total exchange required by these companies for their operations and remittances. This $1 billion remained in Latin American countries for other exchange purposes.

In connection with their total sales of nearly $5 billion, wages and salaries were paid by these companies to 600,000 employees. Moreover, approximately $1 billion was paid to Latin American governments in various forms of taxation. The revenue derived from this source became available for the financing of highways, ports, and other activities which the governments have undertaken.

This special study has, we believe, helped to correct one misconception about the effect of foreign investment upon the financial position of recipient countries. It does not, however, tell the whole story. The advantages of foreign investment do not end with their final effect upon the balance-of-payments position. A chief value of the investment, whether it be domestic or foreign, lies in its capacity to increase the total national production of the country in which it was made. This comes through increased productivity.

We believe in my country that technical improvements and managerial knowledge which lead to increased productivity may be even more important to rising standards of living than growth in the stock of capital. The shortage of managerial skills and technical knowledge may be more real and more pressing than any shortage of capital. Private investment carries with it the most highly developed technical and managerial skill. It brings to bear on the development process this essential and dynamic influence to which we attribute so much of our own growth.

The managerial experience and knowledge of techniques and skills required for the successful development of resources is a prerequisite to the most effective use of increased capital funds. The technical knowledge and managerial skills acquired by citizens of Latin America, both in on-the-job training in plants and enterprises financed by foreign capital as well as through the quite remarkable number of visits to the United States sponsored by both private enterprise and our technical cooperation programs, represent for this hemisphere an ever expanding fund of what might be called managerial wealth—an asset of incalculable value.

As we all realize, the movement of private capital cannot be forced. Private investment flows only where the situation is attractive. Investment opportunities throughout the free world are so numerous that all who seek investment capital must compete for it. Even in the most highly developed countries there is a shortage of savings for investment. Nevertheless, as the figures demonstrate, the Latin American Republics have been successfully competing and obtaining a sharply expanded flow of new capital funds. In this they have been more fortunate than many other areas which have not been able to devote their resources so fully to peaceful and constructive purposes.

The process of private capital investment can of course be facilitated. As you know, my Government believes that toward this end governments should remove tax obstacles that lie in the way of capital formation and private investment. This can be done both through unilateral measures, which would remove unsound tax policies and administrative practices, and through international tax agreements.

We have been engaged in the negotiation of broad tax agreements with a number of countries. In addition to establishing rules in these agreements by which to assure fair tax treatment, we have sought to give recognition to so-called tax-sparing laws which seek to encourage the inflow of capital by granting tax reduction for limited periods of time. The executive departments of our Government are trying to devise a formula by which a credit would be allowed under our laws for the taxes given up by a country seeking fo attract capital, in the same way as a credit is given for taxes actually collected by that country.

Tax agreements are, of course, a matter for negotiation between the executive branches of two governments. Like all treaties, they must, in the United States as in many other countries, obtain the approval of the legislative branches of government before they can become effective. We now have several prospective treaties in varying stages of the procedure. One, which includes a credit for tax-sparing, is now under review by the legislative bodies of the signatory countries.

Economic Development

We realize that much is to be done toward economic development in Latin America. In addition to private capital, credits from public institutions are important sources of capital. Many hundreds of millions of dollars will be involved. We feel a sense of responsibility and will participate in this development. The extent of our effort will be determined by careful planning, by the ability of countries to absorb capital, and by the assurance of realistic benefits to the economy and the people of the republics involved. Here my country acts directly through the Export-Import Bank.

You will recall the policy of the Export-Import Bank, first announced at the Caracas conference, and reaffirmed at the Quitandinha conference. Our Government indicated that our country would be prepared to encourage the financing of all sound economic development projects, including loans in the private sector, in the best interest of the countries involved, and for which private capital was not available. This policy has, I believe, produced impressive results. In the 3-year period ending June 30, 1957, the bank has authorized credits of some $840 million to Latin America.

It is significant that more than 40 percent of the bank's total authorizations in all countries during the last 10 years have been made in the Latin American Republics. Since the Quitandinha conference, the bank has extended in Latin America almost 2½ times as much in development loans as it had extended in the similar period before that conference.

During the last fiscal year, indeed, the Export-Import Bank concentrated even more of its development lending in Latin America. Leaving aside its loans for the purchase of agricultural commodities and livestock and the special loan to the United Kingdom which was made on a secured basis, the bank's total of development loans throughout the world was $482 million during the year. Of this amount no less than $354 million, or 73 percent of the total, was extended in Latin America.

As more and more sound economic projects are developed, the participation of the Export-Import Bank will be intensified so as to meet expanding needs. The International Bank for Reconstruction and Development is also an important source of development loans and the International Finance Coporation is becoming an additional significant source.

As far as we can see ahead, we believe that the adequacy of capital to meet the needs of sound development is not a question of additional institutions but the fuller utilization of those in being so as to keep pace with the expanding needs of constructive projects as they develop.

We are, as well, providing important credits to our Latin American neighbors through the so-called Public Law 480 agreements, under which our Government sells quantities of our agricultural reserves to foreign governments for local currencies. Under these agreements substantial portions of the sales proceeds are lent to the purchasing governments as additional sources of economic development capital. Thus far the amounts allocated for loans, or actually lent, to Latin American countries through this arrangement total about $250 million.

In addition to the expansion of the technical cooperation program in Latin America, which was announced by the United States delegation at the Quitandinha conference in 1954, the United States through the International Cooperation Administration continued its program of emergency economic assistance to Latin America to help resolve problems which were beyond the resources of the individual countries. During the last year a special regional fund authorized by the Congress of the United States was the source of grants amounting to $2 million to the Organization of American States for malaria eradication and for improved research facilities at the Inter-American Institute of Agricultural Sciences in Costa Rica. This fund was also the source of loans totaling nearly $13 million to seven countries for projects in the fields of education, health and sanitation, and land settlement.

All of these are encouraging developments. They are further evidence of a wholesome trend in inter-American cooperation. But let us always remember that economic development in a large and complex area cannot be reduced to easy simplicity. More important than any other factor will be the individual efforts of each people and their dedication to a program of work and savings and the orderly management of their own government and economic affairs.

Heartening as the flow of foreign capital into Latin America may be, we are all fully aware that such capital can, be best, make only a partial contribution to the total investment requirements of an expanding economy. The accumulation of domestic savings and the application of those savings in productive activity are essential to sound economic progress. We must not lose sight of this import fact. We should study with great care the general conditions which are necessary to encourage domestic private savings and to insure that these are used productively in the domestic economy.

You and I, as ministers bearing the principal responsibility for our Governments in this field, can find real encouragement in the current rate of development in our countries. But we must ask ourselves, are we justified in complacency and satisfaction? We are not. The energetic and far-sighted peoples of all of our republics demand that we find effective ways to bring to more and more millions of people throughout the hemisphere those standards of living which are attainable if we make the best use of our human and natural resources and our capital.

It is to consider ways of meeting this challenge that we are here. It will never be simple to put together our natural resources, labor, and capital so as to produce the requirements of a rapidly growing population and, at the same time, raise per capita standards. It will always be a challenging task. It requires unrelenting effort to improve technology. It requires improvement in organization and skills. It will depend upon the people and the leaders of each of our countries and their willingness to work, and save, and encourage efficiency.

The delegation from my country will approach this challenge with sincerity. We shall not underestimate the problems of the future. None of us wishes to encourage unreasonable or impractical expectations. But I hope that we all share the conviction that, when the time comes for us to return to our respective countries, it will be with the knowledge that each of us has made a contribution to the discharge of our historic responsibility to make of these lands a better home for all of our citizens and for our children, and a better inheritance for other generations of Americans.

69. *Organization of American States Economic Conference, Economic Declaration of Buenos Aires**

September 2, 1957

The Economic Conference of the Organization of American States makes the following declaration which shall be known as the "Economic Declaration of Buenos Aires." Since the full realization of the destiny of the Americas is inseparable from the economic and social development of their people, it reiterates: That it is the intention of the governments to maintain conditions which promote the maximum economic growth of each country through the attainment of high and stable levels of real income, employment, and consumption, in order that all their peoples may be adequately fed, housed, clothed, and have access to services necessary for health, education and general well-being, and it declares:

That for the realization of these principles and purposes, and in accordance with provisions of the United Nations Charter and the Charter of the Organization of American States, it is the purpose of the governments to promote:

1. The expansion of the volume of trade among themselves and with other nations, on a mutually advantageous basis, including cooperative measures necessary for its attainment.

2. The reduction of barriers to inter-American and international trade, taking into account the measures which may be necessary in the light of the economic conditions and requirements of each of the American states or of several of them among themselves.

3. International cooperation, either through intergovernmental consultations or through other arrangements which may be agreed upon, relating to the problems of basic or primary commodities whose process may be subject to excessive fluctuations, and relating to the orderly disposal of surpluses in a manner which will not unduly disrupt international trade.

4. The adoption of measures to facilitate the acquisition and exchange, for their mutual benefit, of capital, machinery, raw materials, techniques, and other material elements needed for their economic requirements.

5. The intensification of their efforts, individually or through international financial institutions, to expand the flow of public capital to the countries of the American

*Department of State Bulletin, Sept. 30, 1957, pp. 540-41.

continent through the extension of credits for the sound financing of investments considered essential to development, and to encourage private investment therein, in order to promote their economic development and strengthen mutually beneficial economic relationships among the American countries.

6. The continuation of their efforts toward the achievement of sound monetary and financial conditions.

7. The intensification of their national and international efforts to improve, develop and utilize efficiently their means of transportation and communication.

8. The conclusion of agreements by the interested governments, to facilitate free transit for landlocked countries for the purposes of their trade.

9. Effective support, through the Organization of American States and the appropriate international agencies, or directly between themselves, for technical and scientific cooperation programs which, taking into account the corresponding national or regional plans, may contribute to the acceleration of economic development and the improvement of the standards of living of the peoples of the continent.

10. The strengthening of the Inter-American Economic and Social Council so that it may respond fully to the purposes and functions assigned to it by the Charter of the Organization of American States, act as a coordinating organ of inter-American official activities in the economic and social field, and deal effectively with the consultation which the states may initiate with it for the prevention of difficulties or solution of economic problems.

The terms of this declaration shall be applied by each state to the extent permitted by its resources and requirements, its own laws and its international obligations.

70. Statement by Douglas Dillon, Deputy Under Secretary of State, on the Results of the Economic Conference of the Organization of American States*

September 2, 1957

My delegation is highly gratified at the constructive results of the Economic Conference. The conference faced the economic problems of the hemisphere squarely. We have, all of us, talked frankly, and we have ended by reaching a measure of agreement hitherto unprecedented in our inter-American economic conferences. Resolutions were introduced covering every conceivable practical problem. These resolutions were debated and worked over in committees and with only a single exception were adopted unanimously—thus marking a new high point in hemispheric unity.

The Economic Declaration of Buenos Aires, adopted last night, records and reinforces certain principles which are basic to the inter-American system and which look toward the strengthening of the economies of the participating countries and the improvement of the living standards of the peoples of the Americas.

In the first place, the declaration emphasizes the need of cooperation among the American Republics. Cooperation is the opposite of isolationism. Cooperation means working together for common ends.

In the second place, the declaration stresses that economies are developed and living

*Department of State Bulletin, Sept. 30, 1957, pp. 539-40.

standards are improved to the extent that the countries succeed in developing their natural and human resources and increasing the flow of profitable international trade.

So far as concerns the development of natural resources, the declaration makes clear that both public and private investment are required, and it links these two types of investment together in one paragraph. The United States welcomes this recognition of the close connection between public and private financing. While constantly seeking sound methods of increasing the scope and amount of public international financing within the hemisphere, the United States has continued to stress that the volume of public financing is directly related to the amount of private financing which countries are able to attract and that an expanded flow of private foreign investment is essential if the American Republics are to achieve the degree of development and improvement in living standards to which their peoples rightfully aspire.

I would like to say how impressed we have been by the highly capable manner in which the Argentine Republic, as our host country, has handled the affairs of the conference. I would particularly like to congratulate the conference chairman, Dr. Krieger Vasena, on the way he has guided our work.

We are returning to Washington, firm in the faith that we have added here in Buenos Aires another important block to the great Pan American edifice.

71. Address by Roy R. Rubottom, Jr., Assistant Secretary of State for Inter-American Affairs, before the Council on Foreign Relations, on Developments in Latin America*

October 10, 1957

The definitive book on Latin America can never quite get to press on time. The area is so dynamic, growth in all sectors is so explosively rapid, the political panorama unfolds and then shifts so quickly before our very eyes that the story can only be told in serial form. This is as it should be. The very vitality of Latin America is a great asset. The harnessing of this vast energy, both human and material, is its greatest challenge.

The U.S., due to fortuitous circumstances of history and geography, is indissolubly linked with Latin America. We are proud of our joint heritage of freedom and liberty. We maintain the closest ties of friendship with each of the 20 republics south of us. Of equal importance to the U.S. is the ever closer harmony between the 21 American Republics in the Organization of American States. This concert of the Americas, important as it is to each of the states in it, has rung out all over the world, inspiring the United Nations and other regional groups of states to greater cooperative effort.

The American Republics recently have added a new and important chapter to their record of joint accomplishments. I refer to the Economic Conference of the OAS which was held in Buenos Aires the last half of August and concerning which I shall report to you tonight.

*Department of State Bulletin, Oct. 28, 1957, pp. 675-81.

U.S. Economic Policies in Latin America

Before doing so, I should briefly state or, rather, restate the policies and objectives of our Government in its economic relations with Latin America. There are some rather well-set benchmarks, policies which have been affirmed and reaffirmed by both political parties here.

Our relationship with Latin America has been, and will continue to be, unique in a number of important respects. This relationship has been described as one of "good neighbors" and more recently as "good partners." Both of these appropriately call attention to certain aspects of this relationship. However, I would like to call attention to the high degree of economic interdependence which characterizes our relationship with Latin America, an interdependence which is increasing every year.

In trade, for instance, we exchanged with Latin America last year goods valued in $7.3 billion. In recent years our trade with Latin America has been greater than that with any other area in the world. The importance of this trade to both Latin America and the United States would be hard to overemphasize. The goods valued at $3.6 billion we purchased in Latin America were essential to our well-being and to the maintenance and growth of our industrial plant, while the $3.7 billion which Latin America spent here for a wide variety of manufactured and agricultural products were required for the industrial development which is going ahead so rapidly in Latin America.

In the field of private investment, this economic interdependence is equally manifest. More than one-third of our direct private investment is in Latin America. The value of total long-term U.S. private investment was estimated at more than $7.3 billion as of the end of 1955 (of which direct investment accounted for $6.6 billion). Since that date total long-term private U.S. investment is estimated to have increased by some $1.3 billion. A Department of Commerce survey shows that in 1955 direct private investment provided jobs for over 600,000 persons, paying salaries amounting to a billion dollars. It paid local taxes and royalties to the host countries also estimated at a billion dollars. Of the nearly $4.7 billion worth of goods and services produced in 1955 by the companies making these investments, more than $2 billion worth were sold abroad for dollars, while $2.5 billion worth were sold in local markets, most of them replacing goods which otherwise might have had to be imported. Another somewhat intangible but very important result of these investments has been the great amount of technical knowledge and managerial skills which they have provided for Latin Americans. At the same time, these investments yielded a satisfactory return to their American owners.

A third field in which we are intimately concerned with Latin America is in providing public funds, through the Export-Import Bank, for sound development projects. During the last 10 years over 40 percent of the bank's total authorizations have been made in the 20 Latin American Republics. In the 3-year period ending last June 30th the Export-Import Bank has authorized credits of some $840 million in this area.

With this intensely active and dynamically expanding economic relationship which our country enjoys with Latin America, it is not surprising that our Government maintains a highly sympathetic and intimate concern for the further economic development of our friends who are both good neighbors and good partners. In his address before the first plenary session of the Buenos Aires conference, Secretary of the Treasury Anderson stated our objectives very clearly and simply:

> We want our people all around the Americas to live better; we want them to pursue more healthful lives; we want their lives filled with hope, enriched with progress, and inspired toward the improvement of standards of well-being.

Buenos Aires Economic Conference

This economic interdependence which exists between our country and Latin America makes it essential that there be a greater mutual comprehension of the problems which confront each of our countries in providing for its people the improved standards of living to which we all aspire. Conferences such as the one held recently in Buenos Aires contribute substantially toward the development of this comprehension and understanding of our problems and the means for their solution. The frank and friendly exchange of views which took place there over a period of 3 weeks among men charged with shaping the fiscal and economic policies of their countries could not help but bring about constructive results.

In spite of the positive results of the meeting there was, perhaps, some disillusionment on the part of the press and general public that more was not accomplished. It should be realized, however, that an economic conference cannot in itself create the roads, the factories, the hydroelectric and other projects which will increase productivity and improve standards of living. A conference can only seek ways and means which will expedite the accomplishment of these jobs by the people themselves and their governments. It must be realized, also, that this particular conference, without in any way detracting from its importance, in reality was only part of a continuing process of discussion and consultation of economic problems which is carried on by the American Republics.

At the Buenos Aires conference, with few exceptions each delegation was headed by its Minister of Finance or Economy responsible for policy formulation in the fiscal and economic fields. In the case of the United States, Secretary of the Treasury Anderson was our principal delegate, and upon his return to Washington that position was occupied by the Deputy Under Secretary of State for Economic Affairs, Mr. C. Douglas Dillon. While in Buenos Aires, Secretary Anderson, Mr. Dillon, and I had talks with the head of each of the Latin American delegations. This provided an opportunity not only to discuss matters directly connected with the conference but also those relating to our relations with each country individually. These proved to be mutually advantageous.

The conference adopted 41 resolutions on a wide variety of economic subjects. With a single exception these resolutions were adopted unanimously. The one resolution which the United States voted against is one which looks toward the negotiation of commodity control agreements for price stabilization of Latin America's basic export products. In few instances have international conferences such as this been able to arrive at such a high degree of unanimity.

Interest at the conference was directed chiefly toward four problems: (1) the financing of economic development, (2) terms of trade and commodity agreements, (3) the creation of one or more common-market arrangements in Latin America, and (4) the negotiation of a general economic agreement.

Financing Economic Development

The Latin American countries in general believe that their own savings are not sufficient to finance the rate of economic development which they desire and are therefore anxious to attract foreign funds. Some Latin Americans believe that private investors are not likely to be able to supply the major portion of the foreign funds needed for development. They also have other questions as to the use of private capital. For example, it is sometimes said that the payment of dividends on foreign capital constitutes an unnecessary drain on the foreign-exchange resources of a country. The fear is also expressed at times that foreign private enterprise may exercise an undue influence on the economic and political life of the host country. For these reasons Latin American representatives at inter-American conferences usually press for additional governmental funds for economic development and for new financial institutions to provide such funds.

The United States, which was largely developed with private capital, much of foreign origin, is not disposed to attribute to the use of private capital the disadvantages sometimes ascribed to it in Latin America. In the view of the United States the vast pool of capital for economic development represented by potential private investment is still largely untapped. Such investment is held back by numerous impediments. Some of these are direct restrictions on foreign participation in some fields or limitations on the percentage of ownership. Some are by-products of inflationary financing, multiple exchange rates, and arbitrary import and export taxes and controls. For example, the traditional barrier to increased foreign investment in transportation, communications, and power production has been the unwillingness of the regulatory agencies of many Latin American governments to permit remunerative rates in the face of depreciating currencies and rising costs.

I might add, however, that in some Latin American countries these impediments are being gradually removed, with beneficial results in attracting foreign investments. In 1956 the net outflow of private capital from the United States to Latin America amounted to $521 million and thus established a new record. Substantial amounts of new private capital were also received from Canada, Europe, and Japan.

The fear sometimes expressed regarding the so-called drain of foreign private investment on the foreign exchange earnings of the Latin American countries generally arises from a narrow interpretation of the effect of profit remittances upon the balance of payments. However, the extent to which capacity to produce and employment opportunities have been expanded by private foreign investment cannot appropriately be measured by either the net outflow or the net inflow of capital. United States investments in Latin America are financed not only by the outflow of new capital but by the plowing back of current earnings, by the funds set aside for depreciation, and, in some instances, by local borrowing and equity financing. Gross capital expenditures by United States companies in the area in 1956 were probably in the neighborhood of $1 billion.

Thus the impact of these investments on the growth of the economies of the Latin American countries is much greater than their effects on the balance of payments between the United States and Latin America. Furthermore, investments made by experienced producers create opportunities for local people to acquire the necessary skills to organize and operate business ventures and to become acquainted with opportunities within their own countries for investment in productive enterprises rather than in real estate or foreign securities.

The fear of undue political influence by foreign corporations is, in the view of the United States, not justified. A United States company operating abroad is subject to the laws of the country in which it operates. Those countries are generally in a very good position to prohibit the foreign company from exercising any undue political influence, even if the company should wish to do so. The company as a rule has no desire to interfere in local politics.

Notwithstanding the comments I have made on the subject of private investments, I should not like to give the impression that the United States desires to encourage private capital to go into countries where it is not wanted. We know that it is for countries which need capital, rather than the United States, to take the steps which are needed if the largest potential source of foreign capital is to be tapped.

The United States also recognizes that there are needs for development capital in Latin America which cannot be fully met by private investment funds and therefore has a broad and positive policy toward public investment in Latin America.

It is the view of the United States that the Export-Import Bank, the International Bank for Reconstruction and Development, and the International Finance Corporation are able to meet all demands for ordinary, conventional dollar loans for sound projects. To the extent that private capital is unavailable, these institutions may be relied upon by the Latin American countries to supplement their own resources for the financing of productive economic projects. Among the factors which will influence the volume of foreign lending to any country is the effectiveness of that country's program for combating inflation, encouraging private enterprise, and improving the investment climate.

With regard to Latin American proposals for the establishment of inter-American institutions to finance economic and social development, the United States considers that its participation in such projected institutions would duplicate and interfere with its program for development credits to Latin America and is, therefore, undesirable. It believes that the Latin American countries can make greater progress through use of existing international credit facilities than through efforts to establish inter-American institutions. The limiting factor on further lending is not the lack of lending institutions but the lack of sound projects which are within the capacity of the would-be borrowing countries to service.

The Eximbank's policy regarding loans in Latin America is to assure financing for all appropriate economic development projects for which private capital is not readily available on equitable terms. The bank's lending authority has already been increased several times, and its activities in Latin America have been intensified. It may be noted that new loan authorizations by the Eximbank to Latin American countries in 1956 totaled more than $409 million, a record yearly high.

The International Bank for Reconstruction and Development also has large resources available, and the Latin American countries, all of which are members, have access to its facilities. Loan agreements signed by IBRD with Latin American countries in 1956 totaled $74.4 million. The International Finance Corporation, which was formed in July 1956 with the cooperation and major participation of the United States, is already active in Latin America and is expected to play an increasingly important role in financing the growth of productive private enterprise.

The resolution adopted by the Economic Conference of the Organization of American States on the financing of economic development was formulated against the foregoing background. It declared the necessity of pursuit by the Inter-American Economic and Social Council of studies designed to develop formulas and policies which would permit the expansion of the financing of Latin American economic development in accordance with a resolution previously approved by the Inter-American Committee of Presidential Representatives, which met in Washington in 1956-57. Other portions of the resolution included provisions that the Council convoke a special commission of governmental representatives to carry out this study, which should be brought to the attention of the governments when completed, and that the member states should adopt measures conducive to encouraging the flow of private capital and of techniques toward Latin America to the greatest extent possible.

Terms of Trade and Commodity Agreements

A subject on which there tends to be a common position among the Latin American countries is that relating to "terms of trade" and to the proposal that international commodity agreements be used to help maintain a favorable relationship between prices of the commodities they export and the prices of the products which they import. This is understandable in view of the fact that economic conditions in most of the Latin American countries are influenced to a large degree by the conditions under which a relatively few of their commodities are sold in international trade. For example, Bolivia is highly dependent on tin; Chile on nitrate and copper; Brazil, Ecuador, Colombia, El Salvador, and Guatemala on coffee; Uruguay on meat and wool; Venezuela on petroleum; Mexico and Peru on lead and zinc; and Argentina upon wheat and meat.

The state of the export trade in these few commodities has a large effect upon employment and economic activity generally within these countries. Representatives of such countries have often pointed out that the prices of their raw materials fluctuate widely in relation to the prices of the products they import.

Among the measures most often mentioned for attempting to stabilize such commodity prices are intergovernmental commodity agreements. While the United States fully recognizes that many countries rely heavily upon exports of primary products and do face special problems in the form of relatively wide fluctuations in the world market prices for some of their major products, it does not believe that the cure is to be found in mechanisms for international price support or stabilization. In the view of the United States, there is too strong a probability that such a cure would be at least as harmful as the disease. In general, it is the conviction of the United States that maximum reliance upon competitive forces in free markets will best promote international price relationships conducive to optimum allocation of economic resources and advancement of economic welfare.

It is sometimes alleged that the United States position on this matter is inconsistent with its programs which are aimed at supporting the prices of United States agricultural products in relation to the prices of products which United States farmers buy. It may be noted, however, in partial reply, that the experience which the United States has had with attempting to support agricultural prices domestically, instead of being a recommendation for an international price-support system, indicates strongly that such a system would, in all probability, be unwieldy and unworkable.

The United States Government fully realizes the seriousness of the problems of market instability for primary products but believes that the basic attack on them must be through the maintenance of high levels of economic activity in the industrialized countries and the pursuit of appropriate policies of economic development and expansion elsewhere. Especially since the United States normally takes about 50 percent of all the goods exported from the Latin American countries, as a group, it is evident that to the extent that the United States is successful in its determination to maintain a stable rate of economic growth, considerable mitigation of the price fluctuations which might occur in the absence of this stability can be expected.

United States trade policy is also of great importance to the Latin American countries. It may be pointed out that, while there have been individual exceptions, the tariff treatment accorded by the United States to imports from Latin America is today favorable as a result of tariff reductions under the trade agreements program which was begun in 1934. Some two-thirds of all imports from Latin America are on the free list and are therefore not subject to duty. And under our trade agreements program duties on dutiable imports have been gradually brought down. Measures taken by the United States which tend to relieve or remove impediments to United States foreign trade and which encourage other countries to move in the same direction are, of course, of real benefit to the Latin American countries.

The United States also desires to help the other American countries to diversify their economies and therefore lessen their dependence on a few exports. It attempts to do this in a number of ways. First, it encourages the governments of these countries to pursue policies likely to attract foreign investors to participate in the work of diversification. It also helps encourage such diversification itself through governmental loans in appropriate cases and through its technical cooperation program.

There were two resolutions adopted by the conference which directly related to the subject of basic products. One of these resolutions called for the establishment by the Inter-American Economic and Social Council of a permanent committee on basic products to study and publicize information with respect to the production, distribution, and prospects for basic commodities. The other resolution gives to the committee the task of developing international commodity agreements, in cases deemed appropriate by the committee, for dealing with the problem of price instability. The United States voted for the first resolution and opposed the second in view of its belief that international commodity agreements are not an appropriate or effective means of dealing with the question of price instability.

Regional Latin American Market

Another question discussed at the conference, and on which there is not a common viewpoint among the Latin American countries, relates to the question of the development of a regional market or regional markets among the American countries. There is a general belief that the market provided by individual Latin American countries may be too small in the case of some products to permit the most efficient scale of production. There has accordingly for some time been discussion by the Latin American countries of the possibility of developing one or more regional markets within the Western Hemisphere. Ideas advanced have differed, however, as to the number of countries that should be brought within the purview of the market. For example, it has been suggested that there be one market for all of the American Republics, including the United States. It has also been suggested that there be one Latin American market which would exclude the United States. There have also been proposals that there be a number of regional markets within the Latin American area, each of which would involve a group of countries. Each of these proposals raises serious problems. For example, the proposal that the United States and the Latin American countries form one common market would mean that the infant industries of the Latin American countries would be exposed to direct competition from well-established United States manufacturing concerns. It would also mean that United States producers of such agricultural products as wool and sugar would be in direct competition with the producers of these products in the Latin American countries.

The establishment of one common market for all Latin American countries would mean that the whole area would be developed as an economic unit in which competitive conditions would prevail. However, as has recently been pointed out in a Pan American Union study entitled *Liberalization of Inter-American Trade*, Latin America as a whole is not one region economically but embraces several distinct regions. The development of a common market among a few countries within the region would, however, also raise difficult problems in inter-Latin American relations.

No concrete proposals for specific common-market arrangements were before the conference for consideration. It was agreed, however, that such arrangements, properly devised, could be beneficial. The United States supported the conference resolution on this subject, which declared it to be desirable to establish gradually and progressively a regional Latin American market, in a multilateral and competitive form, and recommended the continuation of studies designed to provide for the development of information essential to the establishment of such a market.

General Economic Agreement

The most publicized conference subject was the proposed general economic agreement. As you know, such an agreement was signed by the American States at Bogotá in 1948, but there were so many objections by so many of the states that only three of them ultimately ratified it. The project was later revived in 1954 at Caracas and also at Rio. Consequently, the secretariat of the Inter-American Economic and Social Council drafted a text of an agreement based on resolutions and declarations made in the inter-American system since 1889. The substance of this draft contained all the

familiar topics in inter-American economic relations, including naturally the controversial ones. It was not possible to arrange for intergovernmental negotiations on the
draft text prior to the opening of the conference, and at Buenos Aires it became clear
to the great majority of the governments that negotiation of such a document in a
period of 3 weeks was manifestly impossible. Accordingly there was unanimous
agreement that the whole problem of an economic treaty should be referred to the
Council of the Organization of American States.

At the same time there was also unanimous agreement on an Economic Declaration
which was drafted by several of the countries and which set forth some of the most
important principles of inter-American economic relations. It sets forth the intention
of governments to maintain conditions that will promote the maximum economic
growth of each country through the attainment of high and stable levels of real
income, employment, and consumption, in order that all their peoples may be
adequately fed, housed, and clothed and have access to the services necessary for
health, education, and general well-being. To realize these objectives it calls on
member governments to promote 10 specific courses of action. Perhaps the most
important of these is that calling for the intensification of efforts, individually and
through international financial institutions, to expand the flow of public capital to the
countries of the Americas, by the granting of credits for the sound financing of
investments considered essential for development, and to stimulate private investment
therein, for the purpose of promoting their economic development and strengthening
mutually beneficial economic relationships among the American nations.

In commenting to the press on the Declaration at the conclusion of the conference,
Mr. Dillon pointed out that it emphasizes the need for cooperation among the
American Republics; it also stresses that economies are developed and living standards
are improved to the extent that the countries succeed in developing their natural and
human resources and in increasing the flow of profitable international trade. In the
development of natural resources, the Declaration makes clear that both public and
private investment are required, linking these two types of investment together in a
single paragraph. The recognition of the close connection between public and private
financing is welcomed by the United States, as we have continued to stress that the
volume of public financing is directly related to the amount of private financing which
countries are able to attract.

In conclusion I would say that the delegations which attended the Buenos Aires
Economic Conference, and the governments which they represented, may be highly
gratified at its constructive results. The economic problems of the hemisphere were
faced squarely and discussed frankly. A measure of agreement was reached hitherto
unprecedented in economic conferences within the inter-American system. The conference was a further manifestation of the accuracy of President Eisenhower's description
of the Organization of American States as "the most successful sustained adventure in
international living that the world has seen."

While much remains to be done before we can fully realize the aspirations expressed
in the Economic Declaration of Buenos Aires, encouragement may be drawn from the
fact that Latin America constitutes one of the most rapidly progressing regions of the
world. The average annual increase of gross national product, in real terms, for the area
as a whole since the end of World War II has been 5.5 percent. This compares

favorably with the rate for Western Europe or the United States. Far from being an undeveloped area, Latin America constitutes an economic frontier where the world's most dramatic economic development is taking place.

The Buenos Aires Economic Conference served to reaffirm our conviction that the people of the Americas will exert themselves to the hard, resourceful work, the self-discipline, and the willingness to grapple with difficult problems in such a way as to achieve their economic goals. The conference restated the determination of our peoples to depend basically on their enterprise to create from their own resources the wealth needed for their growth.

72. Address by Assistant Secretary Roy R. Rubottom on Basic Principles Governing United States Relations with Latin America*

March 21, 1958

Today I would like to state as simply as possible the policy which guides United States relations with Latin America. Our Government has consistently placed the highest priority on maintaining and further extending our excellent relations with this vast neighboring area. This is a bipartisan policy and one which has broad public support throughout the United States. It is a policy which we strongly adhere to and which we keep under continuing study in order that we may be prepared to meet whatever exigency arises. It is one which has already stood the test of time. Yes, and also the vicissitudes of war and economic depression.

Those of us who are charged with the responsibility for the conduct of this policy strive to be as alert as possible to the political, social, and economic developments to which United States policy must respond. Recently there has been more than the usual amount of public attention paid to our relations with Latin America. This is heartening. Early in March the Committee on Foreign Relations of the Senate, which is conducting a review of United States foreign policy, held open hearings to discuss our relations with Latin America. Governor Muñoz Marín of Puerto Rico appeared before the committee, and I was also called to testify. Now let me state the policy.

The United States not only desires, but feels the need, to establish the closest and most friendly relations with the Latin American peoples and their governments. This need arises out of more than self-interest. It is a need that springs from one and the same root and has been a long time growing. It is, in fact, as old as the earliest colonization of the Western Hemisphere. Sometimes we think so much about differences—in language, national origin, aspects of religion and customs—that we forget the identities. However, one of the most striking things about the Americas is how much they have in common. There is no other group of peoples so numerous, no other area of the globe so extensive, of which this could be truthfully said. Here in a world which really was a New World for our forefathers, a tremendous experiment was undertaken with results decisive for human history. We began as groups of explorers and settlers.

Department of State Bulletin, Apr. 14, 1958, pp. 608-14.

We had a period of colonization. We felt the need of independence and won it. Because we believed in the dignity and freedom of man, we established constitutional democracies. And "we" means all of the American Republics—the United States and the 20 sister nations.

In view of this parallel experience, our machinery of inter-American cooperation developed naturally—indeed, almost inevitably. When we speak of the American family of nations, we are voicing a fundamental truth. Since it is truth, it follows that our own cooperation with the other American Republics is based on genuine affection for our friends, which we hope is reciprocated. This affection applies to each of the 20 countries whose considerable differences and distinctive characters we fully recognize while, at the same time, we greatly treasure, as each of them does, our common membership in the Organization of American States, which President Eisenhower has called "the most successfully sustained adventure in international community living that the world has ever seen."

We hold deeply to the belief that the people of the various countries in the hemisphere have the right to choose their own political destiny: The policy of nonintervention, which we strongly uphold, is one of the cornerstones of the inter-American system. Our commitment to this policy, however, does not lessen our own dedication to democracy in its real and, I might add, American sense, and "we are in a position to feel—and we do feel—satisfaction and pleasure when the people of any country determinedly choose the road of democracy and freedom." Here we should remind ourselves of the obligation we have to overcome our own shortcomings and improve upon the example which we are expected to set. We should also recognize that no two governments, any more than two individuals, can be exactly alike. Thus we should not be surprised when the emerging patterns of government differ from country to country.

We acknowledge the high stakes for our neighbors as well as ourselves in maintaining the security of this hemisphere. We hope no aggressor will ever dare attack the nations of the free world, but we cannot rule out this possibility. In addition to recognizing the right of each country to take the measures necessary for self-defense, all 21 of the American Republics are joined together under the Inter-American Treaty of Reciprocal Assistance, known as the Rio Treaty, which is the first of the regional collective-security pacts of the free world. Under this treaty each of the American Republics recognizes that an attack on any one constitutes an attack on all and accepts the obligation to assist in meeting the attack.

Economic Interdependence

In the realm of economic relationships we recognize our interdependence with Latin America. Our own economic well-being, certainly if it is to be lasting, is inextricably intertwined with that of Latin America. This mutual well-being is, I am glad to say, based primarily on trade. This is a proud relationship. More than one-fifth of our exports now go to Latin America, a business worth approximately $4 billion to the United States in 1957 and almost as much in 1956. On the other hand, almost 50 percent of all of Latin America's exports were to the United States last year, the total amount being nearly in balance with the above $4 billion figure. This is big business, and we want to keep it that way; you can rest assured that Latin America feels the same way about it, and would like to see those figures increased. Right now Latin America is observing closely economic trends in the United States, and with ample justification, just as you are. Every Latin American ambassador in Washington is anxiously watching our own efforts to overcome the present problem and is praying that we will be successful in turning business upward again.

There has been a severe decline in prices in some of the goods sold us by Latin America, notably in nonferrous metals, although other products have been affected. Coffee is Latin America's main concern, if one considers that 15 countries produce coffee and that 6 of these are dependent on that product for most of their foreign exchange. However, it makes no difference whether the affected product is coffee, copper, lead, zinc, tin, or something else. When prices drop sharply, people in every walk of life in the producing countries are adversely affected. We can and should be sympathetic to these serious problems in Latin America, just as we know they are to our own problems in the United States. It is in our common interest to find solutions to these common problems.

One of our most important tools in finding mutually beneficial solutions is the Trade Agreements Act. With the authority of this act, first enacted in 1934, behind us, we can negotiate agreements to reduce government-imposed barriers to trade. Without this authority we would find ourselves in an economic jungle in which the only remedy for each injury or fancied injury in the field of trade would be not negotiation but retaliation. Latin America is watching with tremendous interest the debate which is now going on. The effects of the decision ultimately taken by Congress will have far-reaching repercussions in our foreign relations, both psychological and real.

Private Economic Cooperation

But obviously our entire economic relationship is not based on trade alone. United States firms have been investing their capital in Latin America on a constantly increasing scale. This kind of private economic cooperation is helping to speed the development of Latin America, just as foreign investment, mostly European, participated in the growth of our own country. During the last few years United States investors have been pouring approximately one-half billion dollars per year into Latin America, and the total is now more than $8½ billion. Not only have these investments been increasing rapidly, but they are going into diversified manufacturing and service industries as well as the production of vitally needed raw materials. A recent study by the Department of Commerce, using data compiled through 1955, revealed that in that year United States companies operating in Latin America paid salaries totaling $1 billion to 625,000 employees, of whom only 9,000 came from the United States. These companies in the same year paid slightly more than $1 billion in taxes to the host governments in Latin America. Their sales abroad *for dollars* went over the $2-billion mark during that year.

The United States, of course, believes in private enterprise because of its proven success. We also know that private investors are willing to commit large amounts of capital in almost any area where conditions promise mutually beneficial results; it is also self-evident that there is a limited amount of public money available. Therefore, we have recognized, most recently at the Buenos Aires Economic Conference, that the additional great sums required for the development of Latin America can only be supplied through a combination of private and public funds. Thus we say that, if private capital is available in adequate amounts and on reasonable terms for a given project, it is our policy now, as it has been for years, not to have our public lending agencies compete with such capital. This policy is not pointed at any given industry but applies across the board. Notwithstanding our deeply held feeling regarding private enterprise, we recognize the absolute right of any other country to pursue whatever means it deems best for developing its resources.

Other Sources of Capital

In addition to the roles of trade and investment in Latin America, the United States acknowledges the importance of providing loans to our neighbors. During the past decade United States direct loans to Latin America, under the auspices of the Export-Import Bank, have amounted to more than $2 billion. At the same time additional United States public funds have been going to Latin America through our participation in the World Bank, the International Monetary Fund, the technical assistance programs of the United Nations and the Organization of American States, and through other organizations relying heavily upon the United States for financial support. But to speak expressly about the direct United States cooperation through the Export-Import Bank, it is the operating principle of that institution that no economically sound development project in Latin America shall fail for lack of access to capital from other sources to cover its dollar needs. Between 1953 and 1957 the bank authorized credits to governments and private companies in the amount of $1,354,000,000. Recent loans have been as little as $50,000 and as large as one to Brazil of $100 million for the modernization of its railroad system. Every one of our sister Republics shared in these credits during this period, and, I might add, their record of repayment is on the whole excellent.

Another newer source of capital is now provided through the sale for local currency of our surplus agricultural products. Under Public Law 480, adopted by Congress in 1954, the value of loan agreements with Latin American countries signed through 1957 totaled $222 million and the emergency grants of surplus agricultural products aggregated $31 million. An important feature of these loans is the provision that enables the purchasing country to borrow back for its economic development a large part of the money paid to the United States for the products received. Thus the recipient country receives a three-way advantage: (1) the surplus products themselves; (2) the dollar savings, since payments can be made in their own currency; and (3) the loan of a large portion of the sales proceeds over a long period of time and at a low interest rate.

Stabilization credits provide another example of how public funds are used in our economic cooperation with Latin America. These credits, or standbys, as they are called, are made available to countries to help them ease the strain on their reserves and maintain the value of their currencies while they are attempting to achieve financial stability. The standby credits are usually "package" arrangements, with participation by the United States Government, the International Monetary Fund, and, frequently, private United States banks. During 1953–1957 direct participation by the United States Government alone in standby credits aggregated $115½ million.

Another means of extending United States cooperation to Latin American countries has been that of providing emergency grant aid when they were unable to meet their needs with their own resources. These emergencies have arisen from natural disasters such as earthquakes or hurricanes or from unforeseen economic or political situations. Since 1954 this aid, provided under our mutual security program, has totaled $75 million. In addition, easy-term loans were made under Senator Smathers' amendment totaling $12.8 million to seven Latin American countries for certain development projects in the fields of health, sanitation, and education.

Still another type of direct United States Government cooperation is that offered by congressional appropriations for the United States share—which is two-thirds—in the cost of the Inter-American Highway, extending from the Guatemalan border with Mexico down to the Panama Canal. Since 1953 appropriations have amounted to more than $81 million, and Congress is being asked this year to approve another $10 million.

This year for the first time the United States has funds available under the Development Loan Fund. Several applications from Latin American countries are now being considered by the Administrators of this fund, and approval of some of those projects is expected shortly. The fund is designed primarily to extend loans for financing projects in the free world which contribute to economic development and which cannot otherwise be financed by existing international or private institutions. These loans may be repaid in either local currency or dollars and are relatively long-term and at reasonable interest rates.

Technical Cooperation

In speaking of our economic policy toward Latin America I have purposely left until last the mention of our long record of technical cooperation in Latin America. This program, started in 1942, probably yields more human-interest episodes than any of the others, not to mention the long-term practical contribution it is making in our relations with Latin America. In it, scientists, technicians, and other experts from the United States team up with their counterparts in Latin American countries to carry out cooperative programs in agriculture, public health, education, transportation, housing, community development, public administration, and in other areas vital to a country's welfare. A remote tropical jungle can be the setting for one program and a high, arid plateau the location of another. In practically every instance the host government for these projects contributes considerably more to their financing than the United States Government; so you can visualize the constructive work going on when I tell you that in the past 5 years our share alone amounted to $125 million. However, even if we had before us complete figures from all countries, the total, though imposing, would be no index to the accomplishments of this program. The exchange of ideas and technical know-how cannot be reckoned in terms of dollars, and no one can foresee the value of the changes which will follow the improved health conditions, new agricultural techniques, increased productivity, and other positive results growing out of this type of partnership.

Now, having stated the policy and the instruments at our disposal for executing it, I would like to describe briefly some typical problems. Underlying our approach to these, of course, is the most fundamental ingredient of all for constructive foreign relations—the desire to cooperate with our friends. This bears repeating again and again.

The Importance of Coffee

I have already referred to coffee. Let us examine it in more detail.

As important as coffee is to those of us who love both the taste and the aroma of a cup in the morning—or any other time—coffee is even more important to our friends to the south. As I mentioned earlier, 6 of the 15 coffee-producing countries depend on coffee for most of their foreign exchange to buy what they need in the United States. The United States is the principal consumer of coffee.

Except for a period of 6 years, beginning in April 1941, when quotas on imports were first imposed, and continuing through the removal of price controls in 1947, coffee has been subject to the normal laws of supply and demand. There was a time in 1954 when coffee prices in the United States to the consumer rose to such a point as to encounter rather severe resistance. Nobody, certainly not the countries which depend on coffee for their foreign exchange and the livelihood of their people, wants to see coffee priced out of the market. On the other hand, I do not think that the American housewife, any more than the Government of the United States, wants to see a disastrous price decline which would have even more disastrous effects on the countries where coffee is produced and, ultimately, on the quality and quantity of the product that we have come to depend upon to help us get started on our day's work.

Given the importance of coffee, what is going on in this industry? The price of mild coffee fell almost 20 cents a pound between January and October last year, when the new crop came in. Sales were being made at less than 50 cents a pound, which was below the support prices guaranteed producers by their governments and lower than the average prices for any year since 1949. With a large crop coming to market this year and a still larger one forecast for next year, they were understandably worried, and the principal Latin American producing countries met in Mexico City in October of last year to consider what they should do. The chief result of that meeting was a coordinated effort on their part to stabilize coffee prices. This they did by establishing export quotas and agreeing to place on the market only as much as could be sold at what producers regarded as a reasonable price. The plan has been in operation now for about 5 months, and prices are currently about 53 to 54 cents a pound—about what they averaged in 1951 and 1952.

Later, at Rio de Janeiro in January of this year, the American coffee-producing countries met with the African coffee producers to discuss the problem on a world-wide basis. The principal consuming countries of Europe were represented, and the United States sent an official observer. The leading buyers of coffee in the United States, members of the National Coffee Association, were also represented by an observer. The result of that meeting was the establishment of a world coffee organization, the main purposes of which are to promote the increased consumption of coffee, as one method of attacking the problem of overproduction, and to provide a place where the supply-and-demand situation can be kept constantly under review.

Now the United States is searching for the most useful means of cooperating with its Latin American friends on the problem of coffee. In some respects our approach to the problem is different from theirs; in fact, we have quite frankly disagreed with some of their efforts to maintain prices at levels which might operate to reduce consumption. But these disagreements have been in the context of a deep and abiding friendship, and we are searching for means of agreement rather than concentrating on the disagreements. The problem is under urgent and continuing study in the Department of State, and I am confident that we will find a means to work with Latin America on this problem of transcendental importance.

The Problem of Oil

While in Texas, I should not overlook the problem of oil. This, my home State, along with other oil-producing regions of the world, is faced with the problem of reestablishing the petroleum production and marketing relationships which were seriously disrupted when we in the Western Hemisphere expanded to meet the supply deficit created by the Suez crisis. The problem was further complicated by the decline experienced in the United States domestic demand following the Suez crisis and which still continues. We certainly hope that the problem will not be one of long duration.

Meanwhile our Government, with the cooperation of an overwhelming majority of crude-oil importers, instituted a new program of voluntary import limitations last July which has worked very well indeed, even acknowledging the two or three exceptions where cooperation has not been forthcoming. This program, of course, magnifies the fact that the oil problem is not confined to the United States. It is of great significance to two of our Western Hemisphere partners and friends, Venezuela and Canada, on whom we rely for part of our needs for oil and other vital products, both in normal and emergency periods.

Now what do good friends do when they find a common problem? They sit down together to seek a mutually satisfactory solution.

I visited Venezuela about 3 weeks ago and explored this problem with the Provisional Government, certain political and business leaders in the country, and others. I found a disposition on the part of our Venezuelan friends to engage in the kind of frank discussion which should help us find a solution to the problem. The same attitude has been shown by our Canadian friends. I am happy to report that consultations on the technical level have recently been held in Caracas and in Washington in which my outstanding friend and fellow-Texan, General Ernest O. Thompson, took part. This is the essence of the approach that we people of the Americas take to find solutions to problems, and I am sure that this effort will not fail.

Now let us take up another type of problem. Let us assume there is a Latin American country whose exports consist of 50 percent in coffee and 50 percent in nonferrous metals. It finds that because of the decline in prices of one or both of these commodities, and also because of lessening demand abroad, there is a sharp reduction in its income from exports. Its foreign-exchange deficit for the coming year is estimated at about $50 million. Let us also assume that this country has drawn down its reserves in the previous year and that it has only $20 million left with which to meet the anticipated deficit.

In all likelihood a senior official would be sent to Washington to lay this problem before the International Monetary Fund and the United States financial authorities. He would describe his country's situation and work out a program jointly with the IMF staff for dealing with it, subject to the concurrence of his Government and the Board of Directors of the IMF. In general this country would strive for austerity in its imports and would seek to maintain a balanced budget and a tight rein on credit. In some instances where the applicant country's currency has been kept at an artificially low rate of exchange, it may offer to let the rate fluctuate and find its own level, thus reducing some of the drain on foreign exchange.

The measures I just mentioned may show, on examination, that policies to reduce imports and promote exports will only reduce the deficit $25 million instead of $50 million. The International Monetary Fund, having concluded that the program adopted by the country is adequate and that the deficit is temporary in nature, is willing to put up $15 million to help cover that gap. Another $10 million might be obtained from private banking sources in the United States. If so, that makes a package which covers a $25 million deficit.

In some cases, however, the country may not be able to raise an additional $10 million in New York and it may be necessary to turn to other sources to make up this package. The country, for example, because of a local shortage may need wheat and other farm products and be eligible under United States Public Law 480 to obtain $10 million worth of these from our surplus stocks on very long credit terms. In some cases it might even be necessary to ask the Export-Import Bank to make available the last component of the total deficit in order to finance the flow of essential United States imports into that country.

Generally the agencies contributing toward the $25-million gap desire that the IMF contribution come first, since the fund was set up precisely for the purpose of helping countries which have temporary balance-of-payments problems. At times these agencies work out arrangements whereby drawings on them are made in some agreed-upon relationship to the drawings on the IMF and the private banks.

The foregoing represents how the United States Government, in cooperation with international and private financial institutions, assists a country which might otherwise have to reduce imports to such an extent that the economic development of the country would suffer.

I wish to stress that there is deep concern and good will inherent in the United States approach to economic cooperation with Latin America.

Soviet-Bloc Efforts in Latin America

Now to refer briefly to a subject which has received some public notice:

There is evidence that the Soviet Union is intensifying its economic and political offensive in many parts of the world, including Latin America. The Kremlin's propaganda professes sincere interest in trade expansion. Yet, in actual fact, Soviet-bloc trade with Latin America has been declining in recent years, primarily because of the failure of the Soviets to deliver acceptable, competitively priced goods as a counterpart to those raw materials received by them from Latin America.

Although there have been numerous reports of Soviet-bloc "offers" of trade, capital, and technical assistance, it remains to be seen whether these will meet with general acceptance or whether they will actually materialize as serious propositions. This is said because of the vague and illusive character of the offers, as well as because of Latin American governmental prudence based on past experience with Soviet promises.

Nevertheless, I do not wish to minimize the gravity of the challenge for the United States posed by the Soviet-bloc efforts in Latin America or its capacity to choose selected targets for an economic offensive. This will require sustained vigilance and care on the part of the countries approached, and I am confident that our hemisphere partners will not be found lacking.

I have tried today to convey to you a concise idea of the basic principles governing our relations with Latin America. I have endeavored to make clear the needs and situations—the types of problems—to which United States policy must respond. I have spoken of the friendly spirit in which all the American Republics work together to solve our mutual problems. We in Washington are resolved to dedicate our best efforts to insuring that this spirit of inter-American solidarity is further strengthened, and we humbly ask the guidance of Almighty God in our task.

73. Note from Eduardo A. Acosta H., Chargé d'Affaires ad Interim of Venezuela, to Secretary Dulles, Concerning the Caracas Incidents *

May 13, 1958

Excellency: I have the honor to address Your Excellency, in accordance with instructions from my Government, in order to inform you that the Government of Venezuela has taken all the measures necessary for guaranteeing the personal safety of His Excellency Vice President Richard M. Nixon, his wife, and the members of his entourage, and for avoiding repetition of the lamentable occurrences which took place this morning in Caracas and for which I present to the Government of Your Excellency in the name of the Government of Venezuela the most sincere apologies.

I take advantage of this occasion to reiterate to Your Excellency expressions of my highest consideration and respect. . . .

Department of State Bulletin, June 9, 1958, p. 951.

74. *Welcome Speech by President Eisenhower, to Vice-President Richard M. Nixon on his Return from South America**

May 15, 1958

Mr. Vice President, Mrs. Nixon, and our friends: Some weeks ago I asked the Vice President and Mrs. Nixon to go to Argentina to represent me and the Government at the inauguration of their new President. And thereafter he visited seven other countries in Latin America in order to discuss with the leaders some of our common problems and to help in reaching a better understanding of those problems so that our friendships would be solidified—made stronger.

Through this entire trip he has conducted himself effectively, efficiently, and with great dignity and has performed to the satisfaction, not only of us, but of our sister countries that he was sent to.

There have been, during the course of this trip, some unpleasant incidents. Some of them came to the point that there was danger—not only to the Vice President but to Mrs. Nixon—real danger and risk of harm and even worse.

Now I want to make one thing clear: The occurrence of these incidents has in no way impaired the friendship—the traditional friendship—between the United States and any other single one of our sister republics to the south. There could be no more dramatic proof this morning of the truth of this statement than the presence here in this crowd of the ambassadors of our sister republics in the south who have been among the most enthusiastic welcomers of our Vice President and his wife.

And so I repeat America's affection for the peoples of those countries. The governmental relationships between them are as close as ever. And more than this, as one Latin American ambassador said to me this morning, "Really, our whole situation—our situation of cooperation and brotherhood among ourselves—is strengthened because of the fact that we stand together in condemning any kind of Communist leadership of such incidents as endangered our beloved Vice President and his wife."

All America welcomes them home. And in doing so—through its welcome—it means to say to all of our friends and other nations to the south, we send you our warm greetings and hope that some of you will come back to pay to us the call that the Nixons have paid upon you.

75. *Remarks made by Vice-President Nixon, Upon Returning to the United States from South America†*

May 15, 1958

Mr. President and our friends who have so honored us by coming to the airport in such great numbers today: There is very little that I can add to what the President has said so eloquently just now.

**Department of State Bulletin,* June 9, 1958, p. 950.
†*Department of State Bulletin,* June 9, 1958, pp. 950-52.

As you know, we left the United States 18 days ago on a trip which was to take us to eight countries in South America, none of which we had visited before. And may I say that on all the trips that Pat and I have taken around the world we have been tremendously proud to represent the President of the United States—to represent the people of the United States—in what we believe are the real motives of our people in the whole area of foreign policy and our relations with other countries. And we were proud to do so on this trip.

There were occasions, as the President said, when some incidents occurred. (And I remember, before I left, one of my good friends said, "Well, you are very fortunate to get away from the Senate for a nice vacation for 18 days.") But may I say that, as the President just emphasized, while there were incidents—incidents in which a very small, violent, vocal minority were able to enlist the support of some innocent people who were misled as to what the United States' intentions really were—I can tell you, from my observations in each one of the countries we visited, that the great majority of the people—the great majority in all walks of life—are friendly to the United States today. And this is true of every one of the countries.

Now, this doesn't mean that all the people of these countries agree with all the policies of the United States because I can assure you that in country after country, in the great universities, and in conversations with government leaders and labor leaders, I found that there were many areas where people disagreed with what we were doing. And it was my purpose to try to explain to them what our policies were—to try to get away from some of the misapprehensions which existed. Sometimes we were able to do so—sometimes we succeeded, and perhaps sometimes we did not. But may I say in that connection that, as far as this part of the world is concerned, first, there is no area of the world with which we are more closely associated—there is no area of the world which is more important as far as the United States is concerned—than these, our closest neighbors in the American hemisphere. And may I say also that we can be tremendously proud of the fact that they have supported us as partners and friends in the United Nations in vote after vote, as well as in other areas.

Before I left, I said that one rule we must never forget in international relations, as well as in political and business affairs, is that we must never take our friends for granted. We do not take our friends for granted in Latin America. We don't think that we ever have, but some of them may have gotten the impression that we did. And may I say, in that connection, that what we must get across there, as well as in other parts of the world, is this very simple message: that we, the Government and people of the United States, want for other peoples just what we have for ourselves—independence for our country, freedom for our people, and the greatest possibilities for economic progress that can be devised.

In Latin America we have an area which is in a sense in a state of evolution, and as far as the people there are concerned, they are concerned, as they should be, about poverty and misery and disease which exists in so many places. They are determined to do something about it. They are moving toward democracy and freedom—sometimes slowly, but no question surely. They are moving toward economic progress. And the United States is, and should be, proud to work with them as partners in moving toward democracy—toward freedom—and in helping them and working with them for economic progress.

As the President has said, and as I repeated over and over again in every country, at every university that I met with, the only war the people of the United States want to wage is a war against poverty, misery, and disease, wherever it exists in the world.

And now this is not the time, of course, to report on observations and conclusions. I shall have the opportunity to meet with the President and the Secretary of State and others in government at a later time to go into specific matters. But may I say a personal word at this time to those of you who have come here: We have taken many trips over the past 5 years—I think over 40 countries, perhaps 45—but I can tell you that certainly nothing could be more heartwarming than to see this crowd today—the ambassadors who represent the countries that we visited, and others as well, the Members of the Cabinet, and people in the Government, our colleagues in the House and the Senate, and, as well, this wonderful group of students from the universities and colleges in this area.

And may I say that we are always very proud to represent the United States, but I don't think that either of us has ever been as moved as we are at this time, returning as we do.

I remember yesterday, late in the evening, as we drove through the streets of San Juan, Puerto Rico, with Governor Muñoz Marín, that our car was stopped on a couple of occasions by the crowds in the streets. I remember that men and women put their hands to the windows of the car: We finally got out and walked with them, and this is what they said: "Welcome home, Mr. Vice President—or Mr. Nixon—or Mrs. Nixon—God bless the United States."

May I say that we have enjoyed our visits to other countries. It has been a great experience, but certainly there is no greater experience than to return home to see our friends, our family, and to realize how blessed this country is—blessed with freedom, blessed with economic opportunity, blessed with stability in its government, and with fine leadership, whether that leadership is furnished by one of our great parties or by the other. So with that, may I say again, Mr. President, how deeply we have been moved by this reception, by your coming as you have to the airport.

I don't know how adequately to express our thanks. We would like to have the time to shake hands and to add a few thousand to those that we have met in other parts of the world, but that is not possible today.

May I just say, thank you again—and never forget what a great privilege it is to be an American citizen and to live in the United States.

76. *Statement by Robert D. Murphy, Deputy Under Secretary of State, before the U.S. Senate Foreign Relations Committee on Recent Anti-American Demonstrations*

May 19, 1958

In accordance with your invitation of May 16 I am appearing in behalf of the Department of State to discuss with the committee in executive session the recent incidents in Lebanon, South America, and elsewhere. I would say first that the

Department of State Bulletin, June 9, 1958, pp. 952-61.

Department is grateful to the committee for this opportunity both to provide whatever information it can and especially to have the benefit of the committee's wisdom in matters which are of pressing importance to our country. It is my purpose to reply frankly to any questions about which information is immediately available to me. Where I do not have it, effort will be made to supply it promptly.

We all share, I believe, your distress over the indignities suffered by the Vice President of the United states in Peru and Venezuela during the course of his recent tour of eight South American countries. As you know, his tour was incident to the Vice President's attendance at the inauguration of President Frondizi of our sister Republic of the Argentine at Buenos Aires.

It should be said that the purpose of the Vice President's tour was to promote better understanding and good will between this country and our southern neighbors. They had been kind enough to extend invitations, in most instances quite insistent invitations. The Vice President's acceptance was in accordance with practice of long standing to exchange visits of prominent personalities between our countries. It reflected among other things a desire to demonstrate the importance and value this country attaches to close and friendly relations with our sister republics to the south. It was based on an awareness of the importance of firsthand exchanges of views with government officials and other opinion leaders. The Vice President, with tireless energy, successfully made similar trips to Southeast Asia and to Africa and Central America. These trips have gained political advantages of considerable importance to us.

In discussing this subject perhaps you will agree that we should examine the manner in which it fits into the general pattern of world affairs. At present our country is involved in a highly competitive situation. There continues a worldwide wave of nationalism. This has found expression in the creation since the war of some 20 new nations. In other areas additional countries are in the formative stage. In still other areas the old order is in process of change. This fermentation often provokes conflicts and offers opportunity both for constructive effort as well as exploitation by political opportunists. There is evident a worldwide ground swell of desire for a better life. This often generates intense resentments, envy, and even hatreds. There is the inevitable distrust by the have-nots of those who have. There is also the implacable crusade of the ideologists intent on destroying the capitalist system of free enterprise and individual democratic liberties. They are determined to replace it by applying the principles of Marxism-Leninism in the promotion of the totalitarian state. The Soviet Union not without success blends this effort of international communism with skillful promotion of old-fashioned Russian expansionism.

Communist Efforts to Foster Anti-Americanism

The Soviet regime and the world Communist movement since their inception have constantly sought to exploit—in Marxist language—"contradictions" or differences both between "leading imperialist powers" and between "imperialist" and "colonial" or underdeveloped countries. The dominant theme in these provocative efforts since World War II has been anti-Americanism.

Under the leadership of the Soviet Union the world Communist movement has made energetic efforts to organize and exploit hostile sentiments toward the United States. American "ruling circles" are depicted in Communist propaganda as the dominant imperialist force in the world, everywhere seeking to oppress smaller nations and to undermine the influence of other "imperialist" countries—notably France and the Netherlands, but also including the United Kingdom—in order to extend the domination of American capital. The anti-American orientation of the world Communist movement was clearly evidenced in the November 1957 Moscow "Declaration" of 12 Communist parties and "Peace Manifesto" signed by 65 Communist parties, which singled out the United States as the main threat to "peace" and called for united action to fight for "peace," i.e., the interests of the Soviet bloc.

The Soviet Government itself has directly used its propaganda and diplomatic apparatus to foster anti-American sentiments. In areas such as Latin America, where the United States represents the leading outside influence, Soviet efforts have long concentrated on channeling local resentments into resentment against the United States. In South Asia, the Middle East, and North Africa, where other Western countries are prominently involved, the Soviet line has been that the United States is the principal enemy of the local countries, sometimes using other Western powers as its "tools" but always seeking to supplant their positions. Similarly, the Soviet Government has persistently sought to turn French, British, or Italian opinion, as the case may be, against the United States.

In regard to recent manifestations of anti-American sentiments in South America, Algeria, Lebanon, Indonesia, and Burma, the anti-American content in Soviet propaganda directed at these areas has been at a high level for a considerable period of time. There was no marked step-up in Moscow's propaganda immediately prior to the events in these areas, either in the degree of attention to the United States or in the violence of its charges, although in several cases Soviet propaganda media have sought to exploit these events after they occurred to the discredit of the United States.

There is no evidence at present of a Soviet effort to effect a coordinated worldwide demonstration of anti-Americanism coinciding with Vice President Nixon's visit to Latin America. While there is evidence of direct Communist complicity in several of the recent anti-American incidents—in South America, Indonesia, and Burma—the circumstances leading up to these incidents occurred more or less independently of Moscow's will. Thus the coincidence of these outbreaks, so far as their timing is concerned, would seem to be largely accidental. However, all of the recent incidents are related in that there has been a conscious, continuous effort by the Soviet Union to exploit and exacerbate potential or actual misunderstandings in these areas about the United States. These incidents, particularly those in which there was direct Communist involvement, demonstrate the scope and intensity of Soviet long-term efforts to discredit the United States.

Security Measures

Those of you who personally have had experience with mob action and group violence need no reminder that the element of surprise frequently plays an important role. Not so long ago in our own Capital of Washington we witnessed a savage attempt on the life of our President then in residence at Blair House. We also shared the indignation of the Congress over the dastardly shooting in the House of Representatives of several of its distinguished Members. We were aware of the possibility of such dangers. Our security measures were believed adequate. Yet even in our solidly established system grave incidents like those were possible. How much more so is it true in those countries where freshly established governments have not had time or others have been unable for various reasons to develop adequate security organizations. The recent deplorable assassination of the President of our sister Republic of Guatemala is a tragic case in point.

South America

Problems and issues in Latin America were known, and the Vice President was briefed on them. There was nothing in the past history of U.S.–Latin American relations to indicate the possibility of substantial violence against our representatives. In addition, innate Latin American courtesy and their respect for the guest relationship of persons coming to their homes or country were taken into consideration. After Lima and the embarrassment which the incidents there had caused to both the Government and most Peruvians, it was felt that the governments and public opinion in the remaining countries would do their utmost to prevent similar embarrassments. As the tour progressed, and particularly after Peru, the increasing amount of Communist-inspired and directed tactics was known and reported and the increasing possibility of trouble in Venezuela was understood. It was also understood by the governments concerned.

Prior to Lima it was not even deemed necessary to seek any specific assurances of adequate security. After Lima the assurances given by the Ecuadoran, Colombian, and Venezuelan Governments appeared adequate, as they proved to be in Ecuador and Colombia. It seems evident that the trouble in Caracas was caused by the intensive exploitation by Communist and other anti-American elements of grievances against our policies and the failure to take adequate measures to prevent demonstrations and activities of which the Government was fully forewarned by its own security people and by reports from our embassies and investigative agencies.

I think it is important to emphasize that, while there has been a known resentment in Latin America over certain issues and protests concerning them could be expected, this is the first time that minority groups have been able to exploit these issues to incite actual violence against an important American representative. This is something new in Latin America, and therefore it was not expected.

There is considerable evidence that the demonstrations in the various countries visited by the Vice President followed a pattern and were Communist inspired and staged. Slogans on the banners carried by students and others were similar. "Little Rock," "Guatemala," "Yankee Imperialism," "Wall Street Agents," "McCarthyism," "Colonialism," "Nixon Go Home" were among those repeated. The tactics were much the same, with young students urged on by older persons leading the activities. Intelligence reports from Latin American capitals also support the conclusion of a leading Communist role in the demonstrations.

There is no indication of unusual efforts by Radio Moscow to step up its exploitation of anti-American sentiments immediately prior to or during the Vice President's trip. Although Soviet commentaries carried the normal type of anti-American statements and Soviet-bloc propaganda output to Latin America increased somewhat—a normal occurrence during any major event—the demonstrations and scattered violence were not excessively stressed during Mr. Nixon's trip. Moscow Radio warned its Latin audiences of the "exploitative" motives of the Vice President's trip, designed to counter the "discontent over U.S. policies." The majority of the commentaries relied to a great extent on quotations from American newspapers and stressed that even the U.S. press "has been forced to admit" that the anti-U.S. demonstrations are not the intrigues of Communists but the result of U.S. "discriminatory" economic policy toward Latin America. Without attacking the Vice President personally, the Moscow propaganda machine asserted that "Nixon's fiasco was actually the fiasco of U.S. policy toward Latin America."

On May 15, according to FBIS [Foreign Broadcasting Information Service], Radio Moscow began in earnest to exploit the anti-American incidents during the Nixon tour. However, Radio Moscow directed no commentaries at Latin American audiences, the target of most of Moscow's comments prior to the Caracas events. In these latest efforts Moscow is attempting to exploit the incidents to foster anti-Americanism in other areas of the world.

Uruguay

We knew, took into account, and reported to the Vice President before his departure the following matters: information concerning Uruguayan resentment of U.S. economic policies, particularly the countervailing duty on wool tops; the fact that the Soviet-bloc diplomatic missions in Urugay have been active in many sectors of Uruguay; the fact that recent approaches have been made to Uruguay by the Soviets for increased economic intercourse; and finally that there was a possibility of student antipathy or even anti-U.S. demonstrations at the university.

There was no indication that violence would ensue, and there was none. The Vice President was able by debating with the students to win them over, and his visit to the university ended with a resounding ovation and acclaim for his forthrightness in standing up to the students in friendly discussion.

Argentina

The political situation in Argentina and the circumstances surrounding the Frondizi government were explained in briefings to the Vice President. The delicate political situation caused by the coming into power of a new government, the activities outside of Argentina by Peron, and the fact that the Communist Party in Argentina had become the largest in the hemisphere were all included in the briefings and fully discussed. There were rumors that pro-Peron or other groups might stage demonstrations in opposition to the Vice President. The economic difficulties facing President Frondizi, the difficulties with economic problems which might involve the United States, were discussed before the Vice President left and were discussed by him with Argentine leaders in that country.

There was no indication that any violence could be expected, nor did any occur. On the contrary, the reception accorded to the Vice President in Argentina was extremely friendly.

The minor incidents in connection with the late arrival at the swearing-in cere-monies of President Frondizi, in which there were scattered boos for Mr. Nixon, were highlighted in the United States press but were given little importance in Buenos Aires.

Paraguay

Vice President Nixon was aware that in Paraguay there might be some attempt at demonstrations—or in other countries—on the question of a visit to the present Paraguayan Government. Recent attempts by opposition groups to overthrow the Stroessner regime had been the subject of intelligence and embassy reports several weeks before the Vice President departed. These facts were included in briefings, as were matters regarding anti-Paraguayan acts involving the provisional government of Argentina which was in power prior to Frondizi's inauguration. The warm reception given to the Vice President in Paraguay was anticipated, and there were no untoward incidents to mar the visit.

Bolivia

The tense political situation which has existed in Bolivia in recent months and which broke out into disturbances in the mining areas in March, involving mainly the two factions of the governing MNR [Nationalist Revolutionary Movement] Party, were also included in briefings of the Vice President. Bolivia's difficult economic situation, the part which the United States is playing in helping to solve Bolivia's problems, the difficulties involving the mine owners of the expropriated mines (in-cluding U.S. owners) and the Bolivian Government, were well known. The existence of Communist and Trotskyite groups in Bolivia and the dangers which the Vice President's party might possibly encounter in passing through the narrow streets of La Paz were explained in briefings with the Vice President and to the Secret Service. The potential of Communists to incite anti-U.S. actions in Bolivia was considered but not deemed sufficiently strong to cause any change in plans.

There was no violence in Bolivia, and the hostile demonstrations were negligible. The fact that there was no violence there was a factor in considerations concerning the rest of the tour.

Peru

Dissatisfaction in Peru over the U.S. restrictions and tariffs on certain basic agricultural commodities exported by Peru is of long standing. More recently, threat-ened restrictions on lead, zinc, and copper had led to bitter criticism. This was further inflamed by the report of the United States Tariff Commission on lead and zinc. Recent strikes, demonstrations, and lawless acts in various parts of Peru, for which the Communists were in a large measure responsible, had been reported by embassy and intelligence sources and were part of briefings held on Peru. The fact that there had been increased lawlessness within Peru in recent months was also known and considered. The status of the University of San Marcos as an autonomous university, proud of its independence and heritage, was also known. There was, however, nothing in intelligence reports to indicate the real possibility of violence in Peru. Demonstrations were considered possible. The fact that anti-U.S. demonstrations of the nature which occurred have not heretofore been known in Lima and the historic ability of the Peruvian Government to contend with lawlessness were important factors taken into consideration in making decisions on the visit to Peru. Peru's record of close association and ties with the United States is historical.

At the time of the Peruvian visit, mounting evidence of the possibility of student demonstrations was known.

The anti-U.S. demonstrations were the result of a small minority, estimated between 30 and 40 persons, obviously Communist led and inspired. They did not represent the attitude of Peruvians, much less that of the Peruvian Government. The demonstrations seemed to snowball once they were incited, and there is no evidence that large mass demonstrations were planned.

Ecuador

Intelligence reports received prior to the arrival of the Vice President in Ecuador showed that the Communists had undertaken considerable planning and as of May 9 their activities had been limited to fly sheets and wall paintings. It had been expected that anti-Nixon demonstrations might include throwing of water and fruit. Elaborate plans to embarrass the Vice President during his visit to the Central University failed to materialize because the visit was canceled.

Other Communist plans in Ecuador by students were said to include:

1. Presentation of what would appear to be an honorary diploma but actually would portray imperialist domination of Ecuador.

2. A receiving line to turn its back on Mr. Nixon upon his arrival.

3. A Communist student leader to read a list of United States acts of intervention in Latin America during the past 50 years.

4. Students to walk out on Mr. Nixon if there had been any attempt to quiet Communist speakers.

Intelligence reports indicated that other plans, which did not materialize because of the Ecuadoran Government's excellent security efforts and apparent poor Communist organization, included shouting squads along Mr. Nixon's travel route, throwing of water and rotten fruit, and display of derisive signs. Pedro Saad, Secretary General of the Communist Party in Ecuador, ordered no violence, according to reports, but he hoped a riot would occur at the football game.

Mr. Nixon's planned meeting with Communist and other labor leaders was canceled. This cancellation was due in part to the Embassy's decision that such a meeting would not be productive and might give Communist leaders a propaganda weapon. Communist plans to challenge Mr. Nixon to meet labor leaders publicly in Communist-controlled quarters did not materialize.

Two important factors in the failure of any demonstrations in Ecuador are believed to be the excellent security measures adopted by the Ecuadoran Government and the fact that Ecuadorans made an attempt to counteract the incidents in Peru. In any event, the reception in Ecuador was cordial.

Colombia

During the past 10 years Colombia has been the scene of much violence, including the famed *Bogotazo* of 1948. Deaths are reported to have totaled some 200,000 in Colombia during this period, due to guerrilla activities and other political violence. The political situation in Bogotá prior to the start of Vice President Nixon's tour was a confused one. Elections were scheduled for May 4, but no candidate had been chosen one week before the elections. The nomination by both the Conservative and Liberal Parties of Dr. Alberto Lleras Camargo produced a profound effect and gave civilian groups high hopes for political stability. Lleras' nomination, however, evoked a reaction in certain circles. During the last days of April General Rojas Pinilla moved to the Caribbean from Europe, and there was an attempted coup by sympathizers of Rojas on May 2. Details of this attempt were reported to the Vice President in Buenos Aires and elsewhere en route, and the political implications and chances of political turmoil in Colombia were fully explained.

A rumor that an attempt might be made to assassinate the Vice President was reported to Embassy Bogotá prior to the Vice President's arrival. Rumors of possible student and Communist demonstrations were also reported. A detailed report dated May 10 from reliable sources concerning Communist and Communist-front groups' attempts to organize student demonstrations was recorded and the Vice President's party informed. This report included plans to distribute leaflets; plans to demonstrate at wreath-laying ceremonies; alleged plans to throw tomatoes, eggs, etc., and to "duplicate the Lima student incident." There were meetings of Communists to arrange for these demonstrations, and there was some talk of having weapons and a possible assassination attempt. This information was relayed to the Nixon party. It was stated that Communists would play an insignificant part and that the greatest danger came from the followers of ex-dictator Rojas Pinilla in order to discredit the present Government. The assassination talk was assessed as being largely bravado. It was concluded that it was not probable that serious incidents would occur because the Colombian Government was aware of the possible dangers and was well prepared to meet any trouble.

The reports in Colombia centered largely on Colombia's own political turbulence and on rumors which arose following the incidents in Lima. The failure of an attempted coup on May 2 and the subsequent election of President Lleras Camargo on May 4, as scheduled, helped dissipate concern over any serious trouble in Colombia. None occurred. Consideration nevertheless was given to the cumulative chain reaction which seemed to be building up as the tour progressed. This fact was assessed, along with the assurances given by the Colombian authorities. It was decided that there was a possibility of demonstrations but that the Colombian authorities were prepared to keep them under control. The few minor demonstrations were completely over-shadowed by the friendly reception accorded the Vice President. This reception was particularly warm and friendly in the workers' and poorer districts, where some thought trouble might have been anticipated.

Venezuela

From the very start it had been anticipated that there might be more danger of disturbances in Venezuela than in any other place. This was made known to the Secret Service officers accompanying the Vice President prior to the party's departure from the U.S., and it was also made known to the Vice President. The unsettled political situation in Venezuela which has existed since the overthrow of the Perez Jiménez regime in January had been the subject of many reports. The rapid return of the Communists to Venezuela from exile and their intense activity in labor, student, and other civilian sectors following the overthrow of Perez Jiménez were reported and considered in planning the visit. In February a report was received from non-Communist labor leaders that the Communists were back in force in Venezuela and working very assiduously in the labor field. The prominent role played by Communists in organizing opposition to the Perez Jiménez regime and the Communists' efforts to discredit the United States were well known. The many facets of Venezuelan political difficulties, including the delicate balance between the civilian and military power in Venezuela, were also known.

The Venezuelan criticism of U.S. voluntary restrictions on petroleum imports, the inflammability of this issue in Venezuela, the protest by many Venezuelans and particularly leftist groups against the issuance by the United States of visas to ex-President Perez Jiménez and his security chief, Pedro Estrada, were reported to the Nixon party both before and during the trip. The agitation of university students on the visa issue, as well as their criticism of the United States for allegedly supporting the Batista regime in Cuba, were also fully reported and taken into consideration in deciding on the visit to Venezuela and the question of a visit to the university.

On April 22, prior to the departure of the Vice President, a report was received that there might be demonstrations at the University of Caracas.

As Vice President Nixon's tour progressed, and particularly after the events in Lima, increased reports concerning the possibility of serious disturbances at the university in Caracas fomented by the Communists were received. The Embassy consulted with the Venezuelan Government Junta, and the Junta recommended that the Vice President cancel his proposed visit to the university. The Vice President agreed to do this and requested that the Venezuelan Government make public the fact that disturbances might be anticipated.

A report that rumors were being received of a possible assassination attempt at Caracas against the Vice President was sent ahead to the Nixon party by telegram on May 9.

By May 11 rather complete reports concerning preparations being made by students and others in Venezuela for anti-U.S. demonstrations were being received and forwarded on a regular basis to the Nixon party and, through the Embassy, to the Venezuelan Government. Details of these preparations and renewed recommendations that the Vice President not visit the University of Caracas were accompanied by assurances from the Venezuelan Government that it was aware of these plans and was prepared to accord full protection.

On May 13 a report was received that the Minister of Education had received assurances from all political parties, including the Communists, that they would avoid acts of violence during the Vice President's visit to Caracas.

Three reports of possible assassination attempts were forwarded to the Vice President, and the matter was made public by the Secret Service on the eve of the Vice President's departure from Colombia for Caracas.

On May 10 an intelligence report commented that it believed the student manifestations would be limited to a strong verbal harassment without resort to physical violence but that this could not be guaranteed. In a telephone conversation with the Department on May 13, Ambassador Sparks reported that the university visit had been canceled and that, while difficulties in Caracas might be anticipated, the Government was taking security measures.

In view of the total of the foregoing information, it was recognized that demonstrations might occur in Venezuela. The cumulative effect of the demonstrations in Lima among the students was discussed and considered in planning for the visit to Caracas. It was also considered that the events in Lima might cause the Venezuelan Government to take more precautions in order to avoid similar demonstrations. On the basis of assurances by the Venezuelan Government of its security measures, violence in Caracas was not anticipated. The intensity of the demonstrations which followed and the failure of the Venezuelan security forces to act effectively were not foreseen. . . .

77. News Conference Comments by Secretary Dulles on Anti-American Sentiment in Venezuela, the Relations of the United States with Latin American Dictators and the Importance of Latin America to United States Foreign Policy*

May 20, 1958

. . . . *Q. Mr. Secretary, at the time that General Perez Jiménez fell—was ousted from power in Venezuela—in January, our diplomats reported with great pleasure that there was relatively little anti-American sentiment, despite the fact that we had been very friendly in an overt manner to the passing Jiménez regime. That changed at the time Jiménez was admitted to this country about a month ago. Would you explain to us, perhaps, how this change of feeling—how the Venezuelan people were allowed to drift into this anti-American sentiment?*

A. In the first place I would not say that there is any general or preponderant anti-American sentiment among the people of Venezuela. You cannot judge a people on the basis of sporadic, organized outbursts of rowdyism. I am confident that what happened there is not a reflection of the general views of the Venezuelan people.

Now there have been developments which have made it easier for those who want to organize these demonstrations to do so. One of them has been the shift in the oil situation. That is an economic cause. The oil, instead of being in short supply, as it was during the Suez crisis, has come into oversupply, and that has required some voluntary restrictions on oil imports into the United States, including those from Venezuela. As an economic factor, that has come into the situation.

*Department of State Bulletin, June 9, 1958, pp. 942-50.

Then there is a political factor in that, after the overthrow of the 10-year rule of Jiménez, a good many refugees came back to Venezuela and tended to blame their situation on the United States. Furthermore, there was a sort of vacuum of power, which always encourages rowdyist elements to come to the forefront. We know ourselves that, when there is not an adequate police force, as when there is a disaster or something which eliminates the ordinary forces of law and order, rowdyism takes command. I do not think it is sound to judge the basic sentiments of the Venezuelan nation and the Venezuelan people on the basis of what took place when Mr. Nixon was there.

Q. Mr. Secretary, in view of what you have just said, do you think it was wise for the Vice President to have gone into Caracas, especially since he was warned of the possibility of violence and even of assassination?

A. These things, you know, are much simpler to judge after the event than before the event. I believe myself, in the light of what we knew before Vice President Nixon went there, it was a quite correct judgment on his part to go. I think, if we had all known what was going to happen there and had been able to foresee the events, probably he would not have gone. But, you know, if you don't go to places because of threats, you will be locked up at home. I have never gone to any country in the world, hardly, but what I have had threats and there have been demonstrations of one sort or another. It is so with the Vice President, who has also visited a great many countries. If you allow youself to be deterred by threats of that kind, the result is that the Communists will imprison you at home.

I don't accept that at all. The miscalculation in the case of the visit to Caracas was primarily a miscalculation as to the adequacy and efficiency of the police force. It virtually melted away at the sight of trouble. That was't anticipated. I don't know whether it could have been anticipated or not. But if there had been an adequate handling of that situation by the police, such as occurs in most countries, there would not have been any reason whatever to have concluded that the trip was unwise to have undertaken.

Now we can see, in the light of after events, that that might perhaps have been foreseen. The police force that had been maintained under Estrada had been virtually liquidated, and we see now that the substitute police that had been created was inadequate and did not know how to cope with the type of organized rowdy mob such as the Communist agitators put on.

U.S. Policy of Noninterference

Q. On the subject of Latin America, it has been reported that Vice President Nixon feels strongly one of the chief shortcomings of our policy in Latin America is apparently our friendly support of dictator governments. First of all, do you agree with that assessment, and, secondly, is there anything we can do about that?

A. We try to conduct our relations with all the governments of the world on the basis of dealing with the government which is, in fact, in power, unless we have reasons, as we have in Communist China, for not recognizing it. (Laughter)

On the basis of noninterference with the internal affairs of countries and in the case of South America—Latin America—if we tried to deal with those governments on the basis of our appraisal as to whether they were a good government or a bad government, whether they were a dictatorial or not a dictatorial government, we would find ourselves, I am afraid, deeply enmeshed in their internal affairs.

As you know, one of the cardinal doctrines for this hemisphere, which is affirmed and reaffirmed on every occasion by the American Republics, is the doctrine of noninterference in the internal affairs of other countries. Their economic and political interdependence with the United States is such that to a peculiar degree—a greater degree than probably any other area in the world—if we attempted to adjust our relations according to our appraisal of their government, we would become involved in their internal affairs.

I would like to point out there is no clearcut distinction. You can talk about dictators and nondictators, but it isn't quite as easy to classify on that basis. There are quasi-dictators and almost-dictators and "dictators of the proletariat" and all sorts of things in gradations. If you begin to grade and say, if it is a certain type of government, you give 100 percent support, and, if it is not quite as good by our standards, you give 90 percent, and, if it is less good, you give 70 percent support, that would get us involved in an intolerable situation.

It is obvious the American Government and the American nation and the American people like to see governments which rest upon the consent of the governed and where the governed are educated people able to carry the responsibilities of self-government. Wherever that exists, there almost automatically results a closer and more intimate friendly relationship than where that doesn't exist. But any formula whereby we try to apply a sort of slide rule to their governments would be, in fact, an interference in their internal affairs. . . .

Q. Sir, it has been said that our relations with Latin America have been in the category of "always important" and that now since the Nixon incident it has assumed a proportion of "top priority," and I wondered if you would care to spell out any difference in the two categories, if there is such a category?

A. I am not aware of having said what you attribute to me.

Q. No, sir, I didn't attribute it to you—but it has been said that that—

A. I would like to say this: that relations with Latin America have never been in any subordinated category. In many respects we have given them primary importance, particularly over recent years. Now let me give you some examples, first pointing out that the fact that the Organization of American States is centered here in Washington and the cooperation of American states is centered here in Washington means that, when you deal with those problems, it doesn't attract the same attention that it does if I travel to Ankara to a meeting of the Baghdad Pact, or I travel to Copenhagen for a meeting of the NATO, or if I travel to Manila for a meeting of SEATO. These things are done less conspicuously because they are done mostly in Washington. But the fact that they are done in Washington does not mean that they are not done or that they do not have significance.

Now we have developed within that group of American Republics a system of meeting together to discuss the problems of the Americas and of the world which has no parallel anywhere else. Going back now for several years we meet here on fairly frequent occasions—I would say more frequently than do the ministers and ambassadors of most other organizations—to discuss problems of common concern. I have been having these meetings up in my office here. The President has had one or two such meetings at the White House. I remember I had a similar meeting out at San Francisco in 1955 at the time of the tenth anniversary of the founding of the United Nations. Also we have meetings here at the office of the Organization of American States, where I went down and spoke a few weeks ago. I suppose we devote as much time and thought to the problems of the Americas as we do to the problems of any other region in the world. I say it is less conspicuous because it is done quietly here in Washington and does not entail arrival statements and departure statements and all the business that goes with these trips. But there has never been a downgrading.

Now there is another point that I want to make, which is the fact that our relations with the American Republics are more on a basis of private activity and relatively less on a basis of governmental activity than with certain other areas of the world. There is a tremendous private trade.

Now when the Soviets talk about "aid," they include trade. If we included trade, the figures would be massive. There is more private trade between the United States and Latin America than between any of the other—more than Canada and more than any other country in the world, if you lump the Latin American countries together.

There is a big flow of private American capital that goes to these countries, and there are very large loans by the Export-Import Bank. So that the activities in relation to Latin America are not all reflected by activities that take place here in the Department of State. It is a very good thing that that is the case. It is abnormal, under our form of society, to have to deal with other countries through these special grant-aid, Government-sponsored projects, and so forth. It is a healthy thing, and good for both of us, that so much can be done in this other way. But when you are thinking about what is done, the level of interest and concern, don't write off the tremendous volume of private trade, the tremendous volume of private capital, and the loaning facilities of the Export-Import Bank. If you take all those things into account, you will see that the interest and concern of the United States with Latin America is very great indeed.

                    *   *   *

78. Letter from Juscelino Kubitschek, President of Brazil, to President Eisenhower, Suggesting a Mutual Review of Inter-American Policies*

May 28, 1958

Mr. President: I want to convey to Your Excellency, on behalf of the Brazilian people as well as for myself, an expression of sentiments of solidarity and esteem, the affirmation of which is become necessary in view of the aggressions and vexations undergone by Vice President Nixon during his recent visit to countries in Latin America.

The widespread reaction of aversion on the part of the governments and of public opinion in the very nations in which occurred those reprovable acts against the serene

*Department of State Bulletin, June 30, 1958, p. 1091.

and courageous person of the Vice President, constitutes proof that such demonstrations proceeded from a factious minority.

Nonetheless, it would be hardly feasible to conceal the fact that, before world public opinion, the ideal of Pan American unity has suffered serious impairment. Those disagreeable events, which we deplore so much, have nevertheless imparted an inescapable impression that we misunderstand each other on this Continent. The propaganda disseminated by the tools of anti-Americanism is apparently now directed toward presenting such supposed misunderstandings as actual incompatibility and even enmity between the free countries of the American community. Fortunately, this is far from being the truth.

It appears to me, Mr. President, that it would be utterly inconvenient and unfair to allow this false impression to prevail, morally weakening the cause of democracy, to the defense of which we are pledged.

In addressing these words to Your Excellency, my sole purpose is to acquaint you with my deep-seated conviction that something must be done to restore composure to the continental unity. I have no definite and detailed plans to that effect, but rather ideas and thoughts which I could confide to Your Excellency should an early opportunity to do so arise.

I might venture at this juncture, however, that the hour has come for us to undertake jointly a thorough review of the policy of mutual understanding on this Hemisphere and to conduct a comprehensive reappraisal of the proceedings already in motion for the furtherance of Pan American ideals in all their aspects and implications. The time has come for us to ask ourselves the pertinent question as to whether or not all of us are doing our utmost to weld the indestructible union of sentiments, aspirations and interests called for by the graveness of the world situation.

As a soldier who led democracy to victory, as an experienced statesman and, above all as a man sensitive to the ways of truth, Your Excellency is in an unique position to evaluate the seriousness of the question which I postulate with the exclusive purpose of defining and subsequently eliminating an entire range of minunderstandings that are easily capable of being removed at this moment but which may perhaps suffer a malignant growth should we fail to give it proper and timely attention.

It is hoped that the unpleasant memory of the ordeal undergone by Vice President Nixon will be effaced by the results of earnest efforts towards creating something deeper and more durable for the defense and preservation of our common destiny.

As I have already said to Your Excellency, it is advisable that we correct the false impression that we are not behaving in a fraternal way in the Americas; but besides this corrective effort, and in order that it be durable and perfect, we must search our consciences to find out if we are following the right path in regard to Pan Americanism.

It is my earnest hope that Your Excellency will feel that this letter was written under the impulse of a desire to reaffirm the warm and sincere fraternal sentiments which have always bound my Country to the United States of America, in perfect attunement with the ideas outlined by Your Excellency on the occasion of the meeting of the Chief Executives of the American nations in Panama.

May God guard Your Excellency and the people of the United States of America. . . .

79. Response by President Eisenhower, to the Letter of President Kubitschek*

June 5, 1958

This morning your Ambassador delivered to me the letter you wrote under date of May twenty-eighth. I found it intensely interesting.

To my mind you have described accurately both the existing situation and the desirability of corrective action. I am delighted, therefore, that you have taken the initiative in this matter.

While Your Excellency did not suggest any specific program to improve Pan American understanding, it seems to me that our two Governments should consult together as soon as possible with a view to approaching other members of the Pan American community, and starting promptly on measures that would produce throughout the continent a reaffirmation of devotion to Pan Americanism, and better planning in promoting the common interests and welfare of our several countries. There is a wide range of subjects to be discussed and explored, including, for example, the problem of implementing more fully the Declaration of Solidarity of the Tenth Inter-American Conference held at Caracas in 1954.

Because I deem this matter so important, I am instructing Mr. Roy Richard Rubottom, Jr., Assistant Secretary of State for Inter-American Affairs, to deliver my letter to you personally in Rio de Janeiro, to explore with you further your thinking on these matters. Your thoughts and ideas thus obtained at first hand can be the subject of further consultation through normal diplomatic channels, preparatory to a later visit to Brazil by the Secretary of State. With your concurrence, Mr. Rubottom will make final arrangement with your Government for the timing of Secretary Dulles' visit.

With assurance of my highest consideration, and with best wishes for the continued well-being of your Excellency and of the Brazilian people, I remain, ...

80. Report by Personal Representative Milton S. Eisenhower, on a Trip to Central America†

August 1, 1958

My associates and I are deeply moved by your personal reception of us this evening; we recognize that your generous action is inspired by more than brotherly affection; it is also your unmistakable notice to all the world that you, as we, consider firm, abiding relations among the nations of this Hemisphere to be essential to our common future. You sent us on a mission of good will and fact-finding.

At once, upon our return from three weeks in Panama, the five Central American countries, and Puerto Rico, we wish to express our deep appreciation to the Presidents and peoples of the area visited for their friendly reception of us. Everywhere we experienced the warm friendliness which the peoples of this hemisphere have for the United States.

*Department of State Bulletin, June 30, 1958, pp. 1090-91.
†Department of State Bulletin, Aug. 25, 1958, pp. 309-10.

The absence of any unfriendly incident may have confounded those who were looking for sensational headlines, but this very circumstance enabled us, calmly and rationally, to accomplish precisely what we set out to do—to gain a new perspective of the problems, progress, attitudes, and aspirations of the nations visited, as a basis for determining whether new approaches in our own policies and programs might strengthen relations among us.

I re-affirm now all I reported to you, Mr. President, in November 1953 following the fact-finding trip I made to the ten republics of South America.

Now, however, I must add a note of urgency to what I then recommended. I shall make additional suggestions for policy and program improvements which I hope will be found acceptable.

I shall even this evening make a preliminary report. My suggestions will deal with:

1. The imperative need for bankable loans—not grants—in every country visited;

2. The response which I believe the United States should make to the appeal of the Latin American nations for more stable relationships between raw-commodity prices and the prices of manufactured products;

3. The urgent and immediate need to bring about throughout the hemisphere a clear, accurate understanding of United States policies, purposes, programs, and capabilities.

My associates and I met with some 1,200 leaders of government, industry, agriculture, labor, commerce, finance, education, health and social and cultural institutions. We had candid conversations with all of them. They submitted to us some 1,000 pages of data and suggestions.

Now I shall want to hold a series of conferences with numerous individuals and agencies, as I study and integrate this evidence—especially with the Vice President, who recently returned from a trip to South America; officials of the International Bank; the Board of the Export-Import Bank and the Board of Directors of the Development Loan Fund. I shall also want to consult with high officials in the State, Treasury, Labor, Agriculture, Commerce and other Departments.

Since I must do this without neglecting my University duties, I cannot predict when a final brief report will be ready, but the sense of urgency I feel about the problems in the great Central area of this Hemisphere—indeed, about the situation in all the Americas—will impel me to conclude my assignment at the earliest possible moment.

My confidence in the unity, common purpose, and common destiny of the Americas has been strengthened by all I have learned on this trip. The vast majority of the leaders and peoples of Latin America are firm friends of the United States. They do not intend to permit a tiny minority of conspirators and a few misguided associates of such conspirators to confuse and divide us.

May I say in all candor that while, of course, I believe the United States must shore up its policies and programs with respect to Latin America, it is just as essential that all our neighbors to the South re-examine—as I know they will—their policies with respect to the United States. Good relations are never the result of unilateral action. They are the outcome of mutual understanding, mutual respect, shared goals, and a common determination to live, work, and progress together. We are partners in the quest for independence, freedom, democracy, and peace with justice.

I repeat the final words of my 1953 report: "Working together, the nations of this Hemisphere can, if history should so decree, stand firmly against any enemy in war, and prosper mightily together in times of peace."

81. Aide Mémoire from the Brazilian Government, to Governments of other American States, on Operation Panamerica*

August 9, 1958

I. Definition and Objectives

The Brazilian Government considers that a clearer definition of the objectives of Operation Pan America is necessary in order that this movement, which has been initiated at the right time and under the best auspices, may not be impaired or lose its impact.

A *General definition:* Operation Pan America is not an undertaking limited by time, with objectives to be attained in a short period; rather, it is a reorientation of hemisphere policy, intended to place Latin America, by a process of full appraisement, in a position to participate more effectively in the defense of the West, with a growing sense of vitality and a greater development of its capacities. Thus, Operation Pan America is more than a mere program; it is an entire policy.

B. *Strategic political concept:* Operation Pan America must be understood as a corollary of the general strategy of the West, and among its fundamental purposes the following are particularly outstanding: preservation of the democratic system, based on political and religious freedom and on respect for private ownership and free enterprise, and the defense of all areas that concern the security of the free world. Because of its intrinsic, political, economic, social and strategic importance, and because "a threat to the peace in any part of the world is now a threat to the peace of the entire world," it is opportune to re-examine, with a view to strengthening it, the contribution to the resources of the free world that may be made by the nations that are signatories of the Treaty of Rio de Janeiro.

C. *Economic concept:* The more rapid development of Latin America's economic strength will result in a growing sense of vitality and will enable it to increase its contribution to the defense of the West.

II. Characteristics

A. *Joint multilateral action:* Operation Pan America is conceived as involving the joint action of the twenty-one republics of the Western Hemisphere, the preservation of its strictly multilateral nature being indispensable. Bilateral matters will continue to be handled through the channels normally followed in such cases, without becoming part of the aforesaid Operation.

B. *Struggle for democracy:* Within the framework of Operation Pan America, the struggle for democracy becomes identified with the struggle against stagnation and underdevelopment. The underdevelopment that prevails in this Hemisphere morally and materially involves the cause that we are defending. Underdeveloped areas are open to the penetration of antidemocratic ideology. From many standpoints and in all of its implications, the battle of the West is the battle for development. Materialist

*Council of the Organization of American States, Special Committee to Study the Formulation of New Measures for Economic Cooperation, Vol. I: *Report and Documents, First Meeting, Washington, D.C., November 17-December 12, 1958* (Washington, D.C., 1959), pp. 29-31.

ideologies feed upon the poverty and misery that give rise to them in the first place; to combat these factors is the only sure way to combat those ideologies. Where there is poverty, our cause will always be in danger. It is illusory to expect positive action on behalf of a cause embracing such complex factors from peoples whose isolation in the rigors of extreme poverty prevents them from thinking or feeling anything beyond the narrow limits of their urgent needs for survival.

C. *Latin America's participation in world policy:* According to the Brazilian concept, Operation Pan America is a reflection of the need for more active and more vigorous participation and cooperation by the Latin American countries in international policy, and it reveals these countries' full awareness of their moral, political, and demographic importance. Latin America's contribution may become highly significant in the struggle for a balance of power.

III. Western Postwar Policy

A. *Inter-American political reorientation:* The Brazilian Government believes that the time has come for a revision of inter-American policy, with a view to strengthening hemispheric unity in the face of the increasing common danger. A stronger, more courageous, creative, and dynamic initiative is urgently needed in the Western Hemisphere at this time.

It is imperative that the West become ever more conscious of its mission in the modern world. The principal objective of this mission is to defend and to perfect man's spiritual and moral achievements. Spiritual and moral forces should be the ones to guide and regulate a world expanded and profoundly transformed by technology. This is what is important to the West; this is its own Cause.

B. *Economic reorientation of Pan Americanism:* The reasons for underdevelopment are many and complex. One could not in good faith fix responsibility for Latin America's chronic anemic condition and the consequent organic weakening of Pan Americanism. Although it is understood that efforts toward economic development devolve primarily upon each country individually, it is now understood better than ever before that there must be cooperation on international bases.

IV. The Operation's Course of Action

A. *Advance preparation:* The Brazilian Government wishes to clarify the fact that it was never its intention or plan to hold a conference of American Chiefs of State without the most careful advance preparation. Furthermore, the Brazilian Government is not committed to any rigid plans for carrying out the Operation in question, and it believes that only after a series of contacts and consultations among the countries of our community will it be possible to make a definitive determination of the best methods for achieving the common objective.

B. *Preliminary inquiries:* The Brazilian Government would now be willing to assume responsibility for making diplomatic inquiries with a view to the preparation of a basic agenda and toward ascertaining whether the American governments would agree with the idea of reaching informal understanding and carrying out preliminary negotiations in Washington through the embassies accredited to the Government of the United States.

C. *Initiation of the Operation:* The preparatory work could be done at the diplomatic or technical level, and it is anticipated that the participation by members of the delegations accredited to the Organization of American States would be desirable. These informal understandings would become more clearly defined and be better coordinafed if a *Committee of Twenty-one* were created. Brazil does not wish to propose any date, but nonetheless it does state that it would be ready to begin its work in the said committee during the latter part of September.

D. *High-level meeting.* Once the bases for an agreement have been established and significant results obtained that might be looked upon as substantial progress, then the competent organs of the Orgnaization of American States could study the idea of a high-level meeting among the republics of the Hemisphere to approve and to sign that group of resolutions and proclamations that could become the plan of action for achieving Pan American unity; among these would be included, with special emphasis, the preparation of a dynamic and progressive program for the struggle against under-development, and this would be the crowning feature of Operation Pan America.

V. Basic Objectives of the Operation

The following points might be the basic objectives of the Operation:

1. Reaffirmation of the principles of hemispheric solidarity;

2. Recognition of underdevelopment as a problem of common interest;

3. Adaptation of inter-American organs and agencies as necessary to the requirements of more dynamic action to carry on the struggle against underdevelopment;

4. Technical assistance for increased productivity;

5. Measures to stabilize the market for basic commodities;

6. Adaptation to present needs and expansion of the resources of international financial institutions;

7. Reaffirmation of private initiative in the struggle against underdevelopment; and

8. Revision by each country, where necessary, of its fiscal and economic policy, for the purpose of assuring means to promote economic development.

82. *Communiqué Issued by Foreign Ministers of the American Republics on Inter-American Economic Relations and Other Matters* *

September 24, 1958

The Foreign Ministers of the 21 American Republics met informally in Washington on September 23 and 24, at the invitation of the Secretary of State of the United States, and discussed important current questions of common interest. In three sessions, the Foreign Ministers exchanged views regarding inter-American relations and problems, particularly those of an economic nature, and also reviewed the international scene.

*Department of State Bulletin, Oct. 13, 1958, pp. 575-76.

The Ministers recognize that in the history of the world, the solidarity of the American States has been of great importance, and that at the present time it acquires special significance. They reaffirm that solidarity, which is founded on the principles of the Charter of the Organization [of American States]. The present period of evolutionary change in the political, economic and social structure of society calls for a renewed dedication to the inter-American ideals of independence, political liberty, and economic and cultural progress, and for a reaffirmation of the faith of the American nations in their capacity to proceed dynamically toward the realization of those high ideals.

The Ministers are confident that their exchange of views and informal conversations will have fruitful results. They agree to recommend that their governments instruct their representatives on the Council of the Organization of American States to consider the desirability of holding more frequently similar informal meetings of Foreign Ministers and other high-ranking government representatives.

The Ministers are of the opinion that, in keeping with the aspirations and needs of the peoples of America expressed on numerous occasions, action to promote the greatest possible economic development of the continent must be intensified. They are certain that a harmonious and carefully planned joint effort to that end will contribute enormously to strengthening the solidarity of the hemisphere and to the well-being of all Americans.

The Foreign Ministers are deeply gratified at the affirmation made by President Eisenhower, that the Government of the United States is prepared to lend its full cooperation in achieving concrete results in the common effort to promote the economic development of the American countries, for it considers that peace, prosperity and security are in the end, indivisible.

They furthermore consider that this is the proper time to review and strengthen inter-American cooperation in the economic field, as has been suggested by President Kubitschek and in the proposals of various American Governments. The Ministers recommend that, during the coming period before the Eleventh Inter-American Conference, special attention be given to working out additional measures of economic cooperation taking as the point of departure the six topics proposed by the Government of Brazil in its memorandum of August 9, 1958 concerning the plan known as "Operation Pan America", any other specific topics that the other governments of the Republics of the hemisphere may wish to submit in connection with the general topic under consideration, namely, the promotion of economic development, and the following topic proposed by the Foreign Minister of Argentina:

Preparation and immediate execution of a broad hemispheric program to train experts for economic development, chiefly in the fields of engineering, agronomy, industrial engineering, economics, public administration, and business administration.

For this purpose and to facilitate other informal talks, the Ministers are of the opinion that the Council of the Organization of American States should set up a Special Commission of the Council on which the governments of the 21 American Republics would be represented. As the Commission reaches conclusions regarding measures that might be taken, it should submit its reports to the Council of the Organization. Then the necessary action may be taken to have those proposals or measures carried out through the organs of the Organization, or directly by the governments. as may be appropriate.

Also, the Ministers are of the opinion that practical measures may be taken now in connection with certain specific proposals. These are:

1. The establishment of an inter-American economic development institution in which all the American countries would participate. For this purpose the Inter-American Economic and Social Council should convene as soon as possible a specialized committee of government representatives, as recommended in Resolution XVIII of the Buenos Aires Economic Conference. It is recommended that this committee meet in continuous session until it completes draft articles of the agreement for the proposed institution, which will be signed at a later date.

2. Intensification of efforts to establish regional markets in Latin America. It would be well for the governments directly concerned and the international organizations directly interested, chiefly the Organization of American States, the Economic Commission for Latin America, and the Organization of Central American States, to expedite their studies and concrete measures directed toward the establishment of regional markets in Central and South America. The Ministers suggest that a report on this important project be submitted to the members of the OAS not later than the Eleventh Inter-American Conference. In this connection the Ministers note that the United States Government has made known that it is prepared to assist financially in the establishment of solvent industries, through appropriate agencies, under suitable conditions, with a view to promoting enjoyment of the benefits of regional markets through public and private investment.

The Ministers again express their constant concern about the problems of markets for basic products. They are in agreement that the economic structure of the majority of the American Republics requires that solutions to these problems be sought urgently, for which purpose consultations should be carried out between the interested members of the Organization of American States, on bilateral and multilateral bases, as well as with the producer and consumer countries of other geographic areas.

In concluding this communiqué, the Ministers expressed that there prevailed at this meeting an atmosphere of frankness, sincerity, and understanding which contributed greatly to the establishment of a feeling of confidence that the important tasks being started at this time will be completed successfully.

83. Remarks by Douglas Dillon, Under Secretary of State, before the Special Committee of the Council of the Organization of American States, on Inter-American Economic Cooperation*

December 12, 1958

This meeting just prior to our recess is an appropriate time to review, in general terms, the accomplishments of our Committee since we first met here on November 17. This Committee was created to examine the whole complex of economic problems with which the American Republics are presently faced and to devise means for their solution. Our deliberations have been guided by the wise and understanding leadership of our chairman, Dr. Alfonso Lopez of Colombia. We are indebted to him for the

*Department of State Bulletin, Jan. 12, 1959, pp. 48-49.

substantial progress which has been made toward defining and clarifying the various aspects of our task. It is unfortunate that illness keeps him from our midst today. We owe him a vote of thanks for the able manner in which he has directed our discussions.

You will all agree with me, I am sure, that it is fitting that recognition be given to the role played by Brazil in this challenging undertaking. What is now known as Operation Pan America had its inception in the timely and thoughtful letter which President Kubitschek addressed to President Eisenhower in May of this year. President Kubitschek's initiative found a warm response in each of our governments, and the machinery of the inter-American system was promptly set into motion.

Meetings such as this have always contributed greatly to increased understanding between our governments and our peoples. No nation in this hemisphere possesses a monopoly of talent or of ideas. We all learn from each other in a continuing process, for understanding is based upon knowledge of one another's capabilities and motivations. Speaking for my delegation, I can tell you that we have benefited greatly from this exchange of viewpoints.

I believe that there could be no better occasion than this on which to reaffirm our individual and collective support for our inter-American system, in which, as equal partners, we are striving together to advance the economic well-being of our peoples.

The task which faces our Committee is not an easy one. Each of our economies has its own individual problems, which add to the technical difficulties inherent in any group effort in the field of economic relations.

However, we have made real progress in the council chamber. We are now establishing a working group to carry on during our recess period. We are thereby assured that when the Special Committee's meetings are resumed further progress will have been made. The recess also offers an excellent opportunity for a thorough review by each of our delegations of its own country's economic situation in the light of the searching discussions which we have held here. This examination may well result in the conception and implementation of concrete measures which will not only strengthen our individual economies but will also add to the contribution each of us can make to our joint effort in Operation Pan America.

Our discussions have been closely followed by my Government and by a large number of our individual citizens who view United States participation in the inter-American system as a keystone of our international relations. My Government's sincere and continuing interest in helping to advance the economic progress of the other American Republics is expressed in a special message which President Eisenhower has asked me to deliver to you as we close our current deliberations. The President says,

I extend my congratulations to the "Special Committee To Study the Formulation of New Measures for Economic Cooperation," for its perseverance and diligence in carrying out the tasks assigned to it last September by the Foreign Ministers of the American Republics.

My personal interest in what has come to be known as "Operation Pan America" began when President Kubitschek of Brazil wrote to me on May 28 of this year. The Secretary of State thereafter formally expressed the willingness of my Government to cooperate in finding ways of making inter-American economic cooperation more effective. This remains the policy of the United States Government, and I assure you that the United States will lend its warmhearted cooperation to "Operation Pan America."

I am informed that the Special Committee has now completed its general review of the problems of underdeveloped countries and has decided to constitute a working group which, during the time the Special Committee is in recess, will address itself to specific concrete measures that can be taken to promote, by cooperative effort, a greater degree of economic development. I am confident that this work will go forward in the same spirit of mutual understanding and cooperation that has always characterized inter-American relations and that meaningful and constructive measures will be devised to achieve our common objective.

The economic development of Latin America is of vital importance to the strength and well-being of the whole of the free world. I hope that the working group will make rapid progress so that the Special Committee may soon resume its meeting here in Washington. As Americans, I am sure that we all share a confidence in the future of this hemisphere and that we are determined to press forward with the concrete measures necessary to make inter-American cooperation in the economic field as fruitful as it has been in the political field.

There is little I can add to the message from my President, other than to assure you that this policy of the United Sates Government will be carried out as vigorously as is possible and within the framework of our inter-American system.

In conclusion, permit me, Mr. Chairman, to make a personal observation:

I believe that, if we apply to the economic problems we have been discussing the same energy, creativity, and perseverance we have devoted to solving political problems within our framework of nations, they will yield to our determination. What we need is faith in our ability to do what must be done.

It is undeniably true that each of our countries must pursue progress in ways consistent with its own cultural, political, and economic patterns. But no nation in this hemisphere stands alone. The spiritual and material well-being of one country is a matter of continuing and urgent concern to all the members of our family of nations. I say this with deep conviction. But it is more than a conviction. It is an article of faith. For our American community is built upon a bedrock of friendship and mutual respect. And friendship and solidarity have their roots in the human heart.

On behalf of my country and my people, I want to assure you of this: No matter what our commitments in other areas of the world—and you must know that they are many and burdensome and are designed to achieve the same free-world goals to which each of your governments subscribes—the United States will never forget the needs of any of its sister republics. Our feeling of friendship for the citizens of the other Americas is as deep-rooted and enduring as our belief in freedom and the dignity of the human spirit.

84. Declaration on Activities of the Special Committee of the Council of the Organization of American States*

December 12, 1958

At the close of its first meeting, at which the governments of all twenty-one American republics were represented, the Special Committee of the Council of the Organization of American States deems it fitting to state that, from the start of its

*Department of State Bulletin, Jan. 12, 1959, pp. 49-50.

deliberations on November 17, 1958, the representatives of the member states have had full opportunity, in the course of the sessions, to express with all frankness and clarity the views of their governments on the pressing need for strengthening inter-American cooperation.

Opinions were freely exchanged, always in an atmosphere of extreme cordiality and mutual understanding. The members of the committee unanimously reaffirmed their faith in the Organization of American States and their common determination to strengthen the harmonious relations uniting their countries in bonds of brotherhood. They also recognized the urgent necessity of making the best possible use of all the means and the facilities available within the regional system for promoting the economic development of the hemisphere in a way that will bring positive benefits to each and every one of the American republics.

There was a full discussion of each of the topics accepted at the Informal Meeting of American Foreign Ministers, held in Washington last September 23 and 24, and of many other proposals that were presented by the various delegations during the sessions.

Special attention was given the problem of financing the economic development of Latin America, and a draft resolution was adopted endorsing the proposal to establish an inter-American institution for economic development and expressing the hope that the Committee of Experts convoked by the Inter-American Economic and Social Council and scheduled to meet next January 8 will, in the shortest possible time, draw up the draft conventions that are to bring this new instrument of inter-American cooperation into existence.

In regard to the need for creating new incentives to the flow of private capital, all the representatives agreed that it was necessary to supplement such measures as the countries interested in attracting and receiving foreign capital have adopted, or will in the future adopt, by concluding agreements with capital-exporting countries so that the special tax rates that are now offered, or may later be offered, by the former will not be negated by the absence of counterpart measures in those countries in a position to furnish capital.

This matter is one in which the initiative is left to the interested governments, and with respect to which the willingness of the United States Government to conclude the necesssary agreements, as expessed on the very first day of the meeting, can be counted on.

There was general agreement that the heavy reliance of the Latin American economies on the export trade in one or a few primary products poses a serious problem, since abrupt fluctuations and sudden drops in the prices of those commodities give rise to serious disturbances and impair the entire economic and financial outlook.

In this respect, the representatives of all the American countries displayed a willingness to participate in the study of the problems connected with each product in an effort to find satisfactory solutions within a spirit of hemisphere solidarity and an awareness of the mutual benefits that spring from the many and varied relationships linking the countries of the American regional community.

All the representatives at the meeting placed special emphasis on the need for intensifying technical cooperation and providing a new and greater stimulus to the campaigns directed toward increasing technical ability and productivity, which are the principal requirements for economic development.

In this connection, highly constructive suggestions, inspired by a proposal of Argentina, were made. These suggestions are aimed at expanding and intensifying the pertinent programs now being conducted by the OAS and at awakening the interest of and obtaining assistance in this field from other public and private organizations.

The committee is about to suspend its sessions because it feels that, now that the general viewpoints have been expounded, the time has come to proceed without loss of time to the stage of preparing concrete formulas and specific proposals. In order to carry out this technical work, which is essential if useful results are to be obtained, the committee has appointed a working group that will develop the practical arrangements for arriving at the aforesaid objectives. The working group will meet at the Pan American Union beginning January 15, 1959, and will enlist the effective and indispensable services of the IAECOSOC and the General Secretariat of the OAS. When it completes its task, which should be no later than April 1, 1959, the Group will report its conclusions and recommendations to the Special Committee. Thus, the new measures required for more effective inter-American cooperation are already in progress.

When the Special Committee meets again in April, it will examine these specific proposals and submit them to the Council of the Organization of American States, so that the governments may arrive at final agreements and decisions.

Strongly evident was a feeling of gratitude on the part of all the governments to President Juscelino Kubitschek of Brazil for his timely proposal for setting in motion what has come to be known as "Operation Pan America."

The Special Committee is fully aware of the far-reaching importance of the tasks assigned to it by the American governments; in view of what has already been said and done, the Committee feels confident that it will be possible to advance toward the goal set by the governments, namely: the promotion of economic development in their respective countries with a view to raising the standard of living of their peoples, thus paving the way for progress and strengthening democracy in the hemisphere.

85. Report by Personal Representative Milton S. Eisenhower, on United States-Latin American Relations, 1953-1958*

December 27, 1958

Five years ago I submitted to you a report on United States–Latin American Relations following field observations in the ten Republics of South America and subsequent study with the Federal officials who had accompanied me on that fact-finding, good-will trip.

In the 1953 report, I emphasized the vital importance of Latin America and the United States to each other; suggested the principles which should be observed in strengthening hemispheric relations; analyzed those continental conditions which have a direct bearing upon United States policies and programs; and recommended a number of actions which I believed would be helpful in binding the American

*Department of State Bulletin, Jan. 19, 1959, pp. 89-105.

Republics into a cooperative enterprise directed toward the goals of peace, freedom, and rising levels of human well-being.

In the period September 1956 to May 1957, I had an extraordinary opportunity to learn the views of distinguished leaders of the twenty republics of Latin America. It was my privilege to serve as your personal representative on the Inter-American Committee of Presidential Representatives, which unanimously recommended to the Chiefs of State ways in which the Organization of American States might broaden the scope of its activities for the benefit of the peoples of this hemisphere.

In the summer of 1957, several associates and I, at your request, responded to an invitation from President Ruiz Cortines of Mexico, and made a fact-finding good-will visit to that country.

Then, in July of this year, the Assistant Secretary of State for Inter-American Affairs, the Assistant Secretary of the Treasury, the President of the Export-Import Bank, the Managing Director of the Development Loan Fund, a physician of the Johns Hopkins University, and I made a fact-finding trip to the five republics of Central America and to Panama, interrupting it for a few days to participate in Puerto Rico's sixth annual celebration of its having achieved Commonwealth status.

It had been my intention to submit to you soon after my return from this latest mission a report on our findings, and further recommendations for improving United States—Latin American relations. However, I found it desirable to spend all the time I could spare from my University duties in holding extensive discussions with Federal agencies, and one international agency, whose policies and programs have a significant bearing on this central problem. During the past four months I have had helpful conversations with you, the Vice President, the Secretary of State and other officials of the State Department, the Secretary of the Treasury and some of his associates, the National Security Planning Board, the Board of Directors of the Export-Import Bank, the President of the International Bank for Reconstruction and Development, the Managing Director and other officials of the Development Loan Fund, various officials in other Departments, and the heads of some of our industrial enterprises with activities in Latin America. I suspect, therefore, that there have already been set in motion activities which will lead to such results as might be expected from my studies and observations. Hence this report, as an addendum to the one I submitted in 1953, is prepared primarily for the record.

I reaffirm essentially all I said in my report of 1953, but now I must add a note of urgency to my general recommendation that the nations of Latin America and the United States re-examine their attitudes and policies toward one another and constantly seek to strengthen their economic, political, and cultural relations, to their mutual benefit.

Latin America is a continental area in ferment. While its productivity is increasing, so is its population, at an unprecedented rate. A high degree of illiteracy, poverty, and dependence on one-commodity economies with consequent wide fluctuations in income still characterize most of this vast area.

But the people generally, including the most humble of them, now know that low standards of living are neither universal nor inevitable, and they are therefore impatiently insistent that remedial actions be taken. It is perhaps natural for them to look primarily to the United States for assistance.

Neither the people nor their leaders seek financial grants, save in a few isolated and emergency situations. Rather, they want public and private credit in increasing quantities, stable trade relations, greater stability in the prices of raw commodities which they sell, and technical assistance designed to hasten overall development primarily through improvement in education, health, and agricultural and industrial productivity.

The Need for Understanding

It is surely a truism to say that if the governments and peoples of this hemisphere are to cooperate fruitfully in ways that are mutually beneficial—in ways that enable Latin America to achieve its aspirations without requiring an excessive drain upon the over-taxed resources of the United States—there must first be better understanding among them.

I commented at length on this in my previous report. I now must report that misunderstandings seem to me to be even more serious than they were in 1953.

In the United States, the problem stems primarily from a lack of knowledge. We wish to be a good neighbor. We want the Latin American republics to regard us as a faithful friend. But our people generally do not truly comprehend the problems and aspirations of our neighbors, and thus we sometimes take actions which are detrimental to the good relationships we wish to foster. Thus it is possible that the people of the United States would have favored actions different from those that were taken in the area of trade relations if they had been in possession of all relevant facts.

In Latin America, misunderstandings of our policies, programs, and attitudes are pervasive, and are impediments to the development of more fruitful cooperation.

Latin Americans believe that our economic capacity is essentially unlimited and that we are doing much more for other areas of the world than we are for Latin America. This leads them to conclude that their failure to obtain credit in the desired volume is either sheer perversity or discrimination on our part. That this is not so is beside my immediate point. Leaders and peoples think it is so. This persistent misunderstanding, noted in my previous report and found this summer to be even more strongly held, should warn us that new and dramatic action to overcome it is now imperative.

Another serious misconception is that we sometimes fix prices, to the detriment of Latin America. Everywhere one hears it said, among government officials, university students, and business leaders: "We must sell to you at prices you are willing to pay, and we must buy from you at prices you dictate."

Why is this false idea circulated? One of the most vexing problems in Latin America stems from an excessive dependence upon the export of agricultural products and minerals, whose prices are subject to sharp fluctuations in world markets, whereas the prices of industrial commodities they buy are more rigid. That the United States does not fix prices—that raw commodity and industrial prices are determined in the competitive markets of the world, as they should be—is again in one sense beside the point. The erroneous belief noted above is widely held. It causes bitterness, and impedes rational resolution of substantive problems.

I am deeply disturbed by a gross misconception which is evidently fairly recent in origin. At least I did not encounter it in 1953. Based on a distortion of facts, a false impression is now held by certain misinformed individuals and is also being cleverly fostered by communist agitators. Despite our adherence to a policy of non-intervention, we are charged with supporting Latin American dictators in the face of a strong trend toward freedom and democratic government.

It is ironic that this charge is insidiously spread by international conspirators who represent the most vicious dictatorship in modern history.

These three examples of Latin American misunderstanding of our attitudes, policies, and capabilities are only illustrative.

In my previous report, I made nine recommendations for action which I hoped would help solve the problem. I know that since then notable work has been done by the United States Information Agency, the State Department, private businesses with branches in Latin America, and mass media. But the problem grows. New, heroic efforts are required.

I recommend that the United States take the leadership in urging the Organization of American States to place high on its program effective efforts to develop among the governments and peoples of the American Republics that genuine understanding on which fruitful cooperative action must be based.

(a) The OAS should urge each of the American Republics to establish a national commission of distinguished citizens who voluntarily would assume, as their major extramural responsibility, the promotion within each country of the type of broad understanding which is obviously required. Commission membership should include educators; editors; writers; leaders of business, agriculture, and labor; public officials, and prominent individuals from social and cultural institutions. In the larger countries, I would hope that one hundred distinguished citizens would be willing to serve on each National Commission; in the smaller countries, twenty or more might suffice. As your representative, I made this recommendation to the Inter-American Committee of Presidential Representatives and it was there unanimously approved, but the recommendation has not been implemented.

I also recommend that each of the twenty-one governments be urged to assume a large measure of responsibility for promoting the relevant understanding within its own country.

Sometimes, I regret to report, misunderstandings are permitted to prevail or are encouraged for what may seem to be temporary political advantage. Actually nothing could be more self-defeating. Political leaders must in fact be leaders: Each has a profound responsibility for keeping his people informed with respect to those great problems and issues that determine relationships among the family of nations.

Responsibility for informing the people of the United States about Latin American policies, attitudes, and developments—to the extent this is a government duty—rests with the State Department. Responsibility for informing the peoples of Latin America about similar matters in the United States rests with the United States Information Agency.

I recommend that the information facilities of the State Department be increased, that the State Department cooperate continuously with the United States National Commission for Latin American Affairs (as recommended above) and that special efforts be made to induce the mass media of the United States to maintain competent correspondents in Latin America and to carry a steady flow of news and interpretive material from all twenty republics.

I also recommend that leadership, student, and other exchanges of persons be encouraged by every means. Fortunately, the United States official exchange-of-persons program has recently been increased. The OAS has initiated an excellent program of scholarships and fellowships. Private foundations should be urged to grant scholarships to young men and women who wish to study in the United States. American business enterprises with interests in Latin America should be encouraged to bring promising young employees to the United States for travel, training, and education.

I further recommend that the activities of the United States Information Agency in Latin America be increased:

(a) The bi-national center program should be expanded. It costs us little. It is rapidly helping to make English the second language of Latin America, and is enabling many Latin Americans to gain an insight into our total culture.

(b) The USIA publications program should be increased and modified so as to place particular emphasis on reaching students, intellectuals, and workers.

(c) Government, industry, and foundations might well cooperate in establishing, upon request, endowed chairs in leading universities of Latin America, especially in the social sciences and humanities. Initially, these chairs might well be occupied by United States professors, but eventually by national professors who have done advanced work in the United States.

(d) The USIA posts which had to be vacated because of the budgetary cut in 1957 should be filled.

(e) The private effort in Mexico of prominent Mexican and United States business-men to develop mutual understanding should be studied; if found successful, as I am convinced it is, the USIA should arrange for business leaders in the United States to try to duplicate this pilot project in other Latin American countries.

I wish to call attention again to my 1953 suggestion that we should encourage the establishment in the United States of bi-national institutes for the teaching of Spanish. Our goal should be to develop genuine linguistic ability among all classes of our population so that we may communicate effectively and read the literature of Latin America. We are lamentably deficient in this respect. It is a shameful shortcoming in a country which has the burden of free world leadership.

In the National Defense Education Act, the Congress and the Administration have recognized our limitations in languages and knowledge of the cultures of regions of the world, and have made provision, on a matching grant basis to institutions of higher education, for the establishment of institutes to train teachers and promote the teaching of these subjects. This Act provides a good beginning toward the permanent establishment of bi-national institutes, and may indeed provide a source of well trained personnel for them.

The Need for Credit

Though vast opportunities exist in Latin America to increase the efficiency of agricultural production—and each of the countries should intensify its efforts in this area—nonetheless it is clear that a substantial increase in levels of living requires industrialization. This calls for many things, including a steady flow of private and public credit.

The United States drew vast quantities of capital from Europe during the early years of its industrial revolution; so today must the republics of Latin America look to the United States and perhaps to certain European countries for development capital.

Sound loans in impressive volume have been made over a period of years by the Export-Import Bank, and by the International Bank for Reconstruction and Development. Private United States credit and investment have been of powerful help to Latin America. About twenty per cent of outstanding United States investment is public, eighty per cent private.

The granting of public and private credit must be accelerated. This seems to me to require four things: First, each nation of Latin America must do a better job than heretofore in overall economic planning and in determining priorities within its development program; second, we must coordinate the knowledge about programs of the lending institutions, public and private; third, public lending institutions should take a positive attitude in the use of credit as a means of helping Latin America achieve its aspirations, and, fourth, each Latin American Republic must take those actions which will attract private credit, since it cannot and should not be directed.

An imperative first step is more effective economic analysis and planning by nations which desire development capital. Sound planning, with project priorities assigned, and with knowledge of which projects might be eligible for public credit and which for private credit, would be conducive to the receipt of maximum loans. Lending institutions cannot satisfy the total needs of a borrowing nation at one time, nor could a borrowing nation absorb vast sums quickly without causing economic dislocations. Timing is important: One loan, launching a successful enterprise, may make a second development loan feasible. A public loan, such as for a highway into virgin territory, might make possible a new private industry, such as a pulp and paper mill.

Occasionally, confusion has been caused among lending institutions when nations seeking credit have presented conflicting requests, or have suddenly shifted their priorities; these and other shortcomings could be overcome by competent economic analysis and planning.

I recommend that the projected Inter-American development institution subsequently discussed herein, be so organized and staffed as to assist the American Republics in development planning, in the assignment of priorities, and in the preparation of loan projects, and that the United States International Cooperation Administration assist in the financing of this section of the development agency through its technical cooperation funds.

I should also like to see tried a pilot project in joint planning similar to that which was attempted five or six years ago by the United States and Brazil. The only criticism I have heard of that intensive cooperative effort is this: Brazilian officials erroneously developed the belief that the joint planning constituted a commitment on the part of the lending institutions to finance the projects developed; this of course was not and could not have been true; recriminations flowed from the misunderstanding. Otherwise, all seem agreed that the joint effort was remarkably successful. It ought not to be difficult to avoid the recurrence of misunderstanding.

Once a nation has assessed its potentialities and produced a sound program with priorities, it is in a better position to utilize the facilities of lending institutions; initial applications must be well prepared if they are to meet with favorable responses. In the absence of sound planning of this kind applicants for loans may become confused and frustrated.

Effective borrowing by Latin American countries also requires an understanding of the policies and limitations of the International Bank for Reconstruction and Development, the International Finance Corporation, the International Monetary Fund, the Export-Import Bank, the Development Loan Fund, United States Treasury, the International Cooperation Administration (which has made one or two emergency loans in Latin America) and many private institutions.

The development program of a country may require the cooperation of several public and private institutions, first, in determining the credit capacity of a nation and, then, in timing several types of loans in such a way that one supports the other.

I recommend that the proposed inter-American development institution exercise leadership in this field; that it promote more specific planning by Latin America in the utilization of existing credit facilities; that it have broad responsibility for achieving greater understanding and coordination in the whole field of loans to the Republics of Latin America.

I cannot over-emphasize the constructive good that has been done in Latin America by the World Bank and by United States lending institutions. World Bank loans to Latin America now amount to about $150,000,000 a year, and total loans outstanding approximate $800,000,000. Forty per cent of Export-Import Bank loans over a period of years has been made to Latin American nations; in all, it has authorized $3,500,000,000 of such loans, with current outstanding commitments of $1,800,000,000. The last Congress increased the lending authority of the Bank from $5,000,000,000 to $7,000,000,000, so that the Bank now has substantial sums available for lending.

I imply no criticism of these and other lending institutions when I point out that they have pursued the normal procedure of waiting for applications to come to them in proper form and dealing with applications, when presented. So far as United States lending institutions are concerned, I am convinced that the time has arrived for us to take a more positive approach in using credit as an effective means of forwarding American foreign policy; this clearly involves helping Latin America achieve its sound economic goals and thus serving the best interest of the United States itself.

I recommend that United States lending institutions, with the help of IBRD if possible, inform the Republics of Latin America that they stand ready, as a cooperative group, to consider sympathetically the extension of sound, well-timed loans in support of practical development plans, and that they will meet jointly with delegations from each applicant country to determine how credit resources may best be employed to help that nation proceed effectively with its economic program.

Shortly after my return from central America and Panama, the United States notified the leaders of Latin America that it was prepared to consider participation in a new Inter-American Development Institution. This offer was in response to a suggestion which had been advanced persistently by the twenty Republics of Latin America for many years.

Many aspects of the financing of economic development were discussed at length at the meetings of the Committee of Presidential Representatives in 1956 and 1957, including a specific proposal looking toward the establishment of an Inter-American financial agency. The Personal Representatives of the Presidents of the Latin American Republics, while acknowledging the benefits which "existing international (and national) financial agencies have been providing for the development of . . . their countries," nonetheless stated that "it is their firm opinion that those benefits do not cover the entire field and are insufficient to enable the Latin American countries effectively to achieve an adequate rate of investment in projects which they consider essential to their economic improvement and a rise in their standard of living."

As your personal representative, I found it necessary to oppose this recommendation, first, because I felt that the question was outside the mandate which you and the Presidents of the other American Republics had placed upon our Committee, and, second, because I then agreed with the longstanding attitude of the United States which is expressed in this statement in the Committee's report to the Chiefs of State:

> The Representative of the President of the United States maintained that the resources of existing institutions are adequate to meet the effective demand, and that the creation of new credit institutions could therefore not be justified, since greater progress would be made by using the existing ones. He stated that there had been no change in the United States position (as set forth) at the Meeting of Ministers of Finance or Economy at the Fourth Extraordinary Session of the Inter-American Economic and Social Council with respect to proposals for the establishment of new credit institutions.

At the time I took this officially authorized position, the Development Loan Fund had not been established. This Fund was created primarily to replace grants with loans. It has broader authority than the Export-Import Bank. It can, for example, make loans for local currency expenditures, and sometimes loans may be repaid in local currency. The latter are called "soft" loans in the jargon of the banking world. Such loans are not "soft" in the sense that they are unsound or are grants in disguise. They are "soft" only in the sense that the credit extended may be repaid in the currency of the borrower rather than in dollars.

It is important that the people of the United States understand this. No responsible person has suggested that the United States Government make economically unsound loans. Nothing could so undermine the whole field of international credit.

For what it is worth, I applaud the Administration and the Congress for changing from grants to loans in our program of assisting foreign economic development. Except in unusual emergency situations, I believe grants for this purpose yield only temporary benefits and may cause ill will in all countries save those receiving the largest grants.

There can be no doubt that "soft" loans are needed in Latin America. Like most other underdeveloped areas of the world, Latin America suffers from a shortage of domestic savings. Hence, sound development projects may require loans involving both domestic and foreign capital. Further, until underdeveloped countries, including those of Latin America, can increase their productivity and their exports, which can assure favorable balances of trade, they may lack dollars or other borrowed currencies to meet repayment schedules, even though they could meet their obligations in local currencies.

The Development Loan Fund is now operating on a global basis, although its loans to Latin American countries have thus far been relatively limited. However, a conviction is growing that effective cooperative efforts of borrowers on a regional basis should be encouraged whenever desired by the countries concerned. This was implicit in our shift in policy when we announced our willingness to consider in principle the establishment of an Inter-American Bank.

Latin America is a natural region for such an agency, and there can be no doubt about the existence of the desire and ability to cooperate.

An Inter-American development institution, properly conceived, established and operated, can command the cooperative talents of the twenty-one American republics; it can place a high degree of responsibility for the success of the agency on the Latin American nations themselves; it may be able to tap private as well as public sources of credit.

It is essential, of course, that the development agency be set up soundly, with the right policies and limitations.

For example, the new agency, if established, should not be operated in such a way as to diminish the programs in Latin America of the Export-Import Bank and the World Bank.

In its initial stages the new institution could well study the operations of the Export-Import Bank: its impressive record of help to our neighbors, of businesslike management, and of interest and loan repayments. It might draw on Export-Import Bank's competent and efficient management.

I urge that the United States proceed as rapidly as possible to cooperate with leaders of the Latin American Republics in creating an Inter-American bank. Such a new institution should coordinate its operations closely with those of the World Bank, United States lending institutions and private lending agencies to the end that the total flow of development capital into Latin America may be increased.

(a) I believe that the United States should subscribe a significant portion of the paid-in capital of the new institution, the remainder to be provided by the twenty Latin American Republics. The authorized capital of the institution might be somewhat greater than the paid-in capital, the difference representing a guarantee fund which would help the new institution to issue its bonds in private capital markets. Depending upon future developments, and subject to Congressional approval for any increased subscription by the United States, provision might be made for the member governments to propose subsequent increases in paid-in capital on the same basis as that outlined above.

(b) With respect to its hard-loan activities, the United States should urge that the Inter-American Bank adhere to sound lending policy so that in time its securities will become marketable, thus making possible the tapping of private credit markets.

(c) The institution should have limited authority to make soft loans from a portion of its subscribed capital. Any soft-loan activity of the bank, however, should be segregated in some way from the hard-loan operations of the institution. Should the United States agree to subscribe a somewhat higher proportion for any capital authorized for soft-loan purposes, it should maintain an appropriate degree of authority in the direction of the soft-loan operations of the institution.

(d) The initial capital advances made by the United States should be under a new authorization which would permit the Treasury to subscribe the funds directly to the new bank.

(e) Assuming the willingness of the IBRD, the Inter-American development institution should maintain informal methods of credit coordination for Latin America and should provide a source of information and advice to the member nations seeking loans.

(f) The new Bank should use every means at its disposal to encourage each cooperating country to develop local savings, private and public, for participation in development projects.

(g) The Bank should try to obtain an outstanding Latin American, thoroughly familiar with financial matters, as its President. Each country should designate a member of its Board of Governors, each Governor having a weighted vote according to the percentage of capital advanced by his country. A smaller Board of Directors should supervise day-to-day operations of the institution. If the headquarters of the Bank were to be in Washington, daily coordination with other credit institutions would be facilitated.

As I have previously said, about eighty per cent of all United States capital now invested in Latin America is private. In recent years new private capital has flowed from the United States to Latin America at the rate of $600,000,000 a year. Each nation of Latin America should take every feasible step to encourage this capital movement. Private funds will always be available in larger quantities than will public funds, and private loans usually carry with them technical and management skills which may make the difference between success or failure, particularly in the early stages of new developments.

In some Latin American countries, irrational assumptions are made about private capital. It is said that private credit is imperialistic—that it is an expression of "dollar diplomacy." Of course this is not so. Nearly all of the trade between the United States and Latin America, amounting to about eight billion dollars a year, is privately financed, and it does not result in any sort of imperialism. Just as the private loans we obtained from Europe in our early history—and finally paid off with interest by 1918—aided our development and did not impinge upon our freedom, so too will private loans to Latin American enterprises help those countries advance without detriment to their sovereignty.

This problem is largely outside our hands. Private capital cannot be driven. It must be attracted. Attracting private capital to Latin America, in view of the competitive demand for it in the United States and throughout the world, is not an easy matter. It involves the avoidance of discriminatory restraints, the maintenance of stable financial and political policies within each country, the absence of discriminatory labor laws, control of inflationary forces, a reasonable return on the investment, ability to remit dividends to the lending country in the currency of that country, and, above all, a favorable attitude toward private competitive enterprises which are to be financed with the private capital.

I was favorably impressed to observe in Central America and Panama a strong tendency toward financial stability. I noted a genuine concern for keeping budgets balanced, and currency stabilized and convertible. I found greater faith being placed, as contrasted to my observations in 1953, in private competitive enterprise.

The people of the United States are often critical of Latin America for seeming to place greater emphasis on public credit than upon private credit. It is important for us to realize that competitive private enterprise is not precisely the same in each nation to the South as it is in the United States. In this country we have a socially-conscious private enterprise, whose benefits are widespread, and which gives fair returns to capital, management and labor; it is a system that has benefitted all the people, permitting their standards of living to rise to unprecedented heights, with seemingly no end to the advance. In all history its results have not been matched.

But we should be aware of the fact that in some Latin American countries private competitive enterprise may bestow generous benefits upon a relatively few, and only meager benefits upon the masses. Tax systems may not adequately reflect the capacities of different groups to carry their fair shares of the total burden. On the other hand, in several South American countries various controls and regulations have been placed on private enterprise which have hampered its ability to contribute to the benefit of the people as a whole.

With gratification I can report that these shortcomings are gradually being overcome in some countries, perhaps as rapidly as normal cultural and intellectual change will permit; but the narrowly-distributed rewards of private enterprise in certain industries and countries still cause undue emphasis to be placed on public credit which can initiate those types of development which obviously are designed for the benefit of large numbers of people.

I believe that a proper coordination of increasing quantities of public and private credit to Latin America, each type supporting the other, will help the people generally to lift their levels of well-being, and that gradually the benefits of private competitive enterprise will be more widely shared. Thus the degree of reliance on private credit which we deem appropriate will in time be achieved. In the meantime, patience grounded on understanding will be helpful.

As to tax incentives to the flow of private capital, the State Department has recently asked leading businessmen to study this problem. Under Secretary C. Douglas Dillon recently stated that

> There is one new incentive in the field of taxation which we are already prepared to adopt. . . . Under United States law, if a foreign government grants a special income-tax reduction in order to attract the United States investor, that investor has to pay to the United States Government whatever has been waived by the foreign government. We are seeking to correct this situation so that tax benefits granted to induce investment abroad can retain their full effect. . . . the United States Government is prepared to consider conventions which . . . would contain a tax-sparing provision that would cure this situation. The only way to accomplish this is by treaty. We invite negotiations.

The Need for Social Development

It is only natural that most of the dollar credits which have been made available in Latin America have been loans repayable either from tax revenues or from the earnings of the enterprises meriting the loans. Beyond this, however, many leaders in Latin America point out the need for "social development": They contend that the lack of housing constitutes their most serious single social problem. They hope a method can be found to make credit available for home, hospital, and related construction. In one country I visited this summer, I was told that nine persons, on the average, live in each small room. Health conditions are sub-standard. Ill individuals are not productive. It is argued that better housing would improved health, attitudes, and productivity; hence that loans for housing construction are merited.

I feel that we should be prepared to assist other countries in improving their health and sanitation facilities. Loans for these purposes have been available in the past and should continue to be. The problem of housing finance is, however, much more difficult. There are situations where extremely low productivity of the worker and low levels of income do not permit the worker to pay the economic cost of what would be considered adequate housing. Even in advanced countries, housing makes very heavy demands on savings, and absorbs a large share of the income of the workers.

The choice is then between subsidizing housing for the individuals concerned or—and this is, of course, a long-range solution—raising productivity and improving the level of income in order to permit the worker to buy or rent adequate housing. While the second is clearly the better course, it is, as I have mentioned, a long-run solution. As to subsidizing housing in one way or another, this is a decision for each individual government; the social and political implications of such a decision are far-reaching and it does not appear that foreign governments or international institutions should participate in that activity.

A second reason for housing shortages lies in the inflationary conditions existing in some countries. Housing finance is normally long-term financing. In inflationary conditions, a long-term loan, expressed in monetary terms as it must be, will have lost much of its purchasing power by the time the loan is repaid. Under these conditions, domestic lenders are not prepared to put their money into mortages.

A third explanation of the housing problem is found in the rapid growth of cities. In an area where total population is growing rapidly, urban populations are expanding even more sharply. Under the best of economic conditions, a lag in the provision of adequate housing would be expected in these circumstances.

None of these explanations serves to ameliorate the housing conditions. They do indicate, however, that the financial problem is of such an enormous magnitude throughout Latin America, and indeed in other parts of the world, that any attempt to attack it by the use of public international funds would be doomed to failure. At best, the funds available for public lending are limited. If they are to make the greatest possible contribution to the economic development of friendly countries, they must be used primarily in the most productive way. Whatever we may think about the social desirability of improved housing, we cannot assert that investment in housing contributes directly and in the short-term to increased productivity to the same extent as does an investment in transportation, power, irrigation, or manufacturing.

I suggest, therefore, that the nations of Latin America should not look to the United States or to international agencies for significant financial assistance in housing but should pursue vigorously the path of economic development and inflation control in order to enlarge the national product and available savings, and thus widen the margin that can be devoted to improvement of housing.

In a few isolated instances, however, loans for housing might be made by private agencies in the United States. Thus, thousands of Panamanian employees of the Canal Company today recieve sufficiently high wages that they could meet interest and amortization payments on homes at low cost. Local private capital apparently is not now available. The establishment of a Panamanian Housing Agency, with some support from the Panamanian Government, and with substantial credit from one of the private institutions, could quickly initiate a sizeable undertaking, without violating the principles of sound lending.

I refer to this whole matter in this report primarily because housing is high on the agenda of nearly every inter-American conference and in all discussions such as I was privileged to have this summer. Failure to mention the matter now might be misconstrued in Latin America as indifference to the problem.

The Need for Regional Common Markets

Closely related to credit requirements is the need for Latin America to develop a common market.

A special committee under the aegis of the Economic and Social Council of the United Nations recently published an excellent study which sets out the advantages that would accrue to the Latin American nations if they were to develop a common market: the free movement of goods, services, and individuals, without tariffs or other impediments, across national boundaries. But a common market for all twenty republics is at best remote. Hence, I attach great importance to the fact that in Central America, and possibly in Panama, there is today a favorable attitude toward the construction of a regional common market.

I would point out the obvious: If each of the States of the United States were an independent nation, each with tariff and other barriers, the people of this country would today have a very low standard of living. We have a vast common market available to us at all times, enabling each industry to locate at the point of greatest efficiency of production, and to sell in large volume, without restriction, to 176,000,000 people. Over a long period of years, our growing efficiency has enabled us to increase the quality of products and to lower prices (in terms of a stable dollar), so that both essential goods and luxury items are available to most citizens of the United States at reasonable cost.

Many countries of Latin America are smaller than most of our States. It is difficult, if not impossible, for a steel mill, or an aluminum or cement plant, to be successfully operated in one of them, with its market severely restricted; in such circumstances, an industry cannot develop the efficiency which would permit it to sell products in competition with those produced by United States, Canadian, and European industries.

In my judgment, this, more than any other fact, is responsible for the slow rate of industrialization of many Latin American nations, and therefore for their precarious dependence upon the export of a single commodity, such as coffee or tin.

The five nations of Central America have agreed upon certain initial principles, looking to the creation of a regional common market. They will permit free movements of persons; by agreement, they will foster the establishment of a single new industry in each of the five countries, with unrestricted privilege of selling in the entire area; this accomplished, they will proceed to try to establish a second new industry in each country.

This may be a halting and even faulty beginning, but it is a beginning, and deserves open encouragement from the United States.

I recommend that, after careful preparation through appropriate channels, the United States participate with the five republics of Central America, and Panama if possible, in a regional conference, either at the Ministerial or technical level, to stimulate public and private lending institutions, and private industrial enterprises, to take a positive approach in helping Central America and Panama to the end that new industries, guaranteed free access to the entire market of the participating countries, would be established; that every effort be made to have this development serve as a model for all of Latin America; and that such steps as may be deemed appropriate be taken to encourage the northern group of South American countries, and the southern group of South American countries, to consider the creation of common regional markets in those areas.

The Need for Price Stabilization

One of the most complex problems in Latin America derives from the fact that raw commodity prices are continuously changing. I have previously pointed out that this has evoked detrimental misunderstandings; it is a substantive problem of real import.

Fifteen nations of Latin America produce coffee. In several of them, the sale of coffee to the United States accounts for as much as eighty-five per cent of their exports to us; the dollars earned through the sale of coffee are used for the purchase of equipment and manufactured and processed goods. If the price of coffee declines, the economic and political stability of the producing nation may be threatened.

Coffee is now being over-produced. Production is increasing at a faster rate than consumption: Production is growing at an annual rate of more than five per cent, but consumption is increasing only two or three percent a year. Hence raw coffee prices, now deemed by Latin America to be too low, are further threatened. In one country, a one-cent drop in the price of coffee causes a loss of eight million dollars in export earnings. That is catastrophic to a country ridden with debt and suffering from a very low income.

It is not surprising that the producing nations instinctively look to the United States, the largest consumer of coffee, for cooperation and assistance.

The United States, with sympathetic understanding of the seriousness of this problem to the producing nations, has helped to create an international coffee study group which, I am sure, is causing experts in the field to stop chasing shadows—to cease directing criticism where criticism is not due. Now, instead, all the facts about changing production, consumption, quotas, surpluses, and tax impediments are being objectively analyzed, and from these facts possible courses of action are being carefully considered.

Already producing nations of this hemisphere (it would be better of course if the six producing nations of Africa could also be induced to cooperate) have developed an Inter-American coffee marketing agreement. The hope is that the orderly movement of coffee to market in harmony with demand will help to stabilize the market. Brazil is withholding 40 per cent of its coffee from market; Colombia, 15 per cent; smaller producers, 10 per cent; the smallest producers, 5 per cent.

I recommend that the United States, if requested to do so, cooperate to the extent of furnishing such information as laws and regulations permit to assist the producing countries in enforcing agreed-upon marketing quotas.

I do not believe that we should go beyond this. Further, in cooperating, we should make certain facts and possibilities abundantly clear to the producing nations.

We in the United States for twenty-five years have sought through governmental programs to support agricultural prices—to achieve what we call "parity" of relationship between agricultural and industrial prices. We are now spending more than six billion dollars a year on this effort within a single country. The price relationship achieved, while helpful to farmers and hence to our entire economy, has not, save in war-time, reached the goal of "parity." With reasonably satisfactory prices, production control has proved difficult. We have accumulated huge surpluses. The storage charges on them are a million dollars a day. Even with a billion dollars of Federal funds each year (P. L. 480) to help dispose of these surpluses, we find it extremely difficult to do so without causing new problems for other countries. Thus, our recent efforts to reduce the cotton surplus have caused economic difficulty in two Latin American countries, and the shipment of rice to another has hurt one of the smallest South American nations.

This experience, involving only one nation, suggests the difficulty of having stabilization programs succeed when many nations are involved. It should be a pointed warning to the producing nations not to place too great faith on marketing quotas for coffee. If such quotas do for a time stabilize the price of coffee at a fairly good level, this in itself could further stimulate production, cause the accumulation of additional surpluses, and lead eventually to the collapse of world coffee prices.

Any commodity stabilization plan must be accompanied by unrelenting efforts to broaden coffee markets, reduce production costs, increase quality, and divert high-cost acres (in terms of coffee production) from that commodity to other crops for domestic consumption or export.

It is worth point out that if certain nations of the world purchased as much coffee per capita as do the people of the United States, the coffee surplus would quickly disappear. One prosperous European nation now has two types of taxes on coffee, and these greatly diminish the consumption of coffee. If the producing nations could persuade this country to eliminate the regressive taxes, consumption might well increase fully two million bags a year. I mention this in order to emphasize that the producing nations should not look exclusively to the United States for the solution to this problem; more than this, they should not look primarily here for that solution. This must be self-evident. Either they must sell more or produce less.

The problem of price fluctuations in coffee is repeated in varying degrees with respect to nearly every major commodity which Latin America sells to the world. While the relationship of raw commodity and industrial prices is more favorable to Latin America than it once was, especially prior to World War II, nonetheless it must be said that the recent deterioration in Latin America's terms of trade represents a serious problem for the area.

This does not imply that I believe we should participate in a gigantic hemisphere scheme to stabilize prices artificially. Such an effort would violate most of our basic economic tenets; quite apart from principle, the attempt would fail dismally. The Western Hemisphere is not isolated from the rest of the world. Nearly every product produced in Latin America is also produced in other regions.

Some remedial measures in selected situations can be taken by the producing nations of the world, and in many of these situations they do not need to look to the United States for a helping hand. Thus the six or seven producers of tin were cooperating fruitfully for several years in delivering tin ore to world markets in such a fashion as to avoid serious ups and downs in prices. This was of crucial importance to Bolivia, which must earn dollars and sterling through the sale of tin ore in order to buy food for her people, who have an average per capita income of less than one hundred dollars a year. Then Russia, evidently for no other reason than to scuttle this cooperative effort, dumped thousands of tons of tin upon the world market, causing temporary chaos.

Other instances indicate that Russia intends to disrupt markets to the detriment of Latin America whenever she can, and then seek to place the blame on the largest purchaser of Latin America's raw commodities, the United States. Russia has bartered for certain Latin American commodities, only later at strategic times to dump them back on the open markets of the world.

But while the United States should not and cannot become a party to unworkable, artificial plans to stabilize prices of most commodities—and this should always be made clear—nonetheless much is to be gained by having study groups, similar to that for coffee, obtain and analyze all the facts with respect to each major commodity: information about total production, production costs, present and potential market demand; trends in uses of the commodity, and so on. The facts, when developed, should be widely distributed, especially in producing nations, not only among experts, but among the masses of the people, whose understanding is essential.

I recommend that the United States, when requested by producing nations, partici- pate in single-commodity study groups, giving every possible technical assistance, but always making clear that our participation in no way implies subsequent cooperation in plans the producing nations might develop to stabilize prices.

The Need for Technical Cooperation

The technical cooperation program of the United States, now world-wide, origi- nated in our programs with Latin America. They have been helpful to the participating Latin American countries. They have promoted agricultural efficiency and diversifi- cation, brought higher standards of health and thus of productivity, helped foster better education, and promoted more skillful management in many enterprises.

We are now spending about $32,000,000 a year on technical cooperation programs in this hemisphere, not counting payments to the Organization of American States and the United Nations which also have certain specialized technical programs in some of the republics. I recommend a modest increase in these programs.

Theoretically, all United States activities within a country of Latin America (as in other countries of the world) are under the coordinating direction of the United States Ambassador. This is not sufficient.

I recommend that the technical cooperation program for Latin America be under the direct supervision of the Ambassador in each country.

I further recommend that the Assistant Secretary of State for Inter-American affairs be given authority under the general guidance of the Under Secretary of State for Economic Affairs, to coordinate the technical cooperation programs in Latin American nations with the diplomatic, social, cultural and other activities over which he has cognizance.

The Need To Up-Grade U.S. Activities Affecting Latin America

In my formal report to you in 1953, and in informal reports in 1957 and 1958, I have expressed my strong conviction that the American Republics are uniquely important to one another: Our economic interdependence is immense; our political interdependence in a threatened world is notable; our cultural interdependence is growing rapidly, and our shared aspirations for freedom, independence, peace with justice, and rising levels of human well-being assure that the cooperative processes in the community of nations can work here. The American nations for many years have been able to settle their intra-hemisphere disputes by peaceful means. They have developed the most effective regional organization in the world—an organization through which they have espoused principles of mutual security, mutual respect, and cooperation that stand as models for all the world.

I believe that this unique relationship merits special organizational recognition in the structure of our Federal Government. I am persuaded that such recognition could be attained without causing misapprehension among other nations or regions. I understand that the Vice President, following his trip to South America this year, became convinced of this.

Special recognition of the interdependence of the American nations would help overcome a persistent misunderstanding of the United States in Latin America—a misunderstanding which I reported in 1953, and which I found this summer still to exist, now with a trace of bitterness: It is a belief that we consider other areas of the world to be more important to our future than is Latin America. Nothing could be further from the truth.

This feeling results from several circumstances. Most of the publicized statements of our top government officials, executive and legislative, tend to deal with the crisis areas of the world, not with Latin America. Latin America feels that the vast expenditures under the European Recovery Program, in which she did not participate directly, notwithstanding her indirect gains from it, and under the Mutual Security Act, in which she has participated only to a minor degree, demonstrate our preoccupation with other nations, especially since Latin America has not at the same time been able to obtain loans in desired volume. While our attitude toward Latin America with respect to the principles of mutual respect, juridical equality of states, and non-intervention in their internal affairs has been exemplary for twenty-five years, nonetheless they have lingering memories of previous periods when the United States had a patronizing attitude toward their countries, sometimes intervened in internal affairs, and occasionally engaged in outright imperialism. Their apprehensiveness might well disappear, after a quarter of a century of sound policies and relationships, were it not for the other two factors I have just mentioned.

Of course neither of these two factors actually supports what they believe. I have elsewhere pointed out in detail how our world expenditures under the European Recovery and Mutual Security Acts have brought great benefits to Latin America; that there has not been either discrimination or a lack of appreciation of the high importance we attach to continuing good relations in the Western Hemisphere.

But I emphasize that the belief persists throughout Latin America that we do not by words or deeds demonstrate what we profess.

I have sought to find, in discussions with many officials and others, a method by which we could give continuing expression to our sincere recognition of the interdependence of the American Republics.

I recommend that you establish a Council on Inter-American Affairs, whose task would be to advise with the Secretary of State on all matters of hemispheric importance, bringing to him creative ideas for strengthening relations, and constantly emphasizing by its very existence and public statements the importance which the Government and people of the United States attach to good partnership among the American Republics.

(a) The Secretary of State should be the Chairman of the Council and the Assistant Secretary of State the Vice Chairman. Its membership should include three, perhaps five, American citizens from the fields of business and cultural life who are known to have an abiding interest in Latin America; a member of the Senate Committee on Foreign Relations, a member (from the opposite political party) of the House Committee on Foreign Affairs, and consultants from those agencies of the Federal Government which administer programs of importance to Latin America, including the Treasury, the Export-Import Bank, the Department of Agriculture, the Department of Labor, the Department of Commerce, and the Development Loan Fund.

(b) In its first year, the Council might meet bi-monthly. It should explore with the Secretary of State every aspect of inter-American relations; it should be helpful to the Secretary in informing the American people accurately of critical developments; it should bring ideas from the fields of business, banking, education, and cultural life generally to the Secretary where these would be helpful to solutions of central problems; most important, it should be a constant reminder of the special importance the United States attaches to hemispheric relations. After the first year, it might be sufficient for the Council to meet every three or four months.

(c) The Council should be purely advisory. Its members should accept a special responsibility for promoting understanding in those areas of American life which they represent and among our people generally; they should be helpful to the OAS National Commission in this country, previously recommended in this report; informed and dedicated to Pan Americanism, they might well be available to you and to the Secretary of State for special missions to Latin America from time to time.

(d) The Council should be non-partisan. As assurance of this, both major political parties should be about equally represented in its membership.

The Need to Maintain Stable Trade Relations

In my report of 1953 I said:

> I specifically recommend: . . . That the United States adopt and adhere to trade policies with Latin America which possess stability, and with a minimum of mechanisms permitting the imposition of increased tariffs or quotas. I consider this matter of stability and consistency the outstanding requirement.
>
> The nations of Latin America pay for what they obtain from us. Their purchases from us are governed almost wholly by the volume of our purchases from them.
>
> Occasionally the importation of a particular commodity (into the United States) may cause temporary difficulty for one of our industries. But if we raise the tariff on that commodity, the export sale of other United States commodities is certain to decline. The question then becomes: Which United States industry, if any, should be temporarily disadvantaged? And the change in our tariff may seriously weaken the entire economy of a Latin American nation.

The United States Government, in harmony with the prevailing thought in both the Executive and Legislative branches, has sought generally to refrain from making changes in the rules of international trade which would cause harm in a Latin American nation and which, for the reasons I have cited, would not in fact help the United States as a whole, though might temporarily benefit a particular industry.

However, some of our activities in disposing of agricultural surpluses, and in imposing import quotas, have not been in harmony with the general principles for which we stand.

I understand the reasons which impelled us to take each such action.

Partly through the operation of our own stabilization programs, we had lost a share of the world cotton market which we had long enjoyed. We felt entitled to get back that fair share. Few would argue to the contrary. Criticism can be directed not so much toward this final decision, as toward the changing policy. When we held cotton from the world market, production expanded in several nations of the world, including Mexico and Nicaragua. This was not a calculated scheme on their part to take over a market we had previously enjoyed. It was their natural response to a price situation which made it profitable for them to grow and sell cotton. They not only shifted much acreage to cotton, but they developed many facilities, including transportation, to handle and market it. When we changed the rules of the game and decided to export more cotton, Mexico and Nicaragua suffered substantial loss. They then were compelled to reduce their purchases of goods and services from us.

The difficulty with respect to lead and zinc—which are produced by several Latin American nations—was also some years in developing. Similarly, the eventual imposition of quotas caused economic distress, especially in countries with only a few commodities for export, although I understand a concomitant effect has been the firming up of the market for lead and zinc.

Each nation of the world obviously develops policies and programs in its own interest. The nations of Latin America do this. They would be the first to admit it.

The United States perhaps occupies an unusual position in this regard. It is the free world's creditor and leader. It has a mature, diversified, profitable economy. Sudden changes in rules may have little noticeable national effect (though perceptible local effects) on our economy, and thus the public may be unconcerned, but the same changes may have far-reaching and sometimes disastrous effects upon the economy, level of living, and political stability of a friendly nation.

I have no thought or word of criticism for the final actions which in the two cases cited seemed to be essential to the well-being of the United States.

My earnest suggestion is that the United States maintain as firm a policy of stability in trade relations as it possibly can, recognizing that our own long-time interest as a creditor country and free-world leader requires this; and that in those rare instances where a departure from this policy seems unavoidable, we use every means at our disposal to explain in detail and in advance to affected friendly nations of Latin America the compelling reasons for our actions.

The Need for a Modified Attitude Toward Dictators

Everywhere Vice President Nixon went in South America, and everywhere I went in Central America this year, the charge arose that while the United States treasures freedom and democracy for itself, it is indifferent about these in Latin America—indeed, that we support Latin American dictators. I have previously mentioned this as a serious misunderstanding. It is just that. But I now wish to recommend a change in policy which may seem slight, but I think it is important.

In my visit with Panamanian and Central American leaders this summer, I pointed out with candor that from the beginning of our history until 1933, we had not been very consistent in our policies toward Latin America and that some of our actions in that period had clearly strengthened the hands of dictators. But I also pointed out that at Montevideo in 1933, we agreed to a vital change in policy. We agreed thereafter not to intervene in the internal affairs of our sister republics.

Now, obviously, we cannot at one and the same time refrain from intervention and express judgments regarding the degree of democracy our sister republics have achieved.

We had a few months of optimism regarding this knotty problem in 1945 and 1946 when the foreign Minister of Uruguay proposed that the American nations collectively encourage the development of democratic governments by withholding recognition from those which did not measure up to democratic norms. It seemed logical to maintain that the collective judgment could not be construed as internal intervention, at least by a single nation. The United States supported the proposal. But our neighbors overwhelmingly defeated it.

Since the policy of non-intervention was adopted in 1933, dictatorships in Latin America have steadily declined. Whether this is a result of the policy or a coincidence, I leave to others to argue. My own belief is that one is at least partly the result of the other. Today, only a third as many dictators are in power as were in 1933.

What then, other than constantly reaffirming our hope that all peoples may enjoy the blessings of democracy, can we do about the matter?

I believe the suggestion of Vice President Nixon is sound and would be applauded by Latin America itself—that we have an "abrazo" for democratic leaders, and a formal handshake for dictators. Trivial as this may sound, I recommend that it be our official policy in relations with Latin American leaders and nations.

We have made some honest mistakes in our dealings with dictators. For example, we decorated several of them. Most Latin American nations did the same, and in grander style. Whatever reason impelled them and us to take those actions, I think, in retrospect, we were wrong.

I recommend that we refrain from granting special recognition to a Latin American dictator, regardless of the temporary advantage that might seem to be promised by such an act.

I most emphatically do not believe that we should withdraw our programs from Latin American countries which are ruled by dictators. We should not withdraw or diminish our technical assistance programs, diplomatic missions, loans, or other activities. Reasoning which caused one to feel that we should do so would lead logically to the conclusion that throughout the world we should cease cooperating with any nation in which democracy is not complete. Patently, such a policy would paralyze the conduct of all foreign relations.

Non-recognition and non-cooperation would not help another nation achieve democracy. Most peoples want freedom, though many have never experienced it. By cooperating with them, even through dictators—by keeping open the lines of communication—one may hope that a growing understanding of the strength, glory, and basic morality of democracy will enable the people of a harshly ruled country to achieve and maintain democratic institutions of their own design.

We must be careful in deciding which leader deserves a mere handshake and which an "abrazo." In Latin America one finds widely varying degrees of freedom. At least one nation which today is labeled by some a "dictatorship" has greater freedom of the press, of assembly, of speech, of worship, and of research and teaching, than do several others which are generally conceived to be democratic.

An important consideration it seems to me, is the direction a nation is taking. Throughout Latin America, a strong and irresistible trend toward freedom and democracy is evident. We should watch this trend in each country, and encourage it in any way that may be appropriate, without violating the fundamental policy of non-intervention.

Finally, I may say I do not know of a single act the United States has taken since 1954 that could be construed as granting special or even friendly favors to a dictator in this hemisphere. I state this in fairness to our many diplomatic officials who are on the firing line in international affairs, and who, dedicated to democratic ideals, sometimes must suffer quietly under unjustified criticism. It is true that one dictator has fled to the United States since 1954. What is not generally known, apparently, is that the successor government of his country issued him a diplomatic passport and requested permission for him to enter the United States. By such small acts very great misunderstandings are encouraged.

Conclusion

On the 1958 trip to Panama, Central America and Puerto Rico, my associates and I traveled 9,300 miles, and met with more than 1,200 leaders of government, industry, agriculture, labor, commerce, finance, education, health, and social and cultural institutions. We held candid, informative conversations with them, and they submitted to us nearly 11,000 pages of data and suggestions.

I have given to the Department of State the voluminous material which was presented to me in each of the countries my mission visited. Most of this material deals with specific needs for credit or technical assistance and therefore should be handled through normal governmental channels.

In every country we received a warm, friendly reception. The absence of unfriendly incidents may have confounded those who were looking for sensational headlines, but this very circumstance enabled us, calmly and rationally, to accomplish precisely what we set out to do: to gain a new perspective of the problems, progress, attitudes, and aspirations of the nations visited, as a basis for determining whether new approaches in our policies and programs might strengthen relations among us.

My associates and I are grateful for the many courtesies and kindnesses which were extended to us. The cordial welcome given us is proof of the abiding friendship which exists among the governments and the peoples of the American Republics. It certainly would not have provided any comfort to Communists and others who constantly seek to drive a wedge between us and our friends.

The members of the mission are also indebted to you and Secretary Dulles for giving us the opportunity to represent the Government and people of the United

States in furtherance of a sort of continuing mission which you originally assigned to me five years ago, and which I now assume is concluded. We are unanimous in our conviction that no area in the world is of more importance to us than Latin America, and that no other area matches us in our importance to the future of Latin America. We believe our conversations in the countries visited helped dispel some misunderstandings and clarified many issues.

This trip, like the previous ones, was a rewarding experience.

While everything we did was undertaken as a team, and while I have held lengthy conversations with the other members of the mission since our return, I wish to make clear that this report is submitted solely on my own responsibility. It does not speak for any other member of this or previous missions. Needless to say, I trust that most of the views expressed and the recommendations submitted are acceptable, or at least worthy of consideration. . . .

86. Statement Issued by the State Department on Policy Toward Cuba*

January 15, 1959

Recent statements in the Cuban and American press critical of United States policy in Cuba and of Ambassador [Earl E. T.] Smith reflect a widespread lack of understanding of what United States policy toward Cuba has been.

The policy of the United States with respect to the Cuban revolution has been strictly one of non-intervention in Cuban domestic affairs, and the Ambassador's role has conformed always to this policy. Much as the American people, being free themselves, would have liked to have seen a free democratic system in Cuba, the United States Government was pledged in agreements with its sister republics to a course of nonintervention. Like all the other American Republics, the United States maintained normal diplomatic relations with the Batista government. Under established inter-American policy this did not imply judgment in favor of the domestic policy of that government or against the revolutionary forces. From the time when it became evident that Cuba was undergoing a revolution which had the support of a large segment of the population, the United States demonstrated its determination to avoid all possible involvement in Cuba's internal conflict by suspending all sales and shipments of combat arms to the Batista government. This action coincided with the renewed suspension of constitutional guaranties by the Batista government following a 46-day period during which the suspension had been lifted following the appeal of the United States Government through its Ambassador.

The United States military missions to Cuba were established in 1950 and '51 pursuant to agreements between the United States and Cuba, negotiated with the Prio government. These agreements had as their sole purpose cooperation in the common defense of Cuba and the United States, and of the hemisphere as a whole. The function of the missions was to lend technical advice, facilitate access to United States technical military experience, arrange for the admissions of Cubans to United States

*Department of State Bulletin, Feb. 2, 1959, pp. 162-63.

service schools and academies, and facilitate the procurement of equipment and arms as recommended by the missions for common defense as described above. Similar United States missions are maintained in 19 of the other American Republics. In utilizing for the purpose of putting down the Cuban revolution any part of the equipment that had been provided under the agreement prior to the arms suspension or the small unit that had been previously trained and constituted expressly for the common defense, the government of Batista acted in disregard of the agreement and over the reiterated objections of the United States. No napalm was sold or otherwise provided by the United States for use against the Cuban revolutionaries. Eight napalm bombs were sold in 1955 for demonstration purposes. This sale was approved prior to the existence of the recent revolution in Cuba. By agreement between the Departments of State and Defense, none has been supplied to Cuba since. As for the missions themselves, they had no contact whatever with any military operations against the revolutionaries. They trained no personnel for this purpose. No mission personnel were present at any time in the zones of operation. Therefore, the charge that the United States supplied arms for Batista's operations against the rebels or that the missions assisted these operations in any way is completely false.

87. Agreement of American States, Establishing the Inter-American Development Bank *

April 8, 1959

The countries on whose behalf this Agreement is signed agree to create the Inter-American Development Bank, which shall operate in accordance with the following provisions:

Article I
Purpose and Functions

Section 1. Purpose

The purpose of the Bank shall be to contribute to the acceleration of the process of economic development of the member countries, individually and collectively.

Section 2. Functions

(a) To implement its purpose, the Bank shall have the following functions:

(i) to promote the investment of public and private capital for development purposes;

(ii) to utilize its own capital, funds raised by it in financial markets, and other available resources, for financing the development of the member countries, giving priority to those loans and guarantees that will contribute most effectively to their economic growth;

(iii) to encourage private investment in projects, enterprises, and activities contrib-

---

*Inter-American Institute of International Legal Studies, *The Inter-American System: Its Development and Strengthening* (Dobbs Ferry, N.Y., 1966), pp. 407-36.

uting to economic development and to supplement private investment when private capital is not available on reasonable terms and conditions;

(iv) to cooperate with the member countries to orient their development policies toward a better utilization of their resources, in a manner consistent with the objectives of making their economies more complementary and of fostering the orderly growth of their foreign trade; and

(v) to provide technical assistance for the preparation, financing, and implementation of development plans and projects, including the study of priorities and the formulation of specific project proposals.

(b) In carrying out its functions, the Bank shall cooperate as far as possible with national and international institutions and with private sources supplying investment capital.

Article II
Membership in and Capital of the Bank

Section 1. Membership

(a) The original members of the Bank shall be those members of the Organization of American States which, by the date specified in Article XV, Section 1 (a), shall accept membership in the Bank.

(b) Membership shall be open to other members of the Organization of American States at such times and in accordance with such terms as the Bank may determine.

Section 2. Authorized Capital

(a) The authorized capital stock of the Bank, together with the initial resources of the Fund for Special Operations established in Article IV (hereinafter called the Fund), shall total one billion dollars ($1,000,000,000) in terms of United States dollars of the weight and fineness in effect on January 1, 1959. Of this sum, eight hundred fifty million dollars ($850,000,000) shall constitute the authorized capital stock of the Bank and shall be divided into 85,000 shares having a par value of $10,000 each, which shall be available for subscription by members in accordance with Section 3 of this article.

(b) The authorized capital stock shall be divided into paid-in shares and callable shares. The equivalent of four hundred million dollars ($400,000,000) shall be paid in, and four hundred fifty million dollars ($450,000,000) shall be callable for the purposes specified in Section 4 (a) (ii) of this article.

(c) The capital stock indicated in (a) of this section shall be increased by five hundred million dollars ($500,000,000) in terms of United States dollars of the weight and fineness existing on January 1, 1959, provided that:

(i) the date for payment of all subscriptions established in accordance with Section 4 of this article shall have passed; and

(ii) a regular or special meeting of the Board of Governors, held as soon as possible after the date referred to in subparagraph (i) of this paragraph, shall have approved the above-mentioned increase of five hundred million dollars ($500,000,000) by a three-fourths majority of the total voting power of the member countries.

(d) The increase in capital stock provided for in the preceding paragraph shall be in the form of callable capital.

(e) Notwithstanding the provisions of paragraphs (c) and (d) of this section, the authorized capital stock may be increased when the Board of Governors deems it advisable and in a manner agreed upon by a two-thirds majority of the total number of governors representing not less than three-fourths of the total voting power of the member countries.

Section 3. Subscription of Shares

(a) Each member shall subscribe to shares of the capital stock of the Bank. The number of shares to be subscribed by the original members shall be those set forth in Annex A of this Agreement, which specifies the obligation of each member as to both paid-in and callable capital. The number of shares to be subscribed by other members shall be determined by the Bank.

(b) In case of an increase in capital pursuant to Section 2, paragraph (c) or (e) of this article, each member shall have a right to subscribe, under such conditions as the Bank shall decide, to a proportion of the increase of stock equivalent to the proportion which its stock theretofore subscribed bears to the total capital stock of the Bank. No member, however, shall be obligated to subscribe to any part of such increased capital.

(c) Shares of stock initially subscribed by original members shall be issued at par. Other shares shall be issued at par unless the Bank decides in special circumstances to issue them on other terms.

(d) The liability of the member countries on shares shall be limited to the unpaid portion of their issue price.

(e) Shares of stock shall not be pledged or encumbered in any manner, and they shall be transferable only to the Bank.

Section 4. Payment of Subscriptions

(a) Payment of the subscriptions to the capital stock of the Bank as set forth in Annex A shall be made as follows:

(i) Payment of the amount subscribed by each country to the paid-in capital stock of the Bank shall be made in three installments, the first of which shall be 20 per cent, and the second and third each 40 per cent, of such amount. The first installment shall be paid by each country at any time on or after the date on which this Agreement is signed, and the instrument of acceptance or ratification deposited, on its behalf in accordance with Article XV, Section 1, but not later than September 30, 1960. The remaining two installments shall be paid on such dates as are determined by the Bank, but not sooner than September 30, 1961, and September 30, 1962, respectively.

Of each installment, 50 per cent shall be paid in gold and/or dollars and 50 per cent in the currency of the member.

(ii) The callable portion of the subscription for capital shares of the Bank shall be subject to call only when required to meet the obligations of the Bank created under Article III, Section 4 (ii) and (iii) on borrowings of funds for inclusion in the Bank's ordinary capital resources or guarantees chargeable to such resources. In the event of such a call, payment may be made at the option of the member either in gold, in United States dollars, or in the currency required to discharge the obligations of the Bank for the purpose for which the call is made.

Calls on unpaid subscriptions shall be uniform in percentage on all shares.

(b) Each payment of a member in its own currency under paragraph (a) (i) of this section shall be in such amount as, in the opinion of the Bank, is equivalent to the full value in terms of United States dollars of the weight and fineness in effect on January 1, 1959, of the portion of the subscription being paid. The initial payment shall be in such amount as the member considers appropriate hereunder but shall be subject to such adjustment, to be effected within 60 days of the date on which the payment was due, as the Bank shall determine to be necessary to constitute the full dollar value equivalent as provided in this paragraph.

(c) Unless otherwise determined by the Board of Governors by a three-fourths majority of the total voting power of the member countries, the liability of members for payment of the second and third installments of the paid-in portion of their subscriptions to the capital stock shall be conditional upon payment of not less than 90 per cent of the total obligations of the members due for:

(i) the first and second installments, respectively, of the paid-in portion of the subscriptions; and

(ii) the initial payment and all prior calls on the subscription quotas to the Fund.

Section 5. Ordinary Capital Resources

As used in this Agreement, the term "ordinary capital resources" of the Bank shall be deemed to include the following:

(i) authorized capital, including both paid-in and callable shares, subscribed pursuant to Section 2 and 3 of this article;

(ii) all funds raised by borrowings under the authority of Article VII, Section 1 (i) to which the commitment set forth in Section 4 (a) (ii) of this article is applicable;

(iii) all funds received in repayment of loans made with the resources indicated in (i) and (ii) of this section; and

(iv) all income derived from loans made from the afore-mentioned funds or from guarantees to which the commitment set forth in Section 4 (a) (ii) of this article is applicable.

Article III
Operations

Section 1. Use of Resources

The resources and facilities of the Bank shall be used exclusively to implement the purpose and functions enumerated in Article I of this Agreement.

Section 2. Ordinary and Special Operations

(a) The operations of the Bank shall be divided into ordinary operations and special operations.

(b) The ordinary operations shall be those financed from the Bank's ordinary capital resources, as defined in Article II, Section 5, and shall relate exclusively to loans made, participated in, or guaranteed by the Bank which are repayable only in the respective currency or currencies in which the loans were made. Such operations shall be subject to the terms and conditions that the Bank deems advisable, consistent with the provisions of this Agreement.

(c) The special operations shall be those financed from the resources of the Fund in accordance with the provisions of Article IV.

Section 3. Basic Principle of Separation

(a) The ordinary capital resources of the Bank as defined in Article II, Section 5, shall at all times and in all respects be held, used, obligated, invested, or otherwise disposed of entirely separate from the resources of the Fund, as defined in Article IV, Section 3 (h).

The financial statements of the Bank shall show the ordinary operations of the Bank and the operations of the Fund separately, and the Bank shall establish such other administrative rules as may be necessary to ensure the effective separation of the two types of operations.

The ordinary capital resources of the Bank shall under no circumstances be charged with, or used to discharge, losses or liabilities arising out of operations for which the resources of the Fund were originally used or committed.

(b) Expenses pertaining directly to ordinary operations shall be charged to the ordinary capital resources of the Bank. Expenses pertaining directly to special operations shall be charged to the resources of the Fund. Other expenses shall be charged as the Bank determines.

Section 4. Methods of Making or Guaranteeing Loans

Subject to the conditions stipulated in this article, the Bank may make or guarantee loans to any member, or any agency or political subdivision thereof, and to any enterprise in the territory of a member, in any of the following ways:

(i) by making or participating in direct loans with funds corresponding to the unimpaired paid-in capital and, except as provided in Section 13 of this article, to its reserves and undistributed surplus; or with the unimpaired resources of the Fund;

(ii) by making or participating in direct loans with funds raised by the Bank in capital markets, or borrowed or acquired in any other manner for inclusion in the ordinary capital resources of the Bank or the resources of the Fund, and

(iii) by guaranteeing in whole or in part loans made, except in special cases, by private investors.

Section 5. Limitations on Ordinary Operations

(a) The total amount outstanding of loans and guarantees made by the Bank in its ordinary operations shall not at any time exceed the total amount of the unimpaired subscribed capital of the Bank, plus the unimpaired reserves and surplus included in the ordinary capital resources of the Bank, as defined in Article II, Section 5, exclusive of income assigned to the special reserve established pursuant to Section 13 of this article and other income assigned by decision of the Board of Governors to reserves not available for loans or guarantees.

(b) In the case of loans made out of funds borrowed by the Bank to which the obligations provided for in Article II, Section 4 (a) (ii) are applicable, the total amount of principal outstanding and payable to the Bank in a specific currency shall at no time exceed the total amount of principal of the outstanding borrowings by the Bank that are payable in the same currency.

Section 6. Direct Loan Financing

In making direct loans or participating in them, the Bank may provide financing in any of the following ways:

(a) By furnishing the borrower currencies of members, other than the currency of the member in whose territory the project is to be carried out, that are necessary to meet the foreign exchange costs of the project.

(b) By providing financing to meet expenses related to the purposes of the loan in the territories of the member in which the project is to be carried out. Only in special cases, particularly when the project indirectly gives rise to an increase in the demand for foreign exchange in that country, shall the financing granted by the Bank to meet local expenses be provided in gold or in currencies other than that of such member; in such cases, the amount of the financing granted by the Bank for this purpose shall not exceed a reasonable portion of the local expenses incurred by the borrower.

Section 7. Rules and Conditions for Making or Guaranteeing Loans

(a) The Bank may make or guarantee loans subject to the following rules and conditions:

(i) the applicant for the loan shall have submitted a detailed proposal and the staff of the Bank shall have presented a written report recommending the proposal after a study of its merits. In special circumstances, the Board of Executive Directors, by a majority of the total voting power of the member countries, may require that a proposal be submitted to the Board for decision in the absence of such a report;

(ii) in considering a request for a loan or a guarantee, the Bank shall take into account the ability of the borrower to obtain the loan from private sources of financing on terms which, in the opinion of the Bank, are reasonable for the borrower, taking into account all pertinent factors;

(iii) in making or guaranteeing a loan, the Bank shall pay due regard to prospects that the borrower and its guarantor, if any, will be in a position to meet their obligations under the loan contract;

(iv) in the opinion of the Bank, the rate of interest, other charges and the schedule for repayment of principal are appropriate for the project in question;

(v) in guaranteeing a loan made by other investors, the Bank shall receive suitable compensation for its risk, and

(vi) loans made or guaranteed by the Bank shall be principally for financing specific projects, including those forming part of a national or regional development program. However, the Bank may make or guarantee over-all loans to development institutions or similar agencies of the members in order that the latter may facilitate the financing of specific development projects whose individual financing requirements are not, in the opinion of the Bank, large enough to warrant the direct supervision of the Bank.

(b) The Bank shall not finance any undertaking in the territory of a member if that member objects to such financing.

Section 8. Optional Conditions for Making or Guaranteeing Loans

(a) In the case of loans or guarantees of loans to nongovernmental entities, the Bank may, when it deems it advisable, require that the member in whose territory the project is to be carried out, or a public institution or a similar agency of the member acceptable to the Bank, guarantee the repayment of the principal and the payment of interest and other charges on the loan.

(b) The Bank may attach such other conditions to the making of loans or guarantees as it deems appropriate, taking into account both the interests of the members directly involved in the particular loan or guarantee proposal and the interests of the members as a whole.

Section 9. Use of Loans Made or Guaranteed by the Bank

(a) Except as provided in Article V, Section 1, the Bank shall impose no condition that the proceeds of a loan shall be spent in the territory of any particular country nor that such proceeds shall not be spent in the territories of any particular member or members.

(b) The Bank shall take the necessary measures to ensure that the proceeds of any loan made, guaranteed, or participated in by the Bank are used only for the purposes for which the loan was granted, with due attention to considerations of economy and efficiency.

Section 10. Payment Provisions for Direct Loans

Direct loan contracts made by the Bank in conformity with Section 4 (i) or (ii) of this article shall establish:

(a) All the terms and conditions of each loan, including among others, provision for payment of principal, interest and other charges, maturities, and dates of payment; and

(b) The currency or currencies in which payments shall be made to the Bank.

Section 11. Guarantees

(a) In guaranteeing a loan the Bank shall charge a guarantee fee, at a rate determined by the Bank, payable periodically on the amount of the loan outstanding.

(b) Guarantee contracts concluded by the Bank shall provide that the Bank may terminate its liability with respect to interest if, upon default by the borrower and by the guarantor, if any, the Bank offers to purchase, at par and interest accrued to a date designated in the offer, the bonds or other obligations guaranteed.

(c) In issuing guarantees, the Bank shall have power to determine any other terms and conditions.

Section 12. Special Commission

On all loans, participations, or guarantees made out of or by commitment of the ordinary capital resources of the Bank, the latter shall charge a special commission. The special commission, payable periodically, shall be computed on the amount outstanding on each loan, participation, or guarantee and shall be at the rate of one per cent per annum, unless the Bank, by a two-thirds majority of the total voting power of the member countries, decides to reduce the rate of commission.

Section 13. Special Reserve

The amount of commissions received by the Bank under Section 12 of this article shall be set aside as a special reserve, which shall be kept for meeting liabilities of the Bank in accordance with Article VII, Section 3 (b) (i). The special reserve shall be held in such liquid form, permitted under this Agreement, as the Board of Executive Directors may decide.

Article IV
Fund for Special Operations

Section 1. Establishment, Purpose, and Functions

A Fund for Special Operations is established for the making of loans on terms and conditions appropriate for dealing with special circumstances arising in specific countries or with respect to specific projects.

The Fund, whose administration shall be entrusted to the Bank, shall have the purpose and functions set forth in Article I of this Agreement.

Section 2. Applicable Provisions

The Fund shall be governed by the provisions of the present article and all other provisions of this Agreement, excepting those inconsistent with the provisions of the present article and those expressly applying only to the ordinary operations of the Bank.

Section 3. Resources

(a) The original members of the Bank shall contribute to the resources of the Fund in accordance with the provisions of this section.

(b) Members of the Organization of American States that join the Bank after the date specified in Article XV, Section 1 (a) shall contribute to the Fund with such quotas, and under such terms, as may be determined by the Bank.

(c) The Fund shall be established with initial resources in the amount of one hundred fifty million dollars (150,000,000) in terms of United States dollars of the weight and fineness in effect on January 1, 1959, which shall be contributed by the original members of the Bank in accordance with the quotas specified in Annex B.

(d) Payment of the quotas shall be made as follows:

(i) Fifty per cent of its quota shall be paid by each member at any time on or after the date on which this Agreement is signed, and the instrument of acceptance or ratification deposited, on its behalf in accordance with Article XV, Section 1, but not later than September 30, 1960.

(ii) The remaining 50 per cent shall be paid at any time subsequent to one year after the Bank has begun operations, in such amounts and at such times as are determined by the Bank; provided, however, that the total amount of all quotas shall be made due and payable not later than the date fixed for payment of the third installment of the subscriptions to the paid-in capital stock of the Bank.

(iii) The payments required under this section shall be distributed among the members in proportion to their quotas and shall be made one half in gold and/or United States dollars, and one half in the currency of the contributing member.

(e) Each payment of a member in its own currency under the preceding paragraph shall be in such amount as, in the opinion of the Bank, is equivalent to the full value, in terms of United States dollars of the weight and fineness in effect on January 1, 1959, of the portion of the quota being paid. The initial payment shall be in such amount as the member considers appropriate hereunder but shall be subject to such adjustment, to be effected within 60 days of the date on which payment was due, as the Bank shall determine to be necessary to constitute the full dollar value equivalent as provided in this paragraph.

(f) Unless otherwise determined by the Board of Governors by a three-fourths majority of the total voting power of the member countries, the liability of members for payment of any call on the unpaid portion of their subscription quotas to the Fund shall be conditional upon payment of not less than 90 per cent of the total obligations of the members for:

(i) the initial payment and all prior calls on such quota subscriptions to the Fund; and

(ii) any installments due on the paid-in portion of the subscriptions to the capital stock of the Bank.

(g) The resources of the Fund shall be increased through additional contributions by the members when the Board of Governors considers it advisable by a three-fourths majority of the total voting power of the member countries. The provisions of Article II, Section 3 (b), shall apply to such increases, in terms of the proportion between the quota in effect for each member and the total amount of the resources of the Fund contributed by members.

(h) As used in this Agreement, the terms "resources of the Fund" shall be deemed to include the following:

(i) contributions by members pursuant to paragraphs (c) and (g) of this section;

(ii) all funds raised by borrowing to which the commitment stipulated in Article II, Section 4 (a) (ii) is not applicable, i.e., those that are specifically chargeable to the resources of the Fund;

(iii) all funds received in repayment of loans made from the resources mentioned above;

(iv) all income derived from operations using or commiting any of the resources mentioned above; and

(v) any other resources at the disposal of the Fund.

Section 4. Operations

(a) The operations of the Fund shall be those financed from its own resources, as defined in Section 3 (h) of the present article.

(b) Loans made with resources of the Fund may be partially or wholly repayable in the currency of the member in whose territory the project being financed will be carried out. The part of the loan not repayable in the currency of the member shall be paid in the currency or currencies in which the loan was made.

Section 5. Limitation on Liability

In the operations of the Fund, the financial liability of the Bank shall be limited to the resources and reserves of the Fund, and the liability of members shall be limited to the unpaid portion of their respective quotas that has become due and payable.

Section 6. Limitation on Disposition of Quotas

The rights of members of the Bank resulting from their contributions to the Fund may not be transferred or encumbered, and members shall have no right of reimbursement of such contributions except in cases of loss of the status of membership or of termination of the operations of the Fund.

Section 7. Discharge of Fund Liabilities on Borrowings

Payments in satisfaction of any liability on borrowings of funds for inclusion in the resources of the Fund shall be charged:

(i) first, against any reserve established for this purpose; and

(ii) then, against any other funds available in the resources of the Fund.

Section 8. Administration

(a) Subject to the provisions of this Agreement, the authorities of the Bank shall have full powers to administer the Fund.

(b) There shall be a Vice President of the Bank in charge of the Fund. The Vice President shall participate in the meetings of the Board of Executive Directors of the Bank, without vote, whenever matters relating to the Fund are discussed.

(c) In the operations of the Fund the Bank shall utilize to the fullest extent possible the same personnel, experts, installations, offices, equipment, and services as it uses for its ordinary operations.

(d) The Bank shall publish a separate annual report showing the results of the Fund's financial operations, including profits or losses. At the annual meeting of the Board of Governors there shall be at least one session devoted to consideration of this report. In addition, the Bank shall transmit to the members a quarterly summary of the Fund's operations.

Section 9. Voting

(a) In making decisons concerning operations of the Fund, each member country of the Bank shall have the voting power in the Board of Governors accorded to it pursuant to Article VIII, Section 4 (a) and (b), and each Director shall have the voting power in the Board of Executive Directors accorded to him pursuant to Article VIII, Section 4 (a) and (c).

(b) All decisions of the Bank concerning the operations of the Fund shall be adopted by a two-thirds majority of the total voting power of the member countries, unless otherwise provided in this article.

Section 10. Distribution of Net Profits

The Board of Governors of the Bank shall determine what portion of the net profits of the Fund shall be distributed among the members after making provision for reserves. Such net profits shall be shared in proportion to the quotas of the members.

Section 11. Withdrawal of Contributions

(a) No country may withdraw its contribution and terminate its relations with the Fund while it is still a member of the Bank.

(b) The provisions of Article IX, Section 3, with respect to the settlement of accounts with countries that terminate their membership in the Bank also shall apply to the Fund.

Section 12. Suspension and Termination

The provisions of Article X also shall apply to the Fund with substitution of terms relating to the Fund and its resources and respective creditors for those relating to the Bank and its ordinary capital resources and respective creditors.

Article V
Currencies

Section 1. Use of Currencies

(a) The currency of any member held by the Bank, either in its ordinary capital resources or in the resources of the Fund, however acquired, may be used by the Bank and by any recipient from the Bank, without restriction by the member, to make payments for goods and services produced in the territory of such member.

(b) Members may not maintain or impose restrictions of any kind upon the use the Bank or by any recipient from the Bank, for payments in any country, of the following:

(i) gold and dollars received by the Bank in payment of the 50 per cent portion of each member's subscription to shares of the Bank's capital and of the 50 per cent portion of each member's quota for contribution to the Fund, pursuant to the provisions of Article II and Article IV, respectively;

(ii) currencies of members purchased with the gold and dollar funds referred to in (i) of this paragraph;

(iii) currencies obtained by borrowings, pursuant to the provisions of Article VII, Section 1 (i), for inclusion in the ordinary capital resources of the Bank;

(iv) gold and dollars received by the Bank in payment on account of principal, interest, and other charges, of loans made from the gold and dollar funds referred to in (i) of this paragraph; currencies recieved in payment of principal, interest, and other charges, of loans made from currencies referred to in (ii) and (iii) of this paragraph; and currencies received in payment of commissions and fees on all guarantees made by the Bank; and

(v) currencies, other than the member's own currency, received from the Bank pursuant to Article VII, Section 4 (c) and Article IV, Section 10, in distribution of net profits.

(c) A member's currency held by the Bank, either in its ordinary capital resources or in the resources of the Fund, not covered by paragraph (b) of this section, also may be used by the Bank or any recipient from the Bank for payments in any country without restriction of any kind, unless the member notifies the Bank of its desire that such currency or a portion thereof be restricted to the uses specified in paragraph (a) of this section.

(d) Members may not place any restrictions on the holding and use by the Bank, for making amortization payments or anticipating payment of, or repurchasing part or all of, the Bank's own obligations, of currencies received by the Bank in repayment of direct loans made from borrowed funds included in the ordinary capital resources of the Bank.

(e) Gold or currency held by the Bank in its ordinary capital resources or in the resources of the Fund shall not be used by the Bank to purchase other currencies unless authorized by a two-thirds majority of the total voting power of the member countries.

Section 2. Valuation of Currencies

Whenever it shall become necessary under this Agreement to value any currency in terms of another currency, or in terms of gold, such valuation shall be determined by the Bank after consultation with the International Monetary Fund.

Section 3. Maintenance of Value of the Currency Holdings of the Bank

(a) Whenever the par value in the International Monetary Fund of a member's currency is reduced or the foreign exchange value of a member's currency has, in the opinion of the Bank, depreciated to a significant extent, the member shall pay to the Bank within a reasonable time an additional amount of its own currency sufficient to maintain the value of all the currency of the member held by the Bank in its ordinary capital resources, or in the resources of the Fund, excepting currency derived from borrowings by the Bank. The standard of value for this purpose shall be the United States dollar of the weight and fineness in effect on January 1, 1959.

(b) Whenever the par value in the International Monetary Fund of a member's currency is increased or the foreign exchange of such member's currency has, in the opinion of the Bank, appreciated to a significant extent, the Bank shall return to such member within a reasonable time an amount of that member's currency equal to the increase in the value of the amount of such currency which is held by the Bank in its ordinary capital resources or in the resources of the Fund, excepting currency derived from borrowings by the Bank. The standard of value for this purpose shall be the same as that established in the preceding paragraph.

(c) The provisions of this section may be waived by the Bank when a uniform proportionate change in the par value of the currencies of all the Bank's members is made by the International Monetary Fund.

Section 4. Methods of Conserving Currencies

The Bank shall accept from any member promissory notes or similar securities issued by the government of the member, or by the depository designated by each member, in lieu of any part of the currency of the member representing the 50 per cent portion of its subscription to the Bank's authorized capital and the 50 per cent portion of its subscription to the resources of the Fund, which, pursuant to the provisions of Article II and Article IV, respectively, are payable by each member in its national currency, provided such currency is not required by the Bank for the conduct of its operations. Such promissory notes or securities shall be non-negotiable, non-interest-bearing, and payable to the Bank at their par value on demand.

Article VI
Technical Assistance

Section 1. Provision of Technical Advice and Assistance

The Bank may, at the request of any member or members, or of private firms that may obtain loans from it, provide technical advice and assistance in its field of activity, particularly on:

(i) the preparation, financing, and execution of development plans and projects, including the consideration of priorities, and the formulation of loan proposals on specific national or regional development projects; and

(ii) the development and advanced training, through seminars and other forms of instruction, of personnel specializing in the formulation and implementation of development plans and projects.

Section 2. Cooperative Agreements on Technical Assistance

In order to accomplish the purposes of this article, the Bank may enter into agreements on technical assistance with other national or international institutions, either public or private.

Section 3. Expenses

(a) The Bank may arrange with member countries or firms receiving technical assistance, for reimbursement of the expenses of furnishing such assistance on terms which the Bank deems appropriate.

(b) The expenses of providing technical assistance not paid by the recipients shall be met from the net income of the Bank or of the Fund. However, during the first three years of the Bank's operations, up to three per cent, in total, of the initial resources of the Fund may be used to meet such expenses.

Article VII
Miscellaneous Powers and Distribution of Profits

Section 1. Miscellaneous Powers of the Bank

In addition to the powers specified elsewhere in this Agreement, the Bank shall have the power to:

(i) borrow funds and in that connection to furnish such collateral or other security therefor as the Bank shall determine, provided that, before making a sale of its obligations in the markets of a country, the Bank shall have obtained the approval of that country and of the member in whose currency the obligations are denominated. In addition, in the case of borrowings of funds to be included in the Bank's ordinary capital resources, the Bank shall obtain agreement of such countries that the proceeds may be exchanged for the currency of any other country without restriction;

(ii) buy and sell securities it has issued or guaranteed or in which it has invested, provided that the Bank shall obtain the approval of the country in whose territories the securities are to be bought or sold;

(iii) with the approval of a two-thirds majority of the total voting power of the member countries, invest funds not needed in its operations in such obligations as it may determine;

(iv) guarantee securities in its portfolio for the purpose of facilitating their sale; and

(v) exercise such other powers as shall be necessary or desirable in furtherance of its purpose and functions, consistent with the provisions of this Agreement.

Section 2. Warning to be Placed on Securities

Every security issued or guaranteed by the Bank shall bear on its face a conspicuous statement to the effect that it is not an obligation of any government, unless it is in fact the obligation of a particular government, in which case it shall so state.

Section 3. Methods of Meeting Liabilities of the Bank in Case of Defaults

(a) The Bank, in the event of actual or threatened default on loans made or guaranteed by the Bank using its ordinary capital resources, shall take such action as it deems appropriate with respect to modifying the terms of the loan, other than the currency of repayment.

(b) The payments in discharge of the Bank's liabilities on borrowings or guarantees under Article III, Section 4 (ii) and (iii) chargeable against the ordinary capital resources of the Bank shall be charged:

(i) first, against the special reserve provided for in Article III, Section 13; and

(ii) then, to the extent necessary and at the discretion of the Bank, against the other reserves, surplus, and funds corresponding to the capital paid in for shares.

(c) Whenever necessary to meet contractual payments of interest, other charges, or amortization on the Bank's borrowings, or to meet the Bank's liabilities with respect to similar payments on loans guaranteed by it chargeable to its ordinary capital resources, the Bank may call upon the members to pay an appropriate amount of their callable capital subscriptions, in accordance with Article II, Section 4 (a) (ii). Moreover, if the Bank believes that a default may be of long duration, it may call an additional part of such subscriptions not to exceed in any one year one per cent of the total subscriptions of the members, for the following purposes:

(i) to redeem prior to maturity, or otherwise discharge its liability on, all or part of the outstanding principal of any loan guaranteed by it in respect of which the debtor is in default; and

(ii) to repurchase, or otherwise discharge its liability on, all or part of its own outstanding obligations.

Section 4. Distribution of Net Profits and Surplus

(a) The Board of Governors may determine periodically what part of the net profits and of the surplus shall be distributed. Such distributions may be made only when the reserves have reached a level which the Board of Governors considers adequate.

(b) The distributions referred to in the preceding paragraph shall be made in proportion to the number of shares held by each member.

(c) Payments shall be made in such manner and in such currency or currencies as the Board of Governors shall determine. If such payments are made to a member in currencies other than its own, the transfer of such currencies and their use by the receiving country shall be without restriction by any member.

Article VIII
Organization and Management

Section 1. Structure of the Bank

The Bank shall have a Board of Governors, a Board of Executive Directors, a President, an Executive Vice President, a Vice President in charge of the Fund, and such other officers and staff as may be considered necessary.

Section 2. Board of Governors

(a) All the powers of the Bank shall be vested in the Board of Governors. Each member shall appoint one governor and one alternate, who shall serve for five years, subject to termination of appointment at any time, or to reappointment, at the pleasure of the appointing member. No alternate may vote except in the absence of his principal. The Board shall select one of the governors as Chairman, who shall hold office until the next regular meeting of the Board.

(b) The Board of Governors may delegate to the Board of Executive Directors all its powers except power to:

(i) admit new members and determine the conditions of their admission;

(ii) increase or decrease the authorized capital stock of the Bank and contributions to the Fund;

(iii) elect the President of the Bank and determine his remuneration;

(iv) suspend a member, pursuant to Article IX, Section 2;

(v) determine the remuneration of the executive directors and their alternates;

(vi) hear and decide any appeals from interpretations of this Agreement given by the Board of Executive Directors;

(vii) authorize the conclusion of general agreements for cooperation with other international organizations;

(viii) approve, after reviewing the auditors' report, the general balance sheet and the statement of profit and loss of the institution;

(ix) determine the reserves and the distribution of the net profits of the Bank and of the Fund;

(x) select outside auditors to certify to the general balance sheet and the statement of profit and loss of the institution;

(xi) amend this Agreement; and

(xii) decide to terminate the operations of the Bank and to distribute its assets.

(c) The Board of Governors shall retain full power to exercise authority over any matter delegated to the Board of Executive Directors under paragraph (b) above.

(d) The Board of Governors shall, as a general rule, hold a meeting annually. Other meetings may be held when the Board of Governors so provides or when called by the Board of Executive Directors. Meetings of the Board of Governors also shall be called by the Board of Executive Directors whenever requested by five members of the Bank or by members having one fourth of the total voting power of the member countries.

(e) A quorum for any meeting of the Board of Governors shall be an absolute majority of the total number of governors, representing not less than two thirds of the total voting power of the member countries.

(f) The Board of Governors may establish a procedure whereby the Board of Executive Directors, when it deems such action appropriate, may submit a specific question to a vote of the governors without calling a meeting of the Board of Governors.

(g) The Board of Governors, and the Board of Executive Directors to the extent authorized, may adopt such rules and regulations as may be necessary or appropriate to conduct the business of the Bank.

(h) Governors and alternates shall serve as such without compensation from the Bank, but the Bank may pay them reasonable expenses incurred in attending meetings of the Board of Governors.

Section 3. Board of Executive Directors

(a) The Board of Executive Directors shall be responsible for the conduct of the operations of the Bank, and for this purpose may exercise all the powers delegated to it by the Board of Governors.

(b) There shall be seven executive directors, who shall not be governors, and of whom:

(i) one shall be appointed by the member having the largest number of shares in the Bank;

(ii) six shall be elected by the governors of the remaining members pursuant to the provisions of Annex C of this Agreement.

Executive directors shall be appointed or elected for terms of three years and may be reappointed or re-elected for successive terms. They shall be persons of recognized competence and wide experience in economic and financial matters.

(c) Each executive director shall appoint an alternate who shall have full power to act for him when he is not present. Directors and alternates shall be citizens of the member countries. None of the elected directors and their alternates may be of the same citizenship. Alternates may participate in meetings but may vote only when they are acting in place of their principals.

(d) Directors shall continue in office until their successors are appointed or elected. If the office of an elected director becomes vacant more than 180 days before the end of his term, a successor shall be elected for the remainder of the term by the governors who elected the former director. An absolute majority of the votes cast shall be required for election. While the office remains vacant, the alternate shall have all the powers of the former director except the power to appoint an alternate.

(e) The Board of Executive Directors shall function in continuous session at the principal office of the Bank and shall meet as often as the business of the Bank may require.

(f) A quorum for any meeting of the Board of Executive Directors shall be an absolute majority of the total number of directors representing not less than two thirds of the total voting power of the member countries.

(g) A member of the Bank may send a representative to attend any meeting of the Board of Executive Directors when a matter especially affecting that member is under consideration. Such right of representation shall be regulated by the Board of Governors.

(h) The Board of Executive Directors may appoint such committees as it deems advisable. Membership of such committees need not be limited to governors, directors, or alternates.

(i) The Board of Executive Directors shall determine the basic organization of the Bank, including the number and general responsibilities of the chief administrative and professional positions of the staff, and shall approve the budget of the Bank.

Section 4. Voting

(a) Each member country shall have 135 votes plus one vote for each share of capital stock of the Bank held by that country.

(b) In voting in the Board of Governors, each governor shall be entitled to cast the votes of the member country which he represents. Except as otherwise specifically provided in this Agreement, all matters before the Board of Governors shall be decided by a majority of the total voting power of the member countries.

(c) In voting in the Board of Executive Directors:

(i) the appointed director shall be entitled to cast the number of votes of the member country which appointed him;

(ii) each elected director shall be entitled to cast the number of votes that counted toward his election, which votes shall be cast as a unit; and

(iii) except as otherwise specifically provided in this Agreement, all matters before the Board of Executive Directors shall be decided by a majority of the total voting power of the member countries.

Section 5. President, Executive Vice President, and Staff

(a) The Board of Governors, by an absolute majority of the total number of governors representing not less than a majority of the total voting power of the member countries, shall elect a President of the Bank who, while holding office, shall not be a governor or an executive director or alternate for either.

Under the direction of the Board of Executive Directors, the President of the Bank shall conduct the ordinary business of the Bank and shall be chief of its staff. He also shall be the presiding officer at meetings of the Board of Executive Directors, but shall have no vote, except that it shall be his duty to cast a deciding vote when necessary to break a tie.

The President of the Bank shall be the legal representative of the Bank. The term of office of the President of the Bank shall be five years, and he may be reelected to successive terms. He shall cease to hold office when the Board of Governors so decides by a majority of the total voting power of the member countries.

(b) The Executive Vice President shall be appointed by the Board of Executive Directors on the recommendation of the President of the Bank. Under the direction of the Board of Executive Directors and the President of the Bank, the Executive Vice President shall exercise such authority and perform such functions in the administration of the Bank as may be determined by the Board of Executive Directors. In the absence or incapacity of the President of the Bank, the Executive Vice President shall exercise the authority and perform the functions of the President.

The Executive Vice President shall participate in meetings of the Board of Executive Directors but shall have no vote at such meetings, except that he shall cast the deciding vote, as provided in paragraph (a) of this section, when he is acting in place of the President of the Bank.

(c) In addition to the Vice President referred to in Article IV, Section 8 (b), the Board of Executive Directors may, on recommendation of the President of the Bank, appoint other Vice Presidents who shall exercise such authority and perform such functions as the Board of Executive Directors may determine.

(d) The President, officers, and staff of the Bank, in the discharge of their offices, owe their duty entirely to the Bank and shall recognize no other authority. Each member of the Bank shall respect the international character of this duty.

(e) The paramount consideration in the employment of the staff and in the determination of the conditions of service shall be the necessity of securing the highest standards of efficiency, competence, and integrity. Due regard shall be paid to the importance of recruiting the staff on as wide a geographical basis as possible.

(f) The Bank, its officers and employees shall not interfere in the political affairs of any member, nor shall they be influenced in their decisions by the political character of the member or members concerned. Only economic considerations shall be relevant to their decisions, and these considerations shall be weighed impartially in order to achieve the purpose and functions stated in Article I.

Section 6. Publication of Reports and Provision of Information

(a) The Bank shall publish an annual report containing an audited statement of the accounts. It shall also transmit quarterly to the members a summary statement of the financial position and a profit-and-loss statement showing the results of its ordinary operations.

(b) The Bank may also publish such other reports as it deems desirable to carry out its purpose and functions.

Article IX
Withdrawal and Suspension of Members

Section 1. Right to Withdraw

Any member may withdraw from the Bank by delivering to the Bank at its principal office written notice of its intention to do so. Such withdrawal shall become finally effective on the date specified in the notice but in no event less than six months after the notice is delivered to the Bank. However, at any time before the withdrawal becomes finally effective, the member may notify the Bank in writing of the cancellation of its notice of intention to withdraw.

After withdrawing, a member shall remain liable for all direct and contingent obligations to the Bank to which it was subject at the date of delivery of the withdrawal notice, including those specified in Section 3 of this article. However, if the withdrawal becomes finally effective, the member shall not incur any liability for obligations resulting from operations of the Bank effected after the date on which the withdrawal notice was received by the Bank.

Section 2. Suspension of Membership

If a member fails to fulfill any of its obligations to the Bank, the Bank may suspend its membership by decision of the Board of Governors by a two-thirds majority of the total number of governors representing not less than three fourths of the total voting power of the member countries.

The member so suspended shall automatically cease to be a member of the Bank one year from the date of its suspension unless the Board of Governors decides by the same majority to terminate the suspension.

While under suspension, a member shall not be entitled to exercise any rights under this Agreement, except the right of withdrawal, but shall remain subject to all its obligations.

Section 3. Settlement of Accounts

(a) After a country ceases to be a member, it no longer shall share in the profits or losses of the Bank, nor shall it incur any liability with respect to loans and guarantees entered into by the Bank thereafter. However, it shall remain liable for all amounts it owes the Bank and for its contingent liabilities to the Bank so long as any part of the loans or guarantees contracted by the Bank before the date on which the country ceased to be a member remains outstanding.

(b) When a country ceases to be a member, the Bank shall arrange for the repurchase of such country's capital stock as a part of the settlement of accounts pursuant to the provisions of this section; but the country shall have no other rights under this Agreement except as provided in this section and in Article XIII, Section 2.

(c) The Bank and the country ceasing to be a member may agree on the repurchase of the capital stock on such terms as are deemed appropriate in the circumstances, without regard to the provisions of the following paragraph. Such agreement may provide, among other things, for a final settlement of all obligations of the country to the Bank.

(d) If the agreement referred to in the preceding paragraph has not been consummated within six months after the country ceases to be a member or such other time as the Bank and such country may agree upon, the repurchase price of such country's capital stock shall be its book value, according to the books of the Bank, on the date when the country ceased to be a member. Such repurchase shall be subject to the following conditions:

(i) As a prerequisite for payment, the country ceasing to be a member shall surrender its stock certificates, and such payment may be made in such installments, at such times and in such available currencies as the Bank determines, taking into account the financial position of the Bank.

(ii) Any amount which the Bank owes the country for the repurchase of its capital stock shall be withheld to the extent that the country of any of its subdivisions or agencies remains liable to the Bank as a result of loans or guarantee operations. The amount withheld may, at the option of the Bank, be applied on any such liability as it matures. However, no amount shall be withheld on account of the country's contingent liability for future calls on its subscription pursuant to Article II, Section 4 (a) (ii).

(iii) If the Bank sustains net losses on any loans or participations, or as a result of any guarantees, outstanding on the date the country ceased to be a member, and the amount of such losses exceeds the amount of the reserves provided therefor on such date, such country shall repay on demand the amount by which the repurchase price of its shares would have been reduced, if the losses had been taken into account when the book value of the shares, according to the books of the Bank, was determined. In addition, the former member shall remain liable on any call pursuant to Article II, Section 4 (a) (ii), to the extent that it would have been required to respond if the impairment of capital had occurred and the call had been made at the time the repurchase price of its shares had been determined.

(e) In no event shall any amount due to a country for its shares under this section be paid until six months after the date upon which the country ceases to be a member. If within that period the Bank terminates operations all rights of such country shall be determined by the provisions of Article X, and such country shall be considered still a member of the Bank for the purposes of such article except that it shall have no voting rights.

Article X
Suspension and Termination of Operations

Section 1. Suspension of Operations

In an emergency the Board of Executive Directors may suspend operations in respect of new loans and guarantees until such time as the Board of Governors may have an opportunity to consider the situation and take pertinent measures.

Section 2. Termination of Operations

The Bank may terminate its operations by a decision of the Board of Governors by a two-thirds majority of the total number of governors representing not less than three fourths of the total voting power of the member countries. After such termination of operations the Bank shall forthwith cease all activities, except those incident to the conservation, preservation, and realization of its assets and settlement of its obligations.

Section 3. Liability of Members and Payment of Claims

(a) The liability of all members arising from the subscriptions to the capital stock of the Bank and in respect to the depreciation of their currencies shall continue until all direct and contingent obligations shall have been discharged.

(b) All creditors holding direct claims shall be paid out of the assets of the Bank and then out of payments to the Bank on unpaid or callable subscriptions. Before making any payments to creditors holding direct claims, the Board of Executive Directors shall make such arrangements as are necessary, in its judgment, to ensure a pro rata distribution among holders of direct and contingent claims.

Section 4. Distribution of Assets

(a) No distribution of assets shall be made to members on account of their subscriptions to the capital stock of the Bank until all liabilities to creditors shall have been discharged or provided for. Moreover, such distribution must be approved by a decision of the Board of Governors by a two-thirds majority of the total number of governors representing not less than three fourths of the total voting power of the member countries.

(b) Any distribution of the assets of the Bank to the members shall be in proportion to capital stock held by each member and shall be effected at such times and under such conditions as the Bank shall deem fair and equitable. The shares of assets distributed need not be uniform as to type of assets. No member shall be entitled to receive its share in such a distribution of assets until it has settled all of its obligations to the Bank.

(c) Any member receiving assets distributed pursuant to this article shall enjoy the same rights with respect to such assets as the Bank enjoyed prior to their distribution.

Article XI
Status, Immunities and Privileges

Section 1. Scope of Article

To enable the Bank to fulfill its purpose and the functions with which it is entrusted, the status, immunities, and privileges set forth in this article shall be accorded to the Bank in the territories of each member.

Section 2. Legal Status

The Bank shall possess juridical personality and, in particular, full capacity:
(a) to contract;
(b) to acquire and dispose of immovable and movable property; and
(c) to institute legal proceedings.

Section 3. Judicial Proceedings

Actions may be brought against the Bank only in a court of competent jurisdiction in the territories of a member in which the Bank has an office, has appointed an agent for the purpose of accepting service or notice of process, or has issued or guaranteed securities.

No action shall be brought against the Bank by members or persons acting for or deriving claims from members. However, member countries shall have recourse to such special procedures to settle controversies between the Bank and its members as may be prescribed in this Agreement, in the by-laws and regulations of the Bank or in contracts entered into with the Bank.

Property and assets of the Bank shall, wheresoever located and by whomsoever held, be immune from all forms of seizure, attachment or execution before the delivery of final judgment against the Bank.

Section 4. Immunity of Assets

Property and assets of the Bank, wheresoever located and by whomsoever held, shall be considered public international property and shall be immune from search, requisition, confiscation, expropriation or any other form of taking or foreclosure by executive or legislative action.

Section 5. Inviolability of Archives

The archives of the Bank shall be inviolable.

Section 6. Freedom of Assets from Restrictions

To the extent necessary to carry out the purpose and functions of the Bank and to conduct its operations in accordance with this Agreement, all property and other assets of the Bank shall be free from restrictions, regulations, controls and moratoria of any nature, except as may otherwise be provided in this Agreement.

Section 7. Privilege for Communications

The official communications of the Bank shall be accorded by each member the same treatment that it accords to the official communications of other members.

Section 8. Personal Immunities and Privileges

All governors, executive directors, alternates, officers and employees of the Bank shall have the following privileges and immunities:

(a) Immunity from legal process with respect to acts performed by them in their official capacity, except when the Bank waives this immunity.

(b) When not local nationals, the same immunities from immigration restrictions, alien registration requirements and national service obligations and the same facilities as regards exchange provisions as are accorded by members to the representatives, officials, and employees of comparable rank of other members.

(c) The same privileges in respect of traveling facilities as are accorded by members to representatives, officials, and employees of comparable rank of other members.

Section 9. Immunities from Taxation

(a) The Bank, its property, other assets, income, and the operations and transactions it carries out pursuant to this Agreement, shall be immune from all taxation and from all customs duties. The Bank shall also be immune from any obligation relating to the payment, withholding or collection of any tax, or duty.

(b) No tax shall be levied on or in respect of salaries and emoluments paid by the Bank to executive directors, alternates, officials or employees of the Bank who are not local citizens or other local nationals.

(c) No tax of any kind shall be levied on any obligation or security issued by the Bank, including any dividend or interest thereon, by whomsoever held:

(i) which discriminates against such obligation or security solely because it is issued by the Bank; or

(ii) if the sole jurisdictional basis for such taxation is the place or currency in which it is issued, made payable or paid, or the location of any office or place of business maintained by the Bank.

(d) No tax of any kind shall be levied on any obligation or security guaranteed by the Bank, including any dividend or interest thereon, by whomsoever held:

(i) which discriminates against such obligation or security solely because it is guaranteed by the Bank; or

(ii) if the sole jurisdictional basis for such taxation is the location of any office or place of business maintained by the Bank.

Section 10. Implementation

Each member, in accordance with its juridical system, shall take such action as is necessary to make effective in its own territories the principles set forth in this article, and shall inform the Bank of the action which it has taken on the matter.

Article XII
Amendments

(a) This Agreement may be amended only by decision of the Board of Governors by a two-thirds majority of the total number of governors representing not less than three fourths of the total voting power of the member countries.

(b) Notwithstanding the provisions of the preceding paragraph, the unanimous agreement of the Board of Governors shall be required for the approval of any amendment modifying:

(i) the right to withdraw from the Bank as provided in Article IX, Section 1;

(ii) the right to purchase capital stock of the Bank and to contribute to the Fund as provided in Article II, Section 3 (b) and in Article IV, Section 3 (g), respectively; and

(iii) the limitation on liability as provided in Article II, Section 3 (d) and Article IV, Section 5.

(c) Any proposal to amend this Agreement, whether emanating from a member or the Board of Executive Directors, shall be communicated to the Chairman of the Board of Governors, who shall bring the proposal before the Board of Governors. When an amendment has been adopted, the Bank shall so certify in an official communication addressed to all members. Amendments shall enter into force for all members three months after the date of the official communication unless the Board of Governors shall specify a different period.

Article XIII
Interpretation and Arbitration

Section 1. Interpretation

(a) Any question of interpretation of the provisions of this Agreement arising between any member and the Bank or between any members of the Bank shall be submitted to the Board of Executive Directors for decision.

Members especially affected by the question under consideration shall be entitled to direct representation before the Board of Executive Directors as provided in Article VIII, Section 3 (g).

(b) In any case where the Board of Executive Directors has given a decision under (a) above, any member may require that the question be submitted to the Board of Governors, whose decision shall be final. Pending the decision of the Board of Governors, the Bank may, so far as it deems it necessary, act on the basis of the decision of the Board of Executive Directors.

Section 2. Arbitration

If a disagreement should arise between the Bank and a country which has ceased to be a member, or between the Bank and any member after adoption of a decision to terminate the operation of the Bank, such disagreement shall be submitted to arbitration by a tribunal of three arbitrators. One of the arbitrators shall be appointed by the Bank, another by the country concerned, and the third, unless the parties otherwise agree, by the Secretary General of the Organization of American States. If all efforts to reach a unanimous agreement fail, decisions shall be made by a majority vote of the three arbitrators. The third arbitrator shall be empowered to settle all questions of procedure in any case where the parties are in disagreement with respect thereto.

Article XIV
General Provisions

Section 1. Principal Office

The principal office of the Bank shall be located in Washington, District of Columbia, United States of America.

Section 2. Relations with other Organizations

The Bank may enter into arrangements with other organizations with respect to the exchange of information or for other purposes consistent with this Agreement.

Section 3. Channel of Communication

Each member shall designate an official entity for purposes of communication with the Bank on matters connected with this Agreement.

Section 4. Depositories

Each member shall designate its central bank as a depository in which the Bank may keep its holdings of such member's currency and other assets of the Bank. If a member has no central bank, it shall, in agreement with the Bank, designate another institution for such purpose.

Article XV
Final Provisions

Section 1. Signature and Acceptance

(a) This Agreement shall be deposited with the General Secretariat of the Organization of American States, where it shall remain open until December 31, 1959, for signature by the representatives of the countries listed in Annex A. Each signatory country shall deposit with the General Secretariat of the Organization of American States an instrument setting forth that it has accepted or ratified this Agreement in accordance with its own laws and has taken the steps necessary to enable it to fulfill all of its obligations under this Agreement.

(b) The General Secretariat of the Organization of American States shall send certified copies of this Agreement to the members of the Organization and duly notify them of each signature and deposit of the instrument of acceptance or ratification made pursuant to the foregoing paragraph, as well as the date thereof.

(c) At the time the instrument of acceptance or ratification is deposited on its behalf, each country shall deliver to the General Secretariat of the Organization of American States, for the purpose of meeting administrative expenses of the Bank, gold or United States dollars equivalent to one tenth of one per cent of the purchase price of the shares of the Bank subscribed by it and of its quota in the Fund. This payment shall be credited to the member on account of its subscription and quota prescribed pursuant to Articles II, Section 3 (a) (i), and IV, Section 3 (d) (i). At any time on or after the date on which its instrument of acceptance or ratification is deposited, any member may make additional payments to be credited to the member on account of its subscription and quota prescribed pursuant to Articles II and IV. The General Secretariat of the Organization of American States shall hold all funds paid under this paragraph in a special deposit account or accounts and shall make such funds available to the Bank not later than the time of the first meeting of the Board of Governors held pursuant to Section 3 of this article. If this Agreement has not come into force by December 31, 1959, the General Secretariat of the Organization of American States shall return such funds to the countries that delivered them.

(d) On or after the date on which the Bank commences operations, the General Secretariat of the Organization of American States may receive the signature and the instrument of acceptance or ratification of this Agreement from any country whose membership has been approved in accordance with Article II, Section 1 (b).

Section 2. Entry into Force

(a) This Agreement shall enter into force when it has been signed and instruments of acceptance or ratification have been deposited, in accordance with Section 1 (a) of this article, by representatives of countries whose subscriptions comprise not less than 85 per cent of the total subscriptions set forth in Annex A.

(b) Countries whose instruments of acceptance or ratification were deposited prior to the date on which the agreement entered into force shall become members on that date. Other countries shall become members on the dates on which their instruments of acceptance or ratification are deposited.

Section 3. Commencement of Operations

(a) The Secretary General of the Organization of American States shall call the first meeting of the Board of Governors as soon as this Agreement enters into force under Section 2 of this article.

(b) At the first meeting of the Board of Governors arrangements shall be made for the selection of the executive directors and their alternates in accordance with the provisions of Article VIII, Section 3, and for the determination of the date on which the Bank shall commence operations. Notwithstanding the provisions of Article VIII, Section 3, the governors, if they deem it desirable, may provide that the first term to be served by such directors may be less than three years. . . .

88. *Radio-Television Report by President Eisenhower to the Nation on His Trip to Brazil, Argentina, Chile and Uruguay* *

March 8, 1960

Good evening, friends: My first words upon my return from the four American Republics I have just visited must be a heartfelt expression of gratitude for the friendly receptions my associates and I experienced wherever we went.

Millions endured for long hours along the streets the hot summer sun—and occasionally rain—to let us know of the enthusiastic good will they have for the Government and people of the United States. In the nations of Latin America—indeed as I have found in all of the 18 countries I have visited in my trips of recent months—there is a vast reservoir of respect, adminiration, and affection for the United States of America. The expressions of this attitude by Latin American peoples and their leaders were so enthusiastic and so often repeated as to admit no possibility of mistake. Two or three insignificant exceptions to this may have made a headline, but they were only minor incidents, lost in the massed welcome.

This was a good-will trip; but it was also much more. Members of my party and I held serious conversations and exchanged information on bilateral, hemispheric, and global problems with the four heads of states, with cabinet members, with leaders of labor, education, finance, and business.

Two Impressions From Trip

Two impressions are highlighted in my mind.

First, Brazil, Argentina, Chile, and Uruguay treasure as much as we do freedom, human dignity, equality, and peace with justice. In freedom they are determined to progress, to improve and diversify their economies, to provide better housing and education, to work ceaselessly for rising levels of human well being.

Second, while certain problems are continental in scope, nonetheless each of the

Department of State Bulletin, Mar. 28, 1960, pp. 471-74.

countries I visited—indeed, each of the 20 Republics of Latin America—is highly individual. Each has its own unique problems and ideas regarding future development. Hence, our cooperation with each Republic must be tailored to its particular situation.

I was gratified to learn that, as the indispensable basis for their self-improvement, comprehensive surveys of resources, capacities, objectives, and costs have progressed rapidly in recent years. But each nation feels it must do more in this regard and seeks help for this purpose. The United Nations has funds for such predevelopment studies. The new Inter-American Bank also should be able to lend technical help. The studies of each country called for under Operation Pan America will likewise contribute to this end.

Once sound planning has made significant progress, a nation can formulate specific projects for action, with priorities established and with confidence that each development will open still further opportunity to speed the spiral of growth.

The execution of any development program will of course depend primarily upon the dedicated efforts of the peoples themselves. I was impressed, for example, by what I saw in Chile. I visited a low-cost housing project. The Government had provided land and utilities. The homeowners were helping one another build the new houses. They will pay for them monthly, over a period of years. Personal accomplishments brought pride to their eyes, self-reliance to their bearing. Their new homes are modest in size and character, but I cannot possibly describe the intense satisfaction they take in the knowledge that they themselves have brought about this great forward step in their living conditions.

In Argentina and Uruguay I witnessed encouraging sights—men building schools, homes, and roads—and in Brazil, erecting a wholly new capital city.

The people of Latin America know that poverty, ignorance, and ill health are not inevitable. They are determined to have their resources and labors yield a better life for themselves and for their children.

I assured them that, most earnestly, we of the United States want them to succeed. We realize that to speed improvement they need foreign capital. They want sound loans, public and private. Their repayment record on loans previously made is noteworthy.

International and United States lending agencies have recently had their funds greatly increased. The new Inter-American Development Bank will soon be functioning. I believe that each nation which has produced a well-conceived development program will find that these lending institutions will respond to their needs. Should this not be so in a particular situation, we of the United States would want to know the circumstances and do what we could to help to rectify the difficulty.

In our discussions I stressed that all nations—large or small, powerful or weak—should assume some responsibility for the advancement of humankind in freedom. Though we of the United States will, within the framework of our world situation and economic capacity, assist all we can, we look for the time when all the free nations will feel a common responsibilty for our common destiny. Cooperation among free nations is the key to common progress. Aid from one to another, if on a one-way street basis only and indefinitely continued, is not of itself truly productive.

The peoples of Latin America appreciate that our assistance in recent years has reached new heights and that this has required sacrifice on our part.

Misunderstandings That Need To Be Corrected

I must repeat, however, what I said several times during my trip: Serious misunderstandings of the United States do exist in Latin America. And, indeed, we are not as well informed of them as we should be.

Many persons do not realize the United States is just as committed as are the other Republics to the principles of the Rio Treaty of 1947. This treaty declares that an attack on one American Republic will in effect be an attack on all. We stand firmly by this commitment. This mutual security system, proved by time, should now enable some of the American Republics to reduce expenditures for armaments and thus make funds available for constructive purposes.

One editorial alleged that the United States did not accept the principle of nonintervention until 1959. In fact our country has consistently abided by this hemispheric concept for more than a quarter of a century.

Another persistent misunderstanding which I sought to correct wherever I traveled is that we sometimes support dictators. Of course, we abhor all tyrannical forms of government, whether of the left or of the right. This I made clear.

In Brazil I explained another important item of our policy: We believe in the rights of people to choose their own form of government, to build their own institutions, to abide by their own philosophy. But if a tyrannical form of government were imposed upon any of the Americas from outside or with outside support—by force, threat, or subversion—we would certainly deem this to be a violation of the principle of nonintervention and would expect the Organization of American States, acting under pertinent solemn commitments, to take appropriate collective action.

On occasion I heard it said that economic advance in some American Republics only makes the rich richer and the poor poorer, and that the United States should take the initiative in correcting this evil. This is a view fomented by Communists but often repeated by well-meaning people.

If there should be any truth in this charge whatsoever, it is not the fault of the United States. So far as our purpose is involved, projects financed by our institutions are expected to yield widespread benefits to all and, at the same time, to conform to our policy of nonintervention. I know that the Latin American leaders I met also seek this same result.

Moreover, when internal social reform is required, it is purely an internal matter.

One of the most far-reaching problems of continental scope is this: In their exports the Latin American Republics are largely single-commodity countries. The world-market prices of what they sell fluctuate widely, whereas the prices of things they buy keep going up.

We have tried to be helpful in the cooperative study of this vexing situation. Many facts about supply, demand, production are widely comprehended for the first time. Thus, for example, with the facts about coffee understood, producing nations are cooperating in orderly marketing for this commodity with beneficial results.

The real solution is in agricultural and industrial diversification. Here we are encouraged by the progress being made toward the creation of common markets. Large areas, relatively free of trade restrictions, will make for greater efficiency in production and distribution and will attract new capital to speed development.

Despite such problems as these, our relationships with our sister Republics have, with notable—but very few—exceptions, reached an alltime high. Leaders and populations alike attested to this truth. But an even firmer partnership must be our goal.

Special Relationship of the Americas

The Republics of this hemisphere have a special relationship to one another. The United States is important to all of Latin America, as its largest buyer, as the main source of foreign investment capital, and as a bastion of freedom. Our southern neighbors are important to us economically, politically, culturally, militarily. Indeed, no other area of the world is of more vital significance to our own future.

This interdependence must be comprehended by us and by them. Each should know the policies, attitudes, aspirations, and capacities of the other. For, as I have said time and again, all fruitful, abiding cooperation must be based upon genuine mutual understanding of vital facts.

Exchanges of students, teachers, labor leaders, and others are helpful. Newspapers, magazines, all means of communication should accept the responsibility not merely of transmitting spectacular news but of helping build the knowledge on which cooperative action may flourish.

In one respect our neighbors put us to shame. English is rapidly spreading as the second language in Latin America. Business executives, labor leaders, taxi drivers—most speak English well, learned in school or in binational institutes. The study of Spanish is increasing in our schools, but I wish that literally millions of Americans would learn to speak Spanish or Portuguese fluently and to read the literature, histories, and periodicals of our sister Republics.

H. G. Wells once said that civilization is a race between education and catastrophe. His thought is applicable to hemispheric relations. With common dedication to the highest ideals of mankind, including shared aspirations for a world at peace, freedom, and progress, there is no insurmountable impediment to fruitful cooperation, save only insufficiency in mutual understanding. This is something that you and I—every single citizen, simply by informing himself—can do something about.

I hope each of us will do so.

Again, I express my gratitude to President Kubitschek, President Frondizi, President Alessandri, and President Nardone and all their peoples for providing me with a most instructive and rewarding experience.

And I convey to you their best wishes and warm greetings.

Thank you, and good night.

89. Statement by President Eisenhower, on the Reduction of Cuba's Sugar Quota for 1960*

July 6, 1960

I have today [July 6] approved legislation enacted by the Congress which authorizes the President to determine Cuba's sugar quota for the balance of calendar year

*Department of State Bulletin, July 25, 1960, p. 140

1960 and for the 3-month period ending March 31, 1961. In conformity with this legislation I have signed a proclamation which, in the national interest, establishes the Cuban sugar quota for the balance of 1960 at 39,752 short tons, plus the sugar certified for entry prior to July 3, 1960. This represents a reduction of 700,000 short tons from the original 1960 Cuban quota of 3,119,655 short tons.

This deficit will be filled by purchases from other free-world suppliers.

The importance of the United States Government's action relating to sugar quota legislation makes it desirable, I believe, to set forth the reasons which led the Congress to authorize and the Executive to take this action in the national interest.

Normally about one-third of our total sugar supply comes from Cuba. Despite every effort on our part to maintain traditionally friendly relations, the Government of Cuba is now following a course which raises serious question as to whether the United States can, in the long run, continue to rely upon that country for such large quantities of sugar. I believe that we would fail in our obligation to our people if we did not take steps to reduce our reliance for a major food product upon a nation which has embarked upon a deliberate policy of hostility toward the United States.

The Government of Cuba has committed itself to purchase substantial quantities of goods from the Soviet Union under barter arrangements. It has chosen to undertake to pay for these goods with sugar—traded at prices well below those which it has obtained in the United States. The inescapable conclusion is that Cuba has embarked on a course of action to commit steadily increasing amounts of its sugar crop to trade with the Communist bloc, thus making its future ability to fill the sugar needs of the United States ever more uncertain.

It has been with the most genuine regret that this Government has been compelled to alter the heretofore mutually beneficial sugar trade between the United States and Cuba. Under the system which has existed up to this time, the people of Cuba, particularly those who labor in the cane fields and in the mills, have benefited from the maintenance of an assured market in the United States, where Cuban sugar commands a price well above that which could be obtained in the world market. These benefits also reached many others whose livelihood was related to the sugar industry on the island.

The American people will always maintain their friendly feelings for the people of Cuba. We look forward to the day when the Cuban Government will once again allow this friendship to be fully expressed in the relations between our two countries.

90. Proclamation by President Eisenhower on the Determination of the Cuban Sugar Quota*

July 6, 1960

1. Whereas on December 17, 1959, the 1960 sugar quota for Cuba was determined pursuant to the Sugar Act of 1948, as amended (7 U.S.C. 1100 *et seq.*), at 3,119,655 short tons, raw value, of which 2,379,903 short tons, raw value, have heretofore been

*Department of State Bulletin, July 25, 1960, pp. 140-41.

certified for entry, pursuant to regulations issued by the Secretary of Agriculture (7 CFR 817), leaving 739,752 short tons, raw value, not yet so certified; and

2. Whereas section 408(b) (1) of the Sugar Act of 1948, as amended by the act of July 6, 1960, entitled "An Act to Amend the Sugar Act of 1948, as Amended", provides that the President shall determine, notwithstanding any other provision of Title II of the Sugar Act of 1948, as amended, the quota for Cuba for the balance of calendar year 1960 and for the three-month period ending March 31, 1961, in such amount or amounts as he shall find from time to time to be in the national interest: *Provided,* however, That in no event shall such quota exceed such amount as would be provided for Cuba under the terms of Title II of the Sugar Act of 1948, as amended, in the absence of section 408(b); and

3. Whereas section 408(b) (1) of the Sugar Act of 1948, as amended, further provides that determinations made by the President thereunder shall become effective immediately upon publication in the Federal Register; and

4. Whereas, pursuant to section 408(b) (1) of the Sugar Act of 1948, as amended, I find it to be in the national interest that the quota for Cuba under the Sugar Act of 1948, as amended, for the balance of calendar year 1960 shall be 39,752 short tons, raw value, plus the sugar certified prior to July 3, 1960, for entry but not yet entered, or withdrawn from warehouse, for consumption:

Now, therefore, I, Dwight D. Eisenhower, President of the United States of America, acting under and by virtue of the authority vested in me by section 408(b) of the Sugar Act of 1948, as amended, and section 301 of title 3 of the United States Code, and as President of the United States:

1. Do hereby determine that in the national interest the quota for Cuba pursuant to the Sugar Act of 1948, as amended, for the balance of calendar year 1960 shall be 39,752 short tons, raw value, plus the sugar certified prior to July 3, 1960, for entry but not yet entered, or withdrawn from warehouse, for consumption; and

2. Do hereby delegate to the Secretary of Agriculture the authority vested in the President by section 408(b) (2) and section 408(b) (3) of the Sugar Act of 1948, as amended, such authority to be exercised with the concurrence of the Secretary of State.

This proclamation shall become effective immediately upon publication in the Federal Register. . . .

91. *Resolution by the U.N. Security Council, on Cuban-United States Relations* *

July 19, 1960

The Security Council,

Having heard the statements made by the Foreign Minister of Cuba and by members of the Council,

Taking into account the provisions of Articles 24, 33, 34, 35, 36, 52 and 103 of the Charter of the United Nations,

United Nations, Official Records of the Security Council, Fifteenth Year, Supplement for July, August and September, 1960, Document S/4395, English.

Taking into account also Articles 20 and 102 of the Charter of the Organization of American States of which both Cuba and the United States of America are members,

Deeply concerned by the situation existing between Cuba and the United States of America,

Considering that it is the obligation of all Members of the United Nations to settle their international disputes by negotiation and other peaceful means in such a manner that international peace and security and justice are not endangered,

Noting that this situation is under consideration by the Organization of American States,

1. Decides to adjourn the consideration of this question pending the receipt of a report from the Organization of American States;

2. Invites the members of the Organization of American States to lend their assistance toward the achievement of a peaceful solution of the present situation in accordance with the purposes and principles of the Charter of the United Nations;

3. Urges in the meantime all other States to refrain from any action which might increase the existing tensions between Cuba and the United States of America.

92. Organization of American States, Sixth Meeting of Consultation of Ministers of Foreign Affairs, Final Act*

August 21, 1960

The Sixth Meeting of Consultation of Ministers of Foreign Affairs Serving as Organ of Consultation in Application of the Inter-American Treaty of Reciprocal Assistance, was held in the city of San José, Costa Rica, from August 16 to August 21, 1960.

The Meeting was convoked by a resolution of the Council of the Organization of American States approved July 8, 1960, which reads as follows:

Whereas:

At the meeting held on July 6, 1960, the Council took cognizance of the note of the Ambassador Representative of Venezuela, whereby his government requested "that immediately, and as a matter of urgency, the Organ of Consultation be convoked, pursuant to Article 6 of the Inter-American Treaty of Reciprocal Assistance, to consider the acts of intervention and aggression by the Government of the Dominican Republic against the Government of Venezuela, which culminated in the attempt upon the life of the Venezuelan Chief of State"; and

At the same meeting, the Ambassador Representative of Venezuela gave additional information on the facts referred to in the aforesaid note,

The Council of the Organization of American States

Resolves:

1. To convoke the Organ of Consultation, in accordance with the provisions of the Inter-American Treaty of Reciprocal Assistance, which will meet on a date and at a place to be determined in due course.

*Organization of American States, *Official Records*, OEA/Ser. F/II.6 (English).

2. To constitute itself and act provisionally as Organ of Consultation in accordance with Article 12 of the aforesaid Treaty.

3. To authorize the Chairman of the Council to appoint a committee to investigate the facts denounced and their antecedents, and to submit a report thereon.

4. To request the American governments and the Secretary General of the Organization to provide full cooperation in order to facilitate the work of the committee, which shall begin its task immediately after being constituted.

5. To inform the United Nations Security Council of the text of this resolution, and of all activities connected with this matter. . . .

As a result of its deliberations, the Sixth Meeting of Consultation of Ministers of Foreign Affairs approved the following conclusions:

Resolution I

The Sixth Meeting of Consultation of Ministers of Foreign Affairs Serving as Organ of Consultation in Application of the Inter-American Treaty of Reciprocal Assistance,

Having seen the Report of the Investigating Committee appointed pursuant to the provisions of the third paragraph of the resolution approved by the Council of the Organization of American States on July 8, 1960, and

Considering:

That the Charter of the Organization of American States sets forth the principle that international order consists essentially of respect for the personality, sovereignty and independence of states, and the faithful fulfillment of obligations derived from treaties and other sources of international law;

That in connection with the incident denounced by the Government of Venezuela before the Inter-American Peace Committee on November 25, 1959, that organ of the inter-American system reached the conclusion that "the necessary arrangements to carry out the flight from Ciudad Trujillo to Aruba—planned for the purpose of dropping leaflets over a Venezuelan city—and to load these leaflets in Ciudad Trujillo, could not have been carried out without the connivance of the Dominican authorities";

That the Committee of the Council of the Organization of American States acting provisionally as Organ of Consultation that was entrusted with the investigation of the acts denounced by the Government of Venezuela, reached the conclusion that the Government of the Dominican Republic issued diplomatic passports to be used by Venezuelans who participated in the military uprising that took place in April 1960 in San Cristóbal, Venezuela;

That the Committee of the Council of the Organization of American States acting provisionally as Organ of Consultation, which was charged with the investigation of the acts denounced by the Government of the Republic of Venezuela, also reached the conclusions that:

1. The attempt against the life of the President of Venezuela perpetrated on June 24, 1960, was part of a plot intended to overthrow the Government of that country.

2. The persons implicated in the aforementioned attempt and plot received moral support and material assistance from high officials of the Government of the Dominican Republic.

3. This assistance consisted principally of providing the persons implicated facilities to travel and to enter and reside in Dominican territory in connection with their subversive plans; of having facilitated the two flights of the plane of Venezuelan registry to and from the Military Air Base of San Isidro, Dominican Republic; of providing arms for use in the coup against the Government of Venezuela and the electronic device and the explosive which were used in the attempt; as well as of having instructed the person who caused the explosion in the operation of the electronic device of that explosive and of having demonstrated to him the destructive force of the same.

That the aforementioned actions constitute acts of intervention and aggression against the Republic of Venezuela, which affect the sovereignty of that state and endanger the peace of America; and

That in the present case collective action is justified under the provisions of Article 19 of the Charter of the Organization of American States,

Resolves:

To condemn emphatically the participation of the Government of the Dominican Republic in the acts of aggression and intervention against the State of Venezuela that culminated in the attempt on the life of the President of that country, and, as a consequence, in accordance with the provisions of Articles 6 and 8 of the Inter-American Treaty of Reciprocal Assistance,

Agrees:

1. To apply the following measures:

a. Breaking of diplomatic relations of all the member states with the Dominican Republic;

b. Partial interruption of economic relations of all the member states with the Dominican Republic, beginning with the immediate suspension of trade in arms and implements of war of every kind. The Council of the Organization of American States, in accordance with the circumstances and with due consideration for the constitutional or legal limitations of each and every one of the member states, shall study the feasibility and desirability of extending the suspension of trade with the Dominican Republic to other articles.

2. To authorize the Council of the Organization of American States to discontinue, by a two-thirds affirmative vote of its members, the measures adopted in this resolution, at such time as the Government of the Dominican Republic should cease to constitute a danger to the peace and security of the hemisphere.

3. To authorize the Secretary General of the Organization of American States to transmit to the Security Council of the United Nations full information concerning the measures agreed upon in this resolution. . . .

Statement of Cuba Regarding Resolution I

The Delegation of Cuba has voted in favor of the measures agreed upon, with the natural understanding that they will be applied in accordance with the provisions contained in international pacts, agreements, and treaties. We therefore make this observation, in order that it be included in the Final Act. We also make a further observation, for the same purpose, in regard to the limitations contained in part 1.b because we consider them to be obvious in the light of both national and international law. . . .

93. *Organization of American States, Seventh Meeting of Consultation of Ministers of Foreign Affairs, Declaration of San José**

August 29, 1960

The Seventh Meeting of Consultation of Ministers of Foreign Affairs

1. Condemns energetically the intervention or the threat of intervention, even when conditional, by an extracontinental power in the affairs of the American republics and declares that the acceptance of a threat of extracontinental intervention by any American state endangers American solidarity and security, and that this obliges the Organization of American States to disapprove it and reject it with equal vigor.

2. Rejects, also, the attempt of the Sino-Soviet powers to make use of the political, economic, or social situation of any American state, inasmuch as that attempt is capable of destroying hemispheric unity and endangering the peace and security of the hemisphere.

3. Reaffirms the principle of nonintervention by any American state in the internal or external affairs of the other American states, and reiterates that each state has the right to develop its cultural, political, and economic life freely and naturally, respecting the rights of the individual and the principles of universal morality, and as a consequence, no American state may intervene for the purpose of imposing upon another American state its ideologies or its political, economic, or social principles.

4. Reaffirms that the inter-American system is incompatible with any form of totalitarianism and that democracy will achieve the full scope of its objectives in the hemisphere only when all the American republics conduct themselves in accordance with the principles stated in the Declaration of Santiago, Chile, approved at the Fifth Meeting of Consultation of Ministers of Foreign Affairs, the observance of which it recommends as soon as possible.

5. Proclaims that all member states of the regional organization are under obligation to submit to the discipline of the inter-American system, voluntarily and freely agreed upon, and that the soundest guarantee of their sovereignty and their political independence stems from compliance with the provisions of the Charter of the Organization of American States.

6. Declares that all controversies between member states should be resolved by the measures for peaceful solution that are contemplated in the inter-American system.

7. Reaffirms its faith in the regional system and its confidence in the Organization of American States, created to achieve an order of peace and justice that excludes any possible aggression, to promote solidarity among its members, to strengthen their

*Organization of American States, *Official Records,* OEA/Ser. C/II.7.

collaboration, and to defend their sovereignty, their territorial integrity, and their political independence, since it is in this Organization that its members find the best guarantee for their evolution and development.

8. Resolves that this declaration shall be known as "The Declaration of San José, Costa Rica."

94. Press Release by the State Department, Announcing Severance of Relations with the Dominican Republic*

August 26, 1960

A United States Embassy official in Ciudad Trujillo today [August 26] delivered a note to the Dominican Foreign Office advising that Government that the Government of the United States was severing diplomatic relations with the Government of the Dominican Republic and was withdrawing its diplomatic mission. This action is in consonance with the decisions taken at the Sixth Meeting of Consultation of American Foreign Ministers in San José, Costa Rica. At the same time the Dominican Government was requested to recall its diplomatic mission in the United States.

It is expected that consular functions will be continued.

A friendly power has been requested to assume responsibility for diplomatic representation of the United States in the Dominican Republic.

95. Statement by Douglas Dillon, Under Secretary of State, before the Special Committee of the Council of the Organization of American States to Study the Formulation of New Measures for Economic Cooperation, on Promoting Economic and Social Advancement in the Americas†

September 6, 1960

It is a great pleasure to meet with you again in the Committee of 21 to consider how we may best intensify our efforts to further the lofty objectives of Operation Pan America, given to us by the eminent President of Brazil, Juscelino Kubitschek. In beginning our deliberations we have been inspired by the eloquence of His Excellency President Alberto Lleras Camargo, truly an outstanding man of the Americas. To the Government and people of the Republic of Colombia I wish to express our gratitude for the warm hospitality we have received here in the gracious and cultured city of Bogotá. And I should like to say a very special word about the role played at the recent meeting of foreign ministers in San José, where the delegation of Colombia gave forthright leadership to the forces of freedom and democracy in our hemisphere. The remarks at San José of His Excellency Dr. Julio Cesar Turbay Ayala will be recalled in years to come as one of the most important declarations of our time.

*Department of State Bulletin, Sept. 12, 1960, p. 412.
†Department of State Bulletin, Oct. 3, 1960, pp. 533-37.

This third meeting of the Committee of 21 has before it an unprecedented opportunity. By our decisions we can, if we will, launch a far-reaching attack on the poverty, ignorance, and lack of social justice which, even in this 20th-century world of miraculous technical progress, still oppress so many of our fellow citizens in Latin America.

There are those in the world today who are trying to take advantage of this situation for their own selfish ends. They say to the masses, "Come to us, give up your freedom, give up your individuality, and we will lead you to material benefits that you can get in no other way." We must recognize that there is great temptation in this false doctrine. It poses a challenge to all we hold dear—to the very dignity of man as a free and individual being. We do not fear this challenge. We welcome it.

Our fundamental task here at Bogotá is nothing more than to outline the route by which the people of the Americas can achieve the material progress they desire without any sacrifice of fundamental human rights and freedoms. At this meeting we can, if we will, give a powerful impetus to constructive forces of domestic action and international cooperation working hand in hand to promote the common objective of the economic and social advancement of our peoples today.

The Great Imperative of Our Time

More than ever before our governments are aware of the acute need to rescue the underprivileged from their life of misery—to raise the standards of living of the great masses of the people. This is the great imperative of our time. Unless we succeed in this task, democracy, freedom, and spiritual values that we in the Western Hemisphere hold so dear will become the prey of tyrants and demagogs, aided and abetted by external forces which seek nothing less than to rule the world and to extinguish the light of freedom everywhere. We face an hour of danger. To overcome this danger we must prove anew the ability of the free governments of the hemisphere to spread the material benefits of civilization to all of their peoples.

The inspired concept of Operation Pan America has now become an irreversible objective of the Americas. I am sure I speak for us all when I express our warm appreciation to Brazil for having given us this lofty ideal. Operation Pan America has helped us all to address ourselves with great vision and dedication to the task of speeding up the economic growth of the developing nations of Latin America. We have become more conscious of the need for increased development capital to meet the growing requirements for roads and power, for factories and mines, and for all the other productive enterprises essential to healthy and progressive economies.

The countries of Latin America have recognized that the bulk of the development capital required must come from domestic savings, both public and private. Many of them have taken important, and often courageous, actions to increase the rate of savings through effective monetary and fiscal policies, but the mobilization of domestic capital, essential though it is, is only one of the domestic measures which must be taken if rates of national economic growth are to be increased. In the more highly industrialized countries, where there is relatively full employment of resources, the rate of economic growth depends primarily upon the rate of savings and investment and upon new scientific and technological progress. In the developing countries of

Latin America, on the other hand, the rate of economic growth will be influenced importantly by other factors, particularly by the degree to which unemployed or underemployed resources can be put into productive use and by the extent to which already known technological methods can be adopted.

The greatest economic asset of any country is its people. The productivity of a country will vary directly not only with the capability of its management personnel but also and specially with the degree of skills, training, and technical competence of its working people. Here is an enormous resource possessed by all the Latin American countries. To these developments much more effort must be devoted in the years ahead. To bring these latent but powerful economic forces into play requires organization and planning by the developing countries themselves, including the preparation of well-conceived projects and programs and the establishment of priorities in the activities of the government sector. It requires the provision of incentives and encouragement to private enterprise, both local and foreign, to develop the vast potential of Latin American markets. It requires the modernization of the legal and institutional framework, including improvements in fiscal practices designed to produce the larger governmental revenues required to maintain financial stability in an expanding economy. It requires national economic policies directed to the diversification of production, so that precarious dependence on one or a few industries or commodities may be avoided. While greater domestic savings and greater national efforts are indispensable to the further economic development of the Latin American countries, it is also true that much more must be done to enlarge the flow of development capital to Latin America from international sources.

New Sources of Capital for Investment

Last month at San José the American Republics joined in formally recognizing that both collective and national efforts to eradicate underdevelopment have so far been insufficient and that it is necessary to intensify inter-American economic cooperation through a substantial increase of available resources. New sources of international economic development capital for Latin America are rapidly coming into existence.

Within the last 2 years the American Republics have created a new instrument of inter-American financial cooperation, the Inter-American Development Bank. I think we may be confident that the Bank will soon become a vigorous and operative institution for widening the stream of international capital flowing toward Latin America to accelerate economic development. It should also become an invaluable source of technical assistance in the preparation of development plans and projects. The comprehensive and objective judgment which the Bank, because of its multilateral character, can bring to the development problems of Latin America is of key importance. We are indeed fortunate to have in the governors, the executive directors, the president, and the principal officers of the Bank men of outstanding quality, experience, and integrity. Our governments have also made possible by their initiative and support the establishment of the new International Development Association, an affiliate of the World Bank, for the purpose of providing additional capital on flexible terms suited to the many uses of developing countries of the free world which cannot be satisfied by loans subject to normal banking criteria. Similarly our governments have acted to bring about very substantial increases in the resources of the International Monetary Fund and the World Bank.

I should also mention the formation of the Development Assistance Group by 10 important capital-lending countries. The objective of this group is to mobilize better the resources of the industrialized countries for assistance to the less developed areas, including the countries of Latin America.

Finally, in addition to the resources which it has already pledged to the institutions which I have just mentioned, the United States has acted to increase further the provision of assistance for basic economic and industrial development in Latin America on terms suited to the need of the developing countries. In our endeavor to increase the provision of public capital for economic development we must not lose sight of the important role of private capital as a source of funds for development. Private capital will, of course, go only where it is welcome and where it has the expectation of fair and equitable treatment. Arbitrary and punitive actions against foreign private enterprises, such as we have witnessed in one American country in recent months, discourage the private investment community not only in the country which takes such actions but elsewhere as well. It is to be hoped that the noticeable decrease in foreign private investment in Latin America resulting from the past year's events in Cuba will be of short duration. In the interests of rapid economic development we must all take steps to reassure and encourage private investors so that Latin America may benefit from a renewed and increased flow of foreign private capital.

The increased multilateral efforts to provide public capital to which I have referred, the continued support from our Export-Import Bank, further increases in basic development assistance from the United States to Latin America on suitable terms, and the continued investment of private capital should serve to swell substantially the flow of development capital into Latin America for essential projects such as power, transport, industry, agriculture, and mining, thus strengthening the sinews of the Latin American economies and stimulating their rate of growth. But we must do still more.

Expanding Social Development

To our steadily increasing programs of economic development we must add the new and broad dimension of social development in a conscious and determined effort to further social justice in our hemisphere. All of you here are aware of this pervasive problem. But I think it is obvious, in the light of the existing social tensions, that the efforts hitherto undertaken have in many cases been inadequate and must be intensified in order to strike at the root of the problem. We must bring fresh hope to the less privileged people who make up such a large proportion of the population in many of the countries of Latin America. We must open before them the path to a better life of material well-being, equality, and dignity. We must help them to replace a hovel with a home. We must help them to acquire ownership of the land and the means for its productive use. We must help them to enjoy and use the fruits of modern knowledge for themselves, their families, and their country. It is not enough only to construct modern factories, powerplants, and office buildings.

These things are essential to the development process. But it often takes many years for their benefits to reach down to the ordinary citizen. We must therefore broaden our efforts to help all of the people. The task is nothing less than to lift whole segments of the population into the 20th century. We must do this in order to bring increased opportunity to the man in the street and the man on the farm. In doing so we will make it possible for many millions of people to participate more fully in the economic life of their countries and to make increasing contributions to national economic growth, contributions which have often been insignificant in the past.

The Government of the United States is prepared to devote over the years ahead large additional resources to the inauguration and carrying forward of a broad new social development program for Latin America, dedicated to supporting the self-help efforts of the governments and peoples of Latin America. As a first step President Eisenhower has recommended, and our Congress has authorized, the appropriation of $500 million for this purpose. The appropriation itself will be requested at the next session of our Congress in 1961. As progress is made through joint and cooperative efforts in this area of social development, we would expect to continue our support with new and additional funds.

It is the hope of my Government that here at Bogotá we will strengthen the process of economic development in Latin America by reaching agreement on the major elements of a vigorous program of social development and on the necessary instrumentalities to carry it out. Such a program is, in our view, an essential element of Latin American development.

As you know, my delegation has transmitted to your governments a draft agreement for the establishment of an inter-American program of social development. This has been circulated by the secretariat. The draft agreement envisages, first, an overall attack on social problems through improvement in the conditions of rural life, through better use of agricultural land, through better housing and community facilities, and through the modernization and improvement of education. The agreement thus embodies the concept so vividly expressed by President Eisenhower at Newport last July:

> I have in mind the opening of new areas of arable land for settlement and productive use. I have in mind better land utilization, within a system which provides opportunities for free, self-reliant men to own land, without violating the rights of others. I have in mind housing with emphasis, where appropriate, on individual ownership of small homes. And I have in mind other essential minimums for decent living in both urban and rural environments.

The agreement also envisages increased contributions to this effort by Latin American governments, particularly through the modernization of tax systems, more effective use of land resources, and modernized credit institutions.

Secondly, the agreement looks toward the establishment of an inter-American fund for social development to be financed by the United States but to be administered primarily by the Inter-American Development Bank on flexible terms and in accordance with selective criteria established in the light of the resources available. It is the view of the United States that this fund would be made available for loans which could cover costs in local currency and which could also be repaid in the currency of the borrowing country, thus avoiding burdens on the balance of international payments. Loan repayments to the Bank would be available for relending, thus constituting a revolving fund. While this new inter-American fund would not be able to finance massive projects such as large-scale housing, it could assist in a wide variety of social projects within the areas I have just described. I am sure that all would agree that loans from the special fund should only be made in association with projects, programs, or other measures of self-help formulated and adopted by the Latin American countries themselves.

Finally, as one of the ways of strengthening the Inter-American Economic and Social Council, the proposed agreement would authorize it to carry out annual reviews of the progress achieved in the field of economic and social development as a whole and to outline the areas in which future progress should be sought. The United States believes that it is of the greatest importance to build up and fortify the economic institutions of the OAS [Organization of American States] and to assure that they discharge effectively their vital responsibilities. Thus we can further our common goal of providing ever greater strength to the inter-American system. I wish to make it quite clear that this new program to help the people of Latin America is designed to be in addition to, and not in substitution for, assistance for basic economic and industrial development. It is designed to complement efforts for basic economic development by further strengthening progress toward social justice for all. As I have said, the United States will also make every effort to increase its assistance for basic economic and industrial development in Latin America.

We would be glad to hear the views of other delegations on the new social development program which we are proposing. We earnestly hope that out of our discussions in the next several days will come the text of an understanding which we can all support. While the proposed agreement on social development contains separate sections dealing with the several aspects of the program, we believe that it must be viewed as an integrated whole.

Work of the Subcommittee of Nine

I would now like to turn to the work of the Subcommittee of Nine and the report which it has prepared for our consideration. The Subcommittee of Nine, and especially its distinguished chairman, Señor Vicente Sánchez Gavito of Mexico, deserve our thanks for a job well done. Our thanks are also due to the Government of Brazil, which submitted the plan of work on which the discussions of the Subcommittee were based. The Subcommittee's report contains many practical recommendations in the fields of finance, agriculture, education, productivity, technology, and trade which reflect a wide area of agreement among the American states on additional measures of national and international action. These recommendations are now to be examined by the various working groups of the Committee of 21.

The delegation of the United States is ready to support favorable action by the Committee of 21 on all of the recommendations of the Subcommittee of Nine, with the exception of a very few recommendations relating to finance. In the case of these recommendations, to which the United States entered certain reservations, my Government will have suggested changes to propose which we hope will enable us to reach full agreement on the subjects concerned. If at this conference we can act on the report of our Subcommittee, if we can launch a new inter-American program of social development, and if we can give impetus to the provision of increased resources·for basic economic and industrial development in accordance with the spirit of Operation Pan America, we will have opened a new era of inter-American cooperation. In our endeavors here we must be ever conscious of the many millions of our people who desperately need the help that we can give them. Their eyes are upon us; we must not disappoint them. As the distinguished President of Colombia, Alberto Lleras Camargo, said in addressing the Congress of the United States, with reference to the need for intensified inter-American cooperation: ". . . this must be a high operation of reciprocal confidence in a great common destiny, and an act of faith, on your part and on ours, in the political, economic, and social principles that we share."

96. *Organization of American States, Special Committee of the Council to Study the Formulation of New Measures for Economic Cooperation, Act of Bogotá* *

September 13, 1960

Measures for Social Improvement and Economic Development Within the Framework of Operation Pan America

The Special Committee to Study the Formulation of New Measures for Economic Cooperation,

Recognizing that the preservation and strengthening of free and democratic institutions in the American republics requires the acceleration of social and economic progress in Latin America adequate to meet the legitimate aspirations of the peoples of the Americas for a better life and to provide them the fullest opportunity to improve their status;

Recognizing that the interests of the American republics are so interrelated that sound social and economic progress in each is of importance to all and that lack of it in any American republic may have serious repercussions in others;

Cognizant of the steps already taken by many American republics to cope with the serious economic and social problems confronting them, but convinced that the magnitude of these problems calls for redoubled efforts by governments and for a new and vigorous program of inter-American cooperation;

Recognizing that economic development programs, which should be urgently strengthened and expanded, may have a delayed effect on social welfare, and that accordingly early measures are needed to cope with social needs;

Recognizing that the success of a cooperative program of economic and social progress will require maximum self-help efforts on the part of the American republics and, in many cases, the improvement of existing institutions and practices, particularly in the fields of taxation, the ownership and use of land, education and training, health and housing;

Believing it opportune to give further practical expression to the spirit of Operation

---

* *Department of State Bulletin,* Oct. 3, 1960, pp. 537-40.

Pan America by immediately enlarging the opportunities of the people of Latin America for social progress, thus strengthening their hopes for the future;

Considering it advisable to launch a program for social development, in which emphasis should be given to those measures that meet social needs and also promote increases in productivity and strengthen economic development,

Recommends to the Council of the Organization of American States:

I. Measures for Social Improvement

An inter-American program for social development should be established which should be directed to the carrying out of the following measures of social improvement in Latin America, as considered appropriate in each country:

A. *Measures for the improvement of conditions of rural living and land use*

1. The examination of existing legal and institutional systems with respect to:

a. land tenure legislation and facilities with a view to ensuring a wider and more equitable distribution of the ownership of land, in a manner consistent with the objectives of employment, productivity and economic growth;

b. agricultural credit institutions with a view to providing adequate financing to individual farmers or groups of farmers;

c. tax systems and procedures and fiscal policies with a view to assuring equity of taxation and encouraging improved use of land, especially of privately-owned land which is idle.

2. The initiation or acceleration of appropriate programs to modernize and improve the existing legal and institutional framework to ensure better conditions of land tenure, extend more adequate credit facilities and provide increased incentives in the land tax structure.

3. The acceleration of the preparation of projects and programs for:

a. land reclamation and land settlement, with a view to promoting more widespread ownership and efficient use of land, particularly of unutilized or under-utilized land;

b. the increase of the productivity of land already in use; and

c. the construction of farm-to-market and access roads.

4. The adoption or acceleration of other government service programs designed particularly to assist the small farmer, such as new or improved marketing organizations; extension services; research and basic surveys; and demonstration, education, and training facilities.

B. *Measures for the improvement of housing and community facilities*

1. The examination of existing policies in the field of housing and community facilities, including urban and regional planning, with a view to improving such policies, strengthening public institutions and promoting private initiative and participation in programs in these fields. Special consideration should be given to encouraging financial institutions to invest in low-cost housing on a long-term basis and in building and construction industries.

2. The strengthening of the existing legal and institutional framework for mobilizing financial resources to provide better housing and related facilities for the people and to create new institutions for this purpose when necessary. Special consideration

should be given to legislation and measures which would encourage the establishment and growth of:

a. private financing institutions, such as building and loan associations;

b. institutions to insure sound housing loans against loss;

c. institutions to serve as a secondary market for home mortgages;

d. institutions to provide financial assistance to local communities for the development of facilities such as water supply, sanitation and other public works.

Existing national institutions should be utilized, wherever practical and appropriate, in the application of external resources to further the development of housing and community facilities.

3. The expansion of home building industries through such measures as the training of craftsmen and other personnel, research, the introduction of new techniques, and the development of construction standards for low and medium-cost housing.

4. The lending of encouragement and assistance to programs, on a pilot basis, for aided self-help housing, for the acquisition and subdivision of land for low-cost housing developments, and for industrial housing projects.

C. *Measures for the improvement of educational systems and training facilities*

1. The reexamination of educational systems, giving particular attention to:

a. the development of modern methods of mass education for the eradication of illiteracy;

b. the adequacy of training in the industrial arts and sciences with due emphasis on laboratory and work experience and on the practical application of knowledge for the solution of social and economic problems;

c. the need to provide instruction in rural schools not only in basic subjects but also in agriculture, health, sanitation, nutrition, and in methods of home and community improvement;

d. the broadening of courses of study in secondary schools to provide the training necessary for clerical and executive personnel in industry, commerce, public administration, and community service;

e. specialized trade and industrial education related to the commercial and industrial needs of the community;

f. vocational agricultural instruction;

g. advanced education of administrators, engineers, economists, and other professional personnel of key importance to economic development.

D. *Measures for the improvement of public health*

1. The reexamination of programs and policies of public health, giving particular attention to:

a. strengthening the expansion of national and local health services, especially those directed to the reduction of infant mortality;

b. the progressive development of health insurance systems, including those providing for maternity, accident and disability insurance, in urban and rural areas;

c. the provision of hospital and health service in areas located away from main centers of population;

d. the extension of public medical services to areas of exceptional need;

e. the strengthening of campaigns for the control or elimination of communicable diseases with special attention to the eradication of malaria;

f. the provision of water supply facilities for purposes of health and economic development;

g. the training of public health officials and technicians;

h. the strengthening of programs of nutrition for low-income groups.

E. *Measures for the mobilization of domestic resources*

1. This program shall be carried out within the framework of the maximum creation of domestic savings and of the improvement of fiscal and financial practices;

2. The equity and effectiveness of existing tax schedules, assessment practices and collection procedures shall be examined with a view to providing additional revenue for the purpose of this program;

3. The allocation of tax revenues shall be reviewed, having in mind an adequate provision of such revenues to the areas of social development mentioned in the foregoing paragraphs.

II. Creation of a Special Fund for Social Development

1. The delegations of the Governments of the Latin American republics welcome the decision of the Government of the United States to establish a special inter-American fund for social development, with the Inter-American Development Bank to become the primary mechanism for the administration of the fund.

2. It is understood that the purpose of the special fund would be to contribute capital resources and technical assistance on flexible terms and conditions, including repayment in local currency and the relending of repaid funds, in accordance with appropriate and selective criteria in the light of the resources available, to support the efforts of the Latin American countries that are prepared to initiate or expand effective institutional improvements and to adopt measures to employ efficiently their own resources with a view to achieving greater social progress and more balanced economic growth.

III. Measures for Economic Development

The Special Committee, Having in view Resolution VII adopted at the Seventh Meeting of Consultation of Ministers of Foreign Affairs expressing the need for the maximum contribution of member countries in hemisphere cooperation in the struggle against underdevelopment, in pursuance of the objectives of Operation Pan America,

Expresses Its Conviction

1. That within the framework of Operation Pan America the economic development of Latin America requires prompt action of exceptional breadth in the field of international cooperation and domestic effort comprising:

a. additional public and private financial assistance on the part of capital exporting countries of America, Western Europe, and international lending agencies within the framework of their charters, with special attention to:

i. the need for loans on flexible terms and conditons, including, whenever advisable in the light of the balance of payments situation of individual countries, the possibility of repayment in local currency,

ii. the desirability of the adequate preparation and implementation of development projects and plans, within the framework of the monetary, fiscal and exchange policies necessary for their effectiveness, utilizing as appropriate the technical assistance of inter-American and international agencies,

iii. the advisability, in special cases, of extending foreign financing for the coverage of local expenditures;

b. mobilization of additional domestic capital, both public and private;

c. technical assistance by the appropriate international agencies in the preparation and implementation of national and regional Latin American development projects and plans;

d. the necessity for developing and strengthening credit facilities for small and medium private business, agriculture and industry.

Recommends:

1. That special attention be given to an expansion of long-term lending, particularly in view of the instability of exchange earnings of countries exporting primary products and of the unfavourable effect of the excessive accumulation of short- and medium-term debt on continuing and orderly economic development.

2. That urgent attention be given to the search for effective and practical ways, appropriate to each commodity, to deal with the problem of the instability of exchange earnings of countries heavily dependent upon the exportation of primary products.

IV. Multilateral Cooperation for Social and Economic Progress

The Special Committee, Considering the need for providing instruments and mechanisms for the implementation of the program of inter-American economic and social cooperation which would periodically review the progress made and propose measures for further mobilization of resources,

Recommends:

1. That the Inter-American Economic and Social Council undertake to organize annual consultative meetings to review the social and economic progress of member countries, to analyze and discuss the progress achieved and the problems encountered in each country, to exchange opinions on possible measures that might be adopted to intensify further social and economic progress, within the framework of Operation Pan America, and to prepare reports on the outlook for the future. Such annual meetings should begin with an examination by experts and terminate with a session at the ministerial level.

2. That the Council of the Organization of American States convene within 60 days of the date of this Act a special meeting of senior government representatives to find ways of strengthening and improving the ability of the Inter-American Economic and Social Council to render effective assistance to governments with a view to achieving the objectives enumerated below, taking into account the proposal submitted by the delegation of Argentina in Document CECE/III-13:

a. To further the economic and social development of Latin American countries;

b. To promote trade between the countries of the Western Hemisphere as well as between them and extra-continental countries;

c. To facilitate the flow of capital and the extension of credits to the countries of Latin America both from the Western Hemisphere and from extra-continental sources.

3. The special meeting shall:

a. Examine the existing structure of the Inter-American Economic and Social Council, and of the units of the Secretariat of the Organization of American States working in the economic and social fields, with a view to strengthening and improving the Inter-American Economic and Social Council;

b. Determine the means of strengthening inter-American economic and social cooperation by an administrative reform of the Secretariat, which should be given sufficient technical, administrative and financial flexibility for the adequate fulfillment of its tasks;

c. Formulate recommendations designed to assure effective coordination between the Inter-American Economic and Social Council, the Economic Commission for Latin America, the Inter-American Development Bank, the United Nations and its Specialized Agencies and other agencies offering technical advice and services in the Western Hemisphere;

d. Propose procedures designed to establish effective liaison of the Inter-American Economic and Social Council and other regional American organizations with other international organizations for the purpose of study, discussion and consultation in the fields of international trade and financial and technical assistance;

e. And formulate appropriate recommendations to the Council of the Organization of American States.

In approving the Act of Bogotá the Delegations to the Special Committee, convinced that the people of the Americas can achieve a better life only within the democratic system, renew their faith in the essential values which lie at the base of Western civilization, and re-affirm their determination to assure the fullest measure of well-being to the people of the Americas under conditions of freedom and respect for the supreme dignity of the individual.

97. Address by Fidel Castro, Prime Minister of Cuba, before the U.N. General Assembly, on the Purpose of the Revolution in Cuba*

September 26, 1960

Although we have been given the reputation of speaking at great length, the Assembly need not worry. We shall do our best to be brief, saying only what we regard it as our duty to say here. I also intend to speak slowly, in order to co-operate with the interpreters.

Some people may think that we are highly displeased with the treatment meted out to the Cuban delegation. That is not the case. We understand the reason for these things perfectly and so we are not annoyed. No one need be concerned lest Cuba be

*United Nations General Assembly, *Official Records*, 15th Session, Part I, Vol. I (1960), pp. 117-36.

discouraged from making her small contribution to this effort to bring about world understanding. We shall continue to do so and we shall speak frankly.

It costs a great deal to send a delegation to the United Nations. We of the under-developed countries have very little money to spare but what we have we will spend in order to speak frankly at this meeting of representatives of nearly all the countries of the world.

The speakers who took the floor before me expressed their anxiety over problems which are of concern to the whole world. We are also interested in these problems. Moreover, in Cuba's case, there is another special circumstance: at this moment, Cuba itself is of concern to the world, for various representatives have stated here quite rightly that Cuba is one of the many problems existing in the world at the present time.

This is true; in addition to the problems which are today of concern to the whole world, Cuba has problems which are of concern to her, of concern to our people. Reference has been made to the universal desire for peace, which is the desire of all peoples and accordingly the desire of our people also. But this peace which the world wishes to preserve is a peace which we Cubans have been without for a long time. The perils which other peoples of the world may regard as more or less remote are problems and anxieties which are very close to us. It was not easy to come here to lay Cuba's problems before this Assembly. It was not easy for us to get here. I do not know whether we received special treatment. Can it be that we, the members of the Cuban delegation, represent the worst type of government in the world? Can it be that we, the representatives of the Cuban delegation, deserve the bad treatment which we have received? Why our delegation in particular? Cuba has sent many delegations to the United Nations. Cuba has been represented by many different persons, and yet, these exceptional measures were reserved for us: confinement to the island of Manhattan; instructions to all hotels not to rent us rooms, hostility and, on the pretext of security, isolation.

Probably none of the representatives here, who represent not any individual person but their respective countries and who must therefore be concerned over something that applies to any one of them because of what they represent; probably none of them, I say, on their arrival in the city of New York had to endure personal and physical humiliation of the kind which the Chairman of the Cuban delegation had to undergo.

I am not trying to stir up feeling in this Assembly. I am merely telling the truth. It was high time for us to get to our feet and speak out. People have been talking about us for many days now; the newspapers have been talking and we have been silent. We cannot defend ourselves from the attacks made on us here, in this country. Now we have an opportunity to tell the truth and we shall not fail to do so.

Personal humiliation, attempts at extortion, eviction from the hotel in which we were staying, and our removal to another hotel, after doing everything possible to avoid difficulties, refraining absolutely from leaving our lodgings, going nowhere except to this Assembly hall at the United Nations (on the few occasions when we have been present), and to a reception at the Soviet Embassy, in order to avoid problems and difficulties, even all this was not enough for us to be left in peace.

Over the years there has been considerable Cuban immigration into this country. During the last twenty years over 100,000 Cubans have come to this country from their own homeland, where they would have liked to remain always and where they wish to return as do all who are forced for social or economic reasons to leave their country. This Cuban population is employed; they respected and still respect the law and, very naturally, they felt deeply for their country and for the revolution. They never had any problems.

But one day there began to arrive in this country another kind of visitor; war criminals began to arrive; there began to arrive persons who, in some cases, had murdered hundreds of our compatriots. At once they were welcomed by the Press; they were welcomed by the authorities and naturally they reflected this welcome in their conduct and that is the reason for their many clashes with Cuban immigrants who had been working honestly in this country for years.

One of these incidents, provoked by persons who feel themselves strengthened by the systematic campaign against Cuba and the complicity of the authorities, resulted in the death of a little girl. This was a matter for regret, for all of us. But the guilty parties were not the Cubans who live here. Much less was the Cuban delegation guilty, and yet all of you have undoubtedly seen these headlines in the newspapers saying that pro-Castro groups had killed a ten-year-old girl; with the characteristic hypocrisy of all those who have anything to do with relations between Cuba and this country, a spokesman for the White House immediately made a statement drawing the whole world's attention to this act and to all intents and purposes laying the guilt at the door of the Cuban delegation. The United States representative to this Assembly added the crowning touch to the farce by sending a telegram to the Government of Venezuela and another telegram of condolences to the little girl's family, as though he felt obliged to give an explanation from the United Nations for something for which the Cuban delegation was virtually responsible.

But that was not all. When we were forced to leave one of the hotels in this city and come to United Nations Headquarters while other arrangements were being made, a modest hotel here, a Negro hotel in Harlem, offered us accommodation. The offer came during our conversations with the Secretary-General. Nevertheless, an official of the State Department did everything in his power to prevent us from being accommodated in this hotel.

At that moment, as if by magic, hotels began to spring up all over New York, hotels which had previously refused to house the Cuban delegation, offering to do so for nothing. Naturally, out of common courtesy, we agreed to go to the Harlem hotel. We thought that we had a right to hope that we would be left in peace. But we were not left in peace. As it had not been possible to prevent our stay in Harlem, a whispering campaign was started at once and the world was told that the Cuban delegation had taken up residence in a brothel.

No doubt to some gentlemen, a modest hotel in Harlem, where the Negroes of the United States live, could not be anything but a brothel. But besides this it was a matter of trying to cast a slur on the Cuban delegation, thus showing no respect even for the women members of our delegation or of its staff.

If we were the sort of men that they are trying at all costs to depict us as being, imperialism would not have lost its hope, as it did long ago, of buying us off or seducing us in some way. Since that hope was lost a long time ago—and there was never any reason to entertain it—after it was alleged that the Cuban delegation had taken up residence in a brothel, it had to be recognized that imperialist capital is a prostitute who cannot seduce us, and not exactly "the respectful prostitute" of Jean-Paul Sartre.

The problem of Cuba? Some representatives are perhaps well-informed; some of them not so well—it depends on your sources of information—but there is no doubt that for the world as a whole the Cuban problem is one that has arisen in the last two years; it.is a new problem. Formerly the world had little reason to know that Cuba existed. To many people it was rather like an appendix to the United States. Even for many citizens of this country, Cuba was a colony of the United States. It was not so on the map. On the map we were shown in a different colour from the United States; in reality, we were a colony.

How did our country come to be a United States colony? Not through its origins; the United States and Cuba were not colonized by the same people. Cuba has a very different ethnic and cultural background, built up over several hundred years.

Cuba was the last country in America to free herself from Spanish colonialism, the Spanish colonial yoke, if the representative of the Spanish Government will forgive me, and because it was the last, it had to struggle much more desperately. Spain had only one possession in America left and she defended it obstinately and with every means at her disposal. Our little people, numbering hardly more than one million at that time, had for nearly thirty years to fight alone against an army which was regarded as one of the strongest in Europe. Against our small national population the Spanish Government mobilized a force as large as all the forces which had fought against the independence of all the nations in South America put together. Nearly half a million Spanish soldiers fought against our people's heroic and single-minded determination to be free. The Cubans fought alone for their independence for thirty years; thirty years which laid the foundation for our country's love of freedom and independence.

But in the opinion of John Adams, one of the Presidents of the United States in the early years of last century, Cuba was a fruit, an apple, as it were, hanging from the Spanish tree, destined, as soon as it was ripe, to fall into the hands of the United States. Spain's power had wasted away in our country. She had neither men nor money left to continue the war in Cuba. Spain was routed. Apparently the apple was ripe and the United States Government held out its hands. It was not one apple that fell into its hands but several: Puerto Rico fell, heroic Puerto Rico, which had begun its fight for freedom together with the Cubans; so did the Philippine Islands and a number of other possessions.

However, some different pretext had to be found for subjugating our country. Cuba had fought a tremendous fight and world opinion was on its side. The Cubans who fought for our independence, those Cubans who at that time were laying down their lives, trusted completely in the Joint Resolution of the United States Congress, of 20 April 1898, which declared that "The people of the island of Cuba are, and of right ought to be, free and independent". The people of the United States sympathized with the Cubans in their struggle. That joint declaration was an Act of Congress of this nation under which war was declared on Spain.

That illusion ended in cruel disappointment. After two years of military occupation of our country, something unexpected occurred. Just when the Cuban people, through a Constituent Assembly, were drafting the basic law of the Republic, another act was passed by the United States Congress, an act proposed by Senator Platt, of unhappy memory for Cuba, in which it was laid down that a rider was to be attached to the Cuban Constitution whereby the United States Government would be granted the right to intervene in Cuban political affairs and, in addition, the right to lease certain parts of Cuban territory for naval bases or coaling stations; in other words, under a law enacted by the legislative authority of a foreign country, the Cuban Constitution had to contain this provision, and it was made very clear to the members of our Constituent Assembly that if no such amendment was made, the occupation forces would not be withdrawn. In other words, our country was forced by the legislature of a foreign country to grant that country the right to intervene and to hold naval bases or stations.

It is well for countries which have recently become Members of this Organization, countries now beginning their independent life, to bear in mind the history of our country because of the similar conditions that they may encounter along their own paths, or which those who come after them may encounter, or their children, or their children's children, although it seems that we are not going to get as far as that.

The new colonization of our country then began: the best agricultural land was acquired by the United States companies; concessions were granted for exploiting our natural resources and mines, concessions for the operation of public utilities, commercial concessions, concessions of every kind which, combined with the constitutional right, based on force, to intervene in our country transformed it from a Spanish into a United States colony.

Colonies have no voice. Colonies are not recognized in the world as long as they have no opportunity to make themselves heard. That was why the world knew nothing of this colony or of its problems. Another flag, another coat of arms, appeared in the geography books. Another colour appeared on the maps; but there was no independent republic in Cuba. Let no one be deceived because if we are, we shall only make fools of ourselves. Let no one be deceived. There was no independent republic in Cuba. It was a colony where the orders were given by the Ambassador of the United States of America. We have no shame in proclaiming this because any shame is offset by the pride we have in saying that today no embassy rules our people because our people are governed by the people.

Once again the Cuban people had to resort to strife to win their independence and they achieved it. They achieved it after seven years of bloody oppression. By whom were they oppressed? By those in our country who were merely the tools of those who dominated it economically. How can any unpopular régime, inimical to the interests of the people, remain in power except by force? Do we need to explain here to the representatives of our fellow countries of Latin America what military tyrannies are? Do we need to explain to them how they have remained in power? Do we need to explain to them the history of some of these tyrannies which have already become a byword? Do we need to explain to them on what strength these tyrannies rely, from what national and international interests the military group which oppressed our people drew its support? It was supported by the most reactionary circles in the country and most of all by the foreign economic interests which dominated our country's economy. Everyone knows—and we believe that even the United States Government admits this—that it was the type of government preferred by the monopolies. Why? Because by force any demand by the people can be repressed; by force strikes for better living conditions were repressed; with force peasant movements for ownership of the land were repressed; with force the dearest aspirations of the people were repressed.

That is why governments of force were preferred by those directing United States policy. That is why governments of force remained in power for so long and still remain in power in America. Clearly, it all depends on the circumstances whether or not there will be support from the United States Government. For example, the United States Government now says that it is against one of these governments of force, the Trujillo Government, but it does not say that it is against any other such governments, that of Nicaragua or of Paraguay for instance.

In Nicaragua there is now no longer a government of force but a kind of monarchy, which is almost as constitutional as that of the United Kingdom, in which power is handed down from father to son. And the same would have happened in our country. The Government of Fulgencio Batista was a typical government of force, a government which suited the United States monopolies in Cuba. But it was not, of course, the type of government which suited the Cuban people. With great loss of life and much sacrifice the Cuban people overthrew that Government.

What did the revolution find after it succeeded in Cuba? What wonders did it find? It found, first of all, that 600,000 Cubans fit for work were permanently unemployed—a figure which is, in proportion, equal to the number of unemployed in the United States at the time of the great depression which shook this country and almost led to disaster. Three million people, out of a total population of a little over 6 million, had no electric light and enjoyed none of the benefits and comforts of electricity. Three and a half million people, out of a total population of a little over 6 million, were living in hovels and huts unfit for human habitation. In the towns rents accounted for as much as one third of family incomes. Electricity rates and rents were among the highest in the world.

Thirty-seven and half per cent of our population were illiterate, unable to read or write. Seventy per cent of the children in the rural areas were without teachers. Two per cent of our population were suffering from tuberculosis, that is to say, 100,000 people out of a total of a little over 6 million. Ninety-five per cent of the children in rural areas were suffering from diseases caused by parasites. Infant mortality was consequently very high. The average life span was very short. In addition, 85 percent of small farmers were paying rent for their lands amounting to as much as 30 percent of the total gross incomes, while 1½ percent of all the landowners controlled 46 per cent of the total area of the country. The proportion of hospital beds to the number of inhabitants of the country was ludicrous when compared with countries with average medical services. Public utilities, electricity and telephone companies were owned by United States monopolies. A large part of the banking and import business, the oil refineries, the greater part of the sugar production, the best land, and the chief industries of all types in Cuba belonged to United States companies. In the last ten years, the balance of payments between Cuba and the United States has been in the latter's favour to the extent of $1,000 million, and that does not take into account the millions and hundreds of millions of dollars removed from the public treasury by the corrupt and tyrannical rulers and deposited in United States or European banks. One thousand million dollars in ten years! The poor and under-developed country of the

Caribbean, with 600,000 unemployed, contributing to the economic development of the most highly industrialized country in the world!

That was the situation which confronted us; a situation which is not unknown to many of the countries represented in this Assembly because, in the final analysis, what we have said about Cuba is merely a general X-ray photograph, so to speak, which is valid for the majority of countries represented here. What alternative was there for the revolutionary government? To betray the people? Of course, in the eyes of the President of the United States, what we have done for our people is treason to our people; but it would not be so, for sure, if instead of being loyal to our people we had been loyal to the great United States monopolies which were exploiting our country's economy.

Let note at least be taken here of the wonders which the revolution found after it succeeded, wonders which are no more and no less than the usual wonders associated with imperialism, the wonders of the free world for us colonized countries.

No one can blame us if Cuba had 600,000 unemployed, 37½ per cent of its population illiterate, 2 per cent suffering from tuberculosis, and 95 per cent of the children in rural areas suffering from diseases caused by parasites. No; until the revolution none of us had any say in the future of our country; until then the rulers who served the interests of the monopolies controlled its destinies; until then it was the monopolies which determined the fate of our country. Did anyone try to stop them? No, no one. Did anyone place difficulties in their way? No, no one. They were allowed to go about their business and in Cuba we are now enjoying the fruits of their work.

What was the state of the national reserves? When the tyrant Batista came to power there were $500 million in the national reserves—a goodly sum for investing in the industrial development of the country. After the revolution there were $70 million in our reserves. Does this show any concern for the industrial development of our country? None at all; that is why we are so astonished and we continue to be astonished when we hear in the General Assembly of the United States Government's great concern for the future of the countries of Latin America, Africa and Asia. We cannot overcome our astonishment because, after fifty years of such a régime, we now see the results in Cuba.

What has the revolutionary government done? What crime has the revolutionary government committed, that we should receive the treatment we have received here, that we should have such powerful enemies as we have been shown to have here? Did our problems with the United States Government arise immediately? No. When we came to power, were we possessed with the desire to seek international problems? No; no revolutionary government coming to power wants international problems; what it wants is to devote its energies to solving its own problems; what it wants is to carry out a programme, as does any government that is genuinely interested in the progress of its country.

The first occurrence that we considered an unfriendly act was the opening wide of the doors of this country to a whole gang of criminals who had drenched our land with blood. Men who had murdered hundreds of defenceless peasants, who did not tire of torturing prisoners for years who killed right and left, were welcomed here with open arms. To us this seemed strange. Why this unfriendly act by the United States authorities towards Cuba? Why this act of hostility? At that time we did not fully understand; now, we see the reasons perfectly.

Was this policy consistent with correct behaviour towards Cuba—a correct conduct of relations between the United States and Cuba? No, for we were the injured party, because the Batista régime stayed in power with the assistance of the United States Government, the Batista régime stayed in power with the assistance of tanks, aircraft and weapons supplied by the United States Government; the Batista régime stayed in power through the use of an army whose officers were trained by a military mission of the United States Government. And we trust that no official of the United States will try to deny this fact. At the very moment when the rebel army arrived at the city of Havana, the United States military mission was occupying the principal military camp of that city. That was an army that had been overcome; an army that had been defeated and had surrendered. We could quite rightly have treated as prisoners-of-war these foreign officers who were there assisting and training the enemies of the people. However, that was not what we did; we merely requested the members of the mission to return to their own country, because after all we did not need their lessons, and their pupils there had been defeated.

I have with me a document. Let no one be surprised at its appearance, for it is a torn document. It is an old military Agreement, under which the Batista tyranny received generous assistance from the United States Government.

Now it is important to notice what this Agreement says in article I, paragraph 2:

> "The Government of Cuba undertakes to make effective use of assistance received from the Government of the United States of America pursuant to this Agreement for the purpose of implementing defence plans, accepted by the two Governments, under which the two Governments will participate in missions important to the defence of the Western Hemisphere, and will not, without the prior agreement of the Government of the United States of America . . ."—I repeat—" . . . without the prior agreement of the Government of the United States of America, devote such assistance to purposes other than those for which it was furnished."

This assistance was devoted to combating the Cuban revolutionaries. It had therefore the approval of the United States Government. And even when, a few months before the end of the war, there was an embargo in this country on arms sent to Batista, after more than six years of military aid, the rebel army had evidence, documentary evidence, that after the solemn declaration of this arms embargo the forces of tyranny had been newly supplied with 300 rockets, to be fired from aircraft.

When our fellow-countrymen living in the United States set these documents before the public, the United States Government could find no other explanation than to say that we were mistaken, and that they had not sent any fresh supplies to the army of the tyranny, but had merely replaced some rockets of the wrong calibre for its aircraft by some others which were of the right size—and which doubtless were fired at us while we were in the mountains. A novel way of explaining contradictions, when they become inexplicable!

According to this explanation, it was not a question of military aid. It must then have been a kind of technical assistance. Why were these circumstances displeasing to our people? Everyone knows—even the most ingenuous person knows—that in these modern days, with the revolution that has taken place in military equipment, the weapons of the last war are absolutely obsolete for a modern war; that fifty tanks or armoured cars and a few outdated aircraft could not defend any continent or any hemisphere. On the other hand, they are useful for oppressing unarmed peoples; they are useful for intimidating peoples. They are useful for the defence of monopolies. These agreements for the defence of the hemisphere, therefore, should rather be called "agreements for the defence of United States monopolies".

The Revolutionary Government began to make its first reforms. The first thing it did was to reduce rents paid by families by 50 per cent. A very just measure, since, as we said earlier, there were families paying as much as a third of their income. The people had been the victims of large-scale speculation in housing, and there had been tremendous speculation in urban land at the people's expense. But when the Revolutionary Government reduced rents by 50 per cent, there were some who were not pleased, to be sure: those few who owned the apartment buildings. But the people rushed in to the streets rejoicing, as would happen in any country, even here in New York, if rents for all families were reduced by 50 per cent. But this did not involve any difficulty with the monopolies; some United States companies owned large buildings, but they were relatively few.

Then came another law; a law cancelling the concessions which the tyrannical Government of Fulgencio Batista had granted to the telephone company, which was a United States monopoly. It had taken advantage of the people's defencelessness to obtain very favourable concessions. The Revolutionary Government cancelled these concessions and restored the rates for telephone services to the previous level. This was the beginning of the first conflict with the United States monopolies.

The third measure was the reduction of electricity charges, which were among the highest in the world. Thus arose the second conflict with the United States monopolies. By this time we were beginning to look like communists. We began to be painted red, simply because we had clashed with the interests of the United States monopolies.

There followed another law, an inevitable and indispensable law, inevitable for our country and inevitable, sooner or later, for all the peoples in the world, at least for all those peoples of the world who have not yet carried it out: the land reform law. Of course, in theory, everyone is in favour of land reform. No one dares to question it; no informed person dares to deny that land reform is an essential condition for economic development in the under-developed countries of the world. In Cuba too, even the big landowners were in agreement with land reform, provided it was a kind of land reform which suited them, like the land reform proposed by many theorists: a land reform which would not be carried out, for just as long as it could be avoided.

Land reform is something recognized by the economic organs of the United Nations, something which is no longer in dispute. In our country it was indispensable; more than 200,000 families lived in the rural areas of our country without any land on which to grow essential food crops. Without land reform our country would not have been able to take the first step towards development. Well, we took this step. We instituted a land reform. Was it radical? It was a radical reform. Was it very radical? It was not particularly radical. We carried out a land reform appropriate to the needs of our development, appropriate to our capacities for agricultural development; that is to say, a land reform which would solve the problem of landless peasants, solve the problem of the supply of these essential foodstuffs, remedy the fearfully high level of unemployment in rural areas, and put an end to the appalling poverty which we found in our countryside.

Well, it was at that point that the first real difficulty arose. The same thing had happened in the neighbouring Republic of Guatemala. When land reform was carried out in Guatemala, difficulties arose there. And I must in honesty warn the representatives of Latin America, Africa and Asia: when they plan to carry out a just land reform, they must be prepared to face situations similar to ours, especially if the best and largest estates are owned by United States monopolies, as was the case in Cuba.

It may well be that we shall now be accused of giving bad advice in this Assembly. It is certainly not our object to disturb anyone's sleep. We are simply drawing attention to the facts, although the facts are sufficient to keep anyone awake.

The problems of compensation were at once raised. Communications from the American State Department began to pour in. They never asked us about our problems; not even out of pity, or on account of the large share of responsibility they bore in the matter, did they ask us how many of our people were starving to death, how many were suffering from tuberculosis, how many were out of work. No; never an expression of solidarity with us in our needs. The only concern expressed by the United States Government representatives was for the telephone company, the electricity company, and the problem of the lands owned by the United States companies. How were we going to pay? Clearly, the first question to be asked was—what were we going to pay with? "What with?", rather than "how?". Do you imagine, gentlemen, that a poor, under-developed country with 600,000 unemployed, with such a high level of illiteracy and sickness, whose reserves have been used up, and which has contributed 1,000 million dollars in ten years to the economy of a powerful country, could have the wherewithal to pay for the land which was going to be affected by the land reform, or at least pay for it on the terms demanded by the American State Department as compensation for the prejudice to their interests? They demanded three things: prompt, effective and fair compensation. Do you understand this language, gentlemen? Prompt, effective and fair compensation. In other words, pay immediately, in dollars, the amount we ask for our land.

We were still not 150 per cent Communists. We were just becoming a little more tinged with red. We did not confiscate these lands; we merely proposed to pay for them in twenty years, and the only way we could pay for them was in bonds, maturing after twenty years, earning interest at 4½ per cent, which would be gradually redeemed year by year. How could we pay for the land in dollars? How could we pay immediately? How could we pay what they asked for it? It was absurd. Anyone can see that in these circumstances we had to choose between carrying out the land reform and not carrying it out. If we did not carry it out, the appalling economic situation of our country would last indefinitely; but if we did carry it out, we would be exposing ourselves to the enmity of the Government of our powerful northern neighbour.

We went ahead with the land reform. One can be sure that to a representative of the Netherlands, say, or any other European country, the limits we set to land holdings would be quite surprising; they would be surprisingly high. The maximum set by our land reform law was around 400 hectares. In Europe, 400 hectares would constitute a large estate. In Cuba, where there were United States monopolistic companies holding up to around 200,000 hectares (200,000 hectares, in case anyone thinks he has not heard aright), in Cuba, a land reform designed to reduce the maximum holding to 400 hectares was something which these monopolies considered inadmissible. But in our country it was not only the land that was owned by United States monopolies; the principal mines were also the property of these monopolies. Cuba produces a large quantity of nickel, for example. All the nickel was mined by United States concerns. And under the Batista tyranny, a United States company the Moa Bay Company, had obtained such a profitable concession that, in only five years—listen carefully—in only five years it was going to amortize an investment of 120 million dollars. A 120 million-dollar investment to be amortized in five years!

Who was it that gave that concession to the Moa Bay Company, through the intervention of the United States Ambassador? None other than the tyrannical Government of Fulgencio Batista, the Government that was there to defend the interests of the monopolies, and what is more—and this is a fact beyond any doubt whatever—the concession was completely tax-free. What were such undertakings going to leave for the Cubans? Worked-out mines, impoverished land, not even a modest contribution to the economic development of our country. And then the Revolutionary Government enacted a law on mines requiring these monopolies to pay a 25 per cent tax on mineral exports.

The attitude of the Revolutionary Government had already been too daring. It had clashed with the interests of the international electric trust, clashed with the interests of the international telephone trust, clashed with the interests of the international mining trusts, clashed with the interests of the United Fruit Company, clashed, as it were, with the most powerful interests of the United States, which as you know are closely interrelated. That was more than the United States Government, that is to say, the representatives of the monopolies of the United States, could stand.

It was then that a new stage in the harassment of our revolution began. Can anyone who objectively analyses the facts—anyone who is willing to think for himself and not as the United Press or the Associated Press tells him to think, to think with his own head and draw conclusions from his own reasoning and see things as they are without preconceived notions, honestly and fairly—consider that the things which the Revolutionary Government has done were such as to call for the destruction of the Cuban revolution? No. But the interests affected by the Cuban revolution were not concerned about the case of Cuba, they were not being ruined by the measures of the Cuban Revolutionary Government. That was not the problem. The problem was that those same interests were the owners of the wealth and natural resources of the majority of the peoples of the world.

And the Cuban revolution had to be chastised for its attitude. The audacity of the Revolutionary Government had to be castigated by punitive operations of every kind ranging as far as the destruction of the impudent men concerned. On our word of honour we swear that we had not then had occasion even to exchange a letter with the distinguished Prime Minister of the Soviet Union, Mr. Khrushchev. In other words, at the time when, according to the United States Press and the international information agencies, Cuba was already a red Government, a red menace ninety miles from the United States, with a government dominated by Communists, the Revolutionary Government had not even had occasion to establish diplomatic or commercial relations with the Soviet Union.

But hysteria is capable of anything. Hysteria is capable of making the most unlikely and the most absurd assertions. However, let no one think that we are now going to recite a *mea culpa*. There will be no *mea culpa*. We do not have to ask forgiveness of anyone. What we did we did very deliberately and above all fully convinced of our right to do it.

Then began the threats against our sugar quota. The cheap philosophy of imperialism began to demonstrate its nobility, the nobility of the self-seeker and the exploiter, to demonstrate its kindness towards Cuba, saying that we were being paid a preferential price for sugar, which amounted to a subsidy for Cuban sugar, the sugar that was not so sweet for us Cubans since we were not the owners of the best sugar fields or of the biggest sugar mills. What is more, in that assertion lay hidden the true history of Cuban sugar, of the sacrifices my country had had to bear, of the occasions when it had been subjected to economic aggression.

Earlier on, it was not a matter of quotas, but of customs tariffs. The United States, by virtue of one of those laws, or rather one of those agreements between the shark and the sardine which it called a reciprocity agreement, obtained a number of concessions for its products in order that they might be able to compete freely with the products of its friends, the British and the French, and squeeze them out of the Cuban market, as often happens among friends. In exchange, certain tariff concessions were granted for our sugar but the Congress or Government of the United States could modify them unilaterally at will. And that is what happened. When they considered it more in their interests to raise the tariffs, they did so and our sugar could not enter the United States market, or it entered at a disadvantage. When the clouds of war gathered, the tariffs were reduced.

Obviously, Cuba being the nearest source of supply for sugar, that source of supply had to be assured; tariffs were lowered, production was encouraged, and during the war years, when the price of sugar was astronomical throughout the world, we were selling our sugar cheap to the United States, in spite of the fact that we were its only source of supply.

The war ended and our economy collapsed. The mistakes made in this country in the distribution of sugar were paid for by us; prices that had risen enormously by the end of the First World War; tremendous boost to production; a sudden drop in prices, ruining the Cuban sugar mills, which quietly fell into the hands of—guess whom—the United States banks, of course, because when Cuban nationals went bankrupt, United States banks became rich; and so it went on until the 1930's. In the search for a formula which would reconcile its interests in ensuring a source of supply with those of its domestic producers, the United States Government set up a quota system. One would have thought that the quotas would be based on the historic contributions of the various sources of supply to the market, and our country's historic contribution to the United States market had been almost 50 per cent. Nevertheless, when the quotas were established, our share was reduced to 28 per cent and the few advantages granted us by that law were successively withdrawn in subsequent legislation. Naturally, the colony depended on the metropolitan country; the economy of the colony had been organized by the metropolitan country; the colony had to be subject to the metropolitan country and if the colony took steps to free itself, the metropolitan country would take steps to crush it.

Aware of our economy's dependence on the United States market, the United States Government began its series of warnings that it would deprive us of our sugar quota. Concurrently, other activities were taking place in the United States of America, the activities of the counter-revolutionaries.

One afternoon an aircraft coming from the north flew over one of our sugar mills and dropped a bomb. That was a strange, an unusual event, but of course we knew where that aircraft came from.

Another afternoon another aircraft flew over our sugarcane fields and dropped some small incendiary bombs. And what started in a haphazard fashion was then continued systematically.

One afternoon—when a large number of United States tourist agents were visiting Cuba in connexion with a campaign by the Revolutionary Government to encourage tourism as a source of national income—an aircraft of United States manufacture, of a type used in the Second World War, flew over our capital, dropping leaflets and some hand-grenades. Naturally, some anti-aircraft guns went into action. What with the grenades dropped by the aircraft and the anti-aircraft fire, because, as you know, some of the projectiles explode on contact with any hard object, the result was more than forty casualties. There were children and old people with their entrails ripped out. Was this the first time for us? No, children and old people, men and women had often been wiped out in our Cuban villages by bombs of United States manufacture supplied to the tyrant Batista, and on one occasion eighty workers were killed by the all-too-mysterious explosion of a ship loaded with Belgian weapons which had finally reached our country after a major effort by the United States Government to prevent the Belgian Government from selling us arms.

Dozens of war victims; eighty families destroyed by an explosion; forty casualties caused by an aircraft that leisurely flew over our territory. The authorities of the United States Government denied that those aircraft had come from United States territory. What is more, they said the aircraft was standing quietly in a hangar. But when one of our periodicals published a photograph of the aircraft, it was only then that the United States authorities seized it, and immediately issued a statement to the effect that the matter was of no importance and that the casualties had been caused not by bombs but by anti-aircraft fire; and meanwhile those who had committed this foul deed, this crime, were going about the United States undisturbed, and not hindered in any way from continuing to commit such acts of aggression.

I take this opportunity of telling the representative of the United States that there are many mothers in Cuba still waiting for a telegram of condolences from him for their children murdered by United States bombs.

The aircraft went back and forth. There was no evidence; all right, no one knows what evidence means. There it was—the aircraft that had been photographed and captured; but we were told that that particular aircraft had not dropped any bombs. We do not know how it was that the United States authorities were so well informed. Pirate aircraft continued to fly over our territory, dropping incendiary bombs. Millions and millions of pesos were lost in the burning sugarcane fields. Many ordinary people, the little people of our country, who saw this property that was now truly theirs being destroyed, suffered burns and injuries while fighting the persistent and relentless bombing attacks by pirate aircraft.

Finally, one day, while flying over one of our sugar mills, an aircraft was destroyed by the explosion of one of its own bombs and the Revolutionary Government succeeded in collecting the remains of the pilot and in seizing his papers, which showed that he was indeed a United States pilot and the aircraft a United States aircraft, and provided complete evidence as to the place of take-off. The aircraft had passed between two bases in the United States. It could no longer be denied that those aircraft were taking off from the United States.

This time the United States Government, confronted with irrefutable proof, did give an explanation to the Government of Cuba. Its behaviour in this case was not the same as in the case of the U-2. When it was proved that the aircraft were taking off from the United States, the United States Government did not proclaim its right to burn our sugarcane fields. On this occasion it apologized, it said it was sorry. After all, we were lucky, for the United States Government did not apologize after the U-2 incident; instead, it proclaimed its right to fly over Soviet territory. That is bad luck for the Soviets! But our anti-aircraft defences are not very strong and the aircraft continued their raids until the cane was harvested. When there was no cane left in the fields, the bombing stopped.

We were the only country in the world in which this happened, although I do recall that, at the time of his visit to Cuba, President Sukarno told us that we must not think that we were the only ones, that they too had had some problems, that some United States aircraft had also been flying over their territory. I do not know whether I have committed an indiscretion in mentioning this; I hope not. The fact of the matter is that we were the only country in the world, or at least in this peaceful hemisphere, which, without being at war with anyone, had to endure constant harassment by pirate aircraft. And were those aircraft able to enter and leave United States territory with impunity?

We invite representatives to give a little thought to this matter, and we invite the people of the United States—if perchance the people of the United States have an opportunity to learn what is said in this hall—to think about the fact that, according to the United States Government's own statements, the territory of the United States is completely guarded and protected against any air raid and that the defences of United States territory are infallible, that the defences of the world they call "free"—although for us, at least, it was not free before 1 January 1959—are perfect. If that is the case, how does it happen that aircraft—not supersonic aircraft by any means but ordinary light aircraft with a maximum speed of 150 miles an hour—can enter and leave the national territory of the United States as they please, pass close to two bases on both the outward and return flights, without the United States Government's knowing that these aircraft are entering and leaving? This means one of two things: either the United States Government is lying to the people of the United States and the United States is defenceless against air raids, or the United States Government was an accomplice in these raids.

The air raids finally ended, and then came economic aggression. What was one of the arguments used by the enemies of the land reform? They said that the land reform would bring chaos to agricultural production, that production would decline considerably, that the United States Government was concerned lest Cuba might not be able to fulfil its commitments regarding supplies to the United States market.

The first argument, and it is a good thing at least for the new delegations here to become familiar with some of the arguments, because the day may come when they may have to answer similar arguments—that the land reform meant the ruin of the country. That did not happen. Had the land reform meant the ruin of the country, had agricultural production dropped, there would have been no need for the United States Government to intensify its economic aggression.

Did they believe what they were saying when they stated that the land reform was going to cause a drop in production? Perhaps they did. It is understandable that everyone should think in the way his mind has been trained to think. It is possible they imagined that without the all-powerful monopolies we Cubans could not produce sugar. It is possible, perhaps they were even sure that we should ruin the country. But it is obvious that, if the Revolution had ruined the country, there would have been no need for the United States to attack us, they would have left us alone and the United States Government would have been a very noble, a very good Government, and we a group of people who were ruining the nation, providing a living example of the fact that you cannot have revolutions because revolutions ruin countries. But that is not the way things turned out. There is now evidence that revolutions do not ruin countries and that evidence has just been provided by the United States Government. It has proved many things, including the fact that revolutions do not ruin countries and that imperialist governments are indeed capable of trying to do so. Cuba had not ruined itself and so Cuba had to be ruined.

Cuba needed new markets for its products, and we might frankly ask any delegation here which of them does not want its country to sell what it produces, which of them does not want its exports to increase? We wanted our exports to increase. That is what all countries want, that must be a universal law, for only self-interest can oppose the universal interest of trade, which is one of the oldest aspirations and needs of mankind.

We wanted to sell our products and we were looking for new markets. We signed a trade agreement with the Soviet Union under which we were to sell 1 million tons and bought certain quantities of Soviet goods. Surely no one will say that that is wrong. There may be some who would not sign such a treaty because it would be unpalatable to certain interests. But we did not feel under any obligation to ask the State Department's permission to sign a trade treaty with the Soviet Union because we believed, as we still do and always shall, that Cuba is a truly free country.

When sugar stocks began to fall and our economic position was beginning to improve, the blow fell. At the request of the Executive, the United States Congress enacted legislation authorizing the President or Executive to reduce sugar imports from Cuba by whatever amount might be deemed appropriate. The economic weapon was being used against our revolution. The newspapers had already taken it upon themselves to prepare the ground for this policy. They had been carrying on the campaign for some time for it is common knowledge that here the monopolies and the Press are synonymous. The economic weapon was used. At one fell swoop our sugar quota was cut by nearly 1 million tons—although the sugar had been produced for the United States market—in order to deprive our country of the resources it needed for development, in order to reduce it to impotence, and to attain political ends.

That action is specifically prohibited by regional international law. As all the representatives of Latin America in this Assembly know, economic aggression is expressly condemned by regional international law. Yet, the United States Government violated that law; it made use of the economic weapon and simply slashed our sugar quota by almost a million tons. There was nothing to stop them. What could Cuba do to protect itself in such a situation? It could go before the United Nations to complain of political aggression, economic aggression and the aerial incursions by pirate aircraft, to say nothing of the United States Government's continual interference in Cuba's political affairs and the subversive campaigns it is carrying on against the Revolutionary Government.

We had recourse to the United Nations. The United Nations is empowered to deal with questions of this kind. It is the supreme international organization. It has authority over and above that of the Organization of American States. Moreover, we wanted to bring the question before the United Nations because we know that economically the Latin American nations are dependent on the United States.

The United Nations was seized of the question and asked OAS to look into the matter. OAS met. What action was to be expected? That OAS would protect the country that had been attacked; that it would condemn the political aggression, and in particular the economic aggression, against Cuba. That was what we expected. After all, we were a small country in the Latin American community. We were yet another victim of aggression. We were not the first or the last. Mexico had on more than one occasion, been the victim of aggression, including military aggression. The United States seized a large part of Mexican territory after a war during which heroic sons of Mexico wrapped themselves in the Mexican flag and jumped from the ramparts at Chapultepec rather than surrender. Such are the heroic sons of Mexico. And that was not the only act of aggression; that was not the only occasion on which United States forces marched into Mexican territory.

There was also intervention in Nicaragua, and for seven years César Augusto Sandino put up a heroic resistance. There was intervention more than once in Cuba, and in Haiti and Santo Domingo. There was intervention in Guatemala. Is there any one here who could in honesty deny the intervention of the United Fruit Company and the United States Department of State in the overthrow of the lawful Government of Guatemala? I realize that there are some who consider it their duty as officials to be discreet in this matter and who are capable of coming to this rostrum with a denial, but in their heart of hearts they know that what I say is a fact.

Cuba was not the first country to be attacked; it was not the first country in danger of aggression. Everyone in the Americas knows that the United States Government has always laid down the law, the law that might is right, which it has used to destroy the Puerto Rican nation and maintain its dominion over the island, the law by virtue of which it took possession of, and still holds, the Panama Canal. That was nothing new. Our country should have been protected but it was not. Why? At this point we must consider facts and not forms. According to the dead letter of the law, we are protected; in reality we have no protection whatsoever, for the facts count more than the law set forth in international codes and the fact is that a small country attacked by a powerful Government had no defence and could not be protected.

What happened at the meeting in Costa Rica? By a miracle of ingenuity, neither the United States nor the Government of the United States was censured—and may I say at this point that our feelings towards the people of the United States should not be confused with our feelings towards the United States Government. The Government of the United States was not censured for the sixty flights by pirate aircraft; it was not censured for economic aggression and the many other acts of aggression committed. On the contrary, they censured the Soviet Union. It was an extraordinary thing to do. The Soviet Union had not committed aggression against us; no Soviet aircraft had flown over our territory and yet in Costa Rica they censured the Soviet Union for interference. The Soviet Union had merely said that in the event of military aggression against our country, Soviet artillerymen could, figuratively speaking, support the victim of aggression. Since when has support for a small country, in the event of an attack on it by a powerful country, been regarded as interference? In law there is what is called an "impossible condition". If the United States considers that it is incapable of committing a particular crime, it is sufficient to say that since there is no possibility of its attacking Cuba, there is no possibility of the Soviet Union supporting that little country. But that principle was not laid down. The principle laid down was that the Soviet Union should be censured for its interference. There was no mention of the bombing of Cuba, no mention of the aggression against Cuba.

There is, of course, one thing that we should all bear in mind. All of us here, without exception, are actors and participants in a crucial moment in the history of mankind. Sometimes censure does not seem to strike home. Sometimes we do not heed criticism, particularly when we forget that as persons privileged to play a role at this crucial moment in history, we shall some day be judged by history for our acts. When we think how our country found itself without defenders at the meeting in Costa Rica, we smile because that episode will be judged by history. I say so without bitterness. It is difficult to blame men. Men are frequently the playthings of circumstances and we who are familiar with our country's history and know at first hand what it is enduring today, understand how terrible it is when a nation's economy and way of life in general are subordinate to foreign economic power.

I need only note that our country was left undefended and point to the concern that the question should not reach the United Nations. Perhaps it was felt that it would be easier to obtain an automatic majority in the OAS, although it is hard to see why, as automatic majorities have frequently been obtained here in the United Nations. With all due respect to this Organization, I must say that our people, the people of Cuba, have learned much; they are, and I say this with pride, equal to the task they are undertaking, to the heroic struggle they are waging; they have learnt a lesson from recent international events and they know that at the eleventh hour, when their rights have been denied, when the forces of aggression are marshalled against them, when their rights are not protected either in the Organization of American States or in the United Nations, there still remains to them the ultimate and heroic remedy of resistance.

This is why we small countries still do not feel certain that our rights will be preserved. This is why, when we small countries seek to be free, we know that we must become free by our own efforts and at our own risk. When a people is united and is defending a just cause, it can trust in its own strength. In Cuba we are not, as we have been alleged to be, a group of men governing a country. We are a people governing a country, an entire nation resolutely united in an unshakeable revolutionary spirit in defence of its rights. This is something that the enemies of the revolution and of Cuba should know for if they ignore it they are grievously mistaken.

This is the background to the Cuban revolution. What is the state of the country? Why have difficulties arisen? And yet despite these difficulties the Cuban revolution is changing what was yesterday a country without hope, a country of poverty, many of whose people could not read or write, into a country which will soon be one of the most advanced and highly developed in the Americas.

In a scant twenty months the Revolutionary Government has opened 10,000 new schools, that is, double the number of rural schools which had been built in the previous half century, and Cuba is today the first country in the Americas to meet all its school needs, with teachers even in the most remote mountain villages.

In this short space of time the Revolutionary Government has built 25,000 houses in rural and urban areas. Fifty new towns are under construction. The most important military fortresses are being used to house tens of thousands of students and next year our people propose to launch an all-out offensive against illiteracy, with the ambitious goal of teaching every illiterate person to read and write. Organizations of teachers, students and workers—the entire people—are preparing themselves for an intensive campaign and within a few months Cuba will be the first country in the Americas to be able to claim that it has not a single illiterate inhabitant.

Our people now benefit from the services of hundreds of doctors who have been sent to the country districts to fight diseases caused by parasites and improve sanitary conditions in the nation.

In another field, that of the conservation of natural resources, we can point with pride to the fact that in a single year, in the most ambitious plan for the conservation of natural resources being carried out in this continent, including the United States and Canada, we have planted approximately 50 million timber-producing trees.

Young people, for whom there were no jobs or schools, have been organized by the Revolutionary Government and are today being employed in work that is of value to the country and at the same time are being trained for productive employment.

Agricultural production has increased from the very outset. This virtually unique achievement was possible because the Revolutionary Government made over 100,000 small tenant farmers into landowners and at the same time maintained large-scale production by means of agricultural producers' co-operatives. By using co-operatives to maintain large-scale production it was possible to apply the most modern agricultural techniques, and from the very outset production increased. And we have carried through this programme of social betterment and provided teachers, houses and hospitals without sacrificing resources for development.

The Revolutionary Government is already carrying out a programme of industrialization and the first factories are now being built. We have used our country's resources rationally. Thus, Cuba used to import $35 million worth of cars and $5 million worth of tractors. A predominantly agricultural country was importing seven times as many cars as tractors. We have reversed the figures and are importing seven times as many tractors as cars.

Close to $500 million has been recovered from the politicians who had enriched themselves during the tyranny. We have recovered a total of close to $500 million in cash and other assets from the corrupt politicians who had been plundering our country for seven years.

By making proper use of this wealth and these resources, the Revolutionary Government is able to implement a plan for the industrialization of the country and the expansion of agricultural production and at the same time to build houses and schools, send teachers to the most remote villages and provide medical services, in other words to carry out a programme of social development. As you know, at the recent meeting in Bogotá the United States Government put forward a plan. But it was not a plan for economic development. It was a plan for social development, by which is meant, a plan for building houses, schools and roads. Does this solve the problem? How can social problems be solved without a plan for economic development? Do they want to make fools of the people of Latin America? If the houses are built, what are the families who move into them going to live on? Where are the children who are to go to these schools going to get shoes, clothes and food? Surely they realize that parents will not send their children to school without clothes or shoes? Where is the money going to come from to pay the teachers and doctors? Where is the money going to come from to pay for the medicines? One good way of saving money on medicines would be to improve the people's diet. Money spent on feeding the people will not have to be spent on hospitals.

Now, faced with the tremendous reality of underdevelopment, the United States Government comes out with a plan for social development. Of course, the fact that the United States Government is showing an interest in the problems of Latin America is in itself something remarkable. Previously, it had completely ignored them. What a coincidence that these problems are now causing it concern! Any connexion between this concern and the Cuban revolution will, of course, be interpreted as purely fortuitous.

Formerly, the monopolies' sole concern was to exploit the under-developed countries, but with the advent of the Cuban revolution they began to get worried. And at the same time that the United States is attacking us economically and trying to ruin us, it offers charity to the peoples of Latin America, not in the form of resources for general development—which is what Latin America wants—but resources for social development, for houses for men who have no work, for schools which no children will attend and for hospitals which would be not so necessary if there were a little less malnutrition in Latin America.

After all, some of my Latin American colleagues may feel it is their duty to be discreet here, but I myself can welcome a revolution like the Cuban revolution. At least it has forced the monopolies to return a small part of what they have seized from the peoples of Latin America in the form of natural resources and labour.

We are not worried by the fact that we are not included in the United States aid plan. We are not going to get alarmed about that. We have already been settling these problems for a long time. However, some may feel that we are engaging in propaganda here, because the President of the United States said that some Members were going to come to this rostrum for that purpose. Of course, any of our United Nations colleagues is invited to visit Cuba at any time. We do not close the door on anyone; we do not place restrictions on anyone. Any of our colleagues in this Assembly can visit Cuba and see with his own eyes. You all know that chapter in the Bible which speaks of Saint Thomas, who said that he had to see in order to believe. We can invite any journalist or any representative to visit Cuba and see what a people can do with its own resources, when they are invested honestly and rationally.

We are not only settling our housing and educational difficulties but also our development problems because otherwise our social problems would remain unsolved.

But what is happening? Why is the United States Government unwilling to speak of development? The answer is very simple: it is because the United States Government does not want to stand up to the monopolies and the monopolies require natural resources and investment markets for their capital.

That is where the great contradiction lies. That is why the true solution of the problem is not sought; that is why no programmes are being drawn up for the development of the under-developed countries. It is well that this should be stated in all frankness because, in the final analysis, we under-developed countries are in the majority here, in case anyone is unaware of the fact. And, in the final analysis, it is we who can see what is happening in the under-developed countries. However, the real solution is not sought and here there is always talk about the participation of private capital. This of course, means markets for investments of surplus capital, investments of the kind that are amortized in five years.

The United States Government cannot propose a plan for public investment because this would run counter to its very "raison d'être", namely, the United States monopolies. This is quite frankly the real reason why no genuine economic development programme is being put forward: to preserve our lands in Latin America, Africa and Asia for the investment of surplus capital.

Thus far we have referred to the problems of my own country. Why have these problems not been solved? Is it because we do not want to solve them? No; the Government of Cuba has always been ready to discuss its problems with the United States Government but the United States Government has not wished to discuss its problems with Cuba. And it must have its reasons for not wishing to discuss its problems with Cuba.

Mr. Fekini (Libya) Vice-President, took the Chair.

I have here a note sent by the Revolutionary Government of Cuba to the Government of the United States on 27 January 1960. It states:

> "The differences of opinion which may exist between both Governments as subjects for diplomatic negotiations can be settled effectively by such negotiations. The Government of Cuba is ready and willing to discuss all these differences, without reservations and in the broadest possible terms. It states categorically that, in its view, there are no obstacles of any kind which prevent the holding of such negotiations through any of the channels normally used for this purpose. The Government of Cuba wishes to maintain and extend diplomatic and economic relations with the Government and people of the United States, on the basis of mutual respect and reciprocal benefit, and believes that on such a basis the traditional friendship between the Cuban and United States peoples is indestructible."

On 22 February 1960, the Revolutionary Government of Cuba informed the United States Government that

> "... in accordance with its expressed proposal to renew through diplomatic channels the negotiations already begun on matters pending between Cuba and the United States of America, it has decided to name a commission, qualified for the purpose, which could begin its negotiations in Washington on the date which the two parties might agree."

"The Revolutionary Government of Cuba wishes to make clear, however, that the renewal and subsequent development of the said negotiations must necessarily be subject to no unilateral measure being adopted, by the Government or Congress of your country, which might prejudge the results of the aforementioned negotiations or cause harm to the Cuban economy and people. It seems unnecessary to add that the adherence of your Government to this point of view would not only contribute to the improvement in the relations between our respective countries but also reaffirm the spirit of fraternal friendship which has bound and still binds our peoples. It would, moreover, permit both Governments to examine, in a serene atmosphere and with the broadest scope, the traditional relations between Cuba and the United States of America."

What was the reply from the Government of the United States? ". . . the Government of the United States cannot accept the conditions for the negotiations stated in your Excellency's note to the effect that no unilateral measure shall be adopted on the part of the Government of the United States affecting the Cuban economy and people, whether by the legislative or executive branch. As President Eisenhower said in his statement of 26 January, the Government of the United States must remain free, in the exercise of its own sovereignty, to take whatever steps it deems necessary, fully consistent with its international obligations, in the defence of the legitimate rights and interests of its people."

In other words, the United States Government does not condescend to discuss its differences with a small country like Cuba. What hope has the Cuban people for the solution of these problems? All the facts which we have been able to observe here militate against the solution of these problems and the United Nations should take careful account of this because the Cuban Government and people are extremely concerned about the aggressive trend which has developed in the policy of the United States Government towards Cuba.

It is well that we should be properly informed. In the first place, the United States Government considers itself entitled to foster subversion in our country. The United States Government is encouraging the organization of subversive movements against the Revolutionary Government of Cuba, and we are complaining of this policy here in the General Assembly. Specifically, we wish to complain of the fact that a Caribbean island which belongs to Honduras, known as Swan Island, has been forcibly seized by the United States Government. United States Marines are stationed there, despite the fact that the territory belongs to Honduras. On this island, in breach of international law, despoiling a neighbouring country of a portion of its territory and infringing international broadcasting conventions, the United States has set up a powerful radio transmitter which it has entrusted to the war criminals and the subversive groups it maintains in this country. On that island, too, men are being trained in the tactics of subversion and for armed landings in Cuba. It would be well for the Honduran representative to the General Assembly to claim here his country's right to this piece of its territory. However, that is his own affair. What concerns us is that a piece of territory belonging to a neighbouring country should be seized piratically by the United States Government and used as a base for subversion and attacks against Cuba. I request the Assembly to take note of this complaint which we make on behalf of the Government and people of Cuba.

Does the United States Government consider itself entitled to foster subversion in our country, violating all international agreements and encroaching upon our radio wave-lengths to the great detriment of our own broadcasting stations? Does this mean perhaps that the Revolutionary Government of Cuba also has the right to encourage subversion in the United States? Does it perhaps mean that the Government of Cuba also has the right to violate United States radio wave-lengths? What rights can the United States Government have over our people and over our island? How can it behave like that? Let it give back Swan Island to Honduras because it has never had any jurisdiction over that island.

There are other circumstances even more alarming for our people. It is well known that, by virtue of the Platt Amendment, imposed by force on our people, the United States Government assumed the right to establish naval bases on our territory, a right imposed and maintained by force.

The existence of a foreign naval base in the territory of any country is a just reason for concern. We Cubans are concerned because a country which maintains an aggressive and warlike international policy has established such a base in the heart of our island and we are thus exposed to the dangers of an international atomic conflict without being in any way responsible. We have absolutely nothing to do with the problems of the United States Government and with the crises which the United States Government is provoking. And yet there is a base in the heart of our island which involves us in danger should a conflict break out.

However, is this the only danger? No. There is another danger which causes us more concern because it is closer. The Revolutionary Government of Cuba has repeatedly expressed its concern lest the imperialist Government of the United States should use this base on our territory as a pretext for self-aggression which would justify an attack on our country. I repeat, the Revolutionary Government of Cuba is greatly concerned—and makes known its concern here—lest the imperialist Government of the United States use self-aggression as a pretext for an attack on our country. And this concern on our part is increasing because the United States is becoming more aggressive and the signs of that aggressiveness are becoming more alarming.

Mr. Boland (Ireland) resumed the Chair.

I have here, for example, a United Press cable which came to my country, reading as follows: "Admiral Arleigh Burke, United States Chief of Naval Operations, says that if Cuba should attempt to take the Guantánamo Naval Base by force 'we would fight back'. In a copyrighted interview published today in the magazine *U.S. News & World Report*" (forgive me if I do not pronounce it correctly) "Admiral Burke was asked if the Navy is concerned about the situation in Cuba under Castro. 'Yes, our Navy is concerned—not about our base at Guantánamo, but about the whole Cuban situation', Admiral Burke said. He added that all the military services are concerned. 'Is that because of Cuba's strategic position in the Caribbean?' he was asked. 'Not necessarily', Admiral Burke said. 'Here is a country with a people normally very friendly to the United States, people who have liked the people of this country—and we have liked them. Yet, here has come a man with a small hard core of communists determined to change all of that. Castro has taught hatred of the United States, and he has gone far towards wrecking his country.' Admiral Burke said 'we would react very fast' if Castro moved against the Guantánamo base. 'If they would try to take the base by force, we would fight back' he added. To a question whether Soviet Premier Khrushchev's threats about retaliatory rockets give Admiral Burke 'second thoughts about fighting in Cuba', the Admiral said: 'No. Because he is not going to launch his rockets. He knows he will be destroyed if he does—I mean Russia will be destroyed!' "

First of all, I must point out that in this gentleman's view the fact that industrial production in my country has increased by 35 per cent, that more than 200,000 Cubans have been given employment, that many of my country's great social problems have been solved, amounts to wrecking the country. It is because of these facts that these people take upon themselves the right to make preparations for aggression. You have seen what a dangerous estimate he makes, for this gentleman calculates virtually that in the event of an attack on us, we should stand alone. That is entirely Admiral Burke's idea. But let us suppose that Admiral Burke is mistaken; let us suppose that he, although an Admiral, is wrong—then Admiral Burke is gambling irresponsibly with the fate of the world. Admiral Burke and all the other members of his aggressive military group, are gambling with the fate of the world. It would hardly be worth bothering about our own individual fates; but I believe that as representatives of the various peoples of the world, we are in duty bound to worry about the fate of the world and to condemn all those who gamble irresponsibly with it. These people are not only gambling with the fate of my country; they are gambling with the fate of their own country and with the fate of all the peoples of the world. Or does this Admiral Burke believe that he is still living in the age of the blunderbuss? Has this Admiral Burke not realized that we are living in the atomic age, with its catastrophic destructive force which not even Dante or Leonardo da Vinci with all their imagination could foresee, for it surpasses anything that mankind could ever imagine? Nevertheless, he makes this estimate and the United Press has spread it all over the world. The magazine, the *U.S. News & World Report* is about to be published. Already they are starting to prepare the campaign, starting to whip up hysteria, starting to reveal the imaginary danger of some attack by us against the base.

But that is not all. Yesterday, there appeared another dispatch from the United Press containing statements by the United States Senator Styles Bridges who is, I believe, a member of the United States Senate Armed Forces Committee. He said that the United States must be prepared to maintain its naval base at Guantánamo in Cuba at all costs. He said, "We must go as far as necessary to defend the tremendous United States installation. We have naval forces there; we have the Marines and, if we were attacked, I would certainly defend it for I believe that it is the most important base in the Caribbean area."

This member of the Senate Armed Forces Committee, Mr. Bridges, did not entirely rule out the use of atomic weapons in the case of an attack on the base. What does that mean? It means not only that he is trying to create hysteria, not only that he is systematically preparing the ground, but that he is even threatening us with the use of atomic weapons. Really, among many other things, I am inclined to ask this Mr. Bridges if he is not ashamed to threaten a little country like Cuba with atomic weapons.

For my own part, with all due respect I must tell him that the world's problems are not solved by threatening nor by sowing fear, and that our humble little country is there, no matter how much he dislikes it, and that the revolution will go on, no matter how much he dislikes it, and moreover, that our humble little people will resign themselves to their fate and are not frightened at all by his threats to use atomic weapons.

What does this mean? There are many countries here that have United States bases, but at least they are not directed against the very Governments which granted the facilities, at least as far as we know. Our case is the most tragic. There is a base on our island territory which is directed against Cuba and against the Revolutionary Government of Cuba, that is to say, it is in the hands of those who are the declared enemies of our country, our revolution and our people.

Of all the bases scattered today throughout the world, Cuba's is the most tragic case. A base for the use of force, on what is indisputably our territory, far from the coast of the United States, directed against Cuba and the Cuban people, imposed on us by force and constituting a constant threat and cause of anxiety to our people.

We must therefore say here, in the first place, that this talk about attacks is intended to create hysteria and to pave the way for aggression against our country, and that we have never said a single word which would imply any kind of attack on the naval base at Guantánamo, because we are the first to be anxious to avoid giving the imperialists any excuse for attacking us. I say this quite categorically. At the same time, I must say that as soon as this country began to constitute a threat to the peace and security of our country and people, the Revolutionary Government began very seriously to consider requesting, under the rules of international law, the withdrawal of the United States Government's naval and military forces from this portion of our national territory. The imperialist Government of the United States will then have no alternative but to withdraw these forces. For how could it justify to the world its right to install an atomic base or a base which involves danger to our people in part of our national territory, on the island which is the Cuban people's home in this world? How could it justify to the world its right to retain sovereignty over a portion of our territory? How could it stand before the world and justify such an arbitrary procedure? And because it will be unable to justify its right to do so to the world, when our Government makes a request under the rules of international law, the United States Government will have no option but to yield.

It is important for this Assembly to be well informed on Cuban problems because we must all be on the alert against deceit and confusion. We must explain all these matters very clearly because they affect the security and the future of our country. I ask therefore that these words that I have said be noted very carefully, particularly in view of the fact that there seems to be no prospect of correcting the erroneous view which the politicians of this country have in regard to Cuba's problems.

For example, I have here some statements by Mr. Kennedy which are enough to astound anyone. On Cuba he says:

> "We must use all the power of the Organization of American States to prevent Castro from interfering with other Latin American Governments and to return freedom to Cuba."

They are going to restore freedom to Cuba!

> "We must state our intention of not allowing the Soviet Union to turn Cuba into its Caribbean base, and apply the Monroe Doctrine."

More than half way through the twentieth century this Presidential candidate talks about the Monroe Doctrine!

> "We must force Prime Minister Castro to understand that we propose to defend our right to the naval base of Guantánamo."

He is the third one to speak of this problem.

> "And we must show the Cuban people that we sympathize with their legitimate economic aspirations . . ."

Why did they not sympathize before?

> ". . . that we know full well their love for freedom and that we shall never be satisfied until democracy returns to Cuba."

What democracy? The made-in-America democracy of the imperialist monopolies of the United States Government.

In order to understand why there are aircraft flying from United States territory to Cuba, listen carefully to what this candidate has to say:

> "The forces that are struggling for freedom in exile and in the mountains of Cuba must be supplied and assisted and in other countries of Latin America communism must be confined without allowing it to expand or spread."

If Kennedy was not an illiterate and ignorant millionaire, he would understand that it is impossible to carry out a revolution against the peasants in the mountains with the aid of the landowners, and that whenever imperialism has tried to stir up counter-revolutionary groups, within a very short time the peasant militia has put them out of action. However, he would appear to have read in some novel or seen in some Hollywood film some story about guerrillas and he thinks that it is socially possible to carry out a guerrilla war in Cuba today.

However you look at this, it is discouraging, but let nobody think that these remarks on Kennedy's statements indicate any sympathy on our part for the other candidate, Mr. Nixon, who has made similar statements. As far as we are concerned, both of them lack political sense.

The President: I am sorry to have to interrupt the Prime Minister of Cuba, but I am sure that I am faithfully reflecting the feelings of the Assembly as a whole when I ask him to consider whether it is right and proper that the candidates in the current election in this country be discussed at the rostrum of the Assembly of the United Nations.

I am sure that in this matter the distinguished Prime Minister of Cuba will, on reflection, see my point of view, and I feel that I can rely with confidence on his good-will and co-operation. On that basis I would ask him kindly to continue with his remarks.

Mr. Castro, Prime Minister of Cuba, (translated from Spanish): We have no intention of departing in any way from the rules which govern conduct in the United Nations and the President may count on my co-operation in order to prevent anything that I say from being misinterpreted. I have no intention of offending anybody. It is to some extent a question of style and above all, a question of confidence in the Assembly. In any event, I shall try to avoid wrong interpretations of any kind.

Up to now I have been dealing with the problem of Cuba, which is our basic reason for coming to the United Nations. However, we fully realize that it would be somewhat selfish on our part if our concern was limited to our own specific case. Of course, we have spent most of our time in giving the Assembly information about Cuba's case, so there is not much left for the other questions, to which we will refer only briefly.

Cuba's is not an isolated case. It would be a mistake to think so. Cuba's case is that of all the under-developed countries; it resembles that of the Congo, of Egypt, Algeria, West Irian, Panama, which wants its Canal, Puerto Rico, whose national spirit is being destroyed, Honduras, which is being deprived of part of its territory; in short, although we have not referred specifically to the rest, the case of Cuba is that of all the under-developed and colonial countries.

The problems we have described in connexion with Cuba apply equally well to the whole of Latin America. It is the monopolies that control the economic resources of all Latin America. These monopolies, where they do not directly own the mines and control all mining, as in the case of copper in Chile, Peru or Mexico, zinc in Peru and Mexico, and oil in Venezuela, own the public utilities, as in the case of electricity in Argentina, Brazil, Chile, Peru, Ecuador and Colombia, or the telephone service as in Chile, Brazil, Peru, Venezuela, Paraguay and Bolivia; or else they control the marketing of our products, as in the case of coffee in Brazil, Colombia, El Salvador, Costa Rica and Guatemala, or in the case of bananas which are grown and sold, as well as transported, by the United Fruit Company in Guatemala, Costa Rica and Honduras, or in the case of cotton in Mexico or Brazil. This economic control is exercised by United States monopolies, masters of the most important industries in the country, which is thus entirely dependent on the monopolies.

Woe betide these countries on the day when they too wish to engage in land reform! They will be asked for prompt, effective and fair compensation and if, despite all this, they succeed in land reform, the representatives of these sister countries who come to the United Nations will find themselves confined to Manhattan, unable to take a hotel room, covered with insults and possibly even manhandled by the police.

The problem of Cuba is only one example of what is taking place in Latin America. How long will Latin America have to wait for development? Under the policies of the monopolies, it will have to wait till the Greek Calends. Who is going to industrialize Latin America? The monopolies? No. There is a United Nations economic report which explains that instead of going to the countries where it is most needed to establish basic industry to help in development, private investment capital goes preferably to the more industrialized countries because there, according to what is said or believed, it finds greater security. Obviously, the United Nations Department of Economic and Social Affairs has recognized that there is no possibility of development through private investment capital, in other words, through the monopolies.

Development in Latin America will have to take place by means of planned public investment made without political conditions, for, naturally, we all want to represent free countries and none of us wishes to represent a country which does not feel itself free. None of us wants the independence of our country to be subordinated to any interest which is not that of the country. Hence, aid must be without political conditions.

The fact that we are not offered assistance does not matter. We have not requested it. But in the interest of the peoples of Latin America, we feel it our duty, in the interests of solidarity to make it quite plain that aid must be free of political conditions: public investment for economic development, not social development, which is the latest gambit invented to conceal the real need for economic development.

The problems of Latin America resemble those of the rest of the world, of Africa and of Asia. The world is divided among the monopolies. The same monopolies that we see in Latin America are to be found in the Middle East. There, oil is in the hands of monopolistic companies controlled by financial interests of the United States, Great Britain, the Netherlands and France. This is true of Iran, Iraq, Saudi Arabia, Kuwait and Qatar and, all parts of the world. The same thing takes place, for instance, in the Philippines. It is the same in Africa.

The world is divided among monopolistic interests—who would dare deny this historic truth? The monopolistic interests do not want to see the peoples develop; what they want is to exploit the peoples' natural resources and exploit the peoples themselves, and the sooner they can recover or amortize their original investment, the better.

The difficulties which the people of Cuba have had with the imperialist Government of the United States are the same difficulties as Saudi Arabia, or Iran or Iraq, would encounter if they nationalized their oil. The same difficulties were encountered by Egypt when it, quite rightly, nationalized the Suez Canal; the same difficulties were encountered by Indonesia when it wished to become independent. Instances of the nature of these difficulties are provided by the surprise attack upon Egypt, and the surprise invasion of the Congo.

Have the colonialists and imperialists ever lacked excuses for an invasion? Never; they have always been able to find some excuse to their hand. Which are the colonialist countries? Which are the imperialist countries? It is not just four or five countries, but four or five groups of monopolies which possess the world's wealth.

If a person from outer space who had not read either Karl Marx's Communist Manifesto, or the cables of the United Press or the Associated Press, or other monopolistic publications, were to arrive in this Assembly and ask how the world was divided, and then see on the map of the world that the world's wealth was divided between the monopolies of four or five countries, he would say at once, "the world is badly divided, the world is being exploited". Here in this Assembly, where the under-developed countries are in the great majority, he might say that most of the countries represented are exploited and have been exploited for a long time: the form taken by the exploitation has varied, but they have consistently been exploited. That would be the verdict.

There was a statement in Mr. Khrushchev's speech [169th meeting] which particularly attracted our attention because of its intrinsic importance: this was when he said that the Soviet Union had no colonies nor any investments in any country. What a wonderful world it would be, this world of ours now threatened with disaster, if all the representatives of all the nations could say the same: "Our country has no colonies nor any investments in any foreign country."

Why beat about the bush? This is the crux; this is the crux of the question of peace and war, of the arms race or disarmament. From man's earliest days, wars have broken out for one fundamental reason: the desire of one side to rob the other of its wealth. When this philosophy of despoilment disappears, the philosophy of war will have disappeared. Colonies will disappear; the exploitation of the nations by the monopolies will disappear and then mankind will have made a real step forward along the path of progress. Until this step is taken, until this stage is reached, the world must live constantly under the threat of being involved in some crisis, in an atomic conflagration. Why? Because certain parties are interested in maintaining this despoilment; because certain parties are interested in maintaining exploitation.

We have spoken here of the case of Cuba. Our case has taught us a great deal through the problems which we have had with our imperialism; that is to say, the imperialism which is directed against us. In the last resort, however, all imperialisms are alike and all are allied. A country which exploits the peoples of Latin America or any other part of the world allies itself with the exploitation of the other nations of the world.

There was one point which alarmed us very greatly in the speech made by the President of the United States when he said:

> "In the developing areas, we must seek to promote peaceful change, as well as to assist economic and social progress. To do this—to assist peaceful change—the international community must be able to manifest its presence in emergencies through United Nations observers or forces. I should like to see Member countries take positive action on the suggestions in the Secretary-General's report looking to the creation of a qualified staff within the Secretariat to assist him in meeting future needs for United Nations forces."
> [868th meeting, para. 50]

In other words, after considering the developing areas in Latin America, Africa, Asia and Oceania, he advocates the promotion of peaceful change and proposes that United Nations observers or forces should be used to assist it. Yet, the United States came into the world by means of a revolution against its colonizers. The right of the peoples to free themselves by revolution from colonialism or any form of oppression was recognized in the Declaration of Independence adopted at Philadelphia, on 4 July 1776, but today, the Government of the United States advocates the use of United Nations forces to prevent revolutionary changes.

The President of the United States went on to say:

> "The Secretary-General has now suggested that Members should maintain a readiness to meet possible future requests from the United Nations for contributions to such forces. All countries represented here should respond to this need by earmarking national contingents which could take part in United Nations forces in case of need. The time to do it is now—at this Assembly.
>
> "I assure countries which now receive assistance from the United States that we favour use of that assistance to help them maintain such contingents in the state of readiness suggested by the Secretary-General." [*Ibid.* paras. 52 and 53.]

In other words, he proposes that those countries in which there are United States bases and which receive United States assistance should receive further assistance for the formation of these emergency forces.

President Eisenhower added:

> "To assist the Secretary-General's efforts, the United States is prepared to earmark also substantial air and sea transport facilities on a standby basis, to help move contingents requested by the United Nations in any future emergency." [868th meeting, para. 53.]

That is, he offers United States ships and planes for these emergency forces. We would like to say here and now that the Cuban delegation is not in favour of these emergency forces as long as all the peoples of the world cannot feel sure that these forces are not to be placed at the service of colonialism and imperialism; particularly when any of them may at any time be the victim of the use of these forces against the rights of our peoples.

Herein lie a number of problems which have already been referred to by the various delegations. Simply for reasons of time, I should like merely to place on record Cuba's views on the question of the Congo.

In view of our anti-colonialist position and our opposition to the exploitation of the under-developed countries, we naturally condemn the form taken by the intervention of the United Nations forces in the Congo. In the first place, they failed to act against the intervening forces, the purpose for which they had been summoned. They waited long enough for the first disagreement to arise there. When that was not enough, they allowed time and opportunity for the second dissension to arise. Lastly, during the occupation of the radio stations and airfields they made it possible for the so-called "third man" to come forward—we are already only too familiar with the deliverers who arise in such circumstances. In 1934, one of these deliverers sprang up in our country, and his name was Fulgencio Batista. In the Congo, his name is Mobutu. In Cuba, our deliverer visited the United States Embassy every day and apparently the same thing is happening in the Congo. Is this just our allegation? No, it is reported by a magazine which is one of the monopolies' most fervent supporters and as such could never be against the monopolies. It could not be pro-Lumumba because it is against him, and it is pro-Mobutu. Nevertheless, it explains who he is, how he sprang up, how he went to work, and finally in its latest issue, *Time* magazine says that Mobutu became a frequent visitor to the United States Embassy and had long talks with officials there. One afternoon last week, Mobutu conferred with officers at camp Leopold and won their vociferous support. That night he went to Radio Congo—the same Radio Congo that Lumumba had not been allowed to use—and abruptly announced that the Army was assuming power. All this after frequent visits to and lengthy conversations with, officials of the United States Embassy. This is reported by *Time* magazine, defender of the monopolies. In other words, the hand of the colonial interests has been plain and obvious in the Congo, and our view is, consequently, that a mistake has been made, that colonialist interests have been favoured and that all the facts indicate that the people of the Congo, and right in the Congo, are on the side of the only leader who remained there defending his country's interests, namely, Lumumba.

If, despite this state of affairs and the mysterious "third man" who has sprung up in the Congo to oppose not only the lawful interests of the Congolese people but also the legitimate authorities of the Congo, the African and Asian countries succeed in reconciling these lawful authorities in defence of the Congo's interests, so much the better. But if this reconciliation does not take place, reason and right should attach themselves to the man who not only has the support of the people and of Parliament, but also has stood out against the interests of the monopolies and stood by his people.

As regards the problem of Algeria, we are, I need hardly say, 100 per cent on the side of the right of the people of Algeria to independence. It is ridiculous—like so many ridiculous things in the world which have been artificially created by vested interests—to claim that Algeria is part of France. Similar claims have been made by other countries in an attempt to keep their colonies in other days. This so-called "integration" has failed throughout history. Let us turn the question upside down: suppose Algeria was the metropolitan country and it was to declare that part of Europe was an integral part of its territory? Such reasoning is far-fetched and devoid of all meaning. Algeria belongs to Africa as France belongs to Europe. This African people has been fighting a heroic battle against the metropolitan country for many years.

Perhaps even while we are calmly talking here, the machine-guns and bombs of the Government or the French Army are attacking Algerian villages and hamlets. Men may well be dying, in a struggle in which it is perfectly clear where the right lies, a struggle that could be ended without disregarding the interests of that minority which is being used as an excuse for denying nine-tenths of the population of Algeria their right to independence. Yet the United Nations is doing nothing. We were in such a hurry to go into the Congo and we are so unenthusiastic about going into Algeria! If the Algerian Government, which is a Government, for it represents millions of fighting Algerians, were to request the United Nations to send forces there also, should we go with the same enthusiasm? I hope that we should go with the same enthusiasm, but with a very different purpose, that is to say, for the purpose of defending the interests of the colony and not of the colonizers.

We are, therefore, on the side of the Algerian people, as we are on the side of the remaining colonial peoples in Africa and on the side of the Negroes against whom discrimination is exercised in the Union of South Africa. Similarly, we are on the side of those peoples who wish to be free, not only politically—for it is very easy to acquire a flag, a coat of arms, a national anthem and a colour on the map—but also economically free, for there is one truth which we should all recognize as being of primary importance, namely, that there can be no political independence unless there is economic independence; that political independence without economic independence is an illusion; we therefore support their aspiration to be free politically and economically. Freedom does not consist in the possession of a flag, and a coat of arms and representation in the United Nations.

We should like to draw attention here to another right: a right which was proclaimed by the Cuban people at a mass meeting quite recently; the right of the under-developed countries to nationalize their natural resources and the investments of the monopolies in their respective countries without compensation; in other words, we advocate the nationalization of natural resources and foreign investments in the underdeveloped countries, and indeed if industrialized countries wish to do the same thing, we shall not oppose them.

If countries are to be truly free in political matters, they must be truly free in economic matters and we must lend them assistance.

In reply, we shall be asked about the value of the investments and our reply will be to inquire as to the value of the profits from those investments; the profits which have been extracted from the colonized and under-developed peoples for decades, if not for centuries.

There is also a proposal made by the President of the Republic of Ghana, in his speech to the General Assembly [869th meeting], which we should like to support: the proposal that Africa should be cleared of military bases and thus of nuclear weapon bases; in other words the proposal to free Africa from the perils of atomic war. Something has already been done in regard to Antarctica. As we go forward on the path to disarmament, why should we not also go forward towards freeing certain parts of the world from the danger of nuclear war?

If Africa is reborn—that Africa which we are beginning to know today, not the Africa pictured on the map or in novels and Hollywood films, not the Africa of semi-naked tribesmen armed with spears, ready to run away at the first clash with the white hero, that white hero who became more heroic the more African natives he killed, but the Africa we see represented here by leaders like Kwame Nkrumah and Sékou Touré, the Africa of Nasser's Arab world, the true Africa, the oppressed continent, the exploited continent, the continent which was the birthplace of millions of slaves, this Africa whose past is so full of anguish. To this Africa we have a duty: we must save it from the danger of destruction.

Let the other countries make some recompense! Let the West make up a little for what it has made Africa suffer, by preserving it from the danger of atomic war and declaring it a free zone as far as this peril is concerned. Let no atomic bases be established there! Even if we can do nothing else, let this continent at least remain a sanctuary where human life may be preserved! We support this proposal warmly.

On the question of disarmament, we wholeheartedly support the Soviet proposal [A/4505], and we are not ashamed to do so. We regard it as a correct, specific, well-defined and clear proposal. We have carefully studied the speech made here by President Eisenhower—he made no real reference to disarmament, to the development of the under-developed countries or to the colonial problem. Really, it would be worthwhile for the citizens of this country, who are so influenced by false propaganda, to compare objectively the statements of the President of the United States [868th meeting] and of the Prime Minister of the Soviet Union, [869th meeting], so that they could see which speech contains genuine anxiety over the world's problems; so that they could see which one spoke clearly and sincerely and so that they could see who really wants disarmament and who is against it and why. The Soviet proposal could not be clearer. Nothing could be added to the Soviet explanation. Why should there be any reservations when no one has ever before spoken so clearly of so tremendous a problem?

The history of the world has taught us the tragic lesson that arms races always lead to war: at the same time, never has the responsibility been greater, for never has war signified so vast a holocaust for mankind. What did the representative of the Soviet Union say about this problem, which is of so much concern to mankind because mankind's very existence is at stake? He made a proposal for general and complete disarmament. What more can be asked? If more can be asked, let us ask it; if we can ask for more safeguards, let us do so; but the proposal could not be clearer or better defined, and at this stage of history, it cannot be rejected without assuming the responsibility involved in the danger of war and of war itself.

Why should this problem not come before the General Assembly? Why does the United States delegation not wish to discuss this problem here in the Assembly? Have we no judgement? Have we no right to discuss the problem? Must a special commission be convened? Why not adopt the most democratic method? In other words, let the General Assembly, all the representatives, discuss the disarmament problem here, and let everyone lay his cards on the table so that it will become apparent who wants disarmament and who does not; who wants to play at war and who does not, and who it is who is betraying the aspirations of mankind, for mankind must never be dragged into a holocaust by sordid and self-seeking interests.

Our peoples must be saved from this holocaust, so that everything created by human knowledge and intelligence will not be used to destroy mankind itself.

The representative of the Soviet Union has spoken frankly—I say this objectively— and I urge that these proposals be considered and that everybody put their cards on the table. Above all, this is not merely a question of representatives, this is a matter of public opinion. The warmongers and militarists must be exposed and condemned by world public opinion. This is not a problem for minorities only: it concerns the world. The warmongers and militarists must be unmasked, and this is the task of public opinion. This problem must be discussed not only in the General Assembly but before the entire world, before the great assembly of the whole world, because in the event of a war not the leaders only but also hundreds of millions of completely innocent persons will be exterminated.

And it is for this reason that we meet here as representatives of the world, or of a part of the world, since this Assembly is not yet complete; it will not be complete until the People's Republic of China is represented here. Until then, one-quarter of the world's population is absent. But we who are here have the duty to speak frankly and not to evade the issue. We must all discuss it; this problem is too serious to be overlooked. It is more important than economic aid and all other obligations, because this is the obligation to preserve the life of mankind. We must all discuss and speak about this problem, and we must fight to establish peace, or at least to unmask the militarists and warmongers.

And, above all, if we, the under-developed countries, want to have a chance of progress, if we want to have a chance of seeing our peoples enjoying a higher level of living, let us fight for peace, let us fight for disarmament; with a fifth of what the world spends on armaments, we could promote the development of all the under-developed countries at a rate of growth of 10 per cent per annum. With a fifth of the resources which countries spend on armaments, we could surely raise the peoples' level of living.

Now, what are the obstacles to disarmament? Who is interested in being armed? Those who are interested in being armed to the teeth are those who want to keep colonies, those who want to maintain their monopolies, those who want to retain control of the oil of the Middle East, the natural resources of Latin America, of Asia, of Africa and who require military strength to protect their interests. And as everyone knows, these territories were occupied and colonized on the strength of the law of force; by virtue of the law of force millions of men were enslaved, and it is force which sustains such exploitation in the world. Therefore, those most concerned that there should be no disarmament are those interested in maintaining military strength in order to retain control of natural resources, the wealth of the peoples and cheap labour in under-developed countries.

We promised to speak frankly, and there is no other way of telling the truth. The colonialists, therefore, are against disarmament. Using the weapon of world public opinion, we must fight to force disarmament on them as we must force them to respect the right of peoples to economic and political liberation.

The monopolies are against disarmament, because, apart from the fact that they defend their interests with arms, the arms race has always been good business for them. For example, everybody knows that the great monopolies in this country doubled their capital as a result of the Second World War. Like vultures, the monopolies feed on the corpses which are the harvest of war; and war is a business. Those who trade in war, those who enrich themselves by war, must be unmasked. We must open the eyes of the world and show it who are the ones who trade in the future of mankind, in the danger of war, particularly when the war may be so frightful that it leaves no hope of freedom or deliverance.

We small and under-developed countries urge the whole Assembly and especially the other small and under-developed nations, to devote themselves to this task and to have this problem discussed here, because afterwards we should never forgive ourselves for the consequences if, through our neglect or lack of firmness and energy on this basic issue, the world became involved once again in the dangers of war.

There remains one point, which, according to what we have read in some newspapers, was one of the points the Cuban delegation was going to raise. And this, naturally, was the problem of the People's Republic of China.

Other delegations have already spoken about this matter. We wish to say that the fact that this problem has never been discussed is in reality, a denial of the "raison d'être" and of the essential nature of the United Nations. Why has it never been discussed? Because the United States Government wants it so? Why is the United Nations Assembly going to renounce its right to discuss this problem?

Many countries have joined the United Nations in recent years. To oppose discussion of the right to representation here of the People's Republic of China, that is, of 99 per cent of the inhabitants of a country of more than 600 million, is to deny the reality of history, of the facts and of life itself. It is simply an absurdity; it is ridiculous that this problem is never even discussed.

How long are we going to continue this melancholy business of never discussing this problem, when we have here representatives of Franco, for instance?

Will the President allow me to express my opinion most respectfully on this point without offence to anybody?

The President: I think it is only fair to the Prime Minister of Cuba to make clear the position of the Chair. The Chair does not think it is in keeping with the dignity of the Assembly, or the decorum that we like to preserve in our debates, that references of a personal nature should be made to the Heads of States or the Heads of Governments of States Member of the United Nations, whether present here or not. I hope that the Prime Minister will consider that a fair and reasonable rule.

Mr. Castro, Prime Minister of Cuba, (translated from Spanish): We wish to make some comments about the origin of the United Nations. The United Nations arose after the struggle against fascism, after tens of millions of men had died on the battlefields. From that struggle, which cost so many lives, this Organization emerged as a symbol of hope. Nevertheless, extraordinary paradoxes exist. While American soldiers were falling on Guam or Guadalcanal or Okinawa, or one of the many other islands of the Pacific, men were also fighting on the Chinese mainland against the same enemy, and these same men are denied even the right to discuss their entry into the United Nations. Although soldiers of the Spanish Blue Division fought in the Soviet Union in defence of fascism, the People's Republic of China is denied the right to have its case discussed here, in the United Nations. And yet the régime that was born of German nazism and Italian fascism and which took power with the support of Hitler's guns and aircraft and of Mussolini's "blackshirts" was magnanimously admitted to membership of the United Nations.

China contains one-quarter of the world's population. What Government is the true representative of this nation, which is the largest in the world? Plainly, the Government of the People's Republic of China. And there another régime is maintained, in the midst of a civil war which was interrupted by the interference of the United States Seventh Fleet. Here it is appropriate to ask by what right the navy of an extra-continental country (and it is worth repreating this here, when so much is being said about extra-continental interference) intervened in a domestic affair of China. It would be interesting to have an explanation. The sole purpose of this interference was to maintain a group of supporters in that place and to prevent the total liberation of the territory. That is an absurd and unlawful state of affairs from any point of view, and constitutes the reason why the United States Government does not want the question of the People's Republic of China to be discussed.

We want to put it on record here that this is our position and that we support discussion of this item and the seating by the United Nations General Assembly of the legitimate representatives of the Chinese people, namely, the representatives of the Government of the People's Republic of China.

I understand quite well that it is somewhat difficult for anybody here to free himself from the stereotyped concepts by which the representatives of nations are usually judged. I must say that we have come here free from prejudices, to analyse problems objectively, without fear of what people will think and without fear of the consequences of our position. We have been honest, we have been frank without being Francoist, because we do not want to be a party to injustice being committed against a great number of Spanish men and women, still imprisoned in Spain after more than twenty years, who fought together with the Americans of the Lincoln Brigade, as the companions of those same Americans who were there to honour the name of that great patriot.

In conclusion, we are going to place our trust in reason and in the decency of all. We wish to sum up our ideas about which there should be no doubt, concerning some aspects of these world problems. Our problem, which we have set forth here, is a part of the problems of the world. Those who attack us today are those who are helping to attack others in other parts of the world. The United States Government cannot be on the side of the Algerian people; it cannot be on the side of the Algerian people because it is allied to the metropolitan country, France. It cannot be on the side of the Congolese people, because it is allied to Belgium. It cannot be on the side of the Spanish people, because it is allied to Spain. It cannot be on the side of the Puerto Rican people, whose nationality it has been destroying for fifty years. It cannot be on the side of the Panamanians, who claim the Canal. It cannot support the ascendancy of the civil power in Latin America, Germany or Japan. It cannot be on the side of the peasants who want land, because it is allied to the big landowners. It cannot be on the side of the workers who are demanding better living conditions in all parts of the world, because it is allied to the monopolies. It cannot be on the side of the colonies which want their freedom, because it is allied to the colonizers. That is to say, it is for Franco, for the colonization of Algeria, for the colonization of the Congo; it is for the maintenance of its privileges and interests in the Panama Canal, for colonialism throughout the world. It is for German militarism and for the resurgence of German militarism. It is for Japanese militarism and for the resurgence of Japanese militarism.

The United States Government forgets the millions of Jews murdered in European concentration camps by the Nazis, who are today regaining their influence in the German army. It forgets the Frenchmen who were killed in their heroic struggle against the occupation; it forgets the American soldiers who died on Omaha Beach, on the Siegfried Line, in the Ruhr, on the Rhine or on the Asian fronts. The United States Government cannot be for the integrity and sovereignty of nations. Why? Because it must curtail the sovereignty of nations in order to keep its military bases, and each base is a dagger thrust into sovereignty; each base is a limitation on sovereignty. Therefore it has to be against the sovereignty of nations, because it must constantly limit sovereignty in order to maintain its policy of encircling the Soviet Union with bases.

We believe that these problems are not properly explained to the American people. But the American people need only imagine how uneasy it would be if the Soviet Union began to establish a ring of atomic bases in Cuba, Mexico or Canada. The population would not feel secure or calm. World opinion, including American opinion, must be taught to see the other side of a question; to look at problems from the other person's point of view. The under-developed peoples should not always be represented as aggressors; revolutionaries should not be represented as aggressors, as enemies of the American people. We cannot be enemies of the American people, because we have seen United States nationals like Carleton Beals or Waldo Frank, and others, famous and distinguished intellectuals shed tears at the thought of the mistakes that are being made, at the breach of hospitality towards us; there are many Americans, the most humane, the most progressive, and the most esteemed writers, in whom I see the nobility of this country's early leaders, the Washingtons, the Jeffersons and the Lincolns. I say this is no spirit of demogogy, but with the sincere admiration that we feel for those who once succeeded in freeing their people from colonial status and who did not fight in order that their country might today be the ally of all the reactionaries, the gangsters, the big landowners, the monopolists, the exploiters, the militarists, the fascists in the world, that is to say, the ally of the most retrograde and reactionary forces, but rather in order that their country might always be the champion of noble and just ideals. We know well what will be said about us, today, tomorrow and always, to deceive the American people. But it does not matter. We are doing our duty by stating our views in this historic Assembly.

We proclaim the right of the peoples to integrity and nationality; those who plot against nationalism know that nationalism means that the people want to regain their own property, their wealth, their natural resources. In short, we are for all the noble aspirations of all the peoples. That is our position. We are and always shall be for everything just; against colonialism, exploitation, monopolies, militarism, the arms race, and warmongering. We shall always be against those things. That will be our position.

To conclude, in performing what we regard as our duty, I quote to this Assembly the essential part of the Havana Declaration. The Havana Declaration was the Cuban people's answer to the Declaration of San José, Costa Rica. Not ten, nor 100, nor 100,000, but more than 1 million Cubans gathered together. Whoever doubts it may go and count them at the next mass meeting or general assembly that we hold in Cuba, assured that they are going to see the spectacle of a fervent and informed people, which they rarely had the opportunity of seeing, and which is seen only when a people is ardently defending its most sacred interests.

At that assembly, which was convened in response to the Declaration of Costa Rica, these principles were proclaimed, in consultation with the people and by the acclamation of the people, as the principles of the Cuban revolution.

"The national general assembly of the Cuban people condemns large-scale land-owning as a source of poverty for the peasant and a backward and inhuman system of agricultural production; it condemns starvation wages and the iniquitous exploitation of human labour by illegitimate and privileged interests; it condemns illiteracy, the lack of teachers, schools, doctors and hospitals; the lack of assistance to the aged in the American countries; it condemns discrimination against the Negro and the Indian; it condemns the inequality and the exploitation of women; it condemns political and military oligarchies which keep our peoples in poverty, impede their democratic development and the full exercise of their sovereignty; it condemns concessions of our countries' natural resources to foreign monopolies as a policy sacrificing and betraying the peoples' interests; it condemns Governments which turn a deaf ear to the demands of their people so that they may obey orders from abroad; it condemns the systematic deception of the peoples by mass communication media which serve the interests of the oligarchies and the policy of imperialist oppression; it condemns the news monopoly held by monopolist agencies, which are instruments of monopolist trusts and agents of such interests; it condemns repressive laws which prevent the workers, the peasants, the students and the intellectuals, the great majorities in each country, from forming associations and fighting for their social and patriotic demands; it condemns the imperialist monopolies and enterprises which continually plunder our wealth, exploit our workers and peasants, bleed our economies and keep them backward and subordinate Latin American politics to their designs and interests. In short, the national general assembly of the Cuban people condemns the exploitation of man by man and the exploitation of under-developed countries by imperialist capital.

"Consequently, the national general assembly of the Cuban people proclaims before America, and proclaims here before the world, the right of the peasants to the land;

the right of the workers to the fruits of their labour; the right of children to education; the right of the sick to medical care and hospitalization; the right of young people to work; the right of students to free vocational training and scientific education; the right of Negroes and Indians to full human dignity; the right of women to civil, social and political equality; the right of the elderly to security in their old age; the right of intellectuals, artists and scientists to fight through their works for a better world; the right of States to nationalize imperialist monopolies, thus rescuing the national wealth and resources; the right of countries to trade freely with all the peoples of the world; the right of nations to their complete sovereignty; the right of peoples to convert their military fortresses into schools and to arm their workers (because in this we have to be arms-conscious and to arm our people to defence against imperialist attacks), their peasants, their students, their intellectuals, Negroes, Indians, women, young people, old people, all the oppressed and exploited, so that they may themselves defend their rights and their destinies."

Some people wanted to know what the line of the Revolutionary Government of Cuba was. Well then, there you have our line.

98. Announcement by the State Department of the Institution of Controls on Exports to Cuba*

October 19, 1960

Over the course of the past 21 months the United States has been subjected by the Castro regime to an increasing campaign of hostility and slander. Accompanying its words with actions, the Government of Cuba has instituted a series of arbitrary, illegal, and discriminatory economic measures which have injured thousands of American citizens and have drastically altered the hitherto mutually beneficial pattern of trade between the United States and Cuba. Illustrative of what has happened is the fact that the movement of United States exports to Cuba has been reduced to less than 50 percent of the figure in 1958 and that payment has never been received for about a fourth of the goods shipped since Castro came to power. Meanwhile, Cuban exports to the United States remained normal until July of this year, when it became necessary to reduce the Cuban sugar quota in order that the United States Government might comply with its duty to make proper provision for the future sugar needs of the American consumer.

The principal measures taken by the Government of Cuba aimed at reducing the movement of goods and services from the United States to Cuba are listed below. None of these measures can be justified by a need to conserve foreign exchange reserves, which, according to Cuban Government officials, are adequate. Rather they are the result of a deliberate political policy to divert trade away from the United States.

1. In the first months of the Castro regime a variety of taxes and other restrictions were levied against United States flour, potatoes, rice, drugs, cigarettes, shoes, automobile components, and other products. For example, with regard to rice, a commod-

*Department of State Bulletin, Nov. 7, 1960, pp. 715-16.

ity in which the United States has long had a principal trade interest, the Government of Cuba, without providing a hearing for the interested parties, demanded a special "contribution" of $2.75 per hundred pounds from Cuban importers of this American product, and made the American quota for rice almost meaningless by not releasing dollar exchange for its importation while importing large quantities of rice duty free from another supplier country.

2. Over the course of the year 1959, during which American exporters continued to ship in good faith under the generous credit terms which had long been customary in trading with Cuba, the Government of Cuba made it difficult for Cuban importers to pay for United States goods. Surcharges ranging from 30 percent to 100 percent were imposed in September 1959 on remittances of foreign exchange for certain additional categories of imports. Regulations governing the disposition of dollar exchange were gradually tightened until on November 3, 1959, an order was issued which stipulated that all exporters of Cuban products as well as all persons receiving dollar exchange for services rendered in Cuba must surrender their dollars to the National Bank of Cuba. Foreign exchange required to pay for imported goods had to be requested from an agency of this Bank, and approval of applications for legitimate payments of all sorts became subject to long and indefinite delay. At the end of June 1960 the commercial backlog owed to American businessmen had reached over $150 million.

3. Some American exporters have been pressured to continue shipments of their products on a 90-day open account under the threat that only under this condition would dollars be released to pay for earlier shipments. United States—owned financial institutions were refused rediscount facilities with the aim of forcing them to bring in their own funds from abroad, and American firms operating factories in Cuba were threatened with intervention unless they continued to ship in raw materials in a normal manner despite the fact that dollars had not been released to pay for earlier shipments of raw materials or for the remittance of normal earnings.

4. The Castro regime discriminated against the United States in the administration of its trade regulations. It has used import licensing, state trading, and threats of intervention to force the diversion of trade away from the United States. Traditional customers of the United States in Cuba are under continuous official pressure to divert orders. It is well known that refineries of the Texaco and Standard Oil Companies in Cuba, which had been supplied from Venezuela and other Western Hemisphere sources, were presented with demands to refine Soviet petroleum and were seized when they declined to do so. At the time of seizure over $50 million was owed to these companies by Cuba for petroleum products which for over a year they had continued to supply without reimbursement in order to meet Cuba's needs.

5. The Castro regime's seizure of private American factories, mills, lands, retail establishments, service organizations, technical commercial files, and other properties has also served to distort further the traditional pattern of trade between Cuba and the United States.

6. All efforts on the part of the United States to reach a fair and equitable solution of these trade problems have been rebuffed by the Castro regime. United States interests which have suffered injury have found no effective recourse in the Cuban courts.

For these reasons and under the authority of the Export Control Act, the United States Government is today placing into effect general controls, to prohibit American exports to Cuba except for nonsubsidized foodstuffs, medicines, and medical supplies. This step has been reluctantly taken by the United States in the exercise of its sovereignty and in order to carry out the responsibility of this Government to defend the legitimate economic interests of the people of this country against the discriminatory, aggressive, and injurious economic policies of the Castro regime.

The Department of Commerce is issuing the necessary implementing regulations, and copies will be obtainable from that Department.

99. Address by President Kennedy made at a White House Reception for Latin American Diplomats, Members of Congress and their Wives, on an Alliance for Progress*

March 13, 1961

It is a great pleasure for Mrs. Kennedy and for me, for the Vice President and Mrs. Johnson, and for the Members of Congress, to welcome the ambassadorial corps of the hemisphere, our longtime friends, to the White House today. One hundred and thirty-nine years ago this week the United States, stirred by the heroic struggles of its fellow Americans, urged the independence and recognition of the new Latin American Republics. It was then, at the dawn of freedom throughout this hemisphere, that Bolívar spoke of his desire to see the Americas fashioned into the greatest region in the world, "greatest," he said, "not so much by virtue of her area and her wealth, as by her freedom and her glory."

Never, in the long history of our hemisphere, has this dream been nearer to fulfillment, and never has it been in greater danger.

The genius of our scientists has given us the tools to bring abundance to our land, strength to our industry, and knowledge to our people. For the first time we have the capacity to strike off the remaining bonds of poverty and ignorance—to free our people for the spiritual and intellectual fulfillment which has always been the goal of our civilization.

Yet at this very moment of maximum opportunity, we confront the same forces which have imperiled America throughout its history—the alien forces which once again seek to impose the despotisms of the Old World on the people of the New.

I have asked you to come here today so that I might discuss these challenges and these dangers.

Common Ties Uniting the Republics

We meet together as firm and ancient friends, united by history and experience and by our determination to advance the values of American civilization. For this new world of ours is not merely an accident of geography. Our continents are bound together by a common history—the endless exploration of new frontiers. Our nations are the product of a common struggle—the revolt from colonial rule. And our people share a common heritage—the quest for the dignity and the freedom of man.

*Department of State Bulletin, Apr. 3, 1961, pp. 471-74.

The revolutions which gave us birth ignited, in the words of Thomas Paine, "a spark never to be extinguished." And across vast, turbulent continents these American ideals still stir man's struggle for national independence and individual freedom. But as we welcome the spread of the American Revolution to other lands, we must also remember that our own struggle—the revolution which began in Philadelphia in 1776 and in Caracas in 1811—is not yet finished. Our hemisphere's mission is not yet completed. *For our unfulfilled task is to demonstrate to the entire world that man's unsatisfied aspiration for economic progress and social justice can best be achieved by free men working within a framework of democratic institutions.* If we can do this in our own hemisphere, and for our own people, we may yet realize the prophecy of the great Mexican patriot, Benito Juarez, that "democracy is the destiny of future humanity."

As a citizen of the United States let me be the first to admit that we North Americans have not always grasped the significance of this common mission, just as it is also true that many in your own countries have not fully understood the urgency of the need to lift people from poverty and ignorance and despair. But we must turn from these mistakes—from the failures and the misunderstandings of the past—to a future full of peril but bright with hope.

Throughout Latin America—a continent rich in resources and in the spiritual and cultural achievements of its people—millions of men and women suffer the daily degradations of hunger and poverty. They lack decent shelter or protection from disease. Their children are deprived of the education or the jobs which are the gateway to a better life. And each day the problems grow more urgent. Population growth is outpacing economic growth, low living standards are even further endangered, and discontent—the discontent of a people who know that abundance and the tools of progress are at last within their reach—that discontent is growing. In the words of José Figueres, "once dormant peoples are struggling upward toward the sun, toward a better life."

If we are to meet a problem so staggering in its dimensions, our approach must itself be equally bold, an approach consistent with the majestic concept of Operation Pan America. Therefore I have called on all the people of the hemisphere to join in a new Alliance for Progress.—*Alianza para Progreso*—a vast cooperative effort, unparalleled in magnitude and nobility of purpose, to satisfy the basic needs of the American people for homes, work and land, health and schools—*techo, trabajo y tierra, salud y escuela.*

Ten-Year Plan for the Americas

First, I propose that the American Republics begin on a vast new 10-year plan for the Americas, a plan to transform the 1960's into an historic decade of democratic progress. These 10 years will be the years of maximum progress, maximum effort—the years when the greatest obstacles must be overcome, the years when the need for assistance will be the greatest.

And if we are successful, if our effort is bold enough and determined enough, then the close of this decade will mark the beginning of a new era in the American experience. The living standards of every American family will be on the rise, basic education will be available to all, hunger will be a forgotten experience, the need for massive outside help will have passed, most nations will have entered a period of self-sustaining growth, and, although there will be still much to do, every American Republic will be the master of its own revolution and its own hope and progress.

Let me stress that only the most determined efforts of the American nations themselves can bring success to this effort. They, and they alone, can mobilize their resources, enlist the energies of their people, and modify their social patterns so that all, and not just a privileged few, share in the fruits of growth. If this effort is made, then outside assistance will give a vital impetus to progress; without it, no amount of help will advance the welfare of the people.

Thus if the countries of Latin America are ready to do their part—and I am sure they are—then I believe the United States, for its part, should help provide resources of a scope and magnitude sufficient to make this bold development plan a success, just as we helped to provide, against nearly equal odds, the resources adequate to help rebuild the economies of Western Europe. For only an effort of towering dimensions can insure fulfillment of our plan for a decade of progress.

Secondly I will shortly request a ministerial meeting of the Inter-American Economic and Social Council, a meeting at which we can begin the massive planning effort which will be at the heart of the Alliance for Progress.

For if our alliance is to succeed, each Latin nation must formulate long-range plans for its own development—plans which establish targets and priorities, insure monetary stability, establish the machinery for vital social change, stimulate private activity and initiative, and provide for a maximum national effort. These plans will be the foundation of our development effort and the basis for the allocation of outside resources.

A greatly strengthened IA-ECOSOC, working with the Economic Commission for Latin America and the Inter-American Development Bank, can assemble the leading economists and experts of the hemisphere to help each country develop its own development plan and provide a continuing review of economic progress in this hemisphere.

Third, I have this evening signed a request to the Congress for $500 million as a first step in fulfilling the Act of Bogotá. This is the first large-scale inter-American effort—instituted by my predecessor President Eisenhower—to attack the social barriers which block economic progress. The money will be used to combat illiteracy, improve the productivity and use of their land, wipe out disease, attack archaic tax and land-tenure structures, provide educational opportunities, and offer a broad range of projects designed to make the benefits of increasing abundance available to all. We will begin to commit these funds as soon as they are appropriated.

Fourth, we must support all economic integration which is a genuine step toward larger markets and greater competitive opportunity. The fragmentation of Latin American economies is a serious barrier to industrial growth. Projects such as the Central American common market and free-trade areas in South America can help to remove these obstacles.

Fifth, The United States is ready to cooperate in serious, case-by-case examinations of commodity market problems. Frequent violent changes in commodity prices seriously injure the economies of many Latin American countries, draining their resources and stultifying their growth. Together we must find practical methods of bringing an end to this pattern.

Sixth, we will immediately step up our food-for-peace emergency program, help to establish food reserves in areas of recurrent drought, and help provide school lunches for children and offer feed grains for use in rural development. For hungry men and women cannot wait for economic discussions or diplomatic meetings; their need is urgent, and their hunger rests heavily on the conscience of their fellow men.

Seventh, all the people of the hemisphere must be allowed to share in the expanding wonders of science—wonders which have captured man's imagination, challenged the powers of his mind, and given him the tools for rapid progress. I invite Latin American scientists to work with us in new projects in fields such as medicine and agriculture, physics and astronomy, and desalinization, and to help plan for regional research laboratories in these and other fields, and to strengthen cooperation between American universities and laboratories.

We also intend to expand our science-teacher training programs to include Latin American instructors, to assist in establishing such programs in other American countries, and translate and make available revolutionary new teaching materials in physics, chemistry, biology, and mathematics so that the young of all nations may contribute their skills to the advance of science.

Eighth, we must rapidly expand the training of those needed to man the economies of rapidly developing countries. This means expanded technical training programs, for which the Peace Corps, for example, will be available when needed. It also means assistance to Latin American universities, graduate schools, and research institutes.

We welcome proposals in Central America for intimate cooperation in higher education, cooperation which can achieve a regional effort of increased effectiveness and excellence. We are ready to help fill the gap in trained manpower, realizing that our ultimate goal must be a basic education for all who wish to learn.

Ninth, we reaffirm our pledge to come to the defense of any American nation whose independence is endangered. As confidence in the collective security system of the OAS [Organization of American States] spreads, it will be possible to devote to constructive use a major share of those resources now spent on the instruments of war. Even now, as the Government of Chile has said, the time has come to take the first steps toward sensible limitations of arms. And the new generation of military leaders has shown an increasing awareness that armies can not only defend their countries— they can, as we have learned through our own Corps of Engineers, help to build them.

Tenth, we invite our friends in Latin America to contribute to the enrichment of life and culture in the United States. We need teachers of your literature and history and tradition, opportunities for our young people to study in your universities, access to your music, your art, and the thought of your great philosophers. For we know we have much to learn.

In this way you can help bring a fuller spiritual and intellectual life to the people of the United States and contribute to understanding and mutual respect among the nations of the hemisphere.

With steps such as these we propose to complete the revolution of the Americas, to build a hemisphere where all men can hope for a suitable standard of living and all can live out their lives in dignity and in freedom.

Political Freedom and Social Progress

To achieve this goal political freedom must accompany material progress. Our Alliance for Progress is an alliance of free governments—and it must work to eliminate tyranny from a hemisphere in which it has no rightful place. Therefore let us express our special friendship to the people of Cuba and the Dominican Republic— and the hope they will soon rejoin the society of free men, uniting with us in our common effort.

This political freedom must be accompanied by social change. For unless necessary social reforms, including land and tax reform, are freely made, unless we broaden the opportunity of all of our people, unless the great mass of Americans share in increasing prosperity, then our alliance, our revolution, our dream, and our freedom will fail. But we call for social change by free men—change in the spirit of Washington and Jefferson, of Bolívar and San Martín and Martí—not change which seeks to impose on men tyrannies which we cast out a century and a half ago. Our motto is what it has always been—progress yes, tyranny no— *progreso sí, tiranía no!*

But our greatest challenge comes from within—the task of creating an American civilization where spiritual and cultural values are strengthened by an ever-broadening base of material advance, where, within the rich diversity of its own traditions, each nation is free to follow its own path toward progress.

The completion of our task will, of course, require the efforts of all the governments of our hemisphere. But the efforts of governments alone will never be enough. In the end the people must choose and the people must help themselves.

And so I say to the men and women of the Americas—to the *campesino* in the fields, to the *obrero* in the cities, to the *estudiante* in the schools—prepare your mind and heart for the task ahead, call forth your strength, and let each devote his energies to the betterment of all so that your children and our children in this hemisphere can find an ever richer and a freer life.

Let us once again transform the American Continent into a vast crucible of revolutionary ideas and efforts, a tribute to the power of the creative energies of free men and women, an example to all the world that liberty and progress walk hand in hand. Let us once again awaken our American revolution until it guides the struggles of people everywhere—not with an imperialism of force or fear but the rule of courage and freedom and hope for the future of man.

100. Message from President Kennedy to Congress, Requesting the Appropriation of Money for the Inter-American Fund for Social Progress and for Chilean Earthquake Rehabilitation*

March 14, 1961

On September 8, 1960, at the request of the administration, the Congress authorized the sum of $500 million for the Inter-American Fund for Social Progress. On the

---

Department of State Bulletin, Apr. 3, 1961, pp. 474-78.

basis of this authorization the United States, on September 12, 1960, subscribed to the Act of Bogotá along with 18 other American Republics.

In the same bill the Congress authorized $100 million for the long-term reconstruction and rehabilitation of those areas of southern Chile recently devastated by fire and earthquake.

I now request that Congress appropriate the full amount of $600 million.

The Act of Bogotá marks an historic turning point in the evolution of the Western Hemisphere. For the first time the American nations have agreed to join in a massive cooperative effort to strengthen democratic institutions through a program of economic development and social progress.

Such a program is long overdue. Throughout Latin America millions of people are struggling to free themselves from the bonds of poverty and hunger and ignorance. To the north and east they see the abundance which modern science can bring. They know the tools of progress are within their reach. And they are determined to have a better life for themselves and their children.

The people of Latin America are the inheritors of a deep belief in political democracy and the freedom of man—a sincere faith that the best road to progress is freedom's road. But if the Act of Bogotá becomes just another empty declaration—if we are unwilling to commit our resources and energy to the task of social progress and economic development—then we face a grave and imminent danger that desperate peoples will turn to communism or other forms of tyranny as their only hope for change. Well-organized, skillful, and strongly financed forces are constantly urging them to take this course.

A few statistics will illustrate the depth of the problems of Latin America. This is the fastest growing area in the world. Its current population of 195 million represents an increase of about 30 percent over the past 10 years, and by the 1980's the continent will have to support more than 400 million people. At the same time the average per capita annual product is only $280, less than one-ninth that of the United States—and in large areas, inhabited by millions of people, it is less than $70. Thus it is a difficult task merely to keep living standards from falling further as population grows.

Such poverty inevitably takes its toll in human life. The average American can expect to live 70 years, but life expectancy in Latin America is only 46, dropping to about 35 in some Central American countries. And while our rate of infant mortality is less than 30 per thousand, it is more than 110 per thousand in Latin America.

Perhaps the greatest stimulus to our own development was the establishment of universal basic education. But for most of the children of Latin America education is a remote and unattainable dream. Illiteracy extends to almost half the adults, reaching 90 percent in one country. And approximately 50 percent of school-age children have no schools to attend.

In one major Latin American capital a third of the total population is living in filthy and unbearable slums. In another country 80 percent of the entire population is housed in makeshift shacks and barracks, lacking the privacy of separate rooms for families.

It was to meet these shocking and urgent conditions that the Act of Bogotá was signed. This act, building on the concept of Operation Pan America initiated by Brazil in 1958, introduced two important new elements to the effort to improve living standards in South America.

First, the nations of Latin America have recognized the need for an intensive program of self-help—mobilizing their own domestic resources, and undertaking basic reforms in tax structure, in land ownership and use, and in education, health, and housing.

Second, it launches a major inter-American program for the social progress which is an indispensable condition to growth—a program for improved land use, education, health, and housing. This program—supported by the special fund which I am asking Congress to appropriate—will be administered primarily through the Inter-American [Development] Bank, and guided by greatly strengthened regional institutions.

The $500 million Inter-American Fund for Social Progress is only the first move toward carrying out the declarations of the Act of Bogotá; and the act itself is only a single step in our program for the development of the hemisphere—a program I have termed the Alliance for Progress—Alianza para Progreso. In addition to the social fund, hemispheric development will require substantial outside resources for economic development, a major self-help effort by the Latin American nations themselves, inter-American cooperation to deal with the problems of economic integration and commodity markets and other measures designed to speed economic growth and improve understanding among the American nations.

Social Progress and Economic Development

The fund which I am requesting today will be devoted to social progress. Social progress is not a substitute for economic development. It is an effort to create a social framework within which all the people of a nation can share in the benefits of prosperity, and participate in the process of growth. Economic growth without social progress lets the great majority of the people remain in poverty, while a privileged few reap the benefits of rising abundance. In addition, the process of growth largely depends on the existence of beneficial social conditions. Our own experience is witness to this. For much of our own great productivity and industrial development is based on our system of universal public education.

Thus the purpose of our special effort for social progress is to overcome the barriers of geographical and social isolation, illiteracy and lack of educational opportunities, archaic tax and land tenure structures, and other institutional obstacles to broad participation in economic growth.

Self-Help and Internal Reform

It is clear that the Bogotá program cannot have any significant impact if its funds are used merely for the temporary relief of conditions of distress. Its effectiveness depends on the willingness of each recipient nation to improve its own institutions, make necessary modifications in its own social patterns, and mobilize its own domestic resources for a program of development.

Even at the start such measures will be a condition of assistance from the social fund. Priorities will depend not merely on need, but on the demonstrated readiness of each government to make the institutional improvements which promise lasting social progress. The criteria for administration of the funds by the Inter-American Development Bank and the ICA will explicitly reflect these principles.

For example: The uneven distribution of land is one of the gravest social problems in many Latin American countries. In some nations 2 percent of the farms account for three-fourths of the total farm area. And in one Central American country, 40 percent of the privately owned acreage is held in one-fifth of 1 percent of the number of farms. It is clear that when land ownership is so heavily concentrated, efforts to increase agricultural productivity will only benefit a very small percentage of the population. Thus if funds for improving land usage are to be used effectively they should go only to those nations in which the benefits will accrue to the great mass of rural workers.

Examples of Potential Areas of Progress

When each nation demonstrates its willingness to abide by these general principles, then outside resources will be focused on projects which have the greatest multiplying effect in mobilizing domestic resources, contributing to institutional reform, and in reducing the major obstacles to a development in which all can share.

In housing, for example, much can be done for middle income groups through improved credit mechanisms. But, since the great majority of family incomes are only $10 to $50 a month, until income levels as a whole are increased, the most promising means of improving mass housing is through aided self-help projects—projects in which the low-income worker is provided with low-cost materials, land, and some technical guidance; and then builds the house with his own labor, repaying the costs of materials with a long-term mortgage.

Education is another field where self-help efforts can effectively broaden educational opportunities—and a variety of techniques, from self-help school construction where the entire village contributes labor, to the use of local people as part-time teachers can be used.

In the field of land use there is no sharp demarcation between economic and social development. Improved land use and rural living conditions were rightly given top place in the Act of Bogotá. Most of the Latin American peoples live and work on the land. Yet agricultural output and productivity have lagged far behind both industrial development and urgent needs for consumption and export.

As a result poverty, illiteracy, hopelessness, and a sense of injustice—the conditions which breed political and social unrest—are almost universal in the Latin American countryside.

Thus, there is an immediate need for higher and more diversified agricultural production, better distribution of wealth and income, and wider sharing in the process of development. This can be partly accomplished through establishing supervised rural credit facilities, helping to finance resettlement in new lands, constructing access roads to new settlement sites, conducting agricultural surveys and research, and introducing agricultural extension services.

Administration of the Inter-American Fund for Social Progress

It is fundamental to the success of this cooperative effort that the Latin American nations themselves play an important role in the administration of the social fund.

Therefore, the major share of the funds will be administered by the Inter-American Development Bank (IDB)—an organization to which nearly all the American Republics belong.

Of the total of $500 million, $394 million will be assigned to the IDB, to be administered under a special trust agreement with the United States. The IDB will apply most of these funds on a loan basis with flexible terms, including low interest rates or repayment in local currency. The IDB's major fields of activity will be land settlement and improved land use, housing, water supply and sanitation, and technical assistance related to the mobilizing of domestic financial resources.

In order to promote progress in activities which generally are not self-liquidating and therefore not appropriate for loan financing, the sum of $100 million will be administered by the International Cooperation Administration (ICA). These funds will be applied mainly on a grant basis for education and training, public health projects, and the strengthening of general governmental services in fields related to economic and social development. Funds administered by the ICA will also be available to assist projects for social progress in dependent territories which are becoming independent, but are not yet members of the IDB.

Up to $6 million more is to be used to help strengthen the Organization of American States (OAS). To reinforce the movement toward adequate self-help and institutional improvement, the Inter-American Economic and Social Council (IA-ECOSOC) of the OAS is strengthening its secretariat and its staff. It is also working out cooperative arrangements with the United Nations Economic Commission for Latin America (ECLA) and the IDB. These three regional agencies will work together in making region-wide studies, and in sponsoring conferences directed toward bringing about tax reform, improved land use, educational modernization, and sound national development programing.

Many of the nations of the Americas have already responded to the action taken at Bogotá by directing attention to their most pressing social problems. In the brief period since the meeting at Bogotá, U.S. embassies and operations mission, after consultation with Latin American governments, have already reported proposals for social development projects calling for external assistance totaling about $1,225 million. A preliminary selection from this list shows some $800 million worth of projects which are worthy of early detailed examination by the Bank and the ICA.

In the Bank's area of activity these selected projects total $611 million, including $309 million for land use and improved rural living conditions, $136 million in the field of housing, and $146 million for water supply and sanitation.

Selected proposals in fields to be administered by the ICA total $187 million; of which $136 million are for education and training, $36 million for public health, and $15 million for public administration and other assigned responsibilities.

So that each recipient nation will live up to the principles of self-help and domestic reform outlined above, funds will not be allocated until the operating agency receives assurances that the country being aided will take those measures necessary to insure that the particular project brings the maximum social progress. For the same reason we can make no firm forecast of the rate at which the funds will be committed. Thus, if they are to be used most efficiently and economically, they must be made available for obligation without limitation as to time.

Urgency of the Need

Under ideal conditions projects for social progress would be undertaken only after the preparation of integrated country plans for economic and social development. Many nations, however, do not possess even the most basic information on their own resources or land ownership. Revolutionary new social institutions and patterns cannot be designed overnight. Yet, at the same time, Latin America is seething with discontent and unrest. We must act to relieve large-scale distress immediately if free institutions are to be given a chance to work out long-term solutions. Both the Bank and the ICA are ready to begin operation immediately. But they must have the funds in hand if they are to develop detailed projects, and stimulate vital measures of self-help and institutional improvement.

The Bogotá Conference created a new sense of resolve—a new determination to deal with the causes of the social unrest which afflicts much of the hemisphere. If this momentum is lost, through failure of the United States to act promptly and fully, we may not have another chance.

The Role of Private Organizations

Inter-American cooperation for economic and social progress is not limited to the actions of government. Private foundations and universities have played a pioneering role in identifying critical deficiencies and pointing the way toward constructive remedies. We hope they will redouble their efforts in the years to come.

United States business concerns have also played a significant part in Latin American economic development. They can play an even greater role in the future. Their work is especially important in manufacturing goods and providing services for Latin American markets. Technical expertness and management skills in these fields can be effectively transferred to local enterprises by private investment in a great variety of forms—ranging from licensing through joint ventures to ownership.

Private enterprise's most important future role will be to assist in the development of healthy and responsible private enterprise within the Latin American nations. The initiation, in recent years, of strikingly successful new private investment houses, mutual investment funds, savings and loan associations, and other financial institutions are an example of what can be done. Stimulating the growth of local suppliers of components for complex consumer durable goods is another example of the way in which domestic business can be strengthened.

A major forward thrust in Latin American development will create heavy new demands for technical personnel and specialized knowledge—demands which private organizations can help to fill. And, of course, the continued inflow of private capital will continue to serve as an important stimulus to development.

Chilean Reconstruction and Rehabilitation

Last May more than 5,000 Chileans were killed when fire and earthquake devastated the southern part of that Republic. Several of the American Republics, including the United States, provided emergency supplies of food, medicine, and clothing to the victims of this disaster. Our country provided almost $35 million in emergency grants and loans.

However, these emergency efforts did not meet the desperate need to rebuild the economy of an area which had suffered almost $400 million worth of damage. In recognition of this need, Congress authorized $100 million for long-term reconstruction and rehabilitation. Since then the people of Chile have been patiently rebuilding their shattered homes and communications facilities. But reconstruction is severely hampered by lack of funds. Therefore, I am asking the Congress to appropriate the $100 million so that the task of rebuilding the economy of southern Chile can proceed without delay.

101. *Explanation by the State Department of the Challenge Posed by Cuba* *

April 3, 1961

The present situation in Cuba confronts the Western Hemisphere and the inter-American system with a grave and urgent challenge.

This challenge does not result from the fact that the Castro government in Cuba was established by revolution. The hemisphere rejoiced at the overthrow of the Batista tyranny, looked with sympathy on the new regime, and welcomed its promises of political freedom and social justice for the Cuban people. The challenge results from the fact that the leaders of the revolutionary regime betrayed their own revolution, delivered that revolution into the hands of powers alien to the hemisphere, and transformed it into an instrument employed with calculated effect to suppress the rekindled hopes of the Cuban people for democracy and to intervene in the internal affairs of other American republics.

What began as a movement to enlarge Cuban democracy and freedom has been perverted, in short, into a mechanism for the destruction of free institutions in Cuba, for the seizure by international communism of a base and bridgehead in the Americas, and for the disruption of the inter-American system.

It is the considered judgment of the Government of the United States of America that the Castro regime in Cuba offers a clear and present danger to the authentic and autonomous revolution of the Americas—to the whole hope of spreading political liberty, economic development, and social progress through all the republics of the hemisphere.

*Department of State Publication 7171, Inter-American Series 66, Washington D.C., 1961.

I. The Betrayal of the Cuban Revolution

The character of the Batista regime in Cuba made a violent popular reaction almost inevitable. The rapacity of the leadership, the corruption of the government, the brutality of the police, the regime's indifference to the needs of the people for education, medical care, housing, for social justice and economic opportunity—all these, in Cuba as elsewhere, constituted an open invitation to revolution.

When word arrived from the Sierra Maestra of the revolutionary movement headed by Dr. Fidel Castro Ruz, the people of the hemisphere watched its progress with feeling and with hope. The Cuban Revolution could not, however, have succeeded on the basis of guerrilla action alone. It succeeded because of the rejection of the regime by thousands of civilians behind the lines—a rejection which undermined the morale of the superior military forces of Batista and caused them to collapse from within. This response of the Cuban people was not just to the cruelty and oppression of the Batista government but to the clear and moving declarations repeatedly made by Dr. Castro concerning his plans and purposes for post-revolutionary Cuba.

As early as 1953 Dr. Castro promised that the first revolutionary law would proclaim the Constitution of 1940 as "the supreme law of the land." In this and subsequent statements Dr. Castro promised "absolute guarantee of freedom of information, both of newspapers and radio, and of all the individual and political rights guaranteed by the Constitution," and a provisional government that "will hold general elections . . . at the end of one year under the norms of the Constitution of 1940 and the Electoral Code of 1943 and will deliver the power immediately to the candidate elected." Dr. Castro, in short, promised a free and democratic Cuba dedicated to social and economic justice. It was to assure these goals that the Rebel Army maintained itself in the hills, that the Cuban people turned against Batista, and that all elements of the revolution in the end supported the 26th of July Movement. It was because of the belief in the honesty of Dr. Castro's purposes that the accession of his regime to power on January 1, 1959, was followed within a single week by its acceptance in the hemisphere—a recognition freely accorded by nearly all the American Republics, including the United States.

For a moment the Castro regime seemed determined to make good on at least its social promises. The positive programs initiated in the first months of the Castro regime—the schools built, the medical clinics established, the new housing, the early projects of land reform, the opening up of beaches and resorts to the people, the elimination of graft in government—were impressive in their conception; no future Cuban government can expect to turn its back on such objectives. But so far as the expressed political aims of the revolution were concerned, the record of the Castro regime has been a record of the steady and consistent betrayal of Dr. Castro's prerevolutionary promises; and the result has been to corrupt the social achievements and make them the means, not of liberation, but of bondage.

The history of the Castro Revolution has been the history of the calculated destruction of the free-spirited Rebel Army and its supersession as the main military instrumentality of the regime by the new state militia. It has been the history of the calculated destruction of the 26th of July Movement and its supersession as the main political instrumentality of the regime by the Communist Party (*Partido Socialista Popular*). It has been the history of the disillusion, persecution, imprisonment, exile, and execution of men and women who supported Dr. Castro—in many cases fought by his side—and thereafter doomed themselves by trying to make his regime live up to his own promises.

Thus Dr. José Miró Cardona, a distinguished lawyer of Habana, was in 1958 Coordinator of *Frente Cívico Revolucionario,* the coalition of groups opposed to the Batista regime. Dr. Castro made him the Prime Minister of the Revolutionary Government. As the regime embarked on its Communist course, Dr. Miró Cardona went into exile. Today he is chairman of the Revolutionary Council, representing anti-Batista Cubans determined to rescue the Revolution.

Dr. Manuel Urrutia y Lleó, an eminent Cuban judge, had asserted in defiance of Batista and in defense of Castro the right of Cubans to resort to arms to overthrow an unconstitutional government. He became a hero of the Revolution and served as Provisional President of the Revolutionary Government. When he protested the spread of Communist influence, he was compelled to resign. Today Dr. Urrutia is under house arrest in Habana.

Not only the first Prime Minister and the first President of the Revolutionary Government but a large proportion of the Revolution's original political and military leaders now reject Dr. Castro and his course of betrayal. Of the 19 members of the first cabinet of the Revolutionary Government, nearly two-thirds are today in prison, in exile, or in opposition. Manuel Ray Rivero, who organized the anti-Batista underground in Habana and served as Castro's Minister of Public Works, is now a member of the Revolutionary Council. Humberto Sori Marín, who as Castro's first Minister of Agriculture called for agrarian reform in the spirit of the 1940 Constitution, returned to Cuba early this year to resume his fight for the freedom of his people; according to recent reports; he has been shot and captured by the forces of Castro.

Men who fought with Dr. Castro in the hills are today the hunted victims of his revolutionary regime. Major Huber Matos Benítez, revolutionary *comandante* of Camagüey Province, was a hero of the Sierra Maestra. When Major Matos challenged the spread of Communist influence and requested permission to resign from the Army, he was put on trial for conspiracy, sedition, and treason and sentenced to 20 years' imprisonment. Major Matos is only one of the many foes of Batista who now protest Dr. Castro's perversion of the revolution. There are many, many others: Manuel Artime and Nino Díaz who fought valiantly in the Sierra Maestra; Justo Carrillo, a leader of the Montecristi opposition in Habana and Castro's first choice for President of the National Development Bank; Raúl Chibas, who raised much of the funds for the revolution and fought with Castro in the hills; Felipe Pazos, who represented the 26th of July Movement on the Junta of Liberation and was subsequently appointed by Castro as President of the National Bank of Cuba; Major Pedro Díaz Lanz, chief of the Cuban Air Force and Castro's personal pilot; Ricardo Lorie Vals, chief of arms supply for the Rebel Army; Dr. Manuel Antonio de Varona, leader of the *Organización Auténtica,* which was formed to oppose Batista and which supported its own revolutionary group in the Escambray Mountains; Evelio Duque and Osvaldo Ramírez, fighters in the Sierra Escambray first against Batista and today against Castro.

David Salvador, the labor leader, went to jail under Batista because of his work for Castro. After the revolution he became the militantly pro-Castro and "anti-Yanqui" secretary general of the Cuban trade union federation. In November 1959, the 26th of July Movement swept the national congress of the trade unions, defeated the Communist slate, and confirmed David Salvador as secretary general. But Dr. Castro, appearing in person at the congress, demanded acceptance of the Communist program of "unity." Salvador continued his fight for a free labor movement. A year later he was arrested as he tried to escape from Cuba. Today David Salvador is back again in a Cuban jail—this time not Batista's but Castro's.

Editors and commentators who had fought all their lives for freedom of expression found less of it under Castro even than under Batista. Miguel Angel Quevedo, as editor of *Bohemia,* had freely attacked Batista and backed Castro; the January 1959 issue of *Bohemia* hailing the new regime sold nearly a million copies. But a year and a half later Quevedo concluded that it was impossible to put out an honest magazine in the new Cuba. When he fled the country in July 1960, Castro described it as "one of the hard blows which the Revolution has received." Today *Bohemia Libre's* dateline is Caracas. Luis Conte Agüero, the radio and television commentator, wrote the preface to Dr. Castro's revolutionary exhortation *History Will Absolve Me.* When Conte dared criticize Communist infiltration into the regime, Castro turned on him, angry crowds mobbed him, and he was forced to seek refuge in the Argentine Embassy. Today he is in exile. Even José Pardo Llada, notorious for his vitriolic daily attacks on the United States over the Habana radio, recently fled to Mexico City; he declared, "I am breaking with Fidel Castro upon reaching the conviction that in Cuba it is no longer possible to maintain a position that is not in accord with the line of the Popular Socialist [Communist] Party and that any expression of independence, even in defense of the social program of the Revolution, is considered as deviationist, divisive, or counterrevolutionary."

Never in history has any revolution so rapidly devoured its children. The roster of Castro's victims is the litany of the Cuban Revolution. The Rebel Army and the 26th of July Movement expressed the profound and passionate desire of the Cuban people for democracy and freedom, a desire sanctified in the comradeship and sacrifice of the revolutionary struggle. When Dr. Castro decided to betray the promises of the revolution, he had to liquidate the instrumentalities which embodied those promises and to destroy the men who took the promises seriously.

II. The Establishment of the Communist Bridgehead

In place of the democratic spontaneity of the Cuban Revolution, Dr. Castro placed his confidence in the ruthless discipline of the Cuban Communist Party. Today that party is the *only* political party permitted to operate in Cuba. Today its members and those responsive to its influence dominate the government of Cuba, the commissions of economic planning, the labor front, the press, the educational system, and all the agencies of national power.

The Cuban Communist Party has had a long and intricate history. For years it had a working arrangement with the Batista government; indeed, Batista in 1943 appointed to his cabinet the first avowed Communist ever to serve in any cabinet of any American Republic. Later Batista and the Communists fell out. But the Communists were at first slow to grasp the potentialities of the Castro movement. When Castro first went to the hills, the Cuban Communist Party dismissed him as "bourgeois" and "putschist." Only when they saw that he had a chance of winning did they try to take over his movement.

Their initial opposition was quickly forgiven. Dr. Castro's brother, Major Raúl Castro, had himself been active in the international Communist student movement and had made his pilgrimage to the Communist world. Moreover, Major Ernesto (Ché) Guevara, a dominating influence on Dr. Castro, was a professional revolutionary from Argentina who had worked with Communists in Guatemala and Mexico. Through Raúl Castro and Guevara, the Communists, though unable to gain control either of the 26th of July Movement or of the Rebel Army, won ready access to Dr. Castro himself. What was perhaps even more important, the Communist Party could promise Castro not only a clear-cut program but a tough organization to put that program into execution.

The period since has been a steady expansion of Communist power within the regime. Dr. Osvaldo Dorticós Torrado, the present President of Cuba, was regional organization secretary of the Communist Party in Cienfuegos as a law student and has never publicly explained or repudiated his past party membership. Aníbal Escalante, secretary general of the Cuban Communist Party, is a member of the informal group which, under the chairmanship of Raúl Castro, makes policy for the Cuban Government. Raúl Castro himself runs the Ministry for the Revolutionary Armed Forces; and his friend, Major Ramiro Valdés Menéndez, who accompanied him on a tour of the Soviet bloc in 1960, is chief of military intelligence. Major Guevara is Minister of Industry and chief economic planner. The National Agrarian Reform Institute (INRA), with its vast power over the rural life of Cuba, is headed by Major Antonio Núñez Jiménez, a longtime coworker in Communist-front groups and another frequent pilgrim behind the Iron Curtain. The Bank for Foreign Commerce, which until recently controlled all exports and imports, had as its director Jacinto Torras, an oldtime Communist, who served for many years as economic editor of the Communist daily newspaper *Noticias de Hoy.* All centers of economic power have been taken over by the state and to a considerable degree delivered to the Cuban Communist Party.

This process of consolidation has been extended inexorably to every phase of Cuban national life. Political opposition has been extinguished, and all political parties, save the Communist, are effectively denied political activity. In recent months the regime, by completing its purge of the judiciary, has perfected its control over all organized institutions of political power. Justice is now the instrument of tyranny. Laws have been redefined in such a way that any manifestation of disagreement can be branded as "counterrevolutionary" and the accused haled before military tribunals and sentenced to long prison terms or to the firing squad.

Professional groups and civic institutions have lost their autonomy and are systematically integrated into the "revolutionary" discipline of the regime. The remaining vestiges of opposition in the trade unions, represented by union leaders from the 26th of July Movement, have been destroyed. Recently the hand of the dictatorship has been reaching out beyond the middle class to strike down elements in organized labor. When the electrical workers of Habana marched last December from union headquarters to the Presidential Palace to protest against reductions in their standard of living, Dr. Castro himself took an early occasion to denounce them. A power failure in Habana led to the arrest of three workers as suspected saboteurs; on January 18, 1961, these men were executed by the regime as "traitors." Protest demonstrations by workers' wives against the executions were broken up by civilian strong-arm squads while police and militiamen looked on.

In characteristic Communist manner the regime has seized control of the nation's educational system, introduced Communist propaganda into the schools, destroyed academic freedom, and ended the traditional autonomy of the universities. The director of primary education in the Ministry of Education is Dulce María Escalona Almeida, a Communist. Secondary education is in the hands of Pedro Cañas Abril, long associated with pro-Communist groups. The director of the Department of Culture in the Ministry of Education is a veteran Communist, Vicentina Antuña. Well-known Communists served on the committee named by the Ministry of Education to rewrite the textbooks for the public school system. Two-thirds of the faculty of the University of Habana is today in exile. Fermín Peinado, a former professor at the University of the Oriente, recently published the text of a statement issued last December by faculty members and students of that university:

... In the realm of domestic politics we condemn Fidel Castro as a traitor to the Revolution that this university helped to organize and to win. ... The objectives of complete freedom, human rights, and constitutional order, crystallized in the 26th of July Movement, have been crushed by the Castro regime in open treason to the memory of our martyrs Frank País, Pepito Tey, Eduardo Mesa, and many others. ... In the realm of university life we declare Fidel Castro a traitor to the autonomy of the university, defended to the death by a legion of student martyrs, from Trejo to Ramirez and José A. Echevarría. ... We denounce the systematic subordination of the aims of scientific investigation within the universities to the aim of consolidating and maintaining in power the totalitarian tyranny of Castro.

In similar fashion the Castro regime has seized control of the agencies of public communication—the newspapers, the publishing houses, the radio and television networks, the film industry. No Cuban today, whether in field or factory, in school or cafe or home by the radio, can hope to escape the monotonous and implacable din of Communist propaganda.

The Cuba of Castro, in short, offers the Western Hemisphere a new experience—the experience of a modern totalitarian state. Castro's power touches the daily lives of the people of Cuba at every point; governs their access to jobs, houses, farms, schools, all the necessities of life; and subjects opposition to quick and harsh reprisal. The Castro regime is far more drastic and comprehensive in its control than even the most ruthless of the oldtime military dictatorships which have too long disfigured the hemisphere. On January 27 last, Major Núñez Jiménez, the head of INRA, summed up the inner logic of the Castro course. The Cuban Government, Major Núñez threatened, might have to replace its intended slogan for 1961, "Year of Education," with a new slogan, "Año del Paredón"—"Year of the Execution Wall" or, in effect, "Year of the Firing Squad."

By every criterion, it is evident that the permeation and penetration of political and intellectual life by Communist influences and personalities have reached the point of virtual domination. The North American journalist I. F. Stone, initially sympathetic with the Castro regime, reported after a recent trip to Cuba: "For the first time, in talking with the *Fidelista* intellectuals, I felt that Cuba was on its way to becoming a Soviet-style Popular Democracy."

It is for this reason that some of the most devoted and authentic fighters for social and economic democracy in Latin America—men who themselves spent years in prison or in exile and who had hailed the Castro uprising for its promises of deliverance for the Cuban people—have united in rejecting the Communist conquest of Cuba. Victor Raúl Haya de la Torre of Peru may stand as a symbol of this whole tradition of the democratic left. "In the history of Latin America," Haya de la Torre recently said, "there has been a series of sell-outs. Sell-outs are not new to our America. What is new are sell-outs towards the left. Up until now they were only to the political right. We cannot confuse that which was idealistic, authentic and just in the beginning of the Cuban Revolution with the surrender, submission, and homage to something which is anti-American and totalitarian and which is opposed to the traditional sense of our ideal of bread with freedom."

Meeting in Lima at the end of February 1961, representatives of APRA of Peru, Acción Democrática of Venezuela, and similar political groups in other Latin American Republics summed up the situation when they said of Cuba that its "revolutionary process, justified in the beginning, has been deflected by its present agents, converting a brother country into an instrument of the cold war, separating it, with suicidal premeditation, from the community of interests of the Latin American people."

III. The Delivery of the Revolution to the Sino-Soviet Bloc

The official declarations of the Cuban Government amply document the Lima resolution and make clear the subservience of the Castro regime to the world Communist bloc. The joint communique issued in Moscow on December 19, 1960, by Anastas Mikoyan, Deputy Chairman of the Council of Ministers of the U.S.S.R., and Major Guevara, as chief of the Economic Mission of the Revolutionary Government of Cuba, outline the terms of surrender. After announcing a series of trade, technical assistance, and cultural agreements, the communique noted, "During the talks, the two parties discussed problems relating to the present international situation, and they reaffirmed their agreement in attitude toward the principal problems of mankind today." The Cubans agreed that the Soviet Union is "the most powerful nation on earth" and that every Soviet proposal and policy represented a magnificent contribution to world peace. In return for a total acceptance of Soviet leadership, Cuba received pledges of Soviet economic assistance and of "the Soviet Union's willingness to lend Cuba full assistance in maintaining its independence against unprovoked aggression." The joint communique amounts in effect to an alliance between Cuba and the Soviet Union.

Officials of the Castro government have repeatedly made clear their fidelity to this alliance. Major Guevara, endorsing the conclusions of the Moscow Congress of world Communist parties, said "Cuba wants to tread the way of the Soviet Union" and praised the "militant solidarity of the Cuban and Soviet people." In the presence of Dr. Castro, Faure Chomón, the Cuban Ambassador to Moscow, told an audience on March 13, 1961, We Communists together will continue forward with our truth . . . and the students of today and the students of tomorrow will be greatly interested in seeing how a whole people made itself Communist, how even the children, deceived by religious schools, have become Communists, and how this is to follow that truth which unites the Cuban people. Very soon we shall see all the peoples of Latin America become Communists.

On one issue after another, the Castro regime has signified its unquestioning acceptance of the Soviet line on international affairs. After the termination of diplomatic relations with the United States, the Cuban Government turned over its diplomatic and consular representation to the Embassy of Czechoslovakia in Washington. In the United Nations, Cuba votes with the Communist bloc on virtually all major issues.

Though in 1956 Raúl Roa, the Cuban Foreign Minister, attacked "the crimes, disasters and outrages perpetrated" by the Soviet "invaders" in Hungary, the Hungarian revolution, as well as the rebellion in Tibet, are now "reactionary fascist movements." In October 1960, Manuel Yepe, chief of protocol for the Foreign Ministry, gave an orientation lecture on the subject "Imperialist Aggression and the Case of Hungary."

The last few months have seen the rapid consolidation of this relationship in all its aspects—not only ideological, but military, political, economic, and cultural. Sino-Soviet arms, equipment, technicians, and money have moved into Cuba. Diplomatic relations have been established with every Communist country except East Germany; and economic agreements have been concluded with many Communist countries including East Germany. Cuban leaders have visited the Soviet Union and Communist China as honored guests, and a long list of leaders from the Soviet Union, China, and the Communist satellite states have visited Cuba.

It is important to understand the detail and the magnitude of this process of takeover. Since the middle of 1960, more than 30,000 tons of arms with an estimated value of $50 million have poured from beyond the Iron Curtain into Cuba in an ever-rising flood. The 8-hour military parade through Habana and the military maneuvers in January 1961 displayed Soviet JS—2 51-ton tanks, Soviet SU—100 assault guns, Soviet T—34 35-ton tanks, Soviet 76 mm. field guns, Soviet 85 mm. field guns, Soviet 122 mm. field guns. Except for motorized equipment, the Cuban armed forces have been reequipped by the Soviet bloc and are now dependent on the bloc for the maintenance of their armed power. Soviet and Czech military advisers and technicians have accompanied the flow of arms. And the Castro regime has sent Cubans to Czechoslovakia and the Soviet Union for training as jet pilots, ground maintenance crews, and artillerymen.

As a consequence of Soviet military aid, Cuba has today, except for the United States, the largest ground forces in the hemisphere—at least ten times as large as the military forces maintained by previous Cuban Governments, including that of Batista. Estimates of the size of the Cuban military establishment range from 250,000 to 400,000. On the basis of the lower figure, one out of every 30 Cubans is today in the armed forces as against one out of 50 in the Soviet Union and one out of 60 in the United States.

Soviet domination of economic relations has proceeded with similar speed and comprehensiveness. A series of trade and financial agreements has integrated the Cuban economy with that of the Communist world. The extent of Cuban economic dependence on the Communist world is shown by the fact that approximately 75 percent of its trade is now tied up in barter arrangements with Iron Curtain countries. The artificiality of this development is suggested by the fact that at the beginning of

1960 only 2 percent of Cuba's total foreign trade was with the Communist bloc. The Soviet Union, East Germany, Czechoslovakia, and Poland have permanent technical assistance missions in Cuba; and a Communist Chinese delegation will soon arrive in pursuance of the Cuban-Chinese agreement of December 1960. According to Major Guevara, 2,700 Cubans will be receiving technical training in bloc countries in 1961.

The same process is visible in the field of cultural relations. What is involved is not just the visit of concert artists, dance groups, or athletic teams but the Communist conquest of all phases of cultural activity. This is to be seen in the comprehensive cultural agreements with bloc countries, in the reconstruction of the Cuban educational system to serve Communist purposes, in the impediments placed on students wishing to study anywhere except beyond the Iron Curtain, in the ban on books and magazines from the free states, in the affiliation of *Prensa Latina,* the official Cuban press agency, with Tass and other Communist-bloc news agencies. It has meant a deliberate severing of traditional cultural ties with countries of the hemisphere and of Western Europe. It has meant a massive attempt to impose an alien cultural pattern on the Cuban people.

In every area, the action of the Castro regime is steadily and purposefully directed toward a single goal—the transformation of Cuba into a Soviet satellite state.

IV. The Assault on the Hemisphere

The transformation of Cuba into a Soviet satellite is, from the viewpoint of the Cuban leaders, not an end but a beginning. Dr. Castro's fondest dream is a continent-wide upheaval which would reconstruct all Latin America on the model of Cuba. "We promise," he said on July 26, 1960, "to continue making the nation the example that can convert the Cordillera of the Andes into the Sierra Maestra of the hemisphere." "If they want to accuse us of wanting a revolution in all America," he added later, "let them accuse us."

Under Castro, Cuba has already become a base and staging area for revolutionary activity throughout the continent. In prosecuting the war against the hemisphere, Cuban embassies in Latin American countries work in close collaboration with Iron Curtain diplomatic missions and with the Soviet intelligence services. In addition, Cuban expressions of fealty to the Communist world have provided the Soviet Government a long-sought pretext for threats of direct interventions of its own in the Western Hemisphere. "We shall do everything to support Cuba in her struggle," Prime Minister Khrushchev said on July 9, 1960, ". . . Speaking figuratively, in case of necessity, Soviet artillerymen can support with rocket fire the Cuban people if aggressive forces in the Pentagon dare to start intervention against Cuba."

As Dr. Castro's alliance with international communism has grown closer, his determination to export revolution to other American Republics—a determination now affirmed, now denied—has become more fervent. The Declaration of Habana of September 2, 1960, was an open attack on the Organization of American States. Cuban intervention, though couched in terms designed to appeal to Latin American aspirations for freedom and justice, has shown its readiness to do anything necessary to extend the power of *Fidelismo.* Indeed, Dr. Castro has plainly reached the conclusion that his main enemy in Latin America is not dictatorship but democracy—

that he must, above all, strive to discredit and destroy governments seeking peaceful solutions to social and economic problems. Thus in recent months the Cuban Government has abandoned its aggressive campaign against the Trujillo dictatorship in the Dominican Republic and has accelerated its attacks on the progressive democratic government of Rómulo Betancourt in Venezuela.

Cuban interventionism has taken a variety of forms. During 1959 the Castro government aided or supported armed invasions of Panama, Nicaragua, the Dominican Republic, and Haiti. These projects all failed and all invited action by the Organization of American States. In consequence, after 1959 the Castro regime began increasingly to resort to indirect methods. The present strategy of *Fidelismo* is to provoke revolutionary situations in other republics through the indoctrination of selected individuals from other countries, through assistance to revolutionary exiles, through incitement to mass agitation, and through the political and propaganda operations of Cuban embassies. Cuban diplomats have encouraged local opposition groups, harangued political rallies, distributed inflammatory propaganda, and indulged in a multitude of political assignments beyond the usual call of diplomatic duty. Papers seized in a raid on the Cuban Embassy in Lima in November 1960 display, for example, the extent and variety of clandestine *Fidelista* activities within Peru. Documents made public by the Government of El Salvador on March 12, 1961, appear to establish that large sums of money have been coming into El Salvador through the Cuban Embassy for the purpose of financing pro-Communist student groups plotting the overthrow of the government. The regime is now completing construction of a 100,000-watt radio transmitter to facilitate its propaganda assault on the hemisphere.

Most instances of serious civil disturbance in Latin America in recent months exhibit Cuban influence, if not direct intervention. At the time of the November riots in Venezuela, the government announced the discovery of high-powered transmitting and receiving sets in the possession of Cubans in Caracas. In the following weeks about 50 Cubans were expelled from the country. Similar patterns appear to have existed in troubles in El Salvador, Nicaragua, Panama, Colombia, Bolivia, and Paraguay.

To such covert activities have been joined open and direct attacks on the duly elected leaders of the American states. Thus the Cuban Foreign Minister has applied unprintable language to President Frondizi of Argentina. Government broadcasts have denounced President López Mateos as "the betrayer of the Mexican Revolution," President Alessandri as "the corrupter of the faith of the Chilean people," President Lleras Camargo of Colombia as "the intimate friend of exploiting imperialism," President Betancourt of Venezuela as the "revolutionary of Mercurochrome Band-aids," President Eisenhower of the United States as "decrepit" and "bottle-fed," and so on.

In consequence of Dr. Castro's campaign against the hemisphere, seven American states no longer have diplomatic relations with Cuba. Of the states which retain formal relations, several have found it necessary to ask that Cuban Ambassadors and other official representatives be recalled because of their flagrant intervention into domestic affairs. A number of governments have withdrawn their own ambassadors from Habana.

The nations of the hemisphere, including the United States, have made repeated attempts to dissuade Cuba from thus turning its back on its brother Republics. Though the Cuban Government has tried to portray the United States as the sworn and unrelenting enemy of the Cuban Revolution, Dr. Castro was in fact cordially received when he visited the United States in the spring of 1959. American officials made clear to him the willingness of the United States Government to discuss his country's economic needs. For many months thereafter, the United States sought direct consultations with the Castro government. The United States took the initiative in suggesting negotiations as early as the summer of 1959. That offer and many others made subsequently were not accepted. For a long time the United States Ambassador in Habana was unable even to obtain an audience with Dr. Castro.

Dr. Castro had already made clear his contempt for the Organization of American States and for the entire inter-American system. Early in his regime he declared, "I have no faith in the OAS . . . it decides nothing, the whole thing is a lie." Though Cuba signed the Santiago Declaration of August 1959, with its enunciation of free elections, human rights, due process, freedom of information and expression, and hemisphere economic collaboration, it has systematically disregarded and violated each item in the Declaration. In March 1960 Castro publicly stated that the Cuban Government did not regard itself as obligated by the Rio Treaty, the keystone of hemispheric cooperation for defense, because "the revolution" did not sign the document.

In August 1960 the Foreign Ministers of the hemisphere, meeting at San José, Costa Rica, adopted a declaration condemning the threat of extracontinental intervention in the affairs of the hemisphere and condemning also the acceptance of any such threat by an American Republic; rejecting the attempt of the Sino-Soviet powers to exploit the political, economic, or social situation of any American State; and declaring that the inter-American system was incompatible with any form of totalitarianism and that democracy would achieve its full scope only as all American Republics lived up to the Santiago Declaration.

After the San José Declaration the Cuban regime, identifying itself as the object of these pronouncements, launched an all-out attack on the inter-American system. The Declaration of Habana condemned the Declaration of San José. The United States twice proposed that factfinding and good-offices procedures created by the OAS be used as an approach to resolving differences; these proposals were ignored by Cuba. Cuba refused to join with the other American Republics in the effort to bring about economic and social advance through the continent in the spirit of the Bogotá economic meeting of 1960. It refused to support the recommendations made by the November 1960 Special Meeting of Senior Representatives to strengthen the Inter-American Economic and Social Council. It has hurled insults on the whole conception of *Alianza para el Progreso*. It stands today in defiance not only of the Declarations of Santiago and San José and the Treaty of Rio but also of the Charter of the Organization of American States.

No one contends that the Organization of American States is a perfect institution. But it does represent the collective purpose of the American Republics to work together for democracy, economic development, and peace. The OAS has established the machinery to guarantee the safety and integrity of every American Republic, to preserve the principle of nonintervention by any American State in the internal or external affairs of the other American States, and to assure each nation the right to develop its cultural, political, and economic life freely and naturally, respecting the rights of the individual and the principles of universal morality.

The Organization of American States is the expression of the moral and political unity of the Western Hemisphere. In rejecting the OAS, the Castro regime has rejected the hemisphere and has established itself as the outpost in the Americas for forces determined to wreck the inter-American system. Under Castro, Cuba has become the agency to destroy the Bolivarian vision of the Americas as the greatest region in the world, "greatest not so much by virtue of her area and wealth, as by her freedom and glory."

V. Conclusion

It is not clear whether Dr. Castro intended from the start to betray his pledges of a free and democratic Cuba, to deliver his country to the Sino-Soviet bloc, and to mount an attack on the inter-American system; or whether he made his original pledges in all sincerity but, on assuming his new responsibilities, found himself increasingly dependent on ruthless men around him with clear ideas and the disciplined organization to carry those ideas into action. What is important is not the motive but the result.

The first result has been the institution of a repressive dictatorship in Cuba.

The existence of a regime dedicated to so calculated an attack on human decencies would by itself be a sufficient occasion for intense concern within the hemisphere. In recent years the American family of nations has moved steadily toward the conclusion that the safety and welfare of all the American Republics will be best protected by the establishment and guarantee within each republic of what the OAS Charter calls "the essential rights of man."

But Dr. Castro has done more than establish a dictatorship in Cuba; he has committed that dictatorship to a totalitarian movement outside the hemisphere.

Just as the American Republics over 20 years ago, in conferences beginning at Lima in 1938 and culminating at Rio de Janeiro in 1942, proclaimed that they could not tolerate the invasion of the hemisphere and the seizure of the American States by Nazi movements, serving the interests of the German Reich, so today they reject such invasion and seizure by Communist movements serving the interests of the Sino-Soviet bloc.

The people of Cuba remain our brothers. We acknowledge past omissions and errors in our relationship to them. The United States, along with the other nations of the hemisphere, expresses a profound determination to assure future democratic governments in Cuba full and positive support in their efforts to help the Cuban people achieve freedom, democracy, and social justice.

We call once again on the Castro regime to sever its links with the international Communist movement, to return to the original purposes which brought so many gallant men together in the Sierra Maestra, and to restore the integrity of the Cuban Revolution.

If this call is unheeded, we are confident that the Cuban people, with their passion for liberty, will continue to strive for a free Cuba; that they will return to the splendid vision of inter-American unity and progress; and that in the spirit of José Martí they will join hands with the other republics in the hemisphere in the struggle to win freedom.

Because the Castro regime has become the spearhead of attack on the inter-American system, that regime represents a fateful challenge to the inter-American system. For freedom is the common destiny of our hemisphere—freedom *from* domestic tyranny and foreign intervention, *from* hunger and poverty and illiteracy, freedom *for* each person and nation in the Americas to realize the high potentialities of life in the twentieth century.

102. Statement by Adlai E. Stevenson, U.S. Representative to the United Nations, before Committee I of the United Nations General Assembly, on a Cuban Complaint*

April 15, 1961

I am glad to see that Dr. [Raúl] Roa [Cuban representative] has suddenly recovered from his illness. This has been my first opportunity to listen to Dr. Roa on the sins of the United States and on the virtues of Castro's Cuba, and I must say that it is quite an experience. We have heard a number of charges by Dr. Roa, and now, if I may, I should like to impose on the committee long enough to report a few facts.

Prime Minister Castro's Air Force chief and his private pilot have asked for political asylum in the United States. The Air Force chief, Roberto Verdaguer, and his brother Guillermo landed a Cubana Airlines cargo plane at Jacksonville, Florida, on Friday of this week. These men will be given a hearing in Miami on Monday by immigration officials, and their request for political asylum will be considered in accordance with the usual procedures and practices.

There is also the matter of the bombing and rocket attacks which, according to reports, were made this morning on airports in Habana and Santiago and on Cuban Air Force headquarters at San Antonio de los Baños and to which Dr. Roa has referred.

Dr. Roa has made a number of charges that are without any foundation. I reject them categorically, and I should like to make several points quite clear to the committee.

First, as the President of the United States said a few days ago, there will not be under any conditions—and I repeat, any conditions—any intervention in Cuba by the United States armed forces.

Secondly, the United States will do everything it possibly can to make sure that no Americans participate in any actions against Cuba.

Thirdly, regarding the events which have reportedly occurred this morning and yesterday, the United States will consider, in accordance with its usual practices, the request for political asylum. This principle has long been enshrined as one of the fundamental principles of the Americas and, indeed, of the world. Those who believe in freedom and seek asylum from tyranny and oppression will always receive sympathetic understanding and consideration by the American people and the United States Government.

Fourthly, regarding the two aircraft which landed in Florida today, they were piloted by Cuban Air Force pilots. These pilots and certain other crew members have apparently defected from Castro's tyranny. No United States personnel participated. No United States Government airplanes of any kind participated. These two planes to

*Department of State Bulletin, May 8, 1961, pp. 667-68.

the best of our knowledge were Castro's own Air Force planes, and, according to the pilots, they took off from Castro's own Air Force fields.

I have here a picture of one of these planes. It has the markings of Castro's Air Force right on the tail, which everyone can see for himself. The Cuban star and the initials FAR–*Fuerza Aérea Revolucionaria*–are clearly visible. I should be happy to exhibit it to any members of the committee following my remarks.

As it is well known, the United States has long had under careful surveillance United States airfields in the southeastern part of this country in order to prevent alleged takeoffs from our shores to Cuba. We will continue to keep these airfields under perpetual surveillance.

Now, let me read the statement which has just arrived over the wire from the pilot who landed in Miami. He said,

I am one of the twelve B-26 pilots who remained in the Castro Air Force after the defection of Díaz Lanz and the purges that followed. Three of my fellow pilots and I have planned for months how we could escape from Castro's Cuba. Day before yesterday, I heard that one of the three, Lieutenant Alvaro Gallo, who is the pilot of the B-26, No. FAR-915, had been seen talking to an agent of Ramiro Valdes, the G-2 chief. I alerted the other two and we decided that probably Alvaro Gallo, who had always acted somewhat of a coward, had betrayed us. We decided to take action at once. Yesterday morning I was assigned the routine patrol from my base San Antonio de los Baños over a section of Pinar del Rio and around the Isle of Pines. I told my friends at Campo Libertad, and they agreed that we must act at once. One of them was to fly to Santiago. The other made the excuse that he wished to check out his altimeter, and they were to take off from Campo Libertad at 6 a.m. I was airborne at 6:05. Because of Alvaro Gallo's treachery we had agreed to give him a lesson, so I flew back over San Antonio where his plane is stationed and made two strafing runs at his plane and three others parked nearby. On the way out, I was hit by some small-arms fire and took evasive action. My comrades had broken off earlier to hit airfields which we agreed they would strike. Then because I was low on gas I had to go on into Miami because I could not reach our agreed destination. It may be that they went on to strafe another field before leaving, such as Playa Baracoa, where Fidel keeps his helicopter.

Now, I should like members of this committee to know that steps have been taken to impound the Cuban planes which have landed in Florida and they will not be permitted to take off for Cuba.

Let me make one concluding observation of a general character prior to our more extensive discussion of this matter on Monday. As President Kennedy said just a few days ago, the basic issue in Cuba is not between the United States and Cuba; it is between the Cubans themselves. Anyone familiar with the history of Cuba, however, knows one thing in particular—the history of Cuba has been a history of fighting for freedom. Regardless of what happens, the Cubans will fight for freedom. The activities of the last 24 hours are an eloquent confirmation of this historic fact.

*103. Statement by U.S. Representative Stevenson, before
Committee I of the U.N. General Assembly, on a
Cuban Complaint* *

April 17, 1961

Dr. Roa, speaking for Cuba, has just charged the United States with aggression against Cuba and invasion coming from Florida. These charges are totally false, and I deny them categorically. The United States has committed no aggression against Cuba, and no offensive has been launched from Florida or from any other part of the United States.

We sympathize with the desire of the people of Cuba—including those in exile who do not stop being Cubans merely because they could no longer stand to live in today's Cuba—we sympathize with their desire to seek Cuban independence and freedom. We hope that the Cuban people will succeed in doing what Castro's revolution never really tried to do: that is, to bring democratic processes to Cuba.

But as President Kennedy has already said,

> ... there will not under any conditions be ... an intervention in Cuba by United States armed forces. This Government will do everything it possibly can—and I think it can meet its responsibilities—to make sure that there are no Americans involved in any actions inside Cuba.

I wish to make clear also that we would be opposed to the use of our territory for mounting an offensive against any foreign government.

Dr. Roa has also charged my country—which fought for Cuban independence—with literally everything else, including releasing hounds against children and keeping slavery alive and crucifying the mandates of man and God. I must say, if such lurid oratory is a fair example of Dr. Roa's literature, that I shall read more for entertainment if not for enlightenment.

We have heard Dr. Roa's colorful challenges and his denunciation of the United States paper on Cuba as the most low and astigmatic literature he has ever seen. Well, when it comes to astigmatism, I would remind Dr. Roa what the gospel says in the Book of Matthew, "And why beholdest thou the mote that is in thy brother's eye, but considerest not the beam that is in thine own eye?"

It is my privilege now to discuss some of the beams in Cuba's eyes about the United States.

But first let me say that on Saturday Dr. Roa paid me the compliment of saying that he was familiar with my books and writings and was therefore surprised by my attitude about events in Cuba. He said there must be two Stevensons.

Well, I confess that I am flattered that Dr. Roa has read some of my writings, but I am not sure that I equally appreciate his suggestion that I am so versatile that there are two of me. Dr. Roa will find that on the subject of tyranny—be it of the right or the left—be it of the minority or the majority—be it over the mind, or spirit, or body of man—that I have only one view—unalterable opposition. That he evidently has not read what I think on that subject very carefully does not surprise me.

Department of State Bulletin, May 8, 1961, pp. 668-75.

Dr. Roa's Two Views on Hungarian Revolution

But if there are not two Stevensons, I suggest that on the subject of uprisings and communism Dr. Roa seems to have two views. Perhaps there are two Roas. In his book entitled *En Pie,* published in 1959, Dr. Roa included an essay on the Hungarian revolution and its suppression by the Soviet Army. I should like to quote, if I could, certain brief portions of Dr. Roa's essay, in an English translation which, although it may not do justice to the eloquence of the original language, nevertheless indicates Dr. Roa's views at that time. At that time he wrote:

The brutal methods employed by the Soviet Army to suppress the patriotic uprising of the Hungarian people have given rise to the strongest feelings of repulsion on the part of the free world, and the repercussions of these feelings in the intellectual areas subject to the Kremlin are breaking up the dogmatic unity of the Communist movement on the cultural level. The crimes, excesses and outrages perpetrated by the invaders have evoked strong censure and numerous desertions among the trained seals and charlatan lackeys of Moscow. The implacable brainwashing and systematic hardening of the sensibilities to which the heralds and palfreys of Marxist dichotomist doctrine are subject seem to have failed in this case.

Dr. Roa then cited what he called "representative opinions, judgments and pronouncements" of intellectuals in many countries of many political creeds, including the Communist, in condemnation of "Soviet infamies and depredations in Hungary," to use his own words. His essay concluded with this summation:

In Belgium, Holland, Norway, Sweden, England, Denmark and the United States of America, the most elevated men of science and the most eminent writers have closed ranks with the Hungarian patriots. The free voice of our America has already let itself be heard in a ringing document which I had the honor of signing. And also that of the Asiatic and African peoples who are fighting for the advent of a world wherein will reign justice, equality and respect for human rights.

If valor is not always accompanied by good fortune, nevertheless, the battles fought on behalf of liberty and culture against despotism and barbarism are never lost. The case of Hungary once more corroborates the patent validity of this statement.

Now, though it may seem paradoxical, Mr. Chairman and gentlemen, I must tell you that I am in entire agreement with the judgments in Dr. Roa's essay of 1959.

But in October 1960 the Cuban Foreign Ministry, under Dr. Roa's direction, gave an orientation lecture to its employees in which the Hungarian revolution was characterized as follows:

The Hungarian counterrevolution of 1956 was directed by North American imperialism to divert world attention from the Suez aggression: participating in the counterrevolution were fascist elements of the former Nagy government of Hungary, war criminals from West Germany and other foreign countries, leaders of the Roman Catholic Church who had lost lands and political power, and members of the Hungarian labor party, intellectuals and students who desired the restoration of capitalism; Soviet troops entered Hungary at the request of the legitimate government, and the U.S.S.R. also gave economic aid.

Well, gentlemen, for flexibility and agility I am afraid I would have to concede that even two Stevensons are no match for one Roa.

In reading these conflicting characterizations of the Hungary revolution, one by Dr. Roa and the other by his Ministry of Foreign Affairs, I was reminded of certain other parallels between Hungary and Cuba. The Castro regime and its foreign collaborators are using the same methods now to suppress the patriotic uprising of the Cuban people as were used in 1956 to suppress the Hungarian people. Cuban patriots are now called traitors, mercenaries, criminals, and tools of imperialism in the same way as the patriotic Hungarian workers of 1956 were then and are still being slandered by such false allegations.

Patriots become traitors and mercenaries evidently very quickly in the idiom of Dr. Roa. My recollection is that Batista said the same things, using the same, identical words to describe Dr. Castro, Dr. Roa, and their countless associates who had fled from the tyranny in Cuba.

No, Dr. Roa, our great champions of human freedom, Jefferson and Lincoln, will not have to be reburied because of our sympathy for today's freedom fighters, wherever they are.

Castro's Program of Betrayal

Dr. Roa's description of the detailed reports in the United States papers and magazines about the activities of the Cuban refugees illustrates something that I hope no member here will overlook. It illustrates how free the press is in this country. We don't have to wonder what would happen if a newspaper in Habana exercised the same freedom. We don't have to wonder, because it has already happened; the free press of Cuba has long since been crushed.

I want to remind the committee that there was great sympathy in the United States for the proclaimed goals of the Cuban revolution when it took place; that as soon as the Castro regime came to power the United States accorded it prompt recognition; that in the spring of 1959 the United States stood ready to supply the Castro government with economic assistance; that the hope of my fellow citizens has always been that Dr. Castro would live up to the pledges of freedom and democracy that he uttered from Sierra Maestra to the Cuban people. Instead, Dr. Castro chose to embark on a systematic betrayal of these pledges. He has presided over a methodical and shameless corruption of his own revolution. To conceal his program of betrayal, he has followed the classical course of all tyrants: He has raised the specter of a foreign enemy whose alleged malevolence can serve as an excuse for tightening the screws of tyranny at home. And so, in the course of 1959, he began the anti-United States campaign that in recent months has risen to so strident a crescendo. He closed his door to the American Ambassador in Habana. He conjured up the ghost of a *Yanqui* imperialism. By demanding that the American Embassy in Habana be reduced to a handful of persons, he eventually forced our Government to break diplomatic and consular relations with his regime.

What is even more important, Dr. Castro has accompanied his attack on my country by an ever-widening assault on the entire hemisphere. We must not forget that Dr. Roa has described President [Arturo] Frondizi of Argentina in terms so revolting that I will not repeat them. The official Cuban radio has poured shrill invective on the governments and on the leaders throughout the hemisphere; and the more democratic and progressive the government, the more the Castro regime recognizes it as a mortal enemy and the more savage becomes its abuse.

In time his assault has expanded to include the whole conception of the inter-American system and the Organization of American States. Dr. Castro has repeatedly proclaimed his purpose, to quote his own words, "to convert the Cordillera of the Andes into the Sierra Maestra of the hemisphere." He has avowed his ambition to overthrow the free governments of the Americas and to replace them by regimes modeled in his own tyrannical image. If Dr. Castro stands today an outlaw in the hemisphere, it is through his own desire, his own determination, his own decision to establish a new tyranny in Cuba. If the Castro regime is perishing, it is from self-inflicted wounds.

Fears of the Castro Regime

What Dr. Roa seeks from us today is the protection of the Castro regime from the natural wrath of the Cuban people. We have all read the recent newspaper stories about these activities which he has described with such lurid oratory—of men who hope to return to Cuba for the purpose of establishing a free government in their homeland. At least some members of such groups have been captured or imprisoned or executed by Cuban firing squads. We have given asylum to tens of thousands of Cuban citizens who have been forced to flee from their homeland to these shores. These exiles nurse a natural, burning desire to bring freedom to Cuba, and toward that end they work with the dedicated concentration which José Martí and other Cuban exiles in the United States have shown in the tradition which is now nearly 100 years old.

But what does the present Cuban regime have to fear from these groups? What accounts for Dr. Roa's agitation? Is Dr. Roa demanding that the Cuban exiles throughout the Americas be suppressed and controlled in the same ruthless manner as the people within Cuba today?

It cannot be that he fears the armed might of small armed bands of resistance fighters. His Prime Minister has often boasted of the armed strength of Cuba. Cuba has by far the largest ground forces of any country in Latin America, possessed, by Dr. Castro's own admission, with ample supplies of automatic rifles, machineguns, artillery, grenades, tanks, and other modern armament obtained from his new friends. Well over 30,000 tons of Soviet equipment has arrived in the last few months. This includes at least 15 Soviet 50-ton tanks, 19 Soviet assault guns, 15 Soviet 35-ton tanks, 78 Soviet 76-millimeter field guns, 4 Soviet 122-millimeter field guns, and over 100 Soviet heavy machineguns. Over 200 Soviet and Czechoslovak military advisers are in Cuba, and over 150 Cuban military personnel have been sent to the bloc for training.

In view of all of this, we must look for the answer to Castro's fears somewhere else: in the internal situation in Cuba and in Prime Minister Castro's own experience with the difficulties which small dissident groups can cause for a dictator who has betrayed his own revolution, as in the case of Batista.

If the Cuban Government is so deeply concerned about a few isolated groups, it must be because Dr. Castro has lost confidence in his own people. He evidently really believes that small armed groups are likely to find support enough to become dangerous. If this is the case, it seems a remarkable confession of doubt as to whether his own people approve his regime and its practices, and Dr. Castro is surely right to be afraid. Even with full government control of the press, the radio, television, all forms of communication, every evidence, including the daily defections of his close associates and supporters, suggests that the people of Cuba are rejecting this regime.

Challenge to the Hemisphere

Let me make it clear that we do not regard the Cuban problem as a problem between Cuba and the United States. The challenge is not to the United States but to the hemisphere and its duly constituted body, the Organization of American States. The Castro regime has betrayed the Cuban revolution. It is now collaborating in organized attempts by means of propaganda, agitation, and subversion to bring about the overthrow of existing governments by force and replace them with regimes subservient to an extra-continental power. These events help to explain why the Cuban Government continues to bypass the Organization of American States, even if they do not explain why Cuba, which is thus is open violation of its obligations under inter-American treaties and agreements, continues to charge the United States with violations of these same obligations.

Soon after the Castro government assumed power, it launched a program looking to the export of its system to other countries of the hemisphere, particularly in the Caribbean area. The intervention of Cuban diplomatic personnel in the internal affairs of other nations of the hemisphere has become flagrant. Cuban diplomatic and consular establishments are used as distribution points for propaganda material calling on the peoples of Latin America to follow Cuba's example. Even Cuban diplomatic pouches destined for various Latin American countries have been found to contain inflammatory and subversive propaganda directed against friendly governments.

In public support of these activities Prime Minister Castro, President [Osvaldo] Dorticós, Dr. Roa himself, and many other high-ranking members of the revolutionary government have openly stated that "the peoples of Latin America should follow Cuba's example." They have frankly declared that the Cuban system is for export. On August 30, 1960, Prime Minister Castro said: "What happened in Cuba will someday happen in America, and if for saying this we are accused of being continental revolutionaries, let them accuse us." But in case that was not clear enough it was followed 2 days later by Mr. Roa's statement that the Cuban revolution "will act as a springboard for all the popular forces in Latin America following a destiny identical to Cuba."

And as late as March 4th of this year, last month, President Dorticós did not hesitate to urge a group of Latin American agricultural workers meeting in Habana to "initiate similar movements in their own countries" when they returned home. He promised them the "solidarity of a people who have already won their victory and are ready to help other people achieve theirs."

In spite of all of this, Dr. Roa now tells us that the revolutionary government wants only to live in peace, that it does not threaten its neighbors, that it has not attempted nor intends to export its revolution.

Statements of Soviet Russian and Chinese Communist leaders indicate that, by Dr.

Castro's own actions, the Cuban revolution has become an instrument of the foreign policies of these extra-continental powers. The increasingly intimate relationship between Cuba and the Soviet Union, the People's Republic of China, and other countries associated with them, in conjunction with the huge shipments of arms, munitions, and other equipment from the Sino-Soviet bloc, must therefore be matters of deep concern to independent governments everywhere.

The Castro regime has mercilessly destroyed the hope of freedom the Cuban people had briefly glimpsed at the beginning of 1959. Cuba has never witnessed such political persecution as exists today. The arrests, the prisons bulging with political prisoners, and the firing squads testify to this. Since the Castro regime came to power, more than 600 persons have been executed, with a shocking disregard of the standards of due process of law and fair trial generally accepted and practiced in the civilized community of nations. The Government has even threatened to replace its slogan for this year—"the year of education"—with a new slogan—"the year of the execution wall."

There is no democratic participation of the Cuban people in the determination of their destiny. Staged rallies, at which small percentages of the population are harangued and asked to express approval of policies by shouts or show of hands, represent the procedure of a totalitarian demagog and not free and democratic expression of opinion through the secret ballot.

The Cuban farm worker who was promised his own plot of land finds that he is an employee of the state working on collective or state-run farms. The independent labor movement, once one of the strongest in the hemisphere, is today in chains. Freely elected Cuban labor leaders, who as late as the end of 1960 protested the destruction of workers' rights, were imprisoned for their pains, or took asylum in foreign embassies, or fled the country to escape imprisonment.

When in addition the people are confronted, despite aid from the Sino-Soviet bloc, with a drastic reduction in their standard of living, it is not surprising opposition to their present master grows.

Roster of the Disillusioned

Such conditions have led to a steady stream of defections and escapes—not by members of the previous government but by Castro's own officials.

In his speech on Saturday afternoon, Dr. Roa referred to those Cubans fighting to free their homeland from tyranny as "traitors.and mercenaries." The Soviet representative, in supporting Dr. Roa, embellished the characterization by calling these freedom fighters "human beings who are capable of selling their own father and their mother for a consideration." Now, Dr. Roa well knows that the men of whom he speaks are not traitors or mercenaries. He is familiar with their contribution to the revolution. The reasons for their defection are no mystery to him. Many of them are his friends and associates of long standing, both in government service and at the University of Habana. Mr. [Valerian A.] Zorin [Soviet representative], on the other hand, might be excused perhaps for not being familiar with the revolutionary background of some of these Cuban patriots.

I think it might be instructive for him and for the members of the committee to know who some of these people are. They make an impressive list: the first provisional president of the Revolutionary Government, Dr. Manuel Urrutia, who had asserted in defiance of Batista and in defense of Castro the right of Cubans to resort to arms to overthrow an unconstitutional government; the first Prime Minister, Dr. José Miró Cardona, who is chairman of the Revolutionary Council, which seeks the rescue of the betrayed revolution; and the first President of the Supreme Court, Dr. Emilio Menéndez.

It also includes nearly two-thirds of Castro's first Cabinet, such as Minister of Foreign Affairs Roberto Agramonte, Minister of the Treasury Rufo López Fresquet, Minister of Labor Manuel Fernández, Minister of Agriculture Humberto Sorí Marín, and Minister of Public Works Manuel Ray. In other fields a similar compilation can be made: companions in arms of Fidel Castro such as Sierra Maestra commanders Huber Matos, Niño Díaz, and Jorge Sotus; and rebel Air Force leaders such as Pedro Díaz Lanz and the Verdaguer brothers; labor leaders such as David Salvador and Amaury Fraginals; editors and commentators such as *Bohemia* director Miguel Angel Quevedo, Luis Conte Agüero, and the notoriously anti-American José Pardo Llada; and even such confidants as Juan Orta, the head of the Prime Minister's own offices.

The roster of disillusioned, persecuted, imprisoned, exiled, and executed men and women who originally supported Dr. Castro—and who are now labeled as "traitors and mercenaries" by Dr. Roa because they tried to make the Castro regime live up to its own promises—is long and getting longer. These are the men who are now leading the struggle to restore the Cuban revolution to its original premises.

In his letter of February 23, circulated in document A/4701, Dr. Roa claims that it is the policy of the United States "to punish the Cuban people on account of their legitimate aspirations for the political freedom, economic development and social advancement of the under-developed or dependent peoples of Latin America, Africa, Asia and Oceania." Such a ludicrous charge deserves no serious reply. But I should remind Dr. Castro that he had many friends in the United States at the time he took power in Cuba. The ideals which he then expressed of establishing honest and efficient government, perfecting democratic processes, and creating higher standards of living, full employment, and land reform were welcomed warmly both in the United States and in other parts of the Western Hemisphere. I sincerely wish that was still the case.

Problem Created by Cuban Revolution

The problem created in the Western Hemisphere by the Cuban revolution is not one of revolution. As President Kennedy said on March 13,

> ... political freedom must be accompanied by social change. For unless necessary social reforms, including land and tax reform, are freely made, unless we broaden the opportunity of all of our people, unless the great mass of Americans share in increasing prosperity, then our alliance, our revolution, our dream, and our freedom will fail. But we call for social change by free men—change in the spirit of Washington and Jefferson, of Bolívar and San Martín and Martí—not change which seeks to impose on men tyrannies which we cast out a century and a half ago. Our motto is what it has always been—progress yes, tyranny no. . . .

No, the problem is not social change, which is both inevitable and just. The problem is that every effort is being made to use Cuba as a base to force totalitarian ideology into other parts of the Americas.

The Cuban Government has disparaged the plans of the American states to pool their resources to accelerate social and economic development in the Americas. At the Bogotá meeting of the Committee of 21 in September 1960 the Cuban delegation missed few opportunities to insult the representatives of other American states and to play an obstructionist role. They refused to sign the Act of Bogotá and thereby to take part in the hemisphere-wide cooperative effort of social reform to accompany programs of economic development. The Cuban official reaction to President Kennedy's Alliance for Progress program for the Americas was in a similar vein. In a speech on March 12, 1961, Dr. Castro denounced the program, portraying it as a program of "alms" using "usurious dollars" to buy the economic independence and national dignity of the countries which participate in the program. This is insulting to the countries which participate in the program. But equally important, he chose to ignore the underlying premise of the program: a vast cooperative effort to satisfy the basic needs of the American peoples and thereby to demonstrate to the entire world that man's unsatisfied aspiration for economic progress and social justice can best be achieved by free men working within a framework of democratic institutions. The hostility of the Castro regime to these constructive efforts for social and economic progress in the Americas—and even the language—recalls the similar hostility of the U.S.S.R. to the Marshall plan in Europe.

Dr. Castro has carefully and purposefully destroyed the great hope the hemisphere invested in him when he came to power 2 years ago. No one in his senses could have expected to embark on such a course as this with impunity. No sane man would suppose that he could speak Dr. Castro's words, proclaim his aggressive intentions, carry out his policies of intervention and subversion—and at the same time retain the friendship, the respect, and the confidence of Cuba's sister republics in the Americas. He sowed the wind and reaps the whirlwind.

It is not the United States which is the cause of Dr. Castro's trouble: It is Dr. Castro himself. It is not Washington which has turned so many thousands of his fellow countrymen against his regime—men who fought beside him in the Cuban hills, men who risked their lives for him in the underground movements in Cuban cities, men who lined Cuban streets to hail him as the liberator from tyranny, men who occupied the most prominent places in the first government of the Cuban revolution. It is these men who constitute the threat—if threat there is—to Dr. Castro's hope of consolidating his power and intensifying his tyranny.

It is Dr. Castro's own policy which has deprived these men of the hope of influencing his regime by democratic methods of free elections and representative government. It is Dr. Castro who, by denying Cuban citizens constitutional recourse, has driven them toward the desperate alternative of resistance—just as Batista once did.

Let us be absolutely clear in our minds who these men are. They are not supporters of Batista; they fought as passionately and bravely against Batista as Dr. Castro himself. They are not champions of the old order in Cuba; they labored day and night as long as they could to realize the promises of the Cuban revolution. They will not turn the clock back, either to the tyranny of Batista or to the tyranny of Castro. They stand for a new and brighter Cuba which will genuinely realize the pledge which Dr. Castro has so fanatically betrayed—the pledge of bread with freedom.

U.S. Attitude Toward Castro Regime

The problem which the United States confronts today is our attitude toward such men as these. Three years ago many American citizens looked with sympathy on the cause espoused by Castro and offered hospitality to his followers in their battle against the tyranny of Batista. We cannot expect Americans today to look with less sympathy on those Cubans who, out of love for their country and for liberty, now struggle against the tyranny of Castro.

If the Castro regime has hostility to fear, it is the hostility of Cubans, not of Americans. If today Castro's militia are hunting down guerrillas in the hills where Castro himself once fought, they are hunting down Cubans, not Americans. If the Castro regime is overthrown, it will be overthrown by Cubans, not by Americans.

I do not see that it is the obligation of the United States to protect Dr. Castro from the consequences of his treason to the promises of the Cuban revolution, to the hopes of the Cuban people, and to the democratic aspirations of the Western Hemisphere.

It is because Dr. Castro has turned his back on the inter-American system that this debate marks so tragic a moment for all citizens of the Western Hemisphere. It is tragic to watch the historic aspirations of the Cuban people once again thwarted by tyranny. It is tragic to see bitterness rise within a family of nations united by so many bonds of common memory and common hope. It is tragic to watch a despotic regime drive its own people toward violence and bloodshed. The United States looks with distress and anxiety on such melancholy events.

Our only hope is that the Cuban tragedy may awaken the people and governments of the Americas to a profound resolve—a resolve to concert every resource and energy to advance the cause of economic growth and social progress throughout the hemisphere, but to do so under conditions of human freedom and political democracy. This cause represents the real revolution of the Americas. To this struggle to expand freedom and abundance and education and culture for all the citizens of the New World the free states of the hemisphere summon all the peoples in nations where freedom and independence are in temporary eclipse. We confidently expect that Cuba will be restored to the American community and will take a leading role to win social reform and economic opportunity, human dignity and democratic government, not just for the people of Cuba but for all the people of the hemisphere.

[In a further intervention Ambassador Stevenson said:]

I will detain you only a moment because I agree with Mr. Zorin's suggestion that we adjourn until this afternoon.

But I must intervene long enough to say that, while I was not here at the United Nations at that time, I recall no such complaints of aggression against a small country from Mr. Zorin when Castro's followers were organizing their revolt against Batista on the shores of the United States. Why is it that the distinguished representative of the Soviet Union is so concerned about a revolt against Dr. Castro? Cuba is no smaller today than it was then and far more defensible—thanks to the U.S.S.R.

104. Message from Nikita S. Khrushchev, Chairman of the
Council of Ministers of the Union of Soviet Socialist
Republics, to President Kennedy, Concerning
Cuba*

April 18, 1961

I address this message to you at an alarming hour which is fraught with danger against universal peace. An armed aggression has been started against Cuba. It is an open secret that the armed bands which have invaded that country have been prepared, equipped, and armed in the United States. The planes which bomb Cuban towns belong to the United States of America, the bombs which they drop have been put at their disposal by the American Government.

All this arouses in the Soviet Union, the Soviet Government, and the Soviet people an understandable feeling of indignation. Only recently, exchanging views through our representatives, we talked with you about the mutual wish of the parties to exert joint efforts directed toward the improvement of relations between our countries and the prevention of a danger of war. Your statement a few days ago to the effect that the United States of America would not participate in military actions against Cuba created an impression that the leading authorities of the United States are aware of the consequences which aggression against Cuba could have for the whole world and the United States of America itself.

How are we to understand what is really being done by the United States now that the attack on Cuba has become a fact?

It is yet not too late to prevent the irreparable. The Government of the U.S. can still prevent the flames of war kindled by the interventionists on Cuba from spreading into a conflagration which it will be impossible to cope with. I earnestly appeal to you, Mr. President, to call a halt to the aggression against the Republic of Cuba. The military techniques and the world political situation now are such that any so-called "small war" can produce a chain reaction in all parts of the world.

As for the U.S.S.R., there must be no mistake about our position. We will extend to the Cuban people and its Government all the necessary aid for the repulse of the armed attack on Cuba. We are sincerely interested in the relaxation of international tension, but if others go in for its aggravation, then we will answer them in full measure. In general it is impossible to carry on affairs in such a way that in one area the situation is settled and the fire is put out, and in another area a new fire is lit.

I hope that the U.S. Government will take into consideration these reasons, dictated only by concern that steps should not be permitted which might lead the world to a catastrophe of war.

*Department of State Bulletin, May 8, 1961, p. 662.

105. Statement from the Government of the Union of Soviet Socialist Republics, Concerning Cuba*

April 18, 1961

The Government of the Republic of Cuba has announced that in the morning of 15 April airplanes of the U.S. B-26 bomber type subjected separate districts of the capital of Cuba—Havana—and a number of other inhabited localities to barbarous bombing. There were many killed and injured among the inhabitants of the capital.

Following the bombing, early in the morning of 17 April armed forces of the interventionists landed at various places on the Cuban coast. The landing took place under the cover of U.S. aircraft and warships.

Cuban Government troops and the People's Militia are engaged in fighting the invading gangs.

In connection with the invasion of Cuba the Government of the Soviet Union states:

The attack on Cuba is an open challenge to all freedom-loving peoples, a dangerous provocation against peace in the area of the Caribbean Sea, against universal peace. There can be no justification of this criminal invasion. The organizers of the aggression against Cuba are encroaching on the inalienable right of the Cuban people to live freely and independently. They are trampling underfoot the elementary norms of international relations, the principles of peaceful coexistence of states.

The Cuban nation has not threatened and is not threatening anyone. Having overthrown the tyranny of the bloody despot Batista, lackey of the big U.S. monopolies, the Cuban nation has embarked upon the pursuit of an independent policy, of raising its economy, and improving its life. It demands to be left in peace, to be left to build its life in conformity with its national ideals.

Can small Cuba with its population of 6 million threaten anyone—and such a big state as the United States at that? Of course not. Yet since the first days of the victory of the national revolution in Cuba the United States became the center where the counter-revolutionary elements thrown out from Cuba gathered, where they were formed into gangs and armed for struggle against the popular government of Fidel Castro. Recent events show that the present U.S. Government, which declared itself heir to Roosevelt's policy, is in essence pursuing the reactionary imperialist policy of Dulles and Eisenhower so condemned by the nations.

The U.S. Government declared through President Kennedy that the basic controversial question on Cuba is not a matter of a quarrel between the United States and Cuba but concerns the Cubans alone. The President said that he advocated a free and independent Cuba. In fact, however, everything was done on the territory of the United States and the countries dependent on it to prepare an aggressive attack on Cuba. But for the open aggressive policy of the United States towards Cuba would the counterrevolutionary gangs of the hirelings of U.S. capital have been able to create the so-called Cuban Government on U.S. territory? What territory served as a starting point for the piratical attack on Cuba?

It was the territory of the United States and that of the neighboring countries which are under its control. Whose are the arms with which the counterrevolutionary

*Department of State Bulletin, May 8, 1961, pp. 662-63.

gangs are equipped? They are U.S. arms. With whose funds have they been supported and are they being maintained? With funds appropriated by the United States.

It is clear from this that it is precisely the United States which is the inspirer and organizer of the present bandit-like attack on Cuba. Why did the United States organize this criminal attack on the Cuban Republic? Because, after the overthrow of the tyranny of Batista, the Cuban people were finished with the plunder and exploitation of their homeland by foreign monopolies. These monopolies do not wish to concede anything to the people of Cuba, the peoples of Latin America. They fear that Cuba, building its independent life, will become an example for other countries of Latin America. With the hands of base mercenaries they want to take from the Cuban people their right to determine their own fate, as they did with Guatemala.

But every nation has the right to live as it wishes, and no one, no state has the right to impose its own way of life on other nations. The Cuban nation has passed through a long, harsh, and difficult school of struggle for its freedom and independence against foreign oppressors and their accomplices, and it will not be brought to its knees, will not permit the yoke of foreign enslavers to be placed upon its shoulders. All progressive mankind, all upright people are on the side of Cuba.

The Government of the Soviet Union states that the Soviet Union, as other peace-loving countries, will not abandon the Cuban people in their trouble nor will it refuse it all necessary aid and support in the just struggle for the freedom and independence of Cuba.

The Soviet Government, at this crucial moment, for the sake of preserving universal peace, appeals to the Government of the United States to take measures to stop the aggression against Cuba and intervention in Cuba's internal affairs. Protection of and aid to the counterrevolutionary bands must be stopped immediately.

The Soviet Government hopes that it will be understood in the United States that aggression goes against the interests of the American people and is capable of jeopardizing the peaceful life of the population of the United States itself.

The Soviet Government demands urgent study by the U.N. General Assembly of the question of aggressive actions of the United States, which has prepared and unleashed armed intervention against Cuba.

The Government of the U.S.S.R. appeals to the governments of all member states of the United Nations to take all necessary measures for the immediate cessation of aggressive actions against Cuba, the continuation of which may give rise to the most serious consequences for universal peace.

In this hour, when the sovereignty and independence of Cuba, a sovereign member of the United Nations, are in danger, the duty of all countries members of the United Nations is to render it all necessary aid and support.

The Soviet Government reserves the right, if armed intervention in the affairs of the Cuban people is not stopped, to take all measures with other countries to render the necessary assistance to the Republic of Cuba.

106. *Message from President Kennedy to Premier Khrushchev, Concerning Cuba* *

April 18, 1961

You are under a serious misapprehension in regard to events in Cuba. For months there has been evident and growing resistance to the Castro dictatorship. More than 100,000 refugees have recently fled from Cuba into neighboring countries. Their urgent hope is naturally to assist their fellow Cubans in their struggle for freedom. Many of these refugees fought alongside Dr. Castro against the Batista dictatorship; among them are prominent leaders of his own original movement and government.

These are unmistakable signs that Cubans find intolerable the denial of democratic liberties and the subversion of the 26th of July Movement by an alien-dominated regime. It cannot be surprising that, as resistance within Cuba grows, refugees have been using whatever means are available to return and support their countrymen in the continuing struggle for freedom. Where people are denied the right of choice, recourse to such struggle is the only means of achieving their liberties.

I have previously stated, and I repeat now, that the United States intends no military intervention in Cuba. In the event of any military intervention by outside force we will immediately honor our obligations under the inter-American system to protect this hemisphere against external aggression. While refraining from military intervention in Cuba, the people of the United States do not conceal their admiration for Cuban patriots who wish to see a democratic system in an independent Cuba. The United States government can take no action to stifle the spirit of liberty.

I have taken careful note of your statement that the events in Cuba might affect peace in all parts of the world. I trust that this does not mean that the Soviet government, using the situation in Cuba as a pretext, is planning to inflame other areas of the world. I would like to think that your government has too great a sense of responsibility to embark upon any enterprise so dangerous to general peace.

I agree with you as to the desirability of steps to improve the international atmosphere. I continue to hope that you will cooperate in opportunities now available to this end. A prompt cease-fire and peaceful settlement of the dangerous situation in Laos, cooperation with the United Nations in the Congo and a speedy conclusion of an acceptable treaty for the banning of nuclear tests would be constructive steps in this direction. The regime in Cuba could make a similar contribution by permitting the Cuban people freely to determine their own future by democratic processes and freely to cooperate with their Latin American neighbors.

I believe, Mr. Chairman, that you should recognize that free peoples in all parts of the world do not accept the claim of historical inevitability for Communist revolution. What your government believes is its own business; what it does in the world is the world's business. The great revolution in the history of man, past, present and future, is the revolution of those determined to be free.

*Department of State Bulletin, May 8, 1961, pp. 661-62.

107. *Statement by U.S. Representative Stevenson, before
      Committee I of the U.N. General Assembly, on a Cuban
      Complaint**

April 18, 1961

I am grateful to the distinguished representative of Mexico for his thoughtful, scholarly, and temperate address, as I am to others who have attempted to make constructive contributions to this discussion.

This morning I said that I would read to the committee the message of the President of the United States in reply to Mr. Khrushchev's message, which Mr. Zorin read to us this morning. The message was handed to the Soviet Ambassador in Washington at 7 o'clock this evening and was immediately released to the press. I would have delivered it to you before, but this is the first opportunity I have had to speak. The message reads:

> [At this point Ambassador Stevenson read the text of President Kennedy's message to N. S. Khrushchev, Chairman of the Council of Ministers of the U.S.S.R. . . .

I am afraid that the time has now come for me to comment on and correct some of the innuendoes, the half-truths, the falsehoods about the Cuban affair which the committee has heard for many hours. I said yesterday:

> Dr. Roa . . . has just charged the United States with aggression against Cuba and invasion coming from Florida. These charges are totally false, and I deny them categorically. The United States has committed no aggression against Cuba, and no offensive has been launched from Florida or from any other part of the United States.
>
> We sympathize with the desire of the people of Cuba—including those in exile who do not stop being Cubans merely because they could no longer stand to live in today's Cuba—we sympathize with their desire to seek Cuban independence and freedom.

But we hope, as I have also said, that the Cuban people will succeed in doing what Dr. Castro promised to do: to bring to Cuba social reform, free institutions, and honest democratic government. We in the United States regret that Dr. Castro's promises are forgotten and that he is converting that beautiful, rich island into an outpost of the new imperialism. With its history of gallant struggle for freedom, what has happened in Cuba is all the more tragic.

I have listened here to every kind of epithet and abuse of my country. All of the familiar Communist words have been poured in a torrent on a nation that has fought in two world wars to defeat the designs of tyrants and protect your freedom as well as ours; a nation that bore the greatest burden of the first great battle for collective security in Korea and the protection of a small country from cynical and unprovoked attack by its neighbor; a nation that has poured out its treasure to aid the reconstruction and rehabilitation, the defense and prosperity, of friends and foes alike, with a magnanimity without historical precedents. And for our pains the words that reverberate in this chamber are too often "greedy monopolists," "mercenaries," "economic

Department of State Bulletin, May 8, 1961, pp. 675-81.

imperialists," "exploiters," "pirates," "aggressors," and all the familiar Communist jargon, including the worst of all—"counterrevolutionary"—which of course means anti-Communist. And I must say that after listening to this I welcome the healthy and wholesome suggestion of the representative of Ecuador that we declare a moratorium on epithets and poison in our discussion.

Not content with calling us all the names in the glossary of epithets and abuse, not content with confiscating all of our properties, with closing our Embassy, with persecuting our citizens, I have heard the United States denounced over and over for not buying our assailant's sugar—and at a price above the world market. I am reminded of the little boy who killed his mother and his father and then pleaded for clemency on the ground that he was an orphan.

But I assure you that Cuba is no orphan. Cuba has a new and powerful friend, just like Little Red Riding Hood in the fable. And now that their imperialist invasion of Cuba has succeeded and the Cuban revolution has been conformed to their pattern, we hear them deny the right of revolution to another people—the Cubans. I heard no such bitter protests when Mr. Castro was establishing his foothold in the Cuban mountains after returning from abroad with his followers.

Invalidity of Cuba's Charges

But let me comment on the many accusations about activities in the United States. I repeat again what I said yesterday: No invasion has taken place from Florida or any other part of the United States, and we are opposed to the use of our territory for launching a military attack against any foreign country. Dr. Roa has alleged, and others have faithfully repeated, countless instances of United States intervention in Cuba through air actions, arms, supplies, ships, and so forth. A careful examination of his speech will show, however, not one bit of evidence of United States involvement. But the facts, or the want of them, are evidently no deterrent to lurid rhetoric and accusation by some among us.

The whole world knows and no one denies that, since Dr. Castro betrayed his revolution, there has been a rising tide of discontent and resistance by Cubans both inside and outside of Cuba; sabotage, violence, and guerrilla fighting within Cuba have been daily news for many months. But it is not true, as the representative of Rumania claimed yesterday, that this has been caused by aircraft proceeding from United States territory and "piloted by Americans," to quote his words.

It is not true any more than it is true, as Dr. Roa and others have repeated, that an invasion has been launched from Florida.

A few other examples of the invalidity of Dr. Roa's charges against the United States Government may be of interest to the committee in the consideration of this matter. First Dr. Roa asked a series of questions about particular types of armaments, some of which he displayed in photographs. It is true, as Dr. Roa implied, that most of this armament is used by United States armed forces. It is also true, which he did not imply, that most of these types of arms, including 57-millimeter antitank guns, are widely distributed throughout the armies of Latin America, Europe, and other parts of the world. Most, if not all, of these arms, including those which are only sold originally on a government-to-government basis, are freely available on private arms markets. Every one of the weapons has been accessible to many nations on a licensed basis, including Cuba and other Latin American nations. The Castro army itself, further-more, has stocks of many, if not all, of them.

Secondly, Dr. Roa also repeated charges about pirate flights of United States planes from Florida over Cuba, which he says now number 50. I conclude that the story grows in telling, like the fish story. A report that a plane flying over Cuba came from a northerly direction is apparently Dr. Castro's only evidence that it came from the United States.

The Cuban Government, I am sure, knows that the United States has established the most vigorous and elaborate system of controls in peacetime history to prevent the unauthorized flight of aircraft from the United States over Cuba. Where specific evidence has been brought to our attention, we have attempted to investigate, as is clearly set forth in document A/4537. Some of these investigations have demonstrated that some flights did originate in the United States. It was because of this that the United States established this elaborate control system. But the investigations have also demonstrated the hypocrisy and deceit of the Cuban Government. In at least one of these flights—in March 1960—the pilot, William Shergalis, admitted that he was an agent of Castro and had been directed to make the flight in order to fabricate evidence of an alleged United States provocation. Since admitting this he has been held constantly in jail in Cuba. The Shergalis operation was organized through the head of Prime Minister Castro's own offices, Juan Orta, who only last week defected and sought asylum in a Latin American embassy in Habana.

The latest flight of which Dr. Roa complains was the one on 24 March which, he tells us, the Castro government forced down at José Martí Airport. This case is similarly instructive. What Dr. Roa did not say was that this plane was on its way to Nicaragua, that it had received flight clearance from the Cuban authorities, that clearance was revoked—but not until after the plane was already on its way—that it was carrying spare tractor parts and a banana pulping machine, and that the Cuban Government has since released the fliers.

Thirdly, another example of Dr. Roa's charges is that a ship named the *Western Union* was apprehended on 31 March in Cuban waters and that it had on board 180,000 gallons of high-octane gasoline, that planes flew over the Cuban Coast Guard vessel involved and dropped tear gas, and finally that the ship was engaged in anti-Cuban activities.

The circumstances in this case have been carefully investigated, and I am able to report the facts. The *Western Union* had no relation to any United States Government operation; it was engaged in a cable repair job which had no relation to Cuba. The burden of Dr. Roa's charge that the *Western Union* carried 180,000 gallons of high-octane gasoline is also untrue. It was carrying no gasoline except its own fuel. The *Western Union* is a 90-ton schooner. One hundred and eighty thousand gallons of high-octane gasoline weighs 540 tons. Need I say any more?

The *Western Union* was not within Cuban territorial waters. It was fully 6 miles from the Cuban shore when it was intercepted and illegally forced within Cuban coastal waters. American aircraft, which were dispatched in reply to its signals of distress, limited their activities to observation. No tear gas was used.

In the fourth place, Dr. Roa has also alleged that, before the regime of Fidel Castro, Cuba's economic dependence upon the United States was such as to make it a kind of colony of the United States. He cited the Cuban sugar quota in the United States market as an illustration or proof of his charge. In fact the relationship between Cuba, as the privileged foreign supplier of sugar to this country, and the United States, as the principal market for Cuban sugar, has been of considerable mutual advantage to Cuba and the United States. In return for the assurance which Cuba gave of a secure and close source of supply of sugar, Cuba received a quota—a preferential tariff at any rate—and a United States market price which was normally higher than the world market price. Under this agreement Cuba supplied about 71 percent of the United States sugar imports and earned in 1959 alone—the first year of Dr. Castro's regime—$350 million from sugar exports to the United States.

The Castro regime denounced this quota arrangement as "economic bondage," to quote their words. Yet when the United States after long delay finally and reluctantly terminated the arrangement because of Cuban economic policies, its action was attacked as economic aggression. The Castro government cannot have it both ways. If the arrangement was economic bondage, its termination could hardly be economic aggression.

Record of Promises Made by Castro

In the fifth place, Dr. Roa said yesterday that the United States was trying to force Cuba back to the Constitution of 1940, which he described as a political expression of colonial economic structure. I should like to dwell on this charge for a moment. Dr. Roa implies that there was some evil nature in that Constitution; but Dr. Castro himself made the restoration of the Constitution of 1940 a cornerstone of the program he promised the Cuban people after he assumed power.

In 1953 in his celebrated speech entitled "History Will Absolve Me," delivered at his trial following the attack on Cuartel Moncada, Dr. Castro described the program of his revolutionary movement. The first part of his speech read as follows:

> The first revolutionary law would have returned power to the people and would have proclaimed the Constitution of 1940 the supreme law of the land in order to effect its implementation and punish those who had violated it.

Later in the speech he said:

> Recently there has been a violent controversy concerning the validity of the Constitution of 1940. The Court of Social and Constitutional Rights ruled against it in favor of the laws. Nevertheless, honorable magistrates I maintain that the 1940 Constitution is still in power.

This was the attitude Dr. Castro held at least once about the 1940 Constitution. I say this only to set the record straight. But I also wish to say equally directly that what happens constitutionally in Cuba is a Cuban question. We hold no brief for any constitutional solution, 1940 or any other, and this is up to the Cubans, of course. It may also interest the committee to know in connection with this question that at that time Dr. Castro also made the following statement:

> You are well aware that resistance to despots is legitimate. This is a universally recognized principle and our Constitution of 1940 expressly makes it a sacred right, in the second paragraph of article 40: "It is legitimate to use adequate resistance to protect previously granted individual rights."

I ask the committee, then, to ponder the significance of that statement of Dr. Castro in the light of what is happening between Cubans today.

Let us look at the record of promises made by Dr. Castro prior to the fall of Batista and how he has betrayed the Cuban people themselves, for in this lies the reason for the revolution of today. Dr. Roa claimed that Castro is fulfilling, not denying, his revolution. Yesterday Dr. Roa asked why do we in the United States say "betrayed," and then he answers his question by saying, "because we have been true to the revolution." Well, let us see.

The Declaration of Sierra Maestra of July 12, 1957, was the promise held out to the Cuban people. Its principal pledges were, and I quote them for the enlightenment of the committee:

Immediate freedom for all political prisoners, civil and military.

Absolute guarantee of freedom of information, both of newspapers and radio, and of all the individual and political rights guaranteed by the Constitution.

Democratization of union politics, holding free elections in all unions and industrial federations.

Immediate beginning of an intensive campaign against illiteracy and of civic education, emphasizing the duties and rights which the citizen has both in the society and the fatherland.

Establishment of an organization for agrarian reform to promote the distribution of barren lands and the conversion into proprietors of all lessee-planters, partners and squatters who possess small parcels of land, be it property of the state or of private persons, with prior indemnification to the former owners.

And now let us see what has happened according to the record of what I have called "betrayal."

On political prisoners whom he promised to free, the Castro regime now holds a conservatively estimated 15,000 political prisoners. The national prisons, such as the Isle of Pines prison, the Cabaña, and El Principe, are overflowing, as are the smaller provisional prisons, local jails, and places of confinement. Concentration camps have been built. Some 2,000 political prisoners, for example, are being held incommunicado in a special camp at Minas del Frío in the Sierra Maestra mountains. Perhaps some of you have read in the press this morning that the prisoners now include the distinguished Roman Catholic prelate, Auxiliary Bishop of Habana Monsignor Eduardo Boza Masvidal. The news story says that he is accused of the "counterrevolutionary" crime of having United States currency in his possession and hoarding medicine. Monsignor Masvidal was originally a strong supporter of the social reforms of the revolution.

Freedom of Press Obliterated

And now, on the subject of freedom of information, for which Dr. Castro promised an absolute guarantee. Freedom of the press, as we know, has been completely obliterated. Not a single independent newspaper remains in Cuba. And those Cuban newsmen who tried to uphold the principles of freedom have either been dismissed, imprisoned, driven into exile, or silenced in some other way.

The Castro regime began its campaign against a free press at an early date. Five newspapers were confiscated by the Government on 1 January 1959. Two sections of the Code of Special Defense gave the Cuban Government power to act against those who criticized the Government in the press or on the radio or on television.

El País and *Excelsior* became insolvent in February 1960 and on March 15, 1960, were incorporated into a Government printing establishment. *Avance* and *El Mundo* were intervened by the Government in January and February 1960. *Diario de la Marina* and *Prensa Libre* were taken over by force in May of 1960 by a small handful of armed pro-Castro employees. Other papers in Habana and in other parts of the island have met the same fate. By August 1960, *Información* remained as the only daily not in Government hands and, together with a few periodicals of the Catholic Church, constituted the entire free press in Cuba. In December 1960 *Información,* under economic pressure exerted by the Government, was forced to close. In the same month the Government closed down the few remaining Catholic publications. Freedom of the press was dead.

Cuba's radio and television stations have also come under Government control. Not one independent station remains. The last to be taken was the extensive and popular CMQ complex—radio chain, television channels 6 and 7, and the news station *Radio Reloj*—which was not formally intervened until 12 September 1960. With the Government in control of all radio and television stations, the only voice heard in Cuba today is the propaganda of the Castro regime.

Suppression of Civil Liberties

Now let me turn to individual rights, which were also guaranteed. Civil liberties in Cuba have been suppressed. The process has been steady and thorough. It has been accomplished through the standard guise of suppressing so-called "counter-revolutionary" action. When the revolutionary government assumed power on January 1, 1959, it immediately instituted a policy of "social prophylaxis" against elements of the Batista regime. Law number 1 of 21 February 1959 formed the basis for a new system of military justice. Close to 550 so-called "war criminals" were summarily tried and shot, and some 2,000 were sentenced to long prison terms during the first 6 months under this law. Originally the "revolutionary justice" system applied only to military personnel and civilians in the service of tyranny, that is, the Batista regime. Gradually, however, the revolutionary government enlarged the area of competence of the military courts, and on July 8, 1959, an amendment to the fundamental law made "those guilty of counterrevolutionary crimes and those who injure the national economy or the public treasury liable to the death penalty."

The concept of what constitutes a counterrevolutionary crime was not, and has never been, defined. Further amendments and enlargements were made in the law in 1959.

On November 13, 1959, the civil courts were ruled incompetent to receive and judge counterrevolutionary cases. The granting of provisional freedom to those accused of counterrevolutionary crimes was denied where there exists "reasonable evidence of culpability."

The record since then is one of steady expansion of the system of summary military justice based on undefined counterrevolutionary crimes and at the expense of civilian courts.

The suppression of guarantees for civil liberties has also been accomplished through the destruction of the independence of the judiciary. That campaign began early in 1960 with the attacks on the courts by members of the regime who did not like some of the decisions dealing with agrarian reform matters. In July 1960 the Bar Association came under fire. The Habana Bar Association was forcibly taken over by the militia on July 5. The National Bar Association was prevented by a mob from holding its assembly on July 23. Interference with the independence of the judiciary came to a head during November and December 1960. On November 14, 1960, the President of the Supreme Court, Dr. Emilio Menéndez, resigned and took asylum. In a letter addressed to the President of the Republic, Dr. Dorticós, giving his reasons, he stated:

> The government over which you preside has deviated from that initial and salutary root and with the passage of each day it becomes increasingly evident that the executive is absorbing the general functions of government, thereby taking away from the judicial branch the inherent and indispensable functions for the fulfillment of its broad tasks and transcendental mission.

A month later the regime began the purge of the judicial branch. On December 20 the Castro regime put through a decree reducing the number of Supreme Court magistrates from 32 to 15, suspending all tenure rights throughout the judicial branch, giving the Government a free hand to dismiss, transfer, or demote personnel without restriction, and providing for other changes in the Supreme Court. With this measure the last vestiges of an independent judiciary vanished from Cuba.

These are the ways in which civil liberties have been guaranteed by the Castro regime.

Castro has converted the Cuban Confederation of Workers from an independent labor organization for promoting the welfare of the laboring classes to a mechanism of the state for disciplining, indoctrination, and propaganda. Between that time and December 1960, over 200 principal officers of national federations who had been elected during the spring of 1959 from candidates proposed by Castro's own July 26th Movement were deposed under the pretext of being counterrevolutionaries. One of these was the Secretary General of the Cuban Federation of Workers, David Salvador, who went underground to form an opposition group known as the Movement of November 30th. He now languishes in a Castro prison. While the anti-Communist leadership of the CTC was being purged, the basic function of the labor organization was being transformed. In August 1960 the Minister of Labor was empowered to determine wage rates in state-owned and mixed enterprises and to establish production norms or minima which the worker is obliged to meet. This completed the centralization of authority in the Ministry over promotion, hiring and firing of workers, all collective bargaining, and all labor disputes.

Machinery of Indoctrination

On education, where Castro promised an intensive campaign against illiteracy and of civic education, what has happened? The revolutionary government is turning the machinery of enlightenment into machinery of indoctrination. Only doctrines and ideas which agree with the "Castro philosophy" can now be taught, and only teachers who are politically acceptable to the regime can teach them.

University autonomy, a concept respected by even the worst of Cuba's past tyrants, has now been abolished. By January 1961 over 75 percent of the faculty had either been purged or had resigned and fled. At the secondary and primary school levels the Castro regime has also introduced strict control over teachers and subject matter taught. Textbooks have been rewritten to fit the propaganda line of the Government and teachers given the choice of either accepting the new orientation or being ousted. The regime is moving ahead with its plans to establish large communal school-cities where thousands of children will be taken away from their home environment for concentrated education and indoctrination.

In the field of illiteracy Castro has made much of his campaign to teach all Cubans to read and write by the end of 1961. In fact this campaign is being used as an instrument for indoctrination. A teaching manual prepared by the Cuban Ministry of Education for guidance of teachers contains a chapter entitled "Friends and Enemies." Let me quote just one paragraph:

> We consider as our friends those countries who have already succeeded in obtaining absolute liberty, and who help honestly and disinterestedly the nations who fight against the colonialist yoke imposed by the imperialists. Those countries are the Soviet Union, Communist China and the other socialist states.

This is the type of civic education which is being given to the Cuban people under this regime.

Finally, Dr. Castro promised in his agrarian reform to make shareholders and squatters into proprietors of their land and to compensate the former owners. This promise was intended to break up large landholdings and to distribute them among individual farmers. This promise was to answer the aspirations of Cuban farmers who wanted to own and till their own land. It has not been carried out. On the contrary, many small holdings have been consolidated into larger farms. The large farms have not been parceled out but have been converted into cooperatives and state farms. Landholding in Cuba is now more consolidated than it was before the Castro-led revolution. The overwhelming percentage of Cuba's 14.5 million acres of tillable land is owned or administered by the Cuban Government. The National Agrarian Reform Institute has become the sole *latifundista* in Cuba.

With respect to indemnification for seized property, I am not aware that any compensation has been paid to either Cuban or foreign owners.

These are the ways in which this revolution has been betrayed. The regime has seized land promised to the people. It has turned an educational system promised for the people into a system of indoctrination for the state. It has destroyed the free labor movement. It has denied both civil and political rights, purging the judiciary and substituting vague counterrevolutionary crimes under summary military courts for civilian justice. It has abolished the once lively free press of the Cuban people. These are the reasons why Cubans today are seeking to restore the revolution to its original premises. These are the reasons why it is a Cuban and a hemispheric, and not a United States, problem.

What the Republic of Cuba is seeking from us today is the protection of the Castro regime from the wrath of these people. Dr. Castro has the largest land army in Latin America. It is well equipped with large quantities of modern arms from Eastern

Europe. It has hundreds of Soviet and Czech advisers. If, as Dr. Roa claims, the regime has the backing of the people of Cuba, it is difficult to explain Cuban attitudes toward the rest of the Americas for the last 18 months.

The problem which Cuba has created is not one of revolution or of social change. And the leaders of the present opposition to Castro, leaders who were once Dr. Castro's closest supporters—his first President, his first Prime Minister, his first Chief Justice, the head of Castro's own office, two-thirds of his first cabinet, companions-in arms in the Sierra Maestras—they do not want to turn back the clock to a Batista dictatorship but to restore the revolution to its original ideals. Because these people truly desire social justice with freedom, they are now called mercenaries and traitors.

Cuban People's Uprising Against Oppression

The current uprising in Cuba is the product of the progressively more violent opposition of the Cuban people to the policies and practices of this regime. Let us not forget that there have been hundreds of freedom fighters in the mountains of central Cuba for almost a year; that during the last 6 months skirmishes with the Castro police, attacks upon individual members of his armed forces, nightly acts of sabotage by the revolutionaries, have been increasing in number and intensity. Protest demonstrations have taken place by workers whose trade-union rights have been betrayed, by Catholics whose freedom of expression and worship has been circumscribed, by professional men whose right to free association has been violated. The response of the Castro regime has been repression, arrests without warrant, trial without constitutional guarantees, imprisonment without term and without mercy, and, finally, the execution wall.

Let me be absolutely clear: that the present events are the uprising of the Cuban people against an oppressive regime which has never given them the opportunity in peace and by democratic process to approve or to reject the domestic and foreign policies which it has followed.

For our part, our attitude is clear. Many Americans looked with sympathy, as I have said, on the cause espoused by Dr. Castro when he came to power. They look with the same sympathy on the men who today seek to bring freedom and justice to Cuba—not for foreign monopolies, not for the economic or political interests of the United States or any foreign power, but for Cuba and for the Cuban people.

It is hostility of Cubans, not Americans, that Dr. Castro has to fear. It is not our obligation to protect him from the consequences of his treason to the revolution, to the hopes of the Cuban people, and to the democratic aspirations of the hemisphere.

The United States sincerely hopes that any difficulties which we or other American countries may have with Cuba will be settled peacefully. We have committed no aggression against Cuba. We have no aggressive purposes against Cuba. We intend no military intervention in Cuba. We seek to see a restoration of the friendly relations which once prevailed between Cuba and the United States. We hope that the Cuban people will settle their own problems in their own interests and in a manner which will assure social justice, true independence, and political liberty to the Cuban people.

*108. Statement by U.S. Representative Stevenson, before
Committee I of the U. N. General Assembly, on
a Cuban Complaint* *

April 20, 1961

Although I am loathe to speak as often or as long as the representative of the Soviet Union, this is, after all, an item that involves the United States and not the U.S.S.R. So I have some final words that I should like to say in this debate. I am grateful to those of my colleagues who have expressed respect for my country and for the honesty of its spokesmen here and in Washington.

First let me say that we don't deny that the exiles from Cuba have received the sympathy of many people inside and outside the United States—even as Dr. Castro had the sympathy of many in the United States, Mexico, and elsewhere. But the extent to which so many speakers have deliberately confused this with intervention and aggression by the United States Government has exceeded all bounds of fact or fancy.

Obviously the incessant repetition of such charges as though they had been proved reveals a greater anxiety to mislead and to corrupt world opinion than to keep the discussion on the tracks.

Let me commence where I started a couple of days ago. I said at the outset of this debate about Cuba:

"The United States sincerely hopes that any difficulties which we or other American countries may have with Cuba will be settled peacefully. We have committed no aggression against Cuba. We have no aggressive purposes against Cuba. We intend no military intervention in Cuba." I repeat, no military intervention in Cuba. "We seek to see a restoration of the friendly relations which once prevailed between Cuba and the United States. We hope that the Cuban people will settle their own problems in their own interests and in the manner which will assure social justice, true independence, and political liberty to the Cuban people."

Since I said these words, I have heard a torrent—a deluge—of ugly words from Communist speakers here accusing the United States of agression and invasion against Cuba. I will resist the temptation to invite attention to the record of aggression of the countries represented by some of those speakers—or to inquire as to which country has *really* intervened in Cuba, which country has perverted the Cuban revolution, and why these same speakers are so emotional about the revolt of the Cuban refugees against the new tyranny in Cuba and the new imperialism in the world.

Let me just ask—if this was a United States military operation, do you think it would succeed or fail? How long do you think Cuba could resist the military power of the United States? Perhaps the best evidence of the falsity of the shrill charges of American aggression in Cuba is the melancholy fact that this blow for freedom has not yet succeeded. And if the United States had been in charge I submit that fighting would hardly have broken out on the day debate was to start in this committee.

Aside from these loud charges of aggression, I have also heard the Communists echo over and over like parrots the old theme that the United States is trying to impose economic slavery—this time on Cuba.

Some of these speakers are evidently unaware—or perhaps they don't care—about the fact that I have written and talked about the need for economic and social reform

*Department of State Bulletin, May 8, 1961, pp. 681-85.

and political democracy throughout Latin America for years. I would also remind these cold warriors that President Kennedy has recently proposed a large and thoughtful program of social reforms and economic assistance to Latin America.

But I confess I have no hope that the Communist speakers will be any more interested in the truth tomorrow than they were yesterday or today.

There are those who will say that in the last 48 hours the Cuban people have spoken.

Who can doubt the outcome if the events of the last few days had given the Cuban people the opportunity to choose between tyranny and freedom?

The Cuban people have not spoken.

Their yearning to be free of Castro's executions, of his betrayal of the revolution, of his controlled press, and of his yoke and rule by mailed fist has not been extinguished. The more than 100,000 refugees from his tyranny are undeniable proof of the historic aspirations of the Cuban people for freedom. The Cubans will continue to look forward to the day when they can determine their own future by democratic processes and through free institutions.

And what are the lessons to be learned? For those Cuban patriots who gave their lives, the lesson is one of tragic finality. But what of those who live on and will shape the future? The events of the last few days are indelible reminders to all of us in the Western Hemisphere. The penetration of force from outside our hemisphere, dominating a puppet government and providing it with arms, tanks, and fighter aircraft, is already dangerously strong and deep. It is now demonstrably stronger, deeper, and more dangerous to all of us who value freedom than most Americans—and most of our neighbors in the Western Hemisphere—have been willing to think.

If there is hope in the events of the last few days it is that it will awaken all of us in the Americas to a renewed determination to mobilize every resource and energy to advance the cause of economic growth and social progress throughout the hemisphere—to foster conditions of freedom and political democracy. They summon all of us to expand freedom and abundance with education of all peoples. If we dedicate ourselves with renewed resolve to bringing greater social reform, greater economic opportunity, greater human dignity, the sacrifices of the last few days will not have been in vain.

A Problem for the World Community

The world community is also faced with a problem in Cuba.

The United Nations Organization is designed to preserve and defend the territorial integrity and political independence of its members. Perhaps we have learned in the 15 years of our life to deal reasonably well with the problems of maintaining "territorial integrity," that is, with the problem of preventing armies from marching across borders. But what of "political independence"? Here is the challenge of Cuba, of Laos, of the Congo—and, I fear, of other crises yet to come. The free nations of the world cannot permit political conquest any more than they can tolerate military aggression. My Government, for its part, is unwilling to accept such a pattern of international life. And I humbly suggest that new and small states everywhere should seriously ponder this lesson of the Cuban episode.

As the President of the United States said this afternoon, the message of Cuba, of Laos, of the rising din of Communist voices in Asia and Latin America—these messages are all the same. I hope that the lessons which these developments teach us are not lost on all of us here. There are many small countries whose institutions may not yet be so firmly secured that they can be impervious to the insidious type of subversion of which we are speaking. This internal battle is frequently silent but deadly. Can we ignore what is happening in a small country like Viet-Nam, whose freedom is in danger by guerrilla forces operating under Communist direction from the north and seeking to overthrow the freely elected government of that country? In 1960 alone Communist guerrillas killed, wounded, or captured within south Viet-Nam thousands of Vietnamese soldiers and civilians. I say to you with deep humility and firm resolve that whether infiltrations are in Viet-Nam, in Cuba, or in Laos, each such encroachment on the freedom of these people is a threat to the freedom of all peoples. The new states of Africa in particular, with their newly won freedom, can profit by the example of Cuba. Political independence which they cherish can be impaired and lost by subversion. Let all those who value liberty stand guard. The test of freedom is the right to choose—not once but again and again. When this right is lost, freedom is lost, as Castro's Cuba so tragically shows.

The United States then will vote for the resolution introduced by the seven countries of Latin America.

We will vote against the Soviet and Rumanian resolutions.

We also find that the Mexican resolution is unacceptable, particularly because it makes no reference to the Organization of American States or to cooperation in the Western Hemisphere.

On the other hand, we find, as I have said, the seven-power Latin American resolution an appropriate decision of this matter.

I end by paying my respects to the Cuban exiles and to the patriots within Cuba. They have had one aim in view—not to restore the past, not to frustrate Cuba's social revolution, but to prevent its further perversion. They have fought for the revolution they thought they made when they ousted Batista—a revolution based not only on social justice but on personal freedom, civil liberties, and due process of law. They have fought to end the rule of arbitrary arrest, the packed tribunal, and the firing squad. Freedom is the issue, freedom from an alien, imported despotism. It is for this that countless patriots have died for countless years.

As we know from the past, the fortresses of tyranny may not fall at the first blow, least of all when the dictator has piled up arms and vastly expanded his military strength. Even Cuban courage is not enough to counter such brute strength. Not all the passionate desire of Frenchmen to be free, not all the coldblooded courage of the French underground, could roll back the Nazis. Not all the gallantry of Hungary's workers and students, not all the drive and resources of its freedom fighters, could withstand the onslaught of Russia's armed divisions. But their struggle for freedom was not the less authentic because the Russians wiped it out. And so long as any Cuban longs for freedom, Castro's tyranny is not secure.

The longing will not cease. Of this we can be sure. A hundred thousand Cubans have escaped already. Thousands more will follow. To them we say that the door is open and that the United States respects and upholds their right of asylum as one of the most fundamental of the rights of man.

Right of Asylum

How much freedom would any of us have today if the right of asylum had been wiped out? Throughout the 19th century's struggle for freedom and national independence, great leaders of the emergent peoples were sustained and succored by the liberal powers of Europe when the fortunes of politics turned against them. Italy's Garibaldi was a hero in London. So was Hungary's Kossuth.

In this century, it was in America that the father of Czechoslovakia, Thomas Masaryk, not only found asylum but set up the state which for 20 years between the wars enjoyed the freedom of true democracy.

How would France have recovered its splendid sense of identity and history if General de Gaulle had found no refuge from the Nazis in embattled Britain?

Indeed, even those who now mock at the conceptions of human dignity inherent in the right of asylum were saved from disaster by this same right. It was to London that Marx fled from the police. It was in London that Lenin studied out of reach of Czarist autocracy, and such past and contemporary heroes of the Americas as Francisco Miranda, José Martí and Rómulo Betancourt, who all sought and received asylum in the United States. And where did Fidel Castro seek aid and shelter?

So long as Americans remain a free people, just so long will they uphold the right of asylum as a fundamental human right. This will not change. Nor, I profoundly believe, will the pressure to be free stop. I do not deny that since the war the area of tyranny has widened in some parts of the world. In these areas people cannot protest their position publicly or make clear their profound desire for liberty. But it remains a fact that thousands upon thousands have registered their protest in the only way open to them. They have escaped.

Castro's refugees are but a page in this unhappy history. In Korea a great majority, not only of north Korean prisoners but of Chinese prisoners as well, opted not to return to Communist tyranny. Tibetans have streamed across India's frontiers to escape Chinese oppression. Tens of thousands fled from Hungary and now live in many lands here represented. Most revealing of all, over 3 million Germans have escaped from East Germany—"voting with their feet" against the regime. Gentlemen, there is no stream in the opposite sense. People fly to freedom, not away from it.

I would urge you not to be deafened by violent words designed to paint the Cuban freedom fighters as "running dogs of imperialism," "capitalist lackeys," "mercenaries," and all the other familiar and repellent jargon of the Communist world. This evening I am informed that three of the six members of the Cuban Revolutionary Council had sons engaged in this enterprise. Juan Verona had a son, a nephew, and two brothers; Miró Cardona had a son: Hevia his only son. And yet I hear these speakers call this "an adventure of American mercenaries." The Cuban refugees are but a part of a great multitude of men who have left their homes, who have lost their all, who have risked death and disaster sooner than live in chains.

Why? Because they long for security against unpredictable arrest, against the midnight knock on the door. They long to be free from malevolence and informers and spite. They seek a society in which a man may speak his mind; they want for themselves and their children a political system in which the law is a shield, not a trap, and in which the power of an omnipotent state does not exercise over them the terror of a nameless death.

These are not small things. Cubans thought them worth dying for when with Fidel Castro they fought to overthrow Batista. They think so now, when they fight to overthrow the tyranny that Castro has set up in its place. And the struggle for freedom will continue—as it always has and always must. For these are rights so precious to the soul of man that the longing for them cannot be quenched. I believe that men will continue to be ready to die for them—as the Cuban freedom fighters have done this week.

And I believe that no despot will ever finally have quiet sleep because of the human heart's unslumbering desire to be free.

This is our faith. This is the faith of the free society in which we live. And I believe this is and will utimately be the faith of all mankind.

109. Address by President Kennedy, before the American Society of Newspaper Editors, on the Lesson of Cuba*

April 20, 1961

The President of a great democracy such as ours, and the editors of great newspapers such as yours, owe a common obligation to the people: an obligation to present the facts, to present them with candor, and to present them in perspective. It is with that obligation in mind that I have decided in the last 24 hours to discuss briefly at this time the recent events in Cuba.

On that unhappy island, as in so many other areas of the contest for freedom, the news has grown worse instead of better. I have emphasized before that this was a struggle of Cuban patriots against a Cuban dictator. While we could not be expected to hide our sympathies, we made it repeatedly clear that the armed forces of this country would not intervene in any way.

Any unilateral American intervention, in the absence of an external attack upon ourselves or an ally, would have been contrary to our traditions and to our international obligations. But let the record show that our restraint is not inexhaustible. Should it ever appear that the inter-American doctrine of noninterference merely conceals or excuses a policy of nonaction—if the nations of this hemisphere should fail to meet their commitments against outside Communist penetration—then I want it clearly understood that this Government will not hesitate in meeting its primary obligations, which are to the security of our Nation.

Should that time ever come, we do not intend to be lectured on "intervention" by those whose character was stamped for all time on the bloody streets of Budapest. Nor would we expect or accept the same outcome which this small band of gallant Cuban refugees must have known that they were chancing, determined as they were against heavy odds to pursue their courageous attempts to regain their island's freedom.

But Cuba is not an island unto itself; and our concern is not ended by mere expressions of nonintervention or regret. This is not the first time in either ancient or recent history that a small band of freedom fighters has engaged the armor of totalitarianism.

*Department of State Bulletin, May 8, 1961, pp. 659-61.

It is not the first time that Communist tanks have rolled over gallant men and women fighting to redeem the independence of their homeland. Nor is it by any means the final episode in the eternal struggle of liberty against tyranny, anywhere on the face of the globe, including Cuba itself.

Mr. Castro has said that these were mercenaries. According to press reports, the final message to be relayed from the refugee forces on the beach came from the rebel commander when asked if he wished to be evacuated. His answer was: "I will never leave this country." That is not the reply of a mercenary. He has gone now to join in the mountains countless other guerrilla fighters, who are equally determined that the dedication of those who gave their lives shall not be forgotten and that Cuba must not be abandoned to the Communists. And we do not intend to abandon it either.

The Cuban people have not yet spoken their final piece, and I have no doubt that they and their Revolutionary Council, led by Dr. Miró Cardona—and members of the families of the Revolutionary Council, I am informed by the Doctor yesterday, are involved themselves in the islands—will continue to speak up for a free and independent Cuba.

Meanwhile we will not accept Mr. Castro's attempts to blame this Nation for the hatred with which his onetime supporters now regard his repression. But there are from this sobering episode useful lessons for all to learn. Some may be still obscure and await further information. Some are clear today.

First, it is clear that the forces of communism are not to be underestimated, in Cuba or anywhere else in the world. The advantages of a police state—its use of mass terror and arrests to prevent the spread of free dissent—cannot be overlooked by those who expect the fall of every fanatic tyrant. If the self-discipline of the free cannot match the iron discipline of the mailed fist—in economic, political, scientific, and all the other kinds of struggles as well as the military—then the peril to freedom will continue to rise.

Secondly, it is clear that this Nation, in concert with all the free nations of this hemisphere, must take an even closer and more realistic look at the menace of external Communist intervention and domination in Cuba. The American people are not complacent about Iron Curtain tanks and planes less than 90 miles from our shores. But a nation of Cuba's size is less a threat to our survival than it is a base for subverting the survival of other free nations throughout the hemisphere. It is not primarily our interest or our security but theirs which is now, today, in the greater peril. It is for their sake as well as our own that we must show our will.

The evidence is clear—and the hour is late. We and our Latin friends will have to face the fact that we cannot postpone any longer the real issue of the survival of freedom in this hemisphere itself. On that issue, unlike perhaps some others, there can be no middle ground. Together we must build a hemisphere where freedom can flourish and where any free nation under outside attack of any kind can be assured that all of our resources stand ready to respond to any request for assistance.

Third, and finally, it is clearer than ever that we face a relentless struggle in every corner of the globe that goes far beyond the clash of armies or even nuclear armaments. The armies are there, and in large number. The nuclear armaments are there. But they serve primarily as the shield behind which subversion, infiltration, and a host of other tactics steadily advance, picking off vulnerable areas one by one in situations which do not permit our own armed intervention.

Power is the hallmark of this offensive—power and discipline and deceit. The legitimate discontent of yearning peoples is exploited. The legitimate trappings of self-determination are employed. But once in power, all talk of discontent is repressed —all self-determination disappears—and the promise of a revolution of hope is betrayed, as in Cuba, into a reign of terror. Those who staged automatic "riots" in the streets of free nations over the effort of a small group of young Cubans to regain their freedom should recall the long rollcall of refugees who cannot now go back—to Hungary, to north Korea, to north Viet-Nam, to East Germany, or to Poland, or to any of the other lands from which a steady stream of refugees pours forth, in eloquent testimony to the cruel oppression now holding sway in their homelands.

We dare not fail to see the insidious nature of this new and deeper struggle. We dare not fail to grasp the new concepts, the new tools, the new sense of urgency we will need to combat it—whether in Cuba or south Viet-Nam. And we dare not fail to realize that this struggle is taking place every day, without fanfare, in thousands of villages and markets—day and night—and in classrooms all over the globe.

The message of Cuba, of Laos, of the rising din of Communist voices in Asia and Latin America—these messages are all the same. The complacent, the self-indulgent, the soft societies are about to be swept away with the debris of history. Only the strong, only the industrious, only the determined, only the courageous, only the visionary who determine the real nature of our struggle can possibly survive.

No greater task faces this Nation or this Administration. No other challenge is more deserving of our every effort and energy. Too long we have fixed our eyes on traditional military needs, on armies prepared to cross borders or missiles poised for flight. Now it should be clear that this is no longer enough—that our security may be lost piece by piece, country by country, without the firing of a single missile or the crossing of a single border.

We intend to profit from this lesson. We intend to reexamine and reorient our forces of all kinds—our tactics and other institutions here in this community. We intend to intensify our efforts for a struggle in many ways more difficult than war, where disappointment will often accompany us.

For I am convinced that we in this country and in the free world possess the necessary resources, and all the skill, and the added strength that comes from a belief in the freedom of man. And I am equally convinced that history will record the fact that this bitter struggle reached its climax in the late 1950's and early 1960's. Let me then make clear as the President of the United States that I am determined upon our system's survival and success, regardless of the cost and regardless of the peril.

110. U. N. General Assembly Action on a Complaint by Cuba*

April 21, 1961

1616 (XV). Complaint by the Revolutionary Government of Cuba regarding the various plans of aggression and acts of intervention being executed by the Government of the United States of America against the Republic of Cuba, constituting a manifest

*United Nations, *Official Records of the General Assembly,* 15th Session, Supplement No. 16 A (A/4684/Add. I), p. 3.

violation of its territorial integrity, sovereignty and independence, and a clear threat to international peace and security

The General Assembly,

Having heard the statements made by the Minister for External Relations of Cuba, the representative of the United States of America and other representatives,

Deeply concerned over the situation disclosed therein, which is disturbing world public opinion and the continuation of which could endanger world peace,

Recalling the last two paragraphs of the Security Council resolution of 19 July 1960 and the peaceful means of settlement established at the Seventh Meeting of Consultation of Foreign Ministers of the American Republics,

Considering that the States Members of the United Nations are under an obligation to settle their disputes by negotiation and other peaceful means in such a manner that international peace and security, and justice, are not endangered,

Exhorts all Member States to take such peaceful action as is open to them to remove existing tension.

111. Letter from Premier Khrushchev, to President Kennedy, Concerning Cuba*

April 22, 1961

I received your reply of 18 April. You write that the United States does not intend to carry out a military intervention in Cuba. However, numerous facts known to the entire world, and certainly known better by the Government of the United States of America than anybody else—present a different story. However much the opposite is assured, it is now indisputably ascertained that the preparations for the intervention, the financing of armament, and the transfer of hired gangs which have invaded the territory of Cuba were indeed carried out by the United States.

The armed forces of the United States of America have directly participated in implementing the piratic assault on Cuba. American bombers and fighter planes supported the operation of the hirelings who have entered Cuban territory and participated in the military acts against the armed forces of the lawful government and people of Cuba.

Such are the facts. They illustrate the direct participation of the United States of America in the armed aggression against Cuba.

In your message you took the stand of justification and even eulogy of the assault on Cuba, this crime which has shocked the whole world.

The organization of military aggression against Cuba—only because the way of life chosen by its people does not correspond to the tastes of the leading circles in the United States and the North American monopolies acting in Latin America—you seek to justify by reasoning about the devotion of the U.S. Government to the ideals of "freedom." I take the liberty to ask: What freedom do you mean?

The freedom to strangle the Cuban people with the bony hand of starvation by means of economic blockade? Is this freedom? The freedom to send military planes

*Department of State Bulletin, May 8, 1961, pp. 664-67.

over the territory of Cuba, to expose to barbaric bombardment peaceful Cuban cities, to set fire to sugar cane plantations? Is this freedom?

History knows numerous examples when, under the excuse of the defense of freedom, bloody reprisals were carried out against the people, colonial wars were waged, and one country after the other was taken by the throat.

Apparently, in the case given, you mean the aspiration of the U.S. Government to reestablish in Cuba this kind of "freedom" under which the country would dance to the tune of a stronger neighbor, and the foreign monopolies again could plunder the national riches of Cuba and make profit out of the blood and sweat of the Cuban people. But the Cuban people made their revolution against exactly this kind of "freedom," driving out Batista who, perhaps, faithfully served the interests of his foreign masters but who was a foreign element in the body of the Cuban nation.

Thus you, Mr. President, express solicitude about a band of enemies chased out by their nation, who have found refuge under the wing of those who try to hold Cuba under the muzzle of the arms of their cruisers and minesweepers. But why are you not moved by the destiny of the 6-million-strong Cuban nation? Why do you not wish to reckon with its inalienable right to freedom and independent life, with its right to arrange its internal affairs as it thinks fit? Where is the code of international law, or, finally, of human morality, with the aid of which such a position could be justified? In short, they do not exist.

The Cuban people have expressed their will once again with a degree of clarity which could not leave a single doubt even with those who prefer to close their eyes to reality. They have shown that they not only know their interests best, but know also how to defend them. Cuba today is, of course, not the Cuba which you identified with the band of traitors who fought against their own nation. This is the Cuba of workers, peasants, and intelligentsia. This is a nation which has rallied closely round its revolutionary government headed by the national hero, Fidel Castro. And this nation, judging by all things, has met the interventionists in a worthy manner. Surely this is true evidence of the real will of the people of Cuba. I think this is convincing. And if this is so, then surely the time is ripe to draw sober conclusions from it.

As for the Soviet Union, I have said many times and I affirm again: Our Government does not seek any advantages or privileges in Cuba. We have no bases in Cuba and do not intend to establish any. This is well known to you, and to your generals and admirals. If, despite this, they still insist on scaring people with inventions about "Soviet bases" in Cuba, they do it for the benefit of simpletons. However, the number of such simpletons is ever diminishing, including, I hope, in the United States.

I would like to take this opportunity, Mr. President, to express my opinion as to your declarations, and the declarations of some other U.S. statesmen, that rockets and other armaments might be placed on Cuban territory and used against the United States.

From this a conclusion is drawn as if the United States had a right to attack Cuba—either directly or through the enemies of the Cuban people whom you arm with your weapons, train on your territory, maintain with the money of U.S. taxpayers, transport by the transport units of your armed forces, at the same time striving to mask the fact that they are fighting the Cuban people and its legal government.

You also refer to some duty of the United States "to defend the Western Hemisphere against external aggression." But what kind of duty can it be in this case? No one has a duty to defend rebels against the legal government in a sovereign state, which Cuba is.

Mr. President, you are taking a very dangerous path. Think about it. You speak about your rights and obligations. Certainly, everyone can have pretensions to these rights or those rights, but then you must also permit other states to base their acts in analogous instances on the same kind of reasons and considerations.

You declare that Cuba is allegedly able to use its territory for acts against the United States. This is your assumption, and it is not based on any facts. We, however, on our side, are able now to refer to concrete facts and not to assumptions: In some countries bordering directly on the Soviet Union by land and by sea there are now governments which conduct a far from wise policy, governments which have concluded military agreements with the United States and have put their territory at its disposal to accommodate American military bases there.

In addition, your military people openly declare that these bases are directed toward the Soviet Union. Even so, this is clear to all: If you consider yourself to be in the right to implement such measures against Cuba which have lately been taken by the United States of America, you must admit that other countries, also, do not have lesser reason to act in a similar manner in relation to states on whose territories preparations are actually being made which represent a threat against the security of the Soviet Union. If you do not wish to sin against elementary logic, you evidently must admit such a right to other states. We, on our side, do not adhere to such views.

We consider that the reasonings voiced on this subject in the United States are not only a highly free interpretation of international law, but, speaking frankly, a blunt preaching of perfidious policy.

Certainly, a strong state always can, if it wishes, find an excuse to attack a weaker country and then justify the attack, alleging that this country was a potential threat. But is this the morality of the 20th century? This is the morality of colonizers and brigands who were conducting precisely this policy some time ago. Now, in the second half of the 20th century, it is impossible to follow the piratic morality of colonizers anymore. All of us are now witnesses to the fact of how the colonial system falls to the ground and fades away. The Soviet Union, for its part, does its best to contribute to this, and we are proud of it.

Or let us consider U.S. activities in regard to China. In reference to what legal norms can one justify these activities? It is known to all that Taiwan is an integral part of China. This has also been recognized by the U.S. Government, whose signature was put on the Cairo Declaration of 1943. However, later on the United States seized Taiwan or, actually, entered on the path of robbery. The Chinese People's Republic declared its natural aspiration to reunite the territory of Taiwan with the rest of the Chinese territory. But what was the United States reaction to this? It declared that armed force would be used to prevent the reunion of this seized Chinese territory with the rest of China. It threatens war in case China takes steps aiming at the reunification of Taiwan. And this from a country which has officially recognized Taiwan as belonging to China! Is this not perfidy in international policy?

If such methods prevailed in relations between states then there would be no room for law, and instead of it lawlessness and arbitrariness would take its place.

Thus, Mr. President, your sympathies are one thing, and actions against the security and independence of other nations, undertaken on the strength of those sympathies, is quite another matter. Naturally you can express your sympathies toward the imperialist and colonialist countries and this does not astonish anyone. You, for instance, cast your vote with them in the United Nations. This is a question of your morality. But what was done against Cuba—this is not morality. This is warlike action.

I wish to stress that if the United Nations is destined to attain true strength and fulfill the functions for which it was created—at the present time this Organization, unfortunately, represents an organism that is contaminated with the germs of colonialism and imperialism—then the United Nations must resolutely condemn the warlike actions against Cuba.

The question here is not only one of condemning the United States. It is important that the condemnation of aggression should become a precedent, a lesson which should also be learned by other countries with a view to stopping the repetition of aggression. Because if one starts to approve, or even to condone, the morality of aggressors, this can be taken as a guide by other states, and this will inevitably lead to war conflicts, any one of which may suddenly lead to World War III.

The statement which you made in your last speech to the press representatives must greatly alarm the whole world, for, in essence, you speak openly about some right of yours to use military force when you consider it necessary, and to suppress other nations each time you yourself decide that the expression of will by those nations represents "communism." What right to you have, or what right has anyone, to deprive a nation of the possibility of deciding according to its own desire to choose its own social system?

Have you ever thought that other countries could present you with similar demands, and could say that you, in the United States, have a system which gives rise to wars, pursues imperialistic policies, policies of threats and attacks on other states? There are all grounds for such accusations. And if we assume the premises which you yourself proclaim now, then, obviously, we can require the change of the system in the United States.

We, as you know, are not embarking on this road. We support peaceful coexistence among all states and noninterference in the internal affairs of other countries.

You hint at Budapest, but we can tell you straight, without hints, that it is you, the United States, which crushed the independence of Guatemala by sending your hirelings there, as you are trying to do in the case of Cuba as well. It is the United States, indeed, and not any other country which has so far been mercilessly exploiting and keeping in economic dependence the Latin American countries and many other countries of the world. Everyone is aware of that. And according to your logic, Mr. President, obviously, actions could also be organized against your country from without, which would put an end once and for all to this imperialist policy, the policy of threats, and the policy of reprisals against freedom-loving peoples.

As to your anxiety about emigrants, expelled by the Cuban people, I would say the following in this connection:

You, of course, know that in many countries there are emigrants who are not satisfied with the regime prevailing in those countries from which they fled. If such abnormal practices are introduced in the relations between states as for such emigrants to be armed and used against the countries from which they have fled, then we can surely say that this will inevitably lead to conflicts and wars. And, therefore, one should refrain from such unwise activities because this is a slippery and dangerous road which might lead to world war.

In your answer you considered it to be appropriate to touch on problems not related to the theme of my message—among them, in your interpretation, the problem of the historical inevitability of the Communist revolution.

I am only able to evaluate it as a tendency to divert from the main question—the question of the aggression against Cuba. Under suitable conditions we are also ready to exchange views on the question regarding the ways and means for the development of human society, although such a question is not being solved by disputes between groups or individual persons, regardless of the high position they may occupy in the state. The fact of whose system will turn out to be the better will be solved by the peoples.

You, Mr. President, have spoken frequently and much about your wish to see Cuba liberated. But all acts of the United States in regard to this small country contradict this. I do not even mention the last armed assault on Cuba, which was organized with the aim of changing its inner structure by force.

It was no one but the United States indeed, which thrust on Cuba the cabalistic condition of the Havana agreement almost 60 years ago and created on its territory its Guantanamo military base. But the United States of America is the most powerful country in the Western Hemisphere, and no one in this hemisphere is able to threaten you with military invasion. It follows, therefore, that if you continue to maintain your military base on the territory of Cuba against the clearly expressed wish of the Cuban people and government, this base serves not for defense from aggression by any foreign powers, but has the aim of suppressing the will of the Latin American peoples. It has been created for the implementation of gendarmery functions and for keeping the Latin American peoples in political and economic dependence.

The Government of the United States is now thundering against Cuba. But this only shows one thing—your lack of confidence in your own system, in the policy carried out by the United States. And this is understandable since this is a policy of exploitation, the policy of enslaving underdeveloped countries. You have no faith in your system, and this is why you are afraid that the example of Cuba might infect other countries.

But aggressive, bandit acts cannot save your system. In the historical process of developing mankind, every nation has been, and will be, deciding its own destiny on its own. As for the U.S.S.R., the peoples of our country solved this problem over 43 years ago definitely and irrevocably.

We are a socialist state and our social system is the most just of all that have existed to date because by us he who labors is also the master of all means of production. This is indeed an infectious example, and the sooner the necessity for transition to such a system is understood, the sooner all mankind will have a truly just community. At the same time, also, wars will be ended once and for all.

You did not like it, Mr. President, when I said in my previous message that there could be no firm peace in the entire world if the flame of war was raging anywhere. But this is precisely so. Peace is indivisible—whether anyone likes it or not. And I can only affirm what I said: Things cannot be done in such a way that in one region the situation is made easier and the conflagration dampened, and in another one a new conflagration is started.

The Soviet Government has always consequently defended the freedom and independence of all nations. It is obvious, then, that we cannot recognize any U.S. rights to decide the fate of other countries, including the Latin American countries. We regard any interference by one government in the affairs of another—and armed interference, especially—as a breach of all international laws, and of the principles of peaceful coexistence which the Soviet Union has been unfailingly advocating since the first days of its establishment. If it is a duty of all states and their leaders, in our times more than ever before, to refrain from acts which might threaten universal peace, it concerns even more the leaders of great powers. This is my appeal to you, Mr. President.

The Soviet Government's position in international affairs remains unchanged. We wish to build up our relations with the United States in such a manner that the Soviet Union and the United States, as the two most powerful states in the world, would stop sabre-rattling and bringing forward their military or economic advantage, because this will not result in improvement of the international situation, but in its deterioration. We sincerely wish to reach an agreement with you and other countries of the world on disarmament, as well as other problems the solution of which would facilitate peaceful coexistence, recognition of the people's right to the social and political system which they themselves have established in their countries, and would also facilitate true respect for the people's will and noninterference in their internal affairs.

Only under such conditions is it actually possible to speak about coexistence, as coexistence is only possible if states with different social systems submit to international law, and recognize as their highest aim the insuring of peace in the entire world. Only under such circumstances will peace rest on a sound basis.

112. Statement from the State Department to News Correspondents, on Premier Khrushchev's Letter of April 22, 1961*

April 22, 1961

The President has received a long polemical letter from Chairman Khrushchev relating to Cuba.

The United States Government's views and attitudes toward the situation in Cuba and toward Soviet activities there have been set forth clearly and in detail in the President's letter, in his speech of April 20 before the American Society of Newspaper Editors, and in his press conference of April 21. The President will not be drawn into an extended public debate with the Chairman on the basis of this latest exposition of the Communist distortion of the basic concepts of the rights of man.

Mr. Khrushchev's letter asks, "What freedom do you mean?" Our answer is simple. This Nation was committed at its birth to the proposition that the people of all countries should have the right freely to determine their own future by democratic processes and freely to cooperate with their neighbors. The people of the United

*Department of State Bulletin, May 8, 1961, pp. 663-64.

States believe that the right of self-determination is fundamental and should apply throughout the world. We reject the right of any narrow political grouping or any country to arrogate to itself the power to determine "the real will of the people."

People must be free to express their views, free to organize to make their views effective, free to publish and disseminate their views, and free to vote in secret for those whom they would choose to direct their affairs. Where these freedoms are absent, the "will of the people" is an empty phrase.

History records no single case where communism has been installed in any country by the free vote of its people.

Throughout the world everyone knows that, in countries where Communist minorities have taken power, these freedoms have ceased to exist and those who would assert them are mercilessly repressed. Cuba is a tragic example.

The political history of the world has been a long struggle to assert the fundamental rights of the human being and to establish political institutions which make possible the true expression of the popular will. To attain and maintain these goals requires endless creative struggle. That struggle goes forward day by day in every quarter of the globe.

113. Inter-American Economic and Social Council of the Organization of American States, Ministerial Conference, Declaration and Charter of Punta Del Este*

August 17, 1961

DECLARATION TO THE PEOPLES OF AMERICA

Assembled in Punta del Este, inspired by the principles consecrated in the Charter of the Organization of American States, in Operation Pan America and in the Act of Bogotá, the representatives of the American Republics hereby agree to establish an Alliance for Progress: a vast effort to bring a better life to all the peoples of the Continent.

This Alliance is established on the basic principle that free men working through the institution of representative democracy can best satisfy man's aspirations, including those for work, home and land, health and schools. No system can guarantee true progress unless it affirms the dignity of the individual which is the foundation of our civilization.

Therefore the countries signing this declaration in the exercise of their sovereignty have agreed to work toward the following goals during the coming years:

To improve and strengthen democratic institutions through application of the principle of self-determination by the people.

To accelerate economic and social development, thus rapidly bringing about a

*Inter American Institute of International Legal Studies, *The Inter-American System: Its Development and Strengthening* (New York, 1966), pp. 443-58.

substantial and steady increase in the average income in order to narrow the gap between the standard of living in Latin American countries and that enjoyed in the industrialized countries.

To carry out urban and rural housing programs to provide decent homes for all our people.

To encourage, in accordance with the characteristics of each country, programs of comprehensive agrarian reform, leading to the effective transformation, where required, of unjust structures and systems of land tenure and use; with a view to replacing latifundia and dwarf holdings by an equitable system of property so that, supplemented by timely and adequate credit, technical assistance and improved marketing arrangements, the land will become for the man who works it the basis of his economic stability, the foundation of his increasing welfare, and the guarantee of his freedom and dignity.

To assure fair wages and satisfactory working conditions to all our workers; to establish effective systems of labor-management relations and procedures for consultation and cooperation among government authorities, employers' associations, and trade unions in the interests of social and economic development.

To wipe out illiteracy; to extend, as quickly as possible, the benefits of primary education to all Latin Americans; and to provide broader facilities, on a vast scale, for secondary and technical training and for higher education.

To press forward with programs of health and sanitation in order to prevent sickness, combat contagious disease, and strengthen our human potential.

To reform tax laws, demanding more from those who have most, to punish tax evasion severely, and to redistribute the national income in order to benefit those who are most in need, while, at the same time, promoting savings and investment and reinvestment of capital.

To maintain monetary and fiscal policies which, while avoiding the disastrous effects of inflation or deflation, will protect the purchasing power of the many, guarantee the greatest possible price stability, and form an adequate basis for economic development.

To stimulate private enterprise in order to encourage the development of Latin American countries at a rate which will help them to provide jobs for their growing populations, to eliminate unemployment, and to take their place among the modern industrialized nations of the world.

To find a quick and lasting solution to the grave problem created by excessive price fluctuations in the basic exports of Latin American countries on which their prosperity so heavily depends.

To accelerate the integration of Latin America so as to stimulate the economic and social development of the Continent. This process has already begun through the General Treaty of Economic Integration of Central America and, in other countries, through the Latin American Free Trade Association.

This declaration expresses the conviction of the nations of Latin America that these profound economic, social, and cultural changes can come about only through the self-help efforts of each country. Nonetheless, in order to achieve the goals which have been established with the necessary speed, domestic efforts must be reinforced by essential contributions of external assistance.

The United States, for its part, pledges its efforts to supply financial and technical cooperation in order to achieve the aims of the Alliance for Progress. To this end, the United States will provide a major part of the minimum of twenty billion dollars, principally in public funds, which Latin America will require over the next ten years from all external sources in order to supplement its own efforts.

The United States will provide from public funds, as an immediate contribution to the economic and social progress of Latin America, more than one billion dollars during the twelve months which began on March 13, 1961, when the Alliance for Progress was announced.

The United States intends to furnish development loans on a long-term basis, where appropriate running up to fifty years and in general at very low or zero rates of interest.

For their part, the countries of Latin America agree to devote a steadily increasing share of their own resources to economic and social development, and to make the reforms necessary to assure that all share fully in the fruits of the Alliance for Progress.

Further, as a contribution to the Alliance for Progress, each of the countries of Latin America will formulate a comprehensive and well conceived national program for the development of its own economy.

Independent and highly qualified experts will be made available to Latin American countries in order to assist in formulating and examining national development plans.

Conscious of the overriding importance of this declaration, the signatory countries declare that the inter-American community is now beginning a new era when it will supplement its institutional, legal, cultural and social accomplishments with immediate and concrete actions to secure a better life, under freedom and democracy, for the present and future generations.

THE CHARTER OF PUNTA DEL ESTE

Establishing an Alliance for Progress Within the Framework
of Operation Pan America

Preamble

We, the American Republics, hereby proclaim our decision to unite in a common effort to bring our people accelerated economic progress and broader social justice within the framework of personal dignity and political liberty.

Almost two hundred years ago we began in this Hemisphere the long struggle for freedom which now inspires people in all parts of the world. Today, in ancient lands, men moved to hope by the revolutions of our young nations search for liberty. Now we must give a new meaning to that revolutionary heritage. For America stands at a turning point in history. The men and women of our Hemisphere are reaching for the better life which today's skills have placed within their grasp. They are determined for themselves and their children to have decent and ever more abundant lives, to gain access to knowledge and equal opportunity for all, to end those conditions which benefit the few at the expense of the needs and dignity of the many. It is our inescapable task to fulfill these just desires—to demonstrate to the poor and forsaken of our countries, and of all lands, that the creative powers of free men hold the key to their progress and to the progress of future generations. And our certainty of ultimate success rests not alone on our faith in ourselves and in our nations but on the indomitable spirit of free man which has been the heritage of American civilization.

Inspired by these principles, and by the principles of Operation Pan America and the Act of Bogotá, the American Republics hereby resolve to adopt the following program of action to establish and carry forward an Alliance for Progress.

Title I
Objectives of the Alliance for Progress

It is the purpose of the Alliance for Progress to enlist the full energies of the peoples and governments of the American republics in a great cooperative effort to accelerate the economic and social development of the participating countries of Latin America, so that they may achieve maximum levels of well-being, with equal opportunities for all, in democratic societies adapted to their own needs and desires.

The American republics hereby agree to work toward the achievement of the following fundamental goals in the present decade:

1. To achieve in the participating Latin American countries a substantial and sustained growth of per capita income at a rate designed to attain, at the earliest possible date, levels of income capable of assuring self-sustaining development, and sufficient to make Latin American income levels constantly larger in relation to the levels of the more industrialized nations. In this way the gap between the living standards of Latin America and those of the more developed countries can be narrowed. Similarly, presently existing differences in income levels among the Latin American countries will be reduced by accelerating the development of the relatively less developed countries and granting them maximum priority in the distribution of resources and in international cooperation in general. In evaluating the degree of relative development, account will be taken not only of average levels of real income and gross product per capita, but also of indices of infant mortality, illiteracy, and per capita daily caloric intake.

It is recognized that, in order to reach these objectives within a reasonable time, the rate of economic growth in any country of Latin America should be not less than 2.5 per cent per capita per year, and that each participating country should determine its own growth target in the light of its stage of social and economic evolution, resource endowment, and ability to mobilize national efforts for development.

2. To make the benefits of economic progress available to all citizens of all economic and social groups through a more equitable distribution of national income, raising more rapidly the income and standard of living of the needier sectors of the population, at the same time that a higher proportion of the national product is devoted to investment.

3. To achieve balanced diversification in national economic structures, both regional and functional, making them increasingly free from dependence on the export of a limited number of primary products and the importation of capital goods while attaining stability in the prices of exports or in income derived from exports.

4. To accelerate the process of rational industrialization so as to increase the

productivity of the economy as a whole, taking full advantage of the talents and energies of both the private and public sectors, utilizing the natural resources of the country and providing productive and remunerative employment for unemployed or part-time workers. Within this process of industrialization, special attention should be given to the establishment and development of capital-goods industries.

5. To raise greatly the level of agricultural productivity and output and to improve related storage, transportation, and marketing services.

6. To encourage, in accordance with the characteristics of each country, programs of comprehensive agrarian reform leading to the effective transformation, where required, of unjust structures and systems of land tenure and use, with a view to replacing latifundia and dwarf holdings by an equitable system of land tenure so that, with the help of timely and adequate credit, technical assistance and facilities for the marketing and distribution of products, the land will become for the man who works it the basis of his economic stability, the foundation of his increasing welfare, and the guarantee of his freedom and dignity.

7. To eliminate adult illiteracy and by 1970 to assure, as a minimum, access to six years of primary education for each school-age child in Latin America; to modernize and expand vocational, technical, secondary and higher educational and training facilities, to strengthen the capacity for basic and applied research; and to provide the competent personnel required in rapidly-growing societies.

8. To increase life expectancy at birth by a minimum of five years, and to increase the ability to learn and produce, by improving individual and public health. To attain this goal it will be necessary, among other measures, to provide adequate potable water supply and sewage disposal to not less than 70 per cent of the urban and 50 per cent of the rural population; to reduce the present mortality rate of children less than five years of age by at least one-half; to control the more serious communicable diseases, according to their importance as a cause of sickness, disability, and death; to eradicate those illnesses, especially malaria, for which effective techniques are known; to improve nutrition; to train medical and health personnel to meet at least minimum requirements; to improve basic health services at national and local levels; and to intensify scientific research and apply its results more fully and effectively to the prevention and cure of illness.

9. To increase the construction of low-cost houses for low-income families in order to replace inadequate and deficient housing and to reduce housing shortages; and to provide necessary public services to both urban and rural centers of population.

10. To maintain stable price levels, avoiding inflation or deflation and the consequent social hardships and maldistribution of resources, always bearing in mind the necessity of maintaining an adequate rate of economic growth.

11. To strengthen existing agreements on economic integration, with a view to the ultimate fulfillment of aspirations for a Latin American common market that will expand and diversify trade among the Latin American countries and thus contribute to the economic growth of the region.

12. To develop cooperative programs designed to prevent the harmful effects of excessive fluctuations in the foreign exchange earnings derived from exports of primary products, which are of vital importance to economic and social development; and to adopt the measures necessary to facilitate the access of Latin American exports to international markets.

Title II
Economic and Social Development

Chapter I. Basic Requirements for Economic and Social Development

The American republics recognize that to achieve the foregoing goals it will be necessary:

1. That comprehensive and well conceived national programs of economic and social development, aimed at the achievement of self sustaining growth, be carried out in accordance with democratic principles.

2. That national programs of economic and social development be based on the principle of self-help—as established in the Act of Bogotá—and on the maximum use of domestic resources, taking into account the special conditions of each country.

3. That in the preparation and execution of plans for economic and social development, women should be placed on an equal footing with men.

4. That the Latin American countries obtain sufficient external financial assistance, a substantial portion of which should be extended on flexible conditions with respect to periods and terms of repayment and forms of utilization, in order to supplement domestic capital formation and reinforce their import capacity; and that, in support of well-conceived programs, which include the necessary structural reforms and measures for the mobilization of internal resources, a supply of capital from all external sources during the coming ten years of at least 20 billion dollars be made available to the Latin American countries, with priority to the relatively less developed countries. The greater part of this sum should be in public funds.

5. That institutions in both the public and private sectors, including labor organizations, cooperatives, and commercial, industrial, and financial institutions, be strengthened and improved for the increasing and effective use of domestic resources, and that the social reforms necessary to permit a fair distribution of the fruits of economic and social progress be carried out.

Chapter II. National Development Programs

1. Participating Latin American countries agree to introduce or strengthen systems for the preparation, execution, and periodic revision of national programs for economic and social development consistent with the principles, objectives, and requirements contained in this document. Participating Latin American countries should formulate, if possible within the next eighteen months, long-term development programs. Such programs should embrace, according to the characteristics of each country, the elements outlined in the Appendix.

2. National development programs should incorporate self-help efforts directed toward:

a. Improvement of human resources and widening of opportunities by raising general standards of education and health; improving and extending technical education and professional training with emphasis on science and technology; providing adequate remuneration for work performed, encouraging the talents of managers, entrepreneurs, and wage earners; providing more productive employment for underemployed manpower; establishing effective systems of labor relations, and procedures for consultation and collaboration among public authorities, employer associations, and labor organizations; promoting the establishment and expansion of local institutions for basic and applied research; and improving the standards of public administration.

b. Wider development and more efficient use of natural resources, especially those which are now idle or under-utilized, including measures for the processing of raw materials.

c. The strengthening of the agricultural base, progressively extending the benefits of the land to those who work it, and ensuring in countries with Indian populations the integration of these populations into the economic, social, and cultural processes of modern life. To carry out these aims, measures should be adopted, among others, to establish or improve, as the case may be, the following services: extension, credit, technical assistance, agricultural research and mechanization; health and education; storage and distribution, cooperatives and farmers' associations; and community development.

d. More effective, rational and equitable mobilization and use of financial resources through the reform of tax structures, including fair and adequate taxation of large incomes and real estate, and the strict application of measures to improve fiscal administration. Development programs should include the adaptation of budget expenditures to development needs, measures for the maintenance of price stability, the creation of essential credit facilities at reasonable rates of interest, and the encouragement of private savings.

e. Promotion through appropriate measures, including the signing of agreements for the purpose of reducing or eliminating double taxation, of conditions that will encourage the flow of foreign investments and help to increase the capital resources of participating countries in need of capital.

f. Improvement of systems of distribution and sales in order to make markets more competitive and prevent monopolistic practices.

Chapter III. Immediate and Short-Term Action Measures

1. Recognizing that a number of Latin American countries, despite their best efforts, may require emergency financial assistance, the United States will provide assistance from the funds which are or may be established for such purposes. The United States stands ready to take prompt action on applications for such assistance. Applications relating to existing situations should be submitted within the next 60 days.

2. Participating Latin American countries should, in addition to creating or strengthening machinery for long-term development programming, immediately increase their efforts to accelerate their development by giving special emphasis to the following objectives:

a. The completion of projects already under way and the initiation of projects for which the basic studies have been made, in order to accelerate their financing and execution.

b. The implementation of new projects which are designed:

(1) To meet the most pressing economic and social needs and benefit directly the greatest number of people;

(2) To concentrate efforts within each country in the less developed and more depressed areas in which particularly serious social problems exist;

(3) To utilize idle capacity or resources, particularly under-employed manpower; and

(4) To survey and assess natural resources.

c. The facilitation of the preparation and execution of long-term programs through measures designed:

(1) To train teachers, technicians, and specialists;

(2) To provide accelerated training to workers and farmers;

(3) To improve basic statistics;

(4) To establish needed credit and marketing facilities; and

(5) To improve services and administration.

3. The United States will assist in carrying out these short-term measures with a view to achieving concrete results from the Alliance for Progress at the earliest possible moment. In connection with the measures set forth above, and in accordance with the statement of President Kennedy, the United States will provide assistance under the Alliance, including assistance for the financing of short-term measures, totalling more than one billion dollars in the year ending March 1962.

Chapter IV. External Assistance in Support of National Development Programs

1. The economic and social development of Latin America will require a large amount of additional public and private financial assistance on the part of capital-exporting countries, including the members of the Development Assistance Group and international lending agencies. The measures provided for in the Act of Bogotá and the new measures provided for in this Charter, are designed to create a framework within which such additional assistance can be provided and effectively utilized.

2. The United States will assist those participating countries whose development programs establish self-help measures and economic and social policies and programs consistent with the goals and principles of this Charter. To supplement the domestic efforts of such countries, the United States is prepared to allocate resources which, along with those anticipated from other external sources, will be of a scope and magnitude adequate to realize the goals envisaged in this Charter. Such assistance will be allocated to both social and economic development and, where appropriate, will take the form of grants or loans on flexible terms and conditions. The participating countries will request the support of other capital-exporting countries and appropriate institutions so that they may provide assistance for the attainment of these objectives.

3. The United States will help in the financing of technical assistance projects proposed by a participating country or by the General Secretariat of the Organization of American States for the purpose of:

a. Providing experts contracted in agreement with the governments to work under their direction and to assist them in the preparation of specific investment projects and the strengthening of national mechanisms for preparing projects, using specialized engineering firms where appropriate;

b. Carrying out, pursuant to existing agreements for cooperation among the General Secretariat of the Organization of American States, the Economic Commission for Latin America, and the Inter-American Development Bank, field investigations and studies, including those relating to development problems, the organization of national agencies for the preparation of development programs, agrarian reform and rural development, health, cooperatives, housing, education and professional training, and taxation and tax administration; and

c. Convening meetings of experts and officials on development and related problems.

The governments or abovementioned organizations should, when appropriate, seek the cooperation of the United Nations and its specialized agencies in the execution of these activities.

4. The participating Latin American countries recognize that each has in varying degree a capacity to assist fellow republics by providing technical and financial assistance. They recognize that this capacity will increase as their economies grow. They therefore affirm their intention to assist fellow republics increasingly as their individual circumstances permit.

Chapter V. Organization and Procedures

1. In order to provide technical assistance for the formulation of development programs, as may be requested by participating nations, the Organization of American States, the Economic Commission for Latin America, and the Inter-American Development Bank will continue and strengthen their agreements for coordination in this field, in order to have available a group of programming experts whose service can be used to facilitate the implementation of this Charter. The participating countries will also seek an intensification of technical assistance from the specialized agencies of the United Nations for the same purpose.

2. The Inter-American Economic and Social Council, on the joint nomination of the Secretary General of the Organization of American States, the Chairman of the Inter-American Committee on the Alliance for Progress, the President of the Inter-American Development Bank, and the Executive Secretary of the United Nations Economic Commission for Latin America, will appoint a panel of nine high-level experts, exclusively on the basis of their experience, technical ability, and competence in the various aspects of economic and social development. The experts may be of any nationality, though if of Latin American origin an appropriate geographical distribution will be sought. They will be attached to the Inter-American Economic and Social Council, but will nevertheless enjoy complete autonomy in the performance of their assigned duties. For administrative purposes and the purposes of better organization of its work, the Panel shall elect from among themselves a Coordinator. The Secretary General of the Organization of American States and the Coordinator shall conclude the agreements of a technical or administrative nature necessary for operations.

Four, at most, of the nine members may hold other remunerative positions that in the judgment of the officials who propose them, do not conflict with their responsibilities as independent experts. The Coordinator may not hold any other remunerative position. When not serving as members of ad hoc committees, the experts may be requested by the Coordinator to perform high-level tasks in connection with planning; the evaluation of plans; and execution of such plans. The Panel may also be requested to perform other high-level, specific tasks in its advisory capacity to the Inter-American Committee on the Alliance for Progress by the Chairman of that Committee, through the Coordinator of the Panel, provided such tasks are not incompatible with the functions set forth in paragraph 4. In the performance of such tasks the experts shall enjoy unquestioned autonomy in judgments, evaluations and recommendations that they may make.

The experts who perform their duties during only part of the year shall do so for a minimum of 110 days per year and shall receive a standard lump-sum payment in proportion to the annual remuneration, emoluments, and benefits of the other members of the Panel.

That proportion shall be set by the Secretary General within the authorizations provided in the budget of the OAS.

Each time the coordinator requires the services of the members of the Panel, they shall begin to provide them within a reasonable period.

The appointment of the members of the Panel will be for a period of at least one and not more than three years, and may be renewed.

3. Each government, if it so wishes, may present its program for economic and social development for consideration by an ad hoc committee, composed of no more than three members drawn from the Panel of Experts referred to in the preceding paragraph together with one or more experts not on the Panel, if the interested government so desires, provided that the number of such experts shall not exceed the number of those drawn from the Panel. The experts who compose the ad hoc committee will be appointed by the Secretary General of the Organization of American States at the request of the interested government and with its consent. The Chairman of such ad hoc committee shall be one of the members of the Panel of Experts.

4. The Committee will study the development program, exchange opinions with the interested government as to possible modifications and, with the consent of the government, report its conclusions to the Inter-American Committee on the Alliance for Progress, to the Inter-American Development Bank, and to other governments and institutions that may be prepared to extend external financial and technical assistance in connection with the execution of the program. At the request of the interested government, the Panel will also reevaluate the development program.

5. In considering a development program presented to it, the ad hoc committee will examine the consistency of the program with the principles of the Act of Bogotá and of this Charter, taking into account the elements in the Appendix.

6. The General Secretariat of the Organization of American States will provide the technical and administrative services needed by the experts referred to in paragraphs 2 and 3 of this chapter in order to fulfill their tasks, in accordance with the agreements provided for in Point 2. The personnel for these services may be employed specifically for this purpose or may be made available from the permanent staffs of the Organization of American States, the Economic Commission for Latin America, and the Inter-American Development Bank, in accordance with the present liaison arrangements between the three organizations. The General Secretariat of the Organization of American States may seek arrangements with the United Nations Secretariat, its specialized agencies, and the Inter-American Specialized Organizations for the temporary assignment of necessary personnel.

7. A government whose development program has been the object of recommendations made by the ad hoc committee with respect to external financing requirements may submit the program to the Inter-American Development Bank so that the Bank may undertake the negotiations required to obtain such financing, including the organization of a consortium of credit institutions and governments disposed to contribute to the continuing and systematic financing, on appropriate terms, of the

development program. However, the government will have full freedom to resort through any other channels to all sources of financing, for the purpose of obtaining, in full or in part, the required resources.

The ad hoc committee shall not interfere with the right of each government to formulate its own goals, priorities, and reforms in its national development programs.

The recommendations of the ad hoc committee will be of great importance in determining the distribution of public funds under the Alliance for Progress which contribute to the external financing of such programs. These recommendations shall give special consideration to Title I.1.

The participating governments and the Inter-American Committee on the Alliance for Progress will also use their good offices to the end that these recommendations may be accepted as a factor of great importance in the decisions taken, for the same purpose, by inter-American credit institutions, other international credit agencies, and other friendly governments which may be potential sources of capital.

8. The Inter-American Economic and Social Council will review annually the progress achieved in the formulation, national implementation, and international financing of development programs; and will submit to the Council of the Organization of American States such recommendations as it deems pertinent.

Appendix
Elements of National Development Programs

1. The establishment of mutually consistent targets to be aimed at over the program period in expanding productive capacity in industry, agriculture, mining, transport, power and communications, and in improving conditions of urban and rural life, including better housing, education, and health.

2. The assignment of priorities and the description of methods to achieve the targets, including specific measures and major projects. Specific development projects should be justified in terms of their relative costs and benefits, including their contribution to social productivity.

3. The measures which will be adopted to direct the operations of the public sector and to encourage private action in support of the development program.

4. The estimated cost, in national and foreign currency, of major projects and of the development program as a whole, year by year over the program period.

5. The internal resources, public and private, estimated to become available for the execution of the programs.

6. The direct and indirect effects of the program on the balance of payments, and the external financing, public and private, estimated to be required for the execution of the program.

7. The basic fiscal and monetary policies to be followed in order to permit implementation of the program within a framework of price stability.

8. The machinery of public administration—including relationships with local governments, decentralized agencies and nongovernmental organizations, such as labor organizations, cooperatives, business and industrial organizations—to be used in carrying out the program, adapting it to changing circumstances and evaluating the progress made.

Title III
Economic Integration of Latin America

The American republics consider that the broadening of present national markets in Latin America is essential to accelerate the process of economic development in the Hemisphere. It is also an appropriate means for obtaining greater productivity through specialized and complementary industrial production which will, in turn, facilitate the attainment of greater social benefits for the inhabitants of the various regions of Latin America. The broadening of markets will also make possible the better use of resources under the Alliance for Progress. Consequently, the American republics recognize that:

1. The Montevideo Treaty (because of its flexibility and because it is open to the adherence of all of the Latin American nations) and the Central American Treaty on Economic Integration are appropriate instruments for the attainment of these objectives, as was recognized in Resolution No. 11 (III) of the Ninth Session of the Economic Commission for Latin America.

2. The integration process can be intensified and accelerated not only by the specialization resulting from the broadening of markets through the liberalization of trade but also through the use of such instruments as the agreements for complementary production within economic sectors provided for in the Montevideo Treaty.

3. In order to insure the balanced and complementary economic expansion of all of the countries involved, the integration process should take into account, on a flexible basis, the condition of countries at a relatively less advanced stage of economic development, permitting them to be granted special, fair, and equitable treatment.

4. In order to facilitate economic integration in Latin America, it is advisable to establish effective relationships between the Latin American Free Trade Association and the group of countries adhering to the Central American Economic Integration Treaty, as well as between either of these groups and other Latin American countries. These arrangements should be established within the limits determined by these instruments.

5. The Latin American countries should coordinate their actions to meet the unfavorable treatment accorded to their foreign trade in world markets, particularly that resulting from certain restrictive and discriminatory policies of extracontinental countries and economic groups.

6. In the application of resources under the Alliance for Progress, special attention should be given not only to investments for multinational projects that will contribute to strengthening the integration process in all its aspects, but also to the necessary financing of industrial production, and to the growing expansion of trade in industrial products within Latin America.

7. In order to facilitate the participation of countries at a relatively low stage of economic development in multinational Latin American economic cooperation programs, and in order to promote the balanced and harmonious development of the Latin American integration process, special attention should be given to the needs of these countries in the administration of financial resources provided under the Alliance for Progress, particularly in connection with infrastructure programs and the promotion of new lines of production.

8. The economic integration process implies a need for additional investment in various fields of economic activity and funds provided under the Alliance for Progress

should cover these needs as well as those required for the financing of national development programs.

9. When groups of Latin American countries have their own institutions for financing economic integration, the financing referred to in the preceding paragraph should preferably be channeled through these institutions. With respect to regional financing designed to further the purposes of existing regional integration instruments, the cooperation of the Inter-American Development Bank should be sought in channeling extra-regional contributions which may be granted for these purposes.

10. One of the possible means for making effective a policy for the financing of Latin American integration would be to approach the International Monetary Fund and other financial sources with a view to providing a means for solving temporary balance-of-payments problems that may occur in countries participating in economic integration arrangements.

11. The promotion and coordination of transportation and communications systems is an effective way to accelerate the integration process. In order to counteract abusive practices in relation to freight rates and tariffs, it is advisable to encourage the establishment of multinational transport and communication enterprises in the Latin American countries, or to find other appropriate solutions.

12. In working toward economic integration and complementary economies, efforts should be made to achieve an appropriate coordination of national plans, or to engage in joint planning for various economies through the existing regional integration organizations. Efforts should also be made to promote an investment policy directed to the progressive elimination of unequal growth rates in the different geographic areas, particularly in the case of countries which are relatively less developed.

13. It is necessary to promote the development of national Latin American enterprises, in order that they may compete on an equal footing with foreign enterprises.

14. The active participation of the private sector is essential to economic integration and development, and except in those countries in which free enterprise does not exist, development planning by the pertinent national public agencies, far from hindering such participation, can facilitate and guide it, thus opening new perspectives for the benefit of the community.

15. As the countries of the Hemisphere still under colonial domination achieve their independence, they should be invited to participate in Latin American economic integration programs.

Title IV
Basic Export Commodities

The American republics recognize that the economic development of Latin America requires expansion of its trade, a simultaneous and corresponding increase in foreign exchange incomes received from exports, a lessening of cyclical or seasonal fluctuations in the incomes of those countries that still depend heavily on the export of raw materials, and the correction of the secular deterioration in their terms of trade.

They therefore agree that the following measures should be taken:

Chapter I. National Measures

National measures affecting commerce in primary products should be directed and applied in order to:

1. Avoid undue obstacles to the expansion of trade in these products;

2. Avoid market instability;

3. Improve the efficiency of international plans and mechanisms for stabilization; and

4. Increase their present markets and expand their area of trade at a rate compatible with rapid development.

Therefore:

A. Importing member countries should reduce and if possible eliminate, as soon as feasible, all restrictions and discriminatory practices affecting the consumption and importation of primary products, including those with the highest possible degree of processing in the country of origin, except when these restrictions are imposed temporarily for purposes of economic diversification, to hasten the economic development of less developed nations, or to establish basic national reserves. Importing countries should also be ready to support, by adequate regulations, stabilization programs for primary products that may be agreed upon with producing countries.

B. Industrialized countries should give special attention to the need for hastening economic development of less developed countries. Therefore, they should make maximum efforts to create conditions, compatible with their international obligations, through which they may extend advantages to less developed countries so as to permit the rapid expansion of their markets. In view of the great need for this rapid development, industrialized countries should also study ways in which to modify, wherever possible, international commitments which prevent the achievement of this objective.

C. Producing member countries should formulate their plans for production and export, taking account of their effect on world markets and of the necessity of supporting and improving the effectiveness of international stabilization programs and mechanisms. Similarly they should try to avoid increasing the uneconomic production of goods which can be obtained under better conditions in the the less developed countries of the Continent, in which the production of these goods is an important source of employment.

D. Member countries should adopt all necessary measures to direct technological studies toward finding new uses and by-products of those primary commodities that are most important to their economies.

E. Member countries should try to reduce, and, if possible, eliminate within a reasonable time export subsidies and other measures which cause instability in the markets for basic commodities and excessive fluctuations in prices and income.

Chapter II. International Cooperation Measures

1. Member countries should make coordinated, and if possible, joint efforts designed:

a. To eliminate as soon as possible undue protection of the production of basic products;

b. To eliminate taxes and reduce excessive domestic prices which discourage the consumption of imported basic products;

c. To seek to end preferential agreements and other measures which limit world consumption of Latin American basic products and their access to international markets, especially the markets of Western European countries in process of economic integration, and of countries with centrally planned economies; and

d. To adopt the necessary consultation mechanisms so that their marketing policies will not have damaging effects on the stability of the markets for basic commodities.

2. Industrialized countries should give maximum cooperation to less developed countries so that their raw material exports will have undergone the greatest degree of processing that is economic.

3. Through their representation in international financial organizations, member countries should suggest that these organizations, when considering loans for the promotion of production for export, take into account the effect of such loans on products which are in surplus in world markets.

4. Member countries should support the efforts being made by international commodity study groups and by the Commission on International Commodity Trade of the United Nations. In this connection, it should be considered that producing and consuming nations bear a joint responsibility for taking national and international steps to reduce market instability.

5. The Secretary General of the Organization of American States shall convene a group of experts appointed by their respective governments to meet before November 30, 1961 and to report, not later than March 31, 1962 on measures to provide an adequate and effective means of offsetting the effects of fluctuations in the volume and prices of exports of basic products. The experts shall:

a. Consider the questions regarding compensatory financing raised during the present meeting;

b. Analyze the proposal for establishing an international fund for the stabilization of export receipts contained in the Report of the Group of Experts to the Special Meeting of the Inter-American Economic and Social Council, as well as any other alternative proposals;

c. Prepare a draft plan for the creation of mechanisms for compensatory financing. This draft plan should be circulated among the member Governments and their opinions obtained well in advance of the next meeting of the Commission on International Commodity Trade.

6. Member countries should support the efforts under way to improve and strengthen international commodity agreements and should be prepared to cooperate in the solution of specific commodity problems. Furthermore, they should endeavor to adopt adequate solutions for the short- and long-term problems affecting markets for such commodities so that the economic interests of producers and consumers are equally safeguarded.

7. Member countries should request other producer and consumer countries to cooperate in stabilization programs, bearing in mind that the raw materials of the Western Hemisphere are also produced and consumed in other parts of the world.

8. Member countries recognize that the disposal of accumulated reserves and surpluses can be a means of achieving the goals outlined in the first chapter of this Title, provided that, along with the generation of local resources, the consumption of essential products in the receiving countries is immediately increased. The disposal of surpluses and reserves should be carried out in an orderly manner, in order to:

a. Avoid disturbing existing commercial markets in member countries, and

b. Encourage expansion of the sale of their products to other markets.

However, it is recognized that:

a. The disposal of surpluses should not displace commercial sales of identical products traditionally carried out by other countries; and

b. Such disposal cannot substitute for large scale financial and technical assistance programs. . . .

114. Eighth Consultative Meeting of Foreign Ministers of the American States, Final Act*

January 31, 1962

. . . . The Meeting was convoked by a resolution of the Council of the Organization of American States adopted on December 4, 1961, the text of which is as follows:

The Council of the Organization of American States,

Considering:

The note presented by the Delegation of Colombia, dated November 9, 1961, in which it requests the convocation of a Meeting of Consultation of Ministers of Foreign Affairs, in accordance with Article 6 of the Inter-American Treaty of Reciprocal Assistance, to consider the threats to the peace and to the political independence of the American states that might arise from the intervention of extracontinental powers directed toward breaking American solidarity,

Resolves:

1. To convoke a Meeting of Consultation of Ministers of Foreign Affairs to serve as Organ of Consultation, in accordance with Articles 6 and 11 of the Inter-American Treaty of Reciprocal Assistance, in order to consider the threats to the peace and to the political independence of the American states referred to in the preamble of this resolution, and particularly to point out the various types of threats to the peace or certain acts that, in the event they occur, justify the application of measures for the maintenance of the peace and security, pursuant to Chapter V of the Charter of the Organization of American States and the provisions of the Inter-American Treaty of Reciprocal Assistance, and to determine the measures that it is advisable to take for the maintenance of the peace and security of the Continent.

2. To set January 10, 1962, as the date for the inauguration of the Meeting.

3. To authorize the Chairman of the Council to present to the Council, at the appropriate time, after consultation with the representatives of the member states, a recommendation on the site of the Meeting of Consultation.

On December 22, 1961, the same Council modified the provisions as to site and date of the Meeting by a resolution that reads as follows:

*Organization of American States, *Official Records,*OEA/Ser. C/II.8 (English).

The Council of the Organization of American States

Resolves:

1. To thank the National Council of the Government of Uruguay and accept its generous offer to be host, in Punta del Este, Uruguay, to the Eighth Meeting of Consultation of Ministers of Foreign Affairs to Serve as Organ of Consultation in Application of the Inter-American Treaty of Reciprocal Assistance, which was convoked by a resolution of December 4, 1961, of the Council of the Organization.

2. To set the date of January 22, 1962, for the opening of the Meeting.

The Members of the Meeting, in the order of precedence determined by lot, are listed below:. . . .

As a result of their deliberations, the Eighth Meeting of Consultation of Ministers of Foreign Affairs approved the following resolutions:

I
Communist Offensive in America

1. The Ministers of Foreign Affairs of the American republics, convened in their Eighth Meeting of Consultation, declare that the continental unity and the democratic institutions of the hemisphere are now in danger.

The Ministers have been able to verify that the subversive offensive of communist governments, their agents and the organizations which they control, has increased in intensity. The purpose of this offensive is the destruction of democratic institutions and the establishment of totalitarian dictatorships at the service of extracontinental powers. The outstanding facts in this intensified offensive are the declarations set forth in official documents of the directing bodies of the international communist movement, that one of its principal objectives is the establishment of communist regimes in the underdeveloped countries and in Latin America; and the existence of a Marxist-Leninist government in Cuba which is publicly aligned with the doctrine and foreign policy of the communist powers.

2. In order to achieve their subversive purposes and hide their true intentions, the communist governments and their agents exploit the legitimate needs of the less-favored sectors of the population and the just national aspirations of the various peoples. With the pretext of defending popular interests, freedom is suppressed, democratic institutions are destroyed, human rights are violated and the individual is subjected to materialistic ways of life imposed by the dictatorship of a single party. Under the slogan of "anti-imperialism" they try to establish an oppressive, aggressive imperialism which subordinates the subjugated nations to the militaristic and aggressive interests of extracontinental powers. By maliciously utilizing the very principles of the inter-American system, they attempt to undermine democratic institutions and to strengthen and protect political penetration and aggression. The subversive methods of communist governments and their agents constitute one of the most subtle and dangerous forms of intervention in the internal affairs of other countries.

3. The Ministers of Foreign Affairs alert the peoples of the hemisphere to the intensification of the subversive offensive of communist governments, their agents, and the organizations that they control and to the tactics and methods that they employ

and also warn them of the dangers this situation represents to representative democracy, to respect for human rights, and to the self-determination of peoples.

The principles of communism are incompatible with the principles of the inter-American system.

4. Convinced that the integrity of the democratic revolution of the American states can and must be preserved in the face of the subversive offensive of communism, the Ministers of Foreign Affairs proclaim the following basic political principles:

a. The faith of the American peoples in human rights, liberty, and national independence as a fundamental reason for their existence, as conceived by the founding fathers who destroyed colonialism and brought the American republics into being;

b. The principle of nonintervention and the right of peoples to organize their way of life freely in the political, economic, and cultural spheres, expressing their will through free elections, without foreign interference. The fallacies of communist propaganda cannot and should not obscure or hide the difference in philosophy which these principles represent when they are expressed by a democratic American country, and when communist governments and their agents attempt to utilize them for their own benefit;

c. The repudiation of repressive measures which, under the pretext of isolating or combatting communism, may facilitate the appearance or strengthening of reactionary doctrines and methods which attempt to repress ideas of social progress and to confuse truly progressive and democratic labor organizations and cultural and political movements with communist subversion;

d. The affirmation that communism is not the way to achieve economic development and the elimination of social injustice in America. On the contrary, a democratic regime can encompass all the efforts for economic advancement and all of the measures for improvement and social progress without sacrificing the fundamental values of the human being. The mission of the peoples and governments of the hemisphere during the present generation is to achieve an accelerated development of their economies and to put an end to poverty, injustice, illness, and ignorance as was agreed in the Charter of Punta del Este; and

e. The most essential contribution of each American state in the collective effort to protect the inter-American system against communism is a steadily greater respect for human rights, improvement in democratic institutions and practices, and the adoption of measures that truly express the impulse for a revolutionary change in the economic and social structures of the American republics.

II
Special Consultative Committee on Security
Against the Subversive Action of International Communism

Whereas:

International communism makes use of highly complex techniques of subversion in opposing, and in the task of counteracting such techniques which certain states may benefit from mutual advice and support;

The American states are firmly united for the common goal of fighting the subversive action of international communism and for the preservation of democracy in the Americas, as expressed in Resolution XXXII of the Ninth International Conference of American States, held in Bogotá, in 1948, and that for such purpose they can and should assist each other, mainly through the use of the institutional resources of the Organization of American States; and

It is advisable, therefore, to make available to the Council of the Organization of American States a body of an advisory nature, made up of experts, the main purpose of which would be to advise the member governments which, as the case may be, require and request such assistance.

The Eighth Meeting of Consultation of Ministers of Foreign Affairs, Serving as Organ of Consultation in Application of the Inter-American Treaty of Reciprocal Assistance,

Resolves:

1. To request the Council of the Organization of American States to maintain all necessary vigilance, for the purpose of warning against any acts of aggression, subversion, or other dangers to peace and security, or the preparation of such acts, resulting from the continued intervention of Sino-Soviet powers in this hemisphere, and to make recommendations to the governments of the member states with regard thereto.

2. To direct the Council of the Organization to establish a Special Consultative Committee on Security, composed of experts on security matters, for the purpose of advising the member states they may desire and request such assistance, the following procedures being observed:

a. The Council of the Organization shall select the membership of the Special Consultative Committee on Security from a list of candidates presented by the governments, and shall define immediately terms of reference for the Committee with a view to achieving the full purposes of this resolution.

b. The Committee shall submit reports to such member states as may request its assistance; however, it shall not publish these reports without obtaining express authorization from the state dealt with in the report.

c. The Special Consultative Committee on Security shall submit to the Council of the Organization, no later than May 1, 1962, an initial general report, with pertinent recommendations regarding measures which should be taken.

d. The Committee shall function at the Pan American Union, which shall extend to it the technical, administrative, and financial facilities required for the work of the Committee.

e. The Committee shall function for the period deemed advisable by the Council of the Organization.

3. To urge the member states to take those steps that they may consider appropriate for their individual or collective self-defense, and to cooperate, as may be necessary or desirable, to strengthen their capacity to counteract threats or acts of aggression, subversion, or other dangers to peace and security resulting from the continued intervention in this hemisphere of Sino-Soviet powers, in accordance with the obligations established in treaties and agreements such as the Charter of the Organization of American States and the Inter-American Treaty of Reciprocal Assistance.

III
Reiteration of the Principles of Nonintervention and Self-Determination

Whereas:

This Meeting has been convoked by a resolution of the Council of the Organization of American States that invoked Article 6 of the Inter-American Treaty of Reciprocal Assistance;

It is necessary to maintain the principles of nonintervention and self-determination set forth in the Charter of the Organization of American States, because these principles are a basic part of the juridical system that governs relations among the republics of the hemisphere and makes friendly relations among them possible;

In the Charter of the Organization of American States and in the Declaration of Santiago, signed in August 1959, all the governments of the American states agreed voluntarily that they should result from free elections;

The will of the people, expressed through unrestricted suffrage, assures the formation of governments that represent more faithfully and without yielding to the interests of a privileged few the basic aspirations to freedom and social justice, the constant need for economic progress, and the call of brotherhood that all our peoples feel throughout the hemisphere;

Formation by free elections of the governments that comprise the Organization of American States is therefore the surest guarantee for the peace of the hemisphere and the security and political independence of each and every one of the nations that comprise it; and

Freedom to contract obligations is an inseparable part of the principle of the self-determination of nations, and consequently a request by one or more countries that such obligations be complied with does not signify intervention,

The Eighth Meeting of Consultation of Ministers of Foreign Affairs, Serving as Organ of Consultation in Application of the Inter-American Treaty of Reciprocal Assistance

Resolves:

1. To reiterate its adherence to the principles of self-determination and nonintervention as guiding standards of relations among the American nations.

2. To urge that the governments of the member countries of the Organization of American States, bearing in mind the present situation, and complying with the principles and aims set forth in the Charter of the Organization and the Declaration of Santiago, organize themselves on the basis of free elections that express, without restriction, the will of the people.

IV
Holding of Free Elections

Whereas:

The preamble to the Charter of the Organization of American States proclaims that the true significance of American solidarity and good neighborliness can only mean the consolidation on this hemisphere, within the framework of democratic institutions, of a system of individual liberty and social justice based on respect for the essential rights of man;

The same Charter reaffirms, among its principles, the requirement that the political organization of the American states be based on the effective exercise of representative democracy, even as it reasserts the fundamental rights of the individual;

The Charter confirms the right of each state to develop, freely and naturally, its cultural, political, and economic life, while respecting in this free development the rights of the individual and the principles of universal morality;

The Inter-American Treaty of Reciprocal Assistance affirms as a manifest truth, that juridical organization is a necessary prerequisite of security and peace, and that peace is founded on justice and moral order and, consequently, on the international recognition and protection of human rights and freedoms, on the indispensable well-being of the people, and on the effectiveness of democracy for the international realization of justice and security; and

According to the principles and attributes of the democratic system in this hemisphere, as stated in the Declaration of Santiago, Chile, the governments of the American republics should be the result of free elections, and perpetuation in power, or the exercise of power without a fixed term and with the manifest intent of perpetuation, is incompatible with the effective exercise of democracy,

The Eighth Meeting of Consultation of Ministers of Foreign Affairs, Serving as Organ of Consultation in Application of the Inter-American Treaty of Reciprocal Assistance

Resolves:

To recommend that the governments of the American states whose structure or acts are incompatible with the effective exercise of representative democracy hold free elections in their respective countries, as the most effective means of consulting the sovereign will of their peoples, to guarantee the restoration of a legal order based on the authority of the law and respect for the rights of the individual.

V
Alliance for Progress

Whereas:

The American states have the capacity to eradicate the profound evils of economic and social underdevelopment;

Resolution XI of the Fifth Meeting of Consultation of Ministers of Foreign Affairs and Resolution V of the Seventh Meeting of Consultation of Ministers of Foreign Affairs declare that economic cooperation among the American states is necessary for the stability of democracy and the safeguarding of human rights, and that such cooperation is essential to the strengthening of the solidarity of the hemisphere and the reinforcement of the inter-American system in the face of threats that might affect it; and

In view of the fact that all the nations of the Americas have recognized their urgent need for economic and social development, it is necessary that they intensify immediately their self-help and cooperative efforts under the Alliance for Progress and the Charter of Punta del Este, on the basis of the adoption of vigorous reforms and large-scale internal efforts by the developing countries concerned and a mobilization of all the necessary financial and technical resources by the highly developed nations,

The Eighth Meeting of Consultation of Ministers of Foreign Affairs, Serving as Organ of Consultation in Application of the Inter-American Treaty of Reciprocal Assistance

Declares:

1. That the preservation and strengthening of free and democratic institutions in the American republics require, as an essential condition, the prompt, accelerated execution of an unprecedented effort to promote their economic and social development for which effort the public and private, domestic and foreign financial resources necessary to those objectives are to be made available, economic and social reforms are to be established, and every necessary internal effort is to be made in accordance with the provisions of the Charter of Punta del Este.

2. That it is essential to promote energetically and vigorously the basic industries of the Latin American countries, to liberalize trade in raw materials by the elimination of undue restrictions, to seek to avoid violent fluctuations in their prices, to encourage the modernization and expansion of services in order that industrialization may rest on its own appropriate bases, to mobilize unexploited natural resources in order to increase national wealth and to make such increased wealth available to persons of all economic and social groups, and to satisfy quickly, among other aspirations, the needs for work, housing, land, health, and education.

VI
Exclusion of the Present Government of Cuba
from Participation in the Inter-American System

Whereas:

The inter-American system is based on consistent adherence by its constituent states to certain objectives and principles of solidarity, set forth in the instruments that govern it;

Among these objectives and principles are those of respect for the freedom of man and preservation of his rights, the full exercise of representative democracy, nonintervention of one state in the internal or external affairs of another, and rejection of alliances and agreements that may lead to intervention in America by extracontinental powers;

The Seventh Meeting of Consultation of Ministers of Foreign Affairs, held in San José, Costa Rica, condemned the intervention or the threat of intervention of extracontinental communist powers in the hemisphere and reiterated the obligation of the American states to observe faithfully the principles of the regional organization;

The present Government of Cuba has identified itself with the principles of Marxist-Leninist ideology, has established a political, economic, and social system based on that doctrine, and accepts military assistance from extracontinental communist powers, including even the threat of military intervention in America on the part of the Soviet Union;

The Report of the Inter-American Peace Committee to the Eighth Meeting of Consultation of Ministers of Foreign Affairs establishes that:

> The present connections of the Government of Cuba with the Sino-Soviet bloc of countries are evidently incompatible with the principles and standards that govern the regional system, and particularly with the collective security established by the Charter of the Organization of American States and the Inter-American Treaty of Reciprocal Assistance [page 39];

The abovementioned Report of the Inter-American Peace Committee also states that:

> It is evident that the ties of the Cuban Government with the Sino-Soviet bloc will prevent the said government from fulfilling the obligations stipulated in the Charter of the Organization and the Treaty of Reciprocal Assistance [page 40];

Such a situation in an American state violates the obligations inherent in membership in the regional system and is incompatible with that system;

The attitude adopted by the present Government of Cuba and its acceptance of military assistance offered by extracontinental communist powers breaks down the effective defense of the inter-American system; and

No member state of the inter-American system can claim the rights and privileges pertaining thereto if it denies or fails to recognize the corresponding obligations,

The Eighth Meeting of Consultation of Ministers of Foreign Affairs, Serving as Organ of Consultation in Application of the Inter-American Treaty of Reciprocal Assistance

Declares:

1. That, as a consequence of repeated acts, the present Government of Cuba has voluntarily placed itself outside the inter-American system.

2. That this situation demands unceasing vigilance on the part of the member states of the Organization of American States, which shall report to the Council any fact or situation that could endanger the peace and security of the hemisphere.

3. That the American states have a collective interest in strengthening the inter-American system and reuniting it on the basis of respect for human rights and the principles and objectives relative to the exercise of democracy set forth in the Charter of the Organization; and, therefore

Resolves:

1. That adherence by any member of the Organization of American States to Marxism-Leninism is incompatible with the inter-American system and the alignment of such a government with the communist bloc breaks the unity and solidarity of the hemisphere.

2. That the present Government of Cuba, which has officially identified itself as a Marxist-Leninist government, is incompatible with the principles and objectives of the inter-American system.

3. That this incompatibility excludes the present Government of Cuba from participation in the inter-American system.

4. That the Council of the Organization of American States and the other organs and organizations of the inter-American system adopt without delay the measures necessary to comply with this resolution.

VII
Inter-American Defense Board

Whereas:

The Inter-American Defense Board was established pursuant to Resolution 39 of the Third Meeting of Consultation of Foreign Ministers, held in Rio de Janeiro in 1942, recommending the immediate meeting of a commission composed of military and naval technicians appointed by each of the governments to study and to suggest to them measures necessary for the defense of the hemisphere;

The Inter-American Defense Board, on April 26, 1961, resolved that the participation of the Cuban regime in defense planning is highly prejudicial to the work of the Board and to the security of the hemisphere; and the present Government of Cuba is identified with the aims and policies of the Sino-Soviet bloc.

The Eighth Meeting of Consultation of Ministers of Foreign Affairs, Serving as Organ of Consultation in Application of the Inter-American Treaty of Reciprocal Assistance

Resolves:

To exclude immediately the present Government of Cuba from the Inter-American Defense Board until the Council of the Organization of American States shall determine by a vote of two thirds of its members that membership of the Government of Cuba is not prejudicial to the work of the Board or to the security of the hemisphere.

VIII
Economic Relations

Whereas:

The Report of the Inter-American Peace Committee to the Eighth Meeting of Consultation of Ministers of Foreign Affairs states, with regard to the intense subversive activity in which the countries of the Sino-Soviet bloc and the Cuban Government are engaged in America, that such activity constitutes "a serious violation of fundamental principles of the inter-American system"; and,

During the past three years 13 American states have found it necessary to break diplomatic relations with the present Government of Cuba,

The Eighth Meeting of Consultation of Ministers of Foreign Affairs, Serving as Organ of Consultation in Application of the Inter-American Treaty of Reciprocal Assistance

Resolves:

1. To suspend immediately trade with Cuba in arms and implements of war of every kind.

2. To charge the Council of the Organization of American States, in accordance with the circumstances and with due consideration for the constitutional or legal limitations of each and every one of the member states, with studying the feasibility and desirability of extending the suspension of trade to other items, with special attention to items of strategic importance.

3. To authorize the Council of the Organization of American States to discontinue, by an affirmative vote of two thirds of its members, the measure or measures adopted pursuant to the preceding paragraphs, at such time as the Government of Cuba demonstrates its compatibility with the purposes and principles of the system.

IX
Revision of the Statute of the
Inter-American Commission on Human Rights

Whereas:

The Fifth Meeting of Consultation of Ministers of Foreign Affairs, by Resolution VIII, created the Inter-American Commission on Human Rights, and charged it with furthering respect for human rights in the American states;

Notwithstanding the noble and persevering effort carried on by that Commission in the exercise of its mandate, the inadequacy of the faculties and attributions conferred upon it by its Statute have made it difficult for the Commission to fulfill its assigned mission;

There is a pressing need for accelerating development in the hemisphere of the collective defense of human rights, so that this development may result in international legal protection of these rights; and

There is an obvious relation between violations of human rights and the international tensions that work against the harmony, peace, and unity of the hemisphere,

The Eighth Meeting of Consultation of Ministers of Foreign Affairs, Serving as Organ of Consultation in Application of the Inter-American Treaty of Reciprocal Assistance

Resolves:

To recommend to the Council of the Organization of American States that it revise the Statute of the Inter-American Commission on Human Rights, broadening and strengthening the Commission's attributes and faculties to such an extent as to permit it effectively to further respect for these rights in the countries of the hemisphere.

Statements

Statement of Honduras

Honduras wishes to have the explanation of the position it adopted in voting for Resolution VI, Exclusion of the Present Government of Cuba from Participation in the Inter-American System, recorded in the Final Act.

With regard to the observations of a juridical nature made by several distinguished foreign ministers, Honduras maintains the existence of sufficient bases in the letter and in the spirit of the treaties and conventions of the regional system.

In the last analysis, however, in view of the threat to the peace and security of the hemisphere, in view of the threat to the dignity and freedom of the inhabitants of the Americas, and in view of the political presence of the Soviet Union in America, the Delegation of Honduras, aware of the juridical doubt that might arise, has not hesitated to give the benefit of the doubt to the defense of democracy in America.

Statement of Argentina

In view of the statement made by the Representative of Uruguay at the second plenary session, held on January 31, 1962, the Delegation of Argentina wishes to record that it reiterates the juridical views expressed by Dr. Miguel Angel Cárcano, Minister of Foreign Affairs and Worship, at the ninth session of the General Committee, in explanation of his vote on Resolution VI of this Final Act.

Statement of Colombia

The position of Colombia has been defined in the two statements that will be shown in the minutes of the second plenary session of this Eighth Meeting of Consultation, and that refer to general policy and to Resolution VI.

Statement of Mexico

The Delegation of Mexico wishes to make it a matter of record in the Final Act of the Eighth Meeting of Consultation of Ministers of Foreign Affairs, that, in its opinion, the exclusion of a member state is not juridically possible unless the Charter of the Organization of American States is first amended pursuant to the procedure established in Article III.

Statement of Haiti

My country is proud to have participated in these discussions, which have taken place in an atmosphere of calm, of courtesy, and of mutual respect.

Haiti came to Punta del Este with the firm intention of defending the principles of nonintervention and self-determination of peoples with all that they imply. Haiti remains firmly attached to these intangible principles, which guarantee an order of mutual respect in relations among peoples of different languages and cultures.

Here Haiti has become persuaded that "the fallacies of communist propaganda cannot and should not obscure or hide the difference in philosophy which these principles represent when they are expressed by a democratic American country, and when communist governments and their agents attempt to utilize them for their own benefit."

This is the sole reason for the change in the position and attitude of my country, which is honored to have had a modest part in resolving a problem which jeopardized the peace, the solidarity, and the unity of the hemisphere.

Statement of Ecuador

The Delegation of Ecuador wishes to state in the record that the exclusion of a member state from the inter-American system could only be accomplished through the prior amendment of the Charter of the Organization of American States to grant the power to exclude a state.

The Charter is the constitutional juridical statute that prevails over any other inter-American instrument.

With respect to Resolution VIII, Ecuador abstained from voting, inasmuch as sanctions are being applied, by invoking the Treaty of Reciprocal Assistance, sanctions that begin with the suspension of traffic in arms with the possibility of being extended to other items, with special attention to items of strategic importance, a concept that might include basic necessities of which the Cuban people should not be deprived and thus make the present situation more critical.

Of course, Ecuador, as a peace-loving country, reaffirms its faith in peaceful methods to settle controversies between states and condemns illegal traffic in arms.

Statement of Brazil

In view of the statement made by the Representative of Uruguay at the plenary session held on January 31, 1962, the Delegation of Brazil reaffirms the validity of the juridical bases of the position taken by its country with respect to Resolution VI of the Eighth Meeting of Consultation, which position was explained at length by the Minister of Foreign Affairs of Brazil in statements made at the sessions of the General Committee held on January 24 and 30, 1962.

Statement of Uruguay

The Delegation of Uruguay wishes to state in the record that, in adopting its position in the Eighth Meeting of Consultation, far from violating or forgetting the juridical standards applicable to the Cuban case, it adhered strictly to them, as befits its old and honorable tradition of being a defender of legality. The bases for this position were explained at the plenary session held on January 31, as will be shown in the minutes of that session.

In Witness Whereof, the Ministers of Foreign Affairs sign the present Final Act. . . .

115. Announcement by the State Department of the Suspension of Diplomatic Relations with Peru*

July 18, 1962

A Peruvian Joint Armed Forces Command communique has announced that the Peruvian Armed Forces have deposed President [Manuel] Prado and assumed control of the Government. The communique also announced the suspension of the constitutional guarantees.

We must deplore this military coup d'etat which has overthrown the constitutional government of Peru. We are watching developments in this situation closely and are awaiting more complete reports from our Ambassador [James Loeb] on it. We also expect to be exchanging information with other Latin American countries. Meanwhile, our diplomatic relations with Peru have been suspended.

*Department of State Bulletin, Aug. 6, 1962, pp. 213-14.

116. White House Statement on the Peruvian Coup d' Etat*

July 19, 1962

The President has noted developments in Peru with great concern. It is his belief that the action taken by the Peruvian military to depose a democratic, constitutional government has contravened the common purposes inherent in the inter-American system and most recently restated in the Charter of Punta del Este, which the former Government of Peru and other hemisphere Republics pledged themselves to support a year ago. At that historic meeting, the signatories agreed to work together for the social and economic welfare of the hemisphere within a framework of developing democratic institutions.

The Declaration to the Peoples of America adopted at Punta del Este sets forth the aim "to improve and strengthen democratic institutions through application of the principle of self-determination by the people." In the case of Peru, this great cause has suffered a serious setback.

117. Announcement by the State Department of the Suspension of Assistance Programs in Peru[†]

July 19, 1962

In view of the unfortunate developments in Peru, where a military junta has deposed the democratic constitutional government and nullified the constitutional electoral process, diplomatic relations with that country were yesterday suspended, and diplomatic contact between the two countries has ceased. We are, as of today, suspending our various assistance programs, with certain relatively minor exceptions where important humanitarian factors are involved.

118. Statement by the State Department Concerning the Resumption of Relations with Peru[††]

August 17, 1962

The Department of State has cabled our Chargé d'Affaires in Lima, Mr. Douglas Henderson, directing him to acknowledge the communication of July 18 from Foreign Minister [Luis Edgardo] Llosa of the Government of the Military Junta. By means of this acknowledgment we are resuming relations with the Peruvian Government, and thus recognizing the junta as the provisional Government of Peru. This action was taken after consultation with other hemisphere governments in the light of the following facts:

The United States Government has ascertained that the junta is in effective control

*Department of State Bulletin, Aug. 6, 1962, p. 214
[†]Department of State Bulletin, Aug. 6, 1962, p. 214
[††]Department of State Bulletin, Sept. 3, 1962, pp. 348-49.

of the government and the country, and that it has pledged itself to fulfill Peru's international obligations.

In considering this action, and our economic assistance program within the framework of the Charter of Punta del Este, the United States Government notes that the junta has decreed the restoration of constitutional guarantees of civil liberties in Peru. It has set the date June 9, 1963, for the holding of free elections. Furthermore, it has guaranteed that, under the Constitution, all political parties will be accorded full electoral rights and that the results of the elections, whatever they may be, will be respected and defended by the junta and the Armed Forces which it represents. By announcing that on July 28, 1963, power will be turned over to an elected President and Congress, the junta has affirmed the provisional nature of its position.

We note that the Organization of American States has been assured by the junta that it will maintain an open-door policy toward all those desiring to witness the electoral process at close hand and that, in accordance with that policy, the junta is considering inviting in due course appropriate organizations and persons of stature and responsibility in the Americas. The United States Government welcomes this open-door policy which will permit international representatives of stature and responsibility to be present in Peru to observe the carrying out of the electoral process in accordance with the announced terms and conditions.

We attach particular significance not only to the guarantee to respect the results of free elections and the restoration of constitutionally assured civil liberties but also to the fact that the junta government has formally and publicly affirmed its commitment to this program at the August 8 meeting of the OAS Council, thereby demonstrating its belief in the value of the inter-American system. Thus the interim government has taken important steps on the road back to constitutional government in Peru.

In the light of these solemn commitments and since a recognized government succeeds to the agreements entered into by prior governments, performance under previously signed loans, grants and other agreements of our economic assistance programs will, generally speaking, be resumed with the resumption of diplomatic relations. The same will apply to the Peace Corps program.

119. News Conference Statement by President Kennedy on United States Policy Toward Cuba*

September 13, 1962

There has been a great deal of talk on the situation in Cuba in recent days both in the Communist camp and in our own, and I would like to take this opportunity to set the matter in perspective.

In the first place it is Mr. Castro and his supporters who are in trouble. In the last year his regime has been increasingly isolated from this hemisphere. His name no longer inspires the same fear or following in other Latin American countries. He has been condemned by the OAS [Organization of American States], excluded from the Inter-American Defense Board, and kept out of the [Latin American] Free Trade Association. By his own monumental economic mismanagement, supplemented by

*Department of State Bulletin, Oct. 1, 1962, pp. 481-82.

our refusal to trade with him, his economy has crumbled and his pledges for economic progress have been discarded, along with his pledges for political freedom. His industries are stagnating, his harvests are declining, his own followers are beginning to see that their revolution has been betrayed.

So it is not surprising that in a frantic effort to bolster his regime he should try to arouse the Cuban people by charges of an imminent American invasion and commit himself still further to a Soviet takeover in the hope of preventing his own collapse.

Ever since communism moved into Cuba in 1958, Soviet technical and military personnel have moved steadily onto the island in increasing numbers at the invitation of the Cuban government. Now that movement has been increased. It is under our most careful surveillance. But I will repeat the conclusion that I reported last week that these new shipments do not constitute a serious threat to any other part of this hemisphere.

If the United States ever should find it necessary to take military action against communism in Cuba, all of Castro's Communist-supplied weapons and technicians would not change the result or significantly extend the time required to achieve that result.

However, unilateral military intervention on the part of the United States cannot currently be either required or justified, and it is regrettable that loose talk about such action in this country might serve to give a thin color of legitimacy to the Communist pretense that such a threat exists. But let me make this clear once again: If at any time the Communist buildup in Cuba were to endanger or interfere with our security in any way, including our base at Guantanamo, our passage to the Panama Canal, our missile and space activities at Cape Canaveral, or the lives of American citizens in this country, or if Cuba should ever attempt to export its aggressive purposes by force or the threat of force against any nation in this hemisphere, or become an offensive military base of significant capacity for the Soviet Union, then this country will do whatever must be done to protect its own security and that of its allies.

We shall be alert to, and fully capable of dealing swiftly with, any such development. As President and Commander in Chief I have full authority now to take such action, and I have asked the Congress to authorize me to call up reserve forces should this or any other crisis make it necessary.

In the meantime we intend to do everything within our power to prevent such a threat from coming into existence. Our friends in Latin America must realize the consequences such developments hold out for their own peace and freedom, and we shall be making further proposals to them. Our friends in NATO must realize the implications of their ships' engaging in the Cuban trade.

We shall continue to work with Cuban refugee leaders who are dedicated as we are to that nation's future return to freedom. We shall continue to keep the American people and the Congress fully informed. We shall increase our surveillance of the whole Caribbean area. We shall neither initiate nor permit aggression in this hemisphere.

With this in mind, while I recognize that rash talk is cheap, particularly on the part of those who did not have the responsibility, I would hope that the future record will show that the only people talking about a war and invasion at this time are the Communist spokesmen in Moscow and Habana, and that the American people, defending as we do so much of the free world, will in this nuclear age, as they have in the past, keep both their nerve and their head.

*120. Joint Resolution by the U.S. Congress Concerning Cuba**

October 3, 1962

Whereas President James Monroe, announcing the Monroe Doctrine in 1823, declared that the United States would consider any attempt on the part of European powers "to extend their system to any portion of this hemisphere as dangerous to our peace and safety"; and

Whereas in the Rio Treaty of 1947 the parties agreed that "an armed attack by any State against an American State shall be considered as an attack against all the American States, and, consequently, each one of the said contracting parties undertakes to assist in meeting the attack in the exercise of the inherent right of individual or collective self-defense recognized by article 51 of the Charter of the United Nations"; and

Whereas the Foreign Ministers of the Organization of American States at Punta del Este in January 1962 declared: "The present Government of Cuba has identified itself with the principles of Marxist-Leninist ideology, has established a political, economic, and social system based on that doctrine, and accepts military assistance from extracontinental Communist powers, including even the threat of military intervention in America on the part of the Soviet Union"; and

Whereas the international Communist movement has increasingly extended into Cuba its political, economic, and military sphere of influence; Now, therefore, be it

Resolved by the Senate and House of Representatives of the United States of America in Congress assembled, That the United States is determined—

(a) to prevent by whatever means may be necessary, including the use of arms, the Marxist-Leninist regime in Cuba from extending, by force or the threat of force, its aggressive or subversive activities to any part of this hemisphere;

(b) to prevent in Cuba the creation or use of an externally supported military capability endangering the security of the United States; and

(c) to work with the Organization of American States and with freedom-loving Cubans to support the aspirations of the Cuban people for self-determination.

121. Radio-TV Address by President Kennedy on the Soviet Military Buildup in Cuba†

October 22, 1962

Good evening, my fellow citizens. This Government, as promised, has maintained the closest surveillance of the Soviet military buildup on the island of Cuba. Within the past week unmistakable evidence has established the fact that a series of offensive missile sites is now in preparation on that imprisoned island. The purpose of these bases can be none other than to provide a nuclear strike capability against the Western Hemisphere.

*United States Public Law, Public Law 87-7333-76 Stat.
†Department of State Bulletin, Nov. 12, 1962, pp. 715-20.

Upon receiving the first preliminary hard information of this nature last Tuesday morning [October 16 at 9:00 a.m., I directed that our surveillance be stepped up. And having now confirmed and completed our evaluation of the evidence and our decision on a course of action, this Government feels obliged to report this new crisis to you in fullest detail.

The characteristics of these new missile sites indicate two distinct types of installations. Several of them include medium-range ballistic missiles capable of carrying a nuclear warhead for a distance of more than 1,000 nautical miles. Each of these missiles, in short, is capable of striking Washington, D.C., the Panama Canal, Cape Canaveral, Mexico City, or any other city in the southeastern part of the United States, in Central America, or in the Caribbean area.

Additional sites not yet completed appear to be designed for intermediate-range ballistic missiles capable of traveling more than twice as far—and thus capable of striking most of the major cities in the Western Hemisphere, ranging as far north as Hudson Bay, Canada, and as far south as Lima, Peru. In addition, jet bombers, capable of carrying nuclear weapons, are now being uncrated and assembled in Cuba, while the necessary air bases are being prepared.

This urgent transformation of Cuba into an important strategic base—by the presence of these large, long-range, and clearly offensive weapons of sudden mass destruction—constitutes an explicit threat to the peace and security of all the Americas, in flagrant and deliberate defiance of the Rio Pact of 1947, the traditions of this nation and hemisphere, the Joint Resolution of the 87th Congress, the Charter of the United Nations, and my own public warnings to the Soviets on September 4 and 13.

Soviet Contradictions Cited

This action also contradicts the repeated assurances of Soviet spokesmen, both publicly and privately delivered, that the arms buildup in Cuba would retain its original defensive character and that the Soviet Union had no need or desire to station strategic missiles on the territory of any other nation.

The size of this undertaking makes clear that it has been planned for some months. Yet only last month, after I had made clear the distinction between any introduction of ground-to-ground missiles and the existence of defensive antiaircraft missiles, the Soviet Government publicly stated on September 11 that, and I quote, "The armaments and military equipment sent to Cuba are designed exclusively for defensive purposes," and, and I quote the Soviet Government, "There is no need for the Soviet government to shift its weapons for a retaliatory blow to any other country, for instance Cuba," and that, and I quote the Government, "The Soviet Union has so powerful rockets to carry these nuclear warheads that there is no need to search for sites for them beyond the boundaries of the Soviet Union." That statement was false.

Only last Thursday, as evidence of this rapid offensive buildup was already in my hand, Soviet Foreign Minister Gromyko told me in my office that he was instructed to make it clear once again, as he said his Government had already done, that Soviet assistance to Cuba, and I quote, "pursued solely the purpose of contributing to the defense capabilities of Cuba," that, and I quote him, "training by Soviet specialists of

Cuban nationals in handling defensive armaments was by no means offensive," and that "if it were otherwise," Mr. Gromyko went on, "the Soviet Government would never become involved in rendering such assistance." That statement also was false.

No Room for Deception

Neither the United States of America nor the world community of nations can tolerate deliberate deception and offensive threats on the part of any nation, large or small. We no longer live in a world where only the actual firing of weapons represents a sufficient challenge to a nation's security to constitute maximum peril. Nuclear weapons are so destructive and ballistic missiles are so swift that any substantially increased possibility of their use or any sudden change in their deployment may well be regarded as a definite threat to peace.

For many years both the Soviet Union and the United States, recognizing this fact, have deployed strategic nuclear weapons with great care, never upsetting the precarious *status quo* which insured that these weapons would not be used in the absence of some vital challenge. Our own strategic missiles have never been transferred to the territory of any other nation under a cloak of secrecy and deception; and our history, unlike that of the Soviets since the end of World War II, demonstrates that we have no desire to dominate or conquer any other nation or impose our system upon its people. Nevertheless, American citizens have become adjusted to living daily on the bull's eye of Soviet missiles located inside the U.S.S.R. or in submarines.

In that sense missiles in Cuba add to an already clear and present danger—although it should be noted the nations of Latin America have never previously been subjected to a potential nuclear threat.

But this secret, swift, and extraordinary buildup of Communist missiles—in an area well known to have a special and historical relationship to the United States and the nations of the Western Hemisphere, in violation of Soviet assurances, and in defiance of American and hemispheric policy—this sudden, clandestine decision to station strategic weapons for the first time outside of Soviet soil—is a deliberately provocative and unjustified change in the *status quo* which cannot be accepted by this country if our courage and our commitments are ever to be trusted again by either friend or foe.

The 1930's taught us a clear lesson: Aggressive conduct, if allowed to grow unchecked and unchallenged, ultimately leads to war. This nation is opposed to war. We are also true to our word. Our unswerving objective, therefore, must be to prevent the use of these missiles against this or any other country and to secure their withdrawal or elimination from the Western Hemisphere.

Our policy has been one of patience and restraint, as befits a peaceful and powerful nation, which leads a worldwide alliance. We have been determined not to be diverted from our central concerns by mere irritants and fanatics. But now further action is required—and it is underway; and these actions may only be the beginning. We will not prematurely or unnessarily risk the costs of worldwide nuclear war in which even the fruits of victory would be ashes in our mouth— but neither will we shrink from that risk at any time it must be faced.

Initial Steps Proposed

Acting, therefore, in the defense of our own security and of the entire Western Hemisphere, and under the authority entrusted to me by the Constitution as endorsed by the resolution of the Congress, I have directed that the following *initial* steps be taken immediately:

First: To halt this offensive buildup, a strict quarantine on all offensive military equipment under shipment to Cuba is being initiated. All ships of any kind bound for Cuba from whatever nation or port will, if found to contain cargoes of offensive weapons, be turned back. This quarantine will be extended, if needed, to other types of cargo and carriers. We are not at this time, however, denying the necessities of life as the Soviets attempted to do in their Berlin blockade of 1948.

Second: I have directed the continued and increased close surveillance of Cuba and its military buildup. The Foreign Ministers of the OAS [Organization of American States] in their communique of October 3 rejected secrecy on such matters in this hemisphere. Should these offensive military preparations continue, thus increasing the threat to the hemisphere, further action will be justified. I have directed the Armed Forces to prepare for any eventualities; and I trust that, in the interest of both the Cuban people and the Soviet technicians at the sites, the hazards to all concerned of continuing this threat will be recognized.

Third: It shall be the policy of this nation to regard any nuclear missile launched from Cuba against any nation in the Western Hemisphere as an attack by the Soviet Union on the United States, requiring a full retaliatory response upon the Soviet Union.

Fourth: As a necessary military precaution I have reinforced our base at Guantanamo, evacuated today the dependents of our personnel there, and ordered additional military units to be on a standby alert basis.

Fifth: We are calling tonight for an immediate meeting of the Organ of Consultation, under the Organization of American States, to consider this threat to hemispheric security and to invoke articles 6 and 8 of the Rio Treaty in support of all necessary action. The United Nations Charter allows for regional security arrangements—and the nations of this hemisphere decided long ago against the military presence of outside powers. Our other allies around the world have also been alerted.

Sixth: Under the Charter of the United Nations, we are asking tonight that an emergency meeting of the Security Council be convoked without delay to take action against this latest Soviet threat to world peace. Our resolution will call for the prompt dismantling and withdrawal of all offensive weapons in Cuba, under the supervision of U.N. observers, before the quarantine can be lifted.

Seventh and finally: I call upon Chairman Khrushchev to halt and eliminate this clandestine, reckless, and provocative threat to world peace and to stable relations between our two nations. I call upon him further to abandon this course of world domination and to join in an historic effort to end the perilous arms race and transform the history of man. He has an opportunity now to move the world back from the abyss of destruction—by returning to his Government's own words that it had no need to station missiles outside its own territory, and withdrawing these weapons from Cuba—by refraining from any action which will widen or deepen the present crisis—and then by participating in a search for peaceful and permanent solutions.

This nation is prepared to present its case against the Soviet threat to peace, and our own proposals for a peaceful world, at any time and in any forum—in the OAS, in the United Nations, or in any other meeting that could be useful—without limiting our freedom of action.

U.S. Wishes Peace With U.S.S.R.

We have in the past made strenuous efforts to limit the spread of nuclear weapons. We have proposed the elimination of all arms and military bases in a fair and effective disarmament treaty. We are prepared to discuss new proposals for the removal of tensions on both sides—including the possibilities of a genuinely independent Cuba, free to determine its own destiny. We have no wish to war with the Soviet Union, for we are a peaceful people who desire to live in peace with all other peoples.

But it is difficult to settle or even discuss these problems in an atmosphere of intimidation. That is why this latest Soviet threat—or any other threat which is made either independently or in response to our actions this week—must and will be met with determination. Any hostile move anywhere in the world against the safety and freedom of peoples to whom we are committed—including in particular the brave people of West Berlin—will be met by whatever action is needed.

To the People of Cuba

Finally, I want to say a few words to the captive people of Cuba, to whom this speech is being directly carried by special radio facilities. I speak to you as a friend, as one who knows of your deep attachment to your fatherland, as one who shares your aspirations for liberty and justice for all. And I have watched and the American people have watched with deep sorrow how your nationalist revolution was betrayed and how your fatherland fell under foreign domination. Now your leaders are no longer Cuban leaders inspired by Cuban ideals. They are puppets and agents of an international conspiracy which has turned Cuba against your friends and neighbors in the Americas—and turned it into the first Latin American country to become a target for nuclear war, the first Latin American country to have these weapons on its soil.

These new weapons are not in your interest. They contribute nothing to your peace and well-being. They can only undermine it. But this country has no wish to cause you to suffer or to impose any system upon you. We know that your lives and land are being used as pawns by those who deny you freedom.

Many times in the past the Cuban people have risen to throw out tyrants who destroyed their liberty. And I have no doubt that most Cubans today look forward to the time when they will be truly free—free from foreign domination, free to choose their own leaders, free to select their own system, free to own their own land, free to speak and write and worship without fear or degradation. And then shall Cuba be welcomed back to the society of free nations and to the associations of this hemisphere.

U.S. Chooses Difficult Path

My fellow citizens, let no one doubt that this is a difficult and dangerous effort on which we have set out. No one can foresee precisely what course it will take or what costs or casualties will be incurred. Many months of sacrifice and self-discipline lie ahead—months in which both our patience and our will will be tested, months in which many threats and denunciations will keep us aware of our dangers. But the greatest danger of all would be to do nothing.

The path we have chosen for the present is full of hazards, as all paths are; but it is the one most consistent with our character and courage as a nation and our commitments around the world. The cost of freedom is always high—but Americans have always paid it. And one path we shall never choose, and that is the path of surrender or submission.

Our goal is not the victory of might but the vindication of right—not peace at the expense of freedom, but both peace *and* freedom, here in this hemisphere and, we hope, around the world. God willing, that goal will be achieved.

122. Proclamation by President Kennedy on the Interdiction of the Delivery of Offensive Weapons to Cuba*

October 23, 1962

Whereas the peace of the world and the security of the United States and of all American States are endangered by reason of the establishment by the Sino-Soviet powers of an offensive military capability in Cuba, including bases for ballistic missiles with a potential range covering most of North and South America;

Whereas by a Joint Resolution passed by the Congress of the United States and approved on October 3, 1962, it was declared that the United States is determined to prevent by whatever means may be necessary, including the use of arms, the Marxist-Leninist regime in Cuba from extending, by force or the threat of force, its aggressive or subversive activities to any part of this hemisphere, and to prevent in Cuba the creation or use of an externally supported military capability endangering the security of the United States; and

Whereas the Organ of Consultation of the American Republics meeting in Washington on October 23, 1962, recommended that the Member States, in accordance with Articles 6 and 8 of the Inter-American Treaty of Reciprocal Assistance, take all measures, individually and collectively, including the use of armed force, which they may deem necessary to ensure that the Government of Cuba cannot continue to receive from the Sino-Soviet powers military material and related supplies which may threaten the peace and security of the Continent and to prevent the missiles in Cuba with offensive capability from ever becoming an active threat to the peace and security of the continent:

Now, therefore, I, John F. Kennedy, President of the United States of America, acting under and by virtue of the authority conferred upon me by the Constitution

Department of State Bulletin, Nov. 12, 1962, p. 717.

and statutes of the United States, in accordance with the aforementioned resolutions of the United States Congress and of the Organ of Consultation of the American Republics, and to defend the security of the United States, do hereby proclaim that the forces under my command are ordered, beginning at 2:00 p.m. Greenwich time October 24, 1962, to interdict, subject to the instructions herein contained, the delivery of offensive weapons and associated materiel to Cuba.

For the purposes of this Proclamation, the following are declared to be prohibited materiel:

Surface-to-surface missiles; bomber aircraft; bombs, air-to-surface rockets and guided missiles; warheads for any of the above weapons; mechanical or electronic equipment to support or operate the above items; and any other classes of materiel hereafter designated by the Secretary of Defense for the purpose of effectuating this Proclamation.

To enforce this order, the Secretary of Defense shall take appropriate measures to prevent the delivery of prohibited materiel to Cuba, employing the land, sea and air forces of the United States in cooperation with any forces that may be made available by other American States.

The Secretary of Defense may make such regulations and issue such directives as he deems necessary to ensure the effectiveness of this order, including the designation, within a reasonable distance of Cuba, of prohibited or restricted zones and of prescribed routes.

Any vessel or craft which may be proceeding toward Cuba may be intercepted and may be directed to identify itself, its cargo, equipment and stores and its ports of call, to stop, to lie to, to submit to visit and search, or to proceed as directed. Any vessel or craft which fails or refuses to respond to or comply with directions shall be subject to being taken into custody. Any vessel or craft which it is believed is en route to Cuba and may be carrying prohibited materiel or may itself constitute such materiel shall, wherever possible, be directed to proceed to another destination of its own choice and shall be taken into custody if it fails or refuses to obey such directions. All vessels or craft taken into custody shall be sent into a port of the United States for appropriate disposition.

In carrying out this order, force shall not be used except in case of failure or refusal to comply with directions, or with regulations or directives of the Secretary of Defense issued hereunder, after reasonable efforts have been made to communicate them to the vessel or craft, or in case of self-defense. In any case, force shall be used only to the extent necessary. . . .

123. Resolution by the Council of the Organization of American States, Calling for the Dismantling of Offensive Weapons in Cuba*

October 23, 1962

Whereas,

The Inter-American Treaty of Reciprocal Assistance of 1947 (Rio Treaty) recognizes the obligation of the American Republics to "provide for effective reciprocal assistance to meet armed attacks against any American state and in order to deal with threats of aggression against any of them"

Article 6 of the said Treaty states:

"If the inviolability or the integrity of the territory or the sovereignty or political independence of any American State should be affected by an aggression which is not an armed attack or by an extra-continental or intracontinental conflict, or by any other fact or situation that might endanger the peace of America, the Organ of Consultation shall meet immediately in order to agree on the measures which must be taken in case of aggression to assist the victim of the aggression or, in any case, the measures which should be taken for the common defense and for the maintenance of the peace and security of the Continent."

The Eighth Meeting of Consultation of the Ministers of Foreign Affairs of the American Republics in Punta del Este in January, 1962, agreed in Resolution II "To urge the member states to take those steps that they may consider appropriate for their individual and collective self-defense, and to cooperate, as may be necessary or desirable, to strengthen their capacity to counteract threats or acts of aggression, subversion, or other dangers to peace and security resulting from the continued intervention in this hemisphere of Sino-Soviet powers, in accordance with the obligations established in treaties and agreements such as the Charter of the Organization of American States and the Inter-American Treaty of Reciprocal Assistance";

The Ministers of Foreign Affairs of the American Republics meeting informally in Washington, October 2 and 3, 1962, reasserted "the firm intention of the Governments represented and of the peoples of the American Republics to conduct themselves in accordance with the principles of the regional system, staunchly sustaining and consolidating the principles of the Charter of the Organization of American States, and affirmed the will to strengthen the security of the Hemisphere against all aggression from within or outside the Hemisphere and against all developments or situations capable of threatening the peace and security of the Hemisphere through the application of the Inter-American Treaty of Reciprocal Assistance of Rio de Janeiro. It was the view of the Ministers that the existing organizations and bodies of the inter-American system should intensify the carrying out of their respective duties with special and urgent attention to the situation created by the communist regime in Cuba and that they should stand in readiness to consider the matter promptly if the situation requires measures beyond those already authorized."

The same meeting "recalled that the Soviet Union's intervention in Cuba threatens the unity of the Americas and its democratic institutions, and that this intervention

*Department of State Bulletin, Nov. 12, 1962, pp. 722-23.

has special characteristics which, pursuant to paragraph 3 of Resolution II of the Eighth Meeting of Consultation of Ministers of Foreign Affairs, call for the adoption of special measures, both individual and collective";

Incontrovertible evidence has appeared that the Government of Cuba, despite repeated warnings, has secretly endangered the peace of the Continent by permitting the Sino-Soviet powers to have intermediate and middle-range missiles on its territory capable of carrying nuclear warheads;

The Council of the Organization of American States,
Meeting as the Provisional Organ of Consultation,

Resolves:

1. To call for the immediate dismantling and withdrawal from Cuba of all missiles and other weapons with any offensive capability;

2. To recommend that the member states, in accordance with Articles 6 and 8 of the Inter-American Treaty of Reciprocal Assistance, take all measures, individually and collectively, including the use of armed force, which they may deem necessary to ensure that the Government of Cuba cannot continue to receive from the Sino-Soviet powers military material and related supplies which may threaten the peace and security of the Continent and to prevent the missiles in Cuba with offensive capability from ever becoming an active threat to the peace and security of the Continent;

3. To inform the Security Council of the United Nations of this resolution in accordance with Article 54 of the Charter of the United Nations and to express the hope that the Security Council will, in accordance with the draft resolution introduced by the United States, dispatch United Nations observers to Cuba at the earliest moment;

4. To continue to serve provisionally as Organ of Consultation and to request the Member States to keep the Organ of Consultation duly informed of measures taken by them in accordance with paragraph two of this resolution.

*124. White House Statement on the Proposals of the Union
       of Soviet Socialist Republics Concerning the Cuban
       Crisis**

October 27, 1962

Several inconsistent and conflicting proposals have been made by the U.S.S.R. within the last 24 hours, including the one just made public in Moscow. The proposal broadcast this morning involves the security of nations outside the Western Hemisphere. But it is the Western Hemisphere countries and they alone that are subject to the threat that has produced the current crisis—the action of the Soviet Government in secretly introducing offensive weapons into Cuba. Work on these offensive weapons is still proceeding at a rapid pace. The first imperative must be to deal with this immediate threat, under which no sensible negotiations can proceed.

*Department of State Bulletin, Nov. 12, 1962, p. 741.

It is therefore the position of the United States that as an urgent preliminary to consideration of any proposals work on the Cuban bases must stop; offensive weapons must be rendered inoperable; and further shipment of offensive weapons to Cuba must cease—all under effective international verification.

As to proposals concerning the security of nations outside this hemisphere, the United States and its allies have long taken the lead in seeking properly inspected arms limitation, on both sides. These efforts can continue as soon as the present Soviet-created threat is ended.

125. *Message from Premier Khrushchev to President Kennedy Concerning the Cuban Crisis**

October 27, 1962

It is with great satisfaction that I studied your reply to Mr. U Thant on the adoption of measures in order to avoid contact by our ships and thus avoid irreparable fatal consequences. This reasonable step on your part persuades me that you are showing solicitude for the preservation of peace, and I note this with satisfaction.

I have already said that the only concern of our people and government and myself personally as chairman of the Council of Ministers is to develop our country and have it hold a worthy place among all people of the world in economic competition, advance of culture and arts, and the rise in people's living standards. This is the loftiest and most necessary field for competition which will only benefit both the winner and loser, because this benefit is peace and an increase in the facilities by means of which man lives and obtains pleasure.

In your statement, you said that the main aim lies not only in reaching agreement and adopting measures to avert contact of our ships, and, consequently, a deepening of the crisis, which because of this contact can spark off the fire of military conflict after which any talks would be superfluous because other forces and other laws would begin to operate—the laws of war. I agree with you that this is only a first step. The main thing is to normalize and stabilize the situation in the world between states and between people.

I understand your concern for the security of the United States, Mr. President, because this is the first duty of the president. However, these questions are also uppermost in our minds. The same duties rest with me as chairman of the USSR Council of Ministers. You have been worried over our assisting Cuba with arms designed to strengthen its defensive potential—precisely defensive potential—because Cuba, no matter what weapons it had, could not compare with you since these are different dimensions, the more so given up-to-date means of extermination.

Our purpose has been and is to help Cuba, and no one can challenge the humanity of our motives aimed at allowing Cuba to live peacefully and develop as its people desire. You want to relieve your country from danger and this is understandable. However, Cuba also wants this. All countries want to relieve themselves from danger. But how can we, the Soviet Union and our government, assess your actions which, in

*Department of State Bulletin, Nov. 12, 1962, pp. 741-43.

effect, mean that you have surrounded the Soviet Union with military bases, surrounded our allies with military bases, set up military bases literally around our country, and stationed your rocket weapons at them? This is no secret. High-placed American officials demonstratively declare this. Your rockets are stationed in Britain and in Italy and pointed at us. Your rockets are stationed in Turkey.

You are worried over Cuba. You say that it worries you because it lies at a distance of 90 miles across the sea from the shores of the United States. However, Turkey lies next to us. Our sentinels are pacing up and down and watching each other. Do you believe that you have the right to demand security for your country and the removal of such weapons that you qualify as offensive, while not recognizing this right for us?

You have stationed devastating rocket weapons, which you call offensive, in Turkey literally right next to us. How then does recognition of our equal military possibilities tally with such unequal relations between our great states? This does not tally at all.

It is good, Mr. President, that you agreed for our representatives to meet and begin talks, apparently with the participation of U.N. Acting Secretary General U Thant. Consequently, to some extent, he assumes the role of intermediary, and we believe that he can cope with the responsible mission if, of course, every side that is drawn into this conflict shows good will.

I think that one could rapidly eliminate the conflict and normalize the situation. Then people would heave a sigh of relief, considering that the statesmen who bear the responsibility have sober minds, an awareness of their responsibility, and an ability to solve complicated problems and not allow matters to slide to the disaster of war.

This is why I make this proposal: We agree to remove those weapons from Cuba which you regard as offensive weapons. We agree to do this and to state this commitment in the United Nations. Your representatives will make a statement to the effect that the United States, on its part, bearing in mind the anxiety and concern of the Soviet state, will evacuate its analogous weapons from Turkey. Let us reach an understanding on what time you and we need to put this into effect.

After this, representatives of the U.N. Security Council could control on-the-spot the fulfillment of these commitments. Of course, it is necessary that the Governments of Cuba and Turkey would allow these representatives to come to their countries and check fulfillment of this commitment, which each side undertakes. Apparently, it would be better if these representatives enjoyed the trust of the Security Council and ours—the United States and the Soviet Union—as well as of Turkey and Cuba. I think that it will not be difficult to find such people who enjoy the trust and respect of all interested sides.

We, having assumed this commitment in order to give satisfaction and hope to the peoples of Cuba and Turkey and to increase their confidence in their security, will make a statement in the Security Council to the effect that the Soviet Government gives a solemn pledge to respect the integrity of the frontiers and the sovereignty of Turkey, not to intervene in its domestic affairs, not to invade Turkey, not to make available its territory as a place d'armes for such invasion, and also will restrain those who would think of launching an aggression against Turkey either from Soviet territory or from the territory of other states bordering on Turkey.

The U.S. Government will make the same statement in the Security Council with regard to Cuba. It will declare that the United States will respect the integrity of the frontiers of Cuba, its sovereignty, undertakes not to intervene in its domestic affairs, not to invade and not to make its territory available as place d'armes for the invasion of Cuba, and also will restrain those who would think of launching an aggression against Cuba either from U.S. territory or from the territory of other states bordering on Cuba.

Of course, for this we would have to reach agreement with you and to arrange for some deadline. Let us agree to give some time, but not to delay, two or three weeks, not more than a month.

The weapons on Cuba, that you have mentioned and which, as you say, alarm you, are in the hands of Soviet officers. Therefore any accidental use of them whatsoever to the detriment of the United States of America is excluded. These means are stationed in Cuba at the request of the Cuban Government and only in defensive aims. Therefore, if there is no invasion of Cuba, or an attack on the Soviet Union, or other of our allies then, of course, these means do not threaten anyone and will not threaten. For they do not pursue offensive aims.

If you accept my proposal, Mr. President, we would send our representatives to New York, to the United Nations, and would give them exhaustive instructions to order to come to terms sooner. If you would also appoint your men and give them appropriate instructions, this problem could be solved soon.

Why would I like to achieve this? Because the entire world is now agitated and expects reasonable actions from us. The greatest pleasure for all the peoples would be an announcement on our agreement, on nipping in the bud the conflict that has arisen. I attach a great importance to such understanding because it might be a good beginning and, specifically, facilitate a nuclear test ban agreement. The problem of tests could be solved simultaneously, not linking one with the other, because they are different problems. However, it is important to reach an understanding to both these problems in order to make a good gift to the people, to let them rejoice in the news that a nuclear test ban agreement has also been reached and thus there will be no further contamination of the atmosphere. Your and our positions on this issue are very close.

All this, possibly, would serve as a good impetus to searching for mutually acceptable agreements on other disputed issues, too, on which there is an exchange of opinion between us. These problems have not yet been solved but they wait for an urgent solution which would clear the international atmosphere. We are ready for this.

These are my proposals, Mr. President.

126. Message from President Kennedy to Premier Khrushchev, Concerning the Cuban Crisis*

October 27, 1962

I have read your letter of October 26th with great care and welcomed the statement of your desire to seek a prompt solution to the problem. The first thing that needs to be done, however, is for work to cease on offensive missile bases in Cuba and for all

*Department of State Bulletin, Nov. 12, 1962, p. 743.

weapons systems in Cuba capable of offensive use to be rendered inoperable, under effective United Nations arrangements.

Assuming this is done promptly, I have given my representatives in New York instructions that will permit them to work out this weekend—in cooperation with the Acting Secretary General and your representative—an arrangement for a permanent solution to the Cuban problem along the lines suggested in your letter of October 26th. As I read your letter, the key elements of your proposals—which seem generally acceptable as I understand them—are as follows:

1) You would agree to remove these weapons systems from Cuba under appropriate United Nations observation and supervision; and undertake, with suitable safeguards, to halt the further introduction of such weapons systems into Cuba.

2) We, on our part, would agree—upon the establishment of adequate arrangements through the United Nations to ensure the carrying out and continuation of these commitments—(a) to remove promptly the quarantine measures now in effect and (b) to give assurances against an invasion of Cuba. I am confident that other nations of the Western Hemisphere would be prepared to do likewise.

If you will give your representative similar instructions, there is no reason why we should not be able to complete these arrangements and announce them to the world within a couple of days. The effect of such a settlement on easing world tensions would enable us to work toward a more general arrangement regarding "other armaments", as proposed in your second letter which you made public. I would like to say again that the United States is very much interested in reducing tensions and halting the arms race; and if your letter signifies that you are prepared to discuss a detente affecting NATO and the Warsaw Pact, we are quite prepared to consider with our allies any useful proposals.

But the first ingredient, let me emphasize, is the cessation of work on missile sites in Cuba and measures to render such weapons inoperable, under effective international guarantees. The continuation of this threat, or a prolonging of this discussion concerning Cuba by linking these problems to the broader questions of European and world security, would surely lead to an intensification of the Cuban crisis and a grave risk to the peace of the world. For this reason I hope we can quickly agree along the lines outlined in this letter and in your letter of October 26th.

127. Message from Premier Khrushchev to President Kennedy, Concerning the Cuban Crisis*

October 28, 1962

I have received your message of 27 October. I express my satisfaction and thank you for the sense of proportion you have displayed and for realization of the responsibility which now devolves on you for the preservation of the peace of the world.

I regard with great understanding your concern and the concern of the United States people in connection with the fact that the weapons you describe as offensive

*Department of State Bulletin, Nov. 12, 1962, pp. 743-45.

are formidable weapons indeed. Both you and we understand what kind of weapons these are.

In order to eliminate as rapidly as possible the conflict which endangers the cause of peace, to give an assurance to all people who crave peace, and to reassure the American people, who, I am certain, also want peace, as do the people of the Soviet Union, the Soviet Government, in addition to earlier instructions on the discontinuation of further work on weapons constructions sites, has given a new order to dismantle the arms which you described as offensive, and to crate and return them to the Soviet Union.

Mr. President, I should like to repeat what I had already written to you in my earlier messages—that the Soviet Government has given economic assistance to the Republic of Cuba, as well as arms, because Cuba and the Cuban people were constantly under the continuous threat of an invasion of Cuba.

A piratic vessel had shelled Havana. They say that this shelling was done by irresponsible Cuban emigrees. Perhaps so. However, the question is from where did they shoot. It is a fact that these Cubans have no territory, they are fugitives from their country, and they have no means to conduct military operations.

This means that someone put into their hands these weapons for shelling Havana and for piracy in the Caribbean in Cuban territorial waters. It is impossible in our time not to notice a piratic ship, considering the concentration in the Caribbean of American ships from which everything can be seen and observed.

In these conditions, pirate ships freely roam around and shell Cuba and make piratic attacks on peaceful cargo ships. It is known that they even shelled a British cargo ship. In a word, Cuba was under the continuous threat of aggressive forces, which did not conceal their intention to invade its territory.

The Cuban people want to build their life in their own interests without external interference. This is their right, and they cannot be blamed for wanting to be masters of their own country and disposing of the fruits of their own labor. The threat of invasion of Cuba and all other schemes for creating tension over China are designed to strike the Cuban people with a sense of insecurity, intimidate them, and prevent them from peacefully building their new life.

Mr. President, I should like to say clearly once more that we could not remain indifferent to this. The Soviet Government decided to render assistance to Cuba with means of defense against aggression—only with means for defense purposes. We have supplied the defense means which you describe as offensive means. We have supplied them to prevent an attack on Cuba—to prevent rash acts.

I regard with respect and trust the statement you made in your message of 27 October 1962 that there would be no attack, no invasion of Cuba, and not only on the part of the United States, but also on the part of other nations of the Western Hemisphere, as you said in your same message. Then the motives which induced us to render assistance of such a kind to Cuba disappear.

It is for this reason that we instructed our officers—these means as I had already informed you earlier are in the hands of the Soviet officers—to take appropriate measures to discontinue construction of the aforementioned facilities, to dismantle them, and to return them to the Soviet Union. As I had informed you in the letter of 27 October, we are prepared to reach agreement to enable U.N. representatives to verify the dismantling of these means. Thus in view of the assurances you have given and our instructions on dismantling, there is every condition for eliminating the present conflict.

I note with satisfaction that you have responded to the desire I expressed with regard to elimination of the aforementioned dangerous situation, as well as with regard to providing conditions for a more thoughtful appraisal of the international situation, fraught as it is with great dangers in our age of thermonuclear weapons, rocketry, spaceships, global rockets, and other deadly weapons. All people are interested in insuring peace.

Therefore, vested with trust and great responsibility, we must not allow the situation to become aggravated and must stamp out the centers where a dangerous situation fraught with grave consequences to the cause of peace has arisen. If we, together with you, and with the assistance of other people of good will, succeed in eliminating this tense atmosphere, we should also make certain that no other dangerous conflicts, which could lead to a world nuclear catastrophe, would arise.

In conclusion, I should like to say something about a detente between NATO and the Warsaw Treaty countries that you have mentioned. We have spoken about this long since and are prepared to continue to exchange views on this question with you and to find a reasonable solution.

We should like to continue the exchange of views on the prohibition of atomic and thermonuclear weapons, general disarmament, and other problems relating to the relaxation of international tension.

Although I trust your statement, Mr. President, there are irresponsible people who would like to invade Cuba now and thus touch off a war. If we do take practical steps and proclaim the dismantling and evacuation of the means in question from Cuba, in so doing we, at the same time, want the Cuban people to be certain that we are with them and are not absolving ourselves of responsibility for rendering assistance to the Cuban people.

We are confident that the people of all countries, like you, Mr. President, will understand me correctly. We are not threatening. We want nothing but peace. Our country is now on the upsurge. Our people are enjoying the fruits of their peaceful labor. They have achieved tremendous successes since the October Revolution, and created the greatest material, spiritual, and cultural values. Our people are enjoying these values; they want to continue developing their achievements and insure their further development on the way of peace and social progress by their persistent labor.

I should like to remind you, Mr. President, that military reconnaissance planes have violated the borders of the Soviet Union. In connection with this there have been conflicts between us and notes exchanged. In 1960 we shot down your U-2 plane, whose reconnaissance flight over the USSR wrecked the summit meeting in Paris. At that time, you took a correct position and denounced that criminal act of the former U.S. administration.

But during your term of office as president another violation of our border has occurred, by an American U-2 plane in the Sakhalin area. We wrote you about that violation on 30 August. At that time you replied that that violation had occurred as a result of poor weather, and gave assurances that this would not be repeated. We trusted your assurance, because the weather was indeed poor in that area at that time.

But had not your plane been ordered to fly about our territory, even poor weather could not have brought an American plane into our airspace, hence, the conclusion that this is being done with the knowledge of the Pentagon, which tramples on international norms and violates the borders of other states.

A still more dangerous case occurred on 28 October, when one of your reconnaissance planes intruded over Soviet borders in the Chukotka Peninsula area in the north and flew over our territory. The question is, Mr. President: How should we regard this? What is this, a provocation? One of your planes violates our frontier during this anxious time we are both experiencing, when everything has been put into combat readiness. Is it not a fact that an intruding American plane could be easily taken for a nuclear bomber, which might push us to a fateful step; and all the more so since the U.S. Government and Pentagon long ago declared that you are maintaining a continuous nuclear bomber patrol?

Therefore, you can imagine the responsibility you are assuming; especially now, when we are living through such anxious times.

I should also like to express the following wish; it concerns the Cuban people. You do not have diplomatic relations. But through my officers in Cuba, I have reports that American planes are making flights over Cuba.

We are interested that there should be no war in the world, and that the Cuban people should live in peace. And besides, Mr. President, it is no secret that we have our people on Cuba. Under a treaty with the Cuban Government we have sent there officers, instructors, mostly plain people: specialists, agronomists, zootechnicians, irrigators, land reclamation specialists, plain workers, tractor drivers, and others. We are concerned about them.

I should like you to consider, Mr. President, that violation of Cuban airspace by American planes could also lead to dangerous consequences. And if you do not want this to happen, it would be better if no cause is given for a dangerous situation to arise. We must be careful now and refrain from any steps which would not be useful to the defense of the states involved in the conflict, which could only cause irritation and even serve as a provocation for a fateful step. Therefore, we must display sanity, reason, and refrain from such steps.

We value peace perhaps even more than other peoples because we went through a terrible war with Hitler. But our people will not falter in the face of any test. Our people trust their government, and we assure our people and world public opinion that the Soviet Government will not allow itself to be provoked. But if the provocateurs unleash a war, they will not evade responsibility and the grave consequences a war would bring upon them. But we are confident that reason will triumph, that war will not be unleashed, and peace and the security of the peoples will be insured.

In connection with the current negotiations between Acting Secretary General U Thant and representatives of the Soviet Union, the United States, and the Republic of Cuba, the Soviet Government has sent First Deputy Foreign Minister V. V. Kuznetsov to New York to help U Thant in his noble efforts aimed at eliminating the present dangerous situation.

Respectfully yours,

128. Message from President Kennedy to Premier Khrushchev, Concerning the Cuban Crisis*

October 28, 1962

I am replying at once to your broadcast message of October twenty-eight, even though the official text has not yet reached me, because of the great importance I attach to moving forward promptly to the settlement of the Cuban crisis. I think that you and I, with our heavy responsibilities for the maintenance of peace, were aware that developments were approaching a point where events could have become unmanageable. So welcome this message and consider it an important contribution to peace.

The distinguished efforts of Acting Secretary General U Thant have greatly facilitated both our tasks. I consider my letter to you of October twenty-seventh and your reply of today as firm undertakings on the part of both our governments which should be promptly carried out. I hope that the necessary measures can at once be taken through the United Nations, as your message says, so that the United States in turn will be able to remove the quarantine measures now in effect. I have already made arrangements to report all these matters to the Organization of American States, whose members share a deep interest in a genuine peace in the Caribbean area.

You referred in your letter to a violation of your frontier by an American aircraft in the area of the Chukotsk Peninsula. I have learned that this plane, without arms or photographic equipment, was engaged in an air sampling mission in connection with your nuclear tests. Its course was direct from Eielson Air Force Base in Alaska to the North Pole and return. In turning south, the pilot made a serious navigational error which carried him over Soviet territory. He immediately made an emergency call on open radio for navigational assistance and was guided back to his home base by the most direct route. I regret this incident and will see to it that every precaution is taken to prevent recurrence.

Mr. Chairman, both of our countries have great unfinished tasks and I know that your people as well as those of the United States can ask for nothing better than to pursue them free from the fear of war. Modern science and technology have given us the possibility of making labor fruitful beyond anything that could have been dreamed of a few decades ago.

I agree with you that we must devote urgent attention to the problem of disarmament, as it relates to the whole world and also to critical areas. Perhaps now, as we step back from danger, we can together make real progress in this vital field. I think we should give priority to questions relating to the proliferation of nuclear weapons, on earth and in outer space, and to the great effort for a nuclear test ban. But we should also work hard to see if wider measures of disarmament can be agreed and put into operation at an early date. The United States government will be prepared to discuss these questions urgently, and in a constructive spirit, at Geneva or elsewhere.

*Department of State Bulletin, Nov. 12, 1962, pp. 745-46.

129. *Presidents of the Central American Republics,*
     Panama and the United States, Declaration of Central
     *America**

March 19, 1963

The Presidents of the Republics of Central America and Panama are determined to improve the well-being of their peoples, and are aware that such a task demands a dynamic economic and social development program based on the carefully planned use of human, natural and financial resources. It also depends on important changes of the economic, social and administrative structure, within the framework of the principles that govern our democratic institutions. They have met with the President of the United States of America in San José, Costa Rica, to review the difficulties which impede the achievement of these objectives as well as the progress thus far made in the Isthmus since the integration programs began and since the Alliance for Progress was jointly established by the Republics of the Hemisphere in August 1961.

Following an analysis of the situation, the Presidents of the Republics of Central America, convinced that the best hope for the development of the region is through economic integration, and bearing in mind the extraordinary efforts made toward this end in the last decade and of the importance of accelerating over-all economic growth, pledge to their peoples:

—To accelerate establishment of a customs union to perfect the functioning of the Central American Common Market;

—To formulate and implement national economic and social development plans, coordinating them at the Central American level, and progressively to carry out regional planning for the various sectors of the economy;

—To establish a monetary union and common fiscal, monetary and social policies within the program of economic integration;

—To cooperate in programs to improve the prices of primary export commodities;

—To complete as soon as possible the reforms needed to achieve the objectives set forth in the Act of Bogotá and the Charter of Punta del Este especially in the fields of agriculture, taxation, education, public administration, and social welfare;

—To take the above measures with a view to achieving the creation of a Central American Economic Community which will establish relationships with other nations or regional groups having similar objectives.

The Central American Presidents affirm that the economic integration movement in itself constitutes an effort which is laying the groundwork for regional planning in which sectoral plans of common interest to the Isthmian Republics serve as a point of departure. Their governments have already taken measures to coordinate national plans so that their execution will aid rather than impede the achievement of the objectives of the economic integration program. It is intended that the first global plan for harmonious regional development be presented as soon as possible for evaluation in accordance with the procedures set forth in the Charter of Punta del Este. Meanwhile, the Central American Presidents declare their resolve to proceed immediately with their sectoral plans and with projects of interest to the Isthmus. The President of the

**Department of State Bulletin*, Apr. 8, 1963, pp. 515-17.

United States agrees to consider a long-term loan to enable the appropriate Central American regional organizations, principally the Central American Bank for Economic Integration, to conduct economic feasibility surveys relative to this program of regional development.

The Presidents of Central America reaffirm their hope that the Republic of Panama will participate more closely in the economic integration movement, and the President of Panama declares that his Government fully reaffirms its support of the program of Central American economic integration. He further declares that his Government is prepared to initiate immediate negotiations with the Governments of the general treaty of economic integration as a whole with a view to concluding a special agreement to facilitate the association of his country with this program.

The President of the United States is impressed by the determination of the Presidents of the Central American Republics to move as rapidly as possible toward the integration of the economies of their countries, and of their intention to formulate a regional economic development plan within which national plans would be coordinated, and he believes that the coordination of their respective monetary, fiscal, economic and social policies is a great step forward in the achievement of this objective as well as toward the achievement of the goals set forth in the Charter of Punta del Este.

The President of the United States is prepared to offer the greatest cooperation in the preparation and implementation of the regional and national development projects of Central America and Panama and declares that his government will intensify its joint efforts with the governments and appropriate regional organizations in order to extend to them increased technical and financial assistance for this purpose within the framework of the broad regional program entitled "Joint Exposition of the Presidents of Central America" and the development plan being prepared by Panama.

To this end he proposes a fund for Central American economic integration, to be made available through the Central American Bank for Economic Integration, to which the United States would make an immediate substantial initial contribution, to assist in carrying out regional development projects in accordance with various sectoral plans now being developed by the regional organizations.

For the longer term, he also declares that as soon as the Central American Republics have formulated an over-all regional development plan, and as soon as this plan has been evaluated favorably in accordance with the procedures established in the Charter of Punta del Este, the United States will enlarge and expand its participation in the fund and will work with the Central American countries in obtaining other Free World resources so that the agreed plan can be effectively implemented.

The Presidents have discussed the fundamental importance to economic development of a vigorous and freely-competitive private sector, and declare their intention of taking the necessary steps to encourage private investment which is prepared to accept the normal responsibilities compatible with the development of a modern economy. These measures include establishment of regional trade and promotion offices for the specific purpose of attracting private foreign investment. They also agree that development banks or corporations should be established in each country as soon as possible to provide credit on reasonable terms for the growth of private industry, the President of the United States offering financial assistance to their operation.

Concurrently they agree that economic and social conditions should be created to assure labor of an improved living standard through a better distribution of national income. Furthermore they agree to encourage and support free democratic labor organizations as a means of contributing toward greater worker participation in the common effort on behalf of the general welfare.

The Presidents also agree that opportunities should be given to the people of Central America to build and purchase their homes. There exist in Central America national savings and loan institutions which have been assisted under the Alliance for Progress, and others are about to be created. In order to give further support for these national efforts, the Presidents of Central America suggest that a regional home loan department, which would be a secondary source of home mortgage funds, should be created as a division within the Central American Bank for Economic Integration and the President of the United States agrees to offer technical and financial assistance to it.

The Isthmian Presidents indicate that Central American institutions should be strengthened as much as possible to enable them to play a major role in training the personnel who will be needed to put into effect the plans for integration of the Isthmus. A large part of the responsibility for training will devolve on the Superior Council of Central American Universities (CSUCA). Recognizing, moreover, that trained manpower at all levels is needed for economic development, they agree to the proposal of the President of the United States to establish a multi-million dollar scholarship fund for vocational training in agriculture and in industry for young people of outstanding ability who can not afford the normal expenses of such training, to which the United States will offer substantial financial assistance.

The Presidents note the primary role of coffee in the economies of Central America and the importance of the International Coffee Agreement for the achievement of stable and remunerative prices.

They reiterate the intention of their governments to fully support the agreement so that it will serve as an effective instrument to improve the earnings of exporting countries from coffee and to promote their economic development.

Other primary commodity problems exist and the Isthmian Presidents will hand to President Kennedy studies on these problems.

President Kennedy agrees he will have them reviewed immediately on his return to Washington.

The Presidents, notwithstanding the fact that present conditions are favorable to undertake a solution of the economic and social problems of the Isthmus through joint action of the countries of the area, believe that all of them are faced with an externally provoked political problem, which by its very nature can imperil the exercise of representative democracy and the normal development of the plans in which their respective governments are engaged to attain as rapidly as possible the highest levels of economic and social justice and to bring to full realization the plans for Central American integration. Consequently, the Presidents declare that in order to carry out their programs for social and economic betterment, it is essential to reinforce the measures to meet subversive aggression originating in the focal points of Communist agitation which Soviet imperialism may maintain in Cuba or in any other place in America.

The Presidents note that the Council of the Organization of American States is actively engaged in maintaining vigilance over the continued intervention of Sino-Soviet powers in this Hemisphere as requested by the Eighth Meeting of Consultation of Foreign Ministers. They express special interest in early completion by the Council of the OAS of the studies on Castro-Communist subversion in the Hemisphere, and particularly in early action by the Council on recommendations to the governments for counteracting those activities in these areas.

The Presidents agree that Ministers of Government of the seven countries should meet as soon as possible to develop and put into immediate effect common measures to restrict the movement of their nationals to and from Cuba, and the flow of materiel, propaganda and funds from that country.

This meeting will take action, among other things, to secure stricter travel and passport controls, including appropriate limitations in passports and other travel documents on travel to Cuba. Cooperative arrangements among not only the countries meeting here but also among all OAS members will have to be sought to restrict more effectively not only these movements of people for subversive purposes but also to prevent insofar as possible the introduction of money, propaganda, materials, and arms, arrangements for additional sea and air surveillance and interception within territorial waters will be worked out with special cooperation from the United States.

In addition to these measures, a more rapid and complete exchange of intelligence information on the movement of people, propaganda, money and arms between Cuba and our countries is to be developed by the Meeting of Ministers.

The Presidents voice their deep sympathy for the people of Cuba, and reaffirm their conviction that Cuba soon will join the family of free nations. The Presidents recall how, in 1959, the Cuban people were fired with the hope of a purely Cuban revolution that was to bring them freedom and social justice; honest government and free elections; fair sharing of goods; opportunities for all; more schools and jobs, better health and housing, and constructive land reform not collectivization of the land. In sum, a progressive republic which, in the words of Martí, would be *"con todos y para todos"*. The Presidents declare that they have no doubt that the genuine Cuban revolution will live again, and its betrayers will fall into the shadows of history, and the martyred people of the oppressed isle of the Caribbean will be free from foreign Communist domination, free to choose for themselves the kind of government they wish to have, and free to join their brothers of the Hemisphere in the common undertaking to secure for each individual the liberty, dignity, and well-being which are the objectives of all free societies.

Finally the Presidents solemnly reaffirm their adherence to the principles established by the Treaty of Reciprocal Assistance of Rio de Janeiro, the Charter of the OAS, in the Act of Bogotá and in the Charter of Punta del Este.

130. Statement by Secretary Rusk on the Stoppage of Aid to the Dominican Republic and Honduras*

October 4, 1963

We view the recent military coups in the Dominican Republic and Honduras with the utmost gravity. The establishment and maintenance of representative and constitutional government is an essential element in the Alliance for Progress. Stable and effective government, responsive to the popular will, is a critical factor in the attainment of social and economic progress.

Under existing conditions in the Dominican Republic and Honduras there is no opportunity for effective collaboration by the United States under the Alliance for Progress or for normalization of diplomatic relations. Accordingly, we have stopped all economic and military aid to these countries and have commenced orderly reassignment of the personnel involved.

131. Press Conference Statement by President Kennedy on the Recognition of Governments Established by Military Coups†

October 9, 1963

Q. Mr. President, was Assistant Secretary Martin's statement cleared with you, and if so, does it represent a reversal of your policy on dictatorships in Latin America?

The President. No, I was informed generally of what Mr. Martin was saying, and in fact, I re-read it this afternoon. In the first place, our policy is not reversed. If attention could be drawn to Secretary Rusk's statement of Friday evening in regard to the coups in the Dominican Republic and Honduras, we made it very clear that we are opposed to an interruption of the constitutional system by a military coup, not only because we are all committed under the Alliance for Progress to democratic government and progress and progressive government, but also because of course dictatorships are the seedbeds from which communism ultimately springs up.

So we are opposed to military coups, and it is for that reason that we have broken off our relations with the Dominican Republic and Honduras. It is for that reason that we attempted to work on the situation in Peru, which led, I think in part because of the American effort, mostly because of the Peruvian people's effort, to free elections.

Mr. Martin was merely attempting to explain some of the problems in Latin America, why coups take place, and what problems they present us with. But we are opposed to coups, because we think that they are defeating, self-defeating, and defeating for the hemisphere, and we are using our influence and I am sure the other countries of the hemisphere are using their influence in those areas where coups have taken place to provide for an orderly restoration of constitutional processes.

Q. Beyond the immediate action, sir, in relation to the Dominican Republic and Honduras, does the United States plan any general enunciation of policy in regard to

*Department of State Bulletin, Oct. 21, 1963, p. 624.
†United States Government Printing Office, Public Papers of the Presidents, Washington, D.C., 1964, pp. 770-71.

military regimes, or does it contemplate asking any general hemispheric action in regard to this?

The President. Well, I have just described, I have just attempted to describe what our policy is towards coups. And as far as our national policy, it was described on Friday, with the withdrawal of our diplomatic—our Ambassadors, our aid, our military assistance, and all the rest. So I think we have made very clear our policy and our interest in providing for a return to, as I have said, constitutional processes in those two countries.

We are working with the other members of the Organization of American States so that together we can bring about a return to order in those countries and a return to peaceful procedures. That is the policy of the United States. I have just enunciated it again.

Q. I was asking specifically, sir, whether the United States contemplated any broader hemispheric action in terms of general action by the OAS in this respect.

The President. Not at this time. This is a matter which I think all the other countries of the OAS have to decide what they are going to do. I think the United States has made its position very clear.

Q. Mr. President, are you satisfied in retrospect that the United States did all it could, short of the use of force, to prevent the Dominican and Honduran coups?

The President. Yes, I am. I have looked over the conversations, the minutes, of cables and so on, and I think we did. This idea that we ought to send the United States Marines into Honduras, which, of course, we couldn't have done under the conditions, because of the time gap, I think is a very serious mistake. That is not the way, in my opinion, and I think Mr. Martin was attempting to explain that that is not the way for democracy to flourish.

So I think we did the best we could. It may be possible to always do better, but we did the best we could, and we are going to continue to do so. . . .

132. Resolution Creating the Inter-American Committee on the Alliance for Progress (CIAP)*

November 15, 1963

. . . . *Whereas:*

The First Annual Meeting of the Inter-American Economic and Social Council adopted Resolution A-8, calling for a study of the inter-American system in order to ascertain whether its present structure meets the requirements of the Alliance for Progress program;

Resolution A-8 begins by recognizing "that the inter-American system as presently constituted, was in the main established prior to the Alliance for Progress, and, in consequence, may not possess a type of structure permitting of achievement of the objectives of the Charter of Punta del Este in the dynamic and efficient way called for";

That resolution charged two outstanding Latin Americans with studying the struc-

*OAS, Official Records, OEA Sec. H. 5 (English). (São Paulo, Brazil, Oct. 29–Nov. 9, 1963). Washington, D.C., Pan American Union, 1964.

ture and activities of those organizations and agencies of the inter-American system that have responsibilities in regard to the Alliance, and empowered them to make, if necessary, recommendations regarding those structural and procedural changes that are required in the system and in its various organs in order that the Alliance for Progress may take on the efficiency and the dynamic qualities called for by the Charter of Punta del Este;

The Council of the Organizacion, after approving resolution A-8, entrusted the former presidents of Brazil and Colombia, Juscelino Kubitschek and Alberto Lleras, with the preparation of a report and conclusions, to be brought to the attention of the governments of the member states and submitted to the Inter-American Economic and Social Council for consideration, if need be, at a special meeting;

Former presidents Kubitschek and Lleras accepted and carried out the mandate of the Inter-American Economic and Social Council, and rendered their conclusions in separate reports presented to the Council of the Organization, for transmittal to the governments at the Special Meeting held on June 15, 1963;

The reports of former presidents Kubitschek and Lleras, which have been presented to the Second Annual Meetings of the Inter-American Economic and Social Council for consideration, are in agreement regarding the need to create a permanent, multilateral body representing the Alliance for Progress, and for this purpose proposed the creation of an inter-American development committee;

The recommendations of the former presidents, which have been examined by the Inter-American Economic and Social Council, suggest ways of organizing the proposed new body so that the Alliance for Progress may have multilateral representation and possess functional mechanisms and sufficient authority to permit it to discharge its responsibilities with the dynamic qualities and efficiency required; and

Consideration has been given to the views expressed in this regard in the Memorandum of the General Secretariat of the Organizacion of American States (Doc. OEA/Ser.H/X.4, CIES/344), the Report of the Panel of Experts (Doc. OEA/Ser.H/X.4, CIES/370), and the Observations of the Board of Executive Directors of the Inter-American Development Bank.

The Second Annual Meeting of the Inter-American Economic and Social Council at the Ministerial Level,

Resolves:

To create an Inter-American Committee on the Alliance for Progress (ICAP), in accordance with the following provisions:

I. Nature and Purpose

1. The Inter-American Committee on the Alliance for Progress (ICAP) shall be a special, permanent committee of the Inter-American Economic and Social Council for the purpose of representing multilaterally the Alliance for Progress and, in the same way, coordinating and promoting its implementation in accordance with the Charter of Punta del Este, and of carrying out the mandates of this resolution and those it receives from the Council of the Organization of American States or the Inter-American Economic and Social Council.

II. Duties and Functions

2. The Inter-American Committee on the Alliance for Progress shall carry out its duties and functions in keeping with the general orientation and lines of policy established by the Inter-American Economic and Social Council in its meetings at the ministerial level.

3. To fulfill the purpose set forth in the preceding chapter, the Inter-American Committee on the Alliance for Progress shall have the following duties and functions:

a. To study the problems that may arise in connection with the Alliance for Progress and to resolve them or suggest solutions to the competent authority in each case, in accordance with the standards and policies established therefor.

b. To promote continuing improvements in the process of giving the Alliance a more multilateral character.

c. To make an annual estimate of the financing actually needed for Latin American development and of the total funds that may be available from the various domestic and external sources.

d. To make a continuing review of national and regional plans, steps taken, and efforts made within the framework of the Alliance, and to make specific recommendations to the members of the Alliance and to the regional organizations in the Hemisphere concerning those plans, steps and efforts. In discharging this duty, consideration shall be given to the evaluation reports of the ad hoc committees set up under the Charter of Punta del Este or those deriving from steps taken pursuant to paragraph 9 of this resolution.

e. On the basis of the estimates referred to in paragraph 3.c and the review and the recommendations referred to in paragraph 3.d:

(i) To prepare and present proposals on the amount and sort of domestic resources each country would have to utilize to achieve the objectives of the Alliance, and

(ii) To prepare and present annual proposals for determining the distribution among the several countries of public funds under the Alliance for Progress, referred to in Chapter V.7 of Title II of the Charter of Punta del Este, which contribute to the external financing of general plans and specific programs for the development of the Latin American countries, giving special consideration to the progress which, in line with its basic characteristics, each country makes toward reaching the objectives of the Charter of Punta del Este, and being especially mindful of Title I.1 of the Charter.

f. To cooperate with each country and with the Inter-American Development Bank or other financial agents which the country may designate, in their negotiations with governments and with any other source of financing for the purpose of obtaining the external assistance required to finance their development programs and plans.

g. To coordinate those efforts within the Alliance which require multilateral action, such as economic integration, foreign trade policies of the area, and, in general those activities which are related to the economic and social development of Latin America and which are not specifically assigned to any other body.

h. To obtain information on the progress made in multilateral investment programs for integration purposes and, upon request by the countries concerned, to help in obtaining financing for such investments; in accordance with established criteria and procedures.

i. To coordinate the work of the special committees of the Inter-American Economic and Social Council and to decide upon the necessity for their meetings, which shall be convoked by the Chairman of the Inter-American Committee on the Alliance for Progress.

j. To review the budget of the Pan American Union for the Alliance for Progress, the budget of the Program of Technical Cooperation, and that of any other specific multilateral fund, as prepared by the General Secretariat for approval by the Inter-American Economic and Social Council.

k. To review the program and budget prepared by the Secretary General with respect to the regular operations of the Secretariat within the purview of the Inter-American Economic and Social Council—including the items for permanent professional and administrative personnel; for the operation of the Inter-American Economic and Social Council, the Inter-American Committee on the Alliance for Progress, and the Panel of Experts; and for overhead directly related to these operations—for approval by the Inter-American Economic and Social Council, in accordance with Article 19.f of its Statutes.

1. To establish its Regulations and the rules of procedure it considers advisable for the performance of its functions.

4. The member states agree that, when providing financial and technical assistance through their own agencies and when instructing their representatives in the various international organizations that provide such assistance, they shall give special consideration to the recommendations of the Inter-American Committee on the Alliance for Progress, in accordance with paragraph 3. e. (ii), regarding the distribution of external public funds under the Alliance for Progress.

III. Membership and Operation

5. The Inter-American Committee on the Alliance for Progress shall be composed of a chairman and seven representatives of the member states of the Organization of American States. Each representative shall be entitled to one vote.

The chairman shall be elected for a three-year period and shall be eligible for re-election for one term only.

The representatives of the countries, proposed thereby, shall be appointed by the Inter-American Economic and Social Council for a two-year period, on the basis of the same distribution agreed upon for electing the Executive Directors of the Inter-American Development Bank (IDB) at the election immediately prior to each period. Such distribution shall not apply to the five countries of Central America, which, as a group, shall propose one representative.

At the time of the first appointment, three of the six members who represent the Latin American countries shall be selected by lot to serve for one year.

A member of the Inter-American Committee on the Alliance for Progress may be re-elected only in the event that the countries which proposed their appointment indicate to the Inter-American Economic and Social Council that this be done.

When in the exercise of its functions the Inter-American Committee on the Alliance for Progress is to consider matters specifically concerning a given country, it shall invite that country to appoint an ad hoc representative.

6. The Secretary General of the Organization of American States (OAS), the President of the Inter-American Development Bank (IDB), the Coordinator of the Panel of Experts, and the Principal Director of the Economic Commission for Latin America (ECLA) shall serve as permanent advisors to the Inter-American Committee on the Alliance for Progress and in that capacity may attend its meetings.

7. The Panel of Experts shall be the technical arm of the Inter-American Committee on the Alliance for Progress in carrying out its functions of evaluating development plans and programs, in the spirit of the provisions of Title II, Chapter V.3 of the Charter of Punta del Este, and, in general, it may be consulted by the Inter-American Committee on the Alliance for Progress in relation to other matters relating to its functions. The Inter-American Development Bank shall be the technical arm of the Committee in matters concerning the financing of Latin American development.

The Inter-American Committee on the Alliance for Progress may request the technical advise of the Latin American Free Trade Association (LAFTA) and the Permanent Secretariat of the General Treaty on Central American Economic Integration (SIECA) on matters of economic integration.

8. In conformity with existing provisions, the Inter-American Committee on the Alliance for Progress may invite representatives of governmental and non-governmental agencies, who are recognized international authorities and who may have a particular interest in matters to be taken up at given meetings, to attend these meetings as observers. The Organization for Economic Cooperation and Development (OECD) and the European Economic Community (EEC) shall be among the entities to be so invited.

9. Those countries which have only sectoral programs and those which have national development plans but do not request the formation of an ad hoc committee may come to an agreement with the Inter-American Committee on the Alliance for Progress as to the best way of evaluating their programs or plans in consonance with the aims of the Charter of Punta del Este.

10. In order to ensure more frequent information on the progress of the activities of the Inter-American Committee on the Alliance for Progress, the Chairman of the Inter-American Economic and Social Council, pursuant to Article 20 of its Statutes, shall convoke special meetings of the Inter-American Economic and Social Council at the ministerial level, when such shall be considered necessary.

11. The Inter-American Committee on the Alliance for Progress shall submit to the Inter-American Economic and Social Council for consideration an annual report on the fulfillment of its mandate and the draft resolutions that it may agree upon.

IV. Chairman

12. The Inter-American Economic and Social Council at the Ministerial Level shall elect an outstanding personality of the nationality of one of its members to be chairman of the Inter-American Committee on the Alliance for Progress. In addition to the functions and powers normal to the position, and to those which may be entrusted to him by the Inter-American Economic and Social Council and, on occasion, by the

Council of the Organization of American States, the Chairman shall be the permanent representative of the Inter-American Committee on the Alliance for Progress in actions required for rapid and effective execution of its decisions.

In the discharge of his duties, the Chairman shall be responsible only to the Inter-American committee on the Alliance for Progress and the Inter-American Economic and Social Council.

The Chairman shall take office at a special ceremony in the presence of the Council of the Organization of American States.

V. Secretariat and Headquarters

13. The Executive Secretary of the Inter-American Economic and Social Council shall be the Secretary of the Inter-American Committee on the Alliance for Progress. Secretariat services shall be provided by the General Secretariat. Whenever the Chairman of the Inter-American Committee on the Alliance for Progress considers it indispensable to enlist the services of additional personnel in order to carry out the functions of the Committee more efficiently, he may request the Secretary General of the Organization of American States to take the necessary steps to appoint suitable persons.

14. The Inter-American Committee on the Alliance for Progress shall have its headquarters in Washington, D.C., United States of America, but it may hold meetings in any other city in the member states of the Organization of American States.

133. Report from the State Department on the Recognition of the Governments of the Dominican Republic and Honduras*

December 14, 1963

The United States on December 14 recognized the Governments of the Dominican Republic and Honduras, after consultation with other hemisphere governments.

Both the Honduran and the Dominican regimes have issued decrees setting forth election timetables for return to representative and constitutional governments. Both regimes have given public assurances of respect for civil liberties, freedom of action for political parties, and that international obligations will be fulfilled.

In Honduras a decree law was issued November 22 creating an electoral commission representing major parties and civic sectors. It calls for preparation of a new electoral law by March 1, 1964, and revision of voter registrations by January 1, 1965. A constituent assembly election will be held February 16, 1965, and the assembly will be installed on March 16, 1965, at which time the supreme power of the government passes to the assembly. The electoral commission was sworn in on December 2 and has held several meetings.

In the Dominican Republic, a decree law was issued on November 26 setting forth a schedule for five elections, the first to be held between September 1 and November 30

*Department of State Bulletin, Dec. 30, 1963, pp. 997-98.

next year for minor local officials and to serve also as a voter census. Municipal elections will follow on January 15, 1965, a constituent assembly election on March 1, 1965, and congressional elections on June 24, 1965. Presidential elections are scheduled for July 15, 1965, and the elected government will assume office on August 16, 1965.

A new Central Electoral Board was established November 8 to preside over the electoral process. On December 6 a decree was issued requiring legally recognized parties to submit draft constitutions at least 90 days before the constitutional assembly elections are held in order to qualify for participating in these elections.

134. Note from the Government of the Republic of Panama, to the U.S. Government Breaking Off Diplomatic Relations*

January 10, 1964

In the name of the Government and people of Panama, I present to your excellency a formal protest for the unmerciful acts of aggression carried out by the armed forces of the United States of America stationed in the Canal Zone against the territorial integrity of the republic and its undefended civil population during last night and this morning.

The unjustifiable aggression to which I have referred, without parallel in the history of relations between our two countries, has brought to us Panamanians, up to now, a tragic toll of 17 deaths and more than 200 injured. In addition, the buildings and property situated in certain sectors of the City of Panama adjacent to the Canal Zone have suffered damage of major consequence as a result of the controllable acts of aggression by the North American forces.

The inhuman actions—such as that of the police of the Canal Zone, and later the North American armed forces that attacked a group of young students of both sexes that totaled no more than 50, which attempted to display in a calm manner the national flag in that strip of Panamanian territory—are lacking in any justification.

This incomparable incident has revived chapters of the past that we believed would never again occur in American lands.

The acts of violence that motivate this note cannot be ignored nor tolerated by Panama. My Government, conscious of its responsibility, will make use of all measures at its disposal, of those of the American regional system and international organizations with an end to achieve a just indemnification for the dead and for the injured and for the property destroyed.

My Government seeks the application of sanctions for those responsible for such damages and the guarantee that in the future neither the armed forces stationed in the Canal Zone nor the civilian North American population residing in that section of national territory will ever again unloose similar actions of aggression against a weak and unarmed people anxious to come to the defense of its inalienable rights.

*Jules Davids, ed., *Documents on American Foreign Relations, 1964*, (New York, 1965), pp. 301-02.

Finally, I desire to inform your excellency, that due to the events to which I have referred, the Government of Panama considers its diplomatic relations with your illustrious Government broken, and as a result has issued instructions to its Ambassador, Augusto G. Arango, for his immediate return to his country.

I take this opportunity to manifest to your excellency the guarantee of my highest consideration.

135. Communiqué from the Inter-American Peace Committee, on the Panama—United States Crisis*

January 10, 1964

His Excellency the President of the Inter-American Peace Committee convened a special meeting today at 3 p.m. at the joint request of the Governments of Panama and the United States.

The Committee forms part of the inter-American system for the preservation of peace and it met in order to consider the events which had occurred in Panama during the night of 9 to 10 January. It agreed to take up the problem immediately and, with the consent of the interested parties, it decided to study the case and to go to Panama the same evening in order to investigate the situation and recommend measures for the settlement of the dispute.

The Committee, which is composed of Argentina, Colombia, the Dominican Republic, the United States, and Venezuela—the presiding country—decided to request the Organization of American States, under articles 10 and 11 of the Committee's Statutes, to designate a substitute for the United States, which is a party to the dispute.

136. White House Statement on the Panamanian Crisis†

January 10, 1964

The President has this morning reviewed the situation in Panama with his senior advisers. He has ordered the Assistant Secretary of State, Mr. [Thomas C.] Mann, to proceed at once to the Canal Zone. The United States Government greatly regrets the tragic loss of life of Panamanians and Americans. The President has given most earnest instructions to General [Andrew P.] O'Meara, Commander in Chief, Southern Command (CINCSOUTH), to do all that is within his power to restore and to maintain peace and safety in the Canal Zone.

The President has noted President Chiari's appeal to the citizens of Panama to join in the restoration of peace, and the President is making a similar appeal to the residents of the Canal Zone. The path to a settlement can only be through peace and understanding and not through violence.

*Department of State Bulletin, Feb. 3, 1964, p. 152.
†Department of State Bulletin, Feb. 3, 1964, p. 152.

137. Statement by Ambassador Stevenson, to the U.N. Security Council on the Complaint of the Republic of Panama Against the United States*

January 10, 1964

I must confess that it is with a very heavy heart and deep distress that I speak here tonight. The incidents of yesterday and today in the Canal Zone and in the Republic of Panama are a matter of extreme concern to the United States Government.

My Government and the people of this country are distressed at the tragic and the needless loss of human life—both Panamanian and American. The riots and the violence are of special regret since they blot the record of the long and friendly and improving relationship between our Government and that of Panama. Indeed, with the signature of a new treaty between our Governments in 1955 and the continuing discussions which have taken place between our officials since that time, we had embarked on a new, and a more satisfactory, phase of our historical and friendly relationship.

My Government is doing everything humanly possible to restore the situation. Before noon today President Johnson telephoned President Chiari to discuss the situation, and the two Presidents agreed that there had to be a stop to violence in the Canal Zone.

President Johnson also has given more emphatic instructions to United States authorities to do everything within their power to restore and maintain peace and order in the Canal Zone. United States officials are exerting every effort to assure that restraint and good judgment are exercised.

In addition, to prevent further incidents, all of the residents of the Canal Zone not engaged in official duties have been ordered to remain in their homes.

I devoutly hope that the Panamanian authorities are being equally vigorous in their efforts to restrain lawlessness and to maintain order and prevent further incidents of violence and bloodshed.

I also hope that efforts by any lawless elements hostile both to Panama and the United States to exploit this situation for their own special purposes will be fully exposed and thwarted.

As further evidence of our concern and of our desire to do the utmost to restore order and to contribute to a peaceful adjustment of the problem, President Johnson dispatched this morning several of our most expert and competent officials to the area, headed by the Assistant Secretary of State for Latin American Affairs.

In addition, Mr. President, the Organization of American States has moved with great rapidity. This afternoon the Inter-American Peace Commission of the OAS met at the request of Panama and of the United States to consider the situation. The Commission unanimously agreed, pursuant to the request of both Governments to go to Panama immediately to ascertain the facts. I understand that this group leaves for Panama at midnight tonight. Under these circumstances, Mr. President, I will not attempt to give the Council a detailed account of the facts surrounding these riots as we understand them. It is precisely for this purpose that the Inter-American Peace Commission is going to Panama.

*Department of State Bulletin, Feb. 3, 1964, pp. 153-55.

That the distinguished Ambassador of Panama presumes to make charges of aggression, I must say, surprises me, because his knowledge of the facts can be no better than mine. But from what I already do know, I can categorically deny his allegations of aggression by the United States. The incidents of violence, according to our information, started when a group of Panamanian high school students were permitted by United States zone authorities to move peacefully to the Balboa High School within the zone for the purpose of raising the Panamanian flag. On the way out of the zone some of these students got unruly and damaged property by throwing stones and by other means. The zone police continued to escort them to the zonal boundary, and most of the students peacefully withdrew. Subsequently, however, disorderly crowds of people came back into the zone, destroying property and attacking American citizens. At the same time rioters within Panama itself attacked United States citizens and property. These lawless assaults were accompanied by sniper fire across the boundary and the use of Molotov cocktails, those familiar stimulants of mob violence.

The zone police, who were few in number, attempted to stop a further penetration into the Canal Zone by the use of tear gas and eventually by small-caliber fire when it became necessary to protect human life. But still the police were unable to restore order. The Acting Governor then requested the Commander of the Army forces to assume responsibility for the protection of the zone. And thereupon Army elements took up positions along the boundaries of the zone to prevent further incursions from outside.

United States Army forces, I am informed, have acted with the greatest restraint. In fact, they have already suffered many casualties without using the full means of defense available to them.

While I do not purport to know all of the facts—any more, I believe, than does Ambassador [Aquilino] Boyd—I do know that there is no evidence that either the police of the zone or the United States Army ever went outside the zone, that their only use of firearms was inside of the zone to protect the lives and property of American citizens residing there against an onrushing crowd of several thousand and against snipers. And yet my distinguished friend, the Ambassador of Panama, calls this act of self-defense within the boundaries of the Canal Zone an act of aggression.

I mention these facts, as they are reported to me, not as a complete account of these unhappy events but only to show that, instead of aggression by the United States against Panama, the fact is that only the minimum measures have been taken to insure the safety of the zone and its inhabitants.

Moreover, it was the United States that proposed that the Inter-American Peace Commission should move at once to ascertain the facts. We were pleased that the Panamanian Government agreed that this would be the proper step. There is, I am informed, very good cooperation between the Panamanian National Guard and the United States forces, both in controlling sniping and in safeguarding the lives of American citizens.

Looking beyond this tragic day, Mr. President, it is our earnest hope that this episode will constitute only a temporary obstacle in the continuing development of friendly relations between my country and the Republic of Panama. The way to resolve differences, as the Presidents of our two Republics have agreed, is not by violence but by peaceful means. We are ready through direct discussions with the

Panamanian Government to try to resolve such differences as may exist. And, indeed, I am advised that the Assistant Secretary of State for Latin American Affairs and the Secretary of the United States Army [Cyrus R. Vance] have met with the President of Panama this very evening.

Mr. President, we might well, given these circumstances, ask ourselves what the Security Council itself should do with this problem. I believe there will be general agreement around this table that, in view of the fact that the Inter-American Peace Commission is about to leave for Panama, the problem should continue to be pursued in the regional forum which was established precisely to deal with situations arising among states in the Western Hemisphere.

The United Nations Charter, both in article 33 and in article 52, provides for pacific settlement of local disputes through regional agencies as does the Charter of the Organization of American States in article 20. Without derogating from the responsibilities of the Council, we believe that such local disputes can most effectively be dealt with through regional procedures. The decisive and rapid action of the Organization of American States this afternoon indeed shows that this is the case.

I would conclude merely by saying once more how deeply my Government regrets that such a tragic incident has taken place to mar the cordial relations with a good neighbor. There is no question about the old affinity of the people of my country for the people of Panama, and I am confident that transcending this one unhappy chapter there will be a progressive development of cordial relations between our two Governments.

The United States–Panamanian treaty of friendship and cooperation of 1936 defined the overriding goal of our relations as "a perfect, firm and inviolable peace and sincere friendship between the United States of America and the Republic of Panama and between their citizens."

Mr. President, my Government continues unreservedly to adhere to that goal.

138. Statement by Ambassador Stevenson, to the U.N. Security Council on the Complaint of the Republic of Panama Against the United States*

January 10, 1964

Regarding the proposal by our distinguished colleague, the representative of Brazil, that the President of the Security Council address an appeal to the Governments of the United States and of Panama to impose the utmost restraint upon the military forces and civilians of both countries in order to bring an end to the disorder and violence, we welcome this suggestion and think that such an appeal coming from the Security Council would be helpful. I can assure the members of the Security Council that the United States will comply in letter and spirit with any such representation.

And we would respectfully suggest that in his appeal the President of the Security Council take note of the action already taken by the Organization of American States.

Further, Mr. President, I also agree with what the delegate of Brazil said that no further action or resolution of the Security Council is necessary at this time.

*Department of State Bulletin, Feb. 3, 1964, p. 155.

139. Letter from Enrique Tejera Paris, President of the Inter-American Peace Committee to Ambassador Edwin Martin, United States Representative to the Committee, on the Panama-United States Crises*

January 12, 1964

The Inter-American Peace Committee, over which I have the honor of presiding, has received from the Governments of the United States and Panama, assurances that they will intensify their efforts to maintain order within their respective jurisdictions, in the Canal Zone and the Republic of Panama, particularly in the areas contiguous to the boundary line.

To facilitate that objective, I point out the necessity of paying special attention to those places which, while located in the Canal Zone, remain subject to the vigilance of the National Guard of Panama, and which will require special measures.

This Committee suggests the creation of a Joint Cooperation Committee. It would have the specific purpose of ascertaining the problems which might arise in the execution of the task of maintaining order, and it would agree upon measures to prevent and resolve any interruption of the same. It would also designate the places that will be subject to the vigilance of the National Guard of Panama as mentioned in paragraph 2 of this note. The Joint Cooperation Committee would be made up of a civilian and military representative on behalf of each one of the Governments. They would work together with a representative of the Inter-American Peace Committee who will be the president.

I beg Your Excellency to advise me of the acquiescence of your illustrious Government and, at your convenience, to advise me of the names of your representatives.

Said Joint Cooperation Committee will go into session as soon as the favorable replies of both Governments are received and their representatives are designated. Please receive, Excellency, the expression of my highest consideration.

140. Reply from Thomas C. Mann, Assistant Secretary of State to President Paris†

January 13, 1964

Thank you for your letter relating the proposal of the Inter-American Peace Commission, of which you are chairman, to set up a committee for dealing with the public order aspects of the present emergency. On behalf of the United States Government, I accept the proposal to set up such a committee and nominate Mr. William Belton and Brigadier General George L. Mabry, Jr., to serve as the U.S. members.

In doing so, I wish to state that the United States is pleased to continue to cooperate with, and has in fact already invited the cooperation of, the Panamanian

*Department of State Bulletin, Feb. 3, 1964, p. 155.
†Department of State Bulletin, Feb. 3, 1964, pp. 155-56.

authorities for dealing with the problems of public order in certain areas calling for special vigilance.

With respect to the arrangements mentioned in the second paragraph of your letter it is our understanding:

1. Such arrangements in no way change the jurisdiction of either the Government of the Canal Zone or the Panama Government.

2. They are only for the duration of the present emergency.

3. These arrangements will apply to 4th of July Avenue, and its extension as Kennedy Avenue, and Shaler Triangle; and in Colon, part of Eleventh Street, part of Bolivar Avenue; part of Calle 14; part of Avenida Herrera and Boundary Street, and the Colon Corridor, all of which areas are public thoroughfares or gathering places directly adjacent to heavily populated areas of Panama or the Canal Zone.

4. The areas mentioned in the last preceding paragraph can only be extended by unanimous agreement of the joint committee.

It would be helpful to my Government if you could confirm to me in writing that the above arrangements are consistent with the views of the Inter-American Peace Commission.

Very truly yours,

141. White House Press Statement on the Panama Crisis*

January 14, 1964

The President received a full report on the situation in Panama from Mr. Mann. Mr. Mann emphasized that United States forces have behaved admirably under extreme provocation by mobs and snipers attacking the Canal Zone. The President continues to believe that the first essential is the maintenance of peace. For this reason, the United States welcomes the establishment of the Joint Cooperation Committee through the Inter-American Peace Committee.

The United States tries to live by the policy of the good neighbor and expects others to do the same. The United States cannot allow the security of the Panama Canal to be imperiled. We have a recognized obligation to operate the Canal efficiently and securely. And we intend to honor that obligation in the interests of all who depend on it. The United States continues to believe that when order is fully restored it should be possible to have direct and candid discussions between the two governments.

142. Communiqué from the Inter-American Peace Committee, on the Panama-United States Crisis†

January 15, 1964

The Inter-American Peace Committee, based on its statutes which authorize it to offer its good offices to the states requesting them, has carried on conversations with

*Department of State Bulletin, Feb. 3, 1964, p. 156.
†Department of State Bulletin, Feb. 3, 1964, p. 156.

representatives of the Republic of Panama and the United States and notes with satisfaction the re-establishment of peace which is an indispensable condition for understanding and negotiation between the parties.

As a consequence, the Inter-American Peace Committee has invited the parties to re-establish their diplomatic relations as quickly as possible. The parties have agreed to accept this invitation and as a consequence thereof have agreed to begin discussions which will be initiated thirty days after diplomatic relations are re-established by means of representatives who will have sufficient powers to discuss without limitations all existing matters of any nature which may affect the relations between the United States and Panama.

143. Statement by Ellsworth Bunker, United States Representative on the Council of the Organization of American States, before the Council on the Dispute Between Panama and the United States*

January 21, 1964

These obligations cannot be abandoned. But the security of the Panama Canal is not inconsistent with the interests of the Republic of Panama. Both of these objectives can and should be assured by the actions and the agreement of Panama and the United States.

We have taken the position that, while we cannot agree to preconditions which impair existing treaties in advance of discussion and agreement, we are prepared to engage in a full and frank review and reconsideration of all issues—may I repeat, *all* issues between the two countries—including those arising from the canal and from the treaties relating to it, in an effort to find practical solutions to practical problems and to eliminate the cause of tension.

We have made it abundantly clear that in the discussions which we propose, each Government would be free to raise any matters it wished and that each Government must be equally free to take any position it deems necessary on any issue raised by the other.

In short, Mr. Chairman, the United States rejects all charges of aggression.

The United States reiterates its appreciation for the work of the Inter-American Peace Committee and its conviction that the instrumentalities of the OAS are competent to deal with this problem.

The United States is prepared to cooperate in a full investigation of the facts if that is desired.

The United States urges that the Council issue a call to prevent any further violence.

The United States feels that the principal stumbling block at the moment is the insistence of one of the parties on a precondition of treaty revision.

The United States maintains its objective of resuming talks on all issues.

The United States is willing to do this on the basis of the communique of January 15. It is willing to accept the wording of the draft communique which was discussed in

*Department of State Bulletin, Feb. 24, 1964, pp. 300-02.

the sessions of the Inter-American Peace Committee. In any event the United States is prepared to resume meetings with the Peace Committee and with the representatives of Panama to seek to work out a new solution.

And finally, the United States Government and people continue to extend the hand of friendship to Panama and to the Panamanian people.

The Government of the United States regrets that the Government of Panama has chosen to break off not only diplomatic relations and direct talks but discussions which were going on through the Inter-American Peace Committee, and to take instead the course of bringing this matter before the Council to level charges of aggression against the United States.

Both the U.S. Government and our people were profoundly saddened by the unfortunate events which transpired in Panama on January 9, 1964, and on the days immediately following. These events, which have left a tragic balance of dead and wounded on both sides, cannot in any way be considered to have served the best interests of either the United States or Panama but rather have redounded to the sole benefit of those who seek the breakdown of the inter-American system, of those who would sow the seeds of discord among the sister Republics of the New World, of those who seek to reap the bitter harvest that would result from internecine strife in the Americas.

I want to reiterate that the United States remains ready at all times to try to resolve our differences around the conference table. We do not think that violence is the way to settle disputes, nor, may I add, is emotion. This is a time for calm and reason.

The record will show that the Peace Committee has worked tirelessly and selflessly, literally day and night, in Panama and in Washington, and always in the spirit of utmost impartiality and helpfulness in its efforts to bring the two parties together. My Government wishes to express its deep gratification to the Inter-American Peace Committee, and individually to the distinguished members who make it up, for their significant contribution to the peacekeeping tradition of our organization. I shall have occasion to refer again to the Inter-American Peace Committee, Mr. Chairman, but I now wish to turn to the specific charges which have brought us together today.

U.S. Welcomes Investigation

The truth is that the United States has at no time committed any act of aggression against the Government or the people of Panama. There is no basis in fact for the charges which have been made. Since we have not committed aggression, we are obviously not responsible for the damages and injuries to which Panama alludes.

The United States therefore welcomes a full investigation of the charges which have been made by an appropriate body of the Organization of American States and will, of course, cooperate fully in such an investigation.

If an investigation is made it will demonstrate that the civil police and the United States military forces in the Canal Zone never made any attempt to enter Panama itself and, indeed, that they only attempted to protect lives and property in the zone. It will show that, as a result of the attacks which were made on the zone, there were more than 100 American casualties, both civilian and military, including 4 killed. It will show continuous sniping with rifle fire from buildings and the roofs of buildings in

Panama City into the zone and great restraint on the part of United States forces notwithstanding these attacks. It will show that violent mobs, infiltrated and led by extremists, including persons trained in Communist countries for political action of the kind that took place, assaulted the zone on a wide perimeter, setting fire to buildings inside the zone and attacking with incendiary bombs and rocks the people who were inside. It will show that the Government of Panama, instead of attempting to restore order, was, through a controlled press, television, and radio, inciting the people to attack and to violence. It will show a delay for some 36 hours on the part of the Government of Panama in restoring order. It will show looting and burning by violent mobs in Panama City itself. And it will show that no small proportion of the Panamanian casualties were caused by Panamanians themselves, including those who died of fire and suffocation in buildings and in automobiles which were set on fire.

Mr. Chairman, I reserve the right at a future meeting to make specific comments on these details of alleged happenings to which the distinguished representative of Panama referred, which unfortunately do not correspond with the facts.

We also think it important that any investigation include the full story of the efforts of the IAPC in the last 20 days. For we are confident that that will demonstrate that the United States has gone more than halfway in seeking to resolve this matter.

As to the most appropriate mechanism by which such an investigation might be undertaken, my delegation believes that there are several possibilities which might be explored, and certainly it would be essential to have a full investigation before seeking or implying any judgment on the charges. In addition to the present proposal to invoke the Rio Treaty, it is possible, and in the view of my Government would be quite appropriate, for the IAPC itself to undertake an investigation. This has the advantage that its members are thoroughly familiar with so much of the situation. Alternatively, the U.S. would be willing to undertake a joint investigation with representatives of Panama under the chairmanship of a representative of the Council. Perhaps, as an initial step before taking final action on the current proposal, the Council might request one of its own committees to gather the necessary information and evidence.

The U.S. Objective

In determining what action should be taken, however, it seems to me important to bear in mind the principal stumbling block at the moment which has divided the United States and Panama and the real *objective* which we seek. This point was well stated by the distinguished delegate of Panama himself when he said, if I heard him right, that "Since it has not been possible to attain an express manifestation of the intention of the Government of the United States to initiate negotiations for the conclusion of a new treaty . . . the Government of Panama finds itself under the painful necessity of presenting its case to the Council of the OAS."

Whether the Rio Treaty is the proper instrument to seek to force a revision of existing treaties is a question which the Council will, of course, want to consider. However, the most important consideration which guides our deliberations and action is the objective which we seek. So far as the United States is concerned, our consistently held objective remains to restore diplomatic and friendly relations with the Government and people of Panama and to sit down together with them at the conference table to seek to resolve all outstanding issues.

As President Johnson has said,

> Our obligation to safeguard the canal against riots and vandals and sabotage and other interference rests on the precepts of international law, the requirements of international commerce, and the needs of free-world security.

144. News Conference Statement by President Johnson, on the United States Position in the Panama Crisis*

January 23, 1964

I want to take this opportunity to restate our position on Panama and the Canal Zone. No purpose is served by rehashing either recent or ancient events. There have been excesses and errors on the part of both Americans and Panamanians. Earlier this month actions of imprudent students from both countries played into the hands of agitators seeking to divide us. What followed was a needless and tragic loss of life on both sides.

Our own forces were confronted with sniper fire and mob attack. Their role was one of resisting aggression and not committing it. At all times they remained inside the Canal Zone, and they took only those defensive actions required to maintain law and order and to protect lives and property within the canal itself. Our obligation to safeguard the canal against riots and vandals and sabotage and other interference rests on the precepts of international law, the requirements of international commerce, and the needs of free-world security.

These obligations cannot be abandoned. But the security of the Panama Canal is not inconsistent with the interests of the Republic of Panama. Both of these objectives can and should be assured by the actions and the agreement of Panama and the United States. This Government has long recognized that our operation of the canal across Panama poses special problems for both countries. It is necessary, therefore, that our relations be given constant attention.

Over the past few years we have taken a number of actions to remove inequities and irritants. We recognize that there are things to be done, and we are prepared to talk about the ways and means of doing them. But violence is never justified and is never a basis for talks. Consequently, the first item of business has been the restoration of public order. The Inter-American Peace Committee, which I met this morning, deserves the thanks of us all not only for helping to restore order but for its good offices. For the future, we have stated our willingness to engage without limitation or delay in a full and frank review and reconsideration of all issues between our two countries.

We have set no preconditions to the resumption of peaceful discussions. We are bound by no preconceptions of what they will produce. And we hope that Panama can take the same approach. In the meantime, we expect neither country to either foster or yield to any kind of pressure with respect to such discussions. We are prepared, 30 days after relations are restored, to sit in conference with Panamanian officials to seek

*Department of State Bulletin, Feb. 10, 1964, pp. 195-96.

concrete solutions to all problems dividing our countries. Each Government will be free to raise any issue and to take any position. And our Government will consider all practical solutions to practical problems that are offered in good faith.

Certainly solutions can be found which are compatible with the dignity and the security of both countries as well as the needs of world commerce. And certainly Panama and the United States can remain, as they should remain, good friends and good neighbors.

145. Statement by U.S. Representative Bunker, before the Council on a Dispute Between Panama and the United States*

February 4, 1964

Mr. Chairman, I regret that my distinguished colleague from Panama has seen fit to return to these charges which he made at the last meeting. As President Johnson said, it seems rather futile to rehash these past events; what we ought to do is—it seems to me—to be devoting our energies to finding ways of restoring relations between our two countries and getting around to the conference table, where I am sure that with good will and trust on both sides our problems can be resolved.

In my remarks to the Council on January 31 I indicated that at some future meeting I might make some specific comments on the details of alleged happenings to which the distinguished representative of Panama referred in his speech. I had not intended to do so today, but in view of additional inaccuracies and distortions to which we have just listened, Mr. Chairman, I feel it is more than ever important that the world know what really happened.

As I indicated in my statement before this Council at our last meeting, the U.S. firmly rejects the charge of aggression which has been leveled against us and not only welcomes but is indeed most interested in having all of the facts concerning the events of the 9th and 10th of January brought to light. Indeed as we have gone more deeply into our own investigations of the situation, U.S. authorities have developed considerable information concerning the acts of violence and the behavior of the mob, which we may well want to insist be brought to light.

Mr. Chairman, much as I dislike having to question the statements made by the distinguished representative of Panama, the allegation is untrue that U.S. high school students, some of their parents, and the Canal Zone police attacked the Panamanian students who entered the Canal Zone at approximately 4:30 p.m., January 9, and who marched peacefully to the Balboa High School, where a delegation of five Panamanian students displayed the Panamanian flag. There is incontrovertible evidence from photographs which I would be glad to show any interested member of the Council, as well as sworn statements of U.S. officials, indicating that there was no attack by the American students or those parents present on the Panamanian students. The photographs will show that the Canal Zone police kept these groups apart, that the whole affair was orderly, and that the police at no time used firearms on these students or in fact did anything more than escort them out of the zone, despite the fact that the

*Department of State Bulletin, Feb. 24, 1964, pp. 302-04.

Panamanian students did engage in considerable property damage. As a matter of fact, the Canal Zone authorities had several buses brought to the area to the take the Panamanian students back to the Republic of Panama, but the students did not care to use them and departed on foot.

I would be able to show any interested member of the Council a photograph of the Panamanian flag being borne to the school by the students. An examination of this photograph will show that the center top of the flag was already torn prior to the time it was alleged we tore their flag. In other words, the flag was torn before it ever went from Panama into the Canal Zone, and the allegation that the American students, their parents, and the Canal Zone police had anything to do with defiling the Panamanian flag is simply not correct.

Later on in his statement the distinguished representative from Panama indicated that the U.S. Army forces in battle gear used machine-guns, tanks, and long-range automatic weapons in firing on crowds of Panamanians whose only wish was to enter the Canal Zone to raise the Panamanian flag. I am in a position to offer evidence to any member of the Council who is interested that no machineguns were used, that no tanks were used, although I am sure the distinguished representative from Panama has confused the personnel carriers—that were used to bring the troops from their quarters to the area where the mob was running wild—with tanks.

No automatic weapons were ever employed by U.S. personnel during the mob violence. In fact, most of the American soldiers initially were not issued ball ammunition at all, and when it was later used, it was carefully directed at Panamanian snipers in order to avoid casualties. The distinguished members of the Council may recall that the widow of one of the U.S. soldiers killed early in the violence in Colón was recently in Washington when her husband was buried at Arlington Cemetery and that at that time it was stated that this particular sergeant had no ammunition for his rifle when he was shot and killed. This is because it is, I am told, standard procedure for only the leaders to have ammunition in riot control, with the rest of the group equipped with tear gas and instructed to use persuasion.

The distinguished representative from Panama indicated that U.S. helicopters and aircraft violated airspace of Panama and added to the confusion. What he failed to point out was that the helicopters had loudspeakers and Spanish-speaking personnel were urging the mobs to disperse and go home. It is true that the Colón corridor through the Canal Zone on the Atlantic side had to be closed for a short period of time, in keeping with specific treaty provisions, because of the danger of mob elements getting in behind the forces trying to defend the Canal Zone in that general area, but the statement that the Isthmian Highway was closed, thus preventing the shipment of blood plasma and medical help to the Atlantic side, is absurd. The destruction of property by the mob on the Atlantic side was very great. I have, if any member of the Council is interested, photographs of the destruction caused by the mob in that area.

In short, as I stated on January 31, the facts when brought to light will show that what little force the United States used was employed with the greatest restraint and solely within the Canal Zone for the protection of the residents of the zone. Reflection will convince you, I think, that a crisis with Panama could serve no conceivable United States interests, that my country had nothing whatsoever to gain either in causing the crisis or seeing it expand, and that United States interests as well as humanitarian considerations argued for the very minimum use of force. However, my Government could not and should not be expected to order its defensive forces to stand aside and permit violent mobs, the true character and intentions of which are clearly shown by the pillaging, looting, and wanton destruction that took place in Panama City and Colón, to enter the Canal Zone unopposed.

Now, Mr. Chairman, it seems to me not particularly helpful to keep on attempting to present evidence before the Council, evidence which should go to an investigating committee, if we have one. It doesn't seem to me that we are promoting the cause of understanding, which we want to achieve here. I do, however, consider it necessary to say that I again must reserve the privilege of commenting further on statements of my distinguished colleague from Panama, if this is the course which is to be pursued here. But I do hope that we may be able now to get on with the business in hand, and certainly my Government is most appreciative of the strenuous efforts, not only those which the Peace Committee made but also those which the distinguished members of this Council have been making over the last days here to attempt to find some formula that will provide an avenue of approach to these problems.

146. Resolution by the Council of the Organization of American States, on the Panama—United States Dispute*

February 4, 1964

Considering:

That it has taken cognizance of the note of the Ambassador, Representative of Panama, by which his government furnishes information on the situation that has arisen between his country and the United States of America and requests that the Organ of Consultation be convoked for the purposes indicated in that note, in accordance with the Inter-American Treaty of Reciprocal Assistance, and

Having heard the statements made at the meeting held on January 31 and at today's meeting by the Representatives of Panama and of the United States,

Resolves:

1. To convoke the Organ of Consultation in accordance with the provisions of the Inter-American Treaty of Reciprocal Assistance, to meet at a time and place to be decided in due course.

2. To constitute itself and to act provisionally as Organ of Consultation in accordance with Article 12 of the aforementioned treaty.

3. To inform the United Nations Security Council of the text of this resolution.

*Department of State Bulletin, Feb. 24, 1964, p. 304

147. *Resolution by the Council of the Organization of American States, on the Panama—United States Dispute**

February 7, 1964

Whereas:

Article 4 of the Charter of the Organization of American States proclaims the following as the first two essential purposes of the Organization: "To strengthen the peace and security of the continent" and "To prevent possible causes of difficulties and to ensure the pacific settlement of disputes that may arise among the member states";

The Inter-American Treaty of Reciprocal Assistance recognizes the pre-eminent position within the inter-American system of the procedures for the pacific settlement of controversies, and explicitly and especially mentions the principles set forth in the preamble and declarations of the Act of Chapultepec; and

At the special meetings of the Council held on January 31 and February 4, 1964, both the Representative of the Government of Panama and the Representative of the United States Government expressed a desire that the tragic events that occurred in Panama last January 9 and 10 be fully investigated.

The Council of the Organization of American States Acting Provisionally as Organ of Consultation

Resolves:

1. To urge both governments to abstain from committing any act that might result in violating the peace in Panama.

2. To establish a general committee composed of all the members of the Council, acting provisionally as Organ of Consultation, with the exception of the Representatives of the parties in conflict.

3. The general committee shall:

a. Investigate, fully and at once, the acts that occurred in Panama on January 9 and 10, 1964, and thereafter, and submit a report to the Organ of Consultation on the matter and on the efforts exerted by the governments of the United States and Panama during subsequent days to find a solution to the dispute;

b. Propose to the parties procedures intended to ensure that the peace will not be violated while an effort is being made to find a solution to the dispute between them;

c. Bearing in mind the causes of the dispute, to assist the parties in their search for a fair solution thereof and to submit a report to the Organ of Consultation on this phase of the subject; and

d. Create the special committees that it deems necessary for the fulfillment of its task.

4. To request the American governments and the Secretary General of the Organization to furnish full cooperation in order to facilitate the work of the general committee.

**Department of State Bulletin,* Feb. 24, 1964, p. 304.

148. White House Press Release Concerning the Security of the Guantanamo Base*

February 7, 1964

When the Cuban Government shut off the water supply to Guantanamo, it deliberately broke an agreement made in 1938, reasserted in 1947, and personally supported by Fidel Castro in 1958. The United States is determined to guarantee the security of the Guantanamo naval base and does not intend to submit that security or the welfare of the servicemen and their families who live there to further irresponsible actions of the Cuban Government. The President has instructed the Department of Defense to make the Guantanamo base self-sufficient. In response the Secretary of Defense has issued instructions to:

1. Assure the base control over its own water supply both by conversion of sea water to fresh water and by the transportation of water by ship.

2. Reduce the employment of Cuban personnel who are subject to the control of the Cuban Government and whose wages contribute to its foreign exchange.

The reckless and irresponsible conduct of the Cuban Government remains a constant threat to the peace of this hemisphere. The consequences of further provocations by Castro should be carefully weighed by all nations.

These matters are being called to the attention of the members of the Organization of American States for consideration in connection with charges now pending against Cuba in that organization. They will also be discussed with the members of the North Atlantic Treaty Organization in order that those governments can take them into account in connection with their determination of their own policies toward the threats to the security of the Western Hemisphere posed by the Castro regime.

149. News Conference Statement by President Johnson, on the Panama–United States Dispute†

March 21, 1964

The present inability to resolve our differences with Panama is a source of deep regret.

Our two countries are not linked by only a single agreement or a single interest. We are bound together in an inter-American system whose objective is, in the words of the charter, ". . . through their mutual understanding and respect for the sovereignty of each one, to provide for the betterment of all . . . ."

Under the many treaties and declarations which form the fabric of that system, we have long been allies in the struggle to strengthen democracy and enhance the welfare of our people.

Our history is witness to this essential unity of interest and belief. Panama has unhesitatingly come to our side, twice in this century, when we were threatened by aggression. On December 7, 1941, Panama declared war on our attackers even before

*Department of State Bulletin, Feb. 24, 1964, p. 281.
†Department of State Bulletin, Apr. 6, 1964, pp. 538-39.

our own Congress had time to act. Since that war, Panama has wholeheartedly joined with us, and our sister Republics, in shaping the agreements and goals of this continent.

We have also had a special relationship with Panama, for they have shared with us the benefits, the burdens and trust of maintaining the Panama Canal as a lifeline of defense and a keystone of hemispheric prosperity. All free nations are grateful for the effort they have given to this task.

As circumstances change, as history shapes new attitudes and expectations, we have reviewed periodically this special relationship.

We are well aware that the claims of the Government of Panama, and of the majority of the Panamanian people, do not spring from malice or hatred of America. They are based on a deeply felt sense of the honest and fair needs of Panama. It is, therefore, our obligation as allies and partners to review these claims and to meet them, when meeting them is both just and possible.

We are ready to do this.

We are prepared to review every issue which now divides us, and every problem which the Panama Government wishes to raise.

We are prepared to do this at any time and at any place.

As soon as he is invited by the Government of Panama, our Ambassador will be on his way. We shall also designate a special representative. He will arrive with full authority to discuss every difficulty. He will be charged with the responsibility of seeking a solution which recognizes the fair claims of Panama and protects the interests of all the American nations in the canal. We cannot determine, even before our meeting, what form that solution might best take. But his instructions will not prohibit any solution which is fair, and subject to the appropriate constitutional processes of both our Governments.

I hope that on this basis we can begin to resolve our problems and move ahead to confront the real enemies of this hemisphere—the enemies of hunger and ignorance, disease and injustice. I know President Chiari shares this hope. For, despite today's disagreements, the common values and interests which unite us are far stronger and more enduring than the differences which now divide us.

150. Message from President Johnson, to Ranieri Mazzilli, President of the United States of Brazil*

April 2, 1964

Please accept my warmest good wishes on your installation as President of the United States of Brazil. The American people have watched with anxiety the political and economic difficulties through which your great nation has been passing, and have admired the resolute will of the Brazilian community to resolve these difficulties within a framework of constitutional democracy and without civil strife.

The relations of friendship and cooperation between our two governments and peoples are a great historical legacy for us both and a precious asset in the interests of peace and prosperity and liberty in this hemisphere and in the whole world. I look

*Department of State Bulletin, Apr. 20, 1964, p. 609.

forward to the continued strengthening of those relations and to our intensified cooperation in the interests of economic progress and social justice for all and of hemispheric and world peace.

151. Announcement by the Organization of American States, of an Agreement in the Panama–United States Dispute*

April 3, 1964

The Chairman of the General Committee of the Council of the Organization of American States acting provisionally as Organ of Consultation is pleased to announce that the duly authorized Representatives of the governments of the Republic of Panama and of the United States of America have agreed, on behalf of their governments, to a Joint Declaration which in the English and Spanish languages reads as follows:

Joint Declaration

In accordance with the friendly declarations of the Presidents of the United States of America and of the Republic of Panama of the 21st and 24th of March, 1964, respectively, annexed hereto, which are in agreement in a sincere desire to resolve favorably all the differences between the two countries;

Meeting under the Chairmanship of the President of the Council and recognizing the important cooperation offered by the Organization of American States through the Inter-American Peace Committee and the Delegation of the General Committee of the Organ of Consultation, the Representatives of both governments have agreed:

1. To re-establish diplomatic relations.

2. To designate without delay Special Ambassadors with sufficient powers to seek the prompt elimination of the causes of conflict between the two countries, without limitations or preconditions of any kind.

3. That therefore, the Ambassadors designated will begin immediately the necessary procedures with the objective of reaching a just and fair agreement which would be subject to the constitutional processes of each country. . . .

[A Spanish version of the Declaration follows].

The Chairman of the General Committee of the Council of the Organization of American States acting provisionally as Organ of Consultation records that the parties agree that both texts are equally authentic and that the words "agreement" in the English version and "convenio" in the Spanish version cover all possible forms of international engagements.

*Department of State Bulletin, Apr. 27, 1964, p. 656.

152. Organization of American States, Ninth Meeting of Consultation of Ministers of Foreign Affairs, Final Act*

July 26, 1964

The Ninth Meeting of Consultation of Ministers of Foreign Affairs, Serving as Organ of Consultation in Application of the Inter-American Treaty of Reciprocal Assistance, was held at the headquarters of the Organization of American States, the Pan American Union, in Washington, D.C., from July 21 to 26, 1964.

The Council of the Organization of American States convoked the Meeting by a resolution adopted on December 3, 1963, which reads as follows:

Whereas:

The Council has taken cognizance of the note of the Ambassador, Representative of Venezuela, by means of which his government requests that, in accordance with Article 6 of the Inter-American Treaty of Reciprocal Assistance, the Organ of Consultation be immediately convoked to consider measures that must be taken to deal with the acts of intervention and aggression on the part of the Cuban Government affecting the territorial integrity and the sovereignty of Venezuela, as well as the operation of its democratic institutions; and

The Ambassador, Representative of Venezuela, has furnished information to substantiate his requests,

The Council of the Organization of American States

Resolves:

1. To convoke the Organ of Consultation in accordance with the provisions of the Inter-American Treaty of Reciprocal Assistance, to meet on the date and at the place to be fixed in due time.

2. To constitute itself and act provisionally as Organ of Consultation, in accordance with Article 12 of the aforementioned treaty.

3. To inform the Security Council of the United Nations of the text of this resolution.

At the meeting held on the same day, December 3, 1963, the Council of the Organization, acting provisionally as Organ of Consultation, adopted a resolution, whereby a committee was appointed to investigate the acts denounced by Venezuela and to report thereon. The committee, which was composed of representatives of Argentina, Colombia, Costa Rica, the United States of America, and Uruguay, presented its report at the meeting held on February 24, 1964, by the Council, acting provisionally as Organ of Consultation.

With respect to the date and place of the Meeting, the Council of the Organization of American States at its special meeting on June 26, 1964, adopted the following resolution:

Whereas:

On December 3, 1963, the Council of the Organization convoked the Organ of Consultation in accordance with the provisions of the Inter-American Treaty of

*Department of State Bulletin, Aug. 10, 1964, pp. 179-84.

Reciprocal Assistance, stating that it would meet at a place and at a time to be set in due time,

The Council of the Organization of American States

Resolves:

1. That the Ninth Meeting of Consultation of Ministers of Foreign Affairs, Serving as Organ of Consultation in Application of the Inter-American Treaty of Reciprocal Assistance, shall be held at the headquarters of the Organization of American States.

2. To set July 21, 1964, as the date for the opening of the meeting. . . .

As the result of its deliberations, the Ninth Meeting of Consultation of Ministers of Foreign Affairs, Serving as Organ of Consultation in Application of the Inter-American Treaty of Reciprocal Assistance, approved the following resolutions and declarations:

I
Application of Measures
to the Present Government of Cuba

The Ninth Meeting of Consultation of Ministers of Foreign Affairs, Serving as Organ of Consultation in Application of the Inter-American Treaty of Reciprocal Assistance,

Having seen the report of the Investigating Committee designated on December 3, 1963, by the Council of the Organization of American States, acting provisionally as Organ of Consultation, and

Considering:

That the said report establishes among its conclusions that "the Republic of Venezuela has been the target of a series of actions sponsored and directed by the Government of Cuba, openly intended to subvert Venezuelan institutions and to overthrow the democratic Government of Venezuela through terrorism, sabotage, assault, and guerrilla warfare," and

That the aforementioned acts, like all acts of intervention and aggression, conflict with the principles and aims of the inter-American system,

Resolves:

1. To declare that the acts verified by the Investigating Committee constitute an aggression and an intervention on the part of the Government of Cuba in the internal affairs of Venezuela, which affects all of the member states.

2. To condemn emphatically the present Government of Cuba for its acts of aggression and of intervention against the territorial inviolability, the sovereignty, and the political independence of Venezuela.

3. To apply, in accordance with the provisions of Articles 6 and 8 of the Inter-American Treaty of Reciprocal Assistance, the following measures:

a. That the governments of the American states not maintain diplomatic or consular relations with the Government of Cuba;

b. That the governments of the American states suspend all their trade, whether direct or indirect, with Cuba, except in foodstuffs, medicines, and medical equipment that may be sent to Cuba for humanitarian reasons; and

c. That the governments of the American states suspend all sea transportation between their countries and Cuba, except for such transportation as may be necessary for reasons of a humanitarian nature.

4. To authorize the Council of the Organization of American States, by an affirmative vote of two thirds of its members, to discontinue the measures adopted in the present resolution at such time as the Government of Cuba shall have ceased to constitute a danger to the peace and security of the hemisphere.

5. To warn the Government of Cuba that if it should persist in carrying out acts that possess characteristics of aggression and intervention against one or more of the member states of the Organization, the member states shall preserve their essential rights as sovereign states by the use of self-defense in either individual or collective form, which could go so far as resort to armed force, until such time as the Organ of Consultation takes measures to guarantee the peace and security of the hemisphere.

6. To urge those states not members of the Organization of American States that are animated by the same ideals as the inter-American system to examine the possibility of effectively demonstrating their solidarity in achieving the purposes of this resolution.

7. To instruct the Secretary General of the Organization of American States to transmit to the United Nations Security Council the text of the present resolution, in accordance with the provisions of Article 54 of the United Nations Charter.

II
Declaration to the People of Cuba

Whereas:

The preamble to the Charter of the Organization of American States declares that, "the historic mission of America is to offer to man a land of liberty, and a favorable environment for the development of his personality and the realization of his just aspirations"; and that "the true significance of American solidarity and good neighborliness can only mean the consolidation on this continent, within the framework of democratic institutions, of a system of individual liberty and social justice based on respect for the essential rights of man";

The Charter of the Organization declares that the solidarity of the American states and the high purposes toward which it is dedicated demand that the political organization of these states be based on the effective exercise of representative democracy;

The Charter also proclaims "the fundamental rights of the individual" and reaffirms that the "education of peoples should be directed toward justice, freedom, and peace";

The Declaration of Santiago, Chile, adopted by the Fifth Meeting of Consultation of Ministers of Foreign Affairs and signed by the present Cuban Government, proclaimed that the faith of peoples of America in the effective exercise of representative democracy is the best vehicle for the promotion of their social and political progress (Resolution XCV of the Tenth Inter-American Conference), while well-planned and intensive development of the economies of the American countries and improvement in the standard of living of their peoples represent the best and firmest foundation on which the practical exercise of democracy and the stabilization of their institutions can be established;

The Ninth International Conference of American States condemned "the methods of every system tending to suppress political and civil rights and liberties, and in particular the action of international communism or any other totalitarian doctrine";

The present Government of Cuba, identifying itself with the principles of Marxist-Leninist ideology, has established a political, economic, and social system alien to the democratic and Christian traditions of the American family of nations and contrary to the principles of juridical organization upon which rest the security and peaceful harmonious relations of the peoples of the hemisphere; and

The exclusion of the present Government of Cuba from participation in the inter-American system, by virtue of the provisions of Resolution VI of the Eighth Meeting of Consultation of Ministers of Foreign Affairs, by no means signifies any intention to deny the Cuban people their rightful place in the community of American peoples;

The Ninth Meeting of Consultation of Ministers of Foreign Affairs, Serving as Organ of Consultation in Application of the Inter-American Treaty of Reciprocal Assistance,

Declares:

That the free peoples of the Americas are convinced that the inter-American system offers to the Cuban people unequaled conditions for the realization of their ideals of peace, liberty, and social and economic progress;

That the peoples belonging to the inter-American system are in complete sympathy with the Cuban people in all their sufferings, in the face of the total loss of their liberty both in the spiritual domain and in the social and economic field, the denial of their most elementary human rights, the burden of their persecutions, and the destruction of a legal system that was open to improvement and that offered the possibility of stability; and

That, within this spirit of solidarity, the free peoples of America cannot and must not remain indifferent to or uninterested in the fate of the noble Cuban people, which is oppressed by a dictatorship that renounces the Christian and democratic traditions of the American peoples; and in consequence

Expresses:

1. Its profound concern for the fate of the brother people of Cuba.

2. Its deepest hope that the Cuban people, strengthened by confidence in the solidarity with them of the other American peoples and governments, will be able, by their own endeavor, very soon to liberate themselves from the tyranny of the Communist regime that oppresses them and to establish in that country a government freely elected by the will of the people that will assure respect for fundamental human rights.

3. Its firm conviction that the emphatic condemnation of the policy of the present Cuban Government of aggression and intervention against Venezuela will be taken by the people of Cuba as a renewed stimulus for its hope there will come to prevail in that country a climate of freedom that will offer to man in Cuba a favorable environment for the development of his personality and the realization of his just aspirations.

III
Regional and International Economic Coordination

Whereas:

The objectives of liberty and democracy that inspire the inter-American system, threatened as they are by communist subversion, cannot be fully attained if the peoples of the states that compose it lack adequate and sufficient means for bringing about vigorous social progress and better standards of living;

The persistence of a situation in which the world is divided into areas of poverty and plenty is a serious obstacle to any possibility that may present itself in the American hemisphere for achieving an economically more just society;

Harmonious and decisive action is indispensable, in both the regional and the international spheres, to combat the causes of economic underdevelopment and social backwardness, since prosperity and world peace based on the freedom of man cannot be achieved unless all the American countries attain equality in the economic and social field;

In particular, the continued existence of such a state of underdevelopment and poverty among large sectors of mankind, which becomes more acute in spite of the world increase in wealth and the advance of science and technology from which these sectors cannot derive full benefit; encourages the subversive action of international communism;

The countries of Latin America expressed their aspirations in the Charter of Alta Gracia and declared their determined intention to work together to build a better world in which there will be a more equitable distribution of income;

The Conference on Trade and Development, held recently in Geneva, provided a forum for a full discussion of the problems of international economics and established the basis for adequate solutions to problems arising in the fields of raw materials, manufactured products, and international financing; and

The instruments adopted at the two aforementioned meetings supplement and perfect those signed at the Special Meeting of the Inter-American Economic and Social Council held at Punta del Este in August 1961, and especially, the Charter of Punta del Este,

The Ninth Meeting of Consultation of Ministers of Foreign Affairs, Serving as Organ of Consultation in Application of the Inter-American Treaty of Reciprocal Assistance,

Declares:

That the aims of unity and peace with liberty and democracy pursued in the struggle against international communism, which threatens the stability of the institutions of the inter-American system and of the countries that compose it, must be achieved by eliminating those obstacles that hinder social progress and economic development, and

Resolves:

1. To reaffirm the determined will of their peoples to work, in the regional and international spheres, for the achievement of the objectives expressed in the Charter of

Alta Gracia and at the Conference on Trade and Development, which are in line with the aims and purposes of the Alliance for Progress.

2. To request the Inter-American Economic and Social Council to continue the necessary studies in order to find adequate solutions to the problems involved. . . .

Statements

Statement of Chile

The Delegation of Chile abstained from voting on paragraphs 1 and 2 of the operative part of Resolution I, because of its doubts regarding the legality of the use of the term "aggression" in describing the acts. It voted negatively on paragraph 3, because it is firmly convinced that the measures agreed to are not appropriate to the particular case that has brought about the application of the Inter-American Treaty of Reciprocal Assistance. It also voted against paragraph 5, because it believes that there are discrepancies between the provisions of that paragraph and those of Article 51 of the Charter of the United Nations and of Article 3 of the Rio Treaty. With reference to its abstention on paragraph 6, its attitude is consistent with the attitude taken with respect to the measures called for in paragraph 3.

The Delegation of Chile abstained from voting on the Declaration to the People of Cuba since, although agreeing with its basic content, it maintains relations with the Republic of Cuba and since it believes precisely in the principle of nonintervention, it has deemed it preferable not to give positive support to this resolution.

Statement of Mexico

The Delegation of Mexico wishes to make it a matter of record in the Final Act, that the Government of Mexico:

1. Is convinced that the measures provided for in the third paragraph of the operative part of Resolution I (which the Delegation of Mexico voted against) lack foundation inasmuch as the Inter-American Treaty of Reciprocal Assistance does not envisage, in any part, the application of such measures in situations of the kind and nature dealt with by this Meeting of Consultation.

2. Makes a specific reservation to the fifth paragraph of the operative part of the same resolution since it endeavors to extend, in such a way as to be incompatible with the provisions of Articles 3 and 10 of the Inter-American Treaty of Reciprocal Assistance, the right to individual or collective self-defense.

3. Reiterates without reservations its "will to cooperate permanently in the fulfillment of the principles and purposes of a policy of peace," to which "is essentially related" the "obligation of mutual assistance and common defense of the American Republics," in accordance with the provisions of paragraph five of the Preamble of the Inter-American Treaty of Reciprocal Assistance.

In Witness Whereof, the Ministers of Foreign Affairs sign the present Final Act.

Done in the Pan American Union, Washington, D.C., United States of America, in the four official languages of the Organization, on July twenty-six, nineteen hundred sixty-four. The Secretary General shall deposit the original of the Final Act in the archives of the Pan American Union, which will transmit the authenticated copies thereof to the governments of the American republics.

153. White House Press Release by President Johnson
      Concerning United States Plans for a New Sea-Level
      Canal and a New Treaty on the Existing Canal*

December 18, 1964

This Government has completed an intensive review of policy toward the present and the future of the Panama Canal. On the basis of this review I have reached two decisions.

First, I have decided that the United States should press forward with Panama and other interested governments in plans and preparations for a sea-level canal in this area.

Second, I have decided to propose to the Government of Panama the negotiation of an entirely new treaty on the existing Panama Canal.

These decisions reflect the unanimous judgment of the Secretary of State, the Secretary of Defense, the Joint Chiefs of Staff. They are based on the recommendations of Ambassador Robert Anderson, Secretary [of the Army] Stephen Ailes, Secretary Thomas Mann [Assistant Secretary of State for Inter-American Affairs] , and our Ambassador in Panama, Ambassador Jack Vaughn. They have the full support of Mr. Truman and General Eisenhower. They have been reported to, and in most instances sympathetically received by, the leadership of the Congress.

These two steps, I think, are needed now—needed for the protection and the promotion of peaceful trade—for the welfare of the hemisphere—in the true interests of the United States—and in fairness and justice to all.

For 50 years the Panama Canal has carried ships of all nations in peaceful trade between the two great oceans—on terms of entire equality and at no profit to this country. The canal has also served the cause of peace and freedom in two world wars. It has brought great economic contributions to Panama. For the rest of its life the canal will continue to serve trade, and peace, and the people of Panama.

But that life is now limited. The canal is growing old, and so are the treaties for its management, which go back to 1903.

The Panama Canal, with its limiting locks and channels, will soon be inadequate to the needs of our world commerce. Already more than 300 ships built or building are too big to go through with full loads. Many of them—like our own modern aircraft carriers—cannot even go through at all.

So I think it is time to plan in earnest for a sea-level canal. Such a canal will be more modern, more economical, and will be far easier to defend. It will be free of complex, costly, vulnerable locks and seaways. It will serve the future as the Panama Canal we know has served the past and the present.

The Congress has already authorized $17 million for studies of possible sites and of the other practical problems of a sea-level canal. There seem to be four possible routes—two in Panama, one in Colombia, and one which goes through Nicaragua and possibly Costa Rica as well.

I have asked the Secretary of State to begin discussions immediately with all the governments concerned with these possible new routes. In these discussions we will be prepared to work on the terms and the conditions of building and operating a new

**Department of State Bulletin,* Jan. 4, 1965, pp. 5-6.

canal, and if preliminary arrangements can be reached, we will be ready to go ahead with selected site surveys.

Last January there was violence in Panama. As I said then, ". . . violence is never justified and is never a basis for talks.

But while the people of the United States have never made concessions to force, they have always supported fair play and full respect for the rights of others. So from the very first day, as your President, I made it clear that we were ready to sit down and to seek answers, to reason together, and to try to find the answers that would be just, fair, and right, without precondition or without precommitment on either side.

On that basis, relations between our two countries—negotiations—were resumed in April and on that basis I chose Mr. Robert Anderson, the distinguished former Secretary of the Treasury under President Eisenhower, to be my special ambassador on this problem. Since then Ambassador Anderson has been working with the American Ambassador, Mr. Vaughn, with the Secretary of the Army, Mr. Ailes, and with Secretary Mann of the State Department. They have recommended that we should propose a new treaty for the existing canal. After careful review with my senior advisers, I have accepted this recommendation.

Today we have informed the Government of Panama that we are ready to negotiate a new treaty. In such a treaty we must retain the rights which are necessary for the effective operation and the protection of the canal and the administration of the areas that are necessary for these purposes. Such a treaty would replace the treaty of 1903 and its amendments. It should recognize the sovereignty of Panama. It should provide for its own termination when a sea-level canal comes into operation. It should provide for effective discharge of our common responsibilities for hemispheric defense. Until a new agreement is reached, of course, the present treaties will remain in effect.

In these new proposals we will take every possible step to deal fairly and helpfully with the citizens of both Panama and the United States who have served so faithfully through the years in operating and maintaining the canal.

These changes are necessary not because of failure but because of success; not because of backwardness but because of progress. The age before us is an age of larger, faster ships. It is an age of friendly partnership among the nations concerned with the traffic between the oceans. This new age requires new arrangements.

The strength of our American system is that we have always tried to understand and meet the needs of the future. We have been at our best when we have been both bold and prudent in moving forward. The planning of a new canal and the negotiation of a new treaty are just such bold and prudent steps. So let us today in friendship take them together.

154. *Press Release by President Johnson, on United States Intervention in the Dominican Republic**

April 28, 1965

I just concluded a meeting with the leaders of the Congress. I reported to them on the serious situation in the Dominican Republic. I reported the decisions this Government considers necessary in this situation in order to protect American lives.

The members of the leadership expressed their support in these decisions. The United States Government has been informed by military authorities in the Dominican Republic that American lives are in danger. These authorities are no longer able to guarantee their safety, and they have reported that the assistance of military personnel is now needed for that purpose.

I have ordered the Secretary of Defense to put the necessary American troops ashore in order to give protection to hundreds of Americans who are still in the Dominican Republic and to escort them safely back to this country. This same assistance will be available to the nationals of other countries, some of whom have already asked for our help.

Pursuant to my instructions, 400 Marines have already landed. General [Earle G.] Wheeler, the Chairman of the Joint Chiefs of Staff, has just reported to me that there have been no incidents.

We have appealed repeatedly in recent days for a cease-fire between the contending forces of the Dominican Republic in the interests of all Dominicans and foreigners alike.

I repeat this urgent appeal again tonight. The Council of the OAS has been advised of the situation by the Dominican Ambassador [José Antonio Bonilla Atiles] , and the Council will be kept fully informed.

155. *Letter from Ambassador Stevenson, to Abdul Monem Rifa'i, President of the Security Council, Concerning United States Intervention in the Dominican Republic†*

April 29, 1965

I have the honor to inform you that on April 28 the President of the United States ordered American troops ashore in the Dominican Republic in order to protect American citizens still there and escort them to safety from the country. The President acted after he had been informed by the military authorities in the Dominican Republic that American lives were in danger, that their safety could no longer be guaranteed, and that the assistance of United States military personnel was required. The text of the President's statement is enclosed.

At the request of the United States, the Council of the Organization of American States is meeting to consider the situation in the Dominican Republic.

I request that you circulate copies of this letter, together with a copy of the text of

*Department of State Bulletin, May 17, 1965, pp. 738-39.
†Department of State Bulletin, May 17, 1965, p. 739.

the President's statement to the Delegations of all Member States as a Security Council document.

Sincerely yours,

156. Resolution by the Council of the Organization of American States, Convoking a Meeting of Consultation on Armed Strife in the Dominican Republic*

April 30, 1965

Whereas:

The Ambassador Representative of Chile, on April 29, 1965, addressed a note to the Chairman of the Council in which his Government requested "that a Meeting of Consultation of Ministers of Foreign Affairs be convoked for the first day of May 1965";

As the agenda for the aforesaid Meeting, which would be held pursuant to the terms of Article 39 of the Charter of the Organization of American States, the Ambassador Representative of Chile has proposed the following:

"Serious situation created by armed strife in the Dominican Republic"; and

The urgency of the convocation makes it necessary to call attention to the provisions of Article 42 of the Charter of the OAS, adopting as regulations those approved by the Council at the meeting held on March 1, 1951, and designating the Pan American Union, in Washington, D.C. as the site of the Meeting;

The Council of the Organization
of American States

Resolves:

1. To convoke, pursuant to Articles 39 and 40 of the Charter of the Organization of American States, a Meeting of Consultation of Ministers of Foreign Affairs of the American Republics for May 1, 1965.

2. To approve as the agenda of this meeting the following:

"Serious situation created by the armed strife in the Dominican Republic."

3. To approve as the Regulations of the Conference those approved by the Council of the Organization of American States at the meeting held on March 1, 1951.

4. To designate the Pan American Union, Washington, D.C., as the site of the Meeting.

5. To request the Secretary General to inform the governments of the member states of the OAS of this decision, in the most rapid way possible, calling attention to the provisions of Article 42 of the Charter of the Organization of American States.

6. To appoint a committee to begin today to study the preparations for this Meeting, in the more urgent aspects not covered in this resolution.

*Department of State Bulletin, May 17, 1965, p. 739.

157. Statement by Ambassador Bunker, to the Council on United States Intervention in the Dominican Republic*

April 30, 1965

The resolution is adopted. In spite of the lateness of the hour and because of the urgency with which my Government views the situation in the Dominican Republic, I should like to ask the indulgence of the members to make a statement on behalf of my Government.

Since last Saturday afternoon, at the outbreak of hostilities, the Government of the United States has consistently urged on all the parties the necessity of a cease-fire. Several cease-fires have actually been arranged but none of them have been kept. And since the Americans and other foreigners have been in great danger, we have—at the same time that we have been requesting a cease-fire on both sides—we have evacuated some 1,400 citizens of my country and of other nations.

Unfortunately, before the evacuation was completed, there was further deterioration rather than a cease-fire, and an equal number of American citizens and many more nationals of other countries are still in the Dominican Republic. At this time there are some 650 additional persons at the polo grounds awaiting evacuation.

I may say that among those evacuated there have been 150 other nationals—other than the United States citizens—including citizens of the Latin countries, French, Dutch, Swedish, German, Spanish, British, and Canadians. Beginning today the United States Embassy has been under heavy fire throughout the day, and according to our information the diplomatic inviolability of at least five American Embassies has been violated; one of them, I understand, the Embassy of El Salvador, has been sacked and burned, and the Embassies of Mexico, Guatemala, and Peru, as well as that of the United States, have been violated.

We are, therefore, in our summation, faced with an immediate problem of how to restore law and order in order to protect not only the citizens of foreign countries, private and official; not only to proceed with evacuation in an orderly way; but also to stop the excessive vandalism which many people are wreaking on their fellow Dominican citizens, and I promise to keep the Council fully informed of developments.

I want to also state the fact that we are reinforcing our forces in Santo Domingo tonight, with the purpose of adequately protecting the lives of our citizens and the citizens of other countries who are there. Therefore I would request that, as a matter of great importance and urgency, the Council this very night direct an appeal for a cease-fire to all sides. My Government for its part will heartily join in such an appeal.

But if the appeal is made and goes unheeded we are still faced with the problem—because of the solemn duty which each state has to protect its citizens—to protect them from violence in a situation where there are no authorities to insure their protection. The United States must therefore reserve its right to take the necessary measures to protect its own citizens and officials from violence in a situation of anarchy.

There are many precedents for this kind of a situation. None of this is inconsistent with the inter-American obligations. We wholeheartedly subscribe to these obligations, including the doctrine of nonintervention and self-determination.

*Department of State Bulletin, May 17, 1965, pp. 739-41.

We are not talking about intruding in the domestic affairs of other countries; we are talking simply about the elementary duty to save lives in a situation where there is no authority able to accept responsibility for primary law and order. We believe that this is a matter of the greatest urgency for the OAS to deal with within the family of the hemisphere in which all of us have a great stake.

The United States obviously has no candidate for the Government of the Dominican Republic; this is a matter for the Dominican people themselves. It is for the OAS to find the means to assist the Dominican people to constitute a government which reflects their wishes and a government which can undertake the international obligations of the hemisphere.

We therefore request that the organ which has just been created here by this resolution recognize the urgency and the gravity of the situation, issue a call for a cease-fire, and constitute a committee to go at once to the Dominican Republic to arrange such a ceasefire and to consult with responsible Dominican elements as to the means by which they return as quickly as possible to constitutional government.

I must state quite frankly to this Council that events are moving with great rapidity and it may not be easy for the Organization of American States to keep pace with those events, but I can assure you that the United States is prepared to transfer its responsibility to the Organization of American States at the earliest possible moment. If in the hours ahead it is necessary, for the elementary humanitarian protection of the lives of innocent people, for the United States to take any action for the protection of its own nationals, everything that we might be called upon to do would be designed to make it possible for the OAS to carry out its heavy responsibilities and will be subject to such action as the OAS itself may decide to take.

Gentlemen, I should like to suggest and propose a resolution with reference to the cease-fire, which I will take the liberty of reading: [see Document 157]

In support of this resolution and especially of the second paragraph, I want to say to the members that I have been informed tonight of the desperate condition of the hospitals in Santo Domingo and the serious need for the proper care and treatment of the wounded, and I suggest that the Organization of American States call upon all of the contending parties to respect Red Cross personnel, vehicles, and insignia so that the sick and wounded may be properly cared for. This is an additional reason, it seems to me, for the need of speed and for the need of adopting an urgent call for a cease-fire on the part of all of the parties and of all sides engaged in conflict within the country.

158. *Resolution by the Council of the Organization of
     American States, Calling for a Cease-Fire in the
     Dominican Republic**

April 30, 1965

The Council of the Organization
of American States,

Resolves:
   1. To reiterate the call of April 29, 1965 upon all the authorities, the political groupings, and the opposing forces to pursue immediately all possible means by which a cease-fire may be established and all hostilities and military operations suspended in order to prevent any further tragic loss of life or injury as well as material damages in the sister Dominican Republic.
   2. To make an urgent appeal to the same authorities, political groupings, and forces on both sides to permit the immediate establishment of an international neutral zone of refuge, encompassing the geographic area of the city of Santo Domingo immediately surrounding the embassies of foreign governments, the inviolability of which will be respected by all opposing forces and within which nationals of all countries will be given safe haven.
   3. To inform the Security Council of the United Nations of the text of this resolution pursuant to Article 54 of the United Nations Charter.

159 *Radio-TV Network Broadcast by President Johnson,
    on United States Intervention in the Dominican
    Republic*†

April 30, 1965

   Good evening, ladies and gentlemen: For 2 days American forces have been in Santo Domingo in an effort to protect the lives of Americans and the nationals of other countries in the face of increasing violence and disorder. With the assistance of these American forces, over 2,400 Americans and other nationals have been evacuated from the Dominican Republic. We took this step when, and only when, we were officially notified by police and military officials of the Dominican Republic that they were no longer in a position to guarantee the safety of American and foreign nationals and to preserve law and order.
   In the last 24 hours violence and disorder have increased. There is great danger to the life of foreign nationals and of thousands of Dominican citizens, our fellow citizens of this hemisphere. By an outstanding effort of mediation the Papal Nuncio has achieved an agreement on a cease-fire which I have urged all those concerned to take. But this agreement is not now, as I speak, being fully respected. The maintenance

Department of State Bulletin, May 17, 1965, p. 741.
†*Department of State Bulletin,* May 17, 1965, pp. 742-43.

of the cease-fire is essential to the hopes of all for peace and freedom in the Dominican Republic.

Meanwhile there are signs that people trained outside the Dominican Republic are seeking to gain control. Thus the legitimate aspirations of the Dominican people and most of their leaders for progress, democracy, and social justice are threatened and so are the principles of the inter-American system.

The inter-American system, and its principal organ, the Organization of American States, have a grave and immediate responsibility. It is important that prompt action be taken. I am informed that a representative of the OAS is leaving Washington very shortly for the Dominican Republic. It is very important that representatives of the OAS be sent to the Dominican Republic, just as soon as they can be sent there, in order to strengthen the cease-fire and in order to help clear a road to the return of constitutional processes and free elections. Loss of time may mean that it is too late to preserve freedom, which alone can lead to the establishment of true democracy. This, I am sure, is what the people of the Dominican Republic want. Late action, or delay, in such a case could mean a failure to accomplish the agreed objectives of the American states.

The eyes of the hemisphere are now on the OAS, both in its meeting today and on the meeting of its foreign ministers contemplated tomorrow. The wisdom, the statesmanship, and the ability to act decisively of the OAS are critical to the hopes of peoples in every land of this continent.

The United States will give its full support to the work of the OAS and will never depart from its commitment to the preservation of the right of all of the free people of this hemisphere to choose their own course without falling prey to international conspiracy from any quarter.

160. Resolution by the Organization of American States at the Tenth Meeting of Consultation of Ministers of Foreign Affairs, to Establish a Committee to Re-establish Normal Conditions in the Dominican Republic*

May 1, 1965

The Tenth Meeting of Consultation of Ministers of Foreign Affairs

1. Decides to establish a committee composed of representatives of the following five member states: Argentina, Brazil, Colombia, Guatemala, and Panama;

2. Instructs the Committee to go immediately to the city of Santo Domingo, to do everything possible to obtain the re-establishment of peace and normal conditions, and to give priority to the following two functions:

a. To offer its good offices to the Dominican armed groups and political groups and to diplomatic representatives for the purpose of obtaining urgently:

i. a cease-fire; and

ii. the orderly evacuation of the persons who have taken asylum in the embassies and of all foreign citizens who desire to leave the Dominican Republic; and

*Department of State Bulletin, May 17, 1965, p. 741.

b. To carry out an investigation of all aspects of the situation in the Dominican Republic that led to the convocation of this Meeting;

3. Requests the Committee to submit a report to the Meeting on the progress of its work, including the conclusions and recommendations that it may consider appropriate, in the shortest time possible;

4. Requests the American governments and the Secretary General of the Organization of American States to extend their full cooperation in order to facilitate the work of the Committee; and

5. Instructs the Secretary General of the Organization of American States to transmit to the Security Council of the United Nations the text of this resolution, in accordance with the provisions of Article 54 of the Charter of the United Nations.

161. Press Release by President Johnson, on Sending Additional United States Forces to the Dominican Republic*

May 1, 1965

United States forces in the Dominican Republic have the necessary mission of establishing a neutral zone of refuge in the western zone of Santo Domingo in the terms called for by yesterday's resolution of the OAS Council.

This is a means of carrying out the goal of protecting the life, and insuring the safe evacuation, of all foreign nationals.

However, the forces in this area are thinly spread and subject to continuing attack and sniper fire. Their current responsibility extends over 9 square miles of a largely urban area. They also have the responsibility for keeping the port area of Haina free from attack from any side. Under current circumstances their capability is not adequate to this mission. For this reason we are lending additional forces. Those forces consist of two battalions of the 82d Airborne Division comprising approximately 1,500 men and additional detachments of Marines.

These forces are engaged in protecting human life. It is our earnest hope that it will not be necessary for them to defend themselves from attack from any quarter.

162. Press Release by President Johnson Concerning the Organization of American States Committee to Re-establish Peace in the Dominican Republic†

May 1, 1965

The Organization of American States has demonstrated why, as Franklin Roosevelt said, it is the oldest and most successful association of sovereign governments in the history of the world.

Today, faced with a threat to the principles of the inter-American system and the peace of the hemisphere, the OAS acted decisively.

*Department of State Bulletin, May 17, 1965, p. 743.
†Department of State Bulletin, May 17, 1965, pp. 743-44.

A committee made up of five member states will soon be on its way to the Dominican Republic. Its mission is to reestablish peace and normal conditions in that strife-weary island.

The good offices of this commission, representing the entire hemisphere, will be available to every group and party in the Dominican Republic. It will work for a ceasefire. It will try to insure the safe evacuation of foreign nationals. And it will investigate every aspect of the current volatile situation in that island.

We look forward, as do all the American states, to the success of the mission and to any recommendations and suggestions the commission might make.

For our part, the United States is ready to support—with every resource at its command—the inter-American system. We will help carry out the solemn judgments of the assembled American Republics.

And we once again join in the common appeal to put an end to violence. For only when shooting and bloodshed stop will it be possible to work toward the aspirations and hopes of the Dominican people. Progress and justice do not flourish at the point of a gun.

The daily work of the inter-American system is filled with hope for the progress of the American peoples. But it is in moments of crisis such as this we truly test the vitality of our association. We prove that independent and proud nations can work together in the common cause of peace and human liberty.

Our goal in the Dominican Republic is the goal which has been expressed again and again in the treaties and agreements which make up the fabric of the inter-American system. It is that the people of that country must be permitted to freely choose the path of political democracy, social justice, and economic progress. Neither the United States, nor any nation, can want or permit a return to that brutal and oppressive despotism which earned the condemnation and punishment of this hemisphere and of all civilized humanity. We intend to carry on the struggle against tyranny no matter in what ideology it cloaks itself. This is our mutual responsibility under the agreements we have signed and the common values which bind us together.

163. Radio-TV Network Address by President Johnson, on United States Intervention in the Dominican Republic*

May 2, 1965

Good evening, ladies and gentlemen: I have just come from a meeting with the leaders of both parties in the Congress, which was held in the Cabinet Room of the White House. I briefed them on the facts of the situation in the Dominican Republic. I want to make those same facts known to all the American people and to all the world.

There are times in the affairs of nations when great principles are tested in an ordeal of conflict and danger. This is such a time for the American nations.

At stake are the lives of thousands, the liberty of a nation, and the principles and the values of all the American Republics.

*Department of State Bulletin, May 17, 1965, pp. 744-48.

That is why the hopes and the concern of this entire hemisphere are on this Sabbath Sunday focused on the Dominican Republic.

In the dark mist of conflict and violence, revolution and confusion, it is not easy to find clear and unclouded truths.

But certain things are clear. And they require equally clear action. To understand, I think it is necessary to begin with the events of 8 or 9 days ago.

Last week our observers warned of an approaching political storm in the Dominican Republic. I immediately asked our Ambassador [W. Tapley Bennett, Jr.] to return to Washington at once so that we might discuss the situation and might plan a course of conduct. But events soon outran our hopes for peace.

Saturday, April 24–8 days ago—while Ambassador Bennett was conferring with the highest officials of your Government, revolution erupted in the Dominican Republic. Elements of the military forces of that country overthrew their government. However, the rebels themselves were divided. Some wanted to restore former President Juan Bosch. Others opposed his restoration. President Bosch, elected after the fall of Trujillo and his assassination, had been driven from office by an earlier revolution in the Dominican Republic.

Those who opposed Mr. Bosch's return formed a military committee in an effort to control that country. The others took to the street, and they began to lead a revolt on behalf of President Bosch. Control and effective government dissolved in conflict and confusion.

Meanwhile the United States was making a constant effort to restore peace. From Saturday afternoon onward, our Embassy urged a cease-fire, and I and all the officials of the American Government worked with every weapon at our command to achieve it.

On Tuesday the situation of turmoil was presented to the Peace Committee of the Organization of American States.

On Wednesday the entire Council of the Organization of American States received a full report from the Dominican Ambassador.

Meanwhile, all this time, from Saturday to Wednesday, the danger was mounting. Even though we were deeply saddened by bloodshed and violence in a close and friendly neighbor, we had no desire to interfere in the affairs of a sister Republic.

On Wednesday afternoon there was no longer any choice for the man who is your President. I was sitting in my little office reviewing the world situation with Secretary Rusk, Secretary McNamara, and Mr. McGeorge Bundy. Shortly after 3 o'clock I received a cable from our Ambassador, and he said that things were in danger; he had been informed the chief of police and governmental authorities could no longer protect us. We immediately started the necessary conference calls to be prepared.

At 5:14, almost 2 hours later, we received a cable that was labeled "critic," a word that is reserved for only the most urgent and immediate matters of national security.

The cable reported that Dominican law enforcement and military officials had informed our Embassy that the situation was completely out of control and that the police and the government could no longer give any guarantee concerning the safety of Americans or any foreign nationals.

Ambassador Bennett, who is one of our most experienced Foreign Service officers, went on in that cable to say that only an immediate landing of American forces could safeguard and protect the lives of thousands of Americans and thousands of other citizens of some 30 other countries. Ambassador Bennett urged your President to order an immediate landing.

In this situation hesitation and vacillation could mean death for many of our people, as well as many of the citizens of other lands.

I thought that we could not and we did not hesitate. Our forces, American forces, were ordered in immediately to protect American lives. They have done that. They have attacked no one, and although some of our servicemen gave their lives, not a single American civilian or the civilian of any other nation, as a result of this protection, lost their lives.

There may be those in our own country who say that such action was good but we should have waited, or we should have delayed, or we should have consulted further, or we should have called a meeting. But from the very beginning, the United States, at my instructions, had worked for a cease-fire beginning the Saturday the revolution took place. The matter was before the OAS Peace Committee on Tuesday, at our suggestion. It was before the full Council on Wednesday, and when I made my announcement to the American people that evening, I announced then I was notifying the Council.

When that cable arrived, when our entire country team in the Dominican Republic, made up of nine men—one from the Army, Navy, and Air Force, our Ambassador, our AID man, and others—said to your President unanimously: Mr. President, if you do not send forces immediately, men and women—Americans and those of other lands—will die in the streets—well, I knew there was no time to talk, to consult, or to delay. For in this situation delay itself would be decision—the decision to risk and to lose the lives of thousands of Americans and thousands of innocent people from all lands.

I want you to know that it is not a light or an easy matter to send our American boys to another country, but I do not think that the American people expect their President to hesitate or to vacillate in the face of danger, just because the decision is hard when life is in peril.

The revolutionary movement took a tragic turn. Communist leaders, many of them trained in Cuba, seeing a chance to increase disorder, to gain a foothold, joined the revolution. They took increasing control. And what began as a popular democratic revolution, committed to democracy and social justice, very shortly moved and was taken over and really seized and placed into the hands of a band of Communist conspirators.

Many of the original leaders of the rebellion, the followers of President Bosch, took refuge in foreign embassies because they had been superseded by other evil forces, and the Secretary General of the rebel government, Martínez Francisco, appealed for a cease-fire. But he was ignored. The revolution was now in other and dangerous hands.

When these new and ominous developments emerged, the OAS met again, and it met at the request of the United States. I am glad to say they responded wisely and decisively. A five-nation OAS team is now in the Dominican Republic, acting to achieve a cease-fire to insure the safety of innocent people, to restore normal conditions, and to open a path to democratic progress.

That is the situation now.

I plead, therefore, with every person and every country in this hemisphere that would choose to do so, to contact their ambassador in the Dominican Republic directly and to get firsthand evidence of the horrors and the hardship, the violence and the terror, and the international conspiracy from which United States servicemen have rescued the people of more than 30 nations from that war-torn land.

Earlier today I ordered two additional battalions—2,000 extra men—to proceed immediately to the Dominican Republic. In the meeting that I have just concluded with the congressional leaders—following that meeting—I directed the Secretary of Defense and the Chairman of the Joint Chiefs of Staff to issue instructions to land an additional 4,500 men at the earliest possible moment. The distribution of food to people who have not eaten for days, the need of medical supplies and attention for the sick and wounded, the health requirements to avoid an epidemic because there are hundreds that have been dead for days that are now in the streets, and other protection and security of each individual that is caught on that island require the attention of the additional forces which I have ordered to proceed to the Dominican Republic.

In addition, our servicemen have already, since they landed on Wednesday night, evacuated 3,000 persons from 30 countries in the world from this little island. But more than 5,000 people, 1,500 of whom are Americans—the others are foreign nationals—are tonight awaiting evacuation as I speak. We just must get on with that job immediately.

The evidence that we have on the revolutionary movement indicates that it took a very tragic turn. Many of them trained in Cuba, seeing a chance to increase disorder and to gain a foothold, joined the revolution. They took increasing control. What began as a popular democratic revolution that was committed to democracy and social justice moved into the hands of a band of Communist conspirators. Many of the original leaders of the rebellion, the followers of President Bosch, took refuge in foreign embassies and they are there tonight.

The American nations cannot, must not, and will not permit the establishment of another Communist government in the Western Hemisphere. This was the unanimous view of all the American nations when, in January 1962, they declared, and I quote: "The principles of communism are incompatible with the principles of the Inter-American system."

This is what our beloved President John F. Kennedy meant when, less than a week before his death, he told us: "We in this hemisphere must also use every resource at our command to prevent the establishment of another Cuba in this hemisphere. . . ."

This is and this will be the common action and the common purpose of the democratic forces of the hemisphere. For the danger is also a common danger, and the principles are common principles.

So we have acted to summon the resources of this entire hemisphere to this task. We have sent, on my instructions the night before last, special emissaries such as Ambassador [Teodoro] Moscoso of Puerto Rico, our very able Ambassador Averell Harriman, and others to Latin America to explain the situation, to tell them the truth, and to warn them that joint action is necessary. We are in contact with such distinguished Latin American statesmen as Romulo Betancourt [former President of Venezuela] and José Figueres [former President of Costa Rica]. We are seeking their wisdom and their counsel and their advice. We have also maintained communication with President Bosch, who has chosen to remain in Puerto Rico.

We have been consulting with the Organization of American States, and our distinguished Ambassador—than whom there is no better—Ambassador Bunker, has been reporting to them at great length all the actions of this Government, and we have been acting in conformity with their decisions.

We know that many who are now in revolt do not seek a Communist tyranny. We think it is tragic indeed that their high motives have been misused by a small band of conspirators who receive their directions from abroad.

To those who fight only for liberty and justice and progress I want to join with the Organization of American States in saying—in appealing to you tonight to lay down your arms and to assure you there is nothing to fear. The road is open for you to share in building a Dominican democracy, and we in America are ready and anxious and willing to help you. Your courage and your dedication are qualities which your country and all the hemisphere need for the future. You are needed to help shape that future. And neither we nor any other nation in this hemisphere can or should take it upon itself to ever interfere with the affairs of your country or any other country.

We believe that change comes, and we are glad it does, and it should come through peaceful process. But revolution in any country is a matter for that country to deal with. It becomes a matter calling for hemispheric action only—repeat, only—when the object is the establishment of a Communist dictatorship.

Let me also make clear tonight that we support no single man or any single group of men in the Dominican Republic. Our goal is a simple one. We are there to save the lives of our citizens and to save the lives of all people. Our goal, in keeping with the great principles of the inter-American system, is to help prevent another Communist state in this hemisphere. And we would like to do this without bloodshed or without large-scale fighting.

The form and the nature of the free Dominican government, I assure you, is solely a matter for the Dominican people, but we do know what kind of government we hope to see in the Dominican Republic. For that is carefully spelled out in the treaties and the agreements which make up the fabric of the inter-American system. It is expressed, time and time again, in the words of our statesmen and the values and hopes which bind us all together.

We hope to see a government dedicated to social justice for every citizen.

We hope to see a government working, every hour of every day, to feeding the hungry, to educating the ignorant, to healing the sick—a government whose only concern is the progress and the elevation and the welfare of all the people.

For more than three decades the people of that tragic little island suffered under the weight of one of the most brutal and despotic dictatorships of the Americas. We enthusiastically supported condemnation of that government by the Organization of American States. We joined in applying sanctions, and, when Trujillo was assassinated by his fellow citizens, we immediately acted to protect freedom and to prevent a new tyranny, and since that time we have taken the resources from all of our people at some sacrifice to many, and we have helped them with food and with other resources, with the Peace Corps volunteers, with the AID technicians; we have helped them in the effort to build a new order of progress.

How sad it is tonight that a people so long oppressed should once again be the targets of the forces of tyranny. Their long misery must weigh heavily on the heart of every citizen of this hemisphere. So I think it is our mutual responsibility to help the people of the Dominican Republic toward the day when they can freely choose the path of liberty and justice and progress. This is required of us by the agreements that we are party to and that we have signed. This is required of us by the values which bind us together.

Simón Bolívar once wrote from exile: "The veil has been torn asunder. We have already seen the light and it is not our desire to be thrust back into the darkness."

Well, after decades of night the Dominican people have seen a more hopeful light, and I know that the nations of this hemisphere will not let them be thrust back into the darkness.

And before I leave you, my fellow Americans, I want to say this personal word: I know that no American serviceman wants to kill anyone. I know that no American President wants to give an order which brings shooting and casualties and death. I want you to know, and I want the world to know, that as long as I am President of this country, we are going to defend ourselves. We will defend our soldiers against attackers. We will honor our treaties. We will keep our commitments. We will defend our nation against all those who seek to destroy not only the United States but every free country of this hemisphere. We do not want to bury anyone, as I have said so many times before. But we do not intend to be buried.

Thank you. God bless you. Good night.

164. Resolution by the Organization of American States, at the Tenth Meeting of Consultation of Ministers of Foreign Affairs, Establishing an Inter-American Force*

May 6, 1965

Whereas:

This Meeting at its session of May 1, established a Committee to proceed to the Dominican Republic to seek the re-establishment of peace and normal conditions in the territory of that republic;

The said resolution requests the American governments and the General Secretariat of the Organization of American States to extend their full cooperation to facilitate the work of the Committee;

The formation of an inter-American force will signify *ipso facto* the transformation of the forces presently in Dominican territory into another force that will not be that of one state or of a group of states but that of the Organization of American States, which Organization is charged with the responsibility of interpreting the democratic will of its members;

The American states being under the obligation to provide reciprocal assistance to each other, the Organization is under greater obligation to safeguard the principles of the Charter and to do everything possible so that in situations such as that prevailing in the Dominican Republic appropriate measures may be taken leading to the re-establishment of peace and normal democratic conditions;

*Department of State Bulletin, May 31, 1965, pp. 862-63.

The Organization of American States being competent to assist the member states in the preservation of peace and the re-establishment of normal democratic conditions, it is also competent to provide the means that reality and circumstances require and that prudence counsels as adequate for the accomplishment of such purposes; and

The Committee of the Organization of American States that proceeded to the Dominican Republic, in its second report to this Meeting, advises the formation of an inter-American force to achieve the objectives determined by the Meeting of Consultation,

The Tenth Meeting of Consultation
of Ministers of Foreign Affairs

Resolves:

1. To request governments of member states that are willing and capable of doing so to make contingents of their land, naval, air or police forces available to the Organization of American States, within their capabilities and to the extent they can do so, to form an inter-American force that will operate under the authority of this Tenth Meeting of Consultation.

2. That this Force will have as its sole purpose, in a spirit of democratic impartiality, that of cooperating in the restoration of normal conditions in the Dominican Republic, in maintaining the security of its inhabitants and the inviolability of human rights, and in the establishment of an atmosphere of peace and conciliation that will permit the functioning of democratic institutions.

3. To request the commanders of the contingents of forces that make up this Force to work out directly among themselves and with a Committee of this Meeting the technical measures necessary to establish a Unified Command of the Organization of American States for the coordinated and effective action of the Inter-American Armed Force. In the composition of this Force, an effort will be made to see that the national contingents shall be progressively equalized.

4. That at such time as the OAS Unified Command shall have determined that the Inter-American Armed Force is adequate for the purposes contemplated by the resolution adopted by this Meeting on May 1, 1965, the full responsibility of meeting these purposes shall be assumed by that Force.

5. That the withdrawal of the Inter-American Force from the Dominican Republic shall be determined by this Meeting.

6. To continue in session in order to keep the situation under review, to receive the report and recommendations of the Committee, and in the light thereof to take the necessary steps to facilitate the prompt restoration of democratic order in the Dominican Republic.

7. To inform the Security Council of the United Nations of the text of this resolution.

165. *Resolution by the U. N. Security Council, on the Intervention in the Dominican Republic**

May 14, 1965

The Security Council,
Deeply concerned at the grave events in the Dominican Republic,
1. *Calls for* strict cease-fire;
2. *Invites* the Secretary-General to send, as an urgent measure, a representative to the Dominican Republic for the purpose of reporting to the Security Council on the present situation;
    3. *Calls upon* all concerned in the Dominican Republic to co-operate with the representative of the Secretary-General in the carrying out of this task.

166. *Critique by Senator William J. Fullbright, before the Senate, on United States Policy in the Dominican Republic†*

September 15, 1965

Mr. President, the formation of a provisional government in Santo Domingo under the leadership of Dr. Hector Garcia-Godoy is good news. It provides reason for cautious optimism as to the future and testifies as well to the arduous and patient efforts of the OAS mediating team. I wish to pay tribute especially to Ambassador Bunker for his wisdom and patience in handling this difficult affair. The formation of a provisional government is not the end of the Dominican crisis, but it does bring to an end a tragic and dangerous phase of the crisis. Many problems remain, particularly the problem of establishing the authority of a democratic government over the Dominican military. Nonetheless, the situation now seems to be moving into a less dangerous and more hopeful phase. At this time of relative calm it is appropriate, desirable, and, I think, necessary to review events in the Dominican Republic and the U.S. role in those events. The purpose of such a review—and its only purpose—is to develop guidelines for wise and effective policies in the future.

I was in doubt about the advisability of making a statement on the Dominican affair until some of my colleagues made public statements on the floor. Their views on the way in which the committee proceedings were conducted and, indeed, on the Dominican crisis as a whole, are so diametrically opposed to my own that I now consider it my duty to express my personal conclusions drawn from the hearings held by the Committee on Foreign Relations.

The suggestions that have been made that the committee was prejudiced in its approach against the administration's policies are, in my opinion, without merit. The committee was impartial and fair in giving a full and detailed hearing to the administration's point of view, so much so, in fact, that it heard only one witness from outside the Government.

*United Nations Security Council, S/Res/203 (1965), May 14, 1965.
†*Congressional Record Senate*, Sept. 15, 1965, pp. 23855-61.

U.S. policy in the Dominican crisis was characterized initially by overtimidity and subsequently by overreaction. Throughout the whole affair, it has also been characterized by a lack of candor.

These are general conclusions I have reached from a painstaking review of the salient features of the extremely complex situation. These judgments are made, of course, with the benefit of hindsight and, in fairness, it must be conceded there were no easy choices available to the United States in the Dominican Republic. Nonetheless, it is the task of diplomacy to make wise decisions when they need to be made and U.S. diplomacy failed to do so in the Dominican crisis.

It cannot be said with assurance that the United States could have changed the course of events by acting differently. What can be said with assurance is that the United States did not take advantage of several opportunities in which it might have changed the course of events. The reason appears to be that, very close to the beginning of the revolution, U.S. policymakers decided that it should not be allowed to succeed. This decision seems to me to have been based on exaggerated estimates of Communist influence in the rebel movement in the initial stages and on distaste for the return to power of Juan Bosch or of a government controlled by Bosch's party, the PRD—Dominican Revolutionary Party.

The question of the degree of Communist influence is of critical importance and I shall comment on it later. The essential point, however, is that the United States, on the basis of ambiguous evidence, assumed almost from the beginning that the revolution was Communist dominated, or would certainly become so. It apparently never occurred to anyone that the United States could also attempt to influence the course which the revolution took. We misread prevailing tendencies in Latin America by overlooking or ignoring the fact that any reform movement is likely to attract Communist support. We thus failed to perceive that if we are automatically to oppose any reform movement that Communists adhere to, we are likely to end up opposing every reform movement, making ourselves the prisoners of reactionaries who wish to preserve the status quo—and the status quo in many countries is not good enough.

The principal reason for the failure of American policy in Santo Domingo was faulty advice given to the President by his representatives in the Dominican Republic at the time of acute crisis. Much of this advice was based on misjudgment of the facts of the situation; some of it appears to have been based on inadequate evidence or, in some cases, simply inaccurate information. On the basis of the information and counsel he received, the President could hardly have acted other than he did.

I am hopeful, and reasonably confident, that the mistakes made by the United States in the Dominican Republic can be retrieved and that it will be possible to avoid repeating them in the future. These purposes can be served, however, only if the shortcomings of U.S. policy are thoroughly reviewed and analyzed. I make my remarks today in the hope of contributing to that process.

The development of the Dominican crisis, beginning on April 24, 1965, provides a classic study of policymaking in a fast-changing situation in which each decision reduces the range of options available for future decisions so that errors are compounded and finally, indeed, there are few if any options except to follow through on an ill-conceived course of action. Beyond a certain point the Dominican story acquired some of the inevitability of a Greek tragedy.

Another theme that emerges from the Dominican crisis is the occurrence of a striking change in U.S. policy toward the Dominican Republic and the possibility—not a certainty, because the signs are ambiguous, but only the possibility—of a major change as well in the general Latin American policies of the United States. Obviously, an important change in the official outlook on Dominican affairs occurred between September 1963, when the United States was vigorously opposed to the overthrow of Juan Bosch and April 1965, when the United States was either unenthusiastic or actually opposed to his return.

What happened in that period to change the assessment of Bosch from favorable to unfavorable? It is quite true that Bosch as President did not distinguish himself as an administrator, but that was well known in 1963. It is also true, however, and much more to the point as far as the legitimate interests of the United States are concerned, that Bosch had received 58 percent of the votes in a free and honest election and that he was presiding over a reform-minded government in tune with the Alliance for Progress. This is a great deal more than can be said for any other President of the Dominican Republic.

The question therefore remains as to how and why the attitude of the U.S. Government changed so strikingly between September 1963 and April 1965. And the question inevitably arises whether this shift in the administration's attitude toward the Dominican Republic is part of a broader shift in its attitude toward other Latin American countries, whether, to be specific, the U.S. Government now views the vigorous reform movements of Latin America—such as Christian Democracy in Chile, Peru, and Venezuela, APRA in Peru and Accion Democratica in Venezuela—as threatening to the interests of the United States. And if this is the case, what kind of Latin American political movements would now be regarded as friendly to the United States and beneficial to its interests?

I should like to make it very clear that I am raising a question not offering an answer. I am frankly puzzled as to the current attitude of the U.S. Government toward reformist movements in Latin America. On the one hand, President Johnson's deep personal commitment to the philosophy and aims of the Alliance for Progress is clear; it was convincingly expressed, for example, in his speech to the Latin American Ambassadors on the fourth anniversary of the Alliance for Progress—a statement in which the President compared the Alliance for Progress with his own enlightened program for a Great Society at home. On the other hand, one notes a general tendency on the part of our policymakers not to look beyond a Latin American politician's anticommunism. One also notes in certain Government agencies, particularly the Department of Defense, a preoccupation with counterinsurgency, which is to say, with the prospect of revolutions and means of suppressing them. This preoccupation is manifested in dubious and costly research projects, such as the recently discredited Camelot; these studies claim to be scientific but beneath their almost unbelievably opaque language lies an unmistakable military and reactionary bias.

It is of great importance that the uncertainty as to U.S. aims in Latin America be resolved. We cannot successfully advance the cause of popular democracy and at the same time aline ourselves with corrupt and reactionary oligarchies; yet that is what we seem to be trying to do. The direction of the Alliance for Progress is toward social revolution in Latin America; the direction of our Dominican intervention is toward the suppression of revolutionary movements which are supported by Communists or suspected of being influenced by Communists. The prospect of an election in 9 months which may conceivably produce a strong democratic government is certainly reassuring on this score, but the fact remains that the reaction of the United States at the time of acute crisis was to intervene forcibly and illegally against a revolution which, had we sought to influence it instead of suppressing it, might have produced a strong popular government without foreign military intervention. Since just about every revolutionary movement is likely to attract Communist support, at least in the beginning, the approach followed in the Dominican Republic, if consistently pursued, must inevitably make us the enemy of all revolutions and therefore the ally of all the unpopular and corrupt oligarchies of the hemisphere.

We simply cannot have it both ways; we much choose between the Alliance for Progress and a foredoomed effort to sustain the status quo in Latin America. The choice which we are to make is the principal unanswered question arising out of the unhappy events in the Dominican Republic and, indeed, the principal unanswered question for the future of our relations with Latin America.

It is not surprising that we Americans are not drawn toward the uncouth revolutionaries of the non-Communist left. We are not, as we like to claim in Fourth of July speeches, the most truly revolutionary nation on earth; we are, on the contrary, much closer to being the most unrevolutionary nation on earth. We are sober and satisfied and comfortable and rich; our institutions are stable and old and even venerable; and our Revolution of 1776, for that matter, was not much of an upheaval compared to the French and Russian revolutions and to current and impending revolutions in Latin America, Asia, and Africa.

Our heritage of stability and conservatism is a great blessing, but it also has the effect of limiting our understanding of the character of social revolution and sometimes as well of the injustices which spawn them. Our understanding of revolutions and their causes is imperfect not because of any failures of mind or character but because of our good fortune since the Civil War in never having experienced sustained social injustice without hope of legal or more or less peaceful remedy. We are called upon, therefore, to give our understanding and our sympathy and support to movements which are alien to our experience and jarring to our preferences and prejudices.

We must try to understand social revolution and the injustices that give it rise because they are the heart and core of the experience of the great majority of people now living in the world. In Latin America we may prefer to associate with the well-bred, well-dressed businessmen who often hold positions of power, but Latin American reformers regard such men as aliens in their own countries who neither identify with their own people nor even sympathize with their aspirations. Such leaders are regarded by educated young Latin Americans as a "consular bourgeoisie," by which they mean business-oriented conservatives who more nearly represent the interests of foreign businessmen than the interests of their own people. Men like Donald Reid—who is one of the better of this category of leaders—may have their merits, but they are not the force of the future in Latin America.

It is the revolutionaries of the non-Communist left who have most of the popular support in Latin America. The Radical Party in Chile, for example, is full of 19th century libertarians whom many North Americans would find highly congenial, but it was recently crushed in national elections by a group of rambunctious, leftist Christian Democrats. It may be argued that the Christian Democrats are anti-United States, and to a considerable extent some of them are—more so now, it may be noted, than prior to the intervention of the United States in the Dominican Republic—but they are not Communists and they have popular support. They have also come to terms with the American copper companies in Chile; that is something which the predecessor conservative government was unable to do and something which a Communist government would have been unwilling to do.

The movement of the future in Latin America is social revolution. The question is whether it is to be Communist or democratic revolution and the choice which the Latin Americans make will depend in part on how the United States uses its great influence. It should be very clear that the choice is not between social revolution and conservative oligarchy but whether, by supporting reform, we bolster the popular non-Communist left or whether, by supporting unpopular oligarchies, we drive the rising generation of educated and patriotic young Latin Americans to an embittered and hostile form of communism like that of Fidel Castro in Chile.

In my Senate speech of March 25, 1964, I commented as follows on the prospect of revolution:

> I am not predicting violent revolutions in Latin America or elsewhere. Still less am I advocating them. I wish only to suggest that violent social revolutions are a possibility in countries where feudal oligarchies resist all meaningful change by peaceful means. We must not, in our preference for the democratic procedures envisioned by the Charter of Punta del Este, close our minds to the possibility that democratic procedures may fall in certain countries and that where democracy does fail violent social convulsions may occur.

I think that in the case of the Dominican Republic we did close our minds to the causes and to the essential legitimacy of revolution in a country in which democratic procedures had failed. That, I think, is the central fact concerning the participation of the United States in the Dominican revolution and, possibly as well, its major lesson for the future. I turn now to comment on some of the events which began last April 24 in Santo Domingo.

When the Dominican revolution began on Saturday, April 24, the United States had three options available. First, it could have supported the Reid Cabral government; second, it could have supported the revolutionary forces; and third, it could do nothing.

The administration chose the last course. When Donald Reid Cabral asked for U.S. intervention on Sunday morning, April 25, he was given no encouragement. He then resigned, and considerable disagreement ensued over the nature of the government to succeed him. The party of Juan Bosch, the PRD, or Dominican Revolutionary Party, asked for a "U.S. presence" at the transfer of government power but was given no encouragement. Thus, there began at that time a chaotic situation which amounted to civil war in a country without an effective government.

What happened in essence was that the Dominican military refused to support Reid and were equally opposed to Bosch or other PRD leaders as his successor. The PRD, which had the support of some military officers, announced that Rafael Molina Urena, who had been President of the Senate during the Bosch regime, would govern as Provisional President pending Bosch's return. At this point, the military leaders delivered an ultimatum, which the rebels ignored, and at about 4:30 on the afternoon of April 25 the air force and navy began firing at the National Palace. Later in the day, PRD leaders asked the U.S. Embassy to use its influence to persuade the air force to stop the attacks. The Embassy made it clear it would not intervene on behalf of the rebels, although on the following day, Monday, April 26, the Embassy did persuade the military to stop air attacks for a limited time.

This was the first crucial point in the crisis. If the United States thought that Reid was giving the Dominican Republic the best government it had had or was likely to get, why did the United States not react more vigorously to support him? On the other hand, if the Reid government was thought to be beyond salvation, why did not the United States offer positive encouragement to the moderate forces involved in the coup, if not by providing the "U.S. presence" requested by the PRD, then at least by letting it be known that the United States was not opposed to the prospective change of regimes or by encouraging the return of Juan Bosch to the Dominican Republic? In fact, according to available evidence, the U.S. Government made no effort to contact Bosch in the initial days of the crisis.

The United States was thus at the outset unwilling to support Reid and unwilling to support if not positively opposed to Bosch.

Events of the days following April 24 demonstrated that Reid had so little popular support that it can reasonably be argued that there was nothing the United States could have done, short of armed intervention, to save his regime. The more interesting question is why the United States was so reluctant to see Bosch returned to power. This is part of the larger question of why U.S. attitudes had changed so much since 1963 when Bosch, then in power, was warmly and repeatedly embraced and supported as few if any Latin American presidents have ever been supported by the United States.

The next crucial point in the Dominican story came on Tuesday, April 27, when rebel leaders, including Molina Urena and Caamano Deno, called at the U.S. Embassy seeking mediation and negotiations. At that time the military situation looked very bad for the rebel, or constitutionalist, forces. Ambassador Bennett, who had been instructed four times to work for a cease fire and for the formation of a military junta, felt he did not have authority to mediate; mediation, in his view, would have been "intervention." Mediation at that point might have been accomplished quietly and without massive military intervention. Twenty-four hours later the Ambassador was pleading for the marines, and as we know some 20,000 soldiers were landed—American soldiers.

On the afternoon of April 27 General Wessin y Wessin's tanks seemed about to cross the Duarte bridge into the city of Santo Domingo and the rebel cause appeared hopeless. When the rebels felt themselves rebuffed at the American Embassy, some of their leaders, including Molina Urena, sought asylum in Latin American embassies in Santo Domingo. The administration has interpreted this as evidence that the non-Communist rebels recognized growing Communist influence in their movement and were consequently abandoning the revolution. Molina Urena has said simply that he sought asylum because he thought the revolutionary cause hopeless.

An opportunity was lost on April 27. Ambassador Bennett was in a position to bring possibly decisive mediating power to bear for a democratic solution, but he chose not to do so on the ground that the exercise of his good offices at that point would have constituted intervention. In the words of Washington Post writer Murrey Marder—one of the press people who, to the best of my knowledge, has not been assailed as prejudiced:

> It can be argued with considerable weight that late Tuesday, April 27, the United States threw away a fateful opportunity to try to prevent the sequence that produced the American intervention. It allowed the relatively leaderless revolt to pass into hands which it was to allege were Communist.

The overriding reason for this mistake was the conviction of U.S. officials, on the basis of evidence which was fragmentary at best, that the rebels were dominated by Communists. A related and perhaps equally important reason for the U.S. Embassy's refusal to mediate on April 27 was the desire for and, at that point, expectation of an antirebel victory. They therefore passed up an important opportunity to reduce or even eliminate Communist influence by encouraging the moderate elements among the rebels and mediating for a democratic solution.

Owing to a degree of disorganization and timidity on the part of the anti-rebel forces which no one, including the U.S. Embassy and the rebels themselves, antici-pated, the rebels were still fighting on the morning of Wednesday, April 28. Ambas-sador Bennett thereupon urgently recommended that the antirebels under Air Force General de los Santos be furnished 50 walkie-talkies from U.S. Defense Department stocks in Puerto Rico. Repeating this recommendation later in the day, Bennett said that the issue was one between Castroism and its opponents. The antirebels themselves asked for armed U.S. intervention on their side; this request was refused at that time.

During the day, however, the situation deteriorated rapidly, from the point of view of public order in general and of the antirebels in particular. In midafternoon of April 28 Col. Pedro Bartolome Benoit, head of a junta which had been hastily assembled, asked again, this time in writing, for U.S. troops on the ground that this was the only way to prevent a Communist takeover; no mention was made of the junta's inability to protect American lives. This request was denied in Washington, and Benoit was thereupon told that the United States would not intervene unless he said he could not protect American citizens present in the Dominican Republic. Benoit was thus told in effect that if he said American lives were in danger the United States would intervene. And that is precisely what happened.

It was at this point, on April 28, that events acquired something of the predestiny of a Greek tragedy. Subsequent events—the failure of the missions of John Bartlow Martin and McGeorge Bundy, the conversion of the U.S. force into an inter-American force, the enforced stalemate between the rebels under Caamano Deno and the Imbert junta, the OAS mediation and the tortuous negotiations for a provisional government— have all been widely reported and were not fully explored in the committee hearings. In any case, the general direction of events was largely determined by the fateful decision of April 28. Once the Marines landed on that day, and especially after they were heavily reinforced in the days immediately following, the die was cast and the United States found itself deeply involved in the Dominican civil conflict, with no visible way to extricate itself, and with its hemisphere relations complicated in a way that few could have foreseen and no one could have desired.

The danger to American lives was more a pretext than a reason for the massive U.S. intervention that began on the evening of April 28. In fact, no American lives were lost in Santo Domingo until the Marines began exchanging fire with the rebels after April 28; reports of widespread shooting that endangered American lives turned out to be exaggerated.

Nevertheless, there can be no question that Santo Domingo was not a particularly safe place to be in the last days of April 1965. There was fighting in the streets, aircraft were strafing parts of the city, and there was indiscriminate shooting. I think that the United States would have been justified in landing a small force for the express purpose of removing U.S. citizens and other foreigners from the island. Had such a force been landed and then promptly withdrawn when it had completed its mission, I do not think that any fair-minded observer at home or abroad would have considered the United States to have exceeded its rights and responsibilities.

The United States intervened in the Dominican Republic for the purpose of preventing the victory of a revolutionary force which was judged to be Communist dominated. On the basis of Ambassador Bennett's messages to Washington, there is no doubt that the threat of communism rather than danger to American lives was his primary reason for recommending military intervention.

The question of the degree of Communist influence is therefore crucial, but it cannot be answered with certainty. The weight of the evidence is that Communists did not participate in planning the revolution—indeed, there is some indication that it took them by surprise—but that they very rapidly began to try to take advantage of it and to seize control of it. The evidence does not establish that the Communists at any time actually had control of the revolution. There is little doubt that they had influence within the revolutionary movement, but the degree of that influence remains a matter of speculation.

The administration, however, assumed almost from the beginning that the revolution was Communist-dominated, or would certainly become so, and that nothing short of forcible opposition could prevent a Communist takeover. In their apprehension lest the Dominican Republic become another Cuba, some of our officials seem to have forgotten that virtually all reform movements attract some Communist support, that there is an important difference between Communist support and Communist control of a political movement, that it is quite possible to compete with the Communists for influence in a reform movement rather than abandon it to them, and, most important of all, that economic development and social justice are themselves the primary and most reliable security against Communist subversion.

It is, perhaps, understandable that administration officials should have felt some sense of panic; after all, the Foreign Service officer who had the misfortune to be assigned to the Cuban desk at the time of Castro's rise to power has had his career ruined by congressional committees. Furthermore, even without this consideration, the decisions regarding the Dominican Republic had to be made under great pressure and on the basis of inconclusive information. In charity, this can be accepted as a reason why the decisions were mistaken; but it does not change the conclusion that they were mistaken.

The point I am making is not—emphatically not—that there was no Communist participation in the Dominican crisis, but simply that the administration acted on the premise that the revolution was controlled by Communists—a premise which it failed to establish at the time and has not established since. The issue is not whether there was Communist influence in the Dominican revolution but its degree, which is something on which reasonable men can differ. The burden of proof, however, is on those who take action, and the administration has not proven its assertion of Communist control.

Intervention on the basis of Communist participation as distinguished from control of the Dominican revolution was a mistake in my opinion which also reflects a grievous misreading of the temper of contemporary Latin American politics. Communists are present in all Latin American countries, and they are going to inject themselves into almost any Latin American revolution and try to seize control of it. If any group or any movement with which the Communists associate themselves is going to be automatically condemned in the eyes of the United States, then we have indeed given up all hope of guiding or influencing even to a marginal degree the revolutionary movements and the demands for social change which are sweeping Latin America. Worse, if that is our view, then we have made ourselves the prisoners of the Latin American oligarchs who are engaged in a vain attempt to preserve the status quo—reactionaries who habitually use the term "Communist" very loosely, in part out of emotional predilection and in part in a calculated effort to scare the United States into supporting their selfish and discredited aims.

If the United States had really been intervening to save American lives, as it had a moral if not a strictly legal right to do, it could have done so promptly and then withdrawn and the incident would soon have been forgotten. But the United States did not intervene primarily to save American lives; it intervened to prevent what it conceived to be a Communist takeover. That meant, in the terms in which the United States defined the situation, that it was intervening against the rebels, who, however heavily they might or might not have been infiltrated by Communists, were also the advocates of the restoration of a freely elected constitutional government which had been forcibly overthrown. It also meant that the United States was intervening for the military and the oligarchy—to the detriment of the Dominican people and to the bitter disappointment of those throughout Latin America who had placed their hopes in the United States and the Alliance for Progress.

On the basis of the record, there is ample justification for concluding that, at least from the time Reid resigned, U.S. policy was directed toward construction of a military junta which hopefully would restore peace and conduct free elections. That is to say that U.S. policy was directed against the return of Bosch and against the success of the rebel movement.

In this connection it is interesting to recall U.S. policy toward Bosch when he was in power in the Dominican Republic between February and September of 1963. He had been elected, as I have already mentioned, in the only free and honest election ever held in the Dominican Republic, in December 1962, with 58 percent of the votes cast.

The United States placed such importance on his success that President Kennedy sent the then Vice President Johnson and Senator Humphrey, among others, to attend his inauguration in February 1963. In September 1963, when he was overthrown in a military coup, the United States made strenuous efforts—which stopped just short of sending the Marines—to keep him in power, and thereafter the United States waited almost 3 months before recognizing the successor government. Recognition came, by the way, only after the successor government had conducted military operations against a band of alleged Communist guerrillas in the mountains, and there is a suspicion that the extent of the guerrilla activities was exaggerated by the successor government in order to secure U.S. recognition.

It may be granted that Bosch was no great success as President of the Dominican Republic but, when all his faults have been listed, the fact remains that Bosch was the only freely elected President in Dominican history, the only President who had ever tried, however ineptly, to give the country a decent government, and the only President who was unquestionably in tune with the Alliance for Progress.

Despite these considerations, the United States was at the very least unenthusiastic or, more probably, opposed to Bosch's return to power in April 1965. Bosch himself was apparently not eager to return—he vacillated in the very early stages and some well-informed persons contend that he positively refused to return to the Dominican Republic. In any case, he missed a critical opportunity. But the United States was equally adamant against a return to power of Bosch's party, the PRD, which is the nearest thing to a mass-based, well-organized party that has ever existed in the Dominican Republic. The stated reason was that a PRD government would be Communist dominated.

This might conceivably have happened, but the evidence by no means supports the conclusion that it would have happened. We based our policy on a possibility rather than on anything approaching a likelihood. Obviously, if we based all our policies on the mere possibility of communism, then we would have to set ourselves against just about every progressive political movement in the world, because almost all such movements are subject to at least the theoretical danger of Communist takeover. This approach is not in the national interest; foreign policy must be based on prospects that seem probable, hopeful and susceptible to constructive influence rather than on merely possible dangers.

One is led, therefore, to the conclusion that U.S. policymakers were unduly timid and alarmist in refusing to gamble on the forces of reform and social change. The bitter irony of such timidity is that by casting its lot with the forces of the status quo, in the probably vain hope that these forces could be induced to permit at least some reform and social change, the United States almost certainly helped the Communists to acquire converts whom they otherwise could not have won.

How vain the hopes of U.S. policymakers were is amply demonstrated by events since April 28. The junta led by Gen. Antonio Imbert, which succeeded the junta led by Colonel Benoit, proved quite intractable and indeed filled the airwaves daily with denunciations of the United States and the Organization of American States for preventing it from wiping out the Communist rebels. These are the same military forces which on April 28 were refusing to fight the rebels and begging for U.S. intervention. Our aim apparently was to use Imbert as a counterpoise to Caamano Deno in the ill-founded hope that non-Communist liberals would be drawn away from the rebel side.

In practice, instead of Imbert becoming our tractable instrument, we, to a certain extent, became his: he clung tenaciously to the power we gave him and was at least as intransigent as the rebels in the protracted negotiations for a provisional government.

The resignation of Imbert and his junta provides grounds for hope that a strong popular government may come to power in the Dominican Republic, but that hope must be tempered by the fact that the military continues to wield great power in Dominican politics—power which it probably would not now have if the United States had not intervened to save it from defeat last April 28. Even with a provisional government installed in Santo Domingo, and with the prospect of an election in 9 months, there remains the basic problem of a deep and widespread demand for social change. The prospect for such social change is circumscribed by the fact that the military has not surrendered and cannot be expected voluntarily to surrender its entrenched position of privilege and outrageous corruption.

The United States has grossly underestimated the symbolism of the Bosch constitution of 1963. It can be argued that this contains unrealistic promises, but it has stirred the hopes and idealism of the Dominican people. The real objections to it, the part of conservative Dominicans, seem to be that it provides for separation of church and state and that it provides that Dominican citizens have the right to live in the Dominican Republic if they so desire—that is, that Dominican citizens who happen also to be Communists cannot be deported. In passing, one may note a similarity to the U.S. Constitution on both of these points.

The United States has also misread the dedication of the Dominican military to the status quo and to its own powers and privileges. It may be said that the United States has overestimated its ability to influence the military while failing to use to the fullest the influence it does have.

The act of United States massive military intervention in the Dominican Republic was a grievous mistake, but if one is going to cross the bridge of intervention, with all of the historical ghosts which it calls forth throughout Latin America, then one might as well cross all the way and not stop in the middle. It is too late for the United States to refrain from intervention; it is not too late to try to redeem some permanent benefit from that intervention. Specifically, I think that the influence of the United States and the Organization of American States should be used to help the Dominican people free themselves from the oppressive weight of a corrupt and privileged military establishment. It is entirely possible, if not likely, that if the military is allowed to retain its power it will overthrow any future government that displeases it just as it has done in the past. The OAS mediating team made a contribution by bringing about the installation of a provisional government; the OAS can still make a solid contribution to Dominican democracy by urging or insisting that as part of a permanent solution the Dominican military establishment be substantially reduced in size and some of the more irresponsible generals be pensioned off or sent on lengthy diplomatic holidays abroad. If the United States and the OAS are going to impose a solution in the Dominican Republic, they might as well impose a good solution as a bad one.

Since preparing these remarks, I note in this morning's press that General Wessin has been induced to leave the Dominican Republic. This, I believe, is a step in the right direction.

The Foreign Relations Committee's study of the Dominican crisis leads me to draw certain specific conclusions regarding American policy in the Dominican Republic and also suggests some broader considerations regarding relations between the United States and Latin America. My specific conclusions regarding the crisis in Santo Domingo are as follows:

First. The United States intervened forcibly in the Dominican Republic in the last week of April 1965 not primarily to save American lives, as was then contended, but to prevent the victory of a revolutionary movement which was judged to be Communist-dominated. The decision to land thousands of marines on April 28 was based primarily on the fear of "another Cuba" in Santo Domingo.

Second. This fear was based on fragmentary and inadequate evidence. There is no doubt that Communists participated in the Dominican revolution on the rebel side, probably to a greater extent after than before the landing of U.S. marines on April 28, but just as it cannot be proved that the Communists would not have taken over the revolution neither can it be proved that they would have. There is little basis in the evidence offered the committee for the assertion that the rebels were Communist-dominated or certain to become so; on the contrary, the evidence suggests a chaotic situation in which no single faction was dominant at the outset and in which everbody, including the United States, had opportunities to influence the shape and course of the rebellion.

Third. The United States let pass its best opportunities to influence the course of events. The best opportunities were on April 25, when Juan Bosch's party, the PRD, requested a "United States presence," and on April 27, when the rebels, believing themselves defeated, requested United States mediation for a negotiated settlement. Both requests were rejected, in the first instance for reasons that are not entirely clear but probably because of United States hostility to the PRD, in the second instance because the U.S. Government anticipated and desired a victory of the antirebel forces.

Fourth. U.S. policy toward the Dominican Republic shifted markedly to the right between September 1963 and April 1965. In 1963, the United States strongly supported Bosch and the PRD as enlightened reformers; in 1965 the United States opposed their return to power on the unsubstantiated ground that a Bosch or PRD government would certainly, or almost certainly, become Communist dominated. Thus the United States turned its back on social revolution in Santo Domingo and associated itself with a corrupt and reactionary military oligarchy.

Fifth. U.S. policy was marred by a lack of candor and by misinformation. The former is illustrated by official assertions that U.S. military intervention was primarily for the purpose of saving American lives; the latter is illustrated by exaggerated reports of massacres and atrocities by the rebels—reports which no one has been able to verify. It was officially asserted, for example—by the President in a press conference on June 17 according to an official State Department bulletin—that "some 1,500 innocent people were murdered and shot, and their heads cut off." There is no evidence to support this statement. A sober examination of such evidence as is available indicates that the Imbert junta was guilty of at least as many atrocities as the rebels.

Sixth. Responsibility for the failure of American policy in Santo Domingo lies primarily with those who advised the President. In the critical days between April 25 and April 28, these officials sent the President exaggerated reports of the danger of a Communist takeover in Santo Domingo and, on the basis of these, recommended U.S. massive military intervention. It is not at all difficult to understand why, on the basis of such advice, the President made the decisions that he made.

Seventh. Underlying the bad advice and unwise actions of the United States was the fear of another Cuba. The specter of a second Communist state in the Western Hemisphere—and its probable repercussions within the United States and possible effects on the careers of those who might be held responsible—seems to have been the most important single factor in distorting the judgment of otherwise sensible and competent men.

I turn now to some broader and long-term implications of the Dominican tragedy, first to some considerations relating to the Organization of American States and its charter, then to the problem of reaction and revolution in Latin America, finally to a suggestion for a freer and, I believe, healthier relationship between the United States and Latin America.

Article 15 of the Charter of the Organization of American States says that:

No state or group of states has the right to intervene, directly or indirectly, for any reason whatever, in the internal or external affairs of any other state.

Article 17 states that:

The territory of a state is inviolable; it may not be the object, even temporarily, of military occupation or of other measures of force taken by another state, directly or indirectly, on any grounds whatever.

These clauses are not ambiguous. They mean that, with one exception to be noted, all forms of forcible intervention are absolutely prohibited among the American States. It may be that we should never have accepted this commitment at Bogotá in 1948; it is obvious from all the talk one hears these days about the obsoleteness of the principle of nonintervention that some U.S. officials regret our commitment to it. The fact remains that we are committed to it, not partially or temporarily or insofar as we find it compatible with our vital interests but almost absolutely. It represents our word and our bond and our willingness to honor the solemn commitments embodied in a treaty which was ratified by the Senate on August 28, 1950.

There are those who might concede the point of law but who would also argue that such considerations have to do with our ideals rather than our interests and are therefore of secondary importance. I do not believe that is true. We are currently fighting a war in Vietnam, largely, we are told, because it would be a disaster if the United States failed to honor its word and its commitment; the matter, we are told, is one of vital national interest. I do not see why it is any less a matter of vital interest to honor a clear and explicit treaty obligation in the Americas than it is to honor the much more ambiguous and less formal promises we have made to the South Vietnamese.

The sole exception to the prohibitions of articles 15 and 17 is spelled out in article 19 of the OAS Charter, which states that "measures adopted for the maintenance of peace and security in accordance with existing treaties do not constitute a violation of the principles set forth in articles 15 and 17." Article 6 of the Rio Treaty states:

If the inviolability or the integrity of the territory or the sovereignty or political independence of any American State should be affected by an aggression which is not an armed attack or by an extracontinental or intracontinental conflict, or by any other fact or situation that might endanger the peace of America, the Organ of Consultation shall meet immediately in order to agree on the measures which must be taken in case of aggression to assist the victim of the aggression or, in any case, the measures which should be taken for the common defense and for the maintenance of the peace and security of the continent.

The United States thus had legal recourse when the Dominican crisis broke on April 24, 1965. We could have called an urgent session of the Council of the OAS for the purpose of invoking article 6 of the Rio Treaty. But we did not do so. The administration has argued that there was no time to consult the OAS, although there was time to consult—or inform—the congressional leadership. The United States thus intervened in the Dominican Republic unilaterally—and illegally.

Advising the Latin American countries of our action after the fact did not constitute compliance with the OAS Charter or the Rio Treaty; nor, indeed, would advising them before the fact have constituted compliance. One does not comply with the law by notifying interested parties in advance of one's intent to violate it. Inter-American law requires consultation for the purpose of shaping a collective decision. Only on the basis of advance consultation and agreement could we have undertaken a legal intervention in the Dominican Republic.

It is possible, had we undertaken such consultations, that our Latin American partners would have delayed a decision; it is possible that they would have refused to authorize collective intervention. My own feeling is that the situation in any case did not justify military intervention except for the limited purpose of evacuating U.S. citizens and other foreigners, but even if it seemed to us that it did, we should not have undertaken it without the advance consent of our Latin American allies. We should not have done so because the word and the honor of the United States were at stake just as much—at least as much—in the Dominican crisis as they are in Vietnam and Korea and Berlin and all the places around the globe which we have committed ourselves to defend.

There is another important reason for compliance with the law. The United States is a conservative power in the world in the sense that most of its vital interests are served by stability and order. Law is the essential foundation of stability and order both within societies and in international relations. A great conference is taking place here in Washington this week on the subject, World Peace Through Law. As a conservative power the United States has a vital interest in upholding and expanding the reign of law in international relations. Insofar as international law is observed, it provides us with stability and order and with a means of predicting the behavior of those with whom we have reciprocal legal obligations. When we violate the law ourselves, whatever short term advantage may be gained, we are obviously encouraging others to violate the law; we thus encourage disorder and instability and thereby do incalculable damage to our own long term interests.

There are those who defend U.S. unilateral intervention in the Dominican Republic on the ground that the principle of nonintervention as spelled out in the OAS Charter is obsolete. The argument is unfortunate on two grounds. First, the contention of obsoleteness justifies an effort to bring about changes in the OAS Charter by due process of law, but it does not justify violation of the Charter. Second, the view that the principle of nonintervention is obsolete is one held by certain U.S. officials; most Latin Americans would argue that, far from being obsolete, the principle of nonintervention was and remains the heart and core of the inter-American system. Insofar as it is honored, it provided them with something that many in the United States find it hard to believe they could suppose they need: protection from the United States.

Many North Americans seem to believe that, while the United States does indeed participate in Latin American affairs from time to time, sometimes by force, it is done with the best of intentions, usually indeed to protect the Latin Americans from intervention by somebody else, and therefore cannot really be considered intervention.

The trouble with this point of view is that it is not shared by our neighbors to the south. Most of them do think they need protection from the United States and the history of the Monroe Doctrine and the "Roosevelt corollary" suggest that their fears are not entirely without foundation. "Good intentions" are not a very sound basis for judging the fulfillment of contractual obligations. Just about everybody, including the Communists, believes in his own "good intentions." It is a highly subjective criterion of national behavior and has no more than a chance relationship to good results. With whatever justice or lack of it, many Latin Americans are afraid of the United States; however much it may hurt our feelings, they prefer to have their security based on some more objective standard than the good intentions of the United States.

The standard on which they rely most heavily is the principle of nonintervention; however obsolete it may seem to certain U.S. officials, it remains vital and pertinent in Latin America. When we violate it, we are not overriding the mere letter of the law; we are violating what to Latin Americans is its vital heart and core.

The inter-American system is rooted in an implicit contract between the Latin American countries and the United States. In return for our promise not to interfere in their internal affairs they have accepted a role as members of our "sphere" and to support, or at least not to obstruct, our global policies. In the Dominican Republic we violated our part of the bargain; it remains to be seen whether Latin Americans will now feel free to violate theirs.

In the eyes of educated, energetic and patriotic young Latin Americans—which is to say, the generation that will make or break the Alliance for Progress—the United States committed a worse offense in the Dominican Republic than just intervention; it intervened against social revolution and in support, at least temporarily, of a corrupt, reactionary military oligarchy.

It is not possible at present to assess the depth and extent of disillusion with the United States on the part of democrats and reformers in Latin America. I myself think that it is deep and widespread. Nor am I reassured by assertions on the part of administration officials that a number of Latin American governments have secretly expressed sympathy for our actions in the Dominican Republic while explaining that of course they could not be expected to support us openly. Why cannot they support us openly, unless it is because their sympathy does not represent the views of their own people and they do not dare to express it openly? In fact, real enthusiasm for our Dominican venture has been confined largely to military dictators and ruling oligarchies.

The tragedy of Santo Domingo is that a policy that purported to defeat communism in the short run is more likely to have the effect of promoting it in the long run. Intervention in the Dominican Republic has alienated—temporarily or permanently, depending on our future policies—our real friends in Latin America. These, broadly, are the people of the democratic left—the Christian and social democrats in a number of countries, the APRA Party in Peru, the Accion Democratica Party in Venezuela, and their kindred spirits throughout the hemisphere. By our intervention on the side of a corrupt military oligarchy in the Dominican Republic, we have embarrassed before their own people the democratic reformers who have counseled trust and partnership with the United States. We have lent credence to the idea that the United States is the enemy of social revolution in Latin America and that the only choice Latin Americans have is between communism and reaction.

If those are the available alternatives, if there is no democratic left as a third option, then there is no doubt of the choice that honest and patriotic Latin Americans will make: they will choose communism, not because they want it but because U.S. policy will have foreclosed all other avenues of social revolution and, indeed, all other possibilities except the perpetuation of rule by military juntas and economic oligarchies.

The dominant force in Latin America is the aspiration of increasing numbers of people to personal and national dignity. In the minds of the rising generation there are two principal threats to that aspiration—reaction at home and domination from abroad. As a result of its Dominican actions the United States has allowed itself to become associated with both. We have thereby offended the dignity and self-respect of young and idealistic Latin Americans who must now wonder whether the United States will one day intervene against social revolutions in their own countries, whether one day they will find themselves facing U.S. marines across barricades in their own home towns.

I, myself, am sure, as I know President Johnson and, indeed, most U.S. citizens are sure, that our country is not now and will not become the enemy of social revolution in Latin America. We have made a mistake in the Dominican Republic, as we did at the Bay of Pigs in 1961, but a single misjudgment does not constitute a doctrine for the conduct of future policy and we remain dedicated to the goals of the Alliance for Progress.

We know this ourselves but it remains to convince our true friends in Latin America that their social revolutions will have our sympathy and support. It will not be easy to do so, because our intervention in Santo Domingo shook if it did not shatter a confidence in the United States that had been built up over 30 years since the liquidation of the Caribbean protectorates and the initiation of the "good neighbor policy."

It will be difficult but it can be done. President Johnson took a positive step on the long road back in his statement of rededication to the Alliance for Progress to the Latin American Ambassadors on August 17. It remains for us to eliminate the ambiguity between the antirevolutionary approach symbolized by Project Camelot and the preoccupation with problems of counterinsurgency on the one hand and the creative approach of the Alliance for Progress on the other. If we do this—and I am both sure that we can and reasonably hopeful that we will—then I think that the Dominican affair will be relegated in history to the status of a single unhappy episode on the long road toward the forging of a new and creative and dignified relationship between the United States and Latin America.

In conclusion, I suggest that a new and healthier relationship between the United States and Latin America must be a freer relationship than that of the past.

The United States is a world power with world responsibilities and to it the inter-American system represents a sensible way of maintaining law and order in the region closest to the United States. To the extent that it functions as we want it to function, one of the inter-American system's important advantages is that it stabilizes relations within the western hemisphere and thus frees the United States to act on its worldwide responsibilities.

To Latin Americans, on the other hand, the inter-American system is politically and psychologically confining. It has the effect, so to speak, of cooping them up in the

Western Hemisphere, giving them the feeling that there is no way to break out of the usually well-intentioned but often stifling embrace of the United States. In their hearts, I have no doubt, most Latin Americans would like to be free of us, just as a son or daughter coming of age wishes to be free of an over-protective parent. A great many of those Latin Americans for whom Castro still has some appeal—and there are now more, I would guess, than before last April 28—are attracted not, I feel, because they are infatuated with communism, but because Cuba, albeit at the price of almost complete dependency on the Soviet Union, has broken out of the orbit of the United States.

It is the nature of things that small nations do not live comfortably in the shadow of large and powerful nations, regardless of whether the latter are benevolent or overbearing. Belgium has always been uncomfortable about Germany and France; Ireland has never been able to work up much affection for Great Britain. And in recent years some of the Eastern European governments have demonstrated that, despite the Communist ideology which they share with the Soviet Union, they still wish to free themselves as much as they can and as much as they dare from the overbearing power of Russia. It is natural and inevitable that Latin American countries should have some of the same feelings toward the United States.

Perhaps, then, the foremost immediate requirement for a new and more friendly relationship between Latin America and the United States in the long run is not closer ties and new institutional bonds but a loosening of existing ties and institutional bonds. It is an established psychological principle—or, for that matter, just common-sense—that the strongest and most viable personal bonds are those which are voluntary, a voluntary bond being, by definition, an arrangement which one is free to enter or not to enter. I do not see why the same principle should not operate in relations between nations. If it does, it would follow that the first step toward stronger ties between Latin America and the United States would be the creation of a situation in which Latin American countries would be free, and would feel free, to maintain or sever existing ties as they see fit and, perhaps more important, to establish new arrangements, both among themselves and with nations outside the hemisphere, in which the United States would not participate.

President Frei of Chile has taken an initiative to this end. He has visited European leaders and apparently indicated that his Christian Democratic Government is interested in establishing new political, economic, and cultural links with European countries. For the reasons suggested, I think this is an intelligent and constructive step.

I think further that it would be a fine thing if Latin American countries were to undertake a program of their own for "building bridges" to the world beyond the Western Hemisphere—to Europe and Asia and Africa, and to the Communist countries if they wish. Such relationships, to be sure, would involve a loosening of ties to the United States in the immediate future, but in the long run, I feel sure, they would make for both happier and stronger bonds with the United States—happier because they would be free, stronger because they would be dignified and self-respecting as they never had been before.

167. The Act of Rio de Janeiro: Amendments to the Charter of the Organization of American States*

November 30, 1965

Whereas:

The inter-American system is the most expressive manifestation of the will of the American states in that which relates to firm guarantees of peace and security in the hemisphere, to the rule of the principles of law, both internally and in their foreign relations, and to the economic and social development of the people of the hemisphere;

The experience gained since the Charter of the Organization of American States came into effect indicates the need for strengthening the structure and more effectively coordinating the activities of the organs of the system, to attain fully the objectives set forth in the preceding paragraph; and

The inter-American system should be empowered, in accordance with the purposes and principles of the Charter of the Organization of American States, to resolve more effectively the various problems of the hemisphere,

The Second Special Inter-American Conference

Reaffirms:

The principles and standards in effect that are embodied in Part One of the Charter of the Organization of American States;

Declares:

1. That it is essential to forge a new dynamism for the inter-American system and to avoid duplication of efforts and conflicts of jurisdiction among its organs, in order to facilitate cooperation between the American states and obtain a more rational utilization of the resources of the Organization;

2. That it is essential to modify the working structure of the Organization of American States as defined in the Charter; and

Resolves:

1. To convoke, in accordance with articles 36 and 111 of the Charter of the Organization of American States the Third Special Inter-American Conference, to be held in the city of Buenos Aires. The Council of the Organization in agreement with the host country, shall set a day in July 1966 for the opening of the conference.

2. To entrust to a Special Committee, composed of representatives of each of the member states, the preparation of a preliminary draft proposal on amendments to the Charter of the Organization. The Council of the Organization of American States shall convoke the aforesaid Committee to meet in Panama and shall receive its conclusions. The Council shall refer these to the governments together with its observations, if any, at least 60 days before the Inter-American Conference to be convoked in accordance with paragraph 1 is held.

3. The preliminary draft of these amendments shall include additional standards for inter-American cooperation in the economic, social, and cultural fields.

*Organization of American States, Document OEA/Ser. C./I. 13.

4. The Special Committee shall use the following guidelines for the amendment of the Charter of the Organization:

a. An inter-American conference, as the highest body of the Organization of American States, shall be convened annually at a different site and on a fixed date, for the purposes set forth in Article 33 of the Charter and to approve the program and budget of the Organization, to determine the quotas of the member states, and to coordinate the activities of the organs and agencies of the inter-American system.

b. The Meeting of Consultation of Ministers of Foreign Affairs shall be retained in the form established in Article 39 of the Charter.

c. There shall be three Councils, directly responsible to the Inter-American Conference, as follows:

(1) The present Council of the Organization, which shall be permanent in nature and, in addition to the pertinent powers that may be assigned to it in the Charter of the Organization and inter-American treaties and agreements, as well as those relative to the maintenance of peace and the peaceful settlement of disputes that may be assigned to it, shall be the executive body for the decisions the Inter-American Conference or the Meeting of Consultation does not entrust to the Inter-American Economic and Social Council, to the Inter-American Educational, Scientific and Cultural Council, or to other organs;

(2) The Inter-American Economic and Social Council, which shall meet at least once a year and shall have a permanent executive committee with a structure similar to that of CIAP; CIAP shall act as the executive committee of the IA-ECOSOC so long as the Alliance for Progress is in force; and

(3) The Inter-American Educational, Scientific, and Cultural Council, which shall meet when convoked by the Inter-American Conference and shall have as its duties, in addition to promoting educational, scientific, and cultural progress of the peoples of the Americas, those assigned to the present Inter-American Cultural Council in articles 73 and 74 of the OAS Charter, with the exception of the last part of subparagraph (h) of Article 74, where reference is made to the Council of the Organization. The Inter-American Educational, Scientific and Cultural Council shall have a permanent committee, and its activities in the fields of education and training should be closely coordinated, whenever pertinent, with those of the IA-ECOSOC.

d. The Pan American Union shall continue to function as the central and permanent organ of the Organization of American States and the General Secretariat of the Organization, adapting its functions to the needs of the inter-American system.

e. The Secretary General and the Assistant Secretary General of the Organization shall hold office for five years.

f. The present Inter-American Juridical Committee of Rio de Janeiro shall be maintained as an advisory organ with the structure and functions deemed desirable by the Special Committee, and the situation of the Inter-American Council of Jurists shall be studied.

g. A study shall be made of the advisability of locating the permanent headquarters of all the Councils in one place or having them geographically decentralized, as well as a study of the feasibility of proceeding similarly in the case of the other OAS organs and agencies. In both cases all reasons and circumstances for and against one or the other of these solutions shall be considered.

h. The provisions of the Act of Washington, signed at the First Special Inter-American Conference on December 18, 1964, regulating the admission of new members shall be included; and

Decides:

That this resolution shall be known as "The Act of Rio de Janeiro."

168. *Resolution by the Council of the Organization of American States, Concerning the Havana Tricontinental Solidarity Conference**

February 2, 1966

"*Whereas:*

"The Ambassador, representative of Peru, in the note of January 19, 1966, addressed to the Vice-Chairman of the Council, in his capacity as Acting Chairman, requested on behalf of his Government . . . the convocation of a special meeting of the Council of the Organization, to formulate a denunciation on violation of the principle of non-intervention, set forth in the Charter of the Organization of American States and ratified by the General Assembly of the United Nations in its resolution 2131 (XX), adopted at the session held last December 21,

"The aforementioned convocation was seconded by the Ambassadors, representatives of Colombia and Venezuela, in notes dated January 23 and 24, respectively,

"At this special meeting, the Council heard statements by the representatives of Peru, Venezuela, Colombia, Bolivia, the Dominican Republic, the United States, Costa Rica, Haiti, El Salvador, Ecuador, Argentina, Panama, Nicaragua, Honduras, Paraguay, Guatemala, Brazil, Mexico, Uruguay, and Chile, who expressed unanimous support of the denunciation by the Government of Peru,

"In the city of Havana, during the first half of this past January, and under the official sponsorship of the Government of Cuba, a so-called Conference of Solidarity among the Peoples of Asia, Africa, and Latin America was held, with the participation of delegates from the Soviet Union, communist China, Cuba, and other States, as well as communist parties and groups from other countries, the final resolutions of which proclaimed a pledge by the participants to give financial, political, and military aid to communist subversive movements in this hemisphere, the same as in other parts of the world,

"This policy of intervention and aggression in the Western Hemisphere by some of the communist States constitutes a violation of the principle of non-intervention by one State in the internal and external affairs of another and of the self-determination of peoples, which were the object of resolution 2131 (XX) adopted December 21, 1965, by the General Assembly of the United Nations, principles laid down in the Charter of the Organization of American States,

*U.N. Security Council, U.N. Document S/7133, Feb. 11, 1966, English.

"As a result of the so-called Conference of Solidarity among the Peoples of Asia, Africa and Latin America, a permanent committee of twelve members was established in Havana consisting of representatives of communist countries and groups of those three continents, as well as a special organization for the promotion of subversion, terrorism and civil war in Latin America,

"This policy of intervention and aggression endangers the peace and security of the Western Hemisphere, and

"The Eighth Meeting of Consultation of Ministers of Foreign Affairs, held at Punta del Este, Uruguay, in 1962, in paragraph 1 of resolution 11 requested the Council of the Organization of American States . . . to maintain all necessary vigilance, for the purpose of warning against any acts of aggression, subversion, or other danger to peace and security, or the preparation of such acts, resulting from the continued intervention of Sino-Soviet Powers in this hemisphere, and to make recommendations to the Governments of the member States with regard thereto,

"The Council of the Organization of American States

"Resolves:

"1. To condemn emphatically the policy of intervention and aggression of the communist States and other participating countries and groups, manifested in the discussions and decisions of the so-called Conference of Solidarity among the Peoples of Asia, Africa, and Latin America, held in Havana during the first two weeks of January.

"2. To denounce especially, as an act contrary to the peace and security of the hemisphere and in violation of the principles of the Charter of the United Nations and of resolution 2131 (XX), of 21 December 1965, the open participation at the aforesaid Havana Conference of official or officially sponsored delegations of Member States of the United Nations that also voted in favour of the aforementioned resolution.

"3. To declare, in accordance with the Charter of the United Nations and resolution 2131 (XX), of 21 December 1965, adopted by the General Assembly of the United Nations, and also in conformity with the Charter of the Organization of American States and resolutions of the Inter-American Conferences and Meetings of Consultation of Ministers of Foreign Affairs, that a State is responsible not only for the open use of force against another but also for giving support to any of the indirect forms of aggression, such as the promotion of civil strife in another State, or the organization of armed bands and the furnishing of war material or elements of combat and of money with offensive intentions against another.

"4. To proclaim the American States' reiterated adherence to the principles of non-intervention and self-determination of peoples set forth in the Charter of the Organization and in resolution 2131 (XX), of 21 December 1965, of the United Nations General Assembly.

"5. To call upon the 'Special Committee to Study Resolutions i.1 and viii of the Eighth Meeting of Consultation of Ministers of Foreign Affairs' to make an urgent study and investigation of the deliberations, conclusions, and projections of the so-called Conference of Solidarity among the Peoples of Asia, Africa, and Latin

America, held in Havana, and to submit a report to the Council of the Organization along with such recommendations as it deems pertinent.

"6. To request the Secretary General of the Organization of American States to transmit this resolution to the Secretary-General of the United Nations, with a request that he distribute it among the Member States."

169. Resolution by the Organization of American States, at the Tenth Meeting of Consultation of Ministers of Foreign Affairs, Directing the Withdrawal of the Inter-American Peace Force from the Dominican Republic*

June 24, 1966

. . . . *Whereas:*

The fundamental purposes of the Tenth Meeting of Consultation have been fully achieved, inasmuch as popular elections were held in the Dominican Republic on 1 June 1966, whose results have given that sister nation a constitutional and democratic government,

This meeting, by the resolution it adopted on 6 May 1965, established the Inter-American Peace Force, and

The Minister of Foreign Affairs of the Dominican Republic, completing the representations previously initiated by the Provisional President of his country, Dr. Hector Garcia-Godoy, has formally expressed to this Meeting of Consultation the desire of his Government that the Inter-American Peace Force withdraw from Dominican territory and that it begin this withdrawal before 1 July of this year and complete it within ninety days,

The Tenth Meeting of Consultation of Ministers of Foreign Affairs resolves:

(1) To direct that the Inter-American Peace Force withdraw from the territory of the Dominican Republic.

(2) That this withdrawal begin before 1 July 1966, and be completed within ninety days from the date on which it begins.

(3) That the *Ad Hoc* Committee, in agreement with the Dominican Government, give the Inter-American Peace Force the necessary instructions concerning the dates for and the manner of effecting its withdrawal, in accordance with paragraph 2 above.

(4) To inform the Security Council of the United Nations of the text of this resolution, in accordance with the provisions of Article 54 of the Charter of the United Nations.

*U.N. Security Council, U.N. Document S/7379, June 27, 1966, English.

*170. American Chiefs of State, Declaration of the
       Presidents of America**

April 14, 1967

The Presidents of the American States
and the Prime Minister of Trinidad and Tobago
Meeting in Punta Del Este, Uruguay

Resolved to give more dynamic and concrete expression to the ideals of Latin American unity and of solidarity among the peoples of America, which inspired the founders of their countries;

Determined to make this goal a reality within their own generation, in keeping with the economic, social and cultural aspirations of their peoples;

Inspired by the principles underlying the inter-American system, especially those contained in the Charter of Punta del Este, the Economic and Social Act of Rio de Janeiro, and the Protocol of Buenos Aires amending the Charter of the Organization of American States;

Conscious that the attainment of national and regional development objectives in Latin America is based essentially on self-help;

Convinced, however, that the achievement of those objectives requires determined collaboration by all their countries, complementary support through mutual aid, and expansion of external cooperation;

Pledged to give vigorous impetus to the Alliance for Progress and to emphasize its multilateral character, with a view to encouraging balanced development of the region at a pace substantially faster than attained thus far;

United in the intent to strengthen democratic institutions, to raise the living standards of their peoples and to assure their increased participation in the development process, creating for these purposes suitable conditions in the political, economic and social as well as labor fields;

Resolved to maintain a harmony of fraternal relations in the Americas, in which racial equality must be effective;

Proclaim the solidarity of the countries they represent and their decision to achieve to the fullest measure the free, just, and democratic social order demanded by the peoples of the Hemisphere.

I

The Presidents of the Latin American Republics resolve to create progressively, beginning in 1970, the Latin American Common Market, which shall be substantially in operation in a period of no more than fifteen years. The Latin American Common Market will be based on the complete development and progressive convergence of the Latin American Free Trade Association and of the Central American Common Market, taking into account the interests of the Latin American countries not yet affiliated

---

*Pan American Union, *Declaration of the Presidents of America: Meeting of American Chiefs of State, Punta Del Este, Uruguay, Apr. 12-14, 1967*, Washington D.C., 1967.

with these systems. This great task will reinforce historic bonds, will promote industrial development and the strengthening of Latin American industrial enterprises, as well as more efficient production and new opportunities for employment, and will permit the region to play its deservedly significant role in world affairs. The ties of friendship among the peoples of the Continent will thus be strengthened.

The President of the United States of America, for his part, declares his firm support for this promising Latin American initiative.

The Undersigned Presidents Affirm That:

Economic integration demands a major sustained effort to build a land transportation network and to improve transportation systems of all kinds so as to open the way for the movement of both people and goods throughout the Continent; to establish an adequate and efficient telecommunications system; to install inter-connected power systems; and to develop jointly international river basins, frontier regions, and economic areas which include the territory of two or more countries.

To increase substantially Latin American foreign-trade earnings, individual and joint efforts shall be directed toward facilitating non-discriminatory access of Latin American products in world markets, toward increasing Latin American earnings from traditional exports, toward avoiding frequent fluctuations in income from such commodities, and, finally, toward adopting measures that will stimulate exports of Latin American manufactured products.

The living conditions of the rural workers and farmers of Latin America will be transformed, to guarantee their full participation in economic and social progress. For that purpose, integrated programs of modernization, land settlement, and agrarian reform will be carried out as the countries so require. Similarly, productivity will be improved and agricultural production diversified. Furthermore, recognizing that the Continent's capacity for food production entails a dual responsibility, a special effort will be made to produce sufficient food for the growing needs of their own peoples and to contribute toward feeding the peoples of other regions.

To give a decisive impetus to education for development, literacy campaigns will be intensified, education at all levels will be greatly expanded, and its quality improved so that the rich human potential of their peoples may make their maximum contribution to the economic, social, and cultural development of Latin America. Educational systems will be modernized taking full advantage of educational innovations, and exchanges of teachers and students will be increased.

Latin America will share in the benefits of current scientific and technological progress so as to reduce the widening gap between it and the highly industrialized nations in the areas of production techniques and of living conditions. National scientific and technological programs will be developed and strengthened and a regional program will be started; multinational institutes for advanced training and research will be established; existing institutes of this kind in Latin America will at the same time be strengthened and contributions will be made to the exchange and advancement of technological knowledge.

The fundamental role of health in the economic and social development of Latin America demands that the prevention and control of communicable diseases be intensified and that measures be taken to eradicate those which can be completely eliminated by existing techniques. Also programs to supply drinking water and other services essential to urban and rural environmental sanitation will be speeded up.

The Presidents of the Latin American Republics, conscious of the importance of armed forces to the maintenance of security, recognize at the same time that the demands of economic development and social progress make it necessary to devote to those purposes the maximum resources available in Latin America.

Therefore, they express their intention to limit military expenditures in proportion to the actual demands of national security in accordance with each country's constitutional provisions, avoiding those expenditures that are not indispensable for the performance of the specific duties of the armed forces and, where pertinent, of international commitments that obligate their respective governments. With regard to the Treaty on the Banning of Nuclear Arms in Latin America, they express the hope that it may enter into force as soon as possible, once the requirements established by the Treaty are fulfilled.

In facing the problems considered in this meeting, which constitute a challenge to the will of the American governments[1] and peoples, the Presidents proclaim their faith in the basic purpose of the inter-American system: to promote in the Americas free and democratic societies, existing under the rule of law, whose dynamic economies, reinforced by growing technological capabilities, will allow them to serve with ever-increasing effectiveness the peoples of the Continent, to whom they announce the following program.

II
ACTION PROGRAM

Chapter I

Latin American Economic Integration
and Industrial Development

1. Principles, objectives, and goals

Economic integration is a collective instrument for accelerating Latin American development and should constitute one of the policy goals of each of the countries of the region. The greatest possible efforts should be made to bring it about, as a necessary complement to national development plans.

At the same time, the different levels of development and economic and market conditions of the various Latin American countries must be borne in mind, in order that the integration process may promote their harmonious and balanced growth. In this respect, the countries of relatively less economic development, and, to the extent

---

[1]When the term "Latin America" is used in this text, it is to be understood that it includes all the member states of the Organization of American States, except the United States of America. The term "Presidents" includes the Prime Minister of Trinidad and Tobago. The term "Continent" comprises both the continental and insular areas.

required, those of insufficient market, will have preferential treatment in matters of trade and of technical and financial cooperation.

Integration must be fully at the service of Latin America. This requires the strengthening of Latin American enterprise through vigorous financial and technical support that will permit it to develop and supply the regional market efficiently. Foreign private enterprise will be able to fill an important function in assuring achievement of the objectives of integration within the pertinent policies of each of the countries of Latin America.

Adequate financing is required to facilitate the economic restructuring and adjustments called for by the urgent need to accelerate integration.

It is necessary to adopt all measures that will lead to the completion of Latin American integration, above all those that will bring about, in the shortest time possible, monetary stability and the elimination of all restrictions, including administrative, financial, and exchange restrictions, that obstruct the trade of the products of the area.

To these ends, the Latin American Presidents agree to take action on the following points:

a. Beginning in 1970, to establish progressively the Latin American Common Market, which should be substantially in operation within a period of no more than fifteen years.

b. The Latin American Common Market will be based on the improvement of the two existing integration systems: the Latin American Free Trade Association (LAFTA) and the Central American Common Market (CACM). The two systems will initiate simultaneously a process of convergence by stages of cooperation, closer ties, and integration, taking into account the interest of the Latin American countries not yet associated with these systems, in order to provide their access to one of them.

c. To encourage the incorporation of other countries of the Latin American region into the existing integration systems.

2. Measures with regard to the Latin American Free Trade Association (LAFTA)

The Presidents of the member states of LAFTA instruct their respective Ministers of Foreign Affairs, who will participate in the next meeting of the Council of Ministers of LAFTA, to be held in 1967, to adopt the measures necessary to implement the following decisions:

a. To accelerate the process of converting LAFTA into a common market. To this end, starting in 1970, and to be completed in a period of not more than fifteen years, LAFTA will put into effect a system of programmed elimination of duties and all other nontariff restrictions, and also a system of tariff harmonization, in order to establish progressively a common external tariff at levels that will promote efficiency and productivity, as well as the expansion of trade.

b. To coordinate progressively economic policies and instruments and to harmonize national laws to the extent required for integration. These measures will be adopted simultaneously with the improvement of the integration process.

c. To promote the conclusion of sectoral agreements for industrial complementation, endeavoring to obtain the participation of the countries of relatively less economic development.

d. To promote the conclusion of temporary subregional agreements, with provision for reducing tariffs within the subregions and harmonizing treatments toward third nations more rapidly than in the general agreements, in keeping with the objectives of regional integration. Subregional tariff reductions will not be extended to countries that are not parties to the subregional agreement, nor will they create special obligations for them.

Participation of the countries of relatively less economic development in all stages of the integration process and in the formation of the Latin American Common Market will be based on the provisions of the Treaty of Montevideo and its complementary resolutions, and these countries will be given the greatest possible advantages, so that balanced development of the region may be achieved.

To this same end, they have decided to promote immediate action to facilitate free access of products of the LAFTA member countries of relatively less economic development to the market of the other LAFTA countries, and to promote the installation and financing in the former countries of industries intended for the enlarged market.

The countries of relatively less economic development will have the right to participate and to obtain preferential conditions in the subregional agreements in which they have an interest.

The situation of countries characterized as being of insufficient market shall be taken into account in temporary preferential treatments established, to the extent necessary to achieve a harmonious development in the integration process.

It is understood that all the provisions set forth in this section fall within or are based upon the Treaty of Montevideo.

3. Measures with Regard to the Central American
Economic Integration Program

The Presidents of the member states of the Central American Common Market commit themselves:

a. To carry out an action program that will include the following measures, among others:

(1) Improvement of the customs union and establishment of a Central American monetary union;

(2) Completion of the regional network of infrastructure;

(3) Promotion of a common foreign-trade policy;

(4) Improvement of the common market in agricultural products and implementation of a joint, coordinated industrial policy;

(5) Acceleration of the process of free movement of manpower and capital within the area;

(6) Harmonization of the basic legislation required for economic integration.

b. To apply, in the implementation of the foregoing measures, and when pertinent, the temporary preferential treatment already established or that may be established, in accordance with the principle of balanced development among countries.

c. To foster closer ties between Panama and the Central American Common

Market, as well as rapid expansion of trade and investment relations with neighboring countries of the Central American and Caribbean region, taking advantage, to this end, of their geographic proximity and of the possibilities for economic complementation; also, to seek conclusion of subregional agreements and agreements of industrial complementation between Central America and other Latin American countries.

4. Measures Common to Latin American Countries

The Latin American Presidents commit themselves:

a. Not to establish new restrictions on trade among Latin American countries, except in special cases, such as those arising from equalization of tariffs and other instruments of trade policy, as well as from the need to assure the initiation or expansion of certain productive activities in countries of relatively less economic development.

b. To establish, by a tariff cut or other equivalent measures, a margin of preference within the region for all products originating in Latin American countries, taking into account the different degrees of development of the countries.

c. To have the measures in the two preceding paragraphs applied immediately among the member countries of LAFTA, in harmony with the other measures referring to this organization contained in the present chapter and, insofar as possible, to extend them to nonmember countries in a manner compatible with existing international commitments, inviting the latter countries to extend similar preferences to the members of LAFTA, with the same qualification.

d. To ensure that application of the foregoing measures shall not hinder internal readjustments designed to rationalize the instruments of trade policy made necessary in order to carry out national development plans and to achieve the goals of integration.

e. To promote acceleration of the studies already initiated regarding preferences that LAFTA countries might grant to imports from the Latin American countries that are not members of the Association.

f. To have studies made of the possibility of concluding agreements of industrial complementation in which all Latin American countries may participate, as well as temporary subregional economic integration agreements between the CACM and member countries of LAFTA.

g. To have a committee established composed of the executive organs of LAFTA and the CACM to coordinate implementation of the foregoing points. To this end, the committee will encourage meetings at the ministerial level, in order to ensure that Latin American integration will proceed as rapidly as possible, and, in due course, initiate negotiation of a general treaty or the protocols required to create the Latin American Common Market. Latin American countries that are not members shall be invited to send representatives to these meetings and to those of the committee of the executive organs of LAFTA and the CACM.

h. To give special attention to industrial development within integration, and particularly to the strengthening of Latin American industrial firms. In this regard, we reiterate that development must be balanced between investments for economic ends and investments for social ends.

5. Measures Common to Member Countries of the
Organization of American States (OAS)

The Presidents of the member states of the OAS agree:

a. To mobilize financial and technical resources within and without the hemisphere to contribute to the solution of problems in connection with the balance of payments, industrial readjustments, and retraining of the labor force that may arise from a rapid reduction of trade barriers during the period of transition toward the common market, as well as to increase the sums available for export credits in intra-Latin American trade. The Inter-American Development Bank and the organs of both existing integration systems should participate in the mobilization of such resources.

b. To mobilize public and private resources within and without the hemisphere to encourage industrial development as part of the integration process and of national development plans.

c. To mobilize financial and technical resources to undertake specific feasibility studies on multinational projects for Latin American industrial firms, as well as to aid in carrying out these projects.

d. To accelerate the studies being conducted by various inter-American agencies to promote strengthening of capital markets and the possible establishment of a Latin American stock market.

e. To make available to Central America, within the Alliance for Progress, adequate technical and financial resources, including those required for strengthening and expanding the existing Central American Economic Integration Fund, for the purpose of accelerating the Central American economic integration program.

f. To make available, within the Alliance for Progress and pursuant to the provisions of the Charter of Punta del Este, the technical and financial resources needed to accelerate the preparatory studies and work involved in converting LAFTA into a common market.

Chapter II

Multinational Action for Infrastructure Projects

The economic integration of Latin America demands a vigorous and sustained effort to complete and modernize the physical infrastructure of the region. It is necessary to build a land transport network and improve all types of transport systems to facilitate the movement of persons and goods throughout the hemisphere; to establish an adequate and efficient telecommunications system and interconnected power systems; and jointly to develop international watersheds, frontier regions and economic areas that include the territory of two or more countries. In Latin America there are in existence projects in all these fields, at different stages of preparation or implementation, but in many cases the completion of prior studies, financial resources, or merely the coordination of efforts and the decision to bring them to fruition are lacking.

The Presidents of the member states of the OAS agree to engage in determined action to undertake or accelerate the construction of the infrastructure required for the development and integration of Latin America and to make better use thereof. In so doing, it is essential that the groups of interested countries or multinational institutions determine criteria for assigning priorities, in view of the amount of human and material resources needed for the task.

As one basis for the criteria, which will be determined with precision upon consideration of the specific cases submitted for study, they stress the fundamental need to give preferential attention to those projects that benefit the countries of the region that are at a relatively lower level of economic development.

Priority should also be given to the mobilization of financial and technical resources for the preparation and implementation of infrastructure projects that will facilitate the participation of landlocked countries in regional and international trade.

In consequence, they adopt the following decisions for immediate implementation:

1. To complete the studies and conclude the agreements necessary to accelerate the construction of an inter-American telecommunications network.

2. To expedite the agreements necessary to complete the Pan American Highway, to accelerate the construction of the Bolivarian Highway (Carretera Marginal de la Selva) and its junction with the Trans-Chaco Highway and to support the studies and agreements designed to bring into being the new highway systems that will join groups of countries of continental and insular Latin America, as well as the basic works required to develop water and airborne transport of a multinational nature and the corresponding systems of operation. As a complement to these agreements, negotiations should be undertaken for the purpose of eliminating or reducing to a minimum the restrictions on international traffic and of promoting technical and administrative cooperation among land, water, and air transport enterprises and the establishment of multinational transport services.

3. To sponsor studies for preparing joint projects in connection with watersheds, such as the studies commenced on the development of the River Plate basin and that relating to the Gulf of Fonseca.

4. To allocate sufficient resources to the Preinvestment Fund for Latin American Integration of the IDB for conducting studies that will make it possible to identify and prepare multinational projects in all fields that may be of importance in promoting regional integration. In order that the aforesaid Fund may carry out an effective promotion effort, it is necessary that an adequate part of the resources allocated may be used without reimbursement, or with reimbursement conditioned on the execution of the corresponding projects.

5. To mobilize, within and outside the hemisphere, resources in addition to those that will continue to be placed at the disposal of the countries to support national economic development programs, such resources to be devoted especially to the implementation of multinational infrastructure projects that can represent important advances in the Latin American economic integration process. In this regard, the IDB should have additional resources in order to participate actively in the attainment of this objective.

Chapter III

Measures to Improve International Trade Conditions
in Latin America

The economic development of Latin America is seriously affected by the adverse conditions in which its international trade is carried out. Market structures, financial conditions, and actions that prejudice exports and other income from outside Latin America are impeding its growth and retarding the integration process. All this causes particular concern in view of the serious and growing imbalance between the standard of living in Latin American countries and that of the industrialized nations and, at the same time, calls for definite decisions and adequate instruments to implement the decisions.

Individual and joint efforts of the member states of the OAS are essential to increase the incomes of Latin American countries derived from, and to avoid frequent fluctuations in, traditional exports, as well as to promote new exports. Such efforts are also essential to reduce any adverse effects on the external earnings of Latin American countries that may be caused by measures which may be taken by industrialized countries for balance of payments reasons.

The Charter of Punta del Este, the Economic and Social Act of Rio de Janeiro and the new provisions of the Charter of the OAS reflect a hemispheric agreement with regard to these problems, which needs to be effectively implemented; therefore, the Presidents of the member states of the OAS agree:

1. To act in coordination in multilateral negotiations to achieve, without the more highly developed countries' expecting reciprocity, the greatest possible reduction or the elimination of tariffs and other restrictions that impede the access of Latin American products to world markets. The Government of the United States intends to make efforts for the purpose of liberalizing the conditions affecting exports of basic products of special interest to Latin American countries, in accordance with the provisions of Article 37. a) of the Protocol of Buenos Aires.

2. To consider together possible systems of general nonreciprocal preferential treatment for exports of manufactures and semimanufactures of the developing countries, with a view to improving the condition of the Latin American export trade.

3. To undertake a joint effort in all international institutions and organizations to eliminate discriminatory preferences against Latin American exports.

4. To strengthen the system of intergovernmental consultations and carry them out sufficiently in advance, so as to render them effective and ensure that programs for placing and selling surpluses and reserves that affect the exports of the developing countries take into account the interests of the Latin American countries.

5. To ensure compliance with international commitments to refrain from introducing or increasing tariff and nontariff barriers that affect exports of the developing countries, taking into account the interests of Latin America.

6. To combine efforts to strengthen and perfect existing international agreements, particularly the International Coffee Agreement, to obtain favorable conditions for trade in basic products of interest to Latin America and to explore all possibilities for the development of new agreements.

7. To support the financing and prompt initiation of the activities of the Coffee Diversification Fund, and consider in due course the creation of other funds to make it possible to control the production of basic products of interest to Latin America in which there is a chronic imbalance between supply and demand.

8. To adopt measures to make Latin American export products more competitive in world markets.

9. To put in operation as soon as possible an inter-American agency for export promotion that will help to identify and develop new export lines and to strengthen the placing of Latin American products in international markets, and to improve national and regional agencies designed for the same purpose.

10. To initiate such individual or joint action on the part of the member states of the OAS as may be required to ensure effective and timely execution of the foregoing agreements, as well as those that may be required to continue the execution of the agreements contained in the Charter of Punta del Este, in particular those relating to foreign trade.

With regard to joint action, the Inter-American Committee on the Alliance for Progress (CIAP) and other agencies in the region shall submit to the Inter-American Economic and Social Council (IA-ECOSOC), for consideration at its next meeting, the means, instruments, and action program for initiating execution thereof.

At its annual meetings, IA-ECOSOC shall examine the progress of the programs under way with the object of considering such action as may ensure compliance with the agreements concluded, inasmuch as a substantial improvement in the international conditions in which Latin American foreign trade is carried on is a basic prerequisite to the acceleration of economic development.

Chapter IV

Modernization of Rural Life and Increase of Agricultural Productivity, Principally of Food

In order to promote a rise in the standard of living of farmers and an improvement in the condition of the Latin American rural people and their full participation in economic and social life, it is necessary to give greater dynamism to agriculture in Latin America, through comprehensive programs of modernization, land settlement, and agrarian reform when required by the countries.

To achieve these objectives and to carry out these programs, contained in the Charter of Punta del Este, it is necessary to intensify internal efforts and to provide additional external resources.

Such programs will be oriented toward increasing food production in the Latin American countries in sufficient volume and quality to provide adequately for their population and to meet world needs for food to an ever-increasing extent, as well as toward improving agricultural productivity and toward a diversification of crops, which will assure the best possible competitive conditions for such production.

All these development efforts in agriculture must be related to the overall development of the national economies in order to harmonize the supply of agricultural products and the labor that could be freed as a result of the increase in farm productivity with the increase in demand for such products and with the need for labor in the economy as a whole.

This modernization of agricultural activities will furthermore create conditions for a development more in balance with the effort toward industrialization.

To achieve these goals, the Latin American Presidents undertake:

1. To improve the formulation and execution of agricultural policies and to ensure the carrying out of plans, programs, and projects for preinvestment, agricultural development, agrarian reform, and land settlement, adequately coordinated with national economic development plans, in order to intensify internal efforts and to facilitate obtaining and utilizing external financing.

2. To improve credit systems, including those earmarked for the resettlement of rural workers who are beneficiaries of agrarian reform, and for increased productivity, and to create facilities for the production, marketing, storage, transportation, and distribution of agricultural products.

3. To provide adequate incentives, including price incentives, to promote agricultural production under economic conditions.

4. To foster and to finance the acquisition and intensive use of those agricultural inputs which contribute to the improvement of productivity, as well as the establishment and expansion of Latin American industries producing agricultural inputs, particularly fertilizers, pesticides, and agricultural machinery.

5. To ensure the adequacy of tax systems that affect the agricultural sector, so that they may contribute to the increase of productivity, more production, and better land distribution.

6. To expand substantially programs of specialized education and research and of agricultural extension, in order to improve the training of the rural worker and the education of technical and professional personnel, and, also, to intensify animal and plant sanitation campaigns.

7. To provide incentives and to make available financial resources for the industrialization of agricultural production, especially through the development of small and medium industry and the promotion of exports of processed agricultural products.

8. To facilitate the establishment of multinational or international programs that will make it possible for Latin America to supply a larger proportion of world food needs.

9. To foster national programs of community development and of self-help for small-scale farmers, and to promote the creation and strengthening of agricultural cooperatives.

By recognizing the importance of the stated objectives, goals and means, the Presidents of the member states of the OAS undertake, within the spirit of the Alliance for Progress, to combine intensified internal efforts with additional external support especially earmarked for such measures.

They call upon CIAP, when analyzing the agricultural sector as included in national development plans, to bear in mind the objectives and measures indicated herein, giving due attention to agrarian reform programs in those countries that consider these programs an important basis for their agricultural progress and economic and social development.

Chapter V

Educational, Technological, and Scientific
Development and Intensification of Health Programs

A. Education and Culture

Education is a sector of high priority in the overall development policy of Latin American nations.

The Presidents of the member states of the OAS recognize that, during the past decade, there has been development of educational services in Latin America unparalleled in any other period of the history of their countires.

Nevertheless, it must be admitted that:

a. It is necessary to increase the effectiveness of national efforts in the field of education;

b. Educational systems should be more adequately adjusted to the demands of economic, social, and cultural development;

c. International cooperation in educational matters should be considerably intensified, in accordance with the new standards of the Charter of the OAS.

To these ends, they agree to improve educational administrative and planning systems; to raise the quality of education so as to stimulate the creativity of each pupil; to accelerate expansion of educational systems at all levels; and to assign priority to the following activities related to economic, social, and cultural development:

1. Orientation and, when necessary, reorganization of educational systems, in accordance with the needs and possibilities of each country, in order to achieve:

a. The expansion and progressive improvement of preschool education and extension of the period of general education;

b. An increase in the capacity of secondary schools and the improvement of their curricula;

c. An increase in opportunities following general education, including opportunities for learning a trade or a specialty or for continuing general education;

d. The gradual elimination of barriers between vocational and general education;

e. The expansion and diversification of university courses, so that they will include the new professions essential to economic and social development;

f. The establishment or expansion of graduate courses through professional schools;

g. The establishment of refresher courses in all branches and types of education, so that graduates may keep their knowledge up to date in this era of rapid scientific and technological progress;

h. The strengthening and expansion of adult education programs;

i. The promotion of special education for exceptional students.

2. Promotion of basic and advanced training for teachers and administrative personnel; development of educational research and experimentation, and adequate expansion of school building programs.

3. Broadening of the use of educational television and other modern teaching techniques.

4. Improvement of rural elementary schools to achieve a level of quality equal to that of urban elementary schools, with a view to assuring equal educational opportunities to the rural population.

5. Reorganization of vocational education, when necessary, taking into account the structure of the labor force and the foreseeable manpower needs of each country's development plan.

6. An increase in private financing of education.

7. Encouragement of local and regional communities to take an effective part in the construction of school buildings and in civic support to educational development.

8. A substantial increase in national scholarship and student loan and aid programs.

9. Establishment or expansion of extension services and services for preserving the cultural heritage and encouraging intellectual and artistic activity.

10. Strengthening of education for international understanding and Latin American integration.

Multinational Efforts

1. Increasing international resources for the purposes set forth in this chapter.

2. Instructing the appropriate agencies of the OAS to:

a. Provide technical assistance to the countries that so request:

i) In educational research, experimentation, and innovation;

ii) For training of specialized personnel;

iii) In educational television. It is recommended that study be made of the advisability of establishing a multinational training center in this field;

b. Organize meetings of experts to recommend measures to bring national curricula into harmony with Latin American integration goals;

c. Organize regional volunteer teacher programs;

d. Extend inter-American cooperation to the preservation and use of archeological, historic, and artistic monuments.

3. Expansion of OAS programs for fellowships, student loans, and teacher exchange.

National educational and cultural development efforts will be evaluated in coordination by CIAP and the Inter-American Council for Education, Science, and Culture (now the Inter-American Cultural Council).

B. Science and Technology

Advances in scientific and technological knowledge are changing the economic and social structure of many nations. Science and technology offer infinite possibilities for providing the people with the well-being that they seek. But in Latin American countries the potentialities that this wealth of the modern world offers have by no means been realized to the degree and extent necessary.

Science and technology offer genuine instruments for Latin American progress and must be given an unprecedented impetus at this time. This effort calls for inter-American cooperation, in view of the magnitude of the investments required and the level attained in such knowledge. In the same way, their organization and implementation in each country cannot be effected without a properly planned scientific and technological policy within the general framework of development.

For the above reasons the Presidents of the member states of the OAS agree upon the following measures:

Internal Efforts

Establishment, in accordance with the needs and possibilities of each country, of national policies in the field of science and technology, with the necessary machinery and funds, the main elements of which shall be:

1. Promotion of professional training for scientists and technicians and an increase in their numbers.

2. Establishment of conditions favoring full utilization of the scientific and technological potential for solving the economic and social problems of Latin America, and to prevent the exodus of persons qualified in these fields.

3. Encouragement of increased private financial contributions for scientific and technological research and teaching.

Multinational Efforts

1. Establishment of a Regional Scientific and Technological Development Program designed to advance science and technology to a degree that they will contribute substantially to accelerating the economic development and well-being of their peoples and make it feasible to engage in pure and applied scientific research of the highest possible quality. This Program shall complement Latin American national programs in the area of science and technology and shall take special account of the characteristics of each of the countries.

2. The Program shall be oriented toward the adoption of measures to promote scientific and technological research, teaching, and information; basic and advanced training of scientific personnel; and exchange of information. It shall promote intensively the transfer to, and adaptation by, the Latin American countries of knowledge and technologies originating in other regions.

3. The Program shall be conducted through national agencies responsible for scientific and technological policy, through institutions—national or international, public or private—either now existing or to be established in the future.

4. As part of the Program, they propose that multinational technological and scientific training and research institutions at the post-graduate level be established, and that institutions of this nature already existing in Latin America be strengthened. A group, composed of high-ranking, qualified persons, experienced in science, technology, and university education, shall be established to make recommendations to the Inter-American Council for Education, Science, and Culture (now the Inter-American Cultural Council) on the nature of such multinational institutions, including such matters as their organization, the characteristics of their multinational administration, financing, location, coordination of their activities among themselves and with those of pertinent national institutions, and on the other aspects of their operation. The aforementioned group, selected and convoked by the Inter-American Council for Education, Science, and Culture (now the Inter-American Cultural Council) or, failing this, by CIAP, shall meet within 120 days after the close of this meeting.

5. In order to encourage the training of scientific and technological personnel at the higher academic levels, they resolve that an Inter-American Fund for Scientific and

Technological Training shall be established as part of the Program, so that scientists and research workers from Latin American countries may pursue advanced scientific and technological studies, with the obligation to engage in a period of scientific work in Latin America.

6. The Program shall be promoted by the Inter-American Council for Education, Science, and Culture (now the Inter-American Cultural Council), in cooperation with CIAP. They shall coordinate their activities with similar activities of the United Nations and other interested organizations.

7. The Program may be financed by contributions of the member states of the inter-American system, inter-American or international institutions, technologically advanced countries, universities, foundations, and private individuals.

C. Health

Improvement of health conditions is fundamental to the economic and social development of Latin America.

Available scientific knowledge makes it possible to obtain specific results, which, in accordance with the needs of each country and the provisions of the Charter of Punta del Este, should be utilized to attain the following objectives:

a. Control of communicable diseases and eradication of those for which methods for total elimination exist. Pertinent programs shall receive international coordination when necessary.

b. Acceleration of programs for providing drinking-water supplies, sewerage, and other services essential to environmental sanitation in rural and urban areas, giving preference to lower-income groups. On the basis of studies carried out and with the cooperation of international financing agencies, national revolving fund systems shall be used to assure the continuity of such programs.

c. Greater and more rapid progress in improving nutrition of the neediest groups of the population, taking advantage of all possibilities offered by national effort and international cooperation.

d. Promotion of intensive mother and child welfare programs and of educational programs on overall family guidance methods.

e. Priority for basic and advanced training of professional, technical, administrative, and auxiliary personnel, and support of operational and administrative research in the field of health.

f. Incorporation, as early as the preinvestment phase, of national and regional health programs into general development plans.

The Presidents of the member states of the OAS, therefore, decide:

1. To expand, within the framework of general planning, the preparation and implementation of national plans that will strengthen infrastructure in the field of health.

2. To mobilize internal and external resources to meet the needs for financing these plans. In this connection, to call upon CIAP, when analyzing the health sector in national development programs, to take into account the objectives and needs indicated.

3. To call upon the Pan American Health Organization to cooperate with the governments in the preparation of specific programs relating to these objectives.

Chapter VI

Elimination of Unnecessary Military Expenditures

The Latin American Presidents, conscious of the importance of the armed forces in maintaining security, at the same time recognize that the demands of economic development and social progress make it necessary to apply the maximum resources available in Latin America to these ends.

Consequently, they express their intention to limit military expenditures in proportion to the actual demands of national security, in accordance with each country's constitutional provisions, avoiding those expenditures that are not indispensable for the performance of the specific duties of the armed forces and, where pertinent, of international commitments that obligate their respective governments.

With regard to the Treaty on the Banning of Nuclear Arms in Latin America they express the hope that it may enter into force as soon as possible, once the requirements established by the Treaty are fulfilled. . . .

171. Message from President Johnson, to the Senate Requesting Ratification of Amendments to the Charter of the Organization of American States*

June 12, 1967

I request the advice and consent of the Senate to ratification of the protocol of amendment to the Charter of the Organization of American States—the "Protocol of Buenos Aires"—signed at the Third Special Inter-American Conference at Buenos Aires on February 27, 1967.

The signing of the protocol of Buenos Aires was a major development for the inter-American system. The amendments to be effected in the Charter of the Organization of American States by the protocol of amendment, the first such amendments since the adoption of the charter in 1948, will go far toward the necessary modernization of the structure of the Organization and the strengthening of its capacity to act effectively in the interest of hemispheric cooperation and solidarity. The amendments grant certain fuller responsibilities to some of the organs of the Organization, for instance, in the field of peaceful settlement. They establish new and specific objectives and standards for the promotion of economic, social, and cultural development.

Following in general the guidelines prepared at the Second Special Inter-American Conference at Rio de Janeiro in November 1965, and the draft amendments prepared by the OAS Special Committee which met in Panama in March 1966 and by the Inter-American Economic and Social Council which met in Washington in June 1966, the Buenos Aires Conference adopted the amendments which are embodied in the protocol of amendment.

Among the more significant changes in the amendments relating to the structure of the Organization and to the responsibilities of its organs are those concerning (1) the

*Department of State Bulletin, July 17, 1967, pp. 78-79.

provision in the charter of procedures for the Organization to authorize the admission of new members; (2) the replacement of the Inter-American Conference which meets every 5 years by a General Assembly which meets annually and which assumes certain functions now performed by the OAS Council; (3) the redesignation of the OAS Council as the Permanent Council, and the granting of additional responsibilities to the Inter-American Economic and Social Council and Inter-American Council for Education, Science, and Culture—formerly the Inter-American Cultural Council—which become organs directly responsible to the General Assembly as is the Permanent Council; (4) the elimination of the Inter-American Council of Jurists and the upgrading of the Inter-American Juridical Committee; (5) the assignment to the Permanent Council of specific additional authority in the field of peaceful settlement; (6) the incorporation of the Inter-American Commission on Human Rights into the OAS Charter as an organ with functions to be later determined by an inter-American convention on human rights; and (7) the election of the OAS Secretary General and Assistant Secretary General by the General Assembly for 5-year terms, rather than by the OAS Council for 10-year terms as presently provided.

The expanded economic standards underscore the importance of self-help efforts and reiterate the present charter undertaking of members to cooperate with one another in the economic field "as far as their resources permit and laws may provide." The amendments provide that States should make individual and united efforts to bring about improved conditions of trade in basic commodities and a reduction of trade barriers by importing countries. Several articles deal with efforts to accelerate Latin American economic integration.

The social and the educational, scientific, and cultural standards elaborate on the principles in the present charter in these areas.

The various amendments are dealt with in detail in the enclosed report by the Secretary of State and summary of amendments.

I believe it to be in the national interest of the United States to ratify the proposed amendments. I therefore urge that the Senate consent to ratification by the United States of these amendments to the Charter of the Organization of American States.

172. Statement by Secretary Rusk before the Twelfth Meeting of Consultation of the Ministers of Foreign Affairs of the Organization of American States*

September 23, 1967

It is a great personal pleasure for me to meet again with my colleagues, my fellow Foreign Ministers. I have listened with great respect to the statements that have already been made here, especially those made by the distinguished Foreign Ministers of Venezuela and Bolivia. The presentation of the Bolivian Foreign Minister yesterday made clear the extent of Cuban subversion and intervention in the internal affairs of his country.

The task in front of us is a very simple one. It is to make it clear to Castro that

*Department of State Bulletin, Oct. 16, 1967, pp. 490-93.

these activities must stop. Beginning with the Eighth Meeting of Foreign Ministers in January 1962, we have worked together to build up our national and international defenses against Castro's threat to our free institutions and peoples.

We have thus recognized and acted upon the principle of solidarity and mutual security. This same principle of cooperation is inherent in our efforts to develop the hemisphere economically and socially; it undergirds the Alliance for Progress; it was our basic guide at the meeting of our Presidents last April; it is embodied in the revisions of our charter. All of us accept the premise that each country has an obligation to help itself, but all of us have also accepted the obligation for mutual assistance to each other.

Now Venezuela invokes the principle of mutual security to defend itself and the hemisphere against subversive aggression spawned and directed from Cuba. As the problem is a common one to all of us, so must be our response.

The steps we have already taken have not so far prevented Castro from continuing to pursue his objective. But they have been important measures in preventing him from achieving it. The Castro Communist record of the last years does not make pleasant reading: killings, burnings, kidnapings, sabotage, urban terrorism, and guerrilla warfare. However, despite all of Castro's efforts at subversion, despite all his attempts to exploit every real or supposed political, economic, and social weakness in the hemisphere, and despite all of his maneuvering and opportunistic shifting of political alliances, he has not succeeded. The Castro Communists have failed to achieve the general public support they have sought; they have failed to fire the imaginations or capture the allegiance of significant groups of our peoples; they have failed to disrupt the forward march of our economic and social development under the Alliance for Progress: they have failed in their efforts to turn the Andes into the Sierra Maestra of the hemisphere; they have failed to come even close to achieving power outside of Cuba itself.

There is no need, therefore, for us to exaggerate the ability of the present Cuban regime to subvert our peoples or overthrow our institutions.

However, it would be imprudent not to recognize that these Cuba-directed efforts do constitute a problem of common concern to the hemisphere. It would be imprudent to be indifferent to the violence and disruption which such subversive activities can produce. It would be imprudent not to stop these activities at the very beginning before any momentum is achieved.

We are now confronted with the latest examples of Castro's efforts. Venezuela has presented to us a pervasive case of Cuban intervention and subversion, and we have before us the report of Committee I that provides additional information to corroborate the Venezuelan charges. Here we see once more the panorama of Cuban intervention: the training, arming, landing, and support of Venezuelan guerrillas and terrorists, with the assistance of the Cuban armed forces and intelligence services; the maintenance of clandestine networks for communications, travel, sabotage, and espionage; and the constant outpouring of propaganda to incite and encourage armed violence against the democratic government and people of Venezuela.

The Committee concludes that the specific case of the landing of guerrillas in May 1967 was "planned and executed under the direction of the Government of Cuba and with the participation of members of the Cuban Armed Forces."

If there were any question as to Cuban responsibility that question was obviated by the public admission of responsibility by the Central Committee of the Cuban Communist Party, of which Castro is chairman.

And the comments of the report on the general policy of the present Government of Cuba are equally underscored by the repeated declarations by Castro and by the unhappy experience of other countries.

Our distinguished colleague from Bolivia has given us detailed proof of men and equipment and attempts at armed subversion in his country.

In an effort to provide greater international backing and structure for the whole subversive effort, the "Tricontinental Conference" was held in Havana in January 1966 and created the so-called Afro-Asian-Latin American Peoples Solidarity Organization and the so-called Latin American Solidarity Organization, both with the same objective: the overthrow of existing governments. As the recent LASO conference in Havana revealed, that organization is a device for Castro to exert leadership over extremist elements and subversive movements in the hemisphere. Its participants, having endorsed Castro's advocacy of armed struggle, are now filtering back to their countries carrying that message.

Castro and his LASO colleagues not only advocate armed struggle throughout Latin America but are now attempting to relate this thesis to the United States by claiming a kinship with the struggle for Negro rights and by advocating armed violence in our cities. All responsible American Negroes reject these efforts to capitalize on their—and our—grave problems. They want nothing to do with Castro Communist guerrilla, terrorist, or other subversive movements. As in all our countries, the underprivileged peoples of the United States are determined to achieve a better life but reject alien and repugnant ideologies.

We must neither exaggerate nor underestimate the importance of LASO. It is not as "Latin American" as its sponsors claim, nor does it have the "solidarity" that its name implies. It is so far essentially an instrument of the Cuban regime, designed to carry out Havana's program of guerrilla warfare and urban terrorism. The predominance of the violent line at the conference was achieved at the expense of a deepening split between his extremist Marxist adherents and some of the orthodox Moscow-line Communist parties who currently prefer the so-called *via pacifica*.

Nevertheless, we must remember that these are differences over tactics, and sometimes over strategy, but not over final goals. Communist dictatorship remains the final Communist objective.

Seeing these efforts in their true perspective, what measures should we now consider for joint action at this session—in addition, of course, to standing firm in our hemispheric policy of diplomatic, political, and economic isolation of the Cuban regime?

These actions and policies of the present government of Cuba deserve condemnation and denunciation as flagrant violations of international treaties, of the principles of international law and the standards of conduct among nations. This is a matter which is of concern not only to the OAS but to the United Nations.

We should also make clear to those governments actively supporting the present government of Cuba our concern at their policy, particularly as these same governments are actively seeking increased relations with the governments around this table.

If they are interested in relaxing tensions or more normal relations, we may ask why they finance a government publicly committed to our destruction. It would be difficult to imagine that Castro could continue his efforts without the economic support he receives from countries of the Communist world, which is currently estimated at approximately $1 million a day.

We can also seek greater cooperation from our free-world friends in denying to Cuba resources which help it to carry out its subversive activities. In 1964 we appealed to friendly nonmember countries to cooperate in the policy of the OAS, but there is still a substantial flow of free-world trade which helps Castro to release resources to finance subversive activity in Latin America.

We ask our friends abroad to consider whether such assistance to the Cuban government is in their interest and consistent with the close and friendly relationships which ought to bind us to each other. We are not trying to impose our will on the internal affairs of a small country. The Castro regime, as we determined at Punta del Este in 1962, is repugnant to and incompatible with the inter-American system. It has imposed on the Cuban people a police state that tolerates no dissent, that permits no freedom, and whose witnesses are the *"paredón,"* the jails, and the hundreds of thousands of citizens who have fled and continue to flee their motherland. Nevertheless, the reason for our policy of isolating Cuba under its present government is not its internal system but Castro's policies of promoting and assisting subversion and terrorism in the other countries of the hemisphere and of maintaining military arrangements with an extracontinental power—arrangements which at one time brought the world to the point of its highest crisis. Until Castro desists from these policies, the OAS must maintain measures that isolate Cuba from the society of free men.

And there is more we can and should do individually and jointly to strengthen our own defenses and to take practical steps to implement measures which have been recommended to us by competent OAS bodies. We can and should intensify our vigilance along our coasts and frontiers. We can and should intensify the cooperative efforts and arrangements among neighboring countries and especially among those countries most directly affected by the Castro Communist threat.

There may be other threats. But these are reasonable steps tailored to the dimensions of the immediate threat. They are measures necessary for the safety and self-protection of our citizens.

Let us also pause to look at the larger perspective. Hemispheric security is fundamental and requires constant vigilance, but it is only a small part of our overall effort. Let us keep in mind that the nations of Latin America are utilizing only 1½ percent of their total resources for matters of defense, with the remaining 98½ percent being invested in economic and social development and human welfare. While we take serious note of security threats, while we condemn the neighborhood delinquents who are responsible for these threats, we cannot permit this handful of peddlers of violence to distract us from our major task in this hemisphere.

Our number-one purpose remains the realization of peaceful revolution through the Alliance for Progress. We seek not to destroy but through "a vast effort to bring a better life to all the people of the Continent."

If the first 6 years of the Alliance have not seen adequate solutions to many of the problems that still beset us, we now know that this is a good beginning. The Presidents of America in Punta del Este this year gave us new directions and new stimulation. Our intensified dedication, our best talents, will be required. We know the way will not be quick nor easy; as President Johnson has said, and repeated yesterday at our luncheon, "We will persevere. There is no limit to our commitment. We are in this fight to stay all the way."

In this great adventure of the Alliance for Progress we wish the Cuban people could join us, for it must be increasingly clear to them that under the present system there are no prospects for an improvement of living conditions or for greater personal freedom. The tragedy is that were it not for the militancy of Castro and those closest to him, Cuban problems would by no means be insoluble. Men of good will in Cuba and, indeed, in the United States and other countries supported the idea of democratic revolution and effective reforms in the spirit of the Alliance for Progress—reforms which, unlike those imposed by Castro, would give the Cuban people a better way of life and the freedom denied to them under the corrupt and dictatorial governments of the past and the Communist police state of the present. This was the original hope of many who supported that revolution in 1959—that there would be brought about in Cuba a progressive, democratic republic. We are confident that this genuine revolution will live again and that the martyred people of that oppressed island will be free from foreign Communist domination, free to choose their own leaders, and free to join the rest of the peoples of the hemisphere in our common efforts to secure for each person the liberty, dignity, and the well-being which is the rightful heritage of all the citizens of this great hemisphere.

173. Organization of American States, Twelfth Meeting of Consultation of Ministers of Foreign Relations, Final Act*

September 24, 1967

The Twelfth Meeting of Consultation of Ministers of Foreign Affairs, convoked in accordance with the first part of Article 39 and with Article 40 of the Charter of the Organization of American States, was held at the Pan American Union, Washington, D.C., from June 19 to September 24, 1967.

The Meeting was convoked through a resolution of the Council of the Organization of American States adopted on June 5, 1967, which read as follows:

Whereas:

On June 1, 1967, the Ambassador, Representative of Venezuela, addressed a note to the Chairman of the Council, by which his government requested that a Meeting of Consultation be urgently convoked, in accordance with the first part of Article 39 and with Article 40 of the Charter of the Organization of American States, to consider "the serious situation confronting the member states of this Organization as a consequence of the attitude of the present Government of Cuba, which is carrying out a policy of persistent intervention in their internal affairs with violation of their sovereignty and integrity, by fostering and organizing subversive and terrorist activities

*Department of State Bulletin, Oct. 16, 1967, pp. 493-98.

in the territory of various states, with the deliberate aim of destroying the principles of the inter-American system;"

The Ambassador, Representative of Venezuela, has provided the information on which that request was based; and

Article 39 of the Charter provides that "The Meeting of Consultation of Ministers of Foreign Affairs shall be held in order to consider problems of an urgent nature and of common interest to the American States, . . ."

The Council of the Organization of American States

Resolves:

1. To convoke, in accordance with the first part of Article 39 and with Article 40 of the Charter of the Organization of American States, a Meeting of Consultation of Ministers of Foreign Affairs of the American republics to consider the said situation.

2. To appoint a committee of nine members, to be designated by the Chairman of the Council, to make recommendations regarding the agenda, date, place, and regulations for that meeting.

3. To inform the United Nations Security Council of the text of this resolution, in accordance with Article 54 of the Charter of the United Nations.

In accordance with the provisions of paragraph 2 of the operative part of the resolution transcribed above, the Chairman of the Council, on that same day, appointed the delegations of Argentina, Bolivia, Colombia, Guatemala, Peru, Trinidad and Tobago, the United States, Uruguay, and Venezuela to make up that committee, which later elected the Ambassador, Representative of Venezuela, as its chairman.

At the meeting of the Council of the Organization held on June 15, 1967, this committee submitted a report on the agenda, date, place, and regulations for the Meeting (Doc. 5), and a resolution was adopted in which the following agenda was proposed for the Meeting, which agenda was approved by the opening plenary session held on June 19, 1967:

1. The situation confronting the member states of the Organization of American States as a consequence of the attitude of the present Government of Cuba, which is carrying out a policy of persistent intervention in their internal affairs with violation of their sovereignty and integrity, by fostering and organizing subversive and terrorist activities in the territory of various states, with the deliberate aim of destroying the principles of the inter-American system.

In the same resolution adopted on June 15, 1967, the Council set June 19, 1967, as the opening date for the Meeting and designated the Pan American Union as the place for it.

The deliberations of the Meeting were governed by the Regulations of the Meeting of Consultation of Ministers of Foreign Affairs prepared by the Council of the Organization on March 1, 1951, and approved by the Meeting with certain transitory provisions applicable to it.

The Meeting was attended, from June 19 through September 21, 1967, by special delegates of the Ministers of Foreign Affairs (Doc. 17), and beginning September 22, 1967, the following members of the Meeting, listed in the order of precedence established by lot, participated:

          *   *   *

In accordance with the Regulations of the Meeting, the Secretary General of the Organization of American States installed the opening session on the afternoon of June 19, 1967. At this session, His Excellency Eduardo Ritter Aislán, Special Delegate to Panama, was elected President of the Meeting. Also, the agreements reached at the preliminary session with respect to the Agenda and Regulations of the Meeting and the membership of the Committee on Credentials and the Coordinating and Drafting Committee were ratified.

At the same opening session, a resolution was adopted, authorizing appointment of a committee "to go to Venezuela to gather additional information and to make such verification as it considers advisable of the events that took place in Venezuela and that were denounced by the government of that country. . . ." Committee I was composed of the special delegates of Costa Rica (Chairman), Peru (Rapporteur), Colombia, the Dominican Republic, and the United States.

At the plenary session held on July 10, 1967, the Meeting resolved to establish an eight-member committee (Committee II), to prepare a report on events related to the so-called Afro-Asian Latin American Peoples' Solidarity Conference that had occurred since the report of October 24, 1966, presented by the Special Committee to Study Resolutions II.1 and VIII of the Eighth Meeting of Consultation of Ministers of Foreign Affairs.

Committee II of the Meeting of Consultation was composed of the special delegates of Peru (Chairman), Trinidad and Tobago (Rapporteur), and Argentina, Colombia, the Dominican Republic, El Salvador, Guatemala, and the United States.

Committee I, appointed at the opening session, was in Venezuela from June 23 to 27, and on July 26, 1967, at the third plenary session of the Meeting, it presented its report on the events that had occurred in that country.

At the fourth plenary session, held on August 2, Committee II, established by the resolution of July 10, presented a report on events related to the so-called Afro-Asian Latin American Peoples' Solidarity Conference that had occurred since the report of October 24, 1966, represented by the Special Committee of the Council of the Organization.

In accordance with the Regulations, the Meeting appointed a Committee on Credentials, composed of Guatemala, Mexico, and Paraguay. It also appointed a Coordinating and Drafting Committee, made up of Brazil, Colombia, Haiti, and Trinidad and Tobago.

In accordance with the transitory provisions of the Regulations, a General Committee was established, made up of all the members. His excellency Alfredo Vázquez Carrizosa, Special Delegate of Colombia, and His Excellency Ramón de Clairmont Dueñas, Special Delegate of El Salvador, were appointed Chairman and Rapporteur, respectively, of the General Committee. Later, when Mr. Alfredo Vázquez Carrizosa, Special Delegate of Colombia, ceased to represent his country at the Meeting, His Excellency Eduardo Roca, Special Delegate of Argentina, was elected Chairman of the General Committee.

At the meeting of the General Committee held on August 3, there was general agreement that most of the Ministers of Foreign Affairs of the member states would be willing to attend the Meeting personally beginning September 22, 1967.

On that date, a new preliminary session was held, attended by the Ministers of

Foreign Affairs, at which agreement was reached on the new officers of the Meeting. At the Fifth Plenary Session, held on the same day, His Excellency Héctor Luisi, Minister of Foreign Affairs of Uruguay, was elected President of the Meeting.

At the tenth meeting of the General Committee, held on September 23, 1967, His Excellency Nicanor Costa Méndez, Minister of Foreign Affairs and Worship of Argentina, was elected Chairman of the Committee, and His Excellency Alfredo Martínez Moreno, Minister of Foreign Affairs of El Salvador, was elected Rapporteur.

At the same meeting, the General Committee also formed a Working Group made up of the delegations of Costa Rica (Chairman), Bolivia, Brazil, Chile, Colombia, Ecuador, Trinidad and Tobago, the United States, and Venezuela, which undertook a study of the various drafts and resolutions presented and submitted its conclusions to the General Committee.

This Final Act of the Meeting was signed at the closing session, which took place on September 24, 1967. This session was addressed by His excellency Walter Guevara Arze, Minister of Foreign Affairs of Bolivia, who spoke on behalf of the delegations, and His Excellency Héctor Luisi, Minister of Foreign Affairs of Uruguay, President of the Meeting.

As a result of its discussions, the Twelfth Meeting of Consultation of Ministers of Foreign Affairs adopted the following resolutions:

Resolution I

The Twelfth Meeting of Consultation of Ministers of Foreign Affairs,

Considering:

The note dated June 1, 1967, addressed by the Representative of Venezuela to the Chairman of the Council of the Organization and in the statement made by the Special Delegate of Venezuela during the plenary session held today,

Resolves:

1. To authorize its President to appoint a committee to go to Venezuela to gather additional information and to make such verification as it considers advisable of the events that took place in Venezuela and were denounced by the government of that country in its note dated June 1, 1967, to the Chairman of the Council of the Organization of American States, which was considered at the special meeting held by that Organ on June 5.

2. To request the American governments and the Secretary General of the Organization to cooperate with the Committee, which will begin to work as soon as it has been constituted.

3. That the Committee shall render a report to the Meeting of Consultation as soon as possible.

4. To inform the Security Council of the United Nations of the text of the present resolution, in accordance with the provisions of Article 54 of the Charter of the United Nations.

Resolution II

The Twelfth Meeting of Consultation of Ministers of Foreign Affairs,

Resolves:

1. To establish an eight-member committee to prepare a report on events related to the so-called Afro-Asian-Latin American Peoples' Solidarity Conference that have occurred since the report of October 24, 1966, presented by the Special Committee to Study Resolutions II.1 and VIII of the Eighth Meeting of Consultation of Ministers of Foreign Affairs.

2. To authorize the President of the Twelfth Meeting of Consultation to designate the states that should compose the aforementioned committee.

3. To request the Secretary General of the Organization to give the committee the assistance it needs to achieve the objective stated above.

Resolution III

Whereas:

The report of Committee I of the Twelfth Meeting of Consultation of Ministers of Foreign Affairs states among its conclusions that "it is clear that the present Government of Cuba continues to give moral and material support to the Venezuelan guerrilla and terrorist movement and that the recent series of aggressive acts against the Government of Venezuela is part of the Cuban Government's continuing policy of persistent intervention in the internal affairs of other American states by fostering and organizing subversive and terrorist activities in their territories";

Committee II of the Twelfth Meeting of Consultation of Ministers of Foreign Affairs, responsible for preparing a report on events related to the so-called First Afro-Asian-Latin American Peoples' Solidarity Conference, stated that the so-called First Latin American Solidarity Conference, held in Havana from July 31 to August 8, 1967, "represents a further step in the efforts of communism and other subversive forces in the hemisphere to promote, support, and coordinate guerrilla, terrorist, and other subversive activities directed against established governments" and gives "testimony once again to the efforts of the Government of Cuba to control and direct these subversive activities in our hemisphere";

During the course of the Twelfth Meeting of Consultation the Government of Bolivia has presented evidence of intervention by the Government of Cuba in the preparation, financing, and organization of guerrilla activities in its territory;

The difficult social and economic conditions under which the peoples of Latin America live serve communism as a means for arousing the internal subversion that distorts the legitimate longings of our countries for justice and for change;

The affirmation that the democratic system is the proper path for achieving the desires of the Latin American peoples must be supported by suitable actions and programs that will promote the structural changes necessary for progress and for the strengthening of the system;

Economic cooperation among the American states to speed up and harmonize development is essential to the stability of democracy and the consolidation of the inter-American system in the face of the subversive aims of international communism;

Respect for and observance of human rights constitute a basic universal as well as inter-American juridical principle essential to the effective security of the hemisphere; and

In spite of this, in practice events occur that are incompatible with the system of protection and guarantee that all countries are obligated to establish in behalf of the individual,

The Twelfth Meeting of Consultation of Ministers of Foreign Affairs

Resolves:

1. To condemn forcefully the present Government of Cuba for its repeated acts of aggression and intervention against Venezuela and for its persistent policy of intervention in the internal affairs of Bolivia and of other American states, through incitement and active and admitted support of armed bands and other subversive activities directed against the governments of those states.

2. To request the states that are not members of the Organization of American States and that share the principles of the inter-American system to restrict their trade and financial operations with Cuba and sea and air transport to that country, especially transactions and transportation conducted through state agencies, until such time as the Cuban regime ceases its policy of intervention and aggression, and to indicate to them that the granting of state credits or credit guarantees to private firms conducting such transactions cannot be viewed as a friendly gesture by the member states of the Organization; and to this end to recommend to the member states that, individually or collectively, they reiterate this position to the governments of those states.

3. To request the governments that support establishment of the so-called Afro-Asian-Latin American Peoples' Solidarity Organization (AALAPSO) to withdraw their support or adherence from that organization, and also from the "Second Tricontinental Conference," scheduled to be held in Cairo in January 1968; to denounce these activities as contrary to the sovereignty, peaceful relations, and social and economic development of the peoples; and to declare that support by countries outside the hemisphere to activities conducive to subversion in Latin America jeopardizes solidarity among the developing countries, the increasing importance of which is particularly reflected in the efforts being made to reorganize international trade on more equitable bases.

4. To express to the states that are not members of the Organization of American States that support the Government of Cuba the serious concern of the member states of the Organization, inasmuch as that support tends to stimulate the interventionist and aggressive activities of the Cuban regime against the countries of the Western Hemisphere, and since the cause of peaceful relations will be jeopardized so long as those activities continue; and to this end, to recommend to the governments of the member states of the Organization that they carry out joint or individual representations directed to the states that support the Government of Cuba, to manifest this concern to them.

5. To recommend to the governments of the member states of the Organization of American States that they apply strictly the recommendations contained in the first report of the Special Committee to Study Resolutions II.1 and VIII of the Eighth Meeting of Consultation of Ministers of Foreign Affairs, of July 3, 1963, relative to

the prevention of propaganda and of the movement of funds and arms from Cuba and other illegal sources to other American countries, as well as to the strengthening of controls on travel to and from Cuba in order to prevent the movement of subversive persons, and that they coordinate more effectively their efforts aimed at preventing such movements and shipments.

6. To recommend to the governments of the member states of the Organization that, in accordance with their domestic legislation, they adopt or intensify, as appropriate, measures of vigilance and control on their respective coasts and borders, in order to prevent the entry into their own territory, or the exit, of men, arms, or equipment coming from Cuba and intended for purposes of subversion and aggression.

7. To recommend to the member states of the Organization that, in accordance with their constitutional and legal provisions, they maintain, within their territory, the most strict vigilance over the activities of the so-called Latin American Solidarity Organization (LASO) and its national committees.

8. To recommend to the member states of the Organization the application, where necessary, of all the recommendations contained in the Report of the Special Committee to Study Resolutions II.1 and VIII of the Eighth Meeting of Consultation of Ministers of Foreign Affairs, on the so-called First Afro-Asian-Latin American Peoples' Solidarity Conference and its Projections ("Tricontinental Conference of Havana"), dated November 28, 1966.

9. To recommend to the governments of the member states that they take such steps as they deem pertinent in order to coordinate, among neighboring countries, the measures of vigilance, security, and information set forth in paragraphs 5, 6, 7 and 8 above.

10. To recommend to the governments of the member states that they decline to ship any governmental or government-financed cargo in any vessel that, following the date of this resolution, has engaged in the shipment of cargo to or from Cuba, and that, in addition, the governments of the member states take the necessary measures to prohibit the supply of fuel to any such vessel in their ports, with the exception of cases in which shipments are made for humanitarian purposes.

11. To reaffirm that the maintenance of order and of internal and external security is the exclusive responsibility of the government of each member state, without prejudice to its reiterated adherence to the principle of collective and mutual security for the preservation of peace, in accordance with the treaties on this subject.

12. To express concern that the growth rates of the developing countries of Latin America and the degree of their participation in international trade are not equal to the corresponding rates of growth and expansion of trade of the industrialized countries of the world, and that this situation could result in new and more acute social conflicts that Castro-communism could use to advantage to provoke or intensify subversion and violence and to upset the course of development of the hemisphere.

13. To reaffirm that the principal means of achieving security and prosperity in the hemisphere is development by peaceful and democratic methods, and that the subversion promoted by Cuba disturbs that process.

14. To reiterate its conviction that economic and social development can and should be achieved only within a system that respects democrary and human rights, and on the basis of actions and programs that will coordinate domestic efforts with

international cooperation, to satisfy the undeferrable aspirations and needs of the people of the Americas.

15. To instruct the Secretary General of the Organization of American States to transmit to the Security Council of the United Nations the texts of this resolution and of the reports of Committees I and II of this Meeting of Consultation, in accordance with Article 54 of the Charter of the United Nations.

Resolution IV

Whereas:

Article 34 and the first paragraph of Article 35 of the Charter of the United Nations read as follows:

Article 34. The Security Council may investigate any dispute, or any situation which might lead to international friction or give rise to a dispute, in order to determine whether the continuance of the dispute or situation is likely to endanger the maintenance of international peace and security.

Article 35. Any Member of the United Nations may bring any dispute, or any situation of the nature referred to in Article 34, to the attention of the Security Council or of the General Assembly.

Resolution 2131 (XX) of the General Assembly states the following in paragraphs 1 and 2 of its declarative part:

1. No State has the right to intervene, directly or indirectly, for any reason whatever, in the internal or external affairs of any other State. Consequently, armed intervention and all other forms of interference or attempted threats against the personality of the State or against its political, economic and cultural elements are condemned;

2. No State may use or encourage the use of economic, political or any other type of measures to coerce another State in order to obtain from it the subordination of the exercise of its sovereign rights or to secure from it advantages of any kind. Also, no State shall organize, assist, foment, finance, incite or tolerate subversive, terrorist or armed activities directed towards the violent overthrow of the regime of another State, or interfere in civil strife in another State;
and

Under auspices of the present Government of Cuba, the so-called Latin American Solidarity Organization (LASO), meeting recently in Havana, passed resolutions and adopted agreements to promote subversive movements in the Latin American countries,

The Twelfth Meeting of Consultation of Ministers of Foreign Affairs

Resolves:

1. To recommend to the member states of the Organization of American States that they bring to the attention of the competent organ of the United Nations the acts of the present Government of Cuba that run counter to the provisions cited of Resolution 2131 (XX) of the General Assembly.

2. To request, in like manner, of the countries of the Latin American group in the

United Nations that are not members of the Organization of American States, that they cooperate in the implementation of this resolution.

Resolution V

The foreign ministers meeting here reaffirm the dedication of their governments to the cause of economic and social development of their peoples, within a framework of freedom and democracy, and declare that their efforts in this direction will not be deterred by the aim of any state or organization to subvert their institutions—an aim that those meeting here unanimously repudiate.

Resolution VI

Whereas:

This Meeting of Consultation was convoked in accordance with the first part of Article 39 and with Article 40 of the Charter of the Organization; and

The preparation of the Final Act of the Twelfth Meeting of Consultation in the four official languages requires careful coordination which cannot be accomplished satisfactorily in the limited time available,

The Twelfth Meeting of Consultation of Ministers of Foreign Affairs

Resolves:

1. To prepare the Final Act to be signed in only one of the official languages of the Meeting.

2. To recommend to the Council of the Organization of American States that it constitute a committee of four of its members who will represent the four official languages of the Organization to coordinate the texts of the final Act in the other three official languages.

3. To authorize the Council to approve those three texts, which shall be considered official texts of the Final Act and shall become integral parts of it as it is signed by the Ministers of Foreign Affairs.

4. That all the official texts of the Final Act shall be equally authentic.

174. Statement by Secretary Rusk, before the Twelfth Meeting of Consultation of Ministers of Foreign Affairs of the Organization of American States*

September 24, 1967

It seems to me that we have had a very good meeting indeed, demonstrating the solidarity and unity of the hemisphere. Of course, not every delegation has been able to agree on every point with every other delegation. I myself commented on the

**Department of State Bulletin,* Oct. 16, 1967, p. 493.

applicability of international law to paragraph 6 of the principal resolution. But I think that every delegation made a maximum effort to find a common ground; and that common ground was support and solidarity for Venezuela and Bolivia, the targets of guerrilla activity supported by Castro.

First, we have sent a message of support to the people of Venezuela and Bolivia.

We have sent a message to Castro making it clear to him that he must—sooner rather than later—stop his subversive activities in the hemisphere.

We have sent a message to the friendly countries of the free world asking that they show solidarity with those countries that are trying to build a world where free men can live in peace.

We have sent a message to those supporting Castro making it clear that we do not understand how they can pretend to be for peaceful coexistence at a time when they are providing Castro the means to continue his policy of aggression in this hemisphere.

We have sent a message to the people of this hemisphere making it clear that we will persist in our efforts to attain the objectives set forth in the great decisions made by the Presidents of America at Punta del Este to effect social and economic development and to strengthen democracy and the dignity of the individual.

We have sent a message to the Cuban people letting them know that we all look forward to the time when a free Cuban people can return to this table and rejoin the family of the hemisphere.

Looking back on the eventful episodes over the past several years, I would think that today the hemisphere is more united than ever, more determined than ever to assure the peace, security, tranquillity, and human liberty to which all of us aspire.

175. Address by Covey T. Oliver, Assistant Secretary of State for Inter-American Affairs, before the Pan American Society of the United States, on Our Continuing Commitment in the Home Hemisphere*

November 30, 1967

Our nation is nearing the end of a year marked by a singularly intense stocktaking— measuring our physical and moral resources against a multitude of national and international demands.

This survey has, at times, been painful—marked by a fear that perhaps we are not up to our myriad commitments. Some say we cannot continue to dissipate our energies on a number of fronts but must retrench and focus our attention on those problems of a demonstrably immediate nature. Some contend that our international commitments outside of Viet-Nam should be curtailed or postponed until that conflict is ended or until we have solved the immense problems of our own cities and our own poor. President Johnson recently pointed out that there can be no absolute answer as to which claim on our resources should take priority but that each man must make his own assessment and accept the responsibility for the consequences of his decision.

*Department of State Bulletin, Dec. 25, 1967, pp. 868-73.

Tonight I would like to review with you what our commitment is in Latin America and how I believe this undertaking fits into the broad spectrum of commitments to ourselves and to other nations of the world.

In size and grandeur of concept, the task the United States and the other members of the Organization of American States have set for themselves under the Alliance for Progress has rarely, if ever, been equaled in history. But magnitude and nobility do not, by themselves, necessarily justify the expenditure of resources that may be required to finish the task. We in the United States must continually ask ourselves: What are we trying to do in the home hemisphere? Have our past efforts paid off? Is further effort justified when there are other urgent demands?

I will tell you what I believe are the answers to these questions. You, of course, must judge for yourselves. I would only ask that you keep in mind, as you hear other arguments regarding what we can or should be doing, that this hemisphere is our home. This is where we live, and ultimately it is here we must judge our own actions and it is here we will be judged by others.

Just what is our commitment in Latin America?

Our present commitment was formalized in Punta del Este in 1961 and reaffirmed and strengthened by the American Presidents gathered in the same city last April. In the words of the Alliance Charter signed in 1961, we and our Latin American neighbors have pledged:

> ... to enlist the full energies of the peoples and governments of the American republics in a great cooperative effort to accelerate the economic and social development of the participating countries of Latin America, so that they may achieve maximum levels of well-being, with equal opportunities for all, in democratic societies adapted to their own needs and desires.

This is indeed a grand concept. Some would say it is too grand—that it promises more than can be delivered. I contend that, at the time this commitment was undertaken, it was barely enough to overcome the despair and distrust that had been bred into millions of Latin Americans by generations of neglect.

On the other hand, others reading the words of new hope for the hemisphere recalled the great success of our first massive development effort, the Marshall Plan, and thought of finishing the job in Latin America in a decade. But, by the time the American Presidents met in Punta del Este last April, all of us had taken better measure of the problems we faced. I am sure that each President himself had at some time been a little awed as the full extent and intricacies of the problems became apparent. It was no doubt to moments like these President Johnson was referring when he quoted to his colleagues from Ecclesiastes that "he who increaseth wisdom, increaseth sorrow."

But Presidents are, by force of office if not by natural temperament, a singularly positive breed, and it was not the disappointments and moments of doubt that characterized their mood. Instead, they reviewed the first phase of the Alliance—the time of building institutions and defining courses of action—and affirmed that the right way to development had been found. Willingly, they shouldered even greater development burdens on behalf of their peoples and in their final declaration pledged:

... to give vigorous impetus to the Alliance for Progress and to emphasize its multilateral character, with a view to encouraging balanced development of the region at a pace substantially faster than attained thus far.

U.S. Role Is One of Support

The role of the United States in this redoubled effort was delineated in the Presidents' Action Program. We assured the Latin American leaders that we would:

—support with increased resources their own increased efforts in education and agriculture;

—help them build the multinational infrastructure projects that would knit the vast region together;

—back up their concerted efforts to realize their dream of a Latin American Common Market; and

—harness our science and technology to the whole range of their development programs.

Our role, then, is one of support—and rightly so. I cannot emphasize too strongly that phase II of the Alliance for Progress will be carried out *by* Latin America. It was largely they who outlined the Summit Action Program. It is they who drew up the timetable for economic integration. And it is they who will have to exert the major effort to see that the promise of Punta del Este 1967 is brought to fruition.

While the theme of the Alliance is hemispheric cooperation, the final product of our efforts will be uniquely Latin and "other" American. The societies which they are building must function according to the needs and aspirations of their peoples. It follows that some, not all, of the experience of the United States can be applied to the task. Some, not all, of our knowledge and power is needed; it might not even be welcomed. The identification of which experience and what knowledge and how much power we should offer is one of our major continuing studies. We have learned much in our first years of working together; we still have a long way to go. In a way we are working together to build a diverse hemisphere, and I believe this is as it must be. Diversity within our own country helped make us the strong nation we are. The same quality within our hemisphere should present no problem.

There, in brief, are the bounds of our formal commitment in Latin America—a commitment, we must remember, which grew naturally out of geographical incidence, a common heritage of liberty, and our own realization that the continued well-being of the United States depends on the well-being of our neighbors. Now, what does all this cost, and can we continue to support any program at all in view of our other commitments?

Widening Gap in Economic Well-Being

Since the inception of the Alliance in 1961, this country has allocated for Alliance use each year about $1.1 billion, or a total of more than $7 billion. Before leaving for the Summit Meeting, President Johnson recommended to Congress an expanded assistance program to provide an additional $300 million annually for the next 5 years. This additional money would be used to back up our assurances of support for increased Latin American development efforts. Now, $1.1 billion or $1.5 billion a year is a lot of money, and I do not wish to denigrate what any one of those dollars means to the U.S. taxpayer who earned it. I think, however, that when we come to measure our nation's responsibilities against its resources, a broader perspective is called for.

Our gross national product is now approaching $800 billion every year. Our projected program of increased assistance to Latin America of $1.5 billion would have amounted to less than two-tenths of 1 percent of our national wealth. The funds authorized by the Congress this year represent even less. And when we recall that over 80 percent of our assistance to the home hemisphere in 1967 was loaned—not granted—it is clear we are not depriving ourselves by our current efforts. In fact, it is estimated that our current annual assistance to developing countries in the region amounts to less than one-sixth of what we as a nation will spend on gifts to ourselves this Christmas. With this in mind, it is hard to call up the picture of Uncle Sam as munificent donor to the hemisphere.

The total annual GNP for Latin America as a whole is now approximately one-ninth of our own. We continue to develop from this broad base at a rate almost twice as fast as Latin America's. In other words, the gap between the economic well-being in this country and in Latin America continues to widen. Unless we counter this by helping Latin America to build up its capacity to use and benefit from its resources, this nation will soon be the only rich country in a neighborhood of desperately poor. We rejected this course of inaction in 1961 when we joined with Latin America in drawing up the Alliance for Progress.

Accomplishments of the First 5 Years

Nevertheless, we as taxpayers have a right to demand that the dollars we do make available are spent wisely. Let us look at what Latin America did during phase I of the Alliance—how they used $7 billion.

During the first 5 years of the Alliance, and in spite of an increase in population of approximately 3 percent annually, seven of the 19 Latin American members of the Alliance averaged better than the target growth rate established by the Charter of Punta del Este: 2.5 percent annual increase in per capita GNP.

Exports from Latin America in 1966 were 35 percent above the 1961 level, and imports increased by 23 percent during the same period. In an effort to improve Latin America's trade prospects, the United States is currently working with other developed countries to draw up a generalized system of temporary preferences for products from all developing countries.

Trade among the members of the Latin American Free Trade Association in 1966 was 125 percent above the trade level in 1961. In the Central American Common Market, which got on its feet since the Alliance started, intraregional trade mushroomed from $32 million in 1960 to an astonishing and highly encouraging $186 million in 1966. This growth gives us an indication of the incalculable value of economic integration—a glimpse of what we can expect as the Latin American Common Market becomes fully operational by 1985.

These are some of the signs of long-term economic development. What was accomplished in the same period to provide direct assistance to the people? Since 1961:

—746,000 agricultural credit loans were disbursed, primarily to small farmers;
—24,000 classrooms were constructed;
—130,000 teachers received training; and
—13 million textbooks were distributed.

Roughly 75 percent of this work was done from 1964 to 1967. This reflects an increasing ability on the part of the Latin American countries to utilize properly funds for projects that directly improve the standard of living.

Growing Political Stability

Those are just a few indications of progress that readily lend themselves to statistical measurement. The most important effects the Alliance has had—increased understanding and good will and growing political stability—are more difficult to gage. Nevertheless, it is evident that the countries of Latin America, historically dependent on the coup as a solution to difficult problems, are becoming increasingly aware of the value of constitutional change and democratic procedures—this, despite the social strains brought about by basic changes in economic structures, despite the large rural migration to urban areas, and despite the demands of an exploding population.

Since early 1966, 12 countries of the hemisphere have held successful elections, three of which replaced nonconstitutional regimes with constitutional governments. There has been no unconstitutional change of government in Latin America for the past 18 months. Guyana and Barbados have joined the hemispheric family of democratic nations and Trinidad and Tobago and Barbados became the first new members of our inter-American system since the Charter of the OAS was signed in 1948. In 1967 the present democratically elected government of Guatemala celebrated its first anniversary in office despite serious threats from both the right and the left. Paraguay recently adopted a new constitution which was drafted with the participation of all major opposition groups.

And the administration of President Balaguer has given the Dominican Republic the longest period of constitutional government in 40 years. This breathing space has enabled that country to begin the arduous task of solving its basic economic difficulties, and a good start has been made. By any measure, the tremendous achievement of the Dominican people against heavy odds must stand as a shining example of what can be accomplished when dedicated leadership, supported by appropriate assistance from other members of the Alliance, resolutely sets out to bring democratic order and economic stability out of chaos.

The foregoing, I believe, presents a true picture of the progress we have made under the Alliance. To be sure, we have not begun to solve all our problems. Cuba, for example, remains an outcast that has seen its pretensions to Latin American leadership dissipate even faster than its purported economic gains. How best·to meet the continuing threat of Cuba is only one of the many problems that remain. Yet the overall progress has been unmistakable, and it gives us reason for optimism.

Latin American Military Expenditures

If our progress in Latin America is so evident, why is it that some responsible observers still do not seem to be convinced that we should now support an expended development program in Latin America? As I said, the answer to this question is extremely complex and includes many factors outside the area of my responsibility. Some of the criticisms directed against our present program are within my purview, however, and I would like to address myself to two which are often heard: One is the accusation that the United States is contributing to a Latin American "arms race," and the other that our programs emphasize economic development and the reform of public institutions to the detriment of our efforts to improve the social well-being of the people.

First, the so-called arms race. Let me outline some of the reasons for our present military assistance policy in Latin America:

(1) We accept the fact that the responsibility for the defense of any free and independent nation ultimately rests with those chosen by the country to insure its continued existence. This responsibility cannot be delegated, least of all to nationals of another country.

(2) We and the majority of Latin Americans agree that the greatest threat to continued political stability in the hemisphere at this time is posed by internal disorder and subversion. Accordingly, our military assistance to the region is directed toward helping each country assure domestic tranquillity during a time of massive structural change and to counter the activities of alien or alien-supported insurgents. Our programs are also designed to allow for the incorporation of the defense establishment in the development effort during periods of relative peace.

(3) The defense needs will vary from country to country and from time to time, but any country with a defense establishment will have to keep its military equipment operational through expenditures for maintenance and replacement. We support efforts by developing countries to keep these expenditures at a minimum consistent with the relative demands of development and defense.

Within these limits, I believe that our military assistance program has been a success. Today, Latin America spends less on defense than any other area of the world except Africa south of the Sahara. During a period of increased attempts by Cuba and Cuban-supported elements to subvert a number of countries in the region, defense expenditures have actually decreased.

In 1947, military expenditures in Latin America accounted for 23.5 percent of total government expenditures. This dropped to 12.7 percent—almost halved—by 1966. During the same period, defense budgets as a percentage of GNP dropped from 3 to 1.8 percent. Even more germane when considering the so-called arms race is the fact that only about one-tenth of these relatively small defense budgets is spent for military hardware—the rest going for salaries, maintenance, allowances, and other recurrent expenditures.

The defense establishment also provides training to many who might otherwise never have learned to read and write or acquired a skill useful to them in civilian life. Furthermore, it must be remembered that a significant portion of money labeled for defense is spent in the civilian sector for such things as roadbuilding and other projects in the civic action programs undertaken by the military.

I think we can all agree that these figures add little meat to the specter of Latin American countries rushing headlong into debilitating and unnecessary military expansion.

Within this context, let us consider the question of modern military aircraft sales to Latin America.

As is evident from the budget figures I have quoted, these countries have spent comparatively little in recent years to reequip their air forces. This postponement was in line with the desires of all Alliance members to preserve the maximum resources for use in development efforts. Now the military aircraft in some countries are more than 10 years old and are increasingly difficult and expensive to maintain. Technological advances in the field have left them with aircraft for which spare parts are no longer manufactured. Available replacements are, of course, more advanced than the planes they now fly.

Several South American countries have been considering for several years what military aircraft to purchase. They have held discussions with us and others. One possible replacement, the Northrop F-5, made in the United States meets the internal security and counterinsurgency needs of smaller countries. Alternative designs, without exception, are far more advanced and far more expensive. There are some who urge that we refuse to cooperate in assisting Latin American countries meet what these countries regard as their minimum requirement. Some urge that we not have anything to do with the matter because if we do offer a moderate alternative we will not be exerting our maximum influence against diversion of scarce resources from total development.

The question, however, is not susceptible to any simple solution. We are often faced with unhappy options. We can suggest a rule of reason, but we cannot dictate the defense requirements of another country. If we refuse to cooperate, the countries concerned may decide that their replacement needs require that they buy an alternative aircraft, perhaps in Western Europe, at an even higher cost to their development efforts. Introduction of such sophisticated aircraft into the region could well escalate arms spending to a new and much higher level. It could also force the purchase of aircraft with performance characteristics Latin America agrees it does not need just to obtain the more limited performance it believes it requires. These are just the developments we wish to avoid.

We will continue to review this problem, and as the Secretary has explained to members of the Congress, we shall well and faithfully execute the legislative requirement that we insure that aid recipient countries do not significantly sacrifice economic and social development through unnecessary military expenditures.

Furthermore, we welcome recent initiatives by Chile and Colombia to define realistic limits to arms modernization that would be acceptable to all Latin American countries.

Development, as the President has pointed out, is not yet a fully mastered body of knowledge. Perhaps it is a field in which we will never be able to do everything by doctrine. In the home hemisphere we are working and learning together. We have come a long way—especially considering certain historical and psychological aspects of hemispheric relations—we have come an amazingly long way in dealing with each other as if the traditional privacy of national internal affairs did not exist. But there are limits to this approach. These are fixed by human and national dignity; a requirement of modesty since no one nation has all the right answers; and an honest identification, and then suppression, of what Mr. Justice Holmes might have called our continued tendency to play God.

Long-Term Benefits of Institution-Building

A second criticism holds that we and our Alliance partners are so busy with economic manipulations that we ignore the real goal of the Alliance, which is to bring a better life to each person in the hemisphere. This is also fallacious. The decision made by the Latin Americans to work together for rapid development is itself a reflection of considerable growth in political and social consciousness. The impressive national plans drawn up by the countries of this hemisphere presuppose acceptance of the concept that social conditions must be bettered.

But in order to improve social conditions, practically the whole range of national institutions must be reformed and new institutions established. Loans to small farmers cannot be disbursed unless some mechanism is set up to do so; houses cannot be built until the builders, the savers, the investors, and the buyers are all harnessed in a coordinated effort; new hospitals cannot be lit and new factories that offer increased employment cannot function without more power stations to generate the necessary electricity; and no farmer will ever be convinced that He should produce more if the existing transportation system means that the results of his extra effort will rot on his front step.

The full effect of slowly growing infrastructure projects may not be immediately apparent to the millions who wait. But without them, an assistance program twice its present size would have no lasting effect. Let there be no mistake, we in the Alliance are working for people.

These are among the reasons why I am disturbed by recent attempts to ignore our continuing commitment to Latin America on the grounds that we cannot afford to meet it at this time or that Latin America does not deserve our extra effort. I cannot believe these attempts reflect the majority opinion in our country. Coming as they do at a time when we and our neighbors are expecting greater achievements, when the groundwork for rapid advancement has been laid, when the first fruits of our common efforts are beginning to ripen, these efforts to retrench strike a serious blow at the very keystone of our hemispheric relations—the Alliance for Progress. Already, many of my Latin American colleagues have expressed their concern that the United States may be turning its eyes away from Latin America or that this country is returning to the outmoded paths of paternalism and protectionism.

When I accepted my appointment as Assistant Secretary, I told many of my friends that I approached the assignment with wary optimism. After 5 months on the job and after confronting some of the problems of the office, I can say that I am more challenged than ever but no less optimistic. This nation is not perfect, but I firmly believe it is great. I also believe that this greatness rises from basic idealism and willingness to help our neighbor. I do not believe this country will abandon this precept—especially as regards the people of our home hemisphere. I, for one, will do all I can to speak out, to counter misinformation and temporary lapses in fortitude as long as may be necessary to complete the task of building a new hemisphere composed of nations that have at last achieved "the maximum levels of well-being, with equal opportunities for all, in democratic societies adapted to their own needs and desires."

176. White House Press Release on United States Adherence to the Protocol to the Treaty of Tlatelolco*

February 14, 1968

One year ago today, on February 14, 1967, the nations of Latin America gathered in Tlatelolco, Mexico, to sign a treaty for the prohibition of nuclear weapons in Latin America. Twenty-one nations of the region have now joined in this historic undertaking.

The United States considers this treaty to be a realistic and effective arms control measure of unique significance—not only to the peoples of Latin America but to all the peoples of the world.

Today I am pleased to announce that the United States will sign protocol II to this treaty, which calls upon the powers possessing nuclear weapons to respect the status of denuclearization in Latin America and not to use or threaten to use nuclear weapons against the Latin American states party to the treaty. I have appointed Adrian S. Fisher, Deputy Director of the Arms Control and Disarmament Agency, as my emissary to sign the protocol in Mexico with an appropriate statement.

Upon ratification by the Senate, the United States will assume the obligations to those countries within the region which undertake and meet the treaty's requirements. I am pleased to note that the drafters of this treaty have indicated that transit by the United States within the treaty zone will continue to be governed by the principles and rules of international law.

The Treaty of Tlatelolco has been closely related to the long effort to reach worldwide agreement to prevent the further spread of nuclear weapons. It will create a nuclear-free zone in an area of 7½ million square miles inhabited by nearly 200 million people. Like the nonproliferation treaty, this treaty in addition to prohibiting the acquisition of nuclear weapons also prohibits the acquisition of nuclear explosive devices for peaceful purposes. However, it has been drafted in such a way as to make it possible for Latin American parties to the treaty to obtain peaceful nuclear explosion services.

It is indeed fitting that this giant step forward should have had its genesis in Latin America, an area which has come to be identified with regional cooperation. I particularly wish to congratulate our distinguished friend, President Diaz Ordaz of Mexico, for the initiative and leadership which his government has contributed to this treaty and thereby to the peace of this region and the world.

In signing this protocol, the United States once again affirms its special and historic relationship with the peoples of Latin America and its stake in their future. The United States gives this affirmation gladly, in the conviction that the denuclearization of this region enhances the development of its peaceful nuclear potential.

*Department of State Bulletin, Mar. 4, 1968, pp. 313-14.

*177. Excerpts from an Address by Sol M. Linowitz, United
       States Representative to the Organization of American
       States, to the National Press Club, on Our Latin
       American Policy in a Decade of Urgency**

February 14, 1968

There was a period not too long ago when Latin American policy was a makeshift affair, when our chief foreign policy interests focused on virtually every area of the world except the one closest to us geographically, historically, and traditionally. Today our policy is no longer a stopgap action, a hurried response to an explosive situation, but a policy that has taken its place among this nation's most vital commitments. For we know that by helping Latin America to modernize and become economically stable and viable we help ourselves and the entire course of freedom and democracy. In a day of widespread and unprecedented demand on our resources and will, it is second to none anywhere.

When I was last here 10 months ago, I had just returned from Punta del Este, where I had accompanied the President to the Summit Meeting of American Presidents. I said at the time that I thought the decisions taken there to integrate the economy of the continent and to reinvigorate the Alliance for Progress marked a milestone in the development of the inter-American community. In retrospect, I believe I understated it.

It was at Punta del Este that the President, in speaking of the proposed Common Market, reemphasized that if the Latin American states would move with boldness and determination toward that goal, the United States would be at their side. Thus our participation in hemisphere affairs is now projected more fully than ever before as a shared, multilateral, cooperative endeavor in which we are at the side of the people of Latin America as they take the leadership in their struggle against economic and social injustice and in their effort to build democratic societies responsive to the will of the people.

It is a policy which views the Alliance as part of a long and deeply rooted tradition embodying the basic principles of a new society, as set forth in the Charter of Punta del Este.

It is a policy which recognizes that the problems faced by the people of New York, Chicago, and Los Angeles differ only in degree from those confronting the people of the large cities of Latin America and that the Alliance must, therefore, be part of a continentwide effort in which the people of all the countries—North and South alike—learn from each other even as they help each other.

It is a policy in which we are cooperating with a multinational group—the OAS Inter-American Committee on the Alliance for Progress, or CIAP (as it is known from its initials in Spanish)—in laying down criteria for the allocation of Alliance funds, including our own.

It is a policy which recognizes that so long as there remain in the Americas people without jobs, families without roofs, children without schools, there is much for us all to do.

**Department of State Bulletin*, Mar. 4, 1968, pp. 310-13.

It is a policy which seeks to make education the deep concern of all, recognizing, in the words of Edmund Burke, "that a nation which seeks to be both ignorant and free, seeks what never was and never can be."

It is a policy which extends to the political aspect of our relationship as well. United States policy toward Cuba, for example, adheres to the hemisphere policy shaped by the OAS at several meetings of foreign ministers since 1961.

It is a policy which, over and above the Alliance, seeks to broaden the base of friendship, as in the fulfillment of the Chamizal agreement with Mexico, the effort to find an amicable basis for resolving our problem with Panama, the assistance mobilized to help ease floods in Costa Rica.

It is a policy which seeks to resolve disputes by peaceful means and to find a way that will avoid unnecessary military expenditures which divert resources from urgent social and economic purposes.

It is a policy which, in the words of President Johnson, "will not be deterred by those who tenaciously cling to special privileges from the past . . . (or) who say that to risk change is to risk communism."

The Progress of the Alliance

In the light of this, let us take a look at the reports we hear from time to time that the Alliance is not fulfilling its goals; that low standards of living, soaring birth rates, mushrooming slums and urban blight, straggling agricultural development, and erratic industrial advances are still more the rule than the exception; that the people of Latin America therefore are becoming discouraged with its slow rate of progress.

It is certainly true, as my colleagues and I pointed out at a recent CIAP meeting, that Latin America overall is not yet reaching the Punta del Este goal of an increased 2.5 percent in per capita gross product each year and that last year available data indicate the figure was 1.6 percent.

The real point, however, is that gross national product statistics in themselves are a poor measure of development. Figures in this area are mere abstractions which do not reflect whether the mass of people is better or worse off than before. In the United States, for example, our per capita increase in GNP last year was 1.3 percent.

What is the measure of such improvement in Latin America? To me it is the extent to which Latin American nations are helping themselves in creating a viable climate for development. Take government revenues. Since the start of the Alliance, nearly every government of Latin America has reformed and strengthened its tax structure. With only three exceptions, government income is substantially above pre-Punta del Este levels. In some cases, the increases are above the increases in gross product.

What do the governments do with this increased revenue? Our CIAP studies show that Alliance member governments are spending much more today on such items as education, housing, and social services. Such investments in the human sector do not, of course, produce the spectacular results infrastructure investments do. Nor are they reflected in present gross national product growth figures. But they are the surest guarantee of continued development in the years to come. And they do reinforce the deeply significant fact that the development of Latin America is greater than its growth. This to me is the true test.

The Importance of the OAS

I know full well the skepticism being voiced about the OAS today, the questions being raised about its usefulness and whether we should place such emphasis on our membership in an organization which seems to move in languid fashion.

Let me but say that if our emphasis is on peace, if our emphasis is on a hemisphere secure politically and strong economically, if our emphasis is on progress, law, and respect for the rights of others—and I believe our emphasis is on all these things—then our membership in the OAS services both our national and international interests and will continue to serve them in an unmatched manner.

Yesterday the OAS elected a new Secretary General. The fact that it took six ballots elicited some sad commentaries from the Cassandras and prophets of gloom who seemed convinced that this exercise in parliamentary democracy was a regrettable phenomenon.

Were they right? Was it wrong for the OAS to take the time and the ballots required to elect a man who is to fill what is surely one of the most important offices in all international organizations?

If there is one thing we should have learned by now it is that making international cooperation and organization work is tedious, difficult, and unglamorous labor. It does not succeed merely because of good intentions or wishes. It will succeed only if we believe in it and are willing to work at it, recognizing that in international organizations sovereign nations have equal responsibilities. In the OAS these responsibilities must be discharged with full respect to a nation's individuality of choice, an individuality that is the hallmark of its independence.

We have now arrived at a consensus; and a strong, independent Secretary General will lead a strong regional organization in coping with the challenges that confront the hemisphere. We pledge him our cooperation and support.

Today the diversity of opinion that marked the election no longer is an issue, and it will not be permitted to intrude in all the areas of cooperation and trust that bind together the members of the OAS in a common endeavor—an endeavor that is and will remain our prime concern.

All in all, I believe that the election experience has been good for the OAS and the inter-American community. For it demonstrated the importance with which the organization and its leadership is regarded by the countries of Latin America. And it points up a growing conviction and confidence that the Organization of American States is needed today far more than at any previous time in its history to keep inter-American affairs on an even keel and to move toward a hemisphere of peace and democracy.

Democracy in Latin America

I think it is perfectly valid to ask about the state of democracy in Latin America; the answer, after all, is a key to whether we are following a wise policy in and out of the OAS. Democracy is, of course, not all we would like it to be everywhere in Latin

America. But it is not in the United States either. And I would also say that democracy has moved forward in Latin America in a manner not seen on any other continent since the end of the last war.

True enough, we have witnessed the rise of extremism in Cuba; and its lesson is that a despotism that ignores the just needs of the many for the selfish desires of the few offers a perfect breeding ground for communism and extremism. But it is also true that the number of those searching for a violent revolution in Latin America has lessened and the number of those who believe that a peaceful revolution of the Alliance may yet be the answer to the ills of Latin America has increased.

Whether it be Latin America or the United States, or anywhere for that matter, the growth of democracy is related to basic social and economic factors. Indeed, we can see a parallel to some of the problems confronting our Latin American neighbors by looking at the problems in our own cities where, in some cases, desperate citizens have bypassed the democratic process as they seek other avenues toward a better life.

The great lesson is that time—here and in Latin America—is not on our side and that desperate acts, while demanding firm response in upholding the law, demand equally firm measures to correct the causative ills. For if we want to see democracy fulfill its destiny, then we have a responsibility to help create conditions that will allow it to flower—conditions under which economic freedom and social justice are the firm foundation upon which political democracy must rest.

It is true we will not like what we see at times in Latin America, particulary when military governments, no matter how benevolent, interrupt the normal democratic process. We have a serious choice to make on such occasions; for these coups d'etat can never be the appropriate means of a people's self-determination.

We have both the responsibility to the inter-American system and the commitment to our own principles to advance and encourage the growth of representative government and to act so that we make clear our hopes for the secure future of political democracy and self determination in Latin America.

For in the words of the President, ". . . we shall have—and deserve—the respect of the people of other countries only as they know what side we are on."

That too many still do not know—that some feeling against the United States still remains—is evident from time to time. But I am convinced that this sentiment is not a reflection of majority opinion. I am also convinced it will yet disappear, as more and more of the people learn we stand with the men of vision of their hemisphere, with those who believe that hunger and disease and illiteracy can be ended, with those who are convinced that the entrenchment of the oligarchies and the privileged can be modified peacefully, with those who know there is a future in a unified continent in which the various governments are dedicated to democracy, reform, and progress.

Knowing this, they will know our policy is not a sterile and negative anti-Castro, anti-Communist commitment; that we know a man is not a Communist just because he longs for change; that we know his support of social progress does not mean he also supports Castro extremism; and that perhaps, above all, we understand that the possibility of success for insurgency exists in every village, every community, every phase of life where the heritage of neglect is greater than the effort to bring about a better life for the people.

Military Expenditures

From time to time in recent months, efforts have been made among the countries of Latin America to agree to the elimination of unnecessary military expenditures. Prior to the Summit Conference, discussions were undertaken among various countries in order to determine whether a nonreceipt agreement affecting certain types of heavy military equipment might be feasible. Included in the arrangement would have been an undertaking not to acquire supersonic jet aircraft prior to the end of the decade. Although regrettably such a specific agreement could not be achieved, the desire to accomplish some such limitation remains alive and current. In recent weeks President Frei of Chile has spoken out suggesting its urgency, and several other Latin American Presidents have indicated their concurrence.

In the Summit Declaration the Latin American Presidents expressed their resolve to eliminate unnecessary military expenditures in recognition of the fact that "the demands of economic development and social progress make it necessary to apply the maximum resources available in Latin America to these ends." Preliminary discussions about one procedure to help fulfill this intent involved a review of military expenditures within the context of CIAP's annual country reviews; but this did not meet with requisite support on the part of other CIAP members. Accordingly, other ways or another mechanism must be found, under the OAS or elsewhere within the inter-American system, to focus upon the problem and seek agreement on its solution. We are encouraging the exploration of such possibilities.

Taken as a whole, how does our Latin American policy shape up? Bearing in mind all that still remains undone, all the patience and the determination that are still demanded, all the dangers still to be met, with the basic question still unanswered—will the inevitable revolution in Latin America be one of international cooperation and peaceful change or will it be a violent one in which the only ones to gain will be the forces of tyranny?—Latin America stands today as a vivid and exciting example of what can and should be done to strengthen freedom and de-fuse extremism.

In and of itself, of course, the Alliance will not insure the security of the hemisphere, nor will it solve the problems that beset it. Nor will the OAS. Used wisely and appropriately by the peoples of the hemisphere, however, these are the roadmaps to the future that we believe the Americas can and will attain. Then time can be our ally in this Decade of Urgency. To this end our policy is dedicated.

178. Address by Covey T. Oliver, Assistant Secretary of State for Inter-American Affairs, Integration and Trade in the Alliance for Progress, before a Combined Meeting of the San Francisco World Affairs Council, the Pan American Society, and the Council for Latin America*

April 9, 1968

As a nation, we decided some years ago that it was in our own interest to work with other, less developed American nations for their progress in peace and freedom. Adopting a Pan-American ideal, the United States became a part of a hemisphere-wide effort known as the Alliance for Progress.

Since 1961, when the member nations of the Organization of American States formally pledged the close cooperation and intensive effort required to bring a better life to all Americans, the countries of the Alliance have made great advances. This success enabled the American Presidents, meeting last April in Punta del Este, to consider new stimulants to increase the development pace.

Among the stimulants pledged were:

—to speed industrialization;

—to promote trade and increase the volume and value of Latin American exports;

—to harness modern science and technology to the development effort; and

—to create a Latin American Common Market.

Tonight, I would like to discuss with you two of these decisions: the decision to improve trade within and outside this hemisphere and the decision to create a common market according to a fixed timetable—the latter among the most important decisions ever taken collectively by the nations of this hemisphere.

Foreign trade is of major importance to Latin American countries. On an annual average, the sum of regional exports and imports accounts for over one-quarter of the total of Latin American national incomes.

Some of you may have read recently of two of the measures Alliance and other nations are now taking to improve international trade prospects of the Latin American countries. One of these was the discussion that took place at the recent meetings of the United Nations Conference on Trade and Development concerning a formula by which all the industrialized countries would grant temporary nondiscriminatory tariff preferences for the manufactured and semimanufactured products of all developing countries. Up to now, these discussions have only led to agreement on the general principle and a proposed timetable for developing the scheme. We have, however, learned quite a bit about some of the complexities involved.

The tariff reductions which such a preferential system might bring about are, of course, less than they would have been before the Kennedy Round and previous negotiations under the General Agreement on Tariffs and Trade greatly reduced average tariff levels.

As a result, no one should expect that tremendous economic changes will result from the granting or preferences at this time. But such preferences should still assist

*Department of State Bulletin, May 6, 1968, pp. 584-87.

the flow of private investment capital to new and expanded plants in the developing world. Finally, the agreement on such preferences would do much to convince the underdeveloped nations that developed countries are interested in their progress, even to the point of sacrificing traditional trade philosophy to help bring it about.

The second measure which has been in the news recently was the recently concluded Inter-national Coffee Agreement, which is to come into effect this October. The previous agreement proved that violent price fluctuations could be significantly modified to the advantage of producers and consumers alike. In addition, the increased income received allowed producing nations to finance a significant part of their own development programs. The agreement did not, however, generate much progress on the problem of overproduction of coffee.

Under the new agreement, participating nations will establish a coffee diversification fund which over the life of the agreement should generate about $150 million. This money will help coffee-producing countries to develop or expand other exports and reduce their overdependency on coffee. The United States has indicated its willingness to lend $15 million to the fund.

Through these and other arrangements, the United States is cooperating closely with Latin America in hemispheric and world forums to achieve a better distribution of trade advantages throughout the world.

Success of Regional Economic Organizations

Now let us turn to the plans for the Latin American Common Market.

First, a short review of recent history might be appropriate.

After the Second World War, some countries of Latin America made considerable progress in expanding their industrial base. Much of this industry, however, was designed primarily to replace imports from other countries. As a result, local markets, as poor as most of them were, were jealously guarded behind high protective trade barriers. Too often the local industries that were established were qualitatively and quantitatively incapable of competing outside the country in which they were located. Protected as they are from the invigorating winds of competition and having access to markets too small to encourage the economies of large-scale production, many Latin American industries are high in cost and thus debilitate rather than strengthen national economies.

Many Latin Americans were aware of these shortcomings; and following considerable discussion in the 1950's, two regional economic organizations were established in 1961: the Central American Common Market and the Latin American Free Trade Association.

The beneficial effects of the cooperation and regional planning made possible by these organizations were immediately apparent. Markets expanded, attracting new investments which were funneled into complementary industries within the trade blocs. More people were put to work to fill the growing demand for goods. The quality of manufactured goods improved as inefficient industries were replaced.

The growth in intraregional trade in the five-nation Central American market surprised even the most optimistic. That trade has increased over 400 percent since the market began. The Latin American Free Trade Association, which has grown to include all South American Alliance nations plus Mexico, expanded its regional trade by 125 percent. Central America's trade with the rest of the world today is 60 percent above the figure in 1961; and the Free Trade Association's grew 25 percent in the same period.

Building the Latin American Common Market

Against this background of success for partial integration, the American Presidents at their meeting in Punta del Este 1 year ago decided "to create progressively, beginning in 1970, the Latin American Common Market, which shall be substantially in operation in a period of no more than fifteen years."

As projected in the Presidents' Action Program, the common market will be built by improving the two existing integration systems, the Central American Common Market and the Latin American Free Trade Association; encouraging temporary subregional arrangements to allow countries to integrate their economies more rapidly if they wish to do so; and finally by fusing the two major organizations into one market.

This ambitious plan will, of course, be carried out by the Latin Americans themselves. The United States will not be a member of the market. One reason for this is that our industries are so highly developed and experienced by years of competition in world markets that they would swamp the smaller, more protected industries in Latin America..This being the case, why did this country pledge to provide financial support to help attenuate the problems of temporary economic imbalances, industrial readjustments, and retraining of labor that will arise as the barriers fall?

First of all, as I said, we have already concluded that the development of our neighbors to the south is vital to the continued peace and security of this nation. We also are convinced that economic integration is the biggest step our neighbors could take to accelerate that development. It is obvious, then, that we are serving our own national interest by helping our allies during the difficult years ahead.

Furthermore, although we will not be a member of the Latin American Common Market, we will certainly realize important trade benefits once the market comes into effect. This country has already benefited handsomely from the trade-creating effects, particularly in producer goods, brought about by the evolution of the European Economic Community and the European Free Trade Association. As long as the Latin American Common Market is equally outward-looking—and it appears to be developing along these lines—we can expect comparable benefits as our neighbors to the south put their own trade on a more solid footing.

Preliminary Steps Toward Integration

Although the timetable for integration has been fixed and the various steps by which it will come into operation delineated, many obstacles stand in the way of Latin American success. For example:

—Latin American Free Trade Association members must adopt a programed elimination of duties and other trade restrictions and establish a common external tariff to convert their organization into a true common market. Considering the great disparities among member economies, this will be no mean feat.

—Some way must be found to insure that the less developed Latin American countries receive a fair share of the benefits of integration.

—Physical integration—building and linking together national and regional transportation, power, and communications networks—must keep pace with and even precede economic integration.

—A tremendous education program must be undertaken to familiarize Latin American businessmen with the trading opportunities that now exist and with those that will evolve as integration moves forward.

—The already short supply of private capital, both local and foreign, must be increased to finance the great cost of industrial growth.

—And finally, much missionary work must be done to convince many Latin Americans that the benefits expected from economic integration far outweigh the temporary inequalities and dislocations integration will bring. Those who have never had to compete for markets have little confidence they can survive—a defeatist attitude which, if allowed to proliferate, can hamper or stop entirely any government move toward freer regional trade.

None of these problems has an easy solution. I do not expect them to be overcome without considerably more cooperation and good will than many Latin Americans have shown in the past.

As difficult as the road to integration is bound to be, however, some of the preliminary steps taken by Latin American nations give good grounds for optimism that the schedule will be adhered to.

For one thing, the flourishing Central American Common Market stands as a good small-scale example of what can be expected of total regional integration.

A forward-looking group of six Andean nations, all members of the Latin American Free Trade Association, has received approval from the Association to move more quickly toward merging their economies as a preliminary step toward wider integration. The treaty that will govern their move toward rapid subregional trade liberalization and the establishment of a common external tariff is now being drafted. As a first step, the six nations involved in the Andean group have already proposed to eliminate, over a 5-year period, all trade barriers affecting Andean petrochemicals. Potential annual trade in petrochemicals among the Andean group is estimated at about $60 million. In addition, the members have formed a subregional bank, the Andean Development Corporation, capitalized at $100 million, which will help finance infrastructure and industrial projects within the participant countries.

There are reports that other Latin American nations are now considering similar subregional arrangements. If these moves are successful, Latin America may only have to integrate four or five diverse economies as a penultimate step rather than more than 20.

The tremendous work that must be done to achieve physical integration is also moving apace. Recent contributions to the Inter-American Development Bank will enable that organization to finance a minimum of $300 million worth of multinational development projects over a 3-year period. Among the possible projects being studied are the development of vast river basins; improving and expanding air, water, and land transportation networks; a Pan-American communications network that will depend on satellites; and expanding and coordinating regional electric power grids.

At this point, it is true that much of the work that has gone into integrating Latin America has been on paper. We must remember, though, that the decision to integrate—a great psychological step forward—was made only 1 year ago this month. We must remember that it took 2 years for the European Economic Community to move from a similar declaration of interest to agreement on the Treaty of Rome—and Latin Americans face many formidable obstacles to integration that were not so important in Europe.

These hard facts, however, should not be used by Latin Americans to justify delay or over-caution. Nor should they lead us—we in the United States, who are partners in Latin American development and who have so much to offer in terms of finances and experience in world trade—to despair when the integration move appears to falter.

From the advances toward development that have already been made as a result of close cooperation and intensive effort, I believe that a totally developed home hemisphere, including regional integration, is within grasp. To attain this goal, we and our allies have but to practice a virtue for which we are not particularly famous: patient perseverance.

If we persevere, we will have realized the age-old dream of the Americas. If we persevere, American children throughout our home hemisphere today will receive from our hands the legacy of a strong, just, democratic, and peaceful totally New World.

179. Statement by President Johnson, on Signing the United States Ratification of the Protocol of Amendment to the Charter of the Organization of American States*

April 23, 1968

Twenty years ago, our American Republics met in Bogotá to charter the Organization of American States. Our goal was to consolidate peace and solidarity among our nations in the Western Hemisphere.

Eight years ago, we broadened and deepened our commitment. With the Act of Bogotá and the Alliance for Progress, we joined forces to create a social and economic revolution on these continents.

It was 1 year ago that our countries went back to Punta del Este to review our progress—and to declare a new decade of urgency. For we found that, while we had achieved much in the 20 years and in the 8 years, the basic human problems still demanded many new commitments.

The program that we approved a year ago rested on three main pillars: more food, better education, and closer economic integration.

I asked you to come here this morning so I could tell you that we are encouraged by these beginnings:

*Department of State Bulletin, May 13, 1968, pp. 614-15.

—Last year Latin American farms produced food at twice the rate of new mouths to feed.

—Since Punta del Este, funds for education in Latin America have increased by more than 6 percent, to $2 billion.

—The Inter-American Development Bank has loaned $81 million in Latin America just to build new roads and industries and to increase electric power across national boundaries.

—Throughout Latin America manufacturing production has increased by about 7 percent.

—The Andean Development Corporation has joined together six nations—Bolivia, Chile, Colombia, Ecuador, Peru, and Venezuela—in a new step to develop a common market for all of Latin America.

Today we take another step toward perfecting the OAS. The charter amendments we ratify will streamline the political, economic, and cultural machinery of our organization. They will enable the OAS to meet its greatly increased responsibilities— and to meet them far more promptly and efficiently.

Despite all that we have accomplished over these past two decades, no one knows better than those in this room how far we have yet to go.

As I said only a year ago at Punta del Este:

> The pace of change is not fast enough. It will remain too slow unless you join your energies, your skills and commitments, in a mighty effort that extends into the farthest reaches of this hemisphere.
> The time is now. The responsibility is ours.

I believe that we are moving forward in this hemisphere. The dimensions of poverty, ignorance, and disease to be overcome in our Americas are quite sobering— but they are not crushing. Our confidence in what the Alliance can, and will, do should spring from what has been done.

At Punta del Este my fellow Presidents and I called for a bold plan to overcome the physical barriers to Latin American unity. The Latin American countries have too long been isolated from each other. They have looked across the seas to Europe and the United States. They have neglected the sinews of transportation and communications which can bind together a continent—as happened here in the United States.

For example:

—The man in Lima, Peru, who wishes to talk to a man in Rio de Janeiro must do so through the telephone exchange in Miami or New York.

—The traveler from southern Brazil to Buenos Aires—roughly the same distance, I think, as Boston to Washington—may take as much as 2 to 3 days for that route.

—Most of all, the nations throughout the continent have great natural resources which their neighbors cannot or do not use. Locked behind the high mountain ranges and rain forests, forbidding deserts, that divide South America, we find many unknown resources.

Central America has already demonstrated what can be accomplished when such resources are made freely available by an interlocking system of roads and communications. Without these systems, the achievements of the Central American Common Market would have never been made possible.

The new frontiers of the South American heartland beckon to the daring and the determined. A start has already been made. I should like to cite three examples:

A satellite for Latin America will be launched this fall, capable of bringing fast communications for the first time to the entire hemisphere. Chile, Panama, and Mexico will be the first to join the satellite network. Next year Argentina, Brazil, Peru, and Venezuela will join the system.

The marginal highway on the eastern slopes of the Andes is opening a vast new frontier that is offering work and opportunities for hundreds who are living in crowded seaboard cities.

A large dam and powerplant is rising on the Acaray River between Paraguay and Brazil. It will bring electricity into thousands of homes and factories in three countries.

Now, these are just some of the illustrations of what can be done and what is being done. I believe the time is here and the time is now for us to prepare a plan, a specific blueprint for carrying forward this gigantic enterprise—an enterprise that is capable of uniting the continents with roads and river systems, with power grids and pipelines, and with transport and telephone communications.

In order to do this, I would suggest to my fellow Presidents and to those who direct our Alliance for Progress that they establish a high-level task force, the finest collection of planners that we can bring together, under the leadership of a distinguished Latin American, to prepare a 5-year plan for speeding up the physical integration of our own hemisphere. I assure you that the United States will lend its full cooperation and support.

I am reminded of some famous words of Simón Bolívar to the leaders of his own day, when he said:

> Do not forget that you are about to lay the foundations of a new people, which may some day rise to the heights that Nature has marked out for it, provided you make those foundations. . . .

After almost a century and a half, we are still building the foundations of progress for all of the Americas. But I hope and I believe and I want us to be building them together.

This morning I would observe: Let us continue in the spirit of Bolívar who dreamed of an America "sitting on the throne of liberty . . . showing the old world the majesty of the new."

Thank you very much.

180. White House Press Release Summarizing the Amendments to the Charter of the Organization of American States*

April 23, 1968

The charter amendments (which are the first to be adopted since the charter was signed in 1948) provide needed streamlining of the Organization of American States.

*Department of State Bulletin, May 13, 1968, p. 616.

The amendments modernize the machinery of the OAS. They grant certain fuller responsibilities, as in the field of peaceful settlement. They also incorporate the principles of the Alliance for Progress in the charter.

Among the more significant changes called for by the amendments are:

1. Replacement of the Inter-American Conference, which meets every 5 years, by a General Assembly, which will meet annually.

2. Redesignation of the OAS Council as the Permanent Council, and the granting of additional responsibilities to the Inter-American Economic and Social Council and the Inter-American Council for Education, Science, and Culture. The Economic and Cultural Councils become directly responsible to the General Assembly, as is the Permanent Council. These changes are designed to augment the importance given in the OAS structure to economic, social, educational, and scientific activities.

3. Elimination of the Inter-American Council of Jurists and the upgrading of the Inter-American Juridical Committee.

4. Assignment to the Permanent Council and its subsidiary body (the Inter-American Committee on Peaceful Settlement) a role in assisting member states in resolving disputes between them.

5. Incorporation of the Inter-American Commission on Human Rights in the OAS Charter.

6. Inclusion of a procedure for the admission of new members.

7. Election of the OAS Secretary General and Assistant Secretary General by the General Assembly for 5-year terms, rather than by the Council for 10-year terms, as presently provided.

8. Incorporation in the Charter of the principles of the Alliance for Progress in the form of expanded economic and social standards covering self-help efforts and goals, cooperation and assistance in economic development, improvement of trade conditions for basic Latin American exports, economic integration, and principles of social justice and equal opportunity.

The Protocol of Amendment to the OAS Charter was signed at the Third Special Inter-American Conference in Buenos Aires on February 27, 1967. The amendments will enter into force among the ratifying states when the protocol has been ratified by two-thirds of the members. To date, Argentina, Guatemala, Mexico, and Paraguay have deposited their instruments of ratification.

181. Statement by President Johnson, to a Meeting of the Presidents of Central America*

July 6, 1968

I am grateful to you for inviting me to meet with you and to share in the promise and challenge of this great adventure.

I bring with me the best wishes of the people of the United States, their admiration for what you have accomplished in the past 7 years, and their hope that these

*Department of State Bulletin, July 29, 1968, pp. 109-11.

accomplishments will be the foundation of new economic progress and social justice for all of your people.

We are very proud to have been a part of this adventure.

But this was—and this is—your vision. What you have made of it is now a vivid example for all the world to see. In 7 short years:

—You have established a common market.

—You have founded a bank.

—You have created an organization of Central American states, to oversee your joint enterprise.

—You have established a monetary council.

Because of what you have built in these years:

—Trade among your countries has multiplied almost seven times.

—The average annual growth for the region has been 6 percent.

—Investment is already up 65 percent.

—Four thousand miles of roads have opened new marketing for your people.

—Expenditures for education are up 50 percent. There are half again as many children in primary school. Enrollment in secondary schools has doubled.

The effects of what you have done will one day be felt in the most remote mountain hamlet. They will give men and women now bent under the weight of poverty a chance to lead lives of dignity and security.

That is what you build for. That is why we have helped. That is why we will help even more. We believe that no investment we could have made in these years could have been better spent than it has been here.

The total of our assistance since 1961 now reaches $634 million. I am proud that more than two-thirds of that amount came during my administration. For I know that that is yielding rich dividends, not only in the Americas but throughout the world.

For the developing nations, your example is particularly important.

The world can find here a testament to regionalism.

That is an abstract word—but its power is not abstract nor its promise nor its achievement.

We have already learned many of its lessons—here and in other parts of the world.

First, no country in the world is so large or so rich that it cannot benefit from cooperation with its neighbors.

Second, there is no single pattern to regional progress. United effort can be as broad as a common market, or it can be as narrow as a postal union. Integration may be sudden, or it may come in stages.

Third, successful regionalism requires fair sharing of costs. That is the price of progress. Old quarrels must be put aside.

Fourth, regionalism thrives when it includes a solid economic base.

Fifth, regional institutions are vital—as are men of good will and judgment who are necessary to manage them.

Sixth, the benefits of regionalism go far beyond the specific returns of joint projects. It strengthens the sense of community, which is mankind's best hope for peace.

These are the lessons that we—and you of Central America—took to Punta del Este last year. Together we began the historic march toward Latin American economic integration. Six governments have joined to form the Andean Development Corporation as the first step toward Latin integration. They are now approaching the final stage of negotiating a treaty to establish an Andean common market.

This natural cooperation between neighbors—in some cases only a promise, in others taking the first difficult steps toward reality, in still others already forged and working for common progress—is not limited to the Americas.

In Africa, for instance, the last year has brought an East African Economic Community which is in many ways very much like your own. Groundwork has been laid for a West African common market. The African Development Bank has opened its doors and has already made its first loan. Informal groups are being formed all over the continent to begin joint development of water and power resources, transportation, and communications networks.

In free Asia, regional creativity has flourished:

—The Asian Bank, with $1 billion worth of assets, is now in full operation.

—The Asian and Pacific Council has been founded to provide a forum for discussion.

—The Association of Southeast Asian Nations has joined ancient enemies in a common pursuit of security and progress.

—The education ministers of Southeast Asia have joined in an assault on ignorance and illiteracy. Transportation ministers are organizing in the same way.

—The Mekong Coordinating Committee has completed 10 years of survey works on that mighty river. It will soon propose a system of projects which, with those now under construction, will eventually tame and harness this Mekong giant.

So it is our hope that as the nations and peoples of the Middle East find their way to stable peace, they, too, will find dignity and hope in working together on a regional basis. They will have to solve unique problems, but the resources available to them also offer unique possibilities.

These diverse efforts are built on a common understanding among the developing nations. Great powers, however enlightened or benevolent or rich, cannot solve their problems for them. There is no mythical benefactor who will appear out of the mists to spread plenty. Nor is there any all-powerful keeper of the peace who can solve all the family quarrels or offset the effects of prolonging them.

It is a great tribute to the human spirit that the fruit of this understanding is neither despair nor recklessness.

It is, instead, a great outpouring of energy and will to make a better life possible for their people. It is willingness—even the eagerness—to cooperate with neighbors who share the same problems and the same resources and the same destiny. The single strand is weak; the woven strands will endure and clothe the coming generations.

Your example has given hope and guidance to a movement that now reaches every continent. You know better than I that much remains to be done here in Central America. The gap between what exists and what ought to exist is still unacceptably wide. But you are moving—you are moving to close it in the only effective way to move—and that is to move together.

We in the United States want to move with you. We want to help you. I have listened to your plans for strengthening your national economies and common market. I have talked with each of you individually and collectively. Today I have brought with me approval of a $30 million loan to the Central American Fund for Economic

Integration, to assist in completing your regional transportation system and to try to help you create a regional telecommunications system.

I have also approved loans totaling $35 million more to help you carry forward programs of social justice and economic progress. These include:

—In El Salvador, a loan to establish a pilot instructional television station;

—In Guatemala, a loan to improve the primary education system in the cities and rural areas;

—In Nicaragua, a loan to launch a rural electric cooperative program;

—In Honduras, a loan to increase food production and marketing facilities; and

—In Costa Rica, a loan to promote the establishment of agricultural industries.

I believe that each of these loans is needed, and I believe needed in each country where they will be used and will be used profitably. I believe, too, that the power of our assistance in each country has been multiplied because each of you has committed yourself to cooperation for progress.

One day, the material needs of the Central American people will be met. But I believe it can be said that the spirit of Central America has already triumphed and is very much in evidence here today. It is a spirit of accommodation, it is a spirit of confidence, it is a spirit of dedication to humanity that embodies—but also surpasses—the interests of each individual nation.

I consider myself honored to have met with you today. I shall consider it a great privilege to work with you as long as I have that chance.

Thank you very much.

182. Joint Declaration by the Presidents of the Central American Republics and the President of the United States*

July 6, 1968

I

The Presidents of El Salvador, Costa Rica, Honduras, Nicaragua and Guatemala met at the headquarters of the Organization of Central American States (ODECA) in San Salvador, Republic of El Salvador, on July 5, 1968, in order to examine the status of the Central American integration program and to adopt measures aimed at speeding up the economic and social development of their countries and of Central America as a whole.

Being aware of the keen interest that Lyndon B. Johnson, President of the United States, has manifested in the economic and social development and the integration of Latin America, the Presidents of the Central American Republics had the honor of inviting him to meet with them on this occasion. The purpose of the invitation was to exchange impressions with President Johnson on the progress achieved by the five countries in accordance with the guideline and commitments contained in the "Declaration of the Presidents of America" adopted at Punta del Este, Uruguay, in April

*Department of State Bulletin, July 29, 1968, pp. 111-15.

1967, as well as on the current problems of the region and the measures that the Presidents of the Central American Republics have adopted to solve those problems.

The joint meeting was held at the ODECA headquarters on July 6, 1968.

II

The Presidents of the Central American Republics reviewed during their meeting of yesterday, July 5, the progress achieved in the multilateral movement of their countries toward integration. In this connection, they stressed the fact that as a result of the effort made over a period of several years, the Central American countries now have a legal and institutional framework for giving impetus to the process of reconstructing their regional unity; in 1951, through the Charter of San Salvador, they founded the Organization of Central American States; and seven years ago, they established a Common Market that is already at a very advanced stage. Within that process, a complex of political, legal, cultural, educational, economic, social and technical institutions has been set up whose activities together constitute an integral movement toward unification.

Thus, it can be noted that: In less than seven years, trade between the five member states has increased by almost 700 percent, with an equally impressive increase in the size of the investments generated by the Common Market.

The figures for the increase in per capita income that prevailed until recent years have been, for certain member countries, largely the result of the integration process.

In addition to providing a framework for cooperation to its member states in the political field, the Organization of Central American States (ODECA) has, through its organs and its General Secretariat, done valuable work in the cultural, educational, research, legal coordination, public health and labor fields. Likewise, it has carried out important specific programs, such as providing millions of textbooks to elementary school children in the five countries; regional coordination of the efforts to eradicate malaria; providing basic health services to more than a million families in rural areas; initiating efforts to harmonize labor legislation and social security services; and promoting personnel training activities.

The Economic and Executive Councils and the Permanent Secretariat (SIECA) have succeeded in nearly completing the organization of the Central American free trade area and the adoption of a uniform tariff on imports; have begun the coordination of industrial and agricultural development; enforced the regulations governing the Common Market; established the basis for coordinated programming of economic and social development; and promoted a common policy for protecting the balance of payments, fostering trade relations with other countries and harmonizing tax systems.

The Central American Bank for Economic Integration (CABEI), as the financial organ of the integration process, has already mobilized resources totaling more than 200 million Central American pesos (equivalent to US dollars) and has rendered assistance in such important fields as the promotion and financing of multinational private industries, housing for middle-income families, and specific projects for establishing the physical infrastructure required by regional economic unity, particularly with respect to roads and telecommunications.

The Central American Economic Integration Fund of the Central American Bank to which the Central American countries, the Inter-American Development Bank, and, to a much greater extent, the Government of the United States, have contributed, has made it possible to meet the financing requirements of major infrastructure projects, in particular the roads forming part of the Central American highway system.

The Central American Monetary Council, established to coordinate the policy of the central banks of the member countries, has expanded the multilateral compensation mechanism, adopted regulations to expedite the movement of funds and capital within the region, and has begun to establish the basis for a Central American monetary union.

The Central American Institute of Industrial Research and Technology (ICAITI) has contributed to the development of the area through feasibility studies of new industries of regional interest, technological research on the most advantageous use of natural resources, and technical standards for products and raw materials, and it is also seeking to adapt the advances of modern technology to the situation of the Central American countries.

The Central American University Council (CSUCA) is striving to create a modern university system for the region and has sponsored programs to improve the teaching of the physical and social sciences and to establish regional specialized schools.

The Central American Institute for Public Administration (ICAP) has contributed to the training of public officials and has provided technical assistance to the member countries for the improvement of their administrative systems, in keeping with the needs of integration.

The achievements of integration are primarily the result of the internal effort carried out jointly by the people and governments of the five Central American countries. The Presidents of Central America recognized that the responsibility for the success of the integration process rests on that internal effort. However, they believe that because of the international technical and financial cooperation that Central America has received in the last few years, the advances made have been greater than they would otherwise have been. In this connection, the cooperation given by the government of the United States of America through the Alliance for Progress should be stressed.

III

The Presidents of Central America realize that, notwithstanding the substantial progress made in the integration and economic and social development of their countries, there are still great obstacles that must be overcome.

In the economic field, the increase and diversification of exports have been insufficient during the last few years to sustain a satisfactory and stable growth process; industrial and agricultural policies have not reached the necessary level of coordination and adaptation to the new situation in Central America; progress made with respect to the free movement of capital and persons in the area is limited; tax systems have not yet been properly adapted to the needs of the countries; and the difficulties encountered in financing national and regional development are a matter of concern.

In the social field, much remains to be done to increase the participation of low income groups in national life and the integration process. It is essential, among other things, to increase educational and health improvement facilities, and to overcome the limitations affecting housing programs.

In the legal field, integration requires new instruments to give flexibility and drive to its progress and administration. Moreover, there is a large task still to be accomplished in order to harmonize and standardize the legal structure of the member states.

Keenly aware of the need to act urgently to resolve those problems, the Central American Presidents, during their meeting of July 5, took the decisions that appear annexed to this document, among which the following merit special mention:

1. To give their full support to the measures agreed upon by the Economic Council, the Monetary Council, and the Central American Ministers of Finance to protect the balance of payments, and to take all steps within their power to put those measures into effect within the stipulated period;

2. To seek the prompt entry into force of the Central American Agreement on Tax Incentives and the protocol thereto;

3. To support the measures adopted by the Central American Monetary Council to achieve adequate harmonization of national monetary policies, and the studies required to establish the Central American Monetary Stabilization Fund;

4. To encourage the expansion and diversification of agricultural production for domestic consumption and foreign markets and to adopt an industrial policy that will be consistent with the needs of domestic and foreign demand and better coordinated at the regional level;

5. To support measures that will make it possible to complete and improve the Central American Common Market with respect to tariff equalization and the free movement of goods;

6. To accelerate the completion in successive stages of a Central American Capital Market, and the adoption of measures to facilitate the free movement of persons;

7. To recognize the special importance of the regional telecommunications program, as well as the joint utilization of electric power resources and the merging of the various sytems into multinational networks, committing themselves to strengthening the resources of the Central American Economic Integration Fund, which constitutes the basic instrument for building the physical infrastructure of the region;

8. To provide the regional integration institutions with the necessary resources to meet their growing responsibilities;

9. To reaffirm their staunch support of the formation of the Latin American Common Market, and of the development of economic bonds between Central America and other countries and subregional groups;

10. To intensify their efforts to achieve steadily growing participation by the less privileged rural and urban populations in the benefits of development and integration;

11. To give more attention to educational programs for the rural population and, in general, to low income groups, in order to raise their educational level and achieve their full participation in the benefits of economic and political democracy;

12. To pursue with renewed vigor the programs to eradicate those diseases against which effective preventive measures exist; to continue the struggle against child malnutrition; to improve environment conditions; and to strengthen national health services through regional coordination; and

13. To introduce adequate reforms in the legal and administrative structures of the Organization of Central American States, in order to give it the drive that regional development demands and to strengthen its various activities, with a view to maintaining proper balance in the development of integration and promoting reforms in the domestic legislation of the member countries that will expedite the implementation of the common objectives being pursued.

IV

The President of the United States of America expressed his satisfaction at having the opportunity to meet once more with his Central American colleagues and to review with them the progress made in the region in the past few years, particularly since the meeting of American Chiefs of State held at Punta del Este, Uruguay, in April 1967.

He reiterated his support for the integration movement in Latin America generally and in Central America specifically. He expressed admiration for the progress achieved by the Central Americans, and, as he has done on previous occasions, he stated that the Central American integration movement is one of the most advanced in the world, and constitutes a model for other developing areas.

President Johnson showed special interest in the proposal to establish a Central American Monetary Stabilization Fund, and indicated that he was convinced it would be an important step toward a monetary union in the context of integration. He said that his Government would carefully and sympathetically study in coordination with the competent international organizations the proposal for the Fund in order to determine the manner in which the United States could cooperate in its formation.

Together with the Central American Presidents, he examined in detail the problems that the region still faces in the social and economic fields, and the measures that the governments are proposing to take to solve those problems. In this connection, he lauded their decision to intensify their efforts in matters of education and health.

He took note of the important role being played by the regional integration institutions and the intention of the member states to provide them with adequate resources in order that they may develop satisfactorily. He indicated his agreement with the high priority which the Central American Governments have assigned to the creation of infrastructure projects, including the regional telecommunication network, all of which are basic to the area's economic development. He also noted with satisfaction the way in which the Central American Governments have selected the projects to be financed, evaluating them on a basis of regional priority.

He also expressed confidence that the efforts being made by the Central American Governments would contribute in the near future to accelerating their programs of agricultural diversification. He analyzed the serious problem he had in maintaining support of the International Coffee Agreement, both because of the domestic impact of the Agreement on the American consumer and because of the limited progress in some exporting countries toward adjusting production to demand.

The President of the United States recognized that the five countries forming the Central American community can perfect their union only on the basis of processes of development in all the member countries, and he agreed that every government has a special responsibility for the welfare of its people, and that this can only be achieved in Central America at both the national and regional levels. He acknowledged that the financial costs of social progress are high and that the developing countries must make great sacrifices to achieve it, and he stated once again that in such cases the United States was prepared to give its unequivocal cooperation.

The President pledged the continued support of the United States of America for the Central American integration process, recognizing that overcoming the problems enumerated by the Presidents of Central America required not only sustained national efforts but also substantial levels of foreign assistance. He referred to the United States commitment, made in the Declaration of the Presidents of America, to the movement of Central American economic integration, reaffirming it, and to that end he authorized the negotiation of new loans to Central America totaling $65 million.

V

The Presidents of the Central American States expressed their recognition of the United States' support of the Alliance for Progress, which reflects the most advanced Latin American thought in the economic and social fields; and they emphasized that the United States had continued its support despite its serious balance-of-payments problem.

They emphasized President Johnson's efforts to give continuity to the International Coffee Agreement and to establish the Coffee Diversification Fund; his active position in favor of the establishment, by the industrialized nations, of a general system of unilateral and nondiscriminatory tariff preferences for the developing countries; and his efforts to prevent the adoption of restrictive measures on Latin American exports.

Finally, the Presidents of the Central American Republics and the President of the United States of America expressed their awareness of the magnitude of the task to be accomplished; that the programs to be carried out represent only a beginning, and that if the basic changes which are the primary objective of the Alliance for Progress are to be achieved, all sectors of society must cooperate in this effort. In this connection, they called upon their citizens to unite with them in their new commitments and to try to reach together the final goals of political democracy, economic development, and social justice.

*   *   *

183. News Conference Comments by Secretary Rusk, on a Coup d'Etat in Peru*

October 10, 1968

Q. Can you comment, sir, about the reports of the takeover of the IPC [International Petroleum Company] in Peru; and, in general, what is the posture toward recognizing the new Peruvian regime?

A. Well, we were concerned and disappointed about the developments in Peru. Nineteen hundred and sixty-seven was the first year in 25 years without a coup d'etat somewhere in Latin America. So we had a considerable period without this type of unconstitutional action.

So not only we but other members of the hemisphere were disappointed and disturbed by this.

We are now consulting under resolution 26 [adopted by the Second Special Inter-American Conference at Rio de Janeiro on November 30, 1965] with other members of the hemisphere. Under that resolution the obligation is to consult, although the decisions will be made by individual governments individually based upon their own attitudes and their own policies. We are in that process now, and I would not want to anticipate what may be the result of it. But we want to, as far as we are concerned, move in whatever way the hemisphere as a whole is inclined to move. We are trying to discover, to ascertain that now.

We also are concerned about some of the bilateral issues that are involved here. We don't know yet just what this announced move against the IPC will involve. Presumably, the company will be the first to discover that and see what the issues are. But we shall be following that closely at the appropriate time.

184. Statement by the State Department Concerning the Resumption of Relations with Peru†

October 25, 1968

The American Embassy in Lima advised the Peruvian Ministry of Foreign Affairs at noon today [October 25] that the United States Government has resumed diplomatic relations with the Government of Peru.

The United States decision was based on an analysis and study of the consultations we carried on with other OAS [Organization of American States] countries under OAS Resolution 26 [adopted by the Second Special Inter-American Conference at Rio de Janeiro on November 30, 1965], and another consideration: Peru had publicly made the traditional guarantee of its recognition of international obligations and has indicated its intention to return to constitutional government.

Aid programs for Peru remain under review. We have given you figures on those programs in the past.

*Department of State Bulletin, Nov. 4, 1968, p. 481.
†*Department of State Bulletin, Nov. 11, 1968, p. 497.*

*185. Excerpts from a Report by Nelson A. Rockefeller,
      Chairman of the United States Presidential Mission
      for the Western Hemisphere, on the Quality of
      Life in the Americas**

August 30, 1969

Foreword

The following report and recommendations are the outgrowth of what the members of the mission learned in discussions with more than 3000 leaders of the 20 countries which the mission visited.

We found in the course of our travels and talks that our perspective concerning the nations we visited and the hopes of their people was more meaningful when taken in the context of the entire Western Hemisphere. The quality of life in one area of the hemisphere is inseparably linked with all the rest. Moreover, if we do not meet the fundamental needs of our own people at home, we cannot expect to inspire or assist the people of other nations to meet their own needs. The more we understood the situation in the other republics, the more clearly we understood what was happening at home—and the more we appreciated the need for unity of the hemisphere.

We have, accordingly, in this report looked at the challenges and opportunities from the point of view of the hemisphere as a whole. Because of this, we have written this report with the hope that Canada might join with all the American republics in a truly hemisphere response to what are in fact common concerns. We were also moved by the hope that one day Cuba can be restored to the society of free men.

These trips were an enriching experience. To convey some sense of our personal reactions, as a group, to this fruitful opportunity to listen to the responsible people in South and Central America, and the Caribbean, a Preamble is included in our report.

—N.A.R.

Preamble

We went to visit neighbors and found brothers. We went to listen to the spokesmen of our sister republics and heard the voices of a hemisphere.

We went to annotate, to document, and to record. We did so; and we also learned, grew, and changed.

We used the tools of specialists: economists and scientists, artists and architects, agronomists and social workers. But there is not one of us who did not reappraise the uses of his specialty, who did not find his sense of purpose and values renewed.

We thought to study the ways of life in the other American nations, to measure their performance and ours. We rediscovered the quality of life for each person in the hemisphere, and finally the world, as the only measure of lasting consequence.

**Department of State Bulletin,* Dec. 8, 1969, pp. 495-540.

Our country was born and has experienced the greatest flowering of human capacities in all recorded time because one great idea was unloosed. And though many neglect it, and others would suppress it, it has not yet been contained: the noble concept that each person is the reason and each person is the strength for the nation.

In the release of our collective energies, we have produced great systems and organizations, techniques of awesome capabilities, and a mosaic of useful things and objects here in the United States. But we have lost sight of the values which are the real source of our greatness. We have exported our systems, techniques, and objects, but their distribution has not been essentially shaped by the values that inspired our nation at home—nor have we transmitted those values.

In the countries we visited, we had the opportunity to see ourselves through their eyes. Even allowing for the distortions of distance and the biases of incomplete knowledge, one theme resounded throughout the hemisphere: you the people of the United States are strong and you are able, but you lack unifying goals and a clear sense of national purpose.

In our concentrated exposure to 20 nations, during thousands of hours of discussions for which our hosts had painstakingly prepared, during planned and unplanned encounters, in the presence of both hospitality and hostility, our group had a dual experience.

We were given a great deal of information about the many dimensions of life in this hemisphere. We exchanged points of view on mutual problems and explored possible solutions. And we have together formed new hypotheses and found new techniques in the many special areas of our concern.

We have also come to one simple principle and it shapes our report: All that we have seen, all that we think that we understand, all that we will recommend must be tested against the single question—how does this affect the way that men live?

The logistics of travel and work had determined our itinerary. Thus each week of our visits were followed by a week at home. Among us, we live in all quarters of the United States and work in many different situations. This repeated alternation may have contributed to a conviction that grew among us: The variations among all people is our great common wealth; and we share the same human problems.

As individuals and as nations, we must learn from one another, and we need constant collaboration and communication with each other if our species is to thrive—or even to survive.

It is for each individual, each family, each community, each nation, each region to define its own particular aspirations—but these share one splendid bias: That no man be exploited or degraded to enrich another and that we work together so that each can grow.

Some nations have moved further toward this goal than others but all nations, including our own, have more to grow than they have grown and more to do than they have done.

This aspiration, when truly applied, has a hard, fine cutting edge. We must ask what necessary elements must come together, in and around each person, if he is to live and grow. Opportunity for self-realization comes immediately to mind—the chance to grow spiritually, the respect for human dignity and justice, the right to hope that life will get better, not worse. Certain commodities, physical circumstances, material requirements also come to mind. Comfort and safety amidst the changing elements: shelter and clothing. Energy: enough of the necessary kinds of food, water. Safety from violence and intrusion upon privacy, and an environment sufficiently free of noxious influence.

But man is a social, learning, creative, responsible and self-aware creature and he needs—absolutely requires—much more if he is to thrive, to become more fully himself. He needs the ability and freedom to move, the opportunities to learn and contribute, to ornament and create, to share his experiences and his hopes. He needs to be able to influence the forces which impinge upon him, to participate in his own destiny and to be recognized for his own accomplishments.

There is in none of this the blandishment of easy or final success. Even our expanding horizons have limits, substance and energy are finite, hard choices must be made again and again. We are a species that is both giving and acquisitive, creative and indolent, gentle and violent, petty and magnificent. But when we choose, when we commit our energies to a common goal, none yet has been beyond us.

We face today a crisis in human expectations. Individuals and nations expect much for themselves and too little for others. But expectations are powerful moving forces. They change the ways people act. The very anticipation that it is more natural to take than to give, consume than to create, tends to fulfill itself. It is urgent that we acknowledge in all peoples the same capacities for giving and sharing that we ascribe to ourselves.

Each country in the Western Hemisphere has its own special history and tradition, and forms of government which do not give the same kind of recognition to individuals. Neither do individuals in each of our nations regard their social obligations in the same fashion. But it is a basic assumption of this mission that men are more alike than otherwise in their potential for social responsiveness, and that latent in our species and in each of us is a capacity for personal growth through an enlarged concern for others.

The urgent human problems in the Western Hemisphere require that the nations help one another. At the least, the patterns of our cooperation and mutual assistance should reflect the expectation that all of us will move toward broadly participating governmental systems which represent the interests of each citizen. If we couple this expectation with an appreciation for the work and steps that must be undertaken to reach this goal, and for the difficulties in change, we will have embarked on a new direction in which we all begin to raise each other up.

CHAPTER ONE: THE QUALITY OF LIFE
IN THE WESTERN HEMISPHERE

A. The Special Relationship
In the Western Hemisphere

The mission heard many details about relations between the United States and the other American republics from the leaders of the hemisphere, but they can best be summed up in one phrase: The United States has allowed the special relationship it has historically maintained with the other nations of the Western Hemisphere to deteriorate badly.

The United States has allowed a host of narrow special interests, a series of other foreign policy priorities, budgetary and balance of payments constraints, a burgeoning bureaucratic tangle, and well-intentioned but unrealistic rhetoric to submerge this special relationship to the point where many of its neighbors in the hemisphere wonder if the United States really does care. Its assistance and trade policies, so critical to the development process of other nations, have been distorted to serve a variety of purposes in the United States having nothing to do with the aspirations and interests of its neighbors; in fact, all too often, these purposes have been in sharp conflict with the goals of development.

Moreover, in its relations, the United States has all too often demonstrated, at least subconsciously, a paternalistic attitude toward the other nations of the hemisphere. It has tried to direct the internal affairs of other nations to an unseemly degree, thinking, perhaps arrogantly, that it knew what was best for them. It has underestimated the capacities of these nations and their willingness to assume responsibility for the course of future developments. The United States has talked about partnership, but it has not truly practiced it.

At the same time, we found that profound changes are occurring in the hemisphere, changes that have not been fully understood. It is clear that these changes will affect all of us, and that we must get rid of some of our stereotypes and conditioned thinking if we are to understand and respond with intelligence and pragmatism to the forces of change.

We have concluded that the national interest requires the United States to revive its special relationship with the nations of the hemisphere, and that this relationship should be reinvigorated with a new commitment, new forms and new style. Western Hemisphere relationships cannot remain static; the forces of change—and our own best interests as well as those of the entire hemisphere—will not permit it.

B. The Existing Situation

Everywhere in the Western Hemisphere today, including the United States, men and women are enjoying a fuller life, but still for many the realities of life are in sharp contrast with the deepest felt human needs and goals of the people.

Everywhere in the hemisphere we see similar problems—problems of population and poverty, urbanization and unemployment, illiteracy and injustice, violence and disorder.

Although each of the 26 countries in the hemisphere is different, with widely varying stages of development, aspirations are outrunning resources and accomplishments everywhere. All nations of the hemisphere share rising expectations and restlessness among those men and women who do not truly participate in the benefits of the industrial revolution and the standard of living which has come with it.

Even among some who have shared in the benefits, there is an increasing tendency to lose confidence and sureness of purpose. This makes fertile soil for the ever-present disruptive forces ready to exploit those who are uncertain and to stir up those who are restless.

We know from our experience in the United States that those who live in deprived circumstances no longer live out of sight and out of mind. Neither are they resigned— nor should they be resigned—to the fact that their lives are less than they could be.

They have looked at the relative quality of their life and found it wanting.

As a result, in the United States and throughout the Western Hemisphere, the legitimacy of the democratic political system and the individual enterprise economic system are under challenge.

The upheavals in international systems over the past three decades have subjected the member states of the Western Hemisphere to external economic, political and ideological stresses that magnify domestic antagonisms.

At the same time, the issue of political legitimacy has challenged "accepted" systems of government, not only in the United States but particularly in the other American republics. With the disintegration of old orders which lacked a popular base, newly-emerging domestic structures have had difficulty in establishing their legitimacy. This makes the problem of creating a system of political order in the Western Hemisphere more difficult.

Some nations have retained their democratic institutions. In others, when democratic forms of government have not been successful, nations have moved to authoritarian forms as a solution to political and social dilemmas. Governments everywhere are struggling to cope with often conflicting demands for social reform and economic growth. The problem is compounded by the 400-year-old heritage of intense individualism which permeates all phases of life in the Latin countries of the Americas. Nationalism is burgeoning in most of the region with strong anti-United States overtones. Increasing frustration is evidenced over political instability, limited educational and economic opportunities, and the incapacity or slowness of existing government structures to solve the people's problems. Subversive forces working throughout the hemisphere are quick to exploit and exacerbate each and every situation.

Change and the stresses and problems brought about by the processes of change characterize the existing situation in the hemisphere. The momentum of industrialization and modernization has strained the fabric of social and political structures. Political and social instability, increased pressure for radical answers to the problems, and a growing tendency to nationalistic independence from the United States dominate the setting.

The restless yearning of individuals for a better life, particularly when accompanied by a well-developed sense of social responsibility, is chipping away at the very order and institutions by which society makes it possible for man to fulfill his personal dignity. The seeds of nihilism and anarchy are spreading throughout the hemisphere.

C. The Forces of Change

Change is the crucial characteristic of our time. It is erupting, and disrupting, in all cultures. It creates anxiety and uncertainty. It is demanding of all peoples an adjustment and flexibility which test the limits of individual and collective capacities.

Change is everywhere about us: in the explosion of new knowledge, the acceleration of all communication, the massive mobility of people, the multiplicity of human contacts, the pace and diversity of experience, the increasingly transitory nature of all relationships and the uprooting of the values to which differing cultures are anchored.

There is no society today, whether industrialized or developing, that is not coping with these hurricane forces of change. It is plain that, depending on how we respond to the need for change and the demands of these forces, the results can be tremendously constructive or tremendously destructive.

The sweeping change occurring in the hemisphere will affect our interests and our relationships with the other nations of the hemisphere. We must recognize that the United States cannot control the forces of change. However, we can and must try to *understand* the forces at work in the hemisphere—as well as at home—and how they may affect our national interests, if we are to shape intelligently and realistically our relationships.

Throughout the hemisphere, although people are constantly moving out of poverty and degradation in varying numbers, the gap between the advantaged and the disadvantaged, within nations as well as between nations, is ever sharper and ever more difficult to endure. It is made to seem all the worse by the facility of modern communications.

Communications

The transistor radio has brought about a revolution in awareness. Millions who used to be isolated by illiteracy and remote location now know that there is a different way of life which others are privileged to enjoy. Never again will they be content to accept as inevitable the patterns of the past. They want to share the privileges of progress. They want a better world for their children. They have listened too long to unfilled promises. Their expectations have outrun performance. Their frustration is turning to a growing sense of injustice and disillusionment.

Science and Technology

Science and technology have not, however, kept pace with communications in the developing nations of the Western Hemisphere. These nations have lagged seriously in their participation in the scientific and cultural revolution which has been an essential part of the industrialization of the developed nations. Many American republics have not, therefore, shared proportionately in the increased productivity and rising standards of living of their northern neighbors. This has fanned the flames of jealousy, resentment and frustration.

Most of the American republics have not yet mobilized the necessary elements for widespread industrialization of their economies. They need, in varying degrees, more and better education, more effective systems for channeling national savings into capital formation and industrial investment, laws to protect the public's interests while encouraging the spirit of entrepreneurship, and expanding governmental services to support industrial growth.

Population Growth

Another vital force for change is the fact that the population of most American republics is the fastest-growing in the world.

The fact that over 60 percent of the population is now under 24 years of age has greatly increased the demands on government for more schools, more health services, more housing and roads—services beyond their resources to provide. It produces an increasing labor supply which cannot find enough work, and thus adds to the frustrations and tensions. It results in slum growth and a multiplication of the problems of urban life, and it cancels out so much of the economic growth achieved as to make improvement of living standards difficult if not impossible.

Urban Life

With urbanization in the Western Hemisphere have come crowded living conditions and a loss of living space in physical and psychological terms. The urban man tends to become both depersonalized and fragmented in his human relationships. Unemployment is high, especially among the young, ranging as high as 25 to 40 percent in some countries—and as low as four percent in others. The impact of poverty is widespread. These sprawling urban areas of the hemisphere spawn restlessness and anger which are readily exploited by the varying forces that thrive on trouble—and such forces are present in all societies.

The problems of urbanization are multiplied by an increasing migration to the cities of the rural poor, who are least prepared for the stresses of industrial urban society.

One positive force is the political emergence of women. They now have the right to vote in every country of the hemisphere—and are proving to be, by and large, a middle-of-the road influence.

Nationalism

All of this is heightened by the spirit of nationalism which has been an essential element in the emotional make-up of all the American republics since their independence. The curve of nationalist sentiment is generally rising as these societies strive toward greater national identity and self-assertiveness. Since the United States looms so large in the lives of the other nations, and its power and presence is so overwhelming, this nationalism tends more and more to find the United States a tempting and natural target.

Nationalism is not confined to any one country, nor does it spring from any one source. Political and pressure groups of all persuasions lean heavily on the exploitation of nationalistic sentiment.

This national sensitivity has been fed by the fact that, in the other American republics, United States management, capital and highly advertised products have played a disproportionately visible role. A high percentage of overseas investment has come from the United States, principally to seek raw materials or to preserve markets.

The forces of nationalism are creating increasing pressures against foreign private investment. The impetus for independence from the United States is leading toward rising pressures for nationalization of U.S. industry, local control, or participation with U.S. firms. Most economists and businessmen in the other American republics recognize the clear need for U.S. capital and technology, but they want them on terms consistent with their desire for self-determination.

Thus, the rising drive for self-identification is naturally and inevitably leading many nations to seek greater independence from U.S. influence and power. The dilemma posed for the governments is that they know that U.S. cooperation and participation can contribute greatly to accelerating achievement of their development goals, but their sense of political legitimacy may well depend on the degree of independence they can maintain from the United States.

Young People

In view of current conditions, it is natural that growing numbers of people in nations throughout the hemisphere including the United States should be disillusioned with society's failures—and perturbed by a sense of loss of individual identity.

Increasing numbers of young people especially are questioning many of our basic premises. They are searching for new values, new meanings, new importance for the individual's worth and dignity.

Student participation in demonstrations and violence is becoming a major force in all countries. This is so regardless of political ideology, regardless of whether the students are acting spontaneously or have been organized. Man has demonstrated in the past that he can endure regimentation; the test today, perhaps, is whether he can survive his freedom.

The idealism of youth is and should be one of the most promising forces for the future. At the same time, the very fact of their idealism makes some of the young vulnerable to subversive penetration and to exploitation as a revolutionary means for the destruction of the existing order. Above all, it is clear that the young people of the hemisphere will no longer accept slogans as substitutes for solutions. They know a better life is possible.

Labor

Yet it is not only the young who are deeply concerned or seeking instant fulfillment of their aspirations. The same phenomena are present in the ranks of labor. The largest groups in the developing labor movement throughout the hemisphere have democratic leadership. They seek increased productivity for their nations and a fair share of that increased productivity for the workers and their families. But a substantial segment of labor is Communist-led—and less concerned with the nation's productivity than with the overthrow of existing institutions—public and private.

The Cross and the Sword

Although it is not yet widely recognized, the military establishments and the Catholic Church are also among today's forces for social and political change in the other American republics. This is a new role for them. For since the arrival of the Conquistadores more than 400 years ago, the history of the military and the Catholic Church, working hand in hand with the landowners to provide "stability," has been a legend in the Americas.

Few people realize the extent to which both these institutions are now breaking with their pasts. They are, in fact, moving rapidly to the forefront as forces for social, economic and political change. In the case of the Church, this is a recognition of a need to be more responsive to the popular will. In the case of the military, it is a reflection of a broadening of opportunities for young men regardless of family background.

Modern communications and increasing education have brought about a stirring among the people that has had a tremendous impact on the Church, making it a force dedicated to change—revolutionary change if necessary.

Actually, the Church may be somewhat in the same situation as the young—with a profound idealism, but as a result, in some cases, vulnerable to subversive penetration; ready to undertake a revolution if necessary to end injustice but not clear either as to the ultimate nature of the revolution itself or as to the governmental system by which the justice it seeks can be realized.

In many South and Central American countries, the military is the single most powerful political grouping in society. Military men are symbols of power, authority and sovereignty and a focus of national pride. They have traditionally been regarded in most countries as the ultimate arbiters of the nation's welfare.

The tendency of the military to intervene when it judges that the government in office has failed to carry out its responsibilities properly has generally been accepted in Central and South America. Virtually all military governments in the hemisphere have assumed power to "rescue" the country from an incompetent government, or an intolerable economic or political situation. Historically, these regimes have varied widely in their attitudes toward civil liberties, social reform and repression.

Like the Church, the military was traditionally a conservative force resistant to change. Most officers came from the landowner class. In recent years, however, the owners of land have shifted more and more to an urban industrial life. The military service has been less attractive to their sons. As a result, opportunities have opened up for young men of ambition and ability from poor families who have neither land nor professional and business connections. These ambitious sons of the working classes have entered the military to seek an education and the opportunity for advancement.

This pattern has become almost universal throughout the American republics to the south. The ablest of these young officers have gone abroad for education and are now assuming top positions of leadership in almost all of the military groups in the hemisphere. And while their loyalties are with the armed forces, their emotional ties are often with the people. Increasingly, their concern and dedication is to the eradication of poverty and the improvement of the lot of the oppressed, both in rural and urban areas.

In short, a new type of military man is coming to the fore and often becoming a major force for constructive social change in the American republics. Motivated by increasing impatience with corruption, inefficiency, and a stagnant political order, the new military man is prepared to adapt his authoritarian tradition to the goals of social and economic progress.

This new role by the military, however, is not free from perils and dilemmas. There is always the risk that the authoritarian style will result in repression. The temptation to expand measures for security or discipline or efficiency to the point of curtailing individual liberties, beyond what is required for the restoration of order and social progress, is not easy to resist.

Above all, authoritarian governments, bent on rapid change, have an intrinsic ideological unreliability and a vulnerability to extreme nationalism. They can go in almost any doctrinal direction.

The danger for the new military is that it may become isolated from the people with authoritarianism turning into a means to suppress rather than eliminate the buildup of social and political tension.

The critical test, ultimately, is whether the new military can and will move the nation, with sensitivity and conscious design, toward a transition from military control for a social purpose to a more pluralistic form of government which will enable individual talent and dignity to flourish. Or will they become radicalized, statist and anti-U.S.?

In this connection, special mention should be made of the appeal to the new military, on a theoretical level, of Marxism: (1) It justifies, through its elitist-vanguard theories, government by a relatively small group or single institution (such as the

Army) and, at the same time, (2) produces a rationale for state-enforced sacrifices to further economic development.

One important influence counteracting this simplistic Marxist approach is the exposure to the fundamental achievements of the U.S. way of life that many of the military from the other American countries have received through the military training programs which the U.S. conducts in Panama and the United States.

Business

A similar phenomenon is apparent within the business community. Again, there is a dichotomy. On the one hand, long-established self-interests cling to practices of paternalism and monopoly behind high protective tariffs. On the other hand, new enterprises or older businesses with new, young management are bringing to bear a social concern for workers and the public as well as for stockholders.

This new business leadership is a promising and constructive force. And it is a necessary force in the process of change, simply because the technical, managerial and marketing competence of private business must assume a major role in the development of the Western Hemisphere.

Communist Subversion

In every country, there is a restless striving for a better life. Coming as it does at a time of uprooting change, it brings to many a vague unease that all the systems of society are out of control. In such a setting, all of the American nations are a tempting target for Communist subversion. In fact, it is plainly evident that such subversion is a reality today with alarming potential.

Castro has consistently recruited from the other American republics, and trained in Cuba, guerrillas to export the Cuban-type Communist agrarian revolution. Fortunately, the governments of the American republics have gradually improved their capabilities for dealing with Castro-type agrarian guerrillas. However, radical revolutionary elements in the hemisphere appear to be increasingly turning toward urban terrorism in their attempts to bring down the existing order. This type of subversion is more difficult to control, and governments are forced to use increasingly repressive measures to deal with it. Thus, a cycle of terrorist actions and repressive counter-reactions tend to polarize and unsettle the political situation, creating more fertile ground for radical solutions among large segments of the population.

There are also Maoist Communist forces in the hemisphere. Although they are relatively small in numbers they are fanatically dedicated to the use of violence and intimidation to achieve their ends. The mystique of Maoism has appealed most to the idealism of the young and, thus, has been the means for widespread subversion.

Now it appears in some cases that Castro and Maoist forces have joined for acts of subversion, terror and violence in the cities. These forces also concentrate on mass student demonstrations and disruptions of various institutions, public and private, calling on the support of Communist labor front organizations to the degree possible.

Although Castro's propaganda casts him as a leader of the down-trodden who is opposed to United States imperialism and independent of Soviet Communism, it is clear that the Soviet Union presently has an important degree of financial, economic, and military influence over Communist Cuba. The recent visit of the Soviet fleet to Havana is one evidence of growing warmth in their relations.

This Soviet performance in Cuba and throughout the hemisphere is to be contrasted with the official Soviet government and Communist party protestations not only of peaceful coexistence but of disassociation from Castro and his program of terror in the American republics.

Clearly, the opinion in the United States that Communism is no longer a serious factor in the Western Hemisphere is thoroughly wrong.

We found almost universally that the other American republics are deeply concerned about the threat that it poses to them—and the United States must be alert to and concerned about the ultimate threat it poses to the United States and the hemisphere as a whole.

Changes in the Decade Ahead

The nations of the Western Hemisphere in the decade ahead will differ greatly from their present situation. They will reflect the rapid and widespread changes now occurring, which will alter the institutions and processes by which the American republics govern and progress. While it is not possible to predict with any precision the precise course of change, the hemisphere is likely to exhibit the following characteristics in the next few years:

—Rising frustration with the pace of development, intensified by industrialization, urbanization and population growth;

—Political and social instability;

—An increased tendency to turn to authoritarian or radical solutions;

—Continuation of the trend of the military to take power for the purpose of guiding social and economic progress; and,

—Growing nationalism, across the spectrum of political groupings, which will often find expression in terms of independence from U.S. domination and influence.

CHAPTER TWO; THE CHALLENGE
TO POLITICAL AND ECONOMIC FREEDOM

A. The Nature of the Challenge

The pace and intensity of change, imposed on rampant inflation, urban violence, grinding poverty, embittering injustice and flaming nationalism, put the nations of the Western Hemisphere at a crossroads. The question of whether systems of freedom with order and justice will survive and prosper is no longer rhetorical; it is reality.

The key issue is whether government of free peoples can be made effective, and can set the necessary priorities, to cope with the people's present needs and their aspirations for the future; whether political and social institutions can hold the confidence not only of a questioning young generation but of adults as well.

For the United States, the challenge is a double one: First, to demonstrate by its example that a free society can resolve its own internal problems and provide a more rewarding life for all its people; second, to find ways in which its tremendous human and material resources can effectively supplement the efforts of the other American nations themselves, in a climate of growing instability, extremism, and anti-U.S. nationalism.

A new relationship between the United States and the other American republics must be shaped with a recognition that devotion to our long-term community of interests will often require sensitive handling of our short-term differences. In forging this relationship we have the opportunity to demonstrate how sovereign nations, working together, can solve common problems and thus to establish a model for cooperative arrangements for the fulfillment of men and women throughout the world.

It is a fortunate and striking fact of the modern world that, for the first time, the scientific know-how and managerial competence required to meet the economic aspects of the challenge are available. Moreover, we believe the Western Hemisphere possesses the human, material and spiritual resources that are needed for the task in all its aspects—economic, social and political.

B. The United States National Interest

The moral and spiritual strength of the United States in the world, the political credibility of our leadership, the security of our nation, the future of our social and economic progress are now at stake.

Rising frustrations throughout the Western Hemisphere over poverty and political instability have led increasing numbers of people to pick the United States as a scapegoat and to seek out Marxist solutions to their socio-economic problems. At the moment, there is only one Castro among the 26 nations of the hemipshere; there can well be more in the future. And a Castro on the mainland, supported militarily and economically by the Communist world, would present the gravest kind of threat to the security of the Western Hemisphere and pose an extremely difficult problem for the United States.

Just as the other American republics depend upon the United States for their capital equipment requirements, so the United States depends on them to provide a vast market for our manufactured goods. And as these countries look to the United States for a market for their primary products whose sale enables them to buy equipment for their development at home, so the United States looks to them for raw materials for our industries, on which depend the jobs of many of our citizens.

But these forces of economic interdependence are changing, and must change. An increasing flow of two-way trade in industrial products must supplement the present interchange of manufactured goods and primary products.

Today's 250 million people in South and Central America will become 643 million in just 30 years. If the current anti-U.S. trend continues, one can foresee a time when the United States would be politically and morally isolated from part or much of the Western Hemisphere. If this should happen, the barriers to our collective growth would become formidable indeed.

It is plainly evident that the countries of the Western Hemisphere, including the United States, have become increasingly dependent on each other.

Historically, the United States has had a special relationship with the other American republics. It is based upon long association, geography and, above all, on the psychological acceptance of a concept of hemisphere community. It is embodied in the web of organizations, treaties and commitments of the inter-American system.

Beyond conventional security and economic interests, the political and psychological value of the special relationship cannot be overestimated. Failure to maintain that special relationship would imply a failure of our capacity and responsibility as a great power. If we cannot maintain a constructive relationship in the Western Hemisphere, we will hardly be able to achieve a successful order elsewhere in the world. Moreover, failure to maintain the special relationship would create a vacuum in the hemisphere and facilitate the influence in the region of hostile foreign powers.

It is clear, then, that our national interest requires the maintenance of our special relationship which should have as its goal the creation of a community of self-reliant, independent nations linked in a mutually beneficial regional system, and seeking to improve the efficiency of their societies and the quality of life of their peoples.

C. Our National Objective

There is no system in all of history better than our own flexible structure of political democracy, individual initiative, and responsible citizenship in elevating the quality of man's life. It makes the individual of central importance; it subordinates the role of government as a servant of the people; it works with people and for people—it has no other justification.

Our job at home is far from finished. We must keep our emphasis on people, our priority concern for people. This will mean shaping the forces of change and stretching out or deferring those programs not related to the urgent needs of people. Unless human needs are met, democracy will have failed of its purpose and cannot survive.

What is true at home is essentially also true for the hemisphere. Our concern must be for people. What we in the hemisphere have to do is work together, multiplying our relations with the people of the hemisphere nations, helping each other develop more effective societies that can enhance the health, freedom and security of all the people, to the end that the quality of the life of each and every person in the hemisphere is enhanced.

We must work with our fellow Americans to the end that no one is exploited or degraded to enrich another and every man and woman has a full opportunity to make the most of his endowments.

However, we must recognize that the specific forms or processes by which each nation moves towards a pluralistic system will vary with its own traditions and situation. We know that we, in the United States, cannot determine the internal political structure of any other nation, except by example.

Our ability to affect or influence the course of events in other nations is limited. We may find that other nations may perceive their interests in ways which conflict with ours. What we must do is take a long-term view of our interests and objectives, always maintaining a sense of our own priorities and of the special Western Hemisphere relationship we hope to achieve. Such a view will require a high degree of tolerance for diversity and for nationalistic expression often directed against the United States, and a recognition that our style may often have a more important effect than what we actually do in the hemisphere.

The kind of paternalistic relationship the United States has had in the past with other hemisphere nations will be increasingly costly and counter-productive in the years ahead. We believe the United States must move increasingly toward a relationship of true partnership, in which it will cooperate with other nations of the hemisphere in those areas where its cooperation can be helpful and is wanted.

The United States must face several important practical issues in trying to shape this new relationship:

1. The United States should determine its attitude towards internal political developments in a more pragmatic way;

2. The United States should decide how it can shift increasing responsibility to the other American nations (through multi-lateral channels) for the development process; and,

3. The United States should decide how its interests are affected by insurgency and subversion elsewhere in the hemisphere and the extent to which its programs can and should assist in meeting the security requirements of its neighbors.

The task is difficult but by no means impossible. It will require discipline and energy and above all a very clear and consistent sense of purpose at home and abroad. To grasp the opportunity that lies in the hemisphere, the United States must make some major and fundamental changes in, first, the structure of the government mechanisms through which we work with our hemisphere neighbors, and, second, in our policies and programs as they relate to the Western Hemisphere.

*   *   *

CHAPTER THREE: ORGANIZATION

A. Organization of the United States Government

Unless there is a major reorganization of the United States government structure, with clear lines of responsibility and corresponding authority to make policy and direct operations in the Western Hemisphere, the effect of other recommendations would, at best, be marginal. Under the Constitution, the President has the responsibility for the formulation and execution of foreign policy. Where there are conflicting interests and points of view among the government departments and agencies, only the President has the authority to reconcile the differences and make the decisions.

With the present United States government structure, Western Hemisphere policy can neither be soundly formulated nor effectively carried out.

Contrary to popular misconceptions, the State Department does not have effective overall responsibility for foreign policy where the interests of other departments of the government are concerned. In actual fact, the State Department controls less than half the policy decisions directly relating to the Western Hemisphere. Responsibility for policy and operations is scattered among many departments and agencies—for example, Treasury, Commerce, Agriculture, and Defense.

To cope with the diffusion of authority, there has grown up a complex and cumbersome system of interdepartmental committees within which there are interminable negotiations because no one member has the authority to make a final decision. The result is that there are endless delays in decision-making. Too often, agreement is

reached on major subjects only by compromise in the lower echelons of government—
often at the lowest common denominator of agreement.

The result is that we have no clear formulation of United States policy objectives
toward the Western Hemisphere. Nor are there clear policy guide lines relating to
substantive and regional problems which are essential to effective day-to-day decision-
making in our contacts with the other American republics. This in itself leads to
conflicts within the government which are detrimental to the best interests of our
country.

In this maze of bureaucracy and procrastination, the representatives of the Western
Hemisphere governments become frustrated and humiliated because they are referred
from one department to another without finding anyone who can make a final
decision. Delays in Washington of months and even years on decisions of major
importance to their countries were reported to the mission in almost every nation we
visited.

The lack of clear policy direction, the indecision and the resulting frustration are
major factors in preventing the kind of understanding and close working relationships
which are essential in light of our growing interdependence.

Obviously, neither the President nor the Secretary of State has the time for
continuing attention to the concern of 25 other nations in the hemisphere, and no one
else has the authority. As a result, the day-to-day relationships with our friends and
neighbors, including Canada, do not get the constant consideration of our top policy
makers.

But if we are to have a true sense of community within the Western Hemisphere, it
must be possible to establish and maintain high-level contacts with each country on a
basis of frankness and openness that will minimize the danger of misunderstanding and
maximize effective cooperation. Such cooperation depends on the ability of the
United States to respond promptly and decisively. For the United States to organize
itself to make this possible:

1. There must be clearly-defined national objectives consistent with the goals of
the Western Hemisphere community;

2. These objectives must be translated into clear policy positions relating to both
governmental and private activities;

3. To implement these national goals and policies effectively, there must be a
structure with clear lines of responsibility and authority flowing directly from the
President;

4. There must be efficiently-run organizations that can carry out supporting
programs free from political and diplomatic encumbrances which reduce the effectiveness of technical and professional operations; and,

5. There must be a close working relationship with the members of Congress as an
indispensable and integral part of the policy-making process.

Finally, and of overriding importance in our special Western Hemisphere relationships is the psychological factor of personal relationships, so important to the Latins.

A characteristic of the Latin temperament is to put more faith in people than in
institutions. It therefore is important to give stature and dignity to the key position of
leadership in the structure of the United States government that deals with the
Western Hemisphere. One man should symbolize, by the importance of his position,
the President's special interest in and concern for our Western Hemisphere relations.

Creation of such a post must therefore outweigh any traditional objections to a change of government organization.

In this way, we can establish a sense of vitality, openness and effectiveness in our relations with the leaders and peoples of the other nations. This is essential to the unity and security of the Western Hemisphere and will make possible the achievement of our common goals.

Recommendation: National Policy Objective
The President should reorganize the foreign policy and operating structure of United States government dealing with the Western Hemisphere.

Recommendations for Action
1. *A Secretary of Western Hemisphere Affairs should be created to give day-to-day leadership and guidance on behalf of the Secretary of State and the President. He would also coordinate on their behalf all United States government activities in the Western Hemisphere.*

a. He would be the focal point within the United States government of all matters pertaining to Western Hemisphere Affairs, subject to the President and the Secretary of State.

*   *   *

2. *There should be created within the National Security Council a Western Hemisphere Policy Staff Director to service the President, the National Security Council, the Secretary of State, the Secretary of Western Hemisphere Affairs and the various departments and agencies involved, such as Defense, Treasury, Commerce and Agriculture, and economic and social program activities.*

a. The Director would serve the Assistant to the President for National Security Affairs and would thus have experts with competence in the fields represented by the key departments and agencies involved in Western Hemisphere affairs.

b. The purpose of this White House staff would be to help in the formulation of the President's Western Hemisphere goals and policies in consultation with the appropriate councils of government.

*   *   *

3. *An Economic and Social Development Agency should be created in the Executive Office of the President to supersede the present AID administration in the State Department. This move is essential for a number of reasons:*

a. The financial and technical operations of the State Department have gotten all tangled up with the diplomatic responsibilities of the state department—to the detriment of both.

b. Because of the lack of clear administrative responsibility and authority in the AID organization, it is having great difficulty in recruiting quality staff.

c. Economic assistance policy operating decisions are too often made on the basis of political negotiations rather than economic and social realities.

*   *   *

4. *An Institute of Western Hemisphere Affairs should be set up under the Development Agency as the operating corporation to carry out government-to-government economic and social programs in the Western Hemisphere.*

a. The activities of this Western Hemisphere corporate institute would be subject to the President, the Secretary of Western Hemisphere Affairs (on behalf of the Secretary of State), and the Policy Staff Director of the Security Council.

*   *   *

g. This corporation would have the power to set up subsidiaries to give special emphasis in fields of particular concern. Two such subsidiaries are specifically recommended:

−A Western Hemisphere Institute for Education, Science and Culture; and,

−An Inter-American Rural Development Corporation.

Each would be an operating corporation to carry out projects in its respective fields under the policy guidance of the President of the Institute of Western Hemisphere Affairs (further descriptions appear on pages 523, 530, and 532).

5. *We applaud the President's support of legislation now before Congress to create an Overseas Private Investment Corporation; it should be enacted into law.*

a. OPIC would take over the activities relating to private economic development that are now being handled by AID, including insurance, contracts, loans and investment surveys.

b. This would separate administration of government-to-government programs from private enterprise activities—a desirable step since an agency operating primarily at a government-to-government level finds it difficult to get the orientation to handle private enterprise matters.

6. *The President should discuss with the leaders of the Senate and the House of Representatives the possibility of creating a Joint Congressional Committee to coordinate legislative policy concerning the hemisphere.*

a. A broad-based steering committee could work with the appropriate committees of both houses of the Congress to anticipate hemisphere problems, consider new legislation and review existing laws relating to hemisphere affairs.

*   *   *

B. Country-by-Country Relations

*   *   *

Each country in the hemisphere is unique, with its own special problems, its own special relations with other countries and with the United States. It is therefore vital that our diplomacy be geared to close and effective ties with each of these nations.

*   *   *

Recommendations: National Policy Objective
The United States should maintain close, open, intimate and effective ties with each

of the hemisphere nations, on a country-by-country basis, recognizing that each nation is different and that bilateral relations and programs have an important role to play.

C. Regional Organizations

As individual entities, many of the hemisphere countries have such limited resources that they could not promote economic growth and social progress or sustain an acceptable level of economic competition in world markets. Thus they have begun to form regional groupings to coordinate their economic policies.

The first of these regional groupings and the most effective thus far has been the Central American Common Market. It began with a limited list of "free trade" goods, was gradually broadened into fiscal agreements and still later expanded to handle issues of economic and political significance.

An important instrument of the CACM is the Central American Bank for Economic Integration, which makes loans for public works, industry, agriculture, opening new markets and other region-wide projects.

The Caribbean nations have a wide variety of regional organizations and are now forming a Caribbean Free Trade Association and a Caribbean Development Bank.

The treaty creating the Andean Group under the Latin American Free Trade Association was signed this summer. The River Plate countries have been discussing the possibility of a regional organization, but have thus far made no commitment.

The Latin American Free Trade Association, which began in 1961 to reduce tariffs among 11 Latin American countries, is moving slowly because of the complexities of negotiating reciprocal tariff cuts among so many nations.

Recommendation: National Policy Objective
The United States should cooperate with and support fully regional organizations among the nations of the Western Hemisphere.

Recommendations for Action
1. Upon request, the United States should encourage regional organizations with financial and technical assistance and support for industrial, agricultural, educational and scientific programs.

2. To facilitate such cooperation, the United States should appoint Assistant Secretaries of Western Hemisphere Affairs for the CACM nations, LAFTA and the Caribbean nations.

*   *   *

D. Inter-American Organizations

Recommendation: National Policy Objective
The United States should give full support to and work through the Organization of American States and its several Councils in dealing with Western Hemisphere affairs; it should re-affirm its adherence to the principles and policies set forth in the various treaties and conventions which form the general structure of the hemisphere.

Recommendations for Action

1. *Political: The United States should cooperate fully with the Organization of the American States in dealing with the political problems of the hemisphere.*

2. *Economic and Social: The United States should make greater use of the multilateral channels of the OAS to execute technical assistance programs and should propose to the Inter-American Economic and Social Council that CIAP (the Council's executive arm) be assigned greater responsibility in planning, setting priorities for, and allocating development assistance for the nations of the Western Hemisphere, and that its name be changed to the Western Hemisphere Development Committee.*

*   *   *

3. *Education, Science and Culture: When the Inter-American Council for Education, Scientific and Cultural Affairs is ratified, the United States should undertake major programs to support its objectives.*

4. *Security: The United States through appropriate channels should propose a Western Hemisphere Security Council composed of civilian as distinct from military leaders with headquarters outside the United States.*

5. *Migration: The United States should stand ready to support the Organization of American States' initiatives toward facilitating desirable migrations within the hemisphere.*

*   *   *

E. International Organizations

*   *   *

Recommendation: National Policy Objective

The United States should foster a world-wide outlook as complementary to rather than competitive with Western Hemisphere goals.

Recommendations for Action

1. *The United States should make use of international facilities, such as the World Bank and World Health Organization, in developing its regional assistance programs.*

2. *United States policy-makers should be ever mindful of the urgent need to avoid any tendency or even an appearance of a tendency toward isolationism inimical to the best interests of the hemisphere and the world at large.*

CHAPTER FOUR: POLICY AND ACTION

A. United States Political Relations
with the Hemisphere

Throughout the hemisphere, there is growing uncertainty concerning the extent of the United States' commitment to work with the people of the other American republics for their economic and social betterment.

Our neighbors need to be reassured of our conviction that people are, indeed, our basic concern, and that we want to continue to work with them, regardless of the form of their government, to help them raise the level of their lives. In this way, we can help strengthen the forces of democracy.

Commitment to representative, responsive democratic government is deeply imbedded in the collective political consciousness of the American people. We would like to see strong representative government develop in the other nations of the hemisphere for both idealistic and practical reasons:

—Our experience convinces us that representative democratic government and free societies offer the best means of organizing man's social, political and economic life so as to maximize the prospects for improving the individual's dignity and the quality of his life.

—Practically, nations with broadly-based political systems of a democratic type are more likely to have outlooks and concepts compatible with the style of the United States and its people, and more willing to cooperate with us in establishing an effective world order.

*   *   *

Democracy is a very subtle and difficult problem for most of the other countries in the hemisphere. The authoritarian and hierarchical tradition which has conditioned and formed the cultures of most of these societies does not lend itself to the particular kind of popular government we are used to. Few of these countries, moreover, have achieved the sufficiently advanced economic and social systems required to support a consistently democratic system. For many of these societies, therefore, the question is less one of democracy or a lack of it, than it is simply of orderly ways of getting along.

There will often be times when the United States will find itself in disagreement with the particular policies or forms of government of other American nations. However, the fundamental question for the United States is how it can cooperate to help meet the basic needs of the people of the hemisphere despite the philosophical disagreements it may have with the nature of particular regimes. It must seek pragmatic ways to help people without necessarily embracing their governments. It should recognize that diplomatic relations are merely practical conveniences and not measures of moral judgment. This can be done by maintaining formal lines of communication without embracing such regimes.

The U.S. should also recognize that political evolution takes time and that, realistically, its long-term interests will be served by maintaining at least minimal diplomatic relationships with other governments of the hemisphere, while trying to find ways to assist the people of those countries, and to encourage the governments to move toward democratic processes. Such a policy requires a very difficult balance, but is one that must be achieved pragmatically on a case by case basis. The U.S. cannot renege on its commitment to a better life for all of the peoples of the hemisphere because of moral disagreement with regimes which the people themselves did not establish and do not control.

Recommendation: National Policy Objective

The United States should work with and for the people of this hemisphere to assist them in enhancing the quality of their lives and to provide moral leadership as a force for freedom and justice in the Americas.

The United States cannot allow disagreements with the form or the domestic policies of other American governments to jeopardize its basic objective of working with and for their people to our mutual benefit.

Recommendations for Action

The President should reaffirm our national commitment:

a. To work with and for the people of this hemisphere.

b. To recognize hemisphere governments in accordance with article XXXV of the Act of the Ninth International Conference of American States in 1948—where it was stated:

—The establishment or maintenance of diplomatic relations with a government does not imply any judgment upon the domestic policy of that government.

c. To the covenants which bind together the nations of the Western Hemisphere in respect for the sovereignty of nations and opposition to foreign intervention.

*   *   *

B. Western Hemisphere Security

If the quality of life for the individual in this hemisphere is to be meaningful, there must be freedom from fear and full respect for the rights and the personal dignity of individuals—not just one's own rights and dignity, but everyone's.

Unfortunately, far too many people in the hemisphere—including people in the United States—are denied such freedom and respect. Forces of anarchy, terror and subversion are loose in the Americas. Moreover, this fact has too long gone unheeded in the United States.

Doubt and cynicism have grown in the other American nations as to the purposefulness of the United States in facing this serious threat to freedom, democracy and the vital interests of the entire hemisphere.

*   *   *

Many of our neighbors find it incomprehensible that the United States will not sell them military equipment which they feel is required to deal with internal subversion. They have been puzzled by the reduction in U.S. military assistance grants in view of the growing intensity of the subversive activities they face.

They were concerned that their young people were being drawn to Cuba in never-diminishing numbers, for indoctrination and for instruction in the arts of propaganda, the skills of subversion and the tactics of terror.

Castro's recent restatement of his policy indicates no change in objectives. Rather, he reaffirms his revolutionary concepts and establishes a new set of priorities and conditions under which Cuban support for revolutionaries will be given.

The subversive capabilities of these Communist forces are increasing throughout the hemisphere. The inflation, urban terrorism, racial strife, overcrowding, poverty, violence and rural insurgency are all among the weapons available to the enemies of the systems of the free nations of the Western Hemisphere. These forces are quick to exploit for their own ends the freedoms afforded by democratic governments.

The seriousness of these factors when exploited by covert Communist forces is not fully recognized in the United States.

Two decades and more ago, in the presence of an overt and world-wide Soviet threat, the United States response was realistic and flexible. It included in the Western Hemisphere the training and equipping of security forces for hemisphere defense.

Fortuitously, the military capability thus achieved subsequently enabled the individual nations of the hemisphere to deal with the initial impact of a growing, covert Communist threat to their internal security. However, the threat has shifted from one based in the rural areas to one centered around urban terrorism. Realistic efforts to deal with this increasingly dangerous development are necessary, on an effective, hemisphere-wide basis.

In addition, the United States must face more forthrightly the fact that while the military in the other American nations are alert to the problems of internal security, they do not feel that this is their only role and responsibility. They are conscious of the more traditional role of a military establishment to defend the nation's territory, and they possess understandable professional pride which creates equally understandable desires for modern arms; in addition, they are subjected to the sales pressures and blandishments of suppliers from other nations—east and west—eager to sell. The result of all this is a natural resentment on the part of the military of other American nations when the United States refuses to sell modern items of equipment.

Thus, many military leaders in the other American republics see the United States acting to hold them back as second-class citizens, and they are becoming increasingly estranged from us at a time when their political role is on the rise. Our dilemma is how to be responsive to their legitimate desires for modern equipment without encouraging the diversion of scarce resources from development to armaments which, in some cases, may be unrelated to any real security requirement.

Military leaders throughout the hemisphere are frequently criticized here in the United States. However, we will have to give increasing recognition to the fact that many new military leaders are deeply motivated by the need for social and economic progress. They are searching for ways to bring education and better standards of living to their people while avoiding anarchy or violent revolution. In many cases, it will be more useful for the United States to try to work with them in these efforts rather than to abandon or insult them because we are conditioned by arbitrary ideological stereotypes.

In addition, there is not in the United States a full appreciation of the important role played by the police. There is a tendency in the United States to equate the police in the other American republics with political action and repression, rather than with security. There have, unfortunately, been many such instances of the use of police. Yet well-motivated, well-trained police, when present in local communities, enforce the laws, protect the citizenry from terror, and discourage criminal elements. At the present time, however, police forces of many countries have not been strengthened as population and great urban growth have taken place. Consequently they have become increasingly less capable of providing either the essential psychological support or the internal security that is their major function.

Moreover, the people of the United States do not recognize that, as a whole, the other American nations spend a smaller percentage of their Gross National Product on defense than any other area except Africa South of the Sahara. Most of this expenditure, despite much talk of supersonic aircraft, is for personnel and operating costs. Relatively little has been spent on major items of equipment. For this reason, most of the military inventories of these other hemisphere nations consist of equipment acquired shortly after World War II. Such equipment is becoming obsolete and unserviceable and spare parts are becoming increasingly unavailable.

One other point not clearly understood in the United States is that no one country today can effectively protect its own internal security by itself.

The youth that go abroad for training in subversive activities, the money and directives that flow through agents, and the propaganda that comes from outside their borders are all beyond their effective control.

Only through hemisphere cooperation can these problems, which so vitally affect internal security, be adequately dealt with.

Recommendation: National Policy Objective
The United States should cooperate with other nations of the Western Hemisphere in measures to strengthen internal security.

Recommendations for Action
   1. *A Western Hemisphere Security Council*
   a. The United States should work with the other republics to form a civilian-directed Western Hemisphere Security Council to cope with the forces of subversion that operate throughout the Western Hemisphere. The purpose of the Council would be to help the hemisphere countries work together in creating and preserving the kind of orderly environment, free from terror and violence, in which each citizen of each country can build a better life for himself and his family. This Council would supersede the Special Consultative Committee on Security of the Organization of American States.
   b. Although the United States would have membership in the Council, the Council should have its headquarters outside of our country.
   2. *A Western Hemisphere Security Training Assistance Program*
   a. The United States should reverse the recent downward trend in grants for assisting the training of security forces for the other hemisphere countries. (The total amount proposed for fiscal year 1970 is $21.4 million, as against $80.7 million in fiscal year 1966.) In view of the growing subversion against hemisphere governments, the mounting terrorism and violence against citizens, and the rapidly expanding population, it is essential that the training program which brings military and police personnel from the other hemisphere nations to the United States and to training centers in Panama be continued and strengthened.
   b. The name "Military Assistance Program" should be dropped because it no longer reflects the security emphasis we believe important. The program should be renamed the "Western Hemisphere Security Program".
   3. Internal Security Support
   a. The United States should respond to requests for assistance of the police and security forces of the hemisphere nations by providing them with the essential tools to do their job.

b. Accordingly, the United States should meet reasonable requests from other hemisphere governments for trucks, jeeps, helicopters and like equipment to provide mobility and logistical support for these forces; for radios, and other command control equipment for proper communications among the forces; and for small arms for security forces.

c. In furtherance of these objectives, the United States should provide, on request, military and technical training missions but should no longer maintain the permanent military missions in residence in other nations which too often have constituted too large and too visible a United States presence.

4. Military Sales for Defense

a. The Executive Branch should seek modification of the Conte and Symington amendments to permit the United States to sell aircraft, ships and other major military equipment without aid cut penalties to the more developed nations of the hemisphere when these nations believe this equipment is necessary to protect their land, patrol their seacoasts and airspace, and otherwise maintain the morale of their forces and protect their sovereignty. Realistically, if the United States doesn't sell such equipment, it will be purchased from other sources, east or west, and this would not be compatible with the United States' best interests.

b. Each country should be permitted to buy such equipment through purchase orders placed with the United States Defense Department through the Military Assistance Program, in order that each country may get full value for its military investment, more reliable delivery dates, and better maintenance.

C. Economic and Social Development

Our common objective—to improve the quality of life for all individuals in the hemisphere—can only be accomplished by working together to accelerate the rate of economic and social development. Hemisphere interdependence in these matters is more than a theory. It is a fact of life.

The Alliance for Progress was the first formal agreement among Western Hemisphere nations on specific goals related to economic and social development. The goals of the Alliance remain the best expression of our common objectives. To be sure, actual progress under the Alliance has not come up to the grand hopes entertained in 1961 at Punta del este. Yet the broad Alliance objectives of economic and social development to enrich the lives of individuals remain the challenging goals which Western Hemisphere nations seek.

One of the least understood features of the Alliance is the fact that it is a self-help effort in which the principal responsibility for financing and implementation has been with the people of the other hemisphere countries. It is not a bilateral United States aid program, contrary to popular impression. The United States is but one partner in a development effort which is about 90 percent financed by the other American republics.

To say the Alliance has failed is to discount the genuine progress it has made. The fact is that many of the expectations generated at the outset of the Alliance were unrealistic. But the Alliance experience shows that man *can* shape the future along lines which will contribute to broad national and hemispheric objectives, and this is the important fact. To be sure, mistakes are made, but progress frequently involves the process of learning through mistakes.

One of the things learned from the mission was that other nations have deeply resented the way in which the United States has carried out its assistance programs. As part of the aid effort, the United States has intervened, usually with the best of intentions, in almost every aspect of their economic policies and programs. It has too often tried to do things *for* them, because it felt it could do them better. Not only was this subconscious paternalism less effective because it was resented, but also because it did not give the other nations an incentive to assume responsibility and initiative themselves.

It is clear that most of the American republics are psychologically ready to assume direction of their own development efforts. Moreover, the technical capabilities of the individual nations and the international lending institutions are growing steadily. The time has arrived for the United States to move consciously from a paternalistic role to one of partnership. The United States must build on the progress already achieved, and improve and accelerate its efforts, but it also must be willing to help without trying to dominate. Shifting an increasing portion of our assistance through multilateral institutions would help to accomplish this objective.

The other American nations must assume greater responsibility for their own performance in utilizing United States resources. They also must recognize that their performance will influence the extent to which the United States Congress and public will be willing to maintain or increase levels of cooperation with the Western Hemisphere.

The challenge now is to develop pragmatic programs which build on the long experience of hemisphere cooperation and which will accelerate economic and social progress.

The procedure involves:

1. Efforts to improve policies and programs which have produced generally constructive results;

2. A resolve to modify or drop those which have not stood the test of time; and,

3. Most importantly, a willingness throughout the hemisphere to innovate by developing new policies and programs to meet common objectives.

Economic and social development must go hand-in-hand. Economic growth provides the wherewithal to support improved diets, health and sanitation, enhanced educational opportunities, better housing and all the elements which contribute to an improvement in the quality of life. The process, however, is not automatic. Positive policies and actions are called for to make sure that the benefits of economic growth are used effectively to provide expanding horizons of opportunity for all individuals. Thus social development is not only made possible by economic growth but is essential to make sure the benefits of growth are broadly shared.

The rate of overall economic progress in the rest of the Western Hemisphere outside of Canada and the United States compares favorably with other regions of the world so far in the 1960's. Gross National Product in constant prices has advanced at an average annual rate of 4.9 percent.

But in terms of improving the quality of life for individuals, progress has not been satisfactory. The rate of population growth in other Western Hemisphere nations—2.9 percent per annum—is the highest of any major area in the world. Thus, the 4.9

percent annual increase in total production has yielded an increase of 2 percent per annum in production per person. This measure is more meaningful, since it is production per person which supports the rise in living standards for individuals. . . .

While it is true that the main impetus for development must come from within nations, it is also true that hemisphere cooperation must provide the support which is essential for accelerated progress. Trade policies on the part of industrial nations can have a major influence on opportunities for export expansion on the part of the developing nations. Development assistance by the United States and the governments of other industrial nations can provide loans, grants and technical assistance to supplement local efforts, primarily in such fields as public works, education, agriculture and health. Foreign private investment can provide essential technical knowledge and capital.

1. Trade Policies

Trade policy is the central economic issue facing all Western Hemisphere nations. Freer access to markets in the United States and other industrial countries is essential to support accelerated economic progress. Provision of such opportunities poses problems of adjustment for the industrial nations in terms of jobs and investment. The challenge is to work together to develop a practical approach which will be in the best interests of all hemisphere nations.

Expanding export trade is the soundest and most important way the other American republics can finance the imports needed for broad development. In 1967, their export earnings were six times the net inflow of private and public capital from abroad. The great bulk of the area's $10.3 billion of imports consisted of the machinery and equipment needed to support industrialization and to expand governmental services, i.e., power, highways, and communications.

The slow growth in exports in the 1960's has been an important factor limiting the pace of general development. From 1960 to 1968, the value of the area's exports increased 4.7 percent per annum as compared with an increase of 8.2 percent for world exports. Growth in world exports was 75 percent greater than that for other hemisphere nations.

A major problem is that 87 percent of the area's exports consist of primary products—food, natural fibers and industrial raw materials. In contrast, almost two-thirds of the exports of the industrial nations are made up of manufactured products.

While sound policy calls for a maximum effort to diversify and develop exports of primary products, at stable prices, it is unlikely that such exports can expand rapidly enough to support accelerated growth in the area as a whole. Though some nations have favorable opportunities in such fields, most of the countries must look to industrialization and increasing exports of industrial products.

Industrial development requires broad markets for efficient production. Domestic markets in most of the nations of the hemisphere are too limited for broad industrialization. Regional trading arrangements offer one constructive way to broaden markets. But even with a rapid development of regional markets, freer access to markets in industrial nations will be needed to support the industrial growth required to improve the quality of life through the hemisphere.

In the face of this imperative need for expanding trade, the United States imposes formidable barriers against imports from other Western Hemisphere nations:

—Imports of many primary products are subject to quotas.

—United States tariffs are so high on processed raw materials and on the manufactured goods the area could export to the United States that they are serious impediments to trade.

It comes down to the elemental fact that trade expansion is essential to support accelerated economic development in the hemisphere. In the process, individuals throughout the hemisphere can benefit. There will be adjustment problems which must be dealt with in realistic terms. But a broader division of labor on a hemisphere basis can bring lower prices to consumers, higher wages for workers, and satisfactory incentive for saving and investment.

Increasing imports by the United States from other hemisphere nations will help expand United States exports to them. Last year, the United States imported goods valued at $4.3 billion from the area and exported $4.7 billion to these countries, for a favorable trade balance of over $400 million. United States exports to other hemisphere nations have grown 41 percent since 1962, as against an increase of 59 percent in United States exports to the rest of the world.

The problem is not that the United States has lost competitive position—its share of exports to Latin America from all industrial nations has been quite stable in recent years. The fact is that the slow growth in the export earnings of the other countries in the hemisphere restricts their ability to finance imports. The record shows clearly that if the United States buys more from these countries, they will spend more on United States exports.

Recommendation: National Policy Objective

The United States should press for the maximum feasible development of mutually beneficial trade with other nations of the hemisphere. A doubling of such trade by 1976 is a realistic goal. This can only be accomplished by United States action to revise its tariffs and quotas to promote such mutually beneficial increased trade.

Recommendations for Action

1. The United States should work out a balanced approach to the problem of expanding hemisphere trade in industrial products by moving to a system of tariff preferences for imports from all developing nations.

*   *   *

2. Realistic and effective arrangements should be set up to assist United States workers and producers who are adversely affected by increased imports.

*   *   *

3. Where the United States applies import quotas for domestic reasons, as in meat and cotton textiles, the allotments to hemisphere nations should be readjusted to assure that they contribute to the general objectives of hemisphere development.

—As a general principle, the United States should allocate a major part of the growth in its imports to hemisphere nations. Changes in the allocation of quotas, even though relatively small in relation to United Stations consumption, can be of great benefit to some hemisphere nations.

4. *The United States should support commodity agreements which operate to stabilize and maintain prices for primary products at levels that reflect fair wages and other costs of production.*

            *   *   *

5. *The United States should use its voting power in the International Coffee Agreement, together with other Western Hemisphere nations, to make sure that the system works as effectively as possible in terms of its objectives relating to prices and quotas, and that Western Hemisphere nations receive a major share in the growth of the United States market.*

a. It has been estimated that a drop of one cent per pound in the price of coffee means a loss of $55 million in foreign exchange to the 14 coffee-producing countries of the Western Hemisphere.

            *   *   *

6. *Special attention should be directed to the requirements of the Western Hemisphere nations when sugar quotas are reviewed in 1971.*

            *   *   *

7. *The United States should lend its support to regional markets as they develop in the area, including participation in regional development banks.*

8. *The rates set by shipping conferences on the United States trade with other hemisphere nations should be reviewed.*

—In many cases, it costs two to three times as much to ship from a United States port as it does from Europe. This imposes a serious competitive disadvantage on United States exporters.

2. Development Assistance

United States assistance has played a helpful role in hemisphere development, not so much in terms of the amount of aid—which can only be marginal to a country's own resources—but by placing assistance at the right place at the right time. It has, for example, financed the needed education or health projects which could not be funded elsewhere, or made possible a child-feeding program, or supported comprehensive land reform. More significantly, in some cases, United States assistance appears to have supplied the margin of resources that permitted a country to break out of stagnation and bring rampant inflation under control, thus helping millions of people.

In this way the $1 billion a year which represents the United States commitment to the Alliance for Progress has made its contribution. In the process, a number of lessons have been learned:

1) Assistance can be fully effective only where a country is making maximum use of its own productive resources.

2) In some cases, additional assistance from the United States and elsewhere can help a country move into a phase of self-sustaining growth, where ultimately foreign assistance is no longer needed.

3) Distributing United States assistance in small and inadequate amounts to a

country, where it makes little impact on development, can be a misuse and waste of funds.

4) Multi-national and regional lending institutions have made great strides in filling the needs of developing nations for project loans. These organizations have the advantages of drawing on the skills and resources of many countries rather than one, and of being better able to avoid the political frictions that can develop in bilateral programs.

Impediments to AID Program

In addition, certain problems have arisen which reduce the effectiveness of the assistance program:

1) The United States assistance program has become increasingly encumbered with conditions and restrictions which seriously reduce the effectiveness of our assistance. These include requirements to ship half the goods purchased with assistance loans on United States freighters; provision that all imports be purchased in the United States no matter how much more expensive; earmarking of funds contrary to the particular needs of a country; and threats to withhold aid if United States investments are expropriated without appropriate payment, if a nation purchases "sophisticated" weapons, or if United States commercial fishing boats are taken into custody and fined.

2) These encumbrances, when viewed separately, may appear reasonable—and, of course, they are to the advantage of special-interest groups in the United States. Taken together, however, they seriously weaken our efforts to assist developing countries. Some of them appear to violate the sovereignty of other nations. They also increase costs by requiring, for example, that imports for a construction project come from the United States and that United States engineering firms be employed regardless of cost.

To be sure, United States government funds must be expended under the most careful controls. Existing controls are exacting in preventing waste and misuse of assistance funds from the United States point of view. But from the point of view of the recipient country, loading extraneous conditions on development loans amounts to waste and misuse of funds which they must repay with interest.

Recommendation: National Policy Objective

The United States should make a renewed policy commitment to support development in the Western Hemisphere as a means of improving the quality of life for individuals. Assistance should be provided without special-interest considerations and with due attention to self-help and country performance.

Recommendations for Action

1. Development or program loans should be made on a three-to-five-year commitment basis, through the proposed Institute of Western Hemisphere Affairs which should become our most important assistance technique.

                    *   *   *

2. Multi-national and regional lending institutions should finance the bulk of public works projects and project loans should be restricted to agriculture, education, public health, and urban development projects which involve pioneering and testing new approaches.

3. In providing both program and project assistance, the United States should take full cognizance of the recommendations of the proposed Western Hemisphere Development Committee of the Organization of American States, giving full weight to Title 6, Section 251 H of the Foreign Assistance Act of 1966.

4. Development assistance loans should carry low interest rates and lenient repayment terms in order to be effective.

a. The basic concern of the United States lies not in how much interest is paid, but whether the funds "pay off" in helping a country develop.

*   *   *

5. The encumbrances on United States assistance programs should be removed in all cases where they interfere with the process of development or impugn the sovereignty of other countries.

*   *   *

6. Loan restrictions should be broadened so borrowers can spend the funds anywhere in the Western Hemisphere with due consideration to questions of quality, price and delivery dates.

*   *   *

7. The Executive Branch should seek the suspension or modifications of the Pelly, Conte, Hickenlooper, Symington, and Reuss amendments which affect the extension of assistance including cut-offs where countries purchase sophisticated weapons, or seize United States fishing boats operating without a license, or expropriate without due compensation.

8. The provision that half of the goods financed by the United States must go in United States freighters should be repealed.

It has been estimated that this provision reduces the effectiveness of each $1.00 of United States assistance by as much as 20¢. It is one of the major irritants felt in developing countries. This is a disguised subsidy to United States shipping companies. Any necessary subsidy should be given openly and directly by Congressional appropriation.

3. Debt Service Problems

In the effort to support accelerated economic development, the major financial mechanism used has been loans from multi-national and regional agencies, governments and private sources. Many of the loans from multi-national and regional institutions and from governments are "soft" loans in the sense that interest rates are low and terms of repayment are lenient. The concept of soft loans is basically sound—they provide real assistance, while the fact that they must be repaid helps keep the development process realistic.

Nevertheless, interest and amortization payments must be made on schedule on all loans, from public and private sources, if a country is to maintain its credit standing. Heavy borrowings by some Western Hemisphere countries to support development have reached the point where annual repayments of interest and amortization absorb a large share of foreign exchange earnings. Within five years, a number of other nations in the Western Hemisphere could face the same situation. Many of the countries are, in effect, having to make new loans to get the foreign exchange to pay interest and amortization on old loans, and at higher interest rates.

This debt service problem is a major concern. If countries get into a position where interest and amortization payments on foreign loans require a disproportionately large share of available foreign exchange, then the general pace of development will be slowed by the inability to maintain imports of the capital equipment needed to support economic growth.

Recommendation: National Policy Objective

The United States policy for the Western Hemisphere should recognize the multiple advantages of a generous rescheduling of debt service requirements for countries facing balance of payments problems.

Recommendations for Action

1. *Studies of the debt service problem on a country-by-country basis should be initiated by the Western Hemisphere Development Committee (the present CIAP).*

*   *   *

2. *Where dollar payments are suspended or stretched out, the equivalent amounts in local currencies should be paid into a special fund to be used—in consultation with the United States—to meet the general development objectives of the other Western Hemisphere nations. These would include:*

a. Financing exports of capital goods within the region;

b. Financing expanded economic development through national and regional development banks; and

c. Financing local private participation in local joint ventures with foreign capital.

4. Private Savings and Investment

Accelerated economic growth will require increasing flows of private investment, local and foreign. Yet in all too many cases, private savings and investment are held back by high and erratic rates of inflation as well as by complex government controls and restrictions. Moreover, too large a portion of local savings tends to seek safer haven abroad.

Private investment, particularly foreign investment, is regarded with suspicion in many quarters. A great many and probably a majority of the citizens of hemisphere nations regard United States private investment as a form of exploitation or economic colonialism. There is a widespread, mistaken view that such investment takes more out of the area than it contributes to it. Fear of domination by United States companies is expressed frequently.

The central problem is the failure of governments throughout the hemisphere to recognize fully the importance of private investment. Thus, realistic steps have not been taken to encourage private investment, to create a framework within which it can operate and which assures that it will serve the best interests of the entire community. Yet history shows that democratic societies which have provided such encouragement and such a framework have been the most successful in attaining their broad objectives.

United States government tax laws and regulations offer a number of significant barriers to private investment abroad. They make it impossible for local governments to offer effective tax incentives to United States investors. They discourage joint ventures—a form of investment viewed with favor in many parts of the hemisphere. Furthermore, the United States offers little in the way of positive incentives to encourage its investors to engage in enterprises elsewhere in the hemisphere.

Recommendation: National Policy Objective

The United States should provide maximum encouragement for private investment throughout the hemisphere.

Recommendations for Action

1. *The United States should not, for narrow domestic reasons, apply tax rules to United states private overseas investment which controvert efforts by developing nations to encourage private investment and promote joint ventures.*

*   *   *

2. *Greater use should be made of the contract mechanism to bring private investors into ventures with discouragingly high risks but with the potential to make significant contributions to local economies.*

a. The proposed Overseas Private Investment Corporation should have the power to contract with private companies in the Western Hemisphere to create production facilities necessary to meet an important need which is not being filled by private investors. In many cases,the problem is that the combinations of the capital required and the overhead costs involved in establishing a venture during its early years are so high as to make the venture unattractive even though longer term prospects appear favorable. In such cases, the contract with the Overseas Private Investment Corporation would cover these start-up costs through some combination of loans and contract payments, possibly involving participation by multi-national, regional or national development banks.

b. Contracts should be worked out in a flexible fashion and could provide, for instance, that the participating private company would have an option to purchase an agreed-upon percent of the equity once the venture was successful, with the remainder of the equity sold to local investors. Such a contract mechanism offers a direct and flexible approach towards encouraging a greater flow of private investment. It is better than the shotgun approach of tax incentives to U.S. private investment which, in reality, constitutes a form of subsidy.

3. *The proposal to transfer AID functions relating to private investment into a new corporation—the Overseas Private Investment Corporation—should be supported.*

*   *   *

4. *Improved mechanisms should be sought to bring together United States private*

investors and companies elsewhere in the hemisphere which are seeking United States partners.

*   *   *

5. *High priority should be given to the development and training of entrepreneurs, managers, scientists and technicians.*

*   *   *

6. *The United States should support all efforts to encourage local savings and to channel them into productive investment.*

*   *   *

7. *The United States government should work with the proposed Western Hemisphere Development Committee and with representatives from the private sectors to develop a set of uniform rules of conduct for private foreign investment.*
a. Such rules should cover the behavior of both private companies and host governments.

*   *   *

5. Urban Development and Housing

Adequate housing and improved conditions of urban living stand high on the list of factors which contribute to the quality of life throughout the Western Hemisphere. Yet in large part because of a continuing influx of people from rural areas, cities are falling behind in providing the conditions and services which make them reasonably safe and decent places in which to work and live.

Housing needs far exceed the available supply of medium and low cost facilities. Of the population moving into cities, a high percentage live in slums. This not only causes difficult housing and health problems but also unprecedented structural change. Extreme traffic congestion is seen everywhere. Health facilities are inadequate and sanitary and water supply systems are presently insufficient. The very high urban population growth rate (more than 50 percent higher than the rate of growth in total population) exceeds the increase in job opportunities, so unemployment is generally high and rising, particularly among the young.

*   *   *

It is increasingly clear that what is needed is a systems approach to community development. Specific elements—such as transportation, schools, housing, sanitary facilities, administration and finance—must be integrated into a cohesive approach within the context of national, regional and urban planning. Rural and urban development need to be considered as integral partners in overall national development. Factors influencing the migratory flows between rural and urban areas need to be given priority study and attention. Both agricultural and industrial development should proceed on a balanced basis.

*   *   *

Recommendation: National Policy Objective
The United States should give maximum feasible support to urban and rural community development to improve housing and a broad range of community services so as to elevate the quality of the environment in which people live.

Recommendations for Action
1. The United States should undertake a major program for the rehabilitation of its own cities. This will meet the essential needs of our own people; it will demonstrate to other American republics that this job can be done and it will establish the legitimacy of our own system and its ability to set essential priorities.

2. United States assistance efforts in the other American republics must be broadened in orientation to total community development.

3. The U.S. housing loan guarantee and loan programs should be improved.

4. United States programs should stress efforts to join together with local private sector groups, municipal and national governments, and regional and hemisphere organizations in seeking new, ways to improve the environment in both urban and rural areas.

5. The United States should also help in the development of mechanisms which will promote individual savings and direct them into housing and other community facilities.

D. The Division of Labor

In essence, what we the people of the Western Hemisphere really need is a more efficient division of labor among us.

The division of labor is one of the tried and true economic principles that will be as valid in 1976 as it was in 1776 when it was first spelled out by Adam Smith. His example involved the manufacture of dress pins in which some 18 distinct operations were required. When one man had to perform all 18 operations, he "could certainly not make 20 pins a day" said Adam Smith. But if the process could be divided up so that 18 people specialized, with each one performing one particular function of the process, the total output per person could be raised to as much as 4,800 pins per day, according to Adam Smith.

This principle of the division of labor underlies the progress of modern nations. Within national boundaries, the forces of competition in the market lead to specialization—a division of labor. Individuals and companies turn to what they can produce most effectively because that yields the greatest returns. Thus, one company will concentrate on the production of ax handles while another will specialize on producing ax heads. The result will be better axes, lower prices to consumers, and higher returns to workers and employers.

The same principles apply internationally. All participants gain from the freest possible exchange of exports and imports, since that promotes an international division of labor. Each nation concentrates on items it can produce with relatively greater efficiency and lowest costs. It trades these items for those which other nations can produce with selectively greater efficiency. Everyone gains in the process, just as they do in the division of labor within national boundaries.

What is needed now is a broadening division of labor among the nations of the

Western Hemisphere. At present, the United States is producing, at high cost behind tariff walls and quotas, goods which could be produced more economically by other hemisphere nations. The U.S. is short of skilled labor and, if anything, this shortage promises to get worse. The shortage of skilled labor is intensified when the U.S. continues to keep workers in lines which are, by definition, inefficient, since production can only be carried on here behind tariff or quota barriers. National productivity would be enhanced by shifting workers and capital out of protected industries into industries where advanced technology and intensive capital investment permits the U.S. to pay high wages and still remain competitive in world markets. The goods the United States is now producing inefficiently would be imported, mainly from less developed countries. Consumers would gain through lower prices, workers would receive higher wages and the return on capital would be higher.

The less developed countries would also gain. With abundant supplies of labor and wage levels well below those in the United States, they could export processed foods, textiles, apparel, footwear, and other light manufactures, as well as meat and other farm products. This would provide increased employment at higher wages than are now available. Workers could move off farms into higher paid industrial jobs. The increase in income would raise living standards generally, contributing to the improvement in the quality of life. Such nations would become better customers for the high-technology products of the United States.

*   *   *

Recommendation: National Policy Objective
The President should request the Organization of American States to convene a major hemisphere conference to establish a more rational division of labor in the hemisphere.

*   *   *

E. Education, Science, and Culture

The quality of life in any nation today is fundamentally related to the level of its science and the vitality of its culture. Both, in turn, are crucially dependent on education.

A good educational system is absolutely essential to produce the trained leadership required for scholarship, public affairs, the creative arts, management, science, modern agricultural production and skilled industrial labor. No nation ever has had enough highly trained people to meet all of its needs. This lack has been especially severe in the less industrialized nations of the Western Hemisphere.

*   *   *

Recommendation: National Policy Objective
The United States should give full support to the objectives of the new Council for Education, Science and Culture of the Organization of American States.

Recommendations for Action

In order to support the new Organization of American States Council's purposes, the United States should make a major commitment by creating a new corporation, with financing in the magnitude of $100 million annually to start with. The majority of its Board of Directors would be outstanding heads of private institutions. It would be known as the Western Hemisphere Institute for Education, Science and Culture, and would be an operating arm of the Economic and Social Development Agency.

*   *   *

F. Labor

The key to progress in any country is its work force. Organized labor is and will continue to be a major factor in enhancing the quality of life in the Western Hemisphere.

In their own efforts to make economic and social advances, free trade union movements in the hemisphere nations are directing their efforts toward increasing the productivity of industry, and increasing labor's share of industrial productivity.

Opposed to the hemisphere free trade unions are the Communist-dominated unions. These political unions called for general strikes in almost every country the mission visited, to prevent or protest its arrival, but democratic trade unions refused to go along with them.

In most hemisphere countries, labor is now excluded from government planning for development. This has caused wide-spread frustration among labor leaders, who feel their governments show little concern for the role of organized labor and little concern about low wages, poor working conditions, and unemployment. From the nation's standpoint, labor's lack of involvement in planning means that workers and unions cannot make their maximum contribution to economic development.

Except for four hemisphere countries, there are no reliable statistics about unemployment, under-employment, wage levels, costs of living and other data that concern the worker. Unemployment is known to be high in most hemisphere countries, but the lack of precise statistical data handicaps efforts to deal with the problem.

Industrial development is being retarded in many countries because of a shortage of skilled workers, due to the lack of a literate work force and to the shortage of facilities for vocational and technical training.

Recommendation: National Policy Objective

The United States should encourage strong, effective, free trade union movements throughout the Western Hemisphere.

Recommendations for action

1. The United States should encourage governments of the hemisphere to include labor representation in planning their programs for development.

2. The United States should increase its financial and technical assistance, through the American Institute for Free Labor Development, for worker education and vocational training in the other hemisphere countries.

G. Agriculture

To the 24 nations of Central America, the Caribbean and South America, agriculture is a dominant fact of life. For a majority of the peoples of these nations, the quality of life itself is dependent on the farm.

On the average, nearly half the labor force of the other American nations is in agriculture, in fishing, or in forestry.

To those who live as subsistence farmers, life is a struggle for existence on the land—with a burro, a machete, a crude hut and a small hoard of maize and beans patiently coaxed from the soil. These millions live outside any national economy—and they live with the bleak realization that, as things are, there will never be a better life for them.

Yet there is great potential wealth in the good earth of the hemisphere. The grasslands of South America are one of the greatest sources of animal protein in the world. The tropical forests of the hemisphere represent one of the earth's largest remaining timber reserves. A vast expanse of the richest land in all the world lies in a broad belt on the eastern slopes of the Andes. In addition, entire countries and great regions are blessed with good soil and abundant sunshine, ample water and dependable growing seasons. With existing modern scientific and technical knowledge, the other American nations *could* become one of the great food baskets of the world.

*   *   *

Recommendation: National Policy Objective
The United States should recognize that improvement of rural life and increasing agricultural production are basic to improvement of the quality of life in the Western Hemisphere.

Recommendations for Action
1. The United States should make a concerted effort through program and project loans and technical assistance to help our neighbors in their efforts to improve life in rural areas, to expand employment opportunities and to grow more food for themselves and for export.

*   *   *

2. The United States should allocate a major part of future growth in its agricultural consumption to hemisphere nations and re-examine the present limitations on the flow of farm products into the U.S. market from our neighbors to the south.

*   *   *

3. The United States should undertake a series of agricultural demonstration programs at selected sites in different countries to serve both as examples and as a nucleus for further development in transforming subsistence farming into a dynamic factor for economic growth.

*   *   *

H. Conservation

With few exceptions, the countries of Central America, South America and the Caribbean lack effective resource conservation programs. With about three-fourths of the land area of these countries in some form of public ownership, there is up to the present no really effective protection or control over this so-called public domain.

Unless a program of protection and conservation of these resources is undertaken in the next few years, the pressures of a rapidly increasing population and uncontrolled resource exploitation will make it impossible for this to become a region of economically developed and self-supporting nations.

*   *   *

Recommendation: National Policy Objective
The United States, through the combined resources of government and privately supported conservation agencies, should volunteer leadership and assistance for national and regional conservation programs wherever desired and feasible in the American republics.

Recommendations for Action
1. Create an Inter-American Institute of Natural Resource Conservation within the framework of the Organization of American States.

*   *   *

2. The Conservation Institute should make a rapid reconnaissance survey of the American countries to classify and define the problem areas with regard to the destructive exploitation of soil, water, forests, grasslands, wildlife and outstanding natural areas, and the need for conservation practices and controls.

*   *   *

3. A conservation education and information program should be launched, especially through the schools and in the rural areas.
4. A demonstration and training program in natural resource management and conservation should be inaugurated, especially for middle-level (non-university) personnel who will staff conservation projects and help establish control and protective measures over public lands.
5. A conservation public works program should be created incorporating part of the Civilian Conservation Corps and Peace Corps approach with the part-time employment of peasant farmers.

I. Health

The good health of the individual, wherever he lives, is fundamental to the quality of his life.

In the Western Hemisphere, significant improvements in public health have been made in the last quarter of a century. Smallpox, malaria and yellow fever have been radically reduced. Yaws has been all but eradicated. For all these gains, infant mortality is appallingly high in the other American republics, malnutrition is increasing, and the lack of sanitation and water supply systems is the primary cause of intestinal parasites and other origins of sickness.

The population problem exacerbates all the other health problems through overcrowding in urban slums. It is so acute that the people themselves are promoting birth control.

In addition, the great increase of travel between the North and South American continents, the Central American countries and the islands of the Caribbean have increasingly transformed the health problems of one country or region into the health problems of many areas.

Infant Mortality

As the 1968 annual report of the World Health Organization pointed out, as many as 20 percent of the children born in some hemisphere countries die before they are five years old. This is the greatest single problem of health today in too many of the other American republics.

*   *   *

Water is Life

*   *   *

. . . At the present rate of progress, only 40 percent to 50 percent of the urban peoples in the other American republics may have potable water within the decade. For rural peoples, the outlook is that far fewer than 50 percent will have potable water by 1971, the advisers were told.

*   *   *

Legacy of Hunger

The *campesino* goes to bed hungry every night of his life. He will probably never see a doctor, a hospital, a dentist, or a nurse. He has little hope of being vaccinated against smallpox, or inoculated against typhoid, tetanus or yellow fever. If he becomes ill, there is no medicine; he trusts to fate that he will either get better, or die.

The average citizen of Central and South America and the Caribbean can expect a life span of 57 years, compared to 70 years for a North American.

*   *   *

Balance of Growth

Of all the broad concerns of the other hemisphere nations, none is more compelling—in terms of public health, economic growth and social progress—than the increase in population.

At the present extraordinary rate of increase, the number of people in the other American republics will more than double the present population—in less than 30 years.

This prospect—of more people than can be fed, employed, housed or educated with present facilities—has brought a sense of urgency to the leaders of the 20 countries we visited.

*   *   *

Recommendation: National Policy Objective
    The United States should recognize that the health problems of our sister republics are also our problems—for we share them, we are endangered by them, and we are moved to help deal with them.

Recommendations for Action
    1. The United States government should provide leadership in undertaking a special pre-natal and post-natal nutrition program, to be carried out throughout the Western Hemisphere by church, labor, women's, student and other groups.

*   *   *

    2. The United States should support the World Health Organization (WHO) and the Pan American Health Organization (PAHO) as the prime instruments.
    3. The Technical Training Exchange Program set up by AID and the Pan American Health Organization with Public Health Service support should be broadened to provide greater opportunity for U.S. health professions personnel to study tropical medicine in Central, South American and Caribbean countries.

*   *   *

J. Women

One of the most powerful forces for change and improvement in the quality of life in the hemisphere countries is the newly emancipated Latin woman.

Throughout the Western Hemisphere, women are becoming better educated, better informed, and less inclined to follow the tradition that women should be sheltered and subservient. Women's interests in the hemisphere nations cover all aspects of contemporary living, but they are increasingly active in their support of reforms in urban life, rural life, education, health, nutrition, environment, and politics.

To speed the process of change, women in the hemisphere are becoming political activists. They are eager to learn more about the techniques of political organization. And to a substantial degree, they identify themselves with the forces of moderation— the middle-of-the-road.

*   *   *

Recommendation: National Policy Objective
    The United States should recognize fully the expanding role of women in the political and economic, social and cultural development of the nations of the hemisphere.

Recommendation for Action

The United States, working through the proposed Western Hemisphere Institute for Education, Science and Culture, should increase its program of exchange in all fields relating to the role of women in developing the quality of life throughout the Western Hemisphere.

K. Communications

Fundamental to the accomplishment of the objectives and programs of the Western Hemisphere outlined in this report is better understanding among the people of the hemisphere. This in turn rests on better communication between North and South America, and between the various nations themselves. This was a clear consensus of the 350 leading journalists and broadcasters in 20 countries with whom the mission had contact in its travels.

The Latin and Caribbean editors complained that the United States consistently gives them bad press coverage. Then they admitted that they are inclined to play up the negative aspects of the North American scene. They likewise print little news about their immediate neighbors.

It is also clear that the U.S. media have a limited and often uninformed interest in the news of Latin America and the Caribbean. North or south, the result is less than ideal communication among the peoples of the hemisphere.

> *   *   *

Recommendation: National Policy Objective

The United States by its own actions and in consultation and collaboration with its neighbors of the Western Hemisphere should do everything possible to improve communication among the peoples of hemisphere nations.

Recommendations for Action

1. The overall United States information program in the Western Hemisphere should be stepped up substantially.

2. A major effort should be made to make the Voice of America (VOA) at least competitive with Radio Havana in the Central American–Caribbean area, including, improved programming and standard radio band broadcasting by VOA.

3. The President should invite a special team of United States experts on Western Hemisphere affairs to visit United States newspapers, magazines, and television stations, upon request, in order to improve United States media leaders' knowledge of the countries in the south.

4. Greater efforts should be made to send United States journalists, teachers, intellectuals, writers, musicians, artists and other representatives of the United States to other American republics.

> *   *   *

CHAPTER FIVE: CONCLUSION

This report has touched on a whole range of concerns that intrude upon the lives of Americans, in the United States and throughout the hemisphere. The spectrum of these concerns is broad and the patterns are kaleidoscopic. Yet certain concepts emerge as fundamental:

People

The concern of man is man. And man must be the concern not only of his own government, but of all governments and all people. If we are not our brother's keeper, we are at least our brother's brother. If we fail in our awareness or commitment to this essential concept, we will have failed ourselves in a most critical way.

The Western Hemisphere as a Unity

Not only brotherhood but also geography and a common heritage of respect for the worth of man have united our hemisphere. No one can travel through this hemisphere without being keenly conscious of the multiple special links that bind it together. The Western Hemisphere nations are not separate entities; they are sovereign peoples indissolubly bound to one another by mutual hopes and needs, mutual interests, and common goals.

Every problem and opportunity before the hemisphere will yield to a better solution if it is not viewed in terms of "we" here in the United States and "they" in the other countries. The "we-they" approach is bankrupt and will defeat the aims of the policy-makers, and their people, who resort to it in the future.

The Western Hemisphere can achieve the common aspirations of its people only as a cohesive unit of free men.

The Crossroads

There is a convergence of forces and events in the last of this century that is producing a crisis for free men:

—The scientific and technological explosion and the surge of industrialization it has produced;

—The consequent upward push in the standard of living for increasing tens of millions in the industrialized areas of the free world;

—The resulting increase in the gulf between the advantaged and the disadvantaged;

—The awareness both of the gulf and of the fact that it need not exist;

—A tidal wave of population;

—An uneasy nationalism, striving for self-identification;

—And a technology that tears at the fabric of all existing cultures.

However, we have within our reach the means—technical, political and cultural—to shape these forces and to bring to all people in this hemisphere the fulfillment of their capacities and their own sense of worth.

Indeed, the fact that men believe this to be within their reach is one cause of the crisis of our times, since for all too many people in the United States and elsewhere in the hemisphere, indignity and degradation are their intolerable lot.

This crossroads—this challenge to our system of democracy and to the very survival of our values and ourselves—is not rehetorical. It is factual. Either we meet this challenge, or the prospect is for revolutionary changes leading we know not where. We have the values, the ability and the means effectively to meet this crisis in the United States and in the hemisphere. We must employ these means with national dedication and determination, with subtlety and purpose. For the spiritual soil in the hemisphere is fertile for change—and the forces that would nourish revolution are ready and in place.

Interdependence of the Hemisphere

It is clear that the human resources and economic strength of each nation of the Western Hemisphere contribute to the strength of the others; that disease and propaganda cannot be trained to observe the limits of national boundaries; that the physical security of one enhances that of all; that a virus in the tropics will soon strike in the cities—and vice versa—whether that virus is biological or political; that violence in one nation uproots order and trust in its neighbor; that the bitterness and anger of one group erodes the good will of all; that confidence and courage and constructive concern in any one nation are contagious through the hemisphere.

The United States as Example

While specific problems differ from country to country, the fundamental thrust of the issues is the same throughout the Western Hemisphere. It is plain, accordingly, that we in the United States cannot effectively contribute to the forward growth of *our* nation and the hemisphere unless we manage the central problems of our time at home. Unless we are wholly to fail of our purpose as a nation, we must, therefore, meet the hopes of our own people for a decent and dignified life. Only if we do this can we lead, can we inspire, can we add to the quality of life for free men throughout the hemisphere.

A Course of Action

It is in this spirit that this report has recommended reorganization of the United States government's foreign policy structure, fundamental changes of U.S. trade and lending policies, renegotiation of foreign debts, and a more realistic division of labor in the hemisphere.

For the capacity of sovereign nations and free peoples to work together in mutual growth is crucial to survival—and crucial to the quality of life for those who do survive.

The achievement of such cooperation among the people of this hemisphere is the central objective of this report and of all its specific recommendations.

Recommendations for Action

That the President issue a major policy statement on the objectives of our Western Hemisphere relations and seek a joint resolution of the Congress to confirm those objectives so they become our recognized national policy.

—Such a declaration of policy by the Executive and Legislative branches would be a milestone in hemisphere affairs.

—It would have enormous impact throughout the hemisphere.

—It could be written as a first step in legislation to supersede the present encumbrances on Western Hemisphere policies and programs and to discourage similar new measures in the future.

—It should enunciate the principle that United States national interests must supersede those of any domestic special interest group in the conduct of Western Hemisphere relations.

—It would convey a new character and style to our Western Hemisphere relations— one based on partnership, not dominance.

It would help to create the framework for a new era of cooperation, progress, and human dignity in the hemisphere.

No man has ever lived and felt worthy of the gift of life who hasn't also felt tested by his own times. It is our good fortune to be tested in a time of accelerated change and extraordinary opportunity. It is our destiny to determine in our time that dignity for all men is achievable by a free democratic society in our nation, our hemisphere— and our world.

186. Address by President Nixon, before the Inter-American Press Association, on Action for Progress for the Americas*

October 31, 1969

As we stand here on this 25th-anniversary meeting of the Inter American Press Association, I should like to be permitted some personal comments before I then deliver my prepared remarks to you.

I have learned that this is the first occasion in which the remarks of the President of any one of the American nations has been carried and is being carried live by Telstar to all of the nations in the hemisphere. We are proud that it is before the Inter American Press Association. I am sure that those of you, and I know that most of you here are members and publishers of the newspaper profession, will not be jealous if this is on television tonight.

Also, I am very privileged to appear before this organization again. I was reminded it was 15 years ago that I, as Vice President, addressed the organization in New Orleans. It is good to be with you tonight, and particularly as the outgoing President is

United States, *Department of State Bulletin,* Nov. 17, 1969, pp. 409-14.

an old friend, Mr. Edwards [Augustin E. Edwards, president, *El Mercurio*] from Santiago. The new President is also an old friend, Mr. Copley [James Copley, president, Copley Press] from San Diego—sister cities, one in the Northern Hemisphere of the Americas and the other in the Southern Hemisphere.

There is one other remark that Mrs. Edwards brought eloquently to my attention as we heard that magnificent rendition by the Army chorus of "America the Beautiful." She said, "That is for all of us. We are all Americans in this room."

It is in that spirit that I want to address my remarks tonight to our partnership in the Americas. In doing so, I wish to place before you some suggestions for reshaping and reinvigorating that partnership.

Often we in the United States have been charged with an overweening confidence in the rightness of our own prescriptions, and occasionally we have been guilty of the charge. I intend to correct that. Therefore, my words tonight are meant as an invitation by one partner for further interchange, for increased communication, and, above all, for new imagination in meeting our shared responsibilities.

For years, we in the United States have pursued the illusion that we alone could remake continents. Conscious of our wealth and technology, seized by the force of good intentions, driven by habitual impatience, remembering the dramatic success of the Marshall Plan in postwar Europe, we have sometimes imagined that we knew what was best for everyone else and that we could and should make it happen.

Well, experience has taught us better. It has taught us that economic and social development is not an achievement of one nation's foreign policy, but something deeply rooted in each nation's own traditions. It has taught us that aid that infringes pride is no favor to any nation. It has taught us that each nation, and each region, must be true to its own character.

What I hope we can achieve, therefore, is a more mature partnership in which all voices are heard and none is predominant, a partnership guided by a healthy awareness that give-and-take is better than take-it-or-leave it.

My suggestions this evening for new directions toward a more balanced relationship come from many sources.

First, they are rooted in my personal convictions. I have seen the problems of this hemisphere. As those in this room know, I have visited every nation in this hemisphere. I have seen them at first hand. I have felt the surging spirit of those nations—determined to break the grip of outmoded structures, yet equally determined to avoid social disintegration. Freedom, justice, a chance for each of our people to live a better and more abundant life—these are goals to which I am unshakably committed; because progress in our hemisphere is not only a practical necessity, it is a moral imperative.

Second, these new approaches have been substantially shaped by the report of Governor Rockefeller, who, at my request and at your invitation, listened perceptively to the voices of our neighbors and incorporated their thoughts into a set of foresighted proposals.

Third, they are consistent with thoughts expressed in the Consensus of Viña del Mar, which we have studied with great care.

Fourth, they have benefited from the counsel of many persons in government and out, in this country and throughout the hemisphere.

And finally, basically, they reflect the concern of the people of the United States for the development and progress of a hemisphere which is new in spirit and which—through our efforts together—we can make new in accomplishment.

Actions Representing a New Approach

Tonight I offer no grandiose promises and no panaceas.

I do offer action.

The actions I propose represent a new approach. They are based on five principles:

—First, a firm commitment to the inter-American system, to the compacts which bind us in that system, as exemplified by the Organization of American States and by the principles so nobly set forth in its charter.

—Second, respect for national identity and national dignity in a partnership in which rights and responsibilities are shared by a community of independent states.

—Third, a firm commitment to continued United States assistance for hemispheric development.

—Fourth, a belief that the principal future pattern of this assistance must be U.S. support for Latin American initiatives and that this can best be achieved on a multilateral basis within the inter-American system.

—Finally, a dedication to improving the quality of life in this New World of ours—to making people the center of our concerns and to helping meet their economic, social, and human needs.

We have heard many voices from the Americas in their first months of our new administration—voices of hope, voices of concern, and some voices of frustration.

We have listened.

These voices have told us they wanted fewer promises and more action. They have told us that the United States aid programs seemed to have helped the United States more than Latin America. They have told us that our trade policies were insensitive to the needs of other American nations. They have told us that if our partnership is to thrive or even to survive, we must recognize that the nations of the Americas must go forward in their own way under their own leadership.

Now, it is not my purpose here tonight to discuss the extent to which we consider the various charges that I have listed right or wrong. But I recognize the concerns. I share many of them. What I propose tonight is, I believe, responsive to those concerns.

The most pressing concerns center on economic development and especially on the policies by which aid is administered and by which trade is regulated.

In proposing specific changes tonight, I mean these as examples of the actions I believe are possible in a new kind of partnership in the Americas.

Management of Development Assistance

Our partnership should be one in which the United States lectures less and listens more. It should be one in which clear, consistent procedures are established to ensure that the shaping of the future of the nations in the Americas reflects the will of those nations.

I believe this requires a number of changes.

To begin with, it requires a fundamental change in the way in which we manage development assistance in the hemisphere.

That is why I propose that a multilateral inter-American agency be given an increasing share of responsibility for development assistance decisions. CIAP—the Inter-American Committee on the Alliance for Progress—could be given this new function. Or an entirely new agency could be created within the system.

Whatever the form, the objective would be to evolve an effective multilateral framework for bilateral assistance, to provide the agency with an expert international staff, and, over time, to give it major operational and decision-making responsibilities.

The other American nations themselves would thus jointly assume a primary role in setting priorities within the hemisphere, in developing realisitc programs, in keeping their own performance under critical review.

Access to Expanding Markets

One of the areas most urgently in need of new policies is the area of trade. In my various trips to the Latin American countries and other American countries, I have found that this has been uppermost on the minds of the leaders for many, many years. In order to finance their import needs and to achieve self-sustaining growth, the other American nations must expand their exports.

Most Latin American exports now are raw materials and foodstuffs. We are attempting to help the other countries of the hemisphere to stabilize their earnings from these exports, to increase them as time goes on.

Increasingly, however, those countries will have to turn more toward manufactured and semimanufactured products for balanced development and major export growth. Thus they need to be assured of access to the expanding markets of the industrialized world. In order to help achieve this, I have determined to take the following major steps:

—First, to lead a vigorous effort to reduce the nontariff barriers to trade maintained by nearly all industrialized countries against products of particular interest to Latin America and other developing countries.

—Second, to support increased technical and financial assistance to promote Latin American trade expansion.

—Third, to support the establishment within the inter-American system of regular procedures for advance consultation on trade matters. United States trade policies often have a very heavy impact on our neighbors. It seems only fair that in the more balanced realtionship we seek, there should be full consultation within the hemisphere family before decisions affecting its members are taken, not after.

—Finally, and most important, in world trade forums, I believe it is time to press for a liberal system of generalized tariff preferences for all developing countries, including Latin America. We will seek adoption by all of the industrialized nations of a scheme with broad product coverage and with no ceilings on preferential imports. We will seek equal access to industrial markets for all developing countries so as to eliminate the discrimination against Latin America that now exists in many countries. We will also urge that such a system eliminate the inequitable "reverse preferences" that now discriminate against Western Hemisphere countries.

Restrictions on Assistance Loans Reduced

There are three other important economic issues that directly involve the new partnership concept and which a number of our partners have raised. They raised them with me and raised them with Governor Rockefeller, with the Secretary of State and others in our administration.

These are: "tied" loans, debt service, and regional economic integration.

For several years now, virtually all loans made under United States aid programs have been "tied"; that is, as you know, they have been encumbered with restrictions designed to maintain United States exports, including a requirement that the money be spent on purchases in the United States.

These restrictions have been burdensome for the borrowers. They have impaired the effectiveness of the aid. In June I ordered the most cumbersome restrictions removed.

In addition, I announce tonight that I am now ordering that, effective November 1, loan dollars sent to Latin America under AID be freed to allow purchases not only here but anywhere in Latin America.

As a third step, I am also ordering that all other onerous conditions and restrictions on U.S. assistance loans be reviewed with the objective of modifying or eliminating them.

If I might add a personal word, this decision on freeing AID loans is one of those things that people kept saying ought to be done but could not be done. In light of our own balance-of-payments problems, there were compelling arguments against it. I can assure you that within the administration we had a very vigorous session on this subject. But I felt, and the rest of my colleagues within the administration felt, that the needs of the hemisphere had to come first, so I simply ordered it done, showing our commitment in actions rather than only in words. This will be our guiding principle in the future.

We have present many Members of the House and Senate here tonight. I am sure they realize that there are not too many occasions that the President can accomplish something by just ordering it to be done.

Debt Service and Economic Integration

The growing burden of external debt service has increasingly become a major problem of future development. Some countries find themselves making heavy payments in debt service which reduce the positive effects of development aid. Therefore, tonight I suggest that CIAP might appropriately urge the international financial organizations to recommend possible remedies.

We have seen a number of moves in the Americas toward regional economic integration, such as the establishment of the Central American Common Market, the Latin American and Caribbean Free Trade Areas, and the Andean Group. The decisions on how far and how fast this process of integration goes, of course, are not ours to make. But I do want to stress this: We in the United States stand ready to help in this effort if our help is requested and is needed.

On all of these matters, we look forward to consulting further with our hemisphere neighbors and partners. In a major related move, I am also directing our representatives to invite CIAP, as a regular procedure, to conduct a periodic review of U.S. economic policies as they affect the other nations of the hemisphere and to consult with us about them.

Similar reviews are now made of the other hemisphere countries' policies, as you are aware; but the United States has not previously opened its policies to such consultation. I believe that true partnership requires that we should; and henceforth, if our partners so desire—as I gather from your applause you do—we shall.

I would like to turn now to a vital subject in connection with economic development in the hemisphere; namely, the role of private investment. Clearly, each government in the Americas must make its own decision about the place of private investment, domestic and foreign, in its development process. Each must decide for itself whether it wishes to accept or forgo the benefits that private investment can bring.

Advantages of Private Investment

For a developing country, constructive foreign private investment has the special advantage of being a prime vehicle for the transfer of technology. And certainly from no other source is so much investment capital available, because capital from government to government on that basis is not expansible. In fact, it tends to be more restricted, whereas private capital can be greatly expanded.

As we have seen, however, just as a capital-exporting nation cannot expect another country to accept investors against its will, so must a capital-importing country expect a serious impairment of its ability to attract investment funds when it acts against existing investments in a way which runs counter to commonly accepted norms of international law and behavior. Unfortunately and perhaps unfairly, such acts in one of the Americas affect investors in the entire region.

We will not encourage U.S. private investment where it is not wanted or where local conditions face it with unwarranted risks. But I must state my own strong belief, and it is this: I think that properly motivated private enterprise has a vitally important role to play in social as well as economic development in all of the nations. We have seen it work in our own country. We have seen it work in other countries, whether they are developing or developed, other countries that lately have been recording the world's most spectacular rates of economic growth.

Referring to a completely other area of the world, exciting stories of the greatest growth rates are those that have turned toward more private investment rather than less. Japan we all know about, but the story is repeated in Korea, Taiwan, Malaysia, Singapore, and Thailand.

In line with this belief we are examining ways to modify our direct investment controls in order to help meet the investment requirements of developing nations in the Americas and elsewhere. I have further directed that our aid programs place increasing emphasis on assistance to locally owned private enterprise. I am also directing that we expand our technical assistance for establishing national and regional capital markets.

As we all have seen, in this age of rapidly advancing science, the challenge of development is only partly economic. Science and technology increasingly hold the key to our national futures. If the promise of this final third of the 20th century is to be realized, the wonders of science must be turned to the service of man.

In the Consensus of Viña del Mar we were asked for an unprecedented effort to share our scientific and technical capabilities.

To that request we shall respond in a true spirit of partnership.

This I pledge to you tonight: The Nation that went to the moon in peace for all mankind is ready, ready to share its technology in peace with its nearest neighbors.

Coordination of U.S. Government Activities

Tonight I have discussed with you a new concept of partnership. I have made a commitment to act. I have been trying to give some examples of actions we are prepared to take.

But as anyone familiar with government knows, commitment alone is not enough. There has to be the machinery to ensure an effective followthrough.

Therefore, I am also directing a major reorganization and upgrading of the United States Government structure for dealing with Western Hemisphere affairs.

As a key element of this—and this is one of those areas where the President cannot do it and he needs the approval of the Congress—but as a key element of this, I have ordered preparation of a legislative request, which I will submit to the Congress, raising the rank of the Assistant Secretary of State for Inter-American Affairs to Under Secretary, thus giving the hemisphere special representation.

I know that many in this room, 15 years ago, urged that upon me, and I see Mr. Pedro Beltrán here particularly applauding. He urged it upon me just a few years ago, too.

I trust we will be able, through the new Under Secretary of State, to do a more effective job with regard to the problems of the hemisphere; and the new Under Secretary will be given authority to coordinate all United States Government activities in the hemisphere so that there will be one window for all of those activities.

And now, my friends in the American family, I turn to a sensitive subject. Debates have long raged, raged in the United States and elsewhere, as to what our attitude should be toward the various forms of government within the inter-American system.

Dealing With Governments As They Are

Let me sum up my own views very candidly.

First, my own country lives by a democratic system which has preserved its form for nearly two centuries. It has its problems. But we are proud of our system. We are jealous of our liberties. We hope that eventually most, perhaps all, of the world's people will share what we believe to be the blessings of a genuine democracy.

We are aware that most people today in most countries of the world do not share those blessings.

I would be less than honest if I did not express my concern over examples of liberty compromised, of justice denied, or of rights infringed.

Nevertheless, we recognize that enormous, sometimes explosive, forces for change are operating in Latin America. These create instabilities and bring changes in governments. On the diplomatic level, we must deal realistically with governments in the inter-American system as they are. We have, of course—we in this country—a preference for democratic procedures and we hope that each government will help its own people to move forward toward a better, a fuller, and a freer life.

In this connection, however, I would stress one other point. We cannot have a peaceful community of nations if one nation sponsors armed subversion in another's territory. The ninth meeting of American Foreign Ministers clearly enunciated this principle. The "export" of revolution is an intervention which our system cannot condone; and a nation, like Cuba, which seeks to practice it can hardly expect to share in the benefits of this community.

And now, finally, a word about what all this can mean—not just for the Americas but for the world.

Today, the world's most fervent hope is for a lasting peace in which life is secure, progress is possible, and freedom can flourish. In each part of the world we can have lasting peace and progress only if the nations directly concerned take the lead themselves in achieving it, and in no part of the world can there be a true partnership if one partner dictates its direction.

I can think of no assembly of nations better suited than ours to point the way in developing such a partnership. A successfully progressing Western Hemisphere, here in this New World, demonstrating in action mutual help and mutual respect, will be an example for the world. Once again, by this example, we will stand for something larger than ourselves.

For three-quarters of a century, many of us have been linked together in the Organization of American States and its predecessors in a joint quest for a better future. Eleven years ago, Operation Pan America was launched as a Brazilian initiative. More recently, we have joined in a noble Alliance for Progress, whose principles still guide us. Now I suggest our goal for the seventies should be a decade of Action for Progress for the Americas.

As we seek to forge a new partnership, we must recognize that we are a community of widely diverse peoples. Our cultures are different. Our perceptions are often different. Our emotional reactions are often different. May it always be that way. What a dull world it would be if we were all alike. Partnership, mutuality—these do not flow naturally. We have to work at them.

Understandably perhaps, a feeling has arisen in many Latin American countries that the United States really "no longer cares."

My answer to that is very simple.

We do care. I care. I have visited most of your countries, as I have said before. I have met most of your leaders. I have talked with your people. I have seen your great needs as well as your great achievements.

And I know this, in my heart as well as in my mind: If peace and freedom are to endure in this world, there is no task more urgent than lifting up the hungry and the helpless and putting flesh on the dreams of those who yearn for a better life.

Today, we in this American community share an historic opportunity.

As we look together down the closing decades of the century, we see tasks that summon the very best that is in us. But those tasks are difficult, precisely because they do mean the difference between despair and fulfillment for most of the 600 million people who will live in Latin America in the year 2000. Those lives are our challenge. Those lives are our hope. And we could ask no prouder reward than to have our efforts crowned by peace, prosperity, and dignity in the lives of those 600 million human beings in Latin America—and in the United States—each so precious, each so unique— our children and our legacy.

187. Statement by President Nixon, on the Release of the Rockefeller Report*

November 10, 1969

There are two points I want to stress in connection with Governor Rockefeller's report which is being released today:

First, as I said in my October 31 speech, this report constituted a major contribution to the formulation of our policy for this hemisphere. Both our general conceptual approach and the specific lines of action we intend to follow have been substantially shaped by that report.

Secondly, this report is still very much under active consideration. Many of its recommendations which are far-reaching and complex are still being staffed and examined with a view to their implementation. Therefore, a good many of the things we will be doing in the weeks and months ahead will have had their genesis in this report.

Let me give you an example: In his report, Governor Rockefeller recommends a unique and imaginative technique that might be used in cases where this type of action is indicated in the debt service area. He recommended the possibility of maintaining equivalent local currency payments in instances where the dollar repayments are suspended or stretched out. The local currency would be paid into a fund which could in turn be used for development purposes in that country. Now, there are a number of technical points to be clarified; but the concept is an imaginative one, and I believe it is something that can be useful. Accordingly, I have directed the Secretary of the Treasury to undertake an immediate study of this proposal with a view to adopting it as a technique in those cases where it is appropriate. Mr. George Woods, who was a senior adviser to the Governor on his mission and is former President of the World Bank, will be a consultant to the Secretary of the Treasury for this purpose.

Now let me make a more general point. My speech on October 31 was intended as a philosophical foundation for what I envisage as a continuous process of policy formation over the months ahead. It outlined our view of the nature of our relationship with the other states in the hemisphere; the principles which should underlie that relationship; the policies which should implement it; and the directions those policies should take, together with some concrete examples.

I did not want to promise things which would have been unattainable, such as greatly increased aid levels. On the other hand, I want to do the maximum of what is possible and "doable." This is what I meant by an action program, and we intend now to take such concrete measures in conjunction with the other American nations. We intend to propose over the next several months further concrete actions. We will be discussing and exchanging views with our sister nations on key issues and problems,

Department of State Bulletin, Dec. 8, 1969, pp. 493-94.

and jointly we will be developing programs and policies to meet our problems. One of the things I want to explore very carefully when budget considerations make it possible is a program to finish the highway net down the center of the South American Continent. This is a program which I think would have an immense effect economically and be a great boost to integration of the region.

Next week the Inter-American Economic and Social Council will convene here in Washington at the technical level. The United States will be making some specific proposals in a number of fields; we will want to have the views of the other nations, and we will then be developing proposals and lines of action accordingly over the next several months.

Let me give you a concrete example: All of the American nations want to see the early establishment of a liberal worldwide system of generalized trade preferences for all developing countries. I stated in my speech that the United States intended to press vigorously with the developed countries for the adoption of such a system. This week U.S. representatives at OECD [Organization for Economic Cooperation and Development] meetings in Paris took that position. The United States will work actively now for such a system. I want to say, however, that if for any reason we find it not possible to establish a satisfactory system of generalized preferences within a reasonable time, then the United States will be prepared to consider other alternative actions it can take to assure that the American nations will have preferential access to the U.S. market.

As another example, we are also going to propose to the other American nations at the IA-ECOSOC meetings joint initiatives whose costs we are prepared to share:
—expansion of regional science programs, emphasizing research and training;
—promotion of an intensified hemispheric effort in basic and applied food research;
—establishment of an inter-American science information exchange program.

I am, in short, most serious about undertaking an action program and implementing a mature partnership with the countries of this hemisphere. Our fundamental objective, as Governor Rockefeller so eloquently expressed it, is to help improve the quality of life of the people of this hemipshere.

The Governor knows how personally grateful I am for all of the time and energy he spent on this mission and how deeply appreciative I am for his insights and imaginative ideas. Let me once more take this opportunity publicly to express my appreciation.

188. Statement by Secretary of the Treasury, David M. Kennedy to the Board of Governors of the Inter-American Development Bank*

April 23, 1970

The inter-American community is again grateful to the Government and people of Uruguay for providing this beautiful and historic city as the site of our deliberations. Here, where Presidents of the Americas have conferred and contemporary inter-American solidarity has been forged, we have an opportunity this week to give concrete reality to our mature partnership in the framework of this decade's program

*Department of State Bulletin, May 25, 1970, pp. 658-61.

of Action for Progress. We are also fortunate to have here with us for the first time the Governor for Jamaica, whom we welcome as our newest member.

*   *   *

The Bank's First Decade

The world, our hemisphere, and this Bank have undergone extraordinary changes since the first Board of Governors met in San Salvador in early 1960. Ten years ago, foreign assistance had only recently changed focus from the reconstruction of relatively advanced countries to the development of underdeveloped ones. Advanced countries other than the United States were just beginning to make significant contributions to development assistance. The terms of such assistance were often poorly adapted to the prospective balance-of-payments situations of borrowing countries. In the multilateral assistance field there was the World Bank, but its concessional-lending instrument, the International Development Association, was untested. Multilateral financial cooperation for regional development was, until the establishment of the Inter-American Bank, nonexistent.

Today's contrast with 1960 is striking. Development assistance, its form, and its degree of multilateralism have changed markedly. This Bank has emerged as a major element in the inter-American structure. It has demonstrated the validity of the idea of multilateral development cooperation at the regional level. And it can justly regard itself as the trailblazer for other regional institutions, such as the Asian Development Bank.

A second contrast can be found in the ability of a regional institution such as the Bank to reach out and mobilize funds in the world capital markets, using for this purpose the guarantee provided by its members. Its bonds are now widely held and its financial standing highly respected. Through its patient efforts in world financial centers, the Bank itself has been an important instrument in changing the forms and practices of development finance.

A third difference relates to the kinds of activities in which we now think it appropriate for development institutions to engage. This Bank has led the way in directing attention of development agencies to areas that had been relatively neglected or even considered inappropriate for the attention of international financial institutions. These include education, health, and the difficult problems of rural poverty. Lending in these frontier areas of development assistance has gained respectability only within the last 10 years. This Bank—supported in the early years, I am proud to say, by the Social Progress Trust Fund provided by the United States—has played a catalytic role in the emergence of new attitudes.

Ten years of experience has made us all more realistic in our approach to development. We have learned that there is no single formula for development applicable to all countries. Each nation is different, and each requires a different mix of resources. We recognize more clearly now the importance of a sound framework of fiscal, monetary, exchange, and investment policies within which development can take place. And we perceive now more clearly than ever that external assistance can only be efficiently utilized where there is an intense domestic will to develop. This must be accompanied by a readiness to commit domestic resources to the development task in the fullest measure.

Thus, the opening of this decade presents new opportunities to the Bank. It can become more selective, both in terms of the types of activities it finances and the quality of economic performance it expects of borrowers as a condition of its lending. With such selectivity, and a continuation of its distinctive Latin and pioneering spirit, the Bank can make the decade of the seventies a fitting and fruitful successor to the sixties.

Increase in Resources

The main task of this meeting is to make adequate provision for obtaining the capital resources needed by the Bank in the first half of its second decade of lending. I have been authorized by President Nixon to announce that the United States is prepared to join Latin American efforts in accomplishing this task. In the context of a proposal with full Latin American support, we would be prepared to approach the U.S. Congress promptly for increases in both our Ordinary Capital subscription and our contribution to the Fund for Special Operations. Specifically, the United States would be prepared to seek legislative authority for

—an increase in its paid-in Ordinary Capital subscription of $150 million combined with a $674 million increase in its callable Ordinary Capital subscription, both as our established share of a $2 billion overall increase in the Bank's Ordinary Capital resources.

—a substantial contribution to the Fund for Special Operations as part of an overall increase in Fund resources which would reflect the progress Latin economies have made these past 10 years, as well as their commitment to the role of multilateral institutions in development.

Resources should be sought in a magnitude which will cover requirements foreseen for the Bank in a 3- to 5-year period. They should permit the Bank to provide half again as much financing per year as the approximately $600 million which the Bank committed to loans in 1969. Moreover, they should ensure funding for new types and directions of activities that are now under preliminary consideration in the Bank.

But provision for the future requires more than money alone. It requires adaptation to reflect new realities in the seventies. It requires new relationships beyond the hemisphere to reflect Latin America's growing integration into the world economy and the world's growing commitment to multilateral development financing.

I have three major areas in mind where beneficial changes could be made. First, the present practice of extending Fund for Special Operations loans on a local-currency repayable basis involves the potential problem of excess accumulations of such currencies in the Bank's accounts. A shift to a policy of repayment in the currencies lent, combined with an appropriate easing of repayment terms as necessary, would avoid the problem. This would permit the fund ultimately to become a revolving source of hard-currency financing. I understand that a move in this direction already has widespread support.

Second, our concern for achieving more balanced growth in the hemisphere suggests that the financial needs of the least developed members should have first claim on the

Bank's concessional-loan resources. The opposite side of the same coin is that the region's more advanced countries should place relatively greater reliance on Ordinary Capital financing. This could be considered a cooperative contribution on the part of the stronger countries toward self-help in the hemispheric sense. It would also complement the willingness of the larger members to allow a greater usefulness of their local-currency subscriptions to the Fund for Special Operations. In this latter connection an expansion of the group of countries allowing this broader use would be widely applauded.

Finally, I believe that multiple benefits would accrue not only to the Bank but to Latin American development in general if other developed countries—regional and nonregional—could be brought within the Bank's membership. Additional Ordinary Capital resources would become available, and access to capital markets would be easier. Membership would also elicit additional concessional-loan resources more effectively. In the light of experience elsewhere, I am confident that these benefits can be obtained without changing the essentially regional character of the Bank. Indeed, it is my confidence in the permanent Latin character of our Bank which permits this judgment. Serious efforts to move in this desirable direction have important and broadening support, and steps are needed now to move toward the removal of existing barriers. This is the time to begin. I strongly urge that the Board of Governors take the necessary steps which will lead to opening our doors to Canada and others.

The provision of the resources called for and the adoption of the policy changes recommended entail real burdens and real sacrifices for all of us. Nevertheless—and with full consideration of the intense competing demands for budgetary resources—I offer full assurance of President Nixon's readiness to support these financial and policy measures. I believe such support constitutes solid evidence of our commitment to Latin America and to hemispheric development.

Perspectives for the Future

In reviewing the last decade I came across the following statement made by one of my predecessors, Robert B. Anderson, the first Bank Governor for the United States, at the inaugural meeting of this Board:

> The creation of the Bank does not in itself solve any of the problems with which we are all so concerned; yet it does provide us with an effective framework in which men of good will can join with the confidence that through the exercise of thought, diligence, and mutual respect they can achieve great benefit for their peoples.

This judgment is still true today, and it remains the framework within which we will meet the challenges in the decade ahead. Four challenges to the Bank should be noted.

First, multilateral institutions will undoubtedly assume a greater role in providing financial and technical assistance. Within this hemisphere, the Bank is in an excellent position to continue leadership in financing development. But to do so fully will require closer collaboration and coordination with the other bilateral and multilateral financing agencies, and with the Inter-American Committee on the Alliance for

Progress. This will assure that scarce external funds are being most effectively utilized and that the Bank has access to the best hemispheric judgments on whether or not a borrowing country itself is pursuing proper development policies and programs.

Second, the Bank's internal organization, management, and procedures will have to continue to adapt to changing conditions.

Third, the next decade challenges the Bank to participate directly and indirectly in encouraging private initiative and free market forces. While it is clear that each nation must fashion its own policies about the role of public- and private-sector activities and of domestic and foreign private investment in its society, the posture of the Bank will be guided, I hope, by practical considerations of efficient economic development. In this regard, I look forward with interest to the deliberations of the Board on expanding the Bank's role in assisting private productive enterprise. In particular I hope that it will be possible to employ in this effort the existing extensive framework of *financieras* and other financial intermediaries.

Fourth, the next decade should see more countries advancing toward self-sustained institutional, financial, and social growth. This will permit a greater number of the stronger member countries to assist the least developed through both technical and economic assistance. And it will contribute to the strengthening of the multilateral character of the Bank.

These and many other challenges of the seventies lie ahead of us. I am confident that the leadership of this great institution, supported by the Bank's capable staff, will effectively meet these challenges with inventiveness, wisdom, and determination.

The actions we are taking this week to increase the resources of the Inter-American Development Bank make clear our strong support of this inter-American institution. President Nixon, in February, outlined in realistic terms the basis on which we must face this decade of the seventies:

> There are no shortcuts to economic and social progress.
> This is a reality, but also a source of hope. For collaborative effort can achieve much. And it is increasingly understood among developed and developing nations that economic development is an inter-national responsibility.

The Inter-American Development Bank is a fine example of a multilateral institution through which this responsibility is effected. The United States is proud to be a member.

189. Address by Secretary of State William P. Rogers before the OAS General Assembly *

June 26, 1970

On behalf of President Nixon and the people of the United States, I would like to express the warm welcome of our country to the Ministers and other officials attending this first meeting of the General Assembly of the Organization of American

*Department of State Bulletin, July 25, 1970, pp. 115-19.

States under its revised charter. I regret that I will have to leave on Sunday for a previously scheduled visit to the Far East and that because of the changes in dates of this meeting I will be able to be with you only for 2 days. There is no doubt in my mind that the days ahead will be fruitful in organizing the work of our new institutions—and I want to take this opportunity to offer any assistance that you may need while here in Washington.

I should also like to take this opportunity, Mr. President [Fernando Amiano Tio, of the Dominican Republic], to extend my congratulations and very good wishes to you on your election as the President of this first General Assembly.

We in the United States are mindful that the roots of this body extend back to Simón Bolívar's first Congress of American States in 1826 and even before that to the war of liberation which Bolívar led and which had so many ties to our own war of independence. Our task is to apply the principles developed over our long history to making the inter-American system more responsive to the changing needs of the present time.

We have not attained all the goals of the charter, to be sure, though it is worth noting that, on the question of peace, our hemisphere in recent decades has a record unrivaled by that of any other major area. In our quest to provide for the betterment of all, we have many problems. We face, in differing degrees, issues of social unrest, poverty, decaying urban centers, et cetera—in addition to trade and other economic problems.

Added to our other heavy international commitments, these grave domestic problems place new burdens on the people of the United States. Nevertheless, the United States is fully aware of the need for common action to deal with the problems besetting all the peoples of our hemisphere.

To begin with, let me underscore that the United States does not, and will not, consider the interests of Latin America as secondary or of low priority. In no other area of the world are our basic long-range interests more deeply involved than in Latin America. Neither our other international interests nor our domestic concerns will reduce or tarnish the firmness of our commitment to the hemisphere.

It was in that conviction that President Nixon set out the principles of our new approach to Latin America. Let me refer to them again:

—First, a firm commitment to the inter-American system—as exemplified by the Organization of American States.

—Second, respect for national identity and national dignity.

—Third, a firm commitment to continued U.S. assistance for hemisphere development.

—Fourth, a belief that the principal future pattern of this assistance must be U.S. support for Latin American initiatives and that this can best be achieved on a multilateral basis within the inter-American system.

—Fifth, a dedication to improving the quality of life in the Western Hemisphere—to making people the center of our concerns.

In the 8 months which have followed since President Nixon spoke, our aim has been to implement those principles with specific actions. I would like to describe some of the things we have done.

Economic Development and Trade

In economic development and trade, encouraging progress has already been made, which underlines our resolve to work together to realize the goals of the Alliance for Progress.

Our first commitment, in the area of economic development, has been to strengthen the multilateral institutions of the region. As one step we have decided to submit our policies for economic development in the hemisphere for review by the Inter-American Committee on the Alliance for Progress (CIAP). We expect to make our first submission in the late summer or early fall of this year.

We are taking steps to give greater financial support to the Inter-American Development ment Bank, which has just completed its 10th year as a dynamic force for development. The U.S. share of the replenishment fund is $1.8 billion; the President is now asking Congress to approve the necessary implementing legislation. This new fund will permit the bank to increase its lending in the hemisphere by 50 percent in the next 3 to 4 years.

Our trade policies are being adjusted to take into account, and encourage, the economic change in Latin America from an almost total dependence upon imports of manufactured products to a search for markets abroad for products you now manufacture. We want to see Latin American exports become more competitive. In the Special Committee on Consultation and Negotiations, for example, we are working with you to identify obstacles impeding access to the U.S. market of over 800 Latin American products.

During the year we have also made efforts to reach agreement with other developed countries on a generalized system of preferences for the exports of manufactured and semimanufactured products of the less developed nations.

In our assistance programs we are giving priority to support of local private investment and to promotion of Latin American exports both to the more industrialized countries and within Latin America itself. And we have implemented our policy of "untying" AID loans to allow purchases anywhere in the hemisphere.

In addition, we have undertaken to join with you in developing procedures within the inter-American system for advance consultation on trade policy initiatives by any of us that might prejudice the trade interests of other OAS members.

We believe the course of our partnership is the right one. It is adapted to meet the changes taking place in your countries and in mine. It maintains my Government's commitment to assist in the development of the hemisphere, yet takes fully into account the force of nationalism and the policy of each of your nations to bear the principal responsibility for your own destiny. It acknowledges that none of us—neither you in Latin America nor we in the United States—possess all of the answers to our problems. And it emphasizes that these answers must be sought and found by all of us working together, each sharing in the providing as well as the receiving.

Here again the Inter-American Committee on the Alliance for Progress can contribute, not only by guiding and coordinating our efforts but also by stimulating member countries to choose economic and social development goals which have the greatest impact on the most people.

Structure of the OAS

The increased emphasis we wanted to give to nonpolitical matters in the revised charter is reflected in the elevation of the Economic and Social Council and the Council for Education, Science, and Culture to a level of equality with the Permanent Council of the OAS. At the same time the establishment of three Councils of equal level will put a greater management responsibility upon the general Secretariat of the Organization, which must serve all three.

These welcome changes emphasize the need to strengthen the structure of this Organization and of its Secretariat. We believe the Secretary General—no less than the General Assembly to which he is ultimately responsible—must play an increasingly important unifying role. Thus, in order to make the most productive use of the resources of the OAS, it will be all the more necessary to maintain a centralized OAS administration.

In this connection we must also make certain that the member governments receive a continuing appraisal of how programs are being carried out and goals are being met. We should seek adequate mechanisms to provide member governments with adequate inspection, appraisal, and evaluation.

Traditional Concerns and New Problems

I have briefly outlined our views on the promotion of trade and development in the hemisphere and on the structure of the OAS. I would like to touch on four other problems. Two involve traditional concerns: peacekeeping and the need to respond to emergency situations. Two are in different ways products of modern society: pollution of the environment and the issues raised by new forms of political terrorism.

Last year, when conflict broke out between Honduras and El Salvador, the OAS scored a notable achievement in peacemaking. The special OAS committee dispatched to the scene secured a cease-fire within 5 days. Since then the continuing involvement of the OAS has helped preserve the peace and advance the prospect of settlement. We can also take satisfaction from the new frontier pacification plan formulated by the OAS and agreed to with the participation of the Central American Foreign Ministers. These successes underscore that the inter-American system does have the capability of acting in the field of peace and security.

However, the successes should not obscure the need to settle disputes peacefully before they reach the stage of conflict. Upon approval of the statutes of the Inter-American Committee on Peaceful Settlement, together with the new role of the Permanent Council, we will set into motion improved machinery for the pacific settlement of disputes. I know that I express the view of all of us when I say I hope that this machinery will be utilized in as broad and constructive a way as possible.

In the Central American conflict the OAS not only helped in the role of peacemaking but also in the humanitarian tasks of protecting civilians and relieving suffering. More recently the tragedy caused by the earthquake in Peru—to which the Peruvian people have reacted so bravely—has called for another humanitarian response.

As elsewhere in the hemisphere this tragedy has produced great compassion and concern in the United States. I hope you will excuse this personal reference when I say that I am proud of the way the people of the United States have responded with relief assistance and food supplies. We, and I know all the countries represented here, extend our condolences to the people of Peru for the vast loss of life and suffering they have undergone.

In the Peruvian tragedy as well as in Central America, the Inter-American Emergency Aid Fund, created in 1965 at the initiative of our distinguished colleague the Foreign Minister of Mexico, has been helpful. In suggesting the establishment of this fund, Dr. Carrillo Flores proposed that it be used to assist victims of emergency situations, whether earthquakes, floods, or social disturbances.

These experiences suggest the need for reviewing the OAS capability in emergency situations. In particular there is a need for rapid and accurate assessment of requirements and for effective coordination of humanitarian assistance. Today an earthquake is involved. Tomorrow it may be a disturbance of another kind giving rise to the need to help. For example, when emergency evacuation of foreign nationals is necessary, perhaps the OAS could take a leadership role as has been done by other organizations elsewhere in the world.

Another new direction for OAS action might relate to the pollution of the environment, which threatens us all. The United Nations has already directed its attention to this problem. And the North Atlantic Treaty Organization last year formed a committee to coordinate joint pilot projects in environmental problems undertaken for the benefit of all of its member countries.

If the OAS considered initiating such a role, the undertaking would correspond to the greater emphasis we are giving under the revised character to the field of science and technology.

Terrorism and Kidnaping

The fourth issue which demands our immediate attention is on the agenda of this Assembly—the problem of terrorism, and particularly kidnaping and extortion.

We live in an era of increasing violence as a mode of dissent. None of our countries is immune to it. In dealing with the problem we must be most careful to distinguish between criminal acts of terrorism and legitimate expressions of discontent.

Bearing this in mind, I hope this Assembly can deal effectively with terrorism and kidnaping, especially in their international aspects. We support the proposal to brand them as common crimes and to treat them accordingly, both domestically and internationally. I hope the Assembly will address itself particularly to terrorism directed against representatives of foreign states. Such acts clearly and distinctly violate the principles governing the conduct of relations between states. We would suggest that the Assembly initiate steps to prepare a new international agreement defining these acts as international crimes and establishing appropriate measures to deal with them.

Terrorism and kidnaping on this continent affect states from other areas as well. As we all know too well, these crimes have already involved kidnapings of representatives of friendly nations outside the hemisphere. The inspiration for armed struggle and violence in our hemisphere also does not stem solely from forces within our countries. Therefore, I think it would be appropriate to appeal to all facets of world opinion to use their influence to help bring an end to such acts.

Mr. President, in the final analysis our efforts to solve the problems of our hemisphere will be measured by the extent to which what we do helps our people achieve the economic and social justice they desire and deserve. We must constantly look behind the programs, the reports, and the statistics for results—and ask ourselves if conditions of life are improving and if the pace of that improvement is fast enough.

The progress each of us wants should be the result of an effort that reflects, as our charter puts it, "the desire of the American peoples to live together in peace." It is this desire that has motivated one of the most significant recent steps taken in the Americas—a step, it should be emphasized, taken as a result of a Latin American initiative. I refer to the Treaty for the Prohibition of Nuclear Weapons in Latin America.

It was because the United States fully supports the hopes of the Latin American peoples to create a nuclear-free zone in their countries that we signed protocol II.

Since that signing in 1968, the United States has been conducting the necessary technical reviews preparatory to ratification. I am now pleased to announce that this review has been completed and that President Nixon intends in the very near future to submit protocol II to the United States Senate for its advice and consent to ratification.

Mr. President, to achieve the results for mankind that we seek we need to work harmoniously in a partnership in which all members cooperate—and none dominates. My delegation holds the firm conviction that this can be done and that we can move dramatically toward a major goal outlined in the OAS Charter: "the consolidation on this continent, within the framework of democratic institutions, of a system of individual liberty and social justice based on respect for the essential rights of man."

190. Statement by John N. Irwin II, Under Secretary of State, before the Inter-American Committee on the Alliance for Progress (CIAP)*

October 19, 1970

It is a pleasure and honor to have my first public appearance in my new position on the occasion of this first review and consultation with respect to the economic policies of the United States as they affect the other nations of the hemisphere. I am delighted to have this opportunity to review the posture of the United States. Inter-American cooperation has always been and will always be a prime concern to the Government of the United States. I am happy to speak to you today because of my great personal interest in working toward cooperative solutions to inter-American problems.

When President Nixon, in his remarks to the Inter-American Press Association last October, announced the decision of his administration to invite CIAP, as a regular procedure, to conduct this periodic review of United States economic policies, it was

*Department of State Bulletin, Nov. 9, 1970, pp. 561-65.

the hope that the candid and frank deliberations of this Committee would lead to thoughtful and constructive recommendations which can strengthen our common efforts and lead to accelerated development in all the Americas. We welcome the chance to have you review our record and give us the benefit of your views and wisdom.

Under your leadership, Mr. Chairman [Carlos Sanz de Santamaría], the Committee has established its reputation as a forum for thorough, frank discussions among friends. The report prepared by the OAS Secretariat, entitled "United States Cooperation with Latin America within the Framework of the Alliance for Progress," provides an admirable basis for the discussions in the review meetings. It is my hope, and the firm purpose of the U.S. delegation, that the presentations which we make during these meetings will be responsive to the important issues raised in the report and to the questions which may be brought up by the participants during the review.

As we approach this first review, it may be useful to recall the five principles outlined by President Nixon in his remarks last fall as the basis for his administration's actions in this hemisphere:

—First, a firm commitment to the inter-American system, and to the compacts which bind us in that system;

—Second, respect for national identity and national dignity in a partnership in which rights and responsibilities are shared by a community of independent states;

—Third, a firm commitment to continued United States assistance for hemispheric development;

—Fourth, a belief that these objectives can best be achieved by supporting Latin American initiatives on a multilateral basis; and

—Finally, a dedication to improving the quality of life in the Americas.

The nations of this hemisphere have increasingly recognized over the past century the historical, geographical, political, and economic considerations which make for the interdependence of all the Americas. The growing pressures to develop, modernize, and adapt to new challenges have led us all to reflect this interdependence in a variety of evolving organizational patterns, from the Pan American Union, to the Organization of American States, the Alliance for Progress, and, most recently, the approach which has emerged from President Nixon's call last October for further action for progress within a more mature partnership. All of us can take pride in the fact that the formal institutions in this inter-American system represent one of the oldest efforts at international organization in the world.

Trade and Development Assistance

We are aware that the countries of the hemisphere are particularly interested in two major topics of relevance here. They are interested in diversifying and expanding their export trade. At the same time, they retain an interest in accepting and utilizing available bilateral and multilateral foreign developmental assistance.

The United States Government has consistently supported efforts in many world-wide forums, such as the GATT, UNCTAD, and the OECD [General Agreement on Tariffs and Trade; United Nations Conference on Trade and Development; Organization for Economic Cooperation and Development], as well as the many forums of the inter-American system, to facilitate access by the developing countries to the industrialized markets and to improve the terms and level of available developmental assistance.

The ability of the United States to continue to implement trade and economic assistance policies is influenced, however, and ultimately limited, by the strength and stability of its domestic economy and by the state of its balance of payments. Our domestic economy in the past decade has been beset by the difficulty of striking a balance between the often competing goals of full employment and stable prices. Current actions are designed to help the economy regain this balance, and recent indicators demonstrate that these actions are succeeding. Our major balance-of-payments problem in the same period has been that of trying to reduce and progressively eliminate a persistent deficit while continuing to fulfill our international commitments and our objective of contributing to international development.

The four topics I have alluded to above, namely, the United States domestic economy, the United States balance of payments, United States trade policies, and United States developmental assistance programs, will be discussed in further detail by the members of the United States delegation in the coming sessions. Speaking on the major topics will be: Mr. Herbert Stein, who is a member of the President's Council of Economic Advisers; Mr. Edwin M. Cronk, Deputy Assistant Secretary of State; Mr. John R. Petty, Assistant Secretary of Treasury; and Mr. Maurice J. Williams, the Deputy Administrator of the Agency for International Development.

New Approach in U.S. Policy

From the beginning of this administration President Nixon has reaffirmed the long-sustained United States interest in assisting Latin American trade and development and suggested new ways to improve and restructure our continuing relationship. To this end he sought and received the advice of our Latin American neighbors in the Consensus of Viña del Mar. His administration embarked on the series of meetings of the IA–ECOSOC [Inter-American Economic and Social Council] and its subsidiary and associated bodies which are continuing and in which the new, more mature relationship and still-evolving new programs of action for progress are being forged. The advice of Governor Rockefeller was received following his series of visits to Latin America and the preparation of his comprehensive report. The new approach to Latin American trade, development, consultation, and coordination matters was included in the overall foreign policy message which President Nixon submitted to the Congress in February.

Against this background, I would like to review the actions for progress which have been taken during the period of less than 2 years of the Nixon administration.

—President Nixon acted last June to remove one of the principal impediments which had arisen in prior years to the orderly and harmonious administration of our bilateral assistance in Latin America. I refer to the elimination of the so-called "additionality" requirement.

—Then, following the summer of 1969, spent in intensive study of actions which could be taken or begun in response to the Latin American requests contained in the

Consensus of Viña del Mar, the President announced a series of new steps in his October 31 speech, with the following results to date:

(1) The decision of the United States Government to press for a liberal, worldwide system of generalized preferences for all developing countries. The initial list of products which the United States proposed for generalized preferences was subsequently expanded following consultations with our Latin American and other trading partners. Finally, a few days ago, a special committee of UNCTAD endorsed the generalized preferences proposals of the developed countries as mutually acceptable.

(2) Multilateral institutions within the inter-American system have been accorded increased responsibilities for operations and decisions affecting United States bilateral assistance to Latin America. For example, as Dr. Sanz de Santamaría has noted, CIAP representatives now participate directly in AID discussions of loan and development programs, and increased funds have been made available to enable CIAP to expand and improve its own operations.

(3) A comprehensive study of debt servicing problems, embarked under CIAP and IA–ECOSOC initiative, with United States Government support, is well advanced, and the international institutions which are conducting the study are expected to issue their reports within a few weeks.

(4) AID loans were "untied" to permit procurement not only in the United States but anywhere in Latin America. This "untying" has now been extended to all the developing countries. In an associated measure, dollars provided in AID loans for the local costs of projects were completely "untied," thus permitting their use for any purpose.

(5) New initiatives were announced for export development, tourism, and capital market development. Concrete proposals in these areas are already in advanced stages of consideration.

–Finally, among major new actions accomplished or well advanced, United States legislation is now proceeding through the United States Congress to provide an additional $1.8 billion in United States support for the Inter-American Development Bank.

In 1961, the United States pledged an annual contribution of nearly $1 billion to assist in the effort of the Alliance to raise the standards of life in all the Americas and, happily, has exceeded it. The United States official commitment to Latin American economic assistance of over $1.1 billion in fiscal year 1970 represents one of the largest single-year inputs in the history of the Alliance. It is true, and widely publicized, that United States bilateral assistance through the Agency for International Development has decreased from about $570 million annually in the midsixties to about $400 million per year at present. We believe, however, this decrease in bilateral assistance has been compensated, as the report of the Secretariat notes, by an increased transfer of resources through multilateral agencies such as the Inter-American Development Bank. At present, a preponderance of all United States assistance to the hemisphere goes through international agencies.

Transformation of U.S. Assistance Machinery

As to the future–last month President Nixon transmitted to the Congress his recommendations for the reorganization of United States foreign assistance programs.

The report of the President's Task Force on International Development, headed by Rudolph Peterson, former president of the Bank of America, has provided the basis for a major transformation of our assistance machinery. In making these proposals the Peterson task force drew heavily on and profited from the experience of the Alliance for Progress.

A principal thrust of the President's recommendations is to channel even more of our development assistance through multilateral institutions, such as the World Bank, the Inter-American Development Bank and other regional lending associations.

United States bilateral assistance programs would continue through two new agencies. One, an International Development Institute, would concentrate scientific and technological talent on the problems of development, assist other countries to manage their own development programs, support expanded research programs in population, and cooperate in other programs of social development.

The other agency, an International Development Corporation, would administer most of our bilateral lending programs, which would be put on a more businesslike basis.

The recently created Overseas Private Investment Corporation has been charged with the responsibility of operating our investment insurance guaranty programs and other activities to promote private investment in developing countries. These programs will continue to play what we believe to be an important part of overall approach to development assistance—the encouragement of private United States firms to undertake the risks of investing in developing countries.

Of special interest to private nonprofit organizations is the fact that the Foreign Assistance Act of 1969 provided for the creating of the Inter-American Social Development Institute. A major function of the ISDI will be to bring private United States and Latin American nonprofit groups to the fore in development problems and to broaden the participation of individuals in the development process.

Thus, while multilateral assistance programs will be predominant in the future, there will continue to be bilateral programs as well, though mostly in a supporting role and probably diminishing as multilateral programs increase.

As you know there is now pending in the Congress a new trade bill which could have significant impact on our trade with Latin America. The Secretary of State testifying just a week ago on the bill spoke out strongly against a number of provisions in the bill which the administration had not requested. He confirmed his conviction that "a liberal trade policy is essential if the developing countries are to achieve the self-reliance that the Nixon doctrine seeks to encourage." We will watch the progress of this bill carefully, recognizing the dangers of any measures which introduce new restrictions and distortions into the channels of international trade.

All of us know that the statistics of the economic growth rate of Latin America as a whole under the Alliance for Progress and the realities of social progress fall short of the needs of today and tomorrow, though most of yesterday's targets were largely accomplished. These are the same statistics and realities that prompted President Nixon to declare at the Organization of American States last year that "We must do better. We must find the ways and the means whereby we can move forward together in a more effective way." As Dr. Raúl Prebisch emphasized in his report last April to the Inter-American Development Bank, the rapidly expanding population and labor force in Latin America requires a higher rate of economic growth than was formerly considered a reasonable target, if per capita well-being is to be maintained, let alone improved.

We ourselves have been increasingly concerned, as all of you must be, with the problems posed for our societies by the relentless pressure of population on resources. We have been mindful of the recommendations made in Caracas at the Meeting on Population Policies in Relation to Development in Latin America to the effect that population variables be included in CIAP's annual reviews. President Nixon, with the approval of the Congress, has appointed a commission to consider what effects population growth may have on the future of our own country.

We recognize, Mr. Chairman, the serious problems and large obstacles you and we must face. Together we form a community of widely diverse peoples, with differing perceptions of self-interest and reality and different ways of reacting to these perceptions. Practical and serious restraints frequently inhibit our efforts to meet the surging aspirations of our societies. The United States will work vigorously and persistently toward a solution of our mutual problems, making people, with their human, social, and economic needs, the inspiration of our efforts.

191. Press Release by Secretary Rogers, on Chile's Decision on Compensation for the Expropriated United States Copper Investments*

October 13, 1971

The Controller General of Chile announced his findings on October 11 that no compensation would be paid for the U.S. copper mining investments expropriated on July 16 except for modest amounts in the cases of two smaller properties.

The United States Government is deeply disappointed and disturbed at this serious departure from accepted standards of international law. Under established principles of international law, the expropriation must be accompanied by reasonable provision for payment of just compensation. The United States had made clear to the Government of Chile its hope that a solution could be found on a reasonable and pragmatic basis consistent with international law.

It appears that the major factor in the Controller General's decision with respect to the larger producers was the determination on September 28 of alleged "excess profits." The unprecedented retroactive application of the excess profits concept, which was not obligatory under the expropriation legislation adopted by the Chilean Congress, is particularly disquieting. The U.S. companies which are affected by this determination of the Chilean Government earned their profits in Chile in accordance with Chilean law and under specific contractual agreements made directly with the Government of Chile. The excess profits deductions punish the companies today for acts that were legal and approved by the Government of Chile at the time. No claim is being made that these excess profits deductions are based on violations of Chilean law. This retroactive determination has serious implications for the rule of law.

Should Chile fail to meet its international obligations, it could jeopardize flows of private funds and erode the base of support for foreign assistance, with possible

*Department of State Bulletin, Nov. 1, 1971, p. 478.

adverse effects on other developing countries. The course of action which the Chilean Government appears to have chosen, therefore, could have an adverse effect on the international development process.

The United States hopes that the Government of Chile, in accordance with its obligations under international law, will give further careful consideration to this matter.

192. Statement by Charles A. Meyer, Assistant Secretary of State for Inter-American Affairs before the Subcommittee on Inter-American Affairs on Policy Toward Chile*

October 15, 1971

I would like to preface my remarks on our overall policies toward Chile and the specific issue of compensation for expropriated U.S. copper holdings in that country by reading the statement issued on October 13 by Secretary Rogers on the compensation question.

(See Document 191)

News analysts and Chile analysts and foreign policy analysts have already commented on the "moderation" or "hardness" of Secretary Rogers' statement, and the Foreign Minister of Chile has, in his turn, speculated as to the pressure intent of the next to last paragraph.

The statement contains no threat. It is purely factual, and the next to last paragraph alludes to the "ripple effect" that Chile's ultimate action in the compensation process, which has not terminated, could have.

I am sure that the fact that Chile has expropriated U.S.-owned copper interests comes as no surprise to anyone on the subcommittee. The nationalization of copper and other natural resources was a well-advertised part of Dr. Allende's electoral campaign. However, repeated public and private statements were made that expropriated properties would be accorded just compensation.

None of the content of Secretary Rogers' statement can constitute a surprise to the Government of Chile. Through diplomatic channels our serious concern with the expropriation legislation and our valid interest in effective, adequate, and prompt compensation have been expressed continuously, and we have gone to great and sincere lengths to advocate a pragmatic solution to the question of compensation for the copper companies. One of our purposes in this persistent effort has been precisely to avoid the "ripple effect," which by my definition is in its ultimate the growth of public and congressional opinion adverse to authorizing or appropriating or allocating sufficient funds, public and private, for development assistance because of negation of generally accepted rules of international law and equity.

We have no reason or desire to seek or welcome a confrontation with the Government of Chile. The entire thrust of our policy in the past year has been to try our level best to minimize the chances of a confrontation. Nor do we question Chile's right to self-determination. We cannot be expected, however, to be indifferent or to remain silent when established international norms applicable to our nationals are in jeopardy. We believe the acknowledged right of any sovereign state to expropriate property on a nondiscriminatory basis cannot be disassociated from the equally valid right of the expropriated to receive prompt, adequate, and effective compensation. Otherwise, expropriation becomes simple confiscation.

As the Secretary's statement indicates, we regard the retroactive application of the "excess profits" concept as a particularly disturbing departure from legal norms. In effect, the U.S. companies which earned their profits in Chile in accordance with Chilean law and under specific contractual agreements with the Chilean Government are now told after the fact that they will be penalized for making such profits. The deduction of those so-called "excess profits" from the Controller General's valuation of the companies' properties punishes the companies today for actions that were legal and approved by the Chilean Government yesterday. Significantly, no claim is being made that these "excess profits" are being deducted because they resulted from violations of Chilean law. Obviously the deduction of $774 million in "excess profits" from a "book value" of $629 million—in itself a dubious measure of true worth—for three of the five mines involved means there will be no effective compensation at all for these properties unless modifications are made before the compensation process is completed.

In addition to the basic question of compensation, there is considerable ambiguity and uncertainty regarding the Government of Chile's intentions to repay debts owed to the expropriated U.S. copper interests and third parties. These debts are normal obligations of the Chilean Government. We do not have, however, a clear indication of what the Chilean Government intends to do about them.

I wish to make it clear that any differences we may have with Chile are neither political nor ideological in their origin. President Nixon has stated clearly that the United States is prepared to have the kind of relationship with the Chilean Government that it is prepared to have with us. We deal with governments as they are. Our relations depend not on their internal structures or social systems, but on actions which affect us and the inter-American system. In pursuit of this policy we have maintained a correct and positive attitude toward the present Government of Chile since its inception.

We would like to believe that the Chilean Government shares our desire for normal relations, but we cannot ignore the fact that there are some important elements among the political forces within the present Chilean Government which have appeared to welcome a confrontation with the United States for ideological as well as for internal political reasons.

Despite these discouraging signs, we have persisted in our efforts to maintain normality in our relations with Chile and have sought to exhaust every possibility for reaching practical solutions to problems as they have arisen. We have continued bilateral economic and military assistance programs. While these levels are lower than for previous years, the decline reflects the absorption of $500 million of AID loans over recent years and also reflects the internal and external income which accrued to Chile from the very copper operations which Chile now is attacking.

Out positive stance has been further evidenced by the prompt and effective disaster relief assistance totaling approximately $260,000 which we recently extended to

Chile. In this connection we also supported project reallocations by the Inter-American Development Bank (IDB) for earthquake rehabilitation totaling more than $16 million. We have maintained our ongoing cooperative efforts on Antarctic research, satellite tracking, Peace Corps, Food for Peace programs, and cultural exchange activities.

In the multilateral field we have considered Chilean loan applications to the IDB and the World Bank on their merits. Following President Allende's inauguration, we supported IDB loans to two Chilean universities totaling $11.6 million. Despite allegations to the contrary, we have maintained an open position with respect to pending Chilean loan applications before the Eximbank. I would add that this includes the LAN-Chile request for commercial aircraft, which was subject to the normal criteria for such projects.

We have, in short, sought by all available means to make known our genuine desire to maintain normal relations and to resolve bilateral problems pragmatically. To this end, we offered our good offices to aid the search for acceptable solutions to the compensation issue while the basic discussions on nationalized and expropriated U.S. properties were conducted between the Chilean Government and the private companies involved. To date, the results of our efforts can hardly be described as encouraging. We are aware that no amount of reason or good will on our part can by itself create the objective conditions required for an acceptable solution.

As matters stand, the compensation proceedings thus far do not provide for just compensation for the expropriated properties. There is still pending the appeals procedure to a special tribunal, and we will reserve our final judgment until the entire compensation process has been completed. We sincerely hope that the Chilean Government, in accordance with Chilean tradition, will honor its obligations under international law.

193. Address by Assistant Secretary Meyer before the Inter-American Press Association on United States Policy toward Latin America*

October 25, 1971

I was truly pleased when your first vice president, John Watkins, invited me to address you tonight. I admit that I was also intrigued by the topic he assigned to me: where we stand today, 2 years after President Nixon's Latin American policy speech.

I was intrigued because having become so sensitive to complaints that this administration has no Latin American policy, I had wondered whether there was a Latin Americanist left who would admit we had a policy to explain.

I cannot remember how many times I have been tempted to put these complaints in the category of a remark made nearly a century and a half ago by the famous English writer Charles Lamb. Lamb was walking along a London street with a friend, and he stopped and pointed. "Do you see that man over there?" he said. "I hate him." "Hate him?" his friend said. "How can you hate him? You don't even know who he is." "Precisely," Lamb said.

*Department of State Bulletin, Nov. 15, 1971, pp. 559-64.

Lamb's unreasonable reaction to an unknown might be equated with critical assertions by the uninformed that this administration has no Latin American policy or—the common by-product of those complaints—that Latin America ranks so far down our list of priorities that we are "benignly neglecting" our neighbors and partners to the south.

But it was before this group of distinguished publishers and editors of the Inter American Press Association that President Nixon announced his administration's policy toward Latin America 2 years ago, less 1 week.

If any opinion-forming group can be sensitively aware of this administration's Latin American policy, it must be, I have thought, the newspapermen and broadcasters of this hemisphere. I am sure that many of you here tonight were among the President's audience 2 years ago. I am also confident that most of you counted yourselves among the large majority in this hemisphere who applauded the new policy with enthusiasm and with appreciation for its realism. The policy demonstrates the United States is ready to adapt to the changing political, economic, and social environment in Latin America; the policy responds to Latin America's needs and aspirations; and it suggested a series of important actions within the limits of the achievable to follow.

Why in the span of 2 years has such wide-spread support for the President's Latin American policy slipped to expressed doubt that this administration has a policy?

I believe there are four interlocking factors:

First, there has been an obvious and a serious failure to grasp the far-reaching implications inherent in the President's policy.

Second, the fact that the United States has not yet transformed one of the important policy pledges into policy action has led to the erroneous conclusion that an unfulfilled pledge equals no policy or no commitment at all.

Third, the fact that the President has taken a series of decisions within his executive powers in behalf of the hemisphere has been overlooked or even taken for granted.

Fourth, the fact that even the most sophisticated among us interchange bilateral problems with regional objectives and vice versa, depending often on whether we want to accentuate the negative or the positive—and far too often it is the negative—tends to distort relationships between the United States and any one or all of the nations of the Americas.

Mutuality and Shared Responsibility

Let's begin with item one.

The fact is that the President has kept his promise. He has changed our policy radically. The problem is that today's policy is still being measured by yesterday's yardstick.

The essence of the President's new policy was captured in the term "mature partnership," which he used in his address to this association. The term has been repeated so often that it has attained the status of a slogan. Unfortunately, as is so often the case in this era of instant global communications, the slogan overpowered and obscured the message it conveyed and has been negatively interpreted from disengagement through disinterest to abandonment.

The positive message is clear and simple: The United States is dedicated to bringing about a new equilibrium in our relations with Latin America by loosening our long-held paternal grip on the other nations of the hemisphere. Tutelary leadership would be, and has been, replaced by a balanced relationship, including discreet leadership, that respects the sovereign rights of our Latin American partners.

This policy is confirmed by our continuing support to Latin America's drive for economic and social development, but increasingly only in response to Latin America's initiatives. The shift of emphasis from bilateral to multilateral assistance and the arduous but still unfinished business of expanding Latin America's trade opportunities are concrete developments that reflect this policy change.

The new policy also foresaw change in Latin America as a continuing force and the need to live with diversity as one of its outgrowths. We now deal with governments as they are—which is what Latin America wants. We are shaping our relations with governments around the contours of the actions they take affecting us and the inter-American system.

The policy of mature partnership does and should and must emphasize constant progress toward reciprocal understanding. It, in short, strives to develop a true two-way street in bilateral, subregional, and regional relationships. It just may be that Latin America has felt itself at the end of a one-way street for so long that its response to reciprocity or mutuality is initially one of a 180-degree reverse in the one-way street. In such a reverse of direction the interests of the United States would be considered expendable, principally because we are the richest and most powerful nation and therefore should be the givers in a relationship of "give-and-take," not "take-it-or-leave-it," to quote from the President's October 1969 speech.

However, the broad aspect of our policy is one which embodies increased recognition of mutuality and shared responsibility, acceptance of diversity, while pledging continued support for development.

Developments in Trade Policy

The broad policy concept obviously leads to specifics and again to negative interpretation to the degree that any one or more unimplemented specifics can be represented as no policy or no commitment.

Therefore, to present a complete picture I must now turn to both inaction and action in the broad field of trade, in which field some negative developments have adversely affected our relations with Latin America in the past year. I believe these "non-developments" (if I may coin a word) are responsible in part for the simplistic preachment: "U.S. relations with Latin America have reached their lowest point since. . . ."

We have not fulfilled our commitment to implement a system of generalized tariff preferences for the developing countries, which preferences represent Latin America's highest priority objective in its economic relations with the United States. The United States and Latin America agree they are important to development, for as you know, generalized preferences would eliminate tariffs of all major developed countries on a large number of manufactured and semimanufactured products from all LDC's [less developed countries]. Therefore they would stimulate developing countries to diversify their exports and reduce their traditional dependence for foreign exchange earnings on raw materials and commodities and would reduce the high cost of import substitution.

Trade—with good reason—is now considered the unwritten Magna Carta of Latin America's economic development. It offers potential for transferring resources indispensable to development and growth without the real or imagined infringing on national sovereignty that so often conditions bilateral and even multilateral loans and investment, private and public.

In 1969 and early 1970, the United States took the lead in urging the European Common Market countries and Japan to establish with us a system that would benefit the developing countries. The Common Market countries and Japan have since put their generalized preference systems into effect. We have delayed submission of legislation because, concurrent with our negotiations with Latin America, the United States trade and balance of payments position was deteriorating rapidly. This deterioration, coupled with a sluggish economy, created not only an unreceptive mood but a strong protectionist sentiment in Congress. In this unfavorable climate, the administration considered that not only was passage of a preference bill unlikely but that submission of a bill by the executive branch might be unwise.

Our inability to meet a commitment of such importance to Latin America has disappointed and dismayed many Latin American leaders and cast doubt on our sincerity.

I, for one, have tried to explain to our Latin neighbors in these past 2 years that readjustments in global claims on the U.S.A. have become a reality. Our commitments remain firm, but the timing of their implementation is not necessarily determined unilaterally. In today's world, every event everywhere has a ripple effect all over the world, and timing is affected by those ripples.

On August 15, President Nixon announced his new economic policy aimed at reversing the deficit in our worldwide trade account and reviving our economy.

The further dismay expressed by Latin America in the aftermath of the announcement reached its peak at the Inter-American Economic and Social Council meeting in Panama last month. The Latin Americans demanded removal of the 10-percent surcharge on dutiable exports to the United States. They protested that the United States has had a large favorable balance of trade with Latin America for years and that they should not suffer from a program of global readjustment insofar as they were not contributors to the problem.

The United States has stressed that the surcharge is only a temporary measure, that its real impact in Latin America may be slight, and that a robust United States economy—which is the goal of the new program—is in the long-range benefit of all developing countries. Nevertheless, the Latin Americans have not been placated. In addition to its economic impact, the sudden and sweeping nature of the new program along with our inability to consult with the Latin Americans in advance took its toll politically and psychologically. They saw it as dramatic evidence of their impotence and lack of influence on decisions that can crucially affect their own economic planning. In the train of the indefinite timing of the generalized preference legislation, there is no doubt that even if the economic effect is undetermined, the psychological and political shock of the August 15 measures are real, despite their temporary nature and despite the fact that the administration remains wedded to generalized tariff preferences.

Concrete Achievements

The third facet which we must consider is what has been undertaken.

Our policy, as the President has said, is one of give-and-take, not take-it-or-leave-it. Our relationship is a two-way relationship that, in fact, transcends official policy to include ties that have been developed government to government, industry to industry, school to school, scientist to scientist, and volunteer to volunteer. There are so many ties that no one has at hand even a partial catalogue.

And I hasten to add—in the event these remarks are interpreted by some as setting the stage for cutbacks in our official economic commitment to Latin America—that President Nixon has repeatedly reaffirmed our partnership in the development challenge. And he has backed that partnership with resources. Contrary to a popular misconception, economic assistance levels continue to match the annual average during the first 10 years of the Alliance for Progress. The difference is: bilateral aid levels have fallen and multilateral aid contributions have risen, largely in response to Latin American desires.

That leads me to other concrete achievements, not only of this administration's policy but also of the inter-American system which that policy supports. A monetary value can be placed on some. Others can be priced only in terms of the value each of us places on cooperation among the nations of this hemisphere.

We have eased restrictions so that our neighbors may now spend aid dollars elsewhere in Latin America or the developing world. We have submitted U.S. economic policies for annual review to the Inter-American Committee on the Alliance for Progress, an unprecedented step for a donor nation. We have consulted whenever possible with Latin America prior to taking actions that affect their economies. We have participated enthusiastically and generously in inter-American organizations that in the last 2 years have launched programs to develop capital markets, tourism, and export promotion, a vital program regardless of trade preferences. We are studying how best to transfer technology for the hemisphere's social and economic development.

We signed agreements with Colombia and Panama covering the U.S. financing of its share of completion of construction on the Darien Gap, the last unfinished link of the Pan American Highway. The OAS approved a convention on kidnaping and other crimes against foreign officials. We have achieved closer cooperation with Latin American countries in the control of illicit traffic in narcotics and dangerous drugs. Congress passed new sugar legislation which, on the whole, favored Latin American suppliers. And President Nixon exempted Latin America from the 10-percent reduction in foreign economic assistance expenditures called for under the new economic policy.

Regionally, our interlacing of mutual objectives has produced results. Subregionally and bilaterally this is also true, perhaps even more evident.

Subregionally, we have continued our support of the Central American Bank for Economic Integration, formalized our financial support of the Caribbean Development

Bank, held available up to $10 million to assist in loans to the Andean Development Corporation as it develops.

Bilaterally, in the purest sense of a mature partnership, we have abrogated the Bryan-Chamorro Treaty, reformalized bilateral negotiations to modernize the 1903 treaty between the United States and Panama, negotiated a border settlement agreement with Mexico which once and for all settles disputes over the changing course of the Rio Grande. Traditional recurring trade agreements—textiles, meats, fruits, and vegetables—have been successfully negotiated, although obviously in a buyer-seller negotiation neither side reaches its maximum aspirations.

In short, respected friends, neither are our policy objectives stagnant, nor are our relationships sterile.

This, however, leads to the fourth factor—that even the most sophisticated among us inter-change bilateral problems with regional objectives and vice versa, usually with negative distortion.

Bilateral Problems and Regional Objectives

Inherent in President Nixon's policy concept was and is the recognition that differences of priorities, differences of interest, are to be expected but that in the spirit of negotiation not confrontation, differences can be manageable.

There are two significant differences of interest which require this spirit to the fullest. The first of these is what is broadly described as the territorial sea. The second of these is the role of foreign private investment. These differences are not new, are unresolved, and adversely color our total relationship in the minds of all too many of us at home and abroad who, on the one hand, evaluate all of Latin America in the light of the actions of one or more individual nations or who, on the other hand, sadly and inaccurately and negatively evaluate all U.S. interests as "imperialistic" or "exploitative."

I suspect that everyone here tonight has an opinion on the subject of distant fishing in traditional fishing grounds preempted by unilateral claims of maritime sovereignty. And I further suspect that the majority of opinion would be that the interested parties should find a practical solution to the fishing conflict instead of escalating punitive measures, recognizing that the complicated question of the sea and its seabed are both subjects of a U.N. conference scheduled for 1973. Such a practical solution has been sought and is being sought, and it does require give-and-take without compromising the fundamental differences in legal concepts that are involved. What is transcendentally important is that none of us in South or North America allow this specific problem negatively to influence the basic relationships between us nor to spill over into unrelated retribution.

The second important difference which is disruptive to a wholly unnecessary degree is a difference in concept relative to foreign private investment—and to be wholly honest, one would qualify "foreign" as "U.S." private investment.

As many of you will recall, the Presidential address 2 years ago placed balanced emphasis on the importance of the private sector in the total development picture, said private sector to include private foreign investment. And President Nixon urged that the Americas write the rules of the game, rules by which all investors would be governed without the risk of constant change and certainly without the unbelievable risk of retroactivity in the application of whatever rules.

This balanced emphasis reflected and reflects our conviction that development, both economic and social, depends on transfer of resources. This transfer is effected by bilateral and unilateral development loans and grants, by trade, and by direct foreign investment, which may be the one most effective method of transferring the savings of the developed world to the developing world—which is short of savings—at a negligible real cost to the developed world.

This conviction is neither imperialist nor exploitative. It is an honest reflection of the importance of the entrepreneurial instinct and the profit motive in development and an honest evaluation of the mobility of private capital as contrasted with government funds. Yet my Government recognizes the right of a sovereign state to nationalize a foreign-owned property—even though the wisdom, short- and long-range, of some nationalization we would question. The vital point is compensation, prompt, adequate, and effective, for any part or all of a property that is nationalized.

Here is where we of the Americas need the fullest application of mutual under-standing, of give-and-take, of negotiation not confrontation, of third-party adjudication when necessary. For no one can overlook the fact that it is difficult for the American taxpayer to support development assistance or adopt an attitude of "business as usual" with any nation when that very same taxpayer may have lost an important part of his or her savings through uncompensated or inadequately compensated nationalization by that nation.

This is not a "hard-line" reaction nor a "get-tough" reaction; it is merely human—once burned, twice shy.

It is these two areas of difference that develop or that have developed most of the public heat between the United States and Latin America even though these are not regional differences common to all, nor are these differences identical nation by nation where they exist.

So, to restate the fourth aspect in evaluation of this administration's policy and our inter-American relationships, the sad fact is that all of us, north and south, still unconsciously confuse a living, growing, maturing hemispheric relationship with bilateral differences.

Distinguished ladies and gentlemen, the Nixon policy is a living policy. It has been incompletely understood because it is not a pyrotechnic policy conceived for instant impact but a sound policy for now and the future responsive to the nations of Latin America.

The implementation of the trade portion of this policy has been deferred, and this presents a criticism of U.S. policy toward Latin America.

The implementation of scores of initiatives within the authority of the executive branch has proceeded and may, as I have said, have been unnoticed or taken for granted.

Bilateral problems emerging from a subregional concept of maritime jurisdiction and from nationalism as this affects the past, present, and future investment of private capital have been interpreted by some as evidence of deterioration in our inter-American relationships. If my task were to pass around blame, I could suggest that these latter two areas of difference require a better understanding of the U.S.A. on the part of the Latin nations involved.

But to evenly distribute blame or to unevenly distribute blame is not and must not be the basic underpinning of our inter-American convictions, of the U.S. policy for Latin America, nor of the Latin American policy for the United States.

During the balance of this century we simply must build on the concept of mature partnership. All of us face similar problems. No nation among us is developed if one accepts the fact that development is a career, not a destination. It never ends. Our community of interests will not prevent the emergence of differences. The give-and-take, the mutuality, the reciprocity, which we apply to solution of these differences will continue the tradition of the Americas.

In your honor I am proud to close with a message:

"My very best wishes go to the members of the Inter American Press Association as I welcome its delegates to our country.

"I have pleasant memories of the evening 2 years ago when I had the privilege of addressing your last meeting on U.S. soil.

"In the policy statement I made to you then, I told you that the United States hoped to achieve a more mature partnership in which all voices are heard and none predominates. I also expressed our desire to maintain our basic commitment to the hemisphere's social economic development.

"I wish to assure you today that the destiny of every nation within our inter-American system remains of foremost concern to the United States. But I also believe that only through the shared responsibility I called for 2 years ago can we ultimately achieve the equality in our relations that we all seek as partners in the Americas.

"I also want to take this opportunity to say that once the problems to which our new economic program in the United States has been addressed are alleviated, we shall again move forward in many of the basic areas I discussed with you in 1969.

"Meanwhile, I ask for the patience and understanding of our Latin American neighbors during this hopefully brief period in which the imbalances in the U.S. economy are corrected.

"As you are among the most distinguished journalists in our hemisphere, your members have gained the respect, esteem, and trust of countless men and women. You have an awesome responsibility toward them and a role in their continuing well-being. I wholeheartedly applaud your staunch defense of freedom of expression and look forward with the leaders of the countries you represent to your important assistance in bringing into focus the needs of our people and in marshaling the best resources for the sustained progress of our societies."

Richard Nixon

*194. Statement by Assistant Secretary Meyer before the
Subcommittee on Inter-American Affairs on the
Fisheries Disputes**

February 3, 1972

Fisheries disputes between the United States and certain countries of Latin America have been a disturbing element in our relations with the hemisphere for almost 20 years. They have tended to cause periodic problems in the normal conduct of our affairs, which, when the boats went home, often were set aside until the next fishing season. Solutions have been either elusive or, when reached, temporary. The dimensions of these disputes changed significantly in 1971, so significantly that a problem which once could be dealt with primarily as a fisheries problem now forces itself on us as one which involves a range of important interests of the United States.

For this reason and because, in spite of the combined efforts of the Departments concerned, there is still no ready answer, I especially welcome this opportunity to review with you the nature of the disputes, the harm they cause, and the prospects for realizing our continuing hope that they can be resolved. With me today are, representing the Special Assistant to the Secretary for Fisheries and Wildlife and Coordinator for Ocean Affairs, Mr. Wilvan Van Campen, and Mr. Charles J. Pitman, representing the Department's Legal Adviser.

Fisheries disputes arise from differences we have with certain Latin American countries regarding the breadth of the territorial sea and coastal state rights over resources of the waters adjacent to their coasts. The United States recognizes a 3-mile territorial sea and, in addition, claims a 9-mile contiguous zone of exclusive jurisdiction over fisheries. Ecuador, Peru, and Brazil, the countries whose names are most closely associated with the fisheries problem, claim 200 miles of sovereignty or exclusive jurisdiction over the waters off their coasts. Thus, in some ways, fisheries disputes can be seen as the result of a contest between those who believe that the waters beyond 12 miles are high seas and those who claim 200 miles.

This is more than a numbers game, however, as basic to our dispute are differing concepts of how we approach rulemaking with respect to the world's oceans. The United States believes that the question of sovereignty and rights is one which must be settled within the international community in order to avoid the chaos of extensive and conflicting unilateral claims. Certain countries of Latin America, 10 in all, believe that it is the right of each coastal state to determine for itself, on the basis of its own requirements and needs, the extent and nature of its claims over the waters off its coast.

The elements of the fisheries disputes date from the middle and late 1940's. In 1945, when the world was populated by countries claiming less than 12 miles of territorial seas, President Truman issued two proclamations dealing with ocean resources off our own coasts. One of these proclamations stated U.S. policy with respect to the resources of the continental shelf. In reserving for the coastal state the resources of the continental shelf, President Truman carefully reaffirmed the United States view that existing international law provided for a 3-mile territorial sea. We also clearly

*Department of State Bulletin, Feb. 28, 1972, pp. 284-87.

stated that it was not our intention to affect the high-seas character of the waters above the continental shelf and the right thereon to free and unimpeded navigation.

In spite of our intentions, in 1947, Peru and Chile, noting that the United States had acted unilaterally to protect resource interests in an area off its own coast, laid claim to sovereignty and national jurisdiction over the seas adjacent to their coasts extending to a distance of 200 nautical miles. They were joined in 1952 by Ecuador when all three countries signed the Santiago Declaration on the Maritime Zone. It was the thesis of the three nations that the region delineated by this zone constitutes a distinct ecological unit within which a dynamic balance of nature is maintained.

The Declaration of Santiago suggests that the claim of Chile, Ecuador, and Peru is essentially a claim to resources, although in the years since 1952, it has been treated both as a resource claim and as a territorial sea claim. With it, conflict over fisheries resources became inevitable. I say "inevitable" because differences with countries that make claims with which we disagree, and which we protest, cannot always wait on the slow process of writing new international law. Where the American distant-water fishing fleet must continue to operate pending agreement, the differences manifest themselves not only in the exchange of notes protesting juridical positions but, most seriously, in fisheries disputes.

There are, as I said, now 10 Latin American countries with similar claims. In addition to Chile, Ecuador, and Peru, these are El Salvador, Nicaragua, Argentina, Panama, Uruguay, and Brazil. Costa Rica has had a 200-mile conservation zone. Of all of these states, the disputes which concern us today involve only Ecuador, Peru, Chile (because of the tie of the Santiago Declaration), and Brazil.

Two international law-of-the-sea conferences, one in 1958 and one in 1960, have failed to resolve the basic issues on territorial seas and resource jurisdiction. We are now looking to a new conference in 1973 to do so. Our experience with fisheries disputes and the proliferation of 200-mile claims in the hemisphere in the decade of the sixties compel us to conclude that this conference must be successful if we are to insure the navigational rights on the world's oceans which are essential to our security and if we are to resolve existing conflicts or, more, to prevent new conflicts over rights to the oceans' resources. Unfortunately, the necessity for international agreement and the difficulty of waiting for it are being most clearly demonstrated in the hemisphere.

Over the years the elements for a full-scale demonstration of the implications for the United States of disagreements over issues of law of the sea have been gathering, with little obvious relation to each other. The American distant-water fishing fleet, particularly our tuna fleet, has been modernizing and improving its technology. It has sailed to more distant seas in search of tuna for a growing American market. Flying the American flag, vessel owners are not obligated, in our view, to buy licenses to fish waters beyond 12 miles, although we do not object when they decide for themselves that they want to. As a consequence of the seizures which began in 1953, when Ecuador and Peru began enforcing their 200-mile claims against unlicensed American fishing vessels, the Congress acted in 1954 to begin assisting the tunaboat owners to meet the costs to them as individuals of an unresolved dispute between governments. Amended in 1968, the Fishermen's Protective Act now permits reimbursement for fines paid and licenses purchased to obtain release after seizure. Other pieces of legislation have been passed by Congress as the vessel seizures have drawn increasing attention to the problem. This body of legislation calls upon the executive branch to act or consider acting against countries that seize American fishing vessels with respect to military sales, economic assistance, military assistance, and ship loan programs. Other drafts of legislation are periodically put forward which are either more stringent or are intended to add to the list of retaliations available for use against seizing countries. We have opposed punitive legislation consistently. Without exception, it does not address the problem of how we end seizures. Instead, it increases the scope of the problem, either by placing new obstacles in the way of returning to negotiations or by complicating the issue by adding others to it, or both.

Throughout 1967 and 1968, in a new effort to find a solution, we urged Chile, Ecuador, and Peru to join us at a conference table. Seizures in 1969, to which we responded by applying the laws then in force, threatened to lead us to bitter confrontation. At that time, however, perhaps because for a brief moment we all had a glimpse of what could happen in a spiral of escalating action and reaction, the United States, Chile, Ecuador, and Peru agreed at last to convene a Quadripartite Fisheries Conference. Taking note of the fact that by that time we were all engaged in the steps leading to the United Nations resolution of 1970 calling for a new law-of-the-sea conference, the Quadripartite Fisheries Conference was to consider practical solutions that set aside our differences on the broader issues of international law.

The Quadripartite Fisheries Conference met in its first session in Buenos Aires in 1969 and met again in that same city in 1970. It was to have reconvened in a third session no later than July 31, 1971.

As I indicated in the beginning of my statement, 1971 was the year for demonstrating the dimensions of the confrontation that can flow from unresolved fisheries disputes. Between January 11 and March 27 and again in November and December, the Ecuadorean Navy made 51 seizures of American fishing vessels. The vessel owners paid a total of $2.4 million for the forced purchase of licenses and fines to obtain their release. This amount will be reimbursed to them under the terms of the Fishermen's Protective Act. The executive branch, because of the legislation passed throughout the years of the dispute, announced on January 18, 1971, the suspension of military sales and credits to Ecuador under the terms of the Foreign Military Sales Act. All other programs which were the subject of discretionary legislation were placed under review. Given your own experience with the countries of the hemisphere, you will not be surprised when you recall that this step of January 18 was quickly followed by an Ecuadorean appeal to the OAS to consider charges of economic aggression and to the expulsion of the United States Military Group from Ecuador.

Mr. Chairman, we have not yet found a solution to this problem. We have not been able to return to negotiations such as a resumption of the Quadripartite Fisheries Conference, because Ecuador insists that measures first applied in January 1971 must be lifted. We have engaged in private conservations with the Ecuadoreans because they believe as firmly as we that the entire range of our relations must not be allowed to deteriorate. These private conversations were initiated in November by Presidential Counsellor Robert Finch. They were continued when I returned to Quito in December 1971 and again in early January of this year. Ambassador McKernan [Donald L. McKernan, Special Assistant to the Secretary of State for Fisheries and Wildlife] and the Legal Adviser of the Department of State, John R. Stevenson, were with me on both of those trips. On our last visit we were accompanied by representatives of the Department of Defense.

The members of the delegation taken together represented the important U.S. interests which must be respected and reconciled in the course of our search for a temporary solution to our problems with Ecuador, which we would hope also would be acceptable to the signatories of the Santiago Declaration. This west coast fishing problem is not necessarily related to the search for an agreement with Brazil on the issues arising from its new fisheries regulations, which, in effect, could exclude a distant-water American shrimp fleet from operating off Brazil's coast.

We have sought a solution that takes into account all the interests of the United States—our security interests, our distant-water fishing interests, our bilateral political and economic interests, our broader interests in good relations in the hemisphere generally, and our interest in the achievement of United States objectives at the 1973 law-of-the-sea conference.

I would be less than frank if I held out to you and to this subcommittee a falsely optimistic prospect for an interim solution to these disputes. Although the law of the sea, with respect to resources, is evolving in a way which we hope eventually will make it possible to have an end to fisheries disputes in the hemisphere, this is a longer term hope only to be realized in the context of the conference that will begin in 1973. We look to other countries in Latin America that do not have extensive claims to help us identify the elements of an accommodation.

We hope that as our private conversations with Ecuador and our formal negotiations with Brazil continue, we will be able to show convincingly that we appreciate the resource concerns of the developing countries of the hemisphere and have no desire to deprive them of access to the wealth of the oceans in which they, as well as we, have a legitimate interest. In return, we hope they will recognize that for the United States as a major power, the question of how the world's oceans are governed in the years ahead must be answered in terms equally responsive to our national security interests.

195. Excerpts from a Report to Congress by President Nixon on Foreign Affairs*

February 9, 1972

The destiny of every nation within our inter-American system remains of foremost concern to the United States.

*Message to the
Inter-American Press Association
October 25, 1971*

Our association with our sister republics of the Western Hemisphere has always been unique in our foreign relations. Geography, history, a common heritage of self-government, and shared interests in the world at large have traditionally given our hemisphere relations a special durability.

When I came into office, however, the premises of our Latin American policy in the postwar period could no longer be uncritically accepted. The easy assumption of hemispheric community—reinforced by shared experience in the Second World War

*Department of State Bulletin, Mar. 13, 1972, pp. 358-63.

and by the new inter-American system—was being severely challenged by the new intensity of nationalism, pluralism, and pressures for change. The ambitious U.S. undertaking to lead the whole continent to democracy and progress—exemplified by our directive role in the Alliance for Progress—could not be sustained in a new period of accelerating expectations and greater assertion by Latin Americans themselves of their right and capacity to determine their own future.

These challenges were inherent in the new political environment of the 1970's. United States policy was hardly responsible for all the problems our relationship faced; nor could a new U.S. policy solve them. This, in fact, was one of the most obvious lessons we had to learn from our postwar experience. But the United States needed a new approach to hemispheric policy in order to respond to new conditions constructively and to lay the basis of a more mature political relationship with Latin American nations.

We needed, and we undertook, a fundamental rethinking of our premises.

We concluded, first, that geography and history and U.S. interests did give our relationship with Latin America a special—and continuing—importance. We could not treat Latin America as simply another region of the developing world. The hemisphere is unique and our political ties in it are unique.

We could see also that the growing sense of national and regional identity in Latin America was expressing itself increasingly in terms of differentiation from the United States. Henceforth a sense of hemisphere-wide community could be sustained only on a new, more realistic basis. The problems in our relationship were, at their roots, political. Solutions would be found in reconciliation of basic interests, not merely in economic programs. Of course, because of the central importance of development as a common objective, our assistance in that effort would be an essential ingredient in our relationship. In the long run, we hoped that the achievement of progress would boost national self-assurance and reduce the need for foreign scapegoats. Nevertheless, we had to understand that the mobilization of national energies and the frustrations of the development process could be accompanied by greater anti-U.S. sentiment, not less.

In recent years, U.S. policy had fluctuated between taking our neighbors for granted and launching ambitious crusades in which we promised a transformation of the continent. The penalties for taking our neighbors for granted were obvious. Our political ties to our own hemisphere would erode. The United States would become a target, rather than an ally, of legitimate national aspirations. Extremist methods would gain wider acceptance. We would have betrayed our own humanitarian traditions and our national commitment to freedom and human dignity.

The penalties for attempting ambitious crusades were less obvious but almost as serious. Enthusiasm was no substitute for concrete achievement. Pious exhortations for a massive U.S. effort would serve no purpose when the U.S. Congress was barely willing to preserve, let alone increase, our foreign assistance program. Raising unrealistic expectations would ultimately end only in greater frustration and bitterness. History had taught us, moreover, that progress toward development and democracy depended in the first instance upon indigenous capacities, traditions, and leadership. Latin Americans understood this, and so should we.

Therefore, this Administration has adopted a new approach to hemispheric policy, more consistent with modern reality. It reflects the new thrust of United States foreign policy under the Nixon Doctrine. We have changed the manner of our participation in both bilateral and collective efforts. We pretend no monopoly on ideas, but elicit and encourage the initiatives of our partners. The concrete economic steps the United States has taken to assist Latin America have been responses to their ideas and their concerns. We give our active support where it is wanted and where it makes a difference.

Ironically, in an area where the pervasiveness of change is a cliche of political rhetoric, old notions of expected U.S. behavior are proving difficult to throw off. United States performance is still to some extent being measured inappropriately by the yardsticks of the past. We are inevitably a leader, and hemispheric unity remains a fundamental principle. But a hemisphere of nations increasingly assertive of their individual identities is less amenable to U.S. direction and less likely to achieve cohesion automatically. Latin American nations vigorously mobilizing themselves for development should be less dependent on U.S. prescriptions.

This is a more mature relationship.

Our adjustment is thus a positive development of great importance. The United States has assumed a new role of leadership and support that we can sustain over the long term. It does justice to the national dignity of our partners. It is the only basis on which genuine progress in the hemisphere can be achieved.

Our policies over the past three years reflect four positive themes:

—A wider sharing of ideas and responsibility in hemispheric collaboration;

—A mature U.S. response to political diversity and nationalism;

—A practical and concrete U.S. contribution to economic and social development;

—A humanitarian concern for the quality of life in the hemisphere.

Sharing Ideas and Sharing Responsibility

The nations of Latin America are our partners, not our dependents.

A tutelary style of United States leadership is unsuited to today's political conditions. The most effective form of hemispheric collaboration in the 1970's is based on a wider sharing of ideas and a wider devolution of initiative.

In this regard, my face-to-face consultations with Latin American leaders over the past three years have been especially valuable. This past December, I conferred in Washington with President Médici of Brazil, as part of my consultation with our allies and friends in advance of my summit visits to Peking and Moscow. We had an important exchange of views on major issues of global as well as hemispheric concern. In spite of some current disagreements between us, on territorial waters and fishing rights, for example, our discussions confirmed a broad area of shared purposes. I have had important talks also with Presidents Lleras of Colombia, Caldera of Venezuela, and Somoza of Nicaragua, in addition to my frequent meetings with Presidents Diaz Ordaz and Echeverria of Mexico.

This is one function of consultation—to foster a sense of shared objectives and help achieve them. Hemispheric enterprises are most effective—and best help Latin America realize its great promise—when Latin Americans themselves play the major part in designing them. This strengthens the hemisphere-wide community.

However, it has long been obvious to our Latin American neighbors that within the wider community they share certain major interests and viewpoints as a group vis-a-vis the United States. The United States gains nothing by ignoring this or trying to deny it. The differences between us are apparent. What will preserve the hemisphere-wide community is practical cooperation among nations which have much to offer one another.

This Latin American sense of regional identity is now increasingly reflected in hemispheric practice, particularly on economic questions. In the Special Committee on Consultation and Negotiation, for example, a body in the Inter-American Economic and Social Council (IA—ECOSOC) for dealing with trade issues, the Latin Americans increasingly consult among themselves before discussions with the United States. Latin American nations have also formed, on their own, the Special Coordinating Commission for Latin America (CECLA), for concerting their positions on political and economic issues vis-a-vis the United States and the rest of the industrialized world. This group produced the Consensus of Viña del Mar—the set of proposals to the United States which contributed valuably to the program I announced in October 1969.

This new practice of Latin American consultation can be a constructive force for cohesion in the hemisphere as a whole; it can make cooperation between the U.S. and Latin America more effective and more responsive. It will be a challenge to statesmanship to ensure that it never degenerates into hostile confrontation, which would be an obstacle to achievement, and thus self-defeating.

Community, Diversity, and Nationalism

The hemisphere community took shape historically as an association of free republics joining together against domination and interference from tyrannies across the ocean. This sense of unity was reinforced by the Second World War and was embodied in the new institutions and instruments of the inter-American system.

Our cohesion has served many other common purposes since then. It has provided forums for multilateral consideration of issues facing us all. It has afforded mechanisms for peaceful settlement of disputes within the hemisphere. It has enabled Latin Americans to express a collective voice in discussions with the United States and the rest of the world.

In the 1970's, this cohesion is being tested by rapid and turbulent change—more intense nationalism, accelerating expectations, new ideologies and political movements, a new diversity of political systems and expanding ties between Latin American countries and the rest of the world. These new conditions are bound to transform our political relationships.

Our task is to respond constructively with a realistic set of objectives and principles for United States policy. We have done so.

There are hemispheric questions on which our judgments differ from those of some of our partners. As I said in October 1969: "partnership—mutuality—these do not flow naturally. We have to work at them." I do not believe that frank discussion and fair settlements between sovereign nations are inconsistent with national dignity.

Our especially close relationship with Mexico provides striking examples of problems resolved systematically by self-respecting states who feel a preeminent interest in good relations. The closeness reflected in my several meetings in 1969 and 1970 with Presidents Diaz Ordaz and Echeverria resulted in specific agreements on such matters as narcotics control, boundaries, civil air routes, agricultural imports, Colorado River salinity, joint flood control projects, and the return of archaeological treasures.

In addition, in 1971 the United States and Nicaragua abrogated the Bryan-Chamorro Treaty, relinquishing canal-construction rights in Nicaragua which we no longer require. Presidential Counsellor Finch, visiting six Latin American nations on my behalf in November 1971, signed an agreement recognizing Honduran sovereignty over the Swan Islands. We have entered new negotiations with Panama to achieve a mutually acceptable basis for the continuing efficient operation and defense of the Panama Canal.

Our mutual interest also requires that we and our neighbors address in this same cooperative spirit the two significant disputes which flared up last year in our relations with Latin America—the fisheries dispute and the problem of expropriation. Let me state frankly the United States view on these unsettled questions.

In 1971, Ecuador seized and fined a great number of U.S.-owned tuna boats fishing within its claimed 200-mile territorial sea. United States law required me to suspend new military sales and credits to Ecuador as a result; seizures have continued nevertheless. Disagreements over the fisheries question have also arisen with Peru and Brazil.

The technical issue is a dispute over the legal definition of the territorial sea. The central issue is political—how to reconcile conflicting interests in an environment in which national pride and nationalist emotions exacerbate our differences. Fundamental security interests of the United States are involved. We do not believe that a continuing cycle of seizures and sanctions serves anyone's interest. We therefore consider it essential to negotiate at least an interim solution: to halt the seizures and sanctions while preserving the juridical positions of both sides until the 1973 UN Conference on the Law of the Sea, which we hope will reach an international consensus. Counsellor Finch reopened talks on this issue on his visit to Ecuador and Peru, and we have also discussed the problem with Brazil.

Major differences have also arisen in the past three years between the United States and some Latin American countries over expropriation of foreign private investments.

International law permits non-discriminatory nationalization of property for public purposes but it also requries reasonable provision for prompt, adequate, and effective compensation. Although mutually acceptable compensation agreements are negotiated in the majority of instances in Latin America, there have been important cases in which the legitimate interests of private investors have been treated arbitrarily and inequitably.

In our view this only jeopardizes the achievement of the goals in whose name these actions are taken. Latin America needs external capital, because internal savings are simply insufficient for development needs. While every country has the right to determine its own conditions for private investment, a government that rejects or discourages private capital cannot realistically assume that foreign public capital will make up the difference. What is needed now is a frank understanding which protects the legitimate interests of private investors, while being fair to the countries in which they invest. This would restore mutual confidence and maintain the flow of needed resources.

In January of this year, I announced the principles that shall govern U.S. Government policy on this matter worldwide. This policy is set forth in the International Economic Policy chapter of this Report.

In our view, the hemisphere community is big enough, mature enough and tolerant enough to accept a diversity of national approaches to human goals. We therefore deal realistically with governments as they are—right and left. We have strong preferences and hopes to see free democratic processes prevail, but we cannot impose our political structure on other nations. We respect the hemispheric principle of non-intervention. We shape our relations with governments according to their policies and actions as they affect our interests and the interests of the inter-American system, not according to their domestic structures.

Our relations with Chile are an example. Chile's leaders will not be charmed out of their deeply held convictions by gestures on our part. We recognize that they are serious men whose ideological principles are, to some extent, frankly in conflict with ours. Nevertheless, our relations will hinge not on their ideology but on their conduct toward the outside world. As I have said many times, we are prepared to have the kind of relationship with the Chilean Government that it is prepared to have with us.

In this context, its actions thus far on compensation for expropriated U.S.-owned copper companies are not encouraging. The application ex post facto of unprecedented legal rules which effectively nullify compensation is, in our view, inconsistent with international law. We and other public and private sources of development investment will take account of whether or not the Chilean Government meets its international obligations.

The integrity of international law, moreover, is not something only the United States has an interest in. On the contrary, it is a world interest. Smaller nations in particular are the beneficiaries of the restraints and obligations which international law seeks to impose on the conduct of states.

It is a challenge to statesmanship to see to it that nationalism works as a positive force and not as an obstacle to mutually beneficial realtions between states.

Confrontation and extremism are destructive. For this reason the United States continues to assist the efforts of its partners to combat subversive violence, both with material and training support for security programs and with support for building the institutions and processes of democratic, social and economic progress.

Regrettably, Cuba has not abandoned its promotion of subversive violence. There has been some moderation of its rhetoric and more selectivity in its approach to exporting revolution, but these seem to be only a shift in tactics prompted by the consistent failures of its domestic policy and revolutionary adventures. Cuba continues to furnish money, weapons, training, and ideological leadership to revolutionary and terrorist groups. Similarly, Cuba has increased, not diminished, its military ties with the USSR—its receipt of arms and provision of facilities—and thus invited a permanent Soviet military presence into the hemisphere. Cuba isolates itself by these policies, which are an obvious and direct threat to the rest of the community. The United States will consider supporting a change in the OAS sanctions against Cuba only when the evidence demonstrates a real change in Cuba's policies.

A Program of Action for Development

A hemisphere divided by a yawning gulf between wealth and squalor is no community. The commitment of the United States to human dignity implies a commitment to help our neighbors achieve their overriding national objective— economic and social development.

There is no certainty that development contributes directly or immediately to democracy, or peace, or friendlier relations with the United States. In the long run, we hope it will. We will assist in the hemispheric effort with realistic expectations and with a realistic program of action that will have an impact.

Trade opportunities are crucial to Latin American development. Export earnings are the most important long term source of foreign exchange; they are a means of financing development without dependence on external aid and without the real or imagined infringement of national sovereignty that so often complicates bilateral and even multilateral lending and investment.

The growth of these earnings, however, is dependent upon long term trends in world demand for Latin America's raw materials and semi-processed goods. Today, the trends in demand are far from adequate to provide the earnings needed. This has been a major burden on Latin American development and one of our partners' most urgent concerns.

The United States, for its part, has taken steps to provide access for such Latin American products as sugar, coffee and meat to our own market. But the problem is greater than this and has to be attacked on a worldwide basis. Latin America was not included in the arrangements by which many industrialized nations gave preferential treatment to selected countries or regions in the developing world. The answer to this—which the U.S. championed—was to press for a generalized system by which industrial countries gave preferential treatment to the products of all developing countries. We made great progress. The European Community, Japan, and other nations have put generalized tariff preference schemes into effect. As Secretary Rogers announced in December, we expect to submit our own generalized preference legislation to the Congress.

For the past three years, in addition, the United States has maintained the average annual level of development assistance of the first ten years of the Alliance for Progress. I have urged the Congress to move quickly and favorably on our new appropriations, particularly for bilateral aid and for the Inter-American Development Bank (IDB), the principal regional entity for development lending. Over the past three years, this Administration has responded to Latin American proposals and taken concrete steps to assist their efforts for development. For example:

—In my October 1969 address, I announced a milestone reform: the relaxation of restrictions which "tied" U.S. loans to Latin America to the purchase of U.S. exports.

—We have given financial and technical support to enhance the effectiveness of multilateral institutions like IA—ECOSOC, CIAP, and IDB as vehicles for Latin American leadership in planning development assistance and setting development priorities.

—I exempted the hemisphere from the ten percent reduction of bilateral foreign aid which was a part of our August 15 emergency New Economic Policy.

—We have supported efforts to develop capital markets, tourism, and export promotion, and to facilitate the transfer of technology for development needs.

—We have given assistance to the Central American Bank for Economic Integration and the Caribbean Development Bank

—The U.S. signed agreements with Panama and Colombia on the financing of the last unfinished link of the Pan American Highway—the Darien Gap. Construction can now begin this year.

The Quality of Life in the Hemisphere

Our ties with Latin America at the people-to-people level are a tradition unto themselves. They cover the range of human and institutional activities—educational, cultural and professional exchanges; volunteer and other humanitarian programs; counterpart contacts between schools, industries, labor unions, credit unions, foundations, cooperatives, and other non-governmental institutions. These people-to-people contacts have the advantage that they are less politically sensitive and generally can survive uncertainties and fluctuations in official relations. In 1970, the United States created the Inter-American Social Development Institute to assist the growth of non-governmental institutions in Latin America. This is a contribution to pluralism and to the kinds of social organization by which people and communities participate directly in improving their own lives.

The government and people of the United States contribute to human betterment in Latin America in other ways. Our public and private assistance to victims of natural disaster is a well-known and long-standing tradition. Our aid to Peru after the 1970 earthquake, and Mrs. Nixon's visit to the scene, were symbolic of our concern.

The Hemispheric Future

The United States cannot be indifferent to the hemisphere in which it lives. But geography alone does not make a community. Our association will thrive only if our common purposes do. The United States believes it has much to contribute, as well as much to gain, in a continuing close relationship with its fellow inhabitants of the Western Hemisphere. We recognize nevertheless that the difficulties facing United States policy will grow, rather than diminish, as the decade unfolds; there will inevitably be strains and disappointments. This will test our compassion, our tolerance and our maturity.

The new United States policy I first announced in October 1969 was a statement of a new philosophy and a blueprint for concrete action. Our philosophy is one of realism and restraint. This is the approach best suited to the realities of the new era and to history's lesson that we in the U.S., whatever our good intentions, cannot mold the continent to our preferred image. Our program of concrete action, designed for effectiveness rather than glamor, is directly responsive to Latin American ideas and needs.

To realize our purposes, these will be our tasks in the years ahead:

*To Share Initiative and Responsibility More Widely
in Collective Enterprises*

This is a constructive way of responding to a radically new political environment in which our partners are more assertive of their right and capacity to determine their own future. The inter-American system and its practices should reflect this more balanced relationship.

*To Demonstrate in Word and Deed the Vitality of the Common
Aspirations of the Hemisphere.*

We are realistic. Differences in interest and perspective are natural. We need to discuss differences and negotiate solutions, as is proper among sovereign states who share an interest in preserving a constructive relationship.

*To Make an Effective Contribution to Economic
Development in Latin America*

We cannot allow the ferment of the age to immobilize us. We can be responsive to good programs in many practical ways—even given the broad limits on what the United States is capable of providing or accomplishing by itself. We will move forward with our program of action.

*To Tap the Humanitarian Concern of the People
of the United States for the Betterment of
People's Lives in the Hemisphere*

This humane concern for people and people's lives is an enduring commitment and a vast resource. It runs far deeper than foreign policies and political relations, and sustains them all.

*   *   *

196. Statement by Under Secretary Irwin before the Inter-American Committee on the Alliance for Progress (CIAP), on United States Economic Policy*

March 20, 1972

It is a pleasure to welcome CIAP once again to its annual country review of the United States. The first CIAP review, a year ago last October, was a tribute to the more mature relationship among the countries of the Americas which President Nixon first announced in 1969 as the goal of U.S. policy—a goal which the other countries of the hemisphere have universally welcomed. The discussions in that first review session, under your able chairmanship, Dr. [Carlos] Sanz de Santamaría, were thorough, frank, and constructive. Above all, they were discussions among friends. They produced a most helpful report.

We will do our part, and I am confident the other CIAP members will do theirs, to see that this second annual review meets the high standard set by the first. The past year has been a difficult one, difficult for the United States economy and difficult for our economic relations with the Americas. The agenda prepared by the CIAP Secre-

*Department of State Bulletin, Apr. 10, 1972, pp. 539-44.

tariat for this review refers to 1971 as "a year of tension in inter-American relations." To the extent that this is true, I hope that our discussions here can help to defuse this tension. We are prepared to examine as fully as time allows the many issues raised in the several papers which the CIAP Secretariat staff, with their usual thoroughness and professionalism, have prepared for this review.

The other members of the United States delegation, most of whom are here, who will participate in the review are:

Mr. Charles A. Meyer, Assistant Secretary of State for Inter-American Affairs; Mr. Ezra Solomon, member of the President's Council of Economic Advisers, who will speak on the United States domestic economy; Mr. Maurice J. Williams, Deputy Administrator of the Agency for International Development, who will cover United States bilateral aid; Mr. Willis Armstrong, Assistant Secretary of State for Economic Affairs, who will cover United States trade policy; and Mr. John M. Hennessy, Acting Assistant Secretary of Treasury for International Affairs, who will discuss the United States balance of payments, the international monetary system, and multilateral financing.

As background for later remarks about U.S. economic policy, let me sketch some basic concepts which underlie U.S. policy toward the countries of Latin America. The Latin American chapter of President Nixon's latest foreign policy report stated that Latin America is not simply another region of the developing world but is unique for United States interests. We believe not only that Latin America is uniquely important for our own interests but also that our interests and those of the countries of Latin America are consonant. In fact, they are mutually supportive, rather than—as some would maintain—conflicting.

—We all desire economic and social progress for all nations of the hemisphere.

—We all want expanded trade.

—We all want an improved quality of life for our peoples and better understanding of how that improvement may best be achieved.

—We all believe in self-determination and in respect for all nations large or small.

—We all believe in the enhancement of political and civil liberties.

—We all want to negotiate and settle disputes among ourselves peacefully and reasonably, rather than letting them escalate into confrontation or harden into hostility.

It is in our mutual interest to work together toward these common ends through a sharing of ideas and responsibilities. We have the institutions for doing so. CIAP is one. This review process, therefore, is a signal expression of a commitment on the part of all CIAP members to continue a common effort to achieve a better life for all of our peoples.

U.S. Domestic Economy and Balance of Payments

What the United States can do toward this common effort is strongly influenced by the condition of our domestic economy and by our international balance of payments. Adverse trends in unemployment, in the rate of inflation, and in our balance of payments came to a head in 1971. Although the economy was expanding and the increase in prices had slowed, it became increasingly clear as the summer of 1971 went on that output expansion and inflation restraint were not proceeding as rapidly as was desirable. The second quarter of the year brought our deteriorating balance of payments to a position where prompt action was imperative.

On August 15 President Nixon announced a new economic policy designed to deal with both the international and the domestic aspects of our economic problems. At home a wage-price freeze was instituted to check inflation. Fiscal measures were adopted to speed up economic activity and cut unemployment. To restore equilibrium in our balance of payments, the President decided to seek a realignment of currency rates, to impose a temporary 10-percent surcharge on dutiable imports, and to press for negotiations in two areas: (1) to correct what in our view were inequitable trade practices of some of our major trading partners and (2) to modernize the international monetary system. Convertibility of the dollar was suspended.

By the end of 1971 substantial progress had been made. The President's revenue bill was passed, with some modifications. On December 18 the United States and nine other industrial nations agreed to a major realignment of their currencies and to undertake urgent negotiations looking toward short-term measures of trade liberalization; they also agreed to longer term discussions on international trade and on the international monetary system. The 10-percent surcharge was lifted.

First results of the August 15 package were already visible at the end of the year. The rate of increase in domestic prices was sharply slowed. The total output of goods and services increased in the fourth quarter at an annual rate double that of the third quarter. The U.S. balance of payments, however, was still heavily in deficit. Improvement in this area will come only over time as the new monetary relationships and trade measures take effect.

As 1972 began, therefore, there were prospects for rising output, diminishing unemployment, greater price stability, and—eventually—a stronger U.S. balance of payments position.

International Monetary Reform

Two issues relating to the reform of the international monetary system are of obvious concern to Latin America and to this CIAP review: first, the effect on Latin America of the currency realignment already achieved and, second, the reform of the monetary system which we hope to negotiate in the future. The currency realignment should help Latin American exports. Sales in the markets of the revaluing countries should increase as Latin American goods become relatively cheaper. In the United States market, Latin American exports will become more competitive with the suppliers whose countries have appreciated their currency. In addition, as the United States economy expands, our ability to absorb more imports from the hemisphere will increase.

Looking to the future, we recognize that the countries of Latin America will wish to participate in the discussions leading to reform of the international monetary system. The question of negotiating forum for these discussions is very much on our minds. The Smithsonian agreement pointed to the International Monetary Fund as an appropriate forum; certainly any forum we might devise should be linked in some way to such relevant institutions as the IMF. At the same time, effective negotiations will require a forum in which the participants can reach agreement as well as exchange ideas and views. This suggests some limitation on the number of actual participants so that discussion remains manageable and decision is possible.

The Group of Ten has proved to be a useful forum in the past. We recognize, however, that the Group of Ten is limited to the more industrialized and wealthier nations; it is not ideally suited to giving a representative voice to other nations whose interests must be taken into account. A forum modeled on the IMF Executive Board might provide suitably wider representation. Other models are possible. Under Secretary of the Treasury Paul Volcker has now been asked to explore this question with interested governments to see whether a mutually satisfactory solution can be found.

United States Trade Policy

Another focus of the CIAP annual review will be the impact of U.S. trade policies on Latin America. For three decades the United States has played a leadership role in removing trade barriers and liberalizing the international movement of goods, services, and capital. In such institutions as GATT, the OECD, and UNCTAD [General Agreement on Tariffs and Trade; Organization for Economic Cooperation and Development; U.N. Conference on Trade and Development], we have consistently supported freer access of goods from the developing countries into industrialized markets. With respect to agricultural products, such as sugar and meat—on which the United States has felt it necessary to retain import quotas—Latin America has received favorable conditions of access. The Sugar Act extension last year continued generally the benefits to Latin America which it has enjoyed in recent years. United States participation in the International Coffee Agreement, which imposes worldwide quotas on coffee exports, has materially benefited Latin American producers by insuring them equitable prices for their exports. Congress has now approved and sent to the President legislation extending our participation in the International Coffee Agreement until October 1973.

There are undeniably strong and growing protectionist sentiments in the United States. They are manifested in the Congress, in the labor movement, and in several industrial sectors of our society. The administration's objective in the field of international economic policy, however, has not changed. We seek an open world economy in which trade and investment flows are not disturbed by national barriers. President Nixon has strongly endorsed the cautions raised in the report by Mr. Peter Peterson, then Chairman of the Council on International Economic Policy and now Secretary of Commerce, against erecting new barriers to imports. The United States has, as you know, joined with the European Community and Japan in calling for multilateral trade negotiations in 1973. The developing countries should play an important role in these negotiations.

The imposition of the 10-percent surcharge was probably the trade measure which elicited the most debate and criticism from Latin America in 1971. While we recognized that the Latin Americans had not contributed to our trade deficit, we felt compelled to impose the surcharge on a worldwide basis in order to comply with our GATT obligations and to achieve the objectives of the new economic policy designed over the long run to benefit all of us in the hemisphere. The impact of the surcharge was somewhat lessened by the exemption of two categories of goods particularly important to Latin America—nondutiable items and items under quantitative restraints. As had been promised, the surcharge was a temporary measure and has now been eliminated.

Another issue of great interest to Latin America is a system of generalized tariff preferences. Generalized preferences would help the countries of Latin America meet their needs to increase foreign exchange earnings and diversify exports. The United States has strongly supported efforts in recent years to establish generalized preferences for the developing countries. We took the lead in the OECD to develop a generally acceptable system. As a result of our efforts, the European Community, Japan, and the U.K. have already adopted some form of generalized preferences. As all of you know only too well, the United States has not yet been able to put its own plan into effect. The improvement in our balance of payments and trading position which we expect as a result of the Smithsonian agreement should create a more favorable climate for preference legislation. We intend to submit such legislation to Congress the moment we feel it would have a real chance of passage without crippling amendments.

The United States recognizes the importance of export development to the economies of Latin America. A recent meeting of experts in Bogotá brought out that substantial possibilities for assistance exist in this field and should be used. Discussions recently concluded between the United States and Latin American governments brought out that Latin American exports to the United States could be increased if producing countries would give greater attention to quarantine, sanitary, and health regulations designed to protect the consumer and the environment.

United States Economic Assistance

Those participating in the CIAP review will be particularly interested in the assistance which the United States provides through multilateral and bilateral channels. The foreign assistance program had rough going in our Congress during the latter part of 1971. But with continued administration support, foreign aid authorization and appropriations bills were finally enacted this year. In signing the authorizing legislation, the President expressed his serious concern over the large cut made by Congress in his foreign aid requests. In his foreign policy report he reemphasized that the vital role of foreign assistance deserves the continued support of the U.S. Congress and public.

In my remarks to the first annual CIAP review a year ago last October, I outlined the proposals which the President had just transmitted to Congress for reorganizing U.S. bilateral assistance efforts. Legislation embodying these proposals was submitted to the Congress last spring, but to date Congress has been unwilling to act on them.

In the interim, a number of significant changes are being made in the existing Agency for International Development. The changes are designed to give our bilateral assistance programs sharper focus in those areas where the United States continues to have a distinctive bilateral contribution to make. The most significant changes involve separating the administration of security and developmental aid, trying to concentrate on sectors such as education and agriculture judged to have the highest priority, strengthening population and humanitarian efforts, and encouraging private United States organizations to use their technical and scientific capabilities more effective to help the developing world.

The administration continues to emphasize providing assistance through multilateral organizations. Broader cooperation and wider sharing of responsibility for assistance to the developing areas are essential if the common goals I spoke of earlier are ever to be reached. We expect the international organizations to take an effective lead in this common effort. The bill authorizing the United States share of replenishment for the Inter-American Development Bank has now been signed into law, and most of the appropriations we sought for the Bank have been obtained. The administration will continue to seek adequate appropriations in this area. We also plan to continue financial and technical support for multilateral consultative institutions such as IA–ECOSOC [Inter-American Economic and Social Council] and CIAP.

The United States believes strongly that private foreign investment can make a significant contribution to the economic development of Latin America. Such investment not only transfers capital, which domestic savings cannot provide in sufficient quantities, but also contributes technology and creates trade and employment opportunities. Private investment usually concentrates on productive facilities and thereby complements public assistance, which of necessity usually concentrates on infrastructure.

I know that some of you participating in this review have philosophical differences with us on this issue. A frank exchange of views, however, may help us to find a common middle ground. President Nixon's January 19 statement on economic assistance and investment security is a comprehensive and authoritative statement of the attitude of this government toward private foreign investment. As evidenced by the President's statement, the United States is deeply concerned that different philosophical attitudes toward the role of private foreign investment—attitudes which we recognize are entirely legitimate even though we may disagree with them—seem to be leading to actions in the area of governmental expropriations which in our view are not legitimate. I cannot overemphasize how important it is for all of us who are interested in the common development goals for the hemisphere which I outlined at the beginning of these remarks to come to an understanding on this issue. If the U.S. commitment to developmental assistance is to be maintained, we must work together to preserve an investment climate in which investors, whether private or public, can count on investment protection and the fulfillment of contractual obligations in accordance with recognized international legal standards.

As the CIAP review discusses the role of private foreign investment in the overall U.S. economic assistance strategy, I urge you to consider the possible use of multilateral mechanisms for dealing with investment disputes. There are a range of available mechanisms, from consultation with or mediation by the international financial institutions and disinterested governments to formal arbitration in a forum such as the International Center for the Settlement of Investment Disputes. My government hopes that the International Investment Insurance Agency of the World Bank will soon be in a position to provide additional security for foreign investment in a multilateral framework acceptable to both investor and recipient nations.

Mr. Chairman, this has been but a brief sketch of the topics which the members of CIAP will review in much greater depth with my colleagues over the next few days.

Let us hope that the review of the difficult year 1971 will lead all of our governments to the kind of common understanding we need to make 1972 a year of increased cooperation among us and progress toward the concrete goal of a better life for our peoples which remains the underlying purpose of the alliance.

INDEX